The Pocket English
Dictionary & Thesaurus

Published in this edition 1997 by Grandreams Limited,
435/437 Edgeware Road, London W2 1TH

© 1997 Geddes & Grosset Ltd,
David Dale House, New Lanark, Scotland

ISBN 1 85830 499 7

Printed and bound in France

10 9 8 7 6 5 4 3 2 1

abbr	abbreviation
adj	adjective
adv	adverb
aux	auxiliary
cap	capital letter
chem	chemistry
coll	colloquial
comput	computer term
conj	conjunction
demons	demonstrative
e.g.	for example
esp	especially
etc	etcetera
f	feminine
gram	grammar
inf	informal
interj	interjection
math	mathematics
med	medicine
mil	military
mus	music
n	noun
naut	nautical
npl	noun plural
pers	personal
philos	philosophy
pl	plural
pp	past participle
prep	preposition
pr p	present participle
pt	past tense
RC	Roman Catholic
Scot	Scottish term
sing	singular
sl	slang
TV	television
usu	usually
vb	verb
vi	intransitive verb
vt	transitive verb
vti	transitive and intransitive verb

Dictionary

A

a *adj* the indefinite article; one; any; per.

aback *adv* **taken aback** startled.

abandon *vt* to leave behind; to desert. • *n* freedom from inhibitions.

abate *vti* to make or become less.

abattoir *n* a slaughterhouse.

abbey *n* a building occupied by monks or nuns.

abbot *n* the head of an abbey of monks.

abbreviate *vt* to shorten (a word) by omitting letters.—**abbreviation** *n*.

abdicate *vti* to renounce an official position or responsibility, etc.—**abdication** *n*.

abdomen *n* the region of the body below the chest; the belly.—**abdominal** *adj*.

abduct *vt* to carry off (a person) by force.—**abduction** *n*.—**abductor** *n*.

abet *vt* to encourage or assist.

abhor *vt* to detest, despise.

abide *vt* to endure.

ability *n* being able; talent; skill.

ablaze *adj* burning, on fire.

able *adj* having the competence or means (to do); talented; skilled.

abnormal *adj* unusual, not average or typical; irregular.—**abnormality** *n*.

aboard *adv* on or in an aircraft, ship, train, etc.

abolish *vt* to bring to an end, do away with.

abolition *n* the act of abolishing, e.g. slavery.

abominable *adj* despicable; (*inf*) unpleasant.

aborigine *n* any of the first known inhabitants of a region; (*with cap*) one of the original inhabitants of Australia.

abort *vti* to undergo, cause an abortion; to terminate, cause to terminate prematurely.

abortion *n* the premature expulsion of a foetus.

abortive *adj* failing in intended purpose.

abound *vi* to be in abundance.

about *prep* on all sides of; near to; with; on the point of; concerning. • *adv* all around; near.

above *prep* over, on top of; better or more than; beyond the reach of. • *adv* in or to a higher place; (*text*) mentioned earlier.

abrasive *adj* causing abrasion; harsh. • *n* a substance or tool for grinding or polishing.

abreast *adv* side by side; informed (of).

abridge *vt* to shorten (text).

abroad *adv* in or to a foreign country; over a wide area; out in the open; in circulation.

abrupt *adj* sudden; unexpected; curt.

abscess *n* an inflamed area of the body containing pus.

abscond *vi* to flee from punishment.

absence *n* the state of not being present; a lack.

absent[1] *adj* not present; inattentive.

absent[2] *vt* to keep (oneself) away.

absentee *n* a person who is absent.

absenteeism *n* persistent absence.

absent-minded *adj* inattentive; forgetful.

absolute *adj* unrestricted, unconditional; complete; positive; perfect; not relative.

absolutely *adv* completely; certainly.

absolve *vt* to clear from guilt or blame; to free from a duty, obligation, etc.

absorb *vt* to take in; to soak up; to incorporate; to occupy.—**absorption** *n*.

absorbent *adj* capable of absorbing moisture.

abstain *vi* to keep oneself from some indulgence, esp alcohol; to refrain from voting.

abstemious *adj* sparing in consuming food, etc.

abstinence *n* an abstaining or refraining, esp from food or alcohol.—**abstinent** *adj*.

abstract *adj* having no material existence; theoretical; (*art*) non-representational. • *n* (*writing, speech*) a summary. • *vt* to remove or extract; to separate; to summarise.

absurd *adj* ridiculous.—**absurdity** *n*.

abundance *n* a plentiful supply.

abundant *adj* plentiful; rich (in).

abuse *vt* to make wrong use of; to mistreat; to insult, attack verbally.—*also n*.

abusive *adj* insulting.

abysmal *adj* extremely bad, deplorable.

abyss *n* a bottomless depth.

academic *adj* pertaining to a school, college or university; scholarly; purely theoretical. • *n* a member of a college, etc.

academy *n* a school for specialised training; a society of scholars, writers, scientists, etc.

accede *vi* to take office; to agree or assent to.

accelerate *vti* to move faster; to (cause to) happen more quickly.—**acceleration** *n*.

accelerator *n* a device for increasing speed; (*physics*) an apparatus that imparts high velocities to elementary particles.

accent *n* emphasis on a syllable or word; a mark used to indicate this; any way of speaking characteristic of a region, class or an individual.

accept *vt* to receive; to approve; to agree to; to

believe in.—**acceptance** n.

acceptable adj satisfactory; tolerable.

access n the right to enter, use. • vt (comput) to retrieve from a storage device.

accessory n a supplementary part or item, esp of clothing; a person who aids another in a crime.

accident n an unexpected event; a mishap.

accidental adj occurring or done by accident.

acclaim vt to praise publicly; to welcome enthusiastically. • n a shout of approval.

acclimatise vt to adapt to a new climate or environment • vi to become acclimatised.

accommodate vt to provide lodging for; to oblige, supply; to adapt, harmonise.

accommodating adj obliging, helpful.

accommodation n lodgings; the process of adapting; willingness to help.

accompaniment n an instrumental part supporting a solo instrument, a voice or a choir; something that accompanies.

accompany vt (person) to go with; (something) to supplement.

accomplice n a partner, esp in a crime.

accomplish vt to succeed in; to fulfil.

accomplished adj done; completed; skilled.

accomplishment n a skill or talent; the act of accomplishing; completion.

accord vi to agree; to harmonise (with). • vt to grant. • n consent; harmony.

accordance n agreement; conformity.

accordingly adv consequently; therefore.

accordion n a portable keyboard instrument with manually operated folding bellows that force air through metal reeds.

accost vt to approach and speak to.

account n a description; explanatory statement; business record or statement; a credit arrangement with a bank, store, etc; importance. • vt to think of as; consider. • vi to give a financial reckoning (to); (with for) to give reasons (for).

accountable adj liable; responsible.—**accountability** n.

accountancy n the profession or practice of an accountant.—**accountant** n.

accumulate vti to collect together in increasing quantities, to amass.—**accumulation** n.

accurate adj correct; done with care, exact.—**accuracy** n.

accusation n the act of alleging guilt.

accuse vt to charge with a crime, fault, etc; to blame.—**accuser** n.—**accusingly** adv.

accustom vt to make used (to).

accustomed adj usual, customary.

ace n the one spot in dice, playing cards, dominoes, etc. • adj (inf) excellent.

ache n a dull, continuous pain. • vi to suffer such pain; (inf) to yearn.

achieve vt to succeed, accomplish; to gain.

acid adj sharp, sour; bitter. • n (chem) a corrosive substance that turns litmus red; (sl) LSD.

acknowledge vt to admit the truth of; to show recognition.—**acknowledgement** n.

acne n inflammation of the skin glands producing pimples.

acorn n the nut of the oak tree.

acoustic adj of the sense of hearing or sound.

acoustics npl properties governing how clearly sounds can be heard; (sing) the physics of sound.

acquaint vt to make (oneself) familiar (with); to inform.

acquaintance n a person whom one knows only slightly.

acquire vt to gain; to obtain.

acquisition n gaining, acquiring; something that is acquired.

acquisitive adj greedy for possessions.

acquit vt to free from an obligation; to conduct (oneself); to declare innocent.—**acquittal** n.

acre n land measuring 4840 sq yards.

acrimony n bitterness of manner or language.—**acrimonious** adj.

acrobat n a skilful performer of spectacular gymnastic feats.—**acrobatic** adj.

acrobatics npl acrobatic feats.

across prep from one side to the other of; on the other side of. • adv from one side to the other.

act vi to behave; to perform a specific function; to have an effect; to perform on the stage. • vt to portray, esp on the stage. • n something done, a deed; a law; a division of a play, etc; the short repertoire of a comic, etc.

acting n the art of an actor. • adj holding an office or position temporarily.

action n a deed; an operation; a movement of the body, gesture; a lawsuit.

activate vt to make active; to set in motion.—

active adj lively, mobile; energetic, busy; (volcano) liable to erupt; capable of producing an effect; radioactive; (armed forces) in full-time service.

activity n being active; energetic, lively action; specific occupations (indoor activities).

actor n a person who acts in a play, film, etc.—**actress** nf.

actual adj real; existing.—**actually** adv.

acumen n sharpness of mind, perception.

acupuncture n the insertion of needles into the skin at certain points to treat ailments.

acute adj (hearing) sensitive; (pain) severe; very serious; (angles) less than 90 degrees; (disease) severe.—**acuteness** n.

ad abbr = anno Domini (in the year of Our Lord) in dates, indicating the number of years since the birth of Christ.

Adam's apple n the hard projection of cartilage in the front of the neck.

adapt *vti* to fit; to adjust to change.—**adaptability** *n*—**adaptable** *adj*.

adaptation *n* the process or condition of being adapted; something produced by modification; a rearranged version.

adapter, adaptor *n* a device that allows an item of equipment to be put to new use; a device for connecting differing parts.

add *vt* to combine (two or more things together); to remark or write further.

adder *n* the venomous viper.

addict *n* a person who is dependent upon a drug.—**addiction** *n*.

addition *n* the act or result of adding; something extra.—**additional** *adj*.

additive *adj* produced by addition. • *n* a substance added (to food) to improve flavour.

address *vt* to write directions on an envelope; to speak directly to; to direct one's skills or attention (to). • *n* a direction on a letter for delivery; a speech, esp formal; (*comput*) a specific memory location where information is stored.

adenoids *npl* enlarged masses of tissue in the throat behind the nose.

adept *adj* highly proficient.

adequate *adj* sufficient for requirements; barely acceptable.—**adequacy** *n*

adhere *vi* to stick, as by gluing or suction; to give allegiance or support (to); to follow.

adhesion *n* an adhering; the attachment of normally separate tissues in the body.

adhesive *adj* sticky; causing adherence. • *n* a substance used to stick, such as glue.

adjacent *adj* nearby; adjoining.

adjective *n* a word used to add a characteristic to a noun or pronoun.

adjoining *adj* beside, in contact with.

adjourn *vt* to suspend temporarily.

adjust *vt* to arrange in a more satisfactory manner; to regulate by minor changes. • *vi* to adapt oneself.—**adjustable** *adj*.—**adjustment** *n*.

adjutant *n* a military staff officer who assists the commanding officer.

ad-lib *vti* (*speech, etc*) to improvise. • *n* an ad-libbed remark.

administer *vt* to manage, direct; to dispense .

administration *n* management; the people who administer an organisation; government; (*with cap*) the executive officials of a government.—**administrative** *adj*.

administrator *n* a person who manages; (*law*) one appointed to settle an estate.

admiral *n* the commanding officer of a fleet; a naval officer of the highest rank.

admiration *n* a feeling of pleasurable and often surprised respect or approval.

admire *vt* to regard with honour and approval; to express admiration.—**admirer** *n*.

admission *n* an entrance fee; a conceding, confessing; a thing conceded, confessed.

admit *vt* to allow to enter or join; to concede or acknowledge as true. • *vi* (*with* of) to allow.

admittance *n* the right to enter.

admonish *vt* to reprove.—**admonition** *n*.

ado *n* fuss, esp over trivial matters.

adolescent *adj* between childhood and maturity; (*inf*) immature. • *n* an adolescent person.—**adolescence** *n*.

adopt *vt* to take legally into one's family; to take as one's own.—**adoption** *n*.

adore *vt* to worship; to love deeply.

adorn *vt* to decorate.—**adornment** *n*.

adrenalin(e) *n* a hormone that stimulates the heart rate, etc, in response to stress.

adrift *adj, adv* floating, drifting free.

adroit *adj* skilful, clever.—**adroitness** *n*.

adult *adj* fully grown; mature; suitable only for adults. • *n* a mature person, etc.

adulterate *vt* to make impure by adding an improper substance.—**adulteration** *n*.

adultery *n* sexual unfaithfulness of a married person.—**adulterous** *adj*.

advance *vt* to bring or move forward; to promote; (*money*) to lend. • *vi* to go forward; to make progress; to rise in rank, etc. • *n* progress; improvement; payment beforehand; (*pl*) friendly approaches.

advanced *adj* in front; old; superior.

advancement *n* promotion to a higher rank; progress in development.

advantage *n* superiority of position or condition; (*tennis*) the first point won after deuce.

advantageous *adj* beneficial.

advent *n* an arrival or coming.

adventure *n* a strange or exciting undertaking.—**adventurous** *adj*.

adventurer *n* a person who seeks adventure.

adverb *n* a word that modifies and indicates how, why, where, etc.—**adverbial** *adj*.

adversary *n* an enemy or opponent.

adverse *adj* hostile; contrary, unfavourable.

adversity *n* trouble, misery, misfortune.

advertise *vti* to call attention to, esp to sell, by way of the media, etc.—**advertiser** *n*.—**advertising** *n*.

advertisement *n* advertising; a public notice promoting goods or a service.

advice *n* recommendation; formal notice.

advisable *adj* prudent.—**advisability** *n*.

advise *vt* to give advice to; to recommend; to inform. • *vi* to give advice.—**adviser** *n*.

advisory *adj* having or exercising the power to advise; containing or giving advice.

advocate *n* one who argues or defends the cause of another, esp in a court of law; a supporter. • *vt* to plead in favour of.

aegis *n* protection, sponsorship.

aerial *adj* of or existing in the air; of aircraft or flying. • *n* a radio or TV antenna.

aeroplane *n* a power-driven aircraft.

aerosol *n* a suspension of fine solid or liquid particles in gas, held in a container under pressure, with a device for releasing it in a fine spray.

aesthetics *n* the philosophy of art and beauty. —**aesthetic** *adj*.

affable *adj* friendly; approachable.—**affability** *n*.

affair *n* a thing done or to be done; (*pl*) public or private business; (*inf*) an event; a temporary romantic or sexual relationship.

affect[1] *vt* to produce a change in; to act in a way that alters the feelings of.

affect[2] *vt* to pretend or feign (an emotion).

affectation *n* a striving or attempt to assume what is not natural or real; pretence.

affected *adj* (*manner, etc*) assumed artificially.

affection *n* tender feeling; liking.

affectionate *adj* showing liking, loving.

affiliate *vt* to connect; to adopt; to associate (oneself with). • *vi* to join. —**affiliation** *n*.

affinity *n* attraction, liking; a relationship, esp by marriage; similarity; (*chem*) a tendency in certain substances to combine.

affirmation *n* affirming; an assertion; a solemn declaration made by those declining to swear an oath, e.g. on religious grounds.

affix *vt* to fasten; to add; to attach.

afflict *vt* to cause persistent pain or suffering to; to trouble greatly.—**affliction** *n*.

affluent *adj* rich.—**affluence** *n*.

afford *vt* to be able to do or bear easily; to have enough time, money or resources for; to supply.

affront *vt* to insult or offend.—*also n*.

afield *adv* far from home; to, at a distance.

afloat *adj* floating; at sea, on board a ship.

afraid *adj* full of fear; regretful.

afresh *adv* anew, starting again.

aft *adv* at, near or toward the stern.

after *prep* behind; later than; in pursuit of; in imitation of; in view of. • *adv* later. • *conj* at a time later than.

aftermath *n* an (unpleasant) result.

afternoon *n* the time between noon and sunset.

aftershave *n* a lotion for use after shaving.

afterthought *n* a thought occurring later.

afterwards *adv* at a later time.

again *adv* once more; besides.

against *prep* in opposition to; unfavourable to; in contrast to; in preparation for; in contact with.

age *n* the period of time during which someone or something has existed; a stage of life; later years of life; a historical or geological period; (*inf: often pl*) a long time. • *vti* to grow or make old.

aged *adj* very old; of a specified age.

agency *n* action; power; means; a firm, etc, empowered to act for another.

agenda *n* a list of items or matters of business that need to be attended to.

agent *n* a person or thing that acts or has an influence; a substance or organism that is active; one empowered to act for another; a spy.

aggravate *vt* to make worse; (*inf*) to annoy, irritate.—**aggravation** *n*.

aggregate *adj* formed of parts combined into a mass or whole; taking all units as a whole. • *n* a collection or sum of individual parts; sand, stones, etc, mixed with cement to form concrete. • *vt* to collect or form into a mass or whole.

aggression *n* an unprovoked attack.

aggressive *adj* boldly hostile; quarrelsome; self-assertive.—**aggressiveness** *n*.

aghast *adj* utterly horrified.

agile *adj* quick and nimble.—**agility** *n*.

agitate *vt* to shake; to disturb the mind of. • *vi* to stir up interest for a cause.—**agitation** *n*.

ago *adv* in the past. • *adj* gone by; past.

agony *n* extreme suffering.

agree *vi* to be of similar opinion; to consent (to); to come to an understanding about; to suit one's digestion; • *vt* to concede, grant.

agreeable *adj* likeable, pleasing; willing.

agreement *n* harmony in thought or opinion, correspondence; an agreed settlement.

agriculture *n* the practice of producing crops and raising livestock.—**agricultural** *adj*.

aground *adv* on or onto the shore.

ahead *adv* in or to the front; forward; onward.

aid *vti* to help, to assist. • *n* help; a specific means of assistance, e.g. money; a helper.

AIDS, Aids *n* (acquired immune deficiency syndrome) a condition caused by a virus, in which the body loses its immunity to infection.

ailment *n* a slight illness.

aim *vti* to point or direct towards; to direct (one's efforts); to intend.—*also n*.

air *n* the mixture of gases surrounding the earth; the atmosphere; empty, open space; a breeze; appearance, demeanour; (*mus*) a melody; (*pl*) an affected manner. • *vt* to expose to the air for drying, etc; to make public.

airborne *adj* carried by or through the air.

air conditioning *n* regulation of air humidity and temperature in buildings, etc.

air-cooled *adj* cooled by having air passed over.

aircraft *n* any machine for travelling through air.

aircraft carrier *n* a warship with a large flat deck for carrying aircraft.

airgun *n* a gun that fires pellets by compressed air.

air letter *n* a sheet of light writing paper folded and sealed to send by airmail.

airline *n* a system or company for transportation by aircraft.

airlock *n* a blockage in a pipe caused by an air bubble; an airtight compartment giving access to a pressurised chamber.

airmail *n* mail transported by aircraft.

airport *n* a place where aircraft can land and take off, with facilities for repair, etc.

air raid *n* an attack by military aircraft on a surface target.

airship *n* a self-propelled steerable aircraft that is lighter than air.

airstrip *n* an area of land cleared for aircraft to land on; a runway.

airtight *adj* too tight for air or gas to enter or escape; (*alibi, etc*) invulnerable.

airy *adj* open to the air; breezy; light as air; graceful; lighthearted; flippant.—**airiness** *n*.

aisle *n* a passageway, as between rows of seats; a side part of a church.

ajar *adv* partly open, as a door.

alarm *n* an automatic device to arouse from sleep or to attract attention; sudden fright. • *vt* to frighten.

album *n* a book with blank pages for photographs, etc; a record, cassette or CD.

alchemy *n* chemistry as practised during medieval times, with the aim of transmuting base metals into gold.—**alchemist** *n*.

alcohol *n* a liquid, made by distillation and fermentation forming the intoxicant in wine, spirits; a liquid containing alcohol.

alcoholic *adj* of or containing alcohol. • *n* a person overdependent on alcohol.—**alcoholism** *n*.

alcove *n* a recess off a larger room.

ale *n* beer.

alert *adj* watchful; active, brisk. • *n* a danger signal. • *vt* to warn of impending danger.

algebra *n* the branch of mathematics dealing with the properties and relations of numbers.

alias *n* an assumed name.

alibi *n* (*law*) the plea that a person charged with a crime was elsewhere when it was committed.

alien *adj* foreign; strange. • *n* a person of foreign birth who has not been naturalised; a being from outer space.

alienate *vt* to make hostile, unfriendly.

alight[1] *vi* to come down, as from a bus; to descend after a flight.

alight[2] *adj* on fire; lively.

align *vt* to place in a straight line, to bring into agreement, etc. • *vi* to line up.—**alignment** *n*.

alike *adj* like. • *adv* equally; similarly.

alimony *n* an allowance made by a man to his (former) wife after a legal separation.

alive *adj* having life; active, alert; in existence.

alkali *n* (*chem*) any salt or mixture that neutralises acids.—**alkaline** *adj*.

all *adj* the whole amount or number of; every one of. • *adv* wholly; completely. • *n* the whole; everyone; everything.

allay *vt* to lighten, alleviate; to pacify.

allege *vt* to assert or declare, esp without proof. —**allegation** *n*.—**allegedly** *adv*.

allegiance *n* loyalty to country or cause.

allegory *n* a story, etc, used to convey a deeper, meaning.—**allegorical** *adj*.

allergy *n* an abnormal reaction of the body to a harmless substance.—**allergic** *adj*.

alleviate *vt* to lessen or relieve (pain, etc).

alley *n* a narrow street between or behind buildings; a bowling lane.

alliance *n* a union by marriage or treaty; the countries, groups in such an association.

alligator *n* a large reptile similar to the crocodile.

allocate *vt* to distribute in shares; to set apart for a purpose.—**allocation** *n*.

allot *vt* to distribute, allocate.

allotment *n* allotting; a share allotted; a small area of land rented for cultivation.

allow *vt* to permit; to admit as true. • *vi* to admit as possible.

allowance *n* a sum allowed; a discount; income not subject to income tax.

alloy *n* a mixture of two or more metals. • *vt* to make into an alloy.

allude *vi* to refer indirectly to.

allure *vt* to charm. • *n* charm.—**alluring** *adj*.

allusion *n* an implied or indirect reference.

ally *vti* to unite for a specific purpose. • *n* a country or person joined with another for a common purpose.

almighty *adj* all-powerful. • *n* (*with cap*) God.

almond *n* the kernel of the fruit of a tree of the rose family; the tree bearing it. • *adj* (*eyes*) oval and pointed at one or both ends.

almost *adv* all but, nearly but not quite all.

alms *npl* money, food, etc, given to the poor.

alone *adj* isolated; solitary; unassisted; unique. • *adv* exclusively.

along *adv* forward; over the length of; in addition. • *prep* in the direction of the length of.

aloof *adj* cool and reserved.—**aloofness** *n*.

aloud *adv* with a normal voice; loudly.

alphabet *n* the characters used in a language arranged in conventional order.—**alphabetical** *adj*.

alpine *adj* of the Alps. • *n* a mountain plant.

already *adv* by or before the time specified.

also *adv* in addition, besides.

altar *n* a table, etc, for sacred purposes in a place of worship.

alter *vti* to make or become different in a small way; to change.—**alteration** *n*.

alternate[1] *vt* to do or use by turns. • *vi* to act, happen, etc, by turns; to take turns regularly.

alternate[2] *adj* occurring in turns.

alternating current *n* an electric current that reverses its direction at regular intervals.

alternative *adj* presenting a choice between two things. • *n* either of two possibilities.

alternator *n* an electric generator that produces alternating current.

although *conj* though; in spite of that.

altitude *n* height, esp above sea level.

alto *n* the range of the highest male voice; a singer with this range.

altogether *adv* in all; completely.

aluminium *n* a light, silvery-white malleable metallic element.

always *adv* at all times; forever.

a.m. *abbr* = *ante meridiem*, before noon.

amalgamate *vt* to combine, unite.—**amalgamation** *n*.

amass *vt* to bring together in a large quantity; to accumulate.

amateur *n* one who engages in a particular activity as a hobby. • *adj* of amateurs.

amateurish *adj* lacking expertise.

amaze *vt* to fill with wonder, astonish.—**amazement** *n*.—**amazing** *adj*.

ambassador *n* a high-ranking diplomatic representative from one country to another.

amber *n* a hard yellowish fossil resin, used for jewellery, etc; its colour; a yellow traffic light used to signal 'caution'.

ambiguous *adj* capable of two or more interpretations; vague.—**ambiguity** *n*.

ambition *n* desire for power, wealth, success; an object of ambition.—**ambitious** *adj*.

amble *vi* to walk in a leisurely way.

ambulance *n* a special vehicle for transporting the sick or injured.

ambush *n* concealment to make a surprise attack. • *vti* to attack from an ambush.

amenable *adj* easily influenced or led.

amend *vt* to remove errors, esp in a text; to modify, improve; to alter in minor details.

amendment *n* the act of amending, correction; an alteration to a document, etc.

amends *npl* compensation for some loss, harm, etc.

amenity *n* pleasantness, as regards situation or convenience.

amethyst *n* a bluish-violet gemstone.

amiable *adj* friendly in manner, congenial.

amicable *adj* friendly; peaceable.

amid(st) *prep* in the middle of; during.

amiss *adj* wrong, improper.—*also adv*.

ammunition *n* bullets, shells, rockets; etc; any means of attack or defence.

amnesia *n* a partial or total loss of memory.

amnesty *n* a general pardon.

among(st) *prep* in the number of, surrounded by; in the group or class of.

amoral *adj* without moral sense.

amorous *adj* displaying or feeling love.

amorphous *adj* lacking a specific shape.

amount *vi* to be equivalent (to) in total, quantity

or significance. • *n* the total sum; the whole value or effect; a quantity.

ampere *n* the standard SI unit by which an electric current is measured.

amphibious *adj* living on both land and water.

amphitheatre *n* an oval or circular building with rising rows of seats round an arena.

ample *adj* large in size, scope, etc; plentiful.

amplifier *n* a device that increases electric voltage, current, power or loudness.

amplify *vt* to expand more fully, add details to; (*electrical signals, etc*) to strengthen.

amputate *vt* to cut off, esp by surgery.—**amputation** *n*.

amuse *vt* to entertain pleasantly; to cause to laugh or smile.—**amusement** *n*.

an *adj* the indefinite article ('a') used before words beginning with the sound of a vowel.

anaemia *n* a condition in which the blood is low in red cells or haemoglobin, resulting in paleness, weakness, etc.—**anaemic** *adj*.

anaesthetic *n* a drug, gas, etc, that produces insensibility. • *adj* of, producing insensibility.

anaesthetist *n* one who gives anaesthetics.

analogy *n* a similarity or correspondence in certain respects between two things.

analyse *vt* to separate (something) into its components to investigate it; to examine in detail.—**analysis** *n*.—**analytic(al)** *adj*.

analyst *n* a person who analyses; a psychoanalyst.

anarchist *n* one who believes all government is unnecessary.—**anarchism** *n*.

anarchy *n* absence of government; political confusion; lawlessness.—**anarchic** *adj*.

anathema *n* anything greatly detested.

anatomy *n* the science of the physical structure of plants and animals; the dissection of a body.—**anatomical** *adj*.

ancestor *n* one from whom a person is descended, a forefather; something regarded as a forerunner.—**ancestral** *adj*.

ancestry *n* ancestors collectively; lineage.

anchor *n* a heavy metal implement that lodges at the bottom of the sea to hold a ship in position. • *vt* to fix by an anchor; to secure firmly.

anchorage *n* a safe anchoring place for ships.

anchovy *n* a small Mediterranean fish resembling a herring with a very salty taste.

ancient *adj* very old; old-fashioned.

and *conj* in addition to; together with; plus.

anecdote *n* a short entertaining account about an event or person.

anew *adv* afresh; again, once more.

angel *n* a messenger of God; an image of a human figure with wings and a halo; a very beautiful or kind person.—**angelic** *adj*.

anger *n* strong displeasure, often because of opposition, a hurt, etc.—*also vti*.

angina *n* sharp stabbing pains in the chest.

angle[1] *n* a corner; the point from which two lines or planes extend or diverge; a specific viewpoint. • *vt* to bend, move or place at an angle; to present news, etc, from a particular point of view.

angle[2] *vi* to fish with a hook and line; to use hints, etc, to get something.—**angler** *n*.

Anglican *adj* belonging to or of the Church of England.—**Anglicanism** *n*.

angry *adj* full of anger; inflamed.—**angrily** *adv*.

anguish *n* intense distress; agony.

angular *adj* having one or more angles; forming an angle; thin and bony.—**angularity** *n*.

animal *n* any living organism except a plant or bacterium, typically able to move about; a lower animal as distinguished from man, esp mammals; a brutish or bestial person. • *adj* of or like an animal; bestial; sensual.

animate *vt* to give life to; to liven up; to inspire.

animosity *n* strong dislike; hostility.

aniseed *n* the seed of the anise plant, used as a flavouring.

ankle *n* the joint between the foot and leg.

annex *vt* to attach, esp to something larger; to incorporate into a state the territory of (another state).—**annexation** *n*.

annihilate *vt* to destroy, defeat completely.—**annihilation** *n*.

anniversary *n* the yearly return of the date of an event; its celebration.—*also adj*.

annotate *vti* to provide with explanatory notes.—**annotation** *n*.

announce *vt* to bring to public attention.—**announcement** *n*.—**announcer** *n*.

annoy *vt* to vex, irritate.—**annoyance** *n*.

annual *adj* of or measured by a year; coming every year; living only one year. • *n* a plant that lives only one year; a yearly publication.

annuity *n* an investment yielding fixed payments, esp yearly; such a payment.

annul *vt* to cancel; to deprive of legal force, nullify.—**annulment** *n*.

anoint *vt* to rub with oil; to apply oil as a sign of consecration.

anomaly *n* abnormality; anything inconsistent or odd.—**anomalous** *adj*.

anonymous *adj* nameless; written or provided by an unnamed person.—**anonymity** *n*.

anorak *n* a waterproof jacket with a hood.

another *adj* a different (thing or person); one more of the same kind.—*also pron*.

answer *n* a spoken or written reply; a solution; a reaction, response. • *vt* to speak, write in reply; to satisfy (a specific need). • *vi* to reply; to be responsible (for).—**answerable** *adj*.

ant *n* any of a family of small insects living in highly organised groups.

antagonise *vt* to arouse opposition in.

antagonism *n* antipathy, hostility.

antagonist *n* an adversary; an opponent.—**antagonistic** *adj*.

Antarctic *adj* of the South Pole, its surroundings or Ocean.

antelope *n* a fast-running graceful deer-like animal of Africa and Asia.

antenatal *adj* before birth.

antenna *n* either of a pair of feelers on the head of an insect, crab, etc; an aerial.

anthem *n* a song of devotion, as to a nation.

anthill *n* a mound thrown up by ants.

anthology *n* a collection of poetry or prose.

anthropology *n* the scientific study of human beings.—**anthropological** *adj*.—**anthropologist** *n*.

antibiotic *n* any substance used against bacterial or fungal infections.

anticipate *vt* to give prior thought and attention to; to act on in advance; to foresee; to thwart; to expect.—**anticipation** *n*.

anticlimax *n* a sudden drop from the important to the trivial; a disappointing ending to a story.

anticyclone *n* a body of air rotating about an area of high atmospheric pressure.

antidote *n* a remedy that counteracts a poison.

antifreeze *n* a substance used, as in car radiator, to prevent freezing up.

antipathy *n* a fixed dislike; aversion.

antiquated *adj* old-fashioned; obsolete.

antique *adj* from the distant past; old-fashioned. • *n* a relic of the distant past; a piece of furniture, pottery, etc, from an earlier time.

antiquity *n* the far distant past; (*pl*) relics dating from the far distant past.

antiseptic *n* a substance that destroys or halts disease-producing microorganisms.—*also adj*.

antisocial *adj* unsocial; contrary to the interests of society in general.

antler *n* the branched horn of a deer.

anus *n* the excretory orifice of the alimentary canal.

anvil *n* the heavy iron block on which metal objects are shaped with a hammer.

anxiety *n* the state of being worried; eagerness, concern; a cause of worry.—**anxious** *adj*.

any *adj* one out of many, some; every.

anybody *pron* any person.

anyhow *adv* in any way; in any case.

anyone *pron* any person; anybody.

anything *pron* any object, event, fact, etc.

anyway *adv* in any manner; at any rate.

anywhere *adv* in, at or to any place.

apart *adv* at a distance, separately, aside; into two or more pieces.

apartheid *n* a policy of racial segregation formerly implemented in South Africa.

apartment n room(s) in a building; a flat.

apathy n lack of feeling.—**apathetic** adj.

ape n any large monkey; a mimic. • vt to imitate.

apéritif n an alcoholic drink taken before a meal.

aperture n an opening; a hole.

apex n the highest point, the tip.

aphrodisiac adj arousing sexually. • n a food, drug, etc, that excites sexual desire.

aplomb n poise; self-possession.

apologetic adj contrite; presented in defence.

apologise vi to make an apology.

apology n an expression of regret for wrongdoing; a defence or justification of one's beliefs, etc; (with for) a poor substitute.

apoplexy n a sudden loss of consciousness and subsequent partial paralysis, usu caused by a broken or blocked artery in the brain.

apostle n the first supporter of a new belief.

apostrophe n a mark (') showing the omission of letters, also a sign of the possessive case.

appal vt to fill with terror or dismay.—**appalling** adj.

apparatus n the equipment, machines used for a specific task.

apparent adj easily seen, evident; seeming.

apparition n an appearance or manifestation.

appeal vi to take a case to a higher court; to make an earnest request; to arouse pleasure or sympathy. • n the referral of a lawsuit to a higher court for rehearing; the power of attracting; a request for donations to a charity.

appear vi to become visible; to arrive; to seem.

appearance n the act or occasion of appearing; external aspect of a thing or person.

appease vt to pacify; to allay.

appendage n an external part, as a tail.

appendicitis n inflammation of the appendix that grows from the intestine.

appendix n supplementary information at the back of a book, etc; a small tube of outgrowth of the intestine.

appetising adj stimulating the appetite.

appetite n sensation of bodily desire, esp for food; (with for) a strong desire or liking.

applaud vt to show approval, esp by clapping the hands; to praise.—**applause** n.

apple n a round, firm, fleshy, edible fruit.

appliance n a device for household use.

applicable adj appropriate, relevant (to).

applicant n one who applies for a job.

application n the act of applying; diligent effort; (comput) a program.

apply vt to put to practical use; to spread, lay on; to devote (oneself). • vi to make a formal request; to be relevant.

appoint vt to decide officially; to select for a job.

appraise vt to estimate the value or quality of.—**appraisal** n.

appreciable adj capable of being perceived.

appreciate vt to value highly; to recognise gratefully; to understand, be aware of. • vi to rise in value.

appreciation n gratitude, approval; sensitivity to aesthetic values; an assessment of a person or thing; an increase in value.—**appreciative** adj.

apprehend vt to arrest, capture; to understand.

apprehension n anxiety; the act of arresting.

apprehensive adj uneasy; anxious.

apprentice n one being taught a trade or craft.—**apprenticeship** n.

approach vi to draw nearer. • vt to make a proposal to; to set about dealing with; to come near to. • n the act of approaching; a means of entering or leaving; a move to establish relations.—**approachable** adj.

appropriate adj fitting, suitable. • vt to take, esp illegally; to set aside for a purpose.

approval n favourable opinion; permission.

approve vt to express a good opinion of; to authorise. • vi (with of) to consider to be favourable.

approximate adj almost exact or correct. • vi to come close.

approximation n an estimate; a likeness.

apricot n a small, oval orange-pink fruit resembling the plum and peach.

apron n a garment worn to protect clothing; the paved surface on an airfield where aircraft are parked, etc.

apt adj ready or likely (to); suitable, relevant; able to learn easily.—**aptness** n.

aptitude n suitability; natural talent for.

aqualung n portable diving gear comprising air cylinders connected to a face mask.

aquarium n a tank for aquatic animals or plants; a building to exhibit collections of these.

aquatic adj done, living, growing in water.

aqueduct n a large pipe or conduit for carrying water; a bridge supporting this.

arable adj (land) suitable for ploughing or planting crops.

arbitrary adj not bound by rules; capricious, unreasonable.—**arbitrarily** adv.

arbitrate vti to act as an umpire or referee, esp in a dispute.—**arbitrator** n.

arbitration n the settlement of disputes by arbitrating.

arc n a portion of the circumference of a circle or other curve; a luminous discharge of electricity across a gap between two electrodes or terminals.

arcade n a covered area lined with shops.

arch¹ n a curved structure spanning an opening; the curved underside of the foot. • vti to span or cover with an arch; to curve, bend into an arch.

arch² adj (criminal, etc) principal, expert; clever, sly; mischievous.

archaeology n the study of past human societies through their extant remains.—**archaeological** adj.—**archaeologist** n.

archaic adj (language) no longer in common use.

archbishop n a bishop of the highest rank.

archer n a person who shoots with a bow and arrow.—**archery** n.

archetype n the original pattern or model; a prototype.—**archetypal** adj.

archipelago n a group of islands.

architect n a person who designs buildings; someone who plans something.

architecture n the art, profession or science of designing and constructing buildings; the style of a building or buildings.—**architectural** adj.

archives npl the location in which public records are kept; public records.

archway n an arched or vaulted passage.

arctic adj (often with cap) of, near or relating to the North Pole; (inf) very cold, icy.

ardent adj passionate; zealous.

arduous adj difficult, laborious, steep.

area n a total outside surface, measured in square units; a part of a district, etc.

arena n an area within a sports stadium, etc, where events take place; a sphere of contest.

arguable adj debatable; doubtful.

argue vt to try to prove by reasoning; to persuade (into, out of). • vi to offer reasons; to disagree, dispute.

argument n a disagreement; a debate, discussion; a reason offered in debate.

arid adj very dry, parched; dull.—**aridity** n.

arise vi to get up, to rise; to come into being.

aristocracy n (a country with) a government dominated by a privileged minority class; the nobility.

aristocrat n a member of the aristocracy; a nobleman or woman.—**aristocratic** adj.

arithmetic n (math) computation (addition, subtraction, etc) using real numbers; calculation.—**arithmetic(al)** adj.—**arithmetically** adv.

ark n (Bible) Noah's vessel; an enclosure in a synagogue for the scrolls of the Torah.

arm¹ n the upper limb from shoulder to wrist; something arm-shaped, as a support on a chair; an administrative division of an organisation.

arm² n (usu pl) weapon(s); (pl) heraldic bearings. • vt to provide with weapons, etc; to provide with something that protects or strengthens, etc.

armchair n a chair with side rests for the arms. • adj lacking practical experience.

armistice n a truce, preliminary to peace.

armour n any defensive covering.

armpit n the hollow underneath the arm.

army n a large organised body of soldiers for waging war; any large number.

aroma n a pleasant smell.—**aromatic** adj.

around prep on all sides of; in various places in or on; approximately. • adv in a circle; in every direction; to the opposite direction.

arouse vt to awaken; to stir; to evoke.

arrange vt to put in a sequence or row; to settle, make preparations for; (mus) to adapt a composition for different instruments. • vi to come to an agreement; to make plans.—**arrangement** n.

array n an orderly grouping, esp of troops; an impressive display; fine clothes; (comput) an ordered data structure that allows information to be easily indexed. • vt to arrange; to dress.

arrears npl overdue debts; work still to do.

arrest vt to stop; to apprehend by legal authority; to catch the attention of. • n a stoppage; seizure by legal authority.

arrive vi to reach any destination; to come; to achieve success.—**arrival** n.

arrogant adj overbearing; aggressively self-important.—**arrogance** n.

arrow n a pointed weapon to shoot from a bow; a sign to indicate direction.

arsenal n a store for weapons and ammunition.

arsenic n a soft grey metallic element, highly poisonous.

arson n the crime of using fire to destroy property deliberately.—**arsonist** n.

art n human creativity; skill acquired by study and experience; any craft and its principles; the making of things that have form and beauty; any branch of this, as painting, sculpture, etc; drawings, paintings, statues, etc; (pl) the creative and nonscientific branches of knowledge.

artefact n a product of human craftsmanship, e.g. a tool.—also **artifact**.

artery n a tubular vessel that conveys blood from the heart; a main channel of transport, communication.—**arterial** adj.

artful adj skilful at attaining one's ends; crafty.—**artfulness** n.

arthritis n painful inflammation of a joint. —**arthritic** adj.

artichoke n a thistle-like edible plant with a scaly flower head.

article n a separate clause in a document; an item on a particular subject in a newspaper, etc; a particular item; (gram) a word placed before a noun to identify it as definite or indefinite.

articulate adj capable of expressing one's thoughts clearly; jointed. • vti to speak or express clearly; to unite (as) by a joint.

artificial adj man-made.—**artificiality** n.

artillery n large, heavy guns.

artisan n a skilled workman.

artist n one who practises fine art, esp painting; a skilled person.—**artistic** adj.—**artistically** adv.

artistry n artistic quality, ability, work, etc.

artless adj simple, natural; without art or skill.—**artlessness** n.

as adv equally; for instance; when related in a certain way. • conj in the same way that; while; because. • prep in the role of.

asbestos n a fibrous, non-burning mineral.

ascend vti to go up; to succeed to (a throne).

ascendancy, **ascendency** n dominance.

ascent n ascending; an upward slope.

ascertain vt to acquire definite knowledge of.

ascetic adj self-denying, austere. • n a person who practises rigorous self-denial as a religious discipline; any severely abstemious person.

ascribe vt to attribute.—**ascribable** adj.

ash[1] n a tree with silver-grey bark; its wood.

ash[2] n powdery residue of anything burnt.

ashamed adj feeling shame or guilt.

ashen adj like ashes, esp in colour; pale.

ashore adv to or on the shore or land.

aside adv on or to the side; in reserve. • n words uttered and intended as inaudible, esp as spoken by an actor to the audience only.

ask vt to question, inquire of; to request; to invite. • vi to inquire about.

askance adv with a sideways glance.

askew adv to one side; awry.—also adj.

asleep adj, adv sleeping; inactive.

asparagus n a plant cultivated for its edible young shoots.

aspect n the look of a person or thing; a particular feature of a problem, situation, etc; the direction something faces.

aspersions npl slander; an attack on a person's reputation.

asphalt n a hard, black bituminous substance, used for paving roads, etc.

asphyxiate vt to suffocate.—**asphyxiation** n.

aspiration n strong desire; ambition; breathing.

aspire vi to desire eagerly; to aim high.

aspirin n a pain-relieving drug.

ass n a donkey; a silly, stupid person.

assail vt to attack.—**assailant** n.

assassin n a murderer, esp one hired to kill.

assassinate vt to kill (a political figure); to harm (a reputation).—**assassination** n.

assault n a violent attack. • vti to make an assault (on).

assemble vti to bring together; to collect; to fit together the parts of.

assembly n assembling; a gathering; the fitting together to make a whole.

assent vi to consent, agree to.—also n.

assert vt to declare, affirm as true; to maintain or enforce (e.g. rights).—**assertion** n.

assertive adj self-assured, confident.

assess vt to establish the amount of, as a tax; to estimate the worth of.—**assessment** n.

asset n anything owned of value; a desirable thing; (pl) all property, accounts receivable.

assign vt to allot; to appoint to a post or duty; (law) to transfer (a right, property, etc).

assignment n the act of assigning; something assigned, such as a share, task, etc.

assimilate vt to absorb; to digest; to be ascribed; to be like.—**assimilation** n.

assist vti to aid.—**assistance** n.—**assistant** n.

associate vt to join as a friend, partner; to connect in the mind. • vi to come together as friends, partners. • adj connected; having secondary status. • n a companion, partner, etc; a person admitted to an organisation as a subordinate member.—**association** n.

assorted adj miscellaneous.

assortment n a collection of people or things of different sorts.

assume vt to undertake; to usurp; to take as true; to pretend to possess.—**assumption** n.

assurance n a promise; life insurance; confidence.

assure vt to make safe or certain; to give confidence to; to state positively; to ensure.

asterisk n a sign (*) in printing to mark omission of words, etc.

astern adv behind a ship; backwards.

asthma n a chronic respiratory condition causing difficulty with breathing.—**asthmatic** adj.

astir adv moving about; out of bed.

astonish vt to fill with great surprise.—**astonishing** adj.—**astonishment** n.

astound vt to astonish.—**astounding** adj.

astray adv off the right path; into error.

astride adv with a leg on either side. • prep extending across.

astrology n the study of planetary positions and motions to determine their supposed influence on human affairs.—**astrologer** n.

astronaut n one trained to make flights in outer space.

astronomy n the scientific study of the stars and other planets.—**astronomer** n.

astute adj crafty; shrewd.—**astuteness** n.

asylum n a place of safety, a refuge; (formerly) a home for the mentally ill, etc.

at prep on; in; near; by; used to indicate location.

atheism n belief in the nonexistence of God.

athlete n one trained in games or exercises requiring skill, speed, strength, etc.—**athletic** adj.

athletics n (used as sing or pl) running, jumping, throwing sports, games, etc.

atlas n a book of maps, charts, tables.

atmosphere n the gaseous mixture that surrounds the earth or the other stars and planets; any dominant or surrounding influence.—**atmospheric** adj.

atom *n* the smallest particle of a chemical element; a tiny particle, bit.

atomic bomb *n* a bomb with explosive power derived from the atomic energy released during nuclear fission or fusion.

atomiser *n* a device for spraying liquids.

atone *vi* to give satisfaction or make amends.

atrocious *adj* extremely brutal or wicked; (*inf*) very bad, of poor quality.

atrocity *n* a cruel act; wickedness.

attach *vt* to fix, fasten to something; to appoint to a specific group. • *vi* to become attached.

attack *vt* to set upon violently; to assault in speech or writing. • *vi* to make an assault. • *n* an assault; a fit of illness; severe criticism.

attain *vt* to succeed in getting or arriving at; to achieve.—**attainable** *adj*.

attainment *n* an accomplishment.

attempt *vt* to try to accomplish, get, etc. • *n* an endeavour; an attack.

attend *vt* to take care of; to go with; to be present at. • *vi* to deal with.

attendance *n* attending; the people present; the times a person attends.

attendant *n* a person who serves another. • *adj* accompanying, following as a result.

attention *n* the application of the mind to a purpose, aim, etc; awareness, notice; care, consideration; (*usu pl*) an act of courtesy.

attentive *adj* observant, diligent; courteous.

attest *vt* to state as true; to certify, as by oath; to give proof of. • *vi* to testify, bear witness (to).

attic *n* the room or space under the roof.

attire *vt* to clothe; to dress up. • *n* dress.

attitude *n* posture; a manner of thought or feeling; the position of aircraft or spacecraft in relation to certain points.

attorney *n* one legally authorised to act for another; a lawyer.

attract *vt* to pull towards; to get the admiration, attention of. • *vi* to be attractive.

attraction *n* the act of attraction; the power of attracting, esp charm; (*physics*) the mutual action by which bodies tend to be drawn together.

attractive *adj* pleasing in appearance, etc; arousing interest; able to draw or pull.

attribute *vt* to regard as belonging to; to ascribe. • *n* a quality, a characteristic of.—**attributable** *adj*.—**attribution** *n*.

attrition *n* a grinding down by or as by friction; a relentless wearing down.

aubergine *n* the dark purple fruit of the egg plant used as a vegetable; its colour.

auburn *adj* reddish brown.

auction *n* a public sale of items to the highest bidder. • *vt* to sell at an auction.

audacious *adj* daring; bold.—**audacity** *n*.

audible *adj* able to be heard.—**audibility** *n*.

audience *n* a gathering of listeners or spectators; a formal interview or meeting.

audiovisual *adj* using both sound and vision.

audit *n* the inspection and verification of business accounts by an accountant.—*also vt to* make such an inspection.

audition *n* a trial to test a performer.—*also vti*.

auditor *n* a person qualified to audit business accounts.

auditorium *n* the part of a building allotted to the audience; a hall for concerts, etc.

augment *vti* to increase.—**augmentation** *n*.

augur *vti* to prophesy; to be an omen (of).

august *adj* imposing; majestic.

aunt *n* a father's or mother's sister, an uncle's wife.

au pair *n* a person, esp a girl, from abroad who performs domestic chores, child-minding, etc, in return for board and lodging.

aura *n* a particular quality or atmosphere surrounding a person or thing.

auspice *n* an omen; (*pl*) sponsorship.

auspicious *adj* favourable.

austere *adj* stern, forbidding; abstemious; severely simple, plain.—**austerity** *n*.

authentic *adj* genuine; trustworthy, reliable.—**authenticity** *n*.

author *n* the writer of a book, etc.

authorise *vt* to give authority to, to empower; to give official approval to.—**authorisation** *n*.

authoritarian *adj* favouring strict obedience.

authoritative *adj* commanding or possessing authority; accepted as true; official.

authority *n* the power or right to command; (*pl*) officials with this power; influence because of knowledge, prestige, etc; an expert.

autobiography *n* the biography of a person written by himself or herself.—**autobiographer** *n*.—**autobiographical** *adj*.

autocrat *n* an absolute ruler; any domineering person.—**autocratic** *adj*.—**autocratically** *adv*.

autograph *n* one's signature. • *vt* to sign.

automatic *adj* involuntary or reflexive; self-regulating; acting by itself. • *n* an automatic pistol or rifle.

automation *n* the use of automatic methods, machinery, etc, in industry.

automaton *n* a robot.

automobile *n* a motor car.

autonomy *n* independence, self-government.

autopsy *n* a post-mortem examination.

autumn *n* the season between summer and winter.—**autumnal** *adj*.

auxiliary *adj* providing help, subsidiary; supplementary. • *n* a helper; (*gram*) a verb that helps form tenses, moods, voices, etc, of other verbs.

avail *vti* to be of use or advantage to. • *n* benefit.

available *adj* obtainable, accessible.—**availability** *n*.

avalanche n a mass of snow, ice and rock tumbling down a mountainside.

avant-garde n (arts) ideas and practices regarded as in advance of those generally accepted.—also adj.

avarice n greed for wealth.—**avaricious** adj.

avenge vt to get revenge for.—**avenger** n.

avenue n a street, drive, etc, esp when broad.

average n the result of dividing the sum of two or more quantities by the number of quantities. • vt to calculate an average.

averse adj unwilling; opposed (to).

aversion n antipathy; hatred.

avert vt to turn away from; to prevent.

aviation n the art of flying aircraft.

avid adj eager, greedy.

avocado (pear) n a thick-skinned, pear-shaped fruit with yellow pulp.

avoid vt to shun; to refrain from.

await vti to wait for; to be in store for.

awake vti to waken; to become aware. • vt to rouse from sleep; to rouse from inaction. • adj not asleep.

award vt to give, as by a legal decision; to give (a prize, etc); to grant.—also n.

aware adj realising, having knowledge; conscious.—**awareness** n.

awash adj filled or overflowing with water.

away adv from a place; in another place.

awe n a mixed feeling of fear, wonder and dread. • vt to fill with awe.

awesome adj inspiring awe.

awful adj very bad; unpleasant.

awhile adv for a short time.

awkward adj lacking dexterity, clumsy; embarrassed; obstructive.

awning n a structure, as of canvas, extended above or in front of a window, door, etc, to provide shelter.

awry adv twisted to one side.

axe n a tool with a long handle and bladed head for chopping wood, etc.

axiom n a widely held or accepted truth.

axis n (pl **axes**) a straight line about which a body rotates; the centre line of a symmetrical figure; a reference line of a coordinate system.

axle n a rod on which a wheel turns; a bar connecting two opposite wheels, as of a car.

B

babble vi to talk incoherently; to murmur, as a brook. • n incoherent talk; a murmuring sound.

baby n a newborn child. • vt to pamper.

baby-sit vti to look after a baby or child while the parents are out.—**baby-sitter** n.

bachelor n an unmarried man; a person who holds a degree from a university.

bacillus n (pl **bacilli**) any of a genus of rod-shaped bacteria; (loosely) bacteria in general.

back n the rear surface of the human body from neck to hip; the corresponding part in animals; a part that supports the back; the part farthest from the front; (sport) a player or position behind the front line. • adj at the rear; of or for the past. • adv at or toward the rear; to or towards a former condition, time, etc; in return or requital; in reserve or concealment. • vti to go backwards; to support; to bet on; to provide a back for; (with down) to withdraw from; (with out) to withdraw from; (with up) to support; (comput) to make a copy for safekeeping.

backbencher n a member of parliament who does not hold an important office.

backbiting n spiteful talk behind a person's back.

backbone n the spinal column; main support; strength, courage.

backdate vt to declare valid from some previous date.

backdrop n a curtain, often scenic, at the back of a stage; background.

backer n a patron; one who bets on a contestant.

backfire vi (automobiles) to ignite prematurely causing a loud bang from the exhaust; to have the opposite effect from that intended.

backgammon n a board game for two played with dice.

background n the distant part of a picture; an inconspicuous position; social class, education, experience.

backing n support; musical accompaniment to a singer.

backlash n a violent and adverse reaction.

backlog n an accumulation of work to be done.

backpack n a rucksack; an astronaut's equipment. • vi to travel with a backpack.

back-pedal vi to modify or withdraw one's original argument or action.

backslide vi to return to one's (bad) old ways.—**backslider** n.

backstage adv behind the stage of a theatre.

backtrack vi to return along the same path; to reverse or recant one's opinion, etc.

backup n support, reinforcement; (*comput*) a copy of a data file, etc.

backward adj turned toward the rear or opposite way; shy; slow or retarded. • adv backwards.—**backwardness** n.

backwards adv towards the back; with the back foremost; in a way opposite the usual.

backwater n a remote, backward place.

bacon n salted and smoked meat from the back or sides of a pig.

bacteria npl microscopic unicellular organisms.—**bacterial** adj.

bacteriology n the study of bacteria.

bad adj not good; not as it should be; inadequate or unfit; rotten or spoiled; faulty; wicked; immoral; harmful; ill; sorry.—**badness** n.

badge n an emblem, symbol or sign.

badger n a hibernating, burrowing black and white mammal related to the weasel. • vt to pester or annoy persistently.

badminton n a court game played with light rackets and a shuttlecock over a net.

baffle vt to bewilder or perplex; to frustrate.—**baffling** adj.

bag n a container of paper, plastic, etc; a sack; a satchel, suitcase, etc; a handbag; game taken in hunting; (*inf. in pl*) plenty (of). • vti to kill in hunting; (*inf*) to get; to make a claim on; to hang loosely.

baggage n suitcases; luggage.

baggy adj hanging loosely in folds.

bagpipe n (*often pl*) a musical instrument consisting of an air-filled bag and pipes.

bail¹ n money as security that a prisoner, if released, will return to court to stand trial; such a release. • vt to free by providing bail; (*with* out) to help out financially.

bail² vti (usu *with* out) to scoop out (water) from (a boat).

bail³ n (*cricket*) either of two wooden crosspieces that rest on the stumps.

bailiff n the agent of a landlord or landowner; a sheriff's officer who serves writs and summonses.

bait n food attached to a hook to entice fish; any lure or enticement. • vt to put food on a hook to lure; to persecute, worry or tease; to lure.

bake vt (*pottery*) to dry and harden by heating in the sun or by fire; (*food*) to cook by dry heat in an oven. • vi to do a baker's work.

baker n one who bakes and sells bread, etc.

bakery n a room or building for baking; a shop that sells bread, etc.

balance n a device for weighing, consisting of two pans hanging from a pivoted beam; equilibrium; stability; a remainder. • vt to weigh; to compare; to equalise debit and credit sides of an account. • vi to be equal in power or weight, etc; to have debits and credits equal.

balance of payments n the difference between a country's total receipts from abroad and total payments abroad over a period.

balance sheet n a statement of assets and liabilities.

balance wheel n a wheel that regulates the speed of a clock or watch.

balcony n a projecting platform from an upper storey enclosed by a railing; an upper floor of seats in a theatre, etc.

bald adj lacking hair; (*tyre*) having little or no tread; (*truth*) plain or blunt.—**baldness** n.

bale n a large bundle of goods compressed and bound. • vt to make into bales. • vi (*with* out) to parachute from aircraft.

balk vi to stop and refuse to move and act.

ball¹ n a spherical body or mass; a round object for use in tennis, football, etc. • vti to form into a ball.

ball² n a formal social dance; (*inf*) a good time.—**ballroom** n.

ballad n a narrative song or poem; a slow, sentimental, esp pop, song.

ballast n heavy material carried in a ship to stabilise it.

ball bearing n a device for lessening friction by having a rotating part resting on small steel balls; one of these balls.

ballcock n a device that uses a floating ball to regulate flow of water in a cistern.

ballerina n a female ballet dancer.

ballet n a story set to music and performed by dancers; the troupe of dancers.

ballistics n (*used as sing*) the scientific study of projectiles and firearms.

balloon n a large airtight envelope that rises when filled with light gases, fitted with a basket for passengers; a small inflatable rubber pouch used as a toy or for decoration; a balloon-shaped line enclosing speech in a strip cartoon. • vti to inflate; to swell.—**balloonist** n.

ballot n a paper used in voting; the process of voting. • vi to vote.

ballot box n a container for ballot papers.

ballpoint pen n a pen with a tiny ball that rotates against an inking cartridge.

balm n a fragrant ointment used in healing and soothing; anything comforting.

balmy adj having a pleasant fragrance; soothing; mild, warm.

balsa n lightweight wood from a tropical American tree.

balsam n a fragrant, resinous substance or the tree yielding it.

bamboo n any of various, often tropical, woody grasses, used for furniture.

ban n an official prohibition. • vt to prohibit.

banal adj trite, obvious.—**banality** n.

banana n a herbaceous plant bearing its fruit in compact, hanging bunches.

band[1] n a strip of material used for binding; a stripe; (radio) a range of wavelengths.

band[2] n a group of people with a common purpose; a group of musicians.—also vti.

bandage n a strip of cloth for binding wounds, etc. • vt to bind a wound.

bandit n a robber.

bandy[1] vt (often with about) (rumours, etc) to spread freely; to exchange words angrily.

bandy[2] adj having legs curved outward at the knee.—also bandy-legged.

bang n a hard blow; a sudden loud sound. • vt to hit with a loud noise. • vi to make a loud noise. • adv with a bang, abruptly.

bangle n a bracelet for the arm or ankle.

banish vt to exile from a place; to drive away.

ban(n)ister n the railing in a staircase.

banjo n a stringed musical instrument with a drum-like body and a long fretted neck.

bank[1] n a mound or pile; the sloping side of a river; elevated ground in a lake or the sea; a row or series of objects, as of dials, switches. • vti (aircraft) to curve or tilt sideways.

bank[2] n an institution offering financial services; the money held by the banker in a card game; any supply or store. • vti (cash, etc) to deposit in a bank.—**banking** n.

banker n a person who runs a bank; the keeper of the bank at a gaming table.

bankrupt n a person, etc, legally declared unable to pay his debts.—also vt.—**bankruptcy** n.

banner n a flag; a headline running across a newspaper page.

banns npl public declaration of intention to marry.

banquet n a feast; an elaborate, formal dinner.

banter vt to tease good-humouredly.

baptise vt to christen, name.

baptism n the sprinkling of water on the forehead or immersion in water, as a rite of admittance to a Christian church.

bar[1] n a straight length of solid material; a counter where drinks are served; a public house; an oblong piece, as of soap; anything that obstructs or hinders; a band or strip; the legal profession; (mus) a vertical line dividing a staff into measures. • vt to secure as with a bar; to exclude or prevent. • prep except for.

bar[2] n a unit of atmospheric pressure.

barbecue n a metal frame for grilling food over an open fire. • vt to cook this.

barber n one who cuts hair, shaves beards.

barbiturate n a sedative drug.

bare adj naked; unadorned; mere; without furnishings. • vt to uncover.—**bareness** n.

barefaced adj shameless.

barely adv openly; merely, scarcely.

bargain n an agreement laying down conditions; something sold at a price favourable to the buyer.—also vi.

barge n a flat-bottomed vessel, used to transport freight along rivers and canals. • vi (with in) to interrupt rudely; (with into) to enter abruptly.

baritone n the male voice ranging between bass and tenor; a singer with this.

bark[1] n the harsh or abrupt cry of a dog, wolf, etc; a similar sound made by a person.—also vi.

bark[2] n the outside covering of a tree trunk. • vt (inf) to scrape; to skin (the knees, etc).

barley n a grain used in making beer and whisky, and for food.

barmaid n a female serving in a bar.

barman n a man serving in a bar.

barn n a farm building used for storing.

barnacle n a hard-shelled marine animal that adheres to rocks and ship bottoms.

barometer n an instrument for measuring atmospheric pressure and imminent changes in the weather; anything that marks change.

baron n a member of a rank of nobility, the lowest in the British peerage.

barracks n (used as sing) a building for housing soldiers.

barrage n heavy artillery fire; (of protests) continuous delivery.

barrel n a cylindrical container, usu with bulging sides held together with hoops; the amount held by a barrel; a tubular structure, as in a gun.

barrel organ n a mechanical piano or organ played by a revolving cylinder with pins that operate the keys or valves.

barren adj infertile; incapable of producing offspring; unable to bear crops.

barricade n a barrier used in defence to block a street; an obstruction.—also vt.

barrier n anything that bars passage, prevents access, controls crowds, etc.

barrister n a qualified lawyer who has been called to the bar in England.

barrow n a wheelbarrow or hand-cart.

barter vi to haggle or bargain.

base[1] n the bottom part; the support or foundation; the fundamental principle; the centre of operations; (baseball) one of the four corners of the diamond. • vt to use as a basis; to found (on).

base[2] adj low in morality or honour; worthless.

baseball n the US national game, involving two teams that score runs by hitting a ball and running round four bases arranged in a diamond shape on the playing area.

basement n the part of a building that is partly or wholly below ground level.

bash vt (inf) to hit hard.

bashful adj easily embarrassed, shy.

basic *adj* fundamental. • *n* (*often pl*) a basic principle, factor, etc.—**basically** *adv*.

basil *n* an aromatic plant or herb.

basin *n* a wide shallow container for liquid; a large hollow; land drained by a river.

basis *n* a foundation; a principal constituent; a fundamental principle.

bask *vt* to lie in sunshine or warmth.

basket *n* a container of interwoven cane etc; the hoop to throw the ball through in basketball.

basketball *n* a game in which two teams compete to score by throwing the ball through an elevated hoop; this ball.

bass[1] *n* (*mus*) the range of the lowest male voice; a singer or instrument with this range.

bass[2] *n* an freshwater food and game fish.

bassoon *n* a deep-toned woodwind instrument.

bastard *n* one born of unmarried parents; (*offensive*) an unpleasant person.

baste[1] *vt* to drip fat over (roasting meat, etc).

baste[2] *vt* to sew with long loose stitches.

bat[1] *n* a wooden club used in cricket, etc; one who bats; a paddle used in table tennis.—*also vti* .

bat[2] *n* a mouse-like flying mammal.

bat[3] *vt* (*one's eyelids*) to flutter.

batch *n* the quantity of bread, etc, produced at one time; one set, group, etc; work for processing by a computer in a single run.

bath *n* water for washing the body; a tub for bathing; (*pl*) a building with baths; a municipal swimming pool. • *vti* to give a bath to; to bathe.

bathe *vt* to dampen with any liquid. • *vi* to have a bath; to swim.—**bather** *n*.

bathroom *n* a room with a bath and a WC.

baton *n* a thin stick used by a conductor to beat time; a hollow cylinder carried in relay team; a police officer's truncheon.

battalion *n* an army unit consisting of three or more companies; a large group.

batter *vti* to beat repeatedly. • *n* a mixture of flour, egg, and milk or water used in cooking.

battery *n* a set of heavy guns; a small unit of artillery; an electric cell that supplies current; an unlawful beating.

battle *n* a fight between two opposing armies; a contest. • *vti* to fight; to struggle.

battlement *n* a parapet or wall with indentations from which to shoot.

battleship *n* a large, heavily armoured warship.

bawdy *adj* humorously indecent; obscene.

bawl *vti* to shout; to weep loudly. • *n* a loud shout; a noisy weeping.—**bawler** *n*.

bay[1] *n* a type of laurel tree.

bay[2] *n* a wide inlet of a sea or lake.

bay[3] *n* an alcove or recess in a wall.

bay[4] *vti* to bark (at). • *n* the position of one forced to turn and fight.

bay[5] *adj* reddish brown.

bayonet *n* a blade for stabbing attached to the muzzle of a rifle.

bay window *n* a window projecting from the outside wall of a house.

bazaar *n* a market-place; a street full of small shops; a benefit sale for a church, etc.

be *vi* to exist; to live.

beach *n* the shore of the sea. • *vi* to bring (a boat) up on the beach.

beacon *n* a light for warning or guiding.

bead *n* a small ball pierced for stringing; (*pl*) a string of beads; (*pl*) a rosary; a bubble or droplet of liquid; the sight of a rifle.

beading *n* a wooden strip, rounded on one side, used for trimming.

beak *n* a bird's bill; the nose.

beaker *n* a large drinking cup; a cylindrical vessel with a pouring lip used by chemists.

beam *n* a long straight piece of timber or metal; a shaft of light; a radiant smile, etc. • *vt* (*light, etc*) to send out; to smile with pleasure.

bean *n* a plant bearing kidney-shaped seeds; a seed or pod of such a plant.

bear[1] *vt* to carry; to endure; to support, to conduct (oneself); to produce; (*with* out) to confirm. • *vi* (*with* down) to press down; to overwhelm; (*with* on *or* upon) to have reference to; (*with* up) to endure.

bear[2] *n* a large mammal with coarse fur, short legs and strong claws; a teddy bear; a speculator who sells in anticipation of a fall in price.

beard *n* hair covering a man's chin; similar bristles on an animal or plant. • *vt* to defy, oppose openly.—**bearded** *adj*.

bearer *n* a person who bears or presents; a person who carries something (a coffin, etc).

bearing *n* demeanour; a compass direction; (*followed by* to *or* on) relevance; a machine part on which another slides, revolves, etc.

beast *n* a large, wild, four-footed animal; a brutal, vicious person; (*inf*) something difficult, an annoyance.—**beastly** *adj*, *adv*.

beat *vti* to strike, pound repeatedly; to flog; to overcome; to find too difficult for; (*mus*) to mark (time); (*eggs, etc*) to mix by stirring vigorously; (*esp wings*) to move up and down; (*a path, way, etc*) to form by repeated trampling; (*sl*) to baffle; to throb; (*naut*) to sail against the wind. • *n* a recurrent stroke, pulsation, as in a heartbeat; rhythm in music or poetry; the area patrolled by a police officer.

beater *n* an implement for beating, such as an attachment for an electric food mixer.

beating *n* the act of striking or thrashing; throbbing or pulsation; a defeat.

beautician *n* one who offers cosmetic treatments.

beautiful *adj* having beauty; very enjoyable.

beauty *n* a combination of delightful qualities; an attractive woman; good looks.

beaver *n* a large semiaquatic dam-building rodent; its fur. • *vi* to work hard (at).

because *conj* since; for the reason that.

beckon *vti* to summon by a gesture.

become *vi* to come or grow to be. • *vt* to be suitable for.

becoming *adj* proper; seemly; suitable to.

bed *n* a piece of furniture for sleeping on; a plot of soil where plants are raised; the bottom of a river, lake, etc; any flat surface used as a foundation; a stratum. • *vt* to put to bed; to embed.

bedraggle *vt* to make dirty by dragging in the wet or dirt.—**bedraggled** *adj*.

bedridden *adj* confined to bed by illness.

bedroom *n* a room for sleeping in. • *adj* suggestive of sexual relations.

bedsit, bedsitter, bedsitting room *n* a room with sleeping and cooking facilities.

bee *n* a social, stinging four-winged insect that is often kept in hives to make honey.

beech *n* a tree with smooth silvery-grey bark; its wood.

beef *n* the meat of a cow, steer, etc; (*inf*) strength; (*inf*) a complaint.

beeline *n* a direct line or course.

beep *n* the brief, high-pitched sound of a horn or electronic signal.—*also vti*.

beer *n* an alcoholic drink made from malt, sugar, hops and water fermented with yeast.

beet *n* a red, edible root; a source of sugar.

beetle *n* an insect with hard wing covers.

beetroot *n* the fleshy edible root of beet.

befall *vti* to happen or occur to.

before *prep* ahead of; in front of; in the presence of; preceding; in preference to; rather than. • *adv* previously; until now. • *conj* earlier than the time that; rather than.

befriend *vt* to be a friend to, to favour.

beg *vti* to ask for money or food; to ask earnestly; to implore.

beggar *n* a person who lives by begging. • *vt* (*description*) to render inadequate.

begin *vti* to start doing; to originate.

beginner *n* a learner.

beginning *n* source or origin; start.

begrudge *vt* to grudge; to envy.

behalf *n*: in or on behalf of in the interest of; for.

behave *vti* to act in a specified way; to conduct (oneself) properly.—**behaviour** *n*.

behind *prep* at the rear of; concealed by; later than; supporting. • *adv* in the rear; slow; late.

behold *vt* to look at; to observe. • *vi* to see.—**beholder** *n*.

beige *n* a very light brown.

being *n* life; existence; a person or thing that exists; nature or substance.

belated *adj* coming late.

belch *vti* to expel gas from the stomach by the mouth; to eject violently.—*also n*.

belfry *n* the upper part of a tower in which bells are hung.

belie *vt* to show to be a lie; to misrepresent.

belief *n* a principle or idea; faith.

believe *vt* to accept as true; to think. • *vi* to have religious faith.—**believer** *n*.

belittle *vt* to make feel small; to disparage.

bell *n* a hollow metal object that rings when struck; its sound; a bell shape.

belligerent *adj* warlike.—**belligerence** *n*.

bellow *vi* to roar; to make an outcry. • *vt* to utter loudly. • *n* any deep roar.

bellows *n* (*used as pl or sing*) a device for creating and directing a stream of air by compression of its collapsible sides.

belly *n* the lower part of the body between the chest and the thighs; the stomach. • *vti* to swell out.

belong *vi* to have a proper place; to be related (to); (*with* to) to be a member; to be owned.

belongings *npl* personal possessions.

beloved *adj* dearly loved. • *n* a dear one.

below *prep* lower than; unworthy of. • *adv* beneath; later (in a book, etc).

belt *n* a band of leather, etc, worn around the waist; any similar encircling thing; a continuous moving strap passing over pulleys and so driving machinery; a distinctive region. • *vt* to surround with a belt; to thrash with a belt.

bench *n* a long hard seat; a long table for working at; the place where judges sit in court.

bend *vt* to form a curve; to make crooked; to turn. • *vi* to turn, esp from a straight line; (*with over or down*) to curve the body; to give in. • *n* a curve, turn; a bent part; (*pl*) decompression sickness.

beneath *prep* underneath; below. • *adv* in a lower place; underneath.

benefactor *n* a patron.

beneficial *adj* advantageous.

benefit *n* advantage; anything contributing to improvement; (*often pl*) allowances paid by a government, insurance company, etc. *vt* to help. • *vi* to receive advantage.

benevolence *n* inclination to do good; kindness; generosity.—**benevolent** *adj*.

bent *n* aptitude; inclination. • *adj* crooked; (*with on*) determined; (*sl*) dishonest.

bequeath *vt* (*property, etc*) to leave by will.

bequest *n* act of bequeathing; a legacy.

bereave *vt* to deprive (of) a loved one through death.—**bereaved** *adj*.—**bereavement** *n*.

beret *n* a flat, round, soft cap.

berry *n* any small, juicy, stoneless fruit.

berserk *adj* frenzied; destructively violent.

berth n a place in a dock for a ship at mooring; a built-in bed, as in a ship. • vt to moor a ship.

beseech vt to implore.

beset vt to surround; to attack from all sides.

beside prep at, by the side of, next to; in comparison with; in addition to; aside from.

besides prep other than. • adv in addition.

besiege vt to hem in with armed forces; to close in on; to overwhelm, harass, etc.

best adj most excellent; most suitable, desirable, etc; largest; above all others. • n one's utmost effort; the highest state of excellence. • adv in or to the highest degree. • vt to defeat.

best man n the principal attendant of the bridegroom at a wedding.

bestow vt to present.—**bestowal** n.

best seller n a book or other commodity that sells in vast numbers; the author of such a book.—**best-selling** adj.

bet n a wager; a sum staked.—also vti.—**better** n.

betray vt to aid an enemy; to expose treacherously; to be a traitor to; to reveal unknowingly.—**betrayal** n.—**betrayer** n.

better adj more excellent; more suitable; improved in health; larger. • adv in a more excellent manner; in a higher degree; more. • n a person superior in position. • vt to outdo.

between prep the space, time, etc, separating (two things); (bond, etc) connecting.

beverage n a drink.

beware vti to be wary or careful (of).

bewilder vt to perplex; to confuse hopelessly.—**bewilderment** n.

bewitching adj fascinating, enchanting.

beyond prep further on than; later than; outside the reach of. • adv further away.

bias n a slanting line, cut or sewn across the grain in cloth; prejudice. • vt to prejudice.

bib n a cloth or plastic cover tied round a baby to prevent food spillage on clothes; the upper part of dungarees or apron.

Bible n the sacred book of the Christian Church.

bicker vi to squabble, quarrel.—also n.

bicycle n a vehicle with two wheels, driven by pedals and having handlebars and a seat.

bid[1] n an offer of an amount one will pay or accept; (cards) a statement of the number of tricks a player intends to win. • vi to make a bid.—**bidder** n.

bid[2] vt to ask; (farewell) to say.

bide vi to wait; to dwell.

bier n a portable framework for a coffin.

big adj large; important; grown-up; boastful.

bigamy n marrying a second time when one is already married.—**bigamous** adj.

bigot n an intolerant person who blindly supports a particular political view or religion.—**bigoted** adj.—**bigotry** n.

bike n (inf) a bicycle; a motorcycle.

bikini n a two-piece swimsuit for women.

bile n a thick bitter fluid secreted by the liver; bad temper.—**bilious** adj.—**biliousness** n.

bilingual adj written in two languages; able to speak two languages.

bill[1] n a bird's beak.

bill[2] n a statement for goods supplied or services rendered; a list, as a menu or theatre programme; a poster; a draft of a proposed law; a bill of exchange; a piece of paper money; (law) a written declaration of charges and complaints filed. • vt to make out a bill of (items); to present a statement of charges to; to advertise by bills.

billet n (an order for civilian) lodging for troops. • vt to assign to a billet.

billiards n a game played with balls and a cue on a felt-covered table with edges.

billion n a thousand millions, the numeral 1 followed by 9 zeros; (UK) a million million.—**billionaire** n.

bin n a box for storing; a dustbin.

bind vt to tie together; to hold or restrain; to encircle; (often with up) to bandage; to fasten together the pages of (a book) and protect with a cover; to obligate. • n anything that binds.

binding n the covering of a book.

bingo n a game of chance in which players cover numbers on their cards according to the number called aloud.

binoculars npl a viewing device for use with both eyes, consisting of two small telescope lenses joined together.

biochemistry n the chemistry of living organisms.—**biochemist** n.

biography n an account of a person's life written by another; biographical writings.—**biographer** n.—**biographical** adj.

biology n the study of living organisms.—**biological** adj.—**biologist** n.

birch n a tree with smooth white bark; a bundle of birch twigs for thrashing. • vt to flog.

bird n a warm-blooded, egg-laying, feathered vertebrate with wings.

birth n the act of being born; childbirth.

birth control n the use of contraceptive drugs or devices to limit reproduction.

birthday n the day of birth; its anniversary.

biscuit n a small, dry, sweet or plain cake.

bishop n a clergyman governing a diocese; a chessman that moves diagonally.

bit[1] n a small amount or piece; a small part in a play, film, etc.

bit[2] n a mouthpiece in a horse's bridle; a cutting, boring attachment for a brace, drill.

bit[3] n (comput) a unit of information equivalent to either of two digits, 0 or 1.

bitch n a female dog; (sl) a spiteful woman.

bite *vti* to grip or tear with the teeth; to sting, as an insect. • *vi* to press the teeth (into, at, etc.) • *n* the act of biting with the teeth; a sting by an insect.

biting *adj* severe; critical, sarcastic.

bitter *adj* having a sharp taste; resentful.—**bitterness** *n*.

bivouac *n* a temporary camp, esp one without tents.—*also vi*.

bizarre *adj* odd, unusual.

blab *vti* to reveal (a secret); to gossip. • *n* a gossip.—**blabber** *n*.

black *adj* of the darkest colour, having dark-coloured skin and hair, esp Negro; without light; dirty. • *n* black colour; (*often with cap*) a Negro, Australian Aborigine. • *vt* to make black; to boycott; (*with out*) (*lights*) to extinguish. • *vi* (*with out*) to lose consciousness.

blackberry *n* a thorny bush with black or purple edible berries.

blackboard *n* a black or dark green board written on with chalk.

blacken *vt* to make black; to defame.

blackjack *n* another name for pontoon.

blackmail *vt* to extort money by threatening to disclose discreditable facts. • *n* the crime of blackmailing.—**blackmailer** *n*.

black market *n* the illegal buying and selling of goods.—**black marketeer** *n*.

blackout *n* the darkness when all lights are switched off; temporary loss of consciousness.

black sheep *n* a person regarded as disreputable or a disgrace by their family.

blacksmith *n* a metal worker.

bladder *n* a sac that fills with fluid, esp one that holds urine flowing from the kidneys.

blade *n* the cutting edge of a tool or knife; a straight, narrow leaf of grass.

blame *vt* to hold responsible for; to accuse. • *n* responsibility for an error; reproof.

blameless *adj* innocent; free from blame.

bland *adj* mild; gentle; insipid.

blank *adj* (*paper*) bearing no writing or marks; vacant; (*mind*) empty; (*cheque*) signed but with no amount written in. • *n* an empty space, esp one to be filled on a form; an empty place or time; a powder-filled cartridge without a bullet.

blanket *n* a large, soft bed cover; (*of snow, smoke*) a layer. • *adj* applying to a wide variety of cases.

blare *vti* to sound harshly or loudly. • *n* a loud, harsh sound.

blasphemy *n* speaking irreverently of God.

blast *n* a sharp gust of air; an explosion; an outburst of criticism. • *vti* to explode; to criticise. • *vi* to make a loud, harsh sound; to set off explosives; (*with off*) to be launched.

blastoff *n* the launch of a space vehicle.

blatant *adj* noisy; glaringly conspicuous.

blaze *n* an intensive fire; splendour. • *vi* to burn, shine brightly; to be excited with anger.

blazer *n* a lightweight jacket representing membership of a sports club, school, etc.

bleach *vti* to make or become white or colourless. • *n* a substance for bleaching.

bleak *adj* cold; exposed; bare; not hopeful.

bleat *vi* to cry as a sheep.—*also n*.

bleed *vi* to lose blood; to ooze sap, colour or dye. • *vt* (*inf*) to extort money from.

bleep *vi* to emit a high-pitched signal. • *n* a small radio receiver that bleeps to convey a message.—*also* **bleeper**.

blemish *n* a flaw or defect. • *vt* to mar.

blend *vt* to mix or mingle components. • *vi* to mix, merge; to shade into each other, as colours; to harmonise. • *n* a mixture.

bless *vt* to consecrate; to praise; to call upon God's protection; to grant happiness.

blessed *adj* holy, sacred; fortunate; blissful.

blessing *n* a cause of happiness; good wishes; a grace said before or after eating.

blight *n* anything that prevents growth or destroys. • *vt* to destroy; to frustrate.

blind *adj* sightless; unable to understand; not directed by reason; (*exit*) hidden; closed at one end. • *n* a shade for a window. • *vti* to make sightless, to deprive of insight.—**blindness** *n*.

blindfold *n* a cloth used to cover the eyes.—*also vt*.

blind spot *n* a point on the retina insensitive to light; a place where vision is obscured; a subject one is ignorant on.

blink *vi* to open and close the eyes rapidly; (*light*) to flash on and off; (*with at*) to ignore. • *vt* (*with at*) to be amazed. • *n* a glance, a glimpse.

bliss *n* supreme happiness.—**blissful** *adj*.

blister *n* a raised patch on the skin caused by burning or rubbing; a raised bubble. • *vti* to cause, form blisters; to lash with words.

blithe *adj* happy, cheerful, gay.

blitz *n* a sudden destructive attack.

blizzard *n* a severe storm of wind and snow.

bloat *vti* to swell as with water or air; to puff up, as with pride.—**bloated** *adj*.

blob *n* a drop of liquid; a round spot.

block *n* a solid piece of stone or wood, etc; a group of buildings; an obstruction. • *vt* to obstruct; to shape; (*often with out*) to sketch roughly. • *vi* to obstruct in sports.

blockade *n* (*mil*) the obstruction of a port by warships; a strategic barrier.—*also vt*.

blockage *n* an obstruction.

block letter *n* a handwritten capital letter.

blond(e) *adj* having light-coloured hair and skin; light-coloured.—*also n*.

blood *n* the red fluid that circulates in the arteries and veins of animals; kinship; descent.

blood donor n a person who donates blood for transfusion.

blood group n any of the types of human blood.

bloodshed n killing.

bloodshot adj (eye) suffused with blood.

bloodstream n the flow of blood through the blood vessels in the human body.

bloodthirsty adj eager for blood, cruel, war-like.—**bloodthirstiness** n.

bloody adj covered in blood; bloodthirsty; cruel, murderous. • vt to cover with blood.

bloom n a flower or blossom; the period of being in flower; a period of good health, vigour, etc. • vi to blossom; to be in one's prime.

blossom n a flower. • vi to flower; to begin to develop.

blot n a stain, esp of ink. • vt to stain; to absorb with blotting paper.

blotch n a spot or discoloration on the skin. • vt to cover with blotches.—**blotchy** adj.

blotting paper n absorbent paper used to dry freshly written ink.

blouse n a woman's shirt-like garment.

blow[1] n a hard hit, as with the fist; a sudden attack; a sudden misfortune; a setback.

blow[2] vi to cause a current of air; to be moved or carried (by air, the wind, etc); (mus) to make a sound by forcing in air with the mouth. • vt to move along with a current of air; to sound by blowing; (inf) to spend (money) freely; (sl) to bungle; (often with up) to explode; (with out) to extinguish by a gust; (with over) to pass over; (with up) (inf) to lose one's temper.

blowlamp, blowtorch n a gas-powered torch that produces a hot flame for welding.

blowout n (inf) a festive social event; a bursting (as a tyre) by pressure on a weak spot.

blubber[1] n whale fat; excessive fat.

blubber[2] vi to weep loudly.

bludgeon n a short, heavy stick for striking. • vti to strike with a bludgeon; to bully.

blue adj of the colour of the clear sky; depressed; (film) indecent. • n a colour of the spectrum; (pl: with the) (inf) a depressed feeling; (pl: with the) a style of jazz.

bluebottle n a large fly.

blueprint n a blue photographic print of plans; a detailed scheme, template of work.

bluff[1] adj rough in manner; abrupt, outspoken. • n a broad, steep bank or cliff.—**bluffness** n.

bluff[2] vti to mislead by a false, bold front.• n deliberate deception.—**bluffer** n.

blunder vi to make a foolish mistake; to move about clumsily.—also n.

blunt adj not having a sharp edge; rude, outspoken.—also vti.—**bluntness** n.

blur n an ill-defined impression.—also vti .

blurt vt (with out) to utter impulsively.

blush n a red flush of the face caused by embarrassment. • vi (with for, at) to show embarrassment, etc, involuntarily, by blushing.

bluster vi to make a noise like the wind. • n bullying, boastful talk.—**blustery** adj.

boar n a male pig, a wild hog.

board n meals, esp when provided for pay; a long, flat piece of sawn wood, esp for a special purpose; a council; a group of people who supervise a company; the side of a ship. • vt to provide meals and lodging at fixed terms; to come onto the deck of (a ship); to get on (a train, etc). • vi to provide room and/or meals for pay.

boarding house n a house where board is provided.

boardroom n a room where meetings of a company's board are held.

boast vi to brag. • vt to speak proudly of; to possess with pride. • n boastful talk.—**boaster** n.—**boastful** adj.

boat n a small, open craft; a ship. • vi to travel in a boat, esp for pleasure.

boater n a stiff flat straw hat.

bob vi to move abruptly up and down; to curtsey. • vt (hair) to cut short. • n a jerking motion up and down; a woman's short haircut.

bobbin n a reel on which yarn is wound.

bodice n the upper part of a dress.

bodily adj physical. • adv altogether.

body n the whole physical substance of a person, animal or plant; the trunk of a person or animal; a corpse; the principal part; substance; a richness of flavour; a person; a distinct group.

bodyguard n a person or persons assigned to guard someone.

bog n wet, spongy ground.—**boggy** adj.

boggle vi to be surprised; to hesitate (at).

bogus adj counterfeit, spurious.

boil[1] vi to change from a liquid to a vapour by heating; to bubble when boiling; to be aroused with anger; (with down) to reduce by boiling; (with over) to overflow when boiling; to burst out in anger. • vt to heat to boiling point; to cook in boiling water.

boil[2] n an inflamed, pus-filled swelling.

boiler n a storage tank to heat water; a device for providing central heating and hot water.

boisterous adj wild, noisy; exuberant.

bold adj daring; fearless; impudent; striking to the eye.—**boldness** n.

bollard n a strong post on a quay round which mooring lines are secured; one of a line of posts closing off a street to traffic.

bolster n a long pillow; any support. • vt (often with up) to support, strengthen.

bolt n a bar to lock a door, etc; a flash of lightning; a sudden dash. • vt to lock with a bolt; to eat hastily. • vi (horse) to rush away suddenly • adv erectly upright.

bomb *n* a projectile containing explosives or chemicals. • *vt* to attack with bombs.

bombard *vt* to attack with bombs, etc; to attack verbally.—**bombardment** *n*.

bombast *n* pretentious or boastful language.—**bombastic** *adj*.

bomber *n* a person who bombs; an aeroplane that carries bombs.

bombshell *n* a shocking surprise.

bona fide *adj* in good faith; genuine or real.

bond *n* anything that binds, fastens or unites; (*pl*) shackles; an obligation imposed by a contract, promise, etc; an interest-bearing certificate issued by the government or business, redeemable on a specified date; surety against theft, absconding, etc. • *vt* to join, bind or unite; to provide a bond for; to place or hold in bond. • *vi* to hold together by a bond.

bone *n* the hard material making up the skeleton; any constituent part of the skeleton. • *vti* to remove the bones from.—**bony** *adj*.

bonnet *n* a hat with a chin ribbon, a cap.

bonus *n* an amount paid over the sum due as interest, dividend or wages.

booby trap *n* a trap for playing a practical joke.

book *n* a bound set of printed or blank pages; a literary work; (*pl*) records of accounts. • *vt* to reserve in advance; to note a person's name and address for an alleged offence. • *vt* to reserve.

bookcase *n* a piece of furniture with shelves for books.

book-keeping *n* the systematic recording of business accounts.—**book-keeper** *n*.

booklet *n* a small book; a pamphlet.

bookmaker *n* a person who takes bets on horse races, etc, and pays out winnings.

boom[1] *n* a spar on which a sail is stretched; a long pole carrying a microphone.

boom[2] *vi* to make a deep, hollow sound. • *n* a resonant sound, as of the sea.

boom[3] *vi* to prosper suddenly. • *n* a period of vigorous business growth.

boomerang *n* a curved stick that, when thrown, returns to the thrower.—*also vi*.

boon *n* something useful or helpful.

boost *vt* (*sales, etc*) to increase; to encourage, to improve; to push. • *n* a push.

boot *n* a strong covering for the foot and lower leg; the rear compartment of a car used for holding luggage, etc. • *vt* to kick; (*comput*) to bring a program from a disk into the memory.

booth *n* a sales stall; a small enclosure for voting; a public telephone enclosure.

booty *n* spoils obtained as plunder.

border *n* the edge, rim; a frontier; a narrow strip along an edge. • *vi* (*with on*) to be adjacent.

borderline *adj* doubtful, indefinite.

bore to drill to form a hole; to weary by being dull. • *n* a hole made by drilling; the diameter of a gun barrel; a dull person.

boring *adj* dull, tedious; making holes.

born *adj* by birth, natural.

borough *n* a self-governing, incorporated town.

borrow *vt* to obtain (an item) with the intention of returning it; (*an idea*) to adopt as one's own; (*loan*) to obtain at definite rates of interest.

bosom *n* the breast; the seat of the emotions. • *adj* (*friend*) very dear, intimate.

boss *n* (*inf*) the manager or foreman; a powerful local politician. • *vt* to domineer.

botany *n* the study of plants.—**botanical** *adj*.—**botanist** *n*.

botch *n* a poorly done piece of work. • *vt* to put together, mend or patch clumsily.

both *adj*, *pron* the two together; the one and the other. • *conj* together equally.—*also adv*.

bother *vt* to annoy; to take trouble.

bottle *n* a glass or plastic container for liquids; its contents; (*sl*) courage. • *vt* to put in bottles.

bottleneck *n* a narrow stretch of a road where traffic is held up; a congestion in any stage of a process.

bottom *n* the lowest or deepest part; the base or foundation; the lowest position; the buttocks. • *vi* (*with out*) to flatten off after dropping sharply.

bottomless *adj* very deep.

bough *n* a branch of a tree.

boulder *n* a large stone or mass of rock.

bounce *vi* to rebound; (*sl: cheque*) to be returned. • *vt* to cause a ball to bounce.—*also n*.

bound[1] *n* (*usu pl*) the limit or boundary. • *vt* to limit, surround.—**boundless** *adj*.

bound[2] *n* a jump or leap.—*also vi*.

bound[3] *adj* on the way to.

boundary *n* the border of an area; the limit.

bout *n* a spell, a turn, a contest.

bovine *adj* relating to cattle; dull, sluggish.

bow[1] *vi* to lean the head (and chest) forward as a form of greeting or respect; to submit. • *vt* to bend downwards; to weigh down.—*also n*.

bow[2] *n* a weapon for shooting arrows; an implement for playing the strings of a violin; a decorative knot of ribbon, etc.

bow[3] *n* the forward part of a ship.

bowel *n* the intestine; (*pl*) the depths.

bowl[1] *n* a wooden ball used in bowling; (*pl*) a game played on a lawn with bowls. • *vti* to play the game of bowls; (*cricket*) to send a ball to a batsman; to dismiss by hitting the wicket with a bowled ball; (*with over*) (*inf*) to astonish.

bowl[2] *n* a deep, rounded dish; the rounded end of a pipe; a sports stadium.

bowler[1] *n* one who plays bowls, cricket.

bowler[2] *n* a stiff felt hat.

bowling *n* a game in which a heavy wooden ball

is bowled along a bowling alley at ten wooden skittles; the game of bowls.

bowling alley n one of the long narrow wooden lanes designed for bowling.

bowling green n a smooth lawn for bowls.

bow tie n a tie tied in the shape of a bow.

box[1] n a container for holding anything; (*theatre*) a compartment with seats. • vt to enclose.

box[2] vt to hit using the hands or fists. • vi to fight with the fists.—**boxing** n.

boxer n a person who boxes; a breed of dog with smooth hair and a stumpy tail.

box office n a theatre ticket office.

boy n a male child; a son.—**boyish** adj.

boycott vt to refuse to deal with or trade with in order to punish or coerce.—*also* n.

boyfriend n a male friend with whom a person is romantically or sexually involved.

brace n a prop; a support; a hand tool for drilling; a pair; (*pl*) straps for holding up trousers; a dental appliance for straightening teeth. • vt to steady.

bracelet n an ornamental wrist band.

bracing adj refreshing, invigorating.

bracken n a large, coarse fern.

bracket n a projecting metal support for a shelf; a category of people classified according to income; (*pl*) a pair of characters (), [], { }, used as parentheses. • vt to enclose by brackets; to group together.

brag vti to boast.

braid vt to weave three or more strands (of hair, straw, etc) together. • n a narrow band for decorating clothing; a plait.

brain n nervous tissue contained in the skull; intellectual ability; (*often pl*) the chief planner of an enterprise. • vt (*sl*) to hit on the head.

brainwash vt to change a person's ideas or beliefs by conditioning.

brain wave n (*inf*) a bright idea.

braise vt (*meat, vegetables, etc*) to fry lightly and cook slowly in liquid with the lid on.

brake n a device for slowing or stopping the motion of a wheel by friction. • vt to retard or stop by a brake. • vi to apply the brake.

bramble n a prickly shrub; blackberry.

bran n the separated husks of cereal grain.

branch n an offshoot from the trunk of a tree; a separate subsidiary of a business. • vi to divide into branches; (*with* out) to extend one's activities, etc.

brand n a mark imprinted with a hot iron; a mark of disgrace; a make (of goods). • vt to mark with a hot iron; to denounce.

brandish vt (*a weapon, etc*) to wave or flourish in a threatening manner.

brandy n an alcoholic liquor made from distilled wine or fermented fruit juice.

brash adj bold; reckless.—**brashness** n.

brass n an alloy of copper and zinc; nerve; cheek; the brass instruments of an orchestra.

brasserie n a bar and restaurant.

brassiere n a woman's undergarment for supporting the breasts.

brat n an ill-mannered, annoying child.

bravado n pretended confidence; swagger.

brave adj not timid; fearless. • vt to confront boldly.—**bravery** n.

brawl n a loud quarrel.—*also* vi.

brawn n physical strength.—**brawny** adj.

bray n the sound of a donkey; any harsh sound. • vi to make similar sounds.

brazen adj made of brass; shameless. • vt to face a situation boldly and shamelessly.

brazier n a metal container for hot coals.

breach n a break or rupture; violation of a contract, promise etc; a break in friendship. • vt to make an opening in.

bread n a dough, made from flour, yeast and milk, that is baked; nourishment.

breadth n measurement from side to side.

break vt to smash; to tame; (*rules*) to violate; to discontinue; to ruin financially; (*news*) to impart; (*with* down) to analyse; (*with* in) to intervene; to train. • vi to fall apart; (*voice*) to assume a lower tone; to cut off relations with; (*news*) to become public; (*with* down) to fail completely; to succumb emotionally; (*with* even) to suffer neither profit nor loss; (*with* in) to force a way in; (*with* out) to escape; (*with* up) to disperse; to separate; to collapse. • n an interruption; a gap; a change, as in weather; (*snooker*) a continuous run of points; (*sl*) a fortunate opportunity.

breakable adj easily broken.

breakage n something broken.

breakdown n a mechanical failure; failure of health; nervous collapse; an analysis.

breakfast n the first meal of the day.

breakthrough n an important advance.

breakwater n a barrier that protects against the force of the waves.

breast n the chest; one of the two mammary glands; the seat of the emotions. • vt to oppose.

breath n the inhalation and exhalation of air in breathing; life; a slight breeze.

Breathalyser™ n a device for measuring the amount of alcohol in the breath.

breathe vi to inhale and exhale air; to whisper. • vt to exhale; to whisper or speak softly.

breather n a pause for breath.

breathless adj out of breath; panting.

breathtaking adj very exciting.

breed vt to bring forth; (*dogs*) to raise; to give rise to. • vi to produce young; to be generated. • n offspring; race; species.—**breeder** n.

breeze n a light gentle wind.

breezy *adj* windy; nonchalant; light-hearted.

brevity *n* briefness; conciseness.

brew *vt* to make (beer) from malt and hops by boiling and fermenting; to infuse (tea); to plot, scheme. • *n* a brewed drink.

brewer *n* a person who brews, usu beer.—**brewery** *n*.

bribe *n* money, gifts offered illegally to gain favour or influence.—*also vt*.

bribery *n* the giving, taking of bribes.

brick *n* a baked clay block for building; a similar shaped block of other material. • *vt* to lay, wall up with brick.—**bricklayer** *n*.

bridal *adj* relating to a bride or a wedding.

bride *n* a woman about to be married or recently married.

bridegroom *n* a man about to be married or recently married.

bridesmaid *n* a young girl or woman attending the bride during a wedding.

bridge[1] *n* a structure built to convey people or traffic over a river, road, railway line, etc; the platform on a ship where the captain gives directions; the hard ridge of bone in the nose; a mounting for false teeth.—*also vt*.

bridge[2] *n* a card game based on whist.

bridle *n* the headgear of a horse. • *vt* to put a bridle on (a horse). • *vi* to draw one's head back as an expression of anger etc.

brief *n* a summary of a client's case for the instruction of a barrister; an outline of an argument; (*pl*) legless underpants.—*also vt*. • *adj* short, concise.—**briefness** *n*.

briefcase *n* a flat case for documents, etc.

brigade *n* an army unit, smaller than a division.

bright *adj* clear, shining; brilliant; favourable; intelligent.—**brightness** *n*.

brighten *vt* to make or become brighter.

brilliant *adj* sparkling, bright; splendid; very intelligent.—**brilliance** *n*.

brim *n* the rim of a hollow vessel; the outer edge of a hat. • *vti* (*with* **over**) to overflow.

brine *n* salt water.

bring *vt* to fetch, carry or convey 'here'; to cause to happen, to result in; to lead to; to sell for; (*with* **about**) to effect; (*with* **down**) to cause to fall by; (*with* **round**) to restore to consciousness; (*with* **up**) to rear; to raise; to vomit.

brink *n* the verge of a steep place; the point of onset; the threshold of danger.

brisk *adj* alert; vigorous.—**briskness** *n*.

bristle *n* a short, coarse hair. • *vi* to stand up, as bristles; to show anger, indignation.

brittle *adj* easily cracked or broken; fragile.

broach *vt* (*a topic*) to introduce for discussion; to pierce open (a container).

broad *adj* wide; strongly marked in dialect.

broadcast *n* a programme on radio or television. • *vti* to transmit on radio or television; to make known widely.

broaden *vti* to grow or make broad.

brochure *n* a booklet.

broil *vti* to cook by exposure to direct heat.

broke *adj* (*inf*) hard up, having no money.

broken *adj* splintered, fractured; violated; ruined; tamed; (*speech*) imperfect.

broken-down *adj* infirm; worn out.

broker *n* an agent who negotiates contracts of purchase and sale.

bronchitis *n* inflammation of the lining of the windpipe.—**bronchitic** *adj*.

bronze *n* a copper and tin alloy; any object cast in bronze; a reddish-brown colour. • *adj* of, like bronze.

brooch *n* an ornament held by a pin.

brood *vi* to incubate or hatch (eggs); to ponder or worry about. • *n* a group having a common origin, esp children in a family.

brook[1] *n* a freshwater stream.

brook[2] *vt* to tolerate.

broom *n* a bundle of fibres or twigs attached to a long handle for sweeping.

broomstick *n* the handle of a broom.

broth *n* a soup made by boiling meat, etc, in water.

brothel *n* a house where prostitutes work.

brother *n* a male sibling; a close friend; a fellow member of a group; a lay member of a religious order.—**brotherly** *adj*.

brother-in-law *n* the brother of a husband or wife; the husband of a sister.

brow *n* the forehead; the eyebrows; the jutting top of a hill.

browbeat *vt* to intimidate with threats, to bully.

brown *adj* of a dark colour, a mixture of red, black and yellow; tanned. • *vti* to make, become brown.

brownie *n* a square of flat, rich chocolate cake; a helpful elf; (*with cap*) a junior Guide.

browse *vti* to nibble; to read casually.

bruise *vt* to injure and discolour without breaking the skin; to inflict psychological pain on. • *vi* to undergo bruising.—*also n*.

brunette *n* a woman with black or dark-brown hair, often with dark eyes.

brunt *n* the main force or shock of a blow.

brush *n* a device made of bristles set in a handle for grooming the hair, painting or sweeping; a fox's, etc, bushy tail; a light touch. • *vt* to groom, sweep, remove with a brush. • *vi* to touch lightly.

Brussels sprout *n* a plant with a small edible green head.

brutal *adj* savage, violent.—**brutality** *n*.

brute *n* any animal except man; a brutal person. • *adj* (*force*) sheer.

bubble *n* a film of liquid forming a ball around

air or gas. • *vi* to boil; to rise in bubbles; to make a gurgling sound.

buck *n* the male of animals such as the deer, hare; (*sl*) a dollar. • *vti* (*horse*) to rear up; (*with up*) (*inf*) to raise or become cheerful.

bucket *n* a container with a handle for carrying liquid or substances in small pieces.

buckle *n* a fastening or clasp for a strap or band; a bend. • *vi* (*with down*) (*inf*) to apply oneself.

bud *n* an embryo shoot, flower; an early stage of development.—*also vi*.

Buddha *n* an image of Siddharta Gautama, founder of Buddhism.—**Buddhist** *adj, n*.

budding *n* being in an early stage of development; promising.

budge *vti* to shift or move.

budgerigar *n* a small Australian parrot.—*also* (*coll*) **budgie**.

budget *n* an estimate of income and expenditure within specified limits; the total amount of money for a given purpose.—*also vb*.

buff *n* a heavy, soft, brownish-yellow leather; this colour; (*inf*) a devotee, fan; (*inf*) bare skin. • *adj* made of buff; of a buff colour. • *vt* to clean or shine.

buffalo *n* a wild ox of North America.

buffer *n* anything that lessens shock, as of collision; a protective barrier; a temporary storage area in a computer.

buffet[1] *n* a blow with the hand or fist. • *vti* to hit with the hand or fist; to batter (as of the wind).

buffet[2] *n* a bar serving refreshments; a meal at which guests serve themselves.

buffoon *n* a clown, a jester.

bug *n* any insect; (*inf*) a germ, virus; (*sl*) a defect in a machine; (*sl*) a hidden microphone. • *vt* (*sl*) to plant a hidden microphone; (*sl*) to annoy.

bugbear *n* a cause of fear, anxiety.

bugle *n* a brass instrument like a small trumpet.

build *vt* to construct, to establish; (*with up*) to create, develop gradually. • *vi* (*with up*) to grow, intensify; (*health, reputation*) to develop. • *n* the shape of a person.—**builder** *n*.

building *adj* the skill or occupation of constructing; something built with walls and a roof.

building society *n* a company that pays interest on deposits and issues loans to enable people to buy their own houses.

built-in *adj* incorporated as an integral part.

built-up *adj* made higher, stronger, etc, with added parts; having many buildings on it.

bulb *n* the underground bud of plants such as the onion and daffodil; a glass bulb in an electric light.—**bulbous** *adj*.

bulge *n* a swelling. • *vti* to swell out.

bulk *n* magnitude; volume; the main part.

bulkhead *n* a wall-like partition in the interior of a ship, aircraft or vehicle.

bulky *adj* large and unwieldy.—**bulkiness** *n*.

bull[1] *n* an adult male bovine animal; a male whale or elephant; a speculator who buys to resell at a profit; (*sl*) nonsense. • *adj* male.

bull[2] *n* an official edict issued by the pope.

bulldozer *n* an excavator with caterpillar tracks for moving earth.

bullet *n* a small metal missile fired from a gun.

bulletin *n* an announcement; a short statement of news or of a patient's progress.

bullfighting *n* the sport of goading and then killing bulls.—**bullfighter** *n*.

bullion *n* gold or silver in mass.

bullock *n* a gelded bull; steer.

bull's-eye *n* (*darts, archery*) the centre of a target; a direct hit.

bully *n* a person who hurts or intimidates others weaker than himself.—*also vt*.

bumblebee *n* a large, furry bee.

bump *vi* to knock with a jolt. • *vt* to hurt by striking or knocking; (*with off*) (*sl*) to murder. • *n* a jolt; a knock; a swelling or lump.

bumper *n* a shock-absorbing bar fixed to the front and rear of a motor vehicle. • *adj* exceptionally large.

bumptious *adj* offensively conceited.

bun *n* a roll of dough and currants, spices and sugar; a bun-shaped coil of hair.

bunch *n* a cluster; a number of things growing or fastened together.—*also vti*.

bundle *n* a number of things fastened together. • *vt* to put in bundles; to push hurriedly into.

bung *n* a cork or rubber stopper. • *vt* to close up with a bung; (*sl*) to throw, toss.

bungalow *n* a one-storey house.

bungle *n* a mistake or blunder. • *vt* to botch.

bunion *n* a lump on the side of the big toe.

bunk *n* a narrow, shelf-like bed.

bunker *n* a large storage container; a sand pit on a golf course; an underground shelter.

bunting *n* a line of pennants and decorative flags.

buoy *n* an anchored float for mooring. • *vt* to keep afloat; (*usu with up*) to hearten, raise the spirits.

buoyancy *n* ability to float or rise; cheerfulness; resilience.—**buoyant** *adj*.

burden *n* a load; something that is difficult to bear; responsibility. • *vt* to weigh down, to oppress.—**burdensome** *adj*.

bureau *n* a writing desk; a government department.

bureaucracy *n* a system of government administration; excessive paperwork and red tape.

bureaucrat *n* an official in a bureaucracy.—**bureaucratic** *adj*.

burglar *n* a housebreaker.—**burglary** *n*.

burgle, burglarise *vt* to commit burglary.

burial *n* the act of burying.

burly *adj* heavily built; sturdy.—**burliness** *n*.

burn *vt* to destroy by fire; to injure by heat. • *vi* to be on fire; to feel hot; to feel passion. • *n* a scorch mark, injury caused by burning.

burnish *vt* to polish. • *n* lustre; polish.

burp *vti* to (cause to) belch.—*also n*.

burrow *n* an underground tunnel dug by a rabbit, fox, etc. • *vi* to dig, live in a burrow.

bursar *n* a college treasurer.

bursary *n* a student scholarship.

burst *vt* to break open; to cause to explode. • *vi* to emerge suddenly; to explode; to break into pieces. • *n* an explosion; a volley of shots.

bury *vt* (*bone, corpse*) to place in the ground; to conceal, to cover; to blot out of the mind.

bus *n* a motor coach for public transport. • *vti* to carry, travel by bus.

bush *n* a low shrub with many branches; woodland; uncultivated land.

bushy *adj* covered with bushes; (*hair*) thick.

business *n* trade or commerce; occupation or profession; a firm; a factory; one's concern or responsibility; a matter.

businesslike *adj* efficient, methodical.

businessman *n* one who works for a commercial company.—**businesswoman** *nf*.

busker *n* a street entertainer.—**busking** *n*.

bust *n* the chest of a woman; a sculpture of head and chest.

bustle[1] *vi* to move or act noisily or fussily. • *n* noisy activity, stir, commotion.

bustle[2] *n* a pad to puff up the back of a skirt.

busy *adj* occupied; active; industrious; (*telephone*) in use. • *vt* to occupy; to make busy.

busybody *n* a meddlesome person.

but *prep* except. • *conj* on the contrary, other than. • *adv* only; merely; just.

butane *n* an inflammable gas used as a fuel.

butcher *n* a retailer of meat; a murderer. • *vt* to slaughter; to murder; to make a mess of.

butler *n* a household's head servant.

butt[1] *vti* to strike or toss with the head or horns, as a bull, etc.—*also n*.

butt[2] *n* a large cask for wine or beer.

butt[3] *n* a target of ridicule.

butt[4] *n* the thick or blunt end; the stump.

butter *n* a solidified fat made from cream by churning. • *vt* to spread butter on; (*with up*) (*inf*) to flatter.

butterfly *n* an insect with a slender body and brightly coloured wings; a swimming stroke.

buttock *n* either half of the human rump.

button *n* a disc of metal, plastic, etc, as a fastening; a badge.—*also vti*.

buttonhole *n* the slit through which a button is passed; a flower in a buttonhole. • *vt* (*person*) to keep in conversation.

buttress *n* a projecting structure for strengthening a wall. • *vt* to support.

buxom *adj* (*woman*) big-bosomed.

buy *vt* to purchase; to bribe.—**buyer** *n*.

buyer's market *n* one in which, because the supply exceeds the demand, the buyer controls the price.

buzz *vi* to hum like an insect; to gossip; to hover (about). • *vt* to spread gossip secretly.—*also n*.

buzzard *n* a large bird of prey.

by *prep* beside; via; no later than. • *adv* past.

by(e)-election *n* an election held other than at a general election.

by(e)-law *n* a rule or law made by a local authority or a company.

by-line *n* a line under a newspaper article naming its author.

bypass *n* a main road built to avoid a town; (*med*) an operation to redirect the flow of blood to the heart.—*also vt*.

by-product *n* a secondary product in the process of making something else.

bystander *n* a chance onlooker.

byte *n* (*comput*) a set of eight bits as a unit.

byword *n* a familiar saying; a perfect example.

C

cab *n* a taxicab; the place where the driver sits in a truck, crane, etc.

cabaret *n* entertainment given in a restaurant or a nightclub.

cabbage *n* an edible plant with thick leaves formed usu into a compact head.

cabin *n* a small house, a hut; a room in a ship.

cabin cruiser *n* a powerful motorboat with living accommodation.

cabinet *n* a case with drawers or shelves; a case containing a TV, radio, etc; a body of official advisers to a government.

cabinetmaker *n* a person who makes furniture.

cable *n* a strong thick rope often of wire strands; an anchor chain; an insulated cord that carries electric current; a cablegram; a bundle of insulated wires for carrying cablegrams, TV signals, etc. • *vti* to send a message by cablegram.

cable car n a car drawn by a moving cable, as up a steep incline.

cablegram n a message transmitted by telephone line, submarine cable, etc.

cache n a secret hiding place or store.

cackle n the clucking sound of a hen; shrill or silly talk or laughter.—also vti.

cactus n a plant with a thick fleshy stem that stores water and is often studded with prickles.

caddie, caddy[1] n a person who carries a golfer's clubs.—vi to perform as a caddie.

caddy[2] n a small box or tin for storing tea.

cadet n a student at an armed forces academy.

cadge vti to beg, get by begging.

Caesarean section n the surgical removal of a child from the womb.

café n a small restaurant, a coffee bar.

cafeteria n a self-service restaurant.

caffeine n a stimulant in coffee and tea.

cage n a box or enclosure with bars for confining an animal, bird, prisoner, etc; a car for raising or lowering miners. • vt to shut in a cage.

cag(e)y adj (inf) wary, secretive, not frank.

cajole vti to persuade, soothe by flattery.

cake n a mixture of flour, eggs, sugar, etc, baked in small, flat shapes or a loaf; a small block of compacted or congealed matter. • vti to encrust.

calamity n a disastrous event, a great misfortune; adversity.—**calamitous** adj.

calcium n the chemical element prevalent in bones and teeth.

calculate vti to reckon or compute by mathematics; to suppose or believe; to plan.

calculating adj shrewd, scheming.

calculation n the act of calculating; the result obtained from this; an estimate.

calculator n a device, esp a small, electronic one, for mathematical calculations.

calculus n an abnormal, stony mass in the body; (math) a mode of calculation using symbols.

calendar n a chart, table of months, days, seasons; a list of scheduled events.

calf[1] n the young of a cow, seal, elephant.

calf[2] n the back part of the leg below the knee.

calibre n the internal diameter of a gun barrel; capacity, standing, ability.

call vi to cry out; to pay a short visit; to telephone; to ask, to appeal to. • vt to summon; to name; to describe as specified; to awaken; (with **down**) to invoke; (with **in**) to summon for advice, help; to demand payment of (a loan); (with **off**) to cancel; (an animal) to call away in order to stop; (with **out**) to cry aloud; (with **up**) to telephone; to summon to military action. • n a summons; the note of a bird; a vocation, esp religious; a demand; a short visit; the use of a telephone; a cry, a shout.

call box n a booth for a telephone.

caller n one who calls, esp by telephone.

call girl n a prostitute who is called by telephone to assignations.

callous adj (person) unfeeling.—**callousness** n.

calm adj windless; still, quiet, peaceful. • n stillness; tranquillity. • vti to become, make calm.

calorie, calory n a unit of heat; a measure of food energy.

calve vti to give birth to a calf.

camber n a slight upward curve in the surface of a road, etc.—also vti.

camel n a large four-footed, long-necked animal with a humped back; a fawny-beige colour.

cameo n an onyx or other gem carved in relief; an outstanding bit role in a film.

camera n the apparatus used for taking still photographs or television or motion pictures.

cameraman n a camera operator.

camouflage n a method (esp using colouring) of disguise or concealment used to deceive an enemy; a means of putting people off the scent.—also vt.

camp[1] n the ground on which tents, etc, are erected; the supporters of a cause. • vi to pitch tents.—**camper** n.—**camp site** n.

camp[2] adj (sl) theatrical; effeminate.

campaign n a series of military operations; activities with a particular objective, such as an election or promotion of a product. • vi to conduct a campaign.—**campaigner** n.

campus n the grounds, and buildings, of a college or university.

can[1] vt to be able to; to be allowed to.

can[2] n a covered container, usu metal, in which petrol, film, etc, is stored; a hermetically sealed tin; its contents, e.g. food, drinks. • vti to preserve in a can.—**canner** n.

canal n an artificial waterway cut across land; a duct in the body.

canary n a small finch, usu greenish to yellow in colour, kept as a songbird.

cancel vt to cross out; to annul, suppress; to call off; to countermand. —**cancellation** n.

cancer n an abnormal growth, esp a malignant tumour; an undesirable, dangerous power that spreads.—**cancerous** adj.

candela n a unit of luminous intensity.

candid adj frank, outspoken; (photograph) informal.—**candidness** n.

candidate n a person who has nomination for an office; a student taking an examination.—**candidacy** n.—**candidature** n.

candle n a stick of wax with a wick that burns to give light.—**candlelight** n.

candour n sincerity, frankness.

candy n a solid confection of sugar or syrup with flavouring, fruit, etc, a sweet.

candyfloss *n* a confection of spun sugar.

cane *n* the slender, jointed stem of certain plants, as bamboo; a plant with such a stem, as sugar cane; a stick for supporting plants; strips of this used in furniture-making, etc; a walking stick. • *vt* to thrash with a cane.

canine *adj* of a dog; of the family of animals that includes wolves, dogs, foxes; pertaining to a pointed tooth next to the incisors.—*also n*.

canister *n* a small box or container for tea; a tube containing tear gas that explodes and releases its contents on impact.

cannabis *n* a narcotic drug obtained from the hemp plant; the hemp plant.

canned *adj* stored in sealed tins; recorded for reproduction.

cannibal *n* one who eats human flesh; an animal that feeds on its own species. —**cannibalism** *n*.—**cannibalistic** *adj*.

cannon *n* a large mounted piece of artillery; an automatic gun on an aircraft; (*billiards*) a shot in which the cue ball hits two others successively —*also* **carom**. • *vi* to collide with (*with* **into**); to rebound; (*billiards*) to make a cannon.

cannonball *n* the heavy, round shot fired from cannon. • *vi* to move along at speed.

canoe *n* a narrow, light boat propelled by paddles.—*also vi.*—**canoeist** *n*.

canon *n* a decree of the Church; a rule or standard, criterion; the works of an author recognised as genuine; a member of a cathedral chapter; a part of the Mass containing words of consecration; (*mus*) a round.—**canonical** *adj*.

canonise *vt* (*RC Church*) to declare a saint.

canopy *n* a tent-like covering over a bed, throne, etc; any roof-like projection.

cant[1] *n* insincere or hypocritical speech; language specific to a group (e.g. thieves, lawyers).

cant[2] *n* an inclination or tilt. • *vti* to slant, to tilt.

cantaloup(e) *n* a melon with orange flesh.

cantankerous *adj* ill-natured, bad-tempered.

canteen *n* a restaurant attached to a factory, school, etc, catering for large numbers of people; a flask for carrying water; (a box containing) a set of cutlery.

canter *n* a horse's slow gallop.—*also vti.*

cantilever *n* a projecting beam that supports a balcony, etc.

canvas *n* a strong coarse cloth of hemp or flax, used for tents, sails, etc, and for painting on; sails; tent(s); an oil painting.

canvass *vti* to ask for votes, opinions, orders, etc.—*also n.*—**canvasser** *n*.

canyon *n* a deep ravine between cliffs.

cap *n* any close-fitting head gear, usu brimless; a cap-like thing, as an artificial covering for a tooth; a top, a cover; a percussion cap in a toy gun; a contraceptive device; (*sport*) the head

gear presented to a player chosen for a team. • *vt* to put a cap on; to cover (the end of); to outdo; (*sport*) to choose a player for a team.

capable *adj* competent, efficient.—**capability** *n*.

capacity *n* the power of holding or grasping; cubic content; mental ability; legal competence.

cape[1] *n* a headland running into the sea.

cape[2] *n* a sleeveless garment hanging over shoulders and back.

capital[1] *adj* of the head; (*offence*) punishable by death; first-class; of capital or wealth; relating to a large letter. • *n* a city that is the seat of government; a large letter; accumulated wealth used to produce more; stock or money for carrying on a business; a chief city.

capital[2] *n* the top part of a column, pillar.

capital gain *n* the profit made on the sale of an asset.

capitalism *n* the system of individual ownership of wealth; the dominance of such a system.

capitalist *n* a person who has money invested in business for profit; a supporter of capitalism.

capital punishment *n* the death penalty for a crime.

capitulate *vi* to give in.—**capitulation** *n*.

capricious *adj* inconstant; unreliable.

capsize *vti* to upset or overturn.

capstan *n* an upright drum around which cables are wound to haul them in.

capsule *n* a small gelatin case enclosing a drug to be swallowed; a metal or plastic container; (*bot*) a seed case; the orbiting and recoverable part of a spacecraft.

captain *n* a chief; a ship's master; the pilot of an aircraft; a rank of army, navy officer; the leader of a sports team. • *vt* to be captain of.—**captaincy** *n*.

caption *n* a heading in a newspaper, to a chapter, etc; a legend describing an illustration; a subtitle.—*also vt* to provide with a caption.

captivate *vt* to charm.—**captivating** *adj*.

captivity *n* the state of being a captive; a period of imprisonment.

capture *vt* to take prisoner; to seize; to catch; to gain by skill, attraction, etc, to win.—*also n.*

car *n* a self-propelled motor vehicle, an automobile, a motorcar; a railway carriage.

carafe *n* an open-topped bottle for serving water or wine at table.

caramel *n* burnt sugar used in cooking to colour or flavour; a sweet tasting of this.

carat *n* a measure of weight for precious stones; a measure of the purity of gold.

caravan *n* an enclosed vehicle equipped to live in (—*also* **trailer**).—*also vi .*

caraway *n* a biennial plant with pungent aromatic seeds used as a flavouring.

carbohydrate *n* a compound of carbon, hydrogen and oxygen, esp in sugars and starches as components of metallic. • *npl* starchy foods.

carbon *n* a nonmetallic element, a constituent of all organic matter; a duplicate made with carbon paper.

carbon copy *n* a copy of typed or written material made by using carbon paper; an exact copy.

carburettor *n* a device in an internal-combustion engine for making an explosive mixture of air and fuel vapour.

carcass, carcase *n* the dead body of an animal; a framework, skeleton or shell.

card[1] *n* a small piece of cardboard; a piece of this with figures for playing games; a piece of this printed with name, address, greeting, etc; a small piece of plastic identifying a person for banking purposes; (*pl*) card games; card playing.

card[2] *n* a toothed instrument for combing cotton, wool or flax fibres off.—*also vt*.

cardboard *n* thick stiff paper. • *adj* made of this; lacking substance.

cardiac *adj* relating to the heart.

cardigan *n* a knitted sweater fastening up the front.

cardinal *adj* principal, fundamental; of a bright red. • *n* an official appointed by the pope to his councils; bright red.

cardinal numbers *npl* numbers that express how many (1, 2, 3, etc).

care *n* anxiety; concern; heed; consideration; charge, protection; the cause or object of concern. • *vt* to be willing (to do something). • *vi* (*usu with* **for** *or* **about**) to feel affection; to have in one's charge.

career *n* progress through life; a profession, occupation, esp with prospects for promotion. • *vi* to rush rapidly or wildly.

carefree *adj* without cares, lively.

careful *adj* cautious.—**carefulness** *n*.

careless *adj* not careful.—**carelessness** *n*.

caress *vt* to touch lovingly.—*also n*.

caretaker *n* a person put in charge; (*government*) one temporarily in control.

cargo *n* the load carried by a ship, truck, etc.

Caribbean *adj* of or pertaining to the Caribbean Sea and its islands.—*also n*.

caricature *n* a likeness made ludicrous by exaggeration.—*also vt*.—**caricaturist** *n*.

carnal *adj* of the flesh; sexual; sensual.

carnation *n* a garden flower.

carnival *n* public festivities and revelry; a travelling fair with sideshows, etc.

carnivore *n* a flesh-eating mammal.

carnivorous *adj* (*animals*) feeding on flesh.

carol *n* a Christmas hymn.—*also vi* .

carom *see* **cannon**.

carp[1] *vi* to find fault, esp continually.

carp[2] *n* a brown and yellow freshwater fish.

car park *n* land intended for parking cars.

carpenter *n* a person skilled in woodwork.

carpet *n* a woven fabric for covering floors.

carriage *n* transport; deportment; a railway coach; the moving part of a typewriter.

carriageway *n* a road bearing single-line traffic.

carrier *n* one who carries or transports goods, esp for hire; a person, animal transmitting an infectious disease without being affected by it.

carrier bag *n* a bag with handles for shopping.

carrot *n* a plant with edible, orange roots; an inducement.

carry *vt* to convey or transport; to involve; to hold (oneself); to stock; (*with* **off**) to handle successfully; (*with* **out**) to perform (a task, etc). • *vi* (*with* **on**) to persevere; to conduct a business, etc.

carrycot *n* a baby's portable cot.

cart *n* a two-wheeled vehicle; any small vehicle for carrying loads.—*also vt*.

cartilage *n* tough, elastic tissue attached to the bones of animals; gristle.

carton *n* a cardboard box or container.

cartoon *n* a humorous picture dealing with current events; a comic-strip; a full-size preparatory sketch.—**cartoonist** *n*.

cartridge *n* the case that contains the explosive charge and bullet in a gun; a sealed case of film for a camera; the device containing the stylus on the end of the pick-up arm of a record player.

carve *vt* to shape by cutting; to cut up.

carving *n* a design carved from wood etc.

cascade *n* a small, steep waterfall; a shower.

case[1] *n* a covering; a suitcase; its contents.

case[2] *n* an instance; a state of affairs; a condition, circumstance; a lawsuit; an argument for one side; (*med*) a patient under treatment; (*gram*) the relationship between nouns, pronouns and adjectives.

cash *n* money in coins or notes; immediate payment as opposed to that by cheque or on credit. • *vt* to give or get cash for.

cashew *n* the edible nut of a tropical tree.

cashier *n* a person in charge of the paying and receiving of money in a bank, shop, etc.

cashmere *n* a fine wool from Kashmir goats.

cash register *n* an automatic or electronic till showing the amount put in it.

casing *n* a protective or outer covering.

casino *n* a room or building where gambling takes place.

cask *n* a barrel for liquids; its contents.

casket *n* a small box for jewels; a coffin.

casserole *n* a covered dish for cooking and serving; the food so cooked.—*also vt*.

cassette *n* a usu plastic box that holds an audio or video tape.

cast *vti* (*pt* **cast**) to direct; to shape in a mould;

to select actors, etc, for a play; (with off) to untie a ship from its moorings; (knitting) to loop off stitches from a needle; (with on) to loop the first row of stitches onto a needle. • n a plaster for immobilising an injured limb; a mould for casting; a tinge of colour; the actors in a play; a slight squint in the eye.

castanets npl shell-shaped pieces of wood held between the fingers and rattled together.

castaway n a shipwrecked person.

caste n any of the Hindu hereditary social classes; an exclusive social group.

casting vote n the deciding vote of a chairman when votes on each side are equal.

cast iron n iron melted and run into moulds.

castle n a fortified building; a chess piece — also **rook**.

castor n a small perforated container for sprinkling; a small swivelled wheel on a table leg, etc.

castor oil n a vegetable oil used as a purgative.

castor sugar n finely ground sugar.

castrate vt to remove the testicles of.

casual adj unplanned; occasional; informal.

casualty n a person injured or killed in a war.

cat n a small, domesticated feline mammal; a wild animal, e.g. lion, tiger.

catalogue n a list of books, names, etc, in systematic order.—also vti.

catalyst n a substance that accelerates or retards a chemical reaction without itself undergoing any permanent chemical change; a person or thing that produces change.

catapult n a contraption with elastic for shooting small stones; a device for launching aircraft from the deck of an aircraft carrier.—also vt.

cataract n a waterfall; a disease of the eye causing dimming and blindness.

catarrh n inflammation of a mucous membrane.

catastrophe n a great disaster.—**catastrophic** adj.

catch vt to grasp; to capture; to trap; to be on time for; to detect; to apprehend; to become infected with (a disease); (with out) (inf) to detect (a person) in a mistake; (cricket) to catch a ball hit by a batsman before it touches the ground. • vi to become entangled; to begin to burn; (with on) (inf) to become popular; to understand; (with up) to come level with; to make up for lost time. • n a fastening; a hidden difficulty.

catching adj infectious; attractive.

catchment area n a geographic area served by an institution.

catch phrase n a phrase or slogan associated with a group or person.

catchy adj easily remembered, as a tune.

catechism n the principles of religion in question and answer form.

categorical adj unconditional, absolute.

categorise vt to place in a category.

category n a class or division of things.

cater vi (with for, to) to provide with what is needed or desired.—**caterer** n.

caterpillar n the worm-like larvae of a butterfly or moth; the ribbed band in place of wheels on a heavy vehicle.

cathedral n the chief church of a diocese.

Catholic n a member of the Roman Catholic Church. • adj relating to the Roman Catholic Church.—**Catholicism** n.

catholic adj all-embracing; liberal.

cattle npl domesticated bovine mammals such as bulls and cows.

cauliflower n a kind of cabbage with an edible white flower head.

cause n that which produces an effect; reason, motive, a principle. • vt to bring about.

causeway n a raised road across wet ground.

caustic adj burning tissue, etc, by chemical action; corrosive; sarcastic, cutting. • n a caustic substance.

caution n care for safety, prudence; warning. • vt to warn (against); to admonish.

cautious adj careful, circumspect.

cavalry n combat troops mounted on horseback.

cave n a hollow place inside the earth open to the surface. • vti to collapse (with in).

caveman n a prehistoric cave dweller.

cavern n a large cave.—**cavernous** adj.

caviar(e) n pickled roe of the sturgeon.

cavity n a hole; a hollow place.

cavort vi to frolic, prance.

cease vti to stop, to come to an end.

ceasefire n a period of truce.

ceaseless adj without ceasing; incessant.

cedar n a large coniferous evergreen tree.

cede vt to yield to another, give up.

ceiling n the inner roof of a room; an upper limit.

celebrate vt to praise, extol; to perform with proper rites; to mark with ceremony.

celebrated adj famous.

celebration n ceremony to celebrate anything.

celebrity n fame; a famous person.

celery n a vegetable with long edible stalks.

celestial adj in or of the sky; heavenly.

celibacy n complete sexual abstinence.—**celibate** adj.

cell n a small room in a prison or monastery; a small cavity as in a honeycomb; a device that converts chemical energy into electricity; a microscopic unit of living matter; a small group of people bound by common aims within an organisation or political party.—**cellular** adj.

cellar n a basement; a stock of wines.

cello n a large bass instrument of the violin family.—**cellist** n.

cellophane n a thin transparent paper made from cellulose.

cellulose n a starch-like carbohydrate forming the cell walls of plants, used in making paper, textiles, film, etc.

Celsius adj of a scale of a hundred degrees. • n a hundredth part of a grade.

Celtic adj of or relating to the Celts; the language of the Celts.

cement n a powdered substance of lime and clay, mixed with water, etc, to make mortar or concrete, which hardens upon drying; any hard-drying substance. • vt to bind together.

cemetery n a place to bury the dead.

cenotaph n a monument to a person who is buried elsewhere.

censor n an official who examines literature, etc, and removes anything objectionable.

censure n disapproval, blame. • vt to condemn.

cent n a hundredth of a dollar.

centenary n a hundredth anniversary.

centi- prefix one hundredth.

centigrade adj of a scale of a hundred degrees. • n a hundredth part of a grade.

centimetre n one hundredth of a metre.

centipede n a crawling creature with a long body divided into numerous segments each with a pair of legs.

central adj in or forming the centre; main.

central heating n a system of heating interiors by pipes and radiators.

centralise vt to draw to the centre; to place under the control of a central authority.

centre n the middle point or part of anything; a pivot; interior; source; political moderation; (sport) a player at the centre of the field, etc, a centreforward. • adj of or at the centre. • vt to place in the centre; to concentrate; to be fixed.

centre forward n (football, hockey) the central player in the forward attack.

centrifugal adj moving away from the centre of rotation.

century n a period of a hundred years; (cricket) 100 runs made by a batsman in a single innings.

ceramic adj of earthenware, porcelain or brick. • n a thing made of ceramic; (pl) pottery.

cereal n edible grain, e.g. wheat, rice; a breakfast food made from these.

ceremony n a sacred rite; formal observance.

certain adj sure, positive; inevitable; definite; fixed; some; one.—**certainty** n.

certainly adv without doubt; yes.

certificate n a document formally attesting a fact; a testimonial.

certify vt to declare in writing or attest formally; to endorse with authority.

cervix n the neck of the womb.

cessation n a stoppage; a pause.

cesspit, cesspool n a covered cistern for collecting liquid waste or sewage.

chafe vti to make or become sore by rubbing.

chaffinch n a European songbird.

chain n a series of connected links; a continuous series; a series of related events; a bond; a group of shops, hotels, etc, owned by the same company. • vt to fasten with a chain.

chain reaction n a process in which a chemical, atomic or other reaction stimulates further reactions, e.g. combustion or nuclear fission; a series of events, each of which stimulates the next.

chain store n one of a series of shops owned by one company.

chair n a seat for one; a seat of authority; a chairman; a professorship; the electric chair. • vt to preside as chairman.

chair lift n a series of seats suspended from a cable for carrying people uphill.

chairman n a person who presides at a meeting; the president of a board or committee.—**chairwoman** nf.—also **chairperson**.

chalet n a Swiss hut; any similar building used in a holiday camp, as a ski lodge, etc.

chalice n a large cup with a base.

chalk n calcium carbonate, a soft white limestone; such a stone or a substitute used for drawing or writing. • vt to write or draw with chalk; (with **up**) (inf) to score, get; to charge.

challenge vt to summon to a fight; to call in question; to hail and interrogate. • n a summons to a contest; a calling in question; a stimulating task.—**challenger** n.—**challenging** adj.

chamber n a room; a deliberative body or a division of a legislature; a compartment; a cavity in the body of an organism; (pl) a judge's office.

chambermaid n a woman employed to clean bedrooms in a hotel, etc.

chamber music n music for performance by a small group, as a string quartet.

chamois n a small antelope found in Europe and Asia; a piece of chamois leather.

chamois leather n soft, pliable leather.

champagne n a sparkling white wine.

champion n a person who upholds a cause; a succesful competitor. • adj first-class. • vt to defend.

championship n a contest held to find a champion.

chance n fortune; an accident; opportunity; possibility; probability; risk. • vti to risk; to happen. • adj accidental, not planned.

chancel n the part of a church around the altar, for the clergy and the choir.

chancellor n a high government official; a head of state, university.—**chancellorship** n.

chandelier n an ornamental hanging frame with branches for holding lights.

change *vti* to alter; to transform; to exchange; to put fresh clothes on; to continue one's journey by altering means of transport. • *n* alteration, modification; money in small units; the balance of money returned on payment.

changeable *adj* altering rapidly; inconstant.

channel *n* a body of water joining two larger ones; a navigable passage; a means of conveying; a band of radio frequencies reserved for a particular purpose, e.g. television station. • *vt* to direct.

chant *vti* to sing; to recite in a singing manner; to shout (a slogan) rhythmically. • *n* sacred music to which prose is sung; a monotonous song; a rhythmic slogan.

chaos *n* utter confusion, muddle.

chaotic *adj* completely without order.

chap¹ *vti* (*skin*) to make or become rough in cold weather.

chap² *n* (*inf*) a man.

chapel *n* a building for Christian worship.

chaperon(e) *n* a woman who accompanies a girl for propriety.—*also vt.*

chaplain *n* a clergyman serving with armed forces or in a prison, hospital.—**chaplaincy** *n*.

chapter *n* a division of a book; the body of canons of a cathedral, members of a monastic order; a sequence of events.

char *vti* to scorch.

character *n* the combination of qualities that distinguishes a person or thing; moral strength; reputation; disposition; an eccentric; a person in a play or novel; a letter or mark in writing, printing, etc.

characterise *vt* to describe in terms of particular qualities; to designate; to be characteristic of, mark.—**characterisation** *n*.

characteristic *adj* marking or constituting the particular nature (of a person or thing). • *n* a characteristic feature.

charade *n* a game of guessing a word from the acted representation of its syllables and the whole; a travesty; an absurd pretence.

charcoal *n* the black carbon matter obtained by partially burning wood.

charge *vt* to ask as the price; to load, to fill; to lay a task or trust on; to accuse; to attack at a run.—*also n*.

charitable *adj* of or for charity; generous to the needy, kindly.

charity *n* leniency towards others; generosity in giving to the needy; a benevolent institution.

charm *n* an alluring quality; a magic formula; something thought to possess occult power; a trinket on a bracelet. • *vt* to delight, captivate; to influence as by magic.

chart *n* a map, esp for navigation; a table, graph, etc; (*pl with the*) a list of the most popular music recordings. • *vt* to make a chart of.

charter *n* a document granting rights, ownership, etc; the hire of transport.—*also vt.*

charwoman *n* one employed to clean.

chase *vt* to pursue; to drive (away); to hunt.—*also n*.

chasm *n* a gaping hole; a wide difference in opinions.

chassis *n* the frame of a vehicle.

chastity *n* sexual abstinence; virginity.

chat *vi* (*pt* **chatted**) to talk in an easy or familiar way. • *n* informal conversation.

chatter *vi* to talk aimlessly; (*animal, etc*) to utter rapid cries; (*teeth*) to rattle together.

chatterbox *n* an incessant talker.

chatty *adj* talkative, full of gossip.

chauffeur *n* a person who drives a car for someone else.—*also vt.*—**chauffeuse** *nf*.

cheap *adj* inexpensive; inferior.

cheapen *vti* to make or become cheap.

cheat *vti* to defraud; to deceive.—*also n*.

check *vti* to bring or come to a stand; to restrain; to admonish; to verify; (*with* out) to settle the bill and leave a hotel; to investigate. • *n* repulse; a pattern of squares; a control to test accuracy; (*chess*) a threatening of the king.

checkmate *n* (*chess*) the winning position when the king is threatened and unable to move; utter defeat.—*also vt.*

cheek *n* the side of the face below the eye; impudence.

cheeky *adj* disrespectful, impudent.

cheer *n* a shout of applause or welcome; happiness. • *vt* to gladden; to applaud.—**cheerful** *adj*.

cheese *n* the curds of milk pressed into a firm or hard mass.

chef *n* a professional cook.

chemical *n* a substance used in, or arising from, a chemical process. • *adj* of chemistry.

chemist *n* a pharmacy; a manufacturer of medicinal drugs; one skilled in chemistry.

chemistry *n* the science of the properties of substances and their combinations and reactions.

cheque *n* a money order to a bank.

chequebook *n* a book containing blank cheques to be drawn on a bank.

chequered *adj* marked with a variegated pattern; having a career marked by fluctuating fortunes.

cherish *vt* to tend lovingly, foster.

cherry *n* a small red, pitted fruit; the tree bearing it; a bright red colour.

chess *n* a game for two with 32 pieces on a chessboard.

chessboard *n* a board chequered with 64 squares used for playing chess or draughts.

chest *n* a large strong box; the thorax.

chestnut *n* a tree of the beech family; its edible nut; its wood; a horse with chestnut colouring.

chest of drawers *n* a piece of furniture containing several drawers.

chew *vt* to grind between the teeth; to ponder, think over.—*also n.*—**chewing gum** *n*.

chic *n* elegance, style. • *adj* stylish.

chick *n* a young bird.

chicken *n* a young, domestic fowl; its flesh. • *adj* cowardly, timorous.

chicken feed *n* (*inf*) a trifling amount.

chickenpox *n* a contagious viral disease that causes a rash of red spots on the skin.

chicory *n* a salad plant (—*also* **endive**).

chief *adj* principal, most important. • *n* a leader.

chiefly *adv* especially; mainly.

chiffon *n* a thin gauzy material.

chilblain *n* an inflamed swelling on the hands, etc, due to cold.

child *n* a young human being.

childbirth *n* the process of giving birth.

childhood *n* the period between birth and puberty in humans.

childish *adj* of, like a child; foolish.

childlike *adj* like a child; innocent, simple.

child minder *n* a person employed to look after children.

chill *n* a sensation of coldness; an illness caused by exposure to cold and marked by shivering.

chilly *adj* cold; unfriendly.

chime *n* the harmonious sound of a bell; (*pl*) a set of bells or metal tubes, etc, tuned in a scale. • *vti* to ring (a bell); (*with* **with**) to agree.

chimney *n* a passage for smoke, hot air or fumes, a funnel.

chimpanzee *n* an African anthropoid ape.

chin *n* the part of the face below the mouth.

china *n* fine porcelain; articles from this.

chink *n* a narrow opening; a crack or slit.

chip *vt* to knock small pieces off; to shape by chipping. • *n* a small piece cut or broken off; a thin strip of fried potato; a counter used in games; a tiny piece of semi-conducting material, such as silicon, printed with a microcircuit and used as part of an integrated circuit.

chirp *n* the sharp, shrill note of some birds or a grasshopper. • *vi* to make this sound.

chisel *n* a tool with a square cutting end. • *vt* to cut or carve with a chisel.

chit[1] *n* a voucher or a sum owed for drink, food, etc; a note; a requisition.

chit[2] *n* a child; (*derog*) an impudent girl.

chivalry *n* the medieval system of knighthood; knightly qualities, courtesy.—**chivalrous** *adj*.

chive, chives *n* a plant with onion-flavoured leaves used in cooking and salads.

chloride *n* any compound containing chlorine.

chlorine *n* a non-metallic element, a yellowish-green poisonous gas used in bleaches, disinfectants and in industry.

chock *n* a block of wood or other material used as a wedge.

chock-a-block *adj* completely full.

chocolate *n* a powder or edible solid made of the roasted, pounded cacao bean; a drink made by dissolving this powder in boiling water or milk; a sweet with a chocolate coating.

choice *n* act of choosing; the power to choose; selection; alternative; a thing chosen.

choir *n* a group of singers, esp of a church.

choke *vti* to stop the breath of, stifle; to throttle; to suffocate; to block (up). • *n* a fit of choking; a choking sound; a valve that controls the flow of air in a carburettor.

cholera *n* a severe, infectious intestinal disease.

choose *vt* to select. • *vi* to decide.

chop *vt* to cut by striking; to cut into pieces. • *n* a cut of meat and bone from the rib, loin or shoulder; a downward blow or motion.

choppy *adj* (*sea*) running in rough waves.

chopsticks *n* a pair of wooden or plastic sticks for eating Chinese food..

choral *adj* relating to, sung by, or written for, a choir or chorus.

chord[1] *n* (*mus*) three or more notes played simultaneously.

chord[2] *n* a straight line joining the ends of an arc.

chore *n* an item of housework; a tedious task.

choreography *n* the art of devising ballets or dances.—**choreographer** *n*.

chorister *n* a member of a choir.

chortle *vi* to chuckle exultantly.—*also n.*

chorus *n* a group of singers and dancers in a play, musical, etc; a refrain.—*also vt.*

Christ *n* Jesus of Nazareth, regarded by Christians as the Messiah.

christen *vt* to enter the Christian Church by baptism; to give a name to.—**christening** *n*.

Christian *n* a person who believes in Christianity. • *adj* of Christianity; kind, humane.

Christianity *n* the religion based on the teachings of Christ.

Christian name *n* a name given when one is christened; (*loosely*) any forename.

Christmas *n* an annual festival (25 December) in memory of the birth of Christ.

chrome *n* chromium; a chromium pigment; something plated with an alloy of chromium.

chromium *n* a hard metallic element used in making steel alloys and electroplating.

chromosome *n* any of the microscopic rod-shaped bodies bearing genes.

chronic *adj* (*disease*) long-lasting.

chronicle *n* a record of events in chronological order; an account; a history.—*also vt.*

chronological *adj* arranged in order of occurrence.

chrysanthemum *n* a plant with a brightly coloured flower head.

chubby *adj* plump.—**chubbiness** *n*.

chuck[1] *vt* to throw; to toss.

chuck[2] *n* a cut of beef from neck to ribs.

chuckle *vi* to laugh softly; to gloat.—*also n*.

chum *n* (*inf*) a close friend.

chunk *n* a short, thick piece.—**chunky** *adj*.

church *n* a building for public worship, esp Christian worship; the clerical profession.

churchyard *n* the yard around a church often used as a burial ground.

churn *n* a large metal container for milk; a device to turn milk or cream into butter. • *vt* to agitate in a churn; to stir violently.

chute *n* a slide for sending down water, logs, rubbish, etc; a fall of water, a rapid.

cider *n* fermented apple juice as a drink.

cigar *n* a roll of tobacco leaf for smoking.

cigarette *n* shredded tobacco rolled in fine paper for smoking.

cinder *n* a tiny piece of partly burned wood, etc.

cine- *prefix* cinema, as *cinecamera*.

cinema *n* a place where motion pictures are shown; film as an industry or art form.

cinnamon *n* a tree of the laurel family; its aromatic edible bark; a spice made from this.

cipher *n* the numeral 0, zero; a person of no importance; a method of secret writing.—*also* **cypher**.

circle *n* a perfectly round plane figure; the line enclosing it; the curved seating area above the stalls in a theatre; a group, set or class (of people). • *vti* to revolve (round).

circuit *n* a distance round; a route or course; an area so enclosed; the path of an electric current.

circuitous *adj* roundabout, indirect.

circular *adj* shaped like a circle, round; moving round a circle. • *n* an advertisement, etc, addressed to many people.

circulate *vti* to pass from hand to hand or place to place; to spread or be spread about; to move round.—**circulatory** *adj*.

circulation *n* a moving round; the number of copies sold of a newspaper, etc.

circumcise *vt* to cut off the foreskin of (a male) or the clitoris of (a female), esp as a religious rite.—**circumcision** *n*.

circumference *n* the line bounding a circle, a ball, etc; the length of this line.

circumstance *n* an occurrence, an incident; a detail; (*pl*) a state of affairs; condition in life.

circus *n* a large arena for the exhibition of games, feats of horsemanship etc; a travelling show of acrobats, clowns, etc.

cistern *n* a tank for storing water, esp in a WC.

cite *vt* to summon officially to appear in court; to quote; to give as an example.

citizen *n* a member of a city, state or nation.

citrus *n* a genus of trees including the lemon, orange, etc; the fruit of these trees.

city *n* an important or cathedral town; a town created a city by charter; business circles.

civic *adj* of a city or citizenship.

civil *adj* of citizens or the state; not military or ecclesiastical; polite, obliging; (*law*) relating to citizens' private rights.

civil engineer *n* an engineer who designs and constructs roads, bridges, etc.

civilian *n* a person who is not a member of the armed forces.

civilisation *n* the state of being civilised; the process of civilising; an advanced stage of social culture; moral and cultural refinement.

civil service *n* those employed in the service of a state apart from the military.

civil war *n* a war between citizens of the same state or country.

claim *vt* to demand as a right; to require; to profess (to have); to assert. • *n* the act of claiming; a right to something; a thing claimed, esp a piece of land for mining.—**claimant** *n*.

clam *n* an edible marine bivalve mollusc.

clamber *vi* to climb with difficulty.

clammy *adj* damp and sticky.

clamp *n* a device for gripping objects tightly together. • *vt* to grip with a clamp; to attach firmly.

clan *n* a group of people with a common ancestor under a single chief; a party or clique.

clang *n* a loud metallic sound.—*also vti*.

clap *vti* to strike (the hands) together sharply; to applaud in this way.

claret *n* a dry red wine of Bordeaux.

clarify *vti* to make or become clear or intelligible; to free or become free from impurities.—**clarification** *n*.

clarinet *n* a woodwind instrument.

clarity *n* clearness.

clash *n* a loud noise of striking weapons, etc; a disagreement; a collision.—*also vti*.

clasp *n* an embrace; a catch or buckle.—*also vt*.

class *n* a division, a group; a kind; a set of students taught together; a grade of merit or quality; rank. • *vt* to put into a class.

classic *adj* of the highest class or rank, esp in literature; of the best Greek and Roman writers; of music conforming to certain standards of form, etc; traditional; authoritative. • *n* a work of literature, etc of high excellence.

classical *adj* influenced by, of or relating to ancient Roman and Greek art, literature and culture; traditional; serious; refined.

classification *n* the organisation of knowledge into categories; a category or division.

classify *vt* to arrange in classes, to categorise; to restrict for security reasons.

clatter n a rattling noise; noisy talk.—*also* vti.

clause n a single article or stipulation in a treaty, law, contract, etc; (*gram*) a short sentence; a division of a sentence.

claustrophobia n a morbid fear of confined spaces.—**claustrophobic** adj.

claw n the sharp hooked nail of an animal or bird; the pointed end or pincer of a crab, etc. • vti to seize or tear with claws or nails.

clay n a sticky ductile earthy material.

clean adj free from dirt or impurities; unsoiled; morally pure; complete, decisive. • adv entirely; outright. • vti to remove dirt from.

cleaner n a substance, device for cleaning; one employed to clean; (*pl*) a dry cleaner.

cleanse vt to make clean or pure.

cleanser n something that cleanses, esp a detergent, face cream, etc.

clear adj bright, not dim; transparent; without blemish; easily seen or heard; unimpeded, open; plain, obvious. • adv plainly. • vti to make or become clear; to rid (of), remove; to free from suspicion; to disentangle; to pass over without touching; to make as a profit.

clearance n a clearing; permission; the space between two objects in motion.

clearing n a tract of land cleared of trees.

clearly adv in a clear manner; evidently.

clearway n a road where it is illegal for vehicles to stop on the carriageway.

clef n a sign on a music stave that indicates the pitch of the notes.

clench vt (*teeth, fist*) to close tightly; to grasp.

clergy n ministers of the Christian church.

clergyman n a member of the clergy.

clerical adj of or relating to the clergy or a clergyman; of or relating to a clerk.

clerk n an office worker; a public official who keeps records.

clever adj intelligent; ingenious; skilful.

cliché n a hackneyed phrase.

click n a slight, sharp sound.—*also* vi.

client n a person who employs another professionally; a customer.

clientele n clients, customers.

cliff n a high steep rock face.

climate n the weather characteristics of an area; the prevailing attitude.—**climatic** adj.

climax n the highest point; a culmination; sexual orgasm.—*also* vi.—**climactic** adj.

climb vti to mount; to ascend; (*plants*) to grow upwards. • n an ascent.

climber n a mountaineer; a climbing plant.

clinch vt (*argument, etc*) to confirm or drive home. • vi (*boxing*) to grip the opponent with the arms to hinder his punching.—*also* n.

cling vi to adhere; to keep hold.

clinic n a place where outpatients are given medical care; a place where medical specialists practise as a group; a private or specialised hospital.

clinical adj of or relating to a clinic; based on medical observation; plain, simple; detached, cool, objective.

clink n a slight metallic ringing sound. • vti to make or cause to make such a sound.

clip[1] vt to cut or trim with scissors or shears; to punch a small hole in, esp a ticket; (*words*) to shorten. • n the piece clipped off; a yield of wool from sheep; an extract from a film.

clip[2] vt to hold firmly; to secure with a clip. • n any device that grips, clasps or hooks; a piece of jewellery held in place by a clip.

clique n a small exclusive group, a set.

cloak n a loose sleeveless outer garment; a pretext. • vt to cover; to conceal.

cloakroom n a room where coats may be left.

clock n a device for measuring time; any timing device with a dial and displayed figures. • vt to time (a race, etc) using a stopwatch.

clockwise adv moving in the direction of a clock's hands.—*also* adj.

clockwork n the mechanism of a clock or any similar mechanism with springs and gears. • adj mechanically regular.

clog n a wooden-soled shoe. • vt to cause a blockage in; to impede.

cloister n a roofed pillared walk, usu with one side open, in a convent, college, etc. • vt to confine as if in a convent.

close[1] adj near; nearly alike; nearly even or equal; sultry, airless. • adv closely; near by. • n a courtyard; the entrance to a courtyard; the precincts of a cathedral.

close[2] vt to make closed; to stop up (an opening); to draw together; to shut. • vi to come together; to complete; to finish. • n a completion.

closed adj shut up; with no opening; restricted; not open to the public, exclusive.

closet n a small room or a cupboard for clothes, supplies, etc; a small private room. • vt to enclose in a private room for a confidential talk.

close-up n a film or television shot taken from very close range; a close examination.

closure n closing; the condition of being closed; (*parliament, etc*) a decision to end debate and move to an immediate vote.

clot n a thickened mass, esp of blood. • vti to form into clots, to curdle, coagulate.

cloth n woven, knitted or pressed fabric; a piece of this; a tablecloth; clerical dress.

clothe vt to cover with garments; to dress.

clothes npl garments, apparel.

clothing n clothes.

cloud n a visible mass of water vapour floating in the sky; a mass of smoke, etc; a threatening thing. • vt to darken or obscure as with clouds.

cloudburst *n* a sudden rainstorm.

cloudy *adj* of or full of clouds; not clear.

clout *n* a blow; (*sl*) power, influence.

clove[1] *n* a segment of a bulb, as garlic.

clove[2] *n* the dried flower bud of a tropical tree, used as a spice.

clover *n* a low-growing plant with three leaves used as fodder; a trefoil; (*inf*) luxury.

clown *n* a person who entertains with jokes, antics, etc, esp in a circus; a boorish person.

club *n* a heavy stick used as a weapon; a stick with a head for playing golf, etc; an association of people for athletic, social purposes; its premises; a suit of playing cards with black clover-like markings. • *vt* to beat with a club.

clubhouse *n* premises used by a club.

cluck *n* the call of a hen.—*also vi.*

clue *n* a guide to the solution of a mystery.

clump *n* a cluster of trees; a lump; (*of hair*) a handful; the sound of heavy footsteps.

clumsy *adj* unwieldy; awkward; lacking tact

cluster *n* a bunch; a swarm; a group.—*also vti.*

clutch[1] *vt* to seize; to snatch at. • *n* a tight grip; a device for throwing parts of a machine into or out of action; the pedal operating this device.

clutch[2] *n* a nest of eggs; a brood of chicks.

clutter *n* a disordered mess. • *vti* to litter.

coach *n* a long-distance bus; a railway carriage; a covered four-wheeled horse-drawn carriage; a sports instructor; a tutor. • *vti* to teach or train.

coagulate *vti* to change from a liquid to partially solid state, to clot, curdle.

coal *n* a black mineral used for fuel; a piece of this; an ember.

coalition *n* a temporary union of parties.

coarse *adj* rough; large in texture; rude, crude.

coast *n* an area of land bordering the sea; the seashore. • *vi* to travel down a slope without power; to proceed with ease.

coastguard *n* an organisation that monitors the coastline and provides help for ships in difficulties, prevents smuggling, etc.

coat *n* a sleeved outer garment; the natural covering of an animal; a layer. • *vt* to cover with a layer or coating.

coating *n* a surface coat; material for coats.

coat of arms *n* the heraldic bearings of a family, city, institution, etc.

coax *vt* to persuade gently.

cobble[1] *n* a rounded stone for paving.

cobble[2] *vt* to repair, to make (shoes); to put together roughly or hastily.

cobra *n* a venomous hooded snake.

cobweb *n* a spider's web; a flimsy thing.

cocaine *n* an addictive drug obtained from coca leaves, used in anaesthesia.

cock *n* the adult male of the domestic fowl; the male of other birds; the hammer of a gun. • *vt* to set erect, to stick up; to set at an angle; to bring the hammer (of gun) to firing position.

cockerel *n* a young cock.

cockle *n* an edible shellfish with a rounded shell.

cockney *n* a person born in the East End of London; the dialect of this area.

cockpit *n* the compartment of a small aircraft for pilot and crew.

cockroach *n* a nocturnal beetle-like insect.

cocktail *n* an alcoholic drink containing a mixture of spirits or other liqueurs.

cocoa *n* a powder of ground cacao seeds; a drink made from this.

coconut *n* the fruit of the coconut palm.

cocoon *n* a silky case spun by some insect larvae for protection in the chrysalis stage.

cod *n* a large edible fish North Atlantic fish.

code *n* a system of letters, numbers or symbols used to transmit secret messages; a systematic body of laws; a set of rules or conventions; (*comput*) a set of program instructions.—*also vt.*

codify *vt* to collect or arrange (laws, rules, regulations, etc) into a system.

coeducation *n* the teaching of students of both sexes in the same institution.

coerce *vt* to force by threats.—**coercion** *n.*

coexist *vi* to exist together at the same time; to live in peace together.—**coexistence** *n.*

coffee *n* a drink made from the seeds of the coffee tree; a light-brown colour.

coffin *n* a chest for a corpse to be buried in.

cog *n* a tooth-like projection on the rim of a wheel.

cogent *adj* persuasive, convincing.

cogwheel *n* a wheel with a toothed rim for gearing.

coherent *adj* capable of intelligible speech.—**coherence** *n.*

coil *vti* to wind in rings or folds; to twist into a circular or spiral shape. • *n* a coiled length of rope; (*elect*) a spiral wire for the passage of current; an intrauterine contraceptive device.

coin *n* a piece of legally stamped metal used as money. • *vt* to invent (a word, phrase); to mint.

coinage *n* currency; a coined word.

coincide *vi* to happen at the same time; to agree exactly, to correspond.

coincidence *n* the act of coinciding; the occurrence of an event at the same time as another without apparent connection.

coke[1] *n* coal from which gas has been expelled.

coke[2] *n* (*sl*) cocaine.

colander *n* a bowl with holes in the bottom for straining cooked vegetables, pasta, etc.

cold *adj* lacking heat; lacking emotion; unfriendly; (*sl*) unconscious. • *n* absence of heat; cold weather; a virus infection of the respiratory tract.

coleslaw *n* raw shredded cabbage in a dressing, used in salads.

collaborate *vi* to work jointly or together; to side with the invaders of one's country.—**collaboration** *n.*—**collaborator** *n.*

collage *n* art made up from scraps of paper, material and other odds and ends pasted onto a hard surface.

collapse *vi* to fall down; to come to ruin, to fail; to break down physically or mentally.—*also n.*

collar *n* the band of a garment round the neck; a band of leather or chain put round an animal's neck. • *vt* to put a collar on; (*inf*) to seize.

colleague *n* an associate in the same profession or office; a fellow worker.

collect *vti* to gather or assemble; to regain command of (oneself); to concentrate (thoughts, etc).

collected *adj* self-possessed, cool.

collection *n* an accumulation; money collected at a meeting, etc; a group of things collected; the periodic showing of a designer's fashions.

collector *n* a person who collects things as a hobby or so as to inspect them.

college *n* an institution of higher learning; a school offering specialised knowledge.

collide *vi* to come into violent contact (with).

colliery *n* a coal mine.

collision *n* state of colliding together; a violent impact of moving bodies, a crash.

colloquial *adj* used in familiar but not formal talk, not literary.

colon[1] *n* part of the large intestine.

colon[2] *n* a punctuation mark (:).

colonel *n* an army officer junior to a brigadier but senior to a lieutenant colonel.

colonial *adj* of or pertaining to a colony or colonies.

colonise *vt* to establish a colony in.

colony *n* an area of land acquired and settled by a distant state and subject to its control.

colossal *adj* gigantic, immense.

colour *n* the eye's perception of wavelengths of light with different colours corresponding to different wavelengths; the attribute of objects to appear different according to their differing ability to absorb, emit, or reflect light of different wavelengths; colour of the face or skin; dye; paint; (*pl*) a flag. • *vt* to give colour to. • *vi* to blush.

colour bar *n* discrimination based on race.

colour-blind *adj* unable to distinguish colours, esp red and green.

coloured *adj* possessing colour; biased, not objective.

colourful *adj* full of colour; vivid.

colt *n* a young male horse.

column *n* a round pillar; a vertical division of a page; a narrow-fronted deep formation of troops; a feature article appearing regularly in a newspaper, etc.

columnist *n* a journalist who contributes a regular column.

coma *n* deep prolonged unconsciousness.

comb *n* a toothed instrument for separating hair, wool, etc; a cock's crest; a honeycomb.—*also vt.*

combat *vti* to strive against, oppose; to do battle. • *n* a contest; a fight; struggle.

combination *n* a union of separate parts; persons allied for a purpose.

combine *vti* to join together; to unite; to cooperate; (*chem*) to form a compound with. • *n* an association formed for commercial purposes; a machine for harvesting and threshing grain.

combustible *adj* capable of burning; excitable.

combustion *n* the process of burning; the process in which substances react with oxygen in air to produce heat.

come *vi* to approach; to arrive; to reach; to happen (to); to originate; to be derived or descended; to be caused; to result; to be available.

comedian *n* an actor of comic parts; an entertainer who tells jokes.

comedy *n* an amusing play or film; drama consisting of amusing plays; humour.

comet *n* a celestial body that travels round the sun, with a visible nucleus and a luminous tail.

comfort *vti* to bring consolation to; to soothe; to cheer. • *n* consolation; relief; bodily ease.

comfortable *adj* promoting comfort; at ease; adequate; (*inf*) financially well off.

comic *adj* of comedy; causing amusement. • *n* a comedian; an entertaining person; a paper or book with strip cartoons.

comical *adj* funny, laughable; droll.

comic strip *n* a series of drawings that depict a story in stages.

comma *n* a punctuation mark (,) that indicates a slight pause or break in a sentence, or separates items in a list.

command *vti* to order; to bid; to control; to have at disposal; to compel; to look down over; to be in authority (over). • *n* an order; control; disposal; an instruction to a computer.

commandeer *vt* to seize for military purposes; to appropriate for one's own use.

commander *n* a person who commands; a naval officer ranking next below a captain.

commando *n* a member of an elite military force.

commemorate *vt* to keep in the memory by ceremony or writing; to be a memorial of.

commence *vti* to begin.

commend *vt* to praise; to recommend; to entrust.—**commendable** *adj.*

commendation *n* praise; an award.

commensurate *adj* having the same extent or measure; proportionate.

comment *n* a remark, observation.—*also vi.*

commentary *n* a series of explanatory notes or remarks.

commentator *n* one who reports and analyses events, trends, etc, as on television.

commerce *n* trade in goods and services between nations or individuals.

commercial *adj* of or engaged in commerce; profitable. • *n* a broadcast advertisement.

commercialise *vt* to put on a business basis; to exploit for profit.

commiserate *vti* to sympathise (with); to feel pity for.—**commiseration** *n.*

commission *n* authority to act; a document bestowing this; appointment to rank of officer; a body of people appointed for specified duties; business committed to someone; a percentage on sales paid to a salesman or agent; brokerage.—*also vt.*

commissionaire *n* a uniformed attendant at the entrance to a building, shop, etc.

commissioner *n* a person empowered by a commission; various types of civil servant.

commit *vti* to entrust; to consign (to prison); to do, to perpetrate; to pledge.

commitment *n* an engagement that restricts freedom; an obligation.

committee *n* people appointed from a larger body to consider or manage some matter.

commodity *n* an article of trade; (*pl*) goods.

common *adj* belonging equally to more than one; public; usual; widespread; familiar; frequent; not rare; low, vulgar. • *n* a tract of open public land; (*pl*) the House of Commons.

commoner *n* an ordinary persony.

common law *n* law based on custom and judicial precedents as distinct from statute law. • *adj* denoting a marriage recognised in law not by an official ceremony.

Common Market *n* (*with the*) an unofficial name for the European Community.

commonplace *adj* ordinary, unremarkable. • *n* a platitude; an ordinary thing.

common sense *n* practical good sense.

commonwealth *n* a political community; a sovereign state; a federation of states; (*with cap*) an association of sovereign states and dependencies (formerly) ruled by Britain.

commotion *n* a violent disturbance.

communal *adj* shared in common.

commune[1] *n* a group of people living together and sharing possessions.

commune[2] *vi* to converse intimately; to communicate spiritually.

communicate *vti* to impart, to share; to succeed in conveying information.

communication *n* information; a connecting channel; (*pl*) connections of transport; (*pl*) means of imparting information, as in newspapers, radio, television.

communication cord *n* a cord to pull to stop a train in an emergency.

communion *n* common possession, sharing; fellowship; (*with cap*) Holy Communion, the Christian sacrament of the Eucharist.

communiqué *n* an official communication.

communism *n* a social system under which private property is abolished and the means of production are owned by the people; (*with cap*) a political movement seeking the overthrow of capitalism based on the writings of Karl Marx.

communist *n* a supporter of communism; (*with cap*) a member of a Communist party.

community *n* an organised political or social body; a body of people in the same locality; the general public.

community centre *n* a place providing social facilities for a local community.

commute *vti* to travel daily from a suburban home to a city; to reduce (a punishment)—**commuter** *n.*

compact[1] *n* an agreement; a treaty.

compact[2] *adj* closely packed; condensed; terse.—*also vt.* • *n* a small cosmetic case.

companion *n* a partner; a friend; one of a pair of matched things.—**companionship** *n.*

company *n* any assembly of people; an association of people for carrying on a business, etc; a society; a military unit; the crew of a ship; companionship, fellowship.

comparable *adj* able to be compared (*with with*); similar.

comparative *adj* relative, not absolute; (*gram*) expressing more.

compare *vt* to make one thing the measure of another; to liken; to bear comparison. • *vi* to be equal or alike.—**comparison** *n.*

compartment *n* a space partitioned off; a division of a railway carriage; a separate category.

compass *n* an extent, area; an instrument with a magnetic needle indicating north; (*often pl*) an instrument for drawing circles, etc.

compassion *n* pity, sympathy.

compassionate *adj* merciful.

compatible *adj* agreeing or fitting in (with); consistent.—**compatibility** *n.*

compel *vt* to force, constrain; to oblige.

compendium *n* an abridgement; a summary.

compensate *vti* to counterbalance; to recompense.—**compensatory** *adj.*

compensation *n* the act of compensating; a sum given to compensate.

compere, compère *n* a person who introduces cabaret, television acts, etc.—*also vt.*

compete *vi* to strive; to contend.

competence *n* efficiency; capacity.

competent *adj* fit, capable; legally qualified.

competition *n* act of competing; rivalry; a contest in skill or knowledge; a match.

competitive *adj* of, or involving, competition; of sufficient value in terms of price or quality to ensure success against rivals.

competitor *n* a person who competes; a rival.

compile *vt* to collect from various sources; to amass.—**compilation** *n*.

complacent *adj* self-satisfied.—**complacency** *n*.

complain *vi* to find fault, to grumble; to be ill.—**complaint** *n*.

complement *n* something making up a whole; a full allowance (of equipment or number). • *vt* to make complete.

complementary *adj* completing; together forming a balanced whole.

complete *adj* entire; free from deficiency; finished; thorough.—*also vt*.

completely *adv* entirely, utterly.

completion *n* the act of completing; accomplishment; fulfilment.

complex *adj* having more than one part; intricate; difficult. • *n* a collection of interconnected buildings or units; a group of impulses, etc, influencing behaviour.—**complexity** *n*.

complexion *n* colour, texture and look of the skin; aspect, character.

compliance *n* acquiescence.

compliant *adj* yielding, submissive.

complicate *vt* to make intricate or involved.—**complicated** *adj*.

complication *n* a circumstance that makes (a situation) more complex; (*med*) a condition following an original illness.

compliment *n* an expression of praise; (*pl*) a formal greeting or expression of regard.—*also vt*.

complimentary *adj* conveying or expressing a compliment; given free of charge.

comply *vi* to yield, to agree.

component *adj* going to the making of a whole, constituent. • *n* a component part.

compose *vt* to make up, to form; to construct in one's mind, to write; to arrange, to put in order; to settle, to adjust. • *vi* to write music.

composed *adj* calm, self-controlled.

composer *n* one who composes music.

composition *n* the process of composing; a work of literature or music; a short essay; the make-up of something.

compost *n* a mixture of decomposed organic matter for fertilising soil.

composure *n* calmness.

compound *n* something made up of a number of parts or ingredients, a mixture; a compound word. • *vt* to combine into a whole, to mix; to intensify by adding; to settle (debt) by partial payment. • *adj* made up of several parts; not simple.

comprehend *vt* to understand; to include, to embrace.—**comprehension** *n*.

comprehensive *adj* wide in scope or content.

comprehensive school *n* in Britain, a secondary school for pupils of all abilities.

compress *vt* to squeeze together; to condense. • *n* a soft pad for compressing an artery, etc; a wet bandage to relieve inflammation.

compression *n* the act of compressing; the increase in pressure in an engine to compress the gases so that they explode.

comprise *vt* to consist of, to include.

compromise *n* a settlement of a dispute by mutual concession; a middle course or view. • *vti* to adjust by compromise; to lay open to disrepute.

compulsion *n* something that compels; an irresistible urge.—**compulsive** *adj*.

compulsory *adj* enforced, obligatory.

computer *n* an electronic device that processes data in accordance with programmed instructions.

computerise *vt* to equip with computers; to perform (a process) using computers.

comrade *n* a companion; a fellow member of a Communist party.—**comradeship** *n*.

concave *adj* curving inwards, hollow. • *n* a concave line or surface.—**concavity** *n*.

conceal *vt* to hide, to keep from sight; to keep secret.—**concealment** *n*.

concede *vt* to grant; to admit to be true.

conceit *n* an over-high opinion of oneself; vanity; a quaint fancy.

conceited *adj* full of conceit, vain.

conceive *vti* to become pregnant (with); to form in the mind.—**conceivable** *adj*.

concentrate *vt* to bring together to one point; to direct to a single object; to collect one's thoughts; (*chem*) to increase the strength of by diminishing bulk, to condense. • *n* a concentrated product, esp a food reduced in bulk by eliminating fluid; a food relatively high in nutrients.—**concentration** *n*.

concern *vt* to apply to; to fill with anxiety; to interest (oneself) in.—*also n.*.

concerning *prep* about; regarding.

concert *n* a musical entertainment; harmony.

concerted *adj* planned or arranged by mutual agreement; combined.

concertina *n* a musical instrument, similar to an accordion, that produces sound by squeezing bellows that pass air over metal reeds.—*also vi*.

concerto *n* a musical composition for a solo instrument and orchestra.

concession *n* the act of conceding; a reduction

in price granted to certain people.—**concessionary** adj.

conciliate vt to appease; to reconcile.—**conciliation** n.—**conciliatory** adj.

concise adj brief, condensed, terse.

conclave n a secret meeting.

conclude vti to bring or come to an end, to finish; to effect, to settle; to infer; to resolve.

conclusion n the end or close; an inference.

conclusive adj decisive; convincing.

concoct vt to make by combining ingredients; to devise, to plan; to invent (a story).

concourse n an open space or hall where crowds gather, e.g. an airport terminal.

concrete adj having a material existence; (gram) denoting a thing, not a quality. • n a mixture of sand, cement, etc, used in building.

concur vi to happen together, to coincide; to cooperate; to be of the same opinion, to agree.—**concurrence** n.

concurrent adj existing, acting or occurring at the same time; coinciding.

concussion n the violent shock of an impact or explosion; loss of consciousness caused by a violent blow to the head.

condemn vt to express strong disapproval of; to find guilty; to blame or censure; to declare unfit for use.—**condemnation** n.

condense vt to reduce to a smaller compass, to compress; to change from a gas into a liquid; to concentrate; to express in fewer words.—**condensation** n.

condescend vi to deign, to stoop; to act patronisingly.—**condescension** n.

condiment n a seasoning or relish.

condition n anything required for the performance, completion or existence of something else; physical state of health; an illness; a prerequisite; (pl) attendant circumstances. • vt to make accustomed (to).

conditional adj depending on conditions; not absolute; (gram) expressing condition.—also n.

conditioner n a substance for bringing the hair into a glossy condition.

condolence n sympathy.

condone vt to overlook, to forgive.

conducive adj leading, helping to cause.

conduct vti to lead; to direct (an orchestra); to manage (a business); to transmit (electricity, heat); to behave (oneself). • n behaviour.

conductor n a person who conducts an orchestra; one in charge of passengers on a train, or who collects fares on a bus; a substance that conducts heat or electricity.—**conductress** nf.

conduit n a channel that carries water, etc.

cone n a solid pointed figure with a circular or elliptical base; any cone-shaped object; the scaly fruit of the pine, fir, etc.

confectionery n sweets.

confederation n an alliance of individuals, organisations or states.

confer vt to grant or bestow; to consult.

conference n a meeting for discussion.

confess vti to acknowledge or admit; to disclose (sins) to a confessor; (priest) to hear confession of.—**confessor** n.

confession n admission of a fault or sin, esp to a confessor; a thing confessed.

confessional n an enclosure in a church where a priest hears confessions.

confetti npl bits of coloured paper thrown at weddings.

confide vti to entrust; to impart.

confidence n faith; belief in one's abilities; something revealed confidentially.

confidence trick n the persuading of a victim to hand over valuables as proof of confidence.

confident adj positive, assured.

confidential adj spoken or written in confidence, secret.

confine vt to restrict; to keep shut up.

confinement n a being confined; the period of childbirth.

confirm vt to establish firmly; to corroborate.—**confirmed** adj.

confirmation n convincing proof; the rite by which people are admitted to full communion in Christian churches.

confiscate vt to seize by authority.

conflict n a fight; a contest; strife, quarrel; emotional disturbance.—also vi.

conform vti to comply, to be obedient (to); to act in accordance with; to adapt; to make like.

conformist n one who conforms to established rules, etc.

confound vt to mix up, to obscure; to perplex.

confounded adj astonished; confused.

confront vt to face; to oppose.—**confrontation** n.

confuse vt to throw into disorder; to mix up; to mistake one thing for another.

confusion n disorder; embarrassment.

congeal vti to change from a liquid to a solid by cooling, to jell.

congenial adj of a similar disposition or with similar tastes, kindred; suited.

congenital adj existing or dating since birth.

conger eel n a large marine eel.

congestion n overcrowding; (med) excessive accumulation of blood; an accumulation of traffic causing obstruction.

congratulate vt to express pleasure at success.

congratulations npl an expression of joy or pleasure.

congregate vti to flock together, to assemble.

congregation n a body of people assembled for worship.

congress n an association or society; an assembly or conference, esp for discussion and action on some question; (with cap) the legislature of the USA.

conic, conical adj of a cone; cone-shaped.

conifer n any evergreen tree bearing cones.—**coniferous** adj.

conjecture n a guess, guesswork.—also vt.

conjugal adj of or relating to marriage.

conjunction n (gram) a word connecting words, clauses or sentences; a union.

conjunctivitis n inflammation of the membrane that covers the eyelid.

conjure vti to practise magical tricks; to call up, to invoke.—**conjurer, conjuror** n.

connect vti to fasten together, to join; to relate together, to link up; (aeroplanes, trains, buses, etc) to be timed to arrive as another leaves.

connection n a relationship, bond; a train, bus, etc, timed to connect with another; context; a link between components in an electric circuit; a relative; (pl) clients.

connive vi to plot.—**connivance** n.

connoisseur n a trained discriminating judge, esp of the fine arts.

connotation n an implication.

conquer vt to defeat; to acquire by conquest; to master. • vi to be victor.—**conqueror** n.

conquest n the winning of a person's affection; a person or thing conquered.

conscience n the knowledge of right and wrong that affects behaviour; the sense of guilt or virtue induced by actions, behaviour, etc.

conscientious adj scrupulous; careful, thorough.

conscientious objector n a person who refuses to serve in the military forces on moral or religious grounds.

conscious adj aware (of); awake to one's surroundings.

consciousness n the state of being conscious; perception.

conscript n a conscripted person (as a military recruit). • vt to enlist compulsorily.—**conscription** n.

consecrate vt to set apart as sacred, to sanctify; to devote (to).—**consecration** n.

consecutive adj following in regular order; successive; (gram) expressing consequence.

consensus n general agreement.

consent vi to agree (to); to comply; to acquiesce. • n agreement, permission.

consequence n a result, an outcome; importance.

consequent adj occurring as a result.—**consequently** adv.

conservation n conserving; preservation of the environment and natural resources.—**conservationist** n.

conservative adj traditional; cautious; moderate. • n a conservative person; (with cap) a member of the Conservative Party.

conservatory n a greenhouse attached to a house.

conserve vt to keep from loss or injury; to preserve (food) with sugar.—also n.

consider vti to contemplate; to examine; to take into account; to be of the opinion.

considerable adj fairly large.

considerate adj careful of the feelings of others.

consideration n deliberation; a point of importance; an inducement; deference.

considering prep in view of. • adv all in all. • conj seeing that.

consign vt to hand over, to commit.

consignment n goods, etc, consigned.

consist vi to be made up (of).

consistency n degree of density, esp of thick liquids; the state of being consistent.

consistent adj compatible, not contradictory.

consolation n someone or something that offers comfort in distress.

console[1] vt to comfort, to cheer.

console[2] n a desk containing the controls of an electronic system; the part of an organ containing the pedals, stops, etc.

consolidate vti to establish firmly, to strengthen; to combine into a single whole.—**consolidation** n.

consonant n a letter of the alphabet that is not a vowel. • adj consistent, in keeping (with).

consortium n an international banking or financial combination.

conspicuous adj easily seen, prominent.

conspiracy n a secret plan for an illegal act.

conspire vti to combine secretly for an evil purpose; to plot, to devise.

constable n a policeman or policewoman.

constant adj fixed; unchangeable; faithful; continual.—**constancy** n.

constellation n a group of fixed stars.

consternation n surprise and alarm.

constipation n infrequent and difficult movement of the bowels.

constituency n a body of electors; the voters in a particular district.

constituent adj forming part of a whole. • n a component part; a voter in a district.

constitute vt to establish; to make up.

constitution n fundamental physical condition; disposition; structure, composition; the system of basic laws and principles of a government.

constitutional adj of a constitution; legal. • n a walk for the sake of one's health.

constrain vt to compel, to force; to hinder by force; to confine, to imprison.

constrained adj enforced; embarrassed.

constraint n compulsion; forcible confinement; repression of feeling; embarrassment.

constrict vt to squeeze, to compress.

construct vt to make, to build, to fit together.

construction n a structure, building; interpretation; (gram) two or more words grouped together to form a phrase, clause or sentence.

constructive adj helping to improve, promoting development.

construe vti to translate word for word; to analyse grammatically; to interpret.

consul n a government official in a foreign city who attends to the interests of his country's citizens.—**consular** adj.

consulate n the residence of a consul.

consult vti to seek advice from; to confer.

consultant n a specialist who gives professional advice; a senior physician or surgeon.

consultation n the act of consulting; a conference, esp with a doctor or lawyer.

consume vti to use up; to eat or drink up.

consumer n a person who uses goods and services, the end user.

consummate[1] vt to bring to perfection, to be the crown of; (marriage) to complete by sexual intercourse.—**consummation** n.

consummate[2] adj complete, perfect.

consumption n using up; (econ) expenditure on goods and services by consumers; tuberculosis.

contact n touch, touching; connection; an acquaintance, esp in business.—also vti.

contact lens n a thin correctional lens placed over the cornea of the eye.

contagious adj (disease) spread by contact; (influence) catching, infectious.

contain vt to hold, to enclose; to comprise, to include; to restrain within limits.

container n a receptacle, etc, designed to contain goods or substances; a standardised receptacle used to transport commodities.

contaminate vt to render impure, to pollute.

contemplate vti to look at steadily; to meditate; to intend.—**contemplation** n.

contemporary adj living or happening at the same time; of the same age; present day. • n one living at the same time; one of the same age.

contempt n scorn, disgust.

contemptible adj deserving contempt.

contemptuous adj showing or feeling contempt; disdainful.

contend vti to take part in a contest, to strive (for); to quarrel; to assert.

content[1] n (usu pl) what is in a container; (usu pl) what is in a book; substance or meaning.

content[2] adj satisfied (with); happy; pleased. • n satisfaction. • vt to make content; to satisfy.—**contentment** n.

contention n struggling, arguing; a point in dispute; an assertion in an argument.

contest vti to dispute; to compete for; to strive. • n a competition; a dispute.—**contestant** n.

context n writing or speech that precedes and follows, contributing to the full meaning.

continent[1] n one of the main divisions of the earth's land; (with cap) the mainland of Europe, excluding the British Isles.

continent[2] adj able to control urination and defecation.

continental adj of a continent; (with cap) of or relating to Europe, excluding the British Isles. • n an inhabitant of the Continent.

contingency n something dependent on a future event.

contingent adj chance; dependent (on); incidental (to). • n a possibility; a quota of troops.

continual adj frequently repeated, going on all the time.—**continually** adv.

continuation n a continuing; prolongation; resumption; a thing that continues something else.

continue vti to go on (with); to prolong; to carry further, to stay; to last; to preserve.

continuity n uninterrupted succession; a script, scenario in a film or broadcast.

continuous adj continuing; occurring without interruption.

contort vti to twist out of a normal shape, to pull awry.—**contortion** n.

contortionist n a person who can twist his or her body into unusual postures.

contour n the outline of a figure, land, etc; the line representing this outline.

contour line n a line on a map that passes through all points at the same altitude.

contra- prefix against.

contraband n smuggled goods; smuggling.

contraception n birth control.

contraceptive n a contraceptive drug or device.—also adj.

contract vt to draw closer together; to confine; (disease) to become infected by; (word) to shorten by omitting letters. • vi to shrink; to make a contract. • n a bargain; an agreement; a written agreement enforceable by law.

contraction n the act of contracting; a contracted word; a labour pain in childbirth.

contractor n a person who makes a business contract, esp a builder.

contradict vti to assert the contrary of; to deny; to be at variance (with).—**contradiction** n.

contralto n a singing voice having a range between tenor and mezzo-soprano; a person having this voice.

contraption n (inf) a device, a gadget.

contrary adj opposed; opposite in nature; wayward, perverse. • n the opposite.

contrast *vi* to show marked differences. • *vt* to compare so as to point out differences.—*also n.*

contravene *vt* to infringe, to transgress; to conflict with.—**contravention** *n.*

contribute *vti* to give to a common fund; to write (an article) for a magazine or newspaper.—**contribution** *n.*—**contributor** *n.*

contrite *adj* deeply repentant, feeling guilt.—**contrition** *n.*

contrivance *n* something contrived, esp a mechanical device, invention.

contrive *vt* to devise, to design, to achieve, esp by some ploy; to scheme.

control *n* restraint; command, authority; a check; a standard of comparison for checking an experiment. • *vt* to check; to restrain; to regulate.

controversial *adj* causing contrary opinions; open to argument.—**controversy** *n.*

convalesce *vi* to recover health after illness.—**convalescence** *n.*—**convalescent** *adj, n.*

convector *n* a heater that circulates warm air.

convene *vti* to call together for a meeting.

convenience *n* what suits one; a useful appliance; a public lavatory.

convenient *adj* handy; suitable.

convent *n* a house of a religious order, esp an establishment of nuns.

convention *n* a political or ecclesiastical meeting; an agreement between nations, a treaty; established usage, social custom.

conventional *adj* of or based on social custom; not spontaneous; following accepted rules; (*weapons*) non-nuclear.—**conventionality** *n.*

converge *vti* to come or bring together.—**convergence** *n.*—**convergent** *adj.*

conversant *adj* familiar (with).

conversation *n* informal talk or exchange of ideas.—**conversational** *adj.*

converse[1] *vi* to engage in conversation (with). • *n* familiar talk, conversation.

converse[2] *adj* opposite, contrary.—*also n.*

conversion *n* change from one state or one religion to another; something converted from one use to another; an alteration to a building undergoing a change in function; (*rugby*) a score after a try by kicking the ball over the crossbar.

convert *vt* to change from one thing, condition or religion to another; (*rugby*) to make a conversion after a try. • *n* a converted person, esp one who has changed religion.

convertible *adj* able to be converted. • *n* a car with a folding or detachable roof.

convex *adj* curving outward like the surface of a sphere.—**convexity** *n.*

convey *vt* to transport; to conduct, to transmit; to make known, to communicate.

conveyor belt *n* a continuous moving belt for moving objects in a factory.

convict *vt* to pronounce guilty. • *n* a person serving a prison sentence.

conviction *n* act of convicting; a firm belief.

convince *vt* to persuade by argument or evidence; to satisfy by proof.

convincing *adj* compelling belief.

convivial *adj* sociable, jovial.

convulse *vt* to agitate violently; to shake with irregular spasms. • *vi* (*inf*) to cause to shake with uncontrollable laughter.—**convulsion** *n..*

cook *vt* to prepare (food) by heat; to subject to great heat. • *vi* to be a cook.—*also n.*

cooker *n* an electric or gas appliance for cooking.

cookery *n* the art or practice of cooking.

cool *adj* moderately cold; calm; indifferent. • *vti* to make or become cool.

coop *n* a small pen for poultry. • *vt* to confine as in a coop.

cooperate *vi* to work together, to act jointly.—**cooperation** *n.*

cooperative *adj* willing to cooperate. • *n* an organisation or enterprise owned by, and operated for the benefit of, those using its services.

coordinate *vt* to integrate (different elements, etc) into an efficient relationship; to adjust to; to function harmoniously. • *n* any of a series of numbers that, in a given frame of reference, locate a point in space; (*pl*) separate items of clothing intended to be worn together.

coordination *n* being coordinated; balanced and harmonious movement of the body.

cope *vi* to deal successfully with.

copilot *n* a second pilot in an aircraft.

copious *adj* plentiful, abundant.

copper *n* a reddish ductile metallic element; a bronze coin. • *adj* made of copper.

copulate *vi* to have sexual intercourse.—**copulation** *n.*—**copulative** *adj.*

copy *n* a reproduction; a single specimen of a book; a manuscript for printing; text for an advertisement; subject matter for a writer. • *vt* to make a copy of; to imitate.

copyright *n* the exclusive legal right to the publication and sale of a literary, dramatic, musical, or artistic work in any form.

copywriter *n* a writer of advertising copy.

coral *n* the hard skeleton secreted by certain marine polyps.—*also adj.*

cord *n* a thick string or thin rope; a slender electric cable; corduroy; (*pl*) corduroy trousers.

cordial *adj* hearty, warm; friendly; affectionate. • *n* a fruit-flavoured drink.

cordon *n* a chain of police or soldiers preventing access to an area. • *vt* (*with off*) (*area*) to prevent access to.

corduroy *n* a strong cotton fabric with a velvety ribbed surface; (*pl*) trousers of this.

core n the innermost part, the heart; the inner part of an apple, etc, containing seeds; the region of a nuclear reactor containing the fissile material; (*comput*) a form of magnetic memory used to store one bit of information. • vt to remove the core from.

cork n the outer bark of the cork oak used esp for stoppers and insulation; a stopper for a bottle, esp made of cork. • adj made of cork. • vt to give a taste of cork to (wine).

corkage n a charge made by a restaurant for serving wine.

corkscrew n a tool for drawing corks from wine bottles. • adj resembling a corkscrew.

corn[1] n a grain or seed of a cereal plant; maize.

corn[2] n a hard painful growth on the foot.

cornea n the transparent membrane in front of the eyeball.—**corneal** adj.

corner n the point where sides or streets meet; an angle; a difficult or dangerous situation; (*football, hockey*) a free kick from the corner of the pitch. • vt to force into a corner; to monopolise supplies of.

cornerstone n the principal stone, esp one at the corner of a foundation; an indispensable part.

cornet n a valved brass musical instrument; a cone-shaped wafer for ice cream.

cornflour n a type of maize flour used for thickening sauces.

cornice n a plaster moulding round a ceiling.

corollary n an additional inference from a proposition already proved; a result.

coronary adj pertaining to the arteries supplying blood to the heart.—*also n*.

coronation n the ceremony of crowning a sovereign.

coroner n an official who inquires into cause of sudden or accidental death.

coronet n a small crown.

corporal[1] n a non-commissioned officer below the rank of sergeant.

corporal[2] adj of or relating to the body.

corporal punishment n physical punishment.

corporate adj of or having a corporation.

corporation n a group of people authorised to act as one individual; a council.

corps n an organised subdivision of troops; a group with a special function.

corpse n a dead body.

corpuscle n a red or white blood cell.

corral n a pen for livestock; an enclosure with wagons. • vt to put or keep in a corral.

correct vt to set right, to remove errors from; to reprove, to punish; to counteract, to neutralise. • adj free from error; right, true, accurate; conforming to a fixed standard.—**correction** n.

correlate vti to have or to bring into mutual relation; to correspond to one another.

correspond vi to answer, to agree; to be similar (to); to communicate by letter.

correspondence n communication by writing letters; the letters themselves.

correspondent n a person who writes letters; a journalist who gathers news.

corridor n a long passage.

corroborate vt to confirm; to make more certain; to verify.—**corroboration** n.

corrode vti to eat into or wear away gradually, to rust; to disintegrate.—**corrosion** n.

corrugated iron n iron pressed in alternate ridges and grooves and galvanised.

corrupt adj dishonest; taking bribes. • vti to make or become corrupt; to infect; to taint.

corset n a close-fitting undergarment, worn to support the torso.

cortege n a retinue; a funeral procession.

cosmetic n a preparation for improving the beauty, esp of the face.—*also adj.*

cosmonaut n a Russian astronaut.

cosmopolitan adj of all parts of the world.

cosmos n the universe as an ordered whole.

cosset vt to make a pet of; to pamper.

cost vt to involve payment, loss, or sacrifice of; to fix the price of. • n a price; expenditure of time, labour, etc; (*pl*) the expenses of a lawsuit.

costly adj expensive.

costume n a style of dress, esp belonging to a particular period, fashion, etc; clothes worn by actors in a play, etc.

cosy adj warm and comfortable.

cot n a child's bed with sides.

cottage n a small house, esp in the country.

cottage cheese n a soft cheese made from loose milk curds.

cotton n soft white fibre of the cotton plant; fabric or thread made of this; thread.

cotton wool n raw cotton bleached and sterilised for use as a dressing, etc.

couch n a piece of furniture, with a back and armrests, to seat several persons; a bed,. • vt to express in words in a particular way.

cough vi to expel air from the lungs with a sudden effort and noise.—*also n.*

council n an elected or appointed legislative or advisory body; a central body uniting a group of organisations.—**councillor** n.

counsel n advice; consultation; a lawyer or a group of lawyers. • vti to advise; to recommend.

counsellor n an adviser; a lawyer.

count[1] n a European noble.

count[2] vt to number, add up; to reckon; to consider to be; to call aloud (beats). • vi to add up items; to be of importance; to rely (upon). • n numbering, reckoning; the total counted.

countdown n the descending count to zero, e.g. to the moment a rocket lifts off.

countenance n the face; appearance; support. • vt to favour, approve.

counter[1] n a disc used for scoring, a token; a table in a bank or shop across which money or goods are passed.

counter[2] adv contrary; adverse; in an opposite direction; in the wrong way. • adj opposed; opposite. • n a return blow or parry; an answering move. • vti to oppose; to retort; to retaliate.

counteract vt to act in opposition to so as to defeat or hinder; to neutralise.

counterbalance n a weight balancing another. • vt to act as a counterbalance.

counterespionage n spying on or exposing enemy spies.

counterfeit adj made in imitation, forged; feigned, sham. • n an imitation, a forgery.

counterfoil n a detachable section of a cheque or ticket, kept as a receipt or record.

counterpart n a thing exactly like another, a duplicate.

countess n a woman with rank of count or earl; the wife, widow of an earl or count.

countless adj innumerable.

country n a nation's territory; a state; the land of one's birth; rural parts. • adj rural.—**countryman** n.—**countrywoman** n.

countryside n a rural district.

county n an administrative subdivision for local government.—also adj.

coup n a masterstroke; a coup d'état.

coup d'état n the sudden overthrow of a government.

coupé n a closed, four-seater, two-door car.

couple n two of the same kind; a husband and wife. • vt to link together. • vi to copulate.

couplet n two rhyming lines of verse.

coupling n a device for joining parts of a machine or two railway carriages.

coupon n a detachable certificate on a bond, presented for payment of interest; a certificate entitling one to a discount, gift, etc; an entry form, as for a competition.

courage n bravery; fortitude; spirit.—**courageous** adj.

courier n a messenger; a tourist guide; a carrier of illegal goods between countries.

course n a race; a track; a career; a direction; a regular sequence; one portion of a meal; conduct; the direction a ship is steered; a series of studies. • vt to hunt; to move swiftly along an indicated path; to chase with greyhounds.

court n an uncovered space surrounded by buildings or walls; a playing space, as for tennis, etc; the retinue of a sovereign; (law) a hall of justice; the judges, etc, engaged there. • vt to seek the friendship of; to woo.

courteous adj polite; obliging.

courtesy n politeness and kindness; civility.

courthouse n a public building that houses law courts.

courtier n one in attendance at a royal court.

court martial n a court of justice composed of naval or military officers for the trial of offences.—**court-martial** vt.

cousin n the child of an uncle or aunt.

cove n a small sheltered bay on the coast.

covenant n a written agreement; a solemn agreement of fellowship and faith between members of a church.

cover vt to overspread the top of anything with something else; to hide; to save from punishment; to shelter; to clothe; to understudy; to insure against damage, loss, etc; to report for a newspaper. • vi to provide an excuse (for). • n that which is laid on something else; a shelter; an understudy; something used to hide one's real actions, etc; insurance against loss or damage.

coverage n the amount of reporting of an event for newspaper, television, etc.

cover charge n a charge made by a restaurant over and above the cost of the food and service.

covet vt to desire earnestly; to lust after; to long to possess (what belongs to another). —**covetous** adj.—**covetousness** n.

cow[1] n the mature female of domestic cattle, the whale, elephant, etc.

cow[2] vt to take the spirit out of, to intimidate.

coward n one lacking courage; one who is afraid.—**cowardice** n.—**cowardly** adj.

cowboy n a person who tends cattle or horses.—also **cowhand**.

cower vi to crouch down through fear.

coxswain n a person who steers a boat.

coy adj playfully demure.—**coyness** n.

cozy see **cosy**.

crab n any of numerous chiefly marine broadly built crustaceans.

crack vt to burst, break or sever; to injure; to open a bottle; (sl) to make (a joke); (inf) to break open (a safe); to decipher (a code). • vi to make a sharp explosive sound. • n a chink or fissure; a narrow fracture; a sharp blow.

cracker n a firework that explodes with a loud crack; a paper tube that when pulled explodes harmlessly and releases a paper hat and plastic toy; a thin, crisp biscuit.

crackle vi to make a slight, sharp explosive noise.

crackling n the crisp rind of roast pork.

cradle n a baby's crib or small bed, often on rockers.

craft n manual skill; a skilled trade; the members of a skilled trade; cunning; a boat, ship, or aircraft.

craftsman n a person skilled in a particular craft.—**craftsmanship** n.

crag n a rough steep rock or cliff.

cram vt to pack tightly; to fill to overflowing; (inf) to prepare quickly for an examination.

cramp n a spasmodic muscular contraction of the limbs; (pl) abdominal spasms and pain. • vti to affect with muscular spasms; to confine narrowly; to hamper.

cramped adj restricted, narrow; (handwriting) small and irregular.

crampon n a metal frame with spikes attached to boots for walking on ice.

cranberry n a small red sour berry.

crane n a large wading bird with very long legs and neck, and a long straight bill; a machine for raising, shifting heavy weights. • vti to stretch out (the neck).

cranium n the skull.—**cranial** adj.

crank n a right-angled arm attached to a shaft for turning it; (inf) an eccentric person. • vt to turn or wind.

cranny n a fissure, crack, crevice.

crash n a loud, sudden confused noise; a violent fall or impact; a sudden failure, as of a business or a computer; a collapse, as of the financial market. • adj done with great speed or effort. • vti to clash together; to make a loud noise; (aircraft) to land with a crash; (inf) to intrude into (a party).

crash helmet n a cushioned helmet worn by airmen, motorcyclists, etc, for protection.

crash-land vti(aircraft) to land without lowering the undercarriage.

crate n an open box of wooden slats, for shipping. • vt to pack in a crate.

crater n the mouth of a volcano; a cavity caused by the explosion of a bomb, shell, etc.

cravat n a neckcloth.

crave vt to have a strong desire (for); to ask humbly, to beg.—**craving** n.

crawl vi to move along the ground on hands and knees; to move slowly; to creep. • n a slow motion; a stroke in swimming.

crayfish n any of numerous freshwater crustaceans; the spiny lobster.

crayon n a stick or pencil of coloured chalk.

craze n a passing infatuation.

crazy adj (inf) mad, insane; foolish; ridiculous; (paving) composed of irregular pieces.

creak vi to make a shrill grating sound. • n such a sound.—**creaky** adj.

cream n the rich, fatty part of milk; a yellowish white colour; a type of face or skin preparation. • vt to add or apply cream to; to beat into a soft, smooth consistency; to remove the best part of.—**creamy** adj.

crease n a line made by folding; (cricket) a line made by a batsman or bowler marking the limits of their position.—also vti.

create vt to cause to come into existence.

creation n the act of creating; the thing created; the whole world or universe.

creative adj imaginative, original, constructive.-**creativity** n.

creator n one who creates, esp God.

creature n a living being; a created thing.

crèche n a day nursery for infants.

credence n belief or trust.

credentials npl documents proving the identity, honesty or authority of a person.

credible adj believable; trustworthy.—**credibility** n.—**credibly** adv.

credit n belief; trust; honour; good reputation; trust in a person's ability to pay; time allowed for payment; a sum at a person's disposal in a bank; the entry in an account of a sum received; the side of the account on which this is entered; (pl) a list of those responsible for a film, etc. • vt to believe; to trust; to have confidence in; to enter on the credit side of an account.

creditable adj worthy of praise.

credit card n a card issued by a bank, etc, authorising the purchase of goods and services on credit.

creditor n one to whom money is owed.

creed n a system of religious belief or faith; a summary of Christian doctrine; any set of principles or beliefs.

creek n a stream smaller than a river.

creep vi to move slowly along, as a reptile; (plant) to grow along or up; to move stealthily; (flesh) to feel as if things were creeping over it.

creeper n a creeping or climbing plant.

creepy adj causing fear or disgust.

cremate vt to burn (a corpse) to ashes.—**cremation** n.

crematorium n a place where bodies are cremated.

creosote n an oily substance derived from tar used as a wood preservative.

crêpe n thin, crinkled fabric; thin paper like crepe; a thin pancake.

crescendo adv (mus) gradually increasing in loudness or intensity. • n a crescendo passage or effect.

crescent n the figure of the moon in its first or last quarter; a narrow, tapering curve; a curving street.

cress n any of various plants with pungent leaves, used in salads.

crest n a plume of feathers on the head of a bird; the ridge of a wave; the summit of a hill; a distinctive device above the shield on a coat of arms. • vti to mount to the top of.

crestfallen adj dejected.

crevasse n a deep cleft, esp in a glacier.

crevice n a crack, a fissure.

crew n the people operating a ship or aircraft; a group of people working together. • vi to act as a member of a crew.

crib n a rack for fodder, a manger; a child's cot with high sides; (inf) something copied from someone else; (inf) a translation used (usu illicitly) by students.—also vti.

crick n a painful stiffness of neck muscles.

cricket[1] n a leaping grasshopper-like insect.

cricket[2] n a game played with wicket, bats and a ball by eleven players on each side.

crime n a violation of the law; an offence against morality or the public welfare.

criminal adj of, or guilty of, a crime. • n a person who has committed a crime.

crimson n a deep-red colour inclining to purple. • adj crimson-coloured.

cringe vi to shrink in fear or embarrassment.

crinkle vt to wrinkle; to crimp. • vi to curl or be crimped. • n a wrinkle.—**crinkly** adj.

cripple vt to disable. • n a disabled person.

crisis n a turning point; a critical point.

crisp adj dry and brittle; bracing. • n a potato snack. • vt to make crisp.

criterion n a standard, law or rule by which a judgment can be made.

critic n a person skilled in judging the merits of literary or artistic works; a fault-finder.

critical adj skilled in criticism; crucial.

criticise vt to judge; to find fault with.

criticism n a critical comment; a review.

croak vi to make a deep hoarse cry.—also vti.

crochet n knitting done with a hooked needle.

crockery n earthenware vessels, etc.

crocodile n large amphibious reptile, similar to an alligator; its skin.

crocus n a bulbous plant with yellow, purple, or white flowers.

croft n a small plot of land with a rented farmhouse, esp in Scotland.—**crofter** n.

crook n a shepherd's hooked staff; a swindler, a dishonest person.

crooked adj bent, twisted; dishonest.

crop n a year's or a season's produce of any cultivated plant; harvest; a pouch in a bird's gullet; a hunting whip; hair cut close or short. • vti to clip short.

croquet n a game with mallets, balls and hoops.

croquette n a ball of minced meat, fish or potato seasoned and fried brown.

cross n a figure formed by two intersecting lines; a structure consisting of two beams placed across each other; the emblem of the Christian faith; a burden or affliction; a cross-shaped medal; a hybrid. • vti to pass across; to intersect; to make the sign of the cross over; to thwart; to modify (a breed) by intermixture. • adj out of temper.

crossbar n a horizontal bar, as that across goal posts or a bicycle frame.

crossbreed vt to breed animals by mating different varieties.—also n.

cross-country adj across fields.

cross-examine vt (law) to question (a witness) who has already been questioned by counsel on the other side.

cross-eyed adj squinting.

crossing n an intersection of roads or railway lines; a place for crossing a street.

crossroad n a road crossing another; (pl) where two roads cross.

cross section n a cutting at right angles to length;the surface then shown; a random selection of the public.

crossword n a word puzzle with clues in which interlocking words are inserted in a square.

crotch n the region of the body where the legs fork, the genital area; any forked region.

crotchet n (mus) a note equal to a half-minim.

crotchety adj peevish, whimsical.

crouch vi to squat close to the ground.

crow n a large, glossy, black bird; the cry of a cock. • vi to make a sound like a cock; to boast; to cry out with pleasure.

crowbar n an iron bar for use as a lever.

crowd n a number of people or things collected closely together; (inf) a set; a clique. • vti to press closely together; to fill to excess.

crown n a wreath worn on the head; the head covering of a monarch; the sovereign; the top of the head; the part of a tooth above the gum. • vt to invest with a crown; to complete.

crucial adj decisive; severe; critical.

crucifix n a cross with the sculptured figure of Christ.

crucifixion n execution by being nailed or bound to a cross; (with cap) the death of Christ.

crucify vt to put to death on a cross; to cause extreme pain to.

crude adj in a natural state; unfinished, rough; lacking polish; vulgar.

cruel adj merciless; hard-hearted; fierce; painful; unrelenting.—**cruelty** n.

cruet n a small glass bottle for vinegar and oil, used at the table.

cruise vi to sail to and fro; to move at the most efficient speed for sustained travel. • vt to cruise over or about. • n a voyage from place to place.

crumb n a fragment of bread.

crumble vt to break into crumbs; to cause to fall into pieces. • vi to disintegrate.

crumpet n a soft cake, usu eaten toasted.

crumple vti to twist or crush into wrinkles.

crunch vti to crush with the teeth; to tread on with force.

crusade n a medieval Christian military expedition to recover the Holy Land; concerted action for the defence of a cause.

crush vt to press; to squeeze; to break by pressure; to ruin; to quell. • vi to be pressed out of shape or until smaller. • n a violent collision; a dense crowd; a drink from crushed fruit.

crust n a hard external coating or rind; the exterior solid part of the earths surface; a shell or hard covering. • vti to cover or become covered with a crust.—**crusty** adj.

crutch n a staff with a crosswise head to support the weight of a lame person; a prop; the crotch.

crux n the essential or deciding point.

cry vi to call aloud; to proclaim; to exclaim vehemently; to implore; to shed tears. • vt to utter loudly and publicly. • n an inarticulate sound; an exclamation of wonder or triumph; a spell of weeping.

crypt n an underground chamber or vault.

cryptic adj hidden, secret; mysterious.

crystal n very clear, brilliant glass; articles of such glass.—also adj.—**crystalline** adj.

crystallise vti to form crystals; to give definite form.—**crystallisation** n.

cub n a young carnivorous mammal; a young person; (with cap) a junior Scout.

cube n a solid body with six equal square sides or faces; the product of a number multiplied by itself twice. • vt to raise (number) to the third power; to cut into cubes.

cubic adj having the properties of a cube.

cubicle n a separate sleeping compartment.

cuckoo n a bird with a dark plumage, a curved bill and a characteristic call, which lays its eggs in the nests of other birds.

cucumber n a long juicy fruit used in salads.

cud n the food that a ruminating animal brings back into the mouth to chew again.

cuddle vt to hug. • vt to nestle.—also n.

cudgel n a short thick stick for beating.

cue[1] n the last word of a speech in a play, serving as a signal for the next actor to enter or begin to speak; any signal; a hint.—also vt.

cue[2] n a tapering rod used in snooker, billiards and pool to strike the ball.

cuff[1] n a blow with the fist or the open hand. • vt to strike such a blow.

cuff[2] n the end of a sleeve.

cuisine n a style of cooking.

cul-de-sac n a street blocked off at one end.

culinary adj of or relating to cooking.

culminate vti to reach the highest point; to bring to the highest point.—**culmination** n.

culpable adj deserving censure; criminal.

culprit n a person accused, or found guilty.

cult n a system of worship; devotion to a person, principle; a religion regarded as unorthodox or spurious; its adherents.

cultivate vt to till; to improve by care or study; to seek the society of; to refine.—**cultivation** n.

cultural adj pertaining to culture.

culture n appreciation and understanding of the arts; the skills, arts, etc, in a given period; the beliefs, social forms and material traits of a group; improvement of the mind, etc; a growth of bacteria, etc, in a prepared substance. • vt to cultivate bacteria for study.—**cultured** adj.

cumbersome adj heavy, unwieldy.

cunning adj ingenious; sly; designing; subtle. • n slyness, craftiness.

cup n a small, bowl-shaped container for liquids, usu with a handle; an ornamental cup as a trophy. • vt to curve (the hands) into the shape of a cup.

cupboard n a closet or cabinet with shelves.

cupola n a dome.

curate n an assistant of a vicar or rector.

curator n a superintendent of a museum, art gallery, etc.

curb vt to restrain; to check.—also n.

curd n the coagulated part of soured milk, used to make cheese.

curdle vti to turn into curds; to coagulate.

cure n a remedy; restoration to health. • vt to heal; to rid of; to preserve, as by salting, etc.

curfew n a signal, as a bell, at a fixed evening hour as a sign that everyone must be indoors.

curio n an item valued or rare.

curiosity n inquisitiveness; a strange, rare or interesting object.

curious adj anxious to know; prying, inquisitive; strange, remarkable, odd.

curl vti to form into a curve, to coil; to twist into ringlets; to bend; to play at curling. • n a ringlet of hair; a spiral, a twist; a bend.—**curly** adj.

curler n a small pin or roller used for curling the hair; a person who plays curling.

curling n a game in which two teams slide smooth stones on ice into a target circle.

currant n a dried grape.

currency n the time during which a thing is current; the money current in a country.

current adj generally accepted; happening now; presently in circulation. • n a body of water or air in motion, a flow; the transmission of electricity through a conductor; a general tendency.

curriculum n a course of study.

curriculum vitae n a brief survey of one's career.

curry n a spicy dish with a hot sauce.

curse n a calling down of destruction or evil; a profane oath; a swear word; a scourge. • vti to invoke a curse on; to swear; to afflict.

cursory adj hasty, passing; superficial, careless.

curt adj short; abrupt; concise; rudely brief.

curtail vt to cut short; to reduce.

curtain n a cloth hung as a screen at a window, etc; the movable screen separating a stage from the auditorium.—*also vt.*

curts(e)y n bending of the knees made by women as a greeting.—*also vi.*

curve n a bending without angles; a bent form; (*geom*) a line of which no part is straight. • *vti* to form a curve, to bend.

cushion n a case stuffed with soft material for resting on; the border round a snooker table; the air mass supporting a hovercraft. • *vt* to protect by padding.

custard n a sauce of milk, eggs and sugar.

custody n guardianship; imprisonment; security.—**custodial** *adj.*—**custodian** n.

custom n a regular practice; usage; business patronage; (*pl*) duties on imports.

customary *adj* habitual; common.

customer n a person who buys from a shop or business, esp regularly.

cut *vti* to separate with a sharp instrument; to make an incision in; to divide; to trim; to intersect; to abridge; to wound deeply; to grow a new tooth through the gum; to divide (a pack of cards) at random; (*cinema*) to change to another scene. • n an incision or wound made by a sharp instrument; a gash; the shape of a garment. • *adj* divided or separated; gashed; having the surface fashioned.

cutback n a reduction, esp in expenditure.

cute *adj* (*inf*) acute, shrewd; attractive.

cuticle n the skin at the base of the nail.

cutlery n knives, forks, spoons.

cutlet n a neck chop of lamb, etc.

cutting n a piece cut off; an incision; a newspaper clipping; a slip from a plant for propagation; the editing of a film, etc. • *adj* hurtful.

cuttlefish n a marine creature with a flattened body that squirts ink when threatened.

cyanide n a poison.

cyclamen n a plant of the primrose family, with pink, purple or white flowers.

cycle n a recurring series of events or phenomena; a body of epics, etc, with a common theme; a bicycle. • *vi* to ride a bicycle.—**cyclist** n.

cyclone n a violent circular storm.

cygnet n a young swan.

cylinder n a hollow figure or object with parallel sides and circular ends; the piston chamber in an engine.—**cylindrical** *adj.*

cymbal n (*mus*) one of a pair of two brass plates struck together to produce a ringing or clashing sound.—**cymbalist** n.

cynic n a morose, surly or sarcastic person.—**cynicism** n.

cynical *adj* sceptical; sneering at goodness or others' weaknesses.

cypher *see* **cipher**.

cypress n an evergreen tree with hard wood.

cyst n a closed sac developing abnormally in the structure of plants or animals.

czar *see* **tsar**.

Czech n a native, or the language, of the Czech Republic.

D

dab¹ *vt* to touch lightly with something moist or soft. • n a light tap; a small lump of anything moist or soft.

dab² n a species of European flounder.

dabble *vi* to move hands, feet, etc, gently in water; (*usu with* **at, in, with**) to do anything in a superficial way. • *vt* to splash.

dad, daddy n (*inf*) father.

daffodil n a yellow spring flower.

daft *adj* (*inf*) silly, weak-minded; giddy.

dagger n a short weapon for stabbing; a reference mark used in printing (†).

daily *adj, adv* (happening) every day. • n a newspaper published every weekday.

dainty *adj* delicate; fastidious. • n a delicacy.

dairy n a building or room where milk is stored and dairy products made; a shop selling these.

daisy n a flower with a yellow centre and white petals.

dale n a valley.

dally *vi* to lose time by idleness or trifling; to play or trifle (with); to flirt.

dam¹ n an artificial embankment to retain water; water so contained.—*also vt* .

dam² n the mother of a four-footed animal.

damage n injury, harm; loss; (pl) (law) payment in compensation for loss or injury.—also vt.

damn vt to condemn, censure; to ruin; to curse; to consign to eternal punishment.

damp n humidity, moisture. • adj slightly wet, moist. • vt to moisten; (with down) to stifle.

dampen vti to make or become damp.

damson n a small, dark purple plum.

dance vti to move rhythmically to music; to cause to dance or move up and down. • n a piece of dancing; a party with music for dancing.— **dancer** n.

dandelion n a wild plant with ragged leaves, a yellow flower and a fluffy seed head.

dandruff n scales of skin on the scalp.

Dane n a native or citizen of Denmark.

danger n exposure to injury or risk.

dangerous adj involving danger; unsafe.

dangle vti to hang and swing loosely; to display temptingly.

Danish adj of the people or language of Denmark. • n the language of Denmark.

dapper adj neat in appearance, spruce.

dare vti to be bold enough; to venture, to risk; to defy, to challenge. • n a challenge.

daredevil n a rash, reckless person. • adj daring.

daring adj fearless; courageous; unconventional. • n adventurous courage.

dark adj having little or no light; of a shade close to black; (person) having brown or black skin or hair. • n a dark state or colour.

darken vti to make or become dark.

darkroom n a room for processing photographs in darkness or safe light.

darling n a dearly loved person; a favourite. • adj lovable; much admired.

darn vt to mend a hole in fabric or a garment with stitches.—also n.

dart n a small pointed missile; a fold sewn into a garment for shaping it; (pl) a game in which darts are thrown at a target. • vi to move fast.

dartboard n a circular cork or wooden target used in the game of darts.

dash vti to fling violently; to rush; (hopes) to shatter. • n a short run; a small amount of something added to food; a tinge; a punctuation mark (—); vigour, verve.

dashboard n an instrument panel in a car.

dashing adj spirited, stylish.

data npl (often used as sing) facts, information.

data processing n the analysis of information stored in a computer for various uses, e.g. stock control, statistical research, etc.

date¹ n a day or time of occurrence; a period to which something belongs; a duration; an appointment. • vt to affix a date to; to note the date of; to reckon the time of; (inf) to make a date

with. • vi to reckon from a point in time; to show signs of belonging to a particular period.

date² n the sweet fruit of the date palm.

date line n the line running north to south along the 180-degree meridian, east of which is one day earlier than west of it; a line on a newspaper story giving the date and place of writing.

daub vt to smear; to paint incompetently.

daughter n a female child or descendant.

daughter-in-law n the wife of one's son.

dauntless adj intrepid.

dawdle vi to move slowly and waste time.

dawn vi (day) to begin to grow light; to begin to appear. • n daybreak; a first sign.

day n the time when the sun is above the horizon; the twenty-four hours from midnight to midnight; daylight; (usu pl) an epoch.

daybreak n dawn.

daydream n a reverie. • vi to fantasise.

daylight n the light of the sun; a visible gap; sudden understanding.

daytime n the time of daylight.

daze vt to stun, to bewilder. • n confusion.

dazzle vt to be partially blinded by strong light; to overwhelm with brilliance. • n a very strong light; bewilderment.—**dazzling** adj.

dead adj without life; inanimate, inert; no longer used; (fire, etc) extinguished; (limb, etc) numb. • adv completely. • n a dead person; the quietest time.

deaden vt to render numb; to muffle.

dead-end n a cul-de-sac; a hopeless situation.

dead heat n a race in which two or more finish equal, a tie.

deadline n the time by which something must be done.

deadlock n a clash of interests making progress impossible; a standstill.—also vt.

deadly adj fatal; (inf) tedious. • adv intensely.

deaf adj unable to hear; hearing badly; not wishing to hear.—**deafness** n.

deafen vt to deprive of hearing.

deal¹ vb vt (a blow) to deliver, inflict; (cards, etc) to distribute; (with with) to do business with; (problem, task) to solve. • vi to do business (with); to trade (in). • n a portion, quantity; a business transaction.

deal² n fir or pine wood.—also adj.

dealer n a trader; a person who deals cards; a seller of illegal drugs.

dealings npl business transactions.

dean n the head of a cathedral chapter; a college fellow in charge of discipline; the head of a university or college faculty.

dear adj loved, precious; expensive; a form of address in letters. • n a person who is loved.

dearth n scarcity, lack.

death n the end of life, dying.

death certificate n an official document with details of a person's death.

death duties npl taxes paid on an inheritance after a death.

deathly adj like death, pale still; deadly.

debar vt to exclude, bar.

debase vt to lower in character or value.

debat(e)able adj open to question.

debate n a formal argument; a discussion, esp in parliament. • vt to contest. • vi to discuss.

debauchery n depraved over-indulgence.

debit n the entry of a sum owed, opposite to the credit; the left side of a ledger used for this. • vt to charge to the debit side.

debris n broken and scattered remains.

debt n a sum owed; an obligation.

debtor n a person who owes money.

debut n a first appearance as a public performer or in society.

decade n a period of ten years.

decadence n deterioration in standards.

decadent adj deteriorating; self-indulgent.

decay vti to decompose; to wither.—also n.

decease n death. • vi to die.

deceased adj dead. • n the dead person.

deceit n treachery; fraud.—**deceitful** adj.

deceive vt to cheat; to mislead; to delude.

decency n being decent; conforming to accepted standards of proper behaviour.

decent adj respectable, proper, moderate.

decentralise vt (government, organisation) to divide among local centres.

deception n the act of deceiving; fraud.

deceptive adj apt to mislead; ambiguous.

decibel n a unit for measuring sound level.

decide vti to determine, to settle; to resolve.

decided adj unhesitating; clearly marked.

deciduous adj (trees, shrubs) shedding all leaves annually.

decimal adj of numbers written to the base 10.

decimal point n a dot written before the numerator in a decimal fraction.

decimate vt to kill every tenth person; to kill a great number.

decipher vt to decode; to make out (indistinct writing, meaning, etc).

decision n a ruling; a judgment; firmness.

decisive adj positive; conclusive, final.

deck n the floor on a ship, aircraft, bus or bridge; a pack of playing cards; the turntable of a record-player; the playing mechanism of a tape recorder. • vt to adorn.

deck chair n a folding chair made of canvas.

declare vt to proclaim; to admit possession of (dutiable goods). • vi (law) to make a statement; (with **against** or **for**) to announce one's support; (cricket) to choose to close an innings before ten wickets have fallen.—**declaration** n.

decline vi to refuse; to deteriorate; to fail; to diminish. • vt to reject, to refuse; (gram) to give the cases of a declension.—also n.

decode vt to translate a code into plain language.

decompose vti to break up into constituent parts, esp as part of a chemical process; to resolve into elements. • vi to decay.

decontaminate vt to free from (radioactive, etc) contamination.

décor n general decorative effect, e.g. of a room; scenery and stage design.

decorate vt to ornament; to paint or wallpaper; to honour with a badge or medal.

decoration n decorating; an ornament; a badge or an honour.—**decorative** adj.

decorator n a person who decorates.

decoy vt to lure into a trap.—also n.

decrease vti to make or become less. • n a decreasing; the amount of diminution.

decree n a judicial decision. • vt to decide by law.

decrepit adj worn out by the infirmities of old age; in the last stage of decay.

dedicate vt to consecrate (to some sacred purpose); to devote wholly or chiefly; to inscribe (to someone).—**dedication** n.

deduce vt to derive (knowledge, a conclusion) from reasoning; to infer.

deduct vt to take (from); to subtract.

deduction n deducting; the amount deducted; deducing; a conclusion that something is true.

deed n an act; an exploit; a legal document recording a transaction.

deep adj extending or placed far down or far from the outside; fully involved; engrossed; profound, intense; heartfelt; low in pitch; (colour) strong and dark.—also adv. • n the sea.

deepen vt to make deeper; to increase. • vi to become deeper.

deep-freeze vt to freeze (food) so that it keeps for a long time. • n a freezer.

deer n an animal with antlers on the males.

deface vt to disfigure; to obliterate.

default n neglect to do what duty or law requires; failure to fulfil a financial obligation; (comput) a basic setting or instruction to which a program reverts.—also vi.

defeat vt to win a victory over.—also n.

defeatism n disposition to accept defeat.

defect n a deficiency; a blemish, fault. • vi to desert one's country or a cause.

defective adj faulty; incomplete. • n a person lacking physical or mental powers.

defence n resistance or protection against attack; a means of resisting an attack; protection; vindication; (law) a defendant's plea; the defending party in legal proceedings; (sport) de-

fending (the goal, etc) against the attacks of the opposing side; the defending players in a team.
defend vt to guard or protect; to maintain against attack.
defendant n a person accused or sued in a lawsuit.
defensive adj serving to defend; in a state or posture of defence.
defer[1] vt to put off; to delay.
defer[2] vi to yield to another person's wishes, judgment or authority.
deference n a deferring or yielding in judgment or opinion; polite respect.
defiance n the act of defying; wilful disobedience; a challenge.—**defiant** adj.
deficiency n lack, shortage.—**deficient** adj.
deficit n the amount by which an amount falls short of what is required.
defile[1] vt to pollute or corrupt.
defile[2] n a long, narrow pass or way. • vt to march in single file.
define vt to fix the bounds or limits of; to mark the limits or outline of clearly; to describe accurately; to fix the meaning of.
definite adj defined; fixed; exact; clear.
definition n an explanation of a word's meaning; sharpness of outline.
definitive adj limiting; decisive, final.
deflate vt to release gas or air from; to reduce in size or importance.—**deflation** n.
deflect vti to turn or cause to turn aside from a line or proper course.
deform vt to spoil the natural form of.
deformity n the condition of being deformed; a deformed part; a defect.
defraud vt to remove (money, rights, etc) from a person by cheating or deceiving.
defray vt to provide money (to pay expenses, etc).
defrost vti to unfreeze; to free from ice.
deft adj skilful, adept; nimble.
defunct adj no longer being in existence or function or in use.
defuse vt to disarm an explosive (bomb or mine) by removing its fuse; to decrease tension in a (crisis) situation.
defy vt to resist boldly; to challenge (a person) to attempt something considered dangerous.
degenerate adj having declined in physical or moral qualities; sexually deviant. • vi to become or grow worse. • n a degenerate person.
degrading adj humiliating.
degree n a step in an ascending or descending series; a stage in intensity; a unit of measurement in a scale; an academic award.
dehydrate vt to remove water from.—**dehydration** n.
de-ice vt to prevent the formation of or to remove ice from a surface.—**de-icer** n.

deign vi to condescend to do (something).
deity n a god or goddess; the rank or essence of a god; (with cap and the) God.
dejected adj morose, depressed.
dejection n depression; lowness of spirits.
delay vt to postpone; to detain, obstruct. • vi to linger. • n a delaying or being delayed.
delectable adj delightful, delicious.
delegate vt to appoint as a representative; to give powers to (an agent or assembly). • n a deputy or representative.
delegation n the act of delegating; a group of people empowered to represent others.
delete vt to strike out (something written or printed); to erase.—**deletion** n.
deliberate vt to consider carefully. • vi to discuss thoroughly. • adj intentional.
delicacy n sensibility; a luxurious food.
delicate adj fine in texture; fragile, not robust; requiring tactful handling.
delicatessen n a store selling prepared foods, esp imported delicacies.
delicious adj having a pleasurable effect on the senses, esp taste; delightful.
delight vt to please greatly. • vi to have or take great pleasure (in).—also n.
delightful adj giving great pleasure.
delinquent n a person guilty of a misdeed, esp a young lawbreaker.—**delinquency** n.
delirium n a state of mental disorder, esp caused by a feverish illness.—**delirious** adj.
deliver vt (goods, letters, etc) to transport to a destination; to distribute regularly; to liberate, to give birth to; to assist at a birth; (blow) to launch.
delivery n act of delivering; anything delivered or communicated; the manner of delivering (a speech, etc); the manner of bowling in cricket, etc; the act of giving birth.
delta n an alluvial deposit at the mouth of a river.
delude vt to mislead, to deceive.
deluge n a flood; anything happening in a heavy rush. • vt to inundate.
delusion n a false belief; a persistent false belief that is a symptom of mental illness.
delve vti to search deeply; to dig.
demagogue n an orator who derives power from appealing to popular prejudices.
demand vt to ask for in an authoritative manner. • n a request or claim made with authority; an urgent claim; desire for goods and services shown by consumers.
demanding adj constantly making demands; requiring skill, concentration, effort.
demarcation n the marking off of a boundary or setting a limit to; the separation of the type of work done by members of different trade unions.
demean vt to lower in dignity.

demeanour n behaviour; bearing.

demented adj crazy, insane.

demise n (formal) death; termination, end.

demobilise vt to discharge from the armed forces.—**demobilisation** n.

democracy n a form of government by the people through elected representatives; a country governed by its people; political, social or legal equality.

democrat n a person who believes in or promotes democracy; (with cap) a member of the Democratic Party in the US.

democratic adj of, relating to, or supporting the principles of democracy.

demolish vt to knock down.—**demolition** n.

demonstrate vti to indicate clearly; to provide certain evidence of, to prove; to show how something works; to show one's support for a cause, etc, by public protest.—**demonstrator** n.

demonstration n proof by evidence; a display or exhibition; a public manifestation of opinion.

demonstrative adj displaying one's feelings openly; (gram) describing an adjective or pronoun indicating the person or thing referred to.

demoralise vt to lower the morale of.

demote vt to reduce in rank or position.—**demotion** n.

demur vi to raise objections.

den n a cave or lair of a wild beast; a place where people gather for illegal activities; a room in a house for relaxation or study.

denial n a refusal of a request, etc; a refusal to admit a truth.

denigrate vt to belittle.—**denigration** n.

denim n a hard-wearing cotton cloth, esp used for jeans; (pl) denim trousers or jeans.

denomination n a name or title; a religious group larger than a sect; one of a series of related units, esp monetary.

denominator n the part of a fractional expression written below the fraction line.

denote vt to indicate; to mean.

denounce vt to condemn or censure publicly; to inform against.

dense adj difficult to see through; massed closely together; dull-witted, stupid.

density n the ratio of mass to volume.

dent n a depression made by pressure or a blow.
• vt to make a dent.

dental adj of or for the teeth.

dentifrice n toothpowder or toothpaste.

dentist n a person qualified to treat tooth decay, gum disease, etc.—**dentistry** n.

denture n (usu pl) a set of artificial teeth.

deny vt to declare to be untrue; to refuse to acknowledge; to refuse a request.

deodorant n a substance that removes or masks unpleasant odours.

depart vi to go away, leave.

department n a unit of specialised functions into which an organisation or business is divided; a province; a realm of activity.

department store n a large shop divided into departments selling different types of goods.

departure n departing; a new venture.

depend vi to be determined by or connected with anything; to rely (on), put trust (in).

dependable adj able to be relied on.

dependant n a person who is dependent on another, esp financially.

dependence n the state of being dependent; reliance, trust; a physical or mental reliance on a drug, person, etc.

dependent adj relying on another person, thing, etc, for support, money, etc; subordinate.

depict vt to represent pictorially; to describe.

deplete vt to use up a large quantity of.

deplorable adj shocking; extremely bad.

deplore vt to regret deeply; to complain of.

deploy vt (military forces) to distribute and position strategically.—**deployment** n.

depopulate vt to reduce population of.

deport vt to expel (an undesirable person) from a country.—**deportation** n.

deportment n manners; behaviour.

depose vt to remove from power; to testify.

deposit vt to place or lay down; to pay money into a bank, etc, for safekeeping, to earn interest.
• n money put in a bank; money given in part payment or security; material left, e.g. sediment.

depot n a warehouse, storehouse; a place for storing military supplies; a military training centre; a bus or railway station.

deprave vt to pervert; to corrupt morally.

depravity n moral corruption.

depreciate vti to make or become lower in value.

depreciation n a fall in value, esp of an asset through wear and tear.

depress vt to push down; to sadden; to lessen the activity of.—**depressing** adj.

depression n excessive gloom and despondency; an abnormal state of physiological inactivity; a phase of the business cycle characterised by widespread unemployment, etc; a falling in or sinking; a lowering of atmospheric pressure.

deprive vt to take away from; to prevent from using or enjoying.—**deprivation** n.

deprived adj lacking the essentials of life.

depth n deepness; the distance downwards or inwards; intensity of emotion or feeling; profundity of thought; intensity of colour.

deputation n a person or group appointed to represent others.

deputise vi to act as deputy.

deputy n a delegate, representative.

derail vti (train) to cause to leave the rails.

derange vt to throw into confusion; to disturb; to make insane.—**derangement** n.

derelict adj abandoned, deserted and left to decay; negligent.—also n.

deride vt to scorn, mock.—**derision** n.

derisive adj mocking, scornful.

derisory adj deserving of derision.

derivation n the tracing of a word to its root; origin; descent.

derivative adj derived from something else; not original. • n a word formed by derivation; (math) the rate of change of one quantity with respect to another.

derive vt to take or receive from a source; to infer, deduce (from).

derogatory adj disparaging.

derrick n any crane-like apparatus; a tower over oil well holding drilling machinery.

descend vi to come or climb down; (with on or upon) to make a sudden attack upon, or visit unexpectedly; to sink in morals or dignity; to be derived. • vt to go, pass, or extend down.

descendant n a person who is descended from an ancestor.

descent n a descending; a way down; a slope; a raid or invasion; ancestry.

describe vt to give a verbal account of; to trace out.

description n a verbal or pictorial account; sort, kind.—**descriptive** adj.

desecrate vt to violate a sacred place by destructive or blasphemous behaviour.—**desecration** n.

desert[1] n (often pl) a deserved reward or punishment.

desert[2] vt to leave, abandon; to abscond from the armed forces.—**deserter** n.—**desertion** n.

desert[3] n a dry, barren region; a place lacking in some essential quality.

deserve vt to merit.—**deservedly** adv.

deserving adj worthy of support.

design vt to plan; to create; to devise; to make working drawings for; to intend. • n a working drawing; a mental plan; the form of something; a decorative pattern; purpose; (pl) dishonest intent.

designate vt to indicate, specify; to name. • adj appointed but not yet installed.

designation n the act of designating; nomination; a distinguishing name or title.

designer n a person who designs things.

desirable adj arousing (sexual) desire; advisable or beneficial; worth doing.

desire vt to long for; to request. • n a longing for something; sexual craving.

desk n a piece of furniture with a writing surface; a counter.

desolate adj solitary, lonely; laid waste.—**desolation** n.

despair vi to have no hope. • n utter loss of hope; something that causes despair.

despatch see **dispatch**.

desperate adj (almost) hopeless; reckless through lack of hope; urgently requiring (money, etc); (remedy) extreme.—**desperation** n.

despicable adj contemptible, worthless.

despise vt to regard with contempt or scorn.

despite prep in spite of.

despondent adj dejected.—**despondence**, **despondency** n.

dessert n the sweet course at the end of a meal.

dessertspoon n a spoon used for eating desserts.

destination n the place to which a person or thing is going.

destine vt to set aside for some specific purpose; to predetermine; intend.

destiny n the power supposedly determining the course of events; the future to which any person or thing is destined.

destitute adj (with of) very poor.

destroy vt to demolish, ruin; to kill.

destroyer n a fast small warship.

destruction n the act or process of destroying or being destroyed; ruin.

destructive adj causing destruction; (with of or to) ruinous; (criticism) intended to discredit.

detach vt to release; to separate from a larger group.

detachable adj able to be detached.

detached adj separate; (house) not joined to another; aloof; free from bias or emotion.

detachment n indifference; freedom from emotional involvement or bias; a body of troops detached from the main body and sent on special service.

detail vt to describe fully. • n an item; a particular or minute account; (art) a reproduction of a smaller part of a picture, etc.

detain vt to place in custody; to delay.

detect vt to discover the existence or presence of; to notice.—**detection** n.

detective n a person or a police officer employed to find evidence of crimes.

detector n a device for detecting the presence of something.

detention n confinement; being kept in (school after hours) as a punishment.

deter vt to discourage or prevent.

detergent n a cleaning agent—also adj.

deteriorate vti to make or become worse.—**deterioration** n.

determination n a decision resolving a dispute; firm intention; resoluteness.

determine vti to settle officially; to find out.

determined *adj* resolute.

deterrent *n* something that deters; a nuclear weapon that deters attack by fear of retaliation.—*also adj.*—**deterrence** *n.*

detest *vt* to dislike intensely.

detonate *vti* to (cause to) explode rapidly and violently.—**detonation** *n.*

detonator *n* a device that sets off an explosion.

detour *n* a deviation from an intended course, esp one serving as an alternative to a more direct route.—*also vti.*

detract *vi* to take away (from).

detriment *n* (a cause of) damage or injury.—**detrimental** *adj.*

devalue, devaluate *vt* to reduce the exchange value of (a currency).

devastate *vt* to lay waste; to destroy; to overwhelm.—**devastation** *n.*

develop *vt* to evolve; to bring to maturity; to show the symptoms of (e.g. a disease); to reveal a photographic image; to improve value of. • *vi* to grow (into).

developer *n* one who develops; a person or organisation that develops property; a substance for developing photographs.

developing country *n* a poor country in process of improvement.

development *n* the process of growing or developing; a new situation that emerges; land, property that has been developed.

deviate *vi* to diverge from a course, topic, principle, etc.—**deviation** *n.*

device *n* a machine, implement, etc, for a particular purpose; an invention; a scheme.

devil *n* (*with cap*) in Christian and Jewish theology, the supreme spirit of evil, Satan; any evil spirit; an extremely wicked person. • *vb vt* to cook food with a hot seasoning.

devilish *adj* fiendish; mischievous.

devious *adj* underhand, deceitful.

devise *vt* to invent, contrive; to plan.

devoid *adj* (*with of*) lacking; free from.

devote *vt* to give or use for a particular purpose.

devoted *adj* zealous; loyal; loving.

devotion *n* religious worship; piety; strong affection or attachment (to); (*pl*) prayers.

devour *vt* to eat up greedily; to consume.

devout *adj* very religious, pious; sincere.

dew *n* air moisture, deposited on a cool surface, esp at night.

dexterity *n* manual skill, adroitness.

diabetes *n* a medical disorder marked by excessive discharge of urine.—**diabetic** *adj, n.*

diagnose *vt* to ascertain by diagnosis.

diagnosis *n* the identification of a disease from its symptoms; the analysis of the nature of a problem.—**diagnostic** *adj.*

diagonal *adj* slanting from one corner to an opposite corner of a polygon. • *n* a straight line connecting opposite corners.

diagram *n* a plan drawn in outline to illustrate the form or workings of something.

dial *n* the face of a watch or clock; a graduated disc with a pointer used in various instruments; the control on a radio or television set indicating wavelength or station.—*also vt .*

dialect *n* the form of language spoken in a particular region or social class.

dialogue *n* a conversation, esp in a play, etc; an exchange of opinions, negotiation.

diameter *n* a straight line bisecting a circle; the length of this line.

diamond *n* a valuable gem, a crystallised form of pure carbon; (*baseball*) the playing field; a suit of playing cards denoted by a red lozenge.

diaphragm *n* the midriff, a muscular structure separating the chest from the abdomen; a contraceptive cap covering the cervix.

diarrhoea *n* excessive looseness of the bowels.

diary *n* a daily record of thoughts, events, appointments; a book for these.

dice *n* (*pl used as sing*) a small cube with numbered sides used in games of chance. • *vt* to gamble using dice; to cut (food) into small cubes.

dictate *vt* to say, read for another to write or a machine to record; to pronounce. • *vi* to give dictation; to give orders (to). • *n* a rule or command; (*usu pl*) ruling principle.—**dictation** *n.*

dictator *n* a ruler with absolute authority.

dictatorship *n* the office or government of a dictator; a country governed by a dictator.

diction *n* a way of speaking, enunciation.

dictionary *n* a reference book containing the words of a language alphabetically arranged, with their meanings.

die^1 *vi* to cease existence.

die^2 *n* a dice; an engraved stamp for pressing coins; a casting mould.

diesel *n* a vehicle driven by diesel engine.

diesel engine *n* an internal combustion engine in which ignition is produced by the heat of highly compressed air alone.

diet^1 *n* food selected to adjust weight, to control illness, etc; food and drink usu consumed by a person or animal. • *vt* to put on a diet. • *vi* to eat according to a special diet.

diet^2 *n* a legislative assembly in some countries.

differ *vi* to be unlike; to disagree.

difference *n* unlikeness; disparity; a distinguishing feature; the result of the subtraction of one quantity from another; a disagreement or argument.

different *adj* distinct, separate; unlike.

differential *adj* of or showing a difference; (*math*) relating to increments in given functions. • *n* something that marks the difference between comparable things.

differentiate vt to make different; to note differences; (math) to calculate the derivative of.

difficult adj hard to understand; hard to do.

difficulty n being difficult; a problem, etc, that is hard to deal with; an obstacle; a troublesome situation; a disagreement.

diffident adj shy, lacking self-confidence.

diffuse[1] vt to spread widely in all directions. • vti (gases, fluids, etc) to intermingle.

diffuse[2] adj spread widely, not concentrated.

dig vt to use a tool, hands, etc, in making a hole in the ground; to excavate; to investigate; to thrust (into); to nudge. • n an archaeological excavation.

digest[1] vt to convert (food) into assimilable form; to reduce (facts, laws, etc) to convenient form by classifying or summarising; to form a clear view of by reflection.

digest[2] n an abridgment of any written matter.

digestion n the act or process of digesting.

digit n any of the basic counting units of a number system; a human finger or toe.—**digital** adj.

dignified adj possessing dignity; noble.

dignitary n a person in a high position.

dignity n formality of manner and appearance.

digress vi to stray from the main subject in speaking or writing.—**digression** n.

digs npl (inf) lodgings.

dilapidated adj in a state of disrepair.

dilate vti to enlarge or become enlarged.

dilatory adj tardy; causing delay.

dilemma n a situation where each of two alternative courses is undesirable.

diligent adj industrious.—**diligence** n.

dilute vt to thin down, esp by mixing with water; to weaken the strength of. • adj diluted.

dim adj faintly lit; not seen, heard, understood, etc, clearly. • vti to make or cause to become dark.

dime n a US coin worth ten cents.

dimension n any linear measurement of width, length, or thickness; extent; size.

diminish vti to make or become smaller in size, amount, or importance.

diminutive adj very small. • n a word formed by a suffix to mean small (e.g. duckling) or to convey affection (e.g. Freddie).

dimple n a small hollow on cheek or chin.

din n a loud persistent noise. • vt (with into) to instil by continual repetition.

dine vi to eat dinner.

dinghy n a small open boat propelled by oars or sails; a small inflatable boat.

dingy adj dirty-looking, shabby.

dinner n the principal meal of the day; a formal meal.

diocese n the district over which a bishop has authority.—**diocesan** adj.

dip vt to put (something) under the surface (as of a liquid) and lift quickly out again. • vi to go into water and come out quickly; to drop down or sink out of sight; to read superficially; to slope down. • n a dipping; a sudden drop; a mixture in which to dip something.

diphtheria n an acute infectious disease causing inflammation of the throat and breathing difficulties.

diphthong n the union of two vowel sounds pronounced in one syllable.

diploma n a certificate given by a college or university to its graduating students.

diplomacy n the management of relations between nations; skill in handling affairs.—**diplomatic** adj.

diplomat n a person employed in diplomacy.

dipstick n a rod with graduated markings to measure fluid level.

dire adj dreadful; ominous; very urgent.

direct adj straight; in an unbroken line; frank. • vt to manage, to control; to tell, show the way; to organise and supervise; to train and lead performances; to command. • vi to act as a director.

direct current n an electric current that flows in one direction only.

direction n management, control; order, command; any way in which one may face or point; (pl) instructions.

directly adv in a direct manner; immediately.

director n person who directs, esp the production of a show for stage or screen; one of the persons directing the affairs of a company or an institution.

directory n an alphabetical or classified list, as of members of an organisation, charities, etc.

dirt n filth; loose earth; obscenity; scandal.

dirty adj filthy; unclean; dishonest; mean; obscene. • vti to make or become dirty.

disability n a lack of physical, mental or social fitness; a handicap.

disabled adj having a physical handicap.

disadvantage n an unfavourable condition or situation; loss, damage.—also vt.

disagree vi to differ in opinion; (with with) to have a bad effect on.—**disagreement** n.

disagreeable adj nasty, bad tempered.

disallow vt to refuse to allow or accept.

disappear vi to pass from sight completely; to fade into nothing.—**disappearance** n.

disappoint vt to fail to fulfil the hopes of.—**disappointed** adj.—**disappointing** adj.

disappointment n the frustration of one's hopes; annoyance due to failure.

disapprove vti to express or have an unfavourable opinion (of).—**disapproval** n.

disarm vt to deprive of weapons or means of defence; to defuse (a bomb); to conciliate.

disarmament *n* the reduction or abolition of a country's armed forces and weaponry.

disaster *n* a devastating and sudden misfortune; utter failure.—**disastrous** *adj*.

disband *vt* to disperse; to break up and separate.—**disbandment** *n*.

disc *n* a flat, thin circular body; something resembling this, as the sun; a cylindrical pad of cartilage between the vertebrae; a gramophone record; (*comput*) a disk.

discard *vti* to get rid of.

disc brake *n* one in which two flat discs press against a central plate on the wheel hub.

discern *vt* to perceive; to see clearly.

discerning *adj* discriminating; perceptive.—**discernment** *n*.

discharge *vt* to unload; to send out, emit; to release, acquit; to dismiss from employment; to shoot a gun; to fulfil, as duties. • *vi* to unload; (*gun*) to be fired; (*fluid*) to pour out. • *n* the act or process of discharging; something that is discharged; an authorisation for release, acquittal, dismissal, etc.

disciple *n* a person who believes in and helps to spread another's teachings, a follower; one of the twelve apostles of Christ.

disciplinary *adj* of or for discipline.

discipline *n* a field of learning; training to produce obedience and self-control; punishment; the maintenance of order.—*also vt*.

disc jockey *n* (*inf*) one who announces records on radio or in discotheques.

disclaim *vi* to deny connection with.

disclose *vt* to reveal.—**disclosure** *n*.

discolour *vti* to ruin the colour of; to fade, stain.—**discoloration** *n*.

discomfort *n* uneasiness; something causing this.—*also vt*.

disconcert *vt* to confuse; to upset.

disconnect *vt* to separate or break the connection of.

disconsolate *adj* miserable; dejected.

discontent *n* lack of contentment.

discontinue *vti* to stop or come to a stop.

discord *n* lack of agreement; (*mus*) a lack of harmony; harsh clashing sounds.—**discordant** *adj*.

discotheque *n* an occasion where people gather to dance to recorded pop music; a club or party, etc, where this takes place.

discount *n* a reduction in the amount or cost; the percentage charged for doing this. • *vt* to deduct from the amount, cost; to allow for exaggeration; to disregard; to make less effective by anticipation. • *vi* to make and give discounts.

discourage *vt* to deprive of the will or courage (to do something).—**discouragement** *n*.

discourteous *adj* lacking in courtesy, rude.—**discourtesy** *n*.

discover *vt* to see, find or learn of for the first time.—**discoverer** *n*.—**discovery** *n*.

discredit *n* damage to a reputation; disgrace.

discreet *adj* prudent; unobtrusive.

discrepancy *n* difference; a disagreement, as between figures in a total.

discretion *n* the freedom to judge or to choose; prudence; wise judgment; skill.

discriminate *vi* to be discerning in matters of taste or judgment; to make a distinction; to treat differently, esp unfavourably due to prejudice.—**discrimination** *n*.

discriminating *adj* judicious; discerning.

discus *n* a heavy disc with a thickened middle, thrown by athletes.

discuss *vt* to talk over; to investigate by reasoning or argument.—**discussion** *n*.

disdain *n* scorn; a feeling of contemptuous superiority.—**disdainful** *adj*.

disease *n* an unhealthy condition in an organism caused by infection, poisoning, etc.

disembark *vti* to land from a ship, debark.—**disembarkation** *n*.

disembodied *adj* free of the body.

disembowel *vt* to remove the entrails of.

disenchant *vt* to disillusion.

disengage *vt* to separate or free from engagement or obligation; to detach, to release.—**disengagement** *n*.

disentangle *vt* to untangle; to free from complications.

disfavour *n* dislike; disapproval.

disfigure *vt* to spoil the beauty or appearance of.—**disfigurement** *n*.

disgrace *n* loss of trust, favour or honour; something that disgraces. • *vt* to bring disgrace or shame upon.—**disgraceful** *adj*.

disgruntled *adj* dissatisfied, resentful.

disguise *vt* to hide what one is by appearing as something else; to hide what (a thing) really is. • *n* the use of a changed appearance to conceal identity; a false appearance.

disgust *n* sickening dislike.—*also vt*.

dish *n* a shallow vessel to serve food in; the food served; a dish aerial.

dishearten *vt* to discourage.

dishevelled *adj* rumpled, untidy.

dishonest *adj* not honest.—**dishonesty** *n*.

dishonour *n* loss of honour; disgrace, shame. • *vt* to bring shame on, to disgrace.

dishonourable *adj* lacking honour, disgraceful.

dishwasher *n* an appliance for washing dishes; a person employed to wash dishes.

disillusion *vt* to free from ideals or illusions. • *n* the state of being disillusioned.

disinfect *vt* to destroy germs.

disinfectant *n* any chemical agent that inhibits the growth of or destroys germs.

disintegrate *vti* to break or cause to break into separate pieces.—**disintegration** *n*.

disinterested *adj* impartial; objective.

disjointed *adj* incoherent, muddled.

disk *n* an alternative spelling of **disc**; (*comput*) a storage device in a computer.

dislike *vt* to consider unpleasant. • *n* aversion.

dislocate *vt* to put (a joint) out of place.

dislodge *vt* to force or move out of a hiding place, established position, etc.

dismal *adj* gloomy, miserable, sad.

dismantle *vt* to pull down; to take apart.

dismay *n* apprehension, discouragement. • *vt* to fill with dismay.

disobedient *adj* failing or refusing to obey.—**disobedience** *n*.

disobey *vt* to refuse to follow orders.

disorder *n* lack of order; untidiness; a riot; an illness or interruption of the normal functioning of the body or mind.—*also vt*.—**disorderly** *adj*.

disorganise *vt* to confuse or disrupt an orderly arrangement.—**disorganisation** *n*.

disown *vt* to refuse to acknowledge or own.

disparage *vt* to belittle.—**disparagement** *n*.

disparity *n* essential difference; inequality.

dispassionate *adj* impartial.

dispatch *vt* to send off; to perform speedily; to kill. • *n* a sending off (of a letter, a messenger etc); promptness; haste; a written message, esp of news.—*also* **despatch**.

dispel *vt* to drive away and scatter.

dispensary *n* a place in a chemist shop, etc, where medicines are made up and dispensed.

dispense *vt* to deal out, distribute; to prepare and distribute medicines; to administer.

disperse *vt* to scatter in different directions. • *vi* to separate, become dispersed.—**dispersal** *n*.

dispirited *adj* depressed, discouraged.

displace *vt* to take the place of, to oust; to remove from a position of authority.

display *vt* to show, expose to view; to exhibit ostentatiously. • *n* a displaying; an eye-catching arrangement, exhibition; a computer monitor for presenting visual information.

displease *vt* to annoy.—**displeasure** *n*.

disposable *adj* designed to be discarded after use; available for use.—*also n*.

disposal *n* a disposing of something; order.

dispose *vt* to place in order, arrange; to influence. • *vi* to deal with or settle; to give, sell or transfer to another; to throw away.

disposed *adj* inclined (towards something).

disposition *n* a natural way of behaving towards others; tendency; arrangement.

disproportionate *adj* out of proportion.

disprove *vt* to prove to be incorrect.

dispute *vt* to query the validity of. • *vi* to argue. • *n* an argument; a quarrel.

disqualify *vt* to make ineligible because of a violation of rules.—**disqualification** *n*.

disquiet *n* anxiety, worry.—*also vt.*.

disregard *vt* to pay no attention to.—*also n*.

disrepair *n* a worn-out condition through neglect of repair.

disreputable *adj* of bad reputation.

disrespect *n* lack of respect, rudeness.

disrupt *vti* to break up; to create disorder or confusion; to interrupt.—**disruption** *n*.

dissect *vt* to cut apart for scientific examination; to analyse and interpret.—**dissection** *n*.

disseminate *vt* to spread or scatter widely.

dissent *vi* to hold a different opinion; to withhold assent.—*also n*.—**dissenter** *n*.

dissident *n* a person who disagrees strongly with government policies, esp one who suffers harassment or imprisonment as a result.

dissipate *vt* to scatter, dispel; to waste, squander. • *vi* to separate and vanish.

dissipated *adj* indulging in excessive pleasure.

dissociate *vti* to separate or cause to separate the association of (people, things, etc) in consciousness; to repudiate a connection with.

dissolute *adj* lacking moral discipline.

dissolve *vt* to cause to pass into solution; to disperse (assembly); to melt; (*marriage*) to annul. • *vi* to become liquid; to fade away.

dissuade *vt* to prevent or discourage by persuasion.—**dissuasion** *n*.—**dissuasive** *adj*.

distance *n* the amount of space between two points or things; a distant place or point; remoteness, coldness of manner. • *vt* to place at a distance, physically or emotionally.

distant *adj* far off; not friendly, aloof.

distaste *n* aversion; dislike.—**distasteful** *adj*.

distemper *n* an infectious and often fatal disease of dogs; a type of paint made by mixing colour with egg or glue.

distend *vti* to swell or cause to swell.

distil *vti* to purify a substance by heating it until it turns into vapour and then cooling the vapour until it becomes liquid.—**distillation** *n*.

distillery *n* a place where distilling of alcoholic spirits is carried on.

distinct *adj* different, separate (from); easy to perceive by the mind or senses.

distinction *n* discrimination, separation; a distinguishing mark or characteristic; excellence, a mark of honour.

distinctive *adj* clearly marking a person or thing as different; characteristic.

distinguish *vti* to see or recognise as different; to mark as different, characterise; to see or hear clearly; to perceive a difference.

distinguished *adj* eminent, famous; dignified.

distort *vt* to pull or twist out of shape; to misrepresent.—**distortion** *n*.

distract vt to draw (e.g. the mind or attention) to something else; to confuse.

distracted adj bewildered, confused.

distraction n something that distracts the attention; an amusement; agitation.

distraught adj extremely distressed.

distress n physical or emotional suffering, as from pain, illness, etc; .—also vt.

distribute vt to divide and share out; to spread, disperse.—**distribution** n.

distributor n an agent who sells goods, esp wholesale; a device for distributing current to the spark plugs in an engine.

district n a region or area.

distrust n suspicion.—also vt.—**distrustful** adj.

disturb vt to interrupt; to cause to move; to destroy the quiet or composure of.

disturbance n an interruption; an outbreak of disorder and confusion.

ditch n a long narrow trench dug in the ground.

dither vi to hesitate, vacillate.—**ditherer** n.

ditto n the same again, as above.

divan n a long couch without back or sides; a bed of similar design.

dive vi to plunge headfirst into water; (aircraft) to descend or fall steeply; (diver, submarine) to submerge; to plunge (e.g. the hand) suddenly into anything; to dash headlong, lunge.—also n.

diver n a person who dives; an aquatic bird.

diverge vi to branch off in different directions from one point; to differ in character, form, etc.—**divergent** adj.—**divergence** n.

diverse adj different; assorted, various.

diversify vt to vary. • vi to engage in a variety of commercial operations to reduce risk.—**diversification** n.

diversion n a recreation, amusement; a drawing of attention away from the principal activity; a detour when a road is temporarily closed.

diversity n variety.

divert vt to turn aside from one course onto another; to entertain, amuse.

divide vt to break up into parts; to distribute, share out; to sort into categories; to cause to separate from something else; to separate into opposing sides; (Parliament) to vote or cause to vote by division; (math) to ascertain how many times one quantity contains another. • vi to become separated; to diverge; to vote by separating into two sides. • n a watershed; a split.

dividend n a number that is to be divided; the money earned by a company and divided among the shareholders; a bonus.

divine adj of, from or like God or a god. • vt to foretell the future by supernatural means; to discover intuitively; to dowse. • vi to practise divination.—**divination** n.

divinity n any god; theology.

division n a dividing or being divided; a partition, a barrier; a portion or section; a military unit; separation; (Parliament) a separation into two opposing sides to vote; a disagreement; (math) the process of dividing one number by another.—**divisional** adj.

divorce n the legal dissolution of marriage; separation.—also vt.

divulge vt to tell, reveal.—**divulgence** n.

dizzy adj confused; causing giddiness or confusion.—**dizziness** n.

do vt to perform; to work; to end, to complete; to make; to provide; to perform. • vi to act or behave; to be satisfactory; to manage.

docile adj submissive.—**docility** n.

dock[1] vt (an animal's tail) to cut short; (wages, etc) to deduct a portion of.

dock[2] n a wharf; an artificial enclosed area of water for ships to be loaded, repaired, etc; (pl) a dockyard. • vt to come or bring into dock; to join (spacecraft) together in space.

dock[3] n an enclosed area in a court of law reserved for the accused.

docker n a dock labourer.

dockyard n an area with docks and facilities for repairing and refitting ships.

doctor n a person qualified to treat diseases; the holder of the highest academic degree. • vt to treat medically; (machinery, etc) to patch up; to tamper with, falsify.

doctrine n a principle of belief.—**doctrinal** adj.

document n a paper containing information or proof. • vt to provide or prove with documents.

documentary adj consisting of documents. • n a non-fiction film.

dodge vi to move quickly in an irregular course. • vt to evade (a duty) by cunning; to avoid by a sudden movement. • n a sudden movement.

dog n a canine mammal of numerous breeds, commonly kept as a domestic pet; the male of the wolf or fox; a despicable person; a device for gripping things. • vt to pursue relentlessly.

dogma n a belief held as true, esp by a church; a doctrine; a belief.—**dogmatic** adj.

doldrums npl inactivity; depression; boredom; the regions of the ocean about the equator where there is little wind.

dole n money received from the state while unemployed. • vt to give (out) in small portions.

doleful adj sad, gloomy.

doll n a toy in the form of a human figure.

dollar n the unit of money in the USA, Canada, Australia, etc.

dolphin n a marine mammal with a beak-like snout.

domain n an area under the control of a ruler or government; a field of thought, activity, etc.

dome n a large, rounded roof.—*also vt.*

domestic adj belonging to the home or family; not foreign; (*animals*) tame.

domesticate vt to tame; to make home-loving and fond of household duties.

domicile n a house; a person's place of residence.—**domiciliary** adj.

dominant adj commanding, prevailing over others; overlooking from a superior height. • n (*mus*) the fifth note of a diatonic scale.

dominate vt to control by strength; to hold a commanding position; to overlook from a superior height.—**domination** n.

dominion n a territory under one ruler or government; the power to rule, authority.

domino n a flat oblong tile marked with up to 6 dots; (*pl*) a game using a set of 28 dominoes.

don[1] vt to put on.

don[2] n a head, fellow or tutor at Oxford or Cambridge universities.

donate vt to give as a gift or donation, esp to a charity.—**donator** n.

donation n donating; a contribution.

donkey n a small animal like a horse.

donor n a person who donates something, a donator; a person who gives their blood, organs, etc, for medical use.

doom n a grim destiny; ruin. • vt condemn to failure, destruction, etc.

doomsday n the day of God's Last Judgment of mankind.

door n a movable barrier to close an opening in a wall; a doorway; a means of entry.

dope n (*inf*) any illegal drug, such as cannabis or narcotics. • vt to treat with dope. • vi to take addictive drugs.

dormant adj sleeping; inactive.

dormitory n a large room with many beds, as in a boarding school.

dormouse n a small mouse-like creature that hibernates in winter.

dose n the amount of medicine, radiation, etc, administered at one time. • vt to administer a dose (of medicine) to.—**dosage** n.

dot n a small round speck, a point; the short signal in Morse code. • vt to mark with a dot; to scatter (about).

dote vi (*with on*) to show excessive affection.

double adj twice as large, as strong, etc; designed or intended for two; made of two similar parts; having two meanings, characters, etc. • adv twice; in twos. • n a number or amount that is twice as much; a person or thing identical to another; (*film*) a person closely resembling an actor and who takes their place to perform stunts, etc; (*pl*) a game between two pairs of players. • vti to make or become twice as much or as many; to bend; to have an additional purpose.

double bass n the largest instrument of the violin family.

double-cross vt to betray an associate.

doubt vi to be uncertain or undecided. • vt to distrust; to be suspicious of. • n uncertainty; (*often pl*) lack of confidence.—**doubtful** adj.

dough n a mixture of flour and water, milk, etc, used to make bread, pastry or cake.

doughnut n a fried ring-shaped cake.

dove n a small bird of the pigeon family; (*politics, diplomacy*) an advocate of peace.

dovetail n a wedge-shaped joint used in woodwork. • vt to fit or combine together.

dowdy adj poorly dressed, not stylish.

down[1] n soft fluffy feathers or fine hairs.

down[2] adv toward or in a lower physical position; to a lying or sitting position; to or in a lower status or in a worse condition. • adj occupying a low position, esp lying on the ground; depressed. • prep in a descending direction in, on, along or through. • n a low period (as in activity, emotional life, or fortunes). • vti to swallow.

downcast adj dejected; (*eyes*) directed downwards.

downfall n a sudden fall (from power, etc); a sudden or heavy fall of rain or snow.

down payment n a deposit.

downright adv thoroughly.

downward adj moving from a higher to a lower level, position or condition.

downwards adv towards a lower place, etc.

dowry n the money or possessions a woman brings to her husband at marriage.

doze vi to sleep lightly. • n a light sleep, a nap.

dozen n a group of twelve.

drab adj dull, uninteresting.

draft n a rough plan, preliminary sketch; an order for the payment of money by a bank; in USA, conscription.—*also vt.*

drain vt to draw off liquid gradually; to exhaust; to drink the entire contents of a glass. • vi to flow away gradually. • n a sewer, pipe, etc, by which water is drained away; something that causes exhaustion.

drainage n a draining; a system of drains.

drainpipe n a pipe that carries waste liquid, sewage, etc, out of a building.

drama n a play for stage, radio or television; dramatic literature; a dramatic situation.—**dramatic** adj.

dramatist n a person who writes plays.

drape vt to arrange in loose folds; to place loosely or untidily. • n a hanging cloth; (*pl*) curtains.

draper n a seller of cloth.

drastic adj acting with force and violence.—**drastically** adv.

draught n a current of air; a dose of medicine or

liquid; beer, wine, etc, stored in bulk in casks; a flat counter used in the game of draughts.

draughts n a board game for two players using 24 round pieces.

draughtsman[1] n a person who makes detailed drawings or plans.—**draughtsmanship** n.

draughtsman[2] n a flat counter used in the game of draughts.

draw vti to drag; to pull out; to attract; to sketch; to receive (as a salary); to leave (a contest) undecided; to draft (a will); to get information from. • n the drawing of lots; a drawn game.

drawback n a hindrance, handicap.

drawbridge n a bridge (e.g. over a moat) designed to be drawn up.

drawer n a person who draws; a sliding box-like compartment (as in a table, chest, or desk); (pl) knickers, underpants.

drawing n a drawn figure, plan, sketch.

drawing pin n a flat-headed pin used for fastening paper, drawings, etc.

drawing room n a living room.

drawl vt to speak slowly and with elongated vowel sounds.—also n.

drawn adj looking strained because of tiredness or worry.

dread n great fear or apprehension. • vt to fear greatly.—**dreadful** adj.

dream n a stream of thoughts and images experienced during sleep; a reverie; an ambition; an ideal. • vb vi to have a dream; to fantasise. • vt to dream of.—**dreamer** n.

dreary adj dull; cheerless.—**dreariness** n.

dredge[1] n a device for scooping up material from the bottom of a river, etc.—also vt.

dredge[2] vt to coat (food) by sprinkling.

dredger[1] n a vessel fitted with dredging equipment.

dredger[2] n a container with a perforated lid for sprinkling.

dregs npl solid impurities that settle on the bottom of a liquid; residue.

drench vt to soak, saturate.

dress n a one-piece garment worn by women comprising a top and skirt; a style of clothing. • vt to put on or provide with clothing; (wound) to wash and bandage. • vi to put on clothes; to put on formal wear.

dress circle n the first tier of seats in a theatre above the stalls.

dresser n a person who assists an actor to dress; a type of kitchen sideboard.

dressing n a sauce for food; dress, clothes; the bandage, ointment applied to a wound.

dress rehearsal n rehearsal in full costume.

dribble vi to flow in a thin stream or small drips; to let saliva trickle from the mouth. • vt (soccer, etc) to move (the ball) along little by little. • n the act of dribbling; a thin stream of liquid.

drift n a heap of snow, sand, etc, deposited by the wind; natural course, tendency; the general meaning or intention (of what is said); the extent of deviation (of an aircraft, etc) from a course; • vt to cause to drift. • vi to be carried along by water or air currents; to move along aimlessly.

drill[1] n an implement with a pointed end that bores holes; the training of soldiers, etc. • vt to make a hole with a drill; to instruct or be instructed by drilling.

drill[2] n a machine for planting seeds in rows; a furrow in which seeds are planted.—also vt.

drink vb vt to swallow (a liquid). • vi to consume alcoholic liquor, esp to excess. • n liquid to be drunk; alcoholic liquor.

drip vti to fall or let fall in drops. • n a liquid that falls in drops; the sound of falling drops; (med) a device for administering a fluid slowly and continuously into a vein.

drip-dry adj (clothing) drying easily and needing relatively little ironing.—also vti.

dripping n fat that drips from meat during roasting.

drive vb vt to urge, push onwards; to direct the course of; to convey in a vehicle; to impress forcefully; to propel (a ball) with a hard blow. • vi to be forced along; to be conveyed in a vehicle; to strive (at). • n a ride in a vehicle; a golf stroke; a driveway; a military attack; an intensive campaign; dynamic ability.

driver n one who or that which drives; a chauffeur; a wooden golf club.

driveway n a road for vehicles.

drizzle n fine light rain.—also vi.

droll adj oddly amusing; whimsical.

dromedary n a one-humped camel.

drone n a male honey-bee; a deep humming sound; monotonous speech. • vi to make a monotonous humming sound; to speak monotonously.

drool vi to slaver, dribble; to show excessive enthusiasm for.

droop vti to bend or hang down.—also n.

drop n a small amount of liquid in a roundish shape; a tiny quantity; a sudden fall; the distance down. • vb vi to fall in drops; to fall suddenly; to sink; (with **in**) to visit informally. • vt to let fall; to lower; to set down from a vehicle; to mention casually; to give up (an idea).

dropout n a student who abandons a course of study; a person who rejects normal society.

droppings npl animal dung.

dross n a surface scum on molten metal; rubbish, waste matter.

drought n a long period of dry weather.

drove[1] n a group of animals driven in a herd or flock, etc; a large moving crowd of people.

drown vti to die, kill by suffocation in water. • vt

to flood; to drench; to become immersed in; to blot out (a sound) with a louder noise.

drowse vi to be nearly asleep.

drowsy adj sleepy.—**drowsiness** n.

drudge vi to do boring or very menial work.—also n.—**drudgery** n.

drug n any substance used in medicine; a narcotic. • vt to administer drugs to; to stupefy

drum n a round percussion instrument, played by striking a membrane stretched across a hollow cylindrical frame; the sound of a drum; a container shaped like a drum. • vb vi to play a drum; to beat rhythmically. • vt (with **in**) to instil (knowledge) into a person by constant repetition; (with **up**) to summon.

drummer n a person who plays a drum.

drunk[1] adj intoxicated with alcohol. • n a drunk person.

drunkard n an habitual drunk.

drunken adj intoxicated.—**drunkenness** n.

dry adj free from water or liquid; thirsty; matter-of-fact, ironic,terse in manner of expression; uninteresting, wearisome; (wine) not sweet; not selling alcohol. • vti to make or become dry.—**dryness** n.

dry-clean vt to clean with solvents.

dryer n a device for drying, as a tumble-dryer; a clothes horse.

dry rot n decay of timber caused by a fungus; any form of moral decay or corruption.

dual adj double.—**duality** n.

dubious adj doubtful (about, of); uncertain as to result; untrustworthy.

duchess n the wife or widow of a duke; a woman having the same rank as a duke.

duck[1] vt to dip briefly in water; to lower the head suddenly; to avoid, dodge. • vi to dip or dive; to evade a duty, etc.

duck[2] n a water bird related to geese.

duct n a pipe for fluids, electric cable, etc; a tube in the body for fluids to pass through.

due adj owed as a debt; immediately payable; fitting, expected to arrive. • adv directly, exactly. • n something owed; (pl) fees.

duel n combat with weapons between two persons. • vi to fight in a duel.

duet n a musical composition for two.

duke n the highest order of British nobility.

dull adj not sharp or pointed; not bright or clear; stupid; boring; not active. • vti to make or become dull.—**dullness** n.

duly adv properly; suitably.

dumb adj not able to speak; silent.

dumbfound vti to astonish, surprise.

dummy n a figure used to display clothes; a soother for a baby; an imitation.

dump vt to drop or put down carelessly; to deposit as rubbish; to abandon; to refuse; a temporary store. • n a place for

dumpling n a rounded piece of dough cooked by boiling or steaming.

dunce n a stupid person.

dune n a hill of sand piled up by the wind.

dung n excrement; manure.

dungarees npl overalls or trousers made from a coarse cotton cloth.

dungeon n an underground cell.

dupe n one who is cheated. • vt to deceive.

duplicate adj in pairs, double; identical; copied exactly from an original.—also n, vt.—**duplication** n.

durable adj enduring, resisting wear, etc.

duration n the time an event lasts.

duress n compulsion by use of force or threat.

during prep throughout the duration of; at a point in the course of.

dusk n twilight.

dusky adj having a dark colour.

dust n fine particles of solid matter. • vt to free from dust; to sprinkle.

dustbin n a container for rubbish.

dust jacket n a paper cover for a book.

Dutch adj pertaining to Holland, its people, or language. • n the Dutch language.

duty n an obligation that must be performed for moral or legal reasons; actions and responsibilities arising from one's business; a tax on goods or imports, etc.

duty-free adj free from tax or duty.

dwarf n a person, animal or plant of abnormally small size. • vt to cause to appear small.

dwell vi to live (in a place); (with **on**); to think, talk, or write at length about.

dwelling n a house.

dwindle vi to shrink, diminish.

dye vt to give a new colour to. • n a colouring substance, esp in solution; a colour produced by dyeing.

dynamic adj relating to force that produces motion; (person) forceful, energetic.

dynamics n (used as sing) the branch of science that deals with forces and their effect on the motion of bodies.

dynamite n a powerful explosive; a potentially dangerous situation. • vt to blow up with dynamite.

dynamo n a device that generates electric current.

dynasty n a line of hereditary rulers or leaders of any powerful family or similar group.

dysentery n painful inflammation of the large intestine with associated diarrhoea.

E

each *adj* every one of two or more.

eager *adj* enthusiastic, desirous (of); keen (for).

eagle *n* a bird of prey with keen eyes and powerful wings; (*golf*) a score of two strokes under par.

eaglet *n* a young eagle.

ear[1] *n* the organ of hearing; attention.

ear[2] *n* the part of a cereal plant (e.g. corn, maize) that contains the seeds.

earache *n* a pain in the ear.

eardrum *n* the membrane within the ear that vibrates in response to sound waves.

earl *n* a member of the British nobility ranking between a marquis and a viscount.

early *adj* before the expected or normal time; of or occurring in the distant past.—*also adv*.

earmark *vt* to set aside for a specific use.

earn *vt* to gain (money, etc) by work or service; to acquire; to deserve.

earnest *adj* sincere.

earnings *npl* wages or profits.

earring *n* an ornament worn on the ear.

earth *n* the world we inhabit; soil; the burrow of a badger, fox, etc; a connection between an electric device or circuit with the earth. • *vt* to connect an electrical circuit or device to earth.

earthenware *n* pottery made from baked clay.

earthly *adj* material, worldly.

earthquake *n* a violent tremor of the earth's crust.

earthwork *n* an excavation of earth.

earthworm *n* any of various common worms that live in the soil.

earthy *adj* of or like earth; crude.

earwig *n* a small insect with a pincer-like appendage at the end of its body.

ease *n* freedom from pain, discomfort or disturbance; effortlessness. • *vt* to relieve from pain, trouble, anxiety; to relax, loosen. • *vi* (*with* **off**) to become less active.

easel *n* a supporting frame, esp one used by artists to support their canvases.

easily *adv* with ease; by far; probably.

east *n* the direction of the sunrise; the compass point opposite west; (*with cap and* **the**) the area of the world east of Europe. • *adj, adv* in, towards, or from the east.

Easter *n* the Christian festival observed on a Sunday in March or April in commemoration of the resurrection of Christ.

easterly *adj* situated towards, coming from the east. • *n* an east wind.

eastern *adj* of or in the east.

eastward *adj* towards the east.

easy *adj* free from pain, trouble, anxiety; not difficult or requiring effort. • *adv* with ease.

easygoing *adj* placid, tolerant, relaxed.

eat *vt* to take into the mouth, chew and swallow as food; (*also with* **into**) to corrode.

eatable *adj* suitable for eating.

eaves *npl* the overhanging edge of a roof.

eavesdrop *vi* to listen secretly to a private conversation.—**eavesdropper** *n*.

ebb *n* the flow of the tide out to sea; a decline.—*also vi*.

ebony *n* a hard heavy wood. • *adj* black.

ebullient *adj* exuberant, enthusiastic; boiling.

eccentric *adj* unconventional, odd; (*circles*) not concentric. • *n* an eccentric person.—**eccentricity** *n*.

ecclesiastic *n* a member of the clergy. • *adj* of or relating to the Christian Church or clergy.

echo *n* a repetition of sound caused by the reflection of sound waves. • *vi* to produce an echo. • *vt* to repeat; to send back (a sound) by an echo.

echo sounder *n* an instrument for determining the depth beneath a ship using sound waves.

éclair *n* a small oblong shell of pastry covered with chocolate and filled with cream.

eclectic *adj* selecting from, using, composed of various styles, ideas, methods, etc.—*also n*.

eclipse *n* the obscuring of the light of the sun or moon by the intervention of the other; a decline into obscurity. • *vt* to cause an eclipse of; to overshadow.

ecology *n* (the study of) the relationships between living things and their environments.

economic *adj* pertaining to economics or the economy; (*business, etc*) capable of producing a profit.

economical *adj* thrifty.

economics *n* (*used as sing*) the social science concerned with the production, consumption and distribution of goods and services; (*as pl*) financial aspects.—**economist** *n*.

economise *vti* to spend money carefully; to save; to use prudently.

economy *n* careful use of money and resources; the management of the finances and resources of a business; the economic system of a country.

ecstasy *n* intense joy; (*sl*) a synthetic amphetamine-based drug.—**ecstatic** *adj*.

ecumenical *adj* of the whole Christian Church.

eczema *n* inflammation of the skin causing itching.

eddy *n* a swiftly revolving current of air, water, fog, etc. • *vi* to move round and round.

edge *n* the border, brink, verge, margin; the sharp cutting side of a blade; sharpness, keenness; force, effectiveness. • *vt* to supply an edge or border to; to move gradually.

edgeways, edgewise *adv* sideways.

edgy *adj* irritable.—**edginess** *n.*

edible *adj* fit or safe to eat.

edict *n* a decree.

edifice *n* a substantial building; any large or complex organisation or institution.

edify *vt* to improve the moral character or mind of (a person).—**edification** *n.*

edit *vt* to prepare (text) for publication; to be in charge of a publication; (*cinema*) to prepare a final version of a film by selection and arrangement of sequences.

edition *n* a whole number of copies of a book, etc, printed at a time; the form of a particular publication.

editor *n* a person in charge of a newspaper or other publication; a person who edits written material for publication; one who prepares the final version of a film.

editorial *adj* of or produced by an editor. • *n* an article expressing the opinions of a newspaper.

educate *vt* to train the mind, to teach.

education *n* the process of learning and training; instruction as imparted in schools, colleges and universities; the theory and practice of teaching.—**educational** *adj.*

eel *n* a snake-like fish.

eerie *adj* causing fear; weird.—**eeriness** *n.*

efface *vt* to rub out; to make (oneself) humble.

effect *n* the result of a cause or action by some agent; the power to produce some result; the fundamental meaning; an impression on the senses; (*pl*) personal belongings; (*pl: theatre, cinema*) sounds, lighting, etc, to accompany a production. • *vt* to bring about, accomplish.

effective *adj* producing a specified effect; forceful, striking; actual, real; operative.

effectual *adj* able to produce the desired effect.

effeminate *adj* (*man*) displaying feminine qualities.—**effeminacy** *n.*

effervesce *vi* (*liquid*) to froth and hiss as bubbles of gas escape; to be exhilarated.

effete *adj* decadent, weak.—**effeteness** *n.*

efficacious *adj* achieving the desired result.—**efficacy** *n.*

efficient *adj* achieving results competently.—**efficiency** *n.*

effigy *n* a sculpture or portrait; a crude figure of a person, esp for exposure to public ridicule.

effluent *adj* flowing out. • *n* sewage.

effort *n* exertion; an attempt, try.

effortless *adj* done with little effort.

effrontery *n* impudent boldness, insolence.

effusion *n* an unrestrained outpouring.

effusive *adj* gushing, emotionally unrestrained.

egalitarian *adj* upholding the principle of equal rights for all.—**egalitarianism** *n.*

egg[1] *n* the oval hard-shelled reproductive cell laid by birds, reptiles and fish; the egg of the domestic poultry used as food; ovum.

egg[2] *vt* (*with* on) to incite.

egg plant *n* a plant producing a smooth, dark-purple fruit; this fruit used as a vegetable.

eggshell *n* the hard covering of an egg. • *adj* fragile; (*paint*) having a slight sheen.

ego *n* the self; self-image, conceit.

egocentric *adj* self-centred.—**egocentricity** *n.*

egoism *n* self-concern; self-centredness.—**egoist** *n.*—**egoistic** *adj.*

egotism *n* excessive reference to oneself; conceit.—**egotist** *n.*—**egotistic** *adj.*

egregious *adj* outstandingly bad.

eiderdown *n* the down of the eider duck used for stuffing quilts, etc; a thick quilt.

eight *n, adj* one more than seven; the symbol for this (8, VIII, viii); (the crew of) an eight-oared rowing boat.—**eighth** *adj, n.*

eighteen *n, adj* one more than seventeen; the symbol for this (18, XVIII, xviii).—**eighteenth** *adj, n.*

eighty *n* eight times ten; the symbol for this (80, LXXX, lxxx).—**eightieth** *adj, n.*

either *adj, n* the one or the other of two; each of two. • *conj* correlative to *or.*

eject *vt* to turn out, to expel by force. • *vi* to escape from an aircraft or spacecraft using an ejector seat.—**ejection** *n.*

ejector seat *n* an escape seat, esp in combat aircraft, that can be ejected with its occupant by means of explosive bolts.

eke *vt* (*with* out) to supplement; to use frugally.

elaborate *adj* highly detailed; planned with care. • *vt* to explain in detail.

elapse *vi* (*time*) to pass by.

elastic *adj* returning to the original size and shape if stretched or squeezed. • *n* fabric, tape, etc, incorporating elastic thread.—**elasticity** *n.*

elate *vt* to fill with happiness or pride.—**elated** *adj.*—**elation** *n.*

elbow *n* the joint between the forearm and upper arm. • *vt* to jostle.

elder[1] *n* a tree or shrub with flat clusters of white or pink flowers.

elder[2] *n* an older person; an office bearer in some churches.

elderly *adj* quite old.

eldest *n* oldest, first born.

elect *vti* to choose by voting; to make a selection (of); to make a decision on.

election *n* the public choice of a person for office, esp a politician.

electioneer *vi* to work on behalf of a candidate for election.—**electioneering** *n.*

elector *n* a person who may vote.

electoral *adj* of elections or electors.

electorate *n* the whole body of qualified electors.

electric *adj* of, producing or worked by electricity; exciting, thrilling.—**electrical** *adj*.

electrician *n* a person who installs and repairs electrical devices.

electricity *n* energy comprising certain charged particles; an electric current.

electrify *vt* to charge with electricity; to astonish or excite.—**electrification** *n*.

electrocute *vt* to kill or execute by electricity.—**electrocution** *n*.

electrode *n* a conductor through which an electric current enters or leaves a gas discharge tube.

electrolysis *n* the destruction of living tissue, esp hair roots, by an electric current

electrolyte *n* a solution that conducts electricity.

electromagnet *n* a metal core rendered magnetic by the passage of an electric current through a surrounding coil.

electromagnetism *n* magnetism produced by electric current; the science dealing with relations between electricity and magnetism.—**electromagnetic** *adj*.

electron *n* a negatively charged elementary particle that forms the part of the atom outside the nucleus.

electronic *adj* of, worked by streams of electrons flowing through devices, vacuum or gas; of, concerned with electrons or electronics.

electronics *n* (*used as sing*) the study, development and application of electronic devices.

elegant *adj* graceful; refined.—**elegance** *n*.

element *n* a constituent part; any of the 105 known substances composed of atoms with the same number of protons in their nuclei; a favourable environment for a plant or animal; a wire that produces heat in an electric kettle, etc; any of the four substances (earth, air, fire, water) that were once believed to constitute the universe; (*pl*) atmospheric conditions (wind, rain, etc); (*pl*) the basic principles, rudiments.

elementary *adj* concerned with the basic principles of a subject.

elephant *n* a large heavy mammal with a long trunk, thick skin and ivory tusks.

elevate *vt* to lift up; to raise in rank.

elevation *n* a raised place; the height above the earth's surface or above sea level; the angle to which a gun is aimed above the horizon; a drawing that shows the front, rear or side view of something.

elevator *n* a cage or platform for moving something from one level to another; a lift.

eleven *adj, n* one more than ten; the symbol for this (11, XI, xi); (*cricket, football, etc*) a team of eleven players.—**eleventh** *adj, n*.

elf *n* a mischievous fairy.

elicit *vt* to draw out (information, etc).

eligible *adj* suitable to be chosen, legally qualified; desirable, esp as a marriage partner.

eliminate *vt* to get rid of; to eradicate; to exclude from a competition.—**elimination** *n*.

elite *n* a superior group.

elitism *n* leadership or rule by an elite; advocacy of such a system.—**elitist** *n*.

elixir *n* (*alchemy*) a substance thought to have the power of transmuting base metals into gold; any medicine claimed as a cure-all.

ellipse *n* (*geom*) a closed plane figure formed by the plane section of a right-angled cone; a flattened circle.

elm *n* a tall deciduous tree with spreading branches and broad top; its wood.

elocution *n* skill in public speaking.

elongate *vti* to make or become longer.—**elongation** *n*.

elope *vi* to run away secretly with a lover, esp to get married.

eloquence *n* skill in the use of words; speaking with fluency.—**eloquent** *adj*.

else *adv* besides; otherwise.

elucidate *vt* to make clear, to explain.

elude *vt* to avoid stealthily; to escape the understanding or memory of a person.

elusive *adj* baffling; difficult to contact.

emanate *vi* to issue from a source.—**emanation** *n*.

emancipate *vt* to liberate, esp from bondage or slavery.—**emancipation** *n*.

embalm *vt* to preserve (a dead body) with drugs, chemicals, etc.—**embalmment** *n*.

embankment *n* an earth or stone mound to hold back water or carry a roadway.

embargo *n* an order of a government forbidding ships to enter or leave its ports; any ban or restriction on commerce by law; a prohibition, ban.—*also vt*.

embark *vti* to go on board a ship to begin a journey; to make a start in any activity or enterprise.—**embarkation** *n*.

embarrass *vt* to make (a person) feel confused, uncomfortable or disconcerted.—**embarrassment** *n*.

embassy *n* the official residence of an ambassador.

embed *vt* to fix firmly in surrounding matter.

embellish *vt* to decorate, to adorn.

ember *n* a piece of glowing coal or wood in fire.

embezzle *vt* to steal (money, etc, entrusted to one's care).—**embezzlement** *n*.

embitter *vt* to cause to feel bitter.

emblem *n* a symbol; a figure adopted and used as an identifying mark.

embody *vt* to express in definite form.

emboss *vt* to ornament with a raised design.

embrace *vt* to hold tightly and affectionately; to adopt (e.g. faith); to include.—*also n.*

embroider *vt* to ornament with decorative stitches; to embellish (e.g. a story).

embroidery *n* decorative needlework; elaboration or exaggeration (of a story, etc).

embryo *n* an animal during the period of its growth from a fertilised egg up to the third month; a human product of conception up to about the second month of growth.

embryology *n* the study of embryos.

embryonic *adj* existing at an early stage.

emend *vt* to correct mistakes.

emerald *n* a green gemstone; its colour.

emerge *vi* to come into view; to be revealed as the result of investigation.

emergency *n* an unforeseen situation demanding immediate action.

emery *n* a hard granular mineral used for grinding and polishing.

emetic *n* a medicine that induces vomiting.

emigrant *n* a person who emigrates.

emigrate *vi* to leave one's country for residence in another.—*emigration n.*

eminence, eminency *n* high rank or position; (*with cap: RC Church*) the title for a cardinal; a high place.

eminent *adj* famous; distinguished.

emit *vt* to send out (light, heat, etc); to utter.—*emission n.*

emotion *n* a strong feeling of any kind.

emotional *adj* of emotion; inclined to express excessive emotion.

emotive *adj* arousing emotion.

emperor *n* the sovereign ruler over an empire.—*empress nf.*

emphasis *n* stress or prominence given to something.

emphasise *vt* to place stress on.

emphatic *adj* spoken, done or marked with emphasis; forceful, decisive.

emphysema *n* a medical condition marked by the distension of the air sacs in the lungs, causing breathlessness.

empire *n* a large state or group of states under a sovereign, usu an emperor; a large, complex business organisation.

empirical *adj* based on observation, experiment or experience only, not theoretical.

employ *vt* to give work and pay to; to use.

employee *n* a person who is hired by another person for wages.

employer *n* a person, business, etc, that employs people.

employment *n* an employing; a being employed; occupation or profession.

empower *vt* to give official authority to.

empress *see* **emperor**.

empty *adj* containing nothing; not occupied; lacking reality, substance or value; hungry. • *vti* to make or become empty; to transfer or discharge (the contents of something) by emptying; to discharge contents. • *n* empty containers or bottles.—*emptiness n.*

emu *n* a fast-running Australian bird.

emulate *vt* to imitate.—*emulation n.*

emulsion *n* a mixture of mutually insoluble liquids in which one is dispersed in drops throughout the other.

enable *vt* to give the authority or means to do something; to make easy or possible.

enamel *n* a glasslike substance used to coat the surface of metal or pottery; the hard outer layer of a tooth; a usu glossy paint that forms a hard coat.—*also vt*.

enamour *vt* to inspire with love.

enchant *vt* to bewitch.—*enchantment n.*

encircle *vt* to surround; to move or pass completely round.—*encirclement n.*

enclose *vt* to shut up or in; to put in a wrapper or parcel, usu together with a letter.

enclosure *n* an enclosed area; something enclosed with a letter in a parcel.

encore *interj* once more! • *n* a call for the repetition of a performance.—*also vt*.

encounter *vt* to meet, esp unexpectedly; to be faced with (problems, etc). • *n* a meeting.

encourage *vt* to inspire with confidence or hope; to urge, incite.—*encouragement n.*

encroach *vi* to infringe another's territory, rights, etc.

encyclop(a)edia *n* a book or books containing information on all branches of knowledge, or treating comprehensively a particular branch.

end *n* the last part; purpose; result. • *vi* to bring to an end; to destroy. • *vi* to come to an end; to result (in). • *adj* final; ultimate.

endanger *vt* to put in danger.

endear *vt* to make loved or more loved.

endearment *n* a word or words of affection.

endeavour *vi* to try or attempt (to).—*also n.*

ending *n* an end; the final part.

endive *see* **chicory**.

endless *adj* unending; extremely numerous.

endorse *vt* to write one's name, comment, etc, on the back of to approve; to record an offence on a driving licence; to support.

endow *vt* to provide with a special power or attribute.—*endowment n.*

endure *vt* to undergo, tolerate (hardship, etc) esp with patience. • *vi* to continue in existence.—*endurance n.*

enemy *n* a person who hates or dislikes and wishes to harm another; a military opponent.

energetic *adj* lively, active; vigorous.

energy n capacity of acting or being active; vigour, power; (physics) capacity to do work.

enforce vt to compel by threat.

enfranchise vt to grant the vote to.

engage vt to pledge as security; to promise to marry; to keep busy; to hire; to attract and hold; to cause to participate; to enter into conflict; to take part in a venture; to connect, mesh.—**engagement** n.

engaged adj entered into a promise to marry; reserved, occupied or busy.

engaging adj pleasing, attractive.

engender vt to bring into existence.

engine n a machine by which physical power is applied to produce a physical effect; a locomotive.

engineer n a person trained in engineering. • vt to contrive, plan, esp deviously.

engineering n the art or practice of constructing and using machinery; the art and science by which natural forces and materials are utilised in structures or machines.

English adj of, relating to or characteristic of England, the English people or the English language.—also n.

engrained see ingrained.

engrave vt to cut to produce a representation that may be printed from; to lodge deeply (in the mind, etc).

engraving n a print made from an engraved surface.

engross vt to occupy (attention) fully.

engulf vt to flow over and enclose.

enhance vt to increase in value, importance, attractiveness, etc; to heighten.

enigma n someone or something that is puzzling or mysterious.—**enigmatic** adj.

enjoy vt to get pleasure from, take joy in; to experience.—**enjoyable** adj.—**enjoyment** n.

enlarge vti to make or grow larger; to reproduce (a photograph) in larger form; to speak, write at length (on).—**enlargement** n.

enlighten vt to instruct; to inform.—**enlightenment** n.

enlightened adj well-meaning, tolerant.

enlist vt to engage for service in the armed forces; to secure the aid or support of. • vi to register oneself for the armed services.

enmity n hostility, esp mutual hatred.

enormity n great wickedness; a serious crime.

enormous adj extremely large.

enough adj adequate, sufficient. • adv so as to be sufficient; very; quite.

enquire see inquire.

enrage vt to fill with anger

enrich vt to improve in quality by adding to.

enrol vti to become a member of a society, etc; to admit as a member.—**enrolment** n.

en route adv along or on the way.

ensemble n something regarded as a whole; the general effect; the performance of the full number of musicians, dancers, etc; a complete harmonious costume.

ensign n a flag.

enslave vt to make a slave; to subjugate.

ensue vi to occur as a consequence.

en suite adv, adj in a single unit.

ensure vt to make certain, sure, or safe.

entail vt to involve as a result.

enter vti to go or come in or into; to come on stage; to start; (with for) to register as an entrant; to pierce, penetrate; (organisation) to join; to insert; to record (item) in a diary, etc.

enterprise n a difficult or challenging undertaking; a business project; readiness to engage in new ventures.

entertain vt to show hospitality to; to amuse; to consider.—**entertaining** adj.

entertainer n a person who entertains.

entertainment n amusement; an act or show to amuse and interest an audience.

enthusiasm n intense interest or liking.

enthusiast n a person filled with enthusiasm for something.—**enthusiastic** adj.

entice vt to attract by offering some reward.

entire adj whole; complete.—**entirety** n.

entitle vt to give a title to; to give a right (to).

entrance[1] n a means of entering.

entrance[2] vt to put into a trance; to fill with great delight.—**entrancing** adj.

entrant n a person who enters (e.g. a competition, profession).

entreat vt to request earnestly; to implore, beg.—**entreaty** n.

entrench vt to establish (oneself) in a strong defensive position.

entrepreneur n a person who takes the commercial risk of starting up and running a business enterprise.—**entrepreneurial** adj.

entrust vt (with with) to confer as a responsibility, duty, etc; (with to) to place something in another's care.

entry n the act of entering; a place of entrance; an item recorded in a diary, etc; a person, thing taking part in a contest.

entwine vt to twine together or around.

E number n a series of numbers with the prefix E used to identify food additives within the European Community.

enumerate vt to count; to list.

enunciate vt to pronounce clearly.—**enunciation** n.

envelop vt to enclose completely (as if) with a covering.

envelope n something used to wrap or cover, esp a gummed paper container for a letter.

envious adj filled with envy.

environment n conditions and surroundings, esp those that affect the quality of life of plants, animals and human beings.—**environmental** adj.

environmentalist n a person concerned with improving the quality of the environment.

envisage vt to have a mental picture of.

envoy n a diplomatic agent.

envy n resentment or discontent at another's achievements, etc. • vt to feel envy of.

enzyme n a complex protein produced by living cells that induces or speeds chemical reactions in plants and animals.

ephemeral adj existing only for a short time.

epic n a long poem narrating the deeds of a hero; any literary work, film, etc, in the same style.

epidemic adj, n (a disease) attacking many people at the same time.

epigram n a short witty poem or saying.

epigraph n a quotation at the beginning of a book or chapter.

epilepsy n a disorder of the nervous system marked typically by convulsive attacks and loss of consciousness.—**epileptic** adj, n.

epilogue n the concluding section of a book, etc; a short speech by an actor given at the end of a play.

epiphany n a moment of sudden revelation or insight; (with cap) a festival of the Christian Church in commemoration of the coming of the Magi to Christ.

episcopacy n the system of church government by bishops.—**episcopal** adj.

episode n a piece of action in a dramatic or literary work; an incident in a sequence of events.—**episodic** adj.

epistle n (formal) a letter.

epitaph n an inscription in memory of a dead person, usu on a tombstone.

epitome n a typical example; a paradigm.

epoch n an age in history associated with certain characteristics; a unit of geological time.

equable adj level, uniform; even-tempered.

equal adj the same in amount, size, number or value; impartial, regarding or affecting all objects in the same way; capable of meeting a task or situation. • n a person who is equal. • vt to be identical in value.—**equality** n.

equalise vti to make or become equal; (games) to even the score.

equanimity n evenness of temper.

equate vt to make, treat, or regard as comparable. • vi to correspond as equal.

equation n (logic, math) a usu formal statement of equivalence with the relations denoted by the sign =; (chem) an expression representing a reaction by means of symbols.

equator n an imaginary circle passing round the globe, equidistant from the poles.—**equatorial** n.

equerry n an officer in a royal household.

equestrian adj pertaining to horses and riding.

equi- prefix equal.

equidistant adj at equal distances.

equilateral adj having all sides equal.

equilibrium n a state of balance of weight, power, force, etc.

equinox two times of year when night and day are equal in length (around 21 March, 23 September).—**equinoctial** adj.

equip vt to provide with all the necessary tools or supplies.

equipment n the tools, supplies, etc, needed for a task, expedition, etc.

equitable adj just, fair.

equity n fairness; (law) a legal system based on natural justice developed into a body of rules supplementing the common law; (pl) ordinary shares in a company.

equivalent adj equal in amount, force, meaning, etc; virtually identical, esp in effect or function. • n an equivalent thing.

equivocal adj ambiguous; uncertain.

era n an historical period typified by some special feature.

eradicate vt to obliterate.—**eradication** n.

erase vt to rub out, obliterate; to remove a recording from magnetic tape; to remove data from a computer memory or storage medium.

erect adj upright; not leaning or lying down; (sexual organs) rigid and swollen with blood from sexual stimulation. • vt to construct, set up.

erection n construction; swelling, esp of the penis, due to sexual excitement.

ermine n the weasel in its winter coat; its white fur.

erode vt to eat or wear away gradually.—**erosion** n.—**erosive** adj.

erotic adj of sexual love.—**eroticism** n.

err vi to be or do wrong.

errand n a short journey to perform some task, usu on behalf of another; its purpose.

erratic adj capricious; irregular; eccentric.

erroneous adj incorrect; mistaken.

error n a mistake, an inaccuracy.

erudite adj scholarly.—**erudition** n.

erupt vi to burst forth; to break out into a rash; (volcano) to explode, ejecting ash and lava.—**eruption** n.—**eruptive** adj.

escalate vi to increase rapidly in magnitude or intensity.—**escalation** n.

escalator n a motorised set of stairs arranged to ascend or descend continuously.

escapade n a wild or mischievous adventure.

escape vt to free oneself from confinement, etc; to avoid. • vi to be free; (gas, liquid) to leak. • n act of escaping; a leakage; a temporary respite from reality.

escort n a person, group, ship, etc, accompanying a person or thing to give protection, etc. • vt to attend as escort.

espionage n spying or the use of spies to obtain information.

esplanade n a level open space for walking or driving, esp along a shore.

espouse vt to adopt or support a cause.

espresso n coffee brewed by forcing steam through finely ground darkly roasted coffee beans; an apparatus for making espresso.

esquire n a general courtesy title used instead of Mr in addressing letters.

essay n a short prose writing; an attempt.

essence n that which makes a thing what it is; a substance extracted from another substance and having the special qualities of the original.

essential adj of or containing the essence of something; indispensable. • n (often pl) indispensable elements or qualities.

establish vt to set up (e.g. a business) permanently; to settle (a person) in a place or position; to prove as a fact.

established adj (church, religion) recognised as the national church or religion.

establishment n the act of establishing; a commercial organisation or other institution; (with cap) those in power upholding the status quo.

estate n landed property; a large area of residential or industrial development; a person's total possessions, esp at their death.

estate agent n a person whose business is selling and leasing property.

estate car n a car with extra carrying space reached through a rear door.

esteem vt to regard highly.—also n.

estimate vt to judge the value, amount, significance of; to calculate approximately.—also n.

estimation n estimating; esteem.

estuary n an arm of the sea at the mouth of a river.

et cetera, etcetera n and so forth.

etch vti to make lines on (metal, glass) usu by the action of acid; to produce (as a design) by etching; to delineate clearly.

etching n the art or process of producing designs on and printing from etched plates; an impression made from an etched plate.

eternal adj continuing forever, everlasting.

eternity n infinite time; the timelessness thought to constitute life after death.

ether n (chem) a light flammable liquid used as an anaesthetic or solvent; the upper regions of space.

ethic n a moral principle or set of principles.

ethical adj conforming to principles of proper conduct as established by society, a profession, etc.

ethics n (used as sing) the philosophical analysis of human morality and conduct; system of behaviour, moral principles.

ethnic adj of races or large groups classed according to common traits and customs.

etiquette n conduct or behaviour prescribed by custom or authority to be observed in social, official, professional life.

eulogy n a speech or writing in praise or celebration of someone or something.

euphemism n a mild word substituted for a more offensive term.—**euphemistic** adj.

Europe n a continent extending from Asia in the east to the Atlantic Ocean in the west.

European Community n the official name of the European Common Market, whose members aim to eliminate all obstacles to free movement of goods, services, capital, labour between member countries and to set up common external commercial, agricultural, and transport policies.

euthanasia n the act or practice of killing painlessly, esp to relieve incurable suffering.

evacuate vti to move (people, etc) from an area of danger to one of safety; to leave or make empty; to discharge wastes from the body.—**evacuation** n.

evade vt to manage to avoid, esp by dexterity.

evaluate vt to determine the value of.

evangelical adj pertaining to various Christian sects that believe in salvation through personal conversion and faith in Christ.

evangelist n a person who preaches the gospel.

evaporate vti to change into a vapour; to remove water from.—**evaporation** n.

evasion n evading; a means of evading, esp an equivocal reply or excuse.—**evasive** adj.

eve n the day before a festival; the period immediately before an event.

even adj level, flat; smooth; regular, equal; divisible by two. • vti to make or become even; (with up) to balance (debts, etc). • adv at the very time; used as an intensive for emphasis (he looked content, even happy), to indicate something unexpected (she refused even to look), or to stress comparative degree (she did even better).—**evenly** adv.—**evenness** n.

even-handed adj impartial, fair.

evening n the latter part of the day and early part of the night.

event n something that happens; a social occasion; contingency; a contest in a sports programme.—**eventful** adj.

eventual adj ultimate.—**eventuality** n.

ever adv always, at all times; at any time.

evergreen adj (plants, trees) having foliage that remains green all year.—also n.

everlasting *adj* enduring forever.

every *adj* being one of the total.

everybody, everyone *pron* every person.

everyday *adj* happening daily; commonplace.

everything *pron* all things, all.

everywhere *adv* in every place.

evict *vt* to expel from land or from a building by legal process; to expel.—**eviction** *n*.

evidence *n* an outward sign; proof, testimony, esp matter submitted in court to determine the truth of alleged facts. • *vt* to demonstrate clearly; to give proof for.

evident *adj* easy to see or understand.

evil *adj* wicked. • *n* a sin; a source of harm.

evocative *adj* serving to evoke.

evoke *vt* to call forth or up.—**evocation** *n*.

evolution *n* a process of change in a particular direction; the process by which something attains its distinctive characteristics; a theory that existing types of plants and animals have developed from earlier forms.—**evolutionary** *adj*.

evolve *vi* to develop by or as if by evolution.

ewe *n* a female sheep.

ex *prep* out of, from.

ex- *prefix* out, forth; quite, entirely; formerly.

exact *adj* without error, absolutely accurate. • *vt* to compel by force, to extort; to require.—**exactness** *n*.—**exactitude** *n*.

exacting *adj* greatly demanding.

exactly *adv* in an exact manner; precisely.

exaggerate *vt* to enlarge (a statement, etc) beyond what is really so or believable.—**exaggeration** *n*.

exalt *vt* to raise up, esp in rank, power, or dignity.—**exaltation** *n*.

examination *n* a close scrutiny; a set of questions designed to test knowledge; the questioning of a witness on oath.

examine *vt* to look at closely and carefully, to investigate; to test, esp by questioning.

example *n* a representative sample; a model to be followed or avoided.

exasperate *vt* to annoy intensely.

excavate *vt* to form a hole or tunnel by digging.—**excavation** *n*

exceed *vt* to be greater than or superior to; to go beyond the limit of.

exceedingly *adv* very, extremely.

excel *vb* *vt* to outdo, to be superior to. • *vi* (with **in, at**) to do better than.

excellence *n* superior merit or quality; (with *cap*) a title of honour given to certain high officials (—*also* **Excellency**).—**excellent** *adj*.

except *vt* to exclude. • *prep* not including.

exception *n* the act of excepting; something excepted; an objection.

exceptional *adj* unusual; superior.

excerpt *n* an extract from a book, film, etc.

excess *n* the exceeding of established limits; (*pl*) overindulgence; unacceptable conduct.

excessive *adj* greater than what is acceptable.

exchange *vt* to give and take (one thing in return for another); to give to and receive from another person. • *n* the exchanging of one thing for another; the thing exchanged; the conversion of money from one currency to another; the system of settling commercial debts between foreign governments; a marketplace for securities; a centre or device in which telephone lines are interconnected.

exchequer *n* (with *cap*) the British governmental department in charge of finances.

excise[1] *n* a tax on the manufacture, sale, or use of certain articles within a country.

excise[2] *vt* to remove by cutting out.

excitable *adj* easily excited.

excite *vt* to arouse feelings, esp of pleasurable anticipation; to cause to experience strong emotion; to stir up, agitate; to stimulate a response.—**excitement** *n*.

excited *adj* experiencing strong emotion.

exciting *adj* causing excitement.

exclaim *vti* to shout out.—**exclamation** *n*.

exclamation mark *n* the punctuation mark (!).

exclude *vt* to shut out, to keep out; to reject or omit; to eject.—**exclusion** *n*.

exclusive *adj* fashionable, high-class, expensive; unobtainable or unpublished elsewhere.

excommunicate *vt* to bar from association with a church.—**excommunication** *n*.

excrement *n* waste matter discharged from the bowels.—**excremental** *adj*.

excrete *vt* to eliminate or discharge wastes from the body.—**excretion** *n*.

excruciating *adj* intensely painful.

excursion *n* a pleasure trip.

excuse *vt* to pardon; to forgive; to give a reason or apology for.—*also n*.

execute *vt* to carry out, put into effect; to perform; to produce (e.g. a work of art); to put to death by law.—**execution** *n*.

executioner *n* a person who executes a death sentence upon a condemned prisoner.

executive *n* a person or group concerned with administration of a business; the branch of government with the power to put laws, etc, into effect.—*also adj*.

executor *n* a person appointed to see that the terms of a will are implemented.

exemplary *adj* deserving imitation; serving as a warning.

exemplify *vt* to illustrate by example; to be an instance or example of.

exempt *adj* not liable, free from the obligations required of others.—*also vt*.—**exemption** *n*.

exercise *n* the use of a power or right; regular

physical or mental exertion; something performed to develop a specific ability or skill.—also vt.

exert vt to bring (e.g. strength) into use.

exhaust vt to use up completely; to tire out; (subject) to deal with completely. • n the escape of waste gas or steam from an engine; the device through which these escape.—**exhausted** adj.

exhaustion n extreme weariness.

exhaustive adj comprehensive.

exhibit vt to display, esp in public. • n something produced and identified in court for use as evidence.

exhibition n a showing, a (public) display.

exhilarate vt to make very happy; to invigorate.—**exhilaration** n.

exhort vt to urge or advise strongly.

exile n prolonged absence from one's own country, either through choice or as a punishment; an exiled person.—also vt.

exist vi to have being; to just manage a living; to occur in a specific place.

existence n the state or fact of existing; continuance of life; everything that exists.

exit n a way out; death; a departure from a stage. • vi to leave; to go offstage.

exonerate vt to absolve from blame.

exorcise vt to expel an evil spirit (from a person or place) by ritual and prayer.—**exorcism** n.—**exorcist** n.

exotic adj foreign; excitingly unusual.

expand vt to increase in size, bulk, extent, importance; to describe in fuller detail. • vi to become larger; to become more genial and responsive.—**expansion** n.

expanse n a wide area of land, etc.

expatriate adj living in another country. • n an expatriate person.—also vti.

expect vt to anticipate; to regard as likely to arrive or happen; to consider necessary, reasonable or due; to think, suppose.

expectant adj hopeful; full of anticipation; pregnant.—**expectancy** n.

expectation n the act or state of expecting; something that is expected to happen; (pl) prospects for the future, esp of inheritance.

expediency n fitness, suitability.

expedient adj suitable or desirable under the circumstances. • n a means to an end; a means devised or used for want of something better.

expedite vt to carry out promptly; to facilitate.

expedition n a journey to achieve some purpose, as exploration, etc; the party making this journey; speedy efficiency.

expel vt to drive out, to eject; to banish.

expend vt to spend (money, time, energy, etc); to use up, consume.—**expenditure** n.

expense n a payment of money for something;

(pl) money spent on some business activity; reimbursement for this.

expense account n an account of expenses to be reimbursed to an employee.

expensive adj involving great expense; costly.

experience n observation or practice resulting in knowledge; knowledge gained by seeing and doing; a state of being affected from without (as by events); an affecting event. • vt to have experience of.—**experienced** adj.

experiment n any test or trial to find out something; a controlled procedure carried out to discover, test, or demonstrate something.—also vi

experimental adj of, derived from or proceeding by experiment; empirical.

expert adj thoroughly skilled. • n a person with special skills or training.

expertise n expert knowledge or skill.

expire vti to lapse; to breathe out; to die.

explain vt to make clear; to give a reason for.

explanation n an act or process of explaining; a statement that explains.—**explanatory** adj.

explicit adj clearly stated; graphically detailed.

explode vti to burst or cause to blow up with a loud noise, as in the detonation of a bomb; (emotions) to burst out; to expose as false.

exploit n a bold achievement. • vt to utilise, develop (raw materials, etc); to take unfair advantage of.—**exploitation** n.

explore vti to examine or inquire into; to travel through (a country) for the purpose of discovery.—**exploration** n.—**exploratory** adj.

explosion n a sudden loud noise caused by this; an outburst of emotion; a rapid increase.

explosive adj liable to explode; liable to burst out with violence and noise.—also n.

exponent n a person who champions, advocates, or exemplifies; (math) an index of the power to which an expression is raised.

export vt to send out (goods) of one country for sale in another.—also n.

expose vt to deprive of protection or shelter; to subject to an influence (as light, weather); to display, reveal; to uncover.

exposure n an exposing; time during which light reaches and acts on a photographic film, paper or plate; publicity.

expound vt to explain or set forth in detail.

express vt to represent in words; to make known one's thoughts, feelings, etc; to squeeze out. • adj firmly stated, explicit; (train, bus, etc) travelling at high speed. • adv at high speed, by express service. • n an express train, coach, etc.

expression n expressing, esp by words; a word or phrase; a look; a manner of showing feeling in communicating or performing (e.g. music); (math) a collection of symbols serving to express something.—**expressive** adj.

expressly *adv* for a specific purpose.

expulsion *n* expelling, being expelled.

exquisite *adj* very beautiful, refined; sensitive.

extend *vt* to stretch, on or spread out; to stretch fully; to prolong in time; to cause to reach in distance, etc; to enlarge, increase the scope of; to hold out; to accord, grant.

extension *n* act of extending or state of being extended; extent, scope; an added part, e.g. to a building; an extra period; an additional telephone connected to the principal line.

extensive *adj* large; having a wide scope.

extent *n* the range, scope or limit of something.

exterior *adj* of, on or coming from the outside; external. • *n* the external part or surface; outward manner or appearance.

exterminate *vt* to destroy completely.—**extermination**.—**exterminator** *n*.

external *adj* outwardly perceivable; of, relating to, or located on the outside or outer part. • *n* an external feature.

extinct *adj* (*animals*) not alive, no longer existing; (*fire*) not burning, out; (*volcano*) no longer active.—**extinction** *n*.

extinguish *vt* to put out (a fire, light, etc); to bring to an end.—**extinguisher** *n*.

extort *vt* to obtain (money, promises, etc) by force or pressure.—**extortion** *n*.

extortionate *adj* excessively high in price.

extra *adj* additional. • *adv* in addition. • *n* something additional.

extra- *prefix* outside, beyond.

extract *vt* to take or pull out by force; to withdraw by chemical or physical means. • *n* the essence of a substance obtained by extraction; a passage taken from a book, play, film, etc.

extraction *n* lineage; something extracted.

extradite *vt* to surrender (an alleged criminal) to the country where the offence was committed.—**extradition** *n*.

extramarital *adj* occurring outside marriage.

extraneous *adj* not essential.

extraordinary *adj* not usual or regular; remarkable, exceptional.

extravagant *adj* lavish in spending; (*prices*) excessively high; wasteful; (*behaviour, praise, etc*) lacking in restraint.—**extravagance** *n*.

extravert *see* **extrovert**

extreme *adj* of the highest degree or intensity; excessive, immoderate.—*also n*.

extremist *n* a person of extreme views.

extremity *n* the utmost point or degree; the most remote part; the end; (*pl*) the hands or feet.

extricate *vt* to release from difficulties; to disentangle.—**extrication** *n*.

extrovert *n* a person more interested in the external world than his own thoughts and feelings.—*also* **extravert**.

exuberant *adj* lively, high-spirited; profuse.—**exuberance** *n*.

exude *vt* to cause or allow to ooze through pores or incisions, as sweat, pus; to display (confidence, emotion) freely.

exult *vi* to rejoice greatly.—**exultation** *n*.

eye *n* the organ of sight; the external part of the eye; something resembling an eye. • *vt* to look at.

eyeball *n* the ball of the eye.

eyebrow *n* the hairy ridge above the eye.

eye-catching *adj* attractive.

eyelash *n* the fringe of fine hairs along the edge of each eyelid.

eyelid *n* the lid of skin and muscle that moves to cover the eye.

eye-opener *n* something that comes as a shock or surprise.

eye-shadow *n* a coloured powder applied to accentuate or decorate the eyelids.

eyesight *n* the faculty of seeing.

eyesore *n* anything offensive to the sight.

eye-witness *n* a person who sees an event.

eyrie *n* the nest of an eagle or other bird of prey.

F

fable *n* a story, often with animal characters, intended to convey a moral; a legendary story.

fabric *n* cloth; framework, structure.

fabulous *adj* told in fables; incredible.

façade *n* the front of a building; an outward appearance, esp concealing something hidden.

face *n* the front part of the head containing the eyes, nose, mouth, chin, etc; facial expression; the front or outer surface of anything; external show or appearance; impudence, effrontery; a coal face. • *vt* to be confronted by (a problem, etc); to deal with resolutely; to be opposite to; to cover with a new surface. • *vi* to be situated in a specific direction.

face-lift *n* plastic surgery to smooth and firm the face; an improvement or renovation.

facet *n* a small plane surface (as on a cut gem); an aspect of character.

facetious *adj* joking, esp flippantly.

facial *adj* of or pertaining to the face. • *n* a beauty treatment for the face.

facile *adj* easy to do; superficial.

facilitate *vt* to make easier.

facility *n* aptitude, dexterity; a service, equipment that makes it easy to do something.

facsimile *n* an exact copy of a book, document, etc; a method of transmitting text and graphics through the telephone system.—*also* **fax**.

fact *n* a thing known to have happened or to exist; reality; a piece of verifiable information.

faction[1] *n* a small group in an organisation working together against the main body.

faction[2] *n* a book, film, etc, based on facts but presented as a blend of fact and fiction.

factor *n* any circumstance that contributes towards a result; (*math*) any of two or more numbers that, when multiplied together, form a product; an agent.

factory *n* a building or buildings where things are manufactured.

factual *adj* based on facts; actual.

faculty *n* any natural power of a living organism; special aptitude; a teaching department of a college or university; its staff.

fad *n* a personal idiosyncrasy; a craze.

fade *vi* to lose vigour or brightness of colour gradually; to vanish gradually. • *vt* to cause (an image or a sound) to increase or decrease in brightness or intensity gradually.

fag *vti* to become or cause to be tired.

fail *vti* to weaken, to fade; to stop operating; to fall short; to be negligent; (*exam, etc*) to be unsuccessful; to disappoint; to grade (a candidate) as not passing a test, etc. • *n* failure in an examination.

failing *n* a fault, weakness. • *prep* in default of.

failure *n* failing, lack of success; ceasing of normal operation; an unsuccessful person or thing.

faint *adj* dim, indistinct; weak, feeble; timid; on the verge of losing consciousness. • *vi* to lose consciousness temporarily from a decrease in the supply of blood to the brain, as from shock. • *n* an act of fainting.—**faintness** *n*.

faint-hearted *adj* lacking courage.

fair[1] *adj* pleasing to the eye; unblemished; (*hair*) light-coloured; (*weather*) clear and sunny; just and honest; moderately large; average. • *adv* in a fair manner.—**fairness** *n*.

fair[2] *n* a competitive exhibition of goods; a funfair.

fairy *n* an imaginary supernatural being, usu in human form.

fairy story, fairy tale *n* a story about fairies; an incredible story; a fabrication.

faith *n* trust or confidence in a person or thing; a strong conviction, esp a belief in a religion; any system of religious belief.

faithful *adj* loyal; true; true to the original.

fake *vt* to make (an object) appear more real or valuable in order to deceive; to pretend. • *n* a faked article; an impostor. • *adj* counterfeit.

falcon *n* a type of hawk trained for sport or hunting.

fall *vi* to descend by force of gravity; to come as if by falling; to collapse; to become lower, weaker, less; to lose power, status, etc; to lose office; to slope downwards; to be wounded or killed in battle; to pass into a certain state; to become pregnant; to take place, happen; to be directed by chance; to come by inheritance; (*with* **back**) to retreat; (*with* **out**) to quarrel; to leave one's place in a military formation. • *n* act or instance of falling; something that falls; a decline in status, position; a decrease in size, quantity, value; in US, autumn;.

fallacy *n* a false idea; a mistake in reasoning.

fallible *adj* liable to make mistakes.

fall-out *n* a deposit of radioactive dust from a nuclear explosion; a by-product.

fallow[1] *adj* (*land*) ploughed and left unplanted for a season or more.

fallow[2] *adj* yellowish-brown.

false *adj* wrong; deceitful; artificial; disloyal.

falsehood *n* a being untrue; a lie.

falter *vi* to move or walk unsteadily, to stumble; to hesitate or stammer in speech; to be weak or unsure, to waver.

fame *n* the state of being well-known; good reputation.—**famed** *adj*.

familiar *adj* well-acquainted; friendly; common; well-known; presumptuous. • *n* a demon supposed to aid a witch.—**familiarity** *n*.

familiarise *vt* to make well known or acquainted.—**familiarisation** *n*.

family *n* parents and their children; a person's children; a set of relatives; the descendants of a common ancestor; any related group, e.g. of plants, animals.

famine *n* an acute scarcity of food in a particular area; an extreme scarcity of anything.

famous *adj* renowned.

fan[1] *n* a handheld or mechanical device used to set up a current of air. • *vt* to cool, as with a fan; to ventilate; to stir up to excite; to spread out like a fan.

fan[2] *n* an enthusiastic follower.

fanatic *n* a person who is excessively enthusiastic about something.—**fanatical** *adj*.

fan belt *n* the belt that drives the cooling fan in a car engine.

fanciful *adj* imaginary; indulging in fancy; elaborate or intricate in design.

fancy n imagination; a mental image; a whim; fondness. • adj elegant or ornamental. • vt to imagine; to have a liking for.

fancy dress n a costume worn at parties.

fang n a long sharp tooth, as in a canine; the long hollow tooth through which venomous snakes inject poison.

fanlight n a semicircular window with radiating bars like the ribs of a fan.

fantastic adj unrealistic, fanciful; unbelievable.

fantasy n imagination; a product of the imagination; an imaginative poem, play, novel.

far adj remote in space or time. • adv very distant in space, time, or degree; to or from a distance in time or position, very much.

faraway adj distant, remote; dreamy.

farce n a style of light comedy; a ludicrous situation.—**farcical** adj.

fare n money paid for transportation; food. • vi to be in a specified condition.

farewell interj goodbye.—also n.

far-fetched adj unlikely.

farm n an area of land (with buildings) on which crops and animals are raised. • vt to grow crops or breed livestock; (with out) to put out (work, etc) to be done by others.—**farmer** n.

farmhouse n a house on a farm.

farmyard n a yard close to farm buildings.

far-reaching adj having serious consequences.

far-seeing adj having foresight.

farther adj at or to a greater distance. • adv to a greater degree.

farthest adj at or to the greatest distance. • adv to the greatest degree.

fascia n the instrument panel of a vehicle; the flat surface above a shop front.

fascinate vt to hold the attention of, to attract irresistibly.—**fascination** n.

fashion n the current style of dress, conduct, speech, etc; the manner or form of appearance or action. • vt to make in a particular form.

fashionable adj conforming to the current fashion; frequented by people of fashion.

fast[1] adj swift, quick; (clock) ahead of time; firmly fastened, fixed; (colour, dye) non-fading; wild, promiscuous.—also adv.

fast[2] vi to go without all or certain foods. • n a period of fasting.

fasten vti to secure firmly; to attach; to fix or direct (the eyes, attention) steadily.

fastener, fastening n a clip, catch, etc, for fastening.

fastidious adj hard to please; over-refined; oversensitive.—**fastidiousness** n.

fat adj plump; thick; fertile; profitable. • n an oily or greasy material found in animal tissue and plant seeds.—**fatness** n.

fatal adj causing death; disastrous (to).

fatalism n belief that all events are predetermined by fate and therefore inevitable.—**fatalist** n.—**fatalistic** adj.

fatality n a death caused by a disaster or accident; a person killed in such a way.

fate n the ultimate power that predetermines events, destiny; outcome; doom.

fateful adj having unpleasant consequences.

father n a male parent; an ancestor; a founder or originator; (with cap) God; a title of respect applied to monks, priests, etc. • vt to be the father of; to found, originate.—**fatherhood** n.

father-in-law n the father of one's husband or wife.

fathom n a nautical measure of 6 feet (1.83 m). • vt to measure depth; to understand.

fatigue n tiredness from physical or mental effort; the tendency of a material to break under repeated stress; any of the menial or manual tasks performed by military personnel; (pl) the clothing worn on fatigue or in the field. • vti to make or become tired.

fatten vt to make fat, abundant.

fatty adj resembling or containing fat.

fatuous adj foolish, idiotic.

faucet n a fixture for draining off liquid (as from a pipe or cask); a tap.

fault n a failing, defect; a minor offence; (tennis, etc) an incorrect serve or other error; a fracture in the earth's crust causing displacement of strata. • vt to find fault with, blame.

faultless adj without fault.

faulty adj imperfect.

fauna n the animals of a region, period, or specific environment.

favour n goodwill; approval; a kind or helpful act; partiality; a small gift given out at a party; (usu pl) a privilege granted or conceded, esp sexual. • vt to regard or treat with favour; to show support for; to oblige (with).

favourable adj expressing approval; pleasing.

favourite n a favoured person or thing; a competitor expected to win. • adj most preferred.

favouritism n showing of unfair favour.

fawn[1] n a young deer; a yellowish-brown colour. • adj fawn-coloured.

fawn[2] vi to flatter in an obsequious manner.

fax see facsimile.

fear n an unpleasant emotion excited by danger, pain, etc; a cause of fear; anxiety; deep reverence. • vti to feel fear, be afraid (of); to be apprehensive, anxious; to be sorry.—**fearful** adj.—**fearless** adj.

feasible adj able to be done or implemented.

feast n an elaborate meal prepared for a special occasion; a periodic religious celebration. • vti to have, take part in, entertain with a feast.

feat n an action of remarkable strength, skill, or courage.

feather n any of the light outgrowths that form the covering of a bird. • vt to ornament with feathers.—**feathery** adj.

feature n any part of the face; a characteristic trait; a special attraction or distinctive quality; a prominent newspaper article, etc; the main film in a cinema programme. • vti to make or be a feature of.

federal adj designating, or of a union of states, etc, in which each member surrenders some of its power to a central authority; of a central government of this type.—**federalism** n.—**federalist** n.

federation n a union of states, groups, etc, in which each subordinates its power to a central authority.

fee n the price paid for the advice or service of a professional; a membership charge.

feeble adj weak, ineffective.—**feebleness** n.

feeble-minded adj of low intelligence.

feed vb vt to give food to; to supply with necessary material; to gratify. • vi to consume food. • n food for animals.

feedback n a return to the input of part of the output of a system; information about a product, service, etc, returned to the supplier for purposes of evaluation.

feel vb vt to perceive or explore by the touch; to find one's way by cautious trial; to be conscious of, experience; to have a vague or instinctual impression of; to believe, consider. • vi to be able to experience the sensation of touch; to be affected by; to convey a certain sensation when touched.—also n.

feeler n a tactile organ (as a tentacle or antenna) of an animal; a tentative approach or suggestion to test another person's reactions.

feeling n the sense of touch; mental or physical awareness or impression; (pl) emotions.

feign vt to invent; to pretend.

fell[1] vt to cut, beat, or knock down; to kill.

fellow n an associate; an equal in power, rank, or position; the other of a pair, a mate; a member of the governing body in some colleges and universities; a member of a learned society. • adj belonging to the same group or class.

fellowship n companionship; a mutual sharing; a group of people with the same interests; the position held by a college fellow.

felony n (formerly) a grave crime.

felt[2] n a fabric made from woollen fibres, often mixed with fur or hair, pressed together.

female adj of the sex that produces young; of a woman; (pipe, plug, etc) designed with a hollow part for receiving an inserted piece.—also n.

feminine adj of, resembling or appropriate to women; (gram) of words of that gender.—**femininity** n.

feminism n the movement to win political, economic and social equality for women.—**feminist** adj, n.

fence n a barrier put round land to mark a boundary or prevent animals escaping; a receiver of stolen goods. • vt to surround with a fence. • vi to practise fencing; to make evasive answers; to act as a fence for stolen goods.

fencing n the art of fighting with foils or other types of sword.

fend vi (with for) to provide a livelihood for.

fender n anything that protects or fends off as the part of a car body over the wheel.

ferment n an agent causing fermentation, as yeast; excitement, agitation. • vti to (cause to) undergo fermentation; to (cause to) be agitated.—**fermentation** n.

fern n any of a large class of nonflowering plants having roots, stems and fronds.

ferocious adj savage, fierce.—**ferocity** n.

ferry vt to convey (passengers, etc) over water; to transport from one place to another. • n a boat for ferrying; the location of a ferry.

fertile adj able to bear offspring; (land) easily supporting plants and vegetation; (animals) capable of breeding; prolific; (mind, brain) inventive.—**fertility** n.

fertilise vt to make (soil) fertile by adding nutrients; to impregnate; to pollinate.—**fertilisation** n.—**fertiliser** n.

fervent, fervid adj passionate; zealous.

fester vti to become or cause to become infected; to suppurate; to rankle.

festival n a time of celebration; performances of music, plays, etc, given periodically.

festive adj merry, joyous.

fetch vt to go for and bring back; to cause to come; (goods) to sell for (a certain price).

fetching adj attractive.

fête n a festival; a usu outdoor sale, bazaar or entertainment in aid of charity. • vt to entertain.

fetish n an object believed by primitive peoples to have magical properties; any object or activity regarded with excessive devotion.

fetus n the unborn young of an animal, esp in its later stages; in humans, the offspring in the womb from the fourth month until birth.—also **foetus**.—**fetal, foetal** adj.

feud n a state of hostilities, esp between individuals, families, or clans; a dispute.—also vi.

feudal adj pertaining to feudalism.

feudalism n the economic and social system in medieval Europe in which land, worked by serfs, was held by vassals in exchange for service to overlords.

fever n an abnormally increased body temperature; restless excitement.—**fevered** adj.

feverish adj having a fever; restlessly excited.

few adj, n a small number, not many.

fiancé, n a person engaged to be married.—
fiancée nf.

fiasco n a complete and humiliating failure.

fib n a trifling lie.—also vi.—**fibber** n.

fibre n a natural or synthetic thread spun into
yarn; a material composed of such yarn; texture;
strength of character; roughage.—**fibrous** adj.

fibreglass n glass in fibrous form, often bonded
with plastic.

fickle adj inconstant.—**fickleness** n.

fiction n an invented story; any literary work
with imaginary characters and events, as a
novel, play, etc; such works collectively.

fictitious adj imaginary, not real.

fiddle n (inf) a violin; (sl) a swindle. • vt (inf) to
play on a violin; (sl) to swindle. • vi to fidget.

fidelity n faithfulness, loyalty; truthfulness.

fidget vi to (cause to) move restlessly.—also
n.—**fidgety** adj.

field n an area of land cleared of trees and buildings, used for pasture or crops; a sports ground;
an area affected by electrical, magnetic or gravi-
tational influence, etc; the area visible through
an optical lens; a division of activity, knowledge, etc; all competitors in a contest; (comput)
a section of a record in a database. • vt (cricket,
baseball, etc) to catch or stop and return the ball;
to put (e.g. a team) into the field to play.

field glasses npl small, portable binoculars.

fieldwork n research done outside the laboratory or place of work by scientists, archaeolo-
gists, social workers, etc.

fiend n an evil spirit; a wicked person.

fierce adj ferociously hostile; violent; intense.

fiery adj like or consisting of fire; intensely hot;
spicy; passionate.—**fieriness** n.

fifteen adj, n one more than fourteen; the symbol for this (15, XV, xv); the first point scored by
a side in a game of tennis.—**fifteenth** adj, n.

fifth adj, n next after fourth; being one of five
equal parts.

fifty adj, n five times ten; the symbol for this
(50, L, l).—**fiftieth** adj.

fig n a tree yielding a soft, pear-shaped fruit.

fight vi to engage in battle in war or in single
combat; to strive, struggle (for). • vt to engage in
a conflict with. • n a conflict; a boxing match.

fighter n a person who fights; a person who does
not yield easily; an aircraft designed to destroy
enemy aircraft.

figment n something imagined.

figurative adj using figures of speech.

figure n a character representing a number; a
number; value or price; bodily shape; a graphic
representation; a design; a geometrical form; a
statue; appearance; a personage; (dancing, skating) a set of steps or movements; (pl) arithmetic.

• vt to represent in a diagram or outline; to imagine. • vi to take a part (in); to calculate.

figurehead n a carved figure on the bow of a
ship; a nominal head or leader.

filament n a slender thread or strand; a fibre; the
fine wire in a light bulb.

file[1] n a container for keeping papers, etc, in order; an
orderly arrangement of papers; a line of persons;
(comput) a collection of related data. • vt to register;
to put on public record. • vi to move in a line.

file[2] n a tool with a rough surface for smoothing
or grinding. • vt to smooth with a file.

filing n a particle rubbed off with a file.

fill vt to put as much as possible into; to occupy
wholly; to put a person into (a job, etc); to supply the things called for (in an order, etc); to
close or plug (holes, etc). • vi to become full. • n
enough to make full or to satisfy.

fillet n a thin boneless strip of meat or fish. • vt to
bone and slice (fish or meat).

filling n a substance used to fill a tooth cavity;
the contents of a sandwich, pie, etc. • adj (meal,
etc) substantial.

filling station n a place where petrol is sold.

fillip n a stimulus.

film n a fine, thin skin, coating, etc; a flexible
cellulose material covered with a light-sensitive
substance used in photography; a haze or blur; a
motion picture. • vti to cover or be covered as
with a film; to make a film.

filter n a device or substance straining out solid
particles, impurities, etc, from a liquid or gas; a
device for removing or minimising electrical os-
cillations or sound or light waves; a traffic signal
at junctions that allows cars to turn left or right
while the main lights are red. • vti to pass
through a filter; to remove with a filter.

filth n dirt; obscenity.

filthy adj dirty; obscene.—**filthiness** n.

fin n an organ by which a fish steers and swims;
a rubber flipper for underwater swimming.

final adj of or coming at the end; conclusive. • n
(often pl) the last of a series of contests; a final
examination.

finale n the concluding part of a performance;
the last section in a musical composition.

finalise vt to bring to an end.

finalist n a contestant in a final.

finance n the management of money; (pl)
money resources. • vt to supply or raise money
for.—**financial** adj.

financier n a person skilled in finance.

find vt to discover by chance or by searching; to
perceive; to recover (something lost); to reach;
to decide and declare to be. • vi to reach a decision. • n a discovery, something found.

finding n a discovery; the conclusion reached
by a judicial enquiry.

fine¹ *adj* very good; refined; (*weather*) clear and bright; not heavy or coarse; very thin; sharp; subtle. • *adv* in a fine manner.—**fineness** *n*.

fine² *n* a sum of money imposed as a punishment. • *vt* to punish by a fine.

fine arts *npl* painting, sculpture, music, etc.

finery *n* elaborate clothes, jewellery, etc.

finesse *n* subtlety of performance; skilfulness, diplomacy in handling.

finger *n* one of the digits of the hand. • *vt* to touch with fingers; (*mus*) to use the fingers in a certain way when playing.

fingerprint *n* the impression of the ridges on a fingertip.—*also vt*.

finicky, finicking *adj* too particular, fussy.

finish *vt* to bring to an end; to consume entirely; to perfect. • *vi* to come to an end. • *n* the end; anything used to finish a surface; the finished effect; polished manners, speech, etc.

finite *adj* having definable limits.

Finn *n* a native of Finland.

fiord *see* **fjord**.

fir *n* a kind of evergreen, cone-bearing tree.

fire *n* the flame, heat and light of combustion; burning fuel in a grate to heat a room; an electric or gas fire; a destructive burning; a strong feeling. • *vti* to ignite; to bake in a kiln; to excite or become excited; to shoot (a gun, etc); to hurl with force; to dismiss.

fire alarm *n* a device that uses a bell, hooter, etc, to warn of a fire.

firearm *n* a handgun.

fire brigade *n* a body of people trained and equipped for fighting fires.

fire escape *n* a means of exit from a building, esp a stairway, for use in case of fire.

fireplace *n* a place for a fire, esp a recess in a wall; the area surrounding this.

firework *n* a device packed with explosive and combustible material used to produce noisy and colourful displays; (*pl*) a fit of temper.

firing squad *n* a detachment with the task of carrying out an execution.

firm¹ *adj* fixed; solid; steady; resolute. • *vti* to make, become firm.—**firmness** *n*.

firm² *n* a business partnership or company.

first *adj* before all others in a series; earliest; foremost, as in rank, etc. • *adv* before all else; for the first time. • *n* any person, thing that is first; the winning place; low gear; the highest university degree.

first aid *n* emergency treatment for an injury, etc.

first-class *adj* of the highest quality.

firsthand *adj* obtained directly.

firstly *adv* in the first place.

first-rate *adj, adv* of the best quality.

fiscal *adj* of or relating to public revenue. • *n* a prosecuting official.

fish *n* any of a large group of cold-blooded animals living in water, having backbones, gills for breathing and fins; the flesh of fish used as food. • *vi* to catch or try to catch fish; (*with* **for**) to try to obtain by roundabout methods. • *vt* (*often with* **out**) to grope for and bring to view.

fisherman *n* a person who fishes.

fishery *n* the fishing industry; an area where fish are caught.

fish finger *n* a small oblong piece of fish covered in breadcrumbs.

fishmonger *n* a shop that sells fish.

fishy *adj* like a fish in odour, taste, etc.

fission *n* a split or cleavage; the reproductive division of biological cells; the splitting of the atomic nucleus resulting in the release of energy.

fissure *n* a narrow opening or cleft.

fist *n* the hand when tightly closed or clenched.

fit¹ *adj* suited to some purpose; proper; right; healthy. • *n* the manner of fitting. • *vt* to be suitable to; to be the proper size, shape, etc, for; to adjust so as to fit; to equip. • *vi* to be suitable; to have the proper size or shape.—**fitness** *n*.

fit² *n* any sudden, uncontrollable attack, as of coughing; an outburst, as of anger; a short period of impulsive activity; a seizure involving convulsions or loss of consciousness.

fitful *adj* spasmodic.—**fitfulness** *n*.

fitment *n* a piece of equipment, esp fixed furniture.

fitter *n* a person who specialises in fitting clothes; a person skilled in the assembly and operation of a particular piece of machinery.

fitting *adj* appropriate. • *n* an act of one that fits, esp a trying on of altered clothes; a small often standardised electrical part.

five *adj, n* one more than four; the symbol for this (5, V, v).

fix *vt* to fasten firmly; to set firmly in the mind; to direct (one's eyes) steadily at; to make rigid; to make permanent; to establish (a date, etc); to set in order; to repair; to prepare (food or meals); (*inf*) to influence a result of by bribery. • *vi* to become fixed. • *n* (*inf*) a situation that has been fixed; (*inf*) something whose supply becomes continually necessary or greatly desired, as a drug, entertainment, activity, etc.

fixture *n* what is fixed to anything, as to land or a house; a fixed article of furniture; a firmly established person or thing; a fixed time.

fizz *vi* to make a hissing or sputtering sound.—*also n*.—**fizzy** *adj*.—**fizziness** *n*.

fizzle *vi* to make a weak fizzing sound; (*with* **out**) (*inf*) to end feebly, die out.

fjord *n* a long, narrow inlet of the sea between cliffs.—*also* **fiord**.

flabbergast *vt* (*inf*) to astonish, startle.

flabby *adj* fat and soft; weak.—**flabbiness** *n*.

flag¹ *vi* to grow limp, weak.

flag² *n* a piece of cloth, usu with a design, used to show nationality, party, etc, or as a signal. • *vt* to signal; (*usu with* **down**) to signal to stop.

flag³ *n* a hard, flat stone used for paving.

flagon *n* a pottery or metal container for liquids.

flagrant *adj* conspicuous; notorious.

flair *n* natural ability, aptitude; discernment.

flake *n* a small piece of snow; a small thin layer chipped from a larger mass of something. • *vti* to form into flakes.—**flaky** *adj*.

flamboyant *adj* brilliantly coloured; ornate; exuberant.—**flamboyance** *n*.

flame *n* the burning gas of a fire, appearing as a tongue of light; the state of burning with a blaze; an intense emotion. • *vi* to burst into flame.

flamingo *n* a wading bird with rosy-white plumage and long legs and neck.

flammable *adj* easily set on fire.

flan *n* an open case of pastry or sponge cake with a sweet or savoury filling.

flange *n* a projecting or raised edge.

flank *n* the fleshy part of the side from the ribs to the hip; the side of anything; the side of a formation of troops. • *vt* to be at, skirt the side of.

flannel *n* a soft light cotton or woollen cloth; a small cloth for washing the face and hands; (*pl*) trousers of such cloth.

flap *vi* to move up and down, as wings; to sway loosely and noisily; to move or hang like a flap. • *n* the motion or noise of a flap; anything broad and flexible, either hinged or hanging loose; a light blow with a flat object.

flare *vi* to burn with a sudden, bright, unsteady flame; to burst into anger; to widen out gradually. • *n* an unsteady flame; a bright light used as a signal or illumination; a widened part.

flare-up *n* a sudden burst of fire, anger.

flash *n* a sudden, brief light; a brief moment; a sudden brief display; (*TV, radio*) a sudden brief news item about an important event; (*photog*) a device for producing a brief intense light. • *vi* to send out a sudden, brief light; to sparkle; to come or pass suddenly. • *vt* to cause to flash.

flashback *n* an interruption in a story, etc, by telling or showing an earlier episode.

flashbulb *n* a small bulb giving an intense light used in photography.

flashlight *n* a torch.

flashy *adj* pretentious; showy, gaudy.

flask *n* a slim-necked bottle; a vacuum flask.

flat *adj* having a smooth level surface; spread out; broad, even and thin; (*tyre*) deflated; (*drink*) not fizzy; (*battery*) drained of electric current. • *adv* in a flat manner or position; exactly; (*mus*) below true pitch. • *n* anything flat, esp a surface, part, or expanse; a flat tyre; a set of rooms on one floor of a building (—*also* **apartment**).

flatten *vti* to make or become flat.

flatter *vt* to praise excessively or insincerely; to display to advantage; to represent too favourably.—**flattery** *n*.

flaunt *vt* to display.

flavour *n* the taste of something in the mouth; a characteristic quality. • *vt* to give flavour to.

flavouring *n* any substance used to give flavour to food.

flaw *n* a defect; a crack. • *vti* to make or become flawed.—**flawless** *adj*.

flax *n* a blue-flowered plant cultivated for its fibre and seed; the fibre of this plant.

flaxen *adj* made of flax; pale yellow.

flea *n* a small jumping bloodsucking insect.

fledge *vt* (*birds*) to rear until ready to fly.

fledgling *n* a young bird just fledged; an inexperienced person, a trainee.

flee *vti* to run away from danger, etc.

fleece *n* the woollen coat of sheep or similar animal. • *vt* to remove wool from; to defraud.—**fleecy** *adj*.

fleet¹ *n* a number of warships under one command; (*often with cap*) a country's navy; any group of cars, buses, etc, under one control.

fleet² *adj* swift moving; nimble.

fleeting *adj* brief, transient.

Flemish *adj* of the people of Flanders, or their language.

flesh *n* the soft substance of the body, esp the muscular tissue; the pulpy part of fruits and vegetables; meat; the body as distinct from the soul; all mankind; a yellowish-pink colour. • *vt* (*usu with* **out**) to give substance to.—**fleshy** *adj*.

flexible *adj* easily bent; adaptable.

flick *n* a light stroke or blow.—*also vt*.

flicker *vi* to burn unsteadily. • *n* a flickering movement, esp of light or flame.

flier *see* **flyer**.

flight¹ *n* the act, manner, or power of flying; distance flown; a group of creatures or things flying together; a scheduled trip by aircraft; a set of stairs between landings; a mental act of soaring; a set of feathers on a dart or arrow.

flight² *n* an act or instance of fleeing.

flimsy *adj* weak, insubstantial; light and thin; unconvincing.—**flimsiness** *n*.

flinch *vi* to draw back; to wince.

fling *vt* to cast, throw, esp with force. • *n* a lively dance; a period of pleasurable indulgence.

flint *n* a very hard rock that produces sparks when struck with steel; an alloy used for producing a spark in lighters.

flip¹ *n* a drink made from any alcoholic beverage sweetened and mixed with beaten egg.

flip² *vt* to toss with a quick jerk; to snap (a coin) in the air with the thumb; to turn (over).

flippant *adj* impertinent; frivolous.

flirt vi to make insincere amorous approaches; to trifle with. • n a person who flirts.—**flirtation** n.

flit vi to move lightly and rapidly; to vacate (premises).—also n.

float vi to rest on the surface of or be suspended in a liquid; to move lightly; to wander aimlessly. • vt to cause to float; to put into circulation; to start up a business, esp by offering shares for sale. • n a device on a fishing line to signal the bait has been taken; a low flat vehicle; a small sum of money for cash expenditures.

flock[1] n a group of certain animals or birds; a group of people. • vi to travel in a crowd.

flock[2] n a tuft of wool or cotton fibre; woollen or cotton waste used for stuffing.

flog vt to beat with a rod, whip.

flood n an overflowing of water on an area normally dry; the rising of the tide; a great outpouring, as of words. • vt to cover or fill, as with a flood; to put too much water, fuel, etc, on or in.—also vi.

floodlight n a strong beam of light used to illuminate a stage, sports field, etc.—also vt .

floor n the bottom surface of anything, e.g. a room, the ocean; a storey in a building; the area in a legislative assembly where the members debate; the lower limit, the base. • vt to provide with a floor; to knock down (a person) in a fight.

flop vi to move in a heavy, clumsy or relaxed manner; (inf) to fail.—also n.

floppy adj hanging loosely.—**floppiness** n.

flora n the plants of a region or a period.

floral adj pertaining to flowers.

florid adj flowery; elaborate; ruddy.

florist n a person who sells or grows flowers.

flotation n the act or process of floating; the launching of a business venture.

flounce[1] vi to move in an emphatic or impatient manner.—also n.

flounce[2] n a frill of material sewn to a skirt.

flounder[1] vi to move awkwardly; to be clumsy in thinking or speaking.

flounder[2] n a small flatfish used as food.

flour n the finely ground powder of wheat or other grain. • vt to sprinkle with flour.

flourish vi (plants) to grow luxuriantly; to prosper. • vt to brandish dramatically. • n embellishment; a bold stroke of the pen; a sweeping gesture; a musical fanfare.

flout vt to treat with contempt; to disobey.

flow vi (liquids) to move (as if) in a stream; to glide smoothly; to continue effortlessly; to be characterised by smooth and easy movement; to hang free or loosely. • n a flowing; the rate of flow.

flow chart n a diagram representing the sequence of and relationships between different steps or procedures in a complex process.

flower n the seed-producing structure of a flowering plant, a blossom; the best or finest part. • vi to produce blossoms; to reach the best stage.

flowery adj full of or decorated with flowers; (language) full of elaborate expressions.

flu n (inf) influenza.

fluctuate vi (prices, etc) to vary in an irregular way.—**fluctuation** n.

fluent adj able to write and speak a foreign language with ease; speaking and writing easily and smoothly; graceful.—**fluency** n.

fluff n soft, light down; a loose, soft mass, as of hair. • vt to pat or shake until fluffy.—**fluffy** adj.

fluid n a substance able to flow freely.

fluke[1] n a flatfish; a flattened parasitic worm.

fluke[2] n the part of an anchor that fastens in the sea bed, etc; the barbed end of a harpoon.

fluke[3] n a stroke of luck.—**fluky** adj.

flurry n a sudden gust of wind, rain, or snow; a sudden commotion.—also vti.

flush[1] n sudden, vigorous growth; sudden excitement; a blush; a sudden feeling of heat. • vti to flow rapidly; to wash (be washed) out by a sudden flow of water; to (cause to) blush; to excite. • adj level with another surface.

flush[2] vt to make game birds rise suddenly.

flush[3] n a hand of cards all of the same suit.

fluster vti to make or become confused. • n agitation or confusion.

flute n an orchestral woodwind instrument in the form of a straight pipe held horizontally and played through a hole near one end; a decorative groove. • vi to cut grooves in.

flutter vi to flap the wings; to wave about; (heart) to beat irregularly. • vt to cause to flutter. • n rapid, irregular motion; (inf) a small bet.

flux n a continual flowing or changing; a substance used to help metals fuse together.

fly[1] n a two-winged insect; a natural or imitation fly attached to a fish-hook as bait.

fly[2] vi to move through the air on wings; to travel in an aircraft; to control an aircraft; to flee; to pass quickly. • vt to cause to fly, as a kite; to escape; to transport by aircraft. • n a flap that conceals buttons, a zip on trousers.

fly[3] adj (inf) sly, astute.

flyer n something that flies or moves very fast; a pilot.—also **flier**.

flying adj capable of flight; fast-moving. • n the act of flying an aircraft, etc.

flying saucer n an unidentified round flying, purportedly from outer space.

flying start n a start in a race when the competitor is already moving when passing the starting line; a promising beginning.

flyover n a bridge that carries a road or railway over another; a fly-past.

fly-past n a processional flight of aircraft.

flywheel n a heavy wheel that stores energy by inertia, used to regulate machinery.

foal n the young of the horse or a related animal.
• vti to give birth to a foal.

foam n froth or fine bubbles on the surface of liquid; a rigid or springy cellular mass made from liquid rubber, plastic, etc.—also vi.

fob[1] n the chain or ribbon for attaching a watch to a waistcoat.

fob[2] vt (with off) to cheat; to put off.

focus n a point where rays of light, heat, etc, meet after being bent by a lens, curved mirror, etc; correct adjustment of the eye or lens to form a clear image; a centre of activity or interest. • vt to adjust the focus of; to bring into focus; to concentrate.—**focal** adj.

fodder n dried food for cattle, horses, etc.

foe n an enemy, an adversary.

foetus see **fetus**.

fog n (poor visibility caused by) a large mass of water vapour condensed to fine particles just above the earth's surface. • vti to make, become foggy.—**foggy** adj.

foible n a slight failing; an idiosyncrasy.

foil[1] vt to defeat; to frustrate.

foil[2] n a very thin sheet of metal; anything that sets off or enhances another by contrast.

foil[3] n a long, thin, blunted fencing sword.

fold[1] vt to cover by doubling over; to wrap up, envelop; to interlace (arms, hands); to incorporate (an ingredient) gently into a food mixture. • vi to become folded; to fail; to collapse. • n something folded, as a piece of cloth; a crease.

fold[2] n a pen for sheep.

folder n a folded cover or large envelope.

foliage n leaves.

folk n a people of a country or tribe; people in general; relatives; folk music.—also adj.

folklore n traditional beliefs, legends.

folk song n a traditional song.

follow vt to go or come after; to pursue; to go along (a path, etc); to copy; to obey; to adopt, as a opinion; to understand the meaning of; to come after in time; (with through) to pursue to a conclusion; (with up) to pursue further. • vi to go or come after another; to result; (with on) (cricket) to take a second innings immediately after a first.

follower n a disciple or adherent.

following n a body of adherents or believers.
• adj next after; now to be stated.

folly n a lack of sense; a foolish act or idea; an extravagant, impractical building.

fond adj loving, affectionate; indulgent; (with of) having a liking for.—**fondness** n.

fondle vt to caress.

font[1] n a receptacle for baptismal water.

font[2] see **fount**[1].

food n any substance, esp a solid, taken in by a plant or animal to enable it to live and grow.

foodstuff n a substance used as food.

fool n a person lacking wisdom; a jester; a cold dessert made from whipped cream mixed with fruit purée. • vt to deceive. • vi to act jokingly, idly; to tease.—**foolish** adj.

foolhardy adj foolishly bold; rash.

foolproof adj proof against failure; easy to understand; easy to use.

foot n the end part of the leg; the lowest part or edge of something, bottom; a measure of 12 inches (30.48 cm); a group of syllables serving as a unit of metre in verse. • vti to pay the entire cost of (a bill).

football n a field game played with an inflated leather ball by two teams; the ball used.—**footballer** n.

footbridge n a bridge for pedestrians.

foothill n a hill at the foot of higher hills.

foothold n a ledge when climbing.

footing n the basis upon which something rests; status, relationship; a foothold.

footlights npl a row of lights in front of a stage.

footman n a liveried servant or attendant.

footnote n a note at the foot of a page.

footpath n a narrow path for pedestrians.

footwear n shoes and socks, etc.

for prep because of, as a result of; as the price of, or recompense of; in order to be, to serve as; appropriate to, or adapted to; in quest of; in the direction of; on behalf of; in place of; in favour of; with respect to; notwithstanding, in spite of; to the extent of. • conj because.

forage n food for domestic animals; a search for provisions.—also vi.

foray n a sudden raid. • vti to plunder.

forbear vi to endure. • vt to hold oneself back from.

forbid vt to command (a person) not to do something; to render impossible, prevent.

forbidding adj unfriendly, solemn, strict.

force n strength, power, effort; (physics) (the intensity of) an influence that causes movement of a body; a body of soldiers, police, etc; effectiveness; violence, compulsion. • vt to compel or oblige by physical effort, etc; to press or drive against resistance; to break open; to impose.

forceful adj powerful, effective.

forceps n an instrument for grasping firmly.

ford n a shallow crossing place in a river.

fore adj in front. • n the front. • adv in, at, the front. • interj (golf) a warning cry.

forearm[1] n the arm between the elbow and the wrist.

forearm[2] vt to arm in advance.

forecast vt to predict (events, weather, etc) through rational analysis.—also n.

forecourt n an enclosed space in front of a building, as in a filling station.

forefathers npl ancestors.

forefinger n the finger next to the thumb.

forego¹ see **forgo**.

forego² vt to precede.

foreground n the part of a picture or view nearest the spectator's vision.

forehead n the part of the face above the eyes.

foreign adj of, in, or belonging to another country; involving other countries; alien.

foreigner n a person from another country.

foreman n a person who supervises workers in a factory, etc; the spokesperson of a jury.—**forewoman** nf.

foremost adj first in importance.

forensic adj belonging to courts of law.

forensic medicine n the application of medical expertise to legal investigations.

forerunner n a person or thing that comes in advance of another; a portent.

foresee vt to be aware of beforehand.

foresight n foreseeing; the power to foresee; prudent provision for the future.

forest n a thick growth of trees.

forestall vt to prevent by taking action beforehand; to anticipate.

forestry n the science of cultivating forests.

foretell vt to forecast.

for ever, forever adv for all future time.

foreword n a preface to a book.

forfeit n something confiscated or given up as a penalty for a fault.—also vt.

forge¹ n (a workshop with) a furnace in which metals are heated and shaped. • vt to shape by heating and hammering; to counterfeit.

forge² vt to move forward with effort.

forgery n fraudulently copying; a forged copy.

forget vti to be unable to remember.

forgetful adj apt to forget, inattentive.

forgive vt to pardon. • vi to be merciful.—**forgiveness** n.

forgo vt to abstain from.—also **forego**.

fork n a small instrument with two or more prongs set in a handle, used in eating and cooking; a pronged agricultural or gardening tool for digging, etc; one of the branches into which a road or river divides; the point of separation.—also vti.

fork-lift truck n a vehicle with power-operated prongs for raising and lowering loads.

form n general structure; the figure; a mould; a particular mode, kind, type, etc; arrangement; a way of doing something; a printed document with blanks to be filled in; a class in school; condition of mind or body; a chart giving information about racehorses. • vt to shape; to train; to develop (habits); to constitute. • vi to be formed.

formal adj in conformity with established rules or habits; regular; ceremonial; punctilious; stiff.

format n the size, form, shape in which books, etc, are issued; the general presentation of, e.g. a television programme; (comput) the arrangement of data on magnetic disk, etc, for access and storage.—also vt.

formation n form of making or producing; that which is formed; structure; regular array.

formative adj pertaining to formation and development; shaping.

former adj of, in a previous time; the first mentioned (of two).—**formerly** adv.

formidable adj causing fear; difficult to defeat.

formula n a set of symbols expressing the composition of a substance; a general expression in algebraic form for solving a problem; a prescribed form; a list of ingredients, as for a prescription or recipe; a fixed method by which something is to be done.

formulate vt to express in a formula.

forsake vt to desert; to give up.

fort n a fortified place for military defence.

forte¹ n something at which a person excels.

forte² adv (mus) loudly.

forth adv forwards; onwards; out.

forthcoming adj about to appear; responsive.

forthright adv frank, direct, outspoken.

fortification n act or process of fortifying; a wall, barricade, etc, built for defence.

fortify vt to strengthen physically, emotionally, etc; (wine, etc) to add alcohol to.

fortitude n courage in adversity.

fortnight n a period of two weeks.

fortress n a strong fort or fortified town.

fortuitous adj happening by chance.

fortunate adj having good luck.

fortune n luck; destiny; prosperity; vast wealth.

forty n four times ten, the symbol for this (40, XL, xl).—also adj.—**fortieth** adj.

forum n an assembly or meeting to discuss topics of public concern; a medium for public debate, as a magazine.

forward adj at, toward, or of the front; advanced; onward; prompt; bold; presumptuous; of or for the future. • vt to promote; to send on. • n (sport) an attacking player in various games.

fossil n the petrified remains of an animal or vegetable preserved in rock.—also adj.

foster vt to encourage; to bring up (a child that is not one's own).

foul adj stinking, loathsome; extremely dirty; indecent; wicked; (language) obscene; (weather) stormy; (sports) against the rules. • vt to make filthy; to dishonour; to obstruct; to make a foul against in a game. • n (sports) a hit, blow, move, etc, that is foul.

found¹ vt to bring into being; to establish.

found² *vt* to melt and pour (metal) into a mould to produce castings.

foundation *n* an institution; the base of a house, wall, etc; a first layer of cosmetic applied to the skin; an underlying principle, etc.

founder¹ *n* one who founds an institution.

founder² *n* a person who casts metal.

founder³ *vi* to collapse; to fail.

foundry *n* a workshop or factory where metal castings are produced.

fount¹ *n* a set of printing type or characters of one style and size.—*also* **font**.

fount² *n* a source.

fountain *n* a natural spring of water; a source; an artificial jet or flow of water; the basin where this flows; a reservoir, as for ink. • *vti* to (cause to) flow like a fountain.

four *n* one more than three; the symbol for this (4, IV, iv); the fourth in a series or set—*also adj.*

fourteen *n, adj* four and ten; the symbol for this (14, XIV, xiv).—**fourteenth** *adj.*

fourth *adj* next after third. • *n* one of four equal parts of something.

fowl *n* any of the domestic birds used as food, as the chicken, duck, etc.

fox *n* a small wild mammal of the dog family.

foyer *n* an anteroom; an entrance hallway.

fraction *n* a small part, amount; (*math*) a quantity less than a whole, expressed as a decimal or with a numerator and denominator.

fracture *n* the breaking of any hard material, esp a bone.—*also vti.*

fragile *adj* easily broken; frail; delicate.

fragment *n* a piece broken off or detached; an incomplete portion.—*also vti.*

fragmentary *adj* consisting of fragments.

fragrance *n* a pleasant scent, a perfume.—**fragrant** *adj.*

frail *adj* physically or morally weak; fragile.

frame *vt* to form according to a pattern; to construct; to put into words; to enclose (a picture) in a border. • *n* the physical make-up of the body; the framework of a house; the structural case enclosing a window, door, etc; a border, as around a picture; (*snooker*) a triangular mould for setting up balls before play.

framework *n* a structural frame; a basic structure (as of ideas); frame of reference.

franchise *n* the right to vote in public elections; authorisation to sell the goods of a manufacturer in a particular area.—*also vt.*

frank *adj* free and direct in expressing oneself; honest, open. • *vt* to mark letters, etc, with a mark denoting free postage. • *n* a mark indicating free postage.—**frankness** *n.*

frantic *adj* violently agitated; wild.

fraternal *adj* of a brother; brotherly.

fraternise *vt* to associate as a friend.

fraternity *n* brotherly feeling; a society of people with common interests.

fraud *n* deliberate deceit; a deception.

fraudulent *adj* deceiving or intending to deceive; obtained by deceit.—**fraudulence** *n.*

fraught *adj* filled or loaded (with).

fray¹ *n* a fight, a brawl.

fray² *vti* (*fabric, etc*) to (cause to) wear away into threads, esp at the edge; (*nerves, temper*) to make or become irritated or strained.

freak *n* an unusual happening; any abnormal animal, person, or plant; an ardent enthusiast.

freckle *n* a small, brownish spot on the skin.—*also vti.*

free *adj* not under the control or power of another; having social and political liberty; able to move in any direction; not burdened by obligations; not exact; generous; with no cost or charge; clear of obstruction. • *vt* to set free; to clear of obstruction, etc.—**freedom** *n.*

freelance *n* a person who pursues a profession without long-term commitment to any employer. • *vt* to work as a freelance.

Freemason *n* a member of the secretive fraternity (Free and Accepted Masons) dedicated to mutual aid.

free trade *n* trade based on the unrestricted international exchange of goods with tariffs only as a source of revenue.

freewheel *vi* to ride a bicycle with the gear disconnected; to drive a car with the gear in neutral.

free will *n* voluntary choice or decision.

freeze *vi* to be formed into or covered by ice; to become very cold; to become motionless; to be made speechless by strong emotion; to become formal and unfriendly. • *vt* to harden into ice; to convert from a liquid to a solid with cold; to make extremely cold; to anaesthetise by cold; to fix (prices, etc) at a given level by authority.

freezer *n* a compartment or container that freezes and preserves food for long periods.

freezing point *n* the temperature at which a liquid solidifies.

freight *n* the transport of goods by water, land or air; the cost for this; the goods transported.

freighter *n* a ship, aircraft carrying freight.

French *adj* of France, its people, culture, etc. • *n* the language of France.

French windows *npl* a pair of casement windows extending to the floor and acting as doors.

frenzy *n* wild excitement; violent mental derangement.

frequency *n* repeated occurrence; the number of cycles, etc, in a given period.

frequent *adj* coming or happening often. • *vi* to visit often; to resort to.

fresco *n* a picture painted on walls covered with damp freshly laid plaster.

fresh adj recently made, grown, etc; not salted, pickled, etc; not spoiled; lively, not tired; not worn, soiled, faded, etc; new, recent; (wind) brisk; (water) not salt.

freshen vi to make or become fresh.

freshwater adj of a river; not sea-going.

fret¹ vti to make, become anxious; to wear away, roughen by rubbing.

fret² n a running design of interlacing small bars.

fret³ n any of a series of metal ridges along the finger-board of a guitar, banjo, etc, used as a guide for depressing the strings.

friar n a member of certain Roman Catholic religious orders.

friction n a rubbing of one object against another; conflict of opinions, ideas, etc.

friend n a person one knows well and is fond of; an ally, supporter, or sympathiser.—**friendly** adj.—**friendship** n.

frieze n a decorative band along the top of the wall of a room.

frigate n a warship used for escort, antisubmarine and patrol duties.

fright n sudden fear; a shock.—**frightful** adj.

frighten vt to scare; to force by frightening.

frigid adj extremely cold; unresponsive sexually.

frill n a piece of pleated or gathered fabric used for edging; something superfluous, an affectation. • vt to decorate with a frill.

fringe n a decorative border of hanging threads; hair hanging over the forehead; an outer edge. • vt to be or make a fringe for. • adj at the outer edge; additional; minor; unconventional.

frisk vi to leap playfully. • vt (inf) to search.

frisky adj lively, playful.—**friskiness** n.

fritter¹ n a slice of fruit, meat fried in batter.

fritter² vt (with away) to waste.

frivolity n a trifling act, thought, or action.

frivolous adj irresponsible; trifling; silly.

fro adv away from; backward.

frock n a dress.

frog n a small tailless web-footed jumping amphibian; a decorative loop fastening.

frogman n a person who wears rubber suit, flippers, oxygen supply, etc, and is trained in working underwater.

frolic n a lively party or game; merriment, fun. • vi to play happily.

from prep beginning at, starting with; out of; originating with; out of the possibility, use of.

front n outward behaviour; the part facing forward; a leading position; the promenade of a seaside resort; the advanced battle area in warfare; a person or group used to hide another's activity; an advancing mass of cold or warm air. • adj at, to, in, on, or of the front.—also vti.

frontal adj of or belonging to the front.

frontier n the border between two countries; the limit of knowledge of a subject.

frost n a coating of powdery ice particles. • vt to cover (as if) with frost or frosting; to give a frost-like opaque surface to (glass).

frostbite n injury by exposure to cold.

frosty adj cold with frost; reserved in manner.

froth n foam; frivolity.—also vi.—**frothy** adj.

frown vi to contract the brow as in anger or thought; (with upon) to regard with displeasure or disapproval.—also n.

frugal adj economical, thrifty; meagre.

fruit n the seed-bearing part of any plant; the fleshy part of this used as food; the result or product of any action.—**fruitful** adj.

fruition n a coming to fulfilment.

fruit machine n a coin-operated gambling machine, using symbols of fruit.

frustrate vt to prevent from achieving a goal or gratifying a desire; to discourage.

fry¹ vti to cook over direct heat in hot fat. • n a dish of things fried.

fry² n recently hatched fishes.

f-stop see stop.

fuchsia n a decorative flowering shrub.

fudge n a soft sweet made of butter, milk, sugar, flavouring, etc. • vt to refuse to commit oneself.

fuel n material burned to supply heat and power, or as a source of nuclear energy; anything that serves to intensify strong feelings. • vti to supply with fuel.

fugitive n a person who flees. • adj fleeing, as from danger or justice; fleeting.

fugue n a polyphonic musical composition with its theme taken up successively by different voices.

fulfil vt to carry out (a promise); to achieve the completion of; to satisfy.—**fulfilment** n.

full adj having or holding all that can be contained; having eaten all one wants; having a great number (of); complete; having reached the greatest size, extent, etc.

fullback n (football, rugby, hockey, etc) a defensive player at the back; this position.

full-stop n the punctuation mark (.) at the end of a sentence.—also **period**.

fully adv thoroughly; at least.

fumble vi to grope about. • vt to handle clumsily; to act awkwardly; to fail to catch (a ball) cleanly.

fume n (usu pl) smoke, gas or vapour, esp if offensive or suffocating. • vi to express anger.

fumigate vt to disinfect.—**fumigation** n.

fun n amusement and enjoyment.

function n the activity characteristic of a person or thing; a specific purpose; an official ceremony or social entertainment. • vi to perform a function; to act, operate.—**functional** adj.

fund n a sum of money set aside for a purpose; (pl) ready money. • vt to provide funds for.

fundamental adj basic; essential.—also n.

funeral n the ceremony associated with the burial or cremation of the dead.

fungus n any of a major group of lower plants, as mildews, mushrooms, etc, that lack chlorophyll and reproduce by spores.

funnel n an implement, usu a cone with a wide top and tapering to a narrow tube, for pouring fluids, powders, into bottles; a metal chimney for the escape of smoke, steam, etc.—also vti .

funny adj causing laughter; puzzling, odd.

fur n the short, soft, fine hair on the bodies of certain animals; their skins with the fur attached; a garment made of fur;.

furious adj full of anger; intense, violent.

furlong n 220 yards, one-eighth of a mile.

furlough n leave of absence from duty.

furnace n an enclosed chamber in which heat is produced to burn, heat, smelt.

furnish vt to provide (a room, etc) with furniture; to equip; to supply.

furnishings npl furniture, carpets, etc.

furniture n the things in a room, etc, that equip it for living, as chairs, beds, etc.

furrow n the groove in the earth made by a plough; a groove or track resembling this.

furry adj like, made of, or covered with fur.

further adv at or to a greater distance or degree; in addition. • adj more distant, remote; additional. • vt to help forward.

furthermore adv moreover, besides.

furthest adj at or to the greatest distance.

furtive adj stealthy; sly.

fury n intense rage; a frenzy.

fuse vti to join or become joined by melting; to (cause) melt by the application of heat; to equip a plug, circuit, etc, with a fuse; to (cause to) fail by blowing a fuse. • n a tube or wick filled with combustible material for setting off an explosive charge; a piece of thin wire that melts and breaks when an electric current exceeds a certain level.

fuselage n the body of an aircraft.

fusible adj able to be fused.

fusion n the act of melting, blending or fusing; a product of fusion; union, partnership.

fuss n excited activity, bustle; a nervous state. • vi to worry over trifles; to whine.

fussy adj hard to please; over-elaborate.

futile adj useless; ineffective.—**futility** n.

future adj that is to be; of or referring to time yet to come. • n the time to come; future events.

futuristic adj forward-looking in design.

fuzzy adj like fuzz; fluffy; blurred.

G

gable n the triangular upper part of a wall enclosed by the sloping ends of a pitched roof.

gadget n a small tool or device.

gag n something put over or into the mouth to prevent talking; any restraint of free speech; a joke. • vt to keep from speaking. • vi to retch; to tell jokes.

gaiety n happiness, liveliness.

gaily adv in a cheerful manner.

gain vt to obtain, earn, esp by effort; to attract; to get as an addition (esp profit or advantage); to make an increase in. • vi to make progress; to increase in weight. • n an increase esp in profit or advantage; an acquisition.

gainful adj profitable.

gait n a manner of walking or running.

gala n a celebration, festival.

galaxy n any of the systems of stars in the universe; (with cap) the galaxy containing the Earth's solar system.

gale n a strong wind; an outburst.

gallant adj dignified, stately; brave; noble.

gall bladder n a membranous sac attached to the liver in which bile is stored.

gallery n a covered passage for walking; a long narrow outside balcony; an upper area of seating in a theatre; a building for showing works of art; the spectators at a golf tournament, tennis match, etc.

galley n a long, usu low, ship of ancient or medieval times, propelled by oars; the kitchen of a ship, aircraft.

gallon n a unit of liquid measure comprising 277.42 cubic inches.

gallop n the fastest gait of a horse, etc. • vti to (cause to) go at a gallop; to move swiftly.

gallows n a wooden frame used for hanging criminals.

gallstone n a small solid mass in the gall bladder.

gambit n (chess) an opening in which a piece is sacrificed to gain an advantage.

gamble vi to play games of chance for money; to take a risk for some advantage. • vt to risk in gambling, to bet. • *n* a risky venture; a bet.—**gambler** *n*.

game *n* a form of play; activity or sport involving competition; a scheme, a plan; wild birds or animals hunted for sport or food, the flesh of such animals. • *adj* (*inf*) willing.

gamekeeper *n* a person who breeds and takes care of game birds and animals.

gammon *n* cured or smoked ham.

gander *n* an adult male goose.

gang *n* a group of persons, working together; a group of persons acting together for illegal purposes.

gangrene *n* death of body tissue when the blood supply is obstructed.

gangster *n* a member of a criminal gang.

gangway *n* a passageway, esp an opening in a ship's side for loading, etc; a gangplank.

gap *n* a break or opening, as in a wall or fence; an interruption in continuity; disparity.

gape *vi* to open the mouth wide; to stare in astonishment, esp with the mouth open; to open widely.—*also n*.

garage *n* an enclosed shelter for motor vehicles; a place where they are repaired and serviced, and fuel sold.—*also vt*.

garbage *n* rubbish.

garden *n* an area of ground for growing herbs, fruits, flowers, or vegetables, usu attached to a house. • *vi* to make, or work in, a garden.—**gardener** *n*.—**gardening** *n*.

gargle *vti* to rinse the throat by breathing air from the lungs through liquid held in the mouth.—*also n*.

gargoyle *n* a grotesquely carved face or figure, usu acting as a spout.

garish *adj* crudely bright, gaudy.

garland *n* a wreath of flowers or leaves worn or hung as decoration.—*also vt*.

garlic *n* a bulbous herb used in cookery.

garment *n* an item of clothing.

garnish *vt* to decorate; to decorate (food) with something that adds colour or flavour.

garrison *n* troops stationed at a fort.

garrulous *adj* excessively talkative.

garter *n* an elasticated band used to support a stocking or sock.

gas *n* an air-like substance with the capacity to expand indefinitely and not liquefy or solidify at ordinary temperatures; any mixture of flammable gases used for lighting or heating. • *vt* to poison or disable with gas; (*inf*) to talk idly and at length.

gash *n* a long, deep, open cut.—*also vt*.

gasket *n* a piece of rubber, metal, etc, sandwiched between metal surfaces to act as a seal.

gas mask *n* a protective breathing device for the face that filters out poisonous gases.

gasp *vi* to draw in the breath suddenly and audibly, as from shock; to struggle to catch the breath. • *n* the act of gasping.

gastric *adj* of, in, or near the stomach.

gastronomy *n* the art and science of good eating.—**gastronomic** *adj*.

gate *n* a movable structure controlling passage through an opening in a fence or wall; a device (as in a computer) that outputs a signal when specified input conditions are met; the total amount or number of paid admissions to a football match, etc.

gate-crasher *n* a person who attends a party, etc, without being invited.

gateway *n* an opening for a gate.

gather *vt* to bring together in one place or group; to get gradually; to harvest; to pucker fabric by pulling a thread or stitching; to understand, infer. • *vi* to come together in a body; to cluster around a focus of attention.

gathering *n* the act of gathering or assembling together; an assembly; folds made in a garment by gathering.

gauche *adj* socially inept.

gaudy *adj* tastelessly bright.—**gaudiness** *n*.

gauge *n* measurement according to some standard or system; any device for measuring; the distance between rails of a railway; the size of the bore of a shotgun. • *vt* to measure the size, amount, etc, of.

gaunt *adj* excessively thin as from hunger.

gauntlet *n* a knight's armoured glove; a long glove, often with a flaring cuff.

gauze *n* any very thin, loosely woven fabric, as of cotton or silk; a surgical dressing.

gay *adj* joyous and lively; colourful; homosexual.—**gayness** *n*.

gaze *vi* to look steadily. • *n* a steady look.

gazelle *n* a small swift Asian or African antelope.

gazump *vti* to force up a price (esp of a house) after a price has been agreed.

gear *n* clothing; equipment, esp for some task or activity; a toothed wheel designed to mesh with another; (*often pl*) a system of such gears meshed together to transmit motion; a specific adjustment of such a system; a part of a mechanism with a specific function. • *vt* to adapt (one thing) to conform with another.

gearbox *n* a metal case enclosing a system of gears.

gear lever *n* a lever used to engage or change gear, esp in a motor vehicle.

gelatin(e) *n* a tasteless, odourless substance extracted by boiling bones, hooves, etc, and used in food, medicines, etc.

gelignite *n* an explosive consisting of nitroglycerin mixed with sodium or potassium nitrate.

gem n a precious stone cut and polished for use as a jewel.

gender n the classification by which words are grouped as feminine, masculine or neuter.

general adj not local, special, or specialised; widespread, common to many; not specific or precise. • n a commissioned officer above a lieutenant general.

generalise vti to form general conclusions from specific instances; to talk in general terms.—**generalisation** n.

generally adv widely; popularly; usually.

general practitioner n a non-specialist doctor who treats all types of illnesses.

generate vt to bring into existence.

generation n the act or process of generating; a single succession in natural descent; people of the same period; production, as of electric current.

generator n one who or that which generates; a machine that changes mechanical energy to electrical energy.

generous adj of a noble nature; willing to give or share; large, ample.—**generosity** n.

genetic adj of or relating to the origin, development or causes of something; of or relating to genes or genetics.

genial adj kindly, sympathetic and cheerful.

genitals, genitalia npl the (external) sexual organs.

genitive adj (gram) of, belonging to the case of nouns, pronouns and adjectives expressing ownership or relation.—also n.

genius n a person possessing extraordinary intellectual power; (with for) natural ability.

genteel adj polite; affectedly refined.

gentle adj refined, courteous; generous; kind; kindly; patient; not harsh or rough.

gentleman n a man of good family and social standing; a courteous, gracious, honourable man; a polite term of address.

gentry n people of high social standing.

genuine adj not fake, real; sincere.

geography n the science of the physical nature of the earth, such as land and sea masses, climate, vegetation, etc, and their interaction with the human population; the physical features of a region.—**geographic(al)** adj.

geology n the science relating to the history and structure of the earth's crust, its rocks and fossils.—**geologist** n.—**geological** adj.

geometry n the branch of mathematics dealing with the properties, measurement, and relationships of points, lines, planes, and solids.—**geometric(al)** adj.

geranium n a garden plant with red, pink or white flowers.

germ n a simple form of living matter capable of growth and development into an organism.

German adj of or relating to Germany, its people or their language.—also n.

German measles n (used as sing) a mild contagious disease similar to measles.

germinate vti to start developing; to sprout, as from a seed.—**germination** n.

gestate vt to carry (young) in the womb during pregnancy; to develop (a plan, etc) gradually in the mind.—**gestation** n.

gesticulate vi to make expressive gestures.

gesture n movement of part of the body to express or emphasise ideas, emotions, etc. • vi to make a gesture.—**gestural** adj.

get vt to obtain, gain, win; to receive; to acquire; to go and bring; (inf) (with **have** or **has**) to be obliged to; to possess; (inf) (with **out of**) to avoid doing; (with **over**) to communicate effectively. • vi to come; to go; to arrive; to come to be; (with **at**)(inf) to annoy; (inf) to criticise; (inf) to corrupt, bribe; (with **away**) to escape; (with **by**) (inf) to manage, to survive; (with **off**) to come off, down, or out of; to be acquitted; to depart; (with **on**) to go on or into; to put on; to proceed; to grow older; to manage; to succeed; (with **on with**) to establish a friendly relationship; (with **out**) to go out or away; (with **over**) to recover from; to forget; (with **through**) to finish; to manage to survive; (with **up**) to rise to one's feet; to get out of bed; (inf) to dress in a certain style; (inf) to be involved in (mischief, etc).

geyser n a natural spring from which columns of boiling water and steam gush into the air at intervals; a water heater.

ghastly adj terrifying, horrible; (inf) intensely disagreeable; pale, unwell looking.

gherkin n a small cucumber.

ghetto n a section of a city in which members of a minority group live.

ghost n the supposed disembodied spirit of a dead person, appearing as a shadowy apparition.

giant n a huge legendary being of great strength; a person or thing of great size, strength, intellect, etc. • adj incredibly large.

gibberish n unintelligible talk, nonsense.

gibe n a taunt, sneer. • vti to jeer, scoff (at).—also **jibe**.

giblets npl the edible internal organs of a bird.

giddy adj flighty; having a feeling of whirling around as if about to lose balance and fall.

gift n something given; a natural ability.

gifted adj having great natural ability.

gigantic adj exceedingly large.

giggle vi to laugh in a nervous or silly manner. • n a laugh in this manner.

gild vt to coat with gold leaf; to give a deceptively attractive appearance to.

gill[1] n an organ in fish for breathing in water.

gill² n a liquid measure equal to a quarter of a pint.

gills npl the radiating plates under the cap of a mushroom.

gimlet n a small tool with a screw point for boring holes.

gimmick n a trick or device for attracting notice.

gin¹ n an alcoholic spirit distilled from grain and flavoured with juniper berries.

gin² n a trap for catching small animals.

ginger n a tropical plant with fleshy roots used as a flavouring.

gingerbread n a cake flavoured with ginger.

gingerly adv with caution. • adj cautious.

gingham n a cotton fabric with stripes or checks.

giraffe n a large cud-chewing mammal of Africa, with very long legs and neck.

girder n a large steel beam for supporting joists, the framework of a building, etc.

girl n a female child; a young woman.

girlfriend n a female friend.

girth n the thickness round something.

gist n the principal point or essence.

give vt to hand over as a present; to deliver; to hand over in or for payment; to pass (regards etc) along; to act as host of; to supply; to yield; (advice) to offer; (punishment, etc) to inflict; to perform; (with away) to make a gift of; to give (the bride) to the bridegroom; to sell cheaply; to reveal, betray; (with off) to emit (fumes, etc); (with out) to discharge; to distribute; (with over) to devote time to a specific activity; to cease (an activity); (with up) to hand over; to renounce; to cease; to stop trying. • vi to bend, move, etc, from force or pressure. • n capacity or tendency to yield to force or strain; the quality or state of being springy.

glacier n a large mass of snow and ice moving slowly down a mountain.

glad adj happy; causing joy; very willing.

gladden vti to make or become glad.

gladiator n (ancient Rome) a person trained to fight in a public arena.

glamour n charm; allure; attractiveness; beauty.—**glamorous** adj.

glance vi to strike obliquely and go off at an angle; to flash; to look quickly. • n a quick look.

gland n an organ that separates substances from the blood and synthesises them for further use in, or for elimination from, the body.

glare n a harsh uncomfortably bright light, esp painfully bright sunlight; an angry stare. • vi to stare fiercely.

glass n a hard brittle substance, usu transparent; a glass drinking vessel; (pl) spectacles; the amount held by a drinking glass. • adj of or made of glass.

glasshouse n a large greenhouse for the commercial cultivation of plants.

glassware n objects made of glass.

glassy adj resembling glass; smooth; expressionless, lifeless.—**glassiness** n.

glaze vt to provide with glass; to give a hard glossy finish to (pottery, etc); to cover (foods, etc) with a glossy surface. • vi to become glassy or glossy. • n a glassy finish or coating.

glazier n a person who fits glass in windows.

gleam n a subdued or moderate beam of light; a brief show of some quality or emotion, esp hope.—also vi.

glee n joy, gaiety; delight; (mus) a song in parts for three or more male voices.—**gleeful** adj.

glib adj speaking or spoken smoothly, to the point of insincerity; lacking substance.

glide vti to move smoothly and effortlessly; to descend in an aircraft or glider with little or no engine power.—also n.

glider n an engineless aircraft.

gliding n the sport of flying gliders.

glimmer vi to give a faint, flickering light; to appear faintly.—also n.

glimpse n a brief, momentary view. • vt to catch a glimpse of.

glint n a brief flash of light; a brief indication. • vti to (cause to) gleam brightly.

glisten vi to shine, as light reflected from a wet surface.

glitter vi to sparkle; (usu with with) to be brilliantly attractive. • n glamour; tiny pieces of sparkling material used for decoration.

gloat vi to gaze or contemplate with wicked or malicious satisfaction.

global adj worldwide; comprehensive.

globe n anything spherical or almost so; the earth, or a model of the earth.

gloom n near darkness; deep sadness. • vti to look sullen or dejected; to make or become cloudy or murky.

gloomy adj almost dark; depressed, dejected.

glorify vt to worship; to praise, to honour.

glorious adj having or deserving glory; conferring glory or renown; beautiful; delightful.

glory n great honour or fame; great splendour or beauty. • vi (with in) to rejoice proudly.

gloss n the lustre of a polished surface; a superficially attractive appearance. • vt to give a shiny surface to; (with over) to hide (an error, etc).

glossary n a list of specialised or technical words and their definitions.

glossy adj having a shiny surface; superficial; (magazines) lavishly produced.

glove n a covering for the hand.

glow vi to shine (as if) with an intense heat; to emit a steady light without flames; to be full of life and enthusiasm; to flush or redden with emotion. • *n* a light emitted due to intense heat; a steady, even light without flames; a reddening of the complexion; warmth of emotion or feeling.

glower *vi* to scowl; to stare angrily.—*also n.*

glucose *n* a crystalline sugar occurring naturally in fruits, honey, etc.

glue *n* a sticky, viscous substance used as an adhesive. • *vt* to join with glue.

glum *adj* sullen; gloomy.—**glumness** *n*.

glut *vt* to over-supply. • *n* a surfeit.

glutton *n* one who eats and drinks to excess; one who has a tremendous capacity for something.

gnarled *adj* (*tree trunks*) full of knots; (*hands*) rough, knobbly; crabby in disposition.

gnat *n* any of various small, two-winged insects that bite or sting.

gnaw *vti* to bite away bit by bit; to torment, as by constant pain.

gnome *n* (*folklore*) a dwarf who dwells in the earth and guards its treasure.

go *vi* to proceed; to work properly; to act, sound, as specified; to be accepted or valid; to leave, to depart; to die; to be allotted or sold; to fit (into); to be capable of being divided (into); (*with* **about**) to undertake (duties, etc); (*with* **off**) to become stale; to take place as planned; to cease to like; (*with* **slow**) to work at a slow rate as part of an industrial dispute.

goad *n* a sharp-pointed stick for driving cattle, etc; a stimulus to action. • *vt* to drive (as if) with a goad; to irritate, nag persistently.

goal *n* the place at which a race, trip, etc, is ended; an objective; the place over or into which the ball or puck must go to score in some games; the score made.

goalkeeper *n* a player who defends the goal.

goat *n* a mammal related to the sheep that has backward curving horns.

gobble *vt* to eat greedily.

go-between *n* an intermediary.

goblet *n* a large drinking vessel with a base and stem but without a handle.

goblin *n* an evil or mischievous elf.

god *n* a being conceived of as supernatural and immortal; an idol; a person or thing deified; (*with cap*) in monotheistic religions, the creator and ruler of the universe.

godchild *n* the child a godparent sponsors.

godfather *n* a male godparent; the head of a Mafia crime family.

god-forsaken *adj* desolate, wretched.

godmother *n* a female godparent.

godsend *n* anything that comes unexpectedly and when needed or desired.

godson *n* a male godchild.

goggle *vi* to stare with bulging eyes. • *npl* large spectacles, sometimes fitting snugly against the face, to protect the eyes.

going *n* a departure; the state of the ground, e.g. for horse-racing. • *adj* commonly accepted; thriving; existing.

gold *n* a malleable yellow metallic element used esp for coins and jewellery; money, wealth; a yellow colour. • *adj* of, or like, gold.

golden *adj* made of gold; bright yellow.

golden rule *n* a guiding principle.

goldfish *n* a small gold-coloured fish of the carp family.

golf *n* a game in which the player attempts to hit a small ball with clubs around a turfed course into a succession of holes in the smallest number of strokes.

gondola *n* a long, narrow, black boat used on the canals of Venice; an enclosed car suspended from a cable for transporting passengers up a mountain.

gone • *adj* departed; dead; lost.

gong *n* a disk-shaped percussion instrument struck with a usu padded hammer; (*sl*) a medal.

good *adj* having the right or proper qualities; beneficial; valid; healthy or sound; virtuous, honourable; enjoyable, pleasant, etc; skilled; considerable. • *n* something good; benefit; something that has economic utility; (*with* **the**) good persons; (*pl*) personal property; commodities; (*pl*) the desired or required articles.

goodbye *interj* a concluding remark at parting; farewell.—*also n.*

Good Friday *n* the Friday before Easter, commemorating the Crucifixion.

goodness *n* the state of being good; the good element in something; kindness; virtue.

goodwill *n* benevolence; willingness; the custom and reputation of a business.

goose *n* a large, long-necked, web-footed bird related to swans and ducks; its flesh as food; a female goose as distinguished from a gander; (*inf*) a foolish person.

gooseberry *n* the acid berry of a shrub related to the currant.

goose bumps, goose pimples *n* a roughening of the skin caused usu by cold or fear.

gore[1] *n* (clotted) blood from a wound.

gore[2] *n* a tapering section of material used to shape a garment, sail, etc.

gore[3] *vt* to pierce or wound as with horns.

gorge *n* a ravine. • *vt* to swallow greedily.

gorgeous *adj* strikingly attractive; brilliantly coloured; (*inf*) magnificent.

gorilla *n* an anthropoid ape of western equatorial Africa.

gorse *n* a spiny yellow-flowered shrub.

gory *adj* bloodthirsty; causing bloodshed; covered in blood.

go-slow *n* a deliberate slowing of the work rate by employees.

gospel n the life and teachings of Christ contained in the first four books of the New Testament; (with cap) one of these four books; anything proclaimed as the absolute truth.

gossamer n very fine cobwebs; any very light and flimsy material.—also adj.

gossip n one who chatters idly about others; such talk. • vi to take part in or spread gossip.

gout n a disease causing painful inflammation of the joints; esp of the great toe.

govern vti to exercise authority over; to rule; to influence the action of; to determine.

government n the exercise of authority over a state, organisation, etc; those who direct the affairs of a state, etc.

governor n a person appointed to govern a province, etc; the elected head of any state of the US; the director or head of a governing body of an organisation or institution.

gown n a long, flowing robe worn by clergymen, judges, etc; a type of overall worn in the operating room.

grab vt to take or grasp suddenly; (inf) to catch the interest or attention of. • n a sudden clutch or attempt to grasp; a mechanical device for grasping and lifting objects.

grace n beauty or charm of form, movement, or expression; good will; favour; a delay granted for payment of an obligation; a short prayer of thanks for a meal. • vt to decorate; to dignify.

graceful adj having beauty of form, movement, or expression.

gracious adj having or showing kindness, courtesy, etc; compassionate; polite to supposed inferiors; marked by luxury, ease, etc.

gradation n a series of systematic steps in rank, degree, intensity, etc; arranging in such stages; a single stage in a gradual progression.

grade n a stage or step in a progression; a degree in a scale of quality, rank, etc; a group of people of the same rank, merit, etc; a mark or rating in an examination, etc. • vt to arrange in grades; to give a grade to.

gradient n the degree of slope in a road.

gradual adj taking place by degrees.

graduate n a person who has completed a course of study at a school, college, or university.—also adj.

graduation n graduating; the ceremony at which degrees are conferred by a college or university; an arranging or marking in grades or stages.

graft n a shoot or bud of one plant inserted into another; the transplanting of skin, bone, etc; the getting of money or advantage.

grain n the seed of any cereal plant, as wheat, corn, etc; cereal plants; a tiny, solid particle, as of salt or sand; a unit of weight, 0.0648 gram;

the arrangement of fibres, layers, etc, of wood, leather, etc; the markings or texture due to this; natural disposition.—also vti.

gram n the basic unit of weight in the metric system, equal to one thousandth of a kilogram.

grammar n the study of the forms of words and their arrangement in sentences; a system of rules for speaking and writing a language; a grammar textbook.

grammatical adj conforming to the rules of grammar.

gramophone n a record player, esp an old mechanical model with an acoustic horn.

granary n a building for storing grain.

grand adj most important; imposing in size, beauty, etc; distinguished; (inf) very good.

grandchild n the child of one's son or daughter.

granddaughter n the daughter of one's son or daughter.

grandfather n the father of one's father or mother.

grandiose adj having grandeur; imposing.

grandmother n the mother of one's father or mother.

grandson n the son of one's son or daughter.

grandstand n the main structure for seating spectators at a sporting event.

granite n a hard, igneous rock consisting chiefly of feldspar and quartz.

grant vt to consent to; to give or transfer by legal procedure; to admit as true. • n the act of granting; something granted, esp a gift for a particular purpose.

granule n a small grain or particle.

grape n a small round, juicy berry, growing in clusters on a vine; a dark purplish red.

grapefruit n a large, round citrus fruit.

graph n a diagram representing the successive changes in the value of a variable quantity or quantities.—also vt.

graphic adj described in realistic detail; pertaining to a graph, lettering, drawing, painting, etc.

grapple vt to seize or grip firmly. • vi to struggle hand-to-hand with; to deal or contend with.

grasp vt to grip with the hand; to understand. • vi to try to clutch, seize; (with at) to take eagerly. • n a firm grip; comprehension.

grasping adj greedy, avaricious.

grass n any of a large family of plants with jointed stems and long narrow leaves including cereals, bamboo, etc; such plants grown as lawn; pasture; (sl) marijuana; (sl) an informer.

grasshopper n a plant-eating, winged insect with powerful hind legs for jumping.

grassy adj abounding in, covered with or like grass.

grate¹ n a frame of metal bars for holding fuel in a fireplace; a fireplace; a grating.

grate² vt to grind into particles by scraping; to rub against or grind together with a harsh sound. • vi to rub or rasp noisily; to cause irritation.

grateful adj appreciative; welcome.

gratify vt to please; to indulge.

grating¹ n a open framework or lattice of bars placed across an opening.

grating² adj harsh; irritating.

gratitude n a being thankful.

gratuity n money given for a service, a tip.

grave¹ n a hole dug in the ground for burying the dead; any place of burial, a tomb.

grave² adj serious, important; harmful; solemn. • n an accent (ˋ) over a vowel.

gravel n coarse sand with small rounded stones.—also vt.

gravestone n a stone marking a grave.

graveyard n a burial-ground, cemetery.

gravitate vi to move or tend to move under the force of gravitation.

gravity n importance, esp seriousness; weight; the attraction of bodies toward the centre of the earth, the moon, or a planet.

gravy n the juice given off by meat in cooking; the sauce made from this juice.

graze¹ vi to feed on growing grass or pasture. • vt to put (animals) to feed on growing grass or pasture.

graze² vt to touch lightly in passing; to scrape, scratch. • n an abrasion, esp on the skin, caused by scraping on a surface.

grease n melted animal fat. • vt to smear or lubricate with grease.

greasy adj covered with grease; full of grease.

great adj of much more than ordinary size, extent, etc; much above the average; intense; eminent; most important; (often with at) (inf) skilful; (inf) excellent; fine.

greed n excessive desire for food or wealth.

greedy adj wanting more than one needs or deserves; having too strong a desire for food.

Greek adj of Greece, its people, or its language. • n a native of Greece; the language used by Greeks.

green adj of the colour green; unripe; inexperienced, naive; (inf) jealous. • n a colour between blue and yellow in the spectrum; the colour of growing grass; (pl) green leafy vegetables; a grassy plot, esp the end of a golf fairway.

greengrocer n a dealer in vegetables and fruit.—greengrocery n.

greenhouse n a heated building, mainly of glass, for growing plants.

greet vt to address with friendliness; to meet (a person, event, etc) in a specified way.

greeting n the act of welcoming with words or gestures; an expression of good wishes.

gregarious adj (animals) living in flocks and herds; (people) sociable, fond of company.

grenade n a small bomb thrown manually.

grey n any of a series of neutral colours ranging between black and white. • adj grey in colour; having grey-coloured hair; darkish; dreary; vague, indeterminate.

greyhound n a tall, slender dog noted for its speed and keen sight.

grid n a gridiron, a grating; an electrode for controlling the flow of electrons in an electron tube; a network of squares on a map used for easy reference; a national network of transmission lines, pipes, etc, for water, etc.

grief n extreme sorrow, deep distress.

grievance n a circumstance thought to be unjust and cause for complaint.

grieve vti to feel or cause to feel grief.

grill vt to cook by direct heat using a grill; (inf) to question relentlessly. • n a device on a cooker that radiates heat downward for grilling.

grille n an open grating forming a screen.

grim adj hard and unyielding, stern; appearing harsh, forbidding; repellent.

grimace n a contortion of the face.

grime n dirt, rubbed into a surface, as the skin. • vt to soil with grime.—grimy adj.

grin vi to smile broadly. • n a broad smile.

grind vt to reduce to powder or fragments by crushing; to wear down, sharpen, or smooth by friction; to rub (the teeth) harshly together; to oppress, tyrannise. • vi to be crushed, smoothed, or sharpened by grinding; to rotate the hips in an erotic manner.—also n.

grip n a secure grasp; the manner of holding a bat, club, racket, etc; mental grasp; mastery. • vt to take firmly and hold fast.

grisly adj terrifying; ghastly.

gristle n cartilage, esp in meat.

grit n rough particles, as of sand; stubborn courage. • vt to clench or grind together (e.g. the teeth); to spread grit on (e.g. an icy road).

groan vi to utter a deep moan.—also n.

grocer n a dealer in food.

groggy adj (inf) weak and unsteady, usu through illness, exhaustion or alcohol.

groin n the fold marking the junction of the lower abdomen and the thighs.

groom n a person employed to care for horses; a bridegroom. • vt to clean and care for (animals); to make neat and tidy; to train (a person) for a particular purpose.

groove n a long, narrow channel; a settled routine. • vt to make a groove in.

grope vi to search about blindly as in the dark; to search uncertainly for a solution to a problem. • vt to find by feeling; (sl) to fondle sexually. • n the act of groping.

gross adj fat and coarse-looking; flagrant; lacking in refinement; obscene; total, with no deductions. • n an overall total; twelve dozen. • vt to earn as total revenue.

grotesque adj distorted in appearance, shape, etc; absurdly incongruous. • n a grotesque person or thing.

grotto n a cave.

ground n the solid surface of the earth; soil; the background, as in design; the connection of an electrical conductor with the earth; (pl) a basis for belief, action, or argument; the area about and relating to a building; sediment. • vti to (cause to) run aground; to base, found, establish; to instruct in first principles of; to prevent (aircraft) from flying.

grounding n basic knowledge of a subject.

group n a number of persons or things considered as a collective unit; a small musical band. • vti to form into a group or groups.

grouse[1] n a game bird; its flesh as food.

grouse[2] vi (inf) to complain.—**grouser** n.

grove n a small wood.

grovel vi to lie and crawl in a prostrate position as a sign of respect, fear or humility.

grow vi to come into being; to be produced naturally; to develop, as a living thing; to increase in size, quantity, etc. • vt to cause or let grow; to raise, to cultivate.

growl vi to make a rumbling, menacing sound such as an angry dog makes. • vt to express in a growling manner. • n a growling noise.

growth n the act or process of growing; progressive increase, development; something that grows or has grown; an abnormal formation of tissue, as a tumour.

grub vi to dig in the ground. • vt to clear (ground) of roots; to uproot. • n the worm-like larva of a beetle; (sl) food.

grubby adj dirty.—**grubbiness** n.

grudge n a deep feeling of resentment or ill will. • vt to be reluctant to give or admit something.

gruelling adj severely testing, exhausting.

gruesome adj causing horror or loathing.

gruff adj rough or surly; hoarse.

grumble vti to mutter in discontent; to make a rumbling sound.—also n.

grumpy adj bad-tempered, peevish.

grunt vi to make a gruff sound like a pig; to speak in such a manner.—also vi.

guarantee n a pledge or security for another's debt or obligation; a pledge to something if it is substandard, etc; an assurance that something will be done as specified. • vt to give a guarantee for; to promise.

guarantor n a person who gives a guarantee.

guard vt to watch over and protect; to defend. • vi to act as a guard. • n defence; protection; a person or group that guards; a railway official.

guarded adj discreet; cautious.

guardian n a custodian; a person legally in charge of a minor or someone incapable of taking care of their own affairs.

guer(r)illa n a member of a small force of irregular soldiers.—also adj.

guess vt to form an opinion of or state with little or no factual knowledge; to judge correctly by doing this; to think or suppose. • n an estimate based on guessing.

guest n a person entertained at the home, club, etc, of another; a paying customer of a hotel.

guffaw n a crude noisy laugh.—also vi.

guidance n leadership; advice or counsel.

guide vt to point out the way for; to lead; to direct the course of; to control. • n a person who leads or directs others; a person who exhibits and explains points of interest; a book of basic instruction; (with cap) a member of the girls' organisation equivalent to the Scouts.

guided missile n a military missile whose course is controlled by radar or internal instruments, etc.

guide dog n a dog trained to guide people who are blind.

guild n a club, society; an association of people with common interests formed for mutual aid.

guile n craftiness, deceit.

guillotine n an instrument for beheading by a heavy blade descending between grooved posts; a device or machine for cutting paper.—also vt.

guilt n the fact of having done a wrong or committed an offence; a feeling of self-reproach from believing one has done wrong.

guiltless adj innocent.

guilty adj having guilt; feeling guilt.

guinea pig n a rodent-like animal commonly kept as a pet; a person or thing subject to an experiment.

guise n an external appearance, aspect.

guitar n a stringed musical instrument with a long, fretted neck, and a flat body, which is plucked with a plectrum or the fingers.

gulf n a large area of ocean reaching into land; a wide, deep chasm; a vast separation.

gull n any of numerous long-winged web-footed sea birds.

gullet n the oesophagus; the throat.

gullible adj easily deceived.

gully n a narrow trench cut by running water after rain;.

gulp vt to swallow hastily or greedily; to choke back as if swallowing. • n a gulping or swallowing; a mouthful.

gum[1] n the firm tissue surrounding the teeth.

gum[2] n a sticky substance found in certain trees and plants; an adhesive. • vt to coat or unite with gum. • vi to become sticky or clogged.

gun n a weapon with a metal tube from which a

projectile is discharged by an explosive. • *vb vi* to shoot with a gun.

gunman *n* an armed gangster; a hired killer.

gunner *n* a soldier, etc, who helps fire artillery.

gunpowder *n* an explosive powder used in guns, for blasting, etc.

gurgle *vi* (*liquid*) to make a low bubbling sound; to utter with this sound.—*also n.*

gush *vi* to issue plentifully; to talk or write effusively. • *n* a sudden outpouring.

gusset *n* a small triangular piece of cloth inserted in a garment.

gust *n* a sudden brief rush of wind; a sudden outburst. • *vi* to blow in gusts.

gusto *n* great enjoyment, zest.

gut *n* (*often pl*) the bowels or the stomach; the intestine; (*pl*) (*sl*) daring; courage. • *vt* to remove the intestines from; to destroy the interior of.

gutter *n* a channel for carrying off water, esp at a roadside; a channel or groove to direct something (as of a bowling alley); the lowest condition of human life. • *adj* marked by extreme vulgarity. • *vi* to flow in rivulets; (*candle*) to melt unevenly.

guttural *adj* formed or pronounced in the throat; harsh-sounding.

guy[1] *n* a rope, chain, etc, for fixing or steadying.

guy[2] *n* an effigy of Guy Fawkes made from old clothes stuffed with newspapers, etc, burnt on the anniversary of the Gunpowder Plot (5 November).

guzzle *vti* to gulp greedily.

gym *n* (*inf*) a gymnasium.

gymnasium *n* a room or building equipped for physical training and sports.

gymnast *n* a person skilled in gymnastics.

gymnastics *n* (*used as sing*) training in exercises devised to strengthen the body.

gynaecology *n* the branch of medicine that deals with the diseases and disorders of the female reproductive system.

gypsy *n* (*with cap*) a member of a travelling people, orig from India; a person who looks or lives like a Gypsy.

gyrate *vi* to revolve; to whirl or spiral.—**gyration** *n.*

H

haberdasher *n* a dealer in sewing accessories.

habit *n* a distinctive costume; a thing done often and hence easily; a usual way of doing things; an addiction, esp to narcotics.

habitat *n* the normal environment of an animal or plant.

habitual *adj* having the nature of a habit.

hack[1] *vt* to cut or chop (at) violently; (*comput*) to gain illegal access to confidential data. • *n* a gash or notch; a harsh, dry cough.

hack[2] *n* a riding horse for hire; an old worn-out horse; a mediocre writer.

hackles *npl* the hairs on the back that stick out when an animal is angry or afraid.

hackneyed *adj* made banal through overuse.

hacksaw *n* a fine-toothed saw.

haddock *n* an important Atlantic food fish related to the cod.

haemoglobin *n* the red colouring matter of the red blood corpuscles.

haemophilia *n* a hereditary condition in which the blood fails to clot normally.—**haemophiliac** *n, adj.*

haemorrhage *n* heavy bleeding. • *vi* to bleed heavily.

haemorrhoids *npl* swollen or bleeding veins around the anus.—*also* **piles.**

haggard *adj* looking exhausted, untidy.

haggle *vi* to bargain; barter.

hail[1] *vt* to greet; to summon by shouting or signalling, as a taxi; to acclaim. • *vi* to originate from. • *interj* an exclamation of tribute, greeting, etc. • *n* a shout to gain attention; a distance within which one can be heard calling.

hail[2] *n* frozen raindrops; something, as abuse, bullets, etc, sent forcefully in rapid succession. • *vti* to pour down like hail.

hair *n* a threadlike growth from the skin of mammals; a mass of hairs, esp on the human head; a threadlike growth on a plant.

hairdresser *n* a person who cuts, styles, colours, etc, hair.

hairpiece *n* a wig or toupee; an additional piece of hair attached to a person's real hair.

hairpin bend *n* a sharply curving bend in a road, etc.

hair-raising *adj* terrifying, shocking.

hairy *adj* covered with hair.—**hairiness** *n.*

hake *n* a marine food fish related to the cod.

half *n* either of two equal parts of something; (*inf*) a half-price ticket for a bus, etc; (*inf*) half a pint. • *adj* being a half; incomplete; partial. • *adv* to the extent of a half; (*inf*) partly.

halfback *n* (*football, hockey*) a player occupying a position between the forwards and the fullbacks; a player in this position in other sports.

half-caste n a person whose parents are of different races.

half-hearted adj with little enthusiasm, etc.

half-hour n 30 minutes.

half-time n (sport) an interval between two halves of a game.

halfway adj midway between two points.

halibut n a large marine flatfish.

hall n a public building with offices, etc; a large room for exhibits, gatherings, etc; a hallway.

hallmark n a mark used on gold, silver or platinum articles to signify a standard of purity, weight, date of manufacture.

hallucination n the apparent perception of sights, sounds, etc, that are not actually present.

halo n a circle of light; a symbolic ring of light round the head of a saint in pictures; the aura of glory surrounding an idealised person or thing.

halt[1] n a temporary interruption or cessation of progress.—also vti.

halt[2] vi to falter; to hesitate.—**halting** adj.

halve vt to divide equally into two.

ham n the upper part of a pig's hind leg, salted, smoked, etc; the meat from this area.

hamburger n ground beef; a cooked patty of such meat, often in a bread roll.

hamlet n a very small village.

hammer n a tool for pounding, driving nails, etc, having a heavy head and a handle; a thing like this in shape or use, as the part of the gun that strikes the firing pin; a heavy metal ball attached to a wire thrown in athletic contests. • vti to strike repeatedly, as with a hammer.

hamper[1] vt to hinder; to interfere with.

hamper[2] n a large, usu covered, basket for storing or transporting food, etc.

hand n the part of the arm below the wrist, used for grasping; a side or direction; a promise to marry; skill; one having a special skill; handwriting; applause; help; a hired worker; one of a ship's crew; anything like a hand, as a pointer on a clock; the breadth of a hand, four inches when measuring the height of a horse; the cards held by a player at one time; (inf) applause. • adj of, for, or controlled by the hand. • vt to give as with the hand; to help or conduct with the hand. • vi (with on) to pass to the next.

handbag n a woman's small bag for carrying personal items.

handcuff n (usu pl) either of a pair of connected steel rings for shackling the wrists of a prisoner. • vt to manacle.

handful n as much as will fill the hand; a few.

handicap n a mental or physical impairment; a contest in which difficulties are imposed or advantages given to equalise contestants' chances; such a difficulty or advantage; any hindrance. • vt to give a handicap to; to hinder.

handicraft n a skill involving the hands, such as basketwork, pottery, etc.

handkerchief n a small cloth for blowing the nose, etc.

handle vt to touch, hold, or move with the hand; to manage, deal with; to buy and sell (goods). • n a part of anything designed to be held or grasped by the hand.

handlebar n (often pl) the curved metal bar with a grip at each end used to steer a bicycle, etc.

hand-out n an item of food, clothing, etc, given free to the needy; a statement given to the press.

handsome adj good-looking; generous.

handy adj near; skilled with the hands.

hang vt to support from above, esp by a rope, chain, etc, to suspend; (wallpaper) to stick to a wall; to exhibit (works of art); to prevent (a jury) from coming to a decision; to put to execute or kill by suspending by the neck. • vi to be suspended, so as to dangle loosely; to fall or droop; (clothing, etc) to fall or flow in a certain direction; to remain in the air; to die by hanging; (with about or around) to loiter; (with back) to hesitate, be reluctant; (with out) to meet regularly at a particular place.

hangar n a shelter for aircraft.

hanger n a device on which something is hung.

hanger-on n a sycophantic follower.

hang-glider n an unpowered aircraft consisting of a metal frame over which a lightweight material is stretched, with a harness for the pilot suspended below.

hanging n the act of executing a person by suspending them by the neck; (pl) decorative draperies hung on walls. • adj undecided.

hangover n the unpleasant after-effects of excessive consumption of alcohol.

hang-up n an emotional preoccupation.

hank n a coiled bundle of wool, rope, etc.

hanker vi (with after or for) to desire.

haphazard adj not planned; random.

happen vi to take place; to occur by chance.

happening n an occurrence.

happy adj fortunate; having, pleasure or contentment.—**happiness** n.

harass vt to annoy, to irritate.

harbour n a protected inlet for anchoring ships; any place of refuge. • vt to shelter or house; (grudge, etc) to keep in the mind secretly.

hard adj firm, solid, not easily cut or punctured; difficult to comprehend; difficult to accomplish; difficult to bear; severe, unfeeling, ungenerous; indisputable, intractable; (drugs) addictive and damaging to health; (weather) severe; (currency) stable in value; (news) definite, not speculative; (drink) very alcoholic; (water) having a high mineral content that prevents lathering; (colour, sound) harsh. • adv with great effort

or intensity; earnestly, with concentration; close, near by.—hardness n.

hardboard n a stiff board made of compressed wood chips.

hard-boiled adj (eggs) boiled until solid; (inf) unfeeling.

hard cash n payment in coins and notes.

hard core n the stubborn inner group in an organisation that is resistant to change.

harden vti to make or become hard.

hard line n an aggressive, unyielding policy.

hardly adv scarcely; barely; with difficulty.

hardship n something that causes suffering.

hard shoulder n a raised strip of land alongside a motorway for vehicles to make emergency stops.

hard up adj (inf) short of money.

hardware n articles made of metal as tools, nails, etc; (comput) the mechanical and electronic components of a system.

hardy adj bold, resolute; robust; vigorous; able to withstand exposure to hardship.

hare n a timid, swift, long-eared mammal resembling but larger than the rabbit.

harelip n a congenital deformity of the upper lip in the form of a vertical fissure.

harm n hurt; damage; injury. • vt. to inflict hurt, damage, or injury upon.—harmful adj.

harmonic adj (mus) of or in harmony. • n an overtone; (pl) the science of musical sounds.

harmonica n a small wind instrument that produces tones when air is blown or sucked across metal reeds; a mouth-organ.

harmonious adj fitting together in an orderly and pleasing manner; melodious.

harmonise vi to be in harmony; to sing in harmony.

harmonium n a keyboard musical instrument whose tones are produced by thin metal reeds operated by foot bellows.

harmony n a pleasing agreement of parts in colour, size, etc; the pleasing combination of musical tones in a chord.

harness n the leather straps and metal pieces by which a horse is fastened to a vehicle, plough, etc. • vt to put a harness on; to control so as to use the power of.

harp n a stringed musical instrument played by plucking. • vi (with on or upon) to talk persistently (on some subject).—harpist n.

harpoon n a barbed spear with an attached line, for spearing whales, etc.

harpsichord n a musical instrument resembling a piano whose strings are plucked rather than struck.

harrow n a heavy frame with spikes for breaking up and levelling ploughed ground. • vt to draw a harrow over (land); to cause mental distress to.

harsh adj unpleasantly rough; jarring on the senses or feelings; rigorous; cruel.

harvest n (the season of) gathering in the ripened crops; the yield of a particular crop; the reward or product of any exertion or action. • vti to gather in (a crop).

hash n a chopped mixture of reheated cooked meat and vegetables.

hashish n resin derived from the leaves and shoots of the hemp plant, smoked or chewed as an intoxicant.

haste n quickness of motion.

hasten vt to accelerate; to cause to hurry.

hasty adj done in a hurry.—hastiness n.

hat n a covering for the head.

hatch[1] n a small door or opening (as on an aircraft or spaceship); an opening in the deck of a ship or in the floor or roof of a building; a lid for such an opening.

hatch[2] vt to produce (young) from the egg, esp by incubating; to devise (e.g. a plot). • vi to emerge from the egg; to incubate.

hatch[3] vt (drawing, engraving) to shade using closely spaced parallel lines or incisions.

hatchet n a small axe with a short handle.

hate vt to feel intense dislike for. • n a strong feeling of dislike or contempt.

hateful adj deserving or arousing hate.

hatred n intense dislike or enmity.

hat trick n (cricket) the taking of three wickets with three successive bowls; the scoring of three successive goals, etc, in any game.

haughty adj having or expressing arrogance.

haul vti to move by pulling; to transport by truck, etc. • n the act of hauling; the amount gained, caught, etc, at one time.

haulage n the transport of commodities.

haulier n a person or business that transports goods by road.

haunch n the leg and loin of a deer, sheep, etc.

haunt vt to visit continually; to recur repeatedly to. • vi to appear habitually as a ghost. • n a place often visited.

have vt to have in one's possession; to possess as an attribute; to hold in the mind; to experience; to give birth to; to allow, or tolerate; to cause, compel or require to be; to be obliged; to be pregnant with; to consume food, drink, etc; to show some quality.

haven n a harbour; a refuge.

haversack n a canvas bag worn over one shoulder.

havoc n widespread destruction.

hawk[1] n a bird of prey; a person who advocates intimidatory action.

hawk[2] vti to clear the throat (of) audibly.

hawk[3] vt to offer goods for sale.

hay n grass cut and dried for fodder.

hay fever n an allergic reaction to pollen causing irritation of the nose and eyes.

haystack, hayrick n a pile of stacked hay.

haywire adj (inf) out of order; disorganised.

hazard n risk. • vt to risk.—**hazardous** adj.

haze n a thin vapour of fog, smoke, etc.

he pron the male person or animal named before. • n a male person or animal.

head n the part of an animal or human body containing the brain, eyes, ears, nose and mouth; the top part of anything; the foremost part; the chief person; mind; understanding; the topic of a chapter, etc; crisis; the source of a river, etc; froth, as on beer. • adj at the head, top or front; chief, leading. • vt to command; to lead; to set out; to travel (in a particular direction); to strike (a ball) with the head.

headache n a continuous pain in the head.

heading n the title, topic, etc, of a chapter, etc.

headland n a promontory.

headline n printed lines at the top of a newspaper article giving the topic; a brief news summary. • vt to give featured billing or publicity to.

headlong adj with the head first; with uncontrolled speed or force; rashly.—also adv.

headmaster, headmistress n the principal of a school.

headquarters n the centre of operations of one in command, as in an army; the main office in any organisation.

headstrong adj determined to do as one pleases.

headway n forward motion; progress.

headwind n a wind blowing against the direction of a ship or aircraft.

heady adj (alcoholic drinks) intoxicating; exciting; impetuous.

heal vti to make or become healthy; to cure.

health n physical and mental wellbeing; freedom from disease, etc.

healthy adj having or producing good health.

heap n a mass or pile of jumbled things. • vt to throw in a heap; to pile high.

hear vt to perceive by the ear; to listen to; to conduct a hearing of (a law case, etc); to be informed of; to learn. • vi to be able to hear sounds.

hearing n the sense by which sound is perceived by the ear; an opportunity to be heard.

hearsay n rumour, gossip.

hearse n a vehicle for transporting a coffin.

heart n the hollow, muscular organ that circulates the blood; the central, vital or main part; the human heart as the centre of emotions; a suit of playing cards marked with the heart as a symbol in red.

heartache n sorrow or grief.

heart attack n a sudden instance of abnormal heart functioning.

heartbeat n the rhythmic contraction and dilation of the heart.

heartbreak n overwhelming sorrow or grief.—**heartbroken** adj.

heartburn n a burning sensation in the lower chest.

heartfelt adj sincere.

hearth n the floor of a fireplace.

heartily adv vigorously, enthusiastically.

heartless adj unfeeling.

hearty adj warm and friendly; unrestrained.

heat n energy produced by molecular agitation; the quality of being hot; the perception of hotness; hot weather or climate; strong feeling, esp ardour, anger, etc; a single bout, round, or trial in sports; the period of sexual excitement and readiness for mating in female animals; (sl) coercion. • vti to make or become warm or hot.

heated adj made hot; impassioned.

heater n a device that provides heat.

heath n an area of uncultivated land with scrubby vegetation.

heathen n anyone not acknowledging the God of Christian, Jewish or Muslim belief; a person regarded as irreligious, uncivilised, etc.

heather n a common evergreen shrub of northern and alpine regions with small sessile leaves and tiny usu purplish pink flowers.

heating n a system of providing heat.

heave vt to lift or move, esp with great effort; to utter (a sigh, etc) with effort; (inf) to throw. • vi to rise and fall rhythmically; to vomit; (with to) (ship) to come to a stop.

heaven n (usu pl) the visible sky; (sometimes cap) the dwelling place of God and his angels where the blessed go after death; any place of great happiness.—**heavenly** adj.

heavy adj hard to lift or carry; of more than the usual, expected, or defined weight; to an unusual extent; hard to do; stodgy, hard to digest; cloudy; (industry) using massive machinery to produce basic materials, as chemicals and steel; serious.

heavyweight n a professional boxer weighing more than 175 pounds (79 kg) or wrestler weighing over 209 pounds (95 kg).

Hebrew n a member of an ancient Semitic people; a Jew; the ancient Semitic language of the Hebrews; its modern form.—also adj.

heckle vti to harass (a speaker) with questions or taunts.—**heckler** n.

hectic adj involving intense activity.

hedge n a fence consisting of a dense line of bushes or small trees; a barrier or means of protection against something, esp financial loss; an evasive or noncommittal answer or statement. • vt to surround or enclose with a hedge. • vi to avoid giving a direct answer in an argument.

hedgehog n a small insectivorous mammal with sharp spines on the back.

heed vt to pay close attention (to). • n careful attention.—**heedful** adj.

heedless adj inattentive; thoughtless.

heel n the back part of the foot, under the ankle; the part covering or supporting the heel in stockings, socks etc, or shoes; a solid attachment forming the back of the sole of a shoe; (inf) a despicable person. • vt to furnish with a heel; to follow closely; (inf) to provide with money, etc. • vi to follow along at the heels of someone.

heifer n a young cow that has not calved.

height n the topmost point; the highest limit; the distance from the bottom to the top; altitude.

heighten vti to make or come higher.

heir n a person who inherits or is entitled to inherit another's property, title, etc.

heiress n a woman or girl who is an heir, esp to great wealth.

heirloom n any possession handed down from generation to generation.

helicopter n a kind of aircraft lifted and moved, or kept hovering, by large rotary blades mounted horizontally.

hell n (Christianity) the place of punishment of the wicked after death; any place or state of supreme misery or discomfort.

helm n the tiller or wheel used to steer a ship; a position of control, authority.

helmet n protective headgear worn by soldiers, policemen, divers, etc.

helmsman n a person who steers.

help vt to make things better or easier for; to aid; to assist; to remedy; to keep from; to serve or wait on. • n aid; assistance; a person that helps, esp a hired person.—**helper** n.

helpful adj giving help; useful.

helping n a single portion of food.

helpless adj weak and defenceless.

helter-skelter adv in confused haste. • adj disorderly. • n a tall spiral slide.

hem n the edge of a garment, etc, turned back and stitched or fixed. • vt to finish (a garment) with a hem; (with in) to enclose, confine.

hemisphere n any of the halves (northern, southern, eastern, or western) of the earth.

hemp n a widely cultivated Asian herb of the mulberry family; its fibre, used to make rope, sailcloth, etc; a narcotic drug obtained from different varieties of this plant.

hen n the female of many birds, esp the chicken.

hence adv from here; from this time.

henpeck vt to nag and domineer over (one's husband).—**henpecked** adj.

her pron the objective case of she. • adj of or belonging to her.

herald n a person who conveys news.—also vt.

heraldry n the study of genealogies and coats of arms; ceremony.—**heraldic** adj.

herb n any plant used as a medicine, seasoning, etc.

herd n a large number of animals, esp cattle, living and feeding together. • vi to assemble or move animals together. • vt to gather together and move as if a herd.

here adv at or in this place; to or into this place.

hereafter adv in some future time or state. • n (with the) the future, life after death.

hereditary adj descending by inheritance; transmitted to offspring.

heredity n the transmission of genetic material from one generation to another.

heresy n a religious belief regarded as contrary to the orthodox doctrine of a church.

heretic n a dissenter from an established belief or doctrine.—**heretical** adj.

heritage n something inherited at birth; historical sites, traditions, practices, etc, regarded as the valuable inheritance of contemporary society.

hermetic adj closed and airtight.

hermit n a person who lives in complete solitude; a recluse.

hermitage n the dwelling place of a hermit.

hernia n the protrusion of an organ, esp part of the intestine, through an opening in a cavity wall; a rupture.

hero n a person admired for superior qualities and achievements; the central male character in a novel, play, etc.

heroic adj of or like a hero; daring, risky.

heroin n a powerfully addictive drug derived from morphine.

heroine n a woman with the attributes of a hero; the leading female character in a novel, film or play.

heroism n the qualities, conduct of a hero.

heron n a slim long-necked wading bird.

herring n a small food fish.

hers pron something or someone belonging to her.

herself pron the reflexive form of she or her.

hesitant adj hesitating.—**hesitancy** n.

hesitate vi to be slow in acting due to indecision; to be reluctant (to).—**hesitation** n.

heterosexual adj sexually attracted to the opposite sex. • n a heterosexual person.

het-up adj (inf) agitated, annoyed.

hew vt to strike or cut with blows using an axe, etc.

hexagon n a polygon with six sides and six angles.

heyday n a period of greatest success.

hibernate vi to spend the winter in a dormant condition like deep sleep.—**hibernation** n.

hiccup n a sudden short stoppage of the breath producing a characteristic sound; (inf) a minor setback.—also vt.

hide¹ vt to conceal, put out of sight; to keep secret; to screen or obscure from view. • vi to conceal oneself.

hide² n the raw or dressed skin of an animal.

hideous adj visually repulsive; horrifying.

hiding n (inf) a thrashing.

hierarchy n a group of persons or things arranged in order of rank, grade, etc.

high adj lofty, tall; extending upward a (specified) distance; above others in rank, position, etc; greater in size, amount, cost, etc, than usual; raised or acute in pitch; (inf) intoxicated; (inf) under the influence of drugs. • adv in or to a high degree, rank, etc. • n a high level, place, etc; an area of high barometric pressure; (inf) a euphoric condition induced by alcohol or drugs.

highbrow n (inf) an intellectual.—also adj.

high-handed adj overbearing.

highlight n the lightest area of a painting, etc; the most interesting or important feature; (pl) a lightening of areas of the hair using a bleaching agent. • vt to bring to special attention; to give highlights to.

highly adv very much; favourably.

high-powered adj energetic; powerful.

high-rise adj (building) having multiple storeys.—also n.

highway n a public road; a main thoroughfare.

high wire n a high tightrope.

hijack vt to steal (goods in transit) by force; to force (an aircraft) to make an unscheduled flight. • n a hijacking.

hike vi to take a long walk. • vt (inf) to pull up. • n a long walk; a tramp.

hilarious adj very amusing.—**hilarity** n.

hill n a natural rise of land lower than a mountain; a slope in a road, etc.—**hilly** adj.

hilt n the handle of a sword, dagger, tool.

him pron the objective case of he.

himself pron the reflexive or emphatic form of he, him.

hind¹ adj situated at the back; rear.

hind² n a female deer.

hinder vt to prevent the progress of.

hindrance n an obstacle, impediment.

hinge n a joint on which a door, lid, etc, turns; a natural joint, as of a clam; a small piece of gummed paper for sticking stamps in an album. • vti to depend.

hint n an indirect or subtle suggestion; a slight mention; a little piece of practical or helpful advice. • vt to suggest or indicate indirectly. • vi to give a hint.

hinterland n the land behind that bordering a coast or river; a remote area.

hip¹ n either side of the body below the waist and above the thigh.

hip² n the fruit of the wild rose.

hip³ adj (sl) stylish, up-to-date.

hippopotamus n a large mammal with thick dark skin, short legs, and a very large head.

hire vt to pay for the services of (a person) or the use of (a thing). • n the payment for the temporary use of anything.

hire-purchase n a system by which a person takes possession of an article after paying a deposit and becomes the owner after payment of instalments is completed.

his poss pron of or belonging to him.—also adj.

hiss vi to make a sound resembling a prolonged s; to show disapproval by hissing. • vt to say or indicate by hissing.—also n.

historian n a person who writes history.

historic adj important or famous in history.

historical adj belonging to or involving history or historical methods; concerning actual events as opposed to myth or legend.

history n a record or account of past events; the study and analysis of past events; past events in total; the past events or experiences of a specific person or thing; an unusual or significant past.

hit vti to come against (something) with force; to give a blow (to), to strike; (with on) to discover by accident or unexpectedly. • n a blow that strikes its mark; a collision; a successful and popular song, book, etc; (inf) an underworld killing; (sl) a dose of a drug.

hitch vt to move, pull, etc, with jerks; to fasten with a hook, knot, etc; to obtain a ride by hitchhiking. • vi to hitchhike. • n a tug; a hindrance, obstruction; a kind of knot used for temporary fastening.

hitchhike vt to travel by asking for free lifts from motorists along the way.

hive n a shelter for a colony of bees; a beehive. • vi to enter a hive; (with off) to separate from a group.

hoard n an accumulation of food, money, etc, stored away for future use. • vti to accumulate and store away.

hoarding n a temporary screen of boards erected around a construction site; a large board used for advertising.

hoarse adj (voice) rough, as from a cold.

hoax n a deception; a practical joke.—also vt.

hob n a flat surface on a cooker incorporating hot plates or burners.

hobble vi to walk unsteadily, to limp.

hobby n a spare-time activity carried out for personal amusement.

hock¹ vt (sl) to give as security for a loan.

hock² n the joint bending backward on the hind leg of a horse, etc.

hockey n an outdoor game played by two teams of 11 players with a ball and clubs curved at one end; ice hockey.

hoe n a long-handled tool for weeding, etc.

hog n a castrated male pig raised for its meat; (inf) a selfish, greedy, or filthy person. • vt to take more than one's due; to hoard greedily.

hoist vt to raise aloft, esp with a crane, etc. • n a hoisting; an apparatus for lifting.

hold[1] vt to take and keep in one's possession; to grasp; to maintain in a certain position or condition; to contain; to remain firm; to carry on, as a meeting; to believe, to consider; to bear or carry oneself; (with back) to withhold; to restrain; (with down) to restrain; (inf) to manage to retain one's job, etc; (with forth) to offer (e.g. an inducement); (with off) to keep apart; (with up) to delay; to hinder; to commit an armed robbery. • vi to remain unbroken or unyielding; to be valid; (with back) to refrain; (with forth) to speak at length; (with off) to wait, to refrain; (with on) to maintain a grip on; (inf) to keep a telephone line open. • n grip; a dominating force on a person.

hold[2] n the storage space in a ship or aircraft used for cargo.

holding n (often pl) property, esp land, stocks and bonds.

hole n a hollow place; a cavity; a pit; an animal's burrow; an aperture; a perforation; a small, squalid, dingy place; (inf) a difficult situation; (golf) a small cavity into which the ball is hit; the tee, the fairway, etc, leading to this. • vti to make a hole in (something); to drive into a hole; (with up) to hibernate; (inf) to hide oneself.

holiday n a period away from work, school, etc, for travel, rest or recreation; a day of freedom from work. • vi to spend a holiday.

holiness n sanctity; (with cap) the pope.

holism n (philos) the belief that wholes are greater than the sum of the parts; (med) consideration of the whole body in the treatment of disease.—**holistic** adj.

hollow adj having a cavity within or below; recessed, concave; empty or worthless. • n a hole, cavity; a depression, a valley. • vti to make or become hollow.

holly n an evergreen shrub with prickly leaves and red berries.

holocaust n a great destruction of life, esp by fire; (with cap and the) the mass extermination of European Jews by the Nazis.

hologram n an image made without the use of a lens on photographic film by means of interference between two parts of a laser beam, the result appearing as a meaningless pattern until suitably illuminated, when it shows as a three-dimensional image.

holster n a leather case attached to a belt for a pistol.

holy adj dedicated to religious use; without sin.

Holy Ghost n the Holy Spirit.

Holy Spirit n the Third of the Trinity.

homage n a public demonstration of respect.

home n the place where one lives; the city, etc, where one was born or reared; a place thought of as home; a household and its affairs; an institution for the aged, orphans, etc. • adj of one's home or country; domestic. • adv at, to, or in the direction of home; to the point aimed at. • vi (birds) to return home; to be guided onto a target; to head for a destination.

home economics n (sing or pl) the art of household management, nutrition, etc.

home help n a person employed by the local authorities to help the aged, etc, with domestic chores.

homely adj simple; crude; not good-looking.

homeopathy see homoeopathy.

homesick adj longing for home.

homeward adj going towards home.

homework n schoolwork to be done outside the classroom.

homicide n the killing of a person by another; a person who kills another.

homoeopathy n the system of treating disease by small quantities of drugs that cause symptoms similar to those of the disease.—also **homeopathy**. —**homoeopathic** adj.

homogeneous adj composed of parts that are of identical or a similar kind or nature.

homosexual adj sexually attracted towards a person of the same sex. • n a homosexual person.—**homosexuality** n.

honest adj truthful; trustworthy; sincere or genuine; gained by fair means; frank, open.

honesty n the quality of being honest; a plant that forms transparent seed pods.

honey n a sweet sticky yellowish substance that bees make as food from the nectar of flowers.

honeycomb n the structure of six-sided wax cells made by bees to hold their honey, eggs, etc.

honeymoon n the vacation spent together by a newly married couple.—also vi.

honk n (a sound resembling) the call of the wild goose; the sound made by an old-fashioned motor horn.—also vti.

honorary adj given as an honour.

honour n high regard or respect; glory; fame; good reputation; integrity; chastity; high rank; distinction; (with cap) the title of certain officials, as judges. • vt to respect greatly; to do or give something in honour of; to accept and pay (a cheque when due, etc).

honourable adj worthy of being honoured; honest; upright; bringing honour; (with cap) a title of respect for certain officials, as Members of Parliament, when addressing each other.

hood *n* a loose covering to protect the head and back of the neck; any hood-like thing as the (folding) top of a car, etc; a car bonnet.

hoodwink *vt* to mislead by trickery.

hoof *n* the horny covering on the ends of the feet of certain animals, as horses, cows, etc.

hook *n* a piece of bent or curved metal to catch or hold anything; a strike, blow, etc, in which a curving motion is involved. • *vt* to seize, fasten, hold, as with a hook; (*rugby*) to pass the ball backwards from a scrum.

hooligan *n* a lawless young person.

hoop *n* a circular band of metal or wood; an iron band for holding together the staves of barrels; anything like this, as a child's toy.

hoot *n* the sound that an owl makes; a similar sound, as made by a train whistle; a shout of scorn; (*inf*) an amusing person or thing. • *vi* to utter a hoot; to blow a whistle, etc.

hop[1] *vi* to jump up on one leg; to leap with all feet at once, as a frog, etc. • *n* a hopping movement; (*inf*) an informal dance.

hop[2] *n* a climbing plant with small cone-shaped flowers; (*pl*) the dried ripe cones, used for flavouring beer.

hope *n* a feeling that what is wanted will happen; the object of this; a person or thing on which one may base some hope. • *vt* to want and expect. • *vi* to have hope (for).

hopeful *adj* filled with hope; inspiring hope. • *n* a person who looks likely to be a success.

hopeless *adj* without hope; offering no grounds for hope or promise of success; impossible to solve; (*inf*) incompetent.

horde *n* a crowd or throng; a swarm.

horizon *n* the apparent line along which the earth and sky meet; the limit of a person's knowledge, interest, etc.

horizontal *adj* level; parallel to the plane of the horizon.

hormone *n* a product of living cells formed in one part of the organism and carried to another part, where it takes effect; a synthetic compound having the same purpose.—**hormonal** *adj*.

horn *n* a bony outgrowth on the head of certain animals; the hard substance of which this is made; a wind instrument, esp the French horn or trumpet; a device to sound a warning.

hornet *n* a large wasp with a severe sting.

horoscope *n* a chart of the zodiacal signs and positions of planets, etc, by which astrologers profess to predict future events.

horrendous *adj* horrific.

horrible *adj* (*inf*) very bad, unpleasant, etc.

horrid *adj* terrible; horrible.

horrify *vt* to fill with horror.

horror *n* the strong feeling caused by something frightful or shocking; strong dislike.

horse *n* four-legged, hoofed herbivorous mammal with a flowing mane and a tail; cavalry; a vaulting horse.

horsepower *n* a unit for measuring the power of engines, etc, equal to 746 watts or 33,000 foot-pounds per minute.

horseradish *n* a tall herb of the mustard family; a sauce or relish made with its pungent root.

horseshoe *n* a U-shaped metal plate nailed to a horse's hoof; anything shaped like this.

horticulture *n* the art of growing flowers, fruits, vegetables.—**horticultural** *adj*.

hose[1] *n* a flexible tube used to convey fluids.

hose[2] *n* stockings, socks, tights, etc.

hospitable *adj* offering a generous welcome to guests or strangers; sociable.

hospital *n* an institution where the sick or injured are given medical treatment.

hospitality *n* the quality of being hospitable.

host[1] *n* a person who receives or entertains a stranger or guest at his house; an animal or plant on or in which another lives; a compere on a television or radio programme. • *vti* to act as a host (to a party, television programme, etc).

host[2] *n* a very large number of people or things.

host[3] *n* the wafer of bread used in the Eucharist or Holy Communion.

hostage *n* a person given or kept as security until certain conditions are met.

hostel *n* a lodging place for the homeless, travellers, or other groups.

hostess *n* a woman acting as a host.

hostile *adj* of or being an enemy; unfriendly.

hostility *n* enmity, antagonism; (*pl*) deliberate acts of warfare.

hot *adj* of high temperature; very warm; causing a burning sensation on the tongue; following closely; (*inf*) recent, new; (*inf*) radioactive; (*inf*) stolen.

hotel *n* a commercial establishment providing lodging and meals for travellers, etc.

hotelier *n* the owner or manager of a hotel.

hothead *n* an impetuous person.

hothouse *n* a greenhouse for raising plants; an environment that encourages rapid growth.

hotplate *n* a heated surface for cooking or keeping food warm.

hound *n* a dog used in hunting. • *vt* to urge on by harassment.

hour *n* a period of 60 minutes, a 24th part of a day; the time for a specific activity; the time; (*pl*) the customary period for work, etc.—**hourly** *adj*, *adv*.

house *n* a building to live in, esp by one person or family; a household; a family or dynasty including relatives, ancestors and descendants; the audience in a theatre; a legislative assembly. • vt to provide accommodation for; to cover, encase.

house arrest n detention in one's own house, as opposed to prison.

housebreaker n a person who forces his way into a house to steal.

household n all those people living together in the same house. • adj pertaining to running a house and family.

householder n a person who runs a home.

housekeeper n a person who runs a home.

housekeeping n the daily running of a household; (inf) money used for domestic expenses.

housewife n the woman who keeps house.

housework n the cooking, cleaning, etc, involved in running a home.

housing n houses collectively; the provision of accommodation; a casing enclosing a piece of machinery, etc; a slot or groove in a piece of wood, etc, to receive an insertion.

hovel n a small miserable dwelling.

hover vi (bird, etc) to hang in the air stationary; to hang about, to linger.

hovercraft n a land or water vehicle that travels supported on a cushion of air.

how adv in what way or manner; by what means; to what extent; in what condition.

howl vi to utter the wailing cry of wolves, dogs, etc; to utter a similar cry of anger, pain, etc; to shout or laugh in pain, amusement, etc. • n the wailing cry of a wolf, dog, etc; any similar sound.

howler n (inf) a stupid mistake.

hub n the centre part of a wheel; a centre of activity.

huddle vti to crowd together in a confined space; to curl (oneself) up. • n a confused crowd.

hue n colour; a particular shade of a colour.

huff n a state of smouldering resentment.

hug vt to hold tightly with the arms; to keep close to. • vi to embrace one another. • n a strong embrace.

huge adj very large, enormous.

hulk n the body of a ship, esp if old and dismantled; a large, clumsy person or thing.

hulking adj unwieldy, bulky.

hull n the outer covering of a fruit or seed; the framework of a ship. • vt to remove the hulls of.

hum vi to make a low continuous vibrating sound; (inf) to be lively; (sl) to stink. • vt to sing with closed lips. • n a humming sound.

human adj of or relating to people; having the qualities of people as opposed to animals; kind.

humane adj kind, compassionate, merciful.

humanity n the human race; the state or quality of being human or humane; (pl) the study of literature and the arts, as opposed to the sciences.

humble adj having a low estimation of one's abilities; unpretentious; servile. • vt to lower in condition or rank; to humiliate.

humbug n fraud, sham, hoax; an insincere person; a peppermint-flavoured sweet.

humdrum adj dull, ordinary, boring.

humid adj (air) moist, damp.

humidity n dampness in the air.

humiliate vt to cause to feel humble; to lower the pride or dignity of.

humility n the state of being humble.

humorist n a person who writes or speaks in a humorous manner.

humorous adj amusing; causing laughter.

humour n the ability to appreciate or express what is funny, amusing, etc; the expression of this; temperament, disposition; state of mind; (formerly) any of the four fluids of the body (blood, phlegm, yellow and black bile) that were thought to determine temperament. • vt to indulge; to gratify by conforming to the wishes of.

hump n a rounded protuberance; a fleshy lump on the back of an animal (as a camel or whale); a deformity causing curvature of the spine. • vt to hunch; to arch.

hunch n a hump; (inf) an intuitive feeling.

hunchback n a person with curvature of the spine.

hundred adj, n ten times ten; the symbol for this(100, C, c); the hundredth in a series.

hundredweight n a unit of weight, equal to 112 pounds.

hunger n (a feeling weak from) a need for food; a strong desire. • vi to have a strong desire (for).

hungry adj desiring food; greedy.

hunt vti to seek out to kill or capture (game) for food or sport; to search (for); to chase. • n a chase; a search; a party for hunting.

hunter n a person who hunts.

hunting n the practice of one who hunts; a pursuit; a search.

hurdle n a frame of bars for jumping over an obstacle; (pl) a race over hurdles.

hurl vt to throw violently.

hurricane n a violent tropical cyclone with winds of at least 74 miles per hour.

hurried adj performed with great haste.

hurry n rush; urgency. • vt to cause to move or happen more quickly. • vi to move or act with haste.

hurt vt to cause physical pain to; to offend. • vi to feel pain; to cause pain.—**hurtful** adj.

hurtle vti to move or throw with great force.

husband n a man to whom a woman is married. • vt to conserve; to manage economically.

hush vti to make or become silent. • n a silence.

husk n the dry covering of certain fruits and seeds; any dry, rough, or useless covering.

husky[1] adj (voice) hoarse; hefty, strong.

husky[2] n an Arctic sled dog.

hustle vt to jostle or push roughly or hurriedly; (sl) to obtain by rough or illegal means.

hut n a plain little house or cabin.

hutch n a pen or coop for small animals.

hyacinth n a plant of the lily family with spikes of bell-shaped flowers.

hybrid n the offspring of two plants or animals of different species; a mongrel. • adj crossbred.

hydrant n a large pipe with a valve for drawing water from a water main.

hydraulic adj operated by water or other liquid, esp by moving through pipes under pressure; of hydraulics.

hydraulics npl (used as sing) the science dealing with the mechanical properties of liquids.

hydroelectricity n electricity generated by water power.—**hydroelectric** adj.

hydrogen n a flammable, colourless, odourless, tasteless, gaseous chemical element, the lightest substance known.

hyena n a nocturnal, carnivorous, scavenging mammal like a wolf.

hygiene n the principles and practice of health and cleanliness.—**hygienic** adj.

hymn n a song of praise to God or other object of worship.

hyphen n a punctuation mark (-) used to join two syllables or words, or to divide words into parts. • vt to hyphenate.

hypnosis n a relaxed state resembling sleep in which the mind responds to external suggestion.

hypnotise vt to put in a state of hypnosis.

hypnotism n the act of inducing hypnosis; its study and use.—**hypnotist** n.

hypocrisy n a falsely pretending to possess virtues, beliefs, etc.—**hypocrite** n.

hypothesis n something assumed for the purpose of argument; a theory to explain some fact that may or may not prove to be true.—**hypothetical** adj.

hysteria n a mental disorder marked by excitability, anxiety, imaginary organic disorders, etc; frenzied emotion or excitement.

hysteric n (pl) fits of hysteria.

hysterical adj suffering from hysteria; (inf) extremely funny.

I

I pron the person who is speaking or writing, used in referring to himself or herself.

ice n water frozen solid; a sheet of this; a portion of ice cream or water ice. • vti (often with up or over) to freeze; to cover with icing.

iceberg n a great mass of mostly submerged ice floating in the sea.

icebox n a compartment in a refrigerator for making and storing ice.

ice cream adj a sweet frozen food, made from flavoured milk or cream.

ice hockey n a hockey game played on ice by two teams of six skaters with curved sticks and a flat disk called a puck.

icicle n a hanging tapering length of ice.

icing n a semi-solid sugary mixture used to cover cakes, etc.

icon n an image; (Eastern Church) a sacred image, usu on a wooden panel.

icy adj covered with ice; cold in manner.

idea n a mental impression of anything; a vague impression, notion; an opinion or belief.

ideal adj existing in the mind or as an idea; satisfying an ideal, perfect. • n the most perfect conception of anything; a person or thing regarded as perfect; a standard for attainment; an aim or principle.

identical adj exactly the same.

identify vt to establish the identity of; to associ-ate closely; to regard (oneself) as similar to another.—**identification** n.

identity n the distinguishing characteristics of a person.

ideology n the doctrines, beliefs or opinions of an individual, social class, political party, etc.—**ideological** adj.

idiocy n mental deficiency; stupidity.

idiom n an accepted phrase with a different meaning from the literal; the usual way in which the words of a language are used to express thought; the dialect of a people, region, etc; the characteristic style of a school of art, literature, etc—**idiomatic** adj.

idiosyncrasy n a type of behaviour or characteristic peculiar to a person or group; a quirk, eccentricity.—**idiosyncratic** adj.

idiot n a severely mentally retarded adult; (inf) a foolish or stupid person.—**idiotic** adj.

idle adj not employed, unoccupied; not in use; averse to work; useless; worthless. • vt to waste, spend (time) in idleness. • vi to move slowly or aimlessly; (engine) to operate without transmitting power.—**idleness** n.

idol n an image or object worshipped as a god; a person who is intensely loved, admired or honoured.

idolise vt to make an idol of, for worship; to love to excess.—**idolisation** n.

If *conj* on condition that; in the event that; supposing that; even though; whenever; whether.

Igloo *n* an Eskimo house built of blocks of snow.

Ignite *vti* to set fire to; to catch fire; to burn.

Ignition *n* an act or instance of igniting; the mechanism that ignites an internal combustion engine.

Ignorant *adj* lacking knowledge; uninformed, uneducated; resulting from, showing lack of knowledge.—**Ignorance** *n*.

Ignore *vt* to disregard; to deliberately refuse to notice someone.

Ill *adj* not in good health. • *adv* badly, wrongly. • *n* trouble; harm; evil.

Illegal *adj* against the law.

Illegible *adj* impossible to read.

Illegitimate *adj* born of parents not married to each other; contrary to law, rules, or logic.

Illicit *adj* improper; unlawful.

Illiterate *adj* uneducated, esp not knowing how to read or write. • *n* an illiterate person.

Ill-natured *adj* spiteful.

Illness *n* a state of ill-health; sickness.

Illogical *adj* not logical or reasonable.

Ill-treat *vt* to treat unkindly, unfairly, etc.

Illuminate *vt* to light up; to make clear; to decorate as with gold or lights.—**Illumination** *n*.

Illusion *n* a false idea; an unreal image.

Illusory *adj* deceptive; based on illusion.

Illustrate *vt* to explain, as by examples; to provide (books, etc) with explanatory pictures.

Illustration *n* an example that explains or corroborates; a picture or diagram in a book, etc.

Illustrious *adj* distinguished, famous.

Ill-will *n* antagonism, hostility.

Image *n* a representation of a person or thing; the visual impression of something in a lens, mirror, etc; a copy; a likeness; a mental picture; the concept of a person, product, etc, held by the public at large.

Imagery *n* the work of the imagination; mental pictures; figures of speech; images in general.

Imaginary *adj* existing only in the imagination.

Imagination *n* the image-forming power of the mind, or the power of the mind that modifies the conceptions, esp the higher form of this power exercised in art and poetry; creative ability; resourcefulness in overcoming practical difficulties, etc.

Imaginative *adj* having or showing imagination; produced by imagination.

Imagine *vt* to form a mental image of; to believe falsely; (*inf*) to suppose; to guess.

Imbalance *n* a lack of balance, as in proportion.

Imbecile *n* an adult with a mental age of a three-to eight-year-old child. • *adj* stupid.

Imitate *vt* to try to follow as a pattern or model; to mimic humorously, impersonate; to copy.

Imitation *n* an act or instance of imitating; a copy; an act of impersonation.

Immaculate *adj* flawless; morally unblemished.

Immaterial *adj* spiritual as opposed to physical; unimportant.

Immature *adj* not mature.

Immediate *adj* acting or occurring without delay; next in relationship; in close proximity, near to; directly concerning a person or thing.—**Immediacy** *n*.

Immediately *adv* without delay; directly; near, close by. • *conj* as soon as.

Immense *adj* very large; (*inf*) excellent.

Immerse *vt* to plunge into a liquid; to absorb or engross; to baptise by total submergence.

Immigrant *n* a person settled in a country but not born there.

Immigrate *vi* to come into a new country, esp to settle permanently.—**Immigration** *n*.

Imminent *adj* about to happen; impending.

Immobile *adj* not moving, unable to move.

Immoral *adj* against accepted standards of proper behaviour; sexually degenerate; corrupt.

Immortal *adj* living for ever; enduring; having lasting fame. • *n* an immortal being or person.

Immortalise *vt* to render immortal; to bestow lasting fame upon.

Immune *adj* not susceptible to a specified disease through inoculation or natural resistance; exempt from a certain obligation.

Immunise *vt* to make immune, esp against infection.—**Immunisation** *n*.

Impact *n* violent contact; a shocking effect; the force of bodies colliding.—*also vti.*

Impair *vt* to make worse, less, etc.

Impale *vt* to pierce through, with something pointed.

Impartial *adj* not favouring one side more than another, unbiased.

Impassable *adj* (*roads, etc*) incapable of being travelled through or over.

Impatient *adj* lacking patience; intolerant of delay, etc; restless.—**Impatience** *n*.

Impeach *vt* to question a person's honesty; to try (a public official) on a charge of wrongdoing.—**Impeachment** *n*.

Impeccable *adj* without defect; faultless.

Impede *vt* to obstruct or hinder progress.

Impediment *n* something that impedes; an obstruction; a physical defect, as a stammer that prevents fluency of speech.

Impend *vi* to be imminent; to threaten.

Imperative *adj* urgent, pressing; obligatory; designating or of the mood of a verb that expresses a command, entreaty, etc. • *n* a command; (*gram*) the imperative mood of a verb.

Imperceptible *adj* not able to be detected by the mind or senses; slight, minute, gradual.

Imperfect *adj* having faults, flaws, etc; defective; incomplete; (*gram*) designating a verb tense that indicates a past action or state as incomplete or continuous. • (*gram*) an imperfect tense.

Imperfection *n* the state or quality of being imperfect; a defect, fault.

Imperial *adj* of an empire, emperor, or empress; majestic; of the British non-metric system of weights and measures.

Impersonal *adj* not referring to any particular person; cold, unfeeling; not existing as a person; (*verb*) occurring only in the third person singular, usu with 'it' as subject.

Impersonate *vt* to assume the role of another person.—**Impersonation** *n*.

Impertinent *adj* impudent; insolent; irrelevant.—**Impertinence** *n*.

Impervious *adj* incapable of being penetrated, as by water; not readily receptive (to).

Impetuous *adj* acting or done suddenly.

Impetus *n* the force with which a body moves against resistance; driving force.

Impinge *vi* (*with* on, upon) to have an impact.

Implement *n* something used in a given activity. • *vt* to carry out.—**Implementation** *n*.

Implicate *vt* to show to have a part, esp in a crime; to imply.

Implication *n* an implicating or being implicated; that which is implied; an inference not expressed but understood; deduction.

Implicit *adj* implied rather than stated explicitly; unquestioning, absolute.

Implore *vt* to request earnestly; to plead.

Imply *vt* to hint, suggest indirectly; to indicate or involve as a consequence.

Impolite *adj* not polite, rude.

Import *vt* to bring (goods) in from a foreign country for sale or use; to mean; to signify. • *vi* to be of importance, to matter. • *n* something imported; meaning; importance.—**Importer** *n*.

Important *adj* having great significance or consequence.—**Importance** *n*.

Impose *vt* to put (a burden, tax, punishment) on or upon; to force (oneself) on others; to lay pages of type or film and secure them.

Imposing *adj* impressive because of size, appearance, dignity, etc.

Impossible *adj* not capable of existing, being done, or happening; (*inf*) unendurable, outrageous.—**Impossibility** *n*.

Impostor, imposter *n* a person who acts fraudulently by impersonating another.

Impotent *adj* lacking in necessary strength, powerless; (*man*) unable to engage in sexual intercourse.—**Impotence** *n*.

Impound *vt* to take legal possession of; to shut up (an animal) in a pound.

Impoverish *vt* to make poor; to deprive of strength.—**Impoverishment** *n*.

Impracticable *adj* not able to be carried out.

Impractical *adj* not practical; not competent in practical skills.

Imprecise *adj* not precise; ill-defined.

Impregnable *adj* secure against attack.

Impregnate *vt* to cause to become pregnant, to fertilise; to soak (with); to pervade.

Impresario *n* the manager of an opera, a concert series, etc.

Impress *vt* to make a strong, usu favourable, impression on; to fix deeply in the mind; to stamp with a mark; to imprint. • *n* an imprint.

Impression *n* the effect produced in the mind by an experience; a mark produced by imprinting; a vague idea, notion; the act of impressing or being impressed; a notable or strong influence on the mind or senses; the number of copies of a book printed at one go; an impersonation or act of mimicry.

Impressionable *n* easily impressed.

Impressive *adj* arousing wonder.

Imprison *vt* to put in a prison.—**Imprisonment** *n*.

Improbable *adj* unlikely to be true.

Impromptu *adj, adv* unrehearsed, unprepared.

Improper *adj* indecent; incorrect.

Impropriety *n* indecency; an improper act.

Improve *vt* to make or become better.

Improvement *n* the act of improving; an alteration that improves something.

Improvise *vti* to compose, perform, recite, etc, without preparation; to make or do with whatever is at hand.—**Improvisation** *n*.

Impudent *adj* disrespectfully bold; impertinent.—**Impudence** *n*.

Impulse *n* a sudden push or thrust; a stimulus transmitted through a nerve or a muscle; a sudden instinctive urge to act.

Impulsive *adj* tending to act on impulse; forceful, impelling; acting momentarily.

Impunity *n* exemption from punishment or harm.

Impure *adj* unclean; adulterated.

Impurity *n* a being impure; an impure substance.

In *prep* inside; within; at; as contained by; during; at the end of; not beyond; affected by; being a member of; wearing; using; because of; into. • *adv* to or at a certain place; so as to be contained by a certain space, condition, etc; (*games*) batting, in play. • *adj* that is in power; inner; inside; gathered, counted, etc; (*inf*) currently smart, fashionable, etc.

Inability *n* lack of ability.

Inaccessible *adj* unapproachable.

Inaccurate *adj* not accurate, imprecise.

Inactive *adj* not active.

Inadequate *adj* not adequate; not capable.

Inadmissible *adj* not admissible, esp as evidence.

Inadvertent *adj* not attentive or observant.

Inadvisable *adj* not advisable; inexpedient.

Inane *adj* lacking sense, silly.

Inanimate *adj* showing no signs of life; dull.

Inappropriate *adj* unsuitable.

Inarticulate *adj* not expressed in words; incapable of being expressed in words; incapable of coherent expression of ideas, feelings, etc.

Inasmuch *adv* (with **as**) seeing that; because.

Inattentive *adj* not attending; neglectful.

Inaudible *adj* unable to be heard.

Inaugural *n* of or pertaining to an inauguration; a speech made at an inauguration.

Inaugurate *vt* to admit ceremonially into office; to open (a building, etc) formally to the public; to initiate.—**Inauguration** *n*.

Inborn *adj* present from birth; hereditary.

Inbreed *vti* to breed by continual mating of individuals of the same stocks.

Incapable *adj* lacking capability; not able or fit to perform an activity.

Incapacitate *vt* to weaken, to disable.

Incarnate *adj* endowed with a human body; personified. • *vt* to give bodily form to; to be the type or embodiment of.

Incendiary *adj* pertaining to arson; (*bomb*) designed to start fires; tending to stir up or inflame. • *n* an arsonist; an incendiary substance.

Incense[1] *vt* to make extremely angry.

Incense[2] *n* a substance that gives off a fragrant odour when burned; the fumes so produced; any pleasant odour.

Incessant *adj* never ceasing; continual.

Inch *n* a measure of length equal to $\frac{1}{12}$ foot (2.54 cm). • *vti* to move very slowly, or by degrees.

Incidence *n* the degree or range of occurrence.

Incidental *adj* happening in connection with something more important; happening by chance. • *npl* miscellaneous items, minor expenses.

Incidentally *adv* in passing, as an aside.

Incinerator *n* a furnace for burning rubbish.

Incipient *adj* beginning to be or appear.

Incision *n* a cut made into something, esp by a surgeon into a body.

Incisive *adj* penetrating; decisive; biting.

Incite *vt* to urge to action; to rouse.

Inclination *n* a propensity or disposition, esp a liking; a deviation from the horizontal or vertical; a slope; inclining or being inclined; a bending movement, a bow.

Incline *vi* to lean, to slope; to be disposed towards an opinion or action. • *vt* to cause to bend (the head or body) forwards; to cause to deviate, esp from the horizontal or vertical. • *n* a slope.

Include *vt* to contain; to comprise as part or a larger group, amount, etc.—**Inclusion** *n*.

Inclusive *adj* comprehensive; including the limits specified.

Incognito *adj, adv* under an assumed name or identity.

Incoherent *adj* inarticulate in speech or thought.

Income *n* the money, etc, received for labour or services or from investments, etc.

Income tax *n* a tax levied on the net income of a person or business.

Incoming *adj* coming; accruing. • *n* the act of coming in; that which comes in; income.

Incompatible *adj* not able to exist together in harmony; antagonistic; inconsistent.

Incompetent *adj* lacking the necessary ability, skill, etc.—**Incompetence** *n*.

Incomplete *adj* unfinished; lacking a part.

Incomprehensible *adj* not to be understood or grasped by the mind; inconceivable.

Inconclusive *adj* leading to no definite result.

Incongruous *adj* lacking harmony of parts; unsuitable; inappropriate.—**Incongruity** *n*.

Inconsequential *adj* irrelevant.

Inconsiderate *adj* uncaring about others.

Inconsistent *adj* not compatible with other facts; contradictory; irregular, fickle.

Inconspicuous *adj* not conspicuous.

Inconstant *adj* subject to change; unstable; variable; fickle; capricious.—**Inconstancy** *n*.

Incontinent *adj* unable to control the excretion of bodily wastes.—**Incontinence** *n*.

Inconvenience *n* unfitness; disadvantage. • *vt* to put to inconvenience; to annoy.—**Inconvenient** *adj*.

Incorrect *adj* faulty; inaccurate; improper.

Incorruptible *adj* incapable of physical corruption, decay or dissolution; incapable of being bribed; not liable to moral perversion.

Increase *vti* to make or become greater in size, quality, amount, etc. • *n* increasing or becoming increased; the amount by which something increases.—**Increasingly** *adv*.

Incredible *adj* unbelievable; (*inf*) wonderful.

Incredulous *adj* not willing to accept as true; unbelieving.

Increment *n* (the amount of) an increase.

Incriminate *vt* to involve in or indicate as involved in a crime or fault.

Incubator *n* an apparatus in which eggs are hatched by artificial heat; an apparatus for nurturing premature babies until they can survive unaided.

Incur *vt* to bring upon oneself.

Incurable *adj* incapable of being cured; beyond the power of skill or medicine; lacking remedy; incorrigible. • *n* a person diseased beyond cure.

Incursion n an invasion or raid into another's territory, etc.

indebted adj in debt; owing gratitude.

indecent adj offending against accepted standards of decent behaviour.—**indecency** n.

indecision n hesitation.—**indecisive** adj.

indeed adv truly, certainly.

indefinable adj that cannot be defined.

indefinite adj not certain, undecided; imprecise, vague; having no fixed limits.

indelible adj not able to be removed or erased.

indemnify vt to insure against loss, damage, etc; to repay (for damage, loss, etc).

indentation n a being indented; a notch, cut, inlet, etc; a dent; a spacing in from the margin.

independent adj freedom from the influence or control of others; self-governing; self-determined; not adhering to any political party; not depending on another for financial support. • n a person who is independent in thinking, action etc.—**Independence** n.

indescribable adj unable to be described; too beautiful, horrible, etc, for words.

index n an alphabetical list of names, subjects, items, etc, mentioned in a printed book, usu listed alphabetically at the end of the text; a figure showing ratio or relative change, as of prices or wages; any indication or sign; a pointer or dial on an instrument; the exponent of a number. • vt to make an index of or for.

index finger n the forefinger.

index-linked adj (pension, etc) linked directly to changes in the cost-of-living index.

Indian n a native of India.

indicate vt to point out; to show or demonstrate; to state briefly, suggest.—**indication** n.

indicative adj serving as a sign (of); (gram) denoting the verb mood that affirms or denies.

indicator n a thing that indicates or points; a measuring device with a pointer, etc; a device giving updated information, such as a departure board in a railway station or airport; a flashing light used to warn of a change in direction of a vehicle.

indict vt to charge with a crime; to accuse.

indictment n a written statement framed by a prosecuting authority charging a person of a crime.

indifferent adj uninterested; average; mediocre.—**indifference** n.

indigenous adj existing naturally in a particular country or environment; native.

indigestible adj difficult, impossible to digest.

indigestion n a pain caused by difficulty in digesting food.

indignant adj expressing anger, esp at mean or unjust action.

indignation n anger at something regarded as unfair, wicked, etc.

indignity n humiliation; treatment making one feel degraded, undignified.

indirect adj not straight; roundabout; secondary; dishonest.—**indirectly** adv.

indiscreet adj not discreet; tactless.

indiscretion n an indiscreet act; rashness.

indiscriminate adj making no distinctions.

indispensable adj absolutely essential.

indisposed adj ill or sick; disinclined.

indisputable adj unquestionable.

indistinct adj not clearly marked; dim.

individual adj existing as a separate thing or being; of, by, for or relating to a single person or thing. • n a single thing or being; a person.

individualist n a person who thinks or behaves with marked independence.—**individualistic** adj.

individuality n the condition of being individual; separate existence; distinctive character.

indoctrinate vt to instruct systematically in doctrines, ideas, beliefs, etc.

indolent adj idle; lazy.

indoor adj done, used, etc, within a building.

indoors adv in or into a building.

indubitable adj not capable of being doubted.

induce vt to persuade; to bring on; to draw (a conclusion) from particular facts; to bring about (an electric or magnetic effect) in a body by placing it within a field of force.

inducement n something that induces; a stimulus; a motive.

induction n the act or an instance of inducting, e.g. to office; reasoning from particular premises to general conclusions; the inducing of an electric or magnetic effect by a field of force.—**inductive** adj.

indulge vt to satisfy (a desire); to gratify the wishes of. • vi to give way to one's desire.

indulgence n indulging or being indulged; a thing indulged in; a favour or privilege.

indulgent adj indulging or characterised by indulgence; lenient.

industrial adj relating to or engaged in industry; used in industry.

industrialist n a person who owns or manages an industrial enterprise.

industrious adj hard-working.

industry n organised production or manufacture of goods; manufacturing enterprises collectively; a branch of commercial enterprise producing a particular product; any large-scale business activity.

inebriated adj drunken.

inedible adj not fit to be eaten.

ineffective adj not effective.

ineffectual adj not effectual; futile.

inefficiency n the quality of being inefficient; an instance of inefficiency.—**inefficient** adj.

Ineligible adj not eligible.—**Ineligibility** n.

Inept adj awkward; clumsy.—**Ineptitude** n.

Inequality n lack of equality in size, status, etc.

Inert adj without power to move or resist.

Inertia n (physics) the tendency of matter to remain at rest; disinclination to act.

Inestimable adj beyond measure or price.

Inevitable adj sure to happen; unavoidable.

Inexact adj not strictly true or correct.

Inexhaustible adj unfailing; unwearied.

Inexorable adj unable to be persuaded by persuasion or entreaty; relentless.

Inexpensive adj cheap.

Inexperience n want of experience or of the knowledge that comes by experience.

Inexplicable adj not to be accounted for.

Inextricable adj that cannot be disentangled, solved, or escaped from.

Infallible adj incapable of being wrong; dependable; reliable.—**Infallibility** n.

Infamous adj having a bad reputation; notorious; causing a bad reputation.

Infamy n ill fame; public disgrace.

Infancy n early childhood; the beginning or early existence of anything.

Infant n a very young child; a baby.

Infantile adj of infants; like an infanth.

Infantry n soldiers trained to fight on foot.

Infatuate vt to inspire with intense, foolish, or short-lived passion.—**Infatuation** n.

Infect vt to contaminate with disease-causing microorganisms; to taint; to affect, esp so as to harm.—**Infective** adj.

Infection n an infecting or being infected; an infectious disease; a diseased condition.

Infectious adj (disease) able to be transmitted; a disease caused by the spread of bacteria in the body, etc; causing or transmitted by infection; tending to spread to others.

Infer vt to conclude by reasoning from facts or premises, to deduce.

Inference n an inferring; something inferred or deduced; a reasoning from premises to a conclusion.—**Inferential** adj.

Inferior adj lower in position, rank, degree, quality. • n an inferior person.—**Inferiority** n.

Infernal adj hellish; (inf) detestable.

Inferno n hell; intense heat; a devastating fire.

Infertile adj not fertile.—**Infertility** n.

Infest vt to overrun in large numbers, usu so as to be harmful; to be parasitic in or on.

Infidelity n unfaithfulness, esp in marriage.

Infighting n intense competition within an organisation.

Infiltrate vti to filter or pass gradually through or into; to permeate; to penetrate (enemy lines, etc) gradually or stealthily.—**Infiltration** n.

Infinite adj endless, limitless; very great; vast.

Infinitive n (gram) the form of a verb without reference to person, number or tense.

Infinity n the condition or quality of being infinite; an unlimited number, quantity, or period.

Infirmary n a hospital or place for the treatment of the sick.

Infirmity n being infirm; a physical weakness.

Inflame vti to arouse, excite, etc, or to become aroused, excited, etc; to undergo or cause to undergo inflammation.

Inflammable adj able to catch fire, flammable.

Inflammation n redness, pain, heat, and swelling in the body, due to injury or disease.

Inflate vti to fill or become filled with air or gas; to puff up with pride; to increase beyond what is normal, esp the supply of money or credit.

Inflation n an inflating or being inflated; an increase in the currency in circulation or a marked expansion of credit, resulting in a fall in currency value and a sharp rise in prices.

Inflexible adj stiff, rigid; fixed; unyielding.

Inflict vt to impose (pain, a penalty, etc) on a person or thing.—**Infliction** n.

Influence n the power to affect others; the power to produce effects by having wealth, etc. • vt to have influence on.—**Influential** adj.

Influenza n a contagious feverish virus disease marked by muscular pain and inflammation of the respiratory system.

Inform vt to provide knowledge of something to. • vi to give information to the police, etc, esp in accusing another.

Informal adj not formal; not according to fixed rules or ceremony, etc; casual.

Informality n the lack of regular, customary, or legal form; an informal act.

Information n something told or facts learned; news; knowledge; data stored in or retrieved from a computer.—**Informative** adj.

Informer n a person who informs on another, esp to the police for a reward.

Infrared n (radiation) having a wavelength longer than light but shorter than radio waves.

Infrastructure n the basic structure of any system; the basic installations, such as roads, etc, that determine an area's economic power.

Infrequent adj seldom occurring; rare.

Infringe vt to break, esp an agreement or a law.

Infuriate vt to enrage; to make furious.

Infuse vt to instil (qualities, etc); to inspire; to steep (tea leaves, etc) to extract the essence.

Ingenious adj clever, resourceful.—**Ingenuity** n.

Ingot n a brick-shaped mass of cast metal.

Ingrained adj (habits, etc) firmly established; (dirt) deeply embedded.—also **engrained**.

Ingratiate vt to bring oneself into another's favour.

ingratitude n absence of gratitude.

ingredient n something included in a mixture.

inhabit vt to live in; to occupy; to reside.

inhabitant n a person or animal inhabiting a specified place.

inhalant n a medicine, etc, that is inhaled.

inhale vti to breathe in.—**inhalation** n.

inhaler n a device that dispenses medicines in a fine spray for inhalation.

inherent adj existing as an inseparable part of something.—**inherence** n.

inherit vt to receive (property, a title, etc) under a will or by right of legal succession; to possess by genetic transmission. • vi to receive by inheritance; to succeed as heir.

inheritance n the action of inheriting; something inherited.

inhibit vt to restrain; to prohibit.

inhibition n a mental process that restrains or represses an action, emotion, or thought.

inhospitable adj affording no shelter; barren.

inhuman adj lacking in the human qualities of kindness, pity, etc; cruel, brutal, not human.

inhumane adj not humane; inhuman.

inimitable adj impossible to imitate; matchless.

iniquity n wickedness; great injustice.

initial adj of or at the beginning. • n the first letter of each word in a name. • vt to sign with initials.

initiate vt to teach the fundamentals of a subject to; to admit as a member into a club, etc, esp with a secret ceremony. • n an initiated person.—**initiation** n.

initiative n the action of taking the first step; ability to originate new ideas, methods.

inject vt to force (a fluid) into a vein, tissue, etc, esp with a syringe; to introduce (a remark, quality, etc), to interject.

injection n an injecting; a substance that is injected.

injunction n a command; an order; a court order prohibiting or ordering a given action.

injure vt to harm physically or mentally.—**injury** n

injustice n being unfair; an unjust act.

ink n a coloured liquid used for writing, printing, etc; the dark protective secretion of an octopus, etc.—also vt.

inkling n a hint; a vague notion.

inland adj of or in the interior of a country. • adv into or toward this region.

inlay vt to decorate a surface by inserting pieces of metal, wood, etc.

inlet n a narrow strip of water extending into a body of land; an opening; a passage, pipe, etc, for liquid to enter a machine, etc.

inmate n a person confined with others in a prison or institution.

inn n a small hotel; a restaurant or public house.

innate adj existing from birth; inherent.

inner adj inside, internal; private.

innings n (used as sing) (cricket) a turn at bat for a batsman or side.

innocent adj not guilty of a crime; blameless; harmless; inoffensive; simple, credulous, naive. • n an innocent person.—**innocence** n.

innocuous adj harmless.

innovate vi to introduce new methods, ideas, etc; to make changes.—**innovation** n.

innuendo n a hint or sly remark.

inoculate vt to inject a serum or a vaccine into, esp in order to create immunity.

inopportune adj unseasonable; untimely.

inordinate adj excessive.

inorganic adj not having the structure or characteristics of living organisms.

input n what is put in, as data into a computer, etc. • vt to enter (data) into a computer.

inquest n a judicial inquiry held by a coroner, esp into a case of violent or unexplained death.

inquire vi to request information about; (usu with **into**) to investigate. • vt to ask about.—also **enquire**.

inquiry n the act of inquiring; a search by questioning; an investigation.—also **enquiry**.

inquisitive adj eager for knowledge; prying.

insane adj not sane, mentally ill; very foolish.

insanitary adj unclean.

insanity n derangement of the mind or intellect; lunacy; madness.

insatiable adj not easily satisfied; greedy.

inscribe vt to mark or engrave (words, etc) on (a surface); to add (a person's name) to a list; to dedicate (a book) to someone; to autograph; to fix in the mind.

inscription n an inscribing; words, etc, inscribed on a tomb, coin, stone, etc.

inscrutable adj hard to understand, incomprehensible; enigmatic.

insect n any of a class of small arthropods with three pairs of legs, a head, thorax, and abdomen and two or four wings.

insecticide n a substance for killing insects.

insecure adj not safe; feeling anxiety.

insecurity n the condition of being insecure; lack of confidence or sureness; instability.

inseminate vt to fertilise; to impregnate.

insensible adj unconscious; unaware.

inseparable adj not able to be separated; closely attached, as romantically.

insert vt to put or fit (something) into something else. • n something inserted.

inshore adj, adv near or towards the shore.

inside n the inner side, surface, or part; (pl: inf) the internal organs, stomach, bowels. • adj internal; known only to insiders; secret. • adv on or in the inside; within; indoors; (sl) in prison. • prep in or within.

Insidious adj marked by slyness or treachery; more dangerous than seems evident.

Insight n the ability to see and understand clearly the inner nature of things, esp by intuition; an instance of such understanding.—**Insightful** adj.

Insignia n a mark or badge of authority.

Insignificant adj having little or no importance; trivial; inadequate.—**Insignificance** n.

Insincere adj not sincere; hypocritical.

Insinuate vt to introduce or work in slowly, indirectly, etc; to hint.—**Insinuation** n.

Insipid adj lacking any distinctive flavour; uninteresting, dull.

Insist vi (often with on) to maintain a stand. • vt to demand strongly; to declare firmly.

Insistent adj insisting or demanding.

Insole n the inner sole of a shoe, etc; a thickness of material used as an inner sole.

Insolent adj disrespectful; impudent, arrogant; rude.—**Insolence** n.

Insoluble adj incapable of being dissolved; impossible to solve or explain.

Insolvent adj unable to pay one's debts.

Insomnia n abnormal inability to sleep.

Inspect vt to look at carefully; to examine or review officially.—**Inspection** n.

Inspector n an official who inspects in order to ensure compliance with regulations, etc; a police officer ranking below a superintendent.

Inspiration n an inspiring; any stimulus to creative thought; an inspired idea, action, etc.

Inspire vt to stimulate, as to some creative effort; to arouse (a thought or feeling) in (someone).

Install vt to place formally in an office, rank, etc; to establish in a place; to settle in a position or state.—**Installation** n.

Instalment n a sum of money to be paid at regular specified times; any of several parts, as of a television serial.

Instance n an example; a step in proceeding.

Instant adj immediate; (food) concentrated or precooked for quick preparation. • n a moment; a particular moment.

Instantaneous adj happening very quickly.

Instantly adv immediately.

Instead adv in place of the one mentioned.

Instep n the upper part of the arch of the foot.

Instigate vt to urge on, goad; to initiate.

Instil vt to put (an idea, etc) in or into (the mind) gradually.

Instinct n the inborn tendency to behave in a way characteristic of a species; a natural or acquired tendency; a knack.

Instinctive adj of or prompted by instinct.

Institute vt to organise, establish; to start. • n an organisation for the promotion of science, art, etc; a school, college or university department specialising in some field.

Institution n an organisation with a social, educational or religious purpose; (inf) a long-established person or thing.

Institutionalise vt to place in an institution; to make a person dependent on an institutional routine.

Instruct vt to teach; to give instructions to.

Instruction n an order, direction; the act or process of teaching or training; knowledge imparted; (pl) orders, directions; detailed guidance.

Instructive adj containing instructions; giving information, educational.

Instrument n a thing by means of which something is done; a tool; a device for indicating, measuring, etc; a device producing musical sound; a formal document.

Instrumental adj serving as a means of doing something; helpful; of, performed on or written for a musical instrument.

Instrumentalist n a person who plays a musical instrument.

Insubordinate adj not submitting to authority.

Insufferable adj intolerable; unbearable.

Insufficient adj not sufficient.

Insular adj narrow-minded; illiberal.

Insulate vt to isolate; to cover with a nonconducting material in order to prevent the escape of electricity, heat, sound, etc.—**Insulation** n.

Insulin n a hormone that controls absorption of sugar by the body, secreted by islets of tissue in the pancreas.

Insult vt to treat with indignity or contempt; to offend. • n an insulting remark or act.

Insuperable adj unable to be overcome.

Insurance n a contract purchased to guarantee compensation for a specified loss by fire, death, etc; the amount for which something is insured; the business of insuring against loss.

Insure vt to take out or issue insurance on; to ensure. • vi to contract to give or take insurance.

Insurgent adj rebellious, rising in revolt. • n a person who fights against established authority.

Insurrection adj a rising or revolt against established authority.—**Insurrectionist** n.

Intact adj unimpaired; whole.

Intangible adj that cannot be touched; representing value but without material being, as good will; indefinable.

Integer n any member of the set consisting of the positive and negative whole numbers and zero, such as -5, 0, 5.

Integral adj necessary for completeness; whole or complete; made up of parts forming a whole.

Integrate *vti* to make whole or become complete; to bring (parts) together into a whole; to remove barriers imposing segregation upon (racial groups).—**Integration** *n*.

Integrity *n* honesty, sincerity; completeness, wholeness; an unimpaired condition.

Intellect *n* the ability to reason or understand; high intelligence; a very intelligent person.

Intellectual *adj* of, involving, or appealing to the intellect. • *n* an intellectual person.

Intelligence *n* the ability to learn or understand; news or information; those engaged in gathering secret, esp military, information.

Intelligent *adj* having or showing intelligence.

Intelligible *adj* able to be understood; clear.

Intemperate *adj* indulging excessively in alcoholic drink; unrestrained; (*climate*) extreme.

Intend *vt* to mean, to signify; to propose, have in mind as an aim or purpose.

Intense *adj* very strong, concentrated.

Intensify *vti* to make or become more intense.—**Intensification** *n*.

Intensity *n* the state or quality of being intense; the force or energy of any physical agent.

Intensive *adj* thorough; denoting careful attention given to patients right after surgery, etc.

Intent *adj* firmly directed; having one's attention or purpose firmly fixed. • *n* intention; something intended; purpose.

Intention *n* a determination to act in a specified way; anything intended.

Intentional *adj* done purposely.

Inter *vt* to bury.

Interact *vi* to act upon each other.

Intercede *vi* to intervene on another's behalf.

Intercept *vt* to stop or catch in its course. • *n* a point of intersection of two geometric figures; interception by an interceptor.

Interchange *vt* to give and receive one thing for another; to exchange, to put (each of two things) in the place of the other; to alternate. • *n* an interchanging; a junction on a motorway.

Intercourse *n* a connection by dealings or communication between individuals or groups; sexual intercourse, copulation.

Interdict *vt* to restrain from doing or using something. • *n* an official prohibition.

Interest *n* a feeling of curiosity about something; the power of causing this feeling; a share in or a right to, something; anything in which one has a share; benefit; money paid for the use of money; the rate of such payment. • *vt* to excite the attention of; to cause to have a share in; to concern oneself with.

Interested *adj* having or expressing an interest; affected by personal interest.

Interesting *n* engaging the attention.

Interface *n* a surface that forms the common boundary between two things; an electrical connection between one device and another.

Interfere *vi* to clash; to come between.

Interference *n* (*radio, TV*) the interruption of reception by atmospherics or by unwanted signals.

Interim *n* an intervening period of time. • *adj* temporary. • *adv* meanwhile.

Interior *adj* situated within; inner; inland; private. • *n* the interior part, as of a country, etc.

Interjection *n* an interruption; an exclamation.

Interlock *vti* to lock or become locked together.

Interloper *n* a person who meddles; an intruder.

Interlude *n* anything that fills time between two events, as music between acts of a play.

Intermediary *n* a mediator.

Intermediate *adj* in the middle; in between.

Interminable *adj* seeming to last forever; endless.

Intermission *n* an interval of time between parts of a performance.

Intermittent *adj* stopping and starting again at intervals; periodic.

Intern *vt* to detain and confine within an area.

Internal *adj* of or on the inside; domestic.

International *adj* between or among nations; concerned with the relations between nations; for the use of all nations; of or for people in various nations. • *n* a sporting competition between teams from different countries; a member of an international team of players.

Interplay *n* the action of two things on each other, interaction.

Interpret *vt* to explain; to translate; to construe; to give one's own conception of, as in a play or musical composition. • *vi* to translate between speakers of different languages.—**Interpretation** *n*.

Interpreter *n* a person who translates orally for persons speaking in different languages; (*comput*) a program that translates an instruction into machine code.

Interrogate *vti* to question, esp formally.

Interrogative *adj* asking a question. • *n* a word used in asking a question.

Interrupt *vt* to break into (a discussion, etc) or break in upon (a speaker, worker, etc); to make a break in the continuity of. • *vi* to interrupt an action, talk, etc.

Intersect *vti* to cut or divide by passing through.

Intersection *n* an intersecting; the place where two lines, roads, etc, meet or cross.

Intersperse *vt* to scatter or insert among other things.

Interval *n* a space between things; the time between events; (*mus*) the difference of pitch between two notes.

Intervene *vi* to occur or come between; to occur between two events, etc.

interview n a meeting in which a person is asked about his or her views, etc, as by a newspaper or television reporter; a formal meeting at which a candidate for a job is questioned and assessed by a prospective employer.—*also vt.*

intestate adj having made no will.

intestine n the lower part of the alimentary canal between the stomach and the anus.

intimacy n close or confidential friendship; familiarity; sexual relations.

intimate adj most private or personal; very close or familiar, esp sexually. • n an intimate friend. • vt to indicate; to hint or imply.

intimation n a notice, announcement.

intimidate vt to frighten; to discourage, silence, etc, esp by threats.—**intimidation** n.

into prep to the interior or inner parts of; to the middle; to a particular condition; (inf) deeply interested or involved in.

intolerable adj unbearable.

intolerance n lack of toleration of the opinions or practices of others.—**intolerant** adj.

intonation n intoning; an accent.

intoxicate vt to make drunken; to elate.

intractable adj unmanageable, uncontrollable.

intransigent adj unwilling to compromise, irreconcilable.—**intransigence** n.

intransitive adj (gram) denoting a verb that does not take a direct object.

intravenous adj into a vein.

intrepid adj bold; fearless; brave.

intricate adj difficult to understand; complex, complicated; involved, detailed.

intrigue n a secret or underhand plotting; a secret or underhanded plot or scheme; a secret love affair. • vi to carry on an intrigue. • vt to excite the interest or curiosity of.

intrinsic adj belonging to the real nature of a person or thing; inherent.

introduce vt to make (a person) acquainted by name (with other persons); to bring into use or establish; to present (a bill, etc) for consideration or approval (by parliament, etc); to present a radio or television programme; to bring into or insert.

introduction n the presentation of one person to another; preliminary text in a book.

introductory adj serving as an introduction.

introspection n examination of one's own mind and feelings, etc.

introvert n a person who is more interested in his or her own thoughts, feelings, etc, than in external objects or events.

intrude vti to force (oneself) upon others.

intrusion n the act or an instance of intruding.

intuition n a perceiving of the truth of something immediately without reasoning or analysis; a hunch, an insight.

inundate vt to cover as with a flood.

invade vt to enter (a country) with hostile intentions; to encroach upon; to penetrate; to crowd into as if invading.—**invader** n.

invalid[1] adj not valid.

invalid[2] n a person who is ill or disabled. • vt to cause to become an invalid; to disable.

invalidate vt to render not valid.—**invalidation** n.

invaluable adj too valuable to be measured in money.

invariable adj never changing; constant.

invasion n the act of invading with military forces; an encroachment, intrusion.

invective n the use of violent or abusive language or writing.

invent vt to think up; to think out or produce a new device, process, etc); to originate; to fabricate (a lie, etc).—**invention** n.—**inventor** n.

inventive adj pertaining to invention; skilled in inventing.—**inventiveness** n.

inventory n an itemised list of goods, property, etc, as of a business; the store of such goods for such a listing; a list of the property of an individual or an estate.

inverse adj reversed in order or position; opposite, contrary. • n an inverse state or thing.

invert vt to turn upside down or inside out; to reverse in order, position or relationship.

invertebrate adj without a backbone. • n an animal without a backbone.

invest vt to commit (money) to property, stocks and shares, etc, for profit; to devote effort, time, etc, on a particular activity; to install in office with ceremony; to furnish with power, authority, etc. • vi to invest money.

investigate vti to search (into); to inquire, examine.—**investigator** n.

investigation n an inquiry; a search to uncover facts, etc.

investiture n the ceremony of investing a person with an office, robes, title, etc.

investment n the act of investing money productively; the amount invested.

inveterate adj firmly established, ingrained; habitual.

invidious adj tending to provoke ill-will, resentment or envy.

invigorate vt to fill with energy; to refresh.

invincible adj unconquerable.

inviolate adj not violated; unbroken, unharmed.

invisible adj unable to be seen; hidden.

invitation n a message used in inviting.

invite vt to ask to come somewhere or do something; to ask for; to entice. • n (inf) an invitation.

inviting adj attractive, enticing.

invoice n a list of goods dispatched, usu with particulars of their price and quantity. • vt to submit an invoice for or to.

Invoke vt to call on (God, etc) for help; to resort to (a law, etc) as pertinent; to implore.
Involuntary adj not done by choice.
Involve vt to affect or include; to require; to occupy, to make busy.—**involvement** n.
invulnerable adj not capable of being hurt.
inward adj situated within or directed to the inside; relating to or in the mind or spirit. • adv inwards.
inwardly adv within; in the mind or spirit.
inwards adv towards the inside or interior; in the mind or spirit.
iodine n a nonmetallic element, found in seawater and seaweed, whose compounds are used in medicine and photography.
ion n an electrically charged atom or group of atoms formed through the gain or loss of one or more electrons.
iota n the ninth letter of the Greek alphabet; a very small quantity; a jot.
irascible adj easily angered; hot-tempered.
irate adj enraged, furious.
iridescent adj exhibiting a spectrum of shimmering colours, which change as the position is altered.—**iridescence** n.
iris n the round, pigmented membrane surrounding the pupil of the eye; a perennial herbaceous plant with sword-shaped leaves and brightly coloured flowers.
Irish adj of Ireland or its people. • n the Celtic language of Ireland.
irk vt to annoy, irritate.—**irksome** adj.
iron n a metallic element, the most common of all metals; a heavy implement with a heated flat underface for pressing cloth; (pl) shackles of iron; a golf club with an angled metal head. • adj of iron; like iron, strong and firm. • vti to press with a hot iron.
ironic(al) adj of or using irony.
ironmonger n a dealer in metal utensils, tools, etc; a hardware shop.
irony n an expression in which the intended meaning of the words is the opposite of their usual sense; an event or result that is the opposite of what is expected.
irradiate vt to shine upon; to light up; to enlighten; to radiate; to expose to X-rays or other radiation. • vi to emit rays; to shine.
irrational adj not rational, lacking the power of reason; senseless; unreasonable; absurd.
irreconcilable adj not able to be brought into agreement; incompatible.
irredeemable adj not able to be redeemed.
irrefutable adj unable to deny or disprove.
irregular adj not regular, straight or even; not conforming to the rules; imperfect.—**irregularity** n.
irrelevant adj not to the point.—**irrelevance** n.

irreparable adj that cannot be repaired.
irreplaceable adj unable to be replaced.
irrepressible adj unable to be restrained.
irreproachable adj blameless; faultless.
irresistible adj not able to be resisted; fascinating; very charming, alluring.
irresolute adj lacking resolution, uncertain.
irrespective adj (with of) regardless.
irresponsible adj not showing a proper sense of the consequences of one's actions; unable to bear responsibility.—**irresponsibility** n.
irreverent adj not reverent, disrespectful.
irrevocable adj unalterable.
irrigate vt to supply (land) with water as by means of ditches, pipes, etc; (med) to wash out (a cavity, wound, etc).—**irrigation** n.
irritable adj easily annoyed, irritated, or provoked.—**irritability** n.
irritate vt to annoy; to make inflamed or sore.
Islam n the Muslim religion, a monotheistic religion founded by Mohammed.
island n a land mass smaller than a continent and surrounded by water; anything like this in position or isolation.
islander n a native or inhabitant of an island.
isobar n a line on a map connecting places of equal barometric pressure.
isolate vt to set apart from others; to place alone; to quarantine a person or animal with a contagious disease; to separate a constituent substance from a compound.—**isolation** n.
isomer n any of two or more chemical compounds whose molecules contain the same atoms but in different arrangements.
isometrics npl physical exercises in which muscles are contracted against each other or in opposition to fixed objects.
isosceles adj denoting a triangle with two equal sides.
isotope n any of two or more forms of an element having the same atomic number but different atomic weights.
issue n an outgoing; an outlet; a result; offspring; a point under dispute; a sending or giving out; all that is put forth at one time (an issue of bonds, a periodical, etc). • vi to go or flow out; to result (from) or end (in); to be published. • vt to let out; to discharge; to give or deal out, as supplies; to publish.
isthmus n a narrow strip of land having water at each side and connecting two larger bodies of land.
it pron the thing mentioned; the subject of an impersonal verb; a subject or object of indefinite sense in various constructions. • n the player, as in tag, who must catch another.
Italian adj of Italy or its people. • n a native of Italy; the Italian language.

italic *adj* denoting a type in which the letters slant upward to the right (*this is italic type*). • *n* (*usu pl*) italic type or handwriting.

itch *n* an irritating sensation on the surface of the skin causing a need to scratch. • *vi* to have or feel an irritating sensation in the skin.—**itchy** *adj*.

item *n* an article; a unit; a separate thing.

itemise *vt* to specify the items of.

itinerant *adj* travelling from place to place.

itinerary *n* a detailed plan of a journey.

its *poss pron* relating to or belonging to it.

itself *pron* the reflexive and emphatic form of it.

ivory *n* the hard, creamy-white substance forming elephant tusks; a creamy white colour. • *adj* of or like ivory; creamy white.

ivy *n* a climbing or creeping vine with a woody stem and evergreen leaves.

J

jab *vti* to poke or thrust roughly; to punch with short, straight blows. • *n* a sudden thrust or stab; (*inf*) an injection.

jack *n* any of various mechanical or hydraulic devices used to lift something heavy; a playing card with a knave's picture on it, ranking below the queen; (*bowls*) a small white ball used as a target. • *vt* to raise by means of a jack.

jacket *n* a short coat; the removable paper cover of a book.

jackknife *n* a pocket-knife; a dive in which the diver touches his feet with knees straight and then straightens out. • *vi* (*articulated lorry*) to lose control so that trailer and cab swing against each other.

jackpot *n* the accumulated stakes in certain games, as poker.

jade *n* a hard, ornamental semiprecious stone; its light green colour.

jaded *adj* tired, exhausted; satiated.

jagged *adj* having sharp projecting points.

jail *n* a prison. • *vt* to confine in prison.

jam¹ *n* a preserve made from fruit boiled with sugar until thickened.

jam² *vt* to press or squeeze into a confined space; to crowd full with people or things; to cause (machinery) to become wedged and inoperable; to cause interference to a radio signal. • *vi* to become stuck or blocked. • *n* a crowded mass or congestion in a confined space; a blockage caused by jamming; (*inf*) a difficult situation.

jamb *n* the straight vertical side post of a door.

jangle *vi* to make a harsh or discordant sound, as bells. • *vt* to cause to jangle; to irritate.—*also n*.

janitor *n* a person who looks after a building, doing routine maintenance, etc.

Japanese *adj* of Japan, its people or language. • *n* the language of Japan.

jar¹ *vi* to make a harsh, discordant noise; to have an irritating effect (on one); to clash.

jar² *n* a short cylindrical glass vessel with a wide mouth; (*inf*) a pint of beer.

jargon *n* the specialised or technical vocabulary of a science, profession, etc; obscure and usu pretentious language.

jasmine *n* any of a genus of climbing shrubs with fragrant white or yellow flowers.

jaundice *n* a condition characterised by yellowing of the skin, caused by excess of bile in the bloodstream; bitterness; resentment; prejudice.

jaunt *n* a short journey, usu for pleasure. • *vi* to make such a journey.

jaunty *adj* sprightly.—**jauntiness** *n*.

javelin *n* a light spear, esp one thrown some distance in a contest.

jaw *n* one of the bones in which teeth are set; either of two movable parts that grasp or crush something, as in a vice; (*sl*) a friendly chat, gossip. • *vi* (*sl*) to talk boringly and at length.

jaywalk *vi* to walk across a street carelessly without obeying traffic rules or signals.

jazz *n* popular music, characterised by syncopated rhythms. • *vt* (*sl:with* up) to enliven or embellish.—**jazzy** *adj*.

jealous *adj* apprehensive of or hostile towards someone thought of as a rival; envious of.

jealousy *n* suspicious fear or watchfulness.

jeans *npl* trousers made from denim.

jeep *n* a small robust vehicle with heavy duty tyres and four-wheel drive.

jeer *vt* to laugh derisively. • *vi* to scoff (at). • *n* a jeering remark.

jelly *n* a soft, gelatinous food made from fruit syrup or meat juice; a substance like this.

jellyfish *n* a sea creature with a nearly transparent body and long tentacles.

jeopardise *vt* to endanger, put at risk.

jeopardy *n* great danger or risk.

jerk *n* a sudden sharp pull or twist; a sudden muscular contraction or reflex; (*inf*) a stupid person. • *vti* to move with a jerk; to pull sharply; to twitch.—**jerky** *adj*.

jersey *n* any plain machine-knitted fabric of natural or man-made fibres; a knitted sweater.

jest n a joke; a thing to be laughed at. • vi to joke.

jet[1] n a hard, black, compact mineral that can be polished and is used in jewellery.—**jet-black** adj.

jet[2] n a stream of liquid or gas suddenly emitted; a jet-propelled aircraft. • vti to gush out in a stream; (inf) to travel by jet.

jetsam n cargo thrown overboard from a ship in distress to lighten it.

jettison vt to abandon, to throw overboard.

jetty n a wharf; a small pier.

Jew n a person descended, or regarded as descended, from the ancient Hebrews; a person whose religion is Judaism.—**Jewish** adj.

jewel n a precious stone; a gem; a piece of jewellery; someone or something highly esteemed.

jewellery n jewels such as rings, brooches, etc, worn for decoration.

jib n a triangular sail extending from the foremast in a ship; the projecting arm of a crane. • vti to pull (a sail) round to the other side.

jibe see **gibe**.

jigsaw n a saw with a narrow fine-toothed blade for cutting irregular shapes; a picture on wood or board cut into irregular pieces for re-assembling for amusement.

jilt vt to discard (a lover) unfeelingly, esp without warning.

jingle n a metallic tinkling sound like a bunch of keys being shaken together; a catchy verse or song with easy rhythm, simple rhymes, etc.—also vti.

jinx n (inf) someone thought to bring bad luck.

jitter vi (inf) to feel nervous or act nervously. • npl (inf) (with **the**) an uneasy nervous feeling.

job n a piece of work done for pay; a task; a duty; work; employment; (inf) a difficult task.

jobless adj unemployed.

jockey n a person whose job is riding horses in races. • vti to act as a jockey; to manœuvre for a more advantageous position.

jocular adj joking; full of jokes.

jog vt to give a slight shake or nudge to; to rouse, as the memory. • vi to run at a relaxed trot for exercise. • n a slight shake or push; a nudge; a slow walk or trot.

join vti to bring and come together (with); to connect; to unite; to become a part or member of (a club, etc); to participate (in a conversation, etc); (with **up**) to enlist in the armed forces; to unite, connect. • n a joining; a place of joining.

joiner n a carpenter who finishes interior woodwork; (inf) a person who is involved in many clubs and activities, etc.

joint n a place where, or way in which, two things are joined; any of the parts of a jointed whole; the parts where two bones move on one another in an animal; a division of an animal carcass made by a butcher; (sl) a cheap bar or restaurant; (sl) a gambling or drinking den; (sl) a cannabis cigarette. • adj common to two or more; sharing with another. • vt to connect by a joint or joints; to divide (an animal carcass) into parts for cooking.—**jointly** adv.

joist n any of the parallel beams supporting the floor-boards or the laths of a ceiling.

joke n something said or done to cause laughter; a thing done or said merely in fun; a person or thing to be laughed at. • vi to make jokes.

joker n a person who jokes; (sl) a person; an extra playing card used in certain games.

jolly adj merry; delightful; (inf) enjoyable. • vti (inf) to try to make (a person) feel good.

jolt vt to give a sudden shake to; to move along jerkily; to surprise or shock suddenly. • n a sudden jar or knock; an emotional shock.

jostle vti to collide or come into contact (with); to elbow for position.—also n.

journal n a daily record of happenings, as a diary; a newspaper or periodical; (bookkeeping) a book of original entry for recording transactions; that part of a shaft or axle that turns in a bearing.

journalism n the work of gathering news for, or producing a newspaper, magazine or news broadcast.—**journalist** n.

journey n a travelling or going from one place to another. • vi to make a journey.

jowl n the lower jaw; (usu pl) the cheek; the loose flesh around the throat; the similar flesh in an animal, as a dewlap.

joy n intense happiness.

joyful adj filled with, expressing or causing joy.

joyous adj joyful.

joy-ride n (inf) a car ride, often in a stolen vehicle and at reckless speed, for pleasure.

jubilant adj joyful and triumphant; elated.

jubilee n a 50th or 25th anniversary.

judge n a public official with authority to hear and decide cases in a court of law; a person chosen to settle a dispute or decide who wins; a person qualified to decide on the relative worth of anything. • vti to hear and pass judgment (on) in a court of law; to determine the winner of (a contest) or settle (a dispute); to form an opinion about; to criticise or censure; to suppose, think.

judgment, judgement n a legal decision; an opinion; the ability to come to a wise decision; censure.

judicial adj of judges, courts, their functions; jurisdiction; judges, courts collectively.

judicious adj possessing or characterised by sound judgment.

judo n a Japanese system of unarmed combat.

jug n a vessel for holding and pouring liquids, with a handle and curved lip; a pitcher; (sl)

prison. • vt to stew meat (esp hare) in an earthen-ware pot; (sl) to put into prison.

juggernaut n a large heavy truck.

juggle vi to toss up balls, etc, and keep them in the air. • vt to manipulate skilfully; to manipulate so as to deceive.—also n.—**juggler** n.

juice n the liquid part of fruit, vegetables or meat; (inf) electric current.

juicy adj full of juice; (inf) very interesting.

jukebox n a coin-operated automatic record player.

jumble vt (often with up) to mix together in a disordered mass. • n articles for a jumble sale.

jumble sale n a sale of second-hand clothes, books, etc, to raise money.

jumbo n something very large of its kind.

jump vi to spring or leap from the ground, a height, etc; to jerk; (often with at) to act swiftly and eagerly; to pass suddenly, as to a new topic; to rise suddenly, as prices; (sl) to be lively. • vt to leap or pass over (something); to leap upon; to cause (prices, etc) to rise; to fail to turn up (for trial when out on bail); (inf) to attack suddenly; (inf) to react to prematurely; (sl) to leave suddenly. • n a jumping; a distance jumped; a sudden transition; an obstacle; a nervous start.

jumper n a knitted garment for the upper body.

jumpy adj moving in jerks, etc; easily startled.

junction n a place or point where things join; a place where roads or railway lines, etc, meet.

juncture n a junction; a point of time.

jungle n an area overgrown with dense tropical trees and other vegetation, etc; any scene of wild confusion, disorder, or of ruthless competition for survival.

junior adj younger in age; of lower status; of juniors. • n a person who is younger, of lower rank, etc; a young person employed in minor capacity in an office.

juniper n an evergreen shrub that yields purple berries.

junk¹ n a flat-bottomed sailing vessel prevalent in the China Seas.

junk² n discarded useless objects; (inf) rubbish, trash; (sl) any narcotic drug. • vt (inf) to scrap.

junta n a group of people, esp military, who assume responsibility for the government of a country following a revolution.

jurisdiction n the authority to apply the law; the limits of territory over which such authority extends.

jurisprudence n the science or philosophy of law; a division of law.

juror n a member of a jury.

jury n a body of usu 12 people sworn to hear evidence and to deliver a verdict on a case; a committee or panel that decides winners in a contest.

just adj fair, impartial; deserved, merited; proper, exact; conforming strictly with the facts. • adv exactly; nearly; only; barely; a very short time ago; immediately; (inf) really.

justice n justness, fairness; the use of authority to maintain what is just; the administration of law; a judge.

jut vti to stick out; to project.

juvenile adj young; immature. • n a young person.

juxtapose vt to place side by side.

K

kaleidoscope n a small tube containing bits of coloured glass reflected by mirrors to form symmetrical patterns as the tube is rotated.

kangaroo n an Australian mammal with short forelegs and strong, large hind legs for jumping.

keel n one of the main structural members of a ship extending along the bottom from stem to stern to which the frame is attached. • vti (to cause) to turn over.

keen¹ adj eager, enthusiastic; intellectually acute, shrewd; having a sharp point or fine edge; (senses) perceptive, penetrating; (prices) very low so as to be competitive.

keen² vi to lament the dead.

keep vt to celebrate, observe; to protect, guard; to take care of; to preserve; to provide for; to

maintain in a specified state; to hold for the future; to hold and not let go. • vi to stay in a specified condition; to continue, go on; to refrain or restrain oneself; to stay fresh. • n food and shelter; care and custody; the inner stronghold of a castle.

keepsake n something kept in memory of the giver.

kennel n a small shelter for a dog; (often pl) a place where dogs are bred or kept. • vt to keep in a kennel.

kerb n a line of raised stone forming the edge of a pavement.

kernel n the inner edible part of a fruit or nut; the essential part of anything.

kerosene n a fuel oil distilled from petroleum.

ketchup *n* any of various thick sauces, esp one made from puréed tomato, for meat, fish, etc.

kettle *n* a container with a handle and spout for boiling water.

kettledrum *n* a musical instrument consisting of a hollow metal body with a parchment head, the tension of which controls the pitch and is adjusted by screws.

key[1] *n* a device for locking and unlocking something; a thing that explains or solves, as the legend of a map, a code, etc; a controlling position, person, or thing; one of a set of parts or levers pressed in a keyboard or typewriter, etc; (*mus*) a system of related tones based on a keynote and forming a given scale; style or mood of expression; a roughened surface for improved adhesion of plaster, etc; an electric circuit breaker. • *adj* controlling; important.

key[2] *n* a low island or reef.

keyboard *n* a set of keys in a piano, organ, computer, etc.

keynote *n* the basic note of a musical scale; the basic idea or ruling principle.

kick *vt* to strike with the foot. • *vi* to strike out with the foot; to recoil, as a gun; (*with* **off**) (*football*) to give the ball the first kick to start play; (*inf*) to start. • *n* an act or method of kicking; (*inf*) a thrill.

kid *n* a young goat; soft leather made from its skin; (*inf*) a child. • *vti* (*inf*) to tease playfully.

kidnap *vt* to seize and hold to ransom, as of a person.

kidney *n* either of a pair of glandular organs excreting waste products from the blood as urine.

kill *vt* to cause the death of; to spend (time) on trivial matters; (*inf*) to cause pain to. • *n* the act of killing; an animal or animals killed.

killing *adj* (*inf*) tiring; very amusing; causing death, deadly. • *n* the act of killing, murder; (*inf*) a sudden (financial) success.

kiln *n* a furnace or large oven for baking or drying (lime, bricks, etc).

kilo *n* kilogram; kilometre.

kilogram *n* a unit of weight and mass, equal to 1000 grams or 2.2046 pounds.

kilometre *n* a unit of length equal to 1000 metres or 0.62 mile.

kilowatt *n* a unit of electrical power, equal to 1000 watts.

kilt *n* a knee-length skirt made from tartan material pleated at the sides.

kimono *n* a loose Japanese robe.

kin *n* relatives; family.

kind[1] *n* sort; variety; class; essential character.

kind[2] *adj* sympathetic; friendly.—**kindness** *n*.

kindergarten *n* a class or school for very young children.

kindle *vt* to set on fire; to excite (feelings, interest, etc). • *vi* to catch fire; to become excited.

kindly *adj* kind; gracious; agreeable; pleasant. • *adv* in a kind manner; favourably.

kindred *n* a person's family or relatives; family relationship; resemblance.—*also adj*.

kinetic *adj* of or produced by movement.

king *n* the man who rules a country and its people; the chief piece in chess; a playing card with a picture of a king on it, ranking above a queen; (*draughts*) a piece that has been crowned.

kingdom *n* a country headed by a king or queen; a realm, domain; any of the three divisions of the natural world: animal; vegetable, mineral.

kingfisher *n* a short-tailed diving bird that feeds chiefly on fish.

kink *n* a tight twist or curl in a piece of string, hair, etc; an eccentricity of personality. • *vti* to form or cause to form a kink or kinks.

kinky *adj* full of kinks; (*inf*) eccentric.

kiosk *n* a small open structure used for selling newspapers, confectionery, etc; a public telephone booth.

kiss *vti* to touch with the lips as an expression of love, affection or in greeting; to touch the lips with those of another person as a sign of love or desire; to touch lightly. • *n* an act of kissing.

kit *n* clothing and personal equipment, etc; tools and equipment for a specific purpose; a set of parts with instructions ready to be assembled. • *vt* (*usu with* **out**) to provide with kit.

kitbag *n* a strong cylindrical bag carried over one shoulder used for holding kit.

kitchen *n* a place where food is cooked.

kite *n* a bird of prey with long narrow wings and a forked tail; a light frame covered with a thin covering for flying in the wind.

kitten *n* a young cat.

kitty *n* the stakes in a game of poker, etc; a shared fund of money.

kleptomania *n* an uncontrollable impulse to steal.—**kleptomaniac** *n*.

knack *n* an ability to do something easily.

knapsack *n* a bag for carrying equipment or supplies on the back.

knave *n* (*formerly*) a tricky or dishonest man; the jack in a pack of playing cards.

knead *vt* to squeeze and press together (dough, clay, etc) into a uniform lump with the hands; to make (bread, etc) by kneading; to squeeze and press with the hands.

knee *n* the joint between the thigh and the lower part of the human leg; anything shaped like a bent knee.

kneecap *n* the small bone covering and protecting the front part of the knee-joint.

kneel *vi* to go down on one's knee or knees; to remain in this position.

knell *n* the sound of a bell rung slowly and solemnly at a death or funeral; a warning of death, failure, etc. • vi (bell) to ring a knell; to summon, announce, etc, (as if) by a knell.

knife n a flat piece of steel, etc, with a sharp edge set in a handle, used to cut. • vt to cut or stab with a knife.

knight n (Middle Ages) a medieval mounted soldier; a man who for some achievement is given honorary rank entitling him to use "Sir" before his given name; a chessman shaped like a horse's head. • vt to make (a man) a knight.—**knighthood** n.

knit vt to form (fabric or a garment) by interlooping yarn using knitting needles or a machine; to cause (e.g. broken bones) to grow together; to draw (the brows) together. • vi to make knitted fabric from yarn by means of needles; to grow together; united. —**knitting** n.

knob n a handle, usu round, of a door, drawer, etc.

knock vi to strike with a sharp blow; to rap on a door; to bump, collide; (engine) to make a thumping noise; (with **off**) (inf) to finish work. • vt to strike; (inf) to criticise; (with **about** or **around**) to wander around aimlessly; to treat roughly; (with **back**) (inf) to drink, swallow quickly; to reject, refuse; (with **down**) to indicate a sale at an auction; (with **down** or **off**) to hit so as to cause to fall; (with **off**) (inf) to complete hastily; (inf) to reduce in price; (sl) to steal; (with **out**) to make unconscious or exhausted; to

eliminate in a knockout competition; (inf) to amaze. • n a knocking, a hit, a rap.

knocker n a device hinged against a door for use in knocking.

knockout n a punch or blow that produces unconsciousness; a contest in which competitors are eliminated at each round; (inf) an attractive or impressive person or thing.

knot n a lump in a thread, etc, formed by a tightened loop or tangling; a fastening made by tying lengths of rope, etc; a small group, cluster; a hard mass of wood where a branch grows out from a tree, which shows as a roundish, cross-grained piece in a board; a unit of speed of one nautical mile per hour. • vti to make or form a knot (in); to entangle or become entangled.

knotty adj full of knots; hard to solve; puzzling.

know vt to be well-informed about; to be aware of; to be acquainted with.

knowing adj having knowledge; shrewd.

knowledge n what one knows; the body of facts, etc, accumulated over time; fact of knowing; range of information or understanding; the act of knowing.

knowledgeable, knowledgable adj having knowledge or intelligence; well-informed.

knuckle n a joint of the finger, esp at the roots of the fingers. • vi (with **down**) (inf) to start to work hard; (with **under**) to give in.

Koran n the sacred book of the Muslims.

L

label n a slip of paper, cloth, metal, etc, attached to anything to provide information about its nature, contents, ownership, etc; a term of generalised classification. • vt to attach a label to; to classify (as).

laboratory n a room or building where scientific work and research is carried out.

laborious adj requiring much work; hard-working; laboured.

labour n work, physical or mental exertion; all wage-earning workers; workers collectively; childbirth. • vi to work hard; to suffer (delusions, etc); to be in childbirth. • vt to develop in unnecessary detail.

labour camp n a penal colony where forced labour takes place.

labourer n a person who labours, esp a person whose work requires strength rather than skill.

labyrinth n a structure containing winding passages through which it is hard to find one's way.

lace n a cord, etc, used to draw together and fasten parts of a shoe, a corset, etc; a delicate orna-

mental fabric of openwork design using fine cotton, silk, etc. • vt to fasten with a lace or laces; to fortify (a drink, etc) with a dash of spirits.

lack n the fact or state of not having any or not having enough; the thing that is needed. • vti to be deficient in or entirely without.

lackadaisical adj showing lack of interest.

laconic adj using few words; concise.

lacquer n a glossy varnish. • vt to coat with lacquer, to make glossy.

lactic adj of or relating to milk; obtained from sour milk or whey.

lactose n a sugar present in milk.

lacy adj resembling lace.—**laciness** n.

lad n a boy; a young man; a fellow, chap.

ladder n a portable framework with rungs between two vertical supports for climbing up and down; something that resembles a ladder.

laden adj loaded with cargo; burdened.

ladle n a long-handled, cup-like spoon for scooping liquids; a device like this.

lady n a polite term for a woman; (with cap) a

title of honour given to various ranks of women in the British peerage.

ladybird n a small, usu brightly-coloured beetle.

lag[1] vi to fall behind, hang back; to fail to keep pace in movement or development.• n a delay.

lag[2] vt to insulate (pipes, etc) with lagging.

lag[3] n (sl) a convict; a term of imprisonment.

lager n a light beer that has been aged for a certain period.

lagging n insulating material used to lag pipes.

lagoon n a shallow lake or pond, esp one connected with a larger body of water.

lair n the dwelling place of a wild animal.

laity n laymen, as opposed to clergymen.

lake n a large inland body of water.

lamb n a young sheep; its flesh as food; (inf) a gentle person. • vi to give birth to a lamb.

lame adj disabled or crippled, esp in the feet or legs; weak, ineffectual. • vt to make lame.

lament vti to feel or express deep sorrow (for); to mourn. • n a lamenting; an elegy, dirge, etc, mourning some loss or death.

lamentable adj distressing, deplorable.

laminate vt to cover with one or more thin layers; to make by building up in layers. • n a product made by laminating.

laminated adj built in thin sheets or layers.

lamp n any device producing light, either by electricity, gas, or by burning oil, etc; a holder or base for such a device.

lampoon n a piece of satirical writing attacking someone. • vt to ridicule maliciously in a lampoon.

lance n a long wooden spear with a sharp iron or steel head. • vt to pierce (as if) with a lance.

land n the solid part of the earth's surface; ground, soil; a country and its people; property in land. • vt to set (an aircraft) down on land or water; to put on shore from a ship; to bring to a particular place; to catch (a fish); to get or secure (a job, prize, etc); to deliver (a blow). • vi to go ashore from a ship; to come to port; to arrive at a specified place; to come to rest.

landing n the act of coming to shore or to the ground; the place where persons or goods are loaded or unloaded from a ship; a platform at the end of a flight of stairs.

landlady n a woman who owns and rents property; a woman who owns and runs a boarding house, pub, etc.

landlord n a man who owns and rents property; a man who owns and runs a boarding house, pub, etc.

landmark n any prominent feature of the landscape distinguishing a locality; an important event or turning point.

landscape n an expanse of natural scenery seen in one view; a picture of natural, inland scenery.

• vt to make (a plot of ground) more attractive, as by adding lawns, bushes, trees, etc.

lane n a narrow road, path, etc; a path or strip specifically designated for ships, aircraft, cars, etc; one of the narrow strips dividing a running track, swimming pool, etc, for athletes and swimmers; one of the narrow passages along which balls are bowled in a bowling alley.

language n human speech or the written symbols for speech; any means of communicating; a special set of symbols used for programming a computer; the speech of a particular nation, etc; the particular style of verbal expression characteristic of a person, group, profession, etc.

languid adj lacking energy or vitality; apathetic; drooping, sluggish.

languish vi to lose strength and vitality; to pine; to suffer hardship; to assume a pleading or melancholic expression.

lank adj tall and thin; long and limp.

lanky adj lean, tall, and ungainly.

lanolin(e) n wool grease used in cosmetics, etc.

lantern n a portable transparent case for holding a light; a structure with windows on top of a door or roof to provide light and air; the light-chamber of a lighthouse.

lap[1] vti to take in (liquid) with the tongue; (waves) to flow gently with a splashing sound.

lap[2] n the flat area from waist to knees formed by a person sitting.

lap[3] n one circuit of a race track.

lapel n a part of a coat, jacket, etc, folded back and continuous with the collar.

lapse n a small error; a decline or drop to a lower condition, degree, or state; a moral decline; a period of time elapsed; the termination of a legal right or privilege through disuse. • vi to depart from the usual or accepted standard, esp in morals; to pass out of existence or use; to become void or discontinued; (time) to slip away.

larceny n theft.—**larcenous** adj.

lard n melted and clarified pig fat.

larder n a place where food is stored.

large adj great in size, amount, or number; bulky; big; spacious.

lark[1] n any of a family of songbirds.

lark[2] n a playful or amusing adventure.

larva n the immature form of many animals after emerging from an egg before transformation into the adult state, e.g. a caterpillar.

laryngitis n inflammation of the larynx.

larynx n the structure at the upper end of the windpipe, containing the vocal cords.

lascivious adj lecherous, lustful.

laser n a device that produces an intense beam of coherent light or other electromagnetic radiation.

lash vt to strike forcefully (as if) with a lash; to

fasten or secure with a cord, etc; to attack with criticism or ridicule. • *vi* (*rain, waves, etc*) to beat violently against; (*with* out) to attack physically or verbally. • *n* the flexible part of a whip; an eyelash; a stroke (as if) with a whip.

last¹ *n* a shoemaker's model of the foot on which boots and shoes are made or repaired.

last² *vi* to remain in existence, use, etc; to endure. • *vt* to continue during; to be enough for.

last³ *adj* being or coming after all the others in time or place; only remaining; the most recent; least likely; conclusive. • *adv* after all the others; most recently; finally. • *n* the one coming last.

lasting *adj* enduring.

last-minute *adj* at the last possible time.

latch *n* a fastening for a door, gate, or window, esp a bar, etc, that fits into a notch. • *vti* to fasten with a latch.

late *adj, adv* after the usual or expected time; at an advanced stage or age; near the end; far on in the day or evening; just prior to the present; deceased; not long past; until lately; out of office.—**lateness** *n*.

lately *adv* recently, in recent times.

latent *adj* existing but not yet developed.

lateral *adj* of, at, from, towards the side.

latex *n* the milky juice produced by certain plants, used in the manufacture of rubber.

lath *n* a thin narrow strip of wood used in constructing a framework for plaster, etc.

lathe *n* a machine that rotates wood, metal, etc, for shaping.

lather *n* a foam made by soap or detergent mixed with water; a state of agitation.

Latin *adj* of ancient Rome, its people, their language, etc; denoting or of the languages derived from Latin (Italian, Spanish, etc), the peoples who speak them, their countries, etc.—*also n*.

latitude *n* the distance north or south of the equator, measured in degrees; freedom from restrictions on actions or opinions.

latter *adj* later; more recent; nearer the end; being the last mentioned of two.

lattice *n* a network of crossed laths or bars.

laudable *adj* praiseworthy.

laugh *vi* to emit explosive inarticulate vocal sounds expressive of amusement, derision. • *vt* to utter with laughter. • *n* the act or sound of laughing; (*inf*) an amusing person or thing.

laughable *adj* causing laughter; ridiculous.

laughter *n* the act or sound of laughing.

launch¹ *vt* to throw, hurl or propel forward; to cause (a vessel) to slide into the water; (*rocket, missile*) to set off; to put into action; to put a new product onto the market.—*also n*.

launch² *n* an open, or partly enclosed, motor boat.

launder *vti* to wash and iron clothes. • *vt* to le-

gitimise (money) from criminal activity by passing it through foreign banks or investing in legitimate businesses, etc.

launderette *n* an establishment equipped with coin-operated washing machines and driers.

laundry *n* a place where clothes are washed and ironed; clothes sent to be washed and ironed.

laurel *n* an evergreen shrub with large, glossy leaves; the leaves used by the ancient Greeks as a symbol of achievement.

lava *n* molten rock flowing from a volcano.

lavatory *n* a sanitary device for the disposal of faeces and urine; a room for this.

lavender *n* the fragrant flowers of a perennial shrub dried and used in sachets; a pale purple colour.

lavish *vt* to give or spend freely. • *adj* abundant.

law *n* all the rules of conduct in an organised community as upheld by authority; any one of such rules; obedience to such rules; the study of such rules, jurisprudence; the seeking of justice in courts under such rules; the profession of lawyers, judges, etc; (*inf*) the police; a sequence of events occurring with unvarying uniformity under the same conditions.

law-abiding *adj* obeying the law.

lawful *adj* in conformity with the law.

lawless *adj* not regulated by law.

lawn¹ *n* a fine sheer cloth of linen or cotton.

lawn² *n* land covered with closely cut grass.

lawn mower *n* a hand-propelled or power-driven machine to cut lawn grass.

lawsuit *n* a suit between private parties in a law court.

lawyer *n* a person whose profession is advising others in matters of law.

lax *adj* slack; not tight; not strict or exact.

laxative *n* a substance that promotes emptying of the bowels.—*also adj*.

lay *vt* to put down; to allay or suppress; to place in a resting position; to place or set; to place in a correct position; to produce (an egg); (*sl*) to have sexual intercourse with; to devise; to present or assert; to stake a bet; (*with* off) to suspend from work temporarily or permanently; (*with* on) to supply; (*with* out) to plan in detail; to arrange for display; to prepare (a corpse) for viewing; (*inf*) to spend money, esp lavishly.

layabout *n* a loafer, lazy person.

lay-by *n* a place where motorists can stop at the side of a road without obstructing other traffic.

layer *n* a single thickness, fold, etc.

layman *n* a person who is not a member of the clergy; a non-specialist, someone who does not possess professional knowledge.

layout *n* the manner in which anything is laid out, esp arrangement of text and pictures on the pages of a newspaper or magazine, etc.

lazy adj disinclined to work or exertion.

lead[1] vt to show the way, esp by going first; to direct or guide on a course; to direct by influence; to be head of (an expedition, orchestra, etc); to be ahead of in a contest; to live, spend (one's life). • vi to show the way, as by going first; (with **to**) to tend in a certain direction; to be or go first. • n the role of a leader; first place; the amount or distance ahead; anything that leads, as a clue; the leading role in a play, etc; the right of playing first in cards or the card played.

lead[2] n a heavy, soft, bluish-grey, metallic element; a weight for sounding depths at sea, etc; bullets; a stick of graphite, used in pencils. • adj of or containing lead.

leaden adj made of lead; very heavy; gloomy.

leader n the person who goes first; the director of an orchestra; the inspiration or head of a movement, such as a political party; a person whose example is followed; a leading article in a newspaper.

leading[1] adj capable of guiding or influencing; principal; in first position.

leading[2] n a covering of lead; (print) the body of a type, larger than the size, giving space.

leaf n any of the flat, thin (usu green) parts growing from the stem of a plant; a sheet of paper; a very thin sheet of metal; a hinged or removable part of a table top.

leaflet n a sheet of printed information (often folded), esp advertising matter distributed free.

league n an association of nations, groups, etc, for promoting common interests; an association of sports clubs that organises matches between members.

leak n a crack or hole through which liquid or gas may accidentally pass; confidential information made public deliberately or accidentally. • vi to (let) escape though an opening; to disclose information surreptitiously.—**leakage** n.

lean[1] adj thin, with little flesh or fat; spare; meagre. • n meat with little or no fat.

lean[2] vi to bend or slant from an upright position; to rest supported (on or against); to rely or depend for help (on).

leaning n inclination, tendency.

leap vi to jump; (with **at**) to accept something offered eagerly. • vt to pass over by a jump. • n an act of leaping; an abrupt transition.

leapfrog n a game in which one player vaults over another's bent back. • vi to vault in this manner; to advance in alternate jumps.

leap year n a year with an extra day (29 February) occurring every fourth year.

learn vti to gain knowledge of or skill in; to memorise; to realise.—**learner** n.

learned adj having learning; erudite; acquired by study, experience, etc.

learning n a gaining of knowledge; the acquiring of knowledge or skill through study.

lease n a contract by which an owner lets land, property, etc, to another person for a specified period. • vt to grant by or hold under lease.

leaseback n the process of selling an asset, esp a building, and then renting it.

leasehold n the act of holding by lease; the land, buildings, etc, held by lease.

least adj smallest in size, degree, etc; slightest. • adv to the smallest degree. • n the smallest in amount.

leather n material made from the skin of an animal prepared by removing the hair and tanning. • vt to thrash.

leave[1] n permission to do something; official authorisation to be absent; the period covered by this.

leave[2] vt to depart from; to cause or allow to remain in a specified state; to cause to remain behind; to refrain from consuming or dealing with; to have remaining at death, to bequeath; to have as a remainder; to allow to stay or continue doing without interference; to entrust or commit to another; to abandon. • vi to depart.

leaven n a substance to make dough rise, esp yeast; something that changes or enlivens. • vt to raise with leaven; to modify, to enliven.

lecherous adj characterised by lechery.

lecture n an informative talk to a class, etc; a lengthy reprimand. • vti to give a lecture (to); to reprimand.—**lecturer** n.

ledge n a narrow horizontal surface resembling a shelf projecting from a wall, rock face, etc; an underwater ridge of rocks.

ledger n a book in which a record of debits, credits, etc, is kept.

leech n a blood-sucking worm; a person who clings to or exploits another.

leek n a vegetable that resembles a greatly elongated green onion.

leer n a sly or lascivious look.—also vi.

leeway n the distance a ship, etc has strayed sideways of its course; freedom of action as regards expenditure of time, etc.

left[1] adj of or on the side that is towards the west when one faces north; worn on the left hand, foot, etc. • n the left side; (often cap) of or relating to the left in politics; the left hand; (boxing) a blow with the left hand.

left-wing adj of the liberal faction of a political party, organisation, etc.

leg n one of the limbs on which humans and animals support themselves and walk; the part of a garment covering the leg; a thing shaped or used like a leg; a branch of a forked object; a section, as of a trip; any of a series of games or matches in a competition.

legacy n money, property, etc, left to someone in a will; something passed on by an ancestor or remaining from the past.

legal adj of or based on law; permitted by law.

legalise vt to make lawful.

legend n a story handed down from the past; a notable person or the stories of his or her exploits; an inscription on a coin, etc; a caption; an explanation of the symbols used on a map.

legendary adj of, based on, or presented in legends; famous, notorious.

leggings npl protective outer coverings for the lower legs; a leg-hugging fashion garment.

legible adj able to be read.

legion n an infantry unit of the ancient Roman army; a large body of soldiers; a large number; a multitude.

legislate vi to make or pass laws. • vt to bring about by legislation.—**legislation** n.

legislative adj of legislation or a legislature.

legislature n the body of people who have the power of making laws.

legitimate adj lawful; reasonable, justifiable; (child) born of parents married to each other.—**legitimacy** n.

leisure n ease, relaxation, esp freedom from employment or duties.

lemon n (a tree bearing) a small yellow oval fruit with an acid pulp; pale yellow.

lend vt to give the use of something temporarily in expectation of its return; to provide (money) at interest. • vi to make loans.

length n the extent of something from end to end, usu the longest dimension; a specified distance or period of time; something of a certain length taken from a larger piece; (often pl) the degree of effort put into some action.

lengthen vti to make or become longer.

lengthways, lengthwise adv in the direction of the length.

lengthy adj long, esp too long.

lenient adj not harsh or severe; merciful.

lens n a curved piece of transparent glass, plastic, etc, used in optical instruments to form an image; any device used to focus electromagnetic rays, sound waves, etc; a similar transparent part of the eye that focuses light rays on the retina.

Lent n the forty weekdays from Ash Wednesday to Easter, observed by Christians as a period of fasting and penitence.

leopard n a large tawny feline with black spots found in Africa and Asia.

leotard n a skintight one-piece garment.

leper n a person with leprosy.

leprosy n a chronic infectious bacterial disease of the skin, often causing disfigurement.

lesbian n a female homosexual. • adj of or characteristic of lesbians.—**lesbianism** n.

lesion n any change in an organ or tissue caused by injury or disease; an injury.

less adj not so much, not so great, etc. • adv to a smaller extent. • n a smaller amount. • prep minus.

lessen vti to make or become less.

lesson n something that has been learned or studied; a unit of learning or teaching; (pl) a course of instruction.

let[1] n a stoppage; (tennis) a minor obstruction of the ball that requires a point to be replayed.

let[2] vt to allow; to rent; to cause to run out, as blood; as an auxiliary in giving suggestions (let us go); (with down) to lower; to deflate; to disappoint; (with off) to explode (a bomb); to deal leniently with; (with out) to release; to reveal; to make a garment larger; (with up) to relax; to cease. • vi (with on) (inf) to pretend; (inf) to indicate awareness.

lethal adj deadly.

lethargy n sluggishness; apathy.—**lethargic** adj.

letter n a symbol representing a phonetic value in a written language; a character of the alphabet; a written or printed message; (pl) literature; learning; knowledge; literal meaning. • vt to mark with letters.

lettering n letters collectively; an inscription.

lettuce n a plant with succulent leaves used in salads.

leukaemia n a chronic disease characterised by an abnormal increase in the number of white blood cells in body tissues and blood.

level n a horizontal line or plane; a position in a scale of values; a flat area or surface; an instrument for determining the horizontal. • adj horizontal; having a flat surface; at the same height, rank, position, etc. • vti to make or become level; to demolish; to raise and aim (a gun, etc).

level-headed adj having sound judgment.

lever n a bar used for prising or moving something; a means to an end; a device consisting of a bar turning about a fixed point; any device used in the same way, e.g. to operate machinery. • vt to raise or move (as with) a lever.

leverage n the mechanical advantage gained by the use of a lever; power, influence.

levity n excessive frivolity; lack of seriousness.

levy vt to collect by force or authority, as a tax, fine, etc; an amount levied; to enrol or conscript troops; to prepare for or wage war. • n a levying; the amount levied.

lewd adj indecent; lustful; obscene.

lexicography n the process of writing or compiling a dictionary.

lexicon n a dictionary; a special vocabulary.

liability n a being liable; something for which one is liable; (inf) a disadvantage; (pl) debts, obligations, disadvantages.

liable adj legally bound or responsible; subject to; likely (to).

liaison n intercommunication as between units of a military force; an illicit love affair.

liar n a person who tells lies.

libel n any written or printed matter tending to injure a person's reputation unjustly; (*inf*) any defamatory or damaging assertion about a person. • vt to utter or publish a libel against.

liberal adj ample, abundant; not literal or strict; tolerant; favouring reform or progress. • n a person who favours reform or progress.

liberality n generosity; breadth of mind.

liberalise vti to make or become less strict.

liberate vt to set free from foreign occupation, slavery, etc.—**liberation** n.

libertarian n a person who advocates liberty, esp in conduct or thought.

libertine n a dissolute person; a freethinker.

liberty n freedom from slavery, captivity, etc; the right to do as one pleases; freedom; a particular right, freedom, etc, granted by authority; an impertinent attitude; authorised leave granted to a sailor.

librarian n a person in charge of a library.

library n a collection of books, tapes, records, photographs, etc, for reference or borrowing; a room, building or institution containing such a collection; (*comput*) a set of, usu general purpose, programs or subroutines for use in programming.

licence n a formal or legal permission to do something specified; a document granting such permission; freedom to deviate from rule, practice, etc; excessive freedom, an abuse of liberty.

license vt to grant a licence to or for; to permit.

licentious adj morally unrestrained.

lichen n any of various small plants consisting of an alga and a fungus growing on stones, etc.

lick vt to draw the tongue over, esp to taste or clean; (*flames, etc*) to flicker around; (*inf*) to defeat.

lid n a removable cover as for a box, etc; an eyelid.—**lidded** adj.

lie[1] n an untrue statement made with intent to deceive. • vi to speak untruthfully with an intention to deceive.

lie[2] vi to be in a reclining or horizontal position; to rest on a support in a horizontal position; to be situated. • n the way in which something is situated.

lieutenant n a commissioned army officer ranking below a captain; a naval officer next below a lieutenant commander.

life n that property of plants and animals (ending at death) that enables them to use food, grow, reproduce, etc; living things collectively; the time a person or thing exists; one's manner of living; one's animate existence; vigour, liveliness; (*inf*) a life sentence; a biography. • adj of animate being; lifelong; using a living model; of or relating to or provided by life insurance.

lifebelt n an inflatable ring to support a person in the water; a safety belt.

lifeboat n a small rescue boat carried by a ship; a specially designed and equipped rescue vessel that helps those in distress along the coastline.

lifeguard n an expert swimmer employed to prevent drownings.

life jacket n a sleeveless jacket or vest of buoyant material to keep a person afloat.

lifeless adj dead; unconscious; dull.

lifeline n a rope for raising or lowering a diver; a rope for rescuing a person, e.g. as attached to a lifebelt; a vitally important channel of communication or transport.

lift vt to bring to a higher position, raise; to raise in rank, condition, etc; (*sl*) to steal; to revoke. • vi to exert oneself in raising something; to rise; to go up; (*fog, etc*) to disperse; (*with* off) (*rocket, etc*) to take off. • n act or fact of lifting; distance through which a thing is lifted; elevation of mood, etc; elevated position or carriage; a ride in the direction in which one is going; help of any kind; a cage or platform for moving from one level to another; upward air pressure maintaining an aircraft in flight.

ligament n a band of tissue connecting bones.

light[1] n the agent of illumination that stimulates the sense of sight; electromagnetic radiation such as ultraviolet, infrared or X-rays; brightness, illumination; a source of light, as the sun, a lamp, etc; daylight. • adj pale in colour. • vt to ignite; to cause to give off light.

light[2] adj having little weight; not heavy; less than usual in weight, amount, force, etc; of little importance; easy to bear; easy to digest; happy; dizzy, giddy; not serious; moderate; moving with ease; producing small products. • adv lightly. • vi to come to rest after travelling through the air; to dismount, to alight; to come or happen on or upon; to strike suddenly, as a blow.

lighten[1] vti to make or become light or lighter.

lighten[2] vti to make or become lighter in weight; to make or become more cheerful; to mitigate.

lighter[1] n a small device that produces a naked flame to light cigarettes.

lighter[2] n a large barge used in loading or unloading larger ships.

light-headed adj dizzy; delirious.

light-hearted adj carefree.

lighthouse n a tower with a bright light to guide ships.

lighting n the process of giving light; equipment for illuminating a stage, television set, etc; the distribution of light on a work of art.

lightning n a flash of electricity in the sky.

light pen n a pen-shaped photoelectric device used to communicate with a computer by pointing at the monitor; a similar device used for reading bar codes.

lightweight adj of less than average weight; trivial, unimportant. • n a person or thing of less than average weight; a professional boxer weighing 130-135 pounds (59-61 kg); a person of little importance or influence.

light year n the distance light travels in one year.

like[1] adj having the same characteristics; similar; equal. • adv (inf) likely. • prep similar to; characteristic of; in the mood for; indicative of; as for example. • conj (inf) as; as if. • n an equal.

like[2] vt to be pleased with. • vi to be so inclined.

likelihood n probability.

likely adj reasonably to be expected; showing promise of success. • adv probably.

likewise adv the same; also.

liking n fondness; affection; preference.

lilac n a shrub with large clusters of tiny, fragrant flowers; a pale purple.

lilt n a light rhythmic song or tune.

lily n a bulbous plant having typically trumpet-shaped flowers; its flower.

lima bean n a bean that produces flat, edible pale green seeds; its edible seed.

limb n a projecting appendage of an animal body, as an arm, leg, or wing; a large branch of a tree; a participating member, agent.

limber adj flexible, able to bend the body easily. • vti to make or become limber.

lime[1] n a white calcium compound used for making cement and in agriculture. • vt to treat or cover with lime.

lime[2] n a small yellowish-green fruit with a juicy, sour pulp; the tree that bears it; its colour.

lime[3] n the linden tree.

limelight n intense publicity.

limerick n a type of humorous verse consisting of five lines.

limestone n a type of rock composed mainly of calcium carbonate.

limit n a boundary; (pl) bounds; the greatest amount allowed. • vt to set a limit to; to restrict.

limitation n the act of limiting or being limited; a hindrance to ability or achievement.

limited adj confined within bounds.

limp[1] vi to walk with or as with a lame leg. • n a lameness in walking.

limp[2] adj not firm; lethargic; wilted; flexible.

limpet n a mollusc with a low conical shell that clings to rocks.

line[1] vt to put, or serve as, a lining in.

line[2] n a length of cord, rope, or wire; a system of conducting fluid, electricity, etc; a thin thread-like mark; as a wrinkle; edge, limit, boundary; border, outline, contour; a row of persons or things, as printed letters across a page; a succession of persons, lineage; a connected series of things; a whole system of transportation; a person's trade or occupation; a field of experience or interest; (inf) glib, persuasive talk; the forward combat position in warfare; a stock of goods; a short letter, note; (pl) all the speeches of a character in a play. • vt to mark with lines; to arrange in a line. • vi to align.

lineage n direct descent from an ancestor.

linear adj of, made of, or using a line or lines; narrow and long; in relation to length.

linen n thread or cloth made of flax; household articles (sheets, cloths, etc) made of linen or cotton cloth.

linesman n an official in certain games who assists the referee.

linger vi to stay a long time; to delay departure; to dawdle or loiter; to dwell on in the mind; to remain alive though on the point of death.

linguist n a person who is skilled in speaking foreign languages.

linguistic adj of language or linguistics.

linguistics n (used as sing) the science of language.

lining n a material used to cover the inner surface of a garment, etc; any material covering an inner surface.

link n a single loop or ring of a chain; something resembling a loop or ring or connecting piece; a person or thing acting as a connection, as in a communication system, machine or organisation. • vti to connect or become connected.

linkage n a linking; a series or system of links.

linoleum n a floor covering of coarse fabric backing with a smooth, hard decorative coating.

lint n scraped and softened linen used to dress wounds; fluff.

lintel n the horizontal crosspiece spanning a doorway or window.

lion n a large, flesh-eating feline mammal with a shaggy mane in the adult male.

lip n either of the two fleshy flaps that surround the mouth; anything like a lip, as the rim of a jug.

lip service n support expressed but not acted upon.

liqueur n a sweet and variously flavoured alcoholic drink.

liquid n a substance that, unlike a gas, does not expand indefinitely and, unlike a solid, flows readily. • adj in liquid form; (assets) readily convertible into cash.

liquidate vt to settle the accounts of; to close a (bankrupt) business and distribute its assets among its creditors; to convert into cash; to eliminate, kill.—**liquidation** n.

liquidise vt to make liquid.

liquor n an alcoholic drink.

liquorice n a black extract made from the root of a European plant, used in medicine and confectionery.

lisp vi to substitute the sounds th (as in thin) for s or th (as in then) for z; a speech defect or habit involving such pronunciation; to utter imperfectly. • vt to speak or utter with a lisp.—also n.

list¹ n a series of names, numbers, words, etc, written or printed in order. • vt to make a list of; to enter in a directory, etc.

list² vti to tilt to one side, as a ship.—also n.

listen vi to try to hear; to pay attention, take heed; (with **in**) to overhear a conversation, e.g. on the telephone; to tune into a radio broadcast.

listless adj lacking energy or enthusiasm.

litany n a type of prayer in which petitions to God are recited by a priest and elicit set responses by the congregation.

literacy n the ability to read and write.

literal adj in accordance with the exact meaning of a word or text; in a basic or strict sense.

literary adj of or dealing with literature.

literate adj able to read and write; educated.

literature n the writings of a period or of a country, esp those valued for their excellence; of style or form; all the books and articles on a subject; (inf) any printed matter.

lithe adj supple, flexible.

litigate vti to bring or contest in a lawsuit.

litigious adj of or causing lawsuits; fond of engaging in lawsuits; contentious.

litmus n a colouring material obtained from certain lichens that turns red in acid solutions and blue in alkaline solutions.

litre n a measure of liquid capacity in the metric system, equivalent to 1.76 pints.

litter n rubbish scattered about; young animals produced at one time; straw, hay, etc, used as bedding for animals; a stretcher for carrying a sick or wounded person. • vt to make untidy; to scatter about carelessly.

little adj not great or big, small in size, amount, degree, etc; short in duration; narrow-minded. • n small in amount, degree, etc. • adv less, least, slightly.

live¹ vi to have life; to remain alive; to pass life in a specified manner; to enjoy a full life; to reside. • vt to spend; pass.

live² adj having life; of present interest; still burning; unexploded; carrying electric current; broadcast during the actual performance.

livelihood n employment; means of living.

lively adj full of life; spirited; exciting; vivid.

liver n the largest glandular organ in vertebrate animals, which secretes bile, etc, and is important in metabolism; the liver of an animal as food.

livestock n (farm) animals raised for use or sale.

livid adj (skin) discoloured, as from bruising; greyish in colour; (inf) extremely angry.

living adj having life; still in use; true to life, vivid; of life, for living in. • n livelihood.

lizard n a reptile with a slender body, four legs, and a tapering tail.

llama n a South American animal related to the camel.

load n an amount carried at one time; something borne with difficulty; a burden; (often pl) (inf) a great amount. • vt to put into or upon; to burden; to oppress; to supply in large quantities; to alter, as by adding a weight to dice; to put a charge of ammunition into (a firearm); to put film into (a camera); (comput) to install a program in memory. • vi to take on a load.

loaf¹ n a mass of bread of regular shape and standard weight.

loaf² vi to pass time in idleness.—**loafer** n.

loam n rich and fertile soil.—**loamy** adj.

loan n the act of lending; something lent, esp money. • vti to lend.

loath adj unwilling.—also **loth**.

loathe vt to dislike intensely; to detest.

lob vti to toss or hit (a ball) in a high curve.

lobby n an entrance hall of a public building; a person or group that tries to influence legislators. • vti to try to influence (legislators) to support a particular cause or take certain action.

lobe n a rounded projection, as the lower end of the ear; any of the divisions of the lungs or brain.

lobster n an edible sea crustacean with four pairs of legs and a pair of large pincers.

local adj of a particular place; serving the needs of a specific district; of or for a particular part of the body. • n an inhabitant of a specific place; (inf) a pub serving a particular district.

locality n a neighbourhood or a district.

locate vt to determine or indicate the position of something.

location n a specific position or place; a locating or being located; a place outside a studio where a film is (partly) shot; (comput) an area in memory where a single item of data is stored.

lock¹ n a fastening device on doors, etc, operated by a key or combination; part of a canal, dock, etc, in which the level of the water can be changed by the operation of gates; the part of a gun by which the charge is fired; a controlling hold, as used in wrestling. • vt to fasten with a lock; to shut; to fit, link; to jam together so as to make immovable. • vi to become locked.

lock² n a curl of hair; a tuft of wool, etc.

locker n a small cupboard, chest, etc, that can be locked.

locomotive n an electric, steam or diesel engine on wheels, designed to move a railway train.

locust n a type of large grasshopper often travelling in swarms and destroying crops; a type of hard-wooded leguminous tree.

lodge n a small house at the entrance to a park or stately home; a country house for seasonal leisure activities; a resort hotel or motel; the local chapter or hall of a fraternal society; a beaver's lair. • vt to house temporarily; to shoot, thrust, etc, firmly (in); to bring before legal authorities; to confer upon. • vi to live as a paying guest; to come to rest and stick firmly (in).

lodger n a person who lives in a rented room in another's home.

loft n a space under a roof; a storage area under the roof of a barn or stable.

lofty adj (objects) of a great height; (person) noble.

log n a section of a felled tree; a device for ascertaining the speed of a ship; a record of speed, progress, etc, esp one kept on a ship's voyage or aircraft's flight. • vt to record in a log. • vi (with on or off) (comput) to establish or disestablish communication with a computer from a remote terminal in a multiuser system.

logarithm n the exponent of the power to which a fixed number (the base) is to be raised to produce a given number, used to avoid multiplying and dividing when solving mathematical problems.

logic n correct reasoning, or the science of this; way of reasoning.

logical adj conforming to the rules of logic; capable of reasoning according to logic.

logistics n (used as sing)the planning and organisation of any complex activity.—**logistic** adj.

loin n (usu pl) the lower part of the back between the hipbones and the ribs; the front part of an animal's hindquarters used for food.

loiter vi to linger or stand about aimlessly.

lollipop n a flat boiled sweet at the end of a stick.

lone adj by oneself; isolated; solitary.

lonely adj isolated; unhappy at being alone.

loner n a person who avoids company.

long[1] adj measuring much in space or time; having a greater than usual length, quantity, etc; tedious, slow; far-reaching; well-supplied. • adv for a long time; from start to finish.

long[2] vi to desire earnestly, esp for something not likely to be attained.

longing n an intense desire.

longitude n distance east or west of the prime meridian, expressed in degrees or time.

long-sighted adj only seeing distant objects clearly.

long-standing adj having continued for a long time.

long-suffering adj enduring pain, provocation, etc, patiently.

long wave n a radio wave of a frequency less than 300 kHz.

long-winded adj speaking at great length.

loofah n the fibrous skeleton of a type of gourd used as a sponge for scrubbing.

look vi to try to see; to see; to search; to appear, seem; to be facing in a specified direction; (with in) to pay a brief visit; (with up) to improve in prospects. • vt to direct one's eyes on; to have an appearance befitting. • n the act of looking; a gaze, glance; appearance; aspect; (with after) to take care of; (with over) to examine; (with up) to research (for information, etc) in book; to visit.

looking glass n a mirror.

lookout n a place for keeping watch; a person assigned to watch.

loom[1] n a machine or frame for weaving yarn.

loom[2] vi to come into view indistinctly and often threateningly; to come ominously close, as an impending event.

loop n a figure made by a curved line crossing itself; a similar rounded shape in cord, rope, etc, crossed on itself; anything forming this figure; (comput) a set of instructions in a program that are executed repeatedly; an intrauterine contraceptive device; a segment of film or magnetic tape. • vt to make a loop of; to fasten with a loop. • vi to form a loop or loops.

loophole n a means of evading an obligation, etc.

loose adj free from confinement or restraint; not firmly fastened; not tight or compact; not precise; inexact; (inf) relaxed. • vt to release; to unfasten; to untie; to detach.

loosen vti to make or become loose or looser.

loot n goods taken during warfare, civil unrest, etc; (sl) money. • vti to plunder, pillage.

lop vt to sever the branches or twigs from a tree; to cut out as superfluous.

lopsided adj having one side larger in weight, height, or size than the other; badly balanced.

lord n a ruler, master or monarch; a male member of the nobility; (with cap and the) God; a form of address used to certain peers, bishops and judges.

lore n learning, esp of a traditional nature.

lorry n a large motor vehicle for transporting heavy loads.

lose vt to have taken from one by death, accident, removal, etc; to be unable to find; to fail to keep, as one's temper; to fail to win; to wander from (one's way, etc). • vi to suffer (a) loss.

loss n a losing or being lost; the damage, trouble caused by losing; the person or amount lost.

loss leader n an item sold at a price below its value in order to attract customers.

lost adj no longer possessed; missing; not won.

lot n an object, such as a straw, slip of paper, etc, drawn from others at random to reach a decision by chance; one's share by lot; fortune; a plot of ground; a group of persons or things; an item or set of items put up for auction; (*often pl*) (*inf*) a great amount; much; (*inf*) sort.

loth *see* **loath.**

lotion n a liquid for cosmetic or external medical use.

lottery n a system of raising money by selling numbered tickets that offer the chance of winning a prize; an enterprise, etc, which may or may not succeed.

loud adj characterised by or producing great noise; emphatic; (*inf*) obtrusive.

lounge vi to move, sit, lie, etc, in a relaxed way; to spend time idly. • n a room with comfortable furniture for sitting, as a waiting room at an airport, etc; a comfortable sitting room in a hotel or private house.

louse n any of various small wingless insects that are parasitic on humans and animals; (*inf*)a mean, contemptible person.

lousy adj infested with lice; (*sl*) of poor quality, inferior; (*sl*) well supplied (with).

lout n a clumsy, rude person.—**loutish** adj.

love n a strong liking for someone or something; a passionate affection for another person; the object of such affection; (*tennis*) a score of zero. • vti to feel love (for).

lovely adj beautiful; (*inf*) highly enjoyable.

lover n a person in love with another person; a person, having an extramarital sexual relationship; (*pl*) a couple in love with each other.

loving adj affectionate.

low[1] n the sound of a cow, a moo.—*also vi.*

low[2] adj not high or tall; below the normal level; less in size, degree, amount, etc, than usual; deep in pitch; depressed in spirits; humble, of low rank; vulgar, coarse; not loud. • adv in or to a low degree, level, etc. • n a low level, degree, etc; a region of low barometric pressure.

lowdown n (*sl: with* **the**) the true facts

low-down adj (*inf*) mean, contemptible.

lower adj below in place, rank, etc; less in amount, degree, etc. • vt to let or put down; to reduce in height, amount, etc; to bring down in respect, etc. • vi to become lower.

lowly adj humble, of low status; meek.

loyal adj firm in allegiance to a person, cause, country, etc, faithful.

lozenge n a four-sided diamond-shaped figure; a cough drop, sweet, etc.

lubricant n a substance that lubricates.

lubricate vt to coat or treat (machinery, etc) with oil or grease to lessen friction; to make smooth, slippery, or greasy.—**lubrication** n.

lucid adj easily understood; sane.

luck n chance; good fortune.

lucky adj having or bringing good luck.

lucrative adj producing wealth; profitable.

ludicrous adj absurd, laughable.

lug[1] vt to pull or drag along with effort.

lug[2] n an ear-like projection.

luggage n the suitcases and other baggage containing the possessions of a traveller.

lugubrious adj mournful, dismal.

lukewarm adj tepid; lacking enthusiasm.

lull vt to soothe, to calm; to calm the suspicions of, esp by deception. • n a short period of calm.

lullaby n a song to lull children to sleep.

lumbago n rheumatic pain in the lower back.

lumber n timber, logs, beams, boards, etc, roughly cut and prepared for use; articles of unused household furniture that are stored away; any useless articles. • vi to cut down timber and saw it into lumber. • vt to clutter with lumber; to heap in disorder.

lumberjack n a person employed to fell trees and transport and prepare timber.

luminous adj glowing in the dark.

lump n a small, compact mass of something, usu without definite shape; an abnormal swelling; a dull or stupid person. • adj in a lump or lumps. • vt to treat or deal with in a mass.

lumpy adj filled or covered with lumps.

lunacy n insanity; utter folly.

lunar adj of or like the moon.

lunatic adj insane. • n an insane person.

lunch n a light meal, esp between breakfast and dinner. • vi to eat lunch.

luncheon n lunch, esp a formal lunch.

lung n either of the two sponge-like breathing organs in the chest of vertebrates.

lunge n a sudden forceful thrust, as with a sword; a sudden plunge forward. • vti to move, or cause to move, with a lunge.

lurch vi to lean or pitch suddenly to the side.

lure n something that attracts, tempts or entices; a brightly coloured fishing bait; a device used to recall a trained hawk; a decoy for wild animals. • vt to entice, attract, or tempt.

lurid adj glaring; shocking; sensational.

lurk vi to lie hidden in wait; to loiter.

luscious adj delicious; richly sweet.

lush adj tender and juicy; of or showing abundant growth.

lust n strong sexual desire (for); an intense longing for something. • vi to feel lust.

lustre n gloss; sheen; brightness; radiance; brilliant beauty or fame; glory.

lusty adj strong, vigorous; healthy.

lute n an old-fashioned stringed instrument.

luxuriant adj profuse, abundant; ornate; fertile.—**luxuriance** n.

luxuriate vi to enjoy immensely, to revel (in).
luxurious adj rich, comfortable.
luxury n indulgence and pleasure in expensive food, accommodation, clothes, etc; (often pl) something that is costly and enjoyable but not indispensable. • adj relating to or supplying luxury.
lynch vt to murder (an accused person) by mob action, without lawful trial, esp as by hanging.

lynx n a wild feline of Europe and North America with spotted fur.
lyre n an ancient musical instrument of the harp family.
lyric adj denoting or of poetry expressing the writer's emotion. • n a lyric poem; (pl) the words of a popular song.—**lyricist** n.
lyrical adj lyric; (inf) expressing enthusiasm.

M

macaroni n pasta in the form of tubes.
mace[1] n a staff used as a symbol of authority by certain institutions.
mace[2] n an aromatic spice made from the external covering of the nutmeg.
machine n a structure of fixed and moving parts, for doing useful work; an organisation functioning like a machine; the controlling group in a political party; a device, as the lever, etc, that transmits, or changes the application of energy. • vt to shape or finish by machine-operated tools.
machine gun n an automatic gun, firing a rapid stream of bullets.—also vt.
machinery n machines collectively; the parts of a machine.
mackerel n a common oily food fish.
mad adj insane; infatuated; (inf) angry.
madden vti to make angry, or wildly excited.
madly adv in an insane manner; force; (inf) excessively.
madman n an insane person.
madness n insanity; foolishness.
magazine n a military store; a space where explosives are stored, as in a fort; a supply chamber, as in a camera, a rifle, etc; a periodical publication containing articles, fiction, etc.
maggot n a wormlike larva, as of the housefly.—**maggoty** adj.
magic n the use of charms, spells, etc, to supposedly influence events by supernatural means; any mysterious power; the art of producing illusions by sleight of hand, etc. • adj of or relating to magic; possessing supposedly supernatural powers; (inf) wonderful.—**magical** adj.
magician n one skilled in magic; a conjurer.
magistrate n a public officer empowered to administer the law.
magnanimous adj noble and generous.
magnate n a very wealthy or influential person.
magnet n any piece of iron or steel that has the property of attracting iron; anything that attracts.

magnetic adj producing or acting by magnetism; having the ability to attract or charm people.
magnetism n the property, quality, or condition of being magnetic; personal charm.
magnification n magnifying or being magnified; the degree of enlargement of something by a lens, microscope, etc.
magnificent adj splendid, stately or sumptuous in appearance; superb, of very high quality.—**magnificence** n.
magnify vt to exaggerate; to increase the apparent size of (an object) as (with) a lens.
magnitude n greatness of size, extent, etc; importance.
magnolia n a spring-flowering shrub or tree with showy flowers.
magpie n a black and white bird of the crow family; an acquisitive person.
mahogany n the hard, reddish-brown wood of a tropical tree; its colour.
maid n a maiden; a woman servant.
maiden n a girl or young unmarried woman. • adj unmarried or virgin; untried; first.
mail[1] n a body armour made of small metal rings.
mail[2] n letters, packages, etc, transported and delivered by the post office; a postal system. • vt to send by mail.
maim vt to cripple; to mutilate.
main adj chief in size, importance, etc; principal. • n (often pl but used a sing) a principal pipe in a distribution system for water, gas, etc.
mainland n the principal land mass of a continent, as distinguished from nearby islands.
maintain vt to preserve; to support, to sustain.
maintenance n upkeep; (financial) support, esp of a spouse after a divorce.
maisonette n a small house; self-contained living quarters, usu on two floors with its own entrance, as part of a larger house.
maize n corn; a light yellow colour.

majestic *adj* dignified; imposing.

majesty *n* grandeur; (*with cap*) a title used in speaking to or of a sovereign.

major *adj* greater in size, importance, amount, etc; (*surgery*) very serious, life-threatening; (*mus*) higher than the corresponding minor by half a tone. • *vi* to specialise (in a field of study). • *n* an officer ranking just above a lieutenant-colonel; (*mus*) a major key, chord or scale.

majority *n* the greater number or part of; full legal age.

make *vt* to cause to exist, occur, appear; to build, create, produce, manufacture, etc; to amount to; to earn; to cause or force; to arrive at; (*with believe*) to imagine, pretend; (*with good*) to make up for, pay compensation; (*with out*)to complete (a form, etc) in writing; to attempt to understand; (*with up*) to invent, esp to deceive; to make complete; to put together. • *vi* (*with do*) to manage with what is available; (*with for*) to go in the direction of; (*with good*) to become successful or wealthy; (*with off*) to leave in haste; (*with out*) to pretend; (*with up*) to become reconciled; to compensate for; to put on make-up for the stage. • *n* style, brand or origin.

make-up *n* cosmetics; the way something is put together, composition; nature, disposition.

maladjusted *adj* poorly adjusted.

malaria *n* an infectious disease caused by mosquito bites, and characterised by recurring attacks of fevers and chills.

male *adj* denoting or of the sex that fertilises the ovum; of, like or suitable for men and boys; masculine. • *n* a male person, animal or plant.

malevolent *adj* ill-disposed towards others; spiteful, malicious.—**malevolence** *n*.

malfunction *n* faulty functioning. • *vi* to function wrongly.

malice *n* active ill will, intention to inflict injury upon another.—**malicious** *adj*.

malign *adj* harmful; evil. • *vt* to slander.

malignant *adj* having a wish to harm others; injurious; (*disease*) rapidly spreading, resistant to treatment, esp of a tumour.

malinger *vi* to feign illness to evade work.

malleable *adj* capable of being shaped.

mallet *n* a small, usu wooden-headed, short-handled hammer; a long-handled version for striking the ball in polo and croquet.

malnutrition *n* lack of nutrition.

malpractice *n* professional misconduct, esp by a medical practitioner.

malt *n* a cereal grain, such as barley, which is soaked and dried and used in brewing; (*inf*) malt liquor, malt whisky.—**malty** *adj*.

mammal *n* any member of a class of warm-blooded vertebrates that suckle their young with milk.—**mammalian** *adj*.

mammoth *n* an extinct elephant with long, curved tusks. • *adj* enormous.

man *n* a human being, esp an adult male; the human race; an ordinary soldier, as opposed to an officer; a member of a team, etc; a piece in games such as chess, draughts, etc; a husband. • *vt* to provide with men for work, defence, etc.

manage *vt* to control the movement or behaviour of; to have charge of; to succeed in accomplishing. • *vi* to contrive to get along.

management *n* those carrying out the administration of a business; the managers collectively; the technique of managing.

manager *n* a person who manages a company, organisation, etc; an agent who looks after the business affairs of an actor, writer, etc; a person who organises the training of a sports team.—**managerial** *adj*.

mandarin *n* (*formerly*) a high-ranking bureaucrat of the Chinese empire; any high-ranking official, esp one given to pedantic sometimes obscure public pronouncements; (*with cap*) the Beijing dialect that is the official pronunciation of the Chinese language; the fruit of a small spiny Chinese tree that has been developed in cultivation.

mandate *n* an order or command; the authority to act on the behalf of another, esp the will of constituents expressed to their representatives in legislatures. • *vt* to entrust by mandate.

mandatory *adj* compulsory.

mane *n* long hair that grows on the back of the neck of the horse, lion, etc.

manful *adj* showing courage and resolution.

mangle[1] *vt* to crush, mutilate; to spoil, ruin.

mangle[2] *n* a machine for drying and pressing sheets, etc, between rollers.

mango *n* a yellow-red fleshy tropical fruit with a firm central stone.

manhandle *vt* to handle roughly.

manhood *n* the state or time of being a man; virility; courage, etc.

manhunt *n* a hunt for a fugitive.

mania *n* a mental disorder displaying sometimes violent behaviour and great excitement; great excitement or enthusiasm; a craze.

maniac *n* a madman.

manicure *n* trimming, polishing, etc, of fingernails.—*also vt.*—**manicurist** *n*.

manifest *adj* obvious, clearly evident. • *vt* to make clear; to display, to reveal. • *n* a list of a ship's or aircraft's cargo.

manifesto *n* a public printed declaration of intent and policy issued by a government or political party.

manipulate *vt* to work or handle skilfully; to manage shrewdly or artfully, often in an unfair way.—**manipulation** *n*.

mankind n the human race.

manly adj appropriate in character to a man.

man-made adj artificial, synthetic.

manner n a method or way of doing something; behaviour; type or kind; habit; (pl) polite social behaviour.—**mannerly** adj.

mannerism n an idiosyncrasy.

manoeuvre n a planned and controlled movement of troops, warships, etc; a skilful or shrewd move; a stratagem. • vti to perform or cause to perform manoeuvres; to manage or plan skilfully; to move, get, make, etc, by some scheme.

manor n a landed estate; the main house on such an estate; (sl) a police district.

manpower n the collective availability for work of people in a given area.

mansion n a large, imposing house.

manslaughter n the killing of a human being by another, esp when unlawful but without malice.

manual adj operated, done, or used by the hand; involving physical skill or hard work rather than the mind. • n a book of instructions.

manufacture vt to make, esp on a large scale, using machinery; to invent, fabricate. • n the production of goods by manufacturing.—**manufacturer** n.

manure n animal dung used to fertilise soil. • vt to spread manure on.

manuscript n a book or document that is handwritten or typewritten.

many adj numerous. • n a large number of persons or things.

map n a representation of all or part of the earth's surface. • vt to make a map of.

maple n a tree with two-winged fruits; its hard light-coloured wood; the flavour of the syrup made from the sap of the sugar maple.

mar vt to blemish, to spoil.

marathon n a foot race of 26 miles, 385 yards.

marble n a hard limestone rock that takes a high polish; a little ball of stone, glass, etc; (pl) a children's game played with such balls; (pl) (sl) wits. • adj of or like marble.

march vi to walk with regular steps, as in military formation; to advance steadily. • vt to make a person or group march. • n a regular, steady step; a piece of music for marching.

mare n a mature female horse.

margarine n a butter substitute made from vegetable and animal fats, etc.

margin n a border, edge; the blank border of a printed or written page; an amount beyond what is needed; provision for increase, error, etc.

marginal adj written in the margin; very slight, insignificant; (Brit politics) denoting a constituency where the sitting MP has only a small majority. • n a marginal constituency.

marigold n a plant with a yellow or orange flower.

marijuana n a narcotic obtained by smoking the dried flowers and leaves of the hemp plant.

marine adj of, in, near, or relating to the sea; maritime; nautical; naval. • n a soldier trained for service on land or sea.

marital adj of marriage, matrimonial.

maritime adj on, near, or living near the sea.

mark n a spot, scratch, etc, on a surface; a distinguishing sign or characteristic; a cross made instead of a signature; a printed or written symbol, as a punctuation mark; a brand or label on an article showing the maker, etc; an indication of some quality, character, etc; a grade for academic work; a standard of quality; impression, influence, etc; a target; (sl) a potential victim for a swindle. • vt to make a mark or marks on; to identify as by a mark; to show plainly; to heed; to grade, rate; (Brit football) to stay close to an opponent so as to hinder his play.

marked adj having a mark or marks; noticeable.

market n a meeting of people for buying and selling merchandise; a space or building in which a market is held; the chance to sell or buy; demand for (goods, etc); a region where goods can be sold; a section of the community offering demand for goods. • vti to offer for sale; to sell, buy domestic provisions.

marketing n act of buying or selling; all the processes involved in moving goods from the producer to the consumer.

marksman n one who is skilled at shooting.

marmalade n a jam-like preserve made from oranges, sugar and water.

maroon[1] n a dark brownish red (—also adj); a type of distress rocket.

maroon[2] vt to leave helpless and alone.

marquee n a large tent used for entertainment.

marriage n the legal contract by which a woman and man become wife and husband.

marrow n the fatty tissue in the cavities of bones; the best part of anything; a widely grown green fruit eaten as a vegetable.

marry vt to join as wife and husband; to take in marriage; to unite. • vi to get married.

marsh n an area of boggy, poorly drained land.—**marshiness** n.—**marshy** adj.

marshal n in some armies, a general officer of the highest rank. • vt (ideas, troops) to arrange in order; to guide.

martial adj warlike; military.

martyr n a person tortured for a belief or cause. • vt to kill as a martyr.

marvel n anything wonderful; a miracle. • vti to become filled with wonder, surprise, etc.—**marvellous** adj.

marzipan n a paste made from ground almonds, sugar and egg white, used to coat cakes or make confectionery.

mascara *n* a cosmetic for darkening the eyelashes.

mascot *n* a person, animal or thing thought to bring good luck.

masculine *adj* having characteristics of or appropriate to the male sex; (*gram*) of the male gender.—**masculinity** *n*.

mask *n* a covering to conceal or protect the face; a moulded likeness of the face; anything that conceals or disguises; a respirator placed over the nose and mouth to aid or prevent inhalation of a gas. • *vt* to cover or conceal as with a mask; to disguise one's intentions.—**masked** *adj*.

mason *n* a person skilled in working or building with stone; (*with cap*) a Freemason.

masonry *n* stonework.

masquerade *n* a ball or party at which fancy dress and masks are worn; a pretence, false show. • *vi* to pretend to be what one is not.

mass *n* a quantity of matter of indefinite shape and size; a large quantity or number; size; (*physics*) the property of a body expressed as a measure of the amount of material contained in it; (*pl*) the common people, esp the lower social classes; (*with cap*) the celebration of the Eucharist. • *adj* of or for the masses or a large number. • *vti* to gather or form into a mass.

massacre *n* the cruel and indiscriminate killing of many people. • *vt* to kill in large numbers.

massage *n* a kneading and rubbing of the muscles to stimulate the circulation of the blood. • *vt* to give a massage to.

massive *adj* big, solid, or heavy; large and imposing; relatively large in comparison to normal.

mast *n* a tall vertical pole used to support the sails on a ship; a vertical pole from which a flag is flown; a tall structure supporting a television or radio aerial.

master *n* a man who rules others or has control over something, esp the head of a household; an employer; an owner of an animal or slave; the captain of a merchant ship; a male teacher in a private school; an expert craftsman; a writer or painter regarded as great; an original from which a copy can be made, esp a phonograph record or magnetic tape; (*with cap*) a title for a boy; one holding an advanced academic degree. • *vt* to become expert.

masterly *adj* expert; skilful.

mastermind *n* a very clever person, esp one who plans a project.—*also vt*.

masterpiece *n* a work done with great skill; the greatest work of a person or group.

mastery *n* control as by a master; expertise.

masturbate *vi* to stimulate one's sexual organs manually to achieve orgasm without sexual intercourse.—**masturbation** *n*.

mat *n* a piece of material of woven fibres, etc, used for protection, as under a vase, etc, or on the floor; a thick pad used in wrestling, gymnastics, etc. • *vti* to tangle into a thick mass.

match[1] *n* a thin strip of wood or cardboard tipped with a chemical that ignites under friction.

match[2] *n* any person or thing equal or similar to another; two persons or things that go well together; a contest or game; a mating or marriage. • *vt* to put in opposition (with, against); to be equal or similar to; (*one thing*) to suit to another. • *vi* to be equal, similar, suitable, etc.

matchless *adj* unequalled.

mate *n* (*inf*) a friend; one of a matched pair; a marriage partner; the male or female of paired animals; an officer of a merchant ship, ranking below the master. • *vti* to join as a pair; to couple in sexual union.

material *adj* of, derived from, or composed of matter, physical; of the body or bodily needs, comfort, etc, not spiritual; important, essential, etc. • *n* what a thing is, or may be made of; elements or parts; cloth, fabric.

materialise *vi* to become fact; to make an unexpected appearance.

maternal *adj* of, like, from a mother; related through the mother's side of the family.

maternity *n* motherhood; motherliness. • *adj* relating to pregnancy.

mathematic(al) *adj* of, like or concerned with mathematics; exact and precise.

mathematics *n* (*used as sing*) the science dealing with quantities, forms, space, etc, and their relationships by the use of numbers and symbols.—**mathematician** *n*.

matriarch *n* a woman who heads or rules her family or tribe.—**matriarchal** *adj*.

matriculate *vti* to enrol, esp as a student.

matrimony *n* the act or rite of marriage; the married state.—**matrimonial** *adj*.

matron *n* a wife or widow, esp one of mature appearance and manner; a woman in charge of domestic and nursing arrangements in a school, hospital or other institution.—**matronly** *adj*.

matt *adj* without lustre, dull.

matter *n* what a thing is made of; material; whatever occupies space and is perceptible to the senses; a thing or affair; significance; trouble, difficulty; pus. • *vi* to be of importance.

matter-of-fact *adj* relating to facts, not opinions, imagination, etc.

mattress *n* a casing of strong cloth filled with cotton, foam rubber, coiled springs, etc, used on a bed.

mature *adj* mentally and physically well-developed, grown-up; (*fruit, cheese, etc*) ripe. • *vi* to become mature; to become due.

maturity *n* the state of being mature.

maudlin adj foolishly sentimental.

maul vt to bruise or lacerate; to paw.

mausoleum n a large tomb.

mauve n a shade of pale purple.—also adj.

mawkish adj maudlin; insipid.

maxim n a rule of conduct; a precept.

maximum n the greatest quantity, number, etc. • adj highest.

may vb aux expressing possibility; permission.

maybe adv perhaps.

mayhem n violent destruction, confusion.

mayonnaise n a salad dressing made from egg yolks with oil and lemon juice or vinegar.

mayor n the chief administrative officer of a municipality.

mayoress n the wife of a mayor; a female mayor.

maze n a confusing, intricate network of pathways; a confused state.

me pers pron the objective case of I.

meadow n low, level, moist grassland.

meagre adj thin; lacking in quality.

meal[1] n any of the times for eating, as lunch, dinner, etc; the food served at such a time.

meal[2] n any coarsely ground edible grain.

mealy-mouthed adj not outspoken and blunt.

mean[1] adj selfish, ungenerous; despicable.

mean[2] adj halfway between extremes; average. • n what is between extremes.

mean[3] vt to have in mind; to intend; to intend to express; to signify.

meander vi (river) to wind; to wander aimlessly.

meaning n sense; significance; import. • adj significant.—**meaningful** adj.

meantime, meanwhile adv in or during the intervening time; at the same time.—also n.

measles n (used as sing) an acute, contagious viral disease, characterised by small red spots on the skin.

measly adj (inf) slight, worthless.

measure n the extent, dimension, capacity, etc, of anything; a determining of this, measurement; a unit of measurement; any standard of valuation; an instrument for measuring; a definite quantity measured out; a course of action; a statute, law; a rhythmical unit. • vt to find out the extent, dimensions, etc, of, esp by a standard; to mark off by measuring; to be a measure of. • vi to be of specified measurements.

measurement n a measuring or being measured; an extent or quantity determined by measuring; a system of measuring or of measures.

meat n animal flesh; food as opposed to drink; the essence of something.

meaty adj full of meat; full of substance.

mechanic n a person skilled in maintaining or operating machines, cars, etc.

mechanical adj of or using machinery or tools; produced or operated by machinery; done as if by a machine, lacking thought or emotion; of the science of mechanics.

mechanics n (used as sing) the science of motion and the action of forces on bodies; knowledge of machinery; (pl) the technical aspects of something.

mechanism n the working parts of a machine; any system of interrelated parts; any physical or mental process by which a result is produced.

medal n a small, flat piece of inscribed metal, commemorating some event or person or awarded for some distinction.

medallion n a large medal.

meddle vi to interfere in another's affairs.—**meddlesome** adj.

mediate vt to intervene (in a dispute); to bring about agreement. • vi to be in an intermediate position; to be an intermediary.—**mediation** n.

medical adj relating to the practice or study of medicine. • n (inf) a medical examination.

medicine n any substance used to treat or prevent disease; the science of preventing, treating or curing disease.—**medicinal** adj.

medi(a)eval adj of or like the Middle Ages.

mediocre adj average; ordinary; inferior.

meditate vi to think deeply; to reflect.

meditation n the act of meditating; contemplation of spiritual or religious matters.

medium n the middle state or condition; any intervening means, instrument, or agency; a means of communicating information (e.g. newspapers, television, radio); a person claiming to act as an intermediary between the living and the dead. • adj midway; average.

medley n a miscellany; a musical piece made up of various tunes or passages.

meek adj patient, long-suffering.

meet vt to encounter, to make the acquaintance of; to contend with, deal with; to experience; to be perceived by (the eye, etc); (demand, etc) to satisfy. • vi to come into contact; to be introduced. • n a meeting to hunt or for an athletics competition.

meeting n a coming together; a gathering.

megaphone n a device to amplify the voice.

melancholy n gloominess or depression; sadness. • adj sad; depressed.

mellow adj (fruit) sweet and ripe; kind-hearted and understanding. • vti to soften through age.

melodrama n a play, film, etc, filled with overdramatic emotion and action; drama of this genre.—**melodramatic** adj.

melody n a tune.—**melodic** adj.

melon n the large juicy many-seeded fruit of trailing plants, as the cantaloupe.

melt vti to make or become liquid; to dissolve; to soften or be softened emotionally.

meltdown n the melting of the fuel core of a nuclear reactor; the drastic collapse of almost anything.

melting point n the temperature at which a solid melts.

member n a person belonging to a society or club; a part of a body, such as a limb; a representative in a legislative body.

membership n the state of being a member; the number of members of a body; the members collectively.

membrane n a thin pliable sheet or film; the fibrous tissue that covers or lines animal organs.

memento n a reminder, esp a souvenir.

memoir n an historical account based on personal experience; (pl) an autobiographical record.

memorable adj worth remembering.

memorandum n an informal written communication as within an office; a note to help the memory.

memorial n a remembrance; a monument.

memorise vt to learn by heart, to commit to memory.—**memorisation** n.

memory n the process of retaining and reproducing past thoughts and sensations; the sum of things remembered; an individual recollection; commemoration; remembrance; the part of a computer that stores information (—also **store**).

menace n a threat; (inf) a nuisance. • vt to threaten.

menagerie n a collection of wild animals; a place where they are kept.

mend vt to repair; (manners, etc) to reform, improve. • vi to become better. • n the act of mending; a repaired area in a garment, etc.

menial adj consisting of work of little skill; servile. • n a domestic servant; a servile person.

meningitis n inflammation of the membranes enveloping the brain or spinal cord.

menopause n the time of life during which a woman's menstrual cycle ceases permanently.

menstruation n the monthly discharge of blood from the uterus.—**menstrual** adj.

mental adj of, or relating to the mind; occurring or performed in the mind; having a psychiatric disorder; (inf) crazy, stupid.

mentality n intellectual power; disposition.

mention n a brief reference to something in speech or writing; an official recognition or citation. • vt to refer to remark; to honour officially.

menu n the list of dishes served in a restaurant; a list of options on a computer display.

mercantile adj of merchants or trade.

mercenary adj working or done for money. • n a soldier hired to fight for a foreign army.

merchandise n commercial goods. • vti to sell.

merchant n a trader; a retailer; (sl) a person fond of a particular activity.

merchant navy n commercial shipping.

merciful adj compassionate, humane.

merciless adj cruel, pitiless; without mercy.

mercury n a heavy silvery liquid metallic element used in thermometers etc.

mercy n clemency; compassion; pity.

mere adj nothing more than; simple, unmixed.—**merely** adv.

merge vti to blend or cause to fuse together gradually; to (cause to) combine, unite.

merger n a combining together, esp of two or more commercial organisations.

meridian n the imaginary circle on the surface of the earth passing through the North and South Poles.

meringue n a mixture of egg whites beaten with sugar and baked.

merit n excellence; worth; (pl) (of a case) rights and wrongs. • vt to be worthy of, to deserve.

mermaid n (legend) a woman with a fish's tale.

merry adj cheerful; causing laughter; lively.

merry-go-round n a revolving platform of wooden horses, etc, a roundabout.

mesh n a net; a network. • vt to entangle, ensnare. • vi to become entangled or interlocked.

mess n a state of disorder or untidiness, esp if dirty; a muddle; a building where service personnel dine. • vti to make a mess (of), bungle; to eat in company; to potter (about).

message n any spoken, written or other form of communication; the chief idea that the writer, artist, etc, seeks to communicate in a work.

messenger n one who carries a message.

messy adj dirty; confused; untidy.

metabolism n the total processes in living organisms by which tissue is formed, energy produced and waste products eliminated.—**metabolic** adj.

metal n any of a class of chemical elements which are often lustrous, ductile solids, and are good conductors of heat, electricity, etc, such as gold, iron, copper, etc.

metallurgy n the science of separating metals from their ores and preparing them for use by smelting, refining, etc.

metamorphosis n the marked change in some animals at a stage in their growth, e.g. chrysalis to butterfly.

metaphor n a figure of speech in which a word or phrase is used for another of which it is an image.—**metaphorical** adj.

metaphysics n (used as sing) the branch of philosophy that seeks to explain the nature of being and reality.—**metaphysical** adj.

meteor n a small particle of matter which travels at great speed through space and becomes luminous through friction as it enters the earth's atmosphere; a shooting star.

meter n a device for measuring and recording a quantity of gas, water, time, etc, supplied; a parking meter.

method n the mode or procedure of accomplishing something; orderliness of thought.

methodical adj orderly, systematic.

methylated spirit n a form of alcohol, adulterated to render it undrinkable, used as a solvent.

meticulous adj precise about small details.

metre[1] n rhythmic pattern in verse, the measured arrangement of syllables according to stress; rhythmic pattern in music.

metre[2] n the basic unit of length in the metric system, consisting of 100 centimetres (39.37 inches).—**metric** adj.

metrical adj of, relating to, or composed in rhythmic metre.

metrication n conversion of an existent system of units into the metric system.

metric system n a decimal system of weights and measures based on the metre, litre and kilogram.

metropolis n any large and important city.—**metropolitan** adj.

mettle n courage, spirit.

mezzanine n an intermediate storey between others; a theatre balcony.

microbe n a microscopic organism.

microfilm n film on which documents are recorded in reduced scale.—also vt.

microphone n an instrument for transforming sound waves into electric signals.

microscope n an optical instrument for making magnified images of minute objects by means of a lens or lenses.

microscopic adj of, with, like a microscope; visible only through a microscope; very small.

mid adj middle. • prep amid.

midday n the middle of the day, noon.

middle adj halfway between two given points, times, etc; intermediate; central. • n the point halfway between two extremes.

middle age n the time between youth and old age.—**middle-aged** adj.

Middle Ages npl the period of European history between AD 500 and 1500.

middle class n the class between the lower and upper classes, mostly composed of professional and business people.

middling adj of medium quality, size, etc; second-rate. • adv moderately.

midge n a small gnat-like insect with a painful bite.

midget n a very small person.—also adj.

midnight n twelve o'clock at night.

midriff n the middle part of the torso between the abdomen and the chest.

midwife n a person trained to assist women before, during, and after childbirth.

might n power, bodily strength.

mighty adj strong; massive; (inf) very.

migraine n an intense, periodic headache, usu limited to one side of the head.

migrant n a person or animal that moves from one region or country to another. • adj migrating.

migrate vi (birds, animals) to move to another region with the change in season.

mild adj (temper) gentle; (weather) temperate.

mildew n a fungus that attacks some plants or appears on damp cloth, etc, as a whitish coating. • vti to affect or be affected with mildew.

mile n a unit of linear measure equal to 5280 feet (1.61 km); the nautical mile is 6075 feet (1.85 km).

mileage n total miles travelled; an allowance per mile for travelling expenses.

militant adj ready to fight, esp for some cause.

military adj relating to soldiers or to war; warlike. • n the armed forces.

militia n an army composed of civilians called out in time of emergency.

milk n a white nutritious liquid secreted by female mammals for feeding their young. • vt to draw milk from; to extract money, etc, from; to exploit.—**milky** adj.

mill n an apparatus for grinding by crushing between rough surfaces; a building where grain is ground into flour; a factory. • vt to produce or grind in a mill; (coins) to put a raised edge on. • vi to move around confusedly.—**miller** n.

millennium n a period of a thousand years.

millet n a cereal grass used for grain and fodder.

millimetre n a thousandth (0.001) of a metre.

million n a thousand thousands, the number one followed by six zeros: 1,000,000; (inf) a very large number.

millionaire n a person who owns at least a million of money; one who is extremely rich.

millstone n a heavy burden.

mime n a theatrical technique using action without words. • vi to act or express using gestures alone; (singers, musicians) to perform as if singing or playing live to prerecorded music.

mimic n a person who imitates, esp an actor skilled in mimicry. • to imitate or ridicule.—**mimicry** n.

mince vt to chop into small pieces; to moderate one's words. • vi to walk with affected daintiness.

mincemeat n a mixture of chopped apples, raisins, etc, used as a pie filling.

mind n the faculty responsible for intellect, thought, feelings, speech; intellect; sanity. • vt to object to, to pay attention to; to obey; to take care of. • vi to pay attention; to be obedient; to be careful; to object.

mindful *adj* heedful, not forgetful.

mindless *adj* requiring little intellectual effort.

mine[1] *poss pron* belonging to me.

mine[2] *n* an excavation from which minerals are dug; an explosive device concealed in the water or ground to destroy enemy ships, personnel, or vehicles that pass over or near them; a rich supply or source. • *vt* to excavate; to lay explosive mines in an area. • *vi* to dig or work a mine.

miner *n* a person who works in a mine.

mineral *n* an inorganic substance, found naturally in the earth; any substance neither vegetable nor animal. • *adj* containing minerals.

mineralogy *n* the science of minerals.

mineral water *n* water containing mineral salts or gases, often with medicinal properties.

minesweeper *n* a ship for clearing away explosive mines.—**minesweeping** *n*.

mingle *vti* to mix; to combine.

miniature *adj* minute, on a small scale. • *n* a painting or reproduction of a very small scale.

minimal *adj* very minute; least possible.

minimise *vt* to reduce to or estimate at a minimum.—**minimisation** *n*.

minimum *n* the least possible amount; the lowest degree or point.

mining *n* the act, process, or industry of excavating from the earth.

minister *n* a clergyman serving a church; an official heading a government department. • *vi* to give help (to).

ministry *n* the clergy; the profession of a clergyman; a government department headed by a minister; the building housing it.

mink *n* any of several carnivorous weasel-like mammals valued for its durable soft fur.

minnow *n* a small, slender freshwater fish.

minor *adj* lesser in size, importance, degree, extent, etc; (*mus*) lower than the corresponding major by a semitone. • *n* a person under full legal age.

minority *n* the smaller part or number; a political or racial group smaller than the majority group; the state of being under age.

mint[1] *n* the place where money is coined; a large amount of money. • *adj* unused, in perfect condition. • *vt* (*coins*) to imprint; to invent.

mint[2] *n* an aromatic plant whose leaves are used for flavouring.

minus *prep* less; (*inf*) without. • *adj* involving subtraction; negative; less than. • *n* a sign (-), indicating subtraction or negative quantity.

minute[1] *n* the sixtieth part of an hour or a degree; a moment; (*pl*) an official record of a meeting. • *vt* to record or summarise the proceedings.

minute[2] *adj* tiny; detailed; exact.

miracle *n* an extraordinary event attributed to the supernatural; an unusual or astounding event.—**miraculous** *adj*.

mirror *n* a smooth surface that reflects images. • *vt* to reflect faithfully.

mirth *n* merriment, esp with laughter.

misadventure *n* an unlucky accident; bad luck.

misapprehension *n* misunderstanding.

misappropriate *vt* to appropriate dishonestly.

misbehave *vi* to behave badly.

miscalculate *vti* to calculate wrongly.

miscarriage *n* spontaneous expulsion of a fetus prematurely; mismanagement or failure.

miscellaneous *adj* consisting of various kinds.

miscellany *n* a mixed collection; a book comprising miscellaneous writings, etc.

mischief *n* wayward behaviour; damage.

mischievous *adj* harmful, prankish.

misconception *n* a mistaken idea.

misconduct *n* improper behaviour.

misconstrue *vt* to misinterpret.

misdemeanour *n* (*law*) a minor offence.

miser *n* a greedy, stingy person who hoards money for its own sake.—**miserly** *adj*.

miserable *adj* wretched; unhappy; causing misery; bad, inadequate; pitiable.

misery *n* extreme pain, unhappiness, or poverty; a cause of such suffering.

misfire *vi* (*engine, etc*) to fail to ignite, start; to fail to succeed.—*also n*.

misfit *n* something that fits badly; a maladjusted person.

misfortune *n* ill luck; trouble; a mishap.

misguided *adj* foolish; mistaken.

mishap *n* an unfortunate accident.

misjudge *vt* to judge wrongly.

mislay *vt* to lose something temporarily.

mislead *vt* to give wrong information to.

misnomer *n* an incorrect or unsuitable name or description.

misplace *vt* to put in a wrong place; (*trust, etc*) to place unwisely.—**misplacement** *n*.

misprint *vt* to print incorrectly. • *n* an error in printing.

miss[1] *n* a girl; (*with cap*) a title used before the surname of an unmarried woman or girl.

miss[2] *vt* to fail to reach, hit, find, meet, hear; to omit; to fail to take advantage of; to regret or discover the absence or loss of. • *vi* to fail to hit; to fail to be successful; to misfire, as an engine. • *n* a failure to hit, reach, obtain, etc.

misshapen *adj* badly shaped; deformed.

missile *n* an object, as a rock, spear, rocket, etc, to be thrown, fired, or launched.

missing *adj* absent; lost.

mission *n* a group of people sent by a church, government, etc, to carry out a special task; the sending of an aircraft or spacecraft on a special assignment; a vocation.

missionary *n* a person who tries to convert unbelievers to his/her religious faith.

mist n a large mass of water vapour, less dense than a fog; something that dims or obscures.—*vti* to cover or be covered, as with mist.—**misty** adj.

mistake vt to misunderstand; to misinterpret. • vi to make a mistake. • n a wrong idea, answer, etc; an error of judgment.

mistaken adj erroneous, ill-judged.

mister n (inf) sir; (with cap) the title used before a man's surname.

mistletoe n an evergreen parasitic plant with white berries used as a Christmas decoration.

mistreat vt to treat wrongly or badly.

mistress n a woman who is head of a household; a woman with whom a man is having a prolonged affair; a female schoolteacher.

mistrust n lack of trust. • vti to suspect.

misunderstand vt to fail to understand correctly.

misunderstanding n a mistake as to sense; a quarrel or disagreement.

misuse vt to ill-treat, abuse. • n improper or incorrect use.

mitigate vti to become or make less severe.

mitre n the headdress of a bishop; a diagonal joint between two pieces of wood to form a corner.—also vt.

mitt n a glove covering the hand but only the base of the fingers; (sl) a hand; a baseball glove.

mitten n a glove with a thumb but no separate fingers.

mix vt to blend together in a single mass; to make by blending ingredients, as a cake; to combine; (with up) to make into a mixture; to make disordered; to confuse or mistake. • vi to be mixed or blended; to get along together.

mixed adj blended; made up of different parts, classes, races, etc; confused.

mixed-up adj (inf) mentally confused.

mixer n a device that blends or mixes; a person considered in terms of their ability (good or bad) to get on with others; a soft drink added to an alcoholic beverage.

mixture n the process of mixing; a blend made by mixing.

mix-up n a mistake; confusion, muddle.

moan n a low mournful sound as of sorrow or pain. • vti to utter a moan; to complain.

moat n a deep ditch surrounding a fortification or castle, usu filled with water.

mob n a disorderly or riotous crowd; a contemptuous term for the masses; (sl) a gang of criminals. • vt to attack in a disorderly group.

mobile adj movable, not fixed; easily changing; characterised by ease in change of social status; capable of moving freely and quickly; (inf) having transport. • n a suspended structure of wood, metal, etc, with parts that move in air currents.—**mobility** n.

mock vt to imitate or ridicule; (with up) to make a model of. • adj false, sham, counterfeit.

mockery n derision, ridicule, or contempt; imitation, esp derisive; an inadequate person, thing, or action.

mock-up n a full-scale working model of a machine, etc.

mode n a way of acting, doing or existing; a style or fashion.

model n a pattern; an ideal; a standard worth imitating; a representation on a smaller scale, usu three-dimensional; a person who sits for an artist or photographer; a person who displays clothes by wearing them. • adj serving as a model. • vt (with after, on) to create by following a model; to display clothes by wearing.

moderate vti to make or become moderate; to preside over. • adj having reasonable limits; avoiding extremes; mild, calm; of medium quality, amount, etc. • n a person who holds moderate views.

modern adj of the present or recent times; up-to-date.—**modernity** n.

modernise vti to make or become modern.

modest adj moderate; having a humble opinion of oneself; unpretentious.

modify vt to lessen the severity of; to change or alter slightly; (gram) to limit in meaning, to qualify.—**modification** n.

module n a unit of measurement; a self-contained unit, esp in a spacecraft.

mohair n the long, fine hair of the Angora goat; the silk cloth made from it.

moist adj damp; slightly wet.

moisten vti to make or become moist.

moisture n liquid in a diffused, absorbed, or condensed state.

moisturise vt (skin, etc) to add moisture to.—**moisturiser** n.

molasses n (used as sing) the thick brown sugar that is produced during the refining of sugar; treacle.

mole[1] n a spot on the skin, usu dark-coloured and raised.

mole[2] n a small burrowing insectivore with soft dark fur; a spy within an organisation.

mole[3] n a large breakwater.

molecule n the simplest unit of a substance, retaining the chemical properties of that substance; a small particle.

molest vt to annoy; to attack or assault, esp sexually.—**molestation** n.

mollusc n an invertebrate animal usu enclosed in a shell, as oysters, etc.

molten adj melted by heat.

moment n an indefinitely brief period of time.

momentary adj lasting only for a moment.

momentous adj very important.

momentum n the impetus of a moving object, equal to the product of its mass and its velocity.

monarch n a sovereign who rules by hereditary right.—**monarchic(al)** adj.

monarchy n a government headed by a monarch; a kingdom.

monastery n the residence of a group of monks, or nuns.

monastic adj of monks or monasteries.

monetary adj of or relating to money.

money n coins or paper notes authorised by a government as a medium of exchange.

mongrel n an animal or plant of mixed or unknown breed, esp a dog.—also adj.

monitor n a student chosen to help the teacher; a device for regulating the performance of a machine, aircraft, etc; a screen for viewing the image being produced by a television camera; a display screen connected to a computer. • vti to watch or check on.

monk n a member of a religious order living in a monastery.

monkey n any of the primates except man and the lemurs, esp the smaller, long-tailed primates; a mischievous child.

monkey wrench n a large wrench with an adjustable jaw.

monochrome n a painting, drawing, or print in a single colour.

monocle n a single eyeglass held in place by the face muscles.

monogram n the embroidered or printed initials of one's name.

monologue n a long speech.

monopolise vt to get, have, or exploit a monopoly of; to get full control of.

monopoly n exclusive control in dealing in a particular commodity or supplying a service; exclusive use or possession.

monosyllable n a word of one syllable.

monotone n an utterance or musical tone without a change in pitch; a tiresome sameness.

monsoon n a seasonal wind of southern Asia; the rainy season.

monster n any greatly malformed plant or animal; an imaginary beast; a very wicked person; a very large animal or thing. • adj very large, huge.—**monstrosity** n.

monstrous adj enormous; horrible.

month n any of the twelve divisions of the year.

monthly adj continuing for a month; done, happening, payable, etc, every month. • n a monthly periodical. • adv once a month; every month.

monument n an obelisk, statue or building that commemorates a person or an event; an exceptional example.—**monumental** adj.

mood n a temporary state of mind or temper; a gloomy feeling; a predominant feeling or spirit; (gram) that form of a verb indicating mode of action; (mus) mode.

moody adj gloomy; temperamental.

moon n the natural satellite that revolves around the earth and shines by reflected sunlight; any natural satellite of another planet. • vi to behave in an idle or abstracted way.

moonbeam n a ray of moonlight.

moonlight n the light of the moon. • vi (inf) to have a secondary (usu night-time) job.

moor¹ n a tract of open wasteland, usu covered with heather and often marshy.

moor² vti (a ship) to secure or be secured by cable or anchor.

mooring n the place where a ship is moored; (pl) the lines, cables, etc, by which a ship is moored.

moose n the largest member of the deer family, native to North America.

mop n a rag, sponge, etc, fixed to a handle for washing floors or dishes; a thick or tangled head of hair. • vt to wash with a mop.

mope vi to be gloomy and apathetic.

moped n a light, motor-assisted bicycle.

moral adj of or relating to character and human behaviour, particularly as regards right and wrong; virtuous, esp in sexual conduct. • n a moral lesson taught by a fable, event, etc; (pl) principles; ethics.—**moralistic** adj.

morale n moral or mental condition with respect to courage, confidence, etc.

morality n virtue; moral principles.

morbid adj diseased, resulting as from a diseased state of mind; gruesome.

more adj greater; further; additional. • adv to a greater extent or degree.

morgue n a place where the bodies of unknown dead or those dead of unknown causes are temporarily kept prior to burial.

morning n the part of the day from midnight or dawn until noon; the early part of anything.

morose adj sullen, surly; gloomy.

morphine n an alkaloid derived from opium, used as an anaesthetic and sedative.

morsel n a small piece of anything.

mortal adj subject to death. • n a human being.

mortality n state of being mortal; death on a large scale, as from war; number or frequency of deaths in a given period relative to population.

mortar n a mixture of cement or lime with sand and water used in building; an artillery piece that fires shells at low velocities and high trajectories; a bowl in which substances are pounded with a pestle.

mortgage n a transfer of rights to a piece of property usu as security for the payment of a loan or debt.—also vt.

mortify vti to humiliate or shame; to become gangrenous.

mortuary n a place of temporary storage for dead bodies.

mosaic n a surface decoration made by inlaying small pieces (of glass, stone, etc) to form figures or patterns; a design made in mosaic.—*also adj.*

mosque n a place of worship for Muslims.

mosquito n a small two-winged bloodsucking insect.

moss n a very small green plant that grows in clusters on rocks, moist ground, etc.

most adj greatest in number; greatest in amount or degree; in the greatest number of instances. • adv in or to the greatest degree or extent. • n the greatest amount or degree; (*with pl*) the greatest number (of).

mostly adv for the most part; mainly, usually.

moth n a four-winged chiefly night-flying insect related to the butterfly.

mothball n a small ball of camphor or naphtalene used to protect stored clothes from moths.

mother n a female who has given birth to offspring; an origin or source. • adj of or like a mother; native. • vt to be the mother of or a mother to.—**motherhood** n.

mother-in-law n the mother of one's spouse.

motherly adj of a mother; like a mother.

mother-of-pearl n the iridescent lining of the shell of the pearl oyster.

motion n activity, movement; a formal suggestion made in a meeting, law court, or legislative assembly; evacuation of the bowels. • vti to signal or direct by a gesture.

motive n something (as a need or desire) that causes a person to act; a recurrent theme in a musical composition (—*also* **motif**).

motor n a machine for converting electrical energy into mechanical energy; a motor car. • adj producing motion; of or powered by a motor; of, by or for motor vehicles; of or involving muscular movements. • vi to travel by car.

motorboat n a boat propelled by an engine or motor.

motorcycle n a two-wheeled motor vehicle.—**motorcyclist** n.

motorist n a person who drives a car.

motorway n a road with controlled access for fast-moving traffic.

mottled adj marked with blotches of various colours.

motto n a short saying adopted as a maxim or ideal.

mould¹ n a fungus producing a furry growth on the surface of organic matter. —**mouldy** adj.

mould² n a hollow form in which something is cast; something made in a mould. • vt to make in or on a mould; to form, shape, guide.

moult vi to shed hair, skin, horns, etc, prior to replacement of new growth.—*also* n.

mound n a heap or bank of earth.

mount¹ n a high hill.

mount² vi to increase. • vt to climb, ascend; to get up on (a horse, platform, etc); (*a jewel*) to fix on a support; (*a picture*) to frame. • n a horse for riding; (*for a picture*) a backing.

mountain n a land mass higher than a hill.

mountaineer n one who climbs mountains.

mountainous adj having many mountains.

mourn vti (*someone dead*) to grieve for; (*something regrettable*) to feel sorrow for.

mournful adj expressing grief or sorrow.

mourning n the expression of grief; dark clothes worn by mourners.

mouse n a small rodent with a pointed snout, long body and slender tail; a timid person; a hand-held device used to position the cursor and control software on a computer screen.

moustache n the hair on the upper lip.

mouth n the opening in the head through which food is eaten, sound uttered or words spoken; opening, as of a bottle, etc. • vt to form words with the mouth without uttering sound.

mouthful n as much (food) as fills the mouth; a word or phrase that is difficult to say correctly; (*sl*) a pertinent remark.

mouth organ n a harmonica.

mouthwatering adj appetising; tasty.

movable, moveable adj that may be moved. • npl personal property.

move vt to shift or change place; to set in motion; to rouse the emotions; to put (a motion) formally. • vi to go from one place to another; to walk, to carry oneself; to change place; to evacuate the bowels; to propose a motion as in a meeting; to change residence; (*chess, draughts, etc*) to change the position of a piece on the board. • n a movement, esp in board games; one's turn to move.

movement n act of moving; the moving part of a machine, esp a clock; the policy and activities of a group; a trend, e.g. in prices; a division of a musical work; tempo.

moving adj arousing the emotions.

mow vti (*grass, etc*) to cut with a sickle or lawnmower; (*with* **down**) to cause to fall like cut grass.

much adj plenty. • adv considerably; to a great extent.

muck n moist manure; mud, dirt, filth. • vt (*with out*) to clear of muck. • vi (*with about or around*) to engage in useless activity.—**mucky** adj.

mucus n the slimy secretion that keeps mucous membranes moist.

mud n soft, wet earth.

muddle vt to confuse; to mix up. • n mess.

muddy adj like or covered with mud; not bright

or clear; confused. • *vti* to make or become dirty or unclear.

mudguard *n* a screen on a wheel to catch mud splashes.

muff *n* a warm soft fur cover for warming the hands.

muffin *n* baked yeast roll.

muffle *vt* to wrap up for warmth or to hide; (*sound*) to deaden by wrapping up.

muffler *n* a long scarf; any means of deadening sound; the silencer of a motor vehicle.

mug *n* a cylindrical drinking cup, usu of earthenware; its contents; (*sl*) the face; (*sl*) a fool. • *vt* to assault, usu with intent to rob.

muggy *adj* (*weather*) warm, damp and close.

mule[1] *n* the offspring of a male donkey and a female horse; an obstinate person.

mule[2] *n* a slipper without a heel.

mull[1] *vti* (*inf*) to ponder (over).

mull[2] *vt* (*wine, etc*) to heat, sweeten and spice.

multiple *adj* various; complex. • *n* (*math*) a number exactly divisible by another.

multiple sclerosis *n* a disease of the nervous system with loss of muscular coordination, etc.

multiplication *n* the act of multiplying; the process of repeatedly adding a quantity to itself a certain number of times.

multiply *vti* to increase in number, degree, etc; to find the product (of) by multiplication.

multitude *n* a large number (of people).

mumble *vti* to speak indistinctly, mutter. • *n* a mumbled utterance.

mummy *n* a carefully preserved dead body, esp an embalmed corpse of ancient Egypt.

mumps *npl* (*used as sing or pl*) an acute contagious virus disease characterised by swelling of the salivary glands.

munch *vti* to chew steadily.

mundane *adj* routine; banal; worldly.

municipal *adj* of or concerning a city, town, etc, or its local government.

municipality *n* a city or town having corporate status and powers of self-government; the governing body of a municipality.

munitions *npl* war supplies, esp weapons and ammunition.

mural *n* a picture painted directly onto a wall.

murder *n* the intentional and unlawful killing of one person by another; (*inf*) something unusually difficult or dangerous to do or deal with.—*also vt.*—**murderer** *n*.

murky *adj* dark, gloomy; darkly obscure.

murmur *n* a continuous low, indistinct sound; (*med*) an abnormal sound made by the heart. • *vti* to make a murmur; to say in a murmur.

muscle *n* fibrous tissue that contracts and relaxes, producing bodily movement; power. • *vi* (*inf*) to force one's way (in).—**muscular** *adj*.

muse *vti* to ponder, meditate.

museum *n* a building for exhibiting objects of artistic, historic or scientific interest.

mushroom *n* a fleshy fungus with a capped stalk, some varieties of which are edible. • *vi* to spread rapidly, to increase.

music *n* vocal or instrumental sounds having rhythm, melody or harmony.

musical *adj* of or relating to music or musicians; having the pleasant tonal qualities of music; having an interest in or talent for music. • *n* a play or film incorporating dialogue, singing and dancing.—**musically** *adv*.

musician *n* one skilled in music, esp a performer.

Muslim *n* an adherent of Islam.—*also adj.*

muslin *n* a fine cotton cloth.

mussel *n* an edible marine bivalve shellfish.

must *aux vb expressing*: necessity; probability; certainty. • *n* (*inf*) something that must be done.

mustard *n* the powdered seeds of the mustard plant used as a condiment; brownish-yellow.

muster *vt* to assemble or call together, as troops for inspection or duty; to gather. • *vi* to be assembled, as troops. • *n* gathering; review; assembly.

musty *adj* mouldy, damp; stale.

mute *adj* silent; dumb; (*colour*) subdued. • *n* a person who is unable to speak; a device that softens the sound of a musical instrument. • *vt* to lessen the sound of a musical instrument.

mutilate *vt* to maim; to damage by removing an essential part of.—**mutilation** *n*.

mutiny *vi* to revolt against authority in military service.—*also n.*—**mutinous** *adj*.

mutter *vti* to utter in a low tone or indistinctly.

mutton *n* the edible flesh of sheep.

mutual *adj* given and received in equal amount; having the same feelings one for the other.

muzzle *n* the projecting nose or mouth of an animal; a strap fitted over the jaws to prevent biting; the open end of a gun barrel. • *vt* to put a muzzle on; to silence or gag.

my *poss adj* of or belonging to me.

myself *pron* emphatic and reflexive form of I.

mystery *n* something unexplained and secret; a story about a secret crime, etc; secrecy.—**mysterious** *adj*.

mystic *adj* having a meaning beyond normal human understanding; magical. • *n* one who seeks direct knowledge of God or spiritual truths by self-surrender.—**mysticism** *n*.

mystify *vt* to bewilder, confuse.

myth *n* a fable; a traditional story of gods and heroes.—**mythical** *adj*.

mythology *n* myths collectively.

N

nab vt (sl) to catch, arrest.

nag[1] vti to scold constantly; to harass; to be felt persistently. • n a person who nags.

nag[2] (inf) a horse.

nail n a horny plate covering the end of a human finger or toe; a thin pointed metal spike for driving into wood as a fastening or hanging device. • vt to fasten with nails; (inf) to catch or hit.

naive, naïve adj inexperienced; unsophisticated; (argument) simple.

naked adj bare, without clothes.

name n a word or term by which a person or thing is called; a title; reputation; authority. • vt to give a name to; to call by name; to designate; (date, price, etc) to specify.

namely adv that is to say.

namesake n a person or thing with the same name as another.

nap[1] n a short sleep, doze. • vi to take a nap.

nap[2] n a hairy surface on cloth or leather.

napalm n a substance added to petrol to form a jelly-like compound used in firebombs and flame-throwers.

nape n the back of the neck.

napkin n a square of cloth or paper for wiping fingers or mouth or protecting clothes at table, a serviette; a nappy.

nappy n a piece of absorbent material wrapped around a baby to absorb or retain its excreta.

narcotic adj inducing sleep. • n a drug, often addictive, used to relieve pain and induce sleep.

narrate vt (a story) to tell, relate; (film, TV) to provide a spoken commentary for.

narrative n a spoken or written account of a sequence of events, experiences, etc.

narrow adj small in width; limited; with little margin; (views) prejudiced or bigoted. • n (usu pl) the narrow part of a pass, street, or channel. • vti to make or grow narrow.

nasal adj of the nose; sounded through the nose.

nasty adj unpleasant; offensive; (problem) hard to deal with; (illness) serious.

nation n people of common territory, descent, culture, language, or history; people united under a single government.

national adj of a nation; common to a whole nation, general. • n a citizen or subject of a specific country.

nationalise vt to make national; to convert into public or government property.

nationalism n patriotic sentiments, principles, etc; a policy of national independence or self-government.—**nationalist** n.

nationality n the status of belonging to a nation by birth or naturalisation.

native adj inborn; natural to a person; innate; (language, etc) of one's place of birth; relating to the indigenous inhabitants of a country or area. • n a person born in the place indicated; a local inhabitant; an indigenous inhabitant, esp a non-White under colonial rule.

natter vi (inf) to chat aimlessly.—also n.

natural adj of or produced by nature; not artificial; innate, not acquired; lifelike; normal; (mus) not flat or sharp. • n (inf) a person or thing considered to have a natural aptitude (for) or to be an obvious choice (for); (mus) a natural note or a sign indicating one.

naturalise vt to confer citizenship upon (a person of foreign birth); (plants) to become established in a different climate. • vi to become established as if native.

naturalist n a person who studies natural history.

naturally adv in a natural manner; of course.

nature n the phenomena of physical life not dominated by man; the entire material world as a whole, or forces observable in it; the essential character of anything; the innate character of a person, temperament; kind, class; vital force or functions; natural scenery.

naught see **nought**.

naughty adj disobedient; titillating.

nausea n a desire to vomit; disgust.

nauseate vti to arouse feelings of disgust; to feel nausea or revulsion.

nautical adj of ships, sailors, or navigation.

naval adj of the navy; of ships.

nave n the central space of a church.

navel n the small scar in the abdomen caused by severance of the umbilical cord; a central point.

navigable adj (rivers, seas) that can be sailed upon or steered through.

navigate vti to steer or direct a ship, aircraft, etc; to travel through or over (water, etc) in a ship, etc; to find a way through, over, etc, and to keep to a course.—**navigator** n.

navigation n the act, art or science of navigating.

navy n (often with cap) the warships of a nation; a nation's entire sea force, including ships, men, stores, etc; navy blue.

navy blue n an almost black blue.

near adj close, not distant in space or time; (escape, etc) narrow. • adv to or at a little distance; close by. • vti to approach.

nearby adj neighbouring; close by in position.

nearly adv almost, closely.

near-sighted adj short-sighted, myopic.

neat adj clean and tidy; efficiently done; (alcoholic drink) undiluted; (sl) nice, pleasing, etc.

nebulous adj indistinct; formless.

necessarily adv as a natural consequence.

necessary adj indispensable; required; inevitable. • n something necessary.

necessitate vt to make necessary; to compel.

necessity n a prerequisite; something that cannot be done without; compulsion; need.

neck n the part of the body that connects the head and shoulders; that part of a garment nearest the neck; a narrow strip of land; the narrowest part of a bottle; a strait. • vti (sl) to kiss and caress.

necklace n a string or band, often of precious stones, beads, or pearls, worn around the neck.

need n necessity; a lack of something; a requirement; poverty. • vt to have a need for; to require.

needle n a small pointed piece of steel for sewing; a larger pointed rod for knitting or crocheting; a stylus; the pointer of a compass, gauge, etc; the thin, short leaf of the pine, spruce, etc; the sharp, slender metal tube at the end of a hypodermic syringe. • vt to goad, prod, or tease.

needless adj not needed, unnecessary.

needy adj in need, very poor.

negation n a negative statement, denial; the opposite or absence of something; a contradiction.

negative adj expressing or meaning denial or refusal; lacking positive attributes; (math) denoting a quantity less than zero, or one to be subtracted; (photog) reversing the light and shade of the original subject or having the colours replaced by complementary ones; (elect) of the charge carried by electrons; producing such a charge. • n a negative word, reply, etc; something that is the opposite of something else; (photog) a negative image on transparent film or a plate. • vt to contradict.

neglect vt to pay little or no attention to; to disregard; to leave uncared for; to fail to do something. • n disregard; lack of attention or care.

negligence n lack of attention or care; an act of carelessness.—**negligent** adj.

negligible adj unimportant; trifling.

negotiable adj able to be legally negotiated.

negotiate vti to discuss, bargain in order to reach an agreement or settlement; to settle by agreement; (obstacle, etc) to overcome.—**negotiation** n

neighbour n a person who lives near another; a person or thing situated next to another.

neighbourhood n a particular community, area, or district; the people in an area.

neighbouring adj adjoining, nearby.

neighbourly adj characteristic of a neighbour, friendly.—also adv.

neither adj, pron not one or the other (of two); not either. • conj not either; also not.

neon n an inert gaseous element that gives off a bright orange glow, used in lighting and advertisements.

nephew n the son of a brother or sister.

nerve n any of the fibres or bundles of fibres that transmit impulses of sensation or of movement between the brain and spinal cord and all parts of the body; courage, coolness in danger; (inf) audacity, boldness; (pl) nervousness, anxiety. • vt to give strength, courage, or vigour to.

nerve-racking, nerve-wracking adj stressful.

nervous adj excitable, highly strung; anxious, apprehensive.

nervous breakdown n a (usu temporary) period of mental illness resulting from severe emotional strain or anxiety.

nest n a structure or place where birds, fish, mice, etc, lay eggs or give birth to young; a set of tables of different sizes, designed to fit together. • vi to make or occupy a nest.

nestle vti to rest snugly; to lie snugly.

net[1] n an openwork material of string, rope, or twine knotted into meshes; a piece of this used to catch fish, divide a tennis court, etc; a snare. • vti to snare as with a net.

net[2], **nett** adj clear of deductions, allowances or charges. • vt to clear as a profit.

netball n a game for two teams of 7 players, in which points are scored by putting a ball through an elevated horizontal ring.

netting n netted fabric.

nettle n a wild plant with stinging hairs. • vt to irritate, annoy.

network n a group of people who co-operate with each other; a chain of interconnected operations, computers, etc; (radio, TV) a group of broadcasting stations connected to transmit the same programme simultaneously. • vt to broadcast on a network.

neurosis n a mental disorder with symptoms such as anxiety, phobia.

neurotic adj suffering from neurosis; highly strung. • n someone with neurosis.

neuter adj (gram) of gender, neither masculine nor feminine; (biol) having no sex organs. • n a neuter person, word, plant, or animal. • vt to castrate or spay.

neutral adj nonaligned; not taking sides with either party in a dispute or war; having no distinctive characteristics; (colour) dull; (chem) neither acid nor alkaline; (physics) having zero charge. • n a neutral state, person, or colour; a position of a gear mechanism in which power is not transmitted.

never adv at no time, not ever; not at all.

nevertheless adv all the same, notwithstanding; in spite of, however.

new adj recently made, discovered or invented; seen, known or used for the first time; different, changed; fresh; unused; unaccustomed; unfamiliar; recently begun.

newly adv recently, lately.

news npl current events; recent happenings; the mass media's coverage of such events; a programme of news on television or radio; information not known before.

newsagent n a retailer of newspapers, etc.

newspaper n a printed periodical containing news published daily or weekly.

next adj nearest; immediately preceding or following; adjacent. • adv in the nearest time, place, rank, etc; on the first subsequent occasion.

nib n a pen point.

nibble vti to take small bites at (food, etc).

nice adj pleasant, attractive, kind, good, etc; particular, fastidious; delicately sensitive.

niche n a shallow recess in a wall for a statue, etc; a place, use, or work for which a person or thing is best suited.

nick n a small cut, chip, etc, made on a surface; (sl) a police station, prison. • vt to wound superficially; (sl) to steal; (sl) to arrest.

nickel n a silvery-white metallic element used in alloys and plating; a US or Canadian coin worth five cents.

nickname n a substitute name, often descriptive, given in fun; a familiar form of a proper name. • vt to give as a nickname.

nicotine n a poisonous alkaloid in tobacco.

niece n the daughter of a brother or sister.

night n the period of darkness from sunset to sunrise; nightfall.

nightcap n a cap worn in bed; (inf) an alcoholic drink taken just before going to bed.

nightclub n a place of entertainment for drinking, dancing, etc, at night.

nightdress n a loose garment worn in bed by women.

nightfall n the close of the day.

nightingale n a songbird celebrated for its musical song at night.

nightlife n social entertainment at night.

nightly adj, adv done or happening by night or every night.

nightmare n a frightening dream; any horrible experience.—**nightmarish** adj.

night-time n night.

nil n nothing.

nimble adj agile; quick.—**nimbly** adv.

nine adj, n one more than eight. • n the symbol for this (9, IX, ix).

nineteen adj, n one more than eighteen. • n the symbol for this (19, XIX, xix).—**nineteenth** adj.

ninety adj, n nine times ten. • n the symbol for this (90, XC, xc).—**ninetieth** adj.

ninth adj, n next after eighth; one of nine equal parts of a thing.

nip[1] vt to pinch; to squeeze between two surfaces; (dog) to give a small bite. • n a pinch; a bite; severe frost or biting coldness.

nip[2] n a small drink of spirits.

nipple n the small protuberance on a breast or udder through which the milk passes; a teat-like rubber part on the cap of a baby's bottle.

nippy adj (inf) quick, nimble; (weather) frosty.

nitrogen n a gaseous element forming nearly 78 per cent of air.

no[1] adv (used to express denial or disagreement) not so, not at all, by no amount. • adj not any; not a; not one, none; not at all; by no means. • n a denial; a refusal.

nobility n nobleness of character, mind, birth, or rank; the class of people of noble birth.

noble adj famous or renowned; excellent in quality or character.

nobody n a person of no importance. • pron no person.

nod vti to incline the head quickly, esp in agreement or greeting; to let the head drop, be drowsy; (with off) (inf) to fall asleep. • n a quick bob of the head; a sign of assent or command.

noise n a sound, esp a loud, disturbing or unpleasant one; a din; unwanted fluctuations in a transmitted signal; (pl) conventional sounds, words, etc, made in reaction, such as sympathy.

noisy adj turbulent, clamorous.

nomad n one of a people or tribe who move in search of pasture; a wanderer.—**nomadic** adj.

no-man's-land n an unclaimed piece of land; a strip of land, esp between armies, borders.

nominal adj of or like a name; existing in name only; having minimal real worth, token.

nominate vt to appoint to an office or position; (candidate) to propose for election.

nominee n a person who is nominated.

nonchalant adj calm; cool, unconcerned.

noncommittal adj not revealing one's opinion.

nondescript adj hard to classify, indeterminate; lacking individual characteristics.

none pron no one; not anyone; (pl verb) not any; no one. • adv not at all.

nonentity n a person or thing of no significance.

nonplus vt to cause to be so perplexed that one cannot, go, speak, act further.

nonsense n words, actions, etc, that are absurd.—**also adj**.

nook n a secluded corner, a retreat; a recess.

noon n midday; twelve o'clock in the day.

nor conj and not; not either.

norm n a standard or model.

normal adj regular; usual; stable mentally.

north n one of the four points of the compass, opposite the sun at noon, to the right of a person facing the sunset; the direction in which a compass needle points; (often with cap) the northern part of one's country or the earth. • adj in, of, or towards the north; from the north. • adv in or towards the north.

northeast adj, n (of) the direction midway between north and east.

northern adj of or in the north.

northward adj towards or in the north.—**northwards** adv.

northwest adj, n (of) the direction midway between north and west.

Norwegian (adj) n (of or relating to) the language, people, etc, of Norway.

nose n the part of the face above the mouth, used for breathing and smelling. • vt to discover as by smell. • vi to inch forwards; to pry.

nose dive n a swift downward plunge of an aircraft, nose first; any sudden sharp drop.

nostalgia n yearning for past times or places.— **nostalgic** adj.

nostril n one of the two external openings of the nose for breathing and smelling.

nosy adj (inf) inquisitive, snooping.

not adv expressing denial, refusal, or negation.

notable adj worthy of being noted or remembered; remarkable, eminent.

notch n a V-shaped cut in an edge or surface; (inf) a step, degree; a narrow pass with steep sides. • vt to cut notches in.

note n a brief summary or record, written down for future reference; a memorandum; a short letter; notice, attention; an explanation or comment on the text of a book; a musical sound of a particular pitch; a sign representing such a sound; a piano or organ key; the vocal sound of a bird. • vt to notice, observe; to write down; to annotate.

notebook n a book with blank pages for writing in.

noted adj celebrated, well-known.

nothing n no thing; a zero; a person or thing of no importance.

notice n an announcement; a warning; a placard giving information; a short article about a book, play, etc; attention, heed; a formal warning of intention to end an agreement at a certain time. • vt to observe. • vi to be aware of.

noticeable adj easily noticed or seen.

notice board n a board on which notices, bulletins, etc, are pinned for public information.

notify vt to inform; to give notice of.

notion n a general idea; an opinion; a whim;.

notorious adj widely known, esp unfavourably.

notwithstanding prep in spite of. • adv nevertheless. • conj although.

nought n nothing; a zero.—also **naught**.

noun n (gram) a word that names a person, a living being, an object, action etc; a substantive.

nourish vt to feed; to encourage the growth of.

nourishing adj health-giving; beneficial.

nourishment n food; the act of nourishing.

novel n a relatively long prose narrative that is usually fictitious and in the form of a story. • adj new and unusual.—**novelist** n.

novelty n a new or unusual thing; (pl) cheap, small objects for sale.

novice n a person on probation in a religious order before taking final vows; a beginner.

now adv at the present time; at once; nowadays. • conj since; seeing that. • n the present time.

nowadays adv at the present time.

nowhere adv not in, at, or to anywhere.

nozzle n the spout at the end of a hose, pipe, etc.

nuance n a subtle difference in meaning, etc.

nuclear adj of or relating to a nucleus; using nuclear energy; having nuclear weapons.

nuclear energy n energy released as a result of nuclear fission or fusion.

nuclear fission n the splitting of a nucleus of an atom either spontaneously or by bombarding it with particles.

nuclear fusion n the combining of two nuclei into a heavier nucleus, releasing energy in the process.

nuclear reactor n a device in which nuclear fission is maintained and harnessed to produce energy.

nucleus n the central part of core around which something may develop, or be grouped or concentrated; the centrally positively charged portion of an atom.

nude adj naked; bare; undressed. • n a naked human figure, esp in a work of art.—**nudity** n.

nudge vt to touch gently with the elbow to attract attention or urge into action.—also n.

nuisance n a person or thing that annoys.

null adj without legal force; invalid.

numb adj deadened; having no feeling (due to cold, shock, etc). • vt to make numb.

number n a symbol or word indicating how many; a numeral identifying a person or thing by its position in a series; a single issue of a magazine; a song or piece of music, esp as an item in a performance; (inf) an object singled out; a total of persons or things; (gram) the form of a word indicating singular or plural; a telephone number; (pl) arithmetic; (pl) numerical superiority. • vti to count; to give a number to; to include or be included as one of a group.

numberplate n a plate on the front or rear of a motor vehicle that displays its registration number.

numeral n a symbol or group of symbols used to express a number.

numeric(al) adj of or relating to numbers.

numerous adj many, consisting of many.

nun n a woman belonging to a religious order.

nurse n a person trained to care for the sick, injured or aged; a person who looks after another person's child or children. • vt to tend, to care for; (baby) to feed at the breast.

nursery n a room set aside for children; a place where children may be left in temporary care; a place where young trees and plants are raised for transplanting.

nursery rhyme n a short traditional poem or song for children.

nursing n the profession of a nurse.

nursing home n an establishment providing care for chronically ill or disabled people.

nut n a kernel (sometimes edible) enclosed in a hard shell; a metallic threaded block screwed on the end of a bolt; (sl) a devotee, fan.

nutmeg n the aromatic kernel produced by a tree, grated and used as a spice.

nutrition n the act or process by which plants and animals take in and assimilate food in their systems; the study of the human diet.

nutritious adj efficient as food; nourishing.

nylon n any of numerous strong, tough, elastic, synthetic materials used esp in plastics and textiles; (pl) stockings made of nylon.

oak n a tree with a hard durable wood.

oar n a pole with a flat blade for rowing a boat.

oasis n a fertile place in a desert; a refuge.

oath n a solemn declaration to a god or a higher authority that one will speak the truth or keep a promise; a swear word; a blasphemous expression.

oatmeal n ground oats; a porridge of this.

oats npl a cereal grass widely cultivated for its edible grain; the seeds.

obedience n the condition of being obedient; observance of orders, instructions, etc.

obedient adj obeying; compliant; dutiful.

obelisk n a four-sided tapering pillar.

obese adj very fat.—**obesity** n.

obey vti to carry out (orders, instructions).

obituary n an announcement of a person's death, often with a short biography.

object n something that can be recognised by the senses; a person or thing towards which action, feeling, etc, is directed; a purpose or aim; (gram) a noun or part of a sentence governed by a transitive verb or a preposition. • vti to state or raise an objection; to oppose; to disapprove.

objection n the act of objecting.

objective adj relating to an object; not influenced by opinions or feelings; impartial; having an independent existence of its own, real; (gram) of, or appropriate to an object governed by a verb or a preposition. • n the thing or placed aimed at; (gram) the objective case.

obligation n the act of obligating; a moral or legal requirement; a debt; a favour; a commitment to pay a certain amount of money.—**obligate** vt.

obligatory adj not optional; compulsory.

oblige vt to compel by moral, legal, or physical force; (person) to make grateful for some favour; to do a favour for.

obliging adj ready to do favours, agreeable.

oblique adj slanting, at an angle; diverging from the straight; indirect. • n an oblique line.

obliterate vt to wipe out, to erase, to destroy.

oblivion n a state of forgetting or being forgotten; a state of mental withdrawal.

oblivious adj unheeding; unaware (of).

oblong adj rectangular.—also n.

obnoxious adj objectionable; highly offensive.

oboe n an orchestral woodwind instrument having a mouthpiece with a double reed.

obscene adj indecent, lewd.

obscenity n the state or quality of being obscene; an obscene act, word, etc.

obscure adj not clear; dim; indistinct; remote, secret; not easily understood; inconspicuous. • vt to make unclear, to confuse; to hide.

obscurity n the state or quality of being obscure; an obscure thing or person.

obsequious adj subservient; fawning.

observance n the observing of a rule, law, etc; a ceremony or religious rite.

observant adj watchful; attentive.

observation n the act or faculty of observing; a comment or remark; careful noting of the symptoms of a patient, movements of a suspect, etc, prior to diagnosis, analysis or interpretation.

observatory n a building for astronomical observation; an institution whose primary purpose is making such observations.

observe vt to notice; to perceive; (a law, etc) to keep to or adhere to; to arrive at as a conclusion; to examine scientifically. • vi to take notice.

observer n a person who observes; a delegate who attends a formal meeting but may not take part.

obsess vt to possess or haunt the mind of; to preoccupy.—**obsessive** adj, n.

obsession n a fixed idea, often associated with mental illness; a persistent idea or preoccupation; the condition of being obsessed.

obsolete adj disused, out of date.

obstacle n anything that hinders something.

obstetrics n (used as sing) the branch of medicine concerned with the care and treatment of women during pregnancy and childbirth.

obstinate adj stubborn, self-willed; intractable; persistent.—**obstinacy** n.

obstreperous adj unruly, turbulent, noisy.

obstruct vt to block with an obstacle; to impede; to prevent, hinder.

obstruction n that which obstructs; the act or an example of obstructing; a hindrance, obstacle.

obstructive adj tending to obstruct; preventing.

obtain vt to get, to acquire, to gain. • vi to be prevalent, hold good.—**obtainable** adj.

obtrude vti to push (an opinion, oneself) on others uninvited; to intrude.—**obtrusion** n.

obtrusive adj apt to obtrude, pushy; protruding.

obtuse adj mentally slow; not pointed; dull, stupid; (geom) greater than a right angle.

obviate vt to make unnecessary; (danger, difficulty) to prevent, clear away.

obvious adj easily seen or understood.

occasion n a special occurrence or event; a time when something happens; an opportunity; reason or grounds. • vt to cause; to bring about.

occasional adj infrequent, not continuous; intermittent; produced for an occasion.

occasionally adv intermittently; now and then; infrequently.

occupant n a person who occupies, resides in, holds a position or place, etc.

occupation n the act of occupying; the state of being occupied; employment or profession; a pursuit.—**occupational** adj.

occupy vt to live in; (room, office) to take up or fill; (a position) to hold; to engross (one's mind); (city, etc) to take possession of.

occur vi to happen; to come into the mind of.

occurrence n a happening, an incident.

ocean n a large stretch of sea, esp one of the earth's five oceans; a huge quantity or expanse.—**oceanic** adj.

ochre n a yellow to orange-coloured clay used as a pigment.

o'clock adv indicating the hour; indicating a relative direction or position, twelve o'clock being directly ahead or above.

octagon n a plane figure having eight equal sides.—**octagonal** adj.

octane n a hydrocarbon found in petrol.

octave n (mus) the eighth full tone above or below a given tone, the interval of eight degrees between a tone and either of its octaves, or the series of tones within this.

octopus n a mollusc having a soft body and eight tentacles covered with suckers.

odd adj eccentric; peculiar; occasional; not divisible by two; with the other of the pair missing; extra or left over. • npl probability; balance of advantage in favour of one against another; excess of one number over another, esp in betting; likelihood; disagreement; strife; miscellaneous articles, scraps.

oddity n the state of being odd; an odd thing or person; peculiarity.

oddment n an odd piece left over, esp fabric.

ode n a lyric poem marked by lofty feeling and dignified style.

odious adj causing hatred or offence.

odour n smell; scent; aroma.

odourless adj without odour.

of prep from; belonging or relating to; among.

off adv away, from; detached, gone; unavailable; disconnected; out of condition; entirely. • prep away from; not on. • adj distant; no longer operating; cancelled; (food or drink) having gone bad; on the right-hand side; (runners, etc) having started a race.

offal n animal entrails eaten as food.

off-colour adj unwell; risqué.

offence n an illegal action, crime; a sin.

offend vt to affront, displease; to insult. • vi to break a law.—**offender** n.

offensive adj causing offence; repulsive, disagreeable; insulting; aggressive. • n an attack.

offer vt to present for acceptance or rejection; to show willingness (to do something); to present for consideration; to bid; (a prayer) to say. • vi to present itself; to declare oneself willing. • n something offered; a bid or proposal.

offering n a gift, present; a sacrifice.

offhand adv impromptu; without thinking. • adj inconsiderate; curt, brusque; unceremonious.

office n a room or building where business is carried out; the people there; (with cap) the location, staff of authority of a government department, etc; a task or function; a position of authority; a duty; a religious rite.

officer n an official; a person holding a position of authority in a government, business, club, military services, etc; a policeman.

official adj properly authorised; formal. • n a person who holds a public office.

officiate vi to act in an official capacity; to perform the functions of a priest, minister, rabbi, etc.

officious adj interfering, meddlesome.

offing n the near or foreseeable future.

off-licence n a licence to sell alcohol for consumption off the premises; a place so licensed.

off-peak adj denoting use of a service, etc, in a period of lesser demand.

offset vt to compensate for, counterbalance. • n compensation; a method of printing in which an image is transferred from a plate to a rubber surface and then to paper.

offside adj, adv illegally in advance of the ball.

offspring n a child, progeny; a result.

offstage adj, adv out of sight of the audience.

often adv many times, frequently.

ogle vti to gape at; to look at lustfully.

oil n a greasy, combustible liquid substance obtained from animal, vegetable or mineral matter; petroleum; an oil painting; (pl) paint mixed by grinding a pigment in oil • vt to smear with oil.

oil painting n a painting in oils; the art of painting in oils; (inf) a good-looking person.

oilskin n fabric made waterproof by treatment with oil; a waterproof garment of oilskin.

oil slick n a mass of oil floating on the surface of water.

oily adj like or covered with oil; greasy; too suave or smooth, unctuous.—**oiliness** n.

ointment n a fatty substance used on the skin for healing or cosmetic purposes; a salve.

OK, okay adj, adv (inf) all right; correct(ly).

old adj aged; elderly, not young; long used, not new; former; of the past, not modern; experienced.

old-fashioned adj out of date.

olive n an evergreen tree cultivated for its edible hard-stoned fruit and oil; its fruit; a yellow-green colour.—also adj.

ombudsman n an official appointed to investigate citizens' or consumers' complaints.

omelette n eggs beaten and cooked flat in a pan.

omen n a sign or warning of impending happiness or disaster.

ominous adj relating to an omen; foreboding evil; threatening.

omission n something that has been left out or neglected; the act of omitting.

omit vt to leave out; to neglect to do.

omnibus n (formal) a bus; a book containing several works, usu by one author.

omnipotent adj all-powerful, almighty.

omnivorous adj eating any sort of food.

on prep in contact with the upper surface of; supported by, attached to, or covering; directed toward; at the time of; concerning, about; using as a basis, condition or principle; immediately after; (sl) using; addicted to. • adv (so as to be) covering or in contact with something; forward; (device) switched on; continuously in progress; due to take place; (actor) on stage; on duty.

once adv on one occasion only; formerly; at some time. • conj as soon as. • n one time.

oncoming adj approaching.

one adj single; undivided, united; the same; a certain unspecified (time, etc). • n the first and lowest cardinal number; an individual thing or person. • pron an indefinite person, used to apply to many people.

onerous adj oppressive; troublesome.

oneself pron reflex form of one.

one-upmanship n the skill of being one jump ahead of or going one better than.

one-way adj (traffic) restricted to one direction.

ongoing adj progressing, continuing.

onion n an edible bulb with a pungent taste and odour.

only adj alone of its kind; single, sole. • adv solely, merely; just. • conj except that, but.

onset n a beginning; an assault, attack.

onslaught n a fierce attack.

onto prep to a position on.

onus n responsibility, duty; burden.

onward adj advancing, forward.

onwards adv to the front, ahead, forward.

onyx n a limestone similar to marble with layers of colour.

ooze vti to flow or leak out slowly; to seep; to exude. • n soft mud or slime.

opal n a white or bluish stone with a play of iridescent colours.

opaque adj not letting light through.

open adj not closed; accessible; uncovered, unprotected; spread out, unfolded; public; lacking reserve; (a person) forthcoming; generous; liable (to); unrestricted. • vti to make or become accessible; to unfasten; to begin; to expand, unfold; to come into view. • n a wide space; (sport) a competition that any player can enter.—**openness** n.

opening n a gap, aperture; a beginning; a chance; a job opportunity. • adj initial.

openly adv frankly; publicly.

opera n a dramatic work represented through music and song.

operate vi to work, to function; to produce a desired effect; to carry out a surgical operation. • vt (a machine) to work or control; to carry on, run.

operatic adj of or relating to opera.

operation n a procedure; a military action; a surgical procedure.

operational adj of or relating to an operation; functioning; ready for use.

operative adj functioning; in force, effective; of, by surgery. • n a mechanic; a secret agent.

operator n a person who operates or works a machine, esp a telephone switchboard; a person who owns or runs a business.

operetta n a short or light opera.

ophthalmic adj of, or situated near, the eye.

ophthalmology n the branch of medicine dealing with diseases of the eye.

opinion n a belief that is not based on proof; judgment; evaluation; a formal expert judgment.

opinionated adj unduly confident in one's opinions, dogmatic.

opium n a narcotic drug produced from poppy.

opponent n a person who opposes another; an adversary, antagonist.—*also adj.*

opportune adj well-timed; convenient.

opportunist n a person who forms or adapts his or her views or principles to benefit from opportunities; to seize opportunities as they may arise.—**opportunism** n.

opportunity n chance; a favourable combination of circumstances.

oppose vt to put in front of or in the way of; to place in opposition; to resist; to fight against; to balance against.—**opposer** n.

opposite adj placed on opposed sides of; face to face; diametrically different; contrary. • n a person or thing that is opposite; an antithesis. • *prep, adv* across from.

opposition n the act of opposing or the condition of being opposed; resistance; hostility; a political party opposing the government.

oppress vt to treat unjustly; to subjugate; to weigh down in the mind.—**oppressor** n.

oppression n the act of oppressing; the state of being oppressed; persecution.

oppressive adj tyrannical; burdensome; (*weather*) sultry, close.

opt vi to choose, to exercise an option.

optic(al) adj of or relating to the eye or light.

optician n a person who makes or sells optical aids.

optimism n a tendency to take the most cheerful view of things; hopefulness; the belief that good must ultimately prevail.—**optimist** n.—**optimistic** adj.

optimum n the best, most favourable condition.—*also adj.*

option n the power to choose; a choice; the right to buy, sell or lease at a fixed price within a specified time.

optional adj left to choice; not compulsory.

opulent adj wealthy; luxuriant.

or conj denoting an alternative; the last in a series of choices.

oracle n a place in ancient Greece where a deity was consulted; the response given (usu ambiguous); a wise adviser; sage advice.

oral adj of the mouth; (*drugs*) taken by mouth; spoken, not written. • n a spoken examination.

orange n a round, reddish-yellow, juicy, edible citrus fruit; the tree bearing it; its colour. • adj orange-coloured.

oration n a formal or public speech.

orator n an eloquent public speaker.

oratorio n a sacred story set to music for voices and instruments.

orb n a sphere or globe; an ornamental sphere surmounted by a cross, esp as carried by a sovereign at a coronation.

orbit n (*astron*) a curved path along which a planet or satellite moves; (*physics*) the path of an electron around the nucleus of an atom. • vti to circle round.

orchard n land planted with fruit trees.

orchestra n a group of musicians playing together under a conductor; their instruments; the space (or pit) in a theatre where they sit; the stalls of a theatre.

orchid n a plant with flowers in brilliant colours comprising three petals of uneven size.

ordain vti to confer holy orders upon; to appoint; to decree; to order, to command.

ordeal n a severe trial or test.

order n arrangement; sequence; an undisturbed condition; tidiness; rules of procedure; an efficient state; a class, group, or sort; a religious fraternity; a style of architecture; an honour or decoration; an instruction or command; a rule or regulation; a state or condition, esp with regard to functioning; a request to supply something; the goods supplied; (*zool*) divisions between class and family or genus. • vti to put or keep (things) in order; to arrange; to command; to request (something) to be supplied.

orderly adj in good order; well-behaved; methodical. • n a hospital attendant; a soldier attending an officer.—**orderliness** n.

ordinal adj showing position in a series (e.g. first, second, third).

ordinary adj normal, usual; common; plain.

ordination n admission to the ministry.

ore n a substance from which minerals can be extracted.

organ n a usu large and complex musical wind instrument with pipes, stops, and a keyboard; a part of an animal or plant that performs a vital or natural function; a medium of information or opinion, a periodical.

organic adj of or relating to bodily organs; (disease) affecting a bodily organ; of, or derived from, living organisms; (*chem*) of the class of compounds that are formed from carbon; (vegetables, etc) grown without the use of artificial fertilisers or pesticides.

organisation n the act or process of organising; arrangement, structure; an organised body.

organise vt to arrange in an orderly way; to establish; to institute; to persuade to join a group.

organism n an animal or plant, any living thing.

orgasm n the sexual climax.

orgy n a wild party or gathering with excessive drinking and indiscriminate sexual activity.

Orient n the East or Asia, esp the Far East.

orient, orientate vti to adjust (oneself) to a particular situation; to arrange in a direction, esp in relation to the points of the compass.

oriental *adj* of the East, its people or languages.

orifice *n* an opening or mouth of a cavity.

origin *n* the source or beginning of anything; ancestry or parentage.

original *adj* relating to the origin or beginning; earliest; unusual; inventive. • *n* an original work, as of art, etc; something from which copies are made; a creative person; an eccentric.

originate *vti* to initiate or begin; to bring or come into being.—**origination** *n*.

ornament *n* anything that enhances the appearance of a person or thing; a small decorative object. • *vt* to adorn, to decorate with ornaments.

ornamental *adj* decorative, not useful.

ornate *adj* richly adorned; (*style*) highly elaborate.—**ornateness** *n*.

ornithology *n* the study of birds.

orphan *n* a child whose parents are dead. • *vt* to cause to become an orphan.

orphanage *n* a residential institution for the care of orphans.

orthodox *adj* conforming with established behaviour or opinions; generally accepted, conventional; (*with cap*) of or relating to a conservative political or religious group.—**orthodoxy** *n*.

orthopaedics *n* the study and surgical treatment of bone and joint disorders.—**orthopaedic** *adj*.

oscillate *vi* to swing back and forth as a pendulum; to waver.—**oscillation** *n*.

ostensible *adj* apparent; seeming; pretended.

ostentation *n* a showy, pretentious display.—**ostentatious** *adj*.

osteopathy *n* the treatment of disease by manipulation of the bones and muscles.—**osteopath** *n*.

ostracise *vt* to exclude, banish from a group, society, etc.—**ostracism** *n*.

ostrich *n* a large, flightless African bird.

other *adj* second; remaining; different; additional. • *pron* the other one; some other one.

otherwise *adv* if not, or else; differently.

otter *n* a fish-eating mammal with smooth fur and a flat tail.

ought *aux vb* expressing obligation or duty; to be bound, to be obliged (to).

ounce *n* a unit of weight, equal to one sixteenth of a pound or 28.34 grams; one sixteenth of a pint, one fluid ounce.

our *poss adj, pron* relating or belonging to us.

ours *pron* belonging to us.

ourselves *pron* emphatic and reflexive form of we.

oust *vt* to eject, expel, esp by underhand means; to remove forcibly.

out *adv* not in; outside; in the open air; ruled out, no longer considered; no longer included (in a game, fashion, etc); in error; on strike; extinguished; published; revealed; (*radio conversation*) transmission ends. • *prep* out of; out through; outside. • *n* an exit; means of escape.

outboard (*engine*) outside a ship, etc.

outbreak *n* a sudden eruption (of disease, etc).

outburst *n* a spurt; an explosion of anger, etc.

outcast *n* a person rejected by society.

outclass *vt* to surpass or excel greatly.

outcome *n* the result, consequence.

outcry *n* protest; uproar.

outdo *vt* to surpass, to excel.

outdoor *adj* taking place in the open air.

outdoors *adv* in or into the open air; out of doors. • *n* the open air, outside world.

outer *adj* further out or away.

outfit *n* the equipment used in an activity; clothes worn together, an ensemble; a group of people associated in an activity.—*also vt*.

outfitter *n* a supplier of equipment or clothes.

outgoing *adj* departing; retiring; sociable. • *n* an outlay; (*pl*) expenditure.

outing *n* a pleasure trip; an excursion.

outlandish *adj* unconventional; strange.

outlaw *vt* to declare illegal. • *n* an outlawed person; a habitual or notorious criminal.

outlay *n* a spending (of money); expenditure.

outlet *n* an opening or release; a means of expression; a market for goods or services.

outline *n* a profile; a general indication; a rough sketch or draft.—*also vt*.

outlive *vt* to live longer than, outlast; to live through; to survive.

outlook *n* mental attitude; view; prospect.

outlying *adj* detached; remote, distant.

outmoded *adj* old-fashioned.

outpatient *n* a person treated at, but not resident in, a hospital.

outpost *n* (*mil*) a post or detachment at a distance from a main force.

output *n* the quantity (of goods, etc) produced, esp over a given period; information delivered by a computer, esp to a printer; (*elect*) the useful voltage, current, or power delivered.—*also vt*.

outrage *n* an extremely vicious or violent act; a grave insult or offence; great anger.

outright *adv* without restrictions.

outset *n* the start, beginning.

outside *n* the outer part or surface, the exterior. • *adj* outer; outdoor; (*chance, etc*) slight. • *adv* on or to the outside. • *prep* beyond.

outsider *n* a person or thing not included in a set, group, etc, a non-member.

outsize *adj* of a larger than usual size.

outskirts *npl* districts remote from the centre.

outspoken *adj* candid in speech, frank.

outstanding *adj* excellent; unpaid.

outward *adj* directed towards the outside; external; clearly apparent. • *adv* outwards.

outwardly adv externally.

outweigh vt to exceed in value or importance.

outwit vt to defeat by wit or cunning.

oval adj egg-shaped; elliptical.—also n.

ovary n one of the two female reproductive organs producing eggs.—**ovarian** adj.

ovation n enthusiastic applause.

oven n an enclosed, heated compartment for baking or drying.

over prep higher than; on top of; across; to the other side of; above; more than; concerning. • adv above; across; in every part; completed. • n (cricket) the number of balls bowled before changing ends.

overact vti to act in an exaggerated manner.

overall adj including everything. • adv as a whole; generally. • n a loose protective garment; (pl) a one-piece protective garment covering body and legs.

overawe vt to restrain by awe, daunt.

overbalance vti to fall over; to upset.

overbearing adj domineering; overriding.

overboard adv over the side of a ship, etc; (inf) to extremes of enthusiasm.

overcast adj clouded over.

overcharge vt (battery) to overload; to fill to excess; to demand too high a price (from). • n an excessive or exorbitant charge or load.

overcoat n a warm, heavy topcoat.

overcome vti to get the better of, to prevail; to render helpless or powerless, as by tears, laughter, emotion, etc; to surmount obstacles, etc.

overdo vt to do to excess; to overact; to cook (food) too much.

overdose n an excessive dose.—also vti.

overdraft n an amount overdrawn, at a bank.

overdraw vti to draw in excess of a credit balance.

overdrive n a high gear in a motor vehicle to reduce wear for travelling at high speed.

overdue adj past the time for payment, return, performance, etc; in arrears; delayed.

overestimate vt to set too high an estimate on.

overflow vti to flow over, flood; to exceed the bounds (of); to abound (with emotion, etc). • n that which overflows; surplus; an outlet for surplus water, etc.

overgrown adj grown beyond the normal size.

overhaul vt to examine for, or make, repairs.—also n.

overhead adj, adv above the head; in the sky. • n (often pl) the general, continuing costs of a business, as of rent, light, etc.

overhear vt to hear without the knowledge of the speaker.

overjoyed adj highly delighted.

overland adj, adv by, on, or across land.

overlap vt to extend over (a thing or each other) so as to coincide in part.—also n.

overload vt to put too great a burden on; (elect) to charge with too much current.

overlook vt to fail to notice; to look at from above; to excuse.

overnight adv for the night; in the course of the night; suddenly. • adj done in the night.

overpass n a road crossing another road, path, etc, at a higher level.

overpower vt to overcome by superior force, to subdue; to overwhelm.

overpowering adj overwhelming; unbearable.

overrate vt to value or assess too highly.

override vt to ride over; to nullify.

overrule vt to set aside by higher authority.

overseas adj, adv abroad.

overshadow vt to throw a shadow over; to appear more prominent or important than.

overshoot vt to shoot or send beyond (a target, etc); (aircraft) to fly or taxi beyond the end of a runway when landing or taking off.

oversight n a careless mistake or omission.

oversleep vi to sleep beyond the intended time.

overspill vi to spill over, overflow. • n that which overspills; excess.

overt adj openly done, unconcealed.

overtake vt to catch up with and pass; to come upon suddenly.

overthrow vt to throw over, overturn; (government, etc) to bring down by force.—also n.

overtime adv beyond regular working hours. • n extra time worked; payment for this.

overtone n an additional subtle meaning; an implicit quality; (mus) a harmonic.

overture n an initiating of negotiations; (mus) an instrumental introduction to an opera, etc.

overturn vti to upset, turn over; to overthrow.

overweight adj weighing more than the proper amount. • n excess weight.

overwhelm vt to overcome totally; to submerge; to crush; to overpower with emotion.

overwhelming adj irresistible; uncontrollable.

overwork vti to work too hard or too long.

overwrought adj over-excited; too elaborate.

owe vti to be in debt; to be obliged to pay; to feel the need to give, do, etc, as because of gratitude.

owing adj due, to be paid; owed; (with to) because of, on account of.

owl n a nocturnal bird of prey with a large head and eyes; a person of nocturnal habits, solemn appearance, etc.—**owlish** adj.

own[1] vti to possess; to admit; to confess to.

own[2] adj belonging to oneself or itself, often used reflexively (my own, their own).

owner n one who owns, a possessor, a proprietor.—**ownership** n.

ox n a castrated bull.

oxide n a compound of oxygen with another element.

oxidise *vti* to cause to undergo a chemical reaction with oxygen; to rust.

oxtail *n* the tail of an ox, esp skinned and used for stews, soups, etc.

oxygen *n* a colourless, odourless, tasteless, highly reactive gaseous element forming part of air, water, etc, and essential to life and combustion.

oxygen mask *n* an apparatus over the nose and mouth through which oxygen passes from a storage tank.

oyster *n* an edible marine bivalve shellfish.

ozone *n* a condensed form of oxygen; (*inf*) bracing seaside air.

ozone layer *n* a layer of ozone in the upper atmosphere that absorbs ultraviolet rays from the sun.

P

pace *n* a single step; the measure of a single stride; speed of movement. • *vti* to measure by paces; to walk up and down.

pacemaker *n* a person who sets the pace in a race; an electronic device inserted in the heart, used to regulate heartbeat.

pacify *vt* to soothe; to calm.

pack *n* a load or bundle (esp one carried on the back); a set of playing cards; a group or mass; a number of wild animals living together; an organised troop (as of Cub Scouts); a small package used as a container for goods for sale. • *vt* to put together in a bundle or pack; (*suitcase*) to fill; to crowd. • *vi* to assemble one's belongings in suitcases or boxes.—**packer** *n*.

package *n* a parcel, a wrapped bundle; several items, arrangements, etc, offered as a unit. • *vt* to make a parcel of; to group together.

packet *n* a small box or package; (*sl*) a considerable sum.

packing *n* material for protecting packed goods.

pact *n* an agreement or treaty.

pad[1] *vi* to walk, esp with a soft step.

pad[2] *n* a piece of a soft material or stuffing; several sheets of paper glued together at one edge; the cushioned thickening of an animal's sole; a piece of folded absorbent material used as a surgical dressing. • *vt* to stuff with soft material.

padding *n* stuffing.

paddle[1] *vi* to wade about in shallow water.

paddle[2] *n* a short oar with a wide blade at one or both ends. • *vti* to propel by a paddle.

padlock *n* a detachable lock used to fasten doors etc. • *vt* to secure with a padlock.

padre *n* (*sl*) a priest or chaplain.

paediatrics *n* the branch of medicine dealing with children and their diseases.

pagan *n* a heathen.

page[1] *n* a boy attendant at a formal function (as a wedding); a uniformed boy employed to run errands. • *vt* to summon by messenger, loudspeaker, etc.

page[2] *n* a sheet of paper in a book, etc.

pageant *n* a spectacular procession or parade; representation in costume of historical events.—**pageantry** *n*.

pageboy *n* a page; a medium-length hairstyle with ends of hair turned under.

pail *n* a bucket.

pain *n* physical or mental suffering; (*pl*) trouble, exertion. • *vt* to cause distress to.

painful *adj* giving pain, distressing.

painkiller *n* (*inf*) a medicine that relieves pain.

painless *adj* without pain.

painstaking *adj* very careful, laborious.

paint *vt* (*a picture*) to make using oil pigments, etc; to depict with paints; to cover with paint. • *vi* to make a picture. • *n* a colouring pigment.

painter *n* a person who paints, esp an artist.

painting *n* the act or art of applying paint; a painted picture.

pair *n* a set of two things that are equal, suited, or used together; any two persons or animals regarded as a unit. • *vti* to form a pair (of).

pal *n* a close friend.—**pally** *adj*.

palace *n* the official residence of a sovereign, president or bishop.

palatable *adj* (*taste*) pleasant; acceptable.

palate *n* the roof of the mouth.

pale[1] *n* a fence stake; a boundary.

pale[2] *adj* (*complexion*) with less colour than usual; (*colour, light*) faint, wan, dim. • *vti* to make or become pale.

palette *n* a small, wooden board on which coloured paints are mixed.

pall[1] *n* (*of smoke*) a mantle.

pall[2] *vi* to become boring.

pallet *n* a portable platform for lifting and stacking goods.

pallid *adj* wan, pale.

palm[1] *n* the underside of the hand between fingers and wrist. • *vt* (*with off*) to pass off by fraud.

palm[2] *n* a tropical branchless tree with fanshaped leaves.

palpable *adj* tangible; easily perceived.

paltry *adj* almost worthless; trifling.

pamper vt to overindulge; to spoil.

pamphlet n a thin, unbound booklet.

pan[1] n a wide metal container, a saucepan. • vi (with out) (inf) to turn out, esp to turn out well.

pan[2] vti (film camera) to move horizontally to follow an object.

pancake n a round, thin cake made from batter and cooked on a griddle.

panda n a large black and white bear-like herbivore.

pandemonium n uproar; chaos.

pander vi to gratify.

pane n a sheet of glass in a frame of a window, door, etc.

panel n a rectangular section forming part of a wall, door, etc; a board for instruments; a lengthwise strip in a skirt, etc; a group of selected persons for judging, discussing, etc.

panelling n panels collectively.

pang n a sudden sharp pain or feeling.

panic n a sudden overpowering terror. • vti to affect or be affected with panic.—**panicky** adj.

panorama n a complete view in all directions.—**panoramic** adj.

pansy n a garden flower of the violet family, with velvety petals.

pant vi to breathe noisily, gasp.

panther n a leopard, esp black.

panties npl (inf) short underpants.

pantomime n a Christmas theatrical entertainment with music and jokes; a drama without words, using only actions and gestures.

pantry n a small room or cupboard for storing cooking ingredients and utensils, etc.

pants npl trousers; underpants.

papacy n the office or authority of the pope.

papal adj of the pope or the papacy.

paper n the thin, flexible material made from pulped rags, wood, etc, which is used to write on, wrap in, or cover walls; a single sheet of this; an official document; a newspaper; an essay or lecture; a set of examination questions; (pl) personal documents. • adj like or made of paper. • vt to cover with wallpaper.

paperback n a book bound in a flexible paper cover.

paperweight n a small heavy object for keeping papers in place.

paperwork n clerical work of any kind.

papier-mâché n a substance made of paper pulp mixed with size, glue, etc, and moulded into various objects when moist.

paprika n a mild red condiment ground from the fruit of certain peppers.

par n the standard or normal level; (golf) the score for a hole by a perfect player; equality.

parable n a short story using everyday events to illustrate a religious or moral point.

parachute n a fabric umbrella-like canopy used to retard speed of fall from an aircraft.—also vti.

parade n a ceremonial procession; an assembly of troops for review; ostentatious display. • vti to march or walk through, as for display.

paradise n heaven; any place of perfection.

paradox n a self-contradictory statement that may be true; something with seeming contradictory qualities or phases.

paraffin n a distilled oil used as fuel.

paragraph n a subdivision in a piece of writing used to separate ideas, marked by the beginning of a new line.

parallel adj equidistant at every point and extended in the same direction; side by side. • n a parallel line, surface, etc; a likeness.

paralyse vt to affect with paralysis; to bring to a stop.—**paralytic** adj, n.

paralysis n a partial or complete loss of voluntary muscle function or sensation in any part of the body.

paramount adj of great importance.

paranoia n a mental illness characterised by delusions of grandeur and persecution; (inf) unfounded fear, suspicion.—**paranoid** adj, n.

paraphernalia npl personal belongings.

paraphrase n expression of a passage in other words in order to clarify meaning. • vt to restate.

parasite n an organism that lives on and feeds off another without rendering any service in return; a person who sponges off another.

paratroops npl troops dropped by parachute into an enemy area.—**paratrooper** n.

parcel n a wrapped bundle; a package. • vt to wrap up into a parcel.

parch vti to make or become hot and dry.

parchment n the skin of a sheep, etc, prepared as a writing material; paper like parchment.

pardon vt to forgive; to release from penalty. • n forgiveness; remission of penalty.

parent n a father or a mother.—**parental** adj.

parenthesis n an explanatory comment in a sentence contained within brackets and set in a sentence, independently of grammatical sequence; the brackets themselves ().

parish n an ecclesiastical area in the charge of one clergyman.

parity n equality.

park n land kept as a game preserve or recreation area; a piece of ground in an urban area kept for ornament or recreation. • vti (vehicle) to leave in a certain place temporarily.

parking meter n a coin-operated machine that registers the purchase of parking time for a motor vehicle.

parliament n a legislative assembly made up of representatives of a nation or part of a nation.

parliamentary adj of a parliament.

parlour n a room in a house used primarily for conversation or receiving guests.

parochial adj provincial in outlook.

parody n a satirical or humorous imitation of a literary or musical work or style.—also vt.

parole n the release of a prisoner before sentence has expired on condition of future good behaviour.—also vt.

parquet n an inlaid hard wood flooring.

parrot n a tropical or subtropical bird with brilliant plumage and the ability to mimic human speech; one who repeats another's words without understanding. • vt to repeat mechanically.

parry vt to ward off, turn aside. • n a defensive movement in fencing.

parsley n a bright green herb used to flavour or garnish some foods.

parsnip n a long tapered root used as a vegetable.

parson n a vicar; (inf) any clergyman.

part n a section; a portion (of a whole); an essential, separable component of a piece of equipment or a machine; the role of an actor in a play. • vt to separate. • vi to become separated.

partial adj incomplete; (with to) having a liking or preference for.—**partiality** n.

participate vi to join in or take part with others.—**participant** n.—**participation** n.

participle n (gram) a verb form used as an adjective.

particle n a tiny portion of matter; a speck.

particular adj referring or belonging to a specific person or thing; distinct; fastidious. • n a detail, single item; (pl) detailed information.

particularly adv very; especially; in detail.

parting n a departure; a breaking or separating; a dividing line in combing hair.

partisan n a strong supporter of a cause.

partition n division into parts; a dividing wall between rooms. • vt to divide.

partly adv in part; to some extent.

partner n one of two or more persons jointly owning a business; one of a pair who dance or play a game together; either member of a couple. • vt to be a partner.

partnership n a contract between two or more people involved in a joint business venture.

partridge n a stout-bodied game bird.

part-time adj working fewer than the full number of hours.

party n a group of people united for political or other purpose; a social gathering; a person involved in a contract or lawsuit; (inf) an individual. • vi to attend social parties.

pass vi to go past; to go beyond or exceed; to move from one place or state to another; (time) to elapse; to die; (with for) to be considered as; (in exam) to be successful; (cards) to decline to make a bid; (law) to be approved by a legislative assembly. • vt to go past, through, over, etc; (time) to spend; (law) to enact; (judgment) to pronounce; to excrete; (in test, etc) to gain the required marks; to approve. • n a narrow road; a permit; (in a test, etc) success; transfer of (a ball) to another player; (inf) an uninvited sexual approach.

passable adj fairly good, tolerable.

passage n a corridor; a route or crossing; a lapse of time; a piece of text or music.

passenger n a traveller in a conveyance.

passer-by n one who happens to pass or go by.

passing adj transient. • n departure, death.

passion n compelling emotion, such as love, hate, envy; ardent love, esp sexual desire; the object of any strong desire.

passionate adj moved by, showing, strong emotion or desire; intense; sensual.

passive adj acted upon, not acting; submissive; (gram) denoting the voice of a verb whose subject receives the action.

passport n an official document giving the owner the right to travel abroad.

password n a secret term by which a person is recognised and allowed to pass; a sequence of characters required to access a computer system.

past adj completed; ended; in time already elapsed. • prep beyond (in time, place, or amount). • n time that has gone by.

pasta n the flour paste from which spaghetti, noodles, etc, is made; any dish of cooked pasta.

paste n a soft plastic mixture; flour and water forming dough or adhesive. • vt to attach with paste.

pastel n a substance made of chalk, used for drawing; a drawing made with such; a soft, pale colour. • adj delicately coloured.

pasteurise vt (milk, etc) to sterilise by heat or radiation to destroy harmful organisms.

pastime n a hobby; recreation, diversion.

pastoral adj of rural life.

pastry n dough made of flour, water, and fat used for making pies, tarts, etc.

pasture n land covered with grass for grazing livestock; the grass growing on it.

pasty[1] n meat, etc, enclosed in pastry and baked.

pasty[2] adj pallid and unhealthy in appearance.

pat[1] vti to strike gently with the palm of the hand or a flat object. • n a light tap with the palm of the hand.

pat[2] adj apt; exact; glib.—also adv.

patch n a piece of cloth used for mending; a shield for an injured part; an irregular spot on a surface. • vt to repair with a patch.

patchwork n needlework made of pieces sewn together.

patchy adj irregular; uneven.

pâté n a spread made of liver, herbs, etc.

patent adj plain; apparent; protected by a patent. • n a government document, granting the exclusive right to produce and sell an invention, etc, for a certain time; the right so granted.

patent leather n leather with a glossy finish.

paternal adj fatherly in disposition; related through the father.

paternity n fatherhood.

path n a way worn by footsteps; a track for people on foot; a direction; a course of conduct.

pathetic adj inspiring pity; (sl) inadequate.

pathologist n a medical specialist who diagnoses by interpreting the changes in tissue and body fluid caused by a disease.

pathology n the branch of medicine that deals with the nature of disease, esp its functional and structural effects.—**pathological** adj.

patience n the capacity to wait calmly; a card game for one.

patient adj even-tempered; able to wait calmly. • n a person receiving medical, etc, treatment.

patio n a paved area adjoining a house, for outdoor lounging, dining, etc.

patriot n one who strongly supports and serves his or her country.—**patriotic** adj.

patrol vti to walk around a building or area in order to guard. • n the act of going the rounds.

patron n a regular client or customer; a person who sponsors and supports the arts, etc.

patronage n the support given or custom brought by a patron; clientele; business; trade.

patronise vt to treat with condescension; to be a regular customer of.

patter[1] vi to run with light steps. • n the sound of tapping or quick steps.

patter[2] n glib speech; chatter; lingo.

pattern n a decorative arrangement; a model to be copied. • vt to make or do in imitation of a pattern.

paunch n the belly, esp a potbelly.

pauper n a very poor person.

pause n a temporary stop, esp in speech, action or music. • vi to cease in action temporarily.

pave vt (a road, etc) to cover with concrete to provide a hard level surface.—**paving** n.

pavement n a paved path adjacent to a road for pedestrians.

pavilion n a building at a sports ground.

paw n a foot of a mammal with claws; (sl) a hand. • vti to maul; to handle clumsily.

pawn[1] n the piece of lowest value in chess; a person used to advance another's purpose.

pawn[2] vt to deposit an article as security for a loan. • n a thing pawned.

pawnbroker n a person licensed to lend money at interest on personal property left with him as security.

pay vti to give (money) to in payment for a debt, goods or services; to give in compensation; (homage, attention) to give. • n salary, wages.

payee n one to whom money is paid.

payment n the act of paying; amount paid.

payroll n a list of employees and their wages.

pea n the edible, round, green seed of a climbing leguminous annual plant.

peace n tranquillity, freedom from war.

peaceful adj having peace; tranquil; quiet.

peach n a round, sweet, juicy, downy-skinned stone-fruit; its yellowish pink colour.

peacock n a male bird with a large brilliantly coloured fan-like tail (nf **peahen**)

peak n the summit of a mountain; the highest point; maximum value; the eyeshade of a cap. • vti to (cause to) reach the height of power, popularity.

peal n a reverberating sound as of thunder, laughter, bells, etc. • vti to sound in peals.

peanut n a plant with underground pods containing edible seeds; the pod or any of its seeds; (pl: sl) a trifling sum.

peanut butter n a food paste made by grinding roasted peanuts.

pear n a juicy fruit of tapering oval shape.

pearl n the lustrous white round gem produced by oysters; mother-of-pearl; one that is choice and precious.

peasant n an agricultural labourer.

peat n decayed vegetable matter from bogs, which is dried and cut into blocks for fuel.

pebble n a small rounded stone.

peck vt to strike with the beak or a pointed object; to pick at one's food; (inf) to kiss lightly.

peckish adj (sl) hungry.

peculiar adj belonging exclusively (to); strange.

peculiarity n an idiosyncrasy; a characteristic.

pedal n a lever operated by the foot. • vt (pt **pedalled**) to operate, propel by pressing pedals with the foot.

pedant n a person who attaches too much importance to insignificant details.—**pedantic** adj.

peddle vt to go from place to place selling small goods; (drugs) to sell.—**peddler** n.

pedestal n the base that supports a column, statue, etc.

pedestrian adj on foot; dull, commonplace. • n a person who walks.

pedigree n a line of descent of an animal; a recorded purity of breed of an individual.

pedlar n a peddler.

peek vi to look quickly or furtively.—also n.

peel vt to remove skin or rind from. • vi to flake off, as skin or paint. • n rind, esp that of fruit.

peep vi to look hastily or furtively; to look through a slit or narrow opening. • n a furtive or hurried glance, a glimpse.

peer¹ *vi* to look closely; to look with difficulty.

peer² *n* an equal in rank, ability, etc; a nobleman.—**peeress** *nf*.

peerage *n* the rank or title of a peer; peers collectively; a book with a list of peers.

peeved *adj* annoyed, resentful.

peevish *adj* fretful, irritable.

peg *n* a tapered piece (of wood) for securing or hanging things on, for marking position, or for adjusting the strings of an instrument. • *vti* (*a price*) to keep steady.

pejorative *adj* disparaging, derogatory.

Pekingese, Pekinese *n* a breed of small dog with long, silky hair, short legs, and a pug nose.

pelican *n* a large fish-eating waterbird with an expandable pouched bill.

pellet *n* a piece of shot.

pelmet *n* a canopy for a window frame.

pelt¹ *vt* to throw missiles, or words, at. • *vi* (*rain*) to fall heavily.

pelt² *n* a usu undressed skin of an animal with its hair, wool, or fur.

pelvis *n* the bony cavity that joins the lower limbs to the body; the bones forming this.

pen¹ *n* an implement used with ink for writing or drawing. • *vt* to write.

pen² *n* a small enclosure for cattle, poultry, etc. • *vt* to enclose in a pen, shut up.

penal *adj* relating to punishment; punitive.

penalise *vt* to impose a penalty.

penalty *n* a punishment attached to an offence; a disadvantage imposed for breaking a rule, as in football; a fine.

penance *n* voluntary suffering to atone for a sin.

pencil *n* a pointed rod-shaped instrument with a core of graphite or crayon for writing, drawing, etc. • *vt* to write, draw or colour with a pencil; (*with* **in**) to commit tentatively.

pendant *n* a hanging ornament.

pending *adj* undecided. • *prep* awaiting.

pendulum *n* a weight suspended from a fixed point so as to swing freely; such a device regulating the movement of a clock.

penetrate *vti* to thrust, force a way into or through something; to pierce; to permeate.

penetrating *adj* acute, discerning; (*voice*) easily heard through other sounds.

penetration *n* the capability, act, or action of penetrating; acute insight.

pen friend *n* a friend made and kept through exchanging letters.

penguin *n* a flightless, marine bird with black and white plumage, usu found in the Antarctic.

penicillin *n* an antibiotic produced synthetically from moulds.

peninsula *n* a piece of land almost surrounded by sea.—**peninsular** *adj*.

penis *n* the male copulative organ in mammals.

penitent *adj* feeling regret for sin. • *n* a person who atones for sin.—**penitence** *n*.

penitentiary *n* a state or federal prison in the USA.

penknife *n* a small knife, usu with one folding blade, that fits into the pocket.

penniless *adj* having no money; poor.

penny *n* a bronze coin of the UK worth one hundredth of a pound.

pension *n* a periodic payment to a person beyond retirement age or widowed or disabled. • *vt* (*with* **off**) to dismiss or retire from service with a pension.

pensioner *n* a person who receives a pension; a senior citizen.

pensive *adj* thoughtful, musing; wistful.

pentagon *n* (*geom*) a polygon with five sides; (*with cap*) the US military leadership.

penthouse *n* an apartment on the flat roof or in the top floor of a building.

pent-up *adj* (*emotion*) repressed, confined.

penultimate *adj* last but one.

people *n* persons considered indefinitely; human beings; (*pl*) all the persons of a racial or ethnic group. • *vt* to populate with people.

pep *n* (*inf*) energy, vigour.

pepper *n* a sharp, hot condiment made from the fruit of various plants; the fruit of the pepper plant, which can be red, yellow, or green, sweet or hot, and is eaten as a vegetable. • *vt* to hit with small shot.

peppermint *n* a pungent and aromatic mint; a sweet flavoured with peppermint.

pep talk *n* (*inf*) a vigorous talk made with the intention of arousing enthusiasm.

per *prep* for or in each; (*inf*) according to.

per annum *adv* yearly; each year.

perceive *vt* to become aware of, apprehend.

per cent *adv* in, for each hundred.

percentage *n* rate per hundred parts.

perceptible *adj* able to be perceived.

perception *n* the act or faculty of perceiving.

perceptive *adj* able to perceive; observant.

perch¹ *n* a chiefly freshwater edible fish.

perch² *n* a pole on which birds roost or alight. • *vti* to alight on a perch; to balance (oneself) on.

percolator *n* a coffee pot in which boiling water is forced through coffee grounds.

percussion *n* musical instruments played by striking with sticks or hammers, e.g. cymbals.

peremptory *adj* urgent; absolute; dogmatic.

perennial *adj* perpetual; lasting throughout the year.

perfect *adj* faultless; exact; excellent; complete. • *n* (*gram*) a verb form expressing completed action or designating a present state that is the result of an action in the past. • *vt* to improve; to finish; to make fully accomplished in anything.—**perfectly** *adv*.

perfection n the act of perfecting; the quality or condition of being perfect; great excellence; faultlessness.

perfectionist n one who demands the highest standard.

perforate vt to make a hole or row of holes.

perforation n the act of perforating; a row of holes to facilitate tearing.

perform vti to carry out, do; to act before an audience.

performance n the act of performing; a dramatic production.

performer n a person who performs, esp one who entertains an audience.

perfume n a pleasing odour; a mixture containing fragrant essential oils and a fixative. • vt to scent; to put perfume on.

perfunctory adj superficial, hasty.

perhaps adv possibly, maybe.

peril n danger, jeopardy; risk, hazard.

perilous adj dangerous.

perimeter n a boundary around an area..

period n a portion of time; menstruation; an interval of time as in an academic day; an age or era in history, epoch; (gram) a full stop (.).

periodic adj recurring at regular intervals.

periodical adj periodic. • n a magazine, etc, issued at regular intervals.

peripheral adj incidental, superficial.

periphery n the outer surface of an area.

periscope n a device with mirrors that enables the viewer to see objects above or around an obstacle or above water, as from a submarine.

perish vi to be destroyed or ruined; to die.

perishable adj (food) liable to spoil or decay. • n something perishable, esp food.

perjure vt to commit perjury, swear falsely.

perjury n (law) the crime of giving false witness under oath, swearing to what is untrue.

perk n (inf) a privilege incidental to regular wages.

perk up vti to become lively or cheerful.—**perky** adj.

perm vt (inf) (hair) to give a permanent wave.—also n.

permanence n the condition of being permanent.

permanent adj lasting, or intended to last, indefinitely.—**permanently** adv.

permeate vti to fill every part of, saturate; to pervade.—**permeable** adj.

permissible adj allowable.

permission n authorisation; consent.

permissive adj allowing permission; lenient; sexually indulgent.—**permissiveness** n.

permit vti to allow to be done. • n a licence.

permutation n any of the total number of groupings within a group.

pernicious adj destructive; very harmful.

perpendicular adj upright, vertical; (geom) at right angles (to).—also n.

perpetrate vt (something criminal, etc) to do.

perpetual adj continuous; everlasting.—**perpetually** adv.

perpetuity n endless duration, eternity.

perplex vt to puzzle, bewilder, confuse; to complicate.—**perplexity** n.

persecute vt to harass, oppress, esp for reasons of race, religion, etc.—**persecution** n.

persevere vi to persist, maintain effort, steadfastly, esp in face of difficulties.

persist vi to continue in spite of obstacles or opposition; to last.—**persistence** n.

persistent adj persevering; stubborn.

person n a human being, individual; the body (including clothing) of a human being; (gram) one of the three classes of personal pronouns and verb forms, referring to the person(s) speaking, spoken to or spoken of.

personable adj pleasing in personality and appearance.

personal adj concerning a person's private affairs, or his/her character, habits, body, etc; done in person; (gram) denoting person.

personality n one's individual characteristics; a celebrity.

personally adv in person; in one's own opinion.

personify vt to think of, represent, as a person; to typify.—**personification** n.

personnel n the employees of an organisation.

perspective n the art of drawing so as to give an impression of relative distance or solidity; a picture so drawn; relation, proportion between parts.

perspire vi to sweat.—**perspiration** n.

persuade vt to convince.

persuasion n the act of persuading; a conviction or opinion.

persuasive adj influencing the mind.

pert adj impudent, cheeky.

pertinent adj relevant; to the point.

perturb vt to trouble; to agitate.

pervade vt to permeate or spread through; to be rife among.—**pervasive** adj.

perverse adj persisting in error; contrary.

perversion n an abnormal way of obtaining sexual gratification, e.g. sadism.

pervert vt to corrupt; to misuse; to distort. • n a person who is sexually perverted.

pessimism n a tendency to see in the world what is bad rather than good; a negative outlook that always expects the worst.

pest n a plant or animal detrimental to man; a person who pesters or annoys.

pester vt to annoy or irritate persistently.

pesticide n any chemical for killing pests.

pestle n a usu club-shaped tool for pounding or grinding substances in a mortar.

pet n a domesticated animal kept as a companion. • adj kept as a pet; favourite. • vti to caress; (inf) to kiss, embrace, etc, in making love.

petal n any of the leaf-like parts of a flower's corolla.—**petalled** adj.

peter out vi to dwindle to nothing.

petite adj (woman) small and trim in figure.

petition n a written demand for action by a government, etc, signed by a number of people.

petrol n a liquid fuel or solvent distilled from petroleum.

petroleum n a crude oil consisting of hydrocarbons occurring naturally in certain rock strata and distilled to yield petrol, paraffin, etc.

petticoat n an underskirt; a slip.

petty adj trivial; small-minded; minor.

petty officer n a non-commissioned officer in the navy.

petulant adj showing impatience or irritation.

pew n a wooden, bench-like seat in a church.

pewter n an alloy of tin and lead with a silvery-grey colour.

phantom n a spectre or apparition.

pharmacy n the preparation and dispensing of drugs and medicines; a pharmacist's shop.—**pharmacist** n.

phase n an amount of the moon's or a planet's surface illuminated at a given time; a characteristic period in a regularly recurring sequence of events or stage in a development. • vt (with out) (making, using, etc) to stop gradually.

pheasant n a richly coloured game bird.

phenomenon n a fact or event that can be scientifically described; a remarkable thing or person.

phial n a small glass bottle; a vial.

philanthropy n love of mankind, esp as demonstrated by benevolent or charitable actions.

philately n stamp collecting.—**philatelist** n.

philosopher n a person who studies philosophy.

philosophical adj of philosophy; resigned.

philosophy n the study of the principles underlying conduct, thought, and the nature of the universe.

phlegm n a thick mucus discharged from the throat, as during a cold.

phlegmatic adj unemotional, composed.

phobia n an irrational, excessive, and persistent fear of some thing or situation.

phone n, vti (inf) (to) telephone.

phonetics n (used as sing) the science concerned with pronunciation and the representation of speech sounds.

phony, phoney adj (inf) not genuine. • n a fake.

phosphorus n a metalloid element.

photo see **photograph**.

photocopy n a photographic reproduction of written or printed work. • vt to copy in this way.—**photocopier** n.

photogenic adj likely to look attractive in photographs.

photograph n an image produced by photography.—also **photo**.

photography n the art or process of recording images permanently and visibly by the chemical action of light on sensitive material, producing prints, slides or film.—**photographer** n.

phrase n a group of words that does not contain a finite verb but which expresses a single idea by itself; (mus) a short, distinct musical passage.

phrase book n a book containing idiomatic expressions of a foreign language and their translations.

physical adj relating to the world of matter and energy, the human body, or natural science. • n a general medical examination.—**physically** adv.

physician n a doctor of medicine.

physics n the branch of science concerned with matter and energy and their interactions in the fields of mechanics, acoustics, optics, heat, electricity, magnetism, radiation, atomic structure and nuclear phenomena.—**physicist** n.

physiology n the science of the functioning and processes of living organisms.

physiotherapy n the treatment of disorders by physical and mechanical means (as massage, exercise, water, heat, etc).—**physiotherapist** n.

physique n bodily structure and appearance.

pianist n a person who plays the piano.

piano n a large stringed keyboard instrument in which each key operates a felt-covered hammer that strikes a corresponding steel wire or wires.

pick n a heavy tool with a shaft and pointed crossbar for breaking ground; a tool for picking, such as a toothpick or icepick; best (of). • vti to pluck at; to nibble (at); to choose; (fruit, etc) to gather; (lock) to force open; (with up) to lift; to recover; (inf) to make the acquaintance of casually; to learn gradually; to give a lift to.

pickaxe n a pick.

picket n a person posted by strikers outside a place of work to persuade others not to enter. • vt to serve as a picket (at a factory, etc).

pickle n vegetables preserved in vinegar. • vt to preserve in vinegar.

pickpocket n a person who steals from pockets.

pick-up n the act of picking up; a person picked up; the power to accelerate rapidly.

picnic n a usu informal meal taken on an excursion and eaten outdoors.

pictorial adj relating to pictures.

picture n drawing, painting, photography, or other visual representation; an impression or mental image; a cinema film. • vt to portray, describe in a picture; to visualise.

picturesque adj striking, vivid, usu pleasing.

pie n a baked dish of fruit, meat, etc, with an under or upper crust of pastry, or both.

piebald adj covered with patches of two colours. • n a piebald horse, etc.

piece n a distinct part; a literary, dramatic, artistic, or musical composition; a man in chess or draughts. • vt to fit together, join.

piecemeal adv gradually; bit by bit.

piecework n work paid for according to the quantity produced.

pier n a structure built out over water and supported by pillars, used as a landing place.

pierce vt to cut or make a hole through.

piercing adj penetrating; keen.

piety n the characteristic of being pious.

pig n a domesticated animal with a broad snout and fat body raised for food; a greedy person.

pigeon n a bird with a small head and a heavy body; (inf) an object of concern.

pigeonhole n a small compartment for filing papers, etc; a category usu failing to reflect actual complexities. • vt to file, classify.

piggy bank n a container for coins shaped like a pig.

pigheaded adj stupidly stubborn.

piglet n a young pig.

pigment n paint; a naturally occurring substance used for colouring.—**pigmentation** n.

pigmy see pygmy.

pigsty n a pen for pigs; a dirty hovel.

pigtail n a tight braid of hair.

pike n a long-snouted game fish.

pilchard n a fish of the herring family.

pile[1] n a heap or mound; a large amount. • vt (with up, on) to heap or stack. • vi to become heaped up.

pile[2] n a vertical beam driven into the ground as a foundation for a building, etc.

pile[3] n the nap of a fabric or carpet.

pile[4] n a haemorrhoid.

pile-up n (inf) a collision of several vehicles.

pilgrim n a person who makes a pilgrimage.

pilgrimage n a journey to a holy place.

pill n medicine in round balls or tablet form.

pillage n looting, plunder. • vti to plunder.

pillar n a slender, vertical structure used as a support or ornament; a column.

pillar box n a red box for receiving letters for mailing, often columnar.

pillion n a seat behind the driver for a passenger on a motorcycle, etc.

pillory vt to expose to public scorn and ridicule.

pillow n a cushion that supports the head during sleep.

pillowcase, pillowslip n a removable cover for a pillow.

pilot n a person who operates an aircraft; one who directs ships in and out of harbour; a television show produced as a sample of a proposed series.—also vt.

pilot light n a burning gas flame used to light a larger jet; an electric indicator light.

pimp n a prostitute's agent.

pimple n a small, raised swelling of the skin.

pin n a piece of metal or wood used to fasten things together; a small piece of pointed wire with a head. • vt to fasten with a pin; (with down) to get (someone) to commit himself or herself as to plans, etc.

pinafore n a sleeveless garment worn over a dress, blouse, etc.

pincers npl a tool with two handles and jaws used for gripping and drawing out nails, etc; a grasping claw, as of a crab.

pinch vti to squeeze or compress painfully; to press between the fingers; to nip; (sl) to steal. • n a squeeze or nip.

pine[1] n an evergreen coniferous tree with cones.

pine[2] vi (with for) to yearn.

pineapple n a tropical plant; its juicy, fleshy, yellow fruit.

ping n a high-pitched ringing sound.

ping-pong n a name for table tennis.

pink[1] n a garden plant with a fragrant flower; a pale red colour. • adj pink-coloured.

pink[2] vt to stab, pierce.

pinnacle n a rocky peak of a mountain; the highest point, climax.

pinpoint vt to locate or identify exactly.

pinstripe n a narrow stripe in suit fabrics, etc.

pint n a liquid measure equal to half a quart.

pin-up n (sl) a photograph of a naked or partially naked person; a person who has been so photographed.

pioneer n a person who initiates or explores new areas of enterprise, research, etc.—also vti.

pious adj religious; sanctimonious.

pip n the seed in a fleshy fruit, e.g. apple.

pipe n a tube of wood, metal, etc, for making musical sounds; (pl) the bagpipes; a stem with a bowl for smoking tobacco; a long tube or hollow body for conveying water, gas, etc. • vt to play on a pipe; (gas, water, etc) to convey by pipe.

pipeline n a pipe (often underground) used to convey oil, gas, etc; a direct channel for information.

piper n a person who plays a pipe, esp bagpipes.

piping n a length of pipe, pipes collectively; a tube-like fold of material used to trim seams; the art of playing a pipe or bagpipes.

piping hot adj very hot.

pique n resentment, ill-feeling.

piracy n robbery at sea; infringement of copyright; unauthorised use of patented work.

pirate n a person who commits robbery at sea; one who infringes copyright. • vti to publish or reproduce in violation of a copyright.

pirouette n a spin on the toes in ballet.—also vi.

pistol n a small, short-barrelled handgun.

piston n a disc that slides to and fro in a close-fitting cylinder, as in engines, pumps.

pit n a deep hole in the earth; a (coal) mine; a space at the front of the stage for the orchestra; the scar left by smallpox, etc; the stone of a fruit; a place where racing cars refuel. • vti to set in competition; to mark or become marked with pits.

pitch[1] vti (tent, etc) to erect by driving pegs, stakes, etc, into the ground; to set the level of; to express in a style. • n intensity; a musical tone; place where a street trader or performer works; a sports field; sales talk.

pitch[2] n the black, sticky substance from distillation of tar, etc.

pitch-black adj black, or extremely dark.

pitch-dark adj completely dark.

pitcher n a large water jug.

pitchfork n a long-handled fork for tossing hay.

piteous adj arousing pity; heart-rending.

pitfall n concealed danger.

pith n the soft tissue inside the rind of citrus fruits; the gist, essence.

pithy adj concise and full of meaning.

pitiable adj deserving pity, lamentable.

pitiful adj causing pity, touching; contemptible.

pitiless adj without pity, ruthless.

pittance n a very small allowance of money.

pity n sympathy with the distress of others; a regrettable fact. • vt to feel pity for.

pivot n a pin on which a part turns, fulcrum; a key person upon whom progress depends. • vi to run on, or as if on, a pivot.—**pivotal** adj.

pixie n a fairy or elf.

placard n a poster or notice for public display.

placate vt to appease.—**placatory** adj.

place n a locality, spot; a town or village; a building, residence; a short street, a square; space, room; a particular point, part, position, etc; a position or job; a seat; rank. • vt to put; to find a place or seat for; to identify; to rank.

place mat n a small mat serving as an individual table cover for a person at a meal.

placid adj calm, tranquil.

plagiarise vt to appropriate writings from another author.

plague n a highly contagious and deadly disease. • vt (inf) to annoy, harass.

plaice n any of various flatfishes, esp a flounder.

plaid n a long wide piece of woollen cloth used as a cloak in Highland dress.

plain adj level, flat; understandable; obvious; not elaborate; not coloured or patterned; ugly. • n a large tract of level country.

plain clothes n ordinary clothes, not uniform.

plainly adv clearly, intelligibly.

plaintiff n (law) a person who brings a civil action against another.

plait n intertwined strands of hair, straw, etc.

plan n a scheme or idea; a drawing to scale of a building. • vti to make a plan of; to intend.

plane[1] n a tall tree with large broad leaves.

plane[2] n a tool with a steel blade for smoothing level wooden surfaces.—also vi.

plane[3] n any flat surface; an aeroplane.

planet n a celestial body that orbits the sun or other star.

plank n a long, broad, thick board.

plankton n the microscopic organisms that float on seas, lakes, etc.

plant n a living organism with cellulose cell walls, which synthesises its food from carbon dioxide, water and light; a soft-stemmed organism of this kind, as distinguished from a tree or shrub; the machinery, buildings, etc, of a factory, etc. • vt (seeds, cuttings) to put into the ground to grow; (sl) to conceal something in another's possession in order to implicate.

plantation n an estate where tea, rubber, cotton, etc, is grown, cultivated by local labour.

plaque n an ornamental tablet or disc attached to a surface; a film of mucus on the teeth.

plasma n the colourless liquid part of blood, milk or lymph.

plaster n an adhesive dressing for cuts; a mixture of sand, lime and water that sets hard and is used for covering walls and ceilings. • vt to cover as with plaster; to apply like a plaster.

plastered adj (sl) intoxicated.

plaster of Paris n gypsum and water made into a quick-setting paste.

plastic n any of various nonmetallic compounds, synthetically produced, that can be moulded, cast, squeezed, drawn or laminated into objects, films or filaments.

plastic surgery n surgery to repair deformed or destroyed parts of the body.

plate n a full-page illustration separate from text; a coating of metal on another metal; a flat shallow dish from which food is eaten; the part of a denture that fits the palate. • vt (a metal) to coat with a thin film of another metal.

plateau n a flat, elevated area of land.

plate glass n rolled, ground, and polished sheet glass.

platform n a raised floor for speakers, musicians, etc; a place or opportunity for public discussion; the raised area next to a railway track.

platinum n a valuable, silvery-white metal.

platitude n a commonplace remark.

platoon n a military unit consisting of two or more sections.

platter n an oval flat serving dish.

plausible adj apparently truthful or reasonable.

play vi to amuse oneself (with toys, games, etc); to act on the stage or perform a musical instrument. • vt to participate in a sport; to be somebody's opponent in a game; (*instrument*) to produce music on. • n fun, amusement; a literary work for performance by actors.—**playful** adj.

player n a person who plays a specified game or instrument; an actor.

playground n an area outdoors for children's recreation.

playgroup n an organised, regular meeting for the shared supervision of children at play.

playing card n one of a set of 52 cards used for playing games.

playing field n a place for playing sport.

playpen n a portable enclosure in which a young child may be left to play safely.

plaything n a thing or person treated as a toy.

playwright n a writer of plays.

plea n (*law*) an answer to a charge, made by the accused person; a request; an entreaty.

plead vti to beg, implore; to give as an excuse; to answer (guilty or not guilty) to a charge.

pleasant adj agreeable; pleasing.

pleasantry n a polite or amusing remark.

please vti to satisfy; to give pleasure to. • adv as a word to express politeness in a request.

pleasure n enjoyment, recreation.

pleat n a double fold of cloth, etc, pressed or stitched in place.—**also** vt.

plectrum n a thin piece of metal, etc, for plucking the strings of a guitar, etc.

pledge n a solemn promise; security for payment of a debt. • vt to give as security.

plentiful adj abundant, copious.

plenty n an abundance; more than enough.

pleurisy n inflammation of the membranes enclosing the lung.

pliable adj easily moulded; easily influenced.

pliers npl a tool with hinged arms and jaws for cutting, shaping wire.

plight[1] n a predicament.

plight[2] vt to pledge, vow solemnly.

plod vi to walk heavily and slowly, to work or study slowly and laboriously.

plough n a farm implement for turning up soil; any implement like this, as a snowplough. • vt to cut and turn up with a plough; to work at laboriously; (*with* **into**) to run into; (*with* **back**) to reinvest.

plover n a wading bird with a short tail.

ploy n a tactic to outwit an opponent.

pluck vt to strip off feathers; (*fruit, flowers, etc*) to pick; (*person*) to remove from one situation in life and transfer to another. • n heart, courage; dogged resolution.

plucky adj brave, spirited.

plug n a stopper used for filling a hole; a device for connecting an appliance to an electricity supply; (*inf*) a free advertisement usu incorporated in other matter. • vti to stop up with a plug; (*inf*) to seek to advertise by frequent repetition; (*inf*) to work doggedly.

plum n an oval smooth-skinned sweet stonefruit; a reddish-purple colour.

plumb n a lead weight attached to a line, used to determine how deep water is or whether a wall is vertical. • vt to test by a plumb line; to supply with or install as plumbing.

plumber n a person who installs and repairs water or gas pipes.

plumbing n the system of pipes used in water or gas supply or drainage; the plumber's craft.

plume n a large or ornamental bird's feather; something resembling a feather in structure or density. • vt (*feathers*) to preen.

plummet vi to drop sharply and abruptly.

plump adj rounded, chubby. • vti to make or become plump.—**plumpness** n.

plunder vt to steal goods by force, to loot.

plunge vti to immerse, dive suddenly.

plural adj more than one. • n (*gram*) the form referring to more than one.

plus prep added to; in addition to. • adj indicating addition; positive. • n the sign (+) indicating a value greater than zero; an advantage.

plush n a velvet-like fabric with a nap. • adj made of plush; (*inf*) luxurious.

ply[1] vti to work at diligently and energetically; to sell; to go to and fro, run regularly.

ply[2] n a layer or thickness, as of cloth, plywood, etc; any of the twisted strands in a yarn, etc.

plywood n a construction material consisting of several thin layers of wood glued together.

pneumatic adj operated by or filled with compressed air.

pneumonia n acute inflammation of the lungs.

poach[1] vt to cook (an egg without its shell, fish, etc) in or over boiling water.

poach[2] vt to catch game or fish illegally; to steal another's idea, employee, etc.

pocket n a small bag or pouch, usu in a garment, for carrying small articles; a deposit (as of gold, water, or gas). • adj small enough to put in a pocket. • vt to put in one's pocket, to steal.

pocketknife n a penknife.

pocket money n a child's allowance.

pod n a dry fruit or seed vessel, as of peas, beans, etc.

podgy adj short and fat, squat.

poem n an arrangement of words, esp in metre, often rhymed, in a style more imaginative than ordinary speech.

poet n the writer of a poem.

poetic(al) adj of poets or poetry; imaginative.

poet laureate n the official poet of a nation, appointed to write poems celebrating national events, etc.

poetry n poems collectively.

poignant adj piercing; incisive; deeply moving.

point n a dot or tiny mark used in writing or printing (e.g. a decimal point, a full stop); a location; a place in a cycle, course, or scale; a unit in scoring or judging; the sharp end of a knife or pin; a moment of time; one of thirty-two divisions of the compass; a fundamental reason or aim; a railway switch; a headland or cape. • vti to aim (at); to extend the finger (at or to).

point-blank adj aimed straight at a mark; direct.

pointed adj having a point; pertinent.

pointer n a rod or needle for pointing; an indicator; a breed of hunting dogs.

pointless adj without a point; aimless.

poise vt to put into readiness. • n self-possessed assurance of manner; bearing; carriage.

poison n a substance that through its chemical action usu destroys or injures an organism. • vt to administer poison in order to kill or injure; to put poison into; to influence wrongfully.—**poisoner** n.—**poisonous** adj.

poke vt to thrust (at), jab or prod; (hole, etc) to make by poking. • vi to jab (at); to pry or search (about or around). • n a jab; a prod or nudge.

poker¹ n a metal rod for poking or stirring fire.

poker² n a card game in which a player bets that the value of his hand is higher than that of the hands held by others.

poker face n an expressionless face, concealing a person's thoughts.—**poker-faced** adj.

poky adj small and uncomfortable.

polar adj of or near the North or South Pole; directly opposite.

polar bear n a large creamy-white bear that inhabits arctic regions.

polarise vt to break up into opposing factions.

pole¹ n a long slender piece of wood, metal, etc.

pole² n either end of an axis, esp of the earth; either of two opposed forces, parts, etc.

pole vault n a field event in which competitors jump over a high bar using a long flexible pole.

police n the governmental department for keeping order, detecting crime, law enforcement, etc; the members of such a department. • vt to control, protect, etc, with police or a similar force.

policeman n a member of a police force. —**policewoman** nf.

policy¹ n a written insurance contract.

policy² n a course of action selected from among alternatives; an overall plan embracing the general principles of an organisation.

polish vt to make smooth and shiny by rubbing (with a cloth and polish); (with off) (inf:) to finish completely. • n smoothness; elegance of manner; a finish or gloss; a substance used to polish.

polished adj accomplished; smoothly or professionally done or performed.

polite adj courteous; well-bred; refined.

political adj relating to politics.

politician n a person engaged in politics.

politics npl the science and art of government.

polka n a lively dance; the music for this.

polka dot n any of a pattern of small round dots on cloth.

poll n a counting, of persons, esp of voters; the number of votes recorded; an opinion survey. • vti to receive the votes (of).

pollen n the yellow dust, containing male spores, that is formed in the anthers of flowers.

pollination n the transfer of pollen from the anthers of a flower to the stigma, often by insects.

pollute vt to contaminate with harmful substances; to make corrupt.

pollution n the act of polluting; contamination by chemicals, noise, etc.

polo n a game played on horseback by two teams, using a wooden ball and long-handled mallets.

polo neck n a high collar turned over at the top; a sweater with such a collar.

polyester n any of a number of synthetic polymeric resins used for adhesives and textiles.

polygamy n the practice of being married to more than one person at a time.

polytechnic n a college that provides instruction in applied sciences and technical subjects.

polythene n a light, plastic material.

pomegranate n an edible fruit with many seeds.

pomp n stately ceremony; ostentation.

pompous adj stately; self-important.

pond n a body of water smaller than a lake.

ponder vti to consider carefully.

ponderous adj heavy; awkward; dull.

pontiff n the pope.

pontificate vi to speak pompously.

pontoon¹ n a boat or cylindrical float forming a support for a bridge.

pontoon² n a gambling game with cards in which players try to obtain points better than the banker's but not more than 21.

pony n a small horse.

pony tail n a style of arranging hair to resemble a pony's tail.

poodle n a dog with a curly coat.

pool¹ n a small pond.

pool² n a game of billiards played on a table with six pockets; a combination of resources, funds, supplies, people, etc, for some common purpose. • vti to contribute to a common fund.

poor adj having little money, needy; deserving pity; disappointing; inferior.

poorly adv badly. • adj not in good health.

pop[1] n a short, explosive sound; any carbonated, nonalcoholic beverage. • vti to make or cause a pop; to go or come quickly (in, out, up).

pop[2] adj in a popular modern style. • n pop music.

pop[3] n (inf) father.

popcorn n a kind of corn or maize, which when heated pops or puffs up.

pope n bishop of Rome, head of the RC Church.

poplar n a slender tree of the willow family.

poppy n an annual or perennial plant with showy flowers, one of which yields opium.

populace n the common people; the masses.

popular adj of the people; well liked.

popularise vt to make popular.

popularity n the condition of being popular.

population n all the inhabitants or the number of people in an area.

populous adj densely inhabited.

porcelain n hard, white, translucent ceramic ware.

porch n a covered entrance to a building; an open or enclosed room on the outside of a building.

porcupine n a large rodent covered with protective quills.

pore[1] n a tiny opening, as in the skin, plant leaves, stem, etc, for absorbing and discharging fluids.

pore[2] vti to study closely.

pork n the flesh of a pig used as food.

pornography n writings, pictures, films, etc, intended primarily to arouse sexual desire.

porous adj having pores.

porpoise n any of several small whales, esp a black blunt-nosed whale; any of several bottle-nosed dolphins.

porridge n a thick food, usu made by boiling oats or oatmeal in water or milk.

port[1] n a town with a harbour.

port[2] n a porthole; a circuit in a computer for inputting or outputting data.

port[3] n the left of an aircraft or ship looking forward.—also adj.

port[4] n a strong, sweet, fortified dark red wine.

portable adj capable of being carried easily.

portent n an omen, warning.

porter[1] n a doorman or gatekeeper.

porter[2] n a person who carries luggage, etc, for hire at a station, airport, etc.

porthole n an opening (as a window) with a cover or closure, esp in the side of a ship.

portico n a covered walkway with columns supporting the roof.

portion n a part, a share; a helping of food.

portly adj stout.

portrait n a painting, photograph, etc, of a person, esp of the face.

portray vt to make a portrait of; to depict in words; to play the part of in a play, film, etc.

pose n a position or attitude, esp one held for an artist or photographer; an attitude deliberately adopted for effect. • vti to propound; to assume an attitude for effect; to sit for a painting, photograph; to set oneself up (as).

posh adj (inf) elegant; fashionable.

position n place, situation; posture; a job; state of affairs; point of view. • vt to place or locate.

positive adj affirmative; definite; sure; expressed clearly or confidently; constructive; (elect) charged with positive electricity; (math) greater than zero, plus; (photog) having light, shade, colour as in the original. • n a photographic print made from a negative.

possess vt to own; to control the mind of.

possession n ownership; something possessed; (pl) property.

possessive adj (gram) denoting a case, form or construction expressing possession; having an excessive desire to possess or dominate.

possibility n a possible occurrence.

possible adj that may be or may happen; feasible, practicable.—**possibly** adv.

post[1] n a piece of wood, metal, etc, set upright to support a building, etc. • vt to put up.

post[2] n a position or job. • vt to station.

post[3] n the official conveyance of letters and parcels; letters, parcels, etc, so conveyed. • vt to send a letter or parcel; to keep informed.

postage n the charge for sending a letter, etc.

postcard n a card, usu decorative, for sending messages by post.

postdate vt to write a future date on a letter or cheque.

poster n a decorative printed sheet for advertising.

posterity n future generations.

postgraduate n a person pursuing study after obtaining a university degree.

posthumous adj (award, etc) given after one's death.

postman n a person who collects or delivers mail.

postmark n the post office mark cancelling the stamp on a letter by showing the date, place of posting.

postmaster n the manager of a post office.

postmortem n an examination of a corpse to determine the cause of death.

post office n the building where postage stamps are sold and other postal business conducted; (with caps) a government department handling the transmission of mail.

postpone vt to put off, delay to a future date.

postscript n a note added to a letter after completion.

postulate vt to assume to be true.

posture n a pose; a body position; an attitude of mind; an official stand or position. • vti to assume a pose.

posy n a small bunch of flowers.

pot[1] n a deep, round cooking vessel; an earthenware or plastic container for plants; (inf) all the money bet at a single time.

pot[2] n (sl) cannabis.

potato n a starchy, oval tuber eaten as a vegetable.

potency n power; strength.

potent adj powerful; intoxicating.

potential adj possible, but not yet actual. • n the unrealised ability to do something.

pothole n a hole worn in a road by traffic; (geol) a deep hole or cave in rock caused by the action of water.

potholing n an activity involving the exploration of deep underground caves.

potion n a mixture of liquids, such as poison.

pot shot n a random or easy shot.

potter[1] vi to busy oneself idly.

potter[2] n a person who makes pottery.

pottery n earthenware vessels; a workshop where such articles are made.

potty adj (inf) slightly crazy.

pouch n a small bag or sack; a sacklike structure, as that on the abdomen of a kangaroo for carrying young.

poultice n a hot moist dressing applied to a sore part of the body.

poultry n domesticated birds kept for meat or eggs.

pounce vi to swoop or spring suddenly (upon).

pound[1] n a unit of weight equal to 16 ounces; a unit of money in the UK and other countries.

pound[2] vt to beat into a powder or a pulp.

pound[3] n a municipal enclosure for stray animals; a depot for holding impounded personal property, e.g. cars, until claimed.

pour vti to cause to flow in a stream; to flow continuously; to rain heavily; to serve tea, etc.

pout vti to push out (the lips); to look sulky.

poverty n the condition of being poor.

powder n any substance in tiny, loose particles; a specific kind of powder, esp for medicinal or cosmetic use. • vti to reduce to powder.

powdery adj like powder.

power n ability to do something; political, social or financial control or force; physical force; a source of energy; (math) the result of continued multiplication of a quantity by itself a specified number of times. • vt to supply with power.

powerful adj mighty; strong; influential.

powerless adj without power; helpless.

power station n a building where electric power is generated.

powwow n an American Indian ceremony (as for victory in war); (inf) any conference.

pox n a virus disease marked by pustules.

practicable adj able to be practised; possible.

practical adj concerned with action, not theory; workable; suitable; virtual, in effect.

practical joke n a prank intended to embarrass or to cause discomfort.

practically adv in a practical manner; virtually.

practice n action; habit, custom; repetition and exercise to gain skill; the exercise of a profession. • vt to practise.

practise vti to repeat an exercise to acquire skill; to put into practice; (profession) to work at.

practitioner n a person who practises a profession.

pragmatic adj practical; testing the validity of all concepts by their practical results.

prairie n a large area of level or rolling land predominantly in grass; a dry treeless plateau.

praise vt to express approval of, to commend; to glorify, to worship. • n commendation.

pram n a four-wheeled carriage for a baby.

prance vi to walk or ride in a showy manner.

prank n a mischievous trick or joke.

prattle vti to talk in a childish manner.

prawn n an edible marine crustacean.

pray vti to offer prayers to God; to implore.

prayer n entreaty, praise or thanks to God.

preach vi to advocate in an earnest or moralising way.—**preacher** n.

preamble n an introductory part to a document, speech, or story, stating its purpose.

precarious adj dependent on chance; insecure.

precaution n a preventive measure.

precede vti to be, come or go before in time, place, order, rank, or importance.

precedence n priority.

precedent n a previous and parallel case serving as an example.

preceding adj coming or going before.

precept n a rule of moral conduct; a maxim.

precinct n an urban area where traffic is prohibited; (pl) environs.

precious adj of great cost or value; beloved; affected. • adv (sl) very.

precipice n a cliff or overhanging rock face.

precipitate vti to cause to happen too soon.

precipitation n rain, snow, etc.

precipitous adj of or like a precipice; steep.

precis, précis n a summary or abstract.

precise adj clearly defined, exact; accurate.

preclude vt to rule out in advance.

precocious adj prematurely ripe or developed.

preconceive vt to form an idea or opinion of before actual experience.

precondition n a requirement that must be met beforehand, a prerequisite.

precursor n a predecessor.

predator n a person who preys, plunders or devours; a carnivorous animal.

predatory adj living on prey.

predecessor n a former holder of a position or office; an ancestor.

predestine vt to destine beforehand.

predicament n a difficult situation.

predict vt to foretell; to state (what one believes will happen).—**predictable** adj.

prediction n the act of predicting; that which is predicted; a forecast or prophecy.

predominant adj ruling over, controlling.

predominantly adv mainly.

predominate vt to have influence or control over; to be greater in number, intensity, etc.

pre-eminent adj distinguished above others; outstanding.—**pre-eminence** n.

pre-empt vt to take action to check other action beforehand.—**pre-emptive** adj.

preen vti (birds) to clean and trim the feathers; to groom (oneself).

prefab n (inf) a prefabricated building.

preface n an introduction; a foreword.

prefect n a student monitor in a school.

prefer vt to like better

preferable adj superior; more desirable.

preference n that which is preferred.

preferential adj giving or receiving preference.

prefix vt to put at the beginning of or before. • n a syllable or group of syllables placed at the beginning of a word, affecting its meaning.

pregnant adj having a foetus in the womb; significant, meaningful.—**pregnancy** n.

prehistoric adj of the period before written records began.

prejudge vt to pass judgment on before a trial; to form a premature opinion.

prejudice n a judgment or opinion made without adequate knowledge; bias; intolerance or hatred of other races, etc. • vt to affect or injure through prejudice.—**prejudiced** adj.

preliminary adj preparatory; introductory. • n a preliminary step or measure.

prelude n an introductory act or event; (mus) a movement which acts as an introduction.

premarital adj taking place before marriage.

premature adj occurring before the expected or normal time; too early, hasty.—**prematurely** adv.

premier adj principal; first. • n the head of a government, a prime minister.

premiere n the first public performance of a play, film, etc. • vt to give a premiere of. • vi to have a first performance.

premise n a proposition on which reasoning is based; something assumed or taken for granted; (pl) a piece of land and its buildings.

premium n a reward, esp an inducement to buy; a periodical payment for insurance; excess over an original price; a high value or value in excess of expectation. • adj (goods) high quality.

premonition n a foreboding.

preoccupied adj absent-minded, lost in thought.

preparation n the act of preparing; something prepared, as a medicine, cosmetic, etc.

preparatory adj serving to prepare.

preparatory school n a private school that prepares students for an advanced school or college.

prepare vt to make ready in advance; to fit out, equip; to cook. • vi to make oneself ready.

prepared adj subjected to a special process or treatment.

preponderate vi to be greater in number, amount, influence, etc; to predominate, prevail.—**preponderance** n.

preposition n a word used before a noun or pronoun to show its relation to another part of the sentence.

preposterous adj ridiculous; absurd.

prerequisite n a condition, etc, that must be fulfilled prior to something else.

prerogative n a privilege or right accorded through office or hereditary rank.

prescribe vt (rules) to lay down; (medicine, treatment) to order, advise.

prescription n (med) a written instruction to a pharmacist for the preparation of a drug.

presence n being present; impressive bearing, personality, etc; something (as a spirit) felt or believed to be present.

presence of mind n readiness of resource in an emergency, etc.

present[1] adj being at the specified place; existing or happening now; (gram) denoting action or state now or action that is always true. • n the time being; now; the present tense.

present[2] n a gift.

present[3] vt to introduce someone, esp socially; (a play, etc) to bring before the public, exhibit; to make a gift or award; to show; to perform; (weapon) to point in a particular direction. • vi to come forward as a patient.

presentable adj of decent appearance.

presentation n act of presenting; a display.

presently adv in a short while, soon.

preservation n the act of preserving.

preservative n something that preserves or has the power of preserving, esp an additive.

preserve vt to keep safe from danger; to protect; (food) to can, pickle, or prepare for future use. • n (usu pl) fruit preserved by cooking in sugar;

something regarded as reserved for certain persons.

preside vi to take control or exercise authority.

president n the head of state of a republic; the highest officer of a company, club, etc.

press vt to act on with steady force or weight; to push against, squeeze, compress, etc; (clothes, etc) to iron; to force, compel; to entreat; to emphasise; (record) to make from a matrix. • vi to crowd closely; to go forward with determination. • n pressure, urgency, etc; a machine for crushing, stamping, etc; a machine for printing; the gathering and distribution of news and those who perform these functions; newspapers collectively; an upright closet for storing clothes.

press conference n a group interview given to members of the press by a celebrity.

pressing adj urgent. • n a number of records made at one time from a master.

pressure n the act of pressing; a compelling force; a moral force; urgency. • vt to pressurise.

pressure group n a group of people organised to alert public opinion, legislators, etc, to a particular area of interest.

pressurise vt to keep nearly normal atmospheric pressure inside an aeroplane, etc, as at high altitudes; to attempt to compel.

prestige n commanding position in people's minds.

prestigious adj imparting prestige.

presumably adv as may be presumed.

presume vt to take for granted, suppose. • vi to take liberties; (with on) to take advantage of.

presumption n a supposition; a thing presumed; a strong probability; effrontery.

presumptuous adj tending to presume; bold; forward.—**presumptuously** adv.

presuppose vt to assume beforehand.

pretence n a hypocritical show; a fraud, a sham.

pretend vti to claim, represent, or assert falsely; to make believe; to lay claim (to).

pretentious adj claiming great importance.

pretext n a pretended reason to conceal a true one; an excuse.

pretty adj attractive in a dainty, graceful way. • adv (inf) fairly, moderately.

prevail vi to predominate; to be customary.

prevailing adj generally accepted; predominant.

prevalent adj predominant; widely practised or experienced.—**prevalence** n.

prevent vt to keep from happening.

preventive, preventative adj serving to prevent, precautionary.

preview n an advance, restricted showing, as of a film; a showing of scenes from a film to advertise it. • vt to view or show in advance of public presentation.

previous adj coming before in time or order; prior, former.—**previously** adv.

prey n an animal killed for food by another; a victim. • vi (with on, upon) to seize and devour prey; (person) to victimise; to weigh heavily on the mind.

price n the amount, usu in money, paid for anything; the cost of obtaining some benefit. • vt to set the price of something; to estimate a price.

priceless adj invaluable; (inf) very amusing.

prick n a puncture or piercing made by a sharp point; the wound or sensation inflicted; a qualm (of conscience); (inf) penis. • vti to affect with remorse; to pierce slightly; to cause a sharp pain to; (the ears) to erect.

prickle n a thorn, bristle; a pricking sensation.

prickly adj tingling; irritable.

prickly heat n a skin eruption caused by inflammation of the sweat glands.

pride n feeling of self-worth or esteem; excessive self-esteem; a feeling of elation due to success; the cause of this; a herd (of lions).

priest n in various churches, a person authorised to perform sacred rites.

priestess n a priest who is a woman; a woman regarded as a leader (as of a movement).

priesthood n the office of priest; priests collectively.

prig n a smug, self-righteous person.

prim adj proper, precise in manner; demure.

primarily adv mainly.

primary adj first; earliest; original; elementary. • n in USA, a preliminary election at which candidates are chosen for the final election.

primary school n a school for children up to the age of 11 or 12.

primate n an archbishop or the highest ranking bishop in a province, etc; any of the highest order of mammals, including man.

prime¹ adj first in rank, importance, or quality; (math) not divisible, divisible only by itself and 1. • n the best time; the height of perfection.

prime² vt to prepare or make something ready.

prime minister n the head of the government in a parliamentary democracy.

primer n a detonating device; a first coat of paint or oil.

primeval adj of the first age of the world.

primitive adj of the earliest times; crude; simple; basic. • n a primitive person.

primrose n a plant with pale yellow flowers.

prince n the son of a sovereign; the head of a principality.

princess n a daughter of a sovereign; the wife of a prince.

principal adj first in rank or importance; chief. • n a person who organises; the head of a college or school; the leading player in a ballet, opera, etc; a capital sum lent or invested.

principality n the rank and territory of a prince.

principally adv mainly.

principle n a basic truth; a law or doctrine used as a basis for others; a moral code of conduct.

print vti to stamp (a mark, letter, etc) on a surface; to produce (on paper, etc) the impressions of inked type, etc; to produce (a book, etc); to write in letters resembling printed ones. • n a mark made on a surface by pressure; the impression of letters, designs, etc, made from inked type, a plate, or block; a photographic copy, esp from a negative.

printer n a person engaged in printing; a device that produces printout.

printing n the business of producing printed matter; a style of writing using capital letters.

printout n a printed record produced automatically (as by a computer).

prior adj previous; taking precedence (as in importance). • n the superior ranking below an abbot in a monastery.

priority n precedence; preference; something requiring specified attention.

priory n a religious house under a prior.

prise vt to force (open, up) with a lever, etc.

prism n (geom) a solid whose ends are similar, equal, and parallel plane figures and whose sides are parallelograms; a transparent body of this form usu with triangular ends used for dispersing or reflecting light.—**prismatic** adj.

prison n a building used to house convicted criminals for punishment and suspects remanded in custody while awaiting trial.

prisoner n a person held in prison.

pristine adj pure; in an original unspoiled condition.

privacy n being private; seclusion; secrecy.

private adj of or concerning a particular person or group; not open to or controlled by the public; secret. • npl the genitals; an enlisted man of the lowest rank in the army.—**privately** adv.

privet n a white-flowered evergreen shrub used for hedges.

privilege n a right or special benefit enjoyed by a person or a small group.

privileged adj having or enjoying privileges.

privy adj private; having access to confidential information.

prize n an award won in competition or a lottery; a reward given for merit. • vt to value highly.

prizefight n a professional boxing match.—**prizefighter** n.

pro[1] adv, prep in favour of. • n an argument for a proposal or motion.

pro[2] adj,n professional.

probability n that which is probable; likelihood.

probable adj likely; to be expected.

probation n testing of character or skill; release from prison under supervision by a probation officer; the period of being on probation.

probe n a flexible surgical instrument for exploring a wound; an investigation. • vt to examine closely; to investigate.

probity n honesty, integrity, uprightness.

problem n a question for solution; a person, thing or matter difficult to cope with; (math) a proposition stating something to be done.

problematic(al) adj presenting a problem.

procedure n an established mode of conducting business, esp in law or in a meeting; a prescribed course; a step taken as part of an established order of steps.

proceed vi to go on, esp after stopping.

proceeding npl steps, action, in a lawsuit; published records of a society, etc.

proceeds npl the total amount of money brought in.

process n a course or state of going on; a series of events; a method of operation. • vt (food, etc) to prepare by a special process; (film) to develop.

procession n a group of people in marching in order, as in a parade.

proclaim vt to announce publicly; to praise.

proclamation n an official notice.

procrastinate vti to delay.

procreate vt to engender offspring.—**procreation** n.

procure vt to obtain by effort; to get and make available for promiscuous sexual intercourse.

prod vt to poke or jab, as with a pointed stick; to rouse into activity. • n the action of prodding.

prodigal adj wasteful; extravagant.

prodigious adj enormous; amazing.

prodigy n a gifted child.

produce vt to bring about; to bring forward, show; to yield; to cause; to manufacture, make; to give birth to; (play, film) to put before the public. • n that which is produced.

producer n someone who produces, esp a farmer or manufacturer; a person who finances or supervises the putting on of a play or making of a film.

product n a thing produced by nature, industry or art; a result; (math) the number obtained by multiplying two or more numbers together.

production n the act of producing; a thing produced; a work presented on the stage or screen.

productive adj capable of producing; fertile.

productivity n the ratio of the output of a manufacturing business to the input of materials, labour, etc.

profane adj irreverent; blasphemous. • vt to desecrate; to debase by a wrong, unworthy or vulgar use.

profess vt to affirm publicly, declare; to claim.

profession n an act of professing; avowal, esp of religious belief; an occupation requiring specialised knowledge and often long and intensive academic preparation.

professional adj of or following a profession; conforming to the technical or ethical standards of a profession; earning a livelihood in an activity or field often engaged in by amateurs; having a specified occupation as a permanent career; engaged in by persons receiving financial return.—also n.—**professionally** adv.

professor n a faculty member of the highest academic rank at a university.

proficient adj skilled, competent.—**proficiency** n.

profile n a side view of the head as in a portrait, drawing, etc; a biographical sketch. • vt to produce (as by writing, drawing, etc) a profile of.

profit n gain; the excess of returns over expenditure; (pl) excess returns from a business. • vti to be of advantage (to), benefit.

profitable adj lucrative; beneficial; useful.

profiteer vi to make exorbitant profits.

profound adj at great depth; intellectually deep; mysterious.—**profoundly** adv.

profuse adj abundant; generous; extravagant.

profusion n an abundance.

progeny n offspring; descendants.

program n a sequence of instructions fed into a computer. • vti to feed a program into a computer.

programme n a printed list containing details of a ceremony, of the actors in a play, etc; a radio or television broadcast; a plan or schedule. • vt to prepare a plan or schedule.

progress n a movement forwards or onwards, advance; satisfactory growth or development. • vi to move forward, advance; to improve.

progression n advancement by degrees.

progressive adj advancing, improving; proceeding by degrees; continuously increasing; aiming at reforms. • n a person who believes in moderate political change, esp social improvement by government action.

prohibit vt to forbid by law; to prevent.

prohibition n the act of forbidding; a legal ban on the manufacture and sale of alcoholic drinks.

prohibitive adj forbidding; so high as to prevent purchase, use, etc, of something.

project n a plan, scheme; a task carried out by students, etc, involving research. • vt to throw forward; (light, shadow, etc) to produce an outline of on a distance surface; (one's voice) to make heard at a distance; (feeling, etc) to attribute to another; to estimate, plan, or figure for the future. • vi to jut out.

projectile n a missile. • adj throwing forward; capable of being thrown forward.

projection n the act of projecting or the condition of being projected; a thing projecting; a projected image; an estimate of future possibilities based on a current trend.

projector n an instrument that projects images from transparencies or film.

proletariat n the lowest social class of a community; the industrial working class.

proliferate vi to grow or reproduce rapidly.

prolific adj producing abundantly.

prologue n the introductory lines of a play, speech, etc; an introductory event.

prolong vt to extend in space or time.

prom n a promenade.

promenade n an esplanade.

prominence n a projection; fame.

prominent adj jutting, projecting; standing out, conspicuous; widely and favourably known.

promiscuous adj indiscriminate, esp in sexual liaisons.—**promiscuity** n.

promise n an undertaking to do or not to do something; an indication, as of a successful future. • vti to undertake; to give reason to expect.

promising adj likely to turn out well.

promontory n a peak of high land that juts out into a body of water.

promote vt to encourage; to advocate; to raise to a higher rank; (product) to encourage sales by advertising, publicity, or discounting.

promoter n a person who organises and finances a sporting event or pop concert.

promotion n an elevation in position or rank; the furtherance of the sale of merchandise through advertising, publicity, or discounting.

prompt adj without delay; immediate. • vt to urge; to inspire; (actor) to remind of forgotten words, etc (as in a play). • n something that reminds.—**promptly** adv.

prompter n a person who sits offstage and reminds actors of forgotten lines.

promptness n alacrity in action or decision.

prone adj face downwards; lying flat, prostrate; inclined or disposed (to).

prong n a spike of a fork.

pronoun n a word used to represent a noun (e.g. I, he, she, it).

pronounce vt to utter; to declare formally.

pronounced adj marked, noticeable.

pronouncement n a formal announcement.

pronunciation n articulation, the way a word is pronounced.

proof n evidence that establishes the truth; the fact, act, or process of validating; test; demonstration; a sample from type, etc, for correction; a trial print from a photographic negative; the relative strength of an alcoholic liquor. • adj resistant; impervious, impenetrable. • vt to make proof against (water).

prop¹ vt to support by placing something under or against. • n a rigid support.

prop² see property.

propaganda n the organised spread of ideas to promote a cause; the ideas so spread.

propel vt to drive or move forward.

propeller n a device having two or more blades in a revolving hub for propelling a ship or aircraft.

propensity n disposition, tendency.

proper adj own, individual, peculiar; appropriate, fit; correct, conventional; decent, respectable; (sl) thorough.

properly adv in the right way; (sl) thoroughly.

property n a quality or attribute; a distinctive feature or characteristic; one's possessions; real estate, land; a movable article used in a stage setting (—also prop).

prophecy n a message of divine will and purpose; prediction.

prophesy vti to predict with assurance or on the basis of mystic knowledge; to foretell.

prophet n a religious leader regarded as, or claiming to be, divinely inspired; one who predicts the future.—**prophetess** nf.

prophetic adj prophesying events.

proportion n the relationship between things in size, quantity, or degree; ratio; (pl) dimensions. • vt to put in proper relation with something else.

proportional adj of proportion; proportionate.

proportionate adj in due proportion.

proposal n a scheme, plan, or suggestion; an offer of marriage.

propose vt to present for consideration; to intend; (person) to nominate; to move as a resolution. • vi to make an offer (of marriage).

proposition n a proposal for consideration; a plan; a request for sexual intercourse;.

proprietor n an owner.—**proprietorial** adj.

propulsion n the act of propelling.

prosaic adj commonplace, dull.

prose n ordinary language without metre.

prosecute vt to bring legal action against.

prosecution n the act of prosecuting, esp by law; the prosecuting party in a legal case.

prosecutor n a person who prosecutes.

prospect n¹ (pl) measure of future success; future outlook. • vti to search (for).—**prospector** n.

prospective adj likely; expected.

prospectus n a printed statement of the features of a new work, enterprise, etc.

prosper vi to thrive; to flourish; to succeed.

prosperity n wealth.—**prosperous** adj.

prostitute n a person who has sexual intercourse for money; (fig) one who deliberately debases his or her talents (as for money). • vt to offer indiscriminately for sexual intercourse, esp for money; to devote to unworthy purposes.

prostrate adj lying face downwards; overcome; lying prone or supine. • vt to throw oneself down; to lie flat; to humble oneself.

protagonist n the main character in a drama, novel, etc; a supporter of a cause.

protect vt to defend from danger or harm; to guard; to foster or shield from infringement or restriction.—**protector** n.

protection n the act of protecting; the condition of being protected; something that protects; immunity from prosecution or attack obtained by the payment of money.

protective adj serving to protect, shelter.

protégé n a person guided and helped in his career by another person.—**protégée** nf.

protein n a complex organic compound containing nitrogen that is an essential constituent of food.

protest vi to object to. • vt to assert or affirm. • n public dissent; an objection; a complaint.—**protester** n.

Protestant n a member, adherent of one of the Christian churches deriving from the Reformation.—**Protestantism** n.

protocol n the ceremonial etiquette accepted as correct in official dealings, as between heads of state or diplomatic officials.

proton n an elementary particle in the nucleus of all atoms, carrying a unit positive charge of electricity.

prototype n an original model or type from which copies are made.

protracted adj extended; long-drawn-out.

protrude vti to jut out, project.

protuberance n a swelling, prominence.

proud adj having too high an opinion of oneself; arrogant, haughty; having proper self-respect; satisfied with one's achievements.

prove vti to try out, test, by experiment; to establish or demonstrate as true using accepted procedures; to show (oneself) to be worthy or capable; to turn out (to be), esp after trial or test; to rise.

proverb n a short traditional saying expressing a truth or moral instruction.

proverbial adj of or like a proverb.

provide vti to arrange for; to supply; to prepare; to afford (an opportunity); to make provision for (financially).—**provider** n.

provided, providing conj on condition (that).

providence n foresight, prudence; God's care.

province n an administrative district or division of a country; (pl) the parts of a country removed from the main cities.

provincial adj having the way, speech, etc, of a certain province; rustic; unsophisticated. • n an inhabitant of the provinces or country areas; a person lacking sophistication.

provision n a requirement; a stipulation, condition; (pl) supplies of food, stores.

provisional adj temporary; conditional.

proviso n a condition, stipulation.

provocation n the act of provoking or inciting.

provocative adj intentionally provoking, esp to anger or sexual desire.

provoke vt to anger, infuriate; to incite.

prow n the forward part of a ship, bow.

prowess n skill.

prowl vi to move stealthily.

prowler n one that moves stealthily, esp an opportunist thief.

proximity n nearness in place, time, etc.

proxy n the authority to vote or act for another; a person so authorised.

prudence n the quality of being prudent.

prudent adj cautious; sensible.

prune[1] n a dried plum.

prune[2] vti (plant) to remove dead or living parts from; to cut away what is unwanted.

pry vi to snoop into other people's affairs.

psalm n a sacred song or hymn.

pseudo adj false, pretended.

pseudonym n a false named adopted by an author.

psyche n the mind, esp as a functional entity governing the total organism and its interactions with the environment.

psychiatry n the branch of medicine dealing with disorders of the mind.—**psychiatric** adj.—**psychiatrist** n.

psychic adj of the mind; having sensitivity to, or contact with, forces that cannot be explained by natural laws. • n a person apparently sensitive to nonphysical forces; a medium.

psychoanalysis n a method of treating mental disorders by analysing emotional conflicts, repressions, etc.—**psychoanalyse** vt.—**psychoanalyst** n.

psychology n the science that studies the human mind and behaviour.—**psychological** adj.—**psychologist** n.

psychopath n a person suffering from a mental disorder that results in antisocial behaviour and lack of guilt.

pub n a public house, an inn.

puberty n the stage at which the reproductive organs become functional.

public adj of, for, or by the people generally; performed in front of people. • n the people in general.—**publicly** adv.

publication n the printing and distribution of books, magazines, etc; something published as a periodical, book, etc..

public house n a tavern or bar; an inn.

publicity n any information or action that brings a person or cause to public notice.

public relations n relations with the general public of a company, etc, as through publicity.

public school n in England, a private secondary school, usu boarding.

publish vt to announce formally; (book) to issue for sale to the public.

publisher n a person or company that prints and issues books, magazines, etc.

publishing n the business of the production and distribution of books, magazines, etc.

puce n, adj (a) purplish brown.

puck n a hard rubber disc used in ice hockey.

pucker vti to draw together in creases, to wrinkle.

pudding n a dessert.

puddle n a small pool of water, esp stagnant.

puerile adj juvenile; childish.

puff n a sudden short blast or gust; an exhalation of air or smoke; a pad for applying powder. • vti to breathe hard, pant; to put out of breath; to swell; to blow, smoke, etc, with puffs.

puffin n a sea bird that has a short neck and a brightly coloured laterally compressed bill.

puffy adj inflated, swollen; panting.

pugnacious adj fond of fighting, belligerent.

pull vt to tug at; to pluck; to move or draw towards oneself; to drag; (muscle) to strain; (inf: gun, etc) to draw out; (inf) to attract. • n a tug; (inf) influence; (inf) drawing power.

pulley n a wheel with a grooved rim for a cord, etc, used to raise weights by downward pull or change of direction of the pull.

pullover n a buttonless garment with or without sleeves pulled on over the head.

pulp n a soft, moist, sticky mass; the soft, juicy part of a fruit or soft pith of a plant stem; ground-up, moistened fibres of wood, rags, etc, used to make paper.

pulpit n a raised enclosed platform, esp in a church, from which a clergyman preaches.

pulsate vi to beat rhythmically.

pulse[1] n a rhythmic beat or throb, as of the heart; a place where this is felt; an underlying opinion or sentiment or an indication of it; a short radio signal.

pulse[2] n the edible seeds of several leguminous plants, such as beans, peas and lentils.

pulverise vti to reduce to a fine powder.

puma n a cougar or mountain lion.

pummel vt to strike repeatedly with the fists.

pump[1] n a device that forces a liquid or gas into, or draws it out of, something. • vti to move (fluids) with a pump; to remove water, etc, from; to drive air into with a pump; to draw out, move up and down, pour forth, etc, as a pump does; (inf) to obtain information through questioning.

pump[2] n a light low shoe or slipper.

pumpkin n a large, round, orange fruit of the gourd family widely cultivated as food.

pun *n* a play on words of the same sound but different meanings, usu humorous.

punch[1] *vt* to strike with the fist; to stamp, perforate with a tool. • *n* a blow with the fist; (*inf*) vigour; a machine or tool for punching.

punch[2] *n* a hot, sweet drink made with fruit juices, often mixed with wine or spirits.

punctual *adj* being on time; prompt.—**punctuality** *n*.—**punctually** *adv*.

punctuate *vt* to use certain standardised marks in (written matter) to clarify meaning; to interrupt.

punctuation *n* the act of punctuating; a system of punctuation.

puncture *n* a small hole made by a sharp object; the deflation of a tyre caused by a puncture. • *vt* to make useless or ineffective as if by puncture; to deflate.

pundit *n* a learned person; an expert.

pungent *adj* having an acrid smell or a sharp taste; caustic; bitter.

punish *vt* to subject a person to a penalty for a crime or misdemeanour.

punishment *n* a penalty for a crime or misdemeanour; rough treatment.

punt *n* a long flat-bottomed square-ended river boat usu propelled with a pole.

puny *adj* of inferior size, strength, or importance.

pup *n* a young dog, a puppy; a young fox, seal, etc.

pupil[1] *n* a child or young person taught under the supervision of a teacher or tutor.

pupil[2] *n* the round, dark opening in the centre of the iris of the eye through which light passes.

puppet *n* a doll moved by strings attached to its limbs or by a hand inserted in its body; a person controlled by another.

puppy *n* a young domestic dog less than a year old.

purchase *vt* to buy. • *n* an object bought; leverage for raising loads.—**purchaser** *n*.

pure *adj* clean; not contaminated; not mixed; chaste, innocent; mere; that and that only.

purge *vt* to cleanse, purify; (*nation, party, etc*) to rid of troublesome people. • *n* the removal of persons believed to be disloyal from an organisation, esp a political party.

purify *vti* to make pure; to cleanse.

purist *n* a stickler for correctness.

puritan *adj* a person who is extremely strict in religion or morals; (*with cap*) an extreme Protestant of Elizabethan or Stuart times.

purity *n* the state of being pure.

purl *vt* to knit a stitch by drawing its base loop from front to back of the fabric.—*also n*.

purple *n* a dark, bluish red. • *adj* purple-coloured; (*writing style*) over-elaborate.

purport *vt* to claim to be true. • *n* significance.

purpose *n* objective; intention; resolution, determination. • *vti* to intend, design.

purposeful *adj* determined, resolute.

purr *vi* (*cat*) to make a low, murmuring sound of pleasure.

purse *n* a small pouch for money; a sum of money for a present or a prize. • *vt* to pucker.

purser *n* an officer on a passenger ship in charge of accounts, tickets, etc; an airline official responsible for the welfare of passengers.

pursue *vt* to follow; to chase; to seek to attain; to engage in.

pursuit *n* the act of pursuing; a pastime.

pus *n* a yellowish fluid produced by infected sores.

push *vti* to exert pressure so as to move; to press against or forward; (*inf*) to approach an age; (*inf*) to sell drugs illegally • *n* a shove; an effort; (*inf*) energy and drive.

pushchair *n* a wheeled metal and canvas chair for a small child.

pushover *n* (*inf*) something easily done; (*inf*) a person easily taken advantage of.

pushy *adj* (*inf*) assertive; forceful.

puss, pussy *n* an informal name for a cat.

put *vti* to place, set; to bring into a specified state; to submit.

putrid *adj* rotten or decayed and foul-smelling.

putt *vti* (*golf*) to hit (a ball) with a putter. • *n* in golf, a stroke to make the ball roll into the hole.

putter *n* (*golf*) a straight-faced club used in putting.

putty *n* a soft, plastic mixture of powdered chalk and linseed oil used to fill small cracks, etc.

puzzle *vt* to bewilder; to perplex. • *n* a difficult problem; a toy or problem for testing skill.

puzzling *adj* perplexing, bewildering.

pygmy *n* an undersized person.—*also* **pigmy**.

pyjamas *npl* a loosely fitting sleeping suit of jacket and trousers.

pylon *n* a tower-like structure supporting electric power lines.

pyramid *n* (*geom*) a solid figure having a polygon as base, and whose sides are triangles sharing a common vertex; a huge structure of this shape, as a royal tomb of ancient Egypt.

python *n* a large, nonpoisonous snake that kills by constriction.

Q

quack¹ *n* the cry of a duck. • *vi* to make a sound like a duck.

quack² *n* an untrained person who practises medicine fraudulently.

quad *n* quadrangle; quadruplet.

quadrangle *n* a court enclosed by buildings.

quadrant *n* (*geom*) a quarter of the circumference of a circle; a curved street.

quadraphonic, quadrophonic *adj* using four channels to record, reproduce sound.

quadratic *adj* square • *n* a quadratic equation.

quadratic equation *n* an equation in which the highest power of the unknown is the square.

quadruped *n* a four-footed animal.

quadruple *adj* four times as much or as many. • *vti* to make or become four times as many.

quadruplet *n* one of four children born at birth.

quadrilateral *adj* having four sides. • *n* (*geom*) a plane figure of four sides.

quadrille *n* a square dance for four or more couples.

quadriplegia *n* paralysis of all four limbs.

quagmire *n* soft, wet ground; a difficult situation.

quail¹ *vi* to cower, to shrink back with fear.

quail² *n* a small American game bird.

quaint *adj* attractive in an odd style.

quake *vi* to tremble, esp with fear or cold.

Quaker *n* a member of the Society of Friends, a religious sect advocating peace and simplicity.

qualification *n* a quality that makes a person fit for a post, etc; modification; (*pl*) academic achievements.

qualify *vti* to restrict; to describe; to moderate; to modify, limit; to make or become capable or suitable; to fulfil conditions; to pass a final examination; (*gram*) to limit the meaning of.

qualitative *adj* of or depending on quality.

quality *n* a characteristic or attribute; degree of excellence; high standard. • *adj* of high quality.

qualm *n* a doubt; a misgiving.

quandary *n* a predicament; a dilemma.

quantify *vt* to determine the amount of.

quantitative *adj* capable of being measured.

quantity *n* an amount that can be measured, counted or weighed; a large amount; the property by which a thing can be measured.

quantum leap *n* an abrupt transition from one energy state to another; a sudden change.

quarantine *n* a period of isolation imposed to prevent the spread of disease.

quark *n* (*physics*) a hypothetical elementary particle.

quarrel *n* an argument; an angry dispute. • *vi* to argue violently; to find fault (with).

quarrelsome *adj* apt to quarrel.

quarry¹ *n* a place from which stone is excavated. • *vti* to excavate (from) a quarry.

quarry² *n* a hunted animal, prey.

quart *n* a liquid measure equal to a quarter of a gallon or two pints.

quarter *n* a fourth of something; one fourth of a year; one fourth of an hour; a particular district or section; (*pl*) lodgings; a particular source; an unspecified person or group; mercy. • *vti* to share or divide into four; to provide with lodgings. • *adj* constituting a quarter.

quarterfinal *n* one of four matches held before the semifinals in a tournament.

quarterly *adj* occurring, issued, or spaced at three-month intervals.

quartermaster *n* (*mil*) an officer in charge of stores; (*naut*) a petty officer in charge of steering, etc.

quartet *n* a group of four instrumentalists or voices.

quartz *n* a crystalline mineral, a form of silica, usu colourless and transparent.

quasar *n* a distant, starlike, celestial object that emits much light and powerful radio waves.

quash *vt* (*rebellion etc*) to put down.

quasi *adv* seemingly; as if.

quaver *vi* to tremble, vibrate; to speak or sing with a quivering voice. • *n* a trembling sound; (*mus*) a note having half the duration of a crotchet.

quay *n* a loading wharf for vessels.

queasy *adj* nauseous; easily upset.

queen *n* a female sovereign and head of state; the wife or widow of a king; a woman considered pre-eminent; the egg-laying female of bees, wasps, etc; a playing card with a picture of a queen; (*chess*) the most powerful piece; (*sl*) a male homosexual, esp one who ostentatiously takes a feminine role. • *vi* (*with* **it**) to act like a queen, esp to put on airs.

queen mother *n* a queen dowager who is the mother of a ruling sovereign.

queer *adj* strange, odd; (*sl*) homosexual. • *n* a (male) homosexual. • *vt* (*sl*) to spoil the success of.

quell *vt* to suppress; to allay.

quench *vt* (*thirst*) to satisfy; (*fire*) to put out.

querulous *adj* complaining, peevish.

query *n* a question; doubt. • *vti* to question; to doubt the accuracy of.

quest n a search, esp involving a journey.

question n an interrogative sentence; an inquiry; a problem; a doubtful or controversial point; a part of a test or examination. • vti to ask questions (of); to dispute.—**questioner** n.

questionable adj doubtful; not clearly true.

question mark n a punctuation mark (?) used at the end of a sentence to indicate a question.

questionnaire n a series of questions designed to collect statistical information.

queue n a line of people, vehicles, etc, awaiting a turn. • vi to wait in turn.

quibble n a minor objection or criticism. • vi to argue about trifling matters.

quiche n a savoury tart filled with onions and a cheese and egg custard.

quick adj rapid, speedy; eager to learn. • n the sensitive flesh below a fingernail or toenail; the inmost sensibilities.—**quickly** adv.

quicken vti to speed up or accelerate.

quicksand n loose wet sand easily yielding to pressure in which persons, animals, etc, may be swallowed up.

quickstep n a ballroom dance in quick time.

quick-witted adj mentally alert.

quid n (sl) a pound (sterling).

quid pro quo n something equivalent given in exchange for something else.

quiet adj silent, not noisy; gentle, not boisterous; unobtrusive, not showy; placid, calm. • n stillness, peace.—**quietly** adv.—**quietness** n.

quieten vti to make or become quiet.

quill n the hollow stem of a feather; anything made of this, as a pen; a spine of a porcupine.

quilt n a cover of two cloths sewn together with padding between.

quin n a quintuplet.

quinine n a bitter crystalline alkaloid used in medicine; one of its salts used esp as an antimalarial and a bitter tonic.

quintet n a group of five instrumentalists or voices.

quintuple adj five times as much or as many.

quintuplet n one of five offspring produced at one birth.

quip n a witty remark; a gibe. • vt to make a clever remark.

quirk n a peculiarity of character.

quit vti to leave; to stop or cease; to resign; to admit defeat.—**quitter** n.

quite adv completely; somewhat, fairly.

quits adj on equal terms by payment or revenge.

quiver[1] vi to shake; to tremble, shiver.

quiver[2] n a case for holding arrows.

quiz n a form of entertainment where players are asked questions of general knowledge. • vt to interrogate.

quizmaster n a person who puts the questions to a contestant in a quiz show.

quiz show n an entertainment programme on television or radio in which contestants answer questions to win prizes.

quizzical adj humorous and questioning.

quoit n a ring thrown in quoits; (pl) a game in which rings are thrown at or over a peg.

quorum n the minimum number that must be present at a meeting or assembly to make its proceedings valid.

quota n a proportional share.

quotation n the act of quoting; the words quoted; an estimated price.

quotation mark n a punctuation mark to indicate the beginning (' or ") and the end (' or ") of a quoted passage.

quote vt to cite; to repeat the words of a novel, play, poem, speech, etc, exactly. • n (inf) something quoted; a quotation mark.

quotient n (math) the result obtained when one number is divided by another.

R

rabbi n the religious and spiritual leader of a Jewish congregation.

rabbit n a small mammal of the hare family with long ears, a short tail and long hind legs.

rabble n a disorderly crowd, a mob.

rabid adj infected with rabies; fanatical.

rabies n an acute, infectious, viral disease transmitted by the bite of an infected animal.

raccoon n a small nocturnal carnivore of North America that lives in trees.

race[1] n any of the divisions of humankind distinguished esp by colour of skin.

race[2] n a contest of speed or out of control. • vi to run at top speed; to compete in a race. • vt to contest against.

racecourse, racetrack n a track over which races are run, esp an oval track for racing horses.

racehorse n a horse bred and trained for racing.

racial adj of or relating to any of the divisions of humankind distinguished by colour, etc.

racialism n discriminating behaviour towards people of another race.—also **racism**.—**racist** n.

rack n a framework for holding or displaying articles; an instrument for torture by stretching.

racket¹, racquet n a bat strung with nylon, for playing tennis, etc.

racket² n din; any fraudulent business.

racy adj lively, spirited; risqué.

radar n a system or device for detecting objects such as aircraft by using the reflection of radio waves.

radiance n dazzling beauty.

radiant adj shining; beaming with happiness.

radiate vt (light, heat, etc) to emit in rays; (happiness, love, etc) to give forth. • vi to spread out as if from a centre.

radiation n radiant particles emitted as energy; rays emitted in nuclear decay; (med) treatment using a radioactive substance.

radiator n an apparatus for heating a room; a cooling device for a vehicle engine.

radical adj fundamental; favouring basic change. • n a person who advocates fundamental political or social change.

radio n the transmission of sounds or signals by electromagnetic waves through space, without wires, to a receiving set; such a set; broadcasting by radio as an industry, etc.

radioactive adj giving off radiant energy in the form of particles or rays caused by the disintegration of atomic nuclei.—**radioactivity** n.

radiography n the production of X-ray photographs for use in medicine, industry, etc.

radiology n a branch of medicine concerned with the use of radiant energy (as X-rays and radium) in diagnosis and treatment.

radish n a pungent root eaten raw as a salad vegetable.

radium n a highly radioactive metallic element.

radius n (geom) a straight line joining the centre of a circle or sphere to its circumference; (anat) the thicker of the two bones of the forearm.

raffia n a kind of palm; fibre from its leaves used in basket-making, etc.

raffle n a lottery with prizes. • vt to offer as a prize in a raffle.

raft n a platform of logs, planks, etc, strapped together to float on water.

rafter n one of the inclined, parallel beams that support a roof.

rag n a torn or waste scrap of cloth; (inf) a sensationalist newspaper; (pl) tattered clothing.

ragbag n a miscellaneous collection, jumble.

rage n violent anger; fashion, craze.

ragged adj uneven; irregular; worn into rags.

raid n a sudden attack to assault or seize. • vt to make a raid on; to steal from.—**raider** n.

rail n a horizontal bar from one post to another, as in a fence, etc; one of a pair of parallel steel lines forming a track.

railing n a fence of rails and posts.

railroad vt to force unduly.

railway n a track of parallel steel rails along which carriages are drawn by locomotive engines; a complete system of such tracks.

rain n water that falls from the clouds in drops; (pl) the rainy season in the tropics. • vti (of rain) to fall; to fall like rain.

rainbow n the arc containing the colours of the spectrum formed in the sky by the sun's rays in falling rain or mist. • adj many-coloured.

raincoat n a waterproof coat.

rainfall n the amount of rain that falls on a given area in a specified time.

rainproof adj rain-resisting.

rainy adj full of rain; wet.

raise vt to elevate; to lift up; to increase in size, amount, degree, intensity, etc; to breed.

raisin n a sweet, dried grape.

rajah n an Indian or Malay prince or ruler.

rake n a tool with a row of teeth and a handle for gathering, scraping or smoothing. • vt to scrape, gather as with a rake; to sweep with gaze or gunshot; (with in: money, etc) to gather a great amount rapidly.

rakish adj jaunty, dashing.

rally vti to bring or come together; to recover strength, revive. • n a large assembly of people; (tennis) a lengthy exchange of shots; a competitive test of driving and navigational skills.

ram n a male sheep. • vt to force or drive.

ramble vi to wander or stroll about for pleasure; (plant) to straggle; to write or talk aimlessly. • n a leisurely walk in the countryside.—**rambler** n.

rambling adj spread out, straggling; disjointed.

ramification n a consequence.

ramp n a sloping runway joining different levels; a wheeled staircase for boarding a plane.

rampage n angry or violent behaviour.

rampant adj rife, prevalent.

rampart n an embankment surrounding a fortification; a protective wall.

ramshackle adj dilapidated.

ranch n a large farm for raising cattle, horses, or sheep.—also vi

rancid adj having an unpleasant smell and taste, as stale fats or oil.

rancour n bitter hate or spite.

random adj haphazard; left to chance.

randy adj (sl) lustful, sexually aroused.

range n a row; a series of mountains, etc; scope; a large open area for grazing livestock; a place for testing rockets in flight; a place for shooting or golf practice; a cooking stove. • vt to place in order or a row. • vi to vary (inside limits).

ranger n a forest or park warden.

rank¹ n a line of objects; a line of soldiers standing abreast; high standing or position; status; (pl) ordinary members of the armed forces. • vti to arrange in a line; (with **with**) to be counted among.

rank² adj utter, flagrant; offensive in odour or flavour.

rank and file n ordinary soldiers; ordinary members, as distinguished from their leaders.

rankle vi to cause continuous irritation.

ransack vt to plunder; to search thoroughly.

ransom n the release of a captured person or thing; the price paid for this.

rant vi to speak loudly or violently.

rap n a sharp blow; a knock; (sl) a song that is rapped. • vti to knock; (sl) to speak a song accompanied by an insistent electronic rhythm.

rape¹ n the act of forcing a woman to have sexual intercourse against her will. • vti to commit rape (upon).—**rapist** n.

rape² n a bright yellow plant of the mustard family grown for its leaves and oily seeds.

rapid adj at great speed; fast. • npl a part of a river where the current flows swiftly.

rapport n a sympathetic relationship.

rapture n intense delight.—**rapturous** adj.

rare¹ adj unusual; exceptionally good.

rare² adj not completely cooked, partly raw.

rarefy vt to make or become less dense; to thin out.—**rarefied** adj.

rarely adv almost never.

rarity n rareness; a rare person or thing.

rascal n a rogue; a mischievous person.

rash¹ adj reckless; impetuous.—**rashly** adv.

rash² n a skin eruption of spots, etc.

rasher n a thin slice of bacon or ham.

rasp vi to produce a grating sound.

raspberry n a shrub with red berry-like fruits; the fruit produced; (inf) a sound of derision.

rat n a long-tailed rodent similar to a mouse but larger; (sl) a sneaky, contemptible person.

ratchet n a device with a toothed wheel that moves in one direction only.

rate n the amount, degree, etc, of something in relation to units of something else; price, esp per unit; degree. • vt to rank; to regard or consider; (sl) to think highly of.

rather adv more willingly; preferably.

ratify vt to approve formally; to confirm.

rating n (radio, TV) the relative popularity of a programme according to sample polls.

ratio n the number of times one thing contains another; proportion.

ration n (pl) food supply. • vt (food, petrol) to restrict the supply of.

rational adj reasonable; sane.—**rationally** adv.

rationale n the reason for a course of action; an explanation of principles.

rationalise vti to justify one's reasons for an action; to cut down on personnel or equipment.

rat race n continual hectic competitive activity.

rattle vi to clatter. • vt to make a series of sharp, quick noises; to clatter; (inf) to disconcert, fluster. • n a rattling sound; a baby's toy that makes a rattling sound.

rattlesnake n a venomous American snake with a rattle in its tail.

raucous adj hoarse and harsh-sounding.

ravage vt to ruin, destroy. • n destruction; ruin; (pl) the effects of this.

rave vi to speak wildly or as if delirious; (inf) to enthuse.—**raving** adj.

raven n a large crow-like bird with glossy black feathers.

ravenous adj very hungry; greedy.

ravine n a deep, narrow gorge, a large gully.

ravioli n small cases of pasta filled with highly seasoned chopped meat or vegetables.

ravishing adj charming, captivating.

raw adj uncooked; unrefined; in a natural state.

raw material n something out of which a finished article is made.

ray¹ n a beam of light that comes from a bright source; any of several lines radiating from a centre; a beam of radiant energy.

ray² n any of various fishes with a flattened body and the eyes on the upper surface.

rayon n a textile fibre made from a cellulose solution; a fabric of such fibres.

raze vt to level to the ground.

razor n a sharp-edged instrument for shaving.

re prep concerning, with reference to.

reach vti to arrive at; to extend as far as; to extend in influence, etc. • n extent; scope.

react vi to act in response to a person or stimulus; (chem) to undergo a chemical reaction.

reaction n an action in response to a stimulus; exhaustion after excitement, etc; (chem) an action set up by one substance in another.

reactionary adj, n (a person) opposed to political or social change.

reactor n a nuclear reactor.

read vti to understand something written; to speak aloud (from a book); to study by reading.

reader n a person who reads; a person who evaluates manuscripts; a senior lecturer.

readership n all the readers of a certain publication, author, etc.

readily adv willingly, easily.

reading n the act of one who reads; any material to be read; the amount measured by a barometer, meter, etc.

ready adj prepared; willing; inclined. • vt to make ready.—**readiness** n.

ready-made adj made in standard sizes, not to measure.

real adj existing, actual, not imaginary; true, genuine, not artificial. • adv (sl) very; really.

real estate n property; land.

realise vt to become fully aware of; (ambition, etc) to make happen; to be sold for.

realism n practical outlook; (art, literature) the ability to represent things as they really are.

realistic adj matter-of-fact; lifelike; of or relating to realism.—**realistically** adv.

reality n the fact or condition of being real; an actual fact or thing; truth.

really adv in fact, in reality; positively, very.

realm n a domain, region; sphere.

reap vti to harvest; to gain (a benefit).

rear[1] n the back part or position, esp of an army; (sl) the rump. • adj of, at, or in the rear.

rear[2] vt to raise; (children) to bring up. • vi (horse) to stand on the hind legs.

reason n motive or justification (of an action or belief); a cause; moderation; sanity. • vti to think logically (about); to argue or infer.

reasonable adj rational; sensible; not expensive; moderate, fair.—**reasonably** adv.

reassure vt to hearten; to free from anxiety.—**reassurance** n.

rebate n a refund of part of an amount paid.

rebel n a person who refuses to conform with convention. • vi to rise up against authority.—**rebellion** n.—**rebellious** adj.

rebound vi to spring back after impact. • n an emotional reaction.

rebuff vt to snub, repulse.—also n.

rebuke vt to reprimand. • n a reprimand.

rebut vt to disprove or refute by argument, etc.—**rebuttal** n.

recall vt to call back; to bring back to mind, remember. • n remembrance; a summons to return.

recant vti to repudiate or retract a former opinion, declaration, or belief.

recap vti to recapitulate. • n (inf) recapitulation.

recapitulate vt to state again, to summarise.

recapture vt (a lost feeling, etc) to regain.

recce n (sl) reconnaissance.

recede vi to withdraw, retreat; to grow less.

receding adj disappearing from view; (hair) ceasing to grow at the temples.

receipt n the act of receiving; a written proof of this; (pl) amount received from business.

receive vt to acquire; to experience, be subjected to; to admit, allow; to greet on arrival; (stolen goods) to take in; to transfer electrical signals.

receiver n equipment that receives electronic signals, esp on a telephone; (law) a person appointed to manage or hold in trust property in bankruptcy or pending a lawsuit.

recent adj happening lately, fresh; not long established, modern.—**recently** adv.

receptacle n a container.

reception n the act of receiving; a social gathering; a response, reaction; the quality of the sound or image produced by a radio or TV set.

receptionist n a person employed to receive visitors to an office, hotel, hospital, etc.

receptive adj able or quick to take in ideas.

recess n a temporary halting of work; a hidden or inner place; an alcove or niche.

recipe n a list of ingredients and directions for preparing food; a method for achieving an end.

recipient n a person who receives.

reciprocal adj done by each to the other.

reciprocate vti to give in return.

recital n the act of reciting; a detailed account, narrative; (mus) a performance given by an individual musician.

recite vti to repeat aloud from memory.

reckless adj rash, careless, incautious.

reckon vti to count; to regard or consider; to think; (with **with**) to take into account.

reckoning n the settlement of an account.

reclaim vt to recover, win back from a wild state or vice.

recline vti to lie down on the back or side.

recluse n a person who lives in solitude.

recognise vt to know again, identify; to accept, admit.—**recognisable** adj.

recognition n identification; acknowledgment.

recoil vti to spring back, kick, as a gun; to shrink or flinch. • n the act of recoiling, a rebound.

recollect vti to recall; to call something to mind.

recollection n the act of recalling to mind; a memory, impression; something remembered.

recommend vt to counsel or advise; to commend or praise.—**recommendation** n.

recompense vt to reward or pay an equivalent; to compensate. • n repayment; compensation.

reconcile vt to re-establish friendly relations; to bring to agreement.—**reconciliation** n.

recondition vt to restore to working order.

reconnaissance n a survey of an area, esp for obtaining military information about an enemy.

reconnoitre vti to make a reconnaissance (of).

reconsider vt to consider afresh, review.

reconstruct vt to build again; to build up, as from remains, an image of the original; to supply missing parts by conjecture.

record vti to preserve evidence of; to write down; to chart; (sound or visual images) to register on a disc, tape, etc, for later reproduction. • n a written account; a register; a report of proceedings; the known facts about anything or anyone; an outstanding performance or achievement that surpasses others previously recorded; a grooved vinyl disc for playing on a record player; (comput) data in machine-readable form.

recorder n a tape recorder; a wind instrument of the flute family.

recording n what is recorded, as on a disc or tape; the record.

record player n an instrument for playing records through a loudspeaker.

recount vt to narrate the details of, to tell.

re-count vt to count again • n a second counting of votes at an election.

recoup vti to make good (financial losses).

recourse n that to which one turns when seeking help.

recover vti to regain after losing; to regain health or after losing emotional control.

re-cover vt to put a new cover on.

recovery n the act or process of recovering; the condition of having recovered; restoration.

re-create vt to create over again, esp mentally.

recreation n a sport, pastime or amusement.

recruit n a soldier newly enlisted; a member newly joined. • vti to enlist.—**recruitment** n.

rectangle n a four-sided geometric figure with all its angles right angles.—**rectangular** adj.

rectify vt to put right, correct; to amend.

rector n in some churches, a clergyman in charge of a parish; the head of certain schools, colleges, etc.

rectory n the house of a minister or priest.

recuperate vti to get well again; to recover.

recur vi to occur again.—**recurrent** adj.

red adj of the colour of blood; politically left-wing. • n the colour of blood; a communist.

red carpet n a strip of red carpet for dignitaries to walk on; a grand or impressive welcome.

red currant n a cultivated red clustered fruit.

redden vti to make or become red; to blush.

reddish adj tinged with red.

redeem vt to recover by payment; to regain; to deliver from sin; to restore to favour.

redeploy vt (troops, workers) to assign to new positions or activities.—**redeployment** n.

red-handed adj caught in the act of committing a crime.

redhead n a person having red hair.

red herring n something that diverts attention from the real issue.

red-hot adj glowing with heat; very new.

redirect vt to readdress.—**redirection** n.

red light n a warning signal, a cautionary sign.

redolent adj reminiscent (of).

redouble vti to make or become twice as much.

redress vt to put right, adjust. • n compensation.

red tape n rigid adherence to bureaucratic routine and regulations, causing delay.

reduce vt to diminish or make smaller in size, amount, extent, or number; to lower in price.

redundant adj surplus to requirements; deprived of one's job as being no longer necessary.

reed n a tall grass found in marshes; a thin piece of cane in the mouthpiece of a musical instrument.

reef n a ridge of rocks, sand, or coral in water.

reek n a strong smell. • vi to give off smoke.

reel[1] n a winding device; a spool or bobbin; thread wound on this; a length of film, about 300m (1,000ft). • vt to draw in by means of a reel; (with off) to tell, write, etc, with fluency.

reel[2] vi to stagger or sway about; to be dizzy.

reel[3] n a lively Scottish or Irish dance.

refectory n the dining hall of a monastery, college, etc.

refer vti (with to) to direct, have recourse (to); to relate to; to mention or allude to.

referee n an arbitrator; an umpire; a judge.

reference n a mention or allusion; a testimonial; a direction to a passage in a book.

reference book n a book for reference rather than general reading.

referendum n the submission of an issue directly to the vote of the electorate.

refill vt to fill again. • n a replacement pack for an empty permanent container.

refine vti to make free from impurities or coarseness.

refined adj polished, cultured; affected.

refinement n fineness of manners or taste; an improvement; a fine distinction.

refinery n a plant where raw materials, e.g. sugar, oil, are refined.

reflect vt (light, heat, etc) to throw back; to show an image of, as a mirror. • vi to mirror; to meditate; (with on) to discredit.

reflection n a reflecting back, turning aside; the action of changing direction when a ray strikes and is thrown back; a reflected image; meditation, thought; reproach.

reflector n a disc, instrument, strip or other surface that reflects light or heat.

reflex n an involuntary response to a stimulus. • adj (angle) of more than 180 degrees; (camera) with a full-size viewfinder using the main lens.

reflexive adj (pronoun, verb) referring back to the subject.

reform vti to improve; to make or become better by the removal of faults. • n improvement or transformation, esp of an institution; removal of social ills.—**reformed** adj.

reformer n a person who advocates reform.

refrain[1] vi to abstain (from).

refrain[2] n a chorus.

refresh vt to give new energy to; to make cool.

refresher n a training course to renew one's skill or knowledge.

refreshment n (pl) food and drink.

refrigerator n a chamber for keeping food, etc, cool.—also **fridge**.

refuel vti to supply with or take on fresh fuel.

refuge n a protection or shelter from danger; a retreat, sanctuary.

refugee n a person who flees to another country to escape political or religious persecution.

refund vti to repay; to reimburse. • n a refunding or the amount refunded.

refusal n the act or process of refusing.

refurbish vt to renovate or re-equip.

refuse[1] n rubbish, garbage, waste.

refuse[2] vt to decline, reject; to withhold.

refute vt to rebut; to disprove.

regain vt to get back, recover.

regal adj royal; relating to a king or queen.

regalia npl the badges of an order, office or membership.

regard vt to observe; to consider. • n a look; attention; reference; respect, esteem; (pl) good wishes, greetings.

regarding prep with reference to, about.

regardless adv (inf) in spite of everything.

regatta n a meeting for yacht or boat races.

regency n the status or authority of a regent.

regent n a person who rules or administers a country during the sovereign's minority, absence, or incapacity.

regime n a political or ruling system.

regiment n a military unit, smaller than a division, consisting usu of a number of battalions. • vt to organise in a strict manner.—**regimental** adj.

region n a large, indefinite part of the earth's surface; an administrative area of a country.—**regional** adj.

register n an official list; a written record, as for attendance; a tone of voice; a variety of language appropriate to a subject or occasion; (print) exact alignment. • vti to record; to enter in or sign a register; to entrust a letter to the post with special precautions for safety; to express emotion facially.—**registration** n.

registered adj recorded officially; qualified formally or officially.

registrar n a person who keeps records, esp one in an educational institution in charge of student records; a hospital doctor below a specialist in rank.

registry office n an office where civil marriages are held, and births and deaths recorded.

regret vt to feel sorrow, grief, or loss. • n sorrow; grief; (pl) polite refusal.—**regretful** adj.

regrettable adj to be regretted.

regular adj normal; habitual, not casual; at fixed intervals; according to rule, custom, or practice; uniform, consistent; symmetrical. • n a professional soldier; (inf) a person who attends regularly.—**regularity** n.—**regularly** adv.

regulate vt to control according to a rule; to cause to conform to a standard or needs.

regulation n a prescribed rule. • adj normal.

rehabilitate vt (prisoner etc) to help adapt to society after a stay in an institution; (sick person etc) to help to adjust to normal conditions after illness.—**rehabilitation** n.

rehash vt to dish up again.

rehearse vti to practise repeatedly before public performance.—**rehearsal** n.

reign n the rule of a sovereign. • vi to rule.

reimburse vt to repay; to refund.

rein n the strap of a bridle for guiding or restraining a horse; (pl) a means of restraint.

reincarnation n the incarnation of the soul after death in another body.

reindeer n a large deer with branched antlers found in northern regions.

reinforce vt (army etc) to strengthen with fresh troops; (a material) to add to the strength of.—**reinforcement** n.

reinstate vt to restore to a former position, rank, or condition.—**reinstatement** n.

reiterate vt to repeat; to say or do again.

reject vt to throw away, to discard; to refuse to accept, to decline; to rebuff. • n a thing or person rejected.—**rejection** n.

rejoice vi to feel joyful or happy.

rejuvenate vt to give youthful vigour to.

relapse vi to fall back into a worse state after improvement. • n the recurrence of illness after apparent recovery.

relate vt to recount; to show a connection.

related adj connected, allied; akin.

relation n the way in which one thing stands in respect to another, footing; reference; regard; connection by blood or marriage; a relative; (pl) the connections between or among persons, nations, etc; (pl) one's family and in-laws.

relationship n the tie or degree of kinship or intimacy; (inf) an affair.

relative adj corresponding; pertinent; comparative, conditional; respective; (gram) referring to a previous noun, clause, etc. • n a person related by blood or marriage.—**relatively** adv.

relax vti to slacken; to make or become less severe or strict; to make (the muscles) less rigid.

relay n a race between teams, each member of which goes a part of the distance. • vt (news, etc) to spread in stages.

release vt to set free; to let go; (film, etc) to issue for public exhibition; (information) to make available. • n a releasing, as from prison, work, etc; a device to hold or release a mechanism.

relegate vt to demote.—**relegation** n.

relent vi to soften in attitude.

relentless adj pitiless; unremitting.

relevant adj applying to the matter in hand.

reliable adj dependable, trustworthy.—**reliability** n.

relic n an object, fragment, or custom that has survived from the past; part of a saint's body or belongings; (pl) remains of the dead.

relief n the sensation following the easing or lifting of discomfort or stress; release from a duty by another person; the projection of a carved design from its ground • adj providing relief in disasters etc.

relieve vt to release from obligation or duty; (with **oneself**) to empty the bladder or bowels.

religion n a belief in God or gods.

relinquish vt to give up; to renounce.

relish n an appetising flavour; enjoyment of food or an experience; a spicy accompaniment to food; gusto, zest. • vt to enjoy, appreciate.

reluctant adj unwilling.—**reluctance** n.

rely vi to depend on; to trust.

remain vi to stay behind or in the same place; to continue to be. • npl a corpse.

remainder n what is left; (math) the result of subtraction, the quantity left over after division.

remand vt to send back into custody for further evidence.—also n.

remark vti to notice; to observe; to pass a comment (upon). • n a brief comment.

remarkable adj unusual; extraordinary; worthy of comment.—**remarkably** adv.

remedial adj providing a remedy; relating to the teaching of people with learning difficulties.

remedy n a medicine or any means to cure a disease. • vt to cure; to put right.

remember vti to recall.

remembrance n a reminiscence; an honouring of the dead or a past event.

remind vt to cause to remember.

reminder n a thing that reminds, esp a letter from a creditor.

reminisce vi to think, talk, or write about past events.

reminiscence n the recalling of a past experience; (pl) memoirs.

reminiscent adj reminding, suggestive (of).

remission n the reduction in length of a prison term; the lessening of the symptoms of a disease.

remit vti to moderate; to send payment (by post). • n an area of authority.

remittance n the sending of money or a payment (by post); the payment or money sent.

remnant n a small remaining fragment or number; an unsold or unused end of piece goods.

remorse n regret and guilt.

remorseless adj ruthless, cruel; relentless.

remote adj far apart or distant in time or place; out of the way; aloof.—**remotely** adv.

remote control n the control of a device or activity from a distance, usu by means of an electric circuit or the making or breaking of radio waves.

removal n the act of removing; a change of home or office.

remove vti to take away and put elsewhere; to get rid of. • n a stage in gradation.

remunerate vt to pay for a service; to reward.

rend vti to tear, to wrench (apart).

render vt (accounts, etc) to submit, as for approval; to cause to be; (fat) to melt down.

rendezvous n an arranged meeting; a place to meet. • vi to meet by appointment.

renegade n a person who is faithless to a principle, party, religion or cause.

renew vti to restore to freshness or vigour; to make or get anew.—**renewal** n.

renounce vt to abandon formally.

renovate vt to do up, repair.—**renovation** n.

renown n fame, celebrity.

renowned adj famous, illustrious.

rent n regular payment to another for the use of a house, etc. • vti to occupy as a tenant; to hire; to let for rent.

rental n an amount paid or received as rent; a house, car, etc, for rent; an act of renting.

renunciation n formal abandonment.

rep abbr = representative; repertory.

repair vt to mend; to restore to good working order; to make amends for. • n the act of repairing; a place repaired; condition as to soundness.

repartee n a witty reply; skill in making such replies.

repay vt to pay back; to refund.

repeal vt to annul, to rescind; to revoke.

repeat vti to say, write, or do again; to recite after another or from memory. • n a re-broadcast of a TV programme.

repeatedly adv over and over again.

repel vt to drive back; to cause distaste.

repellent adj distasteful, unattractive; capable of repelling. • n a substance that repels, esp a spray for protection against insects.

repent vi to wish one had not done something; to regret and change from evil ways.—**repentance** n.—**repentant** adj.

repercussion n a far-reaching, often indirect reaction to an event.

repertoire n the stock of plays, songs, etc, that a company, singer, etc, can perform.

repertory n the system of alternating several plays through a season with a permanent acting group.

repetition n the act of repeating; something repeated, a copy.—**repetitive** adj.

replace vt to put back; to take the place of.

replenish vt to stock again, refill.

replete adj stuffed, gorged.

replica n an exact copy; a reproduction.

reply vti to answer, respond. • n an answer.

report vti to give an account of; to tell as news; to take down and describe for publication; to complain about or against; to inform against; to present oneself (for duty). • n an account of facts; the formal statement of the findings of an investigation; a newspaper, radio or TV account of an event; a sharp, loud noise, as of a gun.

reporter n a person who gathers and reports news for a newspaper, radio or TV.

reprehensible *adj* blameworthy, culpable.

represent *vt* to portray; to describe; to typify; to stand for, symbolise; to act as an agent for.

representation *n* a portrait, reproduction; (*pl*) a presentation of claims, protests, views, etc.

representative *adj* typical. • *n* a person who acts for another; a delegate, agent, salesman, etc.

repress *vt* to suppress, restrain; (*emotions*) to keep under control.—**repression** *n*.

reprieve *vt* to postpone or commute the punishment of; to give respite to.—*also n*.

reprimand *n* a formal rebuke. • *vt* to reprove formally.

reprisal *n* an act of retaliation for an injury.

reproach *vt* to accuse of a fault; to blame. • *n* a rebuke.—**reproachful** *adj*.

reproduce *vti* to make a copy, duplicate, or likeness of; to produce young.

reproduction *n* the process by which plants and animals breed; a copy.—**reproductive** *adj*.

reprove *vt* to rebuke, censure.

reptile *n* any of a class of cold-blooded, air-breathing vertebrates with horny scales or plates.—**reptilian** *adj*.

republic *n* a government in which the people elect the head of state and in which the people and their elected representatives have supreme power; a country governed in this way.

republican *adj* of or supporting a republic. • *n* an advocate of republican government.

repudiate *vt* to reject, disown; to deny.

repugnant *adj* distasteful, offensive.

repulse *vt* to repel. • *n* a rebuff, rejection.

repulsion *n* a feeling of disgust; aversion.

repulsive *adj* disgusting; detestable.

reputable *adj* of good repute, respectable.

reputation *n* the estimation in which a person or thing is held; good name, honour.

repute *vt* to consider to be. • *n* reputation.

reputed *adj* generally reported; supposed.

reputedly *adv* by repute.

request *n* a demand. • *vt* to ask for earnestly.

requiem *n* a mass for the dead; music for this.

require *vt* to demand; to need, call for; to order.

requirement *n* a need; an essential condition.

requisite *adj* needed; essential, indispensable. • *n* something indispensable.

requisition *n* a formal request, demand, or order, as for military supplies. • *vt* to order.

rescind *vt* to annul, cancel.

rescue *vt* to save (a person, thing) from captivity, danger, or harm.—*also n*.

research *n* a systematic and careful investigation of a particular subject; a scientific study. • *vi* to carry out an investigation; to study.

resemble *vt* to be like.—**resemblance** *n*.

resent *vt* to be indignant about; to begrudge.—**resentful** *adj*.—**resentment** *n*.

reservation *n* (*of tickets, accommodation, etc*) a holding until called for; a limitation or proviso; (*pl*) doubt, scepticism; land set aside for a special purpose.

reserve *vt* to hold back for future use; to have set aside; (*tickets, hotel room, etc*) to book. • *n* something put aside for future use; land set aside for wild animals; (*sport*) a substitute; reticence of feelings.

reserved *adj* booked; uncommunicative.

reservoir *n* a tank or artificial lake for storing water.

reside *vi* to live in a place permanently.

residence *n* the period of residing; the house where one lives permanently.

resident *n* a permanent inhabitant; a junior hospital doctor.

residential *adj* of or relating to residence.

residue *n* a remainder; a part left over.

resign *vti* to give up (employment, etc); to reconcile (oneself).

resignation *n* the resigning of office, etc; the written proof of this; patient endurance.

resigned *adj* accepting the inevitable.

resilient *adj* (*person*) capable of carrying on after suffering hardship.—**resilience** *n*.

resin *n* a sticky substance exuded in the sap of trees and plants and used in medicines, varnishes, etc.

resist *vti* to oppose or withstand.

resistance *n* the act of resisting; the power to resist disease; opposition, esp to an occupying force.

resolute *adj* determined.—**resolutely** *adv*.

resolution *n* determination; a fixed intention; the picture definition in a TV.

resolve *vt* to break into component parts, dissolve; to convert or be converted (into); to determine, make up one's mind; to solve, settle; to vote by resolution. • *n* resolution; courage.

resonant *adj* ringing; resounding, echoing.

resort *n* a popular holiday location; recourse. • *vi* to have recourse to.

resound *vti* to echo; to reverberate.

resounding *adj* echoing; notable.

resource *n* source of help; an expedient; the ability to cope with a situation; (*pl*) wealth; assets; raw materials.

resourceful *adj* able to cope in difficult situations; ingenious.

respect *n* esteem; (*pl*) good wishes; reference; relation. • *vt* to feel or show esteem.

respectable *adj* worthy of esteem; well-behaved; of moderate quality or size.

respective *adj* proper to each, several.

respectively *adv* in the indicated order.

respiration *n* the act or process of breathing.

respite *n* a temporary delay; a period of relief.

resplendent *adj* magnificent.

respond *vti* to answer; to reply; to show a favourable reaction.

response *n* an answer; a reaction.

responsibility *n* a moral obligation or duty; a charge or trust; a thing one is responsible for.

responsible *adj* having control (over); (*with for*) accountable (for); involving responsibility.

responsive *adj* responding; sensitive to influence or stimulus.

rest[1] *n* stillness, sleep; inactivity; the state of not moving; relaxation; tranquility; a support or prop. • *vti* to take a rest; to give rest to; to lie down; to relax; to be fixed (on).

rest[2] *n* the remainder; the others.

restaurant *n* a place where meals can be bought and eaten.

restful *adj* peaceful.

rest home *n* an old people's home.

restitution *n* a reimbursement, as for loss.

restive *adj* impatient; fidgety.

restless *adj* unsettled; agitated.

restoration *n* reconstruction; renovation.

restore *vt* to give or put back; to repair; to renovate; to bring back to the original condition.

restrain *vt* to hold back; to restrict.

restrained *adj* moderate; self-controlled.

restraint *n* the ability to hold back; something that restrains.

restrict *vt* to keep within limits, circumscribe.

restricted *adj* affected by restriction; limited.

restriction *n* restraint; limitation.

result *vi* to have as a consequence; to terminate in. • *n* a consequence; an outcome; (*sport*) the final score; (*pl*) a desired effect.

resume *vti* to begin again; to continue after a stop or pause.—**resumption** *n*.

resurgence *n* a renewal of activity.

resurrection *n* a revival; a rising from the dead.

resuscitate *vti* to revive when apparently dead or unconscious.—**resuscitation** *n*.

retail *n* selling directly to the consumer in small quantities. • *vti* to sell or be sold by retail.

retain *vt* to keep possession of; to remember.

retainer *n* (*formerly*) a servant to a family; a fee to retain the services of.

retaliate *vti* to revenge oneself, usu by returning like for like.—**retaliation** *n*.

retarded *adj* slow in physical or mental development.

retch *vi* to heave as if to vomit.

rethink *vt* to think about again, esp with a change in mind.

reticent *adj* reserved in speech.

retina *n* the innermost part of the eye.

retinue *n* a body of attendants.

retire *vi* to give up one's work when pensionable age is reached; to go to bed.—**retirement** *n*.

retiring *adj* unobtrusive; shy.

retort *vi* to reply sharply or wittily. • *n* a sharp or witty reply; a vessel with a funnel bent downwards used in distilling.

retract *vti* to draw in or back; to withdraw (a statement, opinion, etc).

retreat *vi* to withdraw, retire; to recede. • *n* a withdrawal, esp of troops; seclusion for religious devotion.

retrial *n* a second trial.

retribution *n* something given or exacted in compensation, esp punishment.

retrieve *vt* to recover; to revive; (*a loss*) to make good; (*comput*) to obtain information from data stored in a computer. • *vi* (*dogs*) to retrieve game.—**retrieval** *n*.

retriever *n* any of several breeds of dogs capable of being trained for retrieving.

retrospect *n* a mental review of the past.

return *vi* to come or go back; to reply; to recur. • *vt* to give or send back; to repay; to elect. • *n* something returned; a recurrence; (*pl*) yield, revenue; a form for computing (income) tax.

reunion *n* a meeting following separation.

reunite *vt* to unite again. • *vi* to be reunited.

rev *vt* (*inf: with up*) to increase the speed of an engine. • *n* revolution per minute.

revamp *vt* to renovate, to rework, remodel.

reveal *vt* (*something hidden or secret*) to make known; to expose; to make visible.

reveille *n* a morning bugle call to wake soldiers.

revel *vi* (*with in*) to take pleasure or delight in. • *n* (*pl*) celebration.

revelation *n* the act of revealing; the disclosure of something secret; an illuminating experience.

revenge *vt* to inflict punishment in return for. • *n* retaliation; a vindictive feeling.

revenue *n* the total income produced by taxation; gross income from a business.

reverberate *vi* to be reflected in; to resound, to echo.—**reverberation** *n*.

reverence *n* profound respect; devotion; a gesture of respect (such as a bow).

reverent *adj* feeling or expressing reverence.

reverie *n* a daydream.

reversal *n* the act or process of reversing.

reverse *vti* to turn in the opposite direction; to turn outside in, upside down, etc; to move backwards. • *n* the contrary or opposite of something; the back, esp of a coin. • *adj* opposite, contrary.

reversion *n* return to a former condition or type; right to future possession.

revert *vi* to go back (to a former state).

review *n* an evaluation; a survey; a reconsideration; a critical assessment; a periodical containing critical essays. • *vt* to re-examine; to write an assessment of.

reviewer *n* a person who writes a review.

revise vt to correct and amend; to study again (for an examination).—**revision** n.

revival n the act of reviving; renewed performance (of a play).

revive vti to return to life; to make active again.

revoke vt to cancel; to rescind.

revolt vi to rebel; to shock. • n rebellion.

revolting adj extremely offensive.

revolution n the act of revolting; a motion round a centre or axis; an overthrow of a government, social system, etc.

revolutionary adj of revolution; radically new. • n a person who favours revolution.

revolutionise vt to cause a complete change in.

revolve vt to cause to travel in a circle.

revolver n a handgun with a magazine that revolves to reload.

revue n a musical show with skits, dances, etc, often satirising recent events.

revulsion n disgust; aversion.

reward n something that is given in return for something done; money offered, as for the capture of a criminal. • vt to give a reward.

rewarding adj pleasing, profitable.

rewrite vt to write again; to revise. • n something rewritten; revision.

rhapsody n (mus) an irregular instrumental composition of an epic, heroic or national character.

rhetoric n the art of effective speaking and writing; insincere language.

rhetorical adj of or relating to rhetoric; highflown, bombastic.

rheumatic adj suffering from rheumatism.

rheumatism n a disorder causing pain in muscles and joints.

rhinoceros n a large, thick-skinned mammal with one or two horns on the nose.

rhododendron n an shrub with large flowers.

rhubarb n a plant with large leaves and edible (when cooked) pink stalks.

rhyme n the repetition of sounds usu at the ends of lines in verse; such poetry or verse; a word corresponding with another in end sound. • vti to form a rhyme (with).

rhythm n a regular recurrence of beat, accent or silence in the flow of sound, esp of words and music; a measured flow.—**rhythmic(al)** adj.

rib n one of the curved bones of the chest attached to the spine; a ridge or raised strip, as of knitting. • vt to form vertical ridges in knitting; (inf) to tease or ridicule.

ribald adj irreverent; humorously vulgar.

ribbon n silk, satin, velvet, etc, woven into a narrow band; a piece of this; a strip of cloth, etc, inked for use, as in a typewriter.

rice n an annual cereal grass cultivated in warm climates; its starchy food grain.

rich adj having much money, wealthy; abounding in natural resources, fertile; (food) sweet or oily, highly flavoured; deep in colour.

rickets n a children's disease marked by softening of the bones, caused by vitamin D deficiency.

rickety adj shaky, unsteady.

rickshaw n a light, two-wheeled man-drawn vehicle, orig used in Japan.

ricochet vi (bullet) to rebound or skip along ground or water.—also n.

rid vt to free from; to dispose (of).

riddance n clearance; disposal.

ridden adj oppressed by; full of.

riddle[1] n a puzzling question; an enigma.

riddle[2] vt to perforate with holes.

ride vti to be carried along or travel in a vehicle or on an animal, bicycle, etc. • vt (horse, bicycle etc) to sit on and control. • n a trip or journey in a vehicle or on horseback, etc; a thing to ride at a fairground.

rider n a person who rides; an addition to a document, amending a clause.

ridge n a narrow crest or top; the ploughed earth thrown up between the furrows; a line where two slopes meet.

ridicule n mockery, derision. • vt to mock.

ridiculous adj deserving ridicule; preposterous.

rife adj widespread; prevalent.

riffraff n disreputable persons.

rifle[1] n a shoulder gun with a spirally grooved bore.

rifle[2] vti to steal; to look through (a person's papers or belongings).

rift n a split; a cleft; a fissure.

rig vt to set up in working order; to manipulate fraudulently. • n the way sails, etc, are rigged.

rigging n the ropes for supporting masts and sails.

right adj correct, true; just or good; appropriate; opposite to left; conservative; designating the side meant to be seen. • adv straight; directly; correctly, properly; to or on the right side. • n that which is just or correct; truth; fairness; justice; privilege; just or legal claim. • vti to set or become upright; to correct; to redress.

right angle n an angle of 90 degrees.

righteous adj moral, virtuous.

rightful adj legitimate.

right-hand adj of or towards the right side of a person or thing.

right-handed adj using the right hand.

right-hand man n an important and supportive assistant.

rightly adv in truth; in the right.

right-of-way n a public path over private ground; the right to use this; precedence over other traffic.

right-wing adj of or relating to the conservative faction of a political party, organisation, etc.

rigid adj stiff, strict.—**rigidity** n.

rigmarole n a foolishly involved procedure.

rigour n harsh inflexibility.—**rigorous** adj.

rim n a border or raised edge, esp of something circular; the outer part of a wheel.

rimless adj (glasses) without a frame.

rind n crust; peel; bark.

ring[1] n a circular band, esp of metal, worn on the finger, in the ear, etc; an arena for boxing, etc. • vt to encircle, surround.

ring[2] vti to emit a bell-like sound; to resound; to sound a bell; to telephone. • n a ringing sound.

ringlet n a curling lock of hair.

rink n an expanse of ice for skating; a smooth floor for roller skating.

rinse vt to wash lightly; to flush under clean water to remove soap. • n the act of rinsing; a preparation for tinting the hair.

riot n violent public disorder; uproar; unrestrained profusion; (inf) something very funny. • vi to take part in a riot.—**rioter** n.

riotous adj tumultuous, disorderly; luxurious.

rip vti to cut or tear apart roughly; (with into) to attack, esp verbally. • n a tear.

rip cord n a cord for releasing a parachute.

ripe adj ready to be eaten or harvested.

ripen vt to grow or make ripe.

ripple n a little wave on the surface of water; the sound of this. • vti to have or form little waves on the surface (of).

rise vi to get up; to stand up; to increase in value or size; (voice) to reach a higher pitch. • n an ascent; an increase in price, salary, etc.

risk n chance of loss or injury; hazard; danger, peril. • vt to take the chance of.

risky adj dangerous.

risqué adj verging on indecency.

rissole n a fried cake of minced meat, egg, and breadcrumbs.

rite n a ceremonial practice or procedure.

ritual n a fixed (religious) ceremony.

rival n one of two or more people, organisations or teams competing with each other for the same goal. • adj competing. • vt to strive to equal.

rivalry n emulation; competition.

river n a large natural stream of fresh water.

riverbed n the channel formed by a river.

riverside n the bank of a river.

rivet n a short, metal bolt for holding metal plates together. • vt to fix one's eyes upon.

road n a surfaced track for travelling on.

road block n a barrier erected across a road to halt traffic.

road hog n a car driver who obstructs other vehicles by encroaching on the others' traffic lane.

roadside n the border of a road.—also adj.

roadway n the strip of land over which a road passes; the main part of a road, used by vehicles.

roadworthy adj (vehicle) fit for the road.

roam vti to wander about, to travel.

roar vti to make a loud, full, growling sound.

roaring adj boisterous, noisy.

roast vti to cook with little or no moisture, as in an oven; (coffee, etc) to process by exposure to heat; to expose to great heat; (inf) to criticise severely. • n a cut of meat for roasting.

rob vt to steal from.—**robber** n.

robbery n theft by intimidation.

robe n a long flowing outer garment; the official dress of a judge, academic, etc; a bathrobe or dressing gown. • vti to put on or dress in robes.

robin n a songbird with a dull red breast.

robot n a mechanical device that acts in a seemingly human way.

robust adj strong, sturdy; vigorous.

rock[1] n a large stone or boulder; a hard sweet.

rock[2] vti to move to and fro, or from side to side.

rock and roll n popular music that incorporates country and blues elements and is usu played with a heavily accented beat.

rock bottom n the lowest or most fundamental part or level. • adj very lowest.

rocker n a curved support on which a cradle, etc, rocks.

rockery n a garden among rocks for alpine plants.

rocket n any device driven forward by gases escaping through a rear vent. • vi to soar.

rocking chair n a chair mounted on rockers.

rocking horse n a toy horse fixed on rockers.

rocky adj having many rocks; shaky, unstable.

rod n a thin bar of metal or wood; a fishing rod.

rodent n any of several relatively small gnawing animals with two strong front teeth.

rodeo n a display of cowboy skill.

roe[1] n the eggs or sperm of fish.

roe[2] n a small reddish brown deer.

rogue n a rascal; a mischievous person; a wild animal that lives apart from the herd.

role n a part in a film or play taken by an actor.

roll n anything wound into cylindrical form; a list or register; a small cake of bread. • vi to move by turning over or from side to side. • vt to cause to roll.

roll call n the reading aloud of a list of names to check attendance.

rolled gold n a thin coating of gold attached to another metal by passing through heavy rollers.

roller n a revolving cylinder used for spreading paint; a large wave.

roller skate n a four-wheeled skate.

rolling pin n a wooden, plastic or stone cylinder for rolling out pastry.

rolling stock n all the vehicles of a railway.

Roman adj of or relating to the city of Rome or its ancient empire or the Latin alphabet. • n an inhabitant or citizen of Rome.

Roman Catholic adj belonging to the Christian church that is headed by the Pope.—also n.

romance n a series of unusual adventures; a love story; a love affair.

Roman numerals npl the letters I, V, X, L, C, D and M used to represent numbers in the manner of the ancient Romans.

romantic adj of or given to romance.

romp vi to play boisterously.—also n.

rompers npl a child's one-piece garment.

roof n the upper covering of a building.

roofing n materials for a roof.

rook[1] n a crow-like bird.

rook[2] n (chess) a piece with the power to move horizontally or vertically, a castle.

room n space; unoccupied space; adequate space; a division of a house.

roommate n a person with whom one shares a room or rooms.

roomy adj having ample space; wide.

roost n a bird's perch or sleeping-place.

rooster n an adult male domestic fowl.

root[1] n the part of a plant, usu underground, that anchors the plant, draws water from the soil, etc; the embedded part of a tooth, a hair, etc; (math) the factor of a quantity which multiplied by itself gives the quantity. • vti (with out) to tear up.

root[2] vti to search about, rummage; (with for) (inf) to encourage a team by cheering.

rope n a thick cord or thin cable made of twisted fibres or wires. • vt to tie with a rope.

rosary n a string of beads for keeping count of prayers; a series of prayers.

rose n a prickly-stemmed plant with fragrant flowers of many delicate colours; its flower.

rosé n a pink wine made from skinless red grapes or by mixing white and red wine.

rosemary n a fragrant shrubby mint used in cookery and perfumery.

rosette n a rose-shaped bunch of ribbon; a carving, etc, in the shape of a rose.

roster n a list or roll, as of military personnel; a list of duties.

rostrum n a platform for public speaking.

rosy adj having pink cheeks; optimistic.

rot vti to decompose. • n decay; corruption.

rota n a list or roster of duties.

rotary adj revolving; turning like a wheel.

rotate vti to turn on an axis like a wheel.

rotation n the action of rotating.

rotor n a rotating part of a machine or engine.

rotten adj decayed; corrupt; (inf) bad, nasty.

rotund adj rounded; spherical; plump.

rouble n a coin and monetary unit of Russia.

rouge n a red cosmetic for colouring the cheeks.

rough adj not smooth; ill-mannered; violent; unrefined; crude, unfinished; approximate. • n rough ground; (golf) any part of a course with grass, etc, left uncut. • vt to sketch roughly.

roulette n a gambling game played with a revolving disc and a ball.

round adj circular, spherical, or cylindrical in form; curved; plump; (math) expressed to the nearest ten, hundred, etc. • adv on all sides; here and there; around. • prep encircling; on every side of; around. • n a circuit; a series or sequence; (golf) a circuit of a course; a stage of a contest. • vt to make round or plump; (math) to express as a round number.

roundabout adj indirect, circuitous. • n a merry-go-round; a crossroad where traffic circulates around a traffic island.

rounded adj curved or round.

round trip n a journey to a place and back again.

roundup n a driving together of livestock; a summary, as of news.

rouse vti to provoke; to awaken; to wake up.

rousing adj stirring; vigorous.

rout n a disorderly retreat.

route n a course to be taken; the roads travelled on a journey.

routine n a procedure that is regular and unvarying; a sequence of set movements, as in a dance, skating, etc.—also adj.

row[1] n a line of persons or things; a line of seats (in a theatre, etc).

row[2] vti to propel with oars; to transport by rowing.

row[3] n a noisy quarrel or dispute; a scolding; noise, disturbance. • vi to quarrel.

rowdy adj rough and noisy, disorderly. • n a rowdy person, a hooligan.

royal adj relating to or fit for a king or queen. • n (inf) a member of a royal family.

royalist n a person who advocates monarchy.

royalty n the rank or power of a king or queen; royal persons; a share of the proceeds from a book, song, etc, paid to the owner, author, etc.

RSVP abbr = répondez s'il vous plaît.

rub vti to move (a hand, cloth, etc) over the surface of with pressure; (with away, off or out) to remove or erase by friction; to chafe, grate.

rubber[1] n an elastic substance made synthetically or from the sap of various tropical plants; an eraser.

rubber[2] n a group of three games at whist, bridge, etc.

rubber-stamp vt (inf) to give automatic approval without investigation.

rubbish n refuse; garbage, trash; nonsense.

rubble n rough broken stone or rock.

ruby n a deep red, transparent, precious stone.

rucksack n a bag worn on the back by hikers.

rudder *n* a flat vertical piece of wood or metal hinged to the stern of a ship or boat or the rear of an aircraft to steer by.

ruddy *adj* (*complexion*) of a healthy, red colour.

rude *adj* uncivil, ill-mannered; uncultured, coarse; harsh, brutal; crude, roughly made.

rudiment *n* (*pl*) elements, first principles.

rudimentary *adj* imperfectly developed.

rueful *adj* showing good-humoured self-pity.

ruff *n* a pleated collar or frill worn round the neck; a fringe of feathers or fur round the neck of a bird or animal.

ruffian *n* a brutal lawless person; a villain.

ruffle *vti* to disturb the smoothness of, disarrange; to agitate; to upset. • *n* a frill.

rug *n* a thick heavy fabric used as a floor covering; a thick woollen wrap or coverlet.

Rugby *n* a football game for two teams of 15 players played with an oval ball.

rugged *adj* rocky; rough; strong; stern; robust.

ruin *n* destruction; downfall, wrecked state; a loss of fortune; (*pl*) the remains of something destroyed, decayed, etc. • *vti* to spoil; to bankrupt.

ruinous *adj* causing ruin, disastrous.

rule *n* a straight-edged instrument for drawing lines and measuring; a regulation, an order; habitual practice; a straight line. • *vti* to govern, to exercise authority over; to draw (lines) with a ruler; (*with* out) to eliminate.

ruler *n* a person who governs; a strip of wood, metal, etc, with a straight edge, used in drawing lines, measuring, etc.

ruling *adj* governing; reigning; dominant. • *n* an authoritative pronouncement.

rum *n* a spirit made from sugar cane.

rumble *vti* to make a low heavy rolling noise; to move with such a sound; (*sl*) to see through. • *n* the dull deep vibrating noise of thunder, etc.

rummage *vti* to search thoroughly.

rumour *n* common talk not based on definite knowledge; an unconfirmed report, story. • *vt* to report by way of rumour.

rump *n* the hindquarters of an animal's body.

rumpus *n* a commotion; a din.

run *vi* to go by moving the legs faster than in walking; to hurry; to flow; to operate; to compete in a race, election, etc; (*colours*) to merge. • *vt* (*a car, etc*) to drive; (*a business, etc*) to manage; (*a story*) to publish in a newspaper; (*temperature*) to suffer from a fever; (*with* out) to exhaust a supply; (*inf*) to desert; (*with* over) (*vehicle*) to knock down a person or animal; to

overflow; to exceed a limit; to rehearse quickly; (*with* up) to incur or amass. • *n* an act of running; a trip, a flow; a series; prevalence; a trend; free and unrestricted access to all parts; (*in tights, etc*) a ladder.

runaway *n* a person or animal that has run away.

rundown *n* a summary.

run-down *adj* dilapidated.

rung *n* the step of a ladder; the crossbar of a chair.

runner *n* an athlete; a person who runs; a groove or strip on which something glides.

runner bean *n* a climbing plant that produces long green edible pods.

runner-up *n* the competitor who finishes second in a race, contest, etc.

running *n* the act of moving swiftly; a racing, managing, etc. • *adj* moving swiftly; continuous; discharging pus. • *adv* in succession.

runny *adj* tending to flow.

run-of-the-mill *adj* average, mediocre.

runt *n* an unusually small animal, esp the smallest of a litter of pigs; a person of small stature.

runway *n* a landing strip for aircraft.

rupture *n* a breach; the act of bursting or breaking; hernia. • *vti* to cause or suffer a rupture.

rural *adj* relating to the country or agriculture.

ruse *n* a trick, deception.

rush[1] *vti* to move, push, drive, etc, swiftly or impetuously; to make a sudden attack (on); to do with unusual haste; to hurry. • *n* a sudden surge; a press, as of business, requiring unusual haste; an unedited film print.

rush[2] *n* a marsh plant; its slender pithy stem.

rush hour *n* the time at the beginning and end of the working day when traffic is at its heaviest.

rusk *n* a sweet or plain bread sliced and rebaked until dry and crisp.

rust *n* a reddish oxide coating formed on iron or steel when exposed to moisture; a reddish brown colour; a red mould on plants; the fungus causing this. • *vti* to form rust (on).

rustle *n* a crisp, rubbing sound as of dry leaves, paper, etc. • *vti* to make or move with a rustle; to steal (cattle); (*with* up) (*inf*) to get together.

rusty *adj* coated with rust; out of practice.

rut[1] *n* a track worn by wheels; an undeviating mechanical routine.

rut[2] *n* the seasonal period of sexual excitement in certain male animals, e.g. deer.

ruthless *adj* cruel, merciless.

rye *n* a hardy annual grass; its grain, used for making flour and whiskey.

S

sabbath n a day of rest and worship observed on a Saturday by Jews, Sunday by Christians and Friday by Muslims.

sabbatical n a year's leave from a teaching post, often paid, for research or travel.

sabotage n deliberate damage of machinery, or disruption of public services, by enemy agents, disgruntled employees, etc, to prevent their effective operation. • vt to practise sabotage on.

saccharin n a non-fattening sugar substitute.

saccharine adj excessively sweet.

sack n a large bag made of coarse cloth used as a container; (sl: with the) dismissal. • vt (sl) to dismiss.

sacrament n a religious ceremony forming outward and visible sign of inward and spiritual grace, esp Baptism and the Eucharist.

sacred adj regarded as holy; consecrated to a god or God; connected with religion.

sacrifice n the slaughter of an animal (or person) to please a deity; the surrender of something valuable for the sake of something more important or worthy. • vt to slaughter or give up as a sacrifice; to give up for a higher good.

sacrilege n violation of anything holy or sacred.

sacrosanct adj inviolable; very holy.

sad adj sorrowful; deplorable.—**sadly** adv.

sadden vt to make sad.

saddle n a seat, usu of leather, for a rider on a horse, bicycle, etc. • vt to burden.

saddlebag n a bag hung from the saddle of a horse or bicycle.

sadism n sexual pleasure obtained from inflicting cruelty upon another.—**sadistic** adj.

safari n a journey or hunting expedition.

safe adj unhurt; out of danger; involving no risk. • n a locking metal box for valuables.

safeguard n anything that protects against injury or danger. • vt to protect.

safekeeping n the act of keeping safely.

safety n freedom from danger.

safety belt n a seatbelt in a car.

safety pin n a pin with a guard to cover the point.

saffron n a crocus whose bright yellow stigmas are used as a food colouring and flavouring.

sag vi to droop downwards in the middle; to sink or hang down unevenly.

sage[1] adj wise. • n a person of profound wisdom.

sage[2] n a herb with leaves used for flavouring food; sagebrush.

sago n a type of Asian palm; its starchy pith used in puddings.

sail n a piece of canvas used to catch the wind to propel or steer a vessel; an arm of a windmill; a voyage in a sailing vessel. • vt to navigate. • vi to travel by water.

sailing n the act of sailing.

sailing boat n a boat that is propelled by a sail.

sailor n one of a ship's crew.

saint n a person who is very patient, charitable, etc; a person who is canonised by the Roman Catholic church.—**sainthood** n.

sake n behalf; purpose; benefit; interest.

salad n a dish, usu cold, of vegetables, fruits, meat, eggs, etc; lettuce, etc, used for this.

salad dressing n a sauce of oil, vinegar, spices, etc, to put on a salad.

salary n fixed, regular payment for non-manual work, usu paid monthly.

sale n the act of selling; the disposal of goods at reduced prices.

salesman n a person who sells either in a given territory or in a shop.—**saleswoman** nf.

salesroom n a place where goods are displayed for sale.

salient adj conspicuous; noteworthy.

saliva n the liquid secreted by glands in the mouth that aids digestion.—**salivary** adj.

sallow adj (complexion) a yellow colour.

salmon n a large silvery edible fish that lives in salt water and spawns in fresh water.

saloon n a large cabin for the social use of a ship's passengers; a four-seater car with a boot.

salt n a white crystalline substance used as a seasoning or preservative; (chem) a compound of an acid and a base; (pl) mineral salt as an aperient. • adj containing or tasting of salt. • vt to flavour, pickle or sprinkle with salt.—**salty** adj.

salt cellar n a vessel for salt at the table.

salutary adj beneficial; wholesome.

salute n a gesture of greeting; (mil) a motion of the right hand to the head; a discharge of guns, etc, as a military mark of honour. • vti to make a salute (to); to honour.

salvage n the rescuing of a ship or property from loss at sea, by fire, etc. • vt to save from loss or danger.

salvation n in Christianity, the deliverance from evil; a means of preservation.

salvo n a firing of several guns or missiles simultaneously; spirited verbal attack.

same adj identical; exactly similar. • pron the same person or thing. • adv in like manner.

sample n a specimen. • vt (food, drink) to taste a small quantity of.

sanatorium n an establishment for the treatment of convalescents or the chronically ill.

sanctimonious adj hypocritically pious.

sanction n authorisation; a penalty by which a law is enforced, esp a prohibition on trade with a country that has violated international law. • vt to permit.

sanctity n the condition of being sacred.

sanctuary n a sacred place; a place where one is free from arrest or violence; an animal reserve.

sand n very fine rock particles.

sandal n a shoe consisting of a sole strapped to the foot; a low shoe.

sandpaper n a paper coated on one side with sand or other abrasive, used to polish or smooth.

sandstone n a sedimentary rock of compacted sand.

sandwich n two slices of bread with meat, cheese or other filling between. • vt to place between two things or two layers.

sandy adj of sand; yellowish grey.

sane adj mentally sound, not mad.

sanguine adj confident, hopeful.

sanitary adj relating to the promotion and protection of health; relating to sewage disposal.

sanitary towel n an absorbent pad worn externally during menstruation.

sanitation n drainage and disposal of sewage.

sanity n the condition of being sane.

sap n the vital juice of plants; energy and health; (inf) a fool. • vt to exhaust the energy of.

sapling n a young tree; a youth.

sapphire n a transparent blue precious stone.

sarcasm n a scornful or ironic remark; the use of this.—**sarcastic** adj.

sardine n a small, edible seafish.

sash¹ n a band of satin or ribbon worn around the waist or over the shoulder.

sash² n a frame for holding the glass of a window, esp one that slides vertically.

Satan n the devil.—**satanic** adj.

satchel n a bag with shoulder straps for carrying school books, etc.

satellite n a planet orbiting another; a manmade object orbiting the earth, moon, etc, to gather scientific information or for communication; a nation economically dependent on a more powerful one.

satin n a fabric of woven silk with a smooth, shiny surface on one side..

satire n a literary work in which folly or evil in people's behaviour are held up to ridicule.—**satirical** adj.

satisfaction n the condition of being satisfied.

satisfactory adj adequate; acceptable.

satisfy vt to give enough to; (hunger, desire, etc) to appease; to please; to gratify; to convince.

saturate vt to soak thoroughly; to fill completely.

sauce n a liquid or dressing served with food to enhance its flavour.

saucepan n a deep cooking pan with a handle and lid.

saucer n a round shallow dish placed under a cup.

saucy adj rude, impertinent; sprightly.

saunter vi to walk in a leisurely or idle way.

sausage n minced seasoned meat packed into animal gut or other casing.

savage adj fierce; wild; primitive. • n a member of a primitive society.

savagery n the state of being a savage; an act of violence or cruelty.

save vt to rescue from harm or danger; to keep, to accumulate; to set aside for future use; to avoid the necessity of; (energy etc) to prevent waste of; (theol) to deliver from sin. • vi to store up money or goods; (sports) to keep an opponent from scoring or winning. • n (sports) the act of preventing one's opponent from scoring. • conj, prep except, but.

saving adj thrifty, economical; redeeming. • n what is saved; (pl) money saved for future use.

savings bank n a bank receiving small deposits and holding them in interest-bearing accounts.

saviour n a person who saves another from harm or danger; (with cap) Jesus Christ.

savour n the flavour or smell of something; a distinctive quality. • vti to enjoy; to smack (of).

savoury adj having a good taste or smell; spicy, not sweet. • n (pl) snacks served with drinks.

saw n a tool with a toothed edge for cutting wood, etc. • vti to cut with a saw.

sawdust n fine particles of wood caused by sawing.

sawmill n a mill where timber is cut into logs.

saxophone n a brass wind instrument with a single reed and about twenty finger-keys.

say vt to speak, to utter; to state in words; to affirm, declare; to recite; to estimate; to assume. • n the right or opportunity to speak.

saying n a proverb or adage.

scab n a dry crust on a wound or sore; a worker who refuses to join a strike.—**scabby** adj.

scaffold n a raised platform for the execution of a criminal; scaffolding.

scaffolding n a temporary framework of wood and metal for use by workmen constructing a building, etc.

scald vt to burn with hot liquid or steam. • n an injury caused by hot liquid or steam.

scale¹ n (pl) a machine or instrument for weighing.

scale² n one of the thin plates covering a fish or reptile; an incrustation on teeth, etc. • vti to remove the scales from; to flake off.

scale³ n a graduated measure; an instrument so marked; (mus) a series of tones from the keynote to its octave, in order of pitch; the proportion that a map bears to what it represents. • vt (wall) to go up or over.

scallop n an edible shellfish with two fluted, fan-shaped shells; one of a series of curves in an edging. • vt to cut into scallops.

scalp n the skin covering the skull, usu covered with hair. • vti to cut the scalp from.

scalpel n a short, thin, very sharp knife used esp for surgery.

scamper vi to run away quickly or playfully.

scan vt (page etc) to look through quickly; (med) to examine with a radiological device; (radar) to detect with an electronic beam; (poem) to conform to a rhythmical pattern; to check for recorded data by means of a mechanical or electronic device. • n an instance of being scanned.

scandal n a disgraceful event or action; talk arising from immoral behaviour.

scandalise vt to shock the moral feelings of.

scandalous adj causing scandal; shameful.

scant adj limited; meagre; insufficient.

scanty adj barely adequate.—**scantily** adv.

scapegoat n a person who bears the blame for others.

scar n a mark left after the healing of a wound or sore. • vti to mark with or form a scar.

scarce adj not in abundance; rare.

scarcely adv hardly, only just.

scarcity n the state of being scarce; a dearth.

scare vti to startle; to frighten or become frightened; to drive away by frightening. • n a sudden fear; a false alarm.

scarecrow n a wooden figure dressed in clothes for scaring birds from crops.

scaremonger n a person who causes fear or panic by spreading rumours; an alarmist.

scarf n a rectangular or square piece of cloth worn around the neck, shoulders or head for warmth or decoration.

scarlet n a bright red with a tinge of orange. • adj scarlet coloured; immoral or sinful.

scarlet fever n an acute contagious disease marked by a sore throat, fever and a scarlet rash.

scathing adj bitterly critical; cutting.

scatter vti to throw loosely about; to sprinkle.

scatterbrain n a frivolous, heedless person.

scattered adj dispersed widely, spaced out.

scavenge vi to gather things discarded by others; (animal) to eat decaying matter.

scene n the place in which anything occurs; the place in which the action of a play or a story occurs; a section of a play, a division of an act; an unseemly display of strong emotion; a landscape; (inf) an area of interest or activity (e.g. the music scene).

scenery n painted screens, etc, used to represent places, as in a play, film, etc; an aspect of a landscape, esp of beautiful countryside.

scenic adj picturesque.

scent n a perfume; an odour left by an animal by which it can be tracked; a line of pursuit or discovery. • vt to perfume; to detect.

scented adj perfumed.

sceptic n a person who questions opinions generally accepted; a person who doubts religious doctrines, an agnostic.

sceptical adj doubting; questioning.

scepticism n an attitude of questioning criticism, doubt.

sceptre n the staff of office held by a monarch on a ceremonial occasion.

schedule n a timetable. • vt to plan.

scheme n a plan; a project; a diagram; an underhand plot. • vti to devise or plot.—**schemer** n.

scheming adj cunning; intriguing.

schism n a division into two parties.

schizophrenia n a mental disorder characterised by withdrawal from reality and deterioration of the personality.—**schizophrenic** adj, n.

scholar n a pupil, a student; a learned person.

scholarly adj learned, erudite, academic.

scholarship n an annual grant to a scholar or student, usu won by competitive examination; learning, academic achievement.

school[1] n a shoal of porpoises, whales or other aquatic animals of one kind swimming together.

school[2] n an educational establishment; its teachers and students; a particular division of a university; a group of thinkers, artists, etc, holding similar principles. • vt to train; to teach.

schoolboy n a boy who attends school.

schoolgirl n a girl who attends school.

schooling n instruction in school.

schoolmaster n a man who teaches in school.

schoolmistress n a woman who teaches in school.

schoolteacher n a person who teaches in school.

schooner n a sailing ship with two or more masts rigged with fore-and-aft sails; a large drinking glass for sherry or beer.

sciatica n pain along the sciatic nerve.

science n knowledge gained by systematic experimentation and analysis, and the formulation of general principles; a branch of this.

science fiction n highly imaginative fiction typically involving scientific phenomena.

scientific adj of or concerned with science; based on the principles and methods of science.

scientist n a specialist in a branch of science, as in chemistry, etc.

scintillating adj sparkling; amusing.

scissor vt to cut with scissors, to clip. • npl a tool for cutting consisting of two fastened pivoted blades whose edges slide past each other; a gymnastic feat in which the leg movements resemble the opening and closing of scissors.

scoff¹ *vti* to jeer (at) or mock.

scoff² *vt* (*sl*) to eat quickly and greedily.

scold *vi* to reprove angrily; to tell off.

scone *n* a small, round cake made from flour and fat that is baked and spread with butter, etc.

scoop *n* a small shovel-like utensil as for taking up flour, ice cream, etc; (*inf*) a piece of exclusive news; (*inf*) the advantage gained in being the first to publish or broadcast this. • *vt* to shovel, lift or hollow out with a scoop; (*inf: rival newspaper etc*) to forestall with a news item.

scooter *n* a child's two-wheeled vehicle with a footboard and steering handle; a motor scooter.

scope *n* the opportunity to use one's abilities; extent; range; an instrument for viewing.

scorch *vti* to burn on the surface; to singe.

scorcher *n* (*inf*) a very hot day.

scorching *adj* (*inf: weather*) very hot.

score *n* the total number of points made in a game or examination; a notch or scratch; a line indicating deletion; a group of twenty; the music composed for a film; a grievance for settling; (*inf*) the real facts. • *vt* to mark with cuts; (*mus*) to arrange in a score, to orchestrate; to gain or record points, as in a game. • *vi* to make points, as in a game; (*sl*) to be successful in seduction.

scorn *n* extreme contempt or disdain. • *vt* to reject or refuse as unworthy.—**scornful** *adj.*

scorpion *n* a tropical insect-like animal with pincers and a jointed tail with a poisonous sting.

Scot *n* a native or inhabitant of Scotland.

Scotch *n* whisky made in Scotland.

scotch *vt* (*a rumour*) to stamp out.

Scots *adj* of or pertaining to Scotland. • *n* the dialect of English developed in Lowland Scotland.

Scottish *adj* of or relating to Scotland.

scoundrel *n* a rascal; a dishonest person.

scour¹ *vt* to clean by rubbing with an abrasive cloth.

scour² *vt* to range over, esp in search or pursuit.

scourge *n* a whip; a person who harasses and causes widespread and great affliction; a pest.

scout *n* a person, plane, etc, sent to observe the enemy's strength, etc; a person employed to find new talent or survey a competitor, etc; (*with cap*) a member of the Scouting Association, an organisation for young people. • *vti* to reconnoitre.

scowl *n* a contraction of the brows in an angry or threatening manner. • *vi* to look sullen.

scraggy *adj* thin and bony, gaunt.

scram *vi* (*sl*) to go away at once.

scramble *vi* to scuffle or struggle for something; to move with urgency or panic. • *vt* to mix haphazardly; to stir (slightly beaten eggs)

while cooking; (*transmitted signals*) to make unintelligible in transit. • *n* a motorcycle rally over rough ground.

scrap¹ *n* a small piece; a fragment of discarded material; (*pl*) bits of food. • *vt* to discard.

scrap² *n* (*inf*) a fight or quarrel.—*also vi.*

scrapbook *n* a book for pasting clippings, etc, in.

scrape *vt* to rub with a sharp or abrasive object so as to clean, smooth or remove; to eke out or to be economical; to graze. • *n* an abrasion, scratch; an awkward predicament.

scraper *n* an instrument for scraping.

scrapheap *n* a pile of discarded material or things.

scrappy *adj* disjointed; fragmentary.

scratch *vt* to mark with a sharp point; to scrape with the nails or claws; to rub to relieve an itch. • *vi* to use nails or claws to tear or dig. • *n* a mark or sound made by this; a slight injury.

scrawl *n* careless or illegible handwriting; a scribble. • *vti* to draw or write carelessly.

scrawny *adj* skinny; bony.

scream *vti* to utter a piercing cry, as of pain, fear, etc;. • *n* a sharp, piercing cry; (*inf*) a very funny person or thing.

scree *n* loose shifting stones.

screech *n* a harsh, high-pitched cry. • *vti* to utter a screech, to shriek.

screen *n* a movable partition or framework to conceal, divide or protect; a shelter or shield from heat, danger or view; an electronic display (as in a television set, computer terminal, etc); a surface on which films, slides, etc, are projected; a coarse wire mesh over a window or door to keep out insects. • *vt* to conceal or shelter; to separate according to skill, etc; (*a film*) to show on a screen.

screening *n* a showing of a film.

screenplay *n* a script written for a film.

screenwriter *n* a writer of screenplays.

screw *n* a metal cylinder or cone with a spiral thread around it for fastening things by being turned. • *vt* to fasten, tighten, etc, with a screw; to extort, to cheat out of something due; (*sl, vulg*) to have sexual intercourse with; (*with* up) to gather (courage, etc). • *vi* to go together or come apart by being turned like a screw; (*sl, vulg*) to have sexual intercourse; (*with* up) to bungle.

screwdriver *n* a tool like a blunt chisel for turning screws.

screwy *adj* (*sl*) eccentric, odd.

scribble *vti* to draw or write hastily or carelessly, to scrawl. • *n* hasty writing, a scrawl.

script *n* handwriting; the text of a stage play, screenplay or broadcast. • *vt* to write a script (for).

scriptural *adj* of or based on the Bible.

scripture *n* any sacred writing; (*with cap, often pl*) the Bible.

scriptwriter *n* a writer of scripts for TV, etc.

scroll *n* a roll of parchment with writing on it. • *vti* (*comput*) to move text across a screen.

scrounge *vti* (*inf*) to seek or obtain (something) for nothing.—**scrounger** *n*.

scrub[1] *n* an arid area of stunted trees and shrubs.

scrub[2] *vti* to clean vigorously, to scour; to rub hard; (*inf*) to remove, to cancel.

scruff *n* the back of the neck, the nape.

scruffy *adj* shabby; unkempt.

scrum *n* a scrummage.

scrummage *n* (*Rugby football*) a play consisting of a tussle between rival forwards in a compact mass for possession of the ball.

scruple *n* (*usu pl*) a moral principle or belief causing one to doubt or hesitate about a course of action. • *vi* to hesitate owing to scruples.

scrupulous *adj* careful; conscientious.

scrutinise *vti* to look closely at.

scrutiny *n* a careful examination; a critical gaze.

scuff *vti* to drag the feet, to shuffle; to wear or mark the surface of by doing this.

scuffle *n* a confused fight. • *vi* to fight confusedly.

scullery *n* a room for storage or kitchen work.

sculpt *vt* to carve, adorn or portray with sculptures; to shape, mould or form like sculpture.

sculptor *n* a person skilled in sculpture.

sculpture *n* the art of carving wood or forming clay, stone, etc, into figures, statues, etc.

scum *n* a thin layer of impurities on top of a liquid; despicable people.

scurrilous *adj* grossly offensive.

scurry *vi* to hurry with quick, short steps.

scurvy *n* a disease caused by a deficiency of vitamin C.

scuttle[1] *vi* to run quickly; to hurry away.

scuttle[2] *n* a bucket with a lip for storing coal.

scuttle[3] *vt* to sink a ship by making holes in it.

scythe *n* a two-handed implement with a large curved blade for cutting grass, etc.

sea *n* the ocean; a section of this.

sea breeze *n* a wind that blows from the sea.

seafood *n* edible fish or shellfish from the sea.

seagoing *adj* made for use on the open sea.

seagull *n* a gull.

seal[1] *n* an engraved stamp for impressing wax, lead, etc; a device for closing or securing tightly. • *vt* to fix a seal to; to close tightly or securely.

seal[2] *n* an aquatic mammal with four webbed flippers.

sealant *n* a thing that seals, as wax, etc.

sea level *n* the level of the surface of the sea in relation to the land.

sea lion *n* a large seal of the Pacific Ocean.

seam *n* the line where two pieces of cloth are stitched together; (*geol*) a stratum of coal, oil, etc, between thicker ones.

seaman *n* a sailor; a naval rank.

seamy *adj* unpleasant or sordid.

seance, séance *n* a meeting of spiritualists to try to communicate with the dead.

seaplane *n* an aeroplane with floats that allow it to take off from and land on water.

seaport *n* a port, harbour or town accessible to oceangoing ships.

search *vi* to look around to find something. • *vt* to inspect closely. • *n* an investigation.

searching *adj* keen, piercing.

searchlight *n* a powerful ray of light projected by an apparatus on a swivel; the apparatus.

search warrant *n* a legal document that authorises a police search.

seashore *n* land beside the sea; the beach.

seasick *adj* affected with nausea brought on by the motion of a ship.

seaside *n* seashore.

season *n* one of the four equal parts into which the year is divided: spring, summer, autumn or winter; a time when something is plentiful or in use. • *vt* (*food*) to flavour by adding salt, spices, etc.

seasonal *adj* relating to a particular season.

seasoning *n* salt, spices, etc, used to enhance the flavour of food.

season ticket *n* a ticket valid for a number of concerts, games, journeys, etc.

seat *n* a piece of furniture for sitting on; the part of a chair on which one sits; the buttocks, the part of the trousers covering them; the chief location or centre; a parliamentary constituency. • *vt* to place on a seat.

seatbelt *n* an anchored strap worn in a car or aeroplane to secure one to a seat.

seaweed *n* a mass of plants growing in water.

seaworthy *adj* fit to go to sea.

secluded *adj* private; sheltered.

seclusion *n* privacy, solitude.

second *adj* next after first; alternate; another of the same kind; next below the first in rank, value, etc. • *n* a person or thing coming second; another; one sixtieth of a minute of time or of an angular degree; (*pl*) (*inf*) another helping of food. • *adv* in the second place, group, etc. • *vt* (*a motion, resolution, etc*) to support.

secondary *adj* subordinate; second in rank or importance; in the second stage; relating to secondary school. • *n* that which is secondary.

secondary school *n* a school between primary school and college or university.

second class *n* the class next to the first in a classification. • *adj* (**second-class**) inferior, mediocre; (*seating, accommodation*) next in price and quality to first class; (*mail*) less expensive and handled more slowly (than first class).

second-hand *adj* bought after use by another; not original.—*also adv.*

secondly *adv* in the second place.

second-rate *adj* of inferior quality.

second thought *n* a change in thought or decision after consideration.

secrecy *n* the state of being secret.

secret *adj* not made public; concealed from others. • *n* something hidden.—**secretly** *adv.*

secretary *n* a person employed to deal with correspondence, filing, telephone calls of another or of an association; the head of a state department.—**secretarial** *adj.*

secretive *adj* uncommunicative, reticent.

sect *n* a religious denomination.

section *n* the act of cutting; a division.

sector *n* a distinctive part (as of an economy).

secular *adj* having no connection with religion.

secure *adj* free from danger, safe; stable; firmly held or fixed; confident, assured (of). • *vt* to make safe; to fasten firmly; to protect; to confine; to gain possession of.—**securely** *adv.*

security *n* the state of being secure; a financial guarantee; a pledge for repayment, etc.

sedate[1] *adj* calm; composed.—**sedately** *adv.*

sedate[2] *vt* to calm by the administration of a sedative.

sedation *n* the condition of being calmed, esp by sedatives.

sedative *n* a drug with a soothing, calming effect. • *adj* having a soothing, calming effect.

sediment *n* matter that settles at the bottom of a liquid.

seduce *vt* to lead astray; to entice into unlawful sexual intercourse.—**seduction** *n.*

seductive *adj* enticing, alluring.

see[1] *vt* to perceive with the eyes; to grasp with intelligence; to take care (that). • *vi* to have the faculty of sight; to make inquiry; to understand.

see[2] *n* the diocese of a bishop.

seed *n* the small, hard part (ovule) of a plant from which a new plant grows; sperm or semen; (*tennis*) a seeded tournament player. • *vti* to sow (seed); (*tennis*) to arrange (a tournament) so that the best players cannot meet until later rounds.

seedling *n* a young plant raised from seed.

seedy *adj* out of sorts, indisposed; shabby.

seeing *n* vision, sight. • *adj* having sight. • *conj* in view of the fact that; since.

seek *vti* to search for; to try to find, obtain or achieve; (*with* to) to try to, to endeavour.

seem *vi* to appear (to be); to give the impression of.

seep *vi* to ooze gently, to leak through.

seer *n* a person who sees visions, a prophet.

seesaw *n* a plank balanced across a central support so that it is tilted up and down by a person sitting on each end; an up-and-down movement like this. • *vi* to move up and down; to fluctuate.

seethe *vi* to be very angry inwardly; to swarm (with people).

segment *n* a section; a portion.

segregate *vti* to set apart from others, to isolate; to separate racial or minority groups.

seize *vt* to grasp; to capture; to take hold of suddenly or forcibly; to attack or afflict suddenly. • *vi* (*machinery*) to become jammed.

seizure *n* the act of seizing; a sudden attack of illness, an apoplectic stroke.

seldom *adv* not often, rarely.

select *vti* to choose or pick out. • *adj* exclusive.

selection *n* the act of selecting; what is selected.

selective *adj* having the power of selection; highly specific in activity or effect.

self *n* the identity, character, etc, of any person or thing; one's own person as distinct from all others. • *adj* (*colour*) uniform.

self-assured *adj* confident.

self-catering *adj* catering for oneself.

self-centred *adj* preoccupied with one's own affairs.

self-coloured *adj* of a single colour.

self-confident *adj* sure of one's own powers.

self-conscious *adj* embarrassed or awkward in the presence of others, ill at ease.

self-contained *adj* complete in itself; showing self-control.

self-control *n* control of one's emotions, desires, etc, by the will.

self-defence *n* the act of defending oneself.

self-employed *adj* earning one's living in one's own business or profession.

self-evident *adj* evident without proof.

self-indulgence *n* undue gratification of one's desires, appetites or whims.

self-interest *n* regard to one's own advantage.

selfish *adj* chiefly concerned with oneself; lacking consideration for others.—**selfishly** *adv.*

selfless *adj* unselfish.—**selflessness** *n.*

self-portrait *n* an artist's or author's painting or account of himself or herself.

self-possessed *adj* cool and collected.

self-reliant *adj* relying on one's own powers.

self-respect *n* proper respect for oneself, one's standing and dignity.

self-righteous *adj* thinking oneself better than others.—**self-righteousness** *n.*

self-sacrifice *n* the sacrifice of one's own welfare, etc, to secure that of others.

self-satisfied *adj* smugly conceited.

self-service *adj* serving oneself in a cafe, shop, filling station, etc.

self-sufficient *adj* supporting oneself (e.g. in growing food) without the help of others.

sell vt to exchange for money; to promote. • vi (with out) to betray for money or reward.

sellout n a show, game, etc, for which all the tickets are sold; (inf) a betrayal.

semaphore n a system of visual signalling using the operator's arms, flags, etc.

semen n the fluid that carries sperm in men and male animals.

semibreve n (mus) a note equal to two minims.

semicircle n half of a circle.

semicolon n the punctuation mark (;) of intermediate value between a comma and a full stop.

semiconscious adj not fully conscious.

semi-detached adj (house) with another joined to it on one side.—also n.

semifinal n the match or round before the final in a knockout tournament.

seminar n a group of students engaged in study or research under supervision.

semiquaver n (mus) half a quaver.

semiskilled adj partly skilled or trained.

semitone n (mus) an interval equal to half a tone.

semolina n coarse particles of grain left after the sifting of wheat.

senate n a legislative or governing body; (with cap) the upper branch of a two-body legislature in France, the USA, etc.

senator n a member of a senate.

send vti to cause or enable to go; to dispatch (a message or messenger); to propel; (sl) to move (a person) to ecstasy; (with down) to expel from university; (with for) to order to be brought; to summon; (with up) (inf) to imitate or make fun of.—**sender** n.

send-off n a friendly demonstration at a departure.

senile adj of or relating to old age; weakened, esp mentally, by old age.—**senility** n.

senior adj higher in rank; longer in service; older (when distinguishing between father and son with the same first name). • n one's elder or superior in standing.

seniority n status, priority, etc, in a given job.

sensation n an effect on the senses; a thrill; a state of excited interest; the cause of this.

sensational adj exciting violent emotions; melodramatic.—**sensationally** adv.

sensationalism n the use of sensational writing, language, etc.—**sensationalist** n.

sense n one of the five human and animal faculties by which objects are perceived: sight, hearing, smell, taste and touch; soundness of judgment; meaning. • vt to perceive.

senseless adj stupid, foolish; unconscious.

sensibility n (pl) sensitive awareness.

sensible adj having good sense or judgment.

sensitive adj having the power of sensation;

keenly perceptive; (skin) easily irritated; (wound, etc) still in a painful condition; easily hurt or shocked; highly responsive to slight changes.

sensitivity n the condition of being sensitive; awareness of changes or differences.

sensual adj relating to the senses rather than the mind; arousing sexual desire.

sensuous adj giving pleasure to the mind or body through the senses.

sentence n a court judgment; the punishment imposed; (gram) a series of words conveying a complete thought. • vt (a convicted person) to pronounce punishment on.

sentiment n a feeling or emotion; a tendency to be swayed by feeling rather than reason.

sentimental adj of or arising from feelings; foolishly emotional; nostalgic.

sentry n a soldier on guard to give warning of danger and to prevent unauthorised access.

separate vt to divide or part. • vi to go different ways. • adj divided; individual. • npl articles of clothing designed to be interchangeable with others to form various outfits.—**separately** adv.

separation n the act of separating; a formal arrangement of husband and wife to live apart.

septic adj infected by micro-organisms.

sequel n the continuation of a story begun in an earlier literary work, film, etc.

sequence n order of succession; a single, uninterrupted episode, as in a film.

sequin n a shiny round piece of metal or foil sewn on clothes for decoration.

serenade n music sung or played at night beneath a person's window, esp by a lover. • vt to entertain with a serenade.

serene adj calm; tranquil.—**serenity** n.

sergeant n a noncommissioned officer ranking above a corporal in the army, air force and marine corps; a police officer.

serial adj forming a series. • n a story presented in regular instalments with a connected plot.

series n (sing or pl)a succession of things connected by some likeness; a radio or television serial whose episodes have self-contained plots; a set of books issued by one publisher; (math) a progression of numbers or quantities according to a certain law.

serious adj grave, solemn, not frivolous; meaning what one says, sincere.—**seriously** adv.

sermon n a speech on religion or morals, esp by a clergyman; a long, serious talk of reproof.

serrated adj having an edge notched like the teeth of a saw.

serum n the watery part of bodily fluid, esp liquid that separates out from the blood when it coagulates.

servant n a personal or domestic attendant.

serve vt to work for; to do military or naval service (for); to be useful to; to meet the needs (of), (a *customer*) to wait upon; (*food*, *etc*) to hand round; (a *sentence*) to undergo. • vi to be enough. • n the act of serving in tennis, etc.

service n the state of being a servant; military employment or duty; attendance in a hotel, etc; a facility providing a regular supply of trains, etc; any religious ceremony; an overhaul of a vehicle; (*tennis*) the act or manner of serving. • vt to overhaul.

serviceable adj useful; durable.

serviceman n a member of the armed services.

serviette n a small napkin.

servile adj subservient; submissive.

session n the meeting of a court, legislature, etc; a period of study, classes, etc; a university year.

set vt to put in a specified place, condition, etc; (*trap for animals*) to fix; (*clock*, *etc*) to adjust; (*table*) to arrange for a meal; (*hair*) to fix in a desired style; (*bone*)to put into normal position, etc; (*gems*) to mount; to fit (words to music or music to words); (*type*) to arrange for printing. • vi to become firm, hard or fixed; (*sun*) to sink below the horizon; (*with* **off**) to show up by contrast; (*with* **on**) to urge (as a dog) to attack or pursue; (*with* **up**) to erect; to establish, to found. • adj fixed, established; rigid, firm; obstinate. • n a number of persons or things classed or belonging together; a group, a clique; the scenery for a play, film, etc; assembled equipment for radio or television reception, etc; (*math*) the totality of points, numbers or objects that satisfy a given condition; (*tennis*) a series of games forming a unit of a match; a badger's burrow (—*also* **sett**).

setback n misfortune.

settee n a sofa for two people.

setting n a background, scene; a mounting, as for a gem; the music for a song, etc.

settle vti to put in order; to pay (an account); to make or become quiet or calm; to establish or become established in a place, business, home, etc; to colonise (a country).

settlement n an arrangement; a newly established colony; subsidence (of buildings).

settler n an early colonist.

set-up n the plan, makeup, etc, of equipment used in an organisation; the details of a situation, plan, etc.

seven adj, n one more than six. • n the symbol for this (7, VII, vii).

seventeen adj, n one more than sixteen. • n the symbol for this (17, XVII, xvii).—**seventeenth** adj.

seventh adj, n next after sixth; one of seven equal parts of a thing.

seventy adj, n seven times ten. • n the symbol for this (70, LXX, lxx).—**seventieth** adj.

sever vti to separate, to divide into parts; to break off.—**severance** n.

several adj more than two but not very many; separate, distinct. • pron (*with pl vb*) a few.

severe adj harsh; very strict; exacting, difficult; not slight.—**severely** adv.—**severity** n.

sew vti to stitch together with needle and thread; to make, mend, etc, by sewing; (*with* **up**) (*inf*) to make sure of success in.—**sewing** n.

sewage n waste matter carried away in a sewer.

sewer n an underground pipe or drain for carrying off liquid waste matter, etc.

sewing machine n a machine for sewing usu driven by an electric motor.

sex n the characteristics that distinguish male and female organisms on the basis of their reproductive function; either of the two categories (male and female) so distinguished; (*inf*) sexual intercourse.

sexual adj of sex.—**sexually** adv.

sexy adj (*inf*) exciting sexual desire.

shabby adj (*clothes*) threadbare, worn or dirty; dilapidated; (*act*, *trick*) mean, shameful.

shack n a small, crudely built house or cabin.

shackle n a metal fastening, usu in pairs, for the wrists or ankles of a prisoner; anything that restrains freedom. • vt to hamper, to impede.

shade n relative darkness; shadow; a screen protecting from bright light; a place sheltered from the sun; degree of darkness of a colour, esp when made by the addition of black; a minute difference; (*pl: sl*) sunglasses. • vti to screen from light; to pass by degrees into another colour.

shadow n a patch of shade; darkness, obscurity; the dark shape of an object produced on a surface by intercepted light; an inseparable companion; a slight trace. • vt to cast a shadow over; to cloud; to follow and watch, esp in secret. • adj (*opposition party*) matching a function or position of the party in power.

shadowy adj full of shadows; dim, indistinct.

shady adj sheltered from the sun; (*inf*) of doubtful honesty, disreputable.

shaft n a straight rod, a pole; a stem, a shank; a ray of light; a hole giving access to a mine; a vertical opening through a building, as for a lift.

shaggy adj (*hair*, *fur*, *etc*) long and unkempt.

shake vti to move to and fro with quick short motions, to tremble or vibrate; to jar or jolt; to brandish; to make or become unsteady; to weaken; to unnerve; to clasp (another's hand) as in greeting; (*with* **off**) to get rid of; (*with* **up**) to upset. • n a jolt; a shock; (*pl: inf*) a convulsive trembling.

shake-up n an extensive reorganisation.

shaky adj unsteady; infirm; unreliable.

shale n a kind of clay rock like slate but softer.

shall vb aux used formally to express the future in the 1st person and determination or necessity in the 2nd and 3rd person.

shallow adj having little depth; superficial. • n a shallow area in otherwise deep water.

sham n a pretence; a person or thing that is a fraud. • adj counterfeit; fake.

shambles n a scene of great disorder.

shame n a painful emotion arising from guilt or impropriety; disgrace, dishonour. • vti to bring disgrace on; to force by shame (into).

shamefaced adj sheepish; ashamed.

shameful adj disgraceful; outrageous.

shameless adj immodest; impudent, brazen.

shampoo n a liquid cleansing agent for washing the hair; the process of washing the hair.

shamrock n a three-leaved cloverlike plant, the national emblem of Ireland.

shandy n beer diluted with lemonade.

shanty[1] n a crude hut built from corrugated iron or cardboard.

shanty[2] n a rhythmic working song sung by sailors.

shape n the external appearance, outline or contour of a thing; a figure; a mould or pattern; (inf) condition. • vt to give shape to; to model, to mould; (with up) to develop to a definite or satisfactory form.

shapeless adj lacking definite form.

shapely adj well-proportioned.

share n an allotted portion, a part; one of the parts into which a company's capital stock is divided, entitling the holder to a share of profits. • vti to distribute, to have or experience in common with others.

shareholder n a holder of shares in a company.

shark n a large voracious marine fish.

sharp adj having a keen edge or fine point; pointed, not rounded; clear-cut; piercing; cutting; mentally acute; (mus) raised a semitone in pitch. • adv punctually; (mus) above the right pitch. • n (mus) a note that is a semitone higher than the note denoted by the same letter; the symbol for this (#).—**sharply** adv.—**sharpness** n.

sharpen vti to make or become sharp.

sharpener n something that sharpens.

shatter vti to reduce to fragments suddenly; to smash; to damage severely.

shave vti to remove facial or body hair with a razor; to cut away thin slices, to pare. • n the act or process of shaving; a narrow escape or miss.

shaven adj shaved.

shaver n one who shaves; an instrument for shaving, esp an electrical one.

shaving n the act of using a razor; a thin slice of wood, metal, etc, shaved off.

shawl n a large square or oblong cloth worn as a covering for the head or shoulders or as a wrapping for a baby.

she pron the female person or thing named before or in question. • n a female person or animal.

sheaf n a bundle of reaped corn bound together; a collection of papers, etc, tied in a bundle.

shear vti to clip or cut (through); to remove (a sheep's fleece) by clipping. • npl large scissors; a tool for cutting hedges, etc.

sheath n a close-fitting cover, esp for a blade; a condom.

shed[1] n a hut for storing garden tools.

shed[2] vt (tears) to let fall; (skin, etc) to cast off. • n a parting in the hair.

sheep n a cud-chewing four-footed animal with a fleece and edible flesh called mutton.

sheepdog n a dog trained to tend sheep.

sheepish adj bashful, embarrassed.

sheepskin n the skin of a sheep, esp with the fleece.

sheer[1] adj pure, unmixed; downright, utter; extremely steep; (fabric) transparent.

sheer[2] vt to cause to deviate from a course.

sheet n a broad thin piece of any material, as glass, plywood, metal, etc; a large rectangular piece of cloth used as inner bed clothes; a single piece of paper; a broad, flat expanse.

sheet lightning n lightning that has the appearance of a broad sheet due to reflection and diffusion by the clouds and sky.

sheikh n an Arab chief.

shelf n a board fixed horizontally on a wall or in a cupboard for holding articles.

shell n a hard outside covering of a nut, egg, shellfish, etc; an explosive projectile; an external framework. • vt to remove the shell from.

shellfish n an aquatic animal with a shell.

shelter n a structure that protects, esp against weather; a place giving protection, a refuge; protection. • vti to give shelter to; to take shelter.

shelve vti to place on a shelf; to put aside.

shepherd n a person who looks after sheep. • vt to look after; to marshal in a particular direction.

shepherd's pie n a dish of minced meat covered with a mashed potato crust.

sheriff n in US, the chief law enforcement officer of a county; in Scotland, a judge in an intermediate law court; in England and Wales, the chief officer of the Crown.

sherry n a fortified wine originally made in Spain.

Shetland pony n a breed of small sturdy pony with a shaggy mane.

shield n a broad piece of armour carried for defence; a protective covering; a trophy in the shape of a shield. • vti to defend; to protect.

shift *vti* to change position (of); to transfer. • *n* a change in position; a group of people working in relay with others; the time worked by them.

shifty *adj* artful, tricky; evasive.

shilling *n* a former unit of currency of the UK, worth one twentieth of a pound.

shillyshally *vi* to vacillate, to hesitate.

shimmer *vi* to glisten softly, to glimmer.

shin *n* the front part of the leg from the knee to the ankle. • *vi* (*with* **up**) to climb (a pole, etc) by gripping with legs and hands.

shine *vti* to emit light; to be bright, to glow; to direct the light of. • *n* a lustre, a gloss.

shingle[1] *n* a thin wedge-shaped roof tile.

shingle[2] *n* waterworn pebbles as on a beach.

shingles *npl* a virus disease marked by a painful rash of red spots on the skin.

shiny *adj* glossy, polished; worn smooth.

ship *n* a large vessel navigating deep water. • *vti* to transport by any carrier.

shipbuilder *n* a company that constructs ships.

shipping *n* the business of transporting goods.

shipshape *adj* in good order, tidy.

shipwreck *n* the loss of a vessel at sea; the remains of a wrecked ship. • *vti* to destroy by shipwreck.

shipyard *n* a yard or shed where ships are built.

shirk *vti* to neglect or avoid work; to refuse to face (duty, danger, etc).—**shirker** *n*.

shirt *n* a sleeved garment of cotton, etc, for the upper body, typically having a fitted collar and cuffs and front buttons.

shiver[1] *n* a small fragment, a splinter.

shiver[2] *vi* to tremble with cold or fear.

shoal *n* a large number of fish swimming together.

shock[1] *n* a shaggy mass of hair.

shock[2] *n* a violent impact; a sudden disturbance to the emotions; the event causing this; the nerve sensation caused by an electrical charge through the body. • *vt* to outrage, horrify.

shock absorber *n* a device, as on the springs of a car, that absorbs the force of bumps and jars.

shocking *adj* scandalous; very bad.

shoddy *adj* made of inferior material.

shoe *n* an outer covering for the foot not enclosing the ankle. • *vt* to provide with shoes.

shoehorn *n* a curved piece of plastic, metal or horn used for easing the heel into a shoe.

shoelace *n* a cord that passes through eyelets in a shoe and is tied to keep the shoe on the foot.

shoetree *n* a block of wood, plastic or metal for preserving the shape of a shoe.

shoot *vt* to discharge or fire (a gun etc); to hit or kill with a bullet, etc; (*a film scene*) to photograph; (*sport*) to kick or drive (a ball, etc) at goal; (*with* **down**) to disprove (an argument). • *vi* to move swiftly; to attack or kill indiscrimi-

nately. • *n* a shooting trip; a new growth or sprout.

shooting *n* the act of firing a gun or letting off an arrow.

shooting star *n* a meteor.

shop *n* a building where retail goods are sold or services provided; the details and technicalities of one's own work, and talk about these. • *vti* to visit shops to examine or buy; (*sl*) to inform on (a person) to the police; (*with* **around**) to hunt for the best buy.

shop floor *n* the part of a factory where goods are manufactured; the work force employed there, usu unionised.

shopkeeper *n* a person who owns a shop.

shoplifting *n* stealing from a shop during shopping hours.—**shoplifter** *n*.

shopper *n* a person who shops.

shopping *n* the act of shopping; the goods bought.

shopping centre *n* a complex of shops, restaurants and service establishments.

shopsoiled *adj* faded, etc, from being on display in a shop.

shop steward *n* a union member elected to negotiate with management on behalf of his colleagues.

shore[1] *n* land beside the sea; beach.

shore[2] *n* a prop or beam used for support. • *vt* to prop (up), to support with a shore.

short *adj* not measuring much; brief; curt; abrupt; less than the correct amount; (*pastry*) crisp or flaky; (*drink*) undiluted, neat. • *n* (*pl*) trousers not covering the knee; a short circuit.

shortage *n* a deficiency.

shortbread *n* a rich, crumbly biscuit made with much butter.

short-circuit *n* the deviation of an electric current by a path of small resistance.

shortcoming *n* a defect or inadequacy.

short cut *n* a shorter route.

shorten *vt* to make short or shorter.

shorthand *n* a method of rapid writing using signs or contractions.

short-lived *adj* not lasting or living for long.

shortly *adv* soon; rudely.

short-sighted *adj* not able to see well at a distance; lacking foresight.

shortwave *n* a radio wave 60 metres or less in length.

shot *n* the act of shooting; an attempt; small lead pellets for a shotgun; a marksman; a photograph or a continuous film sequence.

shotgun *n* a smooth-bore gun for firing small shot at close range.

should *vb aux* used to express obligation, duty or probability, or a future condition.

shoulder *n* the joint connecting the arm with the

trunk; the strip of land bordering a road. • *vti* to assume responsibility; to jostle.

shoulder blade *n* the large flat triangular bone on either side of the back part of the human shoulder.

shout *n* a loud call; a yell. • *vti* to call loudly.

shove *vti* to push; to jostle. • *n* a forceful push.

shovel *n* an broad tool like a scoop with a long handle for moving loose material. • *vt* to move or lift with a shovel.

show *vti* to present to view, to exhibit; to demonstrate, to make clear; to prove; to manifest, to disclose; to direct, to guide; to appear, to be visible; (*with off*) to display to advantage; to try to attract admiration; to behave pretentiously; (*with up*) to put in an appearance, to arrive; to expose to ridicule; a display, an exhibition; an entertainment; a theatrical performance; a radio or television programme.

show business *n* the entertainment industry.— *also* **show biz**.

showdown *n* (*inf*) a final conflict.

shower *n* a brief period of rain, hail or snow; a similar fall, as of tears, meteors, arrows, etc; a method of cleansing in which the body is sprayed with water from above; a wash in this. • *vt* to pour copiously; to sprinkle; to bestow (with gifts). • *vi* to cleanse in a shower.

showjumping *n* the competitive riding of horses to demonstrate their skill in jumping.

showroom *n* a room where goods for sale are displayed.

shrapnel *n* an artillery shell filled with small pieces of metal that scatter on impact.

shred *n* a strip cut or torn off; a scrap. • *vt* to cut or tear into small pieces.

shrewd *adj* astute, having common sense.

shriek *n* a loud, shrill cry. • *vti* to screech.

shrill *adj* high-pitched and piercing.

shrimp *n* a small edible shellfish.

shrine *n* a container for sacred relics.

shrink *vti* to become smaller, wetting, etc; to recoil (from). • *n* (*sl*) a psychiatrist.

shrinkage *n* contraction; diminution.

shrivel *vti* to dry up and become wrinkled.

shroud *n* a burial cloth; anything that envelops or conceals. • *vt* to envelop or conceal.

shrub *n* a woody plant smaller than a tree with several stems rising from the same root.

shrubbery *n* an area of land planted with shrubs.

shrug *vti* to draw up and contract (the shoulders) as a sign of doubt, indifference, etc; (*with off*) to brush aside. • *n* the act of shrugging.

shrunken *adj* shrivelled, pinched; reduced.

shudder *vi* to shiver; to feel strong repugnance. • *n* a convulsive shiver of the body; a vibration.

shuffle *vt* to scrape (the feet) along the ground; (*playing cards*) to change the order of, to mix.

shun *vt* to keep away from.

shunt *vti* (*trains*) to switch from one track to another.

shut *vti* to close; (*with down*) to (cause to) stop working or operating; (*with in*) to confine; (*with out*) to exclude; (*with up*) to confine; (*inf*) to stop talking.

shutdown *n* a stoppage of work or activity, as in a factory.

shutter *n* a movable cover for a window; a flap device for regulating the exposure of light to a camera lens.

shuttle *n* a device in a loom for holding the weft thread and carrying it between the warp threads; a bus, aircraft, etc, making back-and-forth trips over a short route.

shuttlecock *n* a cork stuck with feathers, or a plastic imitation, hit with a racket in badminton.

shy *adj* very self-conscious, timid; wary (of). • *vi* to move suddenly, as when startled.

Siamese cat *n* a domestic shorthaired cat with a fawn or grey coat, darker ears, paws, tail and face, and blue eyes.

sick *adj* unhealthy, ill; having nausea, vomiting; thoroughly tired (of); disgusted by; (*inf*) of humour, sadistic, gruesome.—**sickness** *n*.

sick bay *n* an area in a ship used as a hospital; a room used for the treatment of the sick.

sicken *vti* to show signs of illness; to nauseate.

sickening *adj* disgusting.

sickle *n* a tool with a crescent-shaped blade for cutting tall grasses.

sick leave *n* absence from work due to illness.

sickly *adj* inclined to be ill; unhealthy; pale.

side *n* a line or surface bounding anything; the left or right part of the body; the top or underneath surface; the slope of a hill; a party or faction; a team. • *adj* towards or at the side, lateral. • *vi* to associate with a particular faction.

sideboard *n* a long table or cabinet for holding cutlery, crockery, etc; (*pl*) two strips of hair growing down a man's cheeks.

side effect *n* a secondary and usu adverse effect, as of a drug or medical treatment.

sidelight *n* a light on the side of a car, etc.

sideline *n* a subsidiary interest.

sidelong *adj* oblique, not direct.

side-saddle *n* a saddle that enables a rider to sit with both feet on the same side of a horse.

sideshow *n* a minor attraction at a fair, etc.

sidetrack *vt* to prevent action by diversionary tactics.

sideways *adj, adv* towards or from one side.

siding *n* a short line beside a main railway track for use in shunting.

sidle *vi* to move sideways, esp to edge along.

siege *n* the surrounding of a fortified place to cut off supplies and compel its surrender.

sieve *n* a utensil with a meshed wire bottom for sifting and straining. • *vt* to put through a sieve.

sift *vti* to separate coarser parts from finer with a sieve; to sort out.

sigh *vti* to draw deep audible breath as a sign of weariness, relief, etc; to pine or lament (for).

sight *n* the act or faculty of seeing; what is seen or is worth seeing, a spectacle; a view or glimpse; range of vision; a device on a gun, etc, to guide the eye in aiming it; (*inf*) anything that looks unpleasant, odd, etc. • *vti* to catch sight of.

sightseeing *n* the viewing or visiting of places of interest.—**sightseer** *n*.

sign *n* a mark or symbol; a gesture; an indication, trace or symptom (of); a board or placard with publicly displayed information. • *vi* to append one's signature. • *vt* to engage by written contract; to write one's name on; to communicate by sign language.

signal *n* a sign, device or gesture to intimate a warning or to give information, esp at a distance; a message so conveyed; a semaphore system used by railways; in radio, etc, the electrical impulses transmitted or received. • *vti* to make a signal (to).

signature *n* a person's name written by himself or herself; the act of signing one's own name.

signature tune *n* a tune associated with a performer or a TV, radio programme, etc.

signet ring *n* a ring with a seal set in it.

significant *adj* full of meaning, esp a special or hidden one.—**significance** *n*.

silence *n* absence of sound; refusal to speak or make a sound. • *vt* to cause to be silent.

silencer *n* a device for reducing the noise of a vehicle exhaust or gun.

silent *adj* not speaking; noiseless.

silhouette *n* the outline of a shape against light or a lighter background; a solid outline drawing, usu in solid black on white, esp of a profile.

silk *n* a fibre produced by silkworms; lustrous textile cloth, thread or a garment made of silk.

silky *adj* soft and smooth like silk; glossy.

silly *adj* lacking in sense or judgment.

silt *n* a fine-grained sandy sediment carried or deposited by water.

silver *n* a ductile, malleable, greyish-white metallic element used in jewellery, cutlery, tableware, coins, etc; a lustrous, greyish white. • *adj* made of or plated with silver; (*hair*) grey; marking the 25th in a series.

silver paper *n* a metallic paper coated or laminated to resemble silver.

silver plate *n* a plating of silver.

silversmith *n* a worker in silver.

similar *adj* having a resemblance to, like.

simile *n* a figure of speech likening one thing to another by the use of like, as, etc.

simmer *vti* to boil gently; to be in a state of suppressed rage or laughter.

simple *adj* single, uncompounded; plain, not elaborate; clear, not complicated; easy to do, understand or solve; sheer, mere.

simplicity *n* the quality or state of being simple; absence of complications; easiness; lack of ornament, plainness, restraint; artlessness; directness; guilelessness, naivety.

simplify *vt* to make easy to understand.

simply *adv* in a simple way; absolutely.

simulate *vt* to pretend to have or feel, to feign; (*conditions*) to reproduce in order to conduct an experiment.

simulator *n* a device that simulates specific conditions in order to test actions or reactions.

simultaneous *adj* done at the same time.

sin *n* an offence against a religious or moral principle; transgression of the law of God; a misdeed, a fault. • *vi* to commit a sin.

since *adv* from then until now. • *prep* during or continuously from (then) until now; after. • *conj* from the time that; because, seeing that.

sincere *adj* genuine, real.—**sincerely** *adv*.

sincerity *n* the quality of being sincere.

sinew *n* a cord of fibrous tissue, a tendon.

sinful *adj* guilty of sin, wicked.

sing *vti* to utter (words) with musical modulations; (*a song*) to perform.

singe *vt* to burn slightly; to scorch.

single *adj* one only, not double; individual; composed of one part; alone, sole; separate; unmarried; for one. • *n* a single ticket; a game between two players; a record with one tune on each side. • *vt* (*with* out) to pick out, to select.

single file *n* a single column of persons or things, one behind the other.

single-handed *adj*, *adv* unaided.

single-minded *adj* having only one aim.

singlet *n* a vest.

singly *adv* alone; one by one.

singular *adj* remarkable; (*gram*) referring to only one person or thing. • *n* (*gram*) the singular number or form of a word.

sinister *adj* ominous; evil-looking; wicked.

sink *vti* to go under the surface or to the bottom (of a liquid); to submerge in water; to go down slowly; to invest; (*with* in) to penetrate; (*inf*) to be understood in full. • *n* a basin with an outflow pipe, usu in a kitchen.

sinner *n* a person who sins.

sinuous *adj* curving; winding; tortuous.

sinus *n* an air cavity in the skull that opens in the nasal cavities.

sip *vti* to drink in small mouthfuls. • *n* the act of sipping; the quantity sipped.

siphon *n* a bent tube for drawing off liquids from a higher to a lower level by atmospheric pressure; a bottle with an internal tube and tap at the top for aerated water. • vt to draw off with a siphon.

sir n a title of respect used to address a man in speech or correspondence; (*with cap*) a title preceding the first name of a knight or baronet.

siren n a device producing a loud wailing sound as a warning signal; a seductive woman.

sirloin n the upper part of a loin of beef.

sirocco n a hot, oppressive wind that blows across southern Europe from North Africa.

sister n a female sibling, a daughter of the same parents; a senior nurse.

sister-in-law n the sister of a husband or wife; the wife of a brother.

sisterly adj like a sister, kind, affectionate.

sit vti to rest oneself on the buttocks, as on a chair; (*court*) to be in session; to pose, as for a portrait; to be located; to take an examination; to take care of a child, pet, etc, while the parents or owners are away; (*with* up) to straighten the back while sitting.

site n a space occupied or to be occupied by a building. • vt to locate, to place.

sit-in n a strike in which the strikers refuse to leave the premises; civil disobedience in which demonstrators occupy a public place and refuse to leave voluntarily.

sitting n a period of being seated, as for a meal, a portrait; a session, as of a court.

sitting room n a parlour.

situation n a place; a state of affairs; a job.

sit-up n an exercise of sitting up from a prone position without using hands or legs.

six adj, n one more than five. • n the symbol for this (6, VI, vi).

sixteen adj, n one more than fifteen. • n the symbol for this (16, XVI, xvi).—**sixteenth** adj.

sixth n one of six equal parts of a thing; (*mus*) an interval of six diatonic degrees; the sixth tone of a diatonic scale. • adj next after fifth.

sixty n six times ten. • n the symbol for this (60, LX, lx).—**sixtieth** adj.

sizable, sizeable adj of some size; large.

size[1] n magnitude; the dimensions or proportions of something; a graduated measurement, as of clothing or shoes. • vt to sort according to size; (*with* up) (*inf*) to make an estimate of.

size[2] n a thin pasty substance used to glaze paper, stiffen cloth, etc.

sizzle vti to make a hissing spluttering noise, as of frying; to be extremely hot.

skate[1] n a steel blade attached to a boot for gliding on ice; a roller skate. • vi to move on skates.

skate[2] n an edible fish of the ray family with a broad, flat body and short, spineless tail.

skateboard n a short, oblong board with two wheels at each end for standing on and riding.

skeleton n the bony framework of the body of a human, an animal or plant; the bones separated from flesh and preserved in their natural position; a supporting structure, a framework; an outline, an abstract; something shameful kept secret. • adj (*staff, crew, etc*) reduced to the lowest possible level.—**skeletal** adj.

sketch n a rough drawing, quickly made; a preliminary draft; a short literary piece or essay; a short humorous item for a revue, etc; a brief outline. • vti to make a sketch (of); to plan roughly.

sketchy adj incomplete; vague; inadequate.

skewer n a long wooden or metal pin on which pieces of meat and vegetables are cooked. • vt to pierce and fasten on a skewer.

ski n a long narrow runner of wood, metal or plastic that is fastened to a boot for moving across snow; a water-ski. • vi to travel on skis.

skid vti to slide without rotating; to slip sideways; (*vehicle*) to slide sideways out of control.

skilful adj having skill; proficient, adroit.

skill n proficiency; expertness, dexterity; a developed aptitude or ability; a type of work or craft requiring specialist training.

skilled adj fully trained, expert.

skim vti to remove (cream, scum) from the surface of; to glide lightly over; to read superficially.

skimp vti to stint; to be sparing or frugal (with).

skimpy adj small in size; inadequate, scant.

skin n the tissue forming the outer covering of the body; the rind of a fruit; a film on the surface of a liquid. • vti to remove the skin from.

skin-deep adj superficial.

skin diving n the sport of swimming underwater with scuba equipment.—**skin-diver** n.

skinny adj very thin.

skip[1] vti to leap or hop lightly over; to keep jumping over a rope as it is swung under one; to pass over, esp in reading.

skip[2] n a large metal container for holding building debris.

skipper n the captain of a boat, aircraft or team.

skipping rope n a light rope that is swung over the head and under the feet while jumping.

skirmish n a minor fight in a war; a conflict.

skirt n a woman's garment that hangs from the waist; the lower part of a dress or coat. • vti to border; to move along the edge (of); to evade.

skirting board n a narrow panel of wood at the foot of an interior wall.

skit n a short humorous sketch, as in the theatre.

ski tow n a motor-driven device that pulls skiers uphill.

skittles n a game in which a wooden or plastic bottle-shaped pin is knocked down by a ball.—also **ninepins**.

skulk vi to move in a stealthy manner; to lurk.

skull n the bony casing enclosing the brain.

skunk n a small black-and-white mammal that emits a foul-smelling liquid when frightened.

sky n the apparent vault over the earth.

skylight n a window in the roof or ceiling.

skyscraper n a very tall building.

skyward adj, adv towards the sky.

slab n a flat, broad, thick piece.

slack adj loose, relaxed, not tight. • n the part (of a rope, etc) that hangs loose; (pl) trousers for casual wear. • vti to be lazy.—**slackness** n.

slacken vti to make or become less active, brisk, etc; to loosen or relax, as a rope.

slag n the waste product from the smelting of metals..

slam vti to shut with a loud noise; (inf) to criticise severely. • n a bang; (bridge) the taking of 12 or 13 tricks.

slander n a false and malicious statement about another. • vt to utter a slander about, to defame.

slang n words or expressions used in familiar speech but not regarded as standard English.

slant vti to incline, to slope; to tell in such way as to have a bias. • n a slope; a bias.

slap n a smack with the open hand. • vt to strike with something flat.

slapdash adj careless; haphazard.

slapstick n boisterous humour of a knockabout kind.

slash vti to cut gashes in, to slit; to strike fiercely (at) with a sword, etc; to reduce (prices) sharply. • n a cutting blow; a long slit, a gash.

slate[1] vt to criticise or punish severely.

slate[2] n a fine-grained rock easily split into thin layers; a flat plate of this used in roofing.

slaughter n the butchering of animals for food; a wholesale killing, a massacre.—also vt.

slaughterhouse n a place where animals are slaughtered, an abattoir.

slave n a person without freedom or personal rights, who is legally owned by another; a person under domination, esp of a habit or vice.

slavery n the condition of being a slave.

sledge n a framework on runners for travelling over snow or ice. • vt to go by sledge.

sledgehammer n a large, heavy hammer for two hands.

sleek adj smooth, glossy; plausible.

sleep n a natural, regularly recurring rest for the body, with little or no consciousness; a period spent sleeping. • vti to rest in a state of sleep; to provide beds for; (with in) to sleep on the premises; to sleep too long in the morning; (with on) to have a night's rest before making a decision; (with off) to get rid of by sleeping; (with with) to have sexual relations with.

sleeper n a person or thing that sleeps; a sleeping car.

sleeping bag n a padded bag for sleeping in, esp outdoors.

sleeping car n a railway carriage with berths.

sleeping pill n a pill that induces sleep.

sleepwalker n a person who walks while asleep.

sleepy adj drowsy; tired.

sleet n snow or hail mixed with rain.

sleeve n the part of a garment enclosing the arm; an open-ended cover, esp for a record.

sleeveless adj (garment) without sleeves.

sleigh n a light vehicle on runners for travelling over snow; a sledge.

sleight of hand n manual dexterity, such as in conjuring or juggling.

slender adj thin; slim; slight; scanty.

slice n a thin flat piece cut from something; a wedge-shaped piece (of cake, pie, etc); a broad knife for serving fish, cheese, etc; (golf) a stroke that makes the ball curl to the right. • vt to cut into slices; to strike (a ball) so that it curves.

slick adj clever, deft; insincere; wily. • n a patch or area of oil floating on water. **slide** vti to move along in constant contact with a smooth surface, as on ice, to glide; to move (an object) unobtrusively. • n a chute; the glass plate of a microscope; a photographic transparency.

slide rule n a ruler with a graduated sliding part for making calculations.

sliding scale n a schedule for automatically varying one thing (e.g. wages) according to the fluctuations of another thing (e.g. cost of living).

slight adj small; trifling; slim; frail, flimsy. • vt to disregard as insignificant; to snub. • n intentional indifference or neglect.

slightly adv to a small degree; slenderly.

slim adj slender, not stout; slight. • vti to make or become slim.

slime n a sticky slippery, half-liquid substance.

sling n a loop of leather with a string attached for hurling stones; a bandage suspended from the neck for supporting an injured arm. • vt to throw; to hurl.

slip[1] vti to slide, to glide; to lose one's foothold and slide; to go or put quietly or quickly; (with up) to make a slight mistake. • n a mistake, a lapse; a woman's undergarment.

slip[2] n a small piece of paper.

slipped disc n a ruptured cartilaginous disc between vertebrae.

slipper n a light, soft, shoe worn in the house.

slippery adj so smooth as to cause slipping; difficult to hold or catch; evasive, shifty.

slip road n a road that gives access to a main road or motorway.

slipshod adj slovenly, careless.

slip-up n (inf) an error, a lapse.

slipway n an inclined surface for launching or repairing ships; a sloped landing stage.

slit vt to cut open or tear lengthways; to slash or tear into strips. • n a long cut, a slash.

slither vi to slide, as on a loose or wet surface.

slog vti to hit hard and wildly; to work laboriously. • n a hard, boring spell of work.

slogan n a catchy phrase used in advertising or as a motto by a political party, etc.

slop n unappetising semi-liquid food; (pl) liquid kitchen refuse. • vti to spill.

slope n an inclined line or surface. • vti to slant.

sloppy adj (inf) sentimental; (inf) careless.

slot n a long narrow opening in a mechanism for inserting a coin, a slit. • vt to fit into a slot.

slot machine n a machine operated by the insertion of a coin, used for gambling or dispensing drinks, etc.

slouch vti to sit, stand or move in a drooping, slovenly way. • n (inf) an incompetent person.

slovenly adj untidy, dirty; careless.

slow adj moving at low speed; not quick in understanding; backward; (clock) behind in time. • vti (also with **down**) to reduce the speed (of).—**slowly** adv.

slow-motion adj denoting a filmed or taped scene with the original action slowed down.

sludge n soft mud or snow; sewage.

slug¹ n a mollusc resembling a snail but with no outer shell.

slug² n a small bullet; (inf) a hard blow; a drink of spirits. • vt (inf) to hit hard.

sluice n a gate regulating a flow of water.

slum n a squalid, rundown house; (usu pl) an overcrowded area characterised by poverty, etc. • vi to make do with less comfort.

slumber vi to sleep. • n a light sleep.

slump n a sudden fall in value or slackening in demand. • vi to fall or decline suddenly; to sink down heavily; to collapse; to slouch.

slur vti to pronounce or speak indistinctly; (letters, words) to run together; (mus) to produce by gliding without a break. • n (mus) a curved line over notes to be slurred.

slush n melting snow; (inf) sentimental language.—**slushy** adj.

slut n a slovenly or immoral woman.

sly adj secretively cunning.—**slyly** adv.

smack¹ n a taste; a distinctive smell or flavour. • vi to have a slight trace of something.

smack² vt to strike with the open hand.

small adj little in size, number, importance, etc. • n the narrow, curving part of the back.

smallpox n an acute contagious viral disease, now rare, causing the eruption of pustules that leave the skin scarred and pitted.

small talk n light, social conversation.

smart vi to cause a sharp, stinging pain; to feel distress. • adj clever, witty; fashionable; neatly dressed; (equipment, etc) capable of seemingly intelligent action through computer control; (bombs, missiles) guided to the target by lasers ensuring pinpoint accuracy.

smarten vti to make or become smart.

smash vti to break into pieces with noise or violence; to collide or move with force; to destroy or be destroyed. • n a violent, noisy breaking; a violent collision; (inf) a popular success.

smashing adj (inf) excellent.

smattering n a slight superficial knowledge.

smear vt to cover with anything greasy or sticky; to slander. • n a smudge; a slanderous attack; a deposit of blood, secretion, etc, on a glass slide for examination under a microscope.

smell n the sense by which odours are perceived with the nose; a scent or stench. • vti to have or perceive an odour.—**smelly** adj.

smile vti to express amusement, friendship, pleasure, etc, by a slight turning up of the corners of the mouth.—**also** n.

smirk vi to smile in an expression of smugness.

smith n a person who works in metal.

smock n a loose shirtlike outer garment.

smog n a mixture of fog and smoke.

smoke n a cloud or plume of gas and small particles emitted from a burning substance; any similar vapour; an act of smoking tobacco, etc. • vi to give off smoke; to (habitually) draw in and exhale the smoke of tobacco, etc. • vt to cure food by treating with smoke; to darken (e.g. glass) using smoke.

smoker n a person who habitually smokes.

smoky adj emitting smoke, esp excessively; filled with smoke; resembling smoke.

smooth adj having an even or flat surface; silky; not rough or lumpy; hairless; of even consistency. • vti to make smooth; to calm.

smother vt to stifle, suffocate; to hold back, suppress. • vi to undergo suffocation.

smoulder vi to burn slowly or without flame; (feelings) to linger on in a suppressed state.

smudge n a dirty or blurred spot or area. • vt to make a smudge; to smear; to blur. • vi to become smudged.

smug adj complacent, self-satisfied.

smuggle vti to import or export (goods) secretly without paying customs duties.—**smuggler** n.

smut n a speck or smudge of dirt, soot, etc; indecent talk, writing or pictures.—**smutty** adj.

snack n a light meal between regular meals.

snag n a tear, as in cloth; an unexpected or hidden difficulty.—**also** vt .

snail n a mollusc having a wormlike body and a spiral protective shell.

snake n limbless, scaly reptile with a long, tapering body.

snap vti (with **at**) to bite or grasp suddenly; (with **at**) to speak or utter sharply; to break suddenly. • *n* a sharp, cracking sound; a sudden spell of cold weather.

snappy *adj* brisk; lively; smart, fashionable.

snapshot *n* a photograph taken casually with a simple camera.

snare *n* a loop of string or wire for trapping birds or animals. • *vt* to trap using a snare.

snarl[1] *vi* to growl with bared teeth; to speak in a rough, angry manner.—*also n.*

snarl[2] *vti* to make or become entangled.

snatch *vt* to seize suddenly. • *n* a fragment.

sneak *vti* to move, act, etc, stealthily. • *n* (*inf*) a person who tells or informs on others.

sneer *vi* to show scorn or contempt by curling up the upper lip.—*also n.*

sneeze *vi* to expel air through the nose violently and audibly.—*also n.*

snide *adj* malicious.

sniff *vti* to inhale through the nose audibly.

snigger *vti* to laugh disrespectfully.—*also n.*

snip *vti* (*pt* **snipped**) to cut or clip with a single stroke of the scissors, etc. • *n* (*inf*) a bargain.

snipe *n* any of various birds with long straight flexible bills. • *vi* to shoot at individuals from a hidden position; to make sly criticisms of.

snippet *n* a scrap of information.

snob *n* a person who wishes to be associated with those of a higher social status while acting condescendingly to those whom he or she regards as inferior.—**snobbish** *adj.*

snooker *n* a game played on a billiard table with 15 red balls, 6 variously coloured balls and a white cue ball; a position in the game where a ball lies between the cue ball and target ball.

snoop *vi* (*inf*) to pry in a sneaking way. • *n* a person who pries into other people's business.

snooze *vi* (*inf*) to sleep lightly. • *n* (*inf*) a nap.

snore *vi* to breathe roughly and noisily while asleep.—*also n.*

snorkel *n* a breathing tube extending above the water, used in swimming just below the surface.

snort *vi* to exhale noisily through the nostrils. • *vt* to inhale (a drug) through the nose.

snout *n* the nose or muzzle of an animal.

snow *n* frozen water vapour in the form of white flakes. • *vi* to fall as snow.

snowball *n* snow pressed together in a ball for throwing. • *vi* to increase rapidly in size.

snowdrift *n* a bank of drifted snow.

snowfall *n* a fall of snow.

snowman *n* snow piled into the shape of a human figure.

snowplough *n* a vehicle designed for clearing away snow.

snub *vt* to insult by ignoring.

snuff[1] *n* a powdered preparation of tobacco inhaled through the nostrils.

snuff[2] *vt* to extinguish (a candle flame).

snug *adj* cosy; warm; close-fitting.

so *adv* in this way; to such an extent; very.

soak *vt* to submerge in a liquid; to absorb.

soap *n* a substance used with water to produce suds for washing; (*inf*) a soap opera.

soap opera *n* a drama broadcast in instalments and usu concerning the domestic and emotional lives of a group of people.

soar *vi* to rise high in the air; to increase.

sob *vi* to weep with convulsive gasps.

sober *adj* not drunk; serious and thoughtful. • *vt* (*often with* **up**) to make sober.

so-called *adj* commonly known as.

soccer *n* a football game played on a field by two teams of 11 players with a round ball.

sociable *adj* friendly; companionable.

social *adj* living or organised in a community, not solitary; relating to human beings living in society; sociable.—**socially** *adv.*

socialism *n* a political and economic theory advocating state ownership of the means of production and distribution.—**socialist** *n.*

social science *n* the study of human social organisation and relationships using scientific methods.

social security *n* financial assistance for the unemployed, the disabled, etc.

social work *n* professional welfare services to aid the underprivileged in society.

society *n* the social relationships between human beings or animals organised collectively; an interest group or organisation; the fashionable or privileged members of a community.

sociology *n* the study of the development and structure of society and social relationships.

sock[1] *n* a kind of short stocking covering the foot and lower leg.

sock[2] *vt* (*sl*) to punch hard.—*also n.*

socket *n* a hollow part into which something is inserted, such as an eye, an electric plug, etc.

sod[1] *n* a lump of earth covered with grass.

sod[2] *n* (*sl*) an obnoxious person.

soda *n* sodium bicarbonate; soda water.

soda water *n* a fizzy drink made by charging water with carbon dioxide under pressure.

sodden *adj* completely soaked through.

sodium *n* a metallic element.

sofa *n* an upholstered couch or settee.

soft *adj* easily cut, shaped, etc; (*drinks*) nonalcoholic; lenient; (*sound*) gentle, low; (*drugs*) non-addictive.—**softly** *adv.*—**softness** *n.*

soften *vti* to make or become softer.

software *n* the programs used in computers.

soggy *adj* soaked with water; moist and heavy.

soil[1] *n* the earth in which plants grow.

soil[2] *vt* to make dirty or stained.

solar *adj* of the sun; powered by light or heat from the sun.

solder n a metal alloy used when melted to join or patch metal parts, etc.—also vti.

soldier n a person who serves in an army.

sole¹ n the underside of the foot or shoe.

sole² n a flatfish used as food.

sole³ adj only; exclusive.—**solely** adv.

solemn adj serious; formal.—**solemnly** adv.

solicitor n a lawyer.

solid adj not hollow; strongly constructed; neither liquid nor gaseous. • n a solid substance (not liquid or gas); a three-dimensional figure.

solidarity n unity of interest and action.

solidify vti to make or become solid.

solitaire n a single diamond.

solitary adj alone; only; single; lonely.

solitude n the state of being alone.

solo n a musical composition for one voice or instrument; a flight by a single person in an aircraft. • adv alone. • adj unaccompanied.

solstice n either of the two times in the year at which the sun is farthest from the equator (21 June and 21 December).

soluble adj capable of being dissolved.

solution n the act or process of answering a problem; the answer found; the dispersion of one substance in another, usu a liquid, so as to form a homogeneous mixture.

solve vt to work out the answer to.

solvent adj able to pay all debts. • n a liquid that dissolves substances.

sombre adj dark, dull; dismal.

some adj certain but not specified; of a certain unspecified quantity, etc; (inf) remarkable. • pron a certain unspecified quantity, number, etc.

somebody n an unspecified person; an important person.

someday adv at some future day or time.

somehow adv in a way not known.

someone n somebody.

someplace adv somewhere.

somersault n a roll head over heels along the ground or in mid-air.—also vi.

something n, pron a thing not definitely known, understood, etc; an important thing.

sometime adj former.

sometimes adv at times, now and then.

somewhat adv to some extent, degree, etc.

somewhere adv in, to or at some place not known or specified.

son n a male offspring.

song n a piece of music composed for the voice.

sonic adj of or involving sound waves.

son-in-law n a daughter's husband.

sonnet n a rhyming poem in a single stanza of fourteen lines.

soon adv in a short time; before long.

sooner or later adv eventually.

soot n a black powder produced from flames.

soothe vt to calm; to relieve (pain, etc).

sophisticated adj refined; worldly-wise; complex.—**sophistication** n.

soppy adj wet; (inf) sickly sentimental.

sorcerer n a magician or wizard.

sordid adj filthy, squalid; vile.

sore n a painful injury or wound. • adj painful.

sorely adv seriously, urgently.

sorrow n sadness; regret.—**sorrowful** adj.

sorry adj feeling sympathy or regret.

sort n a class, kind or variety. • vt to arrange according to kind.

SOS n an international signal code of distress; an urgent call for help or rescue.

souffle n a baked dish made light and puffy by adding beaten egg whites before baking.

soul n a person's spirit; the seat of the emotions.

soul-destroying adj extremely boring.

soulful adj expressing profound sentiment.

sound¹ adj healthy; free from injury or damage.

sound² n a narrow channel of water.

sound³ n vibrations transmitted through the air and detected by the ear; any audible noise. • vt to cause to make a sound.

sound⁴ vt to measure the depth of.

sound barrier n the increase in air resistance experienced by objects travelling close to the speed of sound.

sounding n measurement of the depth of water; a test, sampling, e.g. of public opinion.

soundproof adj unable to be penetrated by sound. • vt to make soundproof by insulation.

soundtrack n the sound accompanying a film.

soup n a liquid food made from boiling meat, fish, vegetables, etc, in water.

sour adj having a sharp, biting taste; bad-tempered. • vti to make or become sour.

source n an origin or cause; a person, book, etc, that provides information.

south n the direction to one's right when facing the direction of the rising sun; the region, country, etc, lying relatively in that direction. • adj, adv facing towards or situated in the south.

southeast n the point on a compass midway between south and east. • adj, adv at, towards or from the southeast.

southerly adj in, towards or from the south. • n a wind from the south.

southern adj in, towards or from the south.

southward adv towards the south.

southwest n the point on a compass midway between south and west. • adj, adv at, towards or from the southwest.

souvenir n a keepsake, a memento.

sovereign adj supreme in authority or rank; (country, etc) independent. • n a monarch.

sow¹ n an adult female pig.

sow² vt to plant or scatter seed on or in the ground.

soya bean n a type of bean (orig from Asia) used as a source of food and oil.

spa n a mineral spring.

space n the limitless three-dimensional expanse within which all objects exist; room; an unoccupied area or seat. • vt to arrange at intervals.

spacecraft n a vehicle for travel in outer space.

spacious adj large in extent; roomy.

spade¹ n a tool with a broad blade and a handle used for digging.

spade² n a black symbol resembling a stylised spearhead marking one of the four suits of playing cards; a card of this suit.

span n a unit of length equal to a hand's breadth (about 9 inches/23 cm); the full extent between any two limits, such as the ends of a bridge or arch. • vt to extend across.

spaniel n any of various breeds of dog with large drooping ears and a long silky coat.

Spanish adj of or pertaining to Spain. • n the language of Spain and Spanish Americans.

spank vt to slap with the flat of the hand.

spanner n a tool with a hole or (often adjustable) jaws to grip and turn nuts or bolts.

spare vt to refrain from harming or killing; to make (something) available (e.g. time). • adj kept as an extra, additional. • n a spare tyre.

sparing adj frugal.—**sparingly** adv.

spark n a fiery particle thrown off by burning material; a flash of light from an electrical discharge. • vt to activate. • vi to give off sparks.

sparrow n a small brownish songbird.

sparse adj spread out thinly; scanty.

spasm n a sudden, involuntary muscular contraction.

spasmodic adj intermittent.

spastic n a person who suffers from cerebral palsy. • adj affected by muscle spasm.

spate n a sudden outburst (as of words); a sudden flood.

spatter vti to scatter or spurt out in drops.

spatula n a tool with a broad, flexible blade for spreading or mixing foods, paints, etc.

spawn n a mass of eggs deposited by fish, frogs or amphibians. • vti to lay eggs.

speak vi to utter words; to talk; to deliver a speech.

speaker n a person who speaks, esp before an audience; a loudspeaker.

spear n a weapon with a long shaft and a sharp point; a blade or shoot (of grass, broccoli, etc).

special adj distinguished; uncommon; designed for a particular purpose; peculiar to one person or thing.—**specially** adv.

specialise vi to concentrate on a particular area of study or activity.—**specialisation** n.

specialist n a person who concentrates on a particular area of study or activity, esp in medicine.

speciality n a special skill; a special product.

species n a class of plants or animals with the same main characteristics.

specific adj explicit; definite.

specification n a requirement; (pl) detailed description of dimensions, materials, etc.

specify vt to state specifically.

specimen n (plant, animal, etc) an example of a particular species; a sample.

speck n a small spot; a fleck.

speckle n a small mark of a different colour.

spectacle n an unusual or interesting scene; a large public show; (pl) a pair of glasses.

spectacular adj impressive; astonishing.

spectator n an onlooker.

spectre n an apparition or ghost.

spectrum n the range of colour that is produced when a white light is passed through a prism; a broad range.

speculate vi to conjecture; to make investments in the hope of making a profit.—**speculation** n.—**speculator** n.

speculative adj of or based on speculation.

speech n the action or power of speaking; a public address or talk.

speechless adj silent, as from shock.

speed n quickness; (sl) an amphetamine drug. • vi to go quickly; to drive (a vehicle) at an illegally high speed.

speedometer n an instrument in a motor vehicle for measuring its speed.

speedway n the sport of racing light motorcycles around dirt or cinder tracks.

speedy adj quick; prompt.—**speedily** adv.

spell¹ n a sequence of words used to perform magic; fascination.

spell² vt to name or write down in correct order the letters to form a word.

spell³ n a usu indefinite period of time.

spellbound adj entranced, enthralled.

spend vt (pt **spent**) to pay out (money); to concentrate (one's time or energy) on an activity.

spendthrift n a person who spends money wastefully or extravagantly.

spent adj used up; exhausted.

sperm n semen; the male reproductive cell.

spew vti to vomit; to flow or gush forth.

sphere n a perfectly round object; a field of activity or interest.—**spherical** adj.

spice n an aromatic vegetable substance used for flavouring and seasoning food. • vt to flavour with spice; to add zest to.

spicy adj flavoured with spice.

spider n a small wingless creature with eight legs.

spike n long heavy nail; a sharp-pointed projection, as on a shoe to prevent slipping.

spill *vti* to cause, esp unintentionally, to flow out of a container.

spin *vt* to rotate rapidly; to draw out and twist fibres into thread or yarn; (*spiders, etc*) to make a web; (*with* **out**) to prolong, extend. • *vi* (*wheels*) to turn rapidly without imparting forward motion. • *n* a swift rotation; (*inf*) a brief, fast ride in a vehicle.

spinach *n* a plant with green edible leaves.

spinal *adj* of or relating to the spine.

spinal cord *n* the cord of nerves enclosed by the spinal column.

spindly *adj* tall and slender; frail.

spine *n* a sharp, stiff projection; a spinal column; the backbone of a book.

spineless *adj* weak-willed.

spinning wheel *n* a machine with a wheel-driven spindle for spinning yarn from fibre.

spinster *n* an unmarried woman.

spiral *adj* winding round in a continuous curve up or down a centre or pole. • *n* a spiral line or shape; a continuous expansion or decrease. • *vi* to move up or down in a spiral curve; to increase or decrease steadily.

spire *n* the tapering point of a steeple.

spirit *n* soul; a supernatural being, as a ghost, etc; (*pl*) disposition; (*usu pl*) distilled alcoholic liquor. • *vt* to carry (away, off, etc) secretly and swiftly.

spirited *adj* full of life; animated.

spirit level *n* a glass tube filled with liquid containing an air bubble and mounted in a frame, used for testing whether a surface is level.

spiritual *adj* of the soul; religious. • *n* an emotional religious song, originating among the Black slaves in the American South.

spiritualism *n* the belief that the spirits of the dead can communicate with the living.

spit[1] *n* a rod on which meat is roasted.

spit[2] *vt* to eject from the mouth. • *vi* to expel saliva from the mouth.

spite *n* ill will; malice.—**spiteful** *adj*.

spittle *n* saliva ejected form the mouth.

splash *vt* to spatter with liquid; to move with a splash. • *n* something splashed.

spleen *n* a large lymphatic organ in the upper left part of the abdomen that modifies the blood structure; spitefulness; ill humour.

splendid *adj* magnificent; (*inf*) very good.

splendour *n* brilliance; magnificence.

splice *vt* to unite (two ends of a rope) by intertwining the strands.

splint *n* a rigid structure used to immobilise and support a fractured limb.

splinter *n* a thin, sharp piece of wood, glass or metal broken off.

split *vti* to break apart (usu into two pieces); to separate into factions; to burst or tear. • *n* a narrow gap made (as if) by splitting; a dessert consisting of sliced banana with ice cream, nuts, etc; (*pl*) the act of extending the legs in opposite directions and lowering the body to the floor.

splutter *vi* to spit out food or liquid noisily; to utter words confusedly and hurriedly.

spoil *vt* to damage as to make useless, etc; to impair the enjoyment, etc, of; to overindulge (a child). • *npl* booty, valuables seized in war.

spoil-sport *n* (*inf*) a person who spoils the fun of others.

spoke *n* any of the braces extending from the hub to the rim of a wheel.

spokesman *n* a person authorised to speak on behalf of others.—**spokeswoman** *nf*.

sponge *n* a plantlike marine animal with an internal skeleton of elastic interlacing horny fibres; a piece of natural or manmade sponge for washing or cleaning. • *vt* to wipe with a sponge. • *vi* (*inf*) to scrounge.

sponge cake *n* a sweet cake with a light porous texture.

sponsor *n* a person or organisation that pays the expenses connected with an artistic production or sports event in return for advertising.

spontaneous *adj* arising naturally.

spook *n* (*inf*) a ghost.—**spooky** *adj*.

spool *n* a cylinder, bobbin or reel, upon which thread, film, etc, are wound.

spoon *n* utensil with a shallow bowl and a handle, for eating, stirring, etc.

sporadic *adj* intermittent.—**sporadically** *adv*.

sport *n* an athletic game or pastime; (*inf*) a person regarded as fair and abiding by the rules. • *vt* (*inf*) to display, flaunt.

sporting *adj* interested in sport.

sportsman *n* a person engaged in sport; a person who plays by the rules.—**sportswoman** *nf*.—**sportsmanlike** *adj*.

sporty *adj* (*inf*) fond of sport; flashy.

spot *n* a small area differing in colour, etc, from the surrounding area; a stain; a small amount; a locality. • *vt* to mark with spots; to glimpse.

spot check *n* a random examination.

spotless *adj* immaculate.

spotty *adj* marked with spots; intermittent.

spouse *n* (one's) husband or wife.

spout *n* a projecting lip or tube for pouring out liquids.

sprain *n* a wrenching of a joint by sudden twisting or tearing of ligaments.—*also vt*.

sprawl *vi* to lie down with the limbs stretched out in an untidy manner.

spray[1] *n* fine particles of a liquid; mist; an aerosol or atomiser. • *vti* to direct a spray (on).

spray[2] *n* a decorative flower arrangement.

spread *vt* to extend; to disseminate; to distribute; to apply a coating (e.g. butter). • *vi* to expand in all directions. • n an expanse; (inf) a feast; food that can be spread on bread.

spree n (inf) excessive indulgence, e.g. in spending money, drinking alcohol, etc.

sprig n a twig with leaves on it.

sprightly adj full of life or energy.

spring vi to move suddenly, as by elastic force; to originate. • n a leap; the season between winter and summer; a coiled piece of wire that springs back to its original shape when stretched; the source of a stream.

springboard n a flexible board used by divers and in gymnastics to provide added height or impetus.

spring-clean vi to clean (a house) thoroughly.—also n.

sprinkle vt to scatter in droplets or particles.

sprint n a short run or race at full speed. • vi to go at top speed.—**sprinter** n.

sprite n an elf or imp.

sprout n a new shoot on a plant; a small cabbage-like vegetable. • vt to put forth (shoots). • vi to begin to grow.

spruce[1] adj smart, neat. • vt to smarten.

spruce[2] n an evergreen tree with a conical head.

spry adj vigorous, agile.

spur n a small metal wheel on a rider's heel with sharp points for urging on the horse; stimulus.

spurious adj not legitimate or genuine.

spurn vt to reject with disdain.

spurt vt to gush forth in a sudden stream.

spy n a secret agent employed to collect information on rivals. • vt (usu with on) to act as a spy. • vt to catch sight of.

squabble vi to quarrel noisily.

squad n a small group of soldiers that form a working unit; a section of a police force; (sport) a group of players from which a team is selected.

squadron n a unit of warships, cavalry, military aircraft, etc.

squalid adj filthy; sordid.—**squalor** n.

squander vt to spend wastefully.

square n a shape with four sides of equal length and four right angles; an open space in a town, surrounded by buildings; (inf) an old-fashioned person; the product of a number multiplied by itself. • adj square-shaped; (financial account) settled; equal in score; (inf) old-fashioned. • vt to make square; to multiply by itself. • vi to agree.

squash vt to squeeze, press or crush; to suppress. • n a crowd of people pressed together; a fruit-flavoured drink; a game played in a walled court with rackets and rubber ball.

squat vi to crouch down upon the heels; to occupy land or property, without permission or title. • adj short and dumpy.

squatter n a person who squats.

squawk n a loud, raucous call or cry.

squeak vi to make a high-pitched cry. • n a squeaky noise.—**squeaky** adj.

squeal vi to make a shrill and prolonged cry or sound; (sl) to be an informer; to protest.

squeamish adj easily nauseated.

squeeze vt to press firmly, compress; to grasp tightly; to hug; to force (through, into) by pressing; to extract liquid, juice, from by pressure. • n squeezing or being squeezed; a crowding together.

squelch vi to walk through soft, wet ground, making a sucking noise.

squid n an edible mollusc with ten arms.

squint vi to half close or cross the eyes. • n crossed eyes, as caused by a visual disorder. • adj (inf) crooked.

squire n the leading landowner in a district.

squirm vi to wriggle; to feel embarrassed.

squirrel n a bushy tailed rodent with grey or reddish fur that lives in trees.

squirt vt to eject liquid in a jet. • vi to spurt. • n a jet of liquid; (inf) an insignificant person.

stab vt to injure with a pointed weapon. • vi to thrust at (as if) with a pointed weapon. • n an act or instance of stabbing; a sudden sensation, as of emotion, pain, etc; (inf) an attempt.

stabilise vti to make or become stable.

stable[1] adj firmly established.—**stability** n.

stable[2] n a building where horses are kept.

stack n a large neatly arranged pile; (inf) a large amount. • vt to pile, arrange in a stack.

stadium n a sports ground surrounded by tiers of seats.

staff n a strong stick or pole; (mus) one of the five horizontal lines upon which music is written; the workers employed in an establishment. • vt to provide with staff.

stag n a full-grown male deer.

stage n a degree or step in a process; a raised platform, esp for acting on; (with **the**) the theatre; a portion of a journey. • vt to perform a play on the stage.

stage fright n nervousness at appearing before an audience.

stage manager n a person responsible for the stage arrangements prior to and during the performance of a play.

stagger vi to walk unsteadily. • vt to astound.

staggering adj astounding.

stagnant adj (water) standing still with a revolting smell; unchanging, dull.

stagnate vi to be, stagnant.

stagy, stagey adj theatrical, dramatic.

staid adj sober; sedate; old-fashioned.

stain vt to discolour with spots of something that cannot be removed. • vi to become stained. • n a discoloured mark.

stained glass n coloured glass used in windows.

stainless *adj* resistant to staining.

stair *n* a flight of stairs; a step; (*pl*) a stairway.

staircase *n* a flight of stairs with banisters.

stairway *n* a staircase.

stake[1] *n* a sharpened post driven into the ground; a post to which persons were tied for execution by burning. • *vt* to mark out (land) with stakes.

stake[2] *vt* to bet. • *n* a financial interest.

stalactite *n* an icicle-like calcium deposit hanging from the roof of a cave.

stalagmite *n* a cylindrical deposit projecting upwards from the floor of a cave.

stale *adj* deteriorated from age; musty.

stalemate *n* (*chess*) a situation in which a king can only be moved in and out of check, thus causing a draw; a deadlock.

stalk[1] *n* the stem of a plant.

stalk[2] *vi* to stride in a stiff or angry way; to hunt (game, prey) stealthily.—**stalker** *n*.

stall[1] *n* a compartment for one animal in a stable; a table or stand for the display or sale of goods; (*pl*) the seats on the ground floor of a theatre. • *vti* (*car engine*) to stop or cause to stop suddenly, e.g. by misuse of the clutch.

stall[2] *vti* to play for time.

stalwart *adj* resolute. • *n* a loyal supporter.

stamina *n* strength; staying power.

stammer *vti* to falter in speaking; to stutter.

stamp *vt* to imprint with an official seal; to affix a postage stamp; (*with* out) to extinguish by stamping; to suppress by force. • *vi* to bring the foot down heavily. • *n* a postage stamp; a block for imprinting.

stampede *n* an impulsive rush of a panic-stricken herd; a rush of a crowd.—*also vi.*

stance *n* posture; attitude.

stand *vi* to be in an upright position; to remain unchanged; (*with* by) to be available for use if required; (*with* down) to resign; (*with* up) to rise to one's feet. • *vt* to put upright; to endure; (*with* by) to remain loyal to; (*with* up) (*inf*) to fail to keep an appointment with. • *n* a strong opinion; a place for taxis awaiting hire; (*pl*) a structure for spectators; a stall for a small retail business.

standard *n* a flag; a criterion; an established or accepted level of achievement; (*pl*) moral principles.

stand-by *n* a person or thing held in readiness for use in an emergency, etc.

stand-in *n* a substitute; a person who takes the place of an actor during the preparation of a scene or in stunts.

standing *n* status or reputation; duration.

standoffish *adj* aloof, reserved.

standpoint *n* a point of view, opinion.

standstill *n* a complete halt.

stand-up *adj* (*fight*) furious; (*comedian*) telling jokes standing alone in front of an audience.

staple[1] *n* a principal commodity of trade or industry of a nation. • *adj* chief.

staple[2] *n* a U-shaped thin piece of wire for fastening. • *vt* to fasten with a staple.

star *n* any one of the celestial bodies, esp those visible by night that appear as small points of light; a figure with five points; a famous actor, musician, etc. • *vti* to feature or be featured as a star.

starboard *n* the right side of a ship or aircraft when facing the bow.

starch *n* a white, tasteless, food substance found in potatoes, cereal, etc; a fabric stiffener based on this. • *vt* to stiffen with starch.—**starchy** *adj*.

stare *vi* to gaze fixedly. • *n* a fixed gaze.

stark *adj* bare; plain. • *adv* completely.

start *vi* to commence, begin; to jump involuntarily, from fright. • *vt* to begin. • *n* a beginning.

starter *n* a person who starts something; the first course of a meal.

startle *vt* to frighten or surprise.—**startling** *adj*.

starve *vi* to die from a lack of food. • *vt* deprive (a person) of food.—**starvation** *n*.

state *n* condition; frame of mind; ceremonious style; (*with cap*) an area or community with its own government or forming a federation under a sovereign government. • *adj* public; ceremonial. • *vt* to express in words.

stately *adj* dignified; majestic.

statement *n* a formal announcement; a document showing one's bank balance.

statesman *n* a well-known politician.

static *adj* fixed; stationary. • *n* electrical interference causing noise on radio or TV.

station *n* a railway or bus terminal or stop; (*inf*) a TV channel; position in society. • *vt* to assign to a post, place, office.

stationary *adj* not moving.

stationer *n* a dealer in stationery.

stationery *n* writing materials.

statistic *n* a fact obtained from analysing information expressed in numbers.

statistics *n* (*used as sing*) the branch of mathematics dealing with the collection, analysis and presentation of numerical data.—**statistical** *adj*.

statue *n* a representation of a human or animal form that is carved or moulded.

stature *n* the standing height of a person.

status *n* social or professional position.

status quo *n* the existing state of affairs.

statute *n* a law enacted by a legislature.

statutory *adj* established by statute.

staunch *adj* loyal; dependable.

stave *n* a piece of wood of a barrel; (*mus*) a staff. • *vt* (*usu with* in) to smash inwards.

stay *vi* to remain in a place; to wait; to reside temporarily. • *n* a short time spent as a guest.

steadfast *adj* firm, fixed; resolute.

steady *adj* firm, stable; regular, constant. • *vti* to make steady.—**steadily** *adv*.

steak *n* a slice of meat, esp beef or fish, for grilling or frying.

steal *vt* to take from someone dishonestly.

stealth *n* a manner of moving quietly and secretly.

stealthy *adj* acting or performed in a quiet, secret manner.—**stealthily** *adv*.

steam *n* the hot vapour created by boiling water. • *vi* to cook with steam; (*with* **up**) (*glasses, windows*) to become covered in condensation.

steel *n* an alloy of iron and carbon. • *vt* to nerve (oneself).—**steely** *adj*.

steep[1] *adj* sloping sharply; (*inf*) exorbitant.

steep[2] *vti* to soak or be soaked in a liquid.

steeple *n* a tower of a church.

steeplechase *n* a horse race across country or on a course over jumps; a track race over hurdles and water jumps.—**steeplechaser** *n*.

steer *vti* to direct (a vehicle, ship, bicycle, etc).

stem[1] *n* a plant stalk; the upright slender part of anything, such as a wineglass. • *vi* to originate (from).

stem[2] *vt* to stop (the flow).

stench *n* a foul odour.

stencil *n* a pierced sheet of card or metal for reproducing letters by applying paint.

step *n* one movement of the foot ahead in walking, running or dancing; a pace; a degree; a stage towards a goal; one tread of a stair, rung of a ladder. • *vti* to take a step or a number of paces.

step- *prefix* related by remarriage of a spouse or parent.

stepladder *n* a short portable ladder.

stereo *n* a hi-fi with two loudspeakers.

stereophonic *adj* (*sound reproduction system*) using two separate channels for recording and transmission to create a spatial effect.

stereotype *n* a fixed, general image of a person or thing shared by many people.—*also vt*.

sterile *adj* unable to produce offspring, fruit, etc; free from germs.

sterilise *vt* to render incapable of reproduction; to free from germs.—**sterilisation** *n*.

sterling *n* the British system of money. • *adj* of excellent character.

stern[1] *adj* severe; austere, harsh.

stern[2] *n* the rear part of a boat or ship

stethoscope *n* an instrument used to detect body sounds.

stew *n* a meal of cooked meat with vegetables. • *vt* to cook slowly.

steward *n* a person who serves food on an aircraft or ship and looks after passengers.

stewardess *n* a woman steward on an aircraft or ship.

stick[1] *vt* to attach with glue, adhesive tape, etc. • *vi* to cling to, to adhere.

stick[2] *n* a broken off shoot or branch of a tree; a walking stick; a hockey stick; a rod.

sticker *n* an adhesive label or poster.

stickler *n* a person who is scrupulous or obstinate about something.

sticky *adj* covered with adhesive; (*weather*) warm and humid; (*inf*) difficult.

stiff *adj* not flexible or supple; rigid; (*drink*) potent; (*penalty*) severe. • *n* (*sl*) a corpse.

stiffen *vti* to make or become stiff.

stifle *vt* to suffocate; to smother; to suppress.

stifling *adj* excessively hot and stuffy.

stigma *n* a social disgrace; the part of a flower that receives pollen; (*Christianity*) marks resembling the wounds of Christ thought to appear on the bodies of saintly people.

stile *n* a set of steps for climbing over a fence.

still[1] *adj* motionless; (*drink*) not carbonated. • *n* a single photograph taken from a cinema film. • *adv* continuously; nevertheless.—**stillness** *n*.

still[2] *n* an apparatus for distilling liquids.

stillborn *adj* born dead.

still life *n* a painting of inanimate objects.

stilt *n* either of a pair of poles with footrests on which one can walk, as in a circus.

stilted *adj* (*speech, writing*) pompous, unnaturally formal; (*conversation*) forced.

stimulate *vt* to excite, arouse.—**stimulation** *n*.

stimulus *n* something that acts as an incentive.

sting *n* a sharp pointed organ of a bee, wasp, etc, or hair on a plant, used for injecting poison; a skin wound caused by injected poison from an insect or plant. • *vt* to wound with a sting.

stingy *adj* miserly, mean.

stink *vi* to give out an offensive smell; (*sl*) to be extremely bad in quality. • *n* a foul smell.

stipulate *vt* to specify as a condition of an agreement.—**stipulation** *n*.

stir[1] *vt* to mix, as with a spoon; to rouse.

stir[2] *n* (*sl*) prison.

stirring *adj* rousing, exciting.

stirrup *n* a strap and flat-bottomed ring hanging from a saddle, for a rider's foot.

stitch *n* a single in-and-out movement of a threaded needle in sewing; a single loop of a yarn in knitting or crocheting; a sudden, sharp pain, esp in the side. • *vti* to sew.

stock *n* goods on hand; shares of corporate capital; lineage; a store; the broth obtained by boiling meat, bones and vegetables as a foundation for soup, etc. • *vt* to keep in store.

stockade *n* a defensive enclosure or barrier of stakes fixed in the ground.

stockbroker *n* a person who deals in stocks.

stocking *n* a sock; a nylon covering for a woman's leg, supported by suspenders.

stock market, stock exchange *n* the market for dealing in stocks and shares.

stockpile n a reserve supply of essentials.

stocky adj short and sturdy.—**stockiness** n.

stodgy adj (food) thick, heavy and indigestible.

stoke vt to stir and feed (a fire) with fuel.

stole n a long scarf or piece of fur worn on the shoulders.

stolid adj impassive; unemotional.

stomach n the organ where food is digested; the belly. • vt to put up with.

stone n a small lump of rock; a precious stone or gem; the hard seed of a fruit; a unit of weight (14 lb./6.35 kg). • vt to throw stones at; to remove stones (from fruit).

stony adj of, like or full of stones.

stool n a seat with no back or arms; matter evacuated from the bowels.

stoop vti to bend the body forward and downward; to degrade oneself.

stop vt to halt; to prevent. • vi to cease; to come to an end. • n (a knob controlling) a set of organ pipes; a standard setting of the aperture in a camera lens (—also **f-stop**); a stopping place for a bus or train.

stopover n a short break in a journey.

stoppage n stopping or being stopped; a concerted cessation of work by employees, as during a strike.

stopper n a cork or bung.

storage n storing or being stored; (comput) the storing of data in a computer memory or on disk, etc.

store n a large supply of goods for future use. • vt to put in a warehouse; (comput) to put (data) into a computer memory or onto a storage device.

storey n a horizontal division of a building.

stork n a long-necked wading bird.

storm n a heavy fall of rain, snow, etc, with strong winds. • vt to invade. • vi to be angry.

story n a narrative of real or imaginary events.

stout adj strong; short and plump; sturdy. • n strong dark beer.

stove n a cooker; heating apparatus.

stow vt to store, pack in an orderly way

stowaway n a person who hides on a ship, car, aircraft, etc, to avoid paying the fare.

straddle vt to have one leg on either side.

straggle vi to stray; to wander.—**straggly** adj.

straight adj (line) not curved or bent; direct; (sl) heterosexual; (alcoholic drinks) not diluted. • adv directly; without delay.

straighten vti to make or become straight.

straightforward adj honest, open; simple; easy.

strain[1] vt to stretch; to stress; to injure (a muscle) by overstretching; (food) to sieve. • n overexertion; tension; an injury from straining.

strain[2] n a plant or animal within a species having a common characteristic; a trait.

strained adj (mood, atmosphere) tense.

strainer n a sieve or colander.

strait n a channel of sea linking two larger seas; (usu pl) difficulty, distress.

straitjacket n a coat-like device for restraining violent people; something that restricts or limits.

strait-laced adj prim, morally strict.

strand[1] vt to leave without transport or money.

strand[2] n a single piece of thread or wire twisted together to make a rope or cable.

strange adj peculiar; unknown; unfamiliar.

stranger n a person who is unknown; a new arrival to a place; a person who is unfamiliar with or ignorant of something.

strangle vt to kill by compressing the windpipe.

strap n a narrow strip of leather or cloth for carrying a bag, etc; a fastening, as on a shoe. • vti to fasten with a strap.

strapping adj tall, well-built.

strategic(al) adj of, relating to or important in strategy; (weapons) designed to strike at the enemy's homeland, not for use on the battlefield.—**strategically** adv.

strategy n the planning and conduct of war.

stratum n a layer of sedimentary rock; a level (of society).

straw n the stalks of threshed grain; a tube for sucking up a drink.

strawberry n a soft red fruit.

stray vi to wander; to digress. • n a domestic animal that has become lost.

streak n a line of contrasting colour; a characteristic. • vti to mark with streaks; to run naked in public as a prank.

streaky adj marked with streaks; (bacon) having alternate layers of fat and lean.

stream n a small river; a flow of liquid; anything flowing and continuous. • vi to flow.

streamer n a long decorative ribbon.

streamline vt to shape (a car, boat, etc) in a way that lessens resistance through air or water.

street n a public road in a town or city lined with houses.

strength n the state or quality of being physically or mentally strong; power of exerting or withstanding pressure, potency.

strengthen vt to make stronger.

strenuous adj vigorous; requiring exertion.

stress n pressure; mental or physical strain; emphasis. • vt to exert pressure on; to emphasise.

stretch vt to extend, to draw out. • vi to extend, spread; to be capable of expanding, as in elastic material. • n the act of stretching or instance of being stretched; an expanse of time or space; (sl) a period of imprisonment.

stretcher n a portable frame for carrying the sick or injured.

strew vt to scatter.

stricken *adj* suffering (from an illness).

strict *adj* harsh, firm.—**strictly** *adv*.

stride *vi* to walk with long steps.

strident *adj* loud and harsh.

strife *n* a fight, quarrel; struggle.

strike *vt* to hit; to crash into; (*mil*) to attack; to ignite (a match) by friction; to delete; (*clock*) to indicate by sounding; to occur to. • *vi* to cease work to enforce a demand (for higher wages or better working conditions). • *n* a stoppage of work; a military attack.

striker *n* a worker who is on strike; (*soccer*) a forward player whose primary role is to score goals.

striking *adj* impressive.

string *n* a thin length of cord or twine used for tying, fastening, etc; a stretched length of catgut, wire or other material in a musical instrument; (*pl*) the stringed instruments in an orchestra; their players. • *vt* to thread on a string.

stringent *adj* strict.—**stringency** *n*.

strip *vt* to peel off. • *vi* to undress. • *n* a long, narrow piece (of cloth, land, etc).

stripe *n* a narrow band of a different colour form the background; a V-shaped band on a military uniform to indicate rank. • *vt* to mark with a stripe.

stripper *n* a striptease artist; a device or solvent that removes paint.

striptease *n* an erotic show where a person removes clothes seductively to music.

strive *vi* to endeavour earnestly.

stroke[1] *n* a blow; (*med*) a seizure; the sound of a clock; (*sport*) an act of hitting a ball; a manner of swimming; a movement of a pen, pencil or paintbrush.

stroke[2] *vt* to caress.

stroll *vi* to walk leisurely, to saunter.—*also n*.

strong *adj* physically or mentally powerful; potent; intense; healthy; convincing.

stronghold *n* a fortress; a centre of strength or support.

structure *n* organisation; construction; arrangement of parts in an organism; system, framework. • *vt* to organise, to arrange.—**structural** *adj*.

struggle *vi* to move strenuously so as to escape; to strive. • *n* a violent effort.

strum *vt* to play on (a guitar, etc) by moving the thumb across the strings.

strut[1] *vi* to walk in a proud or pompous manner.

strut[2] *n* a brace or structural support.

stub *n* a short piece left after the larger part has been removed or used; the counterfoil of a cheque. • *vt* to knock (one's toe) painfully.

stubble *n* any short, bristly growth, as of beard.—**stubbly** *adj*.

stubborn *adj* obstinate; determined.

stuck-up *adj* (*inf*) conceited; snobbish.

stud[1] *n* a horse kept for breeding.

stud[2] *n* a large-headed nail; an ornamental fastener.

student *n* a person who is enrolled for study at a college, university, etc.

studied *adj* carefully planned.

studio *n* the workshop of an artist, photographer, etc; (*pl*) a building where motion pictures are made; a room where TV or radio programmes are recorded.

studious *adj* given to study.

study *vt* to observe and investigate (e.g. phenomena) closely; to scrutinise; to follow a course (at college, etc). • *n* a detailed investigation and analysis of a subject; a room for studying.

stuff *n* material; matter; personal possessions generally. • *vt* to cram or fill.

stuffing *n* material used to stuff or fill anything; a seasoned mixture put inside poultry, meat, vegetables, etc, before cooking.

stuffy *adj* badly ventilated; dull.

stumble *vi* to trip up when walking; to discover by chance (*with* **across** *or* **on**).—*also n*.

stump *n* the part of a tree remaining in the ground after the tree has been felled; the part of a limb, tooth, that remains after the larger part is cut off or destroyed. • *vt* (*inf*) to confuse, baffle.

stun *vt* to render unconscious due to a fall or heavy blow; to shock.

stunning *adj* (*inf*) strikingly attractive.

stunt[1] *vt* to prevent the growth of.

stunt[2] *n* a daring or spectacular feat.

stupefy *vt* to dull the senses of.

stupendous *adj* wonderful, astonishing.

stupid *adj* lacking in understanding.

stupor *n* extreme lethargy; mental dullness.

sturdy *adj* firm; strong, robust.—**sturdiness** *n*.

stutter *vi* to stammer.—*also n*.

sty[1], **stye** *n* an inflamed swelling on the eyelid.

sty[2] *n* a pen for pigs.

style *n* the manner of writing, painting, composing music peculiar to an individual or group; fashion, elegance. • *vt* to design or shape.

stylise *vt* to give a conventional style to.

stylish *adj* having style; fashionable.

stylus *n* the device attached to the cartridge on the arm of a record-player that rests in the groove of a record and transmits the vibrations that are converted to sound.

suave *adj* charming, polite.

sub *n* (*inf*) a submarine; a substitute.

subconscious *adj* happening without one's awareness. • *n* the part of the mind that is active without one's conscious awareness.

subdue *vt* to dominate; to repress; to soften.

subject *adj* under the power of; liable. • *n* a person under the power of another; a citizen; a topic; a theme. • vt to bring under control; to cause to undergo something.

subjective adj determined by one's own mind or consciousness; personal.

subjunctive adj denoting that mood of a verb that expresses doubt, condition, wish or hope. • n the subjunctive mood.

sublime adj noble; exalted.

submarine n a naval vessel capable of being propelled under water, esp for firing torpedoes.

submerge vt to plunge or sink under water.

submission n an act of submitting; an idea or proposal; the state of being submissive.

submissive adj willing to accept orders,.

submit vt to surrender (oneself) to another person or force; to refer to another for consideration or judgment; to offer as an opinion. • vi to surrender.

subordinate adj lower in order, rank. • n a subordinate person.

subscribe vt to pay to receive regular copies of a magazine, etc); to donate money (to a charity, campaign); to support or agree with (an opinion, faith).—**subscriber** n.—**subscription** n.

subsequent adj occurring or following after.

subside vi to sink or fall to the bottom; to settle; to abate.—**subsidence** n.

subsidiary adj secondary; (company) owned or controlled by another.—also n.

subsidy n government financial aid to a private person or company to assist an enterprise.

subsistence n existence; livelihood.

substance n matter (such as powder, liquid); the essential nature or part.

substantial adj of considerable value or size.

substantiate vt to prove, to verify.

substitute vt (with for) to put or act in place of another person or thing; to replace (by). • n a person or thing that serves in place of another.

subtitle n a printed translation superimposed on a foreign language film.

subtle adj delicate; slight.—**subtlety** n.—

subtract vti to take away or deduct.

suburb n a residential district on the outskirts of a large town or city.—**suburban** adj.

subversive adj liable to subvert established authority. • n a person who engages in subversive activities.

subway n a passage under a street; an underground metropolitan electric railway.

succeed vt to come after, to follow; to take the place of. • vi to accomplish what is attempted.

success n the gaining of wealth, fame, etc; the favourable outcome of (anything attempted).

successful adj having success.

succession n following in sequence; a number of persons or things following in order; the act or process of succeeding to a title, throne, etc.

successive adj following in sequence.

successor n a person who succeeds another.

succinct adj clear, concise.

succulent adj juicy; moist and tasty; (plant) having fleshy tissue. • n a succulent plant.

succumb vi to yield to superior strength or overpowering desire; to die.

such adj of a specified kind (e.g. such people, such a film); so great. • adv so; very.

suck vt to draw (a liquid, air) into the mouth; to dissolve or roll about in the mouth (as a sweet).

sucker n (sl) a person who is easily taken in or deceived; a cup-shaped piece of rubber that adheres to surfaces.

suckle vt to feed at the breast or udder.

sucrose n sugar.

suction n the act or process of sucking.

sudden adj happening quickly and unexpectedly, abrupt.—**suddenly** adv.

sue vt to bring a legal action against.

suede n leather finished with a soft nap.

suet n white, solid fat in animal tissue.

suffer vt to undergo; to endure. • vi to feel pain.

suffice vi to be sufficient, adequate.

sufficient adj enough; adequate.

suffix n a letter, syllable or syllables added to the end of a word to modify its meaning or to form a new derivative.

suffocate vti to kill or be killed by depriving of oxygen or by inhaling a poisonous gas.

sugar n a sweet, white, crystalline substance obtained from a variety of cane and beet.

sugary adj resembling or containing sugar; cloyingly sweet in manner, etc.

suggest vt to put forward for consideration; to evoke.—**suggestion** n.

suggestible adj easily influenced.

suggestive adj evocative; rather indecent.

suicide n a person who kills himself intentionally; the act of killing oneself intentionally.

suit n a set of matching garments, such as a jacket and trousers or skirt; one of the four sets of thirteen playing cards. • vt to be appropriate.

suitable adj fitting; convenient (to, for).

suitcase n a portable, oblong case.

suite n a set, esp of rooms, furniture.

sulk vi to be sullen.

sulky adj bad-tempered, quiet and sullen.

sullen adj moody and silent; gloomy.

sulphur n a yellow nonmetallic element that is inflammable and has a strong odour.

sulphuric acid n a powerfully corrosive acid.

sultana n a dried, white grape; the wife or female relative of a sultan.

sultry adj very hot, humid and close; sensual.

sum n the result of two or more things added together; the total; a quantity of money. • vt to add (usu with **up**); to summarise.

summarise *vt* to make or be a summary of.

summary *adj* concise. • *n* a brief account of the main points of something.

summer *n* the warmest season of the year, between spring and autumn.—**summery** *adj*.

summit *n* the highest point, the peak; a meeting of world leaders.

summon *vt* to order to appear, esp in court; to convene; to gather (strength, enthusiasm, etc).

summons *n* a call to appear (in court).

sump *n* a section of an engine for the oil to drain into.

sumptuous *adj* lavish; luxurious.

sun *n* the star around which the earth and other planets revolve that gives light and heat to the solar system. • *vt* to expose to the sun's rays.

sunbathe *vi* to lie in the rays of the sun to get a suntan.

sunburn *n* inflammation of the skin from exposure to sunlight.—*also vti*.

sundial *n* a device that shows the time by casting a shadow on a graduated dial.

sundry *adj* miscellaneous, various.

sunflower *n* a tall plant with large yellow flowers whose seeds yield oil.

sunglasses *npl* tinted glasses to protect the eyes from sunlight.

sunny *adj* (*weather*) bright with sunshine; (*person, mood*) cheerful.

sunrise *n* dawn.

sunset *n* dusk.

sunshine *n* the light and heat from the sun.

sunstroke *n* illness caused by exposure to the sun.

suntan *n* browning of the skin by the sun.

super *adj* (*inf*) fantastic, excellent.

superannuation *n* regular contributions from wages towards a pension scheme.

superb *adj* excellent.—**superbly** *adv*.

supercilious *adj* arrogant; haughty.

superficial *adj* near the surface; slight.

superfluous *adj* exceeding what is required.

superimpose *vt* to lay upon something else.

superintendent *n* a person who manages or supervises; a British police officer next above the rank of inspector.

superior *adj* higher in place, quality, rank, excellence; greater in number, power. • *n* a person of higher rank.—**superiority** *n*.

superlative *adj* of outstanding quality; (*gram*) denoting the extreme degree of comparison of adjectives and adverbs.

supermarket *n* a large self-service shop selling food and household goods.

supernatural *adj* relating to things that cannot be explained by nature.

superpower *n* a nation with great economic and military strength.

supersede *vt* to take the place of, replace.

supersonic *adj* faster than the speed of sound.

superstition *n* irrational belief based on ignorance or fear.—**superstitious** *adj*.

supervise *vti* to have charge of, direct.

supper *n* a meal taken in the evening.

supple *adj* flexible, easily bent; lithe.

supplement *n* an extra amount (usu of money); an additional section of a book, newspaper. • *vt* to add to.

supply *vt* to provide. • *n* (*pl*) provisions.

support *vt* to hold up; to assist; to provide for (financially). • *n* a means of support.

supporter *n* a person who backs a political party, sports team, etc.

suppose *vt* to assume; to expect.

supposed *adj* believed to be on available evidence.

supposedly *adv* allegedly.

supposition *n* an assumption, hypothesis.

suppress *vt* to put an end to; to restrain.

supreme *adj* of highest power.

surcharge *n* an additional tax or charge.

sure *adj* certain; without doubt; reliable, inevitable; secure; safe; dependable.

surely *adv* certainly; it is to be hoped that.

surety *n* a person who undertakes responsibility for the fulfilment of another's debt.

surf *n* the waves of the sea breaking on the shore.

surface *n* the exterior face of an object; any of the faces of a solid; the uppermost level of sea or land. • *vi* to rise to the surface of water.

surfboard *n* a long, narrow board used in the sport of surfing.

surfeit *n* an excessive amount.

surfing *n* the sport of riding in toward shore on the crest of a wave, esp on a surfboard.

surge *n* a sudden, strong increase, as of power.

surgeon *n* a medical specialist who practices surgery.

surgery *n* the treatment of diseases or injuries by operation; the consulting room of a doctor or dentist; the daily period when a doctor is available for consultation; the regular period when an MP, etc, is available for consultation.—**surgical** *adj*.—**surgically** *adv*.

surmise *n* guess, conjecture.

surmount *vt* to overcome; to rise above.

surname *n* the family name.

surpass *vt* to outdo; to excel; to exceed.

surplus *n* an amount in excess of what is required.

surprise *n* the act of catching unawares; astonishment. • *vt* to cause to feel astonished; to take unawares.—**surprising** *adj*.

surreal *adj* bizarre.

surrender *vt* to relinquish or give up. • *vi* to give oneself up (to an enemy).—*also n*.

surreptitious adj clandestine, secret.

surround vt to encircle on all or nearly all sides. • n a border.

surroundings npl the conditions, objects, etc, around a person or thing.

surveillance n a secret watch over a person.

survey vt to take a general view of; to examine carefully; to measure and make a map of an area. • n a detailed study; the process of surveying an area or a house.

surveyor n a person who surveys buildings.

survival n surviving; a relic.

survive vt to live after the death of another person. • vi to remain alive (after experiencing a dangerous situation).—**survivor** n.

susceptible adj liable to be affected by.

suspect vt to mistrust; to believe to be guilty. • n a person under suspicion.

suspend vt to hang; to debar temporarily.

suspender n a fastener for holding up stockings.

suspense n mental anxiety; excitement.

suspension n a temporary removal from office, privileges, etc; the system of springs, shock absorbers, etc, that support a vehicle on its axles.

suspension bridge n a bridge carrying a roadway suspended by cables anchored to towers at either end.

suspicion n a belief formed or held without sure proof; a trace.—**suspicious** adj.

sustain vt to support; to suffer (e.g. an injury).

sustenance n nourishment.

swab n a wad of absorbent cotton used to clean wounds, take specimens, etc.

swagger vi to strut; to brag loudly.

swallow[1] n a small migratory bird with long wings and a forked tail.

swallow[2] vt to cause food and drink to move from the mouth to the stomach.—also n.

swamp n wet, spongy land; bog. • vt to overwhelm; to flood as with water.

swan n a large, usu white, bird with a very long neck that lives on rivers and lakes.

swap vti (inf) to trade, barter. • n (inf) the act of exchanging one thing for another.—also **swop**.

swarm n a colony of migrating bees; a moving crowd.—also vi.

swarthy adj dark-complexioned.

swat vt (inf) to swipe.

sway vi to swing or move from one side to the other or to and fro. • n influence.

swear vi to make a solemn promise, etc, calling God as a witness; to use obscene language.

sweat n perspiration.—also vti.—**sweaty** adj.

sweater n a knitted pullover.

Swede n a native of Sweden.

swede n a round root vegetable with yellow flesh.

Swedish adj pertaining to Sweden, its people or language. • n the language of Sweden.

sweep vt to clean with a brush. • vi to pass by swiftly. • n a sweepstake.

sweeping adj wide-ranging.

sweet adj having a taste like sugar; gentle; kind. • n a small piece of confectionery; a dessert.

sweetcorn n maize, corn on the cob.

sweeten vti to make or become sweet.

sweetheart n a lover.

swell vi to increase in size or volume; to bulge out. • n the movement of the sea; a bulge.

swelling n inflammation.

swelter vi to suffer from heat.

swerve vi to turn aside suddenly from a course.

swift adj moving with great speed; rapid. • n a swallow-like bird.—**swiftly** adv.

swig vt (inf) to take a long drink, esp from a bottle.—also n.

swill vti to drink greedily. • n liquid refuse fed to pigs.

swim vi to move through water by using limbs or fins. • n the act of swimming.

swimming costume, swimsuit n a one-piece garment for swimming in.

swindle vti to cheat (someone) of money or property.—also n.—**swindler** n.

swine n a pig; (inf) a contemptible person.

swing vi to sway or move to and fro, as an object hanging in air; to shift from one mood or opinion to another; (music) to have a lively rhythm. • vt to whirl; to achieve, bring about. • n a swinging, curving or rhythmic movement; a suspended seat for swinging in.

swinging adj (inf) up-to-date; lively.

swipe n (inf) a hard, sweeping blow. • vt (inf) to hit with a swipe; (sl) to steal.

swirl vti to turn with a whirling motion.—also n.

swish vi to move with a soft, whistling, hissing sound. • adj (inf) smart, fashionable.

Swiss adj of or belonging to Switzerland. • n a native of Switzerland.

switch n a control for turning on and off an electrical device; a sudden change; a swap. • vt to shift, change, swap; to turn on or off.

switchback n a zigzag road in a mountain region.

switchboard n an installation in a building where telephone calls are connected.

swivel vi to turn (as if) on a pin or pivot.

swoon vt to faint.—also vi.

swoop vt to carry off abruptly. • vi to make a sudden attack.—also n.

swop see swap.

sword n a weapon with a long blade and a handle at one end.

swordfish n a large marine fish with a swordlike upper jaw.

swot vi (inf) to study hard for an examination. • n (inf) a person who studies hard.

syllable n word or part of a word uttered by a single sound.

syllabus n a summary of a course of study.

symbol n a representation; an object used to represent something abstract.

symbolic adj of, using or constituting a symbol.

symbolise vt to represent by a symbol.

symbolism n the use of symbols.

symmetrical adj having symmetry.

symmetry n the corresponding arrangement of one part to another in size, shape and position.

sympathetic adj having sympathy.

sympathise vi feel sympathy for.

sympathy n agreement of ideas; compassion.

symphony n an orchestral composition in several movements.—**symphonic** adj.

symptom n a bodily sensation experienced by a patient indicative of a particular disease.

synagogue n the building where Jews assemble for worship and religious study.

synchronise vti (watches) to adjust to show the same time.

syndicate n an association of individuals or corporations formed for a project requiring much capital; any group, as of criminals, organised for some undertaking. • vt to manage, form into a syndicate.

syndrome n a characteristic pattern of signs and symptoms of a disease.

synonym n a word that has the same, or similar, meaning as another in the same language.

synonymous adj having the same meaning.

synopsis n a brief review of a subject.

syntax n (gram) the arrangement of words in the sentences and phrases of language; the rules governing this.—**syntactic** adj.

synthesis n the production of a compound by a chemical reaction.

synthetic adj produced by chemical synthesis.

syphilis n a contagious venereal disease.

syringe n a hollow tube with plunger at one end and a sharp needle at the other by which liquids are injected or withdrawn, esp in medicine.

syrup n a thick sweet substance made by boiling sugar with water.—**syrupy** adj.

system n a method of working or organising by following a set of rules; routine.

systematic adj constituting or based on a system.—**systematically** adv.

systems analysis n analysis of a particular task or operation to determine how computer hardware and software may best perform it.

T

tab n a small tag, label or flap; (inf) a bill, as for expenses. • vt to fix a tab on.

tabby n a domestic cat with a striped coat.

tabernacle n a place of worship.

table n a piece of furniture consisting of a slab or board on legs; a list arranged for reference or comparison. • vt to submit, put forward.

tablecloth n a cloth for covering a table.

table d'hôte n a meal at a fixed price for a set number of courses.

tablespoon n a large serving spoon.

tablet n a medicinal pill; a slab of stone.

table tennis n a game like tennis played on a table with small bats and balls.

tabloid n a newspaper of half-size sheets characterised by emphasis on photographs and news in condensed form.

taboo n a religious or social prohibition.

tabulate vt to arrange in the form of a table.

tacit adj implied without being spoken.

taciturn adj habitually reserved.

tack n a short, flat-headed nail; the course of a sailing ship; a course of action, approach.

tackle n a system of ropes and pulleys for lifting; equipment; (sport) an act of grabbing and stopping an opponent. • vt (task, etc) to attend to, undertake; (a person) to confront; (sport) to challenge with a tackle.

tacky adj (paint, etc) sticky.

tact n discretion in managing the feelings of others.—**tactful** adj.—**tactless** adj.

tactics n sing stratagem; ploy.—**tactical** adj.

tactile adj relating to touch.

tadpole n the larva of a frog or toad.

taffeta n a thin glossy fabric with a silky lustre.

tag[1] n a strip or label for identification. • vt to attach a tag; to mark with a tag.

tag[2] n a children's chasing game.

tail n the appendage of an animal growing from the rear; (pl) the side of a coin without a head on it. • vt to follow closely.

tail coat n a man's black or grey coat with two long tails at the back.

tail-end n the last.

tailgate n the hinged board at the rear of a truck.

tailor n a person who makes and repairs outer garments, esp men's suits. • vt to adapt to fit a particular requirement.

tailor-made *adj* specially designed for a particular purpose or person.

taint *vt* to contaminate; to infect. • *n* a stain.

take *vt* to lay hold of; to grasp or seize; to gain, win; to choose, select; (*attitude, pose*) to adopt; to consume; to lead or carry with one; to use as a means of travel; to steal. • *vi* to become effective. • *n* (*film, TV*) the amount of film used without stopping the camera.

takeoff *n* the process of an aircraft becoming airborne.

takeover *n* the taking over of control.

taking *adj* charming. • *n* (*pl*) profits.

talc *n* a type of smooth mineral used in ceramics and talcum powder; talcum powder.

talcum powder *n* perfumed powdered talc.

tale *n* a narrative or story.

talent *n* special aptitude.—**talented** *adj*.

talk *vti* to speak. • *n* a discussion; a lecture.

talkative *adj* given to talking a great deal.

tall *adj* above average in height.

tallboy *n* a high chest of drawers.

tally *n* a reckoning. • *vi* to correspond.

tambourine *n* a percussion hand instrument made of skin stretched over a circular frame with small jingling metal discs round the edge.

tame *adj* (*animal*) domesticated; compliant; dull. • *vt* (*animal*) to domesticate.

tamper *vi* to meddle (with).

tampon *n* a firm plug of cotton wool inserted in the vagina during menstruation.

tan *n* a yellowish-brown colour; suntan. • *vti* to acquire a suntan; (*hide*) to convert into leather by processing.

tandem *n* a bicycle for two riders.

tang *n* sharp smell or a strong taste.

tangent *n* a line that touches a curve or circle at one point, without crossing it.

tangerine *n* a small, sweet orange.

tangible *adj* capable of being felt, seen or noticed; substantial; real.

tangle *n* a mass of hair, string or wire knotted together confusedly; a complication. • *vi* to become tangled; (*with* **with**) to become involved in argument with.

tango *n* a Latin American dance.

tank *n* a container for storing liquids or gases; an armoured combat vehicle mounted with guns.

tankard *n* a tall, one-handled beer mug.

tanker *n* a large ship or truck for transporting oil.

tannin *n* a yellow or brown chemical found in plants or tea, used in tanning.

tantalise *vt* to torment by presenting something greatly desired, but keeping it inaccessible.

tantamount *adj* equivalent (to) in effect.

tantrum *n* a childish fit of bad temper.

tap¹ *n* a quick, light blow or touch. • *vti* to strike lightly; to make a tapping sound.

tap² *n* a device controlling the flow of liquid through a pipe or from a container. • *vt* to pierce in order to draw fluid from; to connect a secret listening device to a telephone; (*inf*) to ask for money from; (*resources*) to draw on.

tap-dance *vi* to perform a step dance in shoes with taps.

tape *n* a narrow strip of cloth, paper, etc, used for tying, binding, etc; a tape measure; magnetic tape. • *vt* to record on magnetic tape.

tape measure *n* a tape marked in inches or centimetres for measuring.

taper *n* a long thin candle. • *vti* to make or become gradually narrower.

tape recorder *n* a machine for recording and reproducing sounds on magnetic tape.

tapestry *n* a heavy fabric woven with patterns.

tapioca *n* a starch extracted from the root of a tropical plant and used in puddings, etc.

tar *n* a thick, dark substance obtained from wood, coal, etc., used for surfacing roads.

tarantula *n* a large, hairy spider with a poisonous bite.

tardy *adj* slow; later than expected.

target *n* a mark to aim at, esp in shooting.

tariff *n* (*in a hotel*) a list of prices.

Tarmac *n* (*trademark*) a material for surfacing roads made from crushed stones and tar; an airport runway.

tarnish *vi* (*metal*) to discolour due to exposure to the air. • *vt* (*reputation*) to taint.

tarpaulin *n* canvas cloth coated with a waterproof substance.

tart¹ *adj* sour; (*speech*) sharp, severe.

tart² *n* an open pastry case containing fruit, jam or custard; (*inf*) a prostitute.

tartan *n* a woollen cloth with a chequered pattern, having a distinctive design for each Scottish clan.

tartar *n* a hard, yellow, crusty deposit that forms on the teeth.

tartar sauce *n* a mayonnaise sauce with herbs, etc, eaten esp with fish.

task *n* a specific amount of work to be done.

task force *n* a small unit with a specific mission, usu military.

tassel *n* an ornamental tuft of threads decorating soft furnishings, clothes, etc.

taste *vt* to perceive (a flavour) by taking into the mouth. • *vi* to have a specific flavour. • *n* the sense by which flavours are perceived; a small portion; the ability to recognise what is beautiful, attractive, etc.

tasteful *adj* showing good taste.

tasteless *adj* bland; in bad taste.

tasty *adj* having a pleasant flavour.

tatter *n* a torn or ragged piece of cloth.

tattoo¹ *n* a continuous beating of a drum.

tattoo² vt to make permanent patterns or pictures on the skin by pricking and marking with dyes. • n marks made on the skin in this way.

tatty adj shabby, ragged.

taunt vt to provoke with mockery or contempt.

taut adj stretched tight; tense; stressed.

tavern n a pub, an inn.

tawdry adj showy, cheap and of poor quality.

tawny adj yellowish brown.

tax n a rate imposed by the government on property or persons to raise revenues. • vt to impose a tax (upon); to strain.

taxation n the act of levying taxes.

taxi n a car fitted with a meter that may be hired to transport passengers. • vi (aircraft) to move along the runway before takeoff or after landing.

taxpayer n a person that pays taxes.

tea n a shrub growing in China, India, etc; its dried, shredded leaves, which are infused in boiling water for a beverage.

tea bag n a small porous bag containing tea leaves for infusing.

teach vt to impart knowledge to.

teacher n a person who instructs others.

teaching n the profession of being a teacher.

teak n a hard wood from an Indian tree.

team n a group of people participating in a sport together; a group of people working together. • vi (with up) to join in cooperative activity.

teamwork n cooperation of individuals for the benefit of the team.

teapot n a vessel in which tea is made.

tear¹ n a drop of salty liquid appearing in the eyes when crying.

tear² vt to split. • vi to move with speed • n a hole or split.

tearaway n an impetuous, violent person.

tearful adj weeping; sad.—**tearfully** adv.

tear gas n gas that irritates the eyes and nasal passages, used in riot control.

tear-jerker n a sentimental book, film, etc.

tease vt to taunt playfully. • n a person who teases; (inf) a flirt.

tea set n the set of cups and saucers, etc, for serving tea.

teaspoon n a small spoon for use with tea.

teat n the nipple on a breast or udder; the mouthpiece of a baby's feeding bottle.

tea towel n a towel for drying dishes.

technical adj relating to industrial, mechanical or applied sciences.—**technically** adv.

technicality n a petty formality.

technician n a person skilled in practical work with scientific equipment.

technique n method of performing a particular task.

technology n the application of mechanical and applied sciences to industrial use.

teddy bear n a stuffed toy bear.

tedious adj monotonous; boring.

tee n (golf) the place from where the first stroke is played at each hole; a small peg from which the ball is driven.

teem¹ vi (with with) to be abundant in.

teem² vi to pour (with rain).

teenager n (inf) a person in his or her teens.

teens npl the years of one's life from thirteen to nineteen.—**teenage** adj.

teepee see **tepee**.

tee-shirt see **T-shirt**.

teeter vi to move or stand unsteadily.

teethe vi to cut one's first teeth.

teething n the condition in babies of the first growth of teeth.

teething troubles npl problems encountered in the early stages of a project, etc.

teetotaller n a person who abstains from alcoholic drinks.—**teetotal** adj.

telecommunications npl the technology of telephone and radio communication.

telegram n a message sent by telegraph.

telegraph n a system for transmitting messages over long distances using electricity, wires and a code. • vt to transmit by telegraph.

telepathy n the communication between people's minds of thoughts and feelings, without the need for speech or proximity.

telephone n an instrument for transmitting speech at a distance, esp by means of electricity. • vt to call by telephone.

telephonist n a person who operates a telephone switchboard.

telephoto lens n a camera lens that magnifies distant objects.

teleprinter n a telegraph apparatus with a keyboard that transmits and a printer that receives messages over a distance.

Teleprompter™ n a device that displays a TV script for a speaker out of sight of the viewer.

telescope n a tubular optical instrument for viewing objects at a distance.

telescopic adj of or like a telescope.

Teletext™ n written information transmitted non-interactively to television viewers.

televise vt to transmit by television.

television n the transmission of visual images and accompanying sound through electrical and sound waves; a television receiving set; television broadcasting.

telex n a communication system whereby subscribers hire teleprinters for transmitting messages. • vt to transmit by telex.

tell vt to narrate; to distinguish; to disclose. • vi to tell tales; to produce a marked effect.

teller n a bank clerk; one who counts votes.

telling adj having great impact.

telltale n a person who tells tales about others. • adj revealing what is meant to be hidden.

telly n (inf) television.

temerity n rashness.

temp n (inf) a temporary employee.

temper n a frame of mind; a fit of anger.

temperament n one's disposition.

temperamental adj easily irritated.

temperance n abstinence from alcohol.

temperate adj mild or moderate in temperature.

temperature n degree of heat or cold; body heat above the normal.

tempest n a violent storm.

tempestuous adj violent; passionate.

template n a pattern, gauge or mould used as a guide esp in cutting metal, stone or plastic.

temple¹ n a place of worship.

temple² n the region on either side of the head above the cheekbone.

tempo n (mus) the speed at which music is meant to be played.

temporal¹ adj relating to time.

temporal² adj of the temples of the head.

temporary adj lasting or used for a limited time.

tempt vt to entice to do wrong; to invite, attract, induce.—**temptress** nf.

temptation n the act of tempting.

tempting adj attractive, inviting.

ten adj, n the cardinal number next above nine. • n the symbol for this (10, X, x).

tenacious adj grasping firmly; persistent.

tenacity n doggedness, obstinacy.

tenancy n the temporary possession by a tenant of another's property; its period.

tenant n a person who pays rent to occupy a house or flat.

tend¹ vt to take care of; to attend (to).

tend² vi to be inclined.

tendency n an inclination or leaning.

tender¹ vt to present for acceptance. • n an offer to provide goods or services at a fixed price.

tender² adj soft, delicate; sore; sensitive.

tenderise vt (meat) to make more tender, esp by pounding.

tendon n fibrous tissue attaching a muscle to a bone.

tendril n a thread-like shoot of a climbing plant by which it attaches itself for support.

tenement n a building divided into flats.

tenet n any belief or doctrine.

tennis n a game for two or four people, played by hitting a ball over a net with a racket.

tennis court n a court surfaced with clay, asphalt or grass on which tennis is played.

tenor n a general purpose or intent; the highest regular adult male voice; a man who sings tenor.

tense¹ n (gram) the verb form that indicates the time of an action or existence of a state.

tense² adj taut; nervous. • vti to make or become tense.

tensile adj of or relating to tension.

tension n the state of being stretched; stress.

tent n a portable shelter of canvas, plastic or other waterproof fabric erected on poles.

tentacle n a long, slender, flexible growth near the mouth of invertebrates, used for feeling, grasping or handling.

tentative adj provisional; not definite.

tenterhook n (pl: with on) in a tense state.

tenth adj the last of ten; being one of ten equal parts. • n one of ten equal parts.

tenuous adj slight, flimsy, insubstantial.

tenure n the holding of property or a position.

tepee, teepee n a cone-shaped, North American Indian tent formed of skins.

tepid adj slightly warm, lukewarm.

term n a limit; any prescribed period of time; a division of an academic year; a word or expression; (pl) conditions of a contract, etc. • vt to call, designate.

terminal adj (disease) incurable. • n a bus, coach or railway station at the end of the line; the point at which an electrical current enters or leaves a device; a device with a keyboard and monitor for inputting or viewing data from a computer.

terminate vti to bring or come to an end.

terminology n the terms used in any specialised subject.

terminus n the end of a transportation line.

termite n a wood-eating, white insect.

terrace n a row of houses; (pl) unroofed tiers in a football ground.

terracotta n a brownish-red clay used for making flower pots and statues, which is baked but not glazed; a brown-red colour.

terrain n the surface features of a tract of land; (fig) field of activity.

terrible adj (inf) very unpleasant.

terribly adv frighteningly; (inf) very.

terrier n a type of small, active dog.

terrific adj of great size; (inf) excellent.

terrify vt to fill with terror.

territorial adj relating to a territory.

territory n a wide tract of land; an area assigned to a salesman; an area of knowledge.

terror n great fear.

terrorise vt to control by terror.

terrorism n the use of terror and violence to intimidate.— **terrorist** n.

terse adj abrupt, concise.—**tersely** adv.

test n an examination; trial; a chemical reaction to test a substance or to test for an illness. • vt to examine critically.

testament n a will; tribute; (with cap) one of the two main parts of the Bible.

testicle *n* either of the two male reproductive glands that produce sperm.

testify *vti* to give evidence under oath.

testimonial *n* a recommendation of one's character or abilities.

testimony *n* evidence.

testis *n* testicle.

test match *n* one of a series of international cricket or Rugby football matches.

test pilot *n* someone who flies new types of aircraft to test their performance.

test tube *n* a cylinder of thin glass closed at one end, used in scientific experiments.

test-tube baby *n* a baby that develops from an ovum fertilised outside the mother's body and replaced in the womb.

testy *adj* touchy, irritable.

tetanus *n* an intense and painful spasm of muscles, caused by the infection of a wound by bacteria; lockjaw.

tête-à-tête *n* a private conversation between two people.

tether *n* the limit of one's endurance.

text *n* the main part of a printed work; a passage from the Bible.

textbook *n* a book used for instruction.

textile *n* a woven fabric or cloth.

texture *n* the characteristic appearance, arrangement or feel of a thing.

thalidomide *n* a sedative drug withdrawn from use when it was discovered to cause malformation in unborn babies.

than *conj* introducing the second element of a comparison.

thank *vt* to express gratitude to or appreciation for. • *npl* an expression of gratitude.

thankless *adj* unrewarding.

that *demons adj, pron* the (one) there or then. • *rel pron* who or which. • *conj* introducing a noun clause or adverbial clause of purpose or consequence.

thatch *n* roofing straw. • *vt* to cover a roof with thatch.

thaw *vi* to melt; to become friendly. • *n* the melting of ice or snow by warm weather.

the *demons adj* denoting a particular person or thing.

theatre *n* a building where plays and operas are performed; the theatrical world as a whole.

theatrical *adj* relating to the theatre; melodramatic, affected.

theft *n* act or crime of stealing.

their *poss adj* of or belonging to them.

theirs *poss pron* of or belonging to them.

them *pron* the objective case of they.

theme *n* the main subject of a discussion.

themselves *pron* the reflexive form of they or them.

then *adv* at that time; afterwards; immediately.

theologian *n* a person who studies and interprets religious texts, etc.

theology *n* the study of God and of religious doctrine and matters of divinity.

theorem *n* a proposition that can be proved from accepted principles.

theoretical *adj* of or based on theory.

theorise *vi* to speculate.—**theorist** *n*.

theory *n* an explanation or system of anything; ideas and abstract principles of a science or art.

therapeutic *adj* relating to the treatment of disease; beneficial.

therapy *n* the treatment of illness.

there *adv* in, at or to, that place or point.

thereabouts *adv* at or near that place.

thereafter *adv* after that.

therefore *adv* for that or this reason.

therm *n* a measurement of heat.

thermal *adj* hot; warm; (*underwear*) of a knitted material with air spaces for insulation.

thermodynamics *n* the branch of physics concerned with the relationship between heat and other forms of energy.

thermometer *n* an instrument for measuring temperature.

thermonuclear *adj* of nuclear fusion or nuclear weapons that utilise fusion reactions.

Thermos™ *n* a brand of vacuum flask.

thermostat *n* an automatic device for regulating temperatures.

thesaurus *n* a reference book of synonyms.

thesis *n* a detailed essay written as part of a university degree.

they *pers pron, pl of* he, she *or* it.

thick *adj* dense; fat, broad; (*inf*) stupid.

thicken *vti* to make or become thick.

thickset *adj* having a short, stocky body.

thick-skinned *adj* not sensitive.

thief *n* a person who steals.

thigh *n* the thick part of the leg from the hip to the knee.

thimble *n* a cover worn to protect the finger when sewing.

thin *adj* narrow; slim; weak, watery; (*material*) fine. • *vt* to make thin; to water down.

thing *n* an inanimate object; an action; (*pl*) possessions; (*inf*) an obsession.

think *vi* to exercise the mind in order to make a decision; to ponder; to consider; • *vt* to judge, to believe; (*with* **up**) to concoct.

third *adj* the last of three; being one of three equal parts.—*also n*.

thirdly *adv* in the third place.

third party *n* (*insurance*) involving a third person.

third rate *adj* inferior.

Third World *n* the underdeveloped countries of the world.

thirst *n* a craving for drink; a longing.

thirsty *adj* having a desire to drink; longing or craving for.

thirteen *adj*, *n* three and ten.—**thirteenth** *adj*.

thirty *adj*, *n* three times ten. • *n* the symbol for this (30, XXX, xxx).—**thirtieth** *adj*.

this *demons pron or adj* denoting a person or thing near, just mentioned or about to be mentioned.

thistle *n* a wild plant with prickly leaves and a purple flower.

thong *n* a strap of leather to lash things together.

thorax *n* the part of the body enclosed by the ribs; the chest.

thorn *n* a sharp point or prickle on the stem of a plant or the branch of a tree.

thorny *adj* prickly; (*problem*) knotty.

thorough *adj* very detailed and painstaking.

thoroughbred *adj* bred from pure stock.

thoroughfare *n* a public street.

thoroughgoing *adj* out-and-out.

thoroughly *adv* completely, absolutely.

those *adj*, *pron*, *pl* of that.

though *conj* yet, even if; • *adv* however.

thought *n* serious consideration; an idea.

thoughtful *adj* pensive; considerate.

thoughtless *adj* inconsiderate.

thousand *adj* ten times one hundred; (*pl*) denoting any large but unspecified number. • *n* the number 1000.—**thousandth** *adj*.

thrash *vt* to beat soundly; to defeat.

thread *n* a long thin piece of cotton, silk or nylon for sewing; the spiral part of a screw; (*of reasoning*) a line. • *vt* to pass a thread through the eye of a needle; to make one's way (through).

threadbare *adj* worn, shabby.

threat *n* a declaration of an intention to inflict harm or punishment upon another.

threaten *vti* to utter threats to; to be a threat.

three *adj*, *n* the cardinal number next above two. • *n* the symbol (3, III, iii) of this.

three-quarter *adj* being three quarters of the normal size or length. • *n* (*Rugby football*) one of usu four attacking players.

thresh *vti* to beat out (grain) from (husks).

threshold *n* the sill at the door of a building.

thrift *n* careful management of money.

thrill *vti* to tingle with pleasure or excitement. • *n* a sensation of pleasure and excitement; a trembling or quiver.

thriller *n* a novel, film or play depicting an exciting story of mystery and suspense.

thrilling *adj* exciting, gripping.

thrive *vi* to prosper, to be successful.

throat *n* the front part of the neck; the passage from back of the mouth to the top part of the tubes into the lungs and stomach.

throb *vi* to beat or pulsate rhythmically.

throes *npl* violent pangs or pain.

thrombosis *n* the forming of a blood clot in a blood vessel.

throne *n* a chair of state occupied by a monarch.

throng *n* a crowd. • *vti* to crowd.

throttle *n* a valve controlling the flow of fuel or steam to an engine. • *vt* to strangle.

through *prep* from one side or end to the other; into and then out of; by means of.

throughout *prep* in every part of; from beginning to end. • *adv* everywhere; at every moment.

throw *vt* to fling; (*party*) to hold; (*inf*) to disconcert.

throwaway *adj* disposable.

thrush[1] *n* a bird with a brown back and spotted breast.

thrush[2] *n* a fungal disease occurring in the mouths of babies or in women's vaginas.

thrust *vti* to push with force. • *n* a forceful push or stab; the point or basic meaning.

thud *n* a dull, heavy sound, caused by a blow or a heavy object falling. • *vi* to make such a sound.

thug *n* a violent and rough person.

thuggery *n* rough and violent behaviour.

thumb *n* the first, short, thick finger of the human hand.

thumb index *n* a series of semicircular notches cut in the edge of a book for easier reference to particular parts.

thump *n* a heavy blow. • *vt* to strike with something heavy. • *vi* to throb.

thunder *n* the deep rumbling after a flash of lightning.

thunderclap *n* a loud bang of thunder.

thunderous *adj* very loud.

thunderstorm *n* a storm with thunder and lightning.

thundery *adj* indicating thunder.

thus *adv* in this or that way.

thwart *vt* to prevent, to frustrate.

thyme *n* a herb with small leaves used for flavouring savoury food.

thyroid *n* the gland in the neck affecting growth.

tiara *n* a semicircular crown.

tibia *n* the inner and thicker of the two bones between the knee and the ankle.

tic *n* any involuntary, regularly repeated, spasmodic contraction of a muscle.

tick[1] *n* a small bloodsucking insect that lives on people and animals.

tick[2] *vi* to beat, as a clock; (*inf*) to function.

tick[3] *n* (*inf*) account, credit.

tick[4] *vt* (*often with off*) to check off, as items in a list. • *n* a check mark (√) to check off items on a list or to indicate correctness.

ticket *n* a printed card, etc, that gives one a right of travel or entry; a label on merchandise giving size, price, etc.

tickle vt to touch lightly to provoke pleasure or laughter; to please or delight.

ticklish adj tickly; easily offended; difficult.

tickly adj sensitive to being tickled.

tidal adj relating to, or having, tides.

tiddler n (inf) something small.

tiddlywinks npl a game whose object is to flick small plastic discs into a container by snapping them with a larger disc.

tide n the regular rise and fall of the seas twice a day. • vt (with **over**) to help temporarily.

tidings npl news, information.

tidy adj neat. • vt to make neat.

tie vt to fasten with a string or thread. • vi to score the same number of points (as an opponent). • n a long narrow piece of cloth worn with a shirt; an equality in score.

tier n a row or rank in a series.

tiff n a petty quarrel or disagreement.

tiger n a large, fierce animal of the cat family with orange and black stripes.

tight adj taut; fitting closely; constricted.

tighten vti to make or grow tight or tighter

tightrope n a taut rope on which acrobats walk.

tights npl a one-piece garment covering the legs and lower body.

tile n a thin slab of baked clay used for covering roofs, floors, etc.—also vt.

till[1] n a drawer inside a cash register for keeping money.

till[2] prep until. • conj until.

till[3] vt (land) to cultivate for raising crops.

tiller n the handle or lever for turning a rudder.

tilt vi to slope. • vt to raise one end of.—also n.

timber n wood when used as construction material.

timbre n the quality of sound of a voice.

time n the past, present and future; a particular moment; hour of the day; occasion. • vt to measure the duration of.

time bomb n a bomb designed to explode at a predetermined time.

timekeeper n a person or instrument that records or keeps time.—**timekeeping** n.

time lag n the interval between two connected events.

timeless adj eternal; ageless.

timely adj at the right time, opportune.

timer n a device for measuring, recording or controlling time; a device for controlling lights, heating, etc, by an electrical clock.

timeshare n joint ownership of holiday accommodation by several people with each occupying the same premises in turn for short periods.

timetable n a list of times of arrivals and departures or trains, aeroplanes, etc; a schedule showing a planned order.

time zone n a geographical region throughout which the same standard time is used.

timing n the control and expression of speech or actions to create the best effect, esp in the theatre, etc.

timpani npl a set of kettledrums.

tin n a malleable metallic element; a can. • vt to put food into a tin.

tinfoil n baking foil for wrapping food.

tinge vt to tint or colour. • n a slight tint.

tingle vi to feel a prickling sensation.

tinker vi to fiddle with.

tinkle vi to make a sound like a small bell ringing. • n a tinkling sound.

tin plate n thin sheets of iron or steel plated with tin.

tinsel n a shiny Christmas decoration made of long strands of thread wound round with thin strips of metal or plastic foil.

tint n a shade of any colour, esp a pale one; a tinge; a hair dye. • vt to colour or tinge.

tiny adj very small.

tip[1] n the pointed end of anything.

tip[2] vti to tilt; to overturn; to give a gratuity to, as a waiter, etc; (rubbish) to dump. • n a gratuity; a rubbish dump; a helpful hint.

tip-off n a warning based on inside information.

tipple vi to drink alcohol regularly in small quantities. • n an alcoholic drink.

tipsy adj slightly drunk.

tiptoe vi to walk very quietly.

tire vt to exhaust the strength of, to weary. • vi to become weary; to lose patience.

tired adj sleepy; (with **of**) exasperated by.

tiresome adj tedious.

tissue n thin, absorbent paper used as a disposable handkerchief, etc; a very finely woven fabric; a mass of organic cells of a similar structure and function.

tit[1] n a songbird such as a blue tit or great tit.

tit[2] n (vulg) a woman's breast.

titanic adj monumental; huge.

titbit n a tasty morsel of food.

titillate vt to arouse or excite pleasurably.

title n the name of a book, play, piece of music, work of art, etc; a name denoting nobility or rank or office held or attached to a personal name.

title deed n a deed or document proving a right to possession.

title role n the character in a play, film, etc, after whom it is named.

titter vi to giggle. • n a suppressed laugh.

tittle-tattle n idle chat, empty gossip.

to prep in the direction of; toward; as far as; expressing the purpose of an action.

toad n an amphibious reptile, like a frog, but having a drier skin.

toadstool n a mushroom, esp a poisonous one.

toady n a person who flatters insincerely.

toast *vt* to brown under a grill; to warm; to drink to the health of. • *n* toasted bread.

toaster *n* a thing that toasts, esp an electrical appliance.

tobacco *n* a plant whose dried leaves are used for smoking, chewing or snuff.

tobacconist *n* a shop that sells cigarettes.

toboggan *n* a sledge, sled.

today *n* this day; the present age. • *adv* on this day; nowadays.

toddle *vi* to walk with short, unsteady, steps.

toddler *n* a young child.

toddy *n* a drink of whisky, sugar and hot water.

toe *n* one of the five digits on the foot.

toenail *n* the thin, hard, covering on the end of the toes.

toffee *n* a sweet of brittle but tender texture made by boiling sugar and butter.

toga *n* a piece of cloth draped around the body, as worn by citizens in ancient Rome.

together *adv* in one place or group; jointly.

toggle *n* a peg attached to a rope to prevent it from passing through a loop or knot.

toil *vi* to work strenuously. • *n* hard work.

toilet *n* a lavatory.

toilet paper *n* an absorbent paper for cleansing after urination, etc.

toilet roll *n* a cardboard cylinder around which toilet paper is wound.

toiletry *n* a lotion, perfume, etc, used in washing.

toilet water *n* a diluted perfume.

token *n* a symbol, sign; a metal disc for a slot machine; a gift voucher. • *adj* nominal.

tolerable *adj* bearable; fairly good.

tolerant *adj* able to put up with the beliefs, actions, etc, of others; open-minded; (*med*) showing the ability to resist the action of a drug, etc.

tolerate *vt* to endure, put up with, suffer.

toll[1] *n* money levied for passing over a bridge or road; the number of people killed in an accident.

toll[2] *vi* to sound, as a bell.—*also n*.

tomato *n* a plant with red pulpy fruit used as a vegetable.

tomb *n* a vault in the earth for the burial of the dead.

tomboy *n* a girl who likes rough outdoor activities.

tombstone *n* a memorial stone over a grave.

tomcat *n* a male cat.

tomorrow *n* the day after today; the future.

ton *n* a unit of weight equivalent to 2,240 pounds; (*inf: pl*) a great quantity.

tone *n* the quality of a sound; pitch or inflection of the voice; colour, shade. • *vi* to harmonise.

tongs *npl* an instrument consisting of two arms that are hinged, used for grasping.

tongue *n* the soft, moveable organ in the mouth,

used in tasting, swallowing and speech; a language; (*shoe*) a piece of leather under the laces.

tongue-tied *adj* speechless.

tongue-twister *n* a sequence of words that it is difficult to pronounce quickly.

tonic *n* a medicine that improves physical wellbeing; something that imparts vigour; a fizzy mineral water with a bitter taste.

tonight *n* this night; the night or evening of the present day.—*also adv*.

tonne *n* metric ton, 1000 kg.

tonsil *n* one of the two oval organs of soft tissue situated one on each side of the throat.

tonsillitis *n* inflammation of the tonsils.

too *adv* in addition; extremely; very.

tool *n* an implement that is used by hand; a means for achieving any purpose.

toot *vi* to hoot a car horn.—*also vt.*

tooth *n* one of the white, bone-like structures arranged in rows in the mouth; a projection like this on a comb, saw or wheel.

toothache *n* a pain in a tooth.

toothbrush *n* a small brush for cleaning teeth.

toothpaste *n* a paste for cleaning teeth.

toothpick *n* a sliver of wood or plastic for removing food particles from between the teeth.

top[1] *n* the highest, or uppermost, part or surface of anything; the highest in rank; the lid. • *adj* highest. • *vt* to cover on the top; to surpass.

top[2] *n* a child's toy, which is spun on its base.

top hat *n* a man's tall, silk hat.

top-heavy *adj* having an upper part too heavy for the lower, causing instability.

topic *n* a subject for discussion.

topical *adj* of current interest.

topless *adj* (*garment*) revealing the breasts; wearing such a garment.

topmost *adj* nearest the top, highest.

topple *vi* to fall over. • *vt* to overthrow.

topsy-turvy *adj, adv* turned upside down.

torch *n* a portable light powered by batteries.

torment *n* torture, a source of pain. • *vt* to afflict with extreme physical or mental pain.

tornado *n* a violently whirling column of air seen as a funnel-shaped cloud that usu destroys everything in its narrow path.

torpedo *n* a self-propelled submarine weapon carrying an explosive charge.

torpor *n* a state of lethargy.

torrent *n* a rushing stream; a flood of words.

torrid *adj* scorched; passionate.

torso *n* the trunk of the human body.

tortoise *n* a slow-moving reptile with a domeshaped shell into which it can withdraw.

tortoiseshell *n* a brown and yellow colour.

tortuous *adj* full of twists, involved.

torture *n* subjection to severe physical or mental pain to extort a confession or as a punishment.

Tory n a member of the Conservative Party.

toss vt to throw up; (head) to throw back.

toss-up n the throwing of a coin to decide a question.

tot[1] n a child; a small measure of spirits.

tot[2] vt (with up) to add up.

total adj whole, complete; absolute. • n the whole sum. • vt to add up.—**totally** adv.

totalitarian adj relating to a system of government in which one political group maintains complete control, esp under a dictator.

totem n an object regarded as a symbol and treated with respect by a particular group of people.

totter vi to walk unsteadily.

touch vt to come in contact with, esp with the hand or fingers; to affect with emotion; (sl) to ask for money (from). • vi to be in contact. • n the act of touching; the sense by which something is perceived through contact; a trace.

touch-and-go adj precarious, risky.

touchdown n the moment when an aircraft or spaceship lands; (rugby football) a placing of the ball on the ground to score.

touched adj emotionally affected.

touching adj affecting, moving.

touchline n (football, etc) the side boundary of a pitch.

touchstone n a siliceous stone used to test gold and silver from the marks they make on it.

touchy adj irritable.

tough adj strong; rough and violent; difficult.

toupee n a section of hair to cover a bald spot.

tour n a long trip, as for sightseeing. • vti to go on a tour (through).

tourism n travelling for pleasure; the business of catering for people who do this.

tourist n a sightseer, travelling for pleasure.

tourist class n economy accommodation, as on a ship, aeroplane, etc.

tournament n a sporting event involving a series of games.

tourniquet n a device for compressing a blood vessel to stop bleeding.

tousle vt to make untidy, ruffle.

tout vti (inf) to solicit business in a brazen way.

tow vt to pull or drag with a rope.

towards prep in the direction of.

towel n an absorbent cloth for drying the skin.

towelling n cloth for towels.

tower n a tall, narrow building. • vi (with over) to loom.

tower block n a skyscraper.

town n a densely populated urban centre.

townhall n a large building housing the offices of the town council.

towpath n the footpath beside a canal.

towrope n a strong rope or cable for towing a wheeled vehicle, ship, etc.

toxaemia n blood poisoning.

toxic adj poisonous; harmful; deadly.

toy n an object for children to play with.

trace n a mark left by a person, animal or thing; a small quantity. • vt to follow by tracks; to discover the whereabouts of; (map, etc) to copy by following the lines on transparent paper.

trachea n the air passage from the mouth to the lungs, windpipe.

track vt to follow the tracks of. • n a mark left; a footprint; parallel steel rails on which trains run; a course for running or racing; one piece of music on a record.

tracksuit n a loose suit worn by athletes to keep warm.

tract n an expanse of land or water.

traction n (med) the using of weights to pull on a muscle, etc, to correct an abnormal condition.

tractor n a motor vehicle for pulling heavy loads and for working ploughs.

trade n buying and selling (of commodities); commerce; occupation. • vi to exchange.

trade-in n a used item given in part payment when buying a replacement.

trademark n a name used on a product by a manufacturer to distinguish it from its competitors, esp when legally protected.

tradesman n a skilled worker.

trade union n an organised association of employees of any trade or industry for the protection of their income and working conditions.

tradition n the handing down from generation to generation and practices. —**traditional** adj.

traffic n the movement or number of vehicles, pedestrians, etc, along a street, etc. • vi to do business (esp in illegal drugs).

traffic light n one of a set of coloured lights used to control traffic at street crossings, etc.

traffic warden n a person who is authorised to control traffic and to report parking violations.

tragedy n a play or drama that is serious and sad, and the climax a catastrophe; a situation involving death or suffering.—**tragic** adj.

trail vt to drag along the ground. • vi to drag loosely behind; (with away) to grow weaker or dimmer. • n a path or track; the scent of an animal.

trailer n a wagon, van, etc, designed to be towed by a motor vehicle; an advertisement for a film or TV programme.

train vt to teach, to tame for use, as animals; to prepare for racing, etc. • vi to do exercise or preparation. • n a series of railway carriages pulled by a locomotive.

trained adj skilled.

trainee n a person who is being trained.

trainer n a coach or instructor in sports.

training n practical instruction.

trait n a characteristic feature.

traitor n a person who betrays his country, friends, etc.

tram n an electrically powered vehicle for public transport that travels along rails set into the ground.

tramp vti to walk heavily. • n a vagrant.

trample vti to tread under foot.

trampoline n a sheet of strong canvas stretched tightly on a frame, used in acrobatic tumbling.

trance n a state of unconsciousness, induced by hypnosis, in which some of the powers of the waking body, such as response to commands, may be retained.

tranquil adj quiet, calm.—**tranquillity** n.

tranquilliser n a drug that calms.

transact vt (business) to conduct.

transaction n a business deal.

transatlantic adj crossing the Atlantic Ocean.

transcend vt to rise above.

transcript n a written or printed copy made by transcribing.

transcription n the act of transcribing; something transcribed, esp a piece of music.

transept n one of the two wings of a church.

transfer vt to carry, convey, from one place to another. • vi to change to another bus, etc. • n the act of transferring; a design that can be moved from one surface to another.

transform vti to change the shape, appearance or condition of.

transformer n a device for changing alternating current with an increase or decrease of voltage.

transfusion n the injection of blood into the veins of a sick or injured person.

transgress vti to break or violate.

transient adj temporary; of short duration.

transistor n a device for amplifying sound.

transit n a passing over or through.

transition n passage from one place or state to another; change.—**transitional** adj.

transitive adj (gram) denoting a verb that requires a direct object.

transitory adj lasting only a short time.

translate vti to express in another language.

translation n something translated into another language.

translucent adj allowing light to pass through, but not transparent.

transmission n a system using gears, etc, to transfer power from an engine to a moving part, esp wheels of a car; a broadcast.

transmit vt to communicate; (radio or TV signals) to send out.

transmitter n an apparatus for broadcasting television or radio programmes.

transparency n the state of being transparent; (photog) a slide.

transparent adj that may be easily seen through; clear, easily understood.

transplant vt (plant) to remove and plant in another place; (med) to remove an organ from one person and transfer it to another.—also n.

transport vt to convey from one place to another. • n the system of transporting goods or passengers.

transsexual n a person born of one sex who identifies psychologically with the opposite sex.

transverse adj crosswise.

transvestite n a person who gains sexual pleasure from wearing the clothes of the opposite sex.

trap n a mechanical device or pit for snaring animals; an ambush. • vt to catch in a trap.

trapdoor n a hinged or sliding door in a roof, ceiling or floor.

trapeze n a gymnastic apparatus consisting of a horizontal bar suspended by two parallel ropes.

trapper n a person who traps animals.

trappings npl trimmings; additions.

trash n nonsense; refuse; rubbish.

trauma n an emotional shock that may cause long-term psychological damage.

travel vi to journey from one place to another.

travel agency n an agency through which one can book travel.—**travel agent** n.

traveller n a person who travels.

traveller's cheque n a draft purchased from a bank, etc, signed at the time of purchase and again at the time of cashing.

travesty n a poor imitation; a parody.

trawl vti to fish by dragging a large net behind a fishing boat.

trawler n a boat used for trawling.

tray n a flat board of metal or plastic, surrounded by a rim, used for carrying food or drink.

treacherous adj disloyal; dangerous.

treachery n disloyalty, betrayal of trust.

treacle n a thick sticky substance obtained during the refining of sugar.

tread vti to step or walk on; to trample (on). • n a step; the part of a tyre that touches the ground.

treason n the crime of betraying one's government or attempting to overthrow it.

treasure n wealth and riches hoarded up.

treasurer n a person appointed to take charge of the finances of a society, etc.

treasury n the funds of a government.

treat vt to deal with or regard; to apply medical treatment to; to pay for another person's entertainment. • n an entertainment paid for by another person.

treatise n a formal essay in which a subject is treated systematically.

treatment n the application of drugs, etc, to a patient; the manner of dealing with a person or thing, esp in a novel or painting.

treaty n a formal agreement between states.

treble adj triple. • n the highest range of musical notes in singing. • vti to make or become three times as much.

tree n a tall, woody, perennial plant having a single trunk, branches and leaves.

trek vi to travel slowly or laboriously. • n a long and difficult journey.

trellis n a structure of lattice work.

tremble vi to shake from cold or fear.

tremendous adj (inf) wonderful.

tremor n an involuntary shaking.

trench n a long narrow channel in the earth.

trench coat n a waterproof coat.

trend n tendency; a current style or fashion.

trendy adj (inf) fashionable.

trepidation n a state of fear or anxiety.

trespass vi to intrude upon another person's property without their permission.

trestle n a wooden framework for supporting a table top.

trial n a test or experiment; judicial examination.

triangle n (math) a plane figure with three angles and three sides; a percussion instrument consisting of a triangular metal bar beaten with a metal stick.—**triangular** adj.

tribe n a group of people of the same race, sharing the same customs, language or land.

tribulation n distress, difficulty, hardship.

tribunal n a court of justice.

tributary n a stream or river flowing into a larger one.

tribute n a speech, gift or action to show one's respect or thanks to someone.

trick n fraud; deception; a mischievous plan or joke; a magical illusion; a clever feat; the playing cards won in a round. • vt to deceive, cheat.

trickery n the practice of using underhand methods to achieve an aim.

trickle vti to flow in drops.

tricky adj complicated; cunning.

tricycle n a three-wheeled pedal cycle.

trifle vi to treat lightly. • n anything of little value; a dessert of whipped cream, custard, sponge cake, sherry, etc.

trifling adj insignificant.

trigger n a catch that when pulled activates the firing mechanism of a gun. • vt (with off) to initiate; to set (off).

trigonometry n the branch of mathematics concerned with calculating the angles of triangles or the lengths of their sides.

trim adj neat; slim. • vt to cut; to decorate. • n a decorative edging.

trimming n decorative part of clothing; (pl) accompaniments.

trinity n (with cap) in Christianity, the union of Father, Son and Holy Spirit in one God.

trinket n a small or worthless ornament.

trio n a group of three singers or instrumentalists.

trip vi to move or tread lightly; to stumble and fall. • vt (a person: often with up) to cause to stumble. • n a journey; (sl) a hallucinatory experience under the influence of a drug.

tripe n the stomach lining of an ox, prepared for cooking; (inf) rubbish, nonsense.

triple adj three times as many. • vti to treble.

triplet n one of three children born at one birth.

triplicate adj threefold.

tripod n a three-legged stand, as for a camera.

trite adj dull; hackneyed.

triumph n a victory. • vi to win a victory.

triumphant adj feeling or showing triumph.

trivia npl unimportant details.

trivial adj unimportant; commonplace.

trolley n a table on wheels for serving food; a cart for transporting luggage or shopping in a supermarket.

trolleybus n an electric bus powered from an overhead wire.

trombone n a brass wind instrument whose length is varied with a U-shaped sliding section.

troop n a crowd of people; a group of soldiers within a cavalry regiment; (pl) armed forces.

trooper n a cavalryman.

trophy n a cup or shield won as a prize.

tropic n one of the two parallel lines of latitude north and south of the equator.

tropical adj of the tropics; hot and humid.

trot vi (horse) to go, lifting the feet higher than in walking and moving at a faster rate.

trouble vti to worry; to upset; to cause inconvenience; to take pains (to). • n an anxiety; a medical condition causing pain; unrest.

troubleshooter n a person whose work is to locate and eliminate a source of trouble.

trough n a long, narrow container for water or animal feed.

trounce vt to defeat completely.

troupe n a travelling company, esp of actors.

trousers npl an item of clothing covering the body from waist to ankle, with two tubes of material for the legs.

trousseau n the clothes, linen a bride collects for her marriage.

trout n a game fish of the salmon family living in fresh water.

trowel n a hand tool for gardening.

truant n a pupil who is absent from school without permission.—**truancy** n.

truce n an agreement between two armies or states to suspend hostilities.

truck n a heavy motor vehicle for transporting goods.

trudge vti to travel on foot wearily.

true *adj* correct, accurate.

truffle *n* a sweet made with chocolate, butter and sugar.

truly *adv* completely; genuinely.

trump *n* (*cards*) the suit that is chosen to have the highest value in one game.

trumpet *n* a brass wind instrument consisting of a long tube with a flared end and three buttons.—**trumpeter** *n*.

truncate *vt* to shorten.

truncheon *n* a short, thick club carried by a policeman.

trundle *vi* to move along slowly.

trunk *n* the main stem of a tree; the torso; the long nose of an elephant; a strong box or chest.

trunks *npl* a man's pants for swimming.

truss *n* a hernia brace. • *vt* to bind (up).

trust *n* firm belief in the truth of anything; a financial arrangement of investing money for another person. • *vti* to have confidence in; to believe.

trustee *n* a person who has legal control of money or property that they are keeping or investing for another.

trustworthy *adj* reliable, dependable.

trusty *adj* faithful. • *n* a prisoner granted special privileges as a trustworthy person.

truth *n* that which is true or genuine.

truthful *adj* accurate; honest.

try *vb* to determine judicially. • *vi* to attempt. • *n* an attempt; (*Rugby football*) a score made with a touchdown.

trying *adj* exasperating.

tsar *n* the former ruler of Russia.—*also* **czar**.

T-shirt *n* an informal knitted cotton sweater.—*also* **tee-shirt**.

T-square *n* a T-shaped instrument for drawing and determining right angles.

tub *n* a circular container, esp for water.

tuba *n* a large brass instrument of bass pitch.

tubby *adj* plump.

tube *n* a long, thin, hollow pipe; a soft metal or plastic cylinder in which thick liquids or pastes are stored.

tuberculosis *n* an infectious disease of the lungs.—**tubercular** *adj*.

tubing *n* tubes collectively; a length of tube.

tuck *vt* to gather together in a fold. • *vi* (*inf*) (*with* **into**) to eat greedily. • *n* a fold in a garment.

tuft *n* a bunch of grass, hair or feathers.

tug *vti* to pull with effort. • *n* a tugboat.

tugboat *n* a small powerful boat for towing ships.

tug of war *n* a contest in which two teams tug on opposite ends of a rope to pull the opposing team over a central line.

tuition *n* teaching, instruction.

tulip *n* a highly coloured cup-shaped flower.

tumble *vi* to fall over; to roll or to twist the body.

tumble dryer *n* a machine for drying clothes with warm air.

tumbler *n* a large drinking glass.

tummy *n* (*inf*) stomach.

tumour *n* an abnormal growth of tissue in any part of the body.

tumult *n* a commotion; an uproar.

tumultuous *adj* disorderly; rowdy, noisy.

tuna *n* a large ocean fish of the mackerel group.

tune *n* a melody. • *vt* (*musical instrument*) to adjust the notes of; (*radio, TV etc*) to adjust the resonant frequency, etc, to a particular value.

tungsten *n* a hard malleable greyish white metallic element used in lamps, etc.

tunic *n* a hip or knee-length loose, usu belted blouse-like garment.

tunnel *n* an underground passage, esp one for cars or trains.

turban *n* a headdress consisting of cloth wound in folds around the head.

turbine *n* a machine in which power is produced when the forced passage of steam, water, etc, causes the blades to rotate.

turbot *n* a large, flat, round edible fish.

turbulent *adj* in violent commotion.

tureen *n* a large dish for serving soup, etc.

turf *n* the surface layer of grass and its roots.

turgid *adj* swollen; pompous, bombastic.

turkey *n* a large bird farmed for its meat.

Turkish bath *n* a bath with steam.

turmoil *n* agitation; disturbance, confusion.

turn *vi* to revolve; to appeal (to) for help. • *vt* to change the position or direction of by revolving. • *n* a rotation; a place in sequence; a performer's act; an act of kindness or malice.

turning point *n* the point at which a significant change occurs.

turnip *n* a plant with a large white or yellow root, cultivated as a vegetable.

turnout *n* a gathering of people.

turnover *n* a fruit or meat pasty; the rate of replacement of workers.

turnstile *n* a mechanical gate across a footpath or entrance that admits only one person at a time.

turntable *n* a circular, horizontal revolving platform, as in a record player.

turn-up *n* the cuff of a trouser; (*inf*) a surprise.

turpentine *n* an oily resin secreted by coniferous trees, used as a solvent and thinner for paints.—*also* **turps**.

turquoise *n* an opaque greenish-blue mineral, valued as a gem; the colour of turquoise.

turret *n* a small tower on a building.

turtle *n* a land, freshwater or marine reptile with a soft body encased in a hard shell.

turtleneck *n* a high close-fitting neckline.

tusk n a long, projecting tooth on either side of the mouth, as of the elephant.

tussle n a scuffle.

tutor n a teacher who instructs pupils individually; a member of staff responsible for the supervision and teaching of students in a university.

tutorial n a period of tuition by a tutor to an individual or a small group.

TV abbr = television.

twang n a sharp, vibrant sound, as of a taut string when plucked; a nasal tone of voice.

tweed n a twilled woollen fabric.

tweezers n sing small pincers.

twelfth adj the last of twelve; being one of twelve equal parts.

twelve adj the cardinal number next after eleven. • n the symbol for this (12, XII, xii).

twenty adj two times ten. • n the symbol for this (20, XX, xx).—**twentieth** adj.

twice adv two times; two times as much.

twig[1] n a small branch or shoot of a tree.

twig[2] vti (inf) to grasp the meaning of.

twilight n the dim light just after sunset and before sunrise; the final stages of something.

twill n a cloth woven in such a way as to produce diagonal lines across it.

twin n either of two persons born at the same birth.

twine n a string of twisted fibres or hemp. • vti to twist together; to wind around.

twinge n a sudden, stabbing pain.

twinkle vi to sparkle; to flicker.

twirl vt to whirl; to rotate; to wind or twist.

twist vt to coil; to distort (the meaning of). • n an unexpected event.

twitch vt to pull with a sudden jerk. • vi to be suddenly jerked. • n a muscular spasm.

two adj the cardinal number next above one. • n the symbol for this (2, II, ii).

two-faced adj deceitful, hypocritical.

two-piece n a garment consisting of two separate matching bits.—also adj.

twosome n a group of two.

tycoon n a powerful industrialist, etc.

type n a kind, class or group; a block of metal for printing letters; style of print. • vt to write by means of a typewriter.

typecast vt to cast in the same role repeatedly because of physical appearance, etc.

typescript n a typed copy of a book.

typewriter n a keyboard machine for printing characters.

typhoid n an acute infectious disease acquired from contaminated food or water.

typhoon n a violent tropical cyclone.

typhus n a highly contagious acute disease spread by body lice.

typical adj representative of a particular type; characteristic.—**typically** adv.

typify vt to characterise.

typist n a person who uses a typewriter.

tyranny n harshness; oppression.

tyrant n a person who uses his or her power arbitrarily and oppressively.—**tyrannical** adj.

tyre n a protective, usu rubber, covering around the rim of a wheel.

U

ubiquitous adj seeming to exist everywhere at once.

udder n a milk-secreting organ containing two or more teats, as in cows.

UFO abbr unidentified flying object.

ugly adj unsightly; unattractive; ill tempered.

ulcer n an open sore on the surface of the skin.

ulterior adj (motives) hidden, not evident.

ultimate adj last; most significant.

ultimatum n the final proposal, condition or terms in negotiations.

ultraviolet adj of light waves shorter than the wavelengths of visible light and longer than X-rays.

umbilical cord n the vascular tube connecting a foetus with the placenta through which oxygen and nutrients are passed.

umbrage n resentment; offence.

umbrella n a cloth-covered collapsible frame carried for protection from rain or sun.

umpire n an official who enforces the rules in sport.—also vti.

umpteen adj (inf) an undetermined large number.—**umpteenth** adj.

unable adj not able; lacking the strength, skill, power or opportunity (to do something).

unanimous adj showing complete agreement.—**unanimously** adv.

unassuming adj unpretentious; modest.

unattached adj unmarried, not engaged.

unattended adj not accompanied.

unauthorised adj not endorsed by authority.

unavoidable adj bound to happen.

unaware adj ignorant (of).

unawares adv by surprise; unexpectedly.

unbalanced adj mentally unstable; having bias.

unbeliever n a person who does not believe.

unbending adj severe, stern; inflexible.

unbridled adj unrestrained.

unburden vt to reveal one's troubles to another.

uncalled-for adj unwarranted.

uncanny adj odd; suggestive of supernatural powers.

uncertain adj not knowing accurately, doubtful.

uncle n the brother of one's father or mother; the husband of one's aunt.

uncommon adj rare, unusual.

uncompromising adj inflexible.

unconditional adj without restrictions.

unconscious adj lacking normal perception by the senses; unintentional. • n the deepest level of mind containing feelings and emotions which one is unable to control.

uncouth adj lacking in manners; rough.

unctuous adj oily; smarmy; too suave.

undaunted adj fearless; not discouraged.

undecided adj doubtful, hesitant.

under prep lower than. • adv lower down.

undercarriage n the landing gear of an aeroplane; a car's supporting framework.

underclothes npl underwear.

undercoat n a coat of paint, etc, applied as a base below another.

undercover adj done or operating secretly.

undercurrent n a hidden current under water.

undercut vt to charge less than a competitor.

underdog n a person in an inferior position.

underdone adj not sufficiently cooked.

underestimate vti to set too low an estimate on.

underexpose vt (photog) to fail to expose (film) to light sufficiently long to produce a good image.

underfoot adv underneath the foot or feet.

undergo vt to experience, suffer, endure.

undergraduate n a student at a college or university studying for a first degree.

underground adj situated under the surface of the ground; secret; unconventional, radical. • n a secret group working for the overthrow of the government or the expulsion of occupying forces; an underground railway system.

undergrowth n shrubs, plants, etc, growing beneath trees.

underhanded adj sly, secret, deceptive.

underlie vt to form the basis of.

underline vt to put a line underneath.

underling n a person of inferior rank or status.

undermine vt to wear away or weaken.

underneath adv under. • adj lower.

underpants npl pants worn as an undergarment by men and boys.

underpass n a section of road running beneath another road, a railway, etc.

underprivileged adj lacking the basic rights of other members of society; poor.

underrate vt to undervalue.

underside n the lower surface.

underskirt n a woman's undergarment worn beneath the skirt, a petticoat.

understand vt to comprehend; to believe. • vi to comprehend.

understanding n comprehension; compassion, sympathy; mutual agreement. • adj sympathetic.

understate vt to state something in restrained terms; to represent as less than is the case.

understudy vti to learn a role or part so as to be able to replace (the actor playing it).—also n

undertake vt to attempt to; to agree to.

undertaker n a person who arranges funerals.

undertaking n enterprise; task; promise.

underwater adj being, carried on under the surface of the water, esp the sea; submerged.

underwear n garments worn underneath one's outer clothes, next to the skin.

underworld n criminals as an organised group.

undesirable adj not pleasant; objectionable.

undies npl (inf) women's underwear.

undo vt to untie or unwrap; to reverse (what has been done).

undoubted adj definite, certain.

undress vt to remove the clothes from. • vi to take off one's clothes.

undue adj improper; excessive.

unduly adv too; excessively; improperly.

unearth vt to discover; to reveal.

unearthly adj eerie; unreasonable.

uneasy adj uncomfortable; anxious.

uneconomic adj wasteful; unprofitable.

unemployed adj not having a job.

unerring adj sure, unfailing.

uneven adj not level or smooth; not divisible by two without leaving a remainder.

unexpected adj unforeseen.

unfailing adj persistent; constant, dependable.

unfair adj unjust; unequal.—**unfairly** adv.

unfaithful adj disloyal; adulterous.

unfasten vt to undo or become undone.

unfeeling adj callous, hardhearted.

unfinished adj not finished, incomplete.

unfit adj unsuitable; in bad physical condition.

unflappable adj (inf) calm, not easily agitated.

unfold vti to open or spread out; to develop.

unforeseen adj unsuspected.

unfortunate adj unlucky; regrettable.

unfortunately adv regrettably, unluckily.

unfounded adj groundless; baseless.

ungainly adj awkward; clumsy.

ungodly adj sinful; (inf) outrageous.

unguarded adj vulnerable; careless.

unguent n a lubricant or ointment.

unhappy adj not happy or fortunate; sad.

unhealthy adj not healthy or fit, sick; harmful, dangerous.

unicorn n an imaginary creature with a body like a horse and a single horn on the forehead.

uniform adj consistent; identical. • n the distinctive clothes worn by members of the same organisation, such as soldiers.

uniformity n the state of being the same.

unify vt to make into one; to unite.

unilateral adj involving only one of several parties.

uninhibited adj not repressed or restrained.

union n a confederation of individuals or groups; marriage; a trade union.

unique adj the only one of its kind.

unison n accordance of sound, harmony.

unit n the smallest whole number, one; a single or whole entity; a group of people who carry out a specific function; a piece of furniture fitting together with other pieces.

unite vti to join into one, to combine.

unit trust n a company that manages a range of investments on behalf of members of the public whose interests are looked after by an independent trust.

unity n oneness; harmony; concord.

universal adj widespread; general; relating to all the world.—**universally** adv.

universe n the totality of space, stars, planets and other forms of matter and energy.

university n an institution of higher education that confers bachelors' and higher degrees.

unkempt adj slovenly, dishevelled.

unkind adj harsh; cruel.—**unkindly** adv.

unknown adj not known; not famous.

unleash vt to free from restraint.

unless conj if not; except that.

unlikely adj improbable; unpromising.

unlimited adj boundless; not restricted.

unload vti to remove a load from a truck, ship, etc; to relieve of troubles, etc.

unlock vt (door, lock, etc) to unfasten.

unlucky adj not fortunate; regrettable.

unmask vti to expose, show up.

unmitigated adj unqualified, absolute.

unnatural adj abnormal; contrary to nature.

unpack vti to remove the contents of.

unpleasant adj nasty; objectionable.

unpopular adj lacking general approval.

unprecedented adj having no precedent.

unpretentious adj modest, not boasting.

unqualified adj lacking recognised qualifications; not restricted, complete.

unravel vt to disentangle; to solve.

unreasonable adj contrary to reason; lacking reason; immoderate; excessive.

unrelenting adj relentless; continuous.

unremitting adj incessant.

unrest n angry discontent verging on revolt.

unroll vti to open out from a roll; to reveal.

unruly adj hard to control; disobedient.

unsavoury adj distasteful; disagreeable.

unscathed adj unharmed.

unscrew vti (lid, etc) to loosen by turning.

unscrupulous adj without principles.

unseemly adj unbecoming; inappropriate.

unsettled adj changeable; lacking stability.

unsightly adj unattractive; ugly.

unskilled adj without special skill or training.

unspeakable adj bad beyond words.

unsteady adj shaky, reeling; vacillating.

unthinkable adj out of the question.

untidy adj disordered. • vt to make untidy.

untie vt to undo a knot in, unfasten.

until prep up to the time of; before. • conj up to the time when or that; before.

untimely adj premature; inopportune.

untold adj too great to be counted.

untoward adj unseemly; unfavourable.

unusual adj uncommon; rare.

unveil vt to reveal; to disclose.

unwary adj lacking caution; unguarded.

unwelcome adj not welcome, unpleasant.

unwell adj ill, not well.

unwieldy adj not easily moved or handled.

unwilling adj not willing, reluctant.

unwind vt to untangle. • vi to relax.

unwitting adj not knowing; unintentional.

unworldly adj spiritual, not concerned with the material world.

unwritten adj not written or printed; traditional.

up adv to, toward, in or on a higher place. • prep from a lower to a higher point on or along. • vt to raise; to increase.

up-and-coming adj likely to succeed.

upbringing n the process of educating and nurturing (a child).

update vt to bring up to date.

upgrade vt to improve, raise to a higher grade.

upheaval n radical or violent change.

uphill adj ascending, rising; difficult, arduous. • adv up a slope or hill; against difficulties.

uphold vt to defend.

upholstery n materials used to make a soft covering esp for a seat.

upkeep n maintenance; the cost of it.

upon prep on, on top of.

upper adj higher in position, rank, status. • n the part of a boot or shoe above the sole; (sl) a drug used as a stimulant.

upper case n capital letters.

upper class n people occupying the highest social rank.—also adj.

upright adj vertical; honest. • n a vertical post.

uprising n a revolt; a rebellion.

uproar n a noisy disturbance.

uproot vt to remove from established surroundings.

upset¹ vt to overturn; to spill; to disturb; to make physically sick.

upset² n distress or its cause. • adj distressed.

upshot n the conclusion; the result.

upside down adj inverted; the wrong way up; (inf) topsy turvy.

upstairs adv to an upper level or storey.

upstart n a person who has suddenly risen to a position of wealth and power.

up-to-date adj modern; fashionable.

upturn n an upward trend.

upward, upwards adj from a lower to a higher place.—also adv.

uranium n a metallic element used as a source of nuclear energy.

urban adj of or relating to a city.

urbane adj sophisticated; refined.—**urbanity** n.

urchin n a ragged, mischievous child.

urge vt to press, plead with. • n an impulse.

urgency n compelling need; importance.

urgent adj impelling; persistent.

urinate vi to pass urine.

urn n a vase; a receptacle for preserving the ashes of the dead; a large metal container for boiling water for tea or coffee.

us pron the objective case of we.

usage n customary use; practice, custom.

use¹ vt to utilise; to exploit (a person).

use² n act of using or putting to a purpose.

used adj not new; second-hand.

useful adj able to be used to good effect.

useless adj of no use.

usher n one who shows people to their seats in a theatre, church, etc. • vt to escort to seats, etc.

usual adj customary; normal.—**usually** adv.

usurp vt to seize unlawfully.

utensil n an implement, esp one for use in the kitchen.

uterus n the womb.

utilise vt to make practical use of.

utilitarian adj designed to be of practical use.

utility n usefulness; a public service, such as telephone, electricity, etc.

utmost adj of the greatest degree or amount.

utter¹ adj absolute; complete.

utter² vt to say; to speak.—**utterance** n.

V

vacancy n an unoccupied job.

vacant adj empty; unoccupied; blank.

vacate vt to give up possession of.

vacation n a holiday.

vaccinate vt to inoculate with vaccine as a protection against a disease.—**vaccination** n

vaccine n a preparation used for inoculation to give immunity from certain diseases.

vacillate vi to waver, show indecision.

vacuous adj lacking intelligence.

vacuum n a region devoid of all matter; a vacuum cleaner. • vt to clean with a vacuum cleaner.

vacuum cleaner n an electrical appliance for removing dust from by suction.

vacuum flask n a container for keeping liquids hot or cold.

vacuum-packed adj sealed in an airtight packet.

vagabond n a vagrant.

vagina n in female mammals and humans, the canal connecting the uterus and the external sex organs.—**vaginal** adj.

vagrant n a person who has no settled home.

vague adj unclear; indistinct, imprecise.

vain adj excessively concerned with one's appearance; worthless.—**vainly** adv.

valance n a decorative cover for the base of a bed.

valence n (chem) the number of atoms of hydrogen that an atom or group can combine with to form a compound.

valency n the combining power of atoms.

valentine n a sweetheart chosen on St Valentine's Day, 14 February; a card sent on that day.

valet n a manservant.

valiant adj courageous; brave.

valid adj sound; legally acceptable.

validate vt to corroborate; to legalise.

valley n low land between hills.

valour n courage; bravery (in battle).

valuable adj having considerable importance or monetary worth. • npl valuable possessions.

valuation n an estimated price or worth.

value n worth; (pl) moral principles. • vt to estimate the worth of; to regard highly.

value added tax n a tax levied on the difference between production cost and selling price.

valve n a device for controlling the flow of a gas or liquid through a pipe; (anat) a tube allowing blood to flow in one direction only.

vampire n (folklore) a creature which by night leaves its grave to suck the blood of living people.

vampire bat n a blood-sucking bat.

van n a covered motor vehicle for transporting goods, etc.

vandal n a person who damages property.

vane n a blade at the top of a spire, etc, to show wind direction.

vanguard n the front part of an army, the leading position of any movement.

vanilla n extract from the orchid pod used as a flavouring.

vanish vi to disappear; to fade away.

vanity n conceit; worthlessness.

vanity case n a small case for cosmetics.

vanquish vt to conquer; to defeat.

vantage n a favourable position.

vaporise vt to change into vapour.

vapour n particles of water or smoke in the air.

variable adj liable to change; not constant. • n (math) a quantity that varies.

variance n discrepancy.

variant n a different form.—also adj.

variation n diversity; deviation.

varicose adj (veins) abnormally swollen.

variety n diversity; an assortment.

variety show n an entertainment made up of various acts, such as songs, comedy turns, etc.

various adj varied, different; several.

varnish n a sticky liquid which dries and forms a hard, glossy coating. • vt to coat with varnish.

vary vti to change, to diversify.

vase n a vessel for displaying flowers.

vasectomy n male sterilisation involving the cutting of the sperm-carrying tube.

Vaseline™ n petroleum jelly as a lubricant.

vast adj immense.—**vastly** adv.

vat n a large barrel or tank.

Vatican n the residence of the pope.

vault[1] n an arched ceiling or roof; a cellar.

vault[2] vti to jump over an obstacle.

veal n the edible flesh of a calf.

veer vi to swing around.

vegetable n a herbaceous plant grown for food; (inf) a person who has suffered brain damage.

vegetarian n a person who consumes a diet that excludes meat and fish.

vegetate vi to lead a mentally inactive life.

vegetation n plants in general.

vehement adj passionate; forceful.

vehicle n a conveyance, such as a car or truck.

veil n a thin fabric worn over the head or face of a woman; a nun's headdress. • vt to conceal.

vein n one of the vessels that convey the blood back to the heart; a seam of mineral within a rock; a branching rib in a leaf.

Velcro™ n a nylon material made of matching strips of tiny hooks and pile that are easily pressed together or pull apart.

velocity n speed.

velvet n a fabric made from silk, rayon, etc, with a soft, thick pile.—**velvety** adj.

venal adj corrupt.

vendetta n a private feud.

vending machine n a coin-operated machine which dispenses goods.

vendor n a person selling something.

veneer n an overlay of fine wood or plastic.

venerable adj worthy of respect.

venereal adj (disease) resulting from sexual intercourse.

Venetian blind n a window blind formed of long thin horizontal slips of wood that can be pivoted.

vengeance n the act of taking revenge.

venial adj (sin) forgivable, excusable.

venison n the edible flesh of the deer.

venom n poison; malice.—**venomous** adj.

vent n a small opening or slit. • vt (temper) to give expression to.

ventilate vt to supply with fresh air.

ventilator n an appliance for ventilating a room.

ventriloquism n the act or art of speaking so that the sounds appear to come from a source other than the actual speaker.

venture n a risky undertaking. • vti to risk.

venue n the place of an action or event.

veranda(h) n a roofed porch, supported by light pillars.

verb n (gram) the part of speech that expresses an action, a process, state or condition.

verbal adj spoken; literal.

verbatim adv word for word.

verbiage n use of too many words.

verbose adj wordy.

verdict n the decision of a jury at the end of a trial; decision, judgment.

verge n the brink; a grass border beside a road. • vi to border (on).

verger n a church official.

verify vt to confirm the truth of.

vermicelli n a pasta like spaghetti, but thinner.

vermil(l)ion n a bright red colour.—also adj.

vermin n (used as pl) pests, such as insects.

vermouth n a white wine flavoured with herbs.

vernacular n the commonly spoken language or dialect of a country or region.

verruca n a wart on the foot.

versatile adj adaptable.—**versatility** n.

verse n a stanza of a poem.

versed adj skilled or learned in a subject.

version n a particular account or description.

versus prep against; in contrast to.

vertebra n one of the bones of the spinal column.

vertebrate n an animal with a backbone.

vertical adj perpendicular to the horizon.

vertigo n a sensation of dizziness caused by a disorder of the sense of balance.

verve n enthusiasm; liveliness; energy.

very adj same. • adv extremely.

vespers npl (used as sing) an Anglican service held daily in the evening.

vessel n a container; a ship or boat; a tube in the body along which fluids pass.

vest n a sleeveless undergarment. • vt to place or settle (power, authority, etc).

vested interest n a strong reason for acting in a certain way, usu for personal gain.

vestibule n an entrance hall or lobby.

vestige n a hint; a trace.

vestry n a room in a church where vestments, etc, are kept and meetings held.

vet n a veterinary surgeon. • vt to examine.

veteran adj old, experienced. • n a person who has served in the armed forces.

veterinary surgeon n a person trained in treating sick or injured animals.

veto n the right of a person or group to prohibit an action or legislation. • vt to prohibit.

vex vt to annoy.—**vexation** n.

via prep by way of.

viable adj workable; practicable.—**viability** n.

viaduct n a road or railway carried by a bridge with arches over a valley, river, etc.

vibrant adj resonant; bright, lively.

vibrate vti to shake.—**vibration** n.

vibrato n (mus) a pulsating effect obtained by rapid variation of emphasis on the same tone.

vicar n a parish priest.

vicarage n the residence of a vicar.

vice[1] n an evil action or habit.

vice[2] n a clamping device with jaws, used for holding objects firmly.

vice- prefix who acts in place of another.

vice versa adv the other way round.

vicinity n a nearby area; proximity.

vicious adj cruel; malicious.—**viciously** adv.

vicissitudes npl changes of fortune.

victim n a person who has been killed or injured.

victimise vt to make a victim.

victor n a winner; a conqueror.

Victorian adj of the reign of Queen Victoria; prudish.

victorious adj having won in battle or contest.

victory n triumph in battle; success.

video n the transmission or recording of television programmes or films, using a television set and a video recorder and tape.

video recorder n the machine that plays or records on video tape.

video tape n a magnetic tape on which images and sounds can be recorded for reproduction on television.—**video-tape** vt.

vie vi to contend or strive for superiority.

view n sight; range of vision; opinion. • vt to see; to consider.

viewer n a person who views, esp television; an optical device used in viewing.

viewfinder n a device in a camera showing the view to be photographed.

viewpoint n opinion; a place from which something can be viewed.

vigil n keeping watch at night.

vigilance n watchfulness.—**vigilant** adj.

vigilante n a self-appointed law enforcer.

vigour n vitality.—**vigorous** adj.

vile adj wicked; evil; offensive; very bad.

villa n a large country or suburban house.

village n a collection of houses smaller than a town.

villager n an inhabitant of a village.

villain n a scoundrel; the main evil character in a play, film, etc.—**villainous** adj.

vindicate vt to justify; to absolve from blame.

vindictive adj vengeful; spiteful.

vine n a grapevine.

vinegar n a sour-tasting liquid containing acetic acid, used as a condiment.

vineyard n a plantation of grapevines.

vintage n the grape harvest of one season. • adj (cars) classic; (wine) of a specified year and of good quality.

vinyl n a strong plastic used in floor coverings, furniture and records, etc.

viola n a stringed instrument of the violin family.

violate vt to break (an agreement); to rape.

violence n physical force intended to cause injury or destruction; intensity.

violent adj vehement; impetuous; forcible.

violet n a small bluish-purple flower; a bluish-purple colour.

violin n a four-stringed musical instrument, played with a bow.

violinist n a person who plays the violin.

viper n a European venomous snake.

virgin n a person (esp a woman) who has never had sexual intercourse.

virginity n the state of being a virgin.

virile adj manly.—**virility** n.

virtual adj in effect or essence, though not in fact or strict definition.—**virtually** adv.

virtue n moral excellence; any admirable quality.

virtuoso n a person highly skilled in an activity, esp in playing a musical instrument.

virtuous adj righteous; upright; pure.

virulent adj extremely poisonous; vicious.

virus n a simple microorganism capable of replicating within living cells, producing disease.

visa n an endorsement on a passport allowing the bearer to travel in the country of the government issuing it.

vis-à-vis prep opposite to; in face of.

viscount n in Britain, a title of nobility next below an earl.

visibility n clearness of seeing.

visible adj that may be seen; evident.

vision n the power of seeing, sight; a supernatural appearance; foresight; imagination.

visionary adj imaginative; having foresight.

visit vt to go to see. • n act of going to see.

visitor n a person who visits; a caller.

visor n a movable part of a helmet protecting the face; the peak of a cap.

vista n a view, as from a high place.

visual adj relating to vision or sight; visible.

visual aid n a film, slide or overhead projector, etc, used to aid teaching.

visualise vt to form a mental picture of.

vital adj necessary to life; essential; lively.

vitality n vigour; spirits; animation.

vital statistics npl data recording births, deaths, marriages; (inf) the measurements of a woman's figure.

vitamin n an organic substance occurring naturally in foods that is essential for good health.

vivacious adj lively; animated; spirited.

vivid adj brightly coloured; intense.

vivisection n the practice of performing surgical operations on living animals for scientific research.

vocabulary n an alphabetical list of words with their meanings; an individual's use of particular words.

vocal adj relating to the voice; outspoken, noisy.

vocalist n a singer.

vocation n calling to a particular career.

vociferous adj clamorous, noisy.

vodka n a spirit distilled from rye.

vogue n the fashion at a specified time.

voice n sound produced by speaking or singing; the relation between a verb and its subject. • vt to express.

voice-over n the voice of an unseen narrator, esp in a film, TV commercial, etc.

void adj unoccupied, empty; not legally binding. • n an empty space, a vacuum.

volatile adj evaporating very quickly.

vol-au-vent n a case of light puff pastry filled with a savoury sauce.

volcano n a mountain formed by ejection of lava through an opening in the earth's crust.

vole n a small rat-like rodent.

volition n the exercise of the will; choice.

volley n the multiple discharge of many missiles or small arms; a barrage; (tennis, volleyball) the return of the ball before it reaches the ground.

volleyball n a team game played by hitting a large inflated ball over a net with the hands.

volt n the unit of measure of the force of an electrical current.

voltage n electrical force measured in volts.

volume n the space occupied by an object; quantity, amount; intensity of sound; a book.

voluntary adj acting by choice; willing; without remuneration.—**voluntarily** adv.

volunteer n a person who carries out work voluntarily.—also vti.

voluptuous adj having an attractive figure.

vomit vi to eject the contents of the stomach through the mouth.—also vt.

vote n an indication of a choice or opinion as to a matter on which one has a right to be consulted. • vi to cast one's vote.—**voter** n.

vouch vi to guarantee.

voucher n a token that can be exchanged for something else.

vow n a solemn promise. • vt to promise.

vowel n an open speech sound produced by continuous passage of the breath; a letter representing such a sound, as a, e, i, o, u.

voyage n a long journey, esp by ship.

vulgar adj common; coarse.—**vulgarity** n.

vulgarism n a crude expression.

vulnerable adj capable of being wounded.

vulture n a large bird of prey.

W

wad n a small, soft mass, as of cotton or paper.

wade vti to walk through water.

wader n a bird that wades, e.g. the heron.

waffle[1] n a thick, crisp pancake baked in a waffle iron.

waffle[2] vi (inf) to speak or write at length without saying anything substantial.

waft vt to drift or float through the air.—also n.

wag[1] vti to move rapidly from side to side.

wag[2] n a joker, a wit.

wage vt to carry on. • n (often pl) payment.

wager n a bet. • vti to bet.

waggle vti to wag.—also n.

wag(g)on n a four-wheeled vehicle pulled by a horse or tractor for carrying goods.

wail vi to make a long, loud cry of sorrow.

waist n the narrowest part of the human trunk, between the ribs and the hips.

waistcoat n a waist-length, sleeveless garment.

waistline n the narrowest part of the waist.

wait vti to stay in expectation; to remain; (with at or on) to serve food at a meal.

waiter n a man or woman who serves at table, as in a restaurant.—**waitress** nf.

waiting list n a list of people applying for or waiting to obtain something.

waiting room n a room for people to wait in.

waive vt to refrain from enforcing.

wake[1] vi to become awake. • vt to rouse from sleep. — n a vigil beside a corpse.

wake[2] n the waves left in the track of a ship.

waken vt to wake.

walk vi to travel on foot with alternate steps. • n the act of walking; gait; a stroll.

walkie-talkie n a portable two-way radio transmitter and receiver.

walking stick n a stick used in walking.

walkover n an unopposed or easy victory.

wall n a vertical structure of brick, stone, etc, for enclosing, dividing or protecting.

wallet n a flat pocketbook for paper money.

wallflower n a plant with red or yellow flowers; a person who does not dance for lack of a partner.

wallop vt (inf) to strike hard. • n (inf) a hard blow.

wallow vi (animal) to roll about in mud; to indulge oneself in emotion.—also n.

wallpaper n decorated paper for covering the walls of a room.

walnut n (a tree producing) an edible nut with a round shell and wrinkled seed.

walrus n a large aquatic animal with long canine teeth and coarse whiskers.

waltz n a whirling or slowly circling dance.

wan adj pale and sickly.

wand n a magician's rod.

wander vi to ramble; to lose concentration.

wane vi to decrease, esp of the moon; to decline.

want n lack. • vt to need; to wish (for).

wanted adj sought after.

wanting adj lacking.

wanton adj malicious; sexually provocative.

war n military conflict between nations or parties. • vi to make war.

ward n a section of a hospital; an electoral district; a child placed under the supervision of a court.

warden n a prison governor;

warder n a prison officer.

wardrobe n a cupboard for clothes.

ware n (pl) merchandise, goods for sale.

warehouse n a building for storing goods.

warfare n armed hostilities; conflict.

warhead n the section of a missile containing the explosive.

warlike adj hostile.

warm adj moderately hot; friendly, kind; (colours) rich. • vt to make warm.—**warmth** n.

warm-hearted adj kind, sympathetic.

warn vt to notify of danger; to caution or advise (against).—**warning** n.

warp vti to twist out of shape; to distort.

warrant vt to guarantee. • n a writ for arrest.

warranty n a pledge to replace something if it is not as represented, a guarantee.

warrior n a soldier, fighter.

warship n a ship equipped for war.

wart n a small, hard projection on the skin.

wartime adj, n (of) a period or time of war.

wary adj watchful; cautious.—**warily** adv.

wash vti to cleanse with water and soap; to cover with a thin coat of paint. • n a washing; the waves left behind by a boat.

washbasin n a basin, esp a bathroom fixture, for use in washing one's hands, etc.

washed-out adj faded; limp; exhausted.

washer n a flat ring of metal, rubber, etc, to give tightness to joints.

washing n the act of cleansing with water; a number of items washed together.

washing machine n a device for washing clothes.

wasp n a winged insect with a black and yellow striped body, which can sting.

wastage n anything lost by use or decay.

waste adj left over; uncultivated. • vt to use foolishly; to fail to use. • vi to lose strength. • n discarded material, excrement.—**wasteful** adj.

watch n close observation; vigil; a small timepiece worn on the wrist, etc. • vi to look with attention. • vt to tend; to observe closely.

watchdog n a dog that guards property.

water n a clear, thin liquid, lacking taste or smell and essential for life; any body of it, as the ocean, a lake, river, etc. • vt to moisten with water. • vi (eyes) to smart; to salivate.

water-closet n a lavatory.

watercolour n a water-soluble paint.

watercress n a plant growing in ponds and streams, used in a salad.

waterfall n a fall of water over a precipice.

watering can n a container with a spout for watering plants.

water line n a line up to which a ship's hull is submerged.

waterlogged adj saturated with water.

water main n a main pipe for carrying water.

watermark n a line marking the height to which water has risen; a mark impressed on paper which can only be seen when held up to the light.

watermelon n a large fruit with a hard green rind and edible red watery flesh.

waterproof adj impervious to water.

watershed n a turning point.

water-skiing n the sport of planing on water by being towed by a motorboat

watertight adj not allowing water to pass through; foolproof.

waterworks n (as sing) an establishment that supplies water to a district; (pl: inf) the urinary system; (inf) tears.

watt n a unit of electrical power.

wave n an undulation travelling on the surface of water; the form in which light and sound are thought to travel; a hair curl; a movement of the hand in greeting or farewell. • vti to move freely backward and forward.—**wavy** adj.

wavelength n the distance between the crests of successive waves of light or sound; radio frequency.

waver vi to hesitate; to falter.

wax[1] n an oily substance used to make candles.

wax[2] vi to increase in strength, size, etc.

waxwork n a figure or model formed of wax.

way n path, route; road; distance; direction.

waylay vt to lie in wait for.

wayward adj wilful; unpredictable.

WC abbr = water-closet.

we pron pl of I.

weak adj lacking power or strength.

weaken vti to make or grow weaker.

weakling n a person who lacks strength of character.

wealth n a large amount of money.

wean vt (baby, animal) to replace the mother's milk with other nourishment; to dissuade (from indulging a habit).

weapon n any instrument used in fighting.

wear vt to have on the body as clothing; to impair by use. • n deterioration from frequent use.

weary adj tired. • vti to make or become tired.

weasel n a small carnivorous animal with a long slender body and reddish fur.

weather n atmospheric conditions, such as temperature, rainfall, cloudiness, etc. • vt to survive.

weathercock n a weather vane in the form of a cock to show the wind direction.

weave vt to interlace threads in a loom to form fabric. • vi to zigzag.

web n the fine threads spun by a spider.

webbed adj (ducks, etc) having the digits connected by a fold of skin.

wed vti to marry; to join closely.

wedding n the ceremony of marriage.

wedge n a V-shaped block of wood or metal for splitting or fastening; a wedge-shaped object. • vti to thrust (in) tightly.

wedlock n marriage.

wee adj small, tiny.

weed n any undesired plant. • vt to remove weeds.

weedkiller n a substance used to kill weeds.

week n the period of seven consecutive days.

weekday n a day of the week other than Saturday or Sunday.

weekend n the period from Friday night to Sunday night.

weekly adj happening once a week.

weep vti to shed tears, to cry; (wound) to ooze.

weigh vt to measure the weight of; to consider carefully. • vi to have weight.

weight n the amount which anything weighs. • vt to attach a weight to.

weightlessness n the state of having no reaction to gravity, esp in space travel.

weightlifting n the sport of lifting weights.

weighty adj heavy; serious.

weir n a low dam across a river that controls the flow of water.

weird adj mysterious; bizarre.

welcome adj gladly received. • n reception of a person or thing. • vt to greet kindly.

welch see welsh.

weld vt to unite, as metal by heating until fused or soft enough to hammer together.

welfare n wellbeing.

well[1] n a spring; a hole bored in the ground to provide a source of water, oil, gas, etc.

well[2] adj in good health. • adv in a satisfactory or excellent manner; thoroughly.

well-heeled adj (inf) wealthy.

wellies npl (sl) wellingtons.

wellington (boot) n a rubber boot.

well-off adj prosperous.

well-to-do adj prosperous.

Welsh adj relating to the people of Wales or their language.—also n.

welsh vti to avoid paying a gambling debt.—also welch.

west n the direction of the sun at sunset; the region in the west of any country. • adj situated in or towards the west. • adv in or to the west.

westerly adj towards the west; from the west. • n a wind from the west.

western adj of or in the west. • n a film, novel, etc, about the pre-20th century American West.

westward adj towards the west.

wet adj covered or saturated with liquid; rainy. • vti to soak; to moisten.

wet suit n a close-fitting suit worn by divers.

whack vti (inf) to strike sharply.

whale n a very large sea mammal that breathes through a blowhole.

wharf n a platform for loading and unloading ships in harbour.

what adj of what sort, how much, how great. • relative pron that which; as much or many as.

whatever pron anything that.

wheat n a cereal grain usu ground into flour for bread.

wheel n a solid disc or circular rim turning on an axle. • vt to transport on wheels.

wheelbarrow n a cart with one wheel in front and two handles and legs at the rear.

wheelchair n a chair with wheels for invalids.

wheeze vi to breathe with a rasping sound.

when adv at what or which time. • conj at the time at which; although.

where adv at which or what place; to which place. • rel pron in or to which.

whereabouts adv near or at what place. • n approximate location.

wherever adv at or to whatever place.

whet vt (pt **whetted**) to stimulate.

whether conj introducing an alternative possibility or condition.

which adj what one (of). • pron which person or thing; that.

whichever pron whatever one that; no matter which.—also adj.

whiff n a sudden puff of odour.

while n a period of time. • conj during the time that; although. • vt to pass (the time) pleasantly.

whim n a fancy; an irrational thought.

whimper vi to make a low, unhappy cry.

whimsical adj unusual, odd, fantastic.

whine vi (dog) to make a high-pitched cry; (person) to complain childishly. • n a plaintive cry.

whip n a piece of leather attached to a handle used for punishing people or driving on animals; an officer in parliament who maintains party discipline. • vt to strike, as with a lash; (eggs, etc) to beat into a froth.

whip-round n (inf) an appeal among friends for contributions.

whir, whirr n a humming or buzzing sound. • vti to revolve with a buzzing noise.

whirl n commotion; (inf) an attempt. • vti to spin.

whirlpool n a circular current of water.

whirlwind n a whirling column of air.

whisk vt to make a quick sweeping movement; (eggs, etc) to beat. • n a kitchen utensil for whisking.

whisker n any of the sensory bristles on the face of a cat, etc; (pl) the hair growing on a man's face, esp the cheeks.

whiskey n whisky distilled in the US or Ireland.

whisky n a spirit distilled from barley or rye.

whisper vti to speak softly. • n a hushed tone.

whist n a card game for four players in two sides.

whistle vti to make a shrill sound by forcing the breath through the lips; to make a similar sound with a whistle. • n a whistling sound; a metal tube that is blown to make a shrill warning sound.

white adj of the colour of snow; (skin) light-coloured. • n the colour white; the white part of an egg or the eye.

white-collar adj of office workers.

whitewash n a mixture of lime and water, used for whitening walls.—also vt.

whittle vt to pare or cut thin shavings from.

whiz, whizz vi to make a humming sound. • n (inf) an expert.

who pron what or which person; that.

whodunnit n (inf) a detective novel, play, etc.

whoever pron anyone who.

whole adj complete. • n the entire amount.

wholehearted adj sincere, enthusiastic.

wholesale n selling of goods, usu at lower prices and in quantity, to a retailer.

wholesome adj healthy; mentally beneficial.

whom pron objective case of who.

whoop n a loud cry of excitement.

whooping cough n an infectious disease, esp of children, causing coughing spasms.

whore n a prostitute.

whose pron the possessive case of who or which.

why adv for what cause or reason?

wick n a cord in a candle that supplies fuel to the flame.

wicked adj evil, immoral, sinful.

wicker n a long, thin, flexible twig; such twigs woven together, as in making baskets.

wicket n a small door or gate; (cricket) the stumps at which the bowler aims the ball; the area between the bowler and batsman.

wide adj broad; extensive; of a definite distance from side to side; open fully.

wide-angle adj (photog) with an angle of view of 60 degrees or more.

wide-awake adj fully awake; ready, alert.

widen vti to make or grow wide or wider.

widespread adj widely extended; general.

widow n a woman whose husband has died.

widower n a man whose wife has died.

width n breadth.

wield vt to brandish; to exercise power.

wife n a married woman.

wig n an artificial covering of real or synthetic hair for the head.

wiggle vti to move from side to side.

wild adj in its natural state; not tamed.

wilderness n an uncultivated place.

wild-goose chase n a futile pursuit.

wildlife n animals in the wild.

wilful adj stubborn; intentional.

will[1] n power of choosing or determining; desire; a legal document directing the disposal of one's property after death.

will[2] aux vb used with 2nd and 3rd persons; to show futurity, determination, obligation.

willow n a tree with slender, flexible branches.

willpower n the ability to control one's emotions and actions.

wilt vi to become limp, as from heat; to droop.

wily adj crafty; sly.

win vti to gain with effort; to succeed in a contest. • n a success.—**winner** n.

wince vi to shrink back; to flinch.

winch n a hoisting machine. • vt to hoist or lower with a winch.

wind[1] n a current of air; breath; (inf) flatulence. • vt to cause to be short of breath.

wind[2] vt to turn by cranking; to tighten the spring of a clock; to coil. • vi to turn, to twist.

windbreak n a shelter that breaks the force of the wind, as a line of trees.

windfall n any unexpected gain, esp financial.

wind instrument n a musical instrument played by blowing into it.

windmill n a machine operated by the force of the wind turning a set of sails.

window n a framework containing glass in the opening in a wall of a building or in a vehicle.

window box n a narrow box on a windowsill for growing flowers, etc.

windowsill n a sill beneath a window.

windpipe n the air passage from the mouth to the lungs.

windscreen n a protective shield of glass in the front of a vehicle.

windscreen wiper n a metal blade with a rubber edge that removes rain, etc, from a windscreen.

windy adj exposed to the winds; stormy.

wine n fermented grape juice used as an alcoholic beverage.

wineglass n a glass, usu with a stem, for wine.

wing n the forelimb of a bird, bat or insect, by which it flies; the main lateral surface of an aeroplane; a projecting part of a building; the side of a stage; a section of a political party.

wink vi to open and close one eye quickly.

winning n a victory; (pl) money won in gambling. • adj charming.

winter n the coldest season of the year.

wintry adj cold, snowy; unfriendly.

wipe vt to rub a surface with a cloth in order to clean or dry it; (with out) to remove; to erase.

wire n a flexible thread of metal.

wireless n (formerly) a radio.

wiry adj lean, supple and sinewy.

wisdom n sound judgment.

wisdom tooth n one of four teeth set at the end of each side of the upper and lower jaw in humans and grown last.

wise adj learned; prudent.

wish vti to long for. • n desire.

wisp n a thin strand; a small bunch.

wistful adj pensive; sad; yearning.

wit n the facility of combining ideas with humorous effect; a person with this ability.

witch n a woman who practises magic and is considered to a have dealings with the devil.

witchcraft n the practice of magic.

with prep in the company of; by means of.

withdraw vt to draw back or away; to remove. • vi to retreat.—**withdrawal** n.

wither vi to fade or become limp or dry, as of a plant. • vt to cause to dry up or fade.

withhold vt to hold back.

within prep inside; not exceeding.

without prep outside or out of, beyond.

withstand vt to resist, esp successfully.

witness n a person who gives evidence or attests a signing; testimony (of a fact). • vt to have first hand knowledge of; to attest a signing.

witness box n an enclosure for witnesses in a court of law.

witticism n a witty remark.

witty adj full of wit.—**wittily** adv.

wizard n a magician; an expert.

wobble vi to sway unsteadily.—**wobbly** adj.

woe n grief; (pl) misfortune.

wok n a large, metal, hemispherical pan used for Chinese-style cooking.

wolf n a wild animal of the dog family.

woman n an adult human female.

womanly adj having the qualities of a woman.

womb n the female organ in which offspring are developed until birth.

wonder n a feeling of surprise or astonishment; something that excites such a feeling. • vi to be curious; to marvel.

wonderful adj marvellous.—**wonderfully** adv.

woo vt to seek to attract with a view to marriage.

wood n the hard fibrous substance under the bark of trees; a thick growth of trees.

woodpecker n a bird that pecks holes in trees to extract insects.

woodwind n section of an orchestra in which wind instruments, originally made of wood, are played.

woodwork n carpentry.

woodworm n an insect larva that bores into wood.

wool n the fleece of sheep and other animals; thread or yarn spun from the coats of sheep.

woollen adj made of wool.

woolly adj of or covered with wool; muddled.

word n a single unit of language; discussion; (pl) lyrics; (pl) a quarrel. • vt to put into words.

wording n a choice of words.

wordy adj verbose.

work n employment, occupation; a literary composition; (pl) a factory. • vi to have a job; to operate (a machine, etc); to produce effects. • vt to achieve.—**worker** n.

working adj used for work; functioning.

working class n people who work for wages, esp manual workers.—also adj.

workmanship n technical skill.

work-out n a session of physical exercises.

workshop n a room where work is done; a seminar for specified intensive study, work, etc.

world n the planet earth and its inhabitants.

worldly adj material; experienced.

worldwide adj universal.

worm n an earthworm. • vt to work (oneself into a position) slowly; to extract information by persistent means.

worn-out adj depressed, tired.

worry vb to bother, pester. • vi to be anxious. • n a cause or feeling of anxiety.

worse adj not so well as before.—**worsen** vti.

worship n religious adoration; a religious ritual, e.g. prayers. • vt to adore or idolise. • vi to participate in a religious service.

worst adj bad or ill in the highest degree. • adv to the worst degree.

worsted n twisted thread or yarn made from long, combed wool.

worth n value; price; excellence; importance. • adj equal in value to.

worthless adj valueless; useless.

worthwhile adj important or rewarding enough to justify the effort.

worthy adj deserving. • n a local celebrity.

would-be adj aspiring or professing to be.

wound n any injury caused to the skin; hurt feelings. • vt to injure.

wrangle vi to argue; to dispute noisily.

wrap vt to fold (paper) round (a purchase, etc); to enfold. • n a shawl.

wrapper n a book jacket.

wrath n intense anger.—**wrathful** adj.

wreak vt inflict (e.g. vengeance, havoc).

wreath n a twisted ring of leaves, flowers, etc.

wreck n a badly damaged ship; a rundown person or thing. • vt to destroy; to ruin.

wreckage n remnants from a wreck.

wren n small brownish songbird.

wrench vt to give something a violent pull; to injure with a twist. • n a forceful twist; emotional upset caused by parting.

wrestle vti to fight by holding and trying to throw one's opponent down.—**wrestler** n.

wretch n a miserable or despised person.

wretched adj very miserable; despicable.

wriggle vi to move with a twisting motion.

wring vt to twist; to compress by twisting to squeeze water from.

wrinkle n a small crease or fold on a surface. • vti to make or become wrinkled.

wrist n the joint connecting the hand with the forearm.

writ n (law) a written court order.

write vt to form letters on paper with a pen or pencil; to compose (a letter, music, book, etc); to communicate by letter; (with off) to cancel a bad debt as a loss; (inf) to damage (a vehicle) beyond repair. • vi to be a writer.

write-off n a debt cancelled as a loss; (inf) a badly damaged car.

writer n an author.

writhe vi to twist the body violently, as in pain.

writing n the act of forming letters on paper, etc; authorship; (pl) literary works.

writing paper n paper treated to accept ink and used for letters.

wrong adj incorrect; immoral. • n harm; injury done to another. • vt to do wrong to.—**wrongly** adv.

wrongful adj unwarranted, unjust.

wrought adj formed; made; (metals) shaped by hammering, etc.

wry adj twisted, contorted; ironic.—**wryly** adv.

XYZ

Xmas abbr Christmas.

X-ray, x-ray n radiation of very short wavelengths, capable of penetrating solid bodies and printing on a photographic plate a shadow picture of objects not permeable by light rays.

xylophone n a percussion instrument consisting of a series of wooden bars which are struck with small hammers.

yacht n a sailing or mechanically driven vessel, used for pleasure cruises or racing.

Yank, Yankee n (inf) an American.

yank vti to pull suddenly, to jerk.—also n.

yap vi to yelp, bark; (sl) to talk constantly, esp in a noisy manner.

yard¹ n a unit of measure of 0.9144 metres.

yard² n an enclosed concrete area, esp near a building; an enclosure for a commercial activity (e.g. a shipyard).

yardstick n a standard used in judging.

yarn n fibres of wool, cotton, etc, spun into strands for knitting; (inf) a tale.

yawn vi to open the jaws involuntarily and inhale, as from drowsiness.—also n.

yawning adj gaping; wide-open.

year n a period of twelve months.

yearly adj occurring every year; lasting a year.

yearn vi to long for.—**yearning** n.

yeast n a fungus that causes alcoholic fermentation, used in brewing and baking.

yell vti to shout loudly. • n a loud shout.

yellow adj of the colour of lemons; (inf) cowardly. • n the colour yellow.

yelp vti to utter a shrill cry or bark.—also n.

yen[1] n the monetary unit of Japan.

yen[2] n (inf) a yearning, an ambition.

yes adv a word of affirmation or consent.

yesterday n the day before today.

yet adv still; so far; even. • conj nevertheless; however; still.

yew n an evergreen tree or shrub.

Yiddish n a mixed German and Hebrew dialect spoken by European Jews.

yield vt to give forth, to produce. • vi to submit.

yodel vti to sing, alternating from the ordinary voice to falsetto.

yoga n a system of exercises for attaining bodily and mental control and well-being.

yoghurt, yogurt n a semi-liquid food made from milk curdled by bacteria.

yoke n slavery; part of a garment that is fitted below the neck.

yolk n the yellow part of an egg.

yonder adv over there.

you pron 2nd person singular or plural; the person or persons spoken to.

young adj in the early period of life. • n young people; offspring.

youngster n a young person; a youth.

your poss adj of or belonging to you.

yours poss pron of or belonging to you.

yourself pron the emphatic and reflexive form of you.

youth n the period between childhood and adulthood; a young man or boy.—**youthful** adj.

youth hostel n a supervised lodging for usu young travellers.

zany adj comical; eccentric.

zeal n fervent devotion; fanaticism.

zealous adj full of zeal; ardent.

zebra n a black and white striped wild animal related to the horse.

zebra crossing n a street crossing marked by black and white strips on the road.

zero n the symbol 0; nothing; freezing point.

zest n the outer part of the skin of an orange or lemon used to give flavour; enthusiasm.

zigzag n a series of short, sharp angles in alternate directions. • vti to move in a zigzag.

zinc n a bluish-white metallic element used in alloys and batteries.

zip(per) n a slide fastener on clothing, etc, with interlocking teeth. • vt to fasten with a zip.

zither n a stringed instrument played by plucking.

zodiac n an imaginary belt in the heavens along which the sun, moon and planets appear to move, divided into twelve equal areas; a diagram representing this.

zombie n a lifeless and apathetic person.

zone n a region, area.

zoo n a place where a collection of living wild animals is kept for public showing.

zoology n the study of animals with regard to their classification, structure and habits.

zoom vi to go quickly, to speed; (photog) to focus in on an object using a zoom lens.

zoom lens n (photog) a camera lens that makes distant objects appear closer.

Thesaurus

A

abandon *vb* abdicate, abjure, desert, drop, evacuate, forsake, forswear, leave, quit, relinquish, yield; cede, forgo, give up, let go, renounce, resign, surrender, vacate, waive. • *n* careless freedom, dash, impetuosity, impulse, wildness.

abandoned *adj* depraved, derelict, deserted, discarded, dropped, forsaken, left, outcast, rejected, relinquished; corrupt, depraved, dissolute, lost, profligate, reprobate, shameless.

abate *vb* diminish, decrease, lessen, lower, moderate, reduce, relax, remove, slacken; deduct, mitigate, rebate, remit; allay, alleviate, appease, assuage, blunt, calm, compose, dull, mitigate, moderate, mollify, pacify, qualify, quiet, quell, soften, soothe, tranquillise.

abbreviate *vb* abridge, condense, contract, cut, curtail, reduce, retrench, shorten.

abbreviation *n* abridgment, compression, condensation, contraction, curtailment, cutting, reduction, shortening.

abdicate *vb* abandon, cede, forgo, forsake, quit, relinquish, renounce, resign, retire, surrender.

aberration *n* departure, deviation, divergence, rambling, wandering; abnormality, anomaly, eccentricity, inconformity, irregularity, peculiarity, singularity; delusion, disorder, hallucination.

abhor *vb* abominate, detest, disgust, execrate, hate, loathe, nauseate.

abhorrent *adj* hateful, horrifying, horrible, loathsome, nauseating, odious, offensive, repellent, repugnant, repulsive.

abide *vb* lodge, rest, sojourn, stay, wait; dwell, inhabit, live, reside; bear, continue, persevere, persist, remain; endure, last, suffer, tolerate; (*with* **by**) conform to, discharge, fulfil, keep.

ability *n* ableness, adroitness, aptitude, aptness, cleverness, dexterity, efficacy, efficiency, facility, ingenuity, knack, power, readiness, skill, strength, talent, vigour, competency, qualification; calibre, capability, capacity, faculty.

able *adj* accomplished, adroit, apt, clever, expert, ingenious, practical, proficient, qualified, skilful, talented, versed; competent, effective, efficient, fitted; capable, gifted, talented.

abnormal *adj* aberrant, anomalous, divergent, eccentric, exceptional, idiosyncratic, irregular, odd, peculiar, singular, strange, unnatural, unusual, weird.

abolish *vb* annul, cancel, eliminate, invalidate,

nullify, quash, repeal, rescind, revoke; annihilate, destroy, end, eradicate, extirpate, extinguish, obliterate, overthrow, terminate.

abominable *adj* accursed, contemptible, cursed, damnable, detestable, execrable, hellish, horrid, nefarious, odious; abhorrent, detestable, disgusting, foul, hateful, loathsome, nauseous, obnoxious, shocking, revolting, repugnant.

abortive *adj* immature, incomplete, futile, fruitless, idle, ineffectual, inoperative, nugatory, unavailing, unsuccessful, useless, vain.

about *prep* around, encircling, surrounding, round; near; concerning, referring to, regarding, relating to, relative to, respecting, with regard to, with respect to; all over, over, through. • *adv* around, before; approximately, near, nearly.

above *adj* above-mentioned, aforementioned, aforesaid, foregoing, preceding, previous, prior. • *adv* aloft, overhead; before, previously; of a higher rank. • *prep* higher than, on top of; exceeding, greater than, more than, over; beyond.

abrupt *adj* broken, craggy, jagged, rough, rugged; precipitous, steep; hasty, ill-timed, precipitate, sudden, unanticipated, unexpected; blunt, brusque, curt, discourteous; cramped, harsh.

absence *n* nonappearance, nonattendance; abstraction, distraction, inattention, musing, preoccupation, reverie; default, defect, deficiency, lack, privation.

absent *adj* abroad, away, elsewhere, gone, not present; abstracted, dreaming, inattentive, lost, musing, napping, preoccupied.

absolute *adj* complete, ideal, independent, perfect, supreme, unconditional, unconditioned, unlimited, unqualified, unrestricted; arbitrary, authoritative, autocratic, despotic, dictatorial, imperious, irresponsible, tyrannical, tyrannous; actual, categorical, certain, decided, determinate, genuine, positive, real, unequivocal, unquestionable, veritable.

absolutely *adv* completely, definitely, unconditionally; actually, downright, indeed, indubitably, positively, really, truly, unquestionably.

absolution *n* acquittal, clearance, deliverance, discharge, forgiveness, liberation, pardon, release, remission, shrift, shriving.

absorb *vb* appropriate, assimilate, drink in, imbibe, soak up; consume, devour, engorge, engulf, exhaust, swallow up, take up; arrest, engage, engross, fix, immerse, occupy, rivet.

abstain *vb* avoid, cease, deny oneself, desist, forbear, refrain, refuse, stop, withhold.

abstemious *adj* abstinent, frugal, moderate, self-denying, sober, temperate.

abstinence *n* abstemiousness, avoidance, fast, moderation, restraint, self-denial, sobriety.

abstract *vb* detach, disengage, dissociate, disunite, isolate, separate; appropriate, purloin, seize, steal, take; abbreviate, abridge, epitomise. • *adj* isolated, separate, simple, unrelated; abstracted, occult, recondite, refined, subtle, vague; nonobjective, nonrepresentational. • *n* abridgment, condensation, digest, excerpt, extract, précis, selection, summary, synopsis.

abstracted *adj* absent, absent-minded, dreaming, inattentive, lost, musing, preoccupied.

absurd *adj* extravagant, fantastic, fatuous, foolish, idiotic, incongruous, ill-advised, ill-judged, irrational, ludicrous, nonsensical, nugatory, preposterous, ridiculous, self-annulling, senseless, silly, stupid, unreasonable.

abundant *adj* abounding, affluent, ample, bountiful, copious, exuberant, fertile, flowing, full, good, large, lavish, luxuriant, rich, liberal, much, overflowing, plentiful, plenteous, replete, teeming, thick.

abuse *vb* betray, cajole, deceive, desecrate, dishonour, misapply, misemploy, misuse, pervert, pollute, profane, prostitute, violate, wrong; harm, hurt, ill-use, ill-treat, injure, maltreat, mishandle; berate, blacken, calumniate, defame, disparage, lampoon, lash, malign, revile, reproach, satirise, slander, traduce, upbraid, vilify. • *n* desecration, dishonour, ill-use, misuse, perversion, pollution, profanation; ill-treatment, maltreatment, outrage; defamation, disparagement, insult, invective, obloquy, opprobrium, railing, rating, reviling, ribaldry, rudeness, scurrility, upbraiding, vilification, vituperation.

academic *adj* collegiate, lettered, scholastic. • *n* academician, classicist, doctor, fellow, pundit, savant, scholar, student, teacher.

accelerate *vb* dispatch, expedite, forward, hasten, hurry, pick up, precipitate, press on, quicken, speed, step up, urge on.

accentuate *vb* accent, emphasise, mark, point up, punctuate, stress; highlight.

accept *vb* acquire, derive, get, gain, obtain, receive, take; accede to, acknowledge, acquiesce in, admit, agree to, approve, assent to, avow, embrace; estimate, construe, interpret, regard.

acceptable *adj* agreeable, gratifying, pleasant, pleasing, pleasurable, welcome.

access *vb* broach, enter, open, open up. • *n* approach, avenue, entrance, entry, passage, way; admission, admittance, audience, interview; addition, accession, aggrandisement, enlargement, gain, increase, increment.

accessory *adj* abetting, additional, additive, adjunct, aiding, ancillary, assisting, contributory, helping, subsidiary, subordinate, supplemental. • *n* abettor, accomplice, assistant, associate, confederate, helper; accompaniment, attendant, concomitant, detail, subsidiary.

accident *n* calamity, casualty, condition, contingency, disaster, fortuity, incident, misadventure, miscarriage, mischance, misfortune, mishap; affection, alteration, chance, contingency.

accidental *adj* casual, chance, contingent, fortuitous, undesigned, unintended; adventitious, immaterial, incidental.

acclimatise *vb* accustom, adapt, adjust, condition, familiarise, habituate, inure, season.

accommodate *vb* contain, furnish, hold, oblige, serve, supply; adapt, fit, suit; adjust, compose, harmonise, reconcile, settle.

accompany *vb* attend, chaperon, convoy, escort, follow, go with.

accomplice *n* abettor, accessory, ally, assistant, associate, confederate, partner.

accomplish *vb* achieve, acquire, attain, bring about, carry, carry through, complete, compass, consummate, do, effect, execute, fulfil, perform, perfect; conclude, end, finish, terminate.

accomplished *adj* achieved, completed, done, effected, executed, finished, fulfilled, realised; able, adroit, apt, consummate, educated, experienced, expert, finished, instructed, practised, proficient, qualified, ripe, skilful, versed; elegant, fashionable, fine, polished, polite, refined.

accord *vb* admit, allow, concede, deign, give, grant, vouchsafe, yield; agree, assent, concur, correspond, harmonise, quadrate, tally. • *n* agreement, concord, concurrence, conformity, consensus, harmony, unanimity, unison.

accordingly *adv* agreeably, conformably, consistently, suitably; consequently, hence, so, thence, therefore, thus, whence, wherefore.

account *vb* assess, appraise, estimate, evaluate, judge, rate; (*with* **for**) assign, attribute, explain, expound, justify, rationalise, vindicate. • *n* inventory, record, register, score; bill, book, charge; calculation, computation, count, reckoning, score, tale, tally; chronicle, detail, description, narration, narrative, portrayal, recital, rehearsal, relation, report, statement, tidings, word; elucidation, explanation, exposition; consideration, ground, motive, reason, regard, sake; consequence, consideration, dignity, distinction, importance, note, repute, reputation, worth.

accumulate *vb* agglomerate, aggregate, amass, bring together, collect, gather, grow, heap, hoard, increase, pile, store.

accurate *adj* careful, close, correct, exact, faithful, nice, precise, regular, strict, true, truthful.

accuse *vb* arraign, charge, censure, impeach.

ace n atom, bit, grain, iota, jot, particle; expert, master, virtuoso. • adj best, expert, outstanding.

achieve vb accomplish, acquire, attain, complete, consummate, effect, execute, finish, fulfil, perform, realise; acquire, gain, get, obtain, win.

acid adj pungent, sharp, sour, stinging, tart.

acknowledge vb recognise; accept, admit, accept, allow, concede, grant; avow, confess, own.

acquaintance n companionship, familiarity, fellowship, intimacy, knowledge; associate, companion, comrade, friend.

acquire vb achieve, attain, earn, gain, gather, get, have, obtain, procure, realise, secure, win; accomplish, learn thoroughly, master.

acquit vb absolve, clear, discharge, exculpate, excuse, exonerate, forgive, liberate, pardon, pay, quit, release, set free, settle.

acrimonious adj abusive, acrid, bitter, caustic, censorious, churlish, crabbed, harsh, malignant, petulant, sarcastic, severe, sharp, spiteful, testy.

act vb do, execute, function, make, operate, work; enact, feign, perform, play. • n achievement, deed, exploit, feat, performance, proceeding, turn; bill, decree, enactment, law, ordinance, statute; actuality, existence, fact, reality.

acting adj interim, provisional, substitute, temporary. • n impersonation, performance, theatre; dissimulation, imitation, pretence.

action n activity, agency, deed, exertion, exploit, feat; battle, combat, conflict, contest, engagement; lawsuit, prosecution.

active adj effective, efficient, influential, living, operative; assiduous, bustling, busy, industrious; agile, alert, brisk, energetic, lively, nimble, prompt, quick, smart, spirited, sprightly, supple; animated, ebullient, fervent, vigorous.

actual adj certain, decided, genuine, objective, real, substantial, tangible, true, veritable; perceptible, present, sensible; absolute, positive.

acumen n acuteness, astuteness, discernment, ingenuity, keenness, penetration, sagacity, sharpness, shrewdness.

acute adj pointed, sharp; astute, bright, discerning, ingenious, intelligent, keen, quick, penetrating, piercing, sagacious, sage, sharp, shrewd, smart, subtle; distressing, fierce, intense, piercing, pungent, poignant, severe, violent; high, sharp, shrill; (med) sudden, violent.

adapt vb accommodate, adjust, conform, coordinate, fit, qualify, proportion, suit, temper.

add vb adjoin, affix, annex, append, attach, join, tag; sum, sum up, total.

addict vb accustom, apply, devote, habituate. • n devotee, enthusiast, fan; head, junkie, user.

addition n augmentation, accession, enlargement, extension, increase, supplement; adjunct, appendage, appendix, extra.

address vb accost, apply to, court, direct. • n appeal, application, entreaty, invocation, memorial, petition, request, solicitation, suit; discourse, oration, lecture, sermon, speech; ability, adroitness, art, dexterity, expertness, skill.

adequate adj able, adapted, capable, competent, equal, fit, requisite, satisfactory, sufficient.

adhere vb cling, cleave, cohere, hold, stick; appertain, belong, pertain.

adherent adj adhering, clinging, sticking. • n acolyte, dependant, disciple, follower, partisan.

adhesive adj clinging, sticking; glutinous, gummy, sticky, tenacious, viscous. • n binder, cement, glue, paste.

adjacent adj adjoining, bordering, contiguous, near, near to, neighbouring, touching.

adjourn vb delay, postpone, procrastinate; close, dissolve, end, prorogue, suspend.

adjunct n addition, advantage, appendage, appurtenance, attachment, attribute, auxiliary.

adjust vb adapt, arrange, dispose, rectify; regulate, settle, suit; compose, harmonise, reconcile; accommodate, adapt, fit, suit.

administer vb contribute, deal out, dispense, supply; conduct, control, direct, govern, manage, oversee, superintend.

admirable adj astonishing, striking, surprising, wonderful; excellent, fine, rare, superb.

admiration n affection, approbation, approval, astonishment, delight, pleasure, regard.

admire vb approve, esteem, respect; adore, prize, cherish, revere, treasure.

admissible adj allowable, lawful, permissible.

admission n access, admittance, entrance, introduction; acceptance, acknowledgement, allowance, assent, avowal, concession.

admit vb let in, receive; accept, acknowledge, concede, confess; allow, bear, permit.

adopt vb appropriate, assume; accept, approve, maintain, support; affiliate, father, foster.

adore vb worship; esteem, honour, idolise, love.

adult adj grownup, mature, ripe, ripened. • n grown-up person.

adulterate vb alloy, contaminate, corrupt, debase, deteriorate, vitiate.

advance adj beforehand, forward, leading. • vb propel, push, send forward; aggrandise, dignify, elevate, exalt, promote; benefit, forward, further, improve, promote; adduce, allege, assign, offer, propose, propound; augment, increase; proceed, progress; grow, improve, prosper, thrive. • n march, progress; advancement, enhancement, growth, promotion, rise; offer, overture, proffering, proposal, proposition; appreciation, rise.

advantage n ascendancy, precedence, pre-eminence, superiority, upper-hand; benefit, blessing, emolument, gain, profit, return; account, behalf, interest; accommodation, convenience, prerogative, privilege.

advent n accession, approach, arrival, coming.

adventure vb dare, hazard, imperil, peril, risk, venture. • n chance, contingency, experiment, fortuity, hazard, risk, venture; crisis, contingency, event, incident, occurrence, transaction.

adventurous adj bold, chivalrous, courageous, daring, doughty; foolhardy, headlong, precipitate, rash, reckless; dangerous, hazardous.

adversary n antagonist, enemy, foe, opponent.

adverse adj conflicting, contrary, opposing; antagonistic, harmful, hostile, hurtful, inimical, unfavourable, unpropitious; calamitous, disastrous, unfortunate, unlucky, untoward.

advertise vb announce, declare, inform.

advice n admonition, caution, counsel, exhortation, persuasion, suggestion, recommendation; information, intelligence, notice, notification; care, counsel, deliberation, forethought.

advisable adj desirable, prudent.

advise vb counsel, recommend, suggest, urge; acquaint, apprise, inform, notify.

adviser n counsellor, director, guide, instructor.

advocate vb maintain, support, uphold, vindicate. • n apologist, counsellor, defender, maintainer, patron, pleader, supporter; attorney, barrister, counsel, lawyer, solicitor.

affable adj accessible, approachable, cordial, easy, friendly, sociable, courteous, civil, obliging, polite.

affair n business, circumstance, concern, matter, office, question; event, incident, occurrence, performance, proceeding, transaction; battle, combat, conflict, encounter, engagement.

affect vb act upon, alter, change, influence, transform; concern, interest, regard, relate; improve, melt, move, touch; adopt, assume, feign.

affectation n affectedness, airs, artificiality, foppery, pretension, simulation.

affection n bent, bias, feeling, inclination, passion, proclivity, propensity; accident, attribute, character, mark, modification, mode, note, property; attachment, endearment, fondness, goodwill, kindness, partiality, love.

affectionate adj attached, devoted, fond, kind, loving, sympathetic, tender.

affirm vb allege, assert, asseverate, aver, declare, state; approve, confirm, establish, ratify.

affliction n adversity, calamity, disaster, misfortune, stroke, visitation; bitterness, depression, distress, grief, misery, plague, scourge, sorrow, trial, tribulation, wretchedness, woe.

affluent adj abounding, abundant, bounteous, plenteous; moneyed, opulent, rich, wealthy.

afford vb furnish, produce, supply, yield; bestow, communicate, confer, give, grant, impart, offer; bear, endure, support.

affront vb abuse, insult, outrage; displease, offend, pique, provoke, vex. • n abuse, insult, outrage, wrong.

afraid adj aghast, alarmed, anxious, apprehensive, frightened, scared, timid.

after prep later than, subsequent to; behind, following; about, according to; because of, in imitation of. • adj behind, consecutive, ensuing, following, later, succeeding, subsequent; aft, back, hind, rear, rearmost, tail. • adv afterwards, later, next, since, subsequently, then.

again adv afresh, anew, another time, once more; besides, further, in addition, moreover.

against prep adverse to, contrary to, resisting; abutting, close to, facing, fronting, off, opposite to, over; in expectation of; in compensation for, to counterbalance, to match.

age vb decline, grow old, mature. • n aeon, date, epoch, period, time; decline, old age, senility; antiquity, oldness.

agent n actor, doer, executor, operator, performer; active element, cause, force; attorney, broker, commissioner, deputy, factor, intermediary.

aggravate vb heighten, increase, worsen; colour, exaggerate, magnify, overstate; enrage, irritate, provoke, tease.

aggressive adj attacking, invading, offensive; pushing, self-assertive.

aggrieve vb afflict, grieve, pain.

aghast adj appalled, dismayed, frightened, horrified, horror-struck, panic-stricken, terrified.

agile adj active, alert, brisk, lively, nimble.

agitate vb disturb, jar, rock, shake, trouble; disquiet, excite, ferment, rouse, trouble; confuse, discontent, flurry, fluster, flutter.

agitation n commotion, convulsion, disturbance, ferment, jarring, storm, tumult, turmoil; discomposure, distraction, emotion, excitement, flutter, perturbation, tremor, trepidation.

agony n anguish, distress, pangs.

agree vb accord, concur, harmonise, unite; accede, acquiesce, assent, comply, concur, subscribe; bargain, contract, covenant, engage, promise, undertake; chime, cohere, conform, correspond, match, suit, tally.

agreement n accordance, compliance, concord, harmony, union; bargain, compact, contract, pact, treaty.

aid vb assist, help, support; relieve, succour; advance, facilitate, further, promote. • n assistance, help, patronage; subsidy, relief.

ailment n disease, illness, sickness.

aim vb direct, level, point, train; design, intend, mean, purpose, seek. • n bearing, course, direction, tendency; design, object, view, reason.

air vb expose, display, ventilate. • n atmosphere, breeze; appearance, manner; melody, tune.

alarm vb daunt, frighten, scare, startle, terrify. • n alarm-bell, tocsin, warning; apprehension, fear, fright, terror.

alert adj awake, circumspect, vigilant, watchful,

wary; active, brisk, lively, nimble, quick, prompt, ready, sprightly, spry. • *vb* alarm, arouse, caution, forewarn, signal, warn. • *n* alarm, signal, warning.

alien *adj* foreign, not native; differing, estranged, inappropriate, remote, unallied, separated. • *n* foreigner, stranger.

alike *adj* akin, analogous, duplicate, identical, resembling, similar. • *adv* equally.

alive *adj* animate, breathing, live; aware, responsive, sensitive; brisk, cheerful, lively.

allay *vb* appease, calm, check, compose; alleviate, assuage, lessen, moderate, solace, temper.

allege *vb* affirm, assert, declare, maintain, say; adduce, advance, cite, plead, produce, quote.

allegiance *n* duty, homage, fealty, fidelity, loyalty, obligation.

alliance *n* affinity, intermarriage, relation; coalition, combination, confederacy, league, treaty, union; affiliation, connection, relationship.

allow *vb* acknowledge, admit, concede, confess, grant, own; authorise, grant, let, permit; bear, endure, suffer, tolerate; grant, yield, relinquish, spare; approve, justify, sanction; abate, deduct.

allure *vb* attract, beguile, cajole, coax, entice, lure, persuade, seduce, tempt. • *n* appeal, attraction, lure, temptation.

ally *vb* combine, connect, join, league, marry, unite. • *n* aider, assistant, associate, coadjutor, colleague, friend, partner.

alone *adj* companionless, deserted, forsaken, isolated, lonely, only, single, sole, solitary.

along *adv* lengthways, lengthwise; forward, onward; beside, together, simultaneously.

alter *vb* change, conform, modify, shift, vary.

alternate *vb* fluctuate, oscillate, vacillate, vary, waver, wobble; change, exchange, interchange, reciprocate; intermit, revolve; relieve, spell, take turns. • *adj* intermittent, periodic; alternative, equivalent, substitute; reciprocal. • *n* deputy, alternative, proxy, replacement, substitute.

alternative *adj* another, different, second, substitute. • *n* choice, option, preference.

although *conj* albeit, even if, for all that, notwithstanding, though.

altitude *n* elevation, height, loftiness.

altogether *adv* completely, entirely, totally.

always *adv* continually, eternally, evermore, perpetually, unceasingly.

amaze *vb* astonish, astound, bewilder, confound, confuse, dumbfound, perplex, stagger.

ambiguous *adj* dubious, doubtful, enigmatic, equivocal, indefinite, obscure, vague.

ambitious *adj* aspiring, avid, eager, intent.

amenable *adj* acquiescent, agreeable, persuadable, responsive, susceptible.

amend *vb* better, correct, improve, mend, redress, reform.

amends *npl* atonement, compensation, expia-

tion, indemnification, recompense, reparation, restitution.

amiable *adj* attractive, benign, charming, genial, good-natured, harmonious, kind, lovable, pleasant, pleasing, sweet, winning.

amicable *adj* amiable, cordial, friendly, harmonious, kind, kindly, peaceable.

amiss *adj* erroneous, inaccurate, incorrect, faulty, improper, wrong. • *adv* erroneously, inaccurately, incorrectly, wrongly.

amorous *adj* ardent, enamoured, fond, longing, loving, passionate, tender; erotic, impassioned.

amount *n* aggregate, sum, total.

ample *adj* broad, capacious, extended, extensive, great, large, roomy, spacious; abounding, abundant, copious, generous, liberal, plentiful.

amuse *vb* charm, cheer, divert, enliven, entertain, gladden, relax, solace.

analysis *n* decomposition, dissection, resolution, separation.

anarchy *n* chaos, confusion, disorder, misrule, lawlessness, riot.

ancestor *n* forebear, forefather, progenitor.

ancestry *n* family, house, line, lineage; descent, genealogy, parentage, pedigree, stock.

anchor *vb* fasten, fix, secure; cast anchor, take firm hold. • *n* (*naut*) ground tackle; defence, hold, security, stay.

ancient *adj* old, primitive, pristine; antiquated, antique, archaic, obsolete.

angelic *adj* adorable, celestial, cherubic, heavenly, saintly, seraphic; entrancing, enrapturing.

anger *vb* chafe, displease, enrage, gall, infuriate, irritate, madden. • *n* choler, exasperation, fury, gall, indignation, ire, passion, rage, resentment, spleen, wrath.

angry *adj* exasperated, furious, incensed, irritated, nettled, piqued, provoked, resentful.

anguish *n* agony, distress, grief, pang, rack, torment, torture.

animate *vb* quicken, vitalise, vivify; fortify, invigorate, revive; activate, enliven, excite, heat, impel, kindle, rouse, stimulate, stir, waken; elate, embolden, encourage, exhilarate. • *adj* alive, breathing, live, living, organic.

animosity *n* bitterness, enmity, grudge, hatred, hostility, rancour, rankling, spleen, virulence.

annex *vb* affix, append, attach, subjoin, tag, tack; connect, join, unite.

annihilate *vb* abolish, annul, destroy, dissolve, exterminate, extinguish, kill, obliterate, raze.

announce *vb* advertise, communicate, declare, disclose, proclaim, promulgate, publish, report, reveal, trumpet.

annoy *vb* badger, chafe, disquiet, disturb, fret, hector, irk, irritate, molest, pain, pester, plague, trouble, vex, worry, wound.

annul *vb* abolish, abrogate, cancel, countermand, nullify, overrule, quash, repeal, recall, reverse, revoke.

anoint vb consecrate, oil, sanctify, smear.

anonymous adj nameless, unsigned.

answer vb fulfil, rejoin, reply, respond, satisfy. • n rejoinder, reply, response, retort; confutation, rebuttal, refutation.

answerable adj accountable, amenable, correspondent, liable, responsible, suited.

antagonism n contradiction, discordance, disharmony, dissonant, incompatibility, opposition.

anterior adj antecedent, foregoing, preceding, previous, prior; fore, front.

anticipation n apprehension, contemplation, expectation, hope, prospect, trust; expectancy, forecast, foresight, foretaste, preconception.

antipathy n abhorrence, aversion, disgust, detestation, hate, hatred, horror, loathing.

antique adj ancient, archaic, bygone, old.

anxiety n apprehension, care, concern, disquiet, fear, foreboding, misgiving, perplexity, trouble, uneasiness, vexation, worry.

anxious adj apprehensive, restless, solicitous, uneasy, unquiet, worried.

apathetic adj cold, dull, inert, listless, passionless, sluggish, torpid.

aplomb n composure, confidence, equanimity.

apologetic adj exculpatory, excusatory; defensive.

apology n defence, justification, vindication; acknowledgement, excuse, explanation, plea.

apostle n angel, herald, messenger, missionary, preacher; advocate, follower, supporter.

appal vb alarm, daunt, dismay, frighten, horrify, scare, shock.

apparent adj discernible, perceptible, visible; conspicuous, evident, legible, manifest, obvious, open, patent, plain, unmistakable; external, ostensible, seeming, superficial.

apparition n appearance, appearing, epiphany, manifestation; being, form; ghost, phantom.

appeal vb address, entreat, implore, invoke, refer, request, solicit. • n application, entreaty, invocation, solicitation, suit.

appear vb emerge, loom; break, open; arise, occur, offer; look, seem, show.

appearance n advent, arrival, apparition, coming; form, shape; colour, face, fashion, feature, guise, pretence, pretext; air, aspect, complexion, demeanour, manner, mien.

append vb attach, fasten, hang; add, annex.

appetite n craving, desire, longing, lust, passion; gusto, relish, stomach, zest; hunger.

applaud vb acclaim, approve, cheer, clap, commend, compliment, encourage, extol, magnify.

application n emollient, lotion, ointment, poultice, wash; appliance, exercise, practice, use; appeal, petition, request, solicitation, suit; assiduity, constancy, diligence, effort, industry.

apply vb bestow, lay upon; appropriate, convert, employ, exercise, use; addict, address, dedicate, devote, direct, engage.

appoint vb determine, establish, fix, prescribe; bid, command, decree, direct, order, require; allot, assign, delegate, depute, detail, destine, settle; create, name, nominate; equip, furnish.

appreciate vb esteem, estimate, rate, realise, value.

apprehend vb arrest, capture, catch, detain, seize, take; conceive, imagine, regard, view; appreciate, perceive, realise, see, take in.

approach vb advance, approximate, come close; broach; resemble. • n advance, advent; approximation, convergence, nearing, tendency; entrance, path, way.

appropriate vb adopt, arrogate, assume, set apart; allot, apportion, assign, devote; apply, convert, employ, use. • adj adapted, apt, befitting, fit, opportune, seemly, suitable.

approve vb appreciate, commend, like, praise, recommend, value; confirm, countenance, justify, ratify, sustain, uphold.

approximate vb approach, resemble. • adj approaching, proximate; inexact, rough.

apt adj applicable, apposite, appropriate, befitting, fit, felicitous, germane; disposed, inclined, liable, prone, subject; able, adroit, clever, dextrous, expert, ready, skilful.

aptitude n applicability, appropriateness, felicity, fitness, pertinence, suitability; inclination, tendency, turn; ability, adroitness, quickness.

arbitrary adj absolute, autocratic, despotic, domineering, imperious, overbearing, unlimited; capricious, discretionary, fanciful, voluntary.

arch adj cunning, knowing, frolicsome, merry, roguish, shrewd, sly; consummate, chief, leading, pre-eminent, prime, principal.

ardent adj burning, fiery, hot; eager, earnest, fervent, keen, passionate, zealous.

ardour n glow, heat, warmth; eagerness, enthusiasm, fervour, passion, spirit, zeal.

arduous adj high, lofty, steep, uphill; difficult, fatiguing, hard, laborious, onerous.

area n circle, circuit, district, domain, field, range, realm, region, tract.

argue vb plead, reason upon; debate, dispute; denote, evince, imply, indicate, mean, prove; contest, debate, discuss, sift.

arise vb ascend, mount, soar, tower; appear, emerge, rise, spring; begin, originate; rebel, revolt, rise; accrue, come, emanate, ensue, flow, issue, originate, proceed, result.

arm vb equip, furnish; clothe, cover, fortify, guard, protect, strengthen.

army n force, host, legions, troops; multitude, throng, vast assemblage.

around prep about, encircling, encompassing,

round, surrounding. • *adv* about, approximately, generally, near, practically, thereabouts.

arouse *vb* animate, awaken, excite, incite, kindle, provoke, rouse, stimulate, warm, whet.

arrange *vb* array, class, classify, dispose, distribute, group, range, rank; adjust, determine, fix upon, settle; construct, devise, plan, prepare.

array *vb* arrange, dispose, place, range, rank; accoutre, adorn, attire, decorate, dress, enrobe, embellish, equip, garnish, habit, invest. • *n* arrangement, collection, disposition, marshalling, order; apparel, attire, clothes, dress, garments; army, battalions, soldiery, troops.

arrest *vb* check, delay, detain, hinder, hold, interrupt, obstruct, restrain, stay, stop, withhold; apprehend, capture, catch, seize, take; catch, engage, engross, fix, occupy, secure, rivet. • *n* check, checking, detention, hindrance, interruption, obstruction, restraining, stay, staying, stopping; apprehension, capture, detention, seizure.

arrive *vb* attain, come, get to, reach.

arrogance *n* disdain, effrontery, haughtiness, lordliness, presumption, superciliousness.

art *n* business, craft, employment, trade; address, adroitness, aptitude, dexterity, ingenuity, knack, sagacity, skill; artfulness, artifice, astuteness, craft, deceit, duplicity, finesse, subtlety.

artful *adj* crafty, cunning, disingenuous, insincere, sly, tricky, wily.

article *n* branch, clause, division, head, item, member, paragraph, part, point, portion; essay, paper, piece; commodity, substance, thing.

artificial *adj* counterfeit, sham, spurious; assumed, affected, forced, laboured, strained.

artless *adj* ignorant, rude, unskilful, untaught; natural, plain, simple; candid, fair, frank, guileless, honest, plain, unaffected, simple, sincere.

ascend *vb* arise, aspire, climb, mount, soar.

ascertain *vb* certify, define, determine, establish, fix, settle, verify; discover, find out, get at.

ashamed *adj* abashed, confused.

ask *vb* interrogate, inquire, question; adjure, beg, conjure, crave, desire, dun, entreat, implore, invite, inquire, petition, request, solicit, supplicate, seek.

aspect *n* air, bearing, countenance, expression, feature, look, mien, visage; appearance, attitude, condition, light, phase, position, situation, state, view; angle, direction, prospect.

asperity *n* ruggedness, roughness, unevenness; acrimony, corrosiveness, sharpness, sourness, tartness; acerbity, bitterness, churlishness, harshness, sternness, severity, virulence.

aspersion *n* abuse, backbiting, calumny, censure, defamation, detraction, slander, vituperation, reflection, reproach.

aspiration *n* aim, ambition, craving, desire, hankering, hope, longing.

assassinate *vb* dispatch, kill, murder, slay.

assault *vb* assail, attack, charge, invade. • *n* aggression, attack, charge, incursion, invasion, onset, onslaught; storm.

assemble *vb* call, collect, congregate, convene, gather, muster; congregate, forgather.

assembly *n* company, collection, concourse, congregation, gathering, meeting, throng; caucus, congress, conclave, convention, convocation, diet, legislature, parliament, synod.

assent *vb* accede, acquiesce, agree, concur, subscribe, yield. • *n* accord, acquiescence, allowance, approval, approbation, consent.

assertion *n* affirmation, allegation, asseveration, averment, declaration, position, predication, remark, statement, word; defence, emphasis, maintenance, pressing, support, vindication.

assess *vb* appraise, compute, estimate, rate, value; assign, determine, fix, impose, levy.

assign *vb* allot, appoint, apportion; fix, designate, specify; advance, give, grant.

assist *vb* abet, aid, befriend, further, help, patronise, promote, second, speed, support, sustain; aid, relieve, succour; alternate with.

associate *vb* affiliate, combine, conjoin, couple, join, link, relate, yoke; consort, fraternise, mingle. • *n* companion, comrade, mate; ally, confederate, friend, partner, fellow.

association *n* combination, company, confederation, connection, partnership, society.

assort *vb* arrange, class, classify, distribute, group, rank, sort; agree, be adapted, consort.

assume *vb* take, undertake; affect, counterfeit, feign, pretend, sham; arrogate, usurp; beg, hypothesise, imply, postulate, posit, presuppose, suppose, simulate.

assurance *n* assuredness, certainty, conviction, persuasion, pledge, security, surety, warrant; engagement, pledge, promise; averment, assertion, protestation; audacity, confidence, courage, firmness, intrepidity; arrogance, brass, boldness.

astonish *vb* amaze, astound, confound, daze, dumbfound, overwhelm, startle, stun, stupefy, surprise.

astute *adj* acute, cunning, deep, discerning, ingenious, intelligent, penetrating, perspicacious, quick, sagacious, sharp, shrewd.

athletic *adj* brawny, lusty, muscular, powerful, robust, sinewy, stalwart, stout, strapping, strong.

atom *n* bit, molecule, monad, particle, scintilla.

atonement *n* amends, expiation, propitiation, reparation, satisfaction.

atrocity *n* depravity, enormity, flagrancy, ferocity, savagery, villainy.

attach *vb* affix, annex, connect, fasten, join, hitch, tie; charm, captivate, enamour, endear, engage, win; (*legal*) distress, distrain, seize, take.

attack *vb* assail, assault, charge, encounter, invade, set upon, storm, tackle; censure, criticise, impugn. • *n* aggression, assault, charge, offence, onset, onslaught, raid, thrust.

attain *vb* accomplish, achieve, acquire, get, obtain, secure; arrive at, come to, reach.

attempt *vb* assail, assault, attack; aim, endeavour, seek, strive, try. • *n* effort, endeavour, enterprise, experiment, undertaking, venture; assault, attack, onset.

attend *vb* accompany, escort, follow; guard, protect, watch; minister to, serve, wait on; give heed, hear, listen; serve, tend, wait.

attention *n* care, circumspection, heed, mindfulness, observation, regard, watch, watchfulness; application, reflection, study; civility, courtesy, deference, politeness, regard, respect; addresses, courtship, devotion, suit, wooing.

attentive *adj* alive, awake, careful, civil, considerate, courteous, heedful, mindful, observant.

attire *vb* accoutre, apparel, array, clothe, dress, enrobe, equip, rig, robe. • *n* clothes, clothing, costume, dress, garb, gear, habiliment, outfit, toilet, trapping, vestment, vesture, wardrobe.

attitude *n* pose, position, posture; aspect, conjuncture, condition, phase, prediction, situation, standing, state.

attract *vb* draw, pull; allure, captivate, charm, enamour, endear, entice, fascinate.

attribute *vb* ascribe, assign, impute, refer. • *n* characteristic, mark, note, peculiarity, predicate, property, quality.

audacity *n* boldness, courage, daring, fearlessness, intrepidity; assurance, brass, effrontery, face, front, impudence, insolence, presumption, sauciness.

audience *n* assemblage, congregation; hearing, interview, reception.

austere *adj* ascetic, difficult, formal, hard, harsh, morose, relentless, rigid, rigorous, severe, stern, stiff, strict, uncompromising, unrelenting.

authentic *adj* genuine, pure, real, true, unadulterated, uncorrupted, veritable; accurate, authoritative, reliable, true, trustworthy.

authorise *vb* empower, enable, entitle; allow, approve, confirm, permit, ratify, sanction.

authority *n* dominion, empire, government, jurisdiction, power, sovereignty; ascendency, control, influence, rule, supremacy, sway; authorisation, liberty, order, permit, sanction, warranty; testimony, witness; connoisseur, expert.

auxiliary *adj* aiding, ancillary, assisting, helpful, subsidiary. • *n* ally, assistant, confederate, help.

available *adj* accessible, advantageous, applicable, beneficial, profitable, serviceable, useful.

avenge *vb* punish, retaliate, revenge, vindicate.

aversion *n* abhorrence, antipathy, disgust, dislike, hate, hatred, loathing, reluctance.

avid *adj* eager, greedy, voracious.

avoid *vb* dodge, elude, escape, eschew, shun.

awaken *vb* arouse, excite, incite, kindle, provoke, spur, stimulate; wake, waken; begin.

award *vb* adjudge, allot, assign, bestow, decree, grant. • *n* adjudication, allotment, assignment, decision, decree, determination, gift, judgement.

aware *adj* acquainted, apprised, conscious, conversant, informed, knowing, mindful, sensible.

away *adv* absent, not present. • *adj* at a distance.

awe *vb* cow, daunt, intimidate, overawe. • *n* abashment, fear, reverence; dread, terror.

awful *adj* august, awesome, dread, grand, inspired; abashed, alarming, appalled, dire, frightful, tremendous.

awkward *adj* bungling, clumsy, inept, maladroit, unskilful; lumbering, unfit, ungainly, unmanageable; boorish; inconvenient, unsuitable.

B

baby *vb* coddle, cosset, indulge, mollycoddle, pamper, spoil. • *adj* babyish, childish, infantile, puerile; diminutive, doll-like, miniature, pocket, pocket-sized, small-scale. • *n* babe, brat, child, infant, suckling, nursling; chicken, coward, milksop, weakling; miniature; innocent.

back *vb* abet, aid, countenance, favour, second, support, sustain; go back, move back, retreat, withdraw. • *adj* hindmost. • *adv* in return, in consideration; ago, gone, since; aside, away, behind, by; abaft, astern, backwards, hindwards, rearwards. • *n* end, hind part, posterior, rear.

bad *adj* baleful, baneful, detrimental, evil, harmful, hurtful, injurious, noxious, pernicious, unwholesome, vicious; abandoned, corrupt, depraved, immoral, sinful, unfair, unprincipled, wicked; unfortunate, unhappy, unlucky, miserable; disappointing, discouraging, distressing, sad, unwelcoming; abominable, mean, shabby, scurvy, vile, wretched; defective, inferior, imperfect, incompetent, poor, unsuitable; hard, heavy, serious, severe.

badge *n* brand, emblem, mark, sign, symbol.

badger *vb* annoy, bait, bother, hector, harry, pester, tease, torment, trouble, vex, worry.

baffle *vb* balk, baulk, check, circumvent, defeat, foil, frustrate, mar, thwart, undermine, upset; bewilder, confound, disconcert, perplex.

bait *vb* harry, tease, worry. • *n* allurement, decoy, enticement, lure, temptation.

balance *vb* equilibrate, pose, (*naut*) trim; compare, weigh; compensate, counteract, estimate; adjust, clear, equalise, square. • *n* equilibrium, liberation; excess, remainder, residue, surplus.

bald *adj* bare, naked, uncovered, treeless; dull, inelegant, meagre, prosaic, tame, unadorned.

ban *vb* anathematise, curse, execrate; interdict, outlaw. • *n* edict, proclamation; anathema, curse, denunciation, execration; interdiction, outlawry, penalty, prohibition

band[1] *vb* belt, bind, encircle, girdle; ally, associate, combine, connect, join; bar, marble, streak, stripe, striate, vein. • *n* crew, gang, horde, society, troop; ensemble, group, orchestra.

band[2] *n* ligament, ligature, tie; bond, chain, cord, fetter, manacle, shackle, trammel; bandage, belt, binding, cincture, girth, tourniquet.

bang *vb* bat, knock, maul, pommel, pound, strike, thrash, thump; slam; clatter, rattle, resound, ring. • *n* clang, clangour, whang; blow, knock, lick, thump, thwack, whack.

bank[1] *vb* incline, slope, tilt; embank. • *n* dike, embankment, escarpment, heap, knoll, mound; border, bound, brim, brink, margin, rim, strand; course, row, tier.

bank[2] *vb* deposit, keep, save. • *n* depository, fund, reserve, savings, stockpile.

bar *vb* exclude, hinder, obstruct, prevent, prohibit, restrain, stop. • *n* grating, pole, rail, rod; barricade, hindrance, impediment, obstacle, obstruction, stop; bank, sand bar, shallow, shoal, spit; (*legal*) barristers, counsel, court, judgement, tribunal.

barbaric *adj* barbarous, rude, savage, uncivilised, untamed; capricious, coarse, gaudy, riotous, showy, outlandish, uncouth, untamed, wild.

bare *vb* denude, depilate, divest, strip, unsheathe; disclose, manifest, open, reveal, show. • *adj* denuded, exposed, naked, nude, stripped, unclothed, uncovered, undressed, unsheltered; alone, mere, sheer, simple; bald, meagre, plain, unadorned, uncovered, unfurnished, empty.

bargain *vb* agree, contract, covenant, stipulate; convey, sell, transfer. • *n* agreement, compact, contract, covenant, convention, indenture, transaction, stipulation, treaty.

barren *adj* childless, infecund, sterile; (*bot*) acarpous, sterile; bare, infertile, poor, sterile, unproductive; ineffectual, unfruitful, uninstructive.

barricade *vb* block up, fortify, protect, obstruct. • *n* barrier, obstruction, palisade, stockade.

barrier *n* bar, barricade, hindrance, impediment, obstacle, obstruction, stop.

barter *vb* bargain, exchange, sell, trade, traffic.

base[1] *adj* cheap, inferior, worthless; counterfeit, debased, false, spurious; contemptible, degraded, despicable, low, menial.

base[2] *vb* establish, found, ground. • *n* foundation, fundament, substructure, underpinning; pedestal, plinth, stand; centre, headquarters, HQ, seat; starting point; basis, cause, grounds, reason, standpoint; bottom, foot, foundation, ground.

bashful *adj* coy, diffident, shy, timid.

basis *n* base, bottom, foundation, fundament, ground, groundwork.

bastard *adj* adulterated, baseborn, counterfeit, false, illegitimate, sham. • *n* love child.

batch *n* amount, collection, crowd, lot, quantity.

bathe *vb* immerse, lave, wash; cover, enfold, enwrap, drench, flood, suffuse. • *n* bath, shower, swim.

batter *vb* beat, pelt, smite; break, bruise, demolish, destroy, shatter, shiver, smash; abrade, deface, disfigure, indent, mar.

battle *vb* contend, contest, engage, fight, strive, struggle. • *n* action, affair, brush, combat, conflict, contest, engagement, fight, fray.

bawl *vb* clamour, cry, howl, roar, shout, yell.

beam *vb* beacon, gleam, glisten, glitter, shine. • *n* balk, girder, joist, scanting, stud; gleam, pencil, ray, streak.

bear *vb* support, sustain, uphold; carry, convey, transport; abide, brook, endure, stand, suffer, tolerate, undergo; carry on, keep up, maintain; cherish, entertain, harbour; produce; cast, drop, sustain; endure, submit, suffer; act, operate.

bearing *n* air, behaviour, demeanour, deportment, conduct, carriage, conduct, mien; connection, dependency, relation; endurance, patience, suffering; aim, course, direction; bringing forth, producing; bed, socket.

beastly *adj* abominable, brutish, ignoble, low, sensual, vile.

beat *vb* bang, baste, belabour, buffet, cane, cudgel, drub, hammer, hit, knock, maul, pommel, pound, punch, strike, thrash, thump, whack, whip; bruise, pound, pulverise; batter, pelt; conquer, defeat, overcome, rout, subdue, surpass, vanquish; pulsate, throb; dash, strike. • *n* blow, striking, stroke; beating, pulsation, throb; accent, metre, rhythm; circuit, course, round.

beautiful *adj* charming, comely, fair, fine, exquisite, handsome, lovely, pretty.

beauty *n* elegance, grace, symmetry; attractiveness, loveliness; belle.

become *vb* change to, get, go, wax; adorn, befit, set off, suit.

becoming *adj* appropriate, congruous, decent, decorous, fit, proper, right, seemly, suitable.

bed *vb* embed, establish, imbed, implant, infix, inset, plant; harbour, house, lodge. • *n* berth, bunk, cot, couch; channel, depression, hollow; base, foundation, receptacle, support, underlay; accumulation, layer, seam, stratum, vein.

befriend *vb* aid, benefit, countenance, encourage, favour, help, patronise.

beg *vb* adjure, ask, beseech, conjure, crave, entreat, implore, importune, petition, pray, request, solicit, supplicate.

begin *vb* arise, commence, enter, open; inaugurate, institute, originate, start.

beginning *n* arising, commencement, dawn, emergence, inauguration, inception, initiation, opening, outset, start, rise; origin, source.

behaviour *n* air, bearing, carriage, comportment, conduct, demeanour, manners.

behind *prep* abaft, after, following. • *adv* abaft, aft, astern, rearward. • *adj* arrested, backward, checked, detained, retarded; after, behind. • *n* afterpart, rear, stern, tail; back, back side, reverse; bottom, buttocks, posterior, rump.

behold *vb* consider, contemplate, eye, observe, regard, see, survey, view.

being *n* actuality, existence, reality, subsistence; core, essence, heart, root.

belief *n* assurance, confidence, conviction, persuasion, trust; acceptance, assent, credence; creed, doctrine, dogma, faith, opinion, tenet.

bellow *vb* bawl, clamour, cry, howl, yell.

bend *vb* bow, crook, curve, deflect, draw; direct, incline, turn; bend, dispose, influence, mould, persuade, subdue; deflect, deviate, diverge, swerve; bow, lower, stoop; condescend, deign, stoop. • *n* angle, arc, crook, curvature, curve, elbow, flexure, turn.

beneath *prep* below, under, underneath; unbecoming, unbefitting, unworthy. • *adv* below, underneath.

beneficial *adj* advantageous, favourable, helpful, profitable, salutary, useful, wholesome.

benefit *vb* befriend, help, serve; advantage, avail, profit. • *n* favour, good turn, kindness, service; account, advantage, behalf, gain, good, interest, profit, utility.

benevolent *adj* altruistic, benign, charitable, generous, humane, kind, kind-hearted, liberal, obliging, philanthropic, tender, unselfish.

bent *adj* angled, angular, bowed, crooked, curved, deflected, embowed, flexed, hooked, twisted; disposed, inclined, prone, minded; (*with* on) determined, fixed on, resolved, set on. • *n* bias, inclination, leaning, partiality, penchant, predilection, prepossession, propensity

beside, besides *adv* additionally, also, further, furthermore, in addition, more, moreover, over and above, too, yet.

besiege *vb* beset, blockade, encircle, encompass, environ, invest, surround.

best *vb* better, exceed, excel, predominate, rival, surpass; beat, defeat, outdo, worst. • *adj* chief, first, foremost, highest, leading, utmost. • *adv* advantageously, excellently; extremely, greatly. • *n* choice, cream, flower, pick.

bet *vb* gamble, hazard, lay, pledge, stake, wage, wager. • *n* gamble, hazard, stake, wager.

betray *vb* be false to, break, violate; blab, discover, divulge, expose, reveal, show, tell; argue, betoken, display, evince, expose, exhibit, imply, indicate, manifest, reveal; beguile, delude, ensnare, lure, mislead; corrupt, ruin, seduce, undo.

better *vb* advance, amend, correct, exceed, improve, promote, rectify, reform. • *adj* bigger, fitter, greater, larger, less ill, preferable. • *n* advantage, superiority, upper hand, victory; improvement, greater good.

beware *vb* avoid, heed, look out, mind.

bewilder *vb* confound, confuse, daze, distract, embarrass, entangle, muddle, mystify, nonplus, perplex, pose, puzzle, stagger.

bewitch *vb* captivate, charm, enchant, enrapture, entrance, fascinate, spellbind, transport.

beyond *prep* above, before, farther, over, past, remote, yonder.

bias *vb* bend, dispose, incline, influence, predispose, prejudice. • *n* bent, inclination, leaning, partiality, penchant, predilection, prepossession, proclivity, propensity, slant, tendency, turn.

bicker *vb* dispute, jangle, quarrel, spar, spat, squabble, wrangle; play, quiver, tremble.

bid *vb* charge, command, direct, enjoin, order, require, summon; ask, call, invite, pray, request, solicit; offer, propose, proffer, tender. • *n* bidding, offer, proposal.

big *adj* bumper, bulking, bulky, great, huge, large, massive, monstrous; important, imposing; distended, inflated, full, swollen, tumid; fecund, fruitful, productive, teeming.

bigoted *adj* dogmatic, hidebound, intolerant, obstinate, narrow-minded, prejudiced.

bill *vb* charge, dun, invoice; programme, schedule; advertise, boost, plug, promote, publicise. • *n* account, charges, reckoning; score; advertisement, banner, hoarding, placard, poster; playbill, programme, schedule; bill of exchange, certificate, money; account, reckoning, statement.

bind *vb* confine, enchain, fetter, restrain, restrict; bandage, tie up, wrap; fasten, lash, pinion, secure, tie, truss; engage, hold, oblige, obligate, pledge; contract, harden, shrink, stiffen.

birth *n* ancestry, blood, descent, extraction, lineage, race.

bit *n* crumb, fragment, morsel, mouthful, piece, scrap; atom, grain, jot, mite, particle, tittle, whit; instant, minute, moment, second.

bite *vb* champ, chew, crunch, gnaw; burn, make smart, sting; catch, clutch, grapple, grasp, grip. • *n* grasp, hold; punch, relish, spice, pungency, tang, zest; lick, morsel, sip, taste; crick, nip, pain, pang, prick, sting.

bitter *adj* acrid; dire, fell, merciless, relentless, ruthless; harsh, severe, stern; afflictive, calamitous, distressing, galling, grievous, painful, poignant, sore, sorrowful.

black *adj* dark, ebony, inky, jet, sable, swarthy; dingy, dusky, lowering, murky, pitchy; calamitous, dark, depressing, disastrous, dismal, doleful, forbidding, gloomy, melancholy, mournful, sombre, sullen.

blacken *vb* darken; deface, defile, soil, stain, sully; asperse, besmirch, calumniate, defame, malign, revile, slander, traduce, vilify.

blame *vb* accuse, censure, condemn, disapprove, reflect upon, reprehend, reproach, reprove, upbraid. • *n* animadversion, censure, condemnation, disapproval, disapprobation, reprehension, reproach, reproof; defect, demerit, fault, guilt, misdeed, shortcoming, sin, wrong.

bland *adj* balmy, demulcent, gentle, mild, soothing, soft; affable, amiable, kindly.

blank *adj* bare, empty, vacuous, void; amazed, astonished, confounded, confused, dumbfounded, nonplussed.

blasphemy *n* impiousness, sacrilege; cursing, profanity, swearing.

blast *vb* annihilate, blight, destroy, kill, ruin, shrivel, wither; burst, explode, kill. • *n* blow, gust, squall; clang, peal; burst, explosion.

blaze *vb* blazon, proclaim, publish; burn, flame, glow. • *n* flame, flare, flash, glow, light.

bleak *adj* bare, exposed, unprotected, unsheltered, storm-beaten, windswept; biting, chill, cold, piercing, raw; cheerless, comfortless, desolate, dreary, uncongenial.

blemish *vb* blur, injure, mar, spot, stain, sully, taint, tarnish; asperse, calumniate, defame, malign, revile, slander, traduce, vilify. • *n* blot, blur, defect, disfigurement, fault, flaw, imperfection, soil, speck, spot, stain, tarnish; disgrace, dishonour, reproach, stain, taint.

blend *vb* amalgamate, coalesce, combine, fuse, mingle, mix, unite. • *n* amalgamation, combination, compound, fusion, mixture.

bless *vb* beatify, delight, gladden; adore, celebrate, exalt, extol, glorify, magnify, praise.

blind *vb* blear, darken, deprive of sight; blindfold, hoodwink. • *adj* eyeless, sightless, stone-blind, unseeing; benighted, ignorant, injudicious, purblind, undiscerning, unenlightened; concealed, confused, dark, dim, hidden, intricate, involved, labyrinthine, obscure, private, remote; careless, headlong, heedless, inconsiderate, indiscriminate, thoughtless; blank, closed, shut. • *n* cover, curtain, screen, shade, shutter; blinker; concealment, disguise, feint, pretence, pretext, ruse, stratagem, subterfuge.

blink *vb* nictate, nictitate, wink; flicker, flutter, gleam, glitter, intermit, twinkle; avoid, disregard, evade, gloss over, ignore, overlook, pass over. • *n* glance, glimpse, sight, view, wink; gleam, glimmer, sheen, shimmer, twinkle.

bliss *n* beatification, beatitude, blessedness, blissfulness, ecstasy, felicity, happiness, heaven, joy, rapture, transport.

block *vb* arrest, bar, blockade, check, choke, close, hinder, impede, jam, obstruct, stop; form, mould, shape; brace, stiffen. • *n* lump, mass; pulley, tackle; execution, scaffold; jam, obstruction, pack, stoppage.

blood *n* children, descendants, offspring, posterity, progeny; family, house, kin, kindred, line, relations; consanguinity, descent, kinship, lineage, relationship; courage, disposition, feelings, mettle, passion, spirit, temper.

bloom *vb* blossom, blow, flower; thrive, prosper. • *n* blossom, blossoming, blow, efflorescence, florescence, flowering; delicacy, delicateness, flush, freshness, heyday, prime, vigour; flush, glow, rose.

blot *vb* cancel, efface, erase, expunge, obliterate, rub out; blur, deface, disfigure, obscure, spot, stain, sully; disgrace, dishonour, tarnish. • *n* blur, erasure, blemish, spot, stain; disgrace, dishonour.

blow[1] *n* bang, beat, buffet, dab, impact, knock, pat, punch, rap, slam, stroke, thump, wallop, buffet, impact; affliction, calamity, disaster, misfortune, setback.

blow[2] *vb* breathe, gasp, pant, puff; flow, move, scud, stream, waft. • *n* blast, gale, gust, squall, storm, wind.

blue *adj* azure, cerulean, cobalt, indigo, sapphire, ultramarine; ghastly, livid, pallid; dejected, depressed, dispirited, downcast, gloomy, glum, mopey, melancholic, melancholy, sad.

bluff[1] *adj* abrupt, blunt, blustering, coarse, frank, good-natured, open, outspoken; abrupt, precipitous, sheer, steep. • *n* cliff, headland.

bluff[2] *vb* deceive, defraud, lie, mislead. • *n* deceit, deception, feint, fraud, lie.

blunder *vb* err, flounder, mistake: stumble. • *n* error, fault, howler, mistake, solecism.

blunt *adj* dull, obtuse, pointless, unsharpened; insensitive, stolid; abrupt, bluff, downright, plain-spoken, outspoken, unceremonious. • *vb* deaden, dull, numb.

blur *vb* bedim, darken, dim, obscure; blemish, blot, spot, stain, sully, tarnish. • *n* blemish, blot, soil, spot, stain, tarnish; disgrace, smear.

blush *vb* colour, flush, glow, redden. • *n* bloom, flush, glow, colour, reddening, suffusion.

boast *vb* bluster, brag, flourish, crow, vaunt.

body *n* carcass, corpse, remains; stem, torso, trunk; aggregate, bulk, corpus, mass; being, individual, mortal creature, person; assemblage, association, band, company, corporation, corps, coterie, force, party, society, troop; consistency, substance, thickness.

boil *vb* agitate, bubble, foam, froth, rage, seethe.

boisterous adj loud, roaring, stormy, clamouring, obstreperous, turbulent.

bold adj adventurous, audacious, courageous; brave, daring, dauntless, doughty, fearless, gallant, hardy, heroic, intrepid, mettlesome, manly, spirited, stouthearted, undaunted, valiant, valorous; assured, confident, self-reliant; forward, impertinent, impudent, insolent, pushing, rude; conspicuous, projecting, prominent, striking; abrupt, precipitous, prominent, steep.

bond vb bind, connect, fuse, glue, join. • n band, cord, fastening, ligament, ligature, link, nexus; bondage, captivity, chains, constraint, fetters, prison, shackle; attachment, attraction, connection, coupling, link, tie, union; compact, obligation, pledge, promise.

bonus n gift, honorarium, premium, reward.

book vb bespeak, engage, reserve; programme, schedule; list, log, record, register. • n booklet, brochure, compendium, handbook, manual, monograph, pamphlet, textbook, tract, treatise, volume, work.

booty n loot, pillage, plunder, spoil.

border vb bound, edge, fringe, line, march, rim, skirt, verge; abut, adjoin, butt, conjoin, connect, neighbour. • n brim, brink, edge, fringe, hem, margin, rim, skirt, verge; boundary, confine, frontier, limit, march, outskirts.

bore[1] vb annoy, fatigue, plague, tire, trouble, vex, weary, worry. • n bother, nuisance, pest.

bore[2] vb drill, perforate, pierce, sink, tunnel. • n calibre, hole, shaft, tunnel.

borrow vb take and return, use temporarily; adopt, appropriate, imitate; dissemble, feign.

boss vb command, direct, employ, run. • n employer, master, overseer, superintendent.

bother vb annoy, disturb, harass, molest, perplex, pester, plague, tease, trouble, vex, worry. • n annoyance, perplexity, plague, trouble.

bottom vb build, establish, found. • adj base, basic, ground, lowermost, lowest, nethermost, undermost. • n base, basis, foot, foundation, groundwork; dale, meadow, valley; buttocks, fundament, seat; dregs, grounds, lees, sediment.

bounce vb bound, jump, leap, rebound, recoil, spring.

bound[1] adj assured, certain, decided, determined, resolute, resolved; confined, hampered, restricted, restrained; committed, contracted, engaged, pledged, promised; beholden, dutybound, obligated, obliged.

bound[2] vb border, delimit, circumscribe, confine, demarcate, limit, restrict, terminate. • n boundary, confine, edge, limit, march, margin, periphery, term, verge.

bound[3] vb jump, leap, spring; bounce.

boundary n border, bourne, circuit, circumference, confine, limit, periphery, term, verge.

boundless adj endless, immeasurable, infinite, limitless, unbounded, unconfined, undefined.

bow[1] n (naut) beak, prow, stem.

bow[2] vb arc, bend, buckle, crook, curve, droop, flex, yield; crush, depress, subdue; curtsy, genuflect, kowtow, submit. • n arc, bend, bilge, bulge, convex, curve, flexion; bob, curtsy, genuflection, greeting, homage, obeisance; coming out, debut, introduction; curtain call, encore.

box[1] vb fight, hit, mill, spar. • n blow, buffet, fight, hit, spar.

box[2] vb barrel, crate, pack, parcel. • n case, chest, container, crate, portmanteau, trunk.

boy n lad, stripling, youth.

brace vb make tight, tighten; buttress, fortify, reinforce, shore, strengthen, support, truss. • n couple, pair; clamp, girder, prop, shore, stay, support, tie, truss.

branch vb diverge, fork, bifurcate, ramify, spread. • n bough, offset, limb, shoot, sprig, twig; arm, fork, ramification, spur; article, department, member, part, portion, section.

brand vb denounce, stigmatise, mark. • n firebrand, torch; bolt, lightning flash; cachet, mark, stamp, tally; blot, reproach, stain, stigma.

brave vb dare, defy. • adj bold, courageous, fearless, heroic, intrepid, stalwart.

bravery n courage, daring, fearlessness, valour.

brawl vb bicker, dispute, jangle, quarrel, squabble. • n broil, dispute, feud, fracas, fray, jangle, quarrel, row, scuffle, squabble, uproar, wrangle.

brawny adj athletic, lusty, muscular, powerful, robust, stalwart, strapping, strong, sturdy.

breach n break, chasm, crack, disruption, fissure, flaw, fracture, opening, rent, rift, rupture; difference, disagreement, split.

break vb crack, disrupt, fracture, part, rend, rive, sever, batter, burst, crush, shatter, smash, splinter; cashier, degrade, discard, discharge, dismiss; disobey, infringe, transgress, violate; intermit, interrupt, stop; disclose, open, unfold. • n aperture, breach, chasm, fissure, gap, rent, rip, rupture; break-up, crash, debacle.

breath n exhaling, inhaling, pant, sigh, respiration, whiff; animation, existence, life; pause, respite, rest; breathing space, instant, moment.

breathe vb live, exist; emit, exhale, give out; diffuse, express, indicate, manifest, show.

breed vb bear, beget, engender, hatch, produce; bring up, foster, nourish, nurture, raise, rear; discipline, educate, instruct, nurture, rear, school, teach, train; generate, originate. • n extraction, family, lineage, pedigree, progeny, race, strain.

brevity n briefness, compression, conciseness, curtness, pithiness, shortness, terseness.

bribe vb buy, corrupt, influence, pay off, suborn. • n allurement, corruption, enticement, graft, pay-off, subornation.

bridle vb check, curb, control, govern, restrain. • n check, control, curb.

brief vb give directions, direct, instruct; capsulate, summarise, delineate, describe, draft, outline, sketch; (law) retain. • adj concise, curt, inconsiderable, laconic, pithy, short, succinct, terse; fleeting, momentary, short, temporary, transient. • n abstract, breviary, briefing, epitome, compendium, summary, syllabus; (law) precept, writ.

bright adj blazing, brilliant, dazzling, gleaming, glowing, light, luminous, radiant, shining, sparkling, sunny; clear, cloudless, lambent, lucid, transparent; famous, glorious, illustrious; acute, discerning, ingenious, intelligent, keen; auspicious, cheering, encouraging, exhilarating, favourable, inspiring, promising, propitious; cheerful, genial, happy, lively, merry, pleasant, smiling, vivacious.

brilliant adj beaming, bright, effulgent, gleaming, glistening, glittering, lustrous, radiant, resplendent, shining, sparkling splendid; admirable, celebrated, distinguished, famous, glorious, illustrious, renowned; dazzling, decided, prominent, signal, striking, unusual.

brim n border, brink, edge, rim, margin, skirt, verge; bank, border, coast, margin, shore.

bring vb bear, convey, fetch; accompany, attend, conduct, convey, convoy, guide, lead; gain, get, obtain, procure, produce.

brisk adj active, alert, agile, lively, nimble, perky, quick, smart, spirited, spry.

brittle adj brash, breakable, crisp, crumbling, fragile, frangible, frail.

broad adj ample, expansive, extensive, large, spacious, sweeping, vast, wide; enlarged, hospitable, liberal, tolerant; diffused, open, spread; coarse, gross, indecent, indelicate, unrefined.

broken adj fractured, rent, ruptured, separated, severed, shattered, shivered, torn; exhausted, feeble, impaired, shaken, shattered, spent, wasted; defective, halting, hesitating, imperfect, stammering, stumbling; contrite, humble, lowly, penitent; abrupt, craggy, precipitous, rough.

brook vb abide, bear, endure, suffer, tolerate. • n burn, beck, creek, rill, rivulet, run, streamlet.

bruise vb contuse, crunch, squeeze; batter, break, maul, pound, pulverise; batter, deface, indent. • n blemish, contusion, swelling.

brush vb buff, clean, polish, swab, sweep, wipe; curry, groom, rub down; caress, flick, glance, graze, scrape, skim, touch. • n besom, broom; conflict, encounter, fight, skirmish.

brutal adj barbaric, barbarous, brutish, cruel, ferocious, inhuman, ruthless, savage.

brute n barbarian, beast, monster, ogre, savage; animal, beast, creature. • adj carnal, mindless, physical; bestial, coarse, gross.

bubble vb boil, effervesce, foam. • n bead, blob, globule; bagatelle, trifle; cheat, delusion, hoax.

bud vb burgeon, germinate, push, shoot, sprout.

budget vb allocate, cost, estimate. • n account, estimate, funds, resources.

build vb construct, erect, establish, fabricate, fashion, model, raise, rear. • n body, figure, form, frame, physique.

bulk n dimension, magnitude, mass, size, volume; amplitude, bulkiness, massiveness; body, majority, mass.

bully vb browbeat, bulldoze, domineer, hector, intimidate, overbear. • n blusterer, browbeater, bulldozer, swaggerer, tyrant.

bump vb collide, knock, strike, thump. • n blow, jar, jolt, knock, shock, thump; lump, protuberance, swelling.

bunch vb assemble, collect, crowd, group, herd, pack. • n cluster, hand, fascicle; assortment, batch, collection, group, lot, parcel, set.

bundle vb bale, pack, package, parcel, truss, wrap. • n bale, batch, bunch, collection, heap, pack, package, packet, parcel, pile, roll, truss.

burden vb encumber, grieve, load, oppress, overlay, overload, saddle, surcharge, try. • n capacity, cargo, freight, lading, load, tonnage, weight; affliction, charge, clog, encumbrance, impediment, grievance, sorrow, trial, trouble; drift, point, substance, tenor, surcharge.

burn[1] n brook, beck, gill, rill, rivulet, runnel, runlet, stream. water

burn[2] vb blaze, conflagrate, enflame, fire, flame, ignite, kindle, light, smoulder; cremate, incinerate; scald, scorch, singe; boil, broil, cook, roast, seethe, simmer, stew, swelter, toast; bronze, brown, sunburn; bake, desiccate, dry, parch, sear, shrivel, wither; glow, incandesce, tingle. • n scald, scorch, singe; sunburn.

burst vb break open, be rent, explode, shatter, split open. • adj broken, kaput, punctured, ruptured, shattered, split. • n break, breakage, breach, fracture, rupture; blast, blowout, blowup, discharge, detonation, explosion; spurt; blaze, flare, flash; cloudburst, downpour; bang, crack, crash, report, sound; fusillade, salvo, spray, volley, outburst, outbreak flare-up, blaze.

bury vb entomb, inearth, inhume, inter; conceal, hide, secrete, shroud.

business n calling, employment, occupation, profession, pursuit, vocation; commerce, dealing, trade, traffic; affair, concern, engagement, matter, transaction, undertaking; duty, function, office, task, work.

bustle vb fuss, hurry, scurry. • n ado, commotion, flurry, fuss, hustle, stir, tumult.

busy vb devote, employ, engage, occupy, spend, work. • adj employed, engaged, occupied; active, assiduous, diligent, engrossed, industrious, sedulous, working; agile, brisk, nimble, spry, stirring; meddling, officious.

but *conj* except, excepting, further, moreover, still, unless, yet. • *adv* even, notwithstanding, still, yet.

butt¹ *vb* push, shove, shunt, strike; encroach, impose, interfere, intrude, invade, obtrude.

butt² *n* aim, goal, mark, object, point, target; dupe, gull, victim.

butt³ *vb* abut, adjoin, conjoin, connect, neighbour. • *n* end, piece, remainder, stub, stump; buttocks, posterior, rump.

C

cackle *vb* giggle, laugh, snicker, titter; babble, chatter, gabble, palaver, prate, prattle, titter.

cage *vb* confine, immure, imprison, incarcerate. • *n* coop, pen, pound.

calamity *n* adversity, affliction, blow, casualty, cataclysm, catastrophe, disaster, distress, downfall, evil, hardship, mischance, misery, misfortune, mishap, reverse, ruin, stroke, trial.

calculate *vb* cast, compute, count, estimate, figure, rate, reckon, weigh; tell.

calculating *adj* crafty, designing, scheming, selfish; careful, cautious, circumspect, far-sighted, politic, sagacious, wary.

calibre *n* bore, capacity, diameter, gauge; ability, capacity, faculty, parts, scope, talent.

call *vb* christen, denominate, designate, dub, entitle, name, phrase, style, term; bid, invite, summons; assemble, convene, convoke, muster; cry, exclaim; arouse, awaken, proclaim, rouse, shout, waken; appoint, elect, ordain. • *n* cry, outcry, voice; appeal, invitation, summons; claim, demand, summons; appointment, invitation.

callous *adj* hard, hardened, indurated; apathetic, dull, indifferent, insensible, inured, obdurate, obtuse, sluggish, torpid, unfeeling.

calm *vb* allay, becalm, compose, hush, lull, smooth, still, tranquillise; alleviate, appease, assuage, moderate, mollify, pacify, quiet, soften, soothe, tranquillise. • *adj* halcyon, mild, peaceful, placid, quiet, reposeful, serene, smooth, still, tranquil, unruffled; collected, cool, composed, controlled, impassive, imperturbable, sedate, self-possessed, undisturbed, unperturbed, unruffled, untroubled. • *n* lull; equanimity, peace, placidity, quiet, repose, serenity, stillness.

camp¹ *vb* bivouac, encamp, lodge, pitch, tent. • *n* bivouac, encampment, laager; cabal, circle, clique, coterie, faction, group, junta, party, set.

camp² *adj* affected, artificial, effeminate, exaggerated, mannered, theatrical.

cancel *vb* blot, efface, erase, expunge, obliterate; abrogate, annul, countermand, nullify, quash, repeal, rescind, revoke.

candid *adj* fair, impartial, just, unbiased, unprejudiced; artless, frank, free, guileless, honest,

honourable, ingenuous, naive, open, plain, sincere, straightforward.

canvass *vb* agitate, debate, discuss, dispute; consider, examine, investigate, scrutinise, sift, study. • *n* debate, discussion, dispute; examination, scrutiny, sifting.

cap *vb* cover, surmount; complete, crown, finish; exceed, overtop, surpass, transcend; match, parallel, pattern. • *n* beret, head-cover; acme, chief, crown, head, peak, perfection, pitch, summit, top.

capable *adj* adapted, fitted, qualified, suited; able, accomplished, clever, competent, efficient, gifted, ingenious, intelligent, sagacious, skilful.

capacious *adj* ample, broad, comprehensive, expanded, extensive, large, roomy, spacious.

capacity *n* amplitude, dimensions, magnitude, volume; aptitude, aptness, brains, calibre, discernment, faculty, forte, genius, gift, parts, power, talent, turn, wit; ability, capability, calibre, cleverness, competency, efficiency, skill; character, charge, function, office, position, post.

capital *adj* cardinal, chief, essential, important, leading, main, major, pre-eminent, principal, prominent; fatal; excellent, first-class, first-rate, good, prime, splendid. • *n* chief city, metropolis, seat; money, estate, investments, shares, stock.

capsize *vb* overturn, upset.

captivate *vb* allure, attract, bewitch, catch, charm, enamour, enchant, enthral, fascinate, gain, hypnotise, infatuate, win.

captivity *n* confinement, durance, duress, imprisonment; bondage, entralment, servitude, slavery, subjection, thraldom, vassalage.

capture *vb* apprehend, arrest, catch, seize. • *n* apprehension, arrest, catch, catching, imprisonment, seizure; bag, prize.

cardinal *adj* capital, central, chief, essential, first, important, leading, main, pre-eminent, primary, principal, vital.

care *n* anxiety, concern, perplexity, trouble, solicitude, worry; attention, carefulness, caution, circumspection, heed, regard, vigilance, wariness, watchfulness; charge, custody, guardianship, keep, oversight, superintendence, ward; burden, charge, concern, responsibility.

careful adj anxious, solicitous, concerned, troubled, uneasy; attentive, heedful, mindful, regardful, thoughtful; cautious, canny, circumspect, discreet, leery, vigilant, watchful.

careless adj carefree, nonchalant, unapprehensive, undisturbed, unperplexed, unsolicitous, untroubled; disregardful, heedless, inattentive, incautious, inconsiderate, neglectful, negligent, regardless, remiss, thoughtless, unobservant, unconcerned, unconsidered, unthinking.

caress vb cuddle, embrace, fondle, hug, kiss, pet. • n cuddle, embrace, fondling, hug, kiss.

caricature vb burlesque, parody, take off, travesty. • n burlesque, farce, parody, representation, take-off, travesty.

carriage n conveyance, vehicle; air, bearing, behaviour, conduct, demeanour, deportment, front.

carry vb bear, convey, transfer, transmit, transport; impel, push forward, urge; accomplish, compass, effect, gain, secure; bear up, support, sustain; infer, involve, imply, import, signify.

carve vb chisel, cut, divide, engrave, grave, hack, hew, indent, incise, sculpture; fashion, form, mould, shape.

case[1] vb cover, encase, enclose, envelop, protect, wrap; box, pack. • n capsule, covering, sheathe; box, container, holder, receptacle.

case[2] n condition, plight, predicament, situation, state; example, instance, occurrence; circumstance, condition, contingency, event; action, argument, cause, lawsuit, suit, trial.

cast vb fling, hurl, pitch, send, shy, sling, throw, toss; drive, force, impel, thrust; lay aside, put off, shed; calculate, compute, reckon; communicate, diffuse, impart, shed, throw. • n fling, throw, toss; shade, tinge, tint, touch; air, character, look, manner, style, turn; form, mould.

caste n class, grade, lineage, order, race, rank, species, status.

castigate vb beat, chastise, flog, lambaste, lash, thrash, whip; chaste, correct, discipline, punish; criticise, flagellate, upbraid.

casual adj accidental, contingent, fortuitous, incidental, irregular, occasional, random, uncertain, unforeseen, unintentional, unpremeditated.

casualty n chance, contingency, fortuity, mishap; accident, catastrophe, disaster, mischance.

catalogue vb alphabetise, categorise, chronicle, class, classify, codify, file, index, list, record, tabulate. • n enumeration, index, inventory, invoice, list, record, register, roll, schedule.

catastrophe n denouement, end, finale, issue, termination, upshot; adversity, blow, calamity, cataclysm, debacle, disaster, ill, misfortune, mischance, mishap, trial, trouble.

catch vb clutch, grasp, gripe, nab, seize, snatch; apprehend, arrest, capture; overtake; enmesh, ensnare, entangle, entrap, lime, net; bewitch,

captivate, charm, enchant, fascinate, win; surprise, take unawares. • n arrest, capture, seizure; bag, find, haul, plum, prize; drawback, fault, hitch, obstacle, rub, snag; captive, conquest.

categorical adj absolute, direct, downright, emphatic, explicit, express, positive, unconditional, unqualified, unreserved.

category n class, division, head, heading, list, order, rank, sort.

cater vb feed, provide, purvey.

cause vb breed, create, originate, produce; effect, effectuate, occasion, produce. • n agent, creator, mainspring, origin, original, producer, source, spring; account, agency, consideration, ground, incentive, incitement, inducement, motive, reason; aim, end, object, purpose; action, case, suit, trial.

caustic adj acrid, cathartic, consuming, corroding, corrosive, eating, erosive, mordant, virulent; biting, bitter, burning, cutting, sarcastic, satirical, scalding, scathing, severe, sharp.

caution vb admonish, forewarn, warn. • n care, carefulness, circumspection, discretion, forethought, heed, heedfulness, providence, prudence, wariness, vigilance, watchfulness; admonition, advice, counsel, injunction, warning.

cautious adj careful, chary, circumspect, discreet, heedful, prudent, wary, vigilant, wary.

cease vb desist, intermit, pause, refrain, stay, stop; fail; discontinue, end, quit, terminate.

celebrate vb applaud, bless, commend, emblazon, extol, glorify, laud, magnify, praise, trumpet; commemorate, honour, keep, observe.

celebrated adj distinguished, eminent, famed, famous, glorious, illustrious, notable, renowned.

celebrity n credit, distinction, eminence, fame, glory, honour, renown, repute; notable, star.

cement vb attach, bind, join, combine, connect, solder, unite, weld; cohere, stick. • n glue, paste, mortar, solder.

censor vb blue-pencil, bowdlerise, cut, edit, expurgate; classify, kill, quash, squash, suppress.

censure vb abuse, blame, chide, condemn, rebuke, reprehend, reprimand, reproach, reprobate, reprove, scold, upbraid. n animadversion, blame, condemnation, criticism, disapprobation, disapproval, rebuke, remonstrance, reprehension, reproach, reproof, stricture.

ceremonious adj civil, courtly, lofty, stately; formal, studied; exact, formal, punctilious, precise, starched, stiff.

ceremony n ceremonial, etiquette, form, formality, observance, solemnity, rite; parade, pomp, show, stateliness.

certain adj absolute, incontestable, incontrovertible, indisputable, indubitable, positive, inevitable, undeniable, undisputed, unquestionable, unquestioned; assured, confident, convinced, sure, undoubting; infallible, never-failing, unfailing; actual, existing, real; constant, determinate, fixed, settled, stated.

certify vb attest, notify, testify, vouch; ascertain, determine, verify, show.

chafe vb rub; anger, annoy, chagrin, enrage, exasperate, fret, gall, incense, irritate, nettle, offend, provoke, ruffle, tease, vex; fume, rage.

chain vb bind, confine, fetter, manacle, restrain, shackle, trammel; enslave. • n bond, fetter, manacle, shackle, union.

challenge vb brave, call out, dare, defy, dispute; demand, require. • n defiance, interrogation, question; exception, objection.

champion vb advocate, defend, uphold. • n defender, promoter, protector, vindicator; belt-holder, hero, victor, warrior, winner.

chance vb befall, betide, happen, occur. • adj accidental, adventitious, casual, fortuitous, incidental, unexpected, unforeseen. • n accident, cast, fortuity, fortune, hap, luck; contingency, possibility; occasion, opening, opportunity; contingency, fortuity, gamble, peradventure, uncertainty; hazard, jeopardy, peril, risk.

change vb alter, fluctuate, modify, vary; displace, remove, replace, shift, substitute; barter, commute, exchange. • n alteration, mutation, revolution, transition, transmutation, turning, variance, variation; innovation, novelty, variety.

changeable adj alterable, inconstant, modifiable, mutable, uncertain, unsettled, unstable, unsteadfast, unsteady, variable, variant; capricious, fickle, fitful, flighty, giddy, mercurial, vacillating, volatile, wavering.

channel vb chamfer, cut, flute, groove. • n canal, conduit, duct, passage; aqueduct, canal, chute, drain, flume, furrow; chamfer, groove, fluting, furrow, gutter.

chant vb carol, sing, warble; intone, recite.

chaos n anarchy, confusion, disorder.

character n emblem, figure, hieroglyph, ideograph, letter, mark, sign, symbol; bent, constitution, cast, disposition, nature, quality; individual, original, person, personage; reputation, repute; nature, traits; eccentric, trait.

characteristic adj distinctive, peculiar, singular, special, specific, typical. • n attribute, feature, idiosyncrasy, lineament, mark, peculiarity, quality, trait.

charge vb entrust; ascribe, impute, lay; accuse, arraign, blame, criminate, impeach, inculpate, indict, involve; bid, command, exhort, enjoin, order, require, tax; assault, attack. • n care, custody, keeping, management, ward; commission, duty, employment, office, trust; responsibility, trust; command, direction, injunction, mandate, order, precept; exhortation, instruction; cost, debit, expense, expenditure, outlay; price, sum; assault, attack, onset, onslaught.

charitable adj beneficial, beneficent, benignant, bountiful, generous, kind, liberal, open-handed; candid, considerate, lenient, mild.

charity n benevolence, benignity, fellow-feeling, good-nature, goodwill, kind-heartedness, kindness, tenderheartedness; beneficence, bounty, generosity, humanity, philanthropy, liberality.

charm vb allure, attract, bewitch, captivate, catch, delight, enamour, enchant, enrapture, fascinate, transport, win. • n enchantment, incantation, magic, necromancy, sorcery, spell, witchery; amulet, talisman; allurement, attraction, attractiveness, fascination.

chase vb follow, hunt, pursue, track; emboss. • n course, field-sport, hunt, hunting.

chaste adj clean, continent, innocent, modest, pure, pure-minded, undefiled, virtuous.

chasten vb correct, discipline, humble; purify, refine, subdue.

chastise vb castigate, correct, flog, lash, punish, whip; chasten, correct, discipline, punish.

chastity n continence, innocence, modesty, pure-mindedness, purity, virtue; cleanness, decency; chasteness, simplicity, unaffectedness.

chat vb babble, chatter, confabulate, gossip, prate, prattle. • n chit-chat, confabulation, conversation, gossip, prattle.

chatter vb babble, chat, confabulate, gossip, prate, prattle.

cheap adj inexpensive, low-priced; common, indifferent, inferior, mean, meretricious, paltry.

cheat vb cozen, deceive, dissemble, juggle, shuffle; bamboozle, beguile, circumvent, deceive, defraud, delude, dupe, ensnare, entrap, fool, gammon, gull, hoax, hoodwink, inveigle, jockey, mislead, outwit, overreach, trick. • n artifice, beguilement, blind, catch, deceit, deception, fraud, imposition, imposture, juggle, pitfall, snare, stratagem, swindle, trap, trick, wile; counterfeit, deception, delusion, illusion, mockery, sham, tinsel; beguiler, charlatan, cheater, impostor, knave, mountebank, trickster, rogue, sharper, swindler.

check vb block, bridle, control, counteract, curb, hinder, obstruct, repress, restrain; chide, rebuke, reprimand, reprove. • n bar, barrier, block, brake, bridle, clog, control, curb, damper, hindrance, impediment, interference, obstacle, obstruction, rebuff, repression, restraint, stop.

cheer vb animate, encourage, enliven, exhilarate, gladden, incite, inspirit; comfort, console, solace; applaud, clap. • n cheerfulness, gaiety, gladness, glee, hilarity, jollity, joy, merriment, entertainment, repast; acclamation, hurrah.

cheerful adj animated, airy, blithe, buoyant, cheery, gay, glad, gleeful, happy, joyful, jocund, jolly, joyous, light-hearted, lightsome, lively, merry, mirthful, sprightly, sunny; animating, cheering, cheery, encouraging, enlivening, glad, gladsome, inspiriting, jocund, pleasant.

cheerless *adj* dark, dejected, desolate, despondent, disconsolate,discouraged, dismal, doleful, dreary, forlorn, gloomy, joyless, low-spirited, lugubrious, melancholy, mournful, rueful, sad, sombre, spiritless, woe begone.

cherish *vb* comfort, foster, nourish, nurse, nurture, support, sustain; treasure; encourage, entertain, indulge, harbour.

chew *vb* crunch, manducate, masticate, munch; bite, champ, gnaw; meditate, ruminate.

chief *adj* first, foremost, headmost, leading, master, supereminent, supreme, top; capital, cardinal, especial, essential, grand, great, main, master, paramount, prime, principal, supreme, vital. • *n* chieftain, commander; head, leader.

child *n* babe, baby, bairn, brat, chit, infant, suckling, wean; issue, offspring, progeny.

childish *adj* infantile, juvenile, puerile, tender, young; foolish, frivolous, silly, trifling, weak.

childlike *adj* docile, dutiful, gentle, meek, obedient, submissive; confiding, guileless, ingenuous, innocent, simple, trustful, uncrafty.

chill *vb* dampen, depress, deject, discourage, dishearten. • *adj* bleak, chilly, cold, frigid, gelid. • *n* chilliness, cold, coldness, frigidity; ague, rigour, shiver; damp, depression

chip *vb* flake, fragment, hew, pare, scrape. • *n* flake, fragment, paring, scrap.

choice *adj* excellent, exquisite, precious, rare, select, superior, uncommon, unusual, valuable; careful, chary, frugal, sparing. • *n* alternative, election, option, selection; favourite, pick, preference.

choose *vb* adopt, co-opt, cull, designate, elect, pick, predestine, prefer, select.

chop *vb* cut, hack, hew; mince; shift, veer. • *n* slice; brand, quality; chap, jaw.

christen *vb* baptise; call, dub, denominate, designate, entitle, name, style, term, title.

chronic *adj* confirmed, continuing, deep-seated, inveterate, rooted.

chronicle *vb* narrate, record, register. • *n* diary, journal, register; account, annals, history, narration, recital, record.

chuckle *vb* crow, exult, giggle, laugh, snigger, titter. • *n* giggle, laughter, snigger, titter.

churlish *adj* brusque, brutish, cynical, harsh, impolite, rough, rude, snappish, snarling, surly, uncivil, waspish; crabbed, ill-tempered, morose, sullen; close, close-fisted, illiberal, mean, miserly, niggardly, penurious, stingy.

circle *vb* compass, encircle, encompass, gird, girdle, ring; gyrate, revolve, rotate, round, turn. • *n* circlet, corona, hoop, ring; circumference, cordon, periphery; ball, globe, orb, sphere; compass, enclosure; class, clique, company, coterie,

fraternity, set, society; bounds, circuit, compass, field, province, range, region.

circuit *n* ambit, circumambience, cycle, turn; bounds, compass, district, field, range, region, sphere, tract; boundary, compass; course, detour, perambulation, round, tour.

circuitous *adj* ambiguous, devious, indirect, roundabout, tortuous, turning, winding.

circulate *vb* diffuse, disseminate, promulgate, propagate, publish, spread.

circumference *n* bound, boundary, circuit, girth, outline, perimeter, periphery.

circumscribe *vb* bound, define, encircle, enclose, limit, surround; confine, restrict.

circumspect *adj* attentive, careful, cautious, considerate, discreet, heedful, judicious, observant, prudent, vigilant, wary, watchful.

circumstance *n* accident, incident; condition, detail, event, fact, happening, occurrence, position, situation.

circumstantial *adj* detailed, particular; indirect, inferential, presumptive.

citizen *n* burgess, burgher, denizen, dweller, inhabitant, resident, subject, townsman.

civil *adj* civic, municipal, political; domestic, intestine; accommodating, affable, courteous, gracious, obliging, polished, polite, refined, suave, urbane, well-bred, well-mannered.

civilise *vb* cultivate, educate, enlighten, humanise, improve, polish, refine.

claim *vb* ask, assert, challenge, demand, exact, require. • *n* call, demand, lien, requisition; pretension, privilege, right, title.

clandestine *adj* concealed, covert, fraudulent, furtive, hidden, private, secret, sly, stealthy.

clap *vb* pat, slap, strike; force, slam; applaud, cheer. • *n* blow, knock, slap; bang, burst, explosion, peal, slam.

clarify *vb* cleanse, clear, purify, strain.

clash *vb* collide, crash, strike; clang, clank, clatter, crash, rattle; contend, disagree, interfere.

clasp *vb* clutch, entwine, grasp, grapple, grip, seize; embrace, enfold, fold, hug. • *n* buckle, catch, hasp, hook; embrace, hug.

class *vb* arrange, classify, dispose, distribute, range, rank. • *n* form, grade, order, rank, status; group, seminar; breed, kind, sort; category, collection, denomination, division, group, head.

classical *adj* first-rate, master, masterly, model, standard; Greek, Latin, Roman; Attic, chaste, elegant, polished, pure, refined.

classify *vb* arrange, assort, categorise, class, dispose, distribute, group. pigeonhole, rank, systematise, tabulate.

clatter *vb* clash, rattle; babble, clack, gabble, jabber, prate, prattle.

clean *vb* cleanse, clear, purge, purify, rinse, scour, scrub, wash, wipe. • *adj* immaculate, spotless, unsmirched, unsoiled, unspotted, unstained, unsullied, white; clarified, pure, purified, unadulterated, unmixed; adroit, delicate, dextrous, graceful, light, neat, shapely; complete, entire, flawless, faultless, perfect, unabated, unblemished, unimpaired, whole; chaste, innocent, moral, pure, undefiled. • adv altogether, completely, entirely, perfectly, quite, thoroughly.

cleanse vb clean, clear, elutriate, purge, purify, rinse, scour, scrub, wash, wipe.

clear vb clarify, cleanse, purify, refine; emancipate, disenthral, free, liberate, loose; absolve, acquit, discharge, exonerate, justify, vindicate; disembarrass, disengage, disentangle, extricate, loosen, rid; clean up, scour, sweep; balance; emancipate, free, liberate. • adj bright, crystalline, light, limpid, luminous, pellucid, transparent; pure, unadulterated, unmixed; free, open, unencumbered, unobstructed; cloudless, fair, serene, sunny, unclouded, undimmed, unobscured; net; distinct, intelligible, lucid, luminous, perspicuous; apparent, conspicuous, distinct, evident, indisputable, manifest, obvious, palpable, unambiguous, undeniable, unequivocal, unmistakable, unquestionable, visible; clean, guiltless, immaculate, innocent, irreproachable, sinless, spotless, unblemished, undefiled, unspotted, unsullied; unhampered, unimpeded, unobstructed; liquid, mellifluous, musical, silvery, sonorous.

clemency n mildness, softness; compassion, fellow-feeling, forgivingness, gentleness, kindness, lenience, leniency, lenity, long-suffering, mercifulness, mercy, mildness, tenderness.

clever adj able, apt, gifted, talented; adroit, capable, dextrous, discerning, expert, handy, ingenious, knowing, quick, ready, skilful, smart.

climax n acme, consummation, crown, culmination, head, peak, summit, top, zenith.

clinch vb clasp, clutch, grapple, grasp, grip; fasten, secure; confirm, establish, fix. • n catch, clutch, grasp, grip, clamp.

cling vb adhere, stick; clasp, embrace.

clip vb cut, shear, snip; curtail, cut, dock, pare, prune, trim. • n cutting, shearing; blow, knock.

cloak vb conceal, cover, hide, mask, veil. • n mantle; blind, cover, mask, pretext, veil.

clock n chronometer, horologue, timekeeper, timepiece, timer, watch.

clog vb fetter, hamper, shackle, trammel; choke, obstruct; burden, embarrass, encumber, hamper, hinder, impede, load, restrain, trammel. • n deadweight, drag-weight, fetter, shackle, trammel; check, drawback, encumbrance, hindrance, impediment, obstacle, obstruction.

close[1] adj closed, confined, snug, tight; hidden, private, secret; incommunicative, reserved, reticent, secretive, taciturn; concealed, retired, secluded, withdrawn; confined, motionless, stagnant; airless, oppressive, stale, stifling, stuffy, sultry; compact, compressed, dense, form, solid, thick; adjacent, adjoining, approaching, immediately, near, nearly, neighbouring; attached, dear, confidential, devoted, intimate; assiduous, earnest, fixed, intense, intent, unremitting; accurate, exact, faithful, nice, precise, strict; churlish, close-fisted, curmudgeonly, mean, illiberal, miserly, niggardly, parsimonious, penurious, stingy, ungenerous. • n courtyard, enclosure, grounds, precinct, yard.

close[2] vb occlude, seal, shut; choke, clog, obstruct, stop; cease, complete, concede, end, finish, terminate; coalesce, unite; cease, conclude, finish, terminate; clinch, grapple; agree. • n cessation, conclusion, end, finish, termination.

clothe vb array, attire, deck, dress, rig; cover, endow, envelop, invest with, swathe.

clothes n apparel, array, attire, clothing, costume, dress, garb, garments, gear, habiliments, habits, raiment, rig, vestments, vesture.

cloud vb overcast, overspread; befog, darken, dim, obscure, shade, shadow. • n cirrus, cumulus, fog, haze, mist, stratus, vapour; army, crowd, horde, host, multitude, swarm, throng; darkness, eclipse, gloom, obscurity.

cloudy adj clouded, filmy, foggy, hazy, lowering, lurid, murky, overcast; confused, dark, dim, obscure; depressing, dismal, gloomy, sullen; clouded; blurred, dimmed, lustreless, muddy.

club vb combine, unite; beat, bludgeon, cudgel. • n bat, bludgeon, cosh, cudgel, hickory, shillelagh, stick, truncheon; association, company, coterie, fraternity, set, society, sodality.

clump vb assemble, batch, bunch, cluster, group, lump; lumber, stamp, stomp, trudge. • n assemblage, bunch, cluster, collection.

clumsy adj botched, cumbrous, heavy, ill-made, ill-shaped, lumbering, ponderous, unwieldy; awkward, blundering, bungling, elephantine, heavy-handed, inapt, maladroit, unhandy.

cluster vb assemble, batch, bunch, clump, collect, gather, group, lump, throng. • n agglomeration, assemblage, batch, bunch, clump, collection, gathering, group, throng.

clutch vb catch, clasp, clench, grab, grasp, grip, grapple, hold, seize, snatch, squeeze.

clutter vb confuse, disarrange, disarray, disorder, jumble, litter, mess, muss; clatter. • n bustle, clatter, clattering, racket; confusion, disarray, disorder, jumble, litter, mess, muss.

coagulate vb clot, congeal, curdle, thicken.

coalesce vb amalgamate, blend, cohere, combine, commix, incorporate, mix, unite; concur.

coalition n alliance, association, combination, compact, confederacy, conjunction, co-partnership, federation, league, union.

coarse adj crude, impure, rough, unpurified;

broad, gross, indecent, indelicate, ribald, vulgar; bearish, bluff, boorish, brutish, churlish, clownish, gruff, impolite, loutish, rude, unpolished; crass, inelegant.

coast vb flow, glide, roll, skim, sail, slide, sweep. • n littoral, seaboard, sea-coast, seaside, shore, strand; border.

coax vb allure, beguile, cajole, entice, flatter, persuade, soothe, wheedle.

coercion n check, curb, repression, restraint; compulsion, constraint, force.

coexistent adj coetaneous, coeval, simultaneous, synchronous.

coherence n coalition, cohesion, connection, dependence, union; agreement, congruity, consistency, correspondence, harmony, intelligibility, intelligible, meaning, rationality, unity.

coil vb curl, twine, twirl, twist, wind. • n convolution, curlicue, helix, knot, roll, spiral, tendril, twirl, volute, whorl; bustle, clamour, confusion, entanglements, perplexities, tumult, turmoil.

coincide vb cohere, correspond, square, tally; acquiesce, agree, harmonise, concur.

cold adj arctic, biting, bleak, boreal, chill, chilly, cutting, frosty, gelid, glacial, icy, nipping, polar, raw, wintry; frost-bitten, shivering; apathetic, cold-blooded, dead, freezing, frigid, indifferent, lukewarm, passionless, phlegmatic, sluggish, stoical, stony, torpid, unconcerned, unfeeling, unimpressible, unresponsive, unsusceptible, unsympathetic; dead, dull, spiritless, unaffecting, uninspiring, uninteresting. • n chill, coldness.

collapse vb break down, fail, fall. • n depression, exhaustion, failure, faint, prostration, sinking, subsidence.

colleague n aider, ally, assistant, associate, auxiliary, coadjutor, collaborator, companion, confederate, confrere, cooperator, helper, partner.

collect vb assemble, compile, gather, muster; accumulate, aggregate, amass, garner.

collected adj calm, composed, cool, placid, self-possessed, serene, unperturbed.

collection n aggregation, assemblage, cluster, crowd, drove, gathering, group, pack; accumulation, conglomeration, hoard, lot, mass, pile, store; contribution, offering, offertory.

collision n clash, concussion, crash, encounter, impact, impingement, shock; conflict, crashing, interference, opposition.

collusion n connivance, conspiracy, craft, deceit.

colossal adj Cyclopean, enormous, gigantic, Herculean, huge, immense, monstrous, vast.

colour vb discolour, dye, paint, stain, tinge, tint; disguise, varnish; disguise, distort, garble, misrepresent, pervert; blush, colour, flush, redden, show. • n hue, shade, tinge, tint, tone; paint, pigment, stain; redness, rosiness, ruddiness; com-

plexion; appearance, disguise, excuse, guise, plea, pretence, pretext, semblance.

colourless adj achromatic, uncoloured, untinged; blanched, hueless, livid, pale, pallid; blank, characterless, dull, expressionless, inexpressive, monotonous.

comatose adj drowsy, lethargic, sleepy, somnolent, stupefied.

comb vb card, curry, dress, groom, rake, unknot, untangle; rake, ransack, rummage, scour, search. • n card, hatchel, ripple; harrow, rake.

combat vb contend, contest, fight, struggle, war; battle, oppose, resist, struggle, withstand. • n action, affair, battle, brush, conflict, contest.

combination n association, conjunction, connection, union; alliance, cartel, coalition, confederacy, consolidation, league, merger, syndicate; cabal, clique, conspiracy, faction, junta, ring; amalgamation, compound, mixture.

combine vb cooperate, merge, pool, unite; amalgamate, blend, incorporate, mix.

come vb advance, approach; arise, ensue, flow, follow, issue, originate, proceed, result; befall, betide, happen, occur.

comfort vb alleviate, animate, cheer, console, encourage, enliven, gladden, inspirit, invigorate, refresh, revive, solace, soothe, strengthen. • n aid, assistance, countenance, help, support, succour; consolation, solace, encouragement, relief; ease, enjoyment, peace, satisfaction.

comfortable adj acceptable, agreeable, delightful, enjoyable, grateful, gratifying, happy, pleasant, pleasurable, welcome; commodious, convenient, easeful, snug; painless.

comical adj amusing, burlesque, comic, diverting, droll, farcical, funny, humorous, laughable, ludicrous, sportive, whimsical.

coming adj approaching, arising, arriving, ensuing, eventual, expected, forthcoming, future, imminent, issuing, looming, nearing, prospective, ultimate; emergent, emerging, successful; due, owed, owing. • n advent, approach, arrival; forthcomingness, imminence, imminency, nearness; apparition, appearance, disclosure, emergence, manifestation, materialisation, occurrence, presentation, revelation, rising.

command vb bid, charge, direct, enjoin, order, require; control, dominate, govern, lead, rule; claim, challenge, compel, demand, exact. • n behest, bidding, charge, direction, injunction, mandate, order, requirement, requisition; ascendency, authority, dominion, control, power, rule, sway, supremacy.

commander n captain, chief, chieftain, commandment, head, leader.

commence vb begin, inaugurate, initiate, institute, open, originate, start.

commend vb bespeak, recommend, regard for;

commit, entrust, yield; applaud, approve, eulogise, extol, laud, praise.

comment vb animadvert, annotate, criticise, explain, interpret, note, remark. • n annotation, explication, elucidation, explanation, commentary, note, gloss; observation, remark.

commentator n annotator, commentator, critic, expositor, expounder, interpreter.

commerce n business, exchange, dealing, trade, traffic; communication, intercourse.

commercial adj mercantile, trading.

commission vb authorise, empower; delegate, depute. • n doing, perpetration; care, charge, duty, employment, errand, office, task, trust; allowance, compensation, fee, rake-off.

commit vb confide, consign, delegate, entrust, remand; consign, deposit, lay, place, put, relegate, resign; do, enact, perform, perpetrate; imprison; engage, implicate, pledge.

commodity n goods, merchandise, produce.

common adj collective, public; general, useful; commonplace, customary, everyday, familiar, frequent, habitual, usual; banal, hackneyed, stale, threadbare, trite; indifferent, inferior, low, ordinary, plebeian, popular, undistinguished.

commotion n agitation, disturbance, ferment, perturbation; ado, bustle, disorder, disturbance, tumult, turbulence, turmoil.

communicate vb bestow, confer, convey, give, impart, transmit; acquaint, announce, declare, disclose, divulge, publish, reveal, unfold; commune, converse, correspond.

communication n conveyance, disclosure, giving, imparting, transmittal; commence, conference, conversation, converse, correspondence, intercourse; announcement, dispatch, information, message, news.

communicative adj affable, chatty, conversable, free, open, sociable, unreserved.

community n commonwealth, people, public, society; association, brotherhood, college, society; likeness, participancy, sameness.

compact[1] n agreement, arrangement, bargain, concordant, contract, covenant, convention, pact, stipulation, treaty.

compact[2] vb compress, condense, pack, press; bind, consolidate, unite. • adj close, compressed, condensed, dense, firm, solid; brief.

companion n accomplice, ally, associate, comrade, compeer, confederate, consort, crony, friend, fellow, mate; partner, sharer.

company n assemblage, assembly, band, bevy, body, circle, collection, communication, concourse, congregation, coterie, crew, crowd, flock, gang, gathering, group, herd, set, syndicate, troop; party; companionship, fellowship, guests, society, visitors; association, corporation, firm, house, partnership.

compare vb assimilate, balance, collate, parallel; liken, resemble.

compass vb embrace, encompass, enclose, encircle, environ, surround; beleaguer, beset, besiege, block, blockade, invest; accomplish, achieve, attain, carry, consummate, effect, obtain, perform, procure, realise; contrive, devise, intend, meditate, plot, purpose. • n bound, boundary, extent, gamut, limit, range, reach, register, scope, stretch; circuit, round.

compassion n clemency, commiseration, condolence, fellow-feeling, heart, humanity, kindheartedness, kindness, kindliness, mercy, pity, rue, ruth, sorrow, sympathy, tenderheartedness.

compassionate adj benignant, clement, commiserative, gracious, kind, merciful, pitying, ruthful, sympathetic, tender.

compatible adj accordant, agreeable to, congruous, consistent, consonant, suitable.

compel vb constrain, force, coerce, drive, necessitate, oblige; bend, bow, subdue, subject.

compensation n pay, payment, recompense, remuneration, reward, salary; amends, atonement, indemnification, indemnity, reparation, requital, satisfaction; balance, counterpoise.

compete vb contend, contest, cope, emulate, rival, strive, struggle, vie.

competence n ability, capableness, capacity, fitness, qualification, suitableness; adequacy, adequateness, enough, sufficiency.

competent adj able, capable, clever, equal, endowed, qualified; adapted, adequate, convenient, fit, sufficient, suitable.

competition n contest, rivalry, rivals.

competitor n adversary, antagonist, contestant, emulator, opponent.

compile vb compose, prepare, write; arrange, collect, select.

complain vb bemoan, bewail, deplore, grieve, groan, grouch, growl, grumble, lament, moan.

complaint n grievance, grumble, lament, lamentation, plaint, murmur, wail; ail, ailment, annoyance, disease, disorder, illness, indisposition, malady, sickness; accusation, charge.

complete vb accomplish, achieve, conclude, consummate, do, effect, effectuate, end, execute, finish, fulfil, perfect, perform, realise, terminate. • adj clean, consummate, faultless, full, perfect, thorough; all, entire, integral, total, unbroken, undiminished, undivided, unimpaired, whole; accomplished, achieved, completed.

complex adj composite, compound, compounded, manifold, mingled, mixed; complicated, entangled, intricate, involved, knotty, tangled. • n entirety, integration, network, totality, whole; compulsion, fixation, obsession, preoccupation, prejudice.

complication n confusion, entanglement, intricacy.

compliment vb commend, congratulate, eulogise, extol, flatter, laud, praise. • n admiration, commendation, courtesy, encomium, eulogy, favour, flattery, honour, laudation, praise, tribute.

complimentary adj commendatory, congratulatory, encomiastic, eulogistic, laudatory.

component adj composing, constituent, constituting. • n constituent, element, ingredient, part.

compose vb build, compact, compound, constitute, form, make, synthesise; contrive, create, frame, imagine, invent, write; adjust, arrange, regulate, settle; appease, assuage, calm, pacify, quell, quiet, soothe, still, tranquillise.

composed adj calm, collected, cool, imperturbable, placid, quiet, sedate, self-possessed, tranquil, undisturbed, unmoved, unruffled.

composite adj amalgamated, combined, complex, compounded, mixed; integrated, unitary. • n admixture, amalgam, blend, combination, composition, compound, mixture, unification.

composition n constitution, construction, formation, framing, making; compound, mixture; arrangement, combination, conjunction, makeup, synthesis, union; invention, opus, piece, production, writing; agreement, arrangement, compromise.

composure n calmness, coolness, equanimity, placidity, sedateness, quiet, self-possession, serenity, tranquillity.

compound vb amalgamate, blend, combine, mingle, mix, unite; adjust, arrange, compose, compromise, settle. • adj complex, composite. • n combination, composition, mixture; farrago, jumble, medley.

comprehend vb comprise, contain, embrace, embody, enclose, include, involve; apprehend, conceive, discern, grasp, know, imagine, mentally, perceive, see, understand.

comprehension n comprising, embracing, inclusion; compass, domain, embrace, field, limits, province, range, reach, scope, sphere, sweep; connotation, depth, force, intention; conception, grasp, intelligence, understanding; intellect, intelligence, mind, reason, understanding.

comprehensive adj all-embracing, ample, broad, capacious, compendious, extensive, full, inclusive, large, sweeping, wide.

compression n abbreviation, condensation, confining, constriction, contraction, pinching, pressing, squeezing; brevity, pithiness, succinctness, terseness.

comprise vb comprehend, contain, embody, embrace, enclose, include, involve.

compromise vb adjust, arbitrate, arrange, compose, compound, settle; imperil, jeopardise, prejudice; commit, engage, implicate, pledge; agree, compound. • n adjustment, agreement, composition, settlement.

compulsion n coercion, constraint, force, forcing, pressure, urgency.

compulsory adj coercive, compelling, constraining; binding, enforced, imperative, necessary, obligatory, unavoidable.

compute vb calculate, count, enumerate, estimate, figure, measure, number, rate, reckon.

comrade n accomplice, ally, associate, chum, companion, compatriot, crony, fellow, mate.

conceal vb bury, cover, screen, secrete; disguise, dissemble, mask.

concede vb grant, surrender, yield; acknowledge, admit, allow, confess, grant.

conceit n belief, conception, fancy, idea, image, imagination, notion, thought; caprice, illusion, vagary, whim; estimate, estimation, impression, judgement, opinion; conceitedness, egoism, self-complacency, priggishness, vanity; point, quip, quirk.

conceivable adj imaginable, comprehensible, intelligible, rational, thinkable.

conceive vb create, contrive, devise, form, plan, purpose; fancy, imagine; comprehend, fathom, think, understand; assume, imagine, suppose; bear, become pregnant.

concern vb affect, belong to, interest, pertain to, regard, relate to, touch; disquiet, disturb, trouble. • n affair, business, matter, transaction; concernment, consequence, importance, interest, moment, weight; anxiety, care, carefulness, solicitude, worry; business, company, establishment.

concession n acquiescence, assent, cessation, compliance, surrender, yielding; acknowledgement, confession, grant, privilege.

concise adj brief, compact, compendious, comprehensive, compressed, condensed, crisp, laconic, pithy, pointed, pregnant, sententious, short, succinct, summary, terse.

conclude vb close, end, finish, terminate; deduce, gather, infer, judge; decide, determine; complete, settle; bar, hinder, restrain, stop.

conclusion n deduction, inference; decision, determination, judgement; close, completion, end, event, finale, issue, termination, upshot; arrangement, closing, effecting, settlement.

conclusive adj clinching, convincing, decisive, irrefutable, unanswerable; final, ultimate.

concrete adj compact, consolidated, firm, solid, solidified; agglomerated, complex, conglomerated, compound, entire, individualised, total. • n compound, concretion, mixture; cement.

concur vb accede, acquiesce, agree, approve, assent, coincide, consent, harmonise; combine, conspire, cooperate, help.

condemn vb ban, convict, doom, judge, penalise, sentence; disapprove, proscribe; blame, censure, damn, reprehend.

condense vb compress, concentrate, consolidate, thicken; abbreviate, abridge, contract, curtail, epitomise, reduce, shorten, summarise.

condescend vb deign, descend, stoop, submit.

condition vb postulate, specify, stipulate; groom, prepare, qualify, ready, train; acclimatise, accustom, adapt, adjust, familiarise, habituate, naturalise; attune, commission, fix, overhaul, prepare, recondition, repair, service, tune. • n case, circumstances, plight, predicament, situation, state; class, estate, grade, rank, station; arrangement, consideration, provision, proviso, stipulation; necessity, prerequisite.

condole vb commiserate, compassionate, console, sympathise.

conduct vb convoy, direct, escort, lead; administer, command, govern, lead, preside, superintend; manage, operate, regulate; direct, lead. • n administration, direction, guidance, leadership, management; convoy, escort, guard; actions, bearing, behaviour, career, carriage, demeanour, deportment, manners.

confer vb advise, consult, converse, deliberate, discourse, parley, talk; bestow, give, grant.

confess vb acknowledge, admit, avow, own; admit, concede, grant, recognise; attest, exhibit, manifest, prove, show; shrive.

confide vb commit, consign, entrust, trust.

confidence n belief, certitude, dependence, faith, reliance, trust; aplomb, assurance, boldness, cocksureness, courage, firmness, intrepidity, self-reliance; secrecy.

confident adj assured, certain, cocksure, positive, sure; bold, presumptuous. sanguine.

confidential adj intimate, private, secret; faithful, trustworthy.

confine vb restrain, shut in, shut up; immure, imprison, incarcerate, impound, jail, mew; bound, circumscribe, limit, restrict. • n border, boundary, frontier, limit.

confinement n restraint; captivity, duress, durance, immurement, imprisonment, incarceration; childbed, childbirth, delivery, lying-in.

confirm vb assure, establish, fix, settle; strengthen; authenticate, avouch, corroborate, countersign, endorse, substantiate, ratify.

confiscate vb appropriate, forfeit, seize.

conflict vb clash, combat, contend, contest, disagree, fight, interfere, strive, struggle. • n battle, collision, combat, contention, contest, encounter, fight, struggle; antagonism, clashing, disagreement, discord, inconsistency, opposition.

conform vb accommodate, adapt, adjust; agree, comport, correspond, harmonise, square, tally.

conformation n accordance, agreement, compliance, conformity; configuration, figure, form, manner, shape, structure.

confound vb confuse; baffle, bewilder, embarrass, flurry, mystify, nonplus, perplex, pose;

amaze, astonish, astound, bewilder, dumfound, paralyse, petrify, startle, stun, stupefy, surprise; annihilate, demolish, destroy, overthrow, overwhelm, ruin; abash, mortify, shame.

confront vb face; challenge, contrapose, encounter, oppose, threaten.

confuse vb blend, confound, intermingle, mingle, mix; derange, disarrange, disorder, jumble, mess, muddle; darken, obscure, perplex; befuddle, bewilder, embarrass, flabbergast, flurry, fluster, mystify, nonplus, pose; abash, confound, discompose, disconcert, mortify, shame.

confusion n anarchy, chaos, clutter, confusedness, derangement, disarrangement, disarray, disorder, jumble, muddle; agitation, commotion, ferment, stir, tumult, turmoil; astonishment, bewilderment, distraction, embarrassment, fluster, fuddle, perplexity; abashment, embarrassment, mortification, shame; annihilation, defeat, demolition, destruction, overthrow, ruin.

congratulate vb compliment, felicitate, gratulate, greet, hail, salute.

congregate vb assemble, collect, convene, convoke, gather, muster; gather, meet, swarm.

congress n assembly, conclave, conference, convention, convocation, council, diet, meeting.

congruous adj accordant, agreeing, compatible, consistent, consonant, suitable; appropriate, befitting, fit, meet, proper, seemly.

conjecture vb assume, guess, hypothesis, imagine, suppose. surmise, suspect; dare say, fancy, presume. • n assumption, guess, hypothesis, supposition, surmise, theory.

conjure vb adjure, beg, beseech, crave, entreat, implore, invoke, pray, supplicate; bewitch, charm, enchant, fascinate; juggle.

connect vb associate, conjoin, combine, couple, hyphenate, interlink, join, link, unite; cohere.

connection n alliance, association, dependence, junction, union; commerce, communication, intercourse; affinity, relationship; kindred, kinsman, relation, relative.

conquer vb beat, checkmate, crush, defeat, discomfit, humble, master, overcome, overpower, overthrow, prevail, quell, reduce, rout, subdue, subjugate, vanquish; overcome, surmount.

conquest n defeat, discomfiture, mastery, overthrow, reduction, subjection, subjugation; triumph, victor, winning.

conscientious adj careful, exact, fair, faithful, high-principled, honest, honourable, incorruptible, just, scrupulous, straightforward, uncorrupt.

conscious adj intelligent, knowing, percipient, sentient; intellectual, rational, reasoning, reflecting, self-conscious, thinking; apprised, awake, aware, cognisant, percipient, sensible; self-admitted, self-accusing.

consecutive adj following, succeeding.

consent *vb* agree, allow, assent, concur, permit, yield; accede, acquiesce, comply. • *n* approval, assent, concurrence, permission; accord, agreement, consensus, concord, cooperation, harmony, unison; acquiescence, compliance.

consequence *n* effect, end, event, issue, result; conclusion, deduction, inference; concatenation, connection, consecution; concern, distinction, importance, influence, standing, weight.

conservation *n* guardianship, maintenance, preservation, protection.

conservative *adj* conservatory, moderate, moderationist; preservative; reactionary, unprogressive. • *n* die-hard, reactionary, redneck, rightist, right-winger; moderate; preservative.

conserve *vb* keep, maintain, preserve, protect, save, sustain, uphold. • *n* comfit, confection, jam, preserve, sweetmeat.

consider *vb* attend, brood, contemplate, examine, heed, mark, mind, ponder, reflect, revolve, study, weigh; care for, consult, envisage, regard, respect; cogitate, deliberate, muse, ruminate, think; believe, deem, hold, judge.

considerate *adj* circumspect, deliberate, discrete, judicious, provident, prudent, serious, sober, staid, thoughtful; charitable, forbearing.

consideration *n* attention, cogitation, contemplation, deliberation, notice, heed, meditation, pondering, reflection, regard; consequence, importance, important, moment, significant, weight; account, cause, ground, motive, reason.

consistent *adj* accordant, agreeing, comfortable, compatible, congruous, consonant, correspondent, harmonious, logical.

consolation *n* alleviation, comfort, encouragement, relieve, solace.

console *vb* assuage, calm, cheer, comfort, encourage, solace, relieve, soothe.

consolidate *vb* cement, compact, compress, condense, conduce, harden, solidify, thicken; combine, conjoin, fuse, unite.

conspicuous *adj* apparent, clear, discernible, glaring, manifest, noticeable, perceptible, plain, striking, visible; celebrated, distinguished, eminent, famed, famous, illustrious, marked, noted, outstanding. pre-eminent, prominent.

conspiracy *n* cabal, collusion, confederation, intrigue, league, machination, plot, scheme.

conspire *vb* concur, conduce, cooperate; combine, compass, contrive, devise, project; confederate, contrive, hatch, plot, scheme.

constant *adj* abiding, enduring, fixed, immutable, invariable, invariant, permanent, perpetual, stable, unalterable, unchanging, unvaried; certain, regular, stated, uniform; determined, firm, resolute, staunch, steadfast, steady, unanswering, undeviating, unmoved, unshaken, unwavering; assiduous, diligent, persevering, sedulous,

tenacious, unremitting; continual, continuous, incessant, perpetual, sustained, unbroken, uninterrupted; devoted, faithful, loyal, true, trusty.

consternation *n* alarm, amazement, awe, bewilderment, dread, fear, fright, horror, panic.

constituent *adj* component, composing, constituting, forming; appointing, electoral. • *n* component, element, ingredient; elector, voter.

constitute *vb* compose, form, make; appoint, delegate, depute, empower; enact, establish, fix.

constitution *n* establishment, formation, make-up, organisation, structure; character, characteristic, disposition, form, habit, humour, peculiarity, physique, quality, spirit, temper.

constitutional *adj* congenital, connate, inborn, inbred, inherent, innate, natural, organic; lawful, legal, legitimate. • *n* airing, exercise, promenade, stretch, walk.

constrain *vb* coerce, compel, drive, force; chain, confine, curb, enthral, hold, restrain; draw, impel, urge.

constriction *n* compression, constraint.

construct *vb* build, fabricate, erect, raise, set up; arrange, establish, form, found, frame, institute, invent, make, organise, originate.

construction *n* building, erection, fabrication; configuration, conformation, figure, form, formation, made, shape, structure; explanation, interpretation, rendering, version.

consult *vb* advise, ask, confer, counsel, deliberate, interrogate, question; consider, regard.

consume *vb* absorb, decay, destroy, devour, dissipate, exhaust, expend, lavish, lessen, spend, squander, vanish, waste.

consummate[1] *vb* accomplish, achieve, compass, complete, conclude, crown, effect, effectuate, end, execute, finish, perfect, perform.

consummate[2] *adj* complete, done, effected, finished, fulfilled, perfect, supreme.

consumption *n* decay, decline, decrease, destruction, diminution, expenditure, use, waste; atrophy, emaciation.

contact *vb* hit, impinge, touch; approach, be heard, communicate with, reach. • *n* approximation, contiguity, junction, juxtaposition, touch.

contain *vb* accommodate, comprehend, comprise, embody, embrace, enclose, include; check, restrain

contemplate *vb* behold, gaze upon, observe, survey; consider, dwell on, meditate on, muse on, ponder, reflect upon, study, survey, think about; design, intend, mean, plan, purpose.

contemporary *adj* coetaneous, coeval, coexistent, coexisting, coincident, concomitant, concurrent, contemporaneous, current, present, simultaneous, synchronous; advanced, modern, modernistic, progressive, up-to-date. • *n* coeval, coexistent, compeer, fellow.

contempt n contumely, derision, despite, disdain, disregard, misprision, mockery, scorn.

contemptible adj abject, base, despicable, haughty, insolent, insulting, low, mean, paltry, pitiful, scurvy, sorry, supercilious, vile.

contemptuous adj arrogant, contumelious, disdainful, haughty, insolent, insulting, scornful, sneering, supercilious.

contend vb battle, combat, compete, contest, fight, strive, struggle, vie; argue, debate, dispute, litigate; affirm, assert, calm, maintain.

content[1] n essence, gist, meaning, meat, stuff, substance; capacity, measure, space, volume.

content[2] vb appease, delight, gladden, gratify, humour, indulge, please, satisfy, suffice. • adj agreeable, contented, happy, pleased, satisfied. • n contentment, ease, peace, satisfaction.

contest vb argue, contend, controvert, debate, dispute, litigate, question; strive, struggle; compete, cope, fight, vie. • n altercation, contention, controversy, difference, dispute, debate, quarrel; affray, battle, bout, combat, conflict, encounter, fight, match, struggle, tussle; competition.

continual adj constant, perpetual, unceasing, uninterrupted, unremitting; endless, eternal, everlasting, interminable, perennial, permanent, unending.

continue vb endure, last, remain; abide, linger, remain, stay, tarry; endure, persevere, persist, stick; extend, prolong, perpetuate, protract.

continuous adj connected, continued, extended, prolonged, unbroken, uninterrupted.

contract vb abbreviate, abridge, condense, confine, curtail, diminish, epitomize, lessen, narrow, reduce, shorten; absorb, catch, incur, get, make, take; constrict, shrink, shrivel, wrinkle; agree, bargain, covenant, engage, pledge, stipulate. • n agreement, arrangement, bargain, bond, compact, concordat, covenant, convention, engagement, pact, stipulation, treaty.

contradict vb assail, challenge, controvert, deny, dispute, gainsay, impugn, traverse; abrogate, annul, belie, counter, disallow, negative, contravene, counteract, oppose, thwart.

contradictory adj antagonistic, contrary, incompatible, inconsistent, negating, opposed.

contrary adj adverse, counter, discordant, opposed, opposing, opposite; antagonistic, conflicting, contradictory, repugnant, retroactive; forward, headstrong, humoursome, obstinate, refractory, stubborn, unruly, wayward, perverse. • n antithesis, converse, obverse, opposite.

contrast vb compare, differentiate, distinguish, oppose. • n contrariety, difference, opposition; comparison, distinction.

contravene vb abrogate, annul, contradict, counteract, countervail, cross, go against, hinder, interfere, nullify, oppose, set aside, thwart, transgress, traverse, violate.

contribute vb bestow, donate, give, grant, subscribe; afford, aid, furnish, supply; concur, conduce, conspire, cooperate, minister, serve, tend.

contrive vb arrange, brew, concoct, design, devise, effect, form, frame, hatch, invent, plan, project; consider, plan, plot, scheme; manage.

control vb command, direct, dominate, dominate, govern, manage, oversee, sway, regulate, rule, superintend; bridle, check, counteract, curb, check, hinder, repress, restrain. • n ascendency, command, direction, disposition, dominion, government, guidance, mastery, oversight, regulation, rule, supremacy, sway.

controversy n altercation, argument, contention, debate, discussion, disputation, dispute, logomachy, polemics, quarrel, strife; lawsuit.

convenient adj adapted, appropriate, fit, fitted, proper, suitable, suited; advantageous, beneficial, comfortable, commodious, favourable, handy, helpful, serviceable, timely, useful.

convention n assembly, congress, convocation, meeting; agreement, bargain, compact, contract, pact, stipulation, treaty; custom, formality.

conventional adj agreed on, bargained for, stipulated; accustomed, approved, common, customary, everyday, habitual, ordinary, orthodox, regular, standard, traditional, usual, wonted.

conversation n chat, colloquy, communion, confabulation, conference, converse, dialogue, discourse, intercourse, interlocution, parley, talk.

converse[1] vb commune; chat, confabulate, discourse, gossip, parley, talk. • n commerce, communication, intercourse; colloquy, conversation.

converse[2] adj adverse, contradictory, contrary, counter, opposed, opposing, opposite; n antithesis, contrary, opposite, reverse.

conversion n change, reduction, resolution, transformation, transmutation; interchange, reversal, transposition.

convert vb alter, change, transform, transmute; interchange, reverse, transpose; apply, appropriate, convince. • n catechumen, disciple, neophyte, proselyte.

convey vb bear, bring, carry, fetch, transmit, transport, waft; abalienate, alienate, cede, consign, deliver, demise, devise, devolve, grant, sell, transfer.

convict vb condemn, confute, convince, imprison, sentence. • n criminal, culprit, felon, malefactor, prisoner.

convoy vb accompany, attend, escort, guard, protect. • n attendance, attendant, escort, guard.

convulsion n cramp, fit, spasm; agitation, commotion, disturbance, shaking, tumult.

cook vb bake, boil, broil, fry, grill, microwave, roast, spit-roast, steam, stir-fry; falsify, garble.

cool vb chill, ice, refrigerate; abate, allay, calm, damp, moderate, quiet, temper. • adj calm, collected, composed, dispassionate, placid, sedate, self-possessed, quiet, staid, unexcited, unimpassioned, undisturbed, unruffled; cold-blooded, indifferent, lukewarm, unconcerned; apathetic, chilling, freezing, frigid, repellent; bold, impertinent, impudent, self-possessed, shameless. • n chill, chilliness, coolness; calmness, composure, coolheadedness, countenance, equanimity, poise, self-possession, self-restraint.

cooperate vb abet, aid, assist, co-act, collaborate, combine, concur, conduce, conspire, contribute, help, unite.

coordinate vb accord, agree, arrange, equalise, harmonise, integrate, methodise, organise, regulate, synchronise, systematise. • adj coequal, equal, equivalent, tantamount; coincident, synchronous. • n complement, counterpart, like, pendant; companion, fellow, match, mate.

cope vb combat, compete, contend, encounter, engage, strive, struggle, vie.

copious adj abundant, ample, exuberant, full, overflowing, plenteous, plentiful, profuse, rich.

copy vb duplicate, reproduce, trace, transcribe; follow, imitate, pattern. • n counterscript, duplicate, facsimile, off-print, replica, reproduction, transcript; archetype, model, original, pattern; manuscript, typescript.

core n centre, essence, heart, kernel.

corner vb confound, confuse, nonplus, perplex, pose, puzzle. • n angle, bend, crutch, cusp, elbow, joint, knee; niche, nook, recess, retreat.

corps n band, body, company, contingent, division, platoon, regiment, squad, squadron, troop.

corpse n body, carcass, corse, remains.

correct vb adjust, amend, cure, improve, mend, reclaim, rectify, redress, reform, regulate, remedy; chasten, discipline, punish. • adj accurate, equitable, exact, faultless, just, precise, proper, regular, right, true, upright.

correction n amendment, improvement, redress; chastening, discipline, punishment.

correspond vb accord, agree, answer, comport, conform, fit, harmonise, match, square, suit, tally; answer, belong, correlate; communicate.

correspondence n accord, agreement, coincidence, concurrence, conformity, congruity, fitness, harmony, match; correlation, counterposition; communication, letters, writing.

corrode vb canker, erode, gnaw; consume, deteriorate, rust, waste; blight, embitter, poison.

corrosive adj acrid, biting, consuming, cathartic, caustic, corroding, eroding, erosive, violent; consuming, corroding, gnawing, mordant, wasting, wearing; blighting, cankerous, carking, embittering, envenoming, poisoning.

corrupt vb putrefy, putrid, render; contaminate, defile, infect, pollute, spoil, taint, vitiate; degrade, demoralise, deprave, pervert, vitiate;

adulterate, debase, falsify, sophisticate; bribe, entice. • adj contaminated, corrupted, impure, infected, putrid, rotten, spoiled, tainted, unsound; abandoned, debauched, depraved, dissolute, profligate, reprobate, vicious, wicked.

cost n amount, charge, expenditure, expense, outlay, price; costliness, preciousness, richness, splendour, sumptuousness; damage, detriment, loss, plain, sacrifice, suffering.

costly adj dear, expensive, high-priced; gorgeous, luxurious, precious, rich, splendid.

couch vb lie, recline, crouch, squat; bend down, stoop; conceal, cover up, hide; lay, level. • n bed, davenport, divan, seat, settee, settle, sofa.

council n advisers, cabinet, ministry; assembly, congress, conclave, convention, convocation, diet, husting, meeting, parliament, synod.

counsel vb admonish, advise, caution, recommend, warm. • n counsel; admonition, advice, caution, instruction, opinion, recommendation, suggestion; deliberation, forethought; advocate, barrister, counsellor, lawyer.

count vb enumerate, number, score; calculate, cast, compute, estimate, reckon; account, consider, deem, esteem, hold, judge, regard, think; tell. • n reckoning, tally.

countenance vb aid, abet, approve, assist, befriend, encourage, favour, patronise, sanction, support. • n aspect, look, men; aid, approbation, approval, assistance, encouragement, favour, patronage, sanction, support.

counteract vb check, contravene, cross, counter, defeat, foil, frustrate, hinder, oppose, resist, thwart, traverse; annul, countervail, counterbalance, destroy, neutralise, offset.

counterfeit vb forge, imitate; fake, feign, pretend, sham, simulate; copy, imitate. • adj fake, forged, fraudulent, spurious, supposititious; false, feigned, hypocritical, mock, sham, simulated, spurious; copies, imitated, resembling.

counterpart n copy, duplicate; complement, correlate, correlative, reverse, supplement; fellow, mate, match, tally, twin.

country n land, region; countryside; fatherland, home, kingdom, state, territory; nation, people, population. • adj rural, rustic; countrified, rough, rude, uncultivated, unpolished, unrefined.

couple vb pair, unite; copulate, embrace; buckle, clasp, conjoin, connect, join, link, pair, unite, yoke. • n brace, pair, twain, two; bond, coupling.

courage n audaciousness, audacity, boldness, bravery, daring, derring-do, dauntlessness, fearlessness, firmness, fortitude, gallantry, hardihood, heroism, intrepidity, manhood, mettle, nerve, pluck, prowess, resolution, spirit, spunk.

courageous adj audacious, brave, bold, chivalrous, daring, dauntless, fearless, gallant, hardy, heroic, intrepid, lion-hearted, mettlesome, plucky, resolute, reliant, staunch, stout, undismayed, valiant, valorous.

course vb chase, follow, hunt, pursue, race, run. • n career, circuit, race, run; road, route, track, way; bearing, direction, path, tremor, track; ambit, beat, orbit, round; process, progress, sequence; order, regularity, succession, turn.

court vb coddle, fawn, flatter, ingratiate; address, woo; seek, solicit; invite, solicit. • n area, courtyard, patio, quadrangle; addresses, civilities, homage; retinue, palace, tribunal.

courteous adj affable, attentive, ceremonious, civil, complaisant, courtly, debonair, elegant, gracious, obliging, polished, polite, refined.

cover vb overlay, overspread; cloak, conceal, curtain, disguise, hide, mask, screen, secrete, shroud, veil; defend, guard, protect, shelter, shield; case, clothe, envelop, invest, jacket, sheathe; comprehend, comprise, contain, embody, embrace, include. • n capsule, case, covering, integument, tegument, top; cloak, disguise, screen, veil; guard, defence, protection, safeguard, shelter, shield; shrubbery, thicket, underbrush, undergrowth, underwood, woods.

covetous adj acquisitive, avaricious, close-fisted, grasping, greedy, miserly, niggardly.

cow vb abash, break, daunt, discourage, dishearten, frighten, intimidate, overawe, subdue.

coward adj cowardly, timid. • n caitiff, craven, dastard, milksop, poltroon, recreant, skulker, sneak, wheyface.

cowardly adj base, chicken-hearted, coward, craven, dastardly, faint-hearted, fearful, lily-livered, mean, pusillanimous, timid, timorous, white-livered, yellow.

cower vb bend, cringe, crouch, fawn, shrink.

coy adj backward, bashful, demure, diffident, distant, evasive, modest, prim, reserved, retiring, self-effacing, shrinking, shy, timid; affected, arch, coquettish.

crack vb break; chop, cleave, split; snap; craze, madden; boast, brag, bluster, crow, gasconade, vapour, vaunt. • adj capital, excellent, first-class, first-rate, tip-top. • n breach, break, chink, cleft, cranny, crevice, fissure, fracture, opening, rent, rift, split; burst, clap, explosion, pop, report.

craft n ability, aptitude, cleverness, dexterity, expertness, power, readiness, skill, tact, talent; artifice, artfulness, cunning, craftiness, deceitfulness, deception, guile, shrewdness, subtlety; art, avocation, business, calling, employment, handicraft, trade, vocation; vessel.

crafty adj arch, artful, astute, cunning, crooked, deceitful, designing, fraudulent, guileful, insidious, intriguing, scheming, shrewd, sly, subtle, tricky, wily.

cram vb fill, glut, gorge, satiate, stuff; compress, crowd, overcrowd, press, squeeze; coach, grind.

cramp vb convulse; check, clog, confine, hamper, hinder, impede, obstruct, restrain, restrict. • n convulsion, crick, spasm; check, restraint, restrict, obstruction

crash vb break, shatter, shiver, smash, splinter. • adj emergency, fast, intensive, rushed, speeded-up. • n clang, clash, collision concussion, jar.

crave vb ask, beg, beseech, entreat, implore, petition, solicit, supplicate; desire, hanker after, long for, need, want, yearn for.

craving n hungering, longing, yearning.

craze vb bewilder, confuse, dement, derange, madden; disorder, impair, weaken. • n fashion, mania, mode, novelty.

crazy adj broken, rickety, shaky, shattered, tottering; crack-brained, delirious, demented, deranged, distracted, idiotic, insane, lunatic, mad, silly.

create vb originate, procreate; cause, design, fashion, form, invent, occasion, produce; appoint, constitute, make.

creation n formation, invention, origination, production; cosmos, universe; appointment, constitution, establishment, nomination.

creature n animal, beast, being, body, brute, man, person; dependant, hanger- on, minion, parasite, retainer, vassal; miscreant, wretch.

credit vb accept, believe, trust; loan, trust. • n belief, confidence, credence, faith, reliance, trust; esteem, regard, reputableness, reputation; influence, power; honour, merit; loan, trust.

creditable adj creditable, estimable, honourable, meritorious, praiseworthy, reputable.

creed n belief, confession, doctrine, dogma, opinion, profession, tenet.

creep vb crawl; steal upon; cringe, fawn, grovel, insinuate. • n crawl, scrabble, scramble; fawner, groveller, sycophant, toady.

crest n comb, plume, topknot, tuft; apex, crown, head, ridge, summit, top; arms, badge, bearings.

crestfallen adj chap-fallen, dejected, depressed, despondent, discouraged, disheartened, dispirited, downcast, down-hearted, low-spirited, sad.

crew n company, complement, hands; corps, gang, horde, mob, party, posse, set, squad, team.

crime n felony, misdeed, misdemeanour, offence, violation; delinquency, fault, guilt, iniquity, sin, transgression, wrong.

criminal adj culpable, felonious, flagitious, guilty, illegal, immoral, iniquitous, nefarious, unlawful, vicious, wicked, wrong. • n convict, culprit, delinquent, felon, malefactor, offender.

cringe vb bend, bow, cower, crouch, fawn, grovel, kneel, sneak, stoop, truckle.

cripple vb cramp, destroy, disable, enfeeble, impair, lame, maim, mutilate, paralyse, ruin.

crisis n acme, climax, height; conjuncture, emergency, exigency, juncture, pass, pinch, push, rub, strait, urgency.

criterion *n* canon, gauge, measure, principle, proof, rule, standard, test, touchstone.

critic *n* arbiter, caviller, censor, connoisseur, judge, nit-picker, reviewer

critical *adj* accurate, exact, nice; captious, carping, cavilling, censorious, exacting; crucial, decisive, determining, important, turning: dangerous, dubious, exigent, hazardous, imminent, momentous, precarious, ticklish.

criticise *vb* appraise, evaluate, examine, judge.

croak *vb* complain, groan, grumble, moan, mumble, repine; die.

crook *vb* bend, bow, curve, incurvate, turn, wind. • *n* bend, curvature, flexion, turn; artifice, machination, trick; criminal, thief, villain

crooked *adj* angular, bent, bowed, curved, winding, zigzag; askew, aslant, awry, deformed, disfigured, distorted, twisted, wry; crafty, deceitful, devious, dishonest, dishonourable, insidious, intriguing, knavish, tricky, unscrupulous.

crop *vb* gather, mow, pick, pluck, reap; browse, nibble; clip, curtail, lop, reduce, shorten. • *n* harvest, produce, yield.

cross *vb* intersect, pass over, traverse; hinder, interfere, obstruct, thwart; interbred, intermix. • *adj* transverse; cantankerous, captious, crabbed, churlish, crusty, cynical, fractious, fretful, grouchy, ill-natured, ill-tempered, irascible, irritable, morose, peevish, pettish, petulant, snappish, snarling, sour, spleeny, splenetic, sulky, sullen, surly, testy, touchy, waspish. • *n* crucifix, gibbet, rood; affliction, misfortune, trial, trouble, vexation; cross-breeding, hybrid, intermixture.

crouch *vb* cower, cringe, fawn, truckle; crouch, kneel, stoop, squat.

crowd *vb* compress, cram, jam, pack, press; collect, congregate, flock, herd, huddle, swarm. • *n* assembly, company, concourse, flock, herd, horde, host, jam, multitude, press, throng; mob, pack, populace, rabble, rout.

crown *vb* adorn, dignify, honour; recompense, requite, reward; cap, complete, consummate, finish, perfect. • *n* bays, chaplet, coronal, coronet, garland, diadem, laurel, wreath; monarchy, royalty, sovereignty; diadem; dignity, honour, recompense, reward; apex, crest, summit, top.

crucial *adj* intersecting, transverse; critical, decisive, searching, severe, testing, trying.

crude *adj* raw, uncooked, undressed, unworked; harsh, immature, rough, unripe; crass, coarse, unrefined; awkward, immature, indigestible, rude, uncouth, unpolished, unpremeditated.

cruel *adj* barbarous, bloodthirsty, dire, fell, ferocious, inexorable, hard-hearted, inhuman, merciless, pitiless, relentless, ruthless, sanguinary, savage, truculent, uncompassionate, unfeeling, unmerciful, unrelenting; bitter, cold, hard, severe, sharp, unfeeling.

crush *vb* bruise, compress, contuse, squash, squeeze; bray, comminute, crumble, disintegrate, mash; demolish, raze, shatter; conquer, overcome, overpower, overwhelm, subdue.

crust *n* coat, coating, incrustation, outside, shell, surface.

cry *vb* call, clamour, exclaim; blubber, snivel, sob, wail, weep, whimper; bawl, bellow, hoot, roar, shout, vociferate, scream, screech, squawk, squall, squeal, yell; announce, blazon, proclaim, publish. • *n* acclamation, clamour, ejaculation, exclamation, outcry, crying, lament, lamentation, plaint, weeping; bawl, bellow, howl, roar, scream, screech, shriek, yell; announcement, proclamation, publication.

cuddle *vb* cosset, nestle, snuggle, caress, embrace, fondle, hug, pet. • *n* caress, embrace, hug,.

cue *vb* intimate, prompt, remind, sign, signal. • *n* catchword, hint, intimation, nod, prompting, sign, signal, suggestion.

cuff *vb* beat, box, buffet, knock, pummel, punch, slap, smack, strike, thump. • *n* blow, box, punch, slap, smack, strike, thump.

culmination *n* acme, apex, climax, completion, consummation, crown, summit, top, zenith.

culpable *adj* blameable, blameworthy, censurable, criminal, faulty, guilty, remiss, reprehensible, sinful, transgressive, wrong.

culprit *n* delinquent, criminal, evil-doer, felon, malefactor, offender.

cultivate *vb* farm, fertilise, till, work; civilise, develop, discipline, elevate, improve, meliorate, refine, train; investigate, prosecute, pursue, search, study; cherish, foster, nourish, promote.

culture *n* agriculture, cultivation, farming, husbandry, tillage; cultivation, elevation, improvement, refinement

cumbersome *adj* burdensome, clumsy, cumbrous, embarrassing, heavy, inconvenient, oppressive, troublesome, unmanageable, unwieldy, vexatious.

cunning *adj* artful, astute, crafty, crooked, deceitful, designing, diplomatic, foxy, guileful, intriguing, Machiavellian, sharp, shrewd, sly, subtle, tricky, wily; curious, ingenious. • *n* art, artfulness, artifice, astuteness, craft, shrewdness, subtlety; craftiness, chicanery, deceit, deception, intrigue, slyness.

curb *vb* bridle, check, control, hinder, moderate, repress, restrain. • *n* bridle, check, control, hindrance, rein, restraint.

cure *vb* alleviate, correct, heal, mend, remedy, restore; kipper, pickle, preserve. • *n* antidote, corrective, help, remedy, reparative, restorative, specific; alleviation, healing, restorative.

curiosity *n* interest, inquiringness, inquisitiveness; celebrity, curio, marvel, novelty, oddity, phenomenon, rarity, sight, spectacle, wonder.

curious *adj* interested, inquiring, inquisitive, meddling, peering, prying, scrutinising; extraordinary, marvellous, novel, queer, rare, singular, strange, unique, unusual; cunning, elegant, fine, finished, neat, skilful, well-wrought.

curl *vb* coil, twist, wind, writhe; bend, buckle, ripple, wave. • *n* curlicue, lovelock, ringlet; flexure, sinuosity, undulation, wave.

current *adj* common, general, popular, rife; circulating, passing; existing, instant, present, prevalent, widespread. • *n* course, progression, river, stream, tide, undertow.

curse *vb* anathematise, damn, denounce, execrate, imprecate, invoke; blast, blight, destroy, doom; afflict, annoy, harass, injure, plague, scourge, torment, vex; blaspheme. • *n* anathema, ban, denunciation, execration, fulmination, imprecation, malediction; affliction, annoyance, plague, scourge, torment, trouble, vexation; ban, condemnation, penalty.

cursory *adj* brief, careless, desultory, hasty, passing, rapid, slight, summary, superficial, transient, transitory.

curt *adj* brief, concise, laconic, short, terse; rude, snappish, tart.

curtail *vb* abridge, dock, lop, retrench, shorten; abbreviate, contract, decrease, diminish, lessen.

curve *vb* bend, crook, inflect, turn, twist, wind.

cushion *vb* absorb, dampen, deaden, dull, muffle, mute, soften, subdue, suppress; cradle, pillow, support. • *n* bolster, hassock, pad, pillow, woolsack.

custodian *n* curator, guardian, keeper, sacristan, superintendent, warden.

custody *n* care, charge, guardianship, keeping, safe-keeping, protection, watch, ward; confinement, durance, duress, imprisonment, prison.

custom *n* consuetude, convention, fashion, habit, manner, mode, practice, rule, usage, use, way; form, formality, observation; patronage; duty, impost, tax, toll, tribute.

customary *adj* accustomed, common, consuetudinary, conventional, familiar, fashionable, general, habitual, gnomic, prescriptive, regular, usual, wonted.

cut *vb* chop, cleave, divide, gash, incise, lance, sever, slice, slit, wound; carve, chisel, sculpture; hurt, move, pierce, touch, wound; ignore, slight; abbreviate, abridge, curtail, shorten. • *n* gash, groove, incision, nick, slit; channel, passage; piece, slice; fling, sarcasm, taunt; fashion, form, shape, style.

cutting *adj* keen, sharp; acid, biting, bitter, caustic, piercing, sarcastic, sardonic, satirical, severe, trenchant, wounding.

cycle *n* age, circle, era, period, revolution, round.

cynical *adj* captious, carping, censorious, churlish, crabbed, cross, crusty, fretful, ill-natured, ill-tempered, morose, peevish, pettish, petulant, sarcastic, satirical, snappish, snarling, surly, testy, touchy, waspish; contemptuous, derisive, misanthropic, pessimistic, scornful.

D

dabble *vb* dip, moisten, soak, spatter, splash, sprinkle, wet; meddle, tamper, trifle.

daft *adj* absurd, delirious, foolish, giddy, idiotic, insane, silly, simple, stupid, witless; frolicsome, merry, mirthful, playful, sportive.

dainty *adj* delicate, delicious, luscious, nice, palatable, savoury, tender, toothsome; beautiful, charming, choice, delicate, elegant, exquisite, fine, neat; fastidious, finical, finicky, over-nice, particular, scrupulous, squeamish.

damage *vb* harm, hurt, impair, injure, mar. • *n* detriment, harm, hurt, injury, loss, mischief.

damn *vb* condemn, doom, kill, ruin. • *n* bean, curse, fig, hoot, rap, sou, straw.

damp *vb* dampen, moisten; allay, abate, check, depress, discourage, hinder, impede, moderate, repress, restrain; chill, cool, deaden, deject, depress, dispirit. • *adj* dank, humid, moist, wet. • *n* dampness, dank, fog, mist; chill, dejection.

danger *n* jeopardy, insecurity, hazard, peril, risk, venture.

dangerous *adj* critical, hazardous, insecure, perilous, risky, ticklish, unsafe.

dare *vb* challenge, defy, endanger, hazard, provoke, risk. • *n* challenge, defiance, gage.

daring *adj* adventurous, bold, brave, chivalrous, courageous, dauntless, doughty, fearless, gallant, heroic, intrepid, valiant, valorous. • *n* adventurousness, boldness, bravery, courage, dauntlessness, doughtiness, fearlessness, intrepidity, undauntedness, valour.

dark *adj* black, cloudy, darksome, dim, dusky, inky, lightless, lurid, moonless, murky, opaque, overcast, pitchy, rayless, shady, shadowy, starless, sunless, swart, tenebrous, umbrageous, unenlightened, unilluminated; abstruse, cabbalistic, enigmatical, incomprehensible, mysterious, mystic, mystical, obscure, occult, opaque, recondite, transcendental, unillumined, unintelligible; cheerless, despondent, discouraging, dismal, disheartening, funereal, gloomy, joyless; benighted, darkened, ignorant, rude, unlettered, untaught; atrocious, damnable, infamous, flagitious, foul, horrible, infernal, nefarious, vile, wicked; private, secret. • n darkness, dusk, murkiness, obscurity; concealment, privacy, secrecy; blindness, ignorance.

darling adj beloved, cherished, dear, loved, precious, treasured. • n dear, favourite, idol, love.

dart vb ejaculate, hurl, launch, propel, sling, throw; emit, shoot; dash, rush, scoot, spring.

dash vb break, destroy, disappoint, frustrate, ruin, shatter, spoil, thwart; abash, confound, disappoint, surprise; bolt, dart, fly, run, speed, rush. • n blow, stroke; advance, onset, rush; infusion, smack, spice, sprinkling, tincture, tinge, touch; flourish, show.

dashing adj headlong, impetuous, precipitate, rushing; brilliant, gay, showy, spirited.

date n age, cycle, day, generation, time; epoch, era, period; appointment, arrangement, assignation, engagement, interview, rendezvous, tryst; catch, steady, sweetheart.

dawdle vb dally, delay, fiddle, idle, lag, loiter, potter, trifle.

dawn vb appear, begin, break, gleam, glimmer, open, rise. • n daybreak, dawning, cockcrow, sunrise, sun-up.

day n daylight, sunlight, sunshine; age, epoch, generation, lifetime, time.

daze vb blind, dazzle; bewilder, confound, confuse, perplex, stun, stupefy. • n bewilderment, confusion, discomposure, perturbation, pother; coma, stupor, swoon, trance.

dazzle vb blind, daze; astonish, confound, overpower. • n brightness, brilliance, splendour.

dead adj breathless, deceased, defunct, departed, gone, inanimate, lifeless; apathetic, callous, cold, dull, frigid, indifferent, inert, lukewarm, numb, obtuse, spiritless, torpid, unfeeling; flat, insipid, stagnant, tasteless, vapid; barren, inactive, sterile, unemployed, unprofitable, useless. • adv absolutely, completely, downright, fundamentally, quite; direct, directly, due, exactly, just, right, squarely, straight. • n depth, midst; hush, peace, quietude, silence, stillness.

deaden vb damp, dampen, dull, impair, muffle, mute, retard, smother, weaken; benumb, blunt, paralyse.

deadly adj deleterious, destructive, fatal, lethal, malignant, mortal, murderous, noxious, pernicious, poisonous, venomous; implacable, mortal, rancorous, sanguinary.

deal vb allot, apportion, assign, bestow, dispense, distribute, divide, give, reward, share; bargain, trade, traffic, treat with. • n amount, degree, distribution, extent, lot, portion, quantity, share; bargain, transaction.

dear adj costly, expensive, high-priced; beloved, cherished, darling, esteemed, precious, treasured. • n beloved, darling, deary, honey, love, precious, sweet, sweetie, sweetheart.

dearth n deficiency, insufficiency, scarcity; famine, lack, need, shortage, want.

deathless adj eternal, everlasting, immortal, imperishable, undying; boring, dull, turgid.

debase vb adulterate, alloy, depress, deteriorate, impair, injure, lower, pervert, reduce, vitiate; abase, degrade, disgrace, dishonour, humble, humiliate, mortify, shame; befoul, contaminate, corrupt, defile, foul, pollute, soil, taint.

debate vb argue, canvass, contest, discuss, dispute; contend, deliberate, wrangle. • n controversy, discussion, disputation; altercation, contention, contest, dispute, logomachy.

debonair adj affable, civil, complaisant, courteous, easy, gracious, kind, obliging, polite, refined, urbane, well-bred.

debris n detritus, fragments, remains, rubbish, ruble, ruins, wreck, wreckage.

debt n arrears, debit, due, liability, obligation; fault, misdoing, offence, shortcoming, sin, transgression, trespass.

decay vb decline, deteriorate, disintegrate, fail, perish, wane, waste, wither; decompose, putrefy, rot. • n caducity, decadence, declension, decline, decomposition, decrepitude, degeneracy, degeneration, deterioration, dilapidation, disintegration, fading, failing, perishing, putrefaction, ruin, wasting, withering.

deceit n artifice, cheating, chicanery, cozenage, craftiness, deceitfulness, deception, double-dealing, duplicity, finesse, fraud, guile, hypocrisy, imposition, imposture, pretence, sham, treachery, tricky, underhandedness, wile.

deceitful adj counterfeit, deceptive, delusive, fallacious, hollow, illusive, illusory, insidious, misleading; circumventive, cunning, designing, dissembling, dodgy, double-dealing, evasive, false, fraudulent, guileful, hypocritical, insincere, tricky, underhanded, wily.

deceive vb befool, beguile, betray, cheat, chouse, circumvent, cozen, defraud, delude, disappoint, double-cross, dupe, ensnare, entrap, fool, gull, hoax, hoodwink, humbug, mislead, outwit, overreach, trick.

decent adj appropriate, becoming, befitting, comely, seemly, decorous, fit, proper, seemly; chaste, delicate, modest, pure; moderate, passable, respectable, tolerable.

deception n artifice, cheating, chicanery, cozenage, craftiness, deceitfulness, deception, double-dealing, duplicity, finesse, fraud, guile, hoax, hypocrisy, imposition, imposture, pretence, sham, treachery, tricky, underhandedness, wile; cheat, ruse, stratagem, wile.

deceptive *adj* deceitful, deceiving, delusive, disingenuous, fallacious, false, illusive, illusory, misleading.

decide *vb* close, conclude, determine, end, settle, terminate; resolve; adjudicate, award.

decided *adj* determined, firm, resolute, unhesitating, unwavering; absolute, categorical, positive, unequivocal; certain, clear, indisputable, undeniable, unmistakable, unquestionable.

decision *n* conclusion, determination, judgement, settlement; adjudication, award, decree, pronouncement, sentence; firmness, resolution.

decisive *adj* conclusive, determinative, final.

declaration *n* affirmation, assertion, asseveration, averment, avowal, protestation, statement; announcement, proclamation.

declare *vb* advertise, affirm, announce, assert, asseverate, aver, blazon, bruit, proclaim, promulgate, pronounce, publish, state, utter.

decline *vb* incline, lean, slope; decay, droop, fail, flag, languish, pine, sink; degenerate, depreciate, deteriorate; decrease, diminish, dwindle, fade, ebb, lapse, lessen, wane; avoid, refuse, reject; inflect, vary. • *n* decadence, decay, declension, declination, degeneracy, deterioration, diminution, wane; atrophy, consumption, marasmus, phthisis; declivity, hill, incline, slope.

decomposition *n* analysis, break-up, disintegration, resolution; caries, corruption, crumbling, decay, disintegration, dissolution, putrescence, rotting.

decorate *vb* adorn, beautify, bedeck, deck, embellish, enrich, garnish, grace, ornament.

decoration *n* adorning, beautifying, bedecking, decking, enriching, garnishing, ornamentation, ornamenting, adornment, embellishment.

decorous *adj* appropriate, becoming, befitting, comely, decent, fit, suitable, proper, sedate, seemly, staid.

decoy *vb* allure, deceive, ensnare, entice, entrap, inveigle, lure, seduce, tempt. • *n* allurement, lure, enticement.

decrease *vb* abate, contract, decline, diminish, dwindle, ebb, lessen, subside, wane; curtail, diminish, lessen, lower, reduce, retrench. • *n* abatement, contraction, declension, decline, decrement, diminishing, diminution, ebb, ebbing, lessening, reduction, subsidence, waning.

decree *vb* adjudge, appoint, command, decide, determine, enact, enjoin, order, ordain. • *n* act, command, edict, enactment, fiat, law, mandate, order, ordinance, precept, regulation, statute.

decrepit *adj* feeble, effete, shattered, wasted, weak; aged, crippled, superannuated.

dedicate *vb* consecrate, devote, hallow, sanctify; address, inscribe.

deduce *vb* conclude, derive, draw, gather, infer.

deduction *n* removal, subtraction, withdrawal; abatement, allowance, defalcation, discount, rebate, reduction, reprise; conclusion, consequence, corollary, inference.

deed *n* achievement, act, action, derring-do, exploit, feat, performance; fact, truth, reality; charter, contract, document, indenture, instrument.

deep *adj* abysmal, profound; abstruse, difficult, hard, intricate, knotty, mysterious, profound, recondite, unfathomable; astute, cunning, designing, discerning, intelligent, insidious, penetrating, sagacious, shrewd; absorbed, engrossed; bass, grave, low; entire, great, heartfelt, thorough. • *n* main, ocean, water, sea; abyss, depth, profound; enigma, mystery, riddle; silence.

deeply *adv* profoundly; completely, entirely, profoundly, thoroughly; affectingly, distressingly, feelingly, mournfully, sadly.

defeat *vb* beat, checkmate, conquer, discomfit, overcome, overpower, overthrow, repulse, rout, ruin, vanquish; baffle, balk, block, disappoint, disconcert, foil, frustrate, thwart. • *n* discomfiture, downfall, overthrow, repulse, rout, vanquishment; bafflement, checkmate, frustration.

defect *vb* abandon, desert, rebel, revolt. • *n* default, deficiency, destitution, lack, shortcoming, spot, taint, want; blemish, blotch, error, flaw, imperfection, mistake; failing, fault, foible.

defective *adj* deficient, inadequate, incomplete, insufficient; faulty, imperfect, marred.

defence *n* defending, guarding, holding, maintaining, maintenance, protection; buckler, bulwark, fortification, guard, protection, rampart, resistance, shield; apology, excuse, justification, plea, vindication.

defend *vb* cover, fortify, guard, preserve, protect, safeguard, screen, secure, shelter, shield; assert, justify, plead, uphold, vindicate.

defer[1] *vb* adjourn, delay, pigeonhole, procrastinate, postpone, prorogue, protract, shelve, table.

defer[2] *vb* abide by, acknowledge, bow to, give way, submit, yield; admire, esteem, honour.

deference *n* esteem, homage, honour, obeisance, regard, respect, reverence, veneration, complaisance, consideration; obedience.

deferential *adj* respectful, reverential.

defiance *n* challenge, daring; contempt, despite, disobedience, disregard, opposition, spite.

defiant *adj* contumacious, recalcitrant, resistant; bold, courageous, resistant.

deficiency *n* dearth, default, deficit, insufficiency, lack, meagreness, scantiness, scarcity, shortage, shortness, want; defect, error, failing, failing, fault, foible, frailty, imperfection, weakness.

define *vb* bound, circumscribe, designate, delimit, demarcate, determine, explain, specify.

definite *adj* defined, determinate, determined,

fixed, restricted; assured, certain, clear, exact, explicit, positive, precise, specific, unequivocal.

definitive *adj* categorical, determinate, explicit, express, positive, unconditional; conclusive, decisive, final.

deformity *n* abnormality, crookedness, defect, disfigurement, distortion, inelegance, irregularity, malformation, misproportion, misshapenness, monstrosity, ugliness.

defraud *vb* beguile, cheat, chouse, circumvent, deceive, delude, diddle, dupe, embezzle, gull, overreach, outwit, pilfer, rob, swindle, trick.

deft *adj* adroit, apt, clever, dab, dextrous, expert, handy, ready, skilful.

defy *vb* challenge, dare; brave, contemn, despise, disregard, face, flout, provoke, scorn, slight, spurn.

degree *n* stage, step; class, grade, order, quality, rank, standing, station; extent, measure; division, interval, space.

dejected *adj* chap-fallen, crestfallen, depressed, despondent, disheartened, dispirited, doleful, downcast, down-hearted, gloomy, low-spirited, miserable, sad, wretched.

delay *vb* defer, postpone, procrastinate; arrest, detain, check, hinder, impede, retard, stay, stop; prolong, protract; dawdle, linger, loiter, tarry. • *n* deferment, postponement, procrastination; check, detention, hindrance, impediment, retardation, stoppage; prolonging, protraction; dallying, dawdling, lingering, tarrying, stay, stop.

delegate *vb* appoint, authorise, mission, depute, deputise, transfer; commit, entrust. • *n* ambassador, deputy, envoy, representative.

delete *vb* cancel, efface, erase, expunge, obliterate, remove.

deliberate *vb* cogitate, consider, consult, meditate, muse, ponder, reflect, ruminate, think, weigh. • *adj* careful, cautious, circumspect, considerate, heedful, purposeful, methodical, thoughtful, wary; well-advised, well-considered; aforethought, intentional, premeditated, purposed, studied.

deliberation *n* caution, circumspection, cogitation, consideration, coolness, meditation, prudence, reflection, thought, thoughtfulness, wariness; purpose.

delicacy *n* agreeableness, daintiness, deliciousness, pleasantness, relish, savouriness; bonne bouche, dainty, tidbit, titbit; elegance, fitness, lightness, niceness, nicety, smoothness, softness, tenderness; fragility, frailty, slenderness, slightness, tenderness, weakness; carefulness, daintiness, discrimination, fastidiousness, finesse, nicety, scrupulousness, sensitivity, subtlety, tact; purity, refinement, sensibility.

delicate *adj* agreeable, delicious, pleasant, pleasing, palatable, savoury; elegant, exquisite,

fine, nice; careful, dainty, discriminating, fastidious, scrupulous; fragile, frail, slender, slight, tender, delicate; pure, refined.

delicious *adj* dainty, delicate, luscious, nice, palatable, savory; agreeable, charming, choice, delightful, exquisite, grateful, pleasant.

delight *vb* charm, enchant, enrapture, gratify, please, ravish, rejoice, satisfy, transport. • *n* charm, delectation, ecstasy, enjoyment, gladness, gratification, happiness, joy, pleasure, rapture, ravishment, satisfaction, transport.

delightful *adj* agreeable, captivating, charming, delectable, enchanting, enjoyable, enrapturing, rapturous, ravishing, transporting.

delinquent *adj* negligent, offending. • *n* criminal, culprit, defaulter, malefactor, miscreant, misdoer, offender, transgressor, wrong-doer.

deliver *vb* emancipate, free, liberate, release; extricate, redeem, rescue, save; commit, give, impart, transfer; cede, grant, relinquish, resign, yield; declare, emit, promulgate, pronounce, speak, utter; deal, discharge.

delivery *n* conveyance, surrender; commitment, giving, rendering, transference, transferral, transmission; elocution, enunciation, pronunciation, speech, utterance; childbirth, confinement, labour, parturition, travail.

delusion *n* artifice, cheat, clap-trap, deceit, dodge, fetch, fraud, imposition, imposture, ruse, snare, trick, wile; deception, error, fallacy, fancy, hallucination, illusion, mistake, mockery.

demand *vb* challenge, exact, require; claim, necessitate, require; ask, inquire. • *n* claim, draft, exaction, requirement, requisition; call, want; inquiry, interrogation, question.

demolish *vb* annihilate, destroy, dismantle, level, overthrow, overturn, pulverise, raze, ruin.

demon *n* devil, fiend, kelpie, goblin, troll.

demonstrate *vb* establish, exhibit, illustrate, indicate, manifest, prove, show.

demonstration *n* display, exhibition, show.

demonstrative *adj* affectionate, communicative, effusive, emotional, expansive, expressive, extroverted, open, outgoing, passionate, sentimental, suggestive, talkative, unreserved; absolute, apodictic, certain, conclusive, probative; exemplificative, illustrative.

denial *n* contradiction, controverting, negation; abjuration, disavowal, disclaimer, disowning; disallowance, refusal, rejection.

dense *adj* close, compact, compressed, condensed, thick; dull, slow, stupid.

dent *vb* depress, dint, indent, pit. • *n* depression, dint, indentation, nick, notch.

deny *vb* contradict, gainsay, oppose, refute, traverse; abjure, disavow, disclaim, disown, renounce; disallow, refuse, reject, withhold.

depart *vb* absent, disappear, vanish; abandon,

decamp, go, leave, migrate, quit, remove, withdraw; decease, die; deviate, diverge, vary.

department n district, division, part, portion, province; bureau, function, office, province, sphere, station; branch, division, subdivision.

departure n exit, leaving, parting, recession, removal, retirement, withdrawal; abandonment, forsaking; death, decease, demise, exit.

depend vb hang, hinge, turn.

dependant n client, hanger-on, henchman, minion, retainer, subordinate, vassal; attendant, circumstance, concomitant, consequence.

dependent adj hanging, pendent; conditioned, contingent, relying, subject, subordinate.

deplorable adj calamitous, distressful, distressing, grievous, lamentable, melancholy, miserable, mournful, pitiable, regrettable, wretched.

depose vb break, cashier, degrade, dethrone, dismiss, displace, oust, reduce; avouch, declare, depone, testify.

deposit vb drop, dump, precipitate; lay, put; bank, hoard, lodge, put, save, store; commit, entrust. • n diluvium, dregs, lees, precipitate, precipitation, sediment, settlement, settlings, silt; money, pawn, pledge, security, stake.

depraved adj abandoned, corrupt, corrupted, debased, debauched, degenerate, dissolute, evil, graceless, hardened, immoral, lascivious, lewd, licentious, lost, perverted, profligate, reprobate, shameless, sinful, vicious, wicked.

depreciate vb underestimate, undervalue, underrate; belittle, censure, decry, degrade, disparage, malign, traduce.

depress vb bow, detrude, drop, lower, reduce, sink; abase, abash, degrade, debase, disgrace, humble, humiliation; chill, damp, dampen, deject, discourage, dishearten, dispirit, sadden.

depression n cavity, concavity, dent, dimple, dint, excavation, hollow, hollowness, indentation, pit; blues, cheerlessness, dejection, dejectedness, despondency, disconsolateness, disheartenment, dispiritedness, dole, dolefulness, downheartedness, dumps, gloom, gloominess, hypochondria, melancholy, sadness, vapours; inactivity, lowness, stagnation; abasement, debasement, degradation, humiliation.

deprive vb bereave, denude, despoil, dispossess, divest, rob, strip.

depth n abyss, deepness, drop, profundity; extent, measure; middle, midst, stillness; astuteness, discernment, penetration, perspicacity, profoundness, profundity, sagacity, shrewdness.

deputation n commission, delegation; commissioners, deputies, delegates, delegation, embassies, envoys, legation.

deputy adj acting, assistant, vice, subordinate. • n agent, commissioner, delegate, envoy, factor, legate, lieutenant, representative, substitute.

derelict adj abandoned, forsaken, left, relinquished; delinquent, faithless, guilty, neglectful, negligent, unfaithful. • n castaway, castoff, outcast, tramp, vagrant, wreck, wretch.

derision n contempt, mockery, ridicule, scorn.

derisive adj contemptuous, contumelious, mocking, ridiculing, scoffing, scornful.

derivation n descent, extraction, genealogy; etymology; deducing, deriving, drawing, getting, obtaining; beginning, origination, source.

derive vb draw, get, obtain, receive; deduce, follow, infer, trace.

descend vb drop, fall, pitch, plunge, sink, swoop; alight, dismount; go, pass, proceed, devolve; derive, issue, originate.

descendants npl offspring, issue, progeny.

descent n downrush, drop, fall; descending; decline, declivity, dip, pitch, slope; ancestry, derivation, extraction, genealogy, lineage, parentage, pedigree; assault, attack, foray, incursion.

describe vb define, delineate, draw, illustrate, limn, sketch, specify, trace; detail; depict, explain, narrate, portray, recount, relate, represent.

description n delineation; account, depiction, explanation, narration, narrative, portrayal, report, representation; kind, sort, species.

desert[1] n due, excellence, merit, worth; punishment, reward.

desert[2] vb abandon, abscond, forsake, leave, quit, relinquish, renounce, resign, quit, vacate.

desert[3] adj barren, desolate, forsaken, lonely, solitary, uncultivated, uninhabited, unproductive, untilled, waste, wild.

deserve vb earn, gain, merit, procure, win.

design vb brew, concoct, contrive, devise, intend, invent, mean, plan, project, scheme; intend, mean, purpose; delineate, describe, draw, outline, sketch, trace. • n aim, device, drift, intent, intention, mark, meaning, object, plan, proposal, project, purport, purpose, scheme; scope; delineation, draught, drawing, outline, plan, sketch; adaptation, artifice, contrivance.

designing adj artful, astute, crafty, crooked, cunning, deceitful, insidious, intriguing, Machiavellian, scheming, sly, subtle, treacherous, trickish, tricky, unscrupulous, wily.

desirable adj agreeable, beneficial, covetable, eligible, enviable, good, pleasing, preferable.

desire vb covet, crave, desiderate, fancy, hanker after, long for, lust after, want, wish, yearn for; ask, entreat, request, solicit. • n eroticism, lasciviousness, libidinousness, libido, lust, lustfulness, passion; fancy, hope, mind, partiality, penchant, pleasure, volition, want, wish.

desolate vb depopulate, despoil, destroy, devastate, pillage, plunder, ravage, ruin, sack. • adj bare, barren, bleak, desert, forsaken, lonely, solitary, unfrequented, uninhabited, waste, wild;

companionable, lonely, lonesome, solitary; destroyed, devastated, ravaged, ruined; cheerless, comfortless, disconsolate, dreary, forlorn, forsaken, miserable, wretched.

desolation n destruction, devastation, havoc, ravage, ruin; barrenness, bleakness, desolateness, dreariness, loneliness, solitariness, solitude, wildness; gloom, misery, sadness.

despair vb despond, give up, lose hope. • n dejection, desperation, despondency, disheartenment, hopelessness.

desperate adj despairing, despondent, desponding, hopeless; forlorn, hopeless, irretrievable; extreme; audacious, daring, despairing, foolhardy, frantic, furious, headstrong, precipitate, rash, reckless, violent, wild, wretched; extreme, great, monstrous, prodigious, supreme.

despicable adj abject, base, contemptible, degrading, low, mean, paltry, pitiful, shameful.

despise vb contemn, disdain, disregard, neglect, scorn, slight, spurn, undervalue.

despondent adj blue, dejected, depressed, discouraged, disheartened, dispirited, gloomy, low-spirited, melancholy, sad.

despotic adj absolute, arrogant, autocratic, dictatorial, imperious; oppressive, tyrannical.

destination n appointment, decree, destiny, doom, fate, foreordainment, foreordination, fortune, lot, ordination, star; aim, design, drift, end, intention, object, purpose, scope; bourne, goal, harbour, haven, journey's end, terminus.

destitute adj distressed, indigent, moneyless, necessitous, needy, penniless, penurious, pinched, poor, reduced, wanting.

destroy vb demolish, overthrow, overturn, subvert, raze, ruin; annihilate, dissolve, efface, quench; desolate, devastate, devour, ravage, waste; eradicate, extinguish, extirpate, kill.

destruction n demolition, havoc, overthrow, ruin, subversion; desolation, devastation, holocaust, ravage; annihilation, eradication, extinction, extirpation, ruin; death, massacre, murder, slaughter.

destructive adj baleful, baneful, deadly, deleterious, detrimental, fatal, hurtful, injurious, lethal, mischievous, noxious, pernicious, ruinous.

detach vb disengage, disconnect, disjoin, dissever, disunite, divide, part, separate, sever, unfix; appoint, detail, send.

detail vb delineate, depict, describe, enumerate, narrate, particularise, portray, recount, rehearse, relate, specify; appoint, detach, send. • n account, narration, narrative, recital, relation; appointment, detachment; item, part.

detain vb arrest, check, delay, hinder, hold, keep, restrain, retain, stay, stop; confine.

detect vb ascertain, catch, descry, disclose, discover, expose, reveal, unmask.

deter vb debar, discourage, frighten, hinder, prevent, restrain, stop, withhold.

deteriorate vb corrupt, debase, degrade, deprave, disgrace, impair, spoil, vitiate; decline, degenerate, depreciate, worsen.

determination n ascertainment, decision, deciding, determining, fixing, settlement, settling; conclusion, decision, judgement, purpose, resolution, resolve, result; direction, leaning, tendency; firmness, constancy, grit, persistence, stamina, resoluteness, resolution; definition, limitation, qualification.

determine vb adjust, conclude, decide, end, establish, fix, resolve, settle; ascertain, certify, check, verify; impel, incline, induce, influence, condition, define, limit; compel, necessitate.

detest vb abhor, abominate, despise, execrate, hate, loathe, nauseate, recoil from.

detestable adj abhorred, abominable, accursed, cursed, damnable, execrable, hateful, odious; disgusting, loathsome, nauseating, offensive, repulsive, sickening, vile.

detract vb abuse, asperse, belittle, calumniate, debase, decry, defame, depreciate, derogate, disparage, slander, traduce, vilify; deprecate, deteriorate, diminish, lessen.

devastation n despoiling, destroying, harrying, pillaging, plundering, ravaging, sacking, spoiling, stripping, wasting; desolation, destruction, havoc, pillage, rapine, ravage, ruin, waste.

develop vb disentangle, disclose, evolve, exhibit, explicate, uncover, unfold, unravel; cultivate, grow, mature, open, progress.

development n disclosure, disentanglement, exhibition, unfolding, unravelling; growth, increase, maturation, maturing; evolution, growth progression; elaboration, expansion.

deviate vb alter, deflect, digress, diverge, sheer off, slew, tack, turn aside, wheel, wheel about; err, stray, swerve, wander; differ, vary.

device n contraption, contrivance, gadget, invention; design, expedient, plan, project, resort, resource, scheme, shift; artifice, evasion, fraud, manoeuvre, ruse, stratagem, trick, wile; blazon, emblazonment, emblem, sign, symbol, type.

devious adj deviating, erratic, roundabout, wandering; circuitous, confusing, crooked, labyrinthine, mazy, obscure; crooked, disingenuous, misleading, treacherous.

devise vb brew, compass, concert, concoct, contrive, dream up, invent, plan, project, scheme; bequeath, demise, leave, will.

devote vb appropriate, consecrate, dedicate, destine; set apart; addict, apply, give up, resign; consign, doom, give over.

devoted adj affectionate, attached, loving; ardent, assiduous, earnest, zealous.

devotion n consecration, dedication; devotedness, devoutness, godliness, holiness, piety, religion, religiousness, saintliness, sanctity; adoration, prayer, worship; affection, attachment, love; ardour, earnestness, zeal.

devour vb engorge, gorge, gulp down, raven, swallow eagerly, wolf; annihilate, consume, destroy, expend, spend, swallow up, waste.

devout adj devotional, godly, holy, pious, religious, saint-like; serious, sincere, solemn.

dexterity n ability, address, adroitness, aptitude, aptness, art, cleverness, expertness, facility, knack, quickness, readiness, skilfulness, skill.

diabolic, diabolical adj atrocious, barbarous, cruel, devilish, fiendish, hellish, impious, infernal, malevolent, malign, malignant, satanic.

dialogue n colloquy, communication, conference, conversation, converse, intercourse, interlocution; playbook, script, speech, text, words.

dictate vb bid, direct, command, decree, enjoin, ordain, order, prescribe, require.

dictator n autocrat, despot, tyrant.

dictatorial adj absolute, unlimited, unrestricted, authoritative, despotic, dictatory, domineering, imperious, overbearing, peremptory, tyrannical.

die vb decease, demise, depart, expire, pass on; decay, decline, fade, fade out, perish, wither; cease, disappear, vanish; faint, fall, sink.

differ vb deviate, diverge, vary; disagree, dissent; bicker, contend, dispute, quarrel, wrangle.

difference n contrariety, contrast, departure, deviation, disagreement, disparity, dissimilarity, dissimilitude, divergence, diversity, heterogeneity, inconformity, nuance, opposition, unlikeness, variation; alienation, altercation, bickering, breach, contention, contest, controversy, debate, discacord, disharmony, dispute, dissension, falling out, irreconcilability, jarring, misunderstanding, quarrel, rupture, strife, variance, wrangle; discrimination, distinction.

different adj distinct, nonidentical, separate, unlike; contradistinct, contrary, contrasted, deviating, disagreeing, discrepant, dissimilar, divergent, diverse, incompatible, incongruous, unlike, variant, various; divers, heterogeneous, manifold, many, sundry, various.

difficult adj arduous, exacting, hard, Herculean, stiff, tough, uphill; abstruse, complex, intricate, knotty, obscure, perplexing; austere, rigid, unaccommodating, uncompliant, unyielding; dainty, fastidious, squeamish.

difficulty n arduousness, laboriousness; bar, barrier, crux, deadlock, dilemma, embarrassment, emergency, exigency, fix, hindrance, impediment, knot, obstacle, obstruction, perplexity, pickle, pinch, predicament, stand, standstill, thwart, trial, trouble; cavil, objection; complication, controversy, difference, embarrassment, embroilment, imbroglio, misunderstanding.

diffident adj distrustful, doubtful, hesitant, hesitating; bashful, modest, shy, timid.

dig vb channel, delve, excavate, grub, hollow out, quarry, scoop, tunnel. • n poke, punch.

dignified adj august, courtly, decorous, grave, imposing, majestic, noble, stately.

dignity n elevation, eminence, exaltation, excellent, glory, greatness, honour, place, rank, respectability, standing, station; decorum, grandeur, majesty, nobleness, stateliness; preferment; dignitary, magistrate; elevation, height.

dilapidated adj decadent, decayed, ruined.

dilemma n difficulty, fix, plight, predicament, problem, quandary, strait.

diligent adj active, assiduous, attentive, busy, careful, constant, earnest, hard-working, indefatigable, industriousness, laborious, notable, painstaking, persevering, persistent, sedulous.

dim adj cloudy, dark, dusky, faint, ill-defined, indefinite, indistinct, mysterious, obscure, shadowy; dull, obtuse; clouded, confused, darkened, faint, obscured; blurred, dull, tarnished.

diminish vb abate, belittle, contract, decrease, lessen, reduce; curtail, cut, decrease, dwindle, narrow, shrink, shrivel, subside, weaken.

din n bruit, clamour, clash, clatter, crash, crashing, hubbub, hullabaloo, noise, outcry, racket, row, shout, uproar.

dingy adj brown, dun, dusky; bedimmed, colourless, dimmed, dulled, faded, obscure, smirched, soiled, sullied.

dip vb douse, duck, immerse, plunge, souse; bail, ladle; dive, duck, pitch, plunge; bend, incline, slope. • n decline, declivity, descent, drop, fall; concavity, depression, hole, hollow, pit, sink; bathe, dipping, ducking, sousing, swim.

diplomat n diplomatist, envoy, legate, minister, negotiator.

dire adj alarming, awful, calamitous, cruel, destructive, disastrous, dismal, dreadful, fearful, gloomy, horrible, horrid, implacable, inexorable, portentous, shocking, terrible.

direct vb aim, cast, level, point, turn; advise, conduct, control, dispose, guide, govern, manage, regulate, rule; command, bid, enjoin, instruct, order; guide, lead, point, show; address, superscribe. • adj immediate, straight, undeviating; absolute, categorical, express, plain, unambiguous; downright, earnest, frank, open, outspoken, sincere, straightforward, unequivocal.

direction n aim; tendency; bearing, course; administration, conduct, control, government, management, oversight, superintendence; guidance, lead; command, order, prescription; address, superscription.

directly adv absolutely, expressly, openly, unambiguously; forthwith, immediately, instantly, quickly, presently, promptly, soon, speedily.

dirty vb befoul, defile, draggle, foul, pollute, soil, sully. • adj begrimed. defiled, filthy, foul, mucky, nasty, soiled, unclean; clouded, cloudy, dark, dull, muddy, sullied; base, beggarly, contemptible, despicable, grovelling, low, mean, squalid; disagreeable, foul, muddy, nasty, rainy, sloppy, uncomfortable.

disability n disablement, disqualification, impotence, impotency, inability, incapacity, incompetence, incompetency, unfitness, weakness.

disable vb cripple, enfeeble, hamstring, impair, paralyse, unman, weaken; disenable, disqualify, incapacitate, unfit.

disadvantage n disadvantageousness, inconvenience, unfavourableness; damage, detriment, disservice, drawback, harm, hindrance, hurt, injury, loss, prejudice.

disagree vb deviate, differ, diverge, vary; dissent; argue, clash, dispute, quarrel.

disagreeable adj contrary, displeasing, distasteful, nasty, offensive, unpleasant.

disagreement n deviation, difference, discrepancy, dissimilarity, dissimilitude, divergence, diversity, incongruity, unlikeness; disaccord, dissent; argument, bickering, clashing, conflict, contention, dispute, dissension, jarring, misunderstanding, quarrel, strife, variance, wrangle.

disappear vb depart, dissolve, fade, vanish.

disappoint vb baffle, balk, deceive, defeat, delude, disconcert, foil, frustrate, mortify, vex.

disappointment n baffling, balk, failure, foiling, frustration, miscarriage, mortification.

disapprove vb blame, censure, condemn, deprecate, dislike, displeasure; disallow, reject.

disarrange vb confuse, derange, disallow, dishevel, dislike, dislocate, disorder, disturb, jumble, reject, rumple, tumble, unsettle.

disaster n accident, adversity, blow, calamity, casualty, catastrophe, misadventure, mischance, misfortune, mishap, reverse, ruin, stroke.

disastrous adj adverse, calamitous, catastrophic, destructive, hapless, ill-fated, ill-starred, ruinous, unfortunate, unlucky, unpropitious, unprosperous, untoward.

discard vb abandon, cast off, lay aside, reject; banish, break, cashier, discharge, dismiss.

discern vb differentiate, discriminate, distinguish, judge; behold, descry, discover, espy, notice, observe, perceive, recognise, see.

discharge vb disburden, unburden, unload; eject, emit, excrete, expel, void; cash, liquidate, pay; absolve, acquit, clear, exonerate, free, release, relieve; cashier, discard, dismiss, sack; destroy, remove; execute, perform, fulfil, observe; annul, cancel, invalidate, nullify, rescind. • n disburdening, unloading; dismissal, displacement, ejection, emission, evacuation, excretion, expulsion, vent, voiding; blast, burst, explosion, fir-

ing; execution, fulfilment, observance, fulfilment; annulment, clearance, liquidation, payment, satisfaction, settlement; exemption, liberation, release; flow, flux, execration.

disciple n catechumen, learner, pupil, scholar, student; adherent, follower, partisan, supporter.

discipline vb breed, drill, educate, exercise, form, instruct, teach, train; control, govern, regulate, school; chasten, chastise, punish. • n culture, drill, drilling, education, exercise, instruction, training; control, government, regulation, subjection; chastisement, correction, punishment.

disclose vb discover, exhibit, expose, manifest, uncover; bare, betray, blab, communicate, divulge, impart, publish, reveal, show, tell, utter.

discomfiture n confusion, defeat, frustration, overthrow, rout, vexation.

discomfort n disquiet, distress, malaise, trouble, uneasiness, unpleasantness, vexation.

disconcert vb baffle, balk, contravene, defeat, disarrange, frustrate, interrupt, thwart, undo, upset; abash, agitate, bewilder, confuse, demoralise, disturb, embarrass, faze, perplex, perturb, unbalance, worry.

disconsolate adj brokenhearted, cheerless, comfortless, dejected, desolate, forlorn, gloomy, heartbroken, inconsolable, melancholy, miserable, sad, sorrowful, unhappy, woeful, wretched.

discontent n displeasure, dissatisfaction, inquietude, restlessness, uneasiness.

discord n contention, difference, disagreement, dissension, opposition, quarrelling, rupture, strife, variance, wrangling; cacophony, discordance, dissonance, harshness, jangle, jarring.

discount vb allow for, deduct, lower, rebate, reduce, subtract; disregard, ignore, overlook. • n abatement, drawback; allowance, deduction, rebate, reduction.

discourage vb abase, awe, damp, daunt, depress, deject, dismay, dishearten, dispirit, frighten, intimidate; deter, dissuade, hinder.

discouragement n disheartening; dissuasion; damper, deterrent, embarrassment, hindrance, impediment, obstacle, wet blanket.

discover vb communicate, disclose, exhibit, impart, manifest, show, reveal, tell; ascertain, behold, discern, espy, see; descry, detect, determine; contrive, invent, originate.

discredit vb disbelieve, doubt, question; depreciate, disgrace, dishonour, disparage, reproach. • n disbelief, distrust; disgrace, dishonour, disrepute, ignominy, notoriety, obloquy, odium, opprobrium, reproach, scandal.

discreet adj careful, cautious, circumspect, considerate, discerning, heedful, judicious, prudent, sagacious, wary, wise.

discrepancy n contrariety, difference, disagreement, discordance, dissonance, divergence, incongruity, inconsistency, variance, variation.

discretion n care, carefulness, caution, circumspection, considerateness, consideration, heedfulness, judgement, prudence, wariness; discrimination, maturity, responsibility; choice, option, pleasure, will.

discrimination n difference, distinction; acumen, acuteness, discernment, insight, judgement, penetration, sagacity.

discuss vb agitate, argue, canvass, consider, debate, deliberate, examine, sift, ventilate.

disdainful adj cavalier, contemptuous, contumelious, haughty, scornful, supercilious.

disease n affection, affliction, ailment, complaint, disorder, distemper, illness, indisposition, infirmity, malady, sickness.

disengage vb clear, deliver, discharge, disembarrass, disembroil, disencumber, disentangle, extricate, liberate, release; detach, disjoin, dissociate, disunite, divide, separate; wean, withdraw.

disentangle vb loosen, separate, unfold, unravel, untwist; clear, detach, disconnect, disembroil, disengage, extricate, liberate, loose, unloose.

disfigurement n blemishing, defacement, deforming, injury, marring, spoiling; blemish, defect, deformity, injury, spot, stain.

disgrace vb degrade, humble, humiliate; abase, debase, defame, discredit, disfavour, dishonour, disparage, reproach, stain, sully, taint, tarnish. • n abomination, disrepute, humiliation, ignominy, infamy, mortification, shame, scandal.

disgraceful adj discreditable, dishonourable, disreputable, ignominious, infamous, opprobrious, scandalous, shameful.

disguise vb cloak, conceal, cover, dissemble, hide, mask, muffle, screen, secrete, shroud, veil. • n concealment, cover, mask, veil; blind, cloak, masquerade, pretence, pretext, veneer.

disgust vb nauseate, sicken; abominate, detest, displease, offend, repel, repulse, revolt. • n distaste, loathing, nausea; abhorrence, abomination, antipathy, aversion, detestation, dislike, repugnance, revulsion.

dish n bowl, plate, saucer, vessel.

dishearten vb cast down, damp, dampen, daunt, deject, depress, deter, discourage, dispirit.

dishevelled adj disarranged, disordered, messed, tousled, tumbled, unkempt, untidy.

dishonest adj cheating, corrupt, crafty, crooked, deceitful, deceiving, deceptive, designing, faithless, false, falsehearted, fraudulent, guileful, knavish, perfidious, slippery, treacherous, unfair, unscrupulous.

dishonour vb abase, defame, degrade, discredit, disfavour, dishonour, disgrace, disparage, reproach, shame, taint. • n abasement, contempt, degradation, discredit, disfavour, disgrace, dis-

honour, disparagement, disrepute, ignominy, infamy, obloquy, odium, opprobrium, shame.

dishonourable adj discreditable, disgraceful, disreputable, ignominious, infamous, scandalous, shameful; base, false, shameless.

disinfect vb cleanse, deodorise, fumigate, purify, sterilise.

disintegrate vb crumble, decompose, dissolve, disunite, pulverise, separate.

disinterested adj candid, fair, high-minded, impartial, indifferent, unbiased, unselfish, unprejudiced; generous, liberal, magnanimous.

dislike vb abominate, detest, disapprove, hate, loathe. • n antagonism, antipathy, aversion, disapproval, disfavour, disgust, disinclination, displeasure, distaste, loathing, repugnance.

dislocate vb disarrange, displace, disturb; disarticulate, disjoint, luxate, slip.

dislodge vb dismount, dispel, displace, eject, expel, oust, remove.

disloyal adj faithless, false, perfidious, treacherous, treasonable, unfaithful, unpatriotic, untrue.

dismal adj cheerless, dark, dreary, dull, gloomy, lonesome; blue, calamitous, doleful, dolorous, funereal, lugubrious, melancholy, mournful, sad, sombre, sorrowful.

dismantle vb divest, strip, unrig.

dismay vb affright, alarm, appal, daunt, discourage, dishearten, frighten, horrify, intimidate, paralyse, scare, terrify. • n affright, alarm, consternation, fear, fright, horror, terror.

dismiss vb banish, cashier, discard, discharge, disperse, reject, release, remove.

disobey vb infringe, transgress, violate.

disorder vb confound, confuse, derange, disarrange, discompose, disorganise, disturb, unsettle, upset. • n confusion, derangement, disarrangement, disarray, disorganisation, irregularity, jumble, litter, mess; brawl, commotion, disturbance, fight, quarrel, riot, tumult; riotousness, turbulence; ailment, complaint, illness, indisposition, malady, sickness.

disorderly adj chaotic, confused, intemperate, irregular, unmethodical, unsystematic, untidy; lawless, rebellious, riotous, tumultuous, turbulent, ungovernable, unmanageable, unruly.

disown vb disavow, disclaim, reject, renounce, repudiate; abnegate, deny, disallow.

disparage vb belittle, decry, depreciate, derogate from, detract from, doubt, question, run down, underestimate, underpraise, underrate, undervalue; asperse, defame, inveigh against, speak ill of, traduce, vilify.

disparity n difference, disproportion, inequality; dissimilarity, dissimilitude, unlikeness.

dispassionate adj calm, collected, composed; candid, disinterested, fair, impartial, neutral, unbiased.

dispatch, despatch vb assassinate, kill, murder, slaughter, slay; accelerate, conclude, dismiss, expedite, finish, forward, hasten, hurry, quicken, speed. • n dispatching, sending; diligence, expedition, haste, rapidity, speed; communication, document, instruction, message, report.

dispel vb banish, disperse, dissipate, scatter.

dispensation n allotment, apportioning, apportionment, dispensing, distributing, distribution; administration, stewardship; economy, plan, scheme, system; exemption, immunity, indulgence, licence, privilege.

dispirited adj dejected, depressed, discouraged, disheartened, downhearted.

display vb expand, extend, open, spread, unfold; exhibit, show; flaunt, parade. • n exhibition, manifestation, show; flourish, ostentation, pageant, parade, pomp.

displease vb disgruntle, disgust, disoblige, dissatisfy, offend; affront, aggravate, anger, annoy, chafe, chagrin, fret, irritate, nettle, pique, vex.

dispose vb arrange, distribute, marshal, group, place, range, rank, set; adjust, determine, regulate, settle; bias, incline, induce, lead, move, predispose; control, decide, regulate, rule, settle; arrange, bargain, compound; alienate, convey, demise, sell, transfer.

disposed adj apt, inclined, prone, ready.

disposition n arrangement, arranging, classification, disposing, grouping, location, placing; adjustment, control, direction, disposure, disposal, management, ordering, regulation; aptitude, bent, bias, inclination, nature, predisposition, proclivity, proneness, propensity, tendency; character, constitution, humour, nature, temper, temperament, turn; inclination, willingness; bestowal, dispensation, distribution.

disproportion n disparity, inadequacy, inequality, insufficiency, unsuitableness.

dispute vb altercate, argue, debate, litigate, question; bicker, brawl, jangle, quarrel, spar, spat, squabble, tiff, wrangle; agitate, ventilate; challenge, contradict, controvert, deny, impugn; contest, struggle for. • n controversy, debate, discussion, disputation; altercation, argument, dissension.

disqualify vb disable, incapacitate, unfit; disenable, incapacitate, preclude, prohibit.

disregard vb contemn, despise, disdain, disobey, disparage, ignore, neglect, overlook, slight. • n contempt, ignoring, inattention, neglect, oversight, slight; disfavour, indifference.

disreputable adj derogatory, discreditable, dishonourable, disgraceful, infamous, opprobrious, scandalous, shameful; base, contemptible, low, mean, vicious, vile, vulgar.

disrespect n disesteem, disregard, irreverence,

neglect, slight; discourteousness, impertinence, impolite, incivility, rudeness.

dissect vb analyse, examine, explore, investigate, scrutinise, sift.

dissemble vb cloak, conceal, cover, disguise, hide; counterfeit, dissimulate, feign, pretend.

disseminate vb circulate, diffuse, disperse, proclaim, promulgate, propagate, publish, spread.

dissent vb decline, differ, disagree, refuse. • n difference, disagreement, nonconformity, opposition, recusancy, refusal.

dissidence n disagreement, dissent, nonconformity, sectarianism.

dissipate vb dispel, disperse, scatter; consume, expend, lavish, squander, waste; vanish.

dissolute adj abandoned, corrupt, debauched, depraved, disorderly, dissipated, graceless, lax, lewd, licentious, loose, profligate, rakish, reprobate, shameless, vicious, wanton, wild.

dissolve vb liquefy, melt; disorganise, disunite, divide, loose, separate, sever; destroy, ruin; disappear, fade, scatter, vanish; crumble, decompose, disintegrate, perish.

distance vb excel, outdo, outstrip, surpass. • n farness, remoteness; aloofness, coldness, frigidity, reserve, stiffness; absence, separation.

distant adj far, faraway, remote; aloof, ceremonious, cold, cool, frigid, haughty, reserved, stiff, uncordial; faint, indirect, obscure, slight.

distasteful adj disgusting, loathsome, nauseating, nauseous, unpalatable, unsavoury; disagreeable, displeasing, offensive, repugnant.

distinct adj definite, different, discrete, disjunct, individual, separate, unconnected; clear, defined, manifest, obvious, plain, unconfused, unmistakable, well-defined.

distinction n discernment, discrimination, distinguishing; difference; account, celebrity, credit, eminence, fame, name, note, rank, renown, reputation, repute, respectability, superiority.

distinctive adj characteristic, differentiating, discriminating, distinguishing.

distinguish vb characterise, mark; differentiate, discern, discriminate, perceive, recognise, see, single out, tell; demarcate, divide, separate; celebrate, honour, signalise.

distinguished adj celebrated, eminent, famous, illustrious, noted; conspicuous, extraordinary, laureate, marked, shining, superior.

distort vb contort, deform, gnarl, screw, twist, warp, wrest; falsify, misrepresent, pervert.

distract vb divert, draw away; bewilder, confound, confuse, derange, discompose, disconcert, disturb, embarrass, harass, madden, mystify, perplex, puzzle.

distress vb afflict, annoy, grieve, harry, pain, perplex, rack, trouble; distrain, seize, take. • n affliction, calamity, disaster, misery, misfortune, adversity, hardship, perplexity, trial, tribulation; agony, anguish, dolour, grief, sorrow, suffering; gnawing, gripe, griping, pain, torment, torture; destitution, indigence, poverty, straits, want.

distribute vb allocate, allot, apportion, assign, deal, dispense, divide, dole out, give, mete, partition, prorate, share; administer, arrange, assort, class, classify, dispose.

distribution n allocation, allotment, apportionment, assignment, assortment, dispensation, dispensing; arrangement, disposal, disposition, classification, division, dole, grouping, sharing.

district n circuit, department, neighbourhood, province, quarter, region, section, territory, ward.

distrust vb disbelieve, discredit, doubt, misbelieve, mistrust, question, suspect. • n doubt, misgiving, mistrust, question, suspicion.

disturb vb agitate, shake, stir; confuse, derange, disarrange, disorder, unsettle, upset; annoy, discompose, disconcert, disquiet, distract, fuss, incommode, molest, perturb, plague, trouble, ruffle, vex, worry; impede, interrupt, hinder.

disturbance n agitation, commotion, confusion, convulsion, derangement, disorder, perturbation, unsettlement; annoyance, discomposure, distraction, excitement, fuss; hindrance, interruption, molestation; brawl, commotion, disorder, excitement, fracas, riot, turmoil.

disuse n desuetude, discontinuance, disusage, neglect, nonobservance.

ditch vb canalise, dig, excavate, furrow, gouge, trench; abandon, discard, dump, jettison, scrap. • n channel, drain, fosse, moat, trench.

dive vb explore, fathom, penetrate, plunge, sound. • n drop, fall, header, plunge; bar, den, dump, joint, saloon.

diverge vb divide, radiate, separate; divaricate, separate; deviate, differ, disagree, vary.

diverse adj different, differing, dissimilar, divergent, heterogeneous, multifarious, separate, unlike, variant, various, varying.

diversion n deflection, diverting; amusement, delight, distraction, enjoyment, entertainment, game, gratification, pastime, play, pleasure, recreation, sport; detour, digression.

diversity n difference, dissimilarity, dissimilitude, divergence, unlikeness, variation; heterogeneity, manifoldness, multifariousness, multiformity, variety.

divert vb deflect, distract, disturb; amuse, beguile, delight, entertain, exhilarate, gratify, recreate, refresh, solace.

divide vb bisect, cleave, cut, dismember, dissever, disunite, open, part, rend, segregate, separate, sever, shear, split, sunder; allocate, allot, apportion, assign, dispense, distribute, dole, mete, portion, share; compartmentalise, demarcate, partition; alienate, disunite, estrange.

divine vb foretell, predict, presage, prognosticate, vaticinate, prophesy; believe, conjecture, fancy, guess, suppose, surmise, suspect, think. • adj deiform, godlike, superhuman, supernatural; angelic, celestial, heavenly, holy, sacred, seraphic, spiritual; exalted, exalting, rapturous, supreme, transcendent. • n churchman, clergyman, ecclesiastic, minister, parson, pastor, priest.

division n compartmentalisation, disconnection, disjunction, dismemberment, segmentation, separation, severance; category, class, compartment, head, parcel, portion, section, segment; demarcation, partition; alienation, allotment, apportionment, distribution; breach, difference, disagreement, discord, disunion, estrangement, feud, rupture, variance.

divorce vb disconnect, dissolve, disunite, part, put away, separate, sever, split up, sunder. • n disjunction, dissolution, disunion, division, parting, separation, severance.

divulge vb communicate, declare, disclose, discover, exhibit, expose, impart, proclaim, promulgate, publish, reveal, tell, uncover.

dizzy adj giddy; careless, heedless, thoughtless.

do vb accomplish, achieve, act, commit, effect, execute, perform; complete, conclude, end, finish, settle, terminate; conduct, transact; observe, perform, practice; translate, render, cook, prepare; cheat, chouse, cozen, hoax, swindle; serve, suffice. • n banquet, event, feast, function, party.

docile adj amenable, obedient, pliant, teachable, tractable, yielding.

dock[1] vb clip, curtail, cut, deduct, truncate; lessen, shorten.

dock[2] vb anchor, moor; join, meet. • n anchorage, basin, berth, dockage, dockyard, dry dock, harbour, haven, marina, pier, shipyard, wharf.

doctor vb adulterate, alter, cook, falsify, manipulate, tamper with; attend, minister to, cure, heal, remedy, treat; fix, mend, overhaul, repair, service. • n general practitioner, GP, healer, leech, medic, physician; adept, savant.

doctrine n article, belief, creed, dogma, opinion, precept, principle, teaching, tenet.

dodge vb equivocate, evade, prevaricate, quibble, shuffle. • n artifice, cavil, evasion, quibble, subterfuge, trick.

dogma n article, belief, creed, doctrine, opinion, precept, principle, tenet.

dogmatic adj authoritative, categorical, formal, settled; arrogant, confident, dictatorial, imperious, magisterial, opinionated, oracular, overbearing, peremptory, positive; doctrinal.

domain n authority, dominion, jurisdiction, province, sway; dominion, empire, realm, territory; lands, estate; branch, department, province, realm, region.

domestic n charwoman, help, home help, maid,

servant. • *adj* domiciliary, family, home, household, private; domesticated; internal, intestine.

domesticate *vb* tame; adopt, assimilate, familiarise, naturalise.

domicile *vb* domiciliate, dwell, inhabit, live, remain, reside. • *n* abode, dwelling, habitation, harbour, home, house, residence.

dominant *adj* ascendant, ascending, chief, controlling, governing, influential, outstanding, paramount, predominant, pre-eminent, preponderant, presiding, prevailing, ruling.

dominate *vb* control, rule, sway; command, overlook, overtop, surmount.

domineer *vb* rule, tyrannise; bluster, bully, hector, menace, swagger, swell, threaten.

dominion *n* ascendency, authority, command, control, domain, domination, government, jurisdiction, mastery, rule, sovereignty, supremacy, sway; country, kingdom, realm, region, territory.

donation *n* contribution, dole, gift, grant, gratuity, largesse, offering, present, subscription.

done *adj* accomplished, achieved, effected, executed, performed; completed, concluded, ended, finished, terminated; carried on, transacted; rendered, translated; cooked, prepared; cheated, cozened, hoaxed, swindled; (*with* **for**) damned, dished, *hors de combat*, ruined, spoiled.

double *vb* fold, plait; duplicate, geminate, increase, multiply, repeat; return. • *adj* binary, coupled, geminate, paired; dual, twice, twofold; deceitful, dishonest, double-dealing, false, hollow, insincere, knavish, perfidious, treacherous, two-faced. • *adv* doubly, twice, twofold. • *n* doubling, fold, plait; artifice, manoeuvre, ruse, shift, stratagem, trick, wile; copy, counterpart, twin.

doubt *vb* demur, fluctuate, hesitate, vacillate, waver; distrust, mistrust, query, question, suspect. • *n* dubiety, hesitance, hesitation, indecision, irresolution, question, suspense, uncertainty, vacillation; distrust, misgiving, mistrust, scepticism, suspicion.

doubtful *adj* dubious, hesitating, sceptical, undecided, undetermined, wavering; ambiguous, dubious, enigmatical, equivocal, hazardous, obscure, problematical, unsure; indeterminate, questionable, undecided, unquestioned.

dowdy *adj* awkward, dingy, ill-dressed, shabby, slovenly; old-fashioned, unfashionable.

downcast *adj* chapfallen, crestfallen, dejected, depressed, despondent, discouraged, disheartened, dispirited, downhearted, sad, unhappy.

downfall *n* descent, destruction, fall, ruin.

downhearted *adj* chapfallen, crestfallen, dejected, depressed, despondent, discouraged, disheartened, dispirited, downcast, sad, unhappy.

downright *adj* absolute, categorical, clear, explicit, plain, positive, sheer, simple, undisguised, unequivocal; above-board, artless, blunt, direct, frank, honest, ingenuous, open, sincere, straightforward.

doze *vb* drowse, nap, sleep, slumber.

draft *vb* detach, select; commandeer, conscript, impress; delineate, draw, outline, sketch. • *n* conscription, drawing, selection; delineation, outline, sketch; bill, cheque, order.

drag *vb* draw, haul, pull, tow, tug; trail; linger, loiter. • *n* brake, check, curb, lag, resistance, skid, slackening, slack-off, slowing.

drain *vb* milk, sluice, tap; empty, evacuate, exhaust; dry. • *n* channel, culvert, ditch, sewer, sluice, trench, watercourse; exhaustion.

draw *vb* drag, haul, tow, tug, pull; attract; drain, suck, syphon; extract, extort; breathe in, inhale, inspire; allure, engage, entice, induce, influence, lead, move, persuade; extend, protract, stretch; delineate, depict, sketch; deduce, derive, infer; compose, draft, formulate, frame, prepare.

drawback *n* defect, deficiency, detriment, disadvantage, fault, flaw, imperfection, injury; abatement, allowance, deduction, discount.

dread *vb* apprehend, fear. • *adj* dreadful, frightful, horrible, terrible; awful, venerable. • *n* affright, alarm, apprehension, fear, terror; awe.

dreadful *adj* alarming, appalling, awesome, dire, direful, fearful, formidable, frightful, horrible, horrid, terrible.

dream *vb* fancy, imagine, think. • *n* conceit, day-dream, delusion, fancy, fantasy, hallucination, illusion, imagination, reverie, vision.

dreary *adj* cheerless, chilling, dark, depressing, dismal, drear, gloomy, lonely, lonesome, sad, solitary, sorrowful; boring, dull, monotonous, tedious, tiresome, uninteresting, wearisome.

drench *vb* dowse, drown, saturate, soak, souse, steep, wet; physic, purge.

dress *vb* align, straighten; adjust, arrange, dispose; fit, prepare; accoutre, apparel, array, attire, clothe, robe, rig; adorn, bedeck, deck, decorate, drape, embellish, trim. • *n* apparel, attire, clothes, clothing, costume, garb, guise, garments, habiliment, habit, raiment, suit, toilet.

drift *vb* accumulate, drive, float, wander. • *n* bearing, course, direction; aim, design, intent, intention, mark, object, proposal, purpose, scope, tendency; detritus, deposit, diluvium; gallery, passage, tunnel; current, rush, sweep; heap.

drill *vb* bore, perforate, pierce; discipline, exercise, instruct, teach, train. • *n* borer; discipline, exercise, training.

drink *vb* imbibe, sip, swill; carouse, indulge, revel, tipple, tope; swallow, quaff; absorb. • *n* beverage, draught, liquid, potation, potion; dram, nip, sip, snifter, refreshment.

drip *vb* dribble, drop, leak, trickle; distil, filter, percolate; ooze, reek, seep, weep. • *n* dribble, drippings, drop, leak, leakage, leaking, trickle, tricklet; bore, nuisance, wet blanket.

drive *vb* hurl, impel, propel, send, shoot, thrust;

actuate, incite, press, urge; coerce, compel, constrain, force, harass, oblige, overburden, press, rush; go, guide, ride, travel; aim, intend. • n effort, energy, pressure; airing, riding; road.

drivel vb babble, blether, dote, drool, slaver, slobber. • n balderdash, drivelling, fatuity, nonsense, prating, rubbish, slaver, stuff, twaddle.

drizzle vb mizzle, rain, shower, sprinkle. • n haar, mist, mizzle, rain, sprinkling.

drone vb dawdle, drawl, idle, loaf, lounge; hum. • n idler, loafer, lounger, sluggard.

droop vb fade, wilt, wither; decline, fail, faint, flag, languish, sink, weaken; bend, hang.

drop vb distil, drip, shed; decline, depress, descend, dump, lower, sink; abandon, desert, forsake, forswear, leave, omit, relinquish, quit; cease, discontinue, intermit, remit; fall, precipitate. • n bead, globule; earring, pendant.

drought n aridity, drouth, dryness, thirstiness.

drown vb deluge, engulf, flood, immerse, inundate, overflow, sink, submerge, swamp; overcome, overpower, overwhelm.

drowse vb doze, nap, sleep, slumber, snooze.

drowsy adj dozy, sleepy; comatose, lethargic, stupid; lulling, soporific.

drudge vb fag, grub, grind, plod, slave, toil, work. • n fag, grind, hack, hard worker, menial, plodder, scullion, slave, toiler, worker.

drug vb dose, medicate; disgust, surfeit. • n medicine, physic, remedy; poison.

drunk adj drunken, inebriated, intoxicated, maudlin, soaked, tipsy; ablaze, aflame, delirious, fervent, suffused. • n alcoholic, boozer, dipsomaniac, drunkard, inebriate, lush, soak; bacchanal, bender, binge.

dry vb dehydrate, desiccate, drain, exsiccate, parch. • adj desiccated, dried, juiceless, sapless, unmoistened; arid, droughty, parched; drouthy, thirsty; barren, dull, insipid, jejune, plain, pointless, tame, tedious, tiresome, unembellished, uninteresting, vapid; cutting, keen, sarcastic.

dubious adj doubtful, fluctuating, hesitant, uncertain, undecided, unsettled, wavering; ambiguous, equivocal, questionable, uncertain.

duck vb dip, dive, immerse, plunge, submerge, souse; bend, bow, dodge, stoop.

duct n canal, channel, conduit, pipe, tube; blood-vessel.

due adj owed, owing; appropriate, becoming, befitting, bounden, fit, proper, suitable, right.

• adv dead, direct, directly, exactly, just, right, squarely, straight. • n claim, debt, desert, right.

dull vb blunt; benumb, besot, deaden, hebetate, obtund, paralyse, stupefy; dampen, deject, depress, discourage, dishearten, dispirit; allay, alleviate, assuage, mitigate, moderate, quiet, soften; deaden, dim, sully, tarnish. • adj blockish, brutish, doltish, obtuse, stolid, stupid, unintelligent; apathetic, callous, dead, insensible, passionless, phlegmatic, unfeeling, unimpassioned, unresponsive; heavy, inactive, inert, lifeless, slow, sluggish; blunt, obtuse; cheerless, dismal, dreary, gloomy, sad, sombre; dim, lack-lustre, lustreless, matt, obscure, opaque, tarnished; dry, flat, insipid, irksome, jejune, prosy, tedious, tiresome, uninteresting, wearisome.

duly adv befittingly, decorously, fitly, properly, rightly; regularly.

dumb adj inarticulate, mute, silent, soundless, speechless, voiceless.

dumbfound vb amaze, astonish, astound, bewilder, confound, confuse, nonplus, pose.

dupe vb beguile, cheat, chouse, circumvent, cozen, deceive, delude, gull, hoodwink, outwit, overreach, swindle, trick. • n gull, simpleton.

duplicate vb copy, double, repeat, replicate, reproduce. • adj doubled, twofold. • n copy, counterpart, facsimile, replica, transcript.

duplicity n artifice, chicanery, circumvention, deceit, deception, dishonesty, dissimulation, double-dealing, falseness, fraud, guile, perfidy.

durable adj abiding, constant, continuing, enduring, firm, lasting, permanent, stable.

duration n continuance, continuation, permanency, perpetuation, prolongation; period, time.

duress n captivity, confinement, constraint, durance, hardship, restraint; compulsion.

dutiful adj duteous, obedient, submissive; deferential, respectful, reverential.

duty n allegiance, devoirs, obligation, responsibility, reverence; business, engagement, function, office, service; custom, excise, impost, tariff, tax, toll.

dwell vb abide, inhabit, live, lodge, remain, reside, rest, sojourn, stay, stop, tarry, tenant.

dwindle vb decrease, diminish, lessen, shrink; decay, decline, deteriorate, pine, sink.

dye vb colour, stain, tinge. • n cast, colour, hue, shade, stain, tinge, tint.

dynasty n dominion, empire, government, rule.

E

eager adj agog, avid, anxious, desirous, fain, greedy, impatient, keen, longing, yearning; animat-

ed, ardent, earnest, enthusiastic, fervent, forward, glowing, impetuous, sanguine, vehement, zealous.

ear *n* attention, hearing, heed, regard.

early *adj* opportune, seasonable, timely; forward, premature; dawning, matutinal. • *adv* anon, beforehand, betimes, shortly, soon.

earn *vb* acquire, gain, get, obtain, procure, realise, reap, win; deserve, merit.

earnest *adj* animated, ardent, eager, cordial, fervent, fervid, glowing, hearty, impassioned, warm, zealous; fixed, intent, steady; sincere, true, truthful; important, momentous, serious, weighty. • *n* reality, seriousness, truth; foretaste, pledge, promise; handsel, payment.

earnings *npl* emoluments, income, pay, proceeds, profits, remuneration, reward, salary.

earth *n* globe, orb, planet, world; clay, clod, dirt, glebe, ground, humus, land, loam, sod, soil, turf; mankind, world.

earthly *adj* terrestrial; base, carnal, earthborn, low, gross, grovelling, sensual, sordid, unspiritual, worldly; bodily, material, mundane, natural.

earthy *adj* clayey, earth-like, terrene; earthly, terrestrial; coarse, gross, material, unrefined.

ease *vb* disburden, disencumber, pacify, quiet, relieve, still; abate, allay, alleviate, appease, assuage, diminish, mitigate, soothe; loosen, release; facilitate, favour. • *n* leisure, quiescence, repose, rest; calmness, content, contentment, enjoyment, happiness, peace, quiet, quietness, quietude, relief, repose, satisfaction, serenity, tranquillity; easiness, facility, readiness; flexibility, freedom, liberty, unconcern, unconstraint.

easy *adj* light; careless, comfortable, contented, effortless, painless, quiet, satisfied, tranquil, untroubled; accommodating, complaisant, compliant, complying, facile, indolent, manageable, pliant, submissive, tractable, yielding; graceful, informal, natural, unconstrained; flowing, ready, smooth, unaffected; gentle, lenient, mild, moderate; affluent, comfortable, loose, unconcerned.

eat *vb* chew, consume, devour, engorge, ingest, ravage, swallow; consume, corrode, demolish, erode; breakfast, dine, feed, lunch, sup.

ebb *vb* abate, recede, retire, subside; decay, decline, decrease, degenerate, deteriorate, sink, wane. • *n* refluence, reflux, regress, regression, retrocedence, retrocession, retrogression, return; caducity, decay, decline, degeneration, deterioration, wane, waning; abatement, decrease.

eccentric *adj* decentred, parabolic; aberrant, abnormal, anomalous, cranky, erratic, fantastic, irregular, odd, outlandish, peculiar, singular, strange, uncommon, unnatural, wayward, whimsical. • *n* crank, curiosity, original.

echo *vb* reply, resound, reverberate, ring; re-echo, repeat. • *n* answer, repetition, reverberation; imitation.

eclipse *vb* cloud, darken, dim, obscure, overshadow, veil; annihilate, annul, blot out, extinguish. • *n* clouding, concealment, darkening, dimming, disappearance, hiding, obscuration, occultation, shrouding, vanishing, veiling; annihilation, blotting out, destruction, extinction, extinguishment, obliteration.

economise *vb* husband, save; retrench.

economy *n* frugality, husbandry, parsimony, providence, retrenchment, saving, skimping, stinginess, thrift, thriftiness; administration, arrangement, management, method, order, plan, regulation, system; dispensation.

ecstasy *n* frenzy, madness, paroxysm, trance; delight, gladness, joy, rhapsody, rapture.

edge *vb* sharpen; border, fringe, rim. • *n* border, brim, brink, border, bound, crest, fringe, hem, lip, margin, rim, verge; animation, intensity, interest, keenness, sharpness, zest; acrimony, bitterness, gall, sharpness, sting.

edible *adj* eatable, esculent, wholesome.

edict *n* act, command, constitution, decision, decree, law, mandate, manifesto, notice, order, ordinance, proclamation, regulation, statute.

edify *vb* educate, elevate, enlightenment, improve, inform, instruct, nurture, teach, upbuild.

educate *vb* breed, cultivate, develop, discipline, drill, edify, exercise, indoctrinate, inform, instruct, mature, nurture, rear, school, teach, train.

education *n* breeding, cultivation, culture, development, discipline, drilling, indoctrination, instruction, nurture, pedagogics, schooling, teaching, training, tuition.

eerie *adj* awesome, fearful, frightening, strange, uncanny, weird.

effect *vb* cause, create, effectuate, produce; accomplish, achieve, carry, compass, complete, conclude, consummate, contrive, do, execute, force, negotiate, perform, realise, work. • *n* consequence, event, fruit, issue, outcome, result; efficiency, fact, force, power, reality; validity, weight; drift, import, intent, meaning, purport, significance, tenor.

effective *adj* able, active, adequate, competent, convincing, effectual, sufficient; cogent, efficacious, energetic, forcible, potent, powerful.

effectual *adj* operative, successful; active, effective, efficacious, efficient.

efficacious *adj* active, adequate, competent, effective, effectual, efficient, energetic, operative.

efficient *adj* active, capable, competent, effective, effectual, efficacious, operative, potent; able, energetic, ready, skilful.

effort *n* application, attempt, endeavour, essay, exertion, pains, spurt, strain, strife, stretch, struggle, trial, trouble.

effrontery *n* assurance, audacity, boldness, disrespect, hardihood, impudence, incivility, insolence, presumption, rudeness, shamelessness.

effusion *n* discharge, efflux, emission, gush,

outpouring; shedding, spilling, waste; address, speech, talk, utterance.

egotistic(al) *adj* bumptious, conceited, egoistical, opinionated, self-asserting, self-admiring, self-centred, self-important, vain.

eject *vb* belch, discharge, disgorge, emit, evacuate, puke, spew, spit, spout, spurt, void, vomit; bounce, cashier, discharge, dismiss, disposes, eliminate, evict, expel, fire, oust; banish, reject.

elaborate *vb* develop, improve, mature, produce, refine, ripen. • *adj* complicated, decorated, detailed, dressy, laboured, laborious, ornate.

elastic *adj* rebounding, recoiling, resilient, springy; buoyant, recuperative.

elder *adj* older, senior; ranking, senior; ancient, earlier, olden. • *n* ancestor, senior; presbyter, prior, senator, senior.

elect *vb* appoint, choose, cull, designate, pick, prefer, select. • *adj* choice, chosen, picked, selected; appointed, elected; predestinated.

election *n* appointment, choice, preference, selection; alternative, choice, freedom, freewill, liberty; predestination.

elector *n* chooser, constituent, selector, voter.

electrify *vb* charge, galvanise; astonish, enchant, excite, rouse, startle, stir, thrill.

elegant *adj* beautiful, chaste, classical, dainty, graceful, fine, handsome, neat, symmetrical, tasteful, trim, well-made, well-proportioned; accomplished, courtly, cultivated, fashionable, genteel, polished, polite, refined.

element *n* basis, component, constituent, factor, germ, ingredient, part, principle, rudiment, unit; environment, milieu, sphere.

elementary *adj* primordial, simple, uncombined, uncomplicated, uncompounded; basic, component, fundamental, initial, primary, rudimental, rudimentary.

elevate *vb* erect, hoist, lift, raise; advance, aggrandise, exalt, promote; dignify, ennoble, exalt, animate, cheer, elate, excite, exhilarate, rouse.

eligible *adj* desirable, preferable; qualified, suitable, worthy.

eliminate *vb* disengage, eradicate, exclude, expel, eradicate, remove, separate; omit, reject.

elope *vb* abscond, bolt, decamp, disappear.

eloquence *n* fluency, oratory, rhetoric.

elucidate *vb* clarify, demonstrate, explain, expound, illuminate, illustrate, interpret, unfold.

elusive *adj* deceptive, deceitful, delusive, evasive, fallacious, fraudulent, illusory; equivocatory, equivocating, shuffling.

emancipate *vb* deliver, discharge, disenthral, enfranchise, free, liberate, manumit, release, unchain, unfetter, unshackle.

embargo *vb* ban, bar, blockade, debar, exclude, prohibit, proscribe, restrict, stop, withhold. • *n* ban, bar, blockade, exclusion, hindrance, imped-

iment, prohibition, prohibitory, proscription, restraint, restriction, stoppage.

embarrass *vb* beset, entangle, perplex; annoy, clog, bother, distress, hamper, harass, involve, plague, trouble, vex; abash, confound, confuse, discomfit, disconcert, dumbfounded, mortify, nonplus, pose, shame.

embellish *vb* adorn, beautify, bedeck, deck, decorate, emblazon, enhance, enrich, garnish.

embezzle *vb* appropriate, defalcate, filch, misappropriate, peculate, pilfer, purloin, steal.

embitter *vb* aggravate, envenom, exacerbate; anger, enrage, exasperate, madden.

emblem *n* badge, cognisance, device, mark, representation, sign, symbol, token, type.

embrace *vb* clasp; accept, seize, welcome; comprehend, comprise, contain, cover, embody, encircle, enclose, encompass, enfold, hold, include. • *n* clasp, fold, hug.

emerge *vb* rise; emanate, escape, issue; appear.

emergency *n* crisis, difficulty, dilemma, exigency, extremity, necessity, pass, pinch, push, strait, urgency; conjuncture, crisis, pass.

emigration *n* departure, exodus, migration.

eminence *n* elevation, hill, projection, prominence, protuberance; celebrity, conspicuousness, distinction, exaltation, fame, loftiness, note, preferment, prominence, reputation, repute, renown.

eminent *adj* elevated, high, lofty; celebrated, conspicuous, distinguished, exalted, famous, illustrious, notable, prominent, remarkable.

emit *vb* breathe out, dart, discharge, eject, emanate, exhale, gust, jet, shoot, spurt, squirt.

emotion *n* agitation, excitement, feeling, passion, perturbation, sentiment, sympathy.

emphasis *n* accent, stress; force, importance, impressiveness, moment, significance, weight.

emphatic *adj* decided, distinct, earnest, energetic, expressive, forcible, impressive, intensive, positive, significant, strong, unequivocal.

empire *n* domain, dominion, sovereignty, supremacy; authority, command, control, government, rule, sway.

employ *vb* busy, devote, engage, engross, enlist, exercise, occupy, retain; apply, commission, use.

employment *n* avocation, business, calling, craft, employ, engagement, occupation, profession, pursuit, trade, vocation, work.

empty *vb* deplete, drain, evacuate, exhaust; discharge. • *adj* blank, hollow, unoccupied, vacant, vacuous, void; deplete, destitute, devoid, hungry; unfilled, unfurnished, unsupplied; unsatisfactory, unsatisfying, unsubstantial, useless, vain; clear, deserted, desolate, exhausted, free, unburdened, unloaded, waste; foolish, frivolous, inane, senseless, silly.

enable *vb* authorise, capacitate, commission, empower, fit, permit, prepare, qualify, sanction.

enact *vb* authorise, command, decree, establish, decree, ordain, order, sanction; act, perform, personate, play, represent.

enchant *vb* beguile, bewitch, charm, delude, fascinate; captivate, catch, enamour, win; beatify, delight, enrapture, rapture, ravish, transport.

enchantment *n* charm, conjuration, incantation, magic, necromancy, sorcery, spell, witchery; bliss, delight, fascination, rapture, ravishment, transport.

enclose *vb* circumscribe, corral, coop, embosom, encircle, encompass, environ, fence in, hedge, include, pen, shut in, surround; box, cover, encase, envelop, wrap.

encounter *vb* confront, face, meet; attack, combat, contend, engage, strive, struggle. • *n* assault, attack, clash, collision, meeting, onset; action, affair, battle, brush, combat, conflict, contest, dispute, engagement, skirmish.

encourage *vb* animate, assure, cheer, comfort, console, embolden, enhearten, fortify, hearten, incite, inspirit, instigate, reassure, stimulate, strengthen; aid, advance, approve, foster, further, help, patronise, promote, support.

encumbrance *n* burden, clog, deadweight, drag, embarrassment, hampering, hindrance, impediment, incubus, load; claim, debt, liability.

end *vb* abolish, close, conclude, discontinue, dissolve, drop, finish, stop, terminate; annihilate, destroy, kill; cease, terminate. • *n* extremity, tip; cessation, close, denouement, ending, expiration, finale, finis, finish, last, period, stoppage, wind-up; completion, conclusion, consummation; annihilation, catastrophe, destruction, dissolution; bound, limit, termination, terminus; consequence, event, issue, result, settlement, sequel, upshot; fragment, remnant, scrap, stub, tag, tail; aim, design, goal, intent, intention, object, objective, purpose.

endanger *vb* commit, compromise, hazard, imperil, jeopardise, peril, risk.

endear *vb* attach, bind, captivate, charm, win.

endeavour *vb* aim, attempt, essay, labour, seek, strive, struggle, study, try. • *n* aim, attempt, conatus, effort, essay, exertion, trial, struggle, trial.

endless *adj* boundless, illimitable, immeasurable, indeterminable, infinite, interminable, limitless, unlimited; dateless, eternal, everlasting, never-ending, perpetual, unending; deathless, ever-enduring, eternal, ever-living, immortal, imperishable, undying.

endorse *vb* approve, back, confirm, guarantee, indorse, ratify, sanction, superscribe, support, visé, vouch for, warrant; superscribe.

endow *vb* bequeath, clothe, confer, dower, endue, enrich, gift, indue, invest, supply.

endowment *n* bequest, boon, bounty, gift, grant, largesse, present; foundation, fund, property, revenue; ability, aptitude, capability, capacity, faculty, genius, gift, parts, power, qualification, quality, talent.

endurance *n* abiding, bearing, sufferance, suffering, tolerance, toleration; backbone, bottom, forbearance, fortitude, guts, patience.

endure *vb* bear, support, sustain; experience, suffer, undergo, weather; abide, brook, permit, pocket, swallow, tolerate, stomach, submit, withstand; continue, last, persist, remain, wear.

enemy *n* adversary, foe; antagonist, foeman, opponent, rival.

energetic *adj* active, effective, efficacious, enterprising, forceful, forcible, hearty, potent, powerful, strenuous, strong, vigorous.

energy *n* activity, dash, drive, efficacy, efficiency, force, go, impetus, intensity, mettle, might, potency, power, strength, verve, vim; animation, life, manliness, spirit, spiritedness, vigour, zeal.

enforce *vb* compel, constrain, exact, force, oblige, require, urge.

engage *vb* bind, commit, obligate, pledge, promise; affiance, betroth, plight, promise; book, brief, employ, enlist, hire, retain; arrest, allure, attach, draw, entertain, fix, gain, win; busy, employ, engross, occupy; attack, encounter; combat, contend, contest, fight, interlock, struggle; embark, enlist; agree, bargain, promise, stipulate, undertake, warrant.

engagement *n* appointment, assurance, contract, obligation, pledge, promise, stipulation; affiancing, betrothal, plighting; avocation, business, calling, employment, enterprise, occupation; action, battle, combat, encounter, fight.

engrave *vb* carve, chisel, cut, etch, grave, hatch, incite, sculpture; grave, impress, imprint, infix.

engross *vb* absorb, engage, occupy, take up; buy up, forestall, monopolise.

enhance *vb* advance, aggravate, augment, elevate, heighten, increase, intensify, raise, swell.

enigma *n* conundrum, mystery, problem, puzzle, riddle.

enigmatic *adj* ambiguous, dark, doubtful, equivocal, hidden, incomprehensible, mysterious, mystic, obscure, occult, perplexing, puzzling, recondite, uncertain, unintelligible.

enjoyment *n* delight, delectation, gratification, happiness, indulgence, pleasure, satisfaction.

enlarge *vb* amplify, augment, broaden, extend, dilate, distend, expand, increase, magnify, widen; aggrandise, ennoble; expand, extend, increase, swell.

enlighten *vb* illume, illuminate, illumine; counsel, educate, civilise, inform, instruct, teach.

enlist *vb* enrol, levy, recruit, register; enrol, list.

enliven *vb* animate, invigorate, quicken, reanimate, rouse, wake; exhilarate, cheer, brighten, delight, elate, gladden, inspire, inspirit, rouse.

enmity n animosity, aversion, bitterness, hate, hatred, hostility, ill-will, malevolence, rancour.

enormity n atrociousness, atrocity, depravity, flagitiousness, heinousness, nefariousness, outrageousness, villainy, wickedness.

enormous adj abnormal, exceptional, inordinate, irregular; colossal, Cyclopean, elephantine, Herculean, huge, immense, monstrous, vast, gigantic, prodigious, titanic, tremendous.

enough adj abundant, adequate, ample, plenty, sufficient. • adv satisfactorily, sufficiently. • n abundance, plenty, sufficiency.

enrage vb anger, chafe, exasperate, incense, inflame, infuriate, irritate, madden, provoke.

enrich vb endow; adorn, deck, decorate, embellish, grace, ornament.

enrol vb catalogue, engage, engross, enlist, list, register; chronicle, record.

enterprise n adventure, attempt, cause, effort, endeavour, essay, project, undertaking, scheme, venture; activity, adventurousness, daring, dash, energy, initiative, readiness, push.

enterprising adj adventurous, audacious, bold, daring, dashing, venturesome; active, adventurous, alert, efficient, energetic, prompt, resourceful, smart, spirited, stirring, strenuous, zealous

entertain vb fete, receive, regale, treat; cherish, foster, harbour, hold, lodge, shelter; admit, consider; amuse, cheer, divert, please, recreate.

entertainment n hospitality; banquet, collation, feast, festival, reception, treat; amusement, diversion, pastime, recreation, sport.

enthusiasm n ecstasy, exaltation, fanaticism; ardour, earnestness, devotion, eagerness, fervour, passion, warmth, zeal.

enthusiast n bigot, devotee, fan, fanatic, zealot; dreamer, visionary.

entice vb allure, attract, bait, cajole, coax, decoy, inveigle, lure, persuade, prevail on, seduce, tempt, wheedle, wile.

entire adj complete, integrated, perfect, unbroken, undiminished, undivided, unimpaired, whole; complete, full, plenary, thorough, unalloyed; mere, pure, sheer, unalloyed, unmingled, unmitigated, unmixed.

entitle vb call, characterise, christen, denominate, designate, dub, name style; empower, enable, fit for, qualify for.

entrance[1] n access, approach, avenue, incoming, ingress; adit, avenue, aperture, door, doorway, entry, gate, hallway, inlet, lobby, mouth, passage, portal, stile, vestibule; beginning, commencement, debut, initiation, introduction; admission, entrée.

entrance[2] vb bewitch, captivate, charm, delight, enchant, enrapture, fascinate, ravish, transport.

entreaty n adjuration, appeal, importunity, petition, prayer, request, suit, supplication.

entrust vb commit, confide, consign.

enumerate vb calculate, cite, compute, count, detail, mention, number, numerate, reckon, recount, specify, tell.

envelop vb enfold, enwrap, fold, pack, wrap; cover, encircle, encompass, enfold, enshroud, fold, hide, involve, surround.

envelope n capsule, case, covering, integument, shroud, skin, wrapper, veil, vesture, wrap.

envoy n ambassador, legate, minister, plenipotentiary; courier, messenger.

envy vb hate; begrudge, grudge; covet, emulate, desire. • n enviousness, hate, hatred, ill-will, jealousy, malice, spite; grudge, grudging.

ephemeral adj brief, diurnal, evanescent, fleeting, flitting, fugacious, fugitive, momentary, occasional, short-lived, transient, transitory.

epidemic adj general, pandemic, prevailing, prevalent. • n outbreak, pandemia, pestilence, plague, spread, wave.

epigrammatic adj antithetic, concise, laconic, piquant, poignant, pointed, sharp, terse.

epitome n abbreviation, abridgement, abstract, breviary, brief, comment, compendium, condensation, conspectus, digest, summary, synopsis.

epitomise vb abbreviate, abridge, abstract, condense, contract, curtail, cut, reduce, shorten.

equable adj calm, equal, even, even-tempered, regular, steady, uniform, serene, tranquil.

equal vb equalise, even, match. • adj alike, coordinate, equivalent, like, tantamount; even, level, equable, regular, uniform; equitable, even-handed, fair, impartial, just, unbiased; co-extensive, commensurate, corresponding, parallel, proportionate; adequate, competent, fit, sufficient. • n compeer, fellow, match, peer; rival.

equanimity n calmness, composure, coolness, peace, regularity, self-possession, serenity.

equip vb appoint, arm, furnish, provide, rig, supply; accoutre, array, dress.

equitable adj even-handed, candid, honest, impartial, just, unbiased, unprejudiced, upright; adequate, fair, proper, reasonable, right.

equity n fairness, impartiality, justice, rectitude, reasonableness, righteousness.

equivalent adj commensurate, equal, equipollent, tantamount; interchangeable, synonymous. • n complement, coordinate, counterpart, double, equal, fellow, like, match, parallel, pendant.

era n age, date, epoch, period, time.

eradicate vb extirpate, root, uproot; abolish, annihilate, destroy, obliterate.

erase vb blot, cancel, delete, efface, expunge, obliterate, scrape out.

erasure n cancellation, cancelling, effacing, expunging, obliteration.

erect vb build, construct, raise, rear; create, establish, form, found, institute, plant. • adj standing, unrecumbent, uplifted, upright; elevated, vertical, perpendicular, straight; bold, firm, undaunted, undismayed, unshaken, unterrified.

erode vb canker, consume, corrode, destroy, eat away, fret, rub.

erotic adj amorous, amatory, arousing, seductive, stimulating, titillating.

err vb deviate, ramble, rove, stray, wander; blunder, misjudge, mistake; fall, lapse, nod, offend, sin, stumble, trespass, trip.

errand n charge, commission, mandate, message, mission, purpose.

erratic adj nomadic, rambling, roving, wandering; moving, planetary; abnormal, capricious, deviating, eccentric, irregular, odd, queer.

erroneous adj false, incorrect, inaccurate, inexact, mistaken, untrue, wrong.

error n blunder, fallacy, inaccuracy, misapprehension, mistake, oversight; delinquency, fault, iniquity, misdeed, misdoing, misstep, obliquity, offence, shortcoming, sin, transgression.

erudition n knowledge, learning, scholarship.

eruption n explosion, outbreak, outburst; rash.

escape vb avoid, elude, evade, flee from, shun; abscond, bolt, decamp, flee, fly; slip. • n flight; release; passage, passing; leakage.

escort vb convey, guard, protect; accompany, attend, conduct. • n attendant, bodyguard, cavalier, companion, convoy, gallant, guard, squire; protection, safe conduct; attendance, company.

especial adj chief, distinguished, marked, particular, peculiar, principal, special, specific, uncommon, unusual.

espouse vb betroth, plight, promise; marry, wed; adopt, champion, defend, embrace, maintain, support.

essay[1] vb attempt, endeavour, try. • n aim, attempt, effort, endeavour, exertion, struggle, trial.

essay[2] n article, composition, disquisition, dissertation, paper, thesis.

essence n nature, quintessence, substance; extract, part; odour, perfume, scent; being, entity.

essential adj fundamental, indispensable, important, inward, intrinsic, necessary, requisite, vital; diffusible, pure, rectified, volatile.

establish vb fix, secure, set, settle; decree, enact, ordain; build, constitute, erect, form, found, institute, organise, originate, pitch, plant, raise; ensconce, ground, install, place, plant, root, secure; approve, confirm, ratify, sanction; prove, substantiate, verify.

estate n condition, state; position, rank, standing; division, order; effects, fortune, possessions, property; interest.

esteem vb appreciate, estimate, rate, reckon, value; admire, appreciate, honour, like, prize, respect, revere, reverence, value, venerate, worship; account, believe, consider, deem, fancy,

hold, imagine, suppose, regard, think. • n account, appreciation, consideration, estimate, estimation, judgement, opinion, reckoning, valuation; credit, honour, regard, respect, reverence.

estimable adj appreciable, calculable, computable; admirable, credible, deserving, excellent, good, meritorious, valuable, worthy.

estimate vb appraise, appreciate, esteem, prise, rate, value; assess, calculate, compute, count, gauge, judge, reckon. • n estimation, judgement, valuation; calculation, computation.

estimation n appreciation, appeasement, estimate, valuation; esteem, estimate, judgement, opinion; honour, regard, respect, reverence.

estrange vb withdraw, withhold; alienate, divert; disaffect, destroy.

eternal adj absolute, inevitable, necessary; abiding, ceaseless, endless, everlasting, incessant, interminable, never-ending, perennial, perpetual, sempiternal, unceasing, unending; deathless, immortal, imperishable, incorruptible, indestructible, undying; immutable, unchangeable; ceaseless, continual, continuous, persistent, uninterrupted.

eulogy n discourse, eulogium, panegyric, speech; applause, encomium, commendation, eulogium, laudation, praise.

evacuate vb empty; discharge, clean out, clear out, eject, excrete, expel, purge, void; abandon, desert, forsake, leave, quit, relinquish, withdraw.

evade vb elude, escape; avoid, decline, dodge, funk, shun; baffle, elude, foil; dodge, equivocate, fence, palter, prevaricate, quibble, shuffle.

evaporate vb distil, volatilise; dehydrate, dry, vaporise; disperse, dissolve, fade, vanish.

even vb balance, equalise, harmonise, symmetrise; align, flatten, flush, level, smooth, square. • adj flat, horizontal, level, plane, smooth; calm, composed, equable, equal, peaceful, placid, regular, steady, uniform, unruffled; direct, equitable, fair, impartial, just, straightforward. • adv exactly, just, verily; likewise.

evening n dusk, eventide, nightfall, sunset, twilight.

event n circumstance, episode, fact, happening, incident, occurrence; conclusion, consequence, end, issue, outcome, result, sequel, termination.

eventful adj critical, important, memorable, momentous, remarkable, signal, stirring.

eventual adj final, last, ultimate; conditional, contingent, possible. ever adv always, aye, constantly, continually, eternally, evermore, forever, incessantly, perpetually, unceasingly.

everlasting adj ceaseless, constant, continual, endless, eternal, ever-during, incessant, interminable, never-ceasing, never-ending, perpetual, unceasing, unending, uninterrupted.

everyday adj accustomed, common, commonplace, customary, habitual, routine, usual.

evict *vb* dispossess, eject, thrust out.

evidence *vb* evince, manifest, prove, show, testify, vouch. • *n* affirmation, attestation, confirmation, corroboration, deposition, grounds, indication, proof, testimony, token, witness.

evident *adj* apparent, bald, clear, conspicuous, distinct, downright, incontestable, indisputable, manifest, obvious, open, overt, palpable, patent, plain, unmistakable.

evil *adj* bad, ill; bad, base, corrupt, malicious, malevolent, malign, nefarious, perverse, sinful, vicious, vile, wicked, wrong; bad, deleterious, baleful, baneful, destructive, harmful, hurtful, injurious, mischievous, noxious, pernicious; adverse, bad, calamitous, disastrous, unfortunate, unhappy, unpropitious, woeful. • *n* calamity, disaster, ill, misery, misfortune, pain, reverse, sorrow, suffering, woe; badness, baseness, corruption, depravity, malignity, sin, viciousness, wickedness; bale, bane, blast, canker, curse, harm, ill, injury, mischief, wrong.

evolve *vb* develop, educe, exhibit, expand, open, unfold, unroll.

exact *vb* elicit, extort, mulch, require, squeeze; ask, claim, compel, demand, enforce, requisition, take. • *adj* rigid, rigorous, scrupulous, severe, strict; diametric, express, faultless, precise, true; accurate, close, correct, definite, faithful, literal, undeviating; accurate, critical, delicate, fine, nice, sensitive; careful, methodical, precise, punctilious, orderly, punctual, regular.

exacting *adj* critical, difficult, exactive, rigid.

exaggerate *vb* enlarge, magnify, overcharge, overcolour, overstate, romance, strain, stretch.

exalted *adj* elated, elevated, high, highflown, lofty, lordly, magnificent, prove.

examination *n* inspection, observation; exploration, inquiry, inquisition, investigation, perusal, research, search, scrutiny, survey; catechism, probation, review, test, trial.

examine *vb* inspect, observe; canvass, consider, explore, inquire, investigate, scrutinise, study, test; catechise, interrogate.

example *n* archetype, copy, model, pattern, piece, prototype, representative, sample, sampler, specimen, standard; exemplification, illustration, instance, precedent, warning.

exasperate *vb* affront, anger, chafe, enrage, incense, irritate, nettle, offend, provoke, vex.

exasperation *n* annoyance, exacerbation, irritation, provocation; anger, fury, ire, passion, rage, wrath; aggravation, heightening, increase.

exceed *vb* cap, overstep, surpass, transcend; excel, outdo, outstrip, outvie, pass, surpass.

excel *vb* beat, eclipse, outdo, outrival, outstrip, outvie, surpass; cap, exceed, surpass, transcend.

excellent *adj* admirable, choice, crack, eminent, first-rate, prime, sterling, superior, tiptop, transcendent; deserving, estimable, praiseworthy, virtuous, worthy.

except *vb* exclude, leave out, omit, reject. • *conj* unless. • *prep* bar, but, excepting, save.

exceptional *adj* aberrant, abnormal, anomalous, exceptive, irregular, peculiar, rare, special, strange, superior, uncommon, unusual.

excess *adj* excessive, unnecessary, redundant, spare, superfluous, surplus. • *n* disproportion, fulsomeness, glut, oversupply, plethora, redundance, redundancy, surfeit, superabundance, superfluity; overplus, remainder, surplus; debauchery, dissipation, dissoluteness, intemperance, immoderation, overindulgence, unrestraint; extravagance, immoderation, overdoing.

excessive *adj* disproportionate, exuberant, superabundant, superfluous, undue; extravagant, enormous, inordinate, outrageous, unreasonable; extreme, immoderate, intemperate; vehement, violent.

exchange *vb* barter, change, commute, shuffle, substitute, swap, trade, truck; bandy, interchange. • *n* barter, change, commutation, dealing, shuffle, substitution, trade, traffic; interchange, reciprocity; bazaar, bourse, fair, market.

excise[1] *n* capitation, customs, dues, duty, tariff, tax, taxes, toll.

excise[2] *vb* cancel, cut, delete, edit, efface, eradicate, erase, expunge, extirpate, remove.

excitable *adj* impressible, nervous, sensitive, susceptible; choleric, hasty, hot-headed, hot-tempered, irascible, irritable, passionate.

excite *vb* animate, arouse, awaken, brew, evoke, impel, incite, inflame, instigate, kindle, move, prompt, provoke, rouse, spur, stimulate; create, raise; agitate, discompose, disturb, provoke.

excitement *n* excitation, exciting; incitement, motive, stimulus; activity, agitation, bustle, commotion, disturbance, ferment, flutter, perturbation, sensation, stir, tension; choler, heat, irritation, passion, violence, warmth.

exclaim *vb* call, cry, declare, ejaculate, shout.

exclude *vb* ban, bar, blackball, debar, ostracise, preclude, reject; hinder, prevent, prohibit, restrain, withhold; except, omit; eject, eliminate.

exclusive *adj* debarring, excluding; illiberal, narrow, narrow-minded, selfish, uncharitable; aristocratic, choice, clannish, cliquish, fastidious, fashionable, select; only, special.

excursion *n* drive, expedition, jaunt, journey, ramble, ride, sally, tour, trip, voyage, walk; digression, episode.

excuse *vb* absolve, acquit, exculpate, exonerate, forgive, pardon, remit; extenuate, justify; exempt, free, release; overlook. • *n* absolution, apology, defence, extenuation, justification, plea; colour, disguise, evasion, guise, pretence, pretext, makeshift, semblance, subterfuge.

execute vb accomplish, achieve, carry out, complete. consummate, do, effect, effectuate, finish, perform, perpetrate; administer, enforce, seal, sign; behead, electrocute, guillotine, hang.

executive adj administrative, commanding, controlling, directing, managing, ministerial, officiating, presiding, ruling. • n administrator, director, manager.

exemplary adj assiduous, close, exact, faithful, punctual, punctilious, rigid, rigorous, scrupulous; commendable, correct, good, estimable, excellent, praiseworthy, virtuous; admonitory, condign, monitory, warning.

exempt vb absolve, except, excuse, exonerate, free, release, relieve. • adj absolved, excepted, excused, exempted, free, immune, liberated, privileged, released.

exercise vb apply, busy, employ, exert, praxis, use; effect, exert, produce, wield; break in, discipline, drill, habituate, school, train; practise, prosecute, pursue, use; task, test, try; afflict, agitate, annoy, burden, pain, trouble, try. • n appliance, application, custom, employment, operation, performance, play, plying, practice, usage, use, working; action, activity, effort, exertion, labour, toil, work; discipline, drill, drilling, schooling, training; lesson, study, task, test.

exert vb employ, endeavour, exercise, labour, strain, strive, struggle, toil, use, work.

exhaust vb drain, draw, empty; consume, destroy, dissipate, expend, impoverish, lavish, spend, squander, waste; cripple, debilitate, deplete, disable, enervate, overtire, weaken.

exhibit vb demonstrate, disclose, display, evince, expose, express, indicate, manifest, offer, present, reveal, show; offer, present.

exhibition n demonstration, display, exposition, manifestation, representation, spectacle, show; exposition; allowance, benefaction, grant, pension, scholarship.

exhilarate vb animate, cheer, elate, enliven, gladden, inspire, inspirit, rejoice, stimulate.

exhilaration n animating, cheering, elating, enlivening, gladdening, rejoicing, stimulating; animation, cheer, cheerfulness, gaiety, gladness, glee, good spirits, hilarity, joyousness.

exile vb banish, expatriate, expel, ostracise, proscribe. • n banishment, expatriation, expulsion, ostracism, separation; outcast, refugee.

exist vb be, breathe, live; abide, continue, endure, last, remain.

existence n being, subsisting, subsistence, subsisting; being, creature, entity, essence, thing; animation, continuation, life.

exit vb depart, egress, go, leave. • n departure, withdrawal; death, demise, end; egress.

exorbitant adj enormous, excessive, extravagant, inordinate, unreasonable.

exorcise vb cast out, drive away, expel; deliver, purify; address, conjure.

exotic adj extraneous, foreign; extravagant.

expand vb develop, open, spread, unfold, unfurl; diffuse, enlarge, extend, increase, stretch.

expanse n area, expansion, extent, stretch.

expansion n opening, spreading; diastole, dilation, distension, swelling; development, enlargement, increase; expanse, extent, stretch.

expect vb anticipate, await, calculate, contemplate, forecast, foresee, hope, reckon, rely.

expectancy n expectance, expectation; abeyance, prospect.

expectation n anticipation, expectance, expectancy, hope, prospect; assurance, confidence, presumption, reliance, trust.

expedient adj advisable, appropriate, convenient, desirable, fit, proper, politic, suitable; advantageous, profitable, useful. • n contrivance, device, means, method, resort, resource, scheme, shift, stopgap, substitute.

expedite vb accelerate, advance, dispatch, facilitate, forward, hasten, hurry, press, quicken.

expedition n alacrity, alertness, celerity, dispatch, haste, promptness quickness, speed; enterprise, undertaking; campaign, excursion, journey, march, quest, voyage.

expel vb dislodge, egest, eject, eliminate, excrete; discharge, eject, evacuate, void; bounce, discharge, exclude, excind, fire, oust, relegate, remove; banish, disown, excommunicate, exile, expatriate, ostracise, proscribe, unchurch.

expenditure n disbursement, outlay, outlaying, spending; charge, cost, expenditure, outlay.

expensive adj costly, dear, high-priced.

experience vb endure, suffer; feel, know; encounter, suffer, undergo. • n endurance, practice, trial; evidence, knowledge, proof, testimony.

experienced adj able, accomplished, expert, instructed, knowing, old, practised, qualified, skilful, trained, thoroughbred, versed, veteran, wise.

experiment vb examine, investigate, test, try.

expert adj able, adroit, apt, clever, dextrous, proficient, prompt, quick, ready, skilful. • n adept, authority, connoisseur, crack, master.

expertise n adroitness, aptness, dexterity, facility, promptness, skilfulness, skill.

expire vb cease, close, conclude, end, stop, terminate; emit, exhale; decease, depart, die.

explain vb demonstrate, elucidate, expound, illustrate, interpret, resolve, solve, unfold, unravel; account for, justify, solve, warrant.

explanation n clarification, description, elucidation, exegesis, explication, exposition, illustration, interpretation; account, answer, deduction, justification, key, meaning, secret, solution, warrant.

explicit adj absolute, categorical, clear, definite,

determinate, exact, express, plain, positive, precise, unambiguous, unequivocal, unreserved.

explode vb burst, detonate, discharge, shatter, shiver; discard, repudiate, scorn, scout.

exploit n achievement, act, deed, feat.

explore vb examine, fathom, inquire, inspect, investigate, prospect, scrutinise, seek.

explosion n blast, burst, bursting, clap, crack, detonation, discharge, displosion, pop.

exponent n example, illustration, index, indication, specimen, symbol, type; commentator, demonstrator, illustrator, interpreter.

expose vb bare, display, uncover; descry, detect, disclose, unearth; denounce, subject, endanger, jeopardise, risk, venture.

expound vb develop, present, rehearse, reproduce, unfold; clear, elucidate, explain, interpret.

express vb air, assert, asseverate, declare, emit, enunciate, manifest, utter, vent, signify, speak, state, voice; betoken, denote, equal, exhibit, indicate, intimate, present, represent, show, signify, symbolise. • adj categorical, clear, definite, determinate, explicit, outspoken, plain, positive, unambiguous; accurate, close, exact, faithful, precise, true; particular, special; fast, nonstop, quick, rapid, speedy, swift.

expression n assertion, asseveration, communication, declaration, emission, statement, utterance, voicing; language, locution, phrase, remark, saying, term, word; air, aspect, look, mien.

expressive adj indicative, meaningful, significant; demonstrative, eloquent, emphatic, energetic, forcible, lively, strong, vivid; appropriate, sympathetic, well-modulated.

expulsion n discharge, eviction, expelling, ousting; elimination, evacuation, excretion; ejection, excision, excommunication, extrusion, ostracism, separation.

exquisite adj accurate, delicate, discriminating, exact, fastidious, nice, refined; choice, elect, excellent, precious, rare, valuable; complete, consummate, matchless, perfect, acute, keen, intense, poignant.

extant adj existent, existing, present, surviving, undestroyed, visible.

extend vb reach, stretch; continue, elongate, lengthen, prolong, protract, widen; augment, dilate, distend, enlarge, expand, increase; diffuse, spread; give, impart, offer, yield.

extension n augmentation, continuation, delay, dilatation, distension, enlargement, expansion, increase, prolongation, protraction.

extensive adj broad, capacious, comprehensive, expanded, extended, far-reaching, large, wide, widespread.

extent n amplitude, expanse, expansion; amount, bulk, content, degree, magnitude, size, volume; compass, measure, length, proportions, reach, stretch; area, field, latitude, range, scope; breadth, depth, height, width.

exterior adj external, outer, outlying, outside, outward, superficial, surface; extrinsic, foreign. • n outside, surface; appearance.

exterminate vb abolish, annihilate, destroy, eliminate, eradicate, extirpate, uproot.

extinct adj extinguished, quenched; closed, dead, ended, lapsed, terminated, vanished.

extinction n death, extinguishment; abolishment, abolition, annihilation, destruction, excision, extermination, extirpation.

extinguish vb choke, douse, put out, quell, smother, stifle, suffocate, suppress; destroy, nullify, subdue; eclipse, obscure.

extol vb celebrate, exalt, glorify, laud, magnify, praise; applaud, commend, eulogise, panegyrise.

extort vb elicit, exact, extract, force, squeeze, wrench, wrest, wring.

extortion n blackmail, compulsion, demand, exaction, rapacity, tribute; exorbitance.

extortionate adj bloodsucking, exacting, hard, harsh, oppressive, rapacious, rigorous, severe; exorbitant, unreasonable.

extra adj accessory, additional, auxiliary, collateral; another, further, more, new, plus, ulterior; side, spare, supernumerary, supplementary, surplus; extraordinary, extreme, unusual. • adv additionally, also, beyond, furthermore, more, moreover, plus. • n accessory, appendage, collateral, nonessential, special, supernumerary, supplement; bonus, premium; balance, leftover, remainder, spare, surplus.

extract vb extort, pull out, remove, withdraw; derive, distil, draw, express, squeeze; cite, determine, derive, quote, select. • n citation, excerpt, passage, quotation, selection; decoction, distillation, essence, infusion, juice.

extraction n drawing out, derivation, distillation, elicitation, essence, pulling out; birth, descent, genealogy, lineage, origin, parentage.

extraordinary adj abnormal, amazing, distinguished, egregious, exceptional, marvellous, monstrous, particular, peculiar, phenomenal, prodigious, rare, remarkable, signal, singular, special, strange, uncommon, unprecedented, unusual, unwonted, wonderful.

extravagant adj excessive, exorbitant, inordinate, preposterous, unreasonable; absurd, foolish, irregular, wild; lavish, prodigal, profuse, spendthrift, useful.

extreme adj farthest, outermost, remotest, utmost, uttermost; greatest, highest; final, last, ultimate; drastic, egregious, excessive, extravagant, immoderate, intense, outrageous, radical, unreasonable. • n end, extremity, limit; acme, climax, degree, height, pink; danger, distress.

extricate vb clear, deliver, disembarrass, disengage, disentangle, liberate, release, relieve.

exuberant *adj* abounding, abundant, copious, fertile, flowing, luxuriant, prolific, rich; excessive, lavish, overabundant, overflowing, over-luxuriant, profuse, rank, superabundant.

exult *vb* gloat, glory, jubilate, rejoice, triumph.

eye *vb* contemplate, inspect, ogle, scrutinise, survey, view, watch. • *n* estimate, judgement, look, sight, vision, view; inspection, notice, observation, scrutiny, sight, vigilance, watch.

F

fable *n* allegory, legend, myth, parable, story, tale; falsehood, fiction, figment.

fabric *n* building,, edifice, pile, structure; conformation, make, texture, workmanship; cloth, material, stuff, textile, tissue, web.

fabulous *adj* amazing, apocryphal, coined, fabricated, feigned, fictitious, forged, imaginary, invented, legendary, marvellous, mythical, romancing, unbelievable, unreal.

face *vb* confront; beard, buck, brave, dare, defy, front, oppose; dress. level, polish, smooth; cover, incrust, veneer. • *n* cover, facet, surface; breast, escarpment, front; countenance, features, grimace, physiognomy, visage; appearance, expression, look, semblance; assurance, audacity, boldness, brass, confidence, effrontery.

facile *adj* easy; affable, approachable, complaisant, conversable, courteous, mild; compliant, ductile, flexible, fluent, manageable, pliable.

facilitate *vb* expedite, help.

facility *n* ease, easiness; ability, dexterity, expertness, knack, quickness, readiness; ductility, flexibility, pliancy; advantage, appliance, convenience, means, resource.

facsimile *n* copy, duplicate, fax, reproduction.

fact *n* act, circumstance, deed, event, incident, occurrence, performance; actuality, certainty, existence, reality, truth.

faculty *n* ability, capability, capacity, endowment, power, property, quality; ableness, address, adroitness, aptitude, aptness, capacity, clearness, competency, dexterity, efficiency, expertness, facility, forte, ingenuity, knack, power, quickness, readiness, skill, skilfulness, talent, turn; body, department, profession; authority, power, prerogative, license, privilege, right.

fade *vb* disappear, die, evanesce, fall, faint, perish, vanish; decay, decline, droop, fall, languish, wither; bleach, blanch, pale; disperse, dissolve.

fail *vb* break, collapse, decay, decline, fade, sicken, sink, wane; cease, disappear; fall, miscarry, miss; neglect, omit; bankrupt, break.

failing *adj* deficient, lacking, needing, wanting; declining, deteriorating, fading, flagging, languishing, sinking,, waning, wilting; unsuccess-ful. • *prep* lacking, needing, wanting. • *n* decay, decline; failure, miscarriage; defect, deficiency, fault, foible, frailty, imperfection, infirmity, shortcoming, vice, weakness; error, lapse, slip; bankruptcy, insolvency.

failure *n* defectiveness, deficiency, delinquency, shortcoming; fail, miscarriage, negligent, neglect, nonobservance, nonperformance, omission, slip; abortion, botch, breakdown, collapse, fiasco, fizzle; bankruptcy, crash, downfall, insolvency, ruin; decay, declension, decline, loss.

faint *vb* swoon; decline, fade, fail, languish, weaken. • *adj* swooning; drooping, exhausted, feeble, languid, listless, sickly, weak; gentle, inconsiderable, little, slight, small, soft, thin; dim, dull, indistinct, perceptible, scarce, slight; cowardly, dastardly, faint-hearted, fearful, timid, timorous; dejected, depressed, discouraged, disheartened, dispirited. • *n* blackout, swoon.

fair *adj* spotless, unblemished, unspotted, unstained, untarnished; blond, light, lily, white; beautiful, comely, handsome, shapely; clear, cloudless, pleasant, unclouded; favourable, prosperous, hopeful, promising, propitious; clear, distinct, open, plain, unencumbered, unobstructed; candid, frank, honest, honourable, impartial, ingenuous, just, open, unbiased, upright; average, indifferent, moderate, ordinary, passable, reasonable, respectful, tolerable.

faith *n* assurance, belief, confidence, credence, credit, dependence, reliance, trust; creed, doctrines, dogmas, persuasion, religion, tenets; constancy, faithfulness, fidelity, loyalty, truth.

faithful *adj* constant, devoted, loyal, staunch, steadfast, true; honest, upright, reliable, trustworthy, trusty; truthful; accurate, close.

fall *vb* collapse, depend, descend, drop, sink, topple, tumble; abate, decline, decrease, depreciate, ebb, subside; err, lapse, sin, stumble, transgress, trespass, trip; die, perish; befall, chance, come, happen, occur, pass; become, get; come, pass. • *n* collapse, descent, dropping, falling, flop, plop, tumble; cascade, cataract, waterfall; death, destruction, downfall, overthrow, ruin, surrender; comeuppance, degradation; apostasy, declension, failure, lapse, slip; decline, decrease, depreciation, diminution, ebb, sinking, subsidence; cadence, close, sinking; declivity, inclination, slope.

fallible adj erring, frail, ignorant, imperfect.

false adj lying, mendacious; dishonest, dishonourable, disingenuous, disloyal, double-tongued, faithless, false-hearted, perfidious, treacherous, unfaithful; fictitious, forged, made-up, unreliable, untrustworthy; artificial, bastard, bogus, counterfeit, factitious, feigned, forged, hollow, hypocritical, make-believe, pretended, pseudo, sham, spurious, supposititious; erroneous, improper, incorrect, unfounded, wrong; deceitful, deceiving, deceptive, disappointing, fallacious, misleading.

falsehood n fabrication, fib, fiction, lie, untruth.

falsify vb alter, adulterate, belie, cook, counterfeit, doctor, fake, garble, misrepresent.

falter vb hesitate, lisp, quaver, stammer, stutter; stagger, totter, tremble; hesitate.

fame n bruit, hearsay, report, rumour; celebrity, credit, eminence, glory, greatness, honour, illustriousness, kudos, lustre, renown, repute.

familiar adj acquainted, aware, conversant, well-versed; amicable, close, cordial, domestic, fraternal, friendly, homely, intimate, near; affable, accessible, companionable, conversable, courteous, civil, friendly, kindly, sociable, social; easy, free and easy, unceremonious, unconstrained; common, frequent, well-known.

familiarity n acquaintance, knowledge, understanding; fellowship, friendship, intimacy; closeness, friendliness, sociability; freedom, informality, liberty; disrespect, presumption.

familiarise vb accustom, habituate, inure, train.

family n brood, household, people; ancestors, blood, breed, clan, dynasty, kindred, house, lineage, race, stock, tribe; class, genus, group, kind.

famine n dearth, destitution, hunger, scarcity.

famish vb distress, exhaust, pinch, starve.

famous adj celebrated, conspicuous, distinguished, eminent, excellent, fabled, famed, far-famed, great, glorious, heroic, honoured, illustrious, immortal, notable, noted, notorious, remarkable, renowned, signal.

fan[1] vb agitate, beat, move, winnow; blow, cool, refresh, ventilate; excite, fire, increase, rouse.

fan[2] n admirer, buff, devotee, enthusiast, fancier, follower, pursuer, supporter.

fanatic n bigot, devotee, enthusiast, zealot.

fanciful adj capricious, crotchety, imaginary, visionary, whimsical; chimerical, fantastical.

fancy vb apprehend, believe, conjecture, imagine, suppose, think; conceive, imagine. • adj elegant, fine, nice, ornament; extravagant, fanciful, whimsical. • n imagination; apprehension, conceit, conception, impression, idea, image, no-

tion, thought; approval, fondness, inclination, judgement, liking, penchant, taste; caprice, crochet, fantasy, freak, humour, maggot, quirk, vagary, whim, whimsy; apparition, chimera, daydream, delusion, hallucination, reverie.

fantastic adj chimerical, fanciful, imaginary, romantic, unreal, visionary; bizarre, capricious, grotesque, strange, whimsical, wild.

far adj distant, long, protracted, remote; farther, remoter; alienated, estranged, hostile. • adv considerably, extremely, greatly, very much; afar, distantly, far away, remotely.

farcical adj absurd, comic, droll, funny, laughable, ludicrous, ridiculous.

fare vb go, journey, pass, travel; happen, prosper, prove; feed, live, manage, subsist. • n charge, price, ticket money; passenger, traveller; board, commons, food, table, provisions.

farther adj additional; further, remoter, ulterior. • adv beyond, further; besides, furthermore.

fascinate vb affect, bewitch, overpower, spellbind, stupefy, transfix; absorb, captivate, catch, charm, delight, enamour, enchant, entrance.

fascination n absorption, charm, enchantment, magic, sorcery, spell, witchcraft, witchery.

fashion vb contrive, create, design, forge, form, make, mould, pattern, shape; accommodate, adapt, adjust, fit, suit. • n manner, method, sort; custom, fad, mode, style, usage, vogue; breeding, gentility; quality.

fashionable adj modish, stylish; current, modern, prevailing, up-to-date.

fast[1] adj close, fastened, firm, fixed, immovable, tenacious, tight; constant, faithful, permanent, resolute, staunch, steadfast, unswerving, unwavering; fortified, impregnable, strong; deep, profound, sound; fleet, quick, rapid, swift; dissipated, dissolute, extravagant, giddy, reckless, thoughtless, thriftless, wild. • adv firmly, immovably, tightly; quickly, rapidly, swiftly; extravagantly, prodigally, reckless, wildly.

fast[2] vb abstain, go hungry, starve. • n abstension, abstinence, diet, fasting, starvation.

fasten vb attach, bind, bolt, catch, chain, cleat, fix, gird, lace, lock, pin, secure, strap, tether, tie; belay, bend; connect, hold, join, unite.

fat adj adipose, fatty, greasy, oily, oleaginous, unctuous; corpulent, fleshy, gross, obese, paunchy, portly, plump, pudgy, pursy; coarse, dull, heavy, sluggish, stupid; lucrative, profitable, rich; fertile, fruitful, productive, rich. • n adipose tissue, ester, grease, oil; best part, cream, flower; corpulence, fatness, fleshiness, obesity.

fatal adj deadly, lethal, mortal; baleful, baneful, calamitous, catastrophic, destructive, mischievous, pernicious, ruinous.

fate n destination, destiny, fate; doom, experience, lot, fortune, portion.

fathom *vb* comprehend, divine, penetrate, reach, understand; estimate, gauge, measure.

fatigue *vb* exhaust, fag, jade, tire, weaken, weary. • *n* exhaustion, lassitude, tiredness.

fault *n* blemish, defect, flaw, foible, frailty, imperfection, infirmity, negligence, obliquity, offence, shortcoming, spot, weakness; delinquency, error, indiscretion, lapse, misdeed, misdemeanour, offence, peccadillo, slip, transgression, trespass, vice, wrong; blame, culpability.

faulty *adj* bad, defective, imperfect, incorrect; blameable, blameworthy, censurable, culpable.

favour *vb* befriend, countenance, encourage, patronise; approve; ease, facilitate; aid, assist, help, oblige, support; extenuate, humour, indulge, palliate, spare. • *n* approval, benignity, countenance, esteem, goodwill, grace, kindness; benefaction, benefit, boon, dispensation, kindness; championship, patronage, popularity, support; gift, present, token; badge, decoration, knot, rosette; leave, pardon, permission; advantage, cover, indulgence, protection; bias, partiality, prejudice.

favourable *adj* auspicious, friendly, kind, propitious, well-disposed, willing; conducive, contributing, propitious; adapted, beneficial, benign, convenient, fair, good, helpful, suitable.

favourite *adj* beloved, darling, dear; choice, fancied, esteemed, pet, preferred.

fear *vb* apprehend, dread; revere, reverence, venerate. • *n* affright, alarm, apprehension, consternation, dismay, dread, fright, horror, panic, phobia, scare, terror; disquietude, flutter, perturbation, palpitation, quaking, quivering, trembling, tremor, trepidation; anxiety, apprehension, concern, misdoubt, misgiving, qualm, solicitude; awe, dread, reverence, veneration.

fearful *adj* afraid, apprehensive, haunted; chicken-hearted, chicken-livered, cowardly, fainthearted, lily-livered, nervous, pusillanimous, timid, timorous; dire, direful, dreadful, frightful, ghastly, horrible, shocking, terrible.

fearless *adj* bold, brave, courageous, daring, dauntless, gallant, heroic, intrepid, valiant.

feast *n* banquet, repast, revels, symposium, treat; celebration, festival, fete, holiday; delight, enjoyment, pleasure.

feat *n* accomplishment, achievement, act, deed, exploit, performance, stunt, trick.

feature *vb* envisage, envision, picture, visualise imagine; specialise; appear in, headline, star. • *n* appearance, aspect, component; conformation, fashion, make; characteristic, item, mark, particularity, peculiarity, property, point, trait; leader, lead item, special; favour, expression, lineament; article, film, movie, story; highlight.

federation *n* alliance, allying, confederation, federating, leaguing, union, uniting; alliance, coalition, combination, compact, confederacy, entente, federacy, league, copartnership.

fee *vb* pay, recompense, reward. • *n* account, bill, charge, compensation, honorarium, remuneration, reward, tip; benefice, fief, feud.

feeble *adj* anaemic, debilitated, declining, drooping, enervated, exhausted, frail, infirm, languid, languishing, sickly; dim, faint.

feel *vb* apprehend, intuit, perceive, sense; examine, handle, probe, touch; enjoy, experience, suffer; prove, sound, test, try; appear, look, seem, sound; believe, conceive, deem, fancy, infer, opine, suppose, think. • *n* atmosphere, feeling, quality; finish, surface, texture.

feeling *n* consciousness, impression, notion, perception, sensation, sense, sentience, touch; affecting, emotion, heartstrings, impression, passion, sensibility, sentiment, soul, sympathy; sensibility, sentiment, susceptibility, tenderness.

fell *vb* knock down, level, prostrate; cut, hew.

fellow *adj* affiliated, associated, joint, like, mutual, similar, twin. • *n* associate, companion, comrade; compeer, equal, peer; counterpart, mate, match, partner; member; boy, character, individual, man, person.

fellowship *n* brotherhood, companionship, comradeship, familiarity, intimacy; participation; partnership; communion, converse, intercourse; affability, kindliness, sociability.

feminine *adj* affectionate, delicate, gentle, graceful, modest, tender, womanish, womanly.

fence *vb* defend, enclose, fortify, guard, protect, surround; circumscribe, evade, equivocate, hedge, prevaricate; guard, parry. • *n* barrier, hedge, hoarding, palings, palisade, stockade, wall; defence, protection, guard, security, shield; fencing, swordplay, swordsmanship; receiver.

ferocious *adj* fierce, rapacious, ravenous, savage, untamed, wild; barbarous, bloody, bloodthirsty, brutal, cruel, fell, inhuman, merciless, murderous, pitiless, remorseless, ruthless.

fertile *adj* bearing, breeding, fecund, prolific; exuberant, fruitful, luxuriant, plenteous, productive, rich, teeming; female, fruit-bearing.

fervent *adj* burning, hot, glowing, melting, seething; animated, ardent, earnest, enthusiastic, fervid, fierce, fiery, glowing, impassioned. intense, passionate, vehement, warm, zealous.

festival *n* anniversary, carnival, feast, fete, gala, holiday, jubilee; banquet, celebration.

festive *adj* carnival, convivial, festal, festival, gay, jolly, jovial, joyful, merry, mirthful.

festivity *n* conviviality, festival, gaiety, jollity, joviality, joyfulness, joyousness, merrymaking.

fetch *vb* bring, elicit, get; accomplish, achieve, effect, perform; attain, reach. • *n* artifice, dodge, ruse, stratagem, trick.

feud *vb* argue, bicker, clash, contend, dispute,

quarrel. • *n* affray, argument, bickering, broil, clashing, contention, contest, discord, dissension, enmity, fray, grudge, hostility, jarring, quarrel, rupture, strife, vendetta.

fever *n* agitation, excitement, ferment, fire, flush, heat, passion.

fibre *n* filament, pile, staple, strand, texture, thread; stamina, strength, toughness.

fickle *adj* capricious, changeable, faithless, fitful, inconstant, irresolute, mercurial, mutable, shifting, unsettled, unstable, unsteady, vacillating, variable, veering, volatile, wavering.

fiction *n* fancy, fantasy, imagination, invention; novel, romance; fable, fabrication, falsehood, figment, forgery, invention, lie.

fictitious *adj* assumed, fabulous, fanciful, feigned, imaginary, invented, mythical, unreal; artificial, counterfeit, dummy, false, spurious.

fidelity *n* constancy, devotedness, devotion, dutifulness, faithfulness, fealty, loyalty, true-heartedness, truth; accuracy, closeness, exactness, faithfulness, precision.

field *n* clearing, glebe, meadow; expanse, extent, opportunity, range, room, scope, surface; department, domain, province, realm, region.

fierce *adj* barbarous, brutal, cruel, fell, ferocious, furious, ravenous, savage; fiery, impetuous, murderous, passionate, tearing, tigerish, truculent, turbulent, uncurbed, untamed.

fiery *adj* fervent, fervid, flaming, heated, hot, glowing, lurid; ardent, fervent, fervid, fierce, flaming, glowing, impassioned, impetuous, inflamed, passionate, vehement.

fight *vb* battle, combat, contend, war; contest, dispute, oppose, strive, struggle, wrestle; encounter, engage; handle, manage, manoeuvre. • *n* action, battle, brush, combat, conflict, contest, duel, encounter, engagement, quarrel, struggle, war; brawl, riot, row, skirmish; pluck, pugnacity, resistance, spirit.

figure *vb* adorn, diversify, ornament, variegate; delineate, depict, represent, signify, symbolise; typify; conceive, image, imagine, picture, represent; calculate, cipher, compute; act, appear, perform. • *n* configuration, conformation, form, outline, shape; effigy, image, likeness, representative; design, diagram, drawing, pattern; metaphor, trope; emblem, symbol, type; character, digit, number, numeral.

file¹ *vb* order, pigeonhole, record, tidy. • *n* data, dossier, folder, portfolio; column, line, list, range, rank, row, series, tier.

file² *vb* polish, rasp, refine, smooth.

fill *vb* occupy, pervade; dilate, distend, expand, stretch, trim; furnish, replenish, stock, store, supply; cloy, congest, content, cram, glut, gorge, line, pack, pall, sate, satiate, satisfy, saturate, stuff, suffuse, swell; engage, fulfil, hold, occupy.

film *vb* becloud, cloud, coat, cover, darken, fog, mist, obfuscate, obscure, veil; photograph, shoot, take. • *n* cloud, coating, gauze, membrane, nebula, pellicle, scum, skin, veil; thread.

filter *vb* filtrate, strain; exude, ooze, percolate, transude. • *n* diffuser, colander, riddle, sieve.

filth *n* dirt, nastiness, ordure; corruption, defilement, foulness, grossness, impurity, obscenity, pollution, squalor, uncleanness, vileness.

final *adj* eventual, extreme, last, latest, terminal, ultimate; conclusive, decisive, definitive.

finale *n* conclusion, end, termination.

finances *npl* funds, resources, revenues, treasury; income, property.

find *vb* discover, fall upon; gain, get, obtain, procure; ascertain, discover, notice, observe, perceive, remark; catch, detect; contribute, furnish, provide, supply. • *n* acquisition, catch, discovery, finding, plum, prize, strike.

fine¹ *vb* filter, purify, refine. • *adj* comminuted, little, minute, small; capillary, delicate, small; choice, light; exact, keen, sharp; attenuated, subtle, tenuous, thin; exquisite, fastidious, nice, refined, sensitive, subtle; dandy, excellent, superb, superior; beautiful, elegant, handsome, magnificent, splendid; clean, pure, unadulterated.

fine² *vb* penalise, punish. • *n* forfeit, forfeiture, mulct, penalty, punishment.

finish *vb* accomplish, achieve, complete, consummate, execute, fulfil, perform; elaborate, perfect, polish; close, conclude, end, terminate. • *n* elaboration, elegance, perfection, polish; close, end, death, termination, wind-up.

fire *vb* ignite, kindle, light; animate, enliven, excite, inflame, inspirit, invigorate, rouse, stir up; discharge, eject, expel, hurl. • *n* combustion; blaze, conflagration; discharge, firing; animation, ardour, enthusiasm, fervour, fervency, fever, force, heat, impetuosity, inflammation, intensity, passion, spirit, vigour, violence; light, lustre, radiance, splendour; imagination, imaginativeness, inspiration, vivacity.

firm¹ *adj* established, confirmed, consistent, fast, fixed, immovable, inflexible, rooted, secure, stable; compact, compressed, dense, hard, solid; constant, determined, resolute, staunch, steadfast, unshaken; loyal, robust, sturdy, strong.

firm² *n* association, business, company, concern, corporation, house, partnership.

first *adj* capital, chief, foremost, highest, leading, prime, principal; earliest, eldest, original; elementary, primary, rudimentary; aboriginal, primal, primeval, primitive, pristine. • *adv* chiefly, initially, mainly, primarily, principally; before, foremost, headmost; before, rather. • *n* alpha, initial, prime.

fit¹ *vb* adapt, adjust, suit; become, conform; accommodate, equip, prepare, provide, qualify.

•*adj* capacitated, competent, fitted; adequate, appropriate, apt, becoming, befitting, consonant, convenient, pertinent, proper, suitable.

flt² *n* convulsion, fit, paroxysm, qualm, seizure, spasm, spell; fancy, humour, whim; mood, pet, tantrum; interval, period, spell, turn.

fitful *adj* capricious, changeable, convulsive, fanciful, fantastic, fickle, humoursome, impulsive, intermittent, irregular, odd, spasmodic, unstable, variable, whimsical; checkered, eventful.

fix *vb* establish, fasten, place, plant, set; adjust, repair; attach, bind, clinch, connect, fasten, lock, rivet, stay, tie; appoint, decide, define, determine, limit, seal, settle; consolidate, harden, solidify; abide, remain, rest, settle; congeal, harden, solidify, stiffen. • *n* difficulty, dilemma.

flabby *adj* feeble, flaccid, limp, soft, weak.

flag¹ *vb* droop, hang, loose; decline, fail, faint, lag, languish, pine, sink, succumb, weaken.

flag² *vb* indicate, mark, semaphore, sign, signal. • *n* banner, colours, ensign, gonfalon, pennant, pennon, standard, streamer.

flagrant *adj* burning, flaming, glowing, raging; crying, enormous, flagitious, glaring, monstrous, nefarious, notorious, outrageous, shameful, wanton, wicked.

flamboyant *adj* bright, gorgeous, ornate.

flame *vb* blaze, shine; burn, flash, glow, warm. • *n* blaze, brightness, fire, flare, vapour; affection, ardour, enthusiasm, fervour, keenness, warmth.

flap *vb* beat, flutter, shake, vibrate, wave. • *n* apron, fly, lap, lappet, tab; beating, flapping, flop, flutter, slap, shaking, swinging, waving.

flare *vb* blaze, flicker, flutter, waver; dazzle, flame, glare; splay, spread, widen. • *n* blaze, dazzle, flame, glare.

flash *vb* blaze, glance, glare, glisten, light, shimmer, scintillate, sparkle, twinkle. • *n* instant, moment, twinkling.

flat *adj* horizontal, level; even, plane, smooth, unbroken; low, prostrate, overthrow; dull, frigid, jejune, lifeless, monotonous, pointless, prosaic, spiritless, tame, unanimated, uniform, uninteresting; dead, insipid, mawkish, stale, tasteless, vapid; absolute, clear, direct, downright, peremptory, positive. • *n* bar, sandbank, shallow, shoal, strand; lowland, plain; apartment, floor, lodging, storey.

flatter *vb* compliment, gratify, praise; blandish, blarney, butter up, cajole, coax, coddle, court, entice, fawn, humour, inveigle, wheedle.

flavour *n* gust, gusto, relish, savour, seasoning, smack, taste, zest; admixture, lacing, seasoning, aroma, essence, soul, spirit.

flaw *n* break, breach, cleft, crack, fissure, fracture, gap, rent, rift; blemish, defect, fault, fleck, imperfection, speck, spot.

flee *vb* abscond, avoid, decamp, depart, escape, fly, leave, run, skedaddle.

fleece *vb* clip, shear; cheat, despoil, pluck, plunder, rifle, rob, steal, strip.

fleeting *adj* brief, caducous, ephemeral, evanescent, flitting, flying, fugitive, passing, short-lived, temporary, transient, transitory.

flesh *n* food, meat; carnality, desires; kindred, race, stock; man, mankind, world.

fleshly *adj* animal, bodily, carnal, lascivious, lustful, lecherous, sensual.

fleshy *adj* corpulent, fat, obese, plump, stout.

flexible *adj* flexible, limber, lithe, pliable, pliant, supple, willowy; affable, complaisant, ductile, docile, gentle, pliable, pliant, tractable.

flight¹ *n* flying, mounting, soaring, volition; shower, flight; steps, stairs.

flight² *n* departure, fleeing, flying, retreat, rout, stampede; exodus, hegira.

flighty *adj* capricious, deranged, fickle, frivolous, giddy, light-headed, mercurial, unbalanced, volatile, wild, whimsical.

flimsy *adj* slight, thin, unsubstantial; feeble, foolish, frivolous, light, puerile, shallow, superficial, trashy, trifling, trivial, weak; insubstantial.

flinch *vb* blench, flee, recoil, retreat, shirk, shrink, swerve, wince, withdraw.

fling *vb* cast, chuck, dart, emit, heave, hurl, pitch, shy, throw, toss; flounce, wince.

flippant *adj* fluent, glib, talkative, voluble; bold, forward, frivolous, glib, impertinent, inconsiderate, irreverent, malapert, pert, saucy, trifling.

flirt *vb* chuck, fling, hurl, pitch, shy, throw, toss; flutter, twirl, whirl, whisk; coquet, dally, philander. • *n* coquette, jilt, philanderer; jerk.

flit *vb* flicker, flutter, hover; depart, hasten, pass.

float *vb* drift, glide, hang, ride, sail, soar, swim, waft; launch, support.

flock *vb* collect, congregate, gather, group, herd, swarm, throng. • *n* collection, group, multitude; bevy, company, convoy, drove, flight, gaggle, herd, pack, swarm, team, troupe; congregation.

flog *vb* beat, castigate, chastise, drub, flagellate, lash, scourge, thrash, whip.

flood *vb* deluge, inundate, overflow, submerge, swamp. • *n* deluge, freshet, inundation, overflow, tide; bore, downpour, eagre, flow, outburst, spate, rush; abundance, excess.

floor *vb* deck, pave; beat, confound, conquer, overthrow, prevail, prostrate, puzzle; disconcert, nonplus; florid. • *n* storey; bottom, deck, flooring, stage.

flourish *vb* grow, thrive; boast, bluster, brag, gasconade, show off, vaunt, vapour; brandish, flaunt, swing, wave. • *n* dash, display, ostentation, parade, show; brandishing, shake, waving; blast, fanfare.

flout *vb* chaff, deride, fleer, gibe, insult, jeer, mock, ridicule, scoff, sneer, taunt.

flow *vb* pour, run, stream; deliquesce, liquefy, melt; arise, come, emanate, follow, grow, issue, proceed, result, spring; glide; float, undulate, wave, waver; abound, run. • n current, discharge, flood, flux, gush, rush, stream, trickle; abundance, copiousness.

flower vb bloom, blossom, effloresce; develop. • n bloom, blossom; best, cream, elite, essence, pick; freshness, prime, vigour.

flowery adj bloomy, florid; embellished, figurative, florid, ornate, overwrought.

fluent adj current, flowing, gliding, liquid; smooth; affluent, copious, easy, facile, glib, ready, talkative, voluble.

flurry vb agitate, confuse, disconcert, disturb, excite, fluster, hurry, perturb. • n gust, flaw, squall; agitation, bustle, commotion, confusion, disturbance, excitement, flutter, haste, hurry, hurry-scurry, perturbation, ruffle, scurry.

flush[1] vb flow, rush, start; glow, mantle, redden; animate, elate, elevate, erect, excite; cleanse, drench. • adj bright, fresh, glowing, vigorous; abundant, affluent, exuberant, fecund, fertile, generous, lavish, liberal, prodigal, prolific, rich, wealthy, well-supplied; even, flat, level, plane. • adv evenly, flat, level; full, point-blank, right, square, squarely, straight. • n bloom, blush, glow, redness, rosiness, ruddiness.

flush[2] vb disturb, rouse, start, uncover.

flutter vb flap, hover; flirt, flit; beat, palpitate, quiver, tremble; fluctuate, oscillate, vacillate, waver. • n agitation, tremor; agitation, hurry, commotion, confusion, excitement, flurry, fluster, hurry-scurry, perturbation, quivering, tremble, tumult, twitter.

fly[1] vb aviate, hover, mount, soar; flap, float, flutter, play, sail, soar, undulate, vibrate, wave; burst, explode; abscond, decamp, depart, flee, vanish; elapse, flit, glide, pass, slip.

fly[2] adj alert, bright, sharp, smart, wide-awake; astute, cunning, knowing, sly.

foam vb cream, froth, lather, spume; boil, churn, ferment, fume, seethe, simmer, stew.

foe n adversary, antagonist, enemy, opponent.

fog vb bedim, bemist, blear, blur, cloud, dim, enmist, mist; addle, befuddle, confuse, fuddle, muddle. • n blear, blur, dimness, film, fogginess, haze, haziness, mist, smog, vapour; befuddlement, confusion, fuddle, maze, muddle.

foggy adj blurred, cloudy, dim, dimmed, hazy, indistinct, misty, obscure; befuddled, bewildered, confused, dazed, muddled, muddy.

foible n defect, failing, fault, frailty, imperfection, infirmity, penchant, weakness.

foil[1] vb baffle, balk, check, checkmate, circumvent, defeat, disappoint, frustrate, thwart.

foil[2] n film, flake, lamina; background, contrast.

foist vb impose, palm off, thrust.

fold[1] vb bend, cover, double, envelop, wrap; clasp, embrace, enfold, enwrap, gather, infold;

interlace; collapse, fail. • n double, doubling, gather, plait, plicature.

fold[2] n cot, enclosure, pen.

folk n kindred, nation, people.

follow vb ensue, succeed; chase, dog, hound, pursue, run after, trail; accompany, attend; conform, heed, obey, observe; cherish, cultivate, seek; practise, pursue; adopt, copy, imitate; arise, come, flow, issue, proceed, result, spring.

follower n acolyte, attendant, associate, companion, dependant, retainer, supporter; adherent, admirer, disciple, partisan, pupil; imitator.

folly n doltishness, dullness, fatuity, foolishness, imbecility, levity, shallowness; absurdity, extravagance, fatuity, foolishness, imprudence, inanity, indiscretion, ineptitude, nonsense, senseless; blunder, faux pas, indiscretion, unwisdom.

fond adj absurd, baseless, empty, foolish, senseless, silly, vain, weak; affectionate, amorous, doting, loving, overaffectionate, tender.

fondle vb blandish, caress, coddle, cosset, pet.

food n aliment, board, bread, cheer, commons, diet, fare, meat, nourishment, nutriment, nutrition, pabulum, provisions, rations, regimen, subsistence, sustenance, victuals; feed, fodder.

fool vb jest, play, toy, trifle; beguile, cheat, circumvent, cozen, deceive, delude, dupe, gull, hoodwink, overreach, trick. • n blockhead, dolt, driveller, idiot, imbecile, nincompoop, ninny, nitwit, simpleton, buffoon, clown, droll, jester, butt, dupe.

foolhardy adj adventurous, bold, desperate, harebrained, headlong, hot-headed, incautious, precipitate, rash, reckless, venturesome.

foolish adj brainless, daft, fatuous, idiotic, inane, inept, insensate, irrational, senseless, shallow, silly, simple, thick-skulled, vain, weak, witless; absurd, ill-judged, imprudent, indiscreet, nonsensical, preposterous, ridiculous, unreasonable, unwise; childish, contemptible, idle, puerile, trifling, trivial, vain.

footing n foothold, purchase; basis, foundation, groundwork, installation; condition, grade, rank, standing, state, status; settlement, establishment.

forage vb feed, graze, provender, provision, victual; hunt for, range, rummage, search, seek; maraud, plunder, raid. • n feed, fodder, food, pasturage, provender; hunt, rummage, search

foray n descent, incursion, invasion, inroad, irruption, raid.

forbid vb ban, debar, disallow, embargo, enjoin, hinder, inhibit, interdict, prohibit, proscribe, taboo, veto.

forbidding adj abhorrent, disagreeable, displeasing, offensive, threatening, unpleasant.

force vb coerce, compel, constrain, necessitate, oblige; drive, impel, overcome, press, urge; ravish, violate. • n emphasis, energy, head, might, pith, power, strength, stress, vigour, vim; agency, efficacy, efficiency, cogency, potency, validity, virtue; coercion, compulsion, constraint, enforcement, vehemence, violence; army, array, battalion, host, legion, posse, squadron, troop.

forcible adj all-powerful, cogent, impressive, irresistible, mighty potent, powerful, strong, weighty; impetuous, vehement, violent, unrestrained; coerced, coercive, compulsory; convincing, energetic, effective, telling, vigorous.

fore adj anterior, antecedent, first, foregoing, former, forward, preceding, previous, prior; advanced, foremost, head, leading.

foreboding n augury, omen, prediction, premonition, presage, presentiment, prognostication.

forecast vb anticipate, foresee, predict; calculate, contrive, devise, plan, project, scheme. • n anticipation, foresight, forethought, planning, prevision, prophecy, provident.

foregoing adj antecedent, anterior, fore, former, preceding, previous, prior.

foregone adj bygone, former, past, previous.

foreign adj alien, distant, exotic, exterior, external, outward, outlandish, remote, strange, unnative; adventitious, exterior, extraneous, extrinsic, inappropriate, irrelevant, outside, unnatural.

foremost adj first, front, highest, leading, main.

forerunner n herald, precursor, predecessor; omen, precursor, prelude, sign.

foresight n foreknowledge, prescience, prevision; anticipation, care, caution, forecast, forethought, precaution, providence, prudence.

foretell vb predict., prophesy; augur, betoken, forebode, forecast, foreshadow, foreshow, portend, presage, presignify, prognosticate.

forfeit vb alienate, lose. • n amercement, damages, fine, forfeiture, mulct, penalty.

forge vb beat, fabricate, form, frame, hammer; coin, devise, frame, invent; counterfeit, fabricate, falsify. • n furnace, ironworks, smithy.

forgery n counterfeit, fake, imitation.

forgetful adj careless, heedless, inattentive, mindless, neglectful, negligent, unmindful.

forgive vb absolve, acquit, condone, excuse, exonerate, pardon, remit.

form vb fashion model, mould, shape; build, conceive, construct, create, fabricate, make, produce; contrive, devise, frame, invent; compose, constitute, develop, organise; discipline, educate, teach, train. • n body, build, cast, configuration, conformation, contour, cut, fashion, figure, format, mould, outline, pattern, shape; formula, formulary, method, mode, practice, ritual; class, kind, manner, model, order, sort, system, type; arrangement, order, regularity, shapeliness; ceremonial, ceremony, conventionality, etiquette, formality, observance, ordinance, punctilio, rite, ritual; bench, seat; class, rank; arrangement, combination, organisation.

formal adj explicit, express, official, positive, strict; fixed, methodical, regular, rigid, set, stiff; affected, ceremonious, exact, precise, prim, punctilious, starched; constitutive, essential; external, outward, perfunctory; formative, innate, organic, primordial.

formative adj creative, determinative, plastic, shaping; derivative, inflectional, nonradical.

former adj antecedent, anterior, earlier, foregoing, preceding, previous, prior; late, old-time, quondam; by, bygone, foregone, gone, past.

forsake vb abandon, desert, leave, quit; drop, forgo, forswear, relinquish, renounce, surrender.

fortify vb brace, encourage, entrench, garrison, protect, reinforce, stiffen, strengthen; confirm.

fortitude n braveness, bravery, courage, determination, endurance, firmness, hardiness, patience, pluck, resolution, strength, valour.

fortuitous adj accidental, casual, chance, contingent, incidental.

fortunate adj favoured, happy, lucky, prosperous, successful; advantageous, auspicious, favourable, happy, lucky, propitious.

fortune n accident, casualty, chance, contingency, fortuity, hap, luck; estate, possessions, property, substance; affluence, felicity, opulence, prosperity, riches, wealth; destination, destiny, doom, fate, lot, star; event, issue, result; favour.

forward vb advance, aid, encourage, favour, foster, further, help, promote, support; accelerate, dispatch, expedite, hasten, hurry, quicken, speed; dispatch, post, send, ship, transmit. • adj advanced, onward; anterior, front, fore, head; prompt, eager, earnest, hasty, impulsive, quick, ready, willing, zealous; assuming, bold, brazen, brazen-faced, confident, flippant, impertinent, pert, presumptuous, presuming; advanced, early, premature. • adv ahead, onward.

foster vb cosset, feed, nurse, nourish, support, sustain; advance, aid, breed, cherish, cultivate, encourage, favour, foment, forward, further, harbour, patronise, promote, rear, stimulate.

foul vb besmirch, defile, pollute, soil, stain, sully; clog, collide, entangle, jam. • adj dirty, fetid, filthy, impure, nasty, polluted, putrid, soiled, stained, squalid, sullied, rank, tarnished, unclean; disgusting, hateful, loathsome, noisome, odious, offensive; dishonourable, underhand, unfair, sinister; abominable, base, dark, detestable, disgraceful, infamous, scandalous, scurvy, shameful, wile, wicked; coarse, low, obscene, vulgar; abusive, foul-mouthed, foul-spoken, insulting, scurrilous; cloudy, rainy, rough, stormy, wet; feculent, muddy, tangled.

found vb base, fix, ground, place. rest, set; build, construct, erect, raise; colonise, establish, institute, originate, plant; cast, mould.

foundation n base, basis, bed, bottom, footing,

ground, groundwork, substructure, support; endowment, establishment, settlement.

fountain n fount, reservoir, spring, well; jet, upswelling; cause, fountainhead, origin, source.

fracture vb break, crack, split. • n breaking, rupture; breach, break, cleft, crack, fissure, flaw, opening, rift, rent.

fragile adj breakable, brittle, delicate, frangible; feeble, frail, infirm, weak.

fragment vb atomise, break, fracture, pulverise, splinter. • n bit, chip, fraction, fracture, morsel, part, piece, remnant, scrap.

fragrant adj ambrosial, aromatic, balmy, odoriferous, odorous, perfumed, redolent, spicy, sweet, sweet-scented, sweet-smelling.

frail adj breakable, brittle, delicate, fragile, frangible, slight; feeble, fragile, infirm, weak.

frame vb build, compose, constitute, construct, erect, form, make, mould, plan, shape; contrive, devise, fabricate, fashion, forge, invest, plan. • n body, carcass, framework, framing, shell, skeleton; constitution, fabric, form, structure, scheme, system; condition, humour, mood.

frank adj artless, candid, direct, downright, frank-hearted, free, genuine, guileless, ingenuous, naive, open, outspoken, outright, plain, plainspoken, point-blank, sincere, straightforward, truthful, unequivocal, unreserved.

frantic adj crazy, distracted, distraught, frenzied, furious, infuriate, mad. outrageous, phrenetic, rabid, raging, raving, transported, wild.

fraud n artifice, cheat, craft, deception, deceit, duplicity, guile, hoax, humbug, imposition, imposture, sham, stratagem, treachery, trick.

fraudulent adj crafty, deceitful, deceptive, dishonest, false, knavish, treacherous, trickish.

freak adj bizarre, freakish, grotesque, monstrous, odd, unexpected, unforeseen. • n caprice, crotchet, fancy, humour, maggot, quirk, vagary, whim, whimsey; antic, caper, gambol; abnormality, abortion, monstrosity.

free vb deliver, discharge, disenthral, emancipate, enfranchise, enlarge, liberate, manumit, ransom, release, redeem, rescue, save; clear, disencumber, disengage, extricate, rid, unbind, unchain, unfetter, unlock; exempt, immunise, privilege. • adj bondless, independent, loose, unattached, unconfined, unentangled, unimpeded, unrestrained, untrammelled; autonomous, delivered, emancipated, freeborn, liberated, manumitted, ransomed, released, self-governing; clear, exempt, immune, privileged; allowed, open, permitted; devoid, empty, open, unimpeded, unobstructed, unrestricted; affable, artless, candid, frank, ingenuous, sincere, unreserved; bountiful, charitable, free-hearted, generous, hospitable, liberal, munificent, openhanded; immoderate, lavish, prodigal; eager, prompt, ready,

willing; available, gratuitous, spontaneous, willing; careless, lax, loose; bold, easy, familiar, informal, overfamiliar, unconstrained. • adv openly, outright, unreservedly, unrestrainedly, unstintingly; freely, gratis, gratuitously.

freedom n emancipation, independence, liberation, liberty, release; elbowroom, margin, play, range, scope, swing; franchise, immunity, privilege; familiarity, laxity, license, looseness.

freeze vb congeal, harden, stiffen; chill.

frenzy n aberration, delirium, derangement, distraction, fury, insanity, lunacy, madness, mania, paroxysm, rage, raving, transport.

frequent vb attend, haunt, resort, visit. • adj iterating, oft-repeated; common, customary, everyday, familiar, habitual, persistent, usual.

fresh adj new, novel, recent; new, renewed, revived; blooming, flourishing, green, undecayed, unimpaired, unfaded, unobliterated, unwilted, unwithered, well-preserved; sweet; blooming, delicate, fair, fresh-coloured, ruddy, rosy; florid, hardy, healthy, vigorous, strong; active, energetic, unexhausted, unfatigued, unwearied, vigorous; keen, lively, unabated, undecayed, unimpaired, vivid; additional, further; uncured, undried, unsalted, unsmoked; bracing, health-giving, invigorating, refreshing, sweet; brisk, stiff, strong; inexperienced, raw, uncultivated, unpracticed, unskilled, untrained, unused.

fretful adj captious, cross, fractious, ill-humoured, ill-tempered, irritable, peevish, pettish, petulant, querulous, short-tempered, snappish, spleeny, splenetic, testy, touchy, uneasy.

friend adj benefactor, chum, companion, comrade, crony, confidant, intimate; adherent, ally, associate, confrere, partisan; adherent, advocate, defender, encourager, patron, supporter.

friendly adj affectionate, amiable, benevolent, favourable, kind, kind-hearted, kindly, well-disposed; amicable, cordial, fraternal, neighbourly; conciliatory, peaceable, unhostile.

friendship n affection, attachment, benevolence, fondness, goodness, love, regard; fellowship, intimacy; amicability, amicableness, amity, cordiality, familiarity, fellowship, fraternisation.

fright n affright, alarm, consternation, dismay, funk, horror, panic, scare, terror.

frighten vb affright, alarm, appal, daunt, dismay, intimidate, scare, stampede, terrify.

frightful adj alarming, awful, dire, direful, dread, dreadful, fearful, horrible, horrid, shocking, terrible, terrific; ghastly, grim, gruesome.

fringe vb border, bound, edge, hem, march, rim, skirt, verge. • n border, edge, edging, tassel, trimming. • adj extra, unofficial.

frisky adj frolicsome, coltish, lively, playful.

frivolous adj childish, empty, flighty, flimsy, flippant, foolish, giddy, idle, light, paltry. petty, puerile, silly, trashy, trifling, trivial, unimportant, vain, worthless.

frolic vb caper, frisk, gambol, lark, play, romp, sport. • n escapade, gambol, lark, romp, skylark, spree, trick; drollery, fun, play, pleasantry, sport.

front vb confront, encounter, face, oppose. • adj anterior, forward; foremost, frontal, headmost. • n brow, face, forehead; assurance, boldness, brass, effrontery, face, impudence; breast, head, van, vanguard; anterior, face, forepart, obverse; facade, frontage.

frontier n border, boundary, coast, confine, limits, marches.

frosty adj chill, chilly, cold, icy, stinging, wintry; cold, cold-hearted, frigid, indifferent, unaffectionate, uncordial, unimpassioned, unloving; cold, dull-hearted, lifeless, spiritless, unanimated; frosted, grey-haired, hoary, white.

froth vb bubble, cream, foam, lather, spume. • n bubbles, foam, lather, spume; balderdash, flummery, nonsense, trash, triviality.

frown vb glower, lower, scowl.

frugal adj abstemious, careful, chary, choice, economical, provident, saving, sparing, temperate, thrifty, unwasteful.

fruit n crop, harvest, produce, production; advantage, consequence, effect, good, outcome, product, profit, result; issue, offspring, young.

fruitful adj abounding, productive; fecund, fertile, prolific; abundant, exuberant, plenteous, plentiful, rich, teeming.

fruitless adj acarpous, barren, sterile, infecund, unfertile, unfruitful, unproductive, unprolific; abortive, barren, bootless, futile, idle, ineffectual, profitless, unavailing, unprofitable, useless.

frustrate vb baffle, baulk, check, circumvent, defeat, disappoint, disconcert, foil, thwart; check, cross, hinder, outwit.

fugitive adj escaping, fleeing, flying; brief, ephemeral, evanescent, fleeting, flitting, flying, fugacious, momentary, short, short-lived, temporal, temporary, transient, transitory, uncertain, unstable, volatile. • n émigré, escapee, evacuee, fleer, outlaw, refugee, runaway.

fulfil vb accomplish, complete, consummate, effect, effectuate, execute, realise; adhere, discharge, do, keep, obey, observe, perform.

full adj brimful, filled, flush, replete; abounding, replete, well-stocked; bagging, flowing, loose, voluminous; cloyed, crammed, glutted, gorged, overflowing, packed, sated, satiated, saturated, soaked, stuffed, swollen; adequate, complete, entire, mature, perfect; abundant, ample, copious, plenteous, plentiful, sufficient; clear, deep, distinct, loud, rounded, strong; broad, large, capacious, comprehensive, extensive, plump; circumstantial, detailed, exhaustive. • adv completely, fully; directly, exactly, precisely.

fully adv abundantly, amply, completely, copiously, entirely, largely, plentifully, sufficiently.

fume vb reek, smoke, vaporise. • n effluvium exhalation, reek, smell, smoke, steam, vapour; agitation, fret, fry, fury, passion, pet, rage, storm.

fun n amusement, diversion, drollery, frolic, gaiety, humour, jesting, jocularity, jollity, joy, merriment, mirth, play, pranks, sport, waggishness.

function vb act, discharge, go, operate, officiate, perform, run, serve, work. • n discharge, execution, exercise, operation, performance, purpose, use; activity, business, capacity, duty, employment, occupation, office, part, province, role; ceremony, rite; dependant, derivative.

fund vb afford, endow, finance, invest, provide, subsidise, support; garner, hoard, stock, store. • n accumulation, capital, endowment, reserve.

fundamental adj basal, basic, bottom, cardinal, constitutional, elementary, essential, indispensable, organic, principal, primary, radical. • n essential, principal, rule.

funereal adj dark, dismal, gloomy, lugubrious, melancholy, mournful, sad, sepulchral, sombre.

funny adj amusing, comic, comical, diverting, droll, facetious, farcical, humorous, jocose, jocular, laughable, ludicrous, sportive, witty; curious, odd, queer, strange.

furious adj angry, fierce, frantic, frenzied, fuming, infuriated, mad, raging, violent, wild.

furnish vb appoint, endow, provide, supply; decorate, equip, fit; afford, bestow, contribute, give, offer, present, produce, yield.

furniture n chattels, effects, household goods, movables; apparatus, appendages, appliances, equipment, fittings, furnishings; decorations, embellishments, ornaments.

further vb advance, aid, assist, encourage, help, forward, promote, succour, strengthen. • adj additional. • adv also, besides, moreover.

furtive adj clandestine, hidden, secret, sly, skulking, sneaking, stealthy, surreptitious.

fury n anger, frenzy, fit, furore, ire, madness, passion, rage; fierceness, impetuosity, turbulence, turbulency, vehemence; bacchant, bacchante, bedlam, hag, shrew, termagant, virago.

fuse vb dissolve, melt, liquefy, smelt; amalgamate, blend, coalesce, combine, commingle, intermingle, intermix, merge, unite.

fuss vb bustle, fidget; fret, fume, worry. • n ado, agitation, bother, bustle, commotion, disturbance, excitement, fidget, flurry, fluster, fret, hurry, pother, stir, worry.

futile adj frivolous, trifling, trivial; bootless, fruitless, idle, ineffectual, profitless, unavailing, unprofitable, useless, vain, valueless, worthless.

future adj coming, eventual, forthcoming, hereafter, prospective, subsequent. • n hereafter, outlook, prospect.

G

gag vb muffle, muzzle, shackle, silence, stifle, throttle; regurgitate, retch, throw up, vomit; choke, gasp, pant. • n muzzle.

gaiety n animation, blithesomeness, cheerfulness, glee, hilarity, jollity, joviality, merriment.

gain vb achieve, acquire, earn, get, obtain, procure, reap, secure; conciliate, enlist, persuade, prevail, win; arrive, attain, reach; clear, net, profit. • n accretion, addition, gainings, profits, winnings; acquisition, earnings, emolument, lucre; advantage, benefit, blessing, good, profit.

galaxy n assemblage, assembly, cluster, collection, constellation, group.

gale n blast, hurricane, squall, storm, tempest, tornado, typhoon.

gallant adj fine, magnificent, showy, splendid, well-dressed; bold, brave, chivalrous, courageous, daring, fearless, heroic, high-spirited, intrepid, valiant, valorous; chivalrous, fine, honourable, high-minded, lofty, magnanimous.

galling adj chafing, irritating, vexing.

gamble vb bet, dice, game, hazard, plunge, speculate, wager.

gambol vb caper, cut, frisk, frolic, hop, jump, leap, romp, skip. • n frolic, hop, jump, skip.

game[1] vb gamble, sport, stake. • n amusement, contest, diversion, pastime, play, sport; adventure, enterprise, measure, plan, project, scheme, stratagem, undertaking; prey, quarry, victim.

game[2] adj brave, courageous, dauntless, fearless, gallant, heroic, intrepid, plucky, unflinching, valorous; enduring, persevering, resolute, undaunted; ready, eager, willing.

game[3] adj crippled, disabled, injured, lame.

gang n band, cabal, clique, company, coterie, crew, horde, party, set, troop.

gap n breach, break, cavity, chasm, chink, cleft, crack, cranny, crevice, hiatus, hollow, interval, interstice, lacuna, opening, pass, vacancy.

gape vb burst open, dehisce, open, stare, yawn.

garish adj bright, dazzling, flashy, flaunting, gaudy, glaring, loud, showy, staring, tawdry.

garment n clothes, clothing, dress, habit.

garnish vb adorn, beautify, bedeck, decorate, deck, embellish, grace, ornament, prank, trim.

gasp vb blow, choke, pant, puff. • n blow, exclamation, gulp, puff.

gather vb assemble, cluster, collect, convene, group, muster, rally; accumulate, amass, garner, hoard, huddle, lump; bunch, crop, glean, pick, pluck, rake, reap, shock, stack; acquire, gain, get, win; conclude, deduce, derive, infer; fold, pucker, shirr, tuck; condense, grow, increase, thicken.

gathering n acquisition, collecting, earning, gain, heap, pile, procuring; assemblage, assembly, collection, company, concourse, congregation, meeting, muster; abscess, boil, fester, pimple, pustule, sore, suppuration, tumour, ulcer.

gaudy adj bespangled, brilliant, brummagem, cheap, flashy, flaunting, garish, gimcrack, glittering, loud, ostentatious, overdecorated, sham.

gauge vb calculate, check, determine, weigh; assess, estimate, guess, reckon. • n criterion, example, indicator, measure, meter, yardstick; bore, depth, height, size, thickness, width.

gaunt adj angular, attenuated, emaciated, haggard, lank, lean, meagre, scraggy, skinny, slender, spare, thin.

gear vb adapt, equip, fit, suit, tailor. • n apparel, array, clothes, clothing, dress, garb; accoutrements, appliances, appointments, appurtenances, array, harness, goods, movables, subsidiaries; harness, rigging, tackle, trappings; apparatus, machinery, mechanics.

general adj broad, collective, generic, popular, universal, widespread; catholic, ecumenical; common, current, ordinary, usual; inaccurate, indefinite, inexact, vague.

generate vb beget, breed, engender, procreate, propagate, reproduce, spawn; cause, form.

generation n creation, engendering, formation, procreation, production; age, epoch, era, period, time; breed, children, family, kind, offspring, progeny, race, stock.

generous adj high-minded, honourable, magnanimous, noble; beneficent, bountiful, charitable, free, hospitable, liberal, munificent, openhanded; abundant, ample, copious, plentiful.

genius n aptitude, aptness, bent, capacity, endowment, faculty, flair, gift, talent, turn; brains, ingenuity, inspiration, intellect, invention, parts, sagacity, wit; adeptness, master hand, proficiency; character, disposition, naturalness, nature; deity, demon, spirit.

gentle adj amiable, bland, clement, compassionate, humane, indulgent, kind, lenient, meek, merciful, mild, moderate, soft, tender, tender-hearted; docile, pacific, peaceable, placid, quiet, tame, tractable; bland, easy, gradual, light, mild, moderate, slight, soft; high-born, noble, well-born; chivalrous, courteous, cultivated, polished, refined, well-bred.

genuine adj authentic, honest, proper, pure, real, right, true, unadulterated, unalloyed, uncorrupted, veritable; frank, sincere, unaffected.

gesture vb indicate, motion, signal, wave. • n action, attitude, gesticulation, sign, signal.

get vb achieve, acquire, attain, earn, gain, obtain, procure, receive, relieve, secure, win; finish, master, prepare; beget, breed, engender, generate, procreate.

ghastly adj cadaverous, corpse-like, death-like, deathly, ghostly, lurid, pale, pallid, wan; dismal, dreadful, fearful, frightful, grim, grisly, gruesome, hideous, horrible, shocking, terrible.

ghost n soul, spirit; apparition, phantom, revenant, shade, spectre, spook, sprite, wraith.

giant adj colossal, enormous, Herculean, huge, large, monstrous, prodigious, vast. • n colossus, cyclops, Hercules, monster.

gibe, jibe vb deride, fleer, flout, jeer, mock, ridicule, scoff, sneer, taunt. • n ridicule, sneer, taunt.

giddy adj dizzy, head-spinning, vertiginous, careless, changeable, fickle, flighty, frivolous, hare-brained, headlong, heedless, inconstant, irresolute, light-headed, thoughtless, unsteady.

gift n alms, allowance, benefaction, bequest, bonus, boon, bounty, contribution, donation, dowry, endowment, favour, grant, gratuity, honorarium, largesse, legacy, offering, premium, present, prize, subscription, subsidy, tip; faculty, talent.

gifted adj able, capable, clever, ingenious, intelligent, inventive, sagacious, talented.

girl n damsel, lass, lassie, maiden, miss, virgin.

gist n basis, core, essence, force, ground, marrow, meaning, pith, point, substance.

give vb accord, bequeath, bestow, confer, devise, entrust, present; afford, contribute, donate, furnish, grant, proffer, spare, supply; communicate, impart; deliver, exchange, pay, requite; allow, permit, vouchsafe; emit, pronounce, render, utter; produce, yield; cause, occasion; apply, devote, surrender; bend, sink, recede, retire, retreat, yield.

glad adj delighted, gratified, happy, pleased, rejoiced, well-contented; animated, blithe, cheerful, cheery, elated, gladsome, happy, jocund, joyful, joyous, light, light-hearted, merry, playful; animating, bright, cheering, exhilarating, gladdening, gratifying, joyful, joyous, pleasing.

glamour n bewitchment, charm, enchantment, fascination, spell, witchery.

glance vb coruscate, gleam, glisten, glister, glitter, scintillate, shine; dart, flit; gaze, glimpse, look, view. • n gleam, glitter; gleam, look, view.

glare vb dazzle, flame, flare, gleam, glisten, glitter, sparkle; frown, gaze, glower. • n flare, glitter.

gleam vb beam, coruscate, flash, glance, glimmer, glitter, shine, sparkle. • n beam, flash, glance, glimmer, glimmering, glow, ray; brightness, coruscation, flashing, gleaming, glitter, glittering, lustre, splendour.

glee n exhilaration, fun, gaiety, hilarity, jocularity, jollity, joviality, joy, liveliness, merriment, mirth, sportiveness, verve.

glib adj slippery, smooth; artful, facile, flippant, fluent, ready, talkative, voluble.

glide vb float, glissade, roll on, skate, skim, slide, slip; flow, lapse, run, roll.

glimmer vb flash, flicker, gleam, glitter, shine.

glimpse vb espy, look, spot, view. • n flash, glance, glimmering, glint, look, sight.

glitter vb coruscate, flare, flash, glance, glare, gleam, glisten, glister, scintillate, shine, sparkle.

gloat vb exult, gaze, rejoice, stare, triumph.

gloomy adj dark, dim, dusky, obscure; cheerless, dismal, lowering, lurid; crestfallen, dejected, depressed, despondent, disheartened, dispirited, downcast, downhearted, glum, melancholy, morose, sad, sullen; dark, depressing, disheartening, dispiriting, heavy, melancholy, sad.

glorify vb adore, bless, celebrate, exalt, extol, laud, magnify, worship; adorn, brighten, elevate, ennoble, exalt, make bright.

glorious adj celebrated, conspicuous, distinguished, eminent, excellent, famed, famous, illustrious, pre-eminent, renowned; brilliant, bright, grand, magnificent, radiant, resplendent, splendid; consummate, exalted, excellent, high.

glory vb boast, exult, vaunt. • n celebrity, distinction, eminence, fame, honour, illustriousness, praise, renown; brightness, brilliancy, effulgence, lustre, pride, resplendence, splendour; exaltation, exceeding, gloriousness, greatness, grandeur, nobleness; bliss, happiness.

glow vb incandesce, radiate, shine; blush, burn, flush, redden. • n blaze, brightness, brilliance, burning, incandescence, luminosity, reddening; ardour, bloom, enthusiasm, fervency, fervour, flush, impetuosity, vehemence, warmth.

glower vb frown, glare, lower, scowl, stare.

glum adj churlish, crabbed, crest-fallen, cross-grained, crusty, depressed, frowning, gloomy, glowering, moody, morose, sour, sullen.

glut vb block up, cloy, cram, gorge, satiate, stuff. • n excess, saturation, surfeit, surplus.

glutton n gobbler, gorger, gourmand, gormandiser, greedy-guts, lurcher, pig.

go vb advance, move, pass, proceed, repair; act, operate; be about, extravagate, fare, journey, roam, travel, walk, wend; depart, disappear; elapse, extend, lead, reach, run; avail, concur, contribute, tend, serve; eventuate, fare, turn out; accept, approve, bear, endure, swallow, tolerate; afford, bet, risk, wager. • n action, business, case, chance, circumstance, doings, turn; custom, fad, fashion, mode, vague; energy, endurance, power, stamina.

goal n bound, home, limit, mark, mete, post; end, object; aim, design, destination.

goblin n apparition, elf, bogey, demon, gnome, hobgoblin, phantom, spectre, sprite.

god n almighty, creator, deity, divinity, idol, Jehovah, omnipotence, providence.

golden adj aureate, brilliant, bright, gilded, resplendent, shining, splendid; excellent, precious; auspicious, favourable, opportune, propitious; blessed, delightful, glorious, halcyon.

good adj advantageous, beneficial, favourable, profitable, serviceable, useful; adequate, appropriate, becoming, convenient, fit, proper, satisfactory, suitable, well-adapted; decorous, dutiful, honest, just, pious, reliable, religious, righteous, true, upright, virtuous, well-behaved, worthy; admirable, capable, excellent, genuine, healthy, precious, sincere, sound, sterling, valid, valuable; benevolent, favourable, friendly, gracious, humane, kind, merciful, obliging, well-disposed; fair, honourable, immaculate, unblemished, unimpeachable, unimpeached, unsullied, untarnished; cheerful, companionable, lively, genial, social; able, competent, dextrous, expert, qualified, ready, skilful, thorough, well-qualified; competent, credit-worthy; agreeable, cheering, gratifying, pleasant. • n advantage, benefit, boon, favour, gain, profit, utility; interest, prosperity, welfare, weal; excellence, righteousness, virtue, worth.

goodness n excellence, quality, value, worth; honesty, integrity, morality, principle, probity, righteousness, uprightness, virtue; benevolence, beneficence, benignity, good-will, humaneness.

goodwill n benevolence, kindness, good nature; ardour, earnestness, heartiness, willingness, zeal; custom, patronage.

gorgeous adj bright, brilliant, dazzling, fine, glittering, grand, magnificent, resplendent, rich.

gospel n creed, doctrine, message, news, revelation, tidings.

gossip n chat, cackle, clack, gabble, prate, prattle, tattle. • n babbler, busybody, chatterer, gadabout, gossipmonger, newsmonger, quidnunc, tale-bearer, tattler, tell-tale; cackle, chat, chit-chat, prate, prattle, tattle.

gourmet n connoisseur, epicure, epicurean.

govern vb administer, conduct, direct, manage, regulate, reign, rule, superintend, supervise; guide, pilot, steer; bridle, check, command, control, curb, restrain, sway.

government n autonomy, command, conduct, control, direction, discipline, dominion, guidance, management, regulation, restraint, rule, rulership, sway; administration, cabinet, commonwealth, polity, sovereignty, state.

governor n commander, comptroller, director, head, headmaster, manager, overseer, ruler, superintendent, supervisor; chief magistrate, executive; guardian, instructor, tutor.

grab vb capture, clutch, seize, snatch.

grace vb adorn, beautify, deck, decorate, embellish; dignify, honour. • n benignity, condescension, favour, good-will, kindness, love; devotion, efficacy, holiness, love, piety, religion, sanctity, virtue; forgiveness, mercy, pardon, reprieve; accomplishment, attractiveness, charm, elegance, polish, propriety, refinement; beauty, comeliness, ease, gracefulness, symmetry; blessing, petition, thanks.

graceful adj beautiful, becoming, comely, easy, elegant; flowing, natural, rounded, unlaboured; appropriate; felicitous, happy, tactful.

gracious adj beneficent, benevolent, benign, benignant, compassionate, condescending, favourable, friendly, gentle, good-natured, kind, kindly, lenient, merciful, mild, tender; affable, civil, courteous, easy, familiar, polite.

grade vb arrange, classify, group, order, rank, sort. • n brand, degree, intensity, stage, step, rank; gradient, incline, slope.

gradual adj approximate, continuous, gentle, progressive, regular, slow, successive.

graduate vb adapt, adjust, proportion, regulate. • n alumna, alumnus, laureate, postgraduate.

grand adj august, dignified, elevated, eminent, exalted, great, illustrious, lordly, majestic, princely, stately, sublime; fine, glorious, gorgeous, magnificent, pompous, lofty, noble, splendid, sublime, superb; chief, leading, main, pre-eminent, principal, superior.

grant vb accord, admit, allow, cede, concede, give, impart, indulge; bestow, confer, deign, invest, vouchsafe; convey, transfer, yield. • n admission, allowance, benefaction, bestowal, boon, bounty, concession, donation, endowment, gift, indulgence, largesse, present; conveyance, cession.

graphic adj descriptive, diagrammatic, figural, figurative, forcible, lively, pictorial, picturesque, striking, telling, vivid, well-delineated.

grapple vb catch, clutch, grasp, grip, hold, hug, seize, tackle, wrestle.

grasp vb catch, clasp, clinch, clutch, grapple, grip, seize; comprehend understand. • n clasp, grip, hold; comprehension, power, reach, scope.

grasping adj acquisitive, avaricious, covetous, exacting, greedy, rapacious, sordid, tight-fisted.

grate vb abrade, rub, scrape, triturate; comminute, rasp; creak, fret, grind, jar, rasp, vex. • n bars, grating, latticework, screen.

grateful adj appreciative, beholden, indebted, obliged, thankful; acceptable, agreeable, charming, delightful, gratifying, pleasant, pleasing, satisfactory, satisfying, welcome.

gratify vb delight, gladden, please; humour, fulfil, grant, indulge, requite, satisfy.

gratitude n goodwill, thankfulness.

grave adj cogent, heavy, important, momentous, pressing, serious, weighty; dignified, sage, sedate, serious, slow, solemn, staid, thoughtful; dull, plain, quiet, sober, sombre, subdued; cruel, hard, harsh, severe; dire, dismal, gross, heinous, infamous, outrageous, scandalous, shameful, shocking; heavy, hollow, low, sepulchral.

gravity n heaviness, weight; demureness, sedateness, seriousness, sobriety, thoughtfulness; importance, moment, momentousness.

graze vb brush, glance, scrape, scratch, shave, skim; browse, crop, feed, pasture.

great adj ample, big, bulky, Cyclopean, enormous, gigantic, Herculean, huge, immense, large, pregnant, vast; decided, excessive, high, much, pronounced; countless, numerous; chief, considerable, grand, important, leading, main, pre-eminent, principal, superior, weighty; celebrated, distinguished, eminent, exalted, excellent, famed, famous, far-famed, illustrious, noted, prominent, renowned; august, dignified, elevated, exalted, grand, lofty, majestic, noble.

greatness n bulk, dimensions, largeness, magnitude, size; distinction, elevation, eminence, fame, importance, renown; augustness, dignity, grandeur, majesty, loftiness, nobility, nobleness, sublimity; chivalrous, disinterestedness, generosity, magnanimity, spirit.

greed, greediness n gluttony, hunger, omnivorousness, ravenousness, voracity; avidity, covetousness, desire, eagerness, longing; avarice, cupidity, graspingness, rapacity.

green adj aquamarine, emerald, olive, verdant, verdure, viridescent, viridian; blooming, flourishing, fresh, undecayed; fresh, new, recent; immature, unfledged, unripe; callow, crude, inexpert, ignorant, inexperienced, raw, unskilful, untrained, verdant, young; raw, unseasoned. • n common, grass plot, lawn, sward, turf, verdure.

greet vb accost, address, complement, hail, receive, salute, welcome.

greeting n compliment, salutation, welcome.

grief n affliction, agony, anguish, bitterness, distress, dole, heartbreak, misery, regret, sadness, sorrow, suffering, tribulation, woe; distress, grievance, sorrow, trial, woe; disaster, failure.

grievance n burden, complaint, hardship, injury, oppression, wrong; affliction, distress, grief, sorrow, trial, woe.

grieve vb afflict, aggrieve, agonise, discomfort, distress, hurt, oppress, pain, sadden, wound; bewail, deplore, mourn, lament, regret, sorrow.

grievous adj afflicting, afflictive, burdensome, deplorable, distressing, heavy, lamentable, oppressive, painful, sad, sorrowful; baleful, baneful, calamitous, destructive, detrimental, hurtful, injurious, mischievous, noxious, troublesome; aggravated, atrocious, dreadful, flagitious, flagrant, gross, heinous, iniquitous, intense, intolerable, severe, outrageous, wicked.

grim adj cruel, ferocious, fierce, harsh, relentless, ruthless, savage, stern, unyielding; appalling, dire, dreadful, fearful, frightful, grisly, hideous, horrid, horrible, terrific.

grimace vb, n frown, scowl, smirk, sneer.

grimy adj begrimed, defiled, dirty, filthy, foul, soiled, sullied, unclean.

grind vb bruise, crunch, crush, grate, grit, pulverise, rub, triturate; sharpen, whet; afflict, harass, oppress, persecute, plague, trouble. • n chore, drudgery, labour, toil.

grip vb clasp, clutch, grasp, hold, seize.

grit vb clench, grate, grind. • n bran, gravel, pebbles, sand; courage, decision, determination, firmness, perseverance, pluck, resolution, spirit.

groan vb complain, lament, moan; creak. • n moan, whine; complaint; grouse, grumble.

gross vb accumulate, earn, make. • adj big, bulky, burly, fat, great, large; dense, dull, stupid, thick; beastly, broad, carnal, coarse, crass, earthy, impure, indelicate, licentious, low, obscene, unbecoming, unrefined, unseemly, vulgar, rough, sensual; aggravated, brutal, enormous, flagrant, glaring, grievous, manifest, obvious, palpable, plain, outrageous, shameful; aggregate, entire, total, whole. • n aggregate, bulk, total, whole.

grotesque adj bizarre, extravagant, fanciful, fantastic, incongruous, odd, strange, unnatural, whimsical, wild; absurd, antic, burlesque, ludicrous, ridiculous.

ground vb fell, place; base, establish, fix, found, set; instruct, train. • n area, clod, distance, earth, loam, mould, sod, soil, turf; country, domain, land, region, territory; acres, estate, field, property; base, basis, foundation, groundwork, support; account, consideration, excuse, gist, motive, opinion, reason.

groundless adj baseless, causeless, false, gratuitous, idle, unauthorised, unwarranted, unfounded, unjustifiable, unsolicited, unsought.

grounds npl deposit, dregs, grouts, lees, precipitate, sediment, settlings; accounts, arguments, considerations, reasons, support; campus, gardens, lawns, premises, yard.

group vb arrange, assemble, dispose, order. • n aggregation, assemblage, assembly, body, combination, class, clump, cluster, collection, order.

grow vb enlarge, expand, extend, increase, swell; arise, burgeon, develop, germinate, shoot, sprout, vegetate; advance, extend, improve, progress, swell, thrive, wax; cultivate, raise.

growl vb complain, croak, find fault, gnarl, groan, grumble, lament, murmur, snarl. • n croak, grown, snarl; complaint.

growth n augmentation, development, expansion, extension, growing, increase; burgeoning, excrescence, formation, germination, pollution, shooting, sprouting, vegetation; cultivation, produce, product, production; advance, advancement, development, improvement, progress; adulthood, maturity

grudge *vb* begrudge, envy, repine; complain, grieve, murmur. • *n* aversion, dislike, enmity, grievance, hate, hatred, ill-will, malevolence, malice, pique, rancour, resentment, spite.

grumble *vb* croak, complain, murmur, repine; gnarl, growl, snarl; roar, rumble. • *n* growl, murmur, complaint, roar, rumble.

grumpy *adj* crabbed, cross, glum, moody, morose, sour, sullen, surly.

guarantee *vb* assure, insure, pledge, secure, warrant. • *n* assurance, pledge, security, surety, warrant, warranty.

guard *vb* defend, keep, patrol, protect, safeguard, save, secure, shelter, shield, watch. • *n* aegis, bulwark, custody, defence, palladium, protection, rampart, safeguard, security, shield; keeper, guardian, patrol, sentinel, sentry, warden, watch, watchman; conduct, convoy, escort; attention, care, caution, circumspection, heed, watchful.

guarded *adj* careful, cautious, circumspect, reserved, reticent, wary, watchful.

guardian *n* custodian, defender, guard, keeper, preserver, protector, trustee, warden.

guess *vb* conjecture, divine, mistrust, surmise, suspect; fathom, find out, penetrate, solve; believe, fancy, hazard, imagine, reckon, suppose, think. • *n* conjecture, supposition, surmise.

guide *vb* conduct, escort, lead, pilot; control, direct, govern, manage, preside, regulate, rule, steer, superintend, supervise. • *n* cicerone, conductor, director, monitor, pilot; adviser, counsellor, instructor, mentor; clew, directory, index, key, thread; guidebook, itinerary, landmark.

guile *n* art, artfulness, artifice, craft, cunning, deceit, deception, duplicity, fraud, knavery, ruse, subtlety, treachery, trickery, wiles, wiliness.

guilt *n* blame, criminality, culpability, guiltless; ill-desert, iniquity, offensiveness, wickedness, wrong; crime, offence, sin, wrong.

guilty *adj* criminal, culpable, evil, sinful.

guise *n* appearance, aspect, costume, dress, fashion, figure, form, garb, manner, mode, shape; air, behaviour, demeanour, mien; custom, disguise, habit, manner, mode, pretence.

gullible *adj* confiding, credulous, naive, overtrustful, simple, unsophisticated, unsuspicious.

gush *vb* burst, flood, flow, pour, rush, spout, stream; emotionalise, sentimentalise. • *n* flow, jet, onrush, rush, spurt, surge; effusion, effusiveness, loquacity, loquaciousness, talkativeness.

gusto *n* enjoyment, liking, pleasure, relish, zest.

guy *vb* caricature, mimic, ridicule. • *n* boy, man, person; dowdy, eccentric, fright, scarecrow.

H

habit *n* condition, constitution, temperament; addiction, custom, habitude, manner, practice, rule, usage, way, wont; apparel, costume, dress, garb, habiliment.

habitual *adj* accustomed, common, confirmed, customary, everyday, familiar, inveterate, ordinary, regular, routine, settled, usual, wonted.

hackneyed *adj* banal, common, commonplace, overworked, pedestrian, stale, threadbare, trite.

haggard *adj* intractable, refractory, unruly, untamed, wild, wayward; carewom, emaciated, gaunt, ghastly, thin, wasted, worn.

haggle *vb* argue, bargain, cavil, chaffer, dispute, higgle; annoy, badger, bait, fret, harass.

hail[1] *vb* acclaim, greet, salute, welcome; accost, address, call, hallo, signal. • *n* greeting, salute.

hail[2] *vb* assail, bombard, rain, shower, storm, volley. • *n* bombardment, rain, shower, storm.

hale *adj* hardy, healthy, hearty, robust, sound.

hallow *vb* consecrate, dedicate, devote, revere, sanctify, solemnise; enshrine, honour, respect, reverence, venerate.

hallucination *n* blunder, error, fallacy, mistake;

aberration, delusion, illusion, phantasm, phantasy, self-deception, vision.

halo *n* aura, aureole, glory, nimbus.

halt[1] *vb* cease, desist, hold, rest, stand, stop. • *n* end, impasse, pause, standstill, stop.

halt[2] *vb* hesitate, pause, stammer, waver; falter, hobble, limp. • *adj* crippled, disabled, lame.

hammer *vb* beat, forge, form, shape; excogitate, contrive, invent.

hamper *vb* bind, clog, confine, curb, embarrass, encumber, entangle, fetter, hinder, impede, obstruct, prevent, restrain, restrict, shackle, trammel. • *n* basket, box, crate, picnic basket; embarrassment, encumbrance, fetter, handicap, impediment, obstruction, restraint, trammel.

hand *vb* deliver, give, present, transmit; conduct, guide, lead. • *n* direction, part, side; ability, dexterity, faculty, skill, talent; course, inning, management, turn; agency, intervention, participation, share; control, possession, power; artificer, artisan, craftsman, employee, labourer, operative, workman; index, indicator, pointer; chirography, handwriting.

handicap vb encumber, hamper, hinder, restrict. • n disadvantage, hindrance, restriction.

handle vb feel, finger, manhandle, paw, touch; direct, manage, manipulate, use, wield; discourse, discuss, treat. • n haft, helve, hilt, stock.

handsome adj admirable, comely, fine-looking, stately, well-formed, well-proportioned; appropriate, suitable, becoming, easy, graceful; generous, gracious, liberal.

handy adj adroit, clever, dextrous, expert, ready, skilful, skilled; close, convenient, near.

hang vb attach, swing; execute, truss; decline, drop, droop, incline; adorn, drape; dangle, depend, impend, swing, suspend; depend, rely; cling, loiter, rest, stick; float, hover, pay

hanker vb covet, crave, desire, hunger, long.

haphazard adj aimless, chance, random.

happen vb befall, betide, chance, come, occur.

happiness n brightness, cheerfulness, delight, gaiety, joy, light-heartedness, merriment, pleasure; beatitude, blessedness, bliss, felicity, enjoyment, welfare, well-being.

happy adj blessed, blest, blissful, cheerful, contented, joyful, joyous, light-hearted, merry; charmed, delighted, glad, gladdened, gratified, pleased, rejoiced; fortunate, lucky, prosperous, successful; able, adroit, apt, dextrous, expert, ready, skilful; befitting, felicitous, opportune, pertinent, seasonable, well-timed; auspicious, bright, favourable, propitious.

harangue vb address, declaim, spout. • n address, oration, rant, speech, tirade.

harass vb exhaust, fag, fatigue, jade, tire, weary; annoy, badger, distress, gall, heckle, disturb, harry, molest, pester, plague, tantalise, tease, torment, trouble, vex, worry.

harbour vb protect, lodge, shelter; cherish, entertain, foster, indulge. • n asylum, cover, refuge, resting place, retreat, sanctuary, shelter; anchorage, destination, haven, port.

hard adj adamantine, compact, firm, flinty, impenetrable, marble, rigid, solid, resistant, stony, stubborn, unyielding; difficult, intricate, knotty, perplexing, puzzling; arduous, exacting, fatiguing, laborious, toilsome, wearying; austere, callous, cruel, exacting, hard-hearted, incorrigible, inflexible, insensible, insensitive, obdurate, oppressive, reprobate, rigorous, severe, unfeeling, unkind, unsusceptible, unsympathetic; calamitous, disagreeable, distressing, grievous, painful, unpleasant; alcoholic, harsh, rough, sour; excessive, intemperate. • adv close, near; diligently, earnestly, energetically, incessantly, laboriously; distressfully, painfully, rigorously, severely; forcibly, vehemently, violently.

harden vb accustom, discipline, form, habituate, inure, season, train; brace, fortify, indurate, nerve, steel, stiffen, strengthen.

hardened adj annealed, case-hardened, tempered, indurated; abandoned, accustomed, benumbed, callous, confirmed, deadened, depraved, habituated, impenitent, incorrigible, inured, insensible, irreclaimable, lost, obdurate, reprobate, seared, seasoned, steeled, trained.

hardly adv barely, scarcely; cruelly, harshly, rigorously, roughly, severely, unkindly.

hardship n fatigue, toil, weariness; affliction, burden, calamity, grievance, hardness, injury, misfortune, privation, suffering, trial, trouble.

hardy adj enduring, firm, hale, healthy, hearty, inured, lusty, rigorous, robust, rugged, sound, stout, strong, sturdy, tough; bold, brave, courageous, daring, heroic, intrepid, manly, resolute.

harm vb damage, hurt, injure, scathe; abuse, desecrate, ill-use, ill-treat, maltreat, molest. • n damage, detriment, disadvantage, hurt, injury, mischief, misfortune, prejudice, wrong.

harmful adj baneful, detrimental, disadvantageous, hurtful, injurious, mischievous, noxious, pernicious, prejudicial.

harmless adj innocent, innocuous, innoxious; inoffensive, safe, unoffending.

harmonious adj concordant, consonant, harmonic; dulcet, euphonious, mellifluous, melodious, musical, smooth, tuneful; comfortable, congruent, consistent, correspondent, orderly, symmetrical; agreeable, amicable, brotherly, cordial, fraternal, friendly, harmonious, neighbourly.

harmony n euphony, melodiousness, melody; accord, accordance, agreement, chime, concord, concordance, consonance, order, unison; adaptation, congruence, congruity, consistency, correspondence, fairness, smoothness, suitableness; amity, friendship, peace.

harry vb devastate, pillage, plunder, raid, ravage, rob; annoy, chafe, disturb, fret, gall, harass, harrow, incommode, molest, pester, plague, molest, tease, torment, trouble, vex, worry.

harsh adj acid, acrid, astringent, biting, caustic, corrosive, crabbed, hard, rough, sharp, sour, tart; cacophonous, discordant, grating, jarring, metallic, raucous, strident, unmelodious; abusive, austere, crabbed, crabby, cruel, disagreeable, hard, ill-natured, ill-tempered, morose, rigorous, severe, stern, unfeeling; bearish, bluff, blunt, brutal, gruff, rude, uncivil, ungracious.

harvest vb gather, glean, reap. • n crops, produce, yield; consequence, effect, issue, outcome, produce, result.

haste n alacrity, celerity, dispatch, expedition, nimbleness, promptitude, quickness, rapidity, speed, urgency, velocity; flurry, hurry, hustle, impetuosity, precipitateness, precipitation, press, rashness, rush, vehemence.

hasten vb haste, hurry; accelerate, dispatch, expedite, precipitate, press, push, quicken, speed.

hasty adj brisk, fast, fleet, quick, rapid, speedy, swift; cursory, hurried, passing, rapid, slight, superficial; ill-advised, rash, reckless; headlong, helter-skelter, pell-mell, precipitate; abrupt, choleric, excitable, fiery, fretful, hot-headed, irascible, irritable, passionate, peevish, peppery.

hatch vb brew, concoct, contrive, excogitate, design, devise, plan, plot, project, scheme; breed, incubate.

hate vb abhor, abominate, detest, dislike, execrate, loathe, nauseate. • n abomination, animosity, antipathy, detestation, dislike, enmity, execration, hatred, hostility, loathing.

hateful adj malevolent, malicious, malign, malignant, rancorous, spiteful; abhorrent, abominable, accursed, damnable, detestable, execrable, horrid, odious, shocking; abhorrent, disgusting, foul, loathsome, nauseous, obnoxious, offensive, repellent, repugnant, repulsive, revolting.

hatred n animosity, enmity, hate, hostility, ill-will, malevolence, malice, malignity, odium, rancour; abhorrence, abomination, antipathy, aversion, detestation, disgust, execration, horror, loathing, repugnance, revulsion.

haughty adj arrogant, assuming, contemptuous, disdainful, imperious, insolent, lofty, lordly, overbearing, overweening, proud, scornful.

haul vb drag, draw, lug, pull, tow, trail, tug. • n heaving, pull, tug; booty, harvest, takings, yield.

haunt vb frequent, resort; follow, importune; hover, inhabit, obsess. • n den, resort, retreat.

havoc n carnage, damage, desolation, destruction, devastation, ravage, ruin, slaughter, waste.

hazard vb adventure, risk, venture; endanger, imperil, jeopardise. • n accident, casualty, chance, contingency, event, fortuity, stake; danger, jeopardy, peril, risk, venture.

head vb command, control, direct, govern, guide, lead, rule; aim, point, tend; beat, excel, outdo, precede, surpass. • adj chief, first, grand, highest, leading, main, principal; adverse, contrary. • n acme, summit, top; beginning, commencement, origin, rise, source; chief, chieftain, commander, director, leader, master, principal, superintendent, superior; intellect, mind, thought, understanding; branch, category, class, department, division, section, subject, topic; brain, crown, headpiece, intellect, mind, thought, understanding; cape, headland, point.

headlong adj dangerous, hasty, heady, impulsive, inconsiderate, perilous, precipitate, rash, reckless, ruinous, thoughtless; perpendicular, precipitous, sheer, steep.

headstrong adj cantankerous, cross-grained, dogged, forward, headless, heady, intractable, obstinate, self-willed, stubborn, ungovernable.

heady adj hasty, headlong, impetuous, impulsive, inconsiderate, precipitate, rash, reckless,

rushing, stubborn, thoughtless; exciting, inebriating, inflaming, intoxicating, spirituous, strong.

heal vb amend, cure, remedy, repair, restore; compose, harmonise, reconcile, settle, soothe.

health n healthfulness, robustness, salubrity, sanity, soundness, strength, tone, vigour.

healthy adj active, hale, hearty, lusty, sound, vigorous, well; bracing, healthful, health-giving, hygienic, invigorating, nourishing, salubrious.

heap vb accumulate, augment, amass, collect, overfill, pile up, store. • n accumulation, collection, cumulus, huddle, lot, mass, mound, pile.

hear vb eavesdrop, hearken, heed, listen, overhear; ascertain, discover, gather, learn, understand; examine, judge.

heart n bosom, breast; centre, core, essence, interior, kernel, marrow, meaning, pith; affection, benevolence, character, disposition, feeling, inclination, love, mind, passion, purpose, will; affections, ardour, emotion, feeling, love; boldness, courage, fortitude, resolution, spirit.

hearten vb animate, assure, cheer, comfort, console, embolden, encourage, enhearten, incite, inspire, inspirit, reassure, stimulate.

heartless adj brutal, cold, cruel, hard, harsh, merciless, pitiless, unfeeling, unsympathetic; spiritless, timid, timorous, uncourageous.

hearty adj cordial, deep, earnest, heartfelt, profound, sincere, true, unfeigned, warm; active, animated, earnest, energetic, vigorous, warm, zealous; hale, hearty, robust, sound, strong, warm; abundant, full, heavy; nourishing, rich.

heat vb excite, flush, inflame; animate, rouse, stimulate, stir. • n calorie, caloricity, torridity, warmth; excitement, fever, flush, impetuosity, passion, vehemence, violence; ardour, earnestness, fervency, fervour, glow, intensity, zeal; exasperation, fierceness, frenzy, rage.

heath n field, moor, wasteland, plain.

heave vb elevate, hoist, lift, raise; breathe, exhale, raise; cast, fling, hurl, send, throw, toss; breathe, dilate, expand, pant, rise, swell; retch, throw up; strive, struggle.

heaven n empyrean, firmament, sky, welkin; bliss, ecstasy, elysium, felicity, happiness, paradise, rapture, transport.

heavenly adj celestial, empyreal, ethereal; angelic, beatific, beatified, cherubic, divine, elysian, glorious, god-like, sainted, saintly, seraphic; beatific, blissful, celestial, delightful, divine, ecstatic, enrapturing, enravishing, glorious, golden, rapturous, ravishing, seraphic.

heavy adj grave, hard, onerous, ponderous, weighty; afflictive, burdensome, crushing, cumbersome, grievous, oppressive, severe, serious; dilatory, dull, inactive, inanimate, indolent, inert, lifeless, sleepy, slow, sluggish, stupid, torpid; chapfallen, crestfallen, crushed, depressed, dejected, despondent, disconsolate, downhearted, gloomy, low-spirited, melancholy, sad, sobered, sorrowful; difficult, laborious; tedious, tiresome, wearisome, weary; burdened, encumbered, loaded; clammy, clayey, cloggy, miry, muddy, oppressive, soggy; boisterous, deep, energetic, loud, roaring, severe, stormy, strong, tempestuous, violent; cloudy, dark, dense, gloomy, lowering, overcast.

hectic adj animated, excited, fevered, feverish.

hedge vb block, encumber, hinder, obstruct, surround; enclose, fence, fortify, guard, protect; disappear, dodge, evade, hide, skulk, temporise. • n barrier, hedgerow, fence, limit.

heed vb attend, consider, mark, mind, note, notice, observe, regard. • n attention, care, carefulness, caution, circumspection, consideration, heedfulness, mindfulness, notice, observation, regard, wariness, vigilance, watchfulness.

heedful adj attentive, careful, cautious, circumspect, mindful, observant, observing, provident, regardful, watchful, wary.

heedless adj careless, inattentive, neglectful, negligent, precipitate, rash, reckless, thoughtless, unmindful, unminding, unobservant.

height n altitude, elevation, tallness; acme, apex, climax, eminence, head, meridian, pinnacle, summit, top, vertex, zenith; eminence, hill, mountain; dignity, eminence, exaltation, grandeur, loftiness, perfection.

heighten vb elevate, raise; ennoble, exalt, magnify, make greater; augment, enhance, improve, increase, strengthen; aggravate, intensify.

help vb relieve, save, succour; abet, aid, assist, back, cooperate, second, serve, support, sustain, wait; alleviate, ameliorate, better, cure, heal, improve, remedy, restore; control, hinder, prevent, repress, resist, withstand; avoid, forbear, control. • n aid, assistance, succour, support; relief, remedy; assistant, helper, servant.

helpful adj advantageous, assistant, auxiliary, beneficial, contributory, convenient, favourable, kind, profitable, serviceable, useful.

helpless adj disabled, feeble, imbecile, impotent, infirm, powerless, prostrate, resourceless, weak; abandoned, defenceless, exposed, unprotected; desperate, irremediable, remediless.

hem vb border, edge, skirt; beset, confine, enclose, environ, surround, sew.

herald vb announce, proclaim, publish. • n announcer, crier, proclaimer, publisher.

herd vb drive, gather, lead, tend; assemble, associate, flock. • n drover, herder, shepherd; crowd, multitude, populace, rabble; assemblage, assembly, collection, crowd, drove, flock, multitude.

heresy n dissent, error, heterodoxy, impiety.

heretic n dissenter, dissident, nonconformist, recusant, schismatic, sectarian, separatist, unbeliever.

heritage n inheritance, legacy, patrimony.

hermit n anchoress, anchoret, anchorite, anchoritess, ascetic, eremite, monk, recluse, solitary.

heroic adj bold, brave, courageous, daring, dauntless, fearless, gallant, illustrious, intrepid, magnanimous, noble, valiant.

hesitate vb boggle, delay, demur, doubt, pause, scruple, shilly-shally, vacillate, waver; falter, stammer, stutter.

hesitation n halting, misgiving, reluctance; delay, doubt, indecision, suspense, uncertainty, vacillation; faltering, stammering, stuttering.

hidden adj blind, clandestine, cloaked, close, concealed, covered, covert, enshrouded, latent, masked, occult, private, secret, suppressed, undiscovered, veiled; abstruse, cabbalistic, cryptic, dark, esoteric, hermetic, inward, mysterious, mystic, mystical, obscure, occult, oracular.

hide vb bury, conceal, cover, secrete, suppress, withhold; cloak, disguise, eclipse, hoard, mask, screen, shelter, suppress, veil.

hideous adj abominable, appalling, awful, dreadful, frightful, ghastly, ghoulish, grim, grisly, horrible, horrid, repulsive, revolting, shocking, terrible, terrifying.

high adj elevated, high-reaching, lofty, soaring, tall, towering; distinguished, eminent, pre-eminent, prominent, superior; admirable, dignified, elevated, exalted, great, noble; arrogant, haughty, lordly, proud, supercilious; boisterous, strong, tumultuous, turbulent, violent; costly, dear, pricey; acute, high-pitched, piercing, sharp, shrill.

hilarious adj boisterous, cheerful, convivial, exhilarated, happy, jolly, jovial, joyful, merry, mirthful, noisy.

hilarity n cheerfulness, conviviality, exhilarated, gaiety, glee, jollity, joviality, joyousness.

hinder vb bar, check, clog, delay, embarrass, encumber, impede, interrupt, obstruct, oppose, prevent, restrain, retard, stop, thwart.

hindrance n check, deterrent, encumbrance, hitch, impediment, interruption, obstacle, obstruction, restraint, stop, stoppage.

hint vb allude, glance, hint, imply, insinuate, intimate, mention, refer, suggest. • n allusion, implication, innuendo, insinuation, intimation, mention, reminder, suggestion, trace.

hire vb buy, rent, secure; charter, employ, engage, lease, let.

history n account, autobiography, annals, biography, chronicle, genealogy, memoirs, narration, narrative, recital, record, relation, story.

hit vb discomfit, hurt, knock, strike; accomplish, achieve, attain, gain, reach, secure, succeed, win; accord, fit, suit; beat, clash, collide, contact, smite. • n blow, collision, strike, stroke; chance, fortune, hazard, success, venture.

hitch vb catch, impede, stick, stop; attach, connect, fasten, harness, join, tether, tie, unite, yoke. • n catch, check, hindrance, impediment, interruption, obstacle; knot, noose.

hoard vb accumulate, amass, collect, deposit, garner, hive, husband, save, store, treasure. • n accumulation, collection, deposit, fund, mass, reserve, savings, stockpile, store.

hoarse adj discordant, grating, gruff, guttural, harsh, husky, low, raucous, rough.

hoax vb deceive, dupe, fool, gammon, gull, hoodwink, swindle, trick. • n canard, cheat, deception, fraud, joke, trick, swindle.

hoist vb elevate, heave, lift, raise, rear.

hold vb clasp, clinch, clutch, grasp, grip, seize; have, keep, occupy, possess, retain; bind, confine, control, detain, imprison, restrain, restrict; bind, connect, fasten, fix, lock; arrest, check, stay, stop, suspend, withhold; continue, keep up, maintain, manage, prosecute, support, sustain; cherish, embrace, entertain; account, believe, consider, count, deem, entertain, esteem, judge, reckon, regard, think; accommodate, admit, carry, contain, receive, stow; assemble, conduct, convene; continue, endure, last, persist, remain; adhere, cleave, cling, cohere, stick. • n anchor, bite, clasp, control, embrace, foothold, grasp, grip, possession, retention; prop, stay, support; claim, footing, vantage point; castle, fort, fortification, fortress, stronghold, tower; locker, storage, storehouse.

hole n aperture, opening, perforation; abyss, bore, cave, cavern, cavity, chasm, depression, excavation, eye, hollow, pit, pore, void; burrow, cover, den, lair, retreat; den, hovel, kennel.

holiday n anniversary, celebration, feast, festival, festivity, fete, gala, recess, vacation.

holiness n blessedness, consecration, devotion, devoutness, godliness, piety, purity, religiousness, righteousness, sacredness, saintliness.

hollow vb dig, excavate, groove, scoop. • adj cavernous, concave, depressed, empty, sunken, vacant, void; deceitful, faithless, false, false-hearted, hollow-hearted, hypocritical, insincere, pharisaical, treacherous, unfeeling; deep, low, muffled, reverberating, rumbling, sepulchral. • n basin, bowl, depression; cave, cavern, cavity, concavity, dent, dimple, dint, depression, excavation, hole, pit; canal, channel, cup, dimple, dig, groove, pocket, sag.

holocaust n carnage, destruction, devastation, genocide, massacre.

holy adj blessed, consecrated, dedicated, devoted, hallowed, sacred, sanctified; devout, godly, pious, pure, religious, righteous, saintlike, saintly, sinless, spiritual.

homage n allegiance, devotion, fealty, fidelity, loyalty; court, deference, duty, honour, obei-

sance, respect, reverence, service; adoration, devotion, worship.

home adj domestic, family; close, direct, effective, penetrating, pointed. • n abode, dwelling, seat, quarters, residence.

homely adj domestic, familiar; coarse, commonplace, homespun, plain, simple, unpolished, unpretentious.

honest adj equitable, fair, faithful, honourable, open, straightforward; conscientious, equitable, fair, faithful, reliable, sound, square, true, trustworthy, trusty, uncorrupted, upright, virtuous; faithful, genuine, thorough, unadulterated; creditable, decent, honourable, proper, reputable, respectable, suitable; chaste, decent, faithful, virtuous; candid, direct, frank, ingenuous, open, sincere, unreserved.

honorary adj formal, nominal, titular, unofficial, unpaid.

honour vb dignify, exalt, glorify, grace; respect, revere, reverence, venerate; adore, hallow, worship; celebrate, commemorate, keep, observe. • n civility, deference, esteem, homage, respect, reverence, veneration; dignity, distinction, elevation, nobleness; consideration, credit, esteem, fame, glory, reputation; high-mindedness, honesty, integrity, magnanimity, probity, uprightness; chastity, purity, virtue; glory, pride.

honourable adj elevated, famous, great, illustrious, noble; admirable, conscientious, fair, honest, just, magnanimous, true, trustworthy, upright, virtuous, worshipful; creditable, esteemed, proper, respected, reputable, right.

hoodwink vb blind, blindfold; cloak, conceal, cover, hide; cheat, circumvent, cozen, deceive, delete, dupe, fool, gull, impose, overreach, trick.

hoot vb boo, cry, jeer, shout, yell; condemn, decry, denounce, execrate, hiss.

hop vb bound, caper, frisk, jump, leap, skip, spring; dance, trip; halt, hobble, limp. • n bound, caper, dance, jump, leap, skip, spring.

hope vb anticipate, await, desire, expect, long; believe, rely, trust. • n confidence, belief, faith, reliance, sanguineness, sanguinity, trust; anticipation, desire, expectancy, expectation.

hopeful adj anticipatory, confident, expectant, fond, optimistic, sanguine; cheerful, encouraging, promising.

hopeless adj abject, crushed, depressed, despondent, despairing, desperate, disconsolate, downcast, forlorn, pessimistic, woebegone; abandoned, helpless, incurable, irremediable, remediless; impossible, impracticable.

horde n clan, crew, gang, troop; crowd, multitude, pack, throng.

horrid adj alarming, awful, bristling, dire, dreadful, fearful, frightful, harrowing, hideous, horrible, horrific, horrifying, rough, terrible, terrific; abominable, disagreeable, disgusting, odious, offensive, repulsive, revolting, shocking.

horrify vb alarm, frighten, shock, terrify.

horror n alarm, awe, consternation, dismay, dread, fear, fright, panic; abhorrence, abomination, antipathy, aversion, detestation, disgust, hatred, loathing, repugnance, revulsion.

hospitable adj attentive, bountiful, kind; bountiful, cordial, generous, liberal, open, receptive, sociable, unconstrained, unreserved.

host[1] n entertainer, innkeeper, landlord, master of ceremonies, presenter, proprietor, owner.

host[2] n array, army, legion; assemblage, assembly, horde, multitude, throng.

host[3] n bread, consecrated bread, wafer.

hostile adj inimical, unfriendly, warlike; adverse, antagonistic, contrary, opposed, opposite.

hot adj burning, fiery, scalding; boiling, flaming, heated, incandescent, parching, roasting, torrid; heated, oppressive, sweltering, warm; angry, choleric, excitable, furious, hasty, impatient, impetuous, irascible, lustful, passionate, touchy, urgent, violent; animated, ardent, eager, fervent, fervid, glowing, passionate, vehement; acrid, biting, peppery, piquant, pungent, sharp, stinging.

house vb harbour, lodge, protect, shelter. • n abode, domicile, dwelling, habitation, home, mansion, residence; building, edifice, family, household; kindred, race, lineage, tribe; company, concern, firm, partnership; hotel, inn, public house, tavern.

hover vb flutter; hang; vacillate, waver.

however adv but, however, nevertheless, notwithstanding, still, though, yet.

howl vb bawl, cry, lament, ululate, weep, yell.

huddle vb cluster, crowd, gather; crouch, curl up, nestle, snuggle. • n confusion, crowd, disorder, disturbance, jumble, tumult.

hue n cast, colour, complexion, dye, shade, tinge, tint, tone.

hug vb clasp, cling, cuddle, embrace, grasp, grip, squeeze; cherish, nurse, retain. • n clasp, cuddle, embrace, grasp, squeeze.

huge adj bulky, colossal, elephantine, enormous, gigantic, immense, stupendous, vast.

hum vb buzz, drone, murmur; croon, sing.

humane adj accommodating, benevolent, benign, charitable, clement, compassionate, gentle, good-hearted, kind, kind-hearted, lenient, merciful, obliging, tender, sympathetic; cultivating, elevating, humanising, rational, spiritual.

humanise vb civilise, cultivate, educate, enlighten, improve, polish, reclaim, refine, soften.

humanity n benevolence, benignity, charity, fellow-feeling, humaneness, kind-heartedness, kindness, philanthropy, sympathy, tenderness; humankind, mankind, mortality.

humble vb abase, abash, break, crush, debase,

degrade, disgrace, humiliate, lower, mortify, reduce, sink subdue. • adj meek, modest, lowly, simple, submissive, unambitious, unassuming, unobtrusive, unostentatious; low, meek, obscure, mean, plain, poor, small, undistinguished.

humdrum adj boring, dronish, dreary, dry, dull, monotonous, prosy, stupid, tedious, tiresome.

humid adj damp, dank, moist, wet.

humiliate vb abase, abash, debase, degrade, depress, humble, mortify, shame.

humility n diffidence, humbleness, lowliness, meekness, modesty, self-abasement.

humorous adj comic, comical, droll, facetious, funny, humorous, jocose, jocular, laughable, ludicrous, merry, playful, pleasant, sportive, whimsical, witty.

humour vb favour, gratify, indulge. • n bent, bias, disposition, predilection, prosperity, temper, vein; mood, state, temper; caprice, crochet, fancy, freak, maggot, vagary, whim, whimsey, wrinkle; drollery, facetiousness, fun, jocoseness, jocularity, pleasantry, wit; fluid, moisture.

hunch vb arch, jostle, nudge, punch, push, shove. • n bunch, hump, knob, protuberance; nudge, punch, push, shove; feeling, idea, intuition, premonition.

hungry adj covetous, craving, desirous, greedy; famished, starved, starving.

hunt vb chase, drive, follow, hound, pursue, stalk, trap, trail; poach, shoot; search, seek. • n chase, field-sport, hunting, pursuit.

hurl vb cast, fling, pitch, project, send, sling, throw, toss.

hurricane n cyclone, gale, storm, tempest, tornado, typhoon.

hurried adj cursory, hasty, slight, superficial.

hurry vb drive, precipitate, dispatch, expedite, hasten, quicken, speed; haste, scurry. • n agitation, bustle, confusion, flurry, flutter, perturbation, precipitation; celerity, haste, dispatch, expedition, promptitude, promptness, quickness.

hurt vb damage, disable, disadvantage, harm, impair, injure, harm, mar; bruise, pain, wound; afflict, grieve, offend; ache, pain, smart, throb. • n damage, detriment, disadvantage, harm, injury, mischief; ache, bruise, pain, suffering.

hurtful adj baleful, baneful, deleterious, destructive, detrimental, disadvantageous, harmful, injurious, mischievous, noxious, pernicious.

hush vb quiet, repress, silence, still, suppress; appease, assuage, calm, console, quiet, still. • n quiet, quietness, silence, stillness.

hypocrite n deceiver, dissembler, impostor.

hypocritical adj deceiving, dissembling, false, insincere, spurious, two-faced.

hysterical adj frantic, frenzied, overwrought, uncontrollable; comical uproarious.

I

icy adj glacial; chilling, cold, frosty; cold-hearted, distant, frigid, indifferent, unemotional.

idea n archetype, essence, exemplar, ideal, model, pattern, plan, model; fantasy, fiction, image, imagination; apprehension, conceit, conception, fancy, illusion, impression, thought; belief, judgement, notion, opinion, sentiment.

ideal adj intellectual, mental; chimerical, fancied, fanciful, fantastic, illusory, imaginary, unreal, visionary, shadowy; complete, consummate, excellent, perfect; impractical, unattainable, utopian. • n criterion, model, standard.

identical adj equivalent, same, selfsame.

identity n existence, individuality, personality.

idiot n blockhead, booby, dunce, fool, ignoramus, imbecile, simpleton.

idle adj inactive, unemployed, unoccupied, vacant; indolent, inert, lazy slothful, sluggish; abortive, bootless, fruitless, futile, groundless; ineffectual, unavailing, useless, vain; foolish, frivolous, trashy, trifling, trivial, unimportant, unprofitable. • vb dally, dawdle, laze, loiter, potter, waste; drift, shirk, slack.

idol n deity, god, icon, image, pagan, simulacrum, symbol; delusion, falsity, pretender, sham; beloved, darling, favourite, pet.

idolise vb canonise, deify; adore, honour, love, reverence, venerate.

ignoble adj base-born, low, low-born, mean, peasant, plebeian, rustic, vulgar; contemptible, degraded, insignificant, mean, worthless; disgraceful, dishonourable, infamous, low.

ignominious adj discreditable, disgraceful, dishonourable, disreputable, infamous, opprobrious, scandalous, shameful; base, contemptible.

ignorant adj blind, illiterate, nescient, unaware, unconversant, uneducated, unenlightened, uninformed, uninstructed, unlearned, unread, untaught, untutored, unwitting.

ignore vb disregard, neglect, overlook, reject.

ill adj bad, evil, faulty, harmful, iniquitous, naughty, unfavourable, unfortunate, unjust, wicked; ailing, diseased, disordered, indisposed, sick, unwell, wrong; crabbed, cross, hateful, malicious, malevolent, peevish, surly, unkind, ill-bred; ill-favoured, ugly, unprepossessing. • adv badly, poorly, unfortunately. • n badness, depravity, evil, mischief, misfortune, wickedness; affliction, ailment, calamity, harm, misery.

illegal adj contraband, forbidden, illegitimate, illicit, prohibited, unauthorised, unlawful.

illegible adj indecipherable, obscure, undecipherable, unreadable.

illegitimate adj bastard, misbegotten, natural.

illicit adj illegal, illegitimate, unauthorised, unlawful, unlegalised, unlicensed; criminal, guilty, forbidden, improper, wrong.

illiterate adj ignorant, uneducated, uninstructed, unlearned, unlettered, unstructured, untaught.

illness n ailing, ailment, complaint, disease, disorder, indisposition, malady, sickness.

illogical adj absurd, fallacious, inconsistent, inconclusive, inconsequent, incorrect, invalid, unreasonable, unsound.

illuminate vb illume, illumine, light; adorn, brighten, decorate, depict, edify, enlighten, inform, inspire, instruct, make wise.

illusion n chimera, deception, delusion, error, fallacy, false appearance, fantasy, hallucination, mockery, phantasm.

illusive, illusory adj barmecide, deceitful, deceptive, delusive, fallacious, imaginary, make-believe, mock, sham, unsatisfying, unreal, unsubstantial, visionary, tantalising.

illustrate vb clarify, demonstrate, elucidate, enlighten, exemplify, explain; adorn, depict, draw.

illustration n demonstration, elucidation, enlightenment, exemplification, explanation, interpretation; adornment, decoration, picture.

illustrious adj bright, brilliant, glorious, radiant, splendid; celebrated, conspicuous, distinguished, eminent, famed, famous, noble, noted.

image n idol, statue; copy, effigy, figure, form, imago, likeness, picture, resemblance, representation, shape, similitude, simulacrum, statue, symbol; conception, counterpart, embodiment, idea, reflection.

imaginable adj assumable, cogitable, conceivable, conjecturable, plausible, possible.

imaginary adj chimerical, dreamy, fancied, fanciful, fantastic, fictitious, ideal, illusive, illusory, invented, quixotic, shadowy, unreal, utopian, visionary, wild; hypothetical, supposed.

imagination n chimera, conception, fancy, fantasy, invention, unreality; position; contrivance, device, plot, scheme.

imaginative adj creative, dreamy, fanciful, inventive, poetical, visionary.

imagine vb conceive, dream, fancy, imagine, picture, pretend; contrive, create, devise, frame, invent, mould, project; assume, suppose, hypothesise; apprehend, assume, believe, deem, guess, opine, suppose, think.

imbecile adj cretinous, drivelling, fatuous, feeble, feeble-minded, foolish, helpless, idiotic, inane, infirm, witless. • n dotard, driveller.

imitate *vb* copy, counterfeit, duplicate, echo, emulate, follow, forge, mirror, reproduce, simulate; ape, impersonate, mimic, mock, personate; burlesque, parody, travesty.

imitation *adj* artificial, fake, man-made, mock, reproduction, synthetic. • *n* aping, copying, imitation, mimicking, parroting; copy, duplicate, likeness, resemblance; mimicry, mocking; burlesque, parody, travesty.

immaculate *adj* clean, pure, spotless, stainless, unblemished, uncontaminated, undefiled, unpolluted, unspotted, unsullied, untainted, untarnished; faultless, guiltless, holy, innocent, pure, saintly, sinless, stainless.

immaterial *adj* bodiless, ethereal, extramundane, impalpable, incorporeal, mental, metaphysical, spiritual, unbodied, unfleshly, unsubstantial; inconsequential, insignificant, nonessential, unessential, unimportant.

immature *adj* crude, green, imperfect, raw, rudimental, rudimentary, unfinished, unformed, unprepared, unripe, unripened, youthful; hasty, premature, unseasonable, untimely.

immediate *adj* close, contiguous, near, next, proximate; intuitive, primary, unmeditated; direct, instant, instantaneous, present, pressing.

immediately *adv* closely, proximately; directly, forthwith, instantly, presently, presto, pronto.

immense *adj* boundless, illimitable, infinite, interminable, measureless, unbounded, unlimited; colossal, elephantine, enormous, gigantic, huge, large, monstrous, mountainous, prodigious, stupendous, titanic, tremendous, vast.

immerse *vb* baptise, bathe, dip, douse, duck, overwhelm, plunge, sink, souse, submerge; absorb, engage, involve, sink.

imminent *adj* close, impending, near, overhanging, threatening; alarming, dangerous, perilous.

immobile *adj* fixed, immovable, inflexible, motionless, quiescent, stable, static, stationary, steadfast; dull, expressionless, impassive, rigid.

immoderate *adj* excessive, exorbitant, extravagant, extreme, inordinate, intemperate.

immoral *adj* antisocial, corrupt, loose, sinful, unethical, vicious, wicked, wrong; bad, depraved, dissolute, profligate, unprincipled, vicious; abandoned, depraved, dissolute, indecent.

immortal *adj* deathless, ever-living, imperishable, incorruptible, indestructible, indissoluble, never-dying, undying, unfading; ceaseless, continuing, eternal, endless, everlasting, never-ending, perpetual, sempiternal; abiding, enduring, lasting, permanent.

immovable *adj* firm, fixed, immobile, stable, stationary; impassive, steadfast, unalterable.

immunity *n* exemption, exoneration, freedom, release; charter, franchise, liberty, license, prerogative, privilege, right.

imp *n* demon, devil, elf, flibbertigibbet, hobgoblin, scamp, sprite; graft, scion, shoot.

impact *vb* collide, crash, strike. • *n* brunt, impression, impulse, shock, stroke, touch; collision, contact, impinging, striking.

impair *vb* blemish, damage, deface, deteriorate, injure, mar, ruin, spoil, vitiate; decrease, diminish, lessen, reduce; enervate, enfeeble, weaken

impart *vb* bestow, confer, give, grant; communicate, disclose, discover, divulge, relate, reveal.

impartial *adj* candid, disinterested, dispassionate, equal, equitable, even-handed, fair, honourable, just, unbiased, unprejudiced, unwarped.

impassable *adj* blocked, closed, impenetrable, impermeable, impervious, inaccessible.

impassioned *adj* animated, ardent, burning, excited, fervent, fervid, fiery, glowing, impetuous, intense, passionate, vehement, warm, zealous.

impassive *adj* calm, passionless; apathetic, callous, indifferent, insensible, insusceptible, unfeeling, unimpressible, unsusceptible.

impatience *n* disquietude, restlessness, uneasiness; eagerness, haste, impetuosity, precipitation, vehemence; heat, irritability, violence.

impatient *adj* restless, uneasy, unquiet; eager, hasty, impetuous, precipitate, vehement; abrupt, brusque, choleric, fretful, hot, intolerant, irritable, peevish, sudden, vehement, testy, violent.

impeach *vb* accuse, arraign, charge, indict; asperse, censure, denounce, disparage, discredit, impair, impute, incriminate, lessen.

impeccable *adj* faultless, immaculate, incorrupt, innocent, perfect, pure, sinless, stainless.

impede *vb* bar, block, check, clog, curb, delay, encumber, hinder, interrupt, obstruct, restrain, retard, stop, thwart.

impediment *n* bar, barrier, block, check, curb, difficulty, encumbrance, hindrance, obstacle, obstruction, stumbling block.

impel *vb* drive, push, send, urge; actuate, animate, compel, constrain, embolden, incite, induce, influence, instigate, move, stimulate.

impend *vb* approach, menace, near, threaten.

impenetrable *adj* impermeable, impervious, inaccessible; cold, dull, impassive, indifferent, obtuse, senseless, stolid, unsympathetic; dense.

impenitent *adj* hardened, hard-hearted, incorrigible, irreclaimable, obdurate, recusant, relentless, stubborn, unconverted, unrepentant.

imperative *adj* authoritative, commanding, despotic, domineering, imperious, overbearing, peremptory, urgent; binding, obligatory.

imperceptible *adj* inaudible, indistinguishable, invisible, undiscerning; fine, impalpable, inappreciable, gradual, minute.

imperfect *adj* abortive, crude, deficient, garbled, incomplete, poor; defective, faulty.

imperfection *n* defectiveness, deficiency, fault-

iness, incompleteness; blemish, defect, fault, flaw, lack, stain, taint; failing, foible, frailty, limitation, vice, weakness.

Imperial adj kingly, regal, royal, sovereign; august, consummate, exalted, grand, great, kingly, magnificent, majestic, noble, regal, royal, queenly, supreme, sovereign, consummate.

Imperil vb endanger, expose, hazard, jeopardise.

Imperious adj arrogant, authoritative, commanding, compelling, despotic, dictatorial, domineering, haughty, imperative, lordly, magisterial, overbearing, tyrannical, urgent, compelling.

Impersonate vb act, ape, enact, imitate, mimic, mock, personate; embody, incarnate, personify.

Impertinence n irrelevance, irrelevancy, unfitness, impropriety; assurance, boldness, brass, brazenness, effrontery, face, forwardness, impudence, incivility, insolence, intrusiveness, presumption, rudeness, sauciness, pertness.

Impertinent adj inapplicable, inapposite, irrelevant; bold, forward, impudent, insolent, intrusive, meddling, officious, pert, rude, saucy.

Impetuous adj ardent, boisterous, brash, breakneck, fierce, fiery, furious, hasty, headlong, hot, hot-headed, impulsive, overzealous, passionate, precipitate, vehement, violent.

Impetus n energy, force, momentum.

Implacable adj deadly, inexorable, merciless, pitiless, rancorous, relentless, unappeasable, unforgiving, unpropitiating, unrelenting.

Implement vb effect, execute, fulfil. • n appliance, instrument, tool, utensil.

Implicate vb entangle, enfold; compromise, concern, entangle, include, involve.

Implication n entanglement, involvement, involution; connotation, hint, inference, innuendo, intimation; conclusion, meaning, significance.

Implicit adj implied, inferred, understood; absolute, constant, firm, steadfast, unhesitating, unquestioning, unreserved, unshaken.

Implore vb adjure, ask, beg, beseech, entreat, petition, pray, solicit, supplicate.

Imply vb betoken, connote, denote, import, include, infer, insinuate, involve, mean, presuppose, signify.

Impolite adj bearish, boorish, discourteous, disrespectful, ill-bred, insolent, rough, rude, uncivil, uncourteous, ungentle, ungentlemanly, ungracious, unmannerly, unpolished, unrefined.

Import vb bring in, introduce, transport; betoken, denote, imply, mean, purport, signify. • n goods, importation, merchandise; bearing, drift, gist, intention, interpretation, matter, meaning, purpose, sense, signification, spirit, tenor; consequence, importance, significance, weight.

Importance n concern, consequence, gravity, import, moment, momentousness, significance, weight, weightiness; consequence, pomposity.

Important adj considerable, grave, material, momentous, notable, pompous, ponderous, serious, significant, urgent, valuable, weighty; esteemed, influential, prominent, substantial; consequential, pompous, self-important.

Importune vb ask, beset, dun, ply, press, solicit.

Impose vb lay, place, put, set; appoint, charge, dictate, enjoin, force, inflict, obtrude, prescribe, tax; (with on, upon) abuse, cheat, circumvent, deceive, delude, dupe, exploit, hoax, trick.

Imposing adj august, commanding, dignified, exalted, grand, grandiose, impressive, lofty, magnificent, majestic, noble, stately, striking.

Impossible adj hopeless, impracticable, infeasible, unachievable, unattainable; self-contradictory, inconceivable, unthinkable.

Impostor n charlatan, cheat, counterfeiter, deceiver, double-dealer, hypocrite, knave, mountebank, pretender, quack, rogue, trickster.

Impotent adj disabled, enfeebled, feeble, frail, helpless, incapable, incapacitated, incompetent, inefficient, powerless, weak; barren, sterile.

Impoverish vb beggar, pauperise, ruin; deplete, exhaust, ruin.

Impracticable adj impossible, infeasible; intractable, obstinate, recalcitrant, stubborn, unmanageable; impassable, insurmountable.

Impracticality n impossibility, impracticableness, impractibility, infeasibility, unpracticability; irrationality, unreality, unreasonableness.

Impregnable adj immovable, invincible, inviolable, invulnerable, irrefrangible, secure, unconquerable, unassailable.

Impregnate vb fecundate, fertilise, fructify; dye, fill, imbrue, imbue, infuse, permeate, pervade, saturate, soak, tincture, tinge.

Impress vb engrave, imprint, print, stamp; affect, move, strike; fix, inculcate; draft, enlist, levy, press, requisition. • n impression, imprint, mark, print, seal, stamp; cognisance, device.

Impression n edition, imprinting, printing, stamping; brand, dent, impress, mark, stamp; effect, influence, sensation; fancy, idea, instinct, notion, opinion, recollection.

Impressive adj affecting, effective, emphatic, exciting, forcible, moving, overpowering, powerful, solemn, splendid, striking.

Imprison vb confine, jail, immure, incarcerate.

Imprisonment n captivity, commitment, confinement, constraint, durance, duress.

Improbable adj doubtful, uncertain, unlikely, implausible.

Impromptu adj extempore, improvised, offhand, spontaneous, unpremeditated, unprepared, unrehearsed. • adv extemporaneously, extemporarily, extempore, offhand, ad-lib.

Improper adj immodest, inapposite, inappropriate, irregular, unadapted, unapt, unfit, unsuitable,

unsuited; indecent, indecorous, indelicate, unbecoming, unseemly; erroneous, inaccurate.

Improve vb ameliorate, amend, better, correct,
edify, meliorate, mend, rectify, reform, correct,
edify; cultivate; gain, mend, progress; enhance.

Improvement n amelioration, amendment, bet-
tering, improving, advancement, amendment,
betterment, proficiency, progress.

Improvident adj careless, heedless, imprudent,
incautious, inconsiderate, negligent, prodigal,
rash, reckless, shiftless, thoughtless, wasteful.

Improvisation n ad-libbing, contrivance, ex-
temporisation, fabrication, invention; (mus) extempore, impromptu.

Imprudent adj careless, heedless, ill-advised,
ill-judged, improvident, incautious, inconsiderate, indiscreet, rash, unadvised, unwise.

Impudence n assurance, audacity, boldness,
brashness, brass, bumptiousness, cheek, cheeki-
ness, effrontery, face, flippancy, forwardness,
front, gall, impertinence, insolence, jaw, lip,
nerve, pertness, presumption, rudeness, sauciness, shamelessness.

Impudent adj bold, bold-faced, brazen, brazen-
faced, cool, flippant, forward, immodest, impertinent, insolent, insulting, pert, presumptuous,
rude, saucy, shameless.

Impulse n force, impetus, impelling, momentum, push, thrust; appetite, inclination, instinct,
passion, proclivity; incentive, incitement, influence, instigation, motive, instigation.

Impulsive adj impelling, moving, propulsive;
emotional, hasty, heedless, hot, impetuous, mad-
cap, passionate, quick, rash, vehement, violent.

Impunity n exemption, immunity, liberty, licence, permission, security.

Impure adj defiled, dirty, feculent, filthy, foul,
polluted, unclean; bawdy, coarse, immodest,
gross, immoral, indelicate, indecent, lewd.

Impute vb ascribe, attribute, charge, consider,
imply, insinuate, refer.

Inability n impotence, incapacity, incapability,
incompetence, incompetency, inefficiency; disability, disqualification.

Inaccuracy n incorrectness, inexactness; blunder, defect, error, fault, mistake.

Inactive adj inactive; dormant, inert, inoperative, peaceful, quiet, quiescent; dilatory, drowsy,
dull, idle, inanimate, indolent, inert, lazy, lifeless, lumpish, passive, slothful, sleepy, stagnant.

Inadequate adj disproportionate, incapable, insufficient, unequal; defective, imperfect, inapt,
incompetent, incomplete.

Inadmissible adj improper, incompetent, unacceptable, unallowable, unqualified.

Inadvertently adv accidently, carelessly, heed-
lessly, inconsiderately, unintentionally.

Inane adj empty, fatuous, vacuous, void; fool-

ish, frivolous, idiotic, puerile, senseless, silly,
stupid, trifling, vain, worthless.

Inanimate adj breathless, dead, extinct; dead,
dull, inert, lifeless, soulless, spiritless.

Inapplicable adj inapposite, inappropriate, inapt, irrelevant, unfit, unsuitable, unsuited.

Inappropriate adj inapposite, unadapted, unbecoming, unfit, unsuitable, unsullied.

Inattentive adj absent-minded, careless, disregarding, heedless, inadvertent, inconsiderate,
neglectful, remiss, thoughtless, unmindful.

Inaugurate vb induct, install, introduce, invest;
begin, commence, initiate, institute, originate.

Incalculable adj countless, enormous, immense, incalculable, inestimable, innumerable,
sumless, unknown, untold.

Incandescent adj aglow, candent, candescent,
gleaming, glowing, luminous, luminant, radiant.

Incapable adj feeble, impotent, incompetent,
insufficient, unable, unfit, unfitted, unqualified.

Incapacitate vb cripple, disable; disqualify.

Incapacity n disability, inability, incapabilit /,
incompetence; disqualification, unfitness.

Incarnation n embodiment, exemplification,
impersonation, manifestation, personification.

Incense[1] vb anger, chafe, enkindle, enrage, exasperate, excite, heat, inflame, irritate, madden.

Incense[2] n aroma, fragrance, perfume, scent;
admiration, adulation, applause, laudation.

Incentive n cause, encouragement, goad, impulse, incitement, inducement, instigation,
mainspring, motive, provocation, spur, stimulus.

Inception n beginning, commencement, inauguration, initiation, origin, rise, start.

Incessant adj ceaseless, constant, continual,
continuous, eternal, everlasting, never-ending,
perpetual, uninterrupted, unremitting.

Incident n circumstance, episode, event, fact,
happening, occurrence.

Incidental adj accidental, casual, chance, concomitant, contingent, fortuitous, subordinate;
adventitious, extraneous, occasional.

Incipient adj beginning, commencing, inchoate,
inceptive, originating, starting.

Incision n cut, gash, notch, opening.

Incisive adj cutting; acute, biting, sarcastic, satirical, sharp; acute, clear, distinct, penetrating,
sharp-cut, trenchant.

Incite vb actuate, animate, arouse, drive, encourage, excite, foment, goad, hound, impel, instigate, prod, prompt, provoke, push, rouse, spur.

Incivility n discourteousness, discourtesy, disrespect, ill-breeding, ill-manners, impoliteness,
impudence, inurbanity, rudeness.

Inclement adj boisterous, harsh, rigorous,
rough, severe, stormy; cruel, harsh, severe.

Inclination n inclining, leaning, slant, slope;
trending, verging; aptitude, bent, bias, disposi-

tion, penchant, predilection, predisposition, proclivity, proneness, propensity, tendency, turn, twist; desire, fondness, liking, taste, partiality, predilection, wish; bow, nod, obeisance.

incline vb lean, slant, slope; bend, nod, verge; tend; bias, dispose, predispose, turn; bend, bow. • n ascent, descent, grade, gradient, rise, slope.

include vb contain, hold; comprehend, comprise, contain, cover, embody, embrace, incorporate, involve, take in.

incognito, incognita adj camouflaged, concealed, disguised, unknown.

incoherent adj detached, loose, nonadhesive, noncohesive; disconnected, incongruous, inconsequential, inconsistent, uncoordinated; confused, illogical, irrational, rambling, unintelligible, wild.

income n earnings, emolument, gains, interest, pay, perquisite, proceeds, profits, receipts, rents, return, revenue, salary, wages.

incomparable adj matchless, inimitable, peerless, surpassing, transcendent, unequalled.

incompatible adj contradictory, incongruous, inconsistent, inharmonious, irreconcilable, unadapted, unsuitable.

incompetent adj incapable, unable; inadequate, insufficient; disqualified, incapacitated, unconstitutional, unfit, unfitted.

incomplete adj defective, deficient, imperfect, partial; uncompleted, unfinished.

incomprehensible adj inconceivable, inexhaustible, unfathomable, unimaginable; inconceivable, unintelligible, unthinkable.

inconceivable adj incomprehensible, incredible, unbelievable, unimaginable, unthinkable.

inconclusive adj inconsequent, inconsequential, indecisive, unconvincing, illogical, unproved, unproven.

incongruous adj absurd, contradictory, contrary, disagreeing, discrepant, inappropriate, incoherent, incompatible, inconsistent, inharmonious, unfit, unsuitable.

inconsiderable adj immaterial, insignificant, petty, slight, small, trifling, trivial, unimportant.

inconsiderate adj intolerant, uncharitable, unthoughtful; careless, heedless, giddy, harebrained, hasty, headlong, imprudent, inadvertent, inattentive, indifferent, indiscreet, lightheaded, negligent, rash, thoughtless.

inconsistent adj different, discrepant, illogical, incoherent, incompatible, incongruous, inconsequent, inconsonant, irreconcilable, unsuitable; contradictory, contrary; changeable, fickle, inconstant, unstable, unsteady, vacillating.

inconstant adj capricious, changeable, faithless, fickle, fluctuating, mercurial, mutable, unsettled, unsteady, vacillating, variable, varying, volatile, wavering; uncertain, unstable.

incontrovertible adj certain, incontestable, indisputable, indubitable, irrefutable, sure, undeniable, unquestionable.

inconvenience vb discommode; annoy, disturb, molest, trouble, vex. • n annoyance, disadvantage, disturbance, molestation, trouble, vexation; awkwardness, cumbersomeness, incommodiousness, unwieldiness; unfitness, unseasonableness, unsuitableness.

inconvenient adj annoying, awkward, cumbersome, cumbrous, disadvantageous, incommodious, inopportune, troublesome, uncomfortable, unfit, unhandy, unmanageable, unseasonable, unsuitable, untimely, unwieldy, vexatious.

incorporate vb affiliate, amalgamate, associate, blend, combine, consolidate, include, merge, mix, unite; embody, incarnate.

incorrect adj erroneous, false, inaccurate, inexact, untrue, wrong; faulty, improper, mistaken, ungrammatical, unbecoming, unsound.

incorrigible adj abandoned, graceless, hardened, irreclaimable, lost, obdurate, recreant, reprobate, shameless; helpless, hopeless, irremediable, irrecoverable, irreparable, irretrievable.

incorruptible adj honest, unbribable; imperishable, indestructible, immortal, undying.

increase vb accrue, advance, augment, enlarge, extend, grow, intensify, mount, wax; multiply; enhance, greaten, heighten, raise, reinforce; extend, prolong; aggravate, prolong. • n accession, accretion, accumulation, addition, augmentation, crescendo, development, enlargement, expansion, extension, growth, heightening, increment, intensification, multiplication, swelling; gain, produce, product, profit.

incredible adj absurd, inadmissible, nonsensical, unbelievable.

incredulous adj distrustful, doubtful, dubious, sceptical, unbelieving.

increment n addition, augmentation, enlargement, increase.

incriminate vb accuse, blame, charge.

inculcate vb enforce, implant, impress, infix, infuse, ingraft, inspire, instil.

incumbent adj binding, devolved, devolving, laid, obligatory; leaning, prone, reclining, resting. • n holder, occupant.

incur vb acquire, bring, contract.

incurable adj cureless, hopeless, irrecoverable, remediless; helpless, incorrigible, irremediable.

incursion n descent, foray, raid, inroad.

indebted adj beholden, obliged, owing.

indecent adj bold, improper, indecorous, offensive, outrageous, unbecoming, unseemly; coarse, dirty, filthy, gross, immodest, impure, indelicate, lewd, nasty, obscene, pornographic, salacious, shameless, smutty, unchaste.

indecipherable adj illegible, undecipherable,

undiscoverable, inexplicable, obscure, unintelligible, unreadable.

Indecisive *adj* dubious, hesitating, inconclusive, irresolute, undecided, unsettled, vacillating, wavering.

Indecorous *adj* coarse, gross, ill-bred, impolite, improper, indecent, rude, unbecoming, uncivil, unseemly.

Indeed *adv* absolutely, actually, certainly, in fact, in truth, in reality, positively, really, strictly, truly, verily, veritably.

Indefatigable *adj* assiduous, never-tiring, persevering, persistent, sedulous, tireless, unflagging, unremitting, untiring, unwearied.

Indefeasible *adj* immutable, inalienable, irreversible, irrevocable, unalterable.

Indefensible *adj* censurable, defenceless, faulty, unpardonable, untenable; inexcusable, insupportable, unjustifiable, wrong.

Indefinite *adj* confused, doubtful, equivocal, general, imprecise, indefinable, indecisive, indeterminate, indistinct, inexact, inexplicit, lax, loose, nondescript, obscure, uncertain, undefined, undetermined, unfixed, unsettled, vague.

Indelible *adj* fast, fixed, ingrained, permanent.

Indelicate *adj* broad, coarse, gross, indecorous, intrusive, rude, unbecoming, unseemly; broad, coarse, foul, gross, immodest, indecent, lewd, obscene, unchaste, vulgar.

Indemnify *vb* compensate, reimburse, remunerate, requite, secure.

Indent *vb* bruise, jag, notch, pink, scallop, serrate; bind, indenture.

Independence *n* freedom, liberty, self-direction; distinctness, nondependence, separation; competence, ease.

Independent *adj* absolute, autonomous, free, self-directing, uncoerced, unrestrained, unrestricted, voluntary; (*person*) self-reliant, unconstrained, unconventional.

Indestructible *adj* abiding, endless, enduring, everlasting, fadeless, imperishable, incorruptible, undecaying.

Indeterminate *adj* indefinite, uncertain, undetermined, unfixed.

Index *vb* alphabetise, catalogue, codify, earmark, file, list, mark, tabulate. • *n* catalogue, list, register, tally; indicator, lead, mark, pointer, sign, signal, token; contents, table of contents; forefinger; exponent.

Indicate *vb* betoken, denote, designate, evince, exhibit, foreshadow, manifest, mark, point out, prefigure, presage, register, show, signify, specify, tell; hint, imply, intimate, sketch, suggest.

Indication *n* hint, index, manifestation, mark, note, sign, suggestion, symptom, token.

Indicative *adj* significant, suggestive, symptomatic; (*gram*) affirmative, declarative.

Indict *vb* (*law*) accuse, charge, present.

Indictment *n* (*law*) indicting, presentment; accusation, arraignment, charge, impeachment.

Indifference *n* apathy, carelessness, coldness, coolness, heedlessness, inattention, insignificance, negligence, unconcern, unconcernedness, uninterestedness; disinterestedness, impartiality.

Indifferent *adj* apathetic, cold, cool, dead, distant, dull, easy-going, frigid, heedless, inattentive, incurious, insensible, insouciant, listless, lukewarm, nonchalant, perfunctory, regardless, stoical, unconcerned, uninterested, unmindful, unmoved; equal; fair, medium, middling, moderate, ordinary, passable, tolerable; mediocre, so-so; immaterial, unimportant; disinterested, impartial, neutral, unbiased.

Indigent *adj* destitute, distressed, insolvent, needy, penniless, pinched, poor, reduced.

Indignation *n* anger, choler, displeasure, exasperation, fury, ire, rage, resentment, wrath.

Indignity *n* abuse, affront, contumely, dishonour, disrespect, ignominy, insult, obloquy, opprobrium, outrage, reproach, slight.

Indirect *adj* circuitous, circumlocutory, collateral, devious, oblique, roundabout, sidelong, tortuous; deceitful, dishonest, dishonorable, unfair; mediate, remote, secondary, subordinate.

Indiscreet *adj* foolish, hasty, headlong, heedless, imprudent, incautious, inconsiderate, injudicious, rash, reckless, unwise.

Indiscretion *n* folly, imprudence, inconsiderateness, rashness; blunder, faux pas, lapse.

Indiscriminate *adj* confused, heterogeneous, indistinct, mingled, miscellaneous, mixed, promiscuous, undiscriminating, undistinguishable.

Indispensable *adj* essential, expedient, necessary, needed, needful, requisite.

Indisposed *adj* ailing, ill, sick, unwell; averse, backward, disinclined, loath, reluctant.

Indisputable *adj* certain, evident, incontestable, incontrovertible, obvious, undeniable, indubitable, unquestionable.

Indissoluble *adj* abiding, enduring, firm, imperishable, incorruptible, indestructible, lasting, stable, unbreakable.

Indistinct *adj* ambiguous, doubtful, uncertain; blurred, dim, dull, faint, hazy, misty, nebulous, obscure, shadowy, vague; confused, inarticulate, indefinite, undefined, undistinguishable.

Individual *adj* characteristic, distinct, identical, idiosyncratic, marked, one, particular, personal, respective, separate, single, singular, special, unique; peculiar, personal, proper, singular; decided, definite, independent, positive, self-guided, unconventional, unique. • *n* being, character, party, person, personage, somebody, someone.

Individuality *n* definiteness, indentity, personality; characterfulness, originality, self-direction, self-determination, singularity, uniqueness.

indoctrinate vb brainwash, imbue, initiate, instruct, teach.

indolent adj easy, easy-going, inactive, inert, lazy, listless, lumpish, otiose, slothful, supine.

indomitable adj invincible, unconquerable, unyielding.

indubitable adj certain, evident, incontestable, incontrovertible, indisputable, sure, undeniable, unquestionable.

induce vb actuate, allure, bring, draw, drive, entice, impel, incite, influence, instigate, move, persuade, prevail, prompt, spur, urge; bring on, cause, effect, motivate, lead, occasion, produce.

inducement n allurement, draw, enticement, instigation, persuasion; cause, consideration, impulse, incentive, incitement, influence, motive, reason, spur, stimulus.

induct vb inaugurate, initiate, instal, introduce.

indulge vb gratify, license, revel, satisfy, wallow, yield to; coddle, cosset, favour, humour, pamper, pet, spoil; allow, cherish, foster, harbour, permit, suffer.

indulgent adj clement, easy, favouring, forbearing, gentle, humouring, kind, lenient, mild, pampering, tender, tolerant.

industrious adj assiduous, diligent, hard-working, laborious, notable, operose, sedulous; brisk, busy, persevering, persistent.

industry n activity, application, assiduousness, assiduity, diligence; perseverance, persistence, sedulousness, vigour; effort, labour, toil.

ineffectual adj abortive, bootless, fruitless, futile, inadequate, inefficacious, ineffective, inoperative, useless, unavailing, vain; feeble, inefficient, powerless, impotent, weak.

inefficient adj feeble, incapable, ineffectual, ineffective, inefficacious, weak.

ineligible adj disqualified, unqualified; inexpedient, objectionable, unadvisable, undesirable.

inept adj awkward, improper, inapposite, inappropriate, unapt, unfit, unsuitable; null, useless, void, worthless; foolish, senseless, silly.

inequality n disproportion, inequitableness, injustice, unfairness; difference, disparity, disproportion, dissimilarity, diversity, imparity, irregularity, roughness, unevenness; inadequacy, incompetency, insufficiency.

inert adj comatose, dead, inactive, lifeless, motionless, quiescent, passive; apathetic, dronish, dull, idle, indolent, lazy, lethargic, lumpish, phlegmatic, slothful, sluggish, supine, torpid.

inertia n apathy, inertness, lethargy, passiveness, passivity, slothfulness, sluggishness.

inevitable adj certain, necessary, unavoidable.

inexact adj imprecise, inaccurate, incorrect; careless, crude, loose.

inexcusable adj indefensible, irremissible, unallowable, unjustifiable, unpardonable.

inexhaustible adj boundless, exhaustless, indefatigable, unfailing, unlimited.

inexorable adj cruel, firm, hard, immovable, implacable, inflexible, merciless, pitiless, relentless, severe, steadfast, unbending, uncompassionate, unmerciful, unrelenting, unyielding.

inexperienced adj callow, green, raw, strange, unacquainted, unconversant, undisciplined, uninitiated, unpractised, unschooled, unskilled, untrained, untried, unversed, young.

inexpert adj awkward, bungling, clumsy, inapt, maladroit, unhandy, unskilful, unskilled.

inexplicable adj enigmatic, enigmatical, incomprehensible, inscrutable, mysterious, strange, unaccountable, unintelligible.

inexpressible adj indescribable, ineffable, unspeakable, unutterable; boundless, infinite.

inexpressive adj blank, characterless, dull.

inextricable adj entangled, intricate, perplexed.

infallible adj certain, indubitable, oracular, sure, unerring, unfailing.

infamous adj abominable, atrocious, base, damnable, dark, detestable, discreditable, disgraceful, dishonorable, disreputable, heinous, ignominious, nefarious, odious, opprobrious, outrageous, scandalous, shameful, wicked.

infancy n beginning, commencement; babyhood, childhood, minority, nonage, pupillage.

infant n babe, baby, bairn, bantling, brat, chit, minor, nursling, papoose, suckling, tot.

infantile adj childish, infantine, newborn, tender, young; babyish, childish, weak.

infatuate vb befool, besot, captivate, delude, prepossess, stultify.

infect vb affect, contaminate, corrupt, defile, poison, pollute, taint, vitiate.

infection n affection, bane, contagion, contamination, corruption, defilement, pest, poison, pollution, taint, virus, vitiation.

infectious adj catching, communicable, contagious, contaminating, corrupting, defiling, demoralising, pestiferous, pestilential, poisoning, polluting, sympathetic, vitiating.

infer vb collect, conclude, deduce, derive, draw, gather, glean, guess, presume, reason.

inference n conclusion, consequence, corollary, deduction, generalisation, guess, illation, implication, induction, presumption.

inferior adj lower, nether; junior, minor, secondary, subordinate; bad, base, deficient, humble, imperfect, indifferent, mean, mediocre, paltry.

inferiority n subjection, subordination, mediocrity; deficiency, inadequacy, shortcoming.

infernal adj abominable, accursed, atrocious, damnable, dark, devilish, diabolical, fiendish, hellish, nefarious, satanic, Stygian.

infertility n barrenness, infecundity, sterility, unfruitfulness, unproductivity.

Infidel n agnostic, atheist, disbeliever, heathen, heretic, sceptic, unbeliever.
Infidelity n adultery, disloyalty, faithlessness, treachery, unfaithfulness; disbelief, scepticism.
Infiltrate vb absorb, pervade, soak.
Infinite adj boundless, endless, illimitable, immeasurable, inexhaustible, interminable, limitless, measureless, perfect, unbounded, unlimited; enormous, immense, stupendous, vast; absolute, eternal, self-determined, self-existent.
Infinitesimal adj infinitely small.
Infinity n absoluteness, boundlessness, endlessness, eternity, immensity, infiniteness, infinitude, interminateness, self-determination.
Infirm adj ailing, debilitated, feeble, frail, weak; faltering, irresolute, vacillating; insecure, precarious, unsound, unstable.
Inflame vb animate, arouse, excite, enkindle, fire, heat, incite, inspirit, intensify, rouse, stimulate; aggravate, anger, chafe, embitter, enrage, exasperate, incense, infuriate, irritate, madden.
Inflammable adj combustible; excitable.
Inflammatory adj fiery, inflaming; dissentious, incendiary, seditious.
Inflate vb bloat, blow up, distend, expand, swell, sufflate; elate, puff up; enlarge, increase.
Inflation n enlargement, increase, overenlargement, overissue; bloatedness, distension, expansion, sufflation; bombast, conceit, conceitedness, self-conceit, self-complacency, self-importance, self-sufficiency, vainglory.
Inflection n bend, bending, crook, curvature, curvity, flexure; (gram) accidence, conjugation, declension, variation; (mus) modulation.
Inflexible adj rigid, rigorous, stiff, unbending; cantankerous, cross-grained, dogged, headstrong, heady, inexorable, intractable, obdurate, obstinant, pertinacious, refractory, stubborn, unyielding, wilful; firm, immovable, persevering, resolute, steadfast, unbending.
Inflict vb bring, impose, lay on.
Infliction n imposition, judgement, punishment.
Influence vb affect, bias, control, direct, lead, modify, prejudice, prepossess, sway; actuate, arouse, impel, incite, induce, instigate, move, persuade, prevail upon, rouse. • n ascendancy, authority, control, mastery, potency, predominance, pull, rule, sway; credit, reputation, weight; inflow, inflowing, influx; magnetism, power, spell.
Influential adj controlling, effective, effectual, potent, powerful, strong.
Inform vb animate, inspire, quicken; acquaint, advise, apprise, enlighten, instruct, notify, teach, tell, tip, warn.
Informal adj unceremonious, unconventional, unofficial; easy, familiar, natural, simple.
Informant n advertiser, adviser, informer, notifier, relator; accuser, complainant, informer.

Information n advice, intelligence, knowledge, notice; advertisement, advice, enlightenment, instruction, message, tip, word, warning; accusation, complaint, denunciation.
Informer n accuser, complainant, informant.
Infrequent adj rare, uncommon, unusual; occasional, rare, scant, scarce, sporadic.
Infringe vb break, contravene, disobey, intrude, invade, transgress, violate.
Infuriated adj angry, enraged, furious, incensed, maddened, raging, wild.
Infuse vb breathe into, implant, inculcate, ingraft, insinuate, inspire, instil, introduce; steep.
Ingenious adj able, adroit, artful, bright, clever, gifted, inventive, ready, shrewd, witty.
Ingenuity n ability, acuteness, aptitude, aptness, capacity, capableness, cleverness, faculty, genius, gift, ingeniousness, inventiveness, knack, readiness, skill, turn.
Ingenuous adj artless, candid, childlike, downright, frank, generous, guileless, honest, innocent, naive, open, open-hearted, plain, simpleminded, sincere, single-minded, straightforward, transparent, truthful, unreserved.
Ingratitude n thanklessness, ungratefulness.
Ingredient n component, constituent, element.
Inhabit vb abide, dwell, live, occupy, people, reside, sojourn.
Inhabitant n citizen, denizen, dweller, resident.
Inhale vb breathe in, draw in, inbreathe, inspire.
Inherent adj essential, immanent, inborn, inbred, indwelling, ingrained, innate, inseparable, intrinsic, native, natural; adhering, sticking.
Inherit vb get, receive.
Inheritance n heritage, legacy, patrimony.
Inhibit vb bar, check, debar, hinder, obstruct, prevent, repress, restrain, stop; forbid, interdict.
Inhibition n check, hindrance, impediment, obstacle, obstruction, restraint; disallowance, embargo, interdict, interdiction, prevention.
Inhospitable adj cool, forbidding, unfriendly, unkind; bigoted, illiberal, intolerant, narrow, prejudiced, ungenerous, unreceptive; barren.
Inhuman adj barbarous, brutal, cruel, fell, ferocious, merciless, pitiless, remorseless, ruthless, savage, unfeeling; nonhuman.
Inimical adj antagonistic, hostile, unfriendly; adverse, contrary, harmful, hurtful, noxious, opposed, pernicious, repugnant, unfavourable.
Inimitable adj incomparable, matchless, peerless, unequalled, unexampled, unmatched, unparagoned, unparalleled, unrivalled.
Iniquitous adj atrocious, criminal, flagitious, heinous, inequitable, nefarious, sinful, wicked, wrong, unfair, unjust, unrighteous.
Initial adj first; beginning, commencing, incipient, initiatory, introductory, opening, original; elementary, inchoate, rudimentary.

Initiate vb begin, commence, enter upon, inaugurate, introduce, open; ground, indoctrinate, instruct, prime, teach.

Initiation n beginning, commencement, inauguration, opening; admission, entrance, introduction; indoctrinate, instruction.

Initiative n beginning; energy, enterprise.

Inject vb force in, interject, insert, introduce.

Injudicious adj foolish, hasty, ill-advised, illjudged, imprudent, incautious, inconsiderate, indiscreet, rash, unwise.

Injunction n admonition, bidding, command, mandate, order, precept.

Injure vb damage, disfigure, harm, hurt, impair, mar, spoil, sully, wound; abuse, aggrieve, wrong; affront, dishonour, insult.

Injurious adj baneful, damaging, deadly, deleterious, destructive, detrimental, disadvantageous, evil, fatal, hurtful, mischievous, noxious, pernicious, prejudicial, ruinous; inequitable, iniquitous, unjust, wrongful, libellous, slanderous.

Injury n evil, ill, injustice, wrong; damage, detriment, harm, hurt, impairment, loss, mischief.

Injustice n inequity, unfairness; grievance, iniquity, injury, wrong.

Inkling n hint, intimation, suggestion, whisper.

Innate adj congenital, constitutional, inborn, inbred, indigenous, inherent, inherited, instinctive, native, natural, organic.

Inner adj interior, internal.

Innocence n blamelessness, chastity, guilelessness, guiltlessness, purity, simplicity, sinlessness, stainlessness; harmlessness, innocuousness, innoxiousness, inoffensiveness.

Innocent adj blameless, clean, clear, faultless, guiltless, immaculate, pure, sinless, spotless, unfallen, upright; harmless, innocuous, innoxious, inoffensive; lawful, legitimate, permitted; artless, guileless, ignorant, ingenuous, simple. • n babe, child, ingénue, naif, naive, unsophisticate.

Innocuous adj harmless, innocent, inoffensive.

Innovation n change, introduction; novelty.

Innuendo n allusion, hint, insinuation, intimation, suggestion.

Innumerable adj countless, numberless.

Inoffensive adj harmless, innocent, innocuous, innoxious, unobjectionable, unoffending.

Inopportune adj ill-timed, inexpedient, infelicitous, mistimed, unfortunate, unhappy, untimely.

Inordinate adj excessive, extravagant, immoderate, intemperate, irregular.

Inquest n inquiry, inquisition, investigation, quest, search.

Inquire vb ask, catechise, interpellate, interrogate, investigate, query, question, quiz.

Inquiry n examination, exploration, investigation, research, scrutiny, study; interrogation, query, question, quiz.

Inquisition n examination, inquest, inquiry, investigation, search.

Inquisitive adj curious, inquiring, scrutinising; meddlesome, peeping, peering, prying.

Inroad n encroachment, foray, incursion, invasion, irruption, raid.

Insanity n craziness, delirium, dementia, derangement, lunacy, madness, mania, mental aberration, mental alienation.

Insatiable adj greedy, rapacious, voracious; insatiate, unappeasable.

Inscribe vb emblaze, endorse, engrave, enroll, impress, imprint, write; address, dedicate.

Inscrutable adj hidden, impenetrable, incomprehensible, inexplicable, mysterious, undiscoverable, unfathomable, unsearchable.

Insecure adj risky, uncertain, unconfident, unsure; exposed, ill-protected, unprotected, unsafe; dangerous, hazardous, perilous; infirm, shaking, shaky, tottering, unstable, weak, wobbly.

Insensible adj imperceivable, imperceptible, undiscoverable; blunted, brutish, deaf, dull, insensate, numb, obtuse, senseless, sluggish, stolid, stupid, torpid, unconscious; apathetic, callous, phlegmatic, impassive, indifferent, insensitive, insentient, unfeeling, unimpressible.

Inseparable adj close, friendly, intimate; indissoluble, indivisible, inseverable.

Insert vb infix, inject, intercalate, interpolate, introduce, inweave, parenthesise, place, put, set.

Inside adj inner, interior, internal, intimate. • prep in, in the interior of, within. • n inner part, interior; nature.

Insidious adj creeping, deceptive, gradual, secretive; arch, artful, crafty, crooked, cunning, deceitful, designing, foxy, guileful, intriguing, sly, sneaky, subtle, wily.

Insight n discernment, intuition, penetration, perception, perspicuity, understanding.

Insignificant adj contemptible, empty, immaterial, inconsequential, inconsiderable, inferior, meaningless, paltry, petty, small, sorry, trifling, trivial, unessential, unimportant.

Insincere adj deceitful, dishonest, disingenuous, dissembling, dissimulating, double-faced, double-tongued, duplicitous, empty, faithless, false, hollow, hypocritical, pharisaical, untrue.

Insinuate vb hint, inculcate, infuse, ingratiate, instil, intimate, introduce, suggest.

Insipid adj dead, dull, flat, heavy, inanimate, jejune, lifeless, monotonous, pointless, prosaic, prosy, spiritless, stupid, tame, unentertaining, uninteresting; flat, tasteless, vapid.

Insist vb demand, maintain, urge.

Insistence n importunity, solicitousness, urging, urgency.

Insolent adj abusive, contemptuous, contumelious, disrespectful, domineering, insulting, offensive, overbearing, rude, supercilious; cheeky, impertinent, impudent, malapert, pert, saucy; contumacious, disobedient, insubordinate.

Insoluble adj indissoluble, indissolvable, irreducible; inexplicable, insolvable.

Insolvable adj inexplicable.

Insolvent adj bankrupt, broken, failed, ruined.

Inspect vb examine, investigate, look into, pry into, scrutinise; oversee, superintend, supervise.

Inspector n censor, critic, examiner, visitor; boss, overseer, superintendent, supervisor.

Inspire vb breathe, inhale; infuse, instil; animate, cheer, enliven, inspirit; elevate, exalt, stimulate; animate, enliven, fill, imbue, impart, inform, quicken.

Instability n changeableness, fickleness, inconstancy, insecurity, mutability.

Install vb inaugurate, induct, introduce; establish, place, set up.

Instalment n earnest, payment, portion.

Instance vb adduce, cite, mention, specify. • n case, example, exemplification, illustration, occasion; impulse, incitement, instigation, motive, prompting, request, solicitation.

Instant adj direct, immediate, instantaneous, prompt, quick; current, present; earnest, fast, imperative, importunate, pressing, urgent; ready cooked. • n flash, jiffy, moment, second, trice, twinkling; hour, moment, time.

Instantaneous adj abrupt, immediate, instant.

Instead adv in lieu, in place, rather.

Instigate vb actuate, agitate, encourage, impel, incite, influence, initiate, move, persuade, prevail upon, prompt, provoke, rouse, set on, spur on, stimulate, stir up, tempt, urge.

Instil vb enforce, implant, impress, inculcate, ingraft; impart, infuse, insinuate.

Instinct n natural impulse.

Instinctive adj automatic, inherent, innate, intuitive, involuntary, natural, spontaneous; impulsive, unreflecting.

Institute[1] n academy, college, foundation, guild, institution, school; custom, doctrine, dogma, law, maxim, precedent, principle, rule, tenet.

Institute[2] vb begin, commence, constitute, establish, found, initial, install, introduce, organise, originate, start.

Institution n enactment, establishment, foundation, institute, society; investiture; custom, law.

Instruct vb discipline, educate, enlighten, exercise, guide, indoctrinate, inform, initiate, school, teach, train; apprise, bid, command, direct, enjoin, order, prescribe to.

Instruction n breeding, discipline, education, indoctrination, information, nurture, schooling, teaching, training, tuition; advice, counsel, precept; command, direction, mandate, order.

Instrument n appliance, apparatus, contrivance, device, implement, musical instrument, tool,

utensil; agent, means, medium; charter, deed, document, indenture, writing.

Instrumental adj ancillary, assisting, auxiliary, conducive, contributory, helpful, helping, ministerial, ministrant, serviceable, subservient.

Insubordinate adj disobedient, disorderly, mutinous, refractory, riotous, seditious, turbulent, ungovernable, unruly.

Insufferable adj intolerable, unbearable, unendurable, insupportable; abominable, detestable, disgusting, execrable, outrageous.

Insular adj contracted, illiberal, limited, narrow, petty, prejudiced, restricted; isolated, remote.

Insulate vb detach, disconnect, disengage, disunite, isolate, separate.

Insult vb abuse, affront, injure, offend, outrage, slander, slight. • n abuse, affront, indignity, insolence, offence, outrage, slight.

Insuperable adj impassable, insurmountable.

Insupportable adj insufferable, intolerable, unbearable, unendurable.

Insure vb assure, guarantee, indemnify, secure.

Insurgent adj disobedient, insubordinate, mutinous, rebellious, revolting, revolutionary, seditious. • n mutineer, rebel, revolter, revolutionary.

Insurmountable adj impassable, insuperable.

Insurrection n insurgence, mutiny, rebellion, revolt, revolution, rising, sedition, uprising.

Intact adj scatheless, unharmed, unhurt, unimpaired, uninjured, untouched; complete, entire, integral, sound, unbroken, undiminished, whole.

Intangible adj dim, impalpable, imperceptible, indefinite, insubstantial, intactile, shadowy, vague; aerial, phantom, spiritous.

Integral adj complete, component, entire, integrant, total, whole.

Integrity n goodness, honesty, principle, probity, purity, rectitude, soundness, uprightness, virtue; completeness, entireness, entirety.

Intellect n brains, cognitive faculty, intelligence, mind, rational faculty, reason, reasoning faculty, sense, thinking principle, understanding.

Intellectual adj cerebral, intelligent, mental, scholarly, thoughtful. • n academic, scholar.

Intelligence n acumen, apprehension, brightness, discernment, imagination, insight, penetration, quickness, sagacity, shrewdness, understanding, wits; information, knowledge; advice, instruction, news, notice, notification, tidings; brains, intellect, mentality, sense, spirit.

Intelligent adj acute, alert, apt, astute, brainy, bright, clear-headed, clear-sighted, clever, discerning, keen-eyed, keen-sighted, knowing, long-headed, quick, quick-sighted, sagacious, sensible, shrewd, understanding.

Intelligible adj clear, comprehensible, distinct, evident, lucid, manifest, obvious, patent, perspicuous, plain, transparent, understandable.

Intemperate *adj* drunken; excessive, extravagant, extreme, immoderate, inordinate, unbridled, uncontrolled; self-indulgent.

Intend *vb* aim at, contemplate, design, determine, drive at, mean, meditate, propose.

Intense *adj* ardent, earnest, fervid, passionate, vehement; close, intent, severe, strained, stretched, strict; energetic, forcible, keen, potent, powerful, sharp, strong, vigorous, violent; acute, deep, extreme, exquisite, grievous, poignant.

Intensify *vb* aggravate, concentrate, deepen, enhance, heighten, quicken, strengthen, whet.

Intensive *adj* emphatic, intensifying.

Intent *adj* absorbed, attentive, close, eager, earnest, engrossed, occupied, pre-occupied, zealous; bent, determined, decided, resolved, set. • *n* aim, design, drift, end, import, intention, mark, meaning, object, plan, purport, purpose, purview, scope, view.

Intention *n* aim, design, drift, end, import, intent, mark, meaning, object, plan, purport, purpose, purview, scope, view.

Intentional *adj* deliberate, designed, intended, preconcerted, predetermined, premeditated, purposed, studied, voluntary, wilful.

Intercede *vb* arbitrate, interpose, mediate; entreat, plead, supplicate.

Intercept *vb* cut off, interrupt, obstruct, seize.

Intercession *n* interposition, intervention, mediation; entreaty, pleading, prayer, supplication.

Interchange *vb* alternate, change, exchange.

Intercourse *n* commerce, communication, communion, connection, converse, correspondence, dealings; acquaintance, intimacy.

Interdict *vb* debar, forbid, inhibit, prohibit, prescribe, proscribe, restrain from. • *n* ban, decree, interdiction, prohibition.

Interest *vb* affect, concern, touch; absorb, attract, engage, enlist, excite, grip, hold, occupy. • *n* advantage, benefit, good, profit, weal; attention, concern, regard, sympathy; part, participation, portion, share, stake; discount, profit.

Interested *adj* attentive, concerned, involved, occupied; biased, partial, prejudiced; selfish, self-seeking.

Interesting *adj* attractive, engaging, entertaining, pleasing.

Interfere *vb* meddle; clash, collide, conflict.

Interim *n* intermediate time, interval, meantime.

Interior *adj* inmost, inner, internal, inward; inland, remote; domestic, home. • *n* inner part, inland, inside.

Interject *vb* comment, inject, insert, interpose.

Intermediary *n* go-between, mediator.

Intermediate *adj* interjacent, interposed, intervening, mean, median, middle, transitional.

Interminable *adj* boundless, endless, illimitable, immeasurable, infinite, limitless, unbounded, unlimited; long-drawn-out, tedious.

Intermission *n* cessation, interruption, interval, lull, pause, remission, respite, rest, stop.

Intermittent *adj* broken, capricious, discontinuous, fitful, flickering, intermitting, periodic, recurrent, remittent, spasmodic.

Internal *adj* inner, inside, interior, inward; incorporeal, mental, spiritual; deeper, emblematic, hidden, higher, metaphorical, secret, spiritual, symbolical, under; genuine, inherent, intrinsic, real, true; domestic, home, inland, inside.

International *adj* cosmopolitan, universal.

Interpolate *vb* add, foist, insert, interpose; (*math*) intercalate, introduce.

Interpret *vb* decipher, decode, define, elucidate, explain, expound, solve, unfold, unravel; construe, render, translate.

Interpretation *n* meaning, sense, signification; elucidation, explanation, explication, exposition; construction, rendering, rendition, version.

Interpreter *n* expositor, expounder, translator.

Interrogate *vb* ask, catechise, examine, inquire of, interpellate, question.

Interrupt *vb* break, check, disturb, hinder, intercept, interfere with, obstruct, pretermit, stop; break, cut, disconnect, disjoin, dissever, dissolve, disunite, divide, separate, sever, sunder; break off, cease, discontinue, suspend.

Interruption *n* hindrance, impediment, obstacle, obstruction, stop, stoppage; cessation, discontinuance, intermission, pause, suspension; break, breaking, disconnecting, disconnection, disjunction, dissolution, disunion, disuniting, division, separation, severing, sundering.

Intersect *vb* cross, cut, decussate, divide.

Intersperse *vb* intermingle, scatter, sprinkle; diversify, interlard, mix.

Interval *n* interim, interlude, interregnum, pause, period, recess, season, space, spell, term; interstice, skip, space.

Intervene *vb* come between, interfere, mediate; befall, happen, occur.

Intervention *n* interference, interposition; agency, mediation.

Interview *n* conference, consultation, parley; meeting.

Intimate[1] *adj* close, near; familiar, friendly; bosom, chummy, close, dear, homelike, special; confidential, personal, private, secret; detailed, exhaustive, first-hand, immediate, penetrating, profound; cosy, friendly, warm. • *n* chum, confidant, companion, crony, friend.

Intimate[2] *vb* allude to, express, hint, impart, indicate, insinuate, signify, suggest, tell.

Intimidate *vb* abash, affright, alarm, appal, browbeat, bully, cow, daunt, dishearten, dismay, frighten, overawe, scare, subdue, terrify.

Intolerable *adj* insufferable, insupportable, unbearable, unendurable.

intolerant *adj* bigoted, narrow, proscriptive; dictatorial, impatient, imperious, overbearing, supercilious.

intonation *n* cadence, modulation, tone; musical recitation.

intoxication *n* drunkenness, inebriation, inebriety; excitement, exhilaration, infatuation.

intractable *adj* cantankerous, contrary, contumacious, cross-grained, dogged, froward, headstrong, indocile, inflexible, mulish, obdurate, obstinate, perverse, pig-headed, refractory, restive, stubborn, tough, uncontrollable, ungovernable, unmanageable, unruly, unyielding, wilful.

intrepid *adj* bold, brave, chivalrous, courageous, daring, dauntless, doughty, fearless, gallant, heroic, unappalled, unawed, undaunted, undismayed, unterrified, valiant, valorous.

intricate *adj* complicated, difficult, entangled, involved, mazy, obscure, perplexed.

intrigue *vb* connive, conspire, machinate, plot, scheme; beguile, bewitch, captivate, charm, fascinate. • *n* artifice, cabal, conspiracy, deception, finesse, Machiavelianism, machination, manoeuvre, plot, ruse, scheme, stratagem, wile; amour, liaison, love affair.

intriguing *adj* arch, artful, crafty, crooked, cunning, deceitful, designing, diplomatic, foxy, Machiavelian, insidious, politic, sly, sneaky, subtle, tortuous, trickish, tricky, wily.

intrinsic *adj* essential, genuine, real, sterling, true; inborn, inbred, ingrained, inherent, internal, inward, native, natural.

introduce *vb* bring in, conduct, import, induct, inject, insert, lead in, usher in; present; begin, broach, commence, inaugurate, initiate, start.

introduction *n* exordium, preface, prelude, proem; introducing, ushering in; presentation.

intrude *vb* encroach, impose, infringe, interfere, interlope, obtrude, trespass.

intrusive *adj* obtrusive, trespassing.

intuition *n* apprehension, cognition, insight, instinct; clairvoyance, divination, presentiment.

intuitive *adj* instinctive, intuitional, natural; clear, distinct, full, immediate.

inundate *vb* deluge, drown, flood, glut, overflow, overwhelm, submerge.

inure *vb* accustom, discipline, familiarise, habituate, harden, toughen, train, use.

invade *vb* encroach upon, infringe, violate; attack, enter in, march into.

invalid[1] *adj* baseless, fallacious, false, inoperative, nugatory, unfounded, unsound, untrue, worthless; (*law*) null, void.

invalid[2] *adj* ailing, bedridden, feeble, frail, ill, infirm, sick, sickly, valetudinary, weak, weakly. • *n* convalescent, patient, valetudinarian.

invalidate *vb* abrogate, annul, cancel, nullify, overthrow, quash, repeal, reverse, undo.

invalidity *n* baselessness, fallaciousness, fallacy, falsity, unsoundness.

invaluable *adj* inestimable, priceless.

invariable *adj* changeless, constant, unchanging, uniform, unvarying; changeless, immutable, unalterable, unchangeable.

invasion *n* encroachment, incursion, infringement, inroad; aggression, assault, attack, foray.

invective *n* abuse, censure, contumely, denunciation, diatribe, railing, satire, vituperation.

inveigle *vb* contrive, devise; concoct, conceive, create, design, excogitate, frame, imagine, originate; coin, fabricate, forge, spin.

invent *vb* concoct, contrive, design, devise, discover, fabricate, find out, frame, originate.

invention *n* creation, discovery, ingenuity, inventing, origination; contrivance, design, device; coinage, fabrication, fiction, forgery.

inventive *adj* creative, fertile, ingenious.

inventor *n* author, contriver, creator, originator.

inversion *n* inverting, reversing, transposal.

invert *vb* capsize, overturn; reverse, transpose.

invest *vb* put at interest; confer, endow, endue; (*mil*) beset, besiege, enclose, surround; array, clothe, dress.

investigate *vb* canvass, consider, dissect, examine, explore, follow up, inquire into, look into, overhaul, probe, question, research, scrutinze, search into, search out, sift, study.

investigation *n* examination, exploration, inquiry, inquisition, overhauling, research, scrutiny, search, sifting, study.

investiture *n* habilitation, induction, installation, ordination.

investment *n* money invested; endowment; (*mil*) beleaguerment, siege; clothes, dress, garments, habiliments, robe, vestment.

inveterate *adj* accustomed, besetting, chronic, confirmed, deep-seated, habitual, habituated, hardened, ingrained, long-established, obstinate.

invidious *adj* disagreeable, envious, hateful, odious, offensive, unfair.

invigorate *vb* animate, brace, energise, fortify, harden, nerve, quicken, refresh, stimulate.

invincible *adj* impregnable, indomitable, ineradicable, insuperable, insurmountable, irrepressible, unconquerable, unyielding.

inviolable *adj* hallowed, holy, inviolate, sacramental, sacred, sacrosanct, stainless.

inviolate *adj* unbroken, unviolated; pure, stainless, unblemished, undefiled, unhurt, uninjured, unpolluted, unprofaned, unstained; sacred.

invisible *adj* impalpable, imperceptible, indistinguishable, intangible, unapparent, undiscernable, unperceivable, unseen.

invitation *n* bidding, call, challenge, solicitation, summons.

invite *vb* ask, bid, call, challenge, request, solicit, summon; allure, attract, draw on, entice, lead, persuade, prevail upon.

Inviting *adj* alluring, attractive, bewitching, captivating, engaging, fascinating, pleasing, winning; prepossessing, promising.

Invoke *vb* adjure, appeal to, beseech, beg, call upon, conjure, entreat, implore, importune, pray, pray to, solicit, summon, supplicate.

Involuntary *adj* automatic, blind, instinctive, mechanical, reflex, spontaneous, unintentional; compulsory, reluctant, unwilling.

Involve *vb* comprise, contain, embrace, imply, include, lead to; complicate, compromise, embarrass, entangle, implicate, incriminate, inculpate; cover, envelop, enwrap, surround, wrap; blend, conjoin, connect, join, mingle; entwine, interlace, intertwine, interweave, inweave.

Invulnerable *adj* incontrovertible, invincible, unassailable, irrefragable.

Iota *n* atom, bit, glimmer, grain, jot, mite, particle, scintilla, scrap, shadow, spark, tittle, trace.

Irascible *adj* choleric, cranky, hasty, hot, hotheaded, impatient, irritable, nettlesome, peevish, peppery, pettish, petulant, quick, splenetic, snappish, testy, touchy, waspish.

Irate *adj* angry, incensed, ireful, irritated.

Irksome *adj* annoying, burdensome, humdrum, monotonous, tedious, tiresome, wearisome, weary, wearying.

Ironic, Ironical *adj* mocking, sarcastic.

Irony *n* mockery, raillery, ridicule, satire.

Irradiate *vb* brighten, illume, illuminate, illumine, light up, shine upon.

Irrational *adj* absurd, extravagant, foolish, injudicious, preposterous, ridiculous, silly, unwise; unreasonable, unreasoning, unthinking; brute, brutish; aberrant, alienated, brainless, crazy, demented, fantastic, idiotic, imbecilic, insane.

Irreconcilable *adj* implacalbe, inexorable, inexpiable, unappeasable; incompatible, incongruous, inconsistent.

Irrecoverable *adj* hopeless, incurable, irremediable, irreparable, irretrievable, remediless.

Irrefutable *adj* impregnable, incontestable, incontrovertible, indisputable, invincible, irrefragable, irresistibe, unanswerable, undeniable.

Irregular *adj* aberrant, abnormal, anomalistic, anomalous, crooked, devious, eccentric, erratic, exceptional, heteromorphous, raged, tortuous, unconformable, unusual; capricious, changeable, desultory, fitful, spasmodic, uncertain, unpunctual, unsettled, variable; disordered, disorderly, improper, uncanonical, unparliamentary, unsystematic; asymmetric, uneven, unsymmetrical; disorderly, dissolute, immoral, loose, wild.

Irrelevant *adj* extraneous, foreign, illogical, impertinent, inapplicable, inapposite, inappropriate, inconsequent, unessential, unrelated.

Irreligious *adj* godless, ungodly, undevout; blasphemous, disrespectful, impious, irreverent, profane, ribald, wicked.

Irreparable *adj* irrecoverable, irremediable, irretrievable, remediless.

Irrepressible *adj* insuppressible, uncontrollable, unquenchable, unsmotherable.

Irreproachable *adj* blameless, faultless, inculpable, innocent, irreprehensible, irreprovable.

Irresistible *adj* irrefragable, irrepressible, overpowering, overwhelming, resistless.

Irresolute *adj* changeable, faltering, fickle, hesitant, hesitating, inconstant, mutable, spineless, uncertain, undecided, unsettled, unstable, unsteady, vacillating, wavering.

Irrespective *adj* independent, regardless.

Irresponsible *adj* unaccountable; untrustworthy.

Irretrievable *adj* incurable, irrecoverable, irremediable, irreparable, remediless.

Irreverent *adj* blasphemous, impious, irreligious, profane; disrespectful, slighting.

Irreversible *adj* irrevocable, unalterable, unchangeable; changeless, immutable, invariable.

Irrevocable *adj* irrepealable, irreversible, unalterable, unchangeable.

Irritable *adj* captious, choleric, excitable, fiery, fretful, hasty, hot, irascible, passionate, peppery, peevish, pettish, petulant, snappish, splenetic, susceptible, testy, touchy, waspish.

Irritate *vb* anger, annoy, chafe, enrage, exacerbate, exasperate, fret, incense, jar, nag, nettle, offend, provoke, rasp, rile, ruffle, vex; gall, tease; *(med)* excite, inflame, stimulate.

Isolate *vb* detach, dissociate, insulate, quarantine, segregate, separate, set apart.

Isolation *n* detachment, disconnection, insulation, quarantine, segregation, separation; loneliness, solitariness, solitude.

Issue *vb* come out, flow out, flow forth, gush, run, rush out, spout, spring, spurt, well; arise, come, emanate, ensue, flow, follow, originate, proceed, spring; end, eventuate, result, terminate; appear, come out, deliver, depart, debouch, discharge, emerge, emit, put forth, send out; distribute, give out; publish, utter. • *n* conclusion, consequence, consummation, denouement, end, effect, event, finale, outcome, result, termination, upshot; antagonism, contest, controversy; debouchment, delivering, delivery, discharge, emergence, emission; flux, outflow, outpouring, stream; copy, edition, number; egress, exit, outlet, vent, way out; escape, sally, sortie; children, offspring, progeny.

Itch *vb* tingle. • *n* itching; burning, importunate craving, teasing desire, uneasy hankering.

Item *n* article, detail, entry, point.

Itinerant *adj* nomadic, peripatetic, roaming, roving, travelling, unsettled, wandering.

J

jaded adj dull, exhausted, fatigued, satiated.

jagged adj cleft, divided, indented, notched, serrated, ragged, uneven.

jam vb block, crowd, crush, press.

jangle vb bicker, chatter, dispute, gossip, jar, quarrel, spar, spat, squabble, tiff, wrangle. • n clang, clangour, clash, din, dissonance.

jar vb clash, grate, interfere, shake; bicker, contend, jangle, quarrel, spar, spat, squabble, tiff, wrangle; agitate, jolt, jounce, shake. • n clash, conflict, disaccord, dicord, jangle, dissonance; agitation, jolt, jostle, shake, shaking, shock.

jargon n gabble, gibberish, nonsense, rigmarole: argot, cant, lingo, slang

jaundiced adj biased, envious, prejudiced.

jaunt n excursion, ramble, tour, trip.

jaunty adj airy, cheery, garish, gay, fine, fluttering, showy, sprightly, unconcerned.

jealous adj distrustful, envious, suspicious; anxious, apprehensive, intolerant, solicitous.

jeer vb deride, despise, flout, gibe, jape, jest, mock, scoff, sneer, spurn, rail, ridicule, taunt. • n abuse, derision, mockery, sneer, ridicule, taunt.

jeopardy n danger, hazard, peril, risk, venture.

jerk vb, n flip, hitch, pluck, tweak, twitch, yank.

jest vb banter, joke, quiz. • n fun, joke, pleasantry, raillery, sport.

jilt vb break, coquette, deceive, disappoint, discard, flirt. • n coquette, flirt, light-o'-love.

jingle vb chink, clink, jangle, rattle, tinkle; chorus, ditty, melody, song.

join vb add, annex, append, attach; cement, combine, conjoin, connect, couple, dovetail, link, unite, yoke; amalgamate, assemble, associate, confederate, consolidate, meagre, unite.

joint vb fit, join, unite. • adj combined, concerted, concurrent, conjoint. • n connection, junction, juncture, hinge, splice.

joke vb banter, jest, frolic, rally. • n crank, jest, quip, quirk, witticism.

jolly adj airy, blithe, cheerful, frolicsome, gamesome, facetious, funny, gay, jocular, jocund, jovial, joyous, merry, mirthful, jocular, jocund, playful, sportive, sprightly, waggish; bouncing, chubby, lusty, plump, portly, stout.

jolt vb jar, jolt, shake, shock.

jostle vb collide, elbow, hustle, joggle, shake, shoulder, shove.

jot n ace, atom, bit, corpuscle, iota, grain, mite, particle, scrap, whit.

journey vb ramble, roam, rove, travel: fare, go, proceed. • n excursion, expedition, jaunt, passage, pilgrimage, tour, travel, trip, voyage.

jovial adj airy, convivial, festive, jolly, joyous, merry, mirthful

joy n beatification, beatitude, delight, ecstasy, exultation, gladness, glee, mirth, pleasure, rapture, ravishment, transport, beatification, beatitude; bliss, felicity, happiness.

jubilant adj exultant, rejoicing, triumphant.

judge vb conclude, decide, decree, determine, pronounce; adjudicate, arbitrate, condemn, doom, sentence, try, umpire; account, apprehend, believe, consider, decide, deem, esteem, guess, hold, imagine, measure, reckon, regard, suppose, think; appreciate, estimate. • n adjudicator, arbiter, arbitrator, bencher, justice, magistrate, moderator, referee, umpire, connoisseur, critic.

judgment, judgement n brains, ballast, circumspection, depth, discernment, discretion, discrimination, intelligence, judiciousness, penetration, prudence, sagacity, sense, sensibility, taste, understanding, wisdom, wit; conclusion, consideration, decision, determination, estimation, notion, opinion, thought; adjudication, arbitration, award, censure, condemnation, decree, doom, sentence.

judicious adj cautious, considerate, cool, critical, discriminating, discreet, enlightened, provident, politic, prudent, rational, reasonable, sagacious, sensible, sober, solid, sound, staid, wise.

juicy adj lush, moist, sappy, succulent, watery; entertaining, exciting, interesting, lively, racy, spicey.

jumble vb confound, confuse, disarrange, disorder, mix, muddle. • n confusion, disarrangement, disorder, medley, mess, mixture, muddle.

jump vb bound, caper, clear, hop, leap, skip, spring, vault. • n bound, caper, hop, leak, skip, spring, vault; fence, hurdle, obstacle; break, gap, interruption, space; advance, boost, increase, rise; jar, jolt, shock, start, twitch.

junction n combination, connection, coupling, hook-up, joining, linking, seam, union; conjunction, joint, juncture.

just adj equitable, lawful, legitimate, reasonable, right, rightful; candid, even-handed, fair, fair-minded, impartial; blameless, conscientious, good, honest, honourable, pure, square, straightforward, virtuous; accurate, correct, exact, normal, proper, regular, true; condign, deserved, due, merited, suitable.

justice n accuracy, equitableness, equity, fairness, honesty, impartiality, justness, right; judge, justiciary

justification *n* defence, exculpation, excuse, exoneration, reason, vindication, warrant.
justify *vb* approve, defend, exculpate, excuse, exonerate, maintain, vindicate, support, warrant.

juvenile *adj* childish, immature, puerile, young, youthful. • *n* boy, child, girl, youth.
juxtaposition *n* adjacency, contiguity, contact.

K

keen[1] *adj* ardent, eager, earnest, fervid, intense, vehement, vivid; acute, sharp; cutting; acrimonious, biting, bitter, caustic, poignant, pungent, sarcastic, severe; astute, discerning, intelligent, quick, sagacious, sharp-sighted, shrewd.
keen[2] *vb* bemoan, bewail, deplore, grieve, lament, mourn, sorrow, weep.
keep *vb* detain, hold, retain; continue, preserve, confine, detain, reserve, restrain, withhold; attend, guard, preserve, protect; adhere to, fulfil; celebrate, commemorate, honour, observe, perform, solemnise; maintain, support, sustain; husband, save, store; abide, dwell, lodge, stay, remain; endure, last. • *n* board, maintenance, subsistence, support; dungeon, stronghold, tower.
keeper *n* caretaker, conservator, curator, custodian, defender, gaoler, governor, guardian, jailer, superintendent, warden, warder, watchman.
keeping *n* care, charge, custody, guard, possession; feed, maintenance, support; agreement, conformity, congruity, consistency, harmony.
key *adj* basic, crucial, essential, important, major, principal. • *n* lock-opener, opener; clue, elucidation, explanation, guide, solution, translation; (*mus*) keynote, tonic; clamp, lever, wedge.
kick *vb* boot, punt; oppose, rebel, resist, spurn. • *n* force, intensity, power, punch, vitality; excitement, pleasure, thrill.
kidnap *vb* abduct, capture, carry off, remove.
kill *vb* assassinate, butcher, dispatch, destroy, massacre, murder, slaughter, slay.
kin *adj* akin, allied, cognate, kindred, related. • *n* affinity, consanguinity, relationship; connections, kindred, kinsfolk, relations; relatives.
kind[1] *adj* accommodating, amiable, beneficent, benevolent, benign, bland, bounteous, brotherly, charitable, clement, compassionate, complaisant, gentle, good, good-natured, forbearing, friendly, generous, gracious, humane, indulgent, lenient, mild, obliging, sympathetic, tender.
kind[2] *n* breed, class, family, genus, race, set, species, type; brand, character, colour, denomination, description, form, make, manner, nature, persuasion, sort, stamp, strain, style,
kindle *vb* fire, ignite, inflame, light; animate,

awaken, bestir, exasperate, excite, foment, incite, provoke, rouse, stimulate, stir, thrill, warm.
kindly *adj* appropriate, congenial, kindred, natural, proper; benevolent, considerate, friendly, gracious, humane, sympathetic, well-disposed.
kindness *n* benefaction, charity, favour; amiability, beneficence, benevolence, benignity, charity, clemency, generosity, goodness, grace, humanity, kindliness, mildness, philanthropy, sympathy, tenderness,
kindred *adj* akin, allied, congenial, connected, related, sympathetic. • *n* affinity, consanguinity, flesh, relationship; folks, kin, relations, relatives.
king *n* majesty, monarch, sovereign.
kingdom *n* dominion, empire, monarchy, rule, sovereignty, supremacy; region, tract; division, department, domain, province, realm.
kink *n* cramp, crick, curl, entanglement, knot, loop, twist; crochet, whim, wrinkle.
kinsfolk *n* kin, kindred, kinsmen, relatives.
knack *n* ability, address, adroitness, aptitude, aptness, dexterity, dextrousness, expertness, facility, quickness, readiness, skill.
knell *n* chime, peal, ring, toll.
knife *vb* cut, slash, stab. • *n* blade, jackknife.
knit *vb* connect, interlace, join, unite, weave.
knob *n* boss, bunch, hunch, lump, protuberance.
knock *vb* clap, cuff, hit, rap, rattle, slap, strike, thump; beat, blow, box, cuff, rap, slap. • *n* blow, slap, smack, thump; blame, criticism, rejection.
knot *vb* complicate, entangle, gnarl, kink, tie, weave. • *n* complication, entanglement; connection, tie; joint, node, knag; bunch, rosette, tuft; band, cluster, clique, crew, gang, group, pack, set, squad.
knotty *adj* gnarled, hard, knaggy, knurled, knotted, rough, rugged; complex, difficult, hard, harassing, intricate, involved, perplexing.
know *vb* apprehend, comprehend, cognise, discern, perceive, recognise, see, understand; discriminate, distinguish.
knowing *adj* accomplished, competent, experienced, intelligent, proficient, qualified, skilful, well-informed; aware, conscious, intelligent, percipient, sensible, thinking; cunning, expressive, significant.
knowingly *adv* consciously, intentionally, purposely, wittingly.

knowledge n apprehension, command, comprehension, discernment, judgement, perception, understanding, wit; acquaintance, acquirement, attainments, enlightenment, erudition, information, learning, lore, mastery, scholarship, science; cognition, cognisance, consciousness, information, ken, notice, prescience, recognition.

knowledgeable adj aware, conscious, experienced; intelligent, learned, scholarly.

L

laborious adj assiduous, diligent, hardworking, indefatigable, industrious, painstaking, sedulous, toiling; arduous, difficult, fatiguing, hard, onerous, tiresome, toilsome, wearisome.

labour vb drudge, endeavour, exert, strive, toil, travail, work. • n drudgery, effort, exertion, industry, pains, toil, work; childbirth, delivery.

lace vb attach, bind, fasten, intertwine, tie, twine. • n filigree, lattice, mesh, net, netting, network, openwork, web.

lack vb need, want. • n dearth, default, defectiveness, deficiency, deficit, destitution, insufficiency, need, scantiness, scarcity, shortcoming, shortness, want.

laconic adj brief, compact, concise, pithy, sententious, short, succinct, terse.

lad n boy, schoolboy, stripling, youth.

lag vb dawdle, delay, idle, linger, loiter, saunter.

lair n burrow, couch, den, form, resting place.

lame vb cripple, disable, hobble. • adj crippled, defective, disabled, halt, hobbling, limping; feeble, insufficient, poor, unsatisfactory, weak.

lament vb complain, grieve, keen, moan, mourn, sorrow, wail, weep; bemoan, bewail, deplore, regret. • n complaint, lamentation, moan, moaning, plaint, wailing; coronach, dirge, elegy, keen, monody, requiem, threnody.

lamentable adj deplorable, grievous, lamented, melancholy, woeful; contemptible, miserable.

land vb debark, disembark. • n earth, ground, soil; country, district, province, region, reservation, territory, tract, weald.

language n dialect, speech, tongue, vernacular; conversation, speech; expression, idiom, jargon, parlance, phraseology, slang, style, terminology; expression, utterance, voice.

languid adj drooping, exhausted, faint, feeble, flagging, languishing, pining, weak; dull, heartless, heavy, inactive, listless, lukewarm, slow, sluggish, spiritless, torpid.

languish vb decline, droop, fade, fail, faint.

lank adj attenuated, emaciated, gaunt, lean, meagre, scraggy, slender, skinny, slim.

lap¹ vb drink, lick, mouth, tongue; plash, ripple, splash, wash; quaff, sip, sup, swizzle, tipple. • n draught, dram, drench, drink, gulp, lick, swig, swill, quaff, sip, sup, suck; plash, splash, wash.

lap² vb cover, enfold, fold, turn, twist, swaddle, wrap; distance, pass, outdistance, overlap. • n fold, flap, lappet, lapel, ply, plait; ambit, beat, circle, circuit, cycle, loop, orbit, revolution, round, tour, walk.

lapse vb glide, sink, slide, slip; err, fail, fall. • n course, flow, gliding; declension, decline, fall; error, fault, indiscretion, shortcoming, slip.

large adj big, broad, bulky, colossal, elephantine, enormous, heroic, great, huge, immense, vast; broad, expanded, extensive, spacious, wide; abundant, ample, copious, full, liberal, plentiful; capacious, comprehensive.

lash¹ vb belay, bind, strap, tie; fasten, join, moor, pinion, secure.

lash² vb beat, castigate, chastise, flagellate, flail, flay, flog, goad, scourge, swinge, thrash, whip; assail, castigate, censure, excoriate, lampoon, satirise, trounce.

last¹ vb abide, carry on, continue, dwell, endure, extend, maintain, persist, prevail, stay, survive.

last² adj hindermost, hindmost, latest; conclusive, final, terminal, ultimate; eventual, endmost, extreme, farthest, ultimate; greatest, highest, maximal, maximum, most, supreme, superlative, utmost; latest, newest; aforegoing, foregoing, latter, preceding; departing, farewell, final, leaving, parting, valedictory. • n conclusion, consummation, culmination, end, ending, finale, finis, finish, termination.

lasting adj abiding, durable, enduring, fixed, perennial, permanent, perpetual, stable.

lastly adv conclusively, eventually, finally.

late adj behindhand, delayed, overdue, slow, tardy; deceased, former; recent. • adv lately, recently, sometime; tardily.

latent adj abeyant, concealed, hidden, invisible, occult, secret, unseen, veiled.

latitude n amplitude, breadth, compass, extent, range, room, scope; freedom, liberty; laxity.

latter adj last, latest, modern, recent.

laugh vb cackle, chortle, chuckle, giggle, guffaw, snicker, snigger, titter. • n chortle, chuckle, giggle, guffaw, laughter, titter.

laughter n cackle, chortle, chuckle, glee, giggle, guffaw, laugh, laughing.

launch vb cast, dart, dispatch, hurl, lance, project, throw; descant, dilate, enlarge, expiate; begin, commence, inaugurate, open, start.

lavish vb dissipate, expend, spend, squander, waste. • adj excessive, extravagant, generous, immoderate, overliberal, prodigal, profuse, thriftless, unrestrained, unstinted, unthrifty.

law n act, code, canon, command, commandment, covenant, decree, edict, enactment, order, precept, principle, statute, regulation, rule; jurisprudence; litigation, process, suit.

lawful adj constitutional, constituted, legal, legalised, legitimate; allowable, authorised, permissible, warrantable; equitable, rightful, just.

lawless adj anarchic, disorderly, insubordinate, rebellious, riotous, seditious, wild.

lax adj loose, relaxed, slow; drooping, flabby, relaxed, soft; neglectful, negligent, remiss; dissolute, immoral, licentious, seditious, wild.

lay[1] vb deposit, establish, leave, place, plant, posit, put, set, settle, spread; arrange, dispose, locate, organise, position; bear, deposit, produce; advance, lodge, offer, submit; allocate, allot, ascribe, assign, attribute, charge, impute; concoct, contrive, design, plan, plot, prepare; apply, burden, encumber, impose, saddle, tax; bet, gamble, hazard, risk, stake, wager; allay, alleviate, appease, assuage, calm, relieve, soothe, still, suppress; disclose, divulge, explain, reveal, show, unveil; acquire, grab, grasp, seize; assault, attack, beat up; discover, find, unearth; bless, confirm, consecrate, ordain. • n arrangement, array, form, formation; attitude, aspect, bearing, direction, lie, pose, position, posture, set.

lay[2] adj amateur, inexpert, nonprofessional; civil, laic, laical, nonclerical, nonecclesiastical, nonreligious, secular, temporal, unclerical.

layer n bed, course, lay, seam, stratum.

lazy adj idle, inactive, indolent, inert, slack, slothful, slow, sluggish, supine, torpid.

lead vb conduct, deliver, direct, draw, escort, guide; front, head, precede; advance, excel, outstrip, pass; allure, entice, induce, persuade, prevail; conduce, contribute, serve, tend. • adj chief, first, foremost, main, primary, prime, principal. • n direction, guidance, leadership; advance; precedence, priority.

leader n conductor, director, guide; captain, chief, chieftain, commander, head.

leading adj governing, ruling; capital, chief, first, foremost, highest, principal, superior.

league vb ally, associate, band, combine, confederate, unite. • n alliance, association, coalition, combination, combine, confederacy, confederation, consortium, union.

leak vb drip, exude, ooze, pass, percolate. • n chink, crack, crevice, hole, fissure, hole, oozing; leakage, leaking, percolation.

lean[1] adj bony, emaciated, gaunt, lank, meagre, poor, skinny, thin; dull, barren, jejune, meagre, tame; inadequate, pitiful, scanty, slender; bare, barren, infertile, unproductive.

lean[2] vb incline, slope; bear, recline, repose, rest; confide, depend, rely, trust.

leaning n aptitude, bent, bias, disposition, inclination, liking, predilection, proneness, propensity, tendency.

leap vb bound, clear, jump, spring, vault; caper, frisk, gambol, hop, skip.

learn vb acquire, ascertain, attain, collect, gain, gather, hear, memorise.

learned adj erudite, lettered, literate, scholarly, well-read; expert, experienced, knowing, skilled, versed, well-informed.

learner n beginner, novice, pupil, student, tyro.

learning n acquirements, attainments, culture, education, knowledge, scholarship.

least adj meanest, minutest, smallest, tiniest.

leave[1] vb abandon, decamp, go, quit, vacate, withdraw; desert, forsake, relinquish, renounce; commit, consign, refer; cease, desist from, discontinue, refrain, stop; allow, cease, let, let alone, permit; bequeath, demise, desist, will.

leave[2] n allowance, liberty, permission, licence, sufferance; departure, retirement, withdrawal; adieu, farewell, goodbye.

lecture vb censure, chide, reprimand, reprove, scold, sermonise; address, harangue, teach. • n censure, lecturing, lesson, reprimand, reproof, scolding; address, discourse, prelection.

left adj larboard, leftward, sinistral.

leg n limb, prop.

legacy n bequest, gift, heirloom; heritage.

legal adj allowable, authorised, constitutional, lawful, legalised, legitimate, proper, sanctioned.

legalise vb authorise, legitimate, sanction.

legend n fable, fiction, myth, narrative, romance, story, tale.

legendary adj fabulous, fictitious, mythical.

legible adj clear, decipherable, fair, distinct, plain, readable.

legion n army, body, cohort, column, corps, detachment, detail, division, force, maniple, phalanx, platoon; squad; army, horde, host, multitude, number, swarm, throng. • adj many, multitudinous, myriad, numerous.

legislate vb enact, ordain.

legitimate adj authorised, lawful, legal, sanctioned; genuine, valid; correct, justifiable, logical, reasonable, warrantable, warranted.

leisure n convenience, ease, freedom, liberty, opportunity, recreation, retirement, vacation.

lend vb advance, afford, bestow, confer, furnish, give, grant, impart, loan, supply.

lengthen vb elongate, extend, produce, prolong, stretch; continue, protract.

lenient adj assuasive, lenitive, mitigating, mitigative, softening, soothing; clement, easy, forbearing, gentle, humouring, indulgent, long-suffering, merciful, mild, tender, tolerant.

less adj baser, inferior, lower, smaller; decreased, fewer, lesser, reduced, smaller, shorter; • adv barely, below, least, under; decreasingly. • prep excepting, lacking, minus, without.

lessen vb abate, abridge, contract, curtail, decrease, diminish, narrow, reduce, shrink; degrade, lower; dwindle, weaken.

lesson n exercise, task; instruction, precept; censure, chiding, lecture, lecturing, rebuke, reproof, scolding.

let[1] vb admit, allow, authorise, permit, suffer; charter, hire, lease, rent.

let[2] vb hinder, impede, instruct, prevent. • n hindrance, impediment, interference, obstacle.

lethal adj deadly, destructive, fatal, mortal.

lethargic adj apathetic, comatose, drowsy, dull, heavy, inactive, inert, sleepy, stupid, stupefied.

letter n epistle, missive, note.

level vb equalise, flatten, horizontalise, smooth; demolish, destroy, raze; aim, direct, point. • adj equal, even, flat, flush, horizontal, plain, plane, smooth. • n altitude, degree, equality, evenness, plain, plane, smoothness; deck, floor, layer, stage, storey, tier.

levity n buoyancy, facetiousness, fickleness, flippancy, frivolity, giddiness, inconstancy.

levy vb collect, exact, gather, tax; call, muster, raise, summon. • n duty, tax.

liability n accountableness, accountability, duty, obligation, responsibility, tendency; exposedness; debt, indebtedness, obligation.

liable adj accountable, amenable, answerable, bound, responsible; exposed, likely, subject.

libel vb calumniate, defame, lampoon, satirise, slander, vilify. • n calumny, defamation, lampoon, satire, slander, vilification, vituperation.

liberal adj beneficent, bountiful, charitable, disinterested, free, generous, munificent, openhearted, princely, unselfish; broad-minded, catholic, chivalrous, enlarged, high-minded, honourable, magnanimous, tolerant, unbiased, unbigoted; abundant, ample, large, plentiful, unstinted; humanising, refined, refining.

liberate vb deliver, discharge, disenthral, emancipate, free, manumit, ransom, release.

liberty n emancipation, freedom, independence, liberation, self-direction; franchise, immunity, privilege; leave, licence, permission.

licence n authorisation, leave, permission, privilege, right; certificate, charter, dispensation, imprimatur, permit, warrant; anarchy, disorder, freedom, lawlessness, laxity, liberty.

license vb allow, authorise, grant, permit, warrant; suffer, tolerate.

lie[1] vb couch, recline, remain, repose, rest.

lie[2] vb equivocate, falsify, fib, prevaricate, romance. • n equivocation, falsehood, falsification, fib, misrepresentation, prevarication, untruth; delusion, illusion.

life n activity, alertness, animation, briskness, energy, sparkle, spirit, sprightliness, verve, vigour, vivacity; behaviour, conduct, deportment; being, duration, existence, lifetime; autobiography, biography, curriculum vitae, memoirs.

lifeless adj dead, deceased, defunct, extinct, inanimate; cold, dull, flat, frigid, inert, lethargic, passive, pulseless, slow, sluggish, tame, torpid.

lift vb elevate, exalt, hoist, raise, uplift. • n aid, assistance, help; elevator.

light[1] vb alight, land, perch, settle. • adj porous, sandy, spongy, well-leavened; loose; free, portable, unburdened, unencumbered; inconsiderable, moderate, negligible, slight, small, trifling, trivial, unimportant; ethereal, feathery, flimsy, gossamer, insubstantial, weightless; easy, effortless, facile; fickle, frivolous, unsettled, unsteady, volatile; airy, buoyant, carefree.

light[2] vb conflagrate, fire, ignite, inflame, kindle; brighten, illume, illuminate, illumine, luminate, irradiate, lighten. • adj bright, clear, fair, lightsome, luminous, pale, pearly, whitish. • n dawn, day, daybreak, sunrise; blaze, brightness, effulgence, gleam, illumination, luminosity, phosphorescence, radiance, ray; candle, lamp, lantern, lighthouse, taper, torch; comprehension, enlightenment, information, insight, instruction, knowledge; elucidation, explanation, illustration; attitude, construction, interpretation, observation, reference, regard, respect, view.

lighten[1] vb allay, alleviate, ease, mitigate, palliate; disburden, disencumber, relieve, unburden.

lighten[2] vb brighten, gleam, shine; light, illume, illuminate, irradiate; enlighten, inform; flash.

like[1] vb approve, please; cherish, enjoy, love, relish; esteem, fancy, regard; choose, desire, elect, list, prefer, select, wish. • n liking, partiality, preference.

like[2] adj alike, allied, analogous, cognate, corresponding, parallel, resembling, similar; equal, same; likely, probable.

likelihood n probability, verisimilitude.

likely adj credible, liable, possible, probable; agreeable, appropriate, convenient, likable, pleasing, suitable, well-adapted, well-suited. • adv presumably, probably.

likeness n appearance, form, parallel, resemblance, semblance, similarity, similitude; copy, counterpart, effigy, facsimile, image, picture, portrait, representation.

liking n desire, fondness, partiality, wish; appearance, bent, bias, disposition, inclination, leaning, penchant, predisposition, proneness.

limit vb bound, circumscribe, define; check, condition, hinder, restrain, restrict. • n bound, boundary, bourn, confine, frontier, march, precinct, term, termination, terminus; check, hindrance, obstruction, restraint, restriction.

limitation n check, constraint, restraint.

limp¹ vb halt, hitch, hobble, totter. • n hitch, hobble, shamble, shuffle, totter.

limp² adj drooping, droopy, floppy, sagging.

limpid adj bright, clear, crystal, crystalline, lucid, pellucid, pure, translucent, transparent.

line vb align, line up, range, rank, regiment; border, bound, edge, fringe, hem, interline, march, rim, verge; seam, stripe, streak, striate, trace; carve, chisel, crease, cut, crosshatch; define, delineate, describe. • n mark, streak, stripe; cable, cord, rope, string, thread; rank, row; ancestry, family, lineage, race, succession; course, method; business, employment, job, occupation.

linger vb dally, dawdle, delay, idle, lag, loiter, remain, saunter, stay, tarry, wait.

link vb bind, conjoin, connect, fasten, join, tie, unite. • n bond, connection, connective, coupler, joint, juncture; division, member, part.

liquefy vb dissolve, fuse, melt, thaw.

liquid adj fluid; clear, dulcet, flowing, mellifluous, mellifluent, melting, soft. • n fluid, liquor.

list¹ vb alphabetise, catalogue, chronicle, codify, docket, enumerate, file, index, inventory, record, register, tabulate, tally; enlist, enroll; choose, desire, elect, like, please, prefer, wish. • n catalogue, enumeration, index, inventory, invoice, register, roll, schedule, scroll, series, table, tally.

list² vb cant, heel, incline, keel, lean, pitch, tilt, tip. • n cant, inclination, incline, leaning, pitch, slope, tilt, tip.

listen vb attend, eavesdrop, hark, hear, hearken, heed, obey, observe.

listless adj apathetic, careless, heedless, impassive, inattentive, indifferent, indolent, languid.

literally adv actually, really; exactly, precisely.

literary adj bookish, book-learned, erudite, instructed, learned, lettered, literate, scholarly.

lithe adj flexible, flexile, limber, pliable, pliant.

litter vb derange, disarrange, disorder, scatter, strew; bear. • n bedding, couch, palanquin, sedan, stretcher; confusion, disarray, disorder, mess, untidiness; fragments, rubbish, shreds.

little adj diminutive, infinitesimal, minute, small, tiny, wee; brief, short, small; feeble, inconsiderable, insignificant, moderate, petty, scanty, slender, slight, trivial, unimportant, weak; contemptible, illiberal, mean, narrow, niggardly, paltry, selfish, stingy. • n handful, jot, modicum, pinch, pittance, trifle, whit.

live¹ vb be, exist; continue, endure, last, remain,

survive; abide, dwell, reside; fare, feed, nourish, subsist, support; continue, lead, pass.

live² adj alive, animate, living, quick; burning, hot, ignited; bright, brilliant, glowing, lively, vivid; active, animated, earnest, wide-awake.

livelihood n living, maintenance, subsistence.

lively adj active, agile, alert, brisk, energetic, nimble, quick, smart, stirring, supple, vigorous, vivacious; airy, animated, blithe, blithesome, buoyant, buxom, frolicsome, gleeful, jocund, jolly, merry, spirited, sportive, sprightly, spry; bright, brilliant, clear, fresh, glowing, strong, vivid; energetic, forcible, glowing, impassioned, keen, nervous, piquant, racy, sparkling, strong.

living adj alive, breathing, existing, live, organic, quick; active, lively, quickening. • n livelihood, maintenance, support; benefice.

load vb freight, lade; burden, cumber, encumber, oppress, weigh. • n burden, freightage, pack, weight; cargo, freight, lading; clog, deadweight, encumbrance, incubus, oppression, pressure.

loathe vb abhor, abominate, detest, dislike, hate.

loathsome adj disgusting, nauseating, nauseous, offensive, repulsive, revolting.

local adj limited, neighbouring, provincial, regional, restricted, sectional, territorial, topical.

locality n location, neighbourhood, place, position, site, situation, spot.

locate vb determine, establish, fix, place, set.

lock¹ vb bolt, fasten, padlock, seal; confine; clog, impede, restrain, stop; clasp, embrace, encircle, enclose, grapple, hug, join, press. • n bolt, fastening, padlock; embrace, grapple, hug.

lock² n curl, ringlet, tress, tuft.

lodge vb deposit, fix, settle; fix, place, plant; accommodate, cover, entertain, harbour, quarter, shelter; abide, dwell, inhabit, live, reside, rest; remain, rest, sojourn, stay, stop. • n cabin, cot, cottage, hovel, hut, shed; cave, den, haunt, lair; assemblage, assembly, association club, group.

lofty adj elevated, high, tall, towering; arrogant, haughty, proud; elevated, exalted, sublime; dignified, imposing, majestic, stately.

logical adj close, coherent, consistent, dialectical, sound, valid; discriminating, rational.

loiter vb dally, dawdle, delay, dilly-dally, idle, lag, linger, saunter, stroll, tarry.

lonely adj apart, dreary, isolated, lonesome, remote, retired, secluded, sequestrated, solitary; alone, lone, companionless, friendless, solitary, unaccompanied; deserted, desolate.

long¹ vb anticipate, await, expect; aspire, covet, crave, desire, hanker, lust, pine, wish, yearn.

long² adj drawn-out, extended, extensive, far-reaching, lengthy, prolonged, protracted, stretched; diffuse, lengthy, long-winded, prolix, tedious, wearisome; backward, behindhand, slack, slow, tardy.

longing n aspiration, coveting, craving, desire, hankering, hunger, pining, yearning.

look vb behold, examine, notice, see, search; consider, examine, inspect, investigate, observe, study, contemplate, gaze, regard, scan, survey, view; anticipate, await, expect; consider, heed, mind, watch; face, front; appear, seem. • n examination, gaze, glance, peep, peer, search; appearance, aspect, complexion; air, aspect, manner.

loose vb free, liberate, release, unbind, undo, unfasten, unlash, unlock, untie; ease, loosen, relax, slacken; detach, disconnect, disengage. • adj unbound, unconfined, unfastened, unsewn, untied; disengaged, free, unattached; relaxed, slack; ill-defined, indefinite, indeterminate, indistinct, vague; careless, heedless, negligent, lax, slack; debauched, dissolute, immoral.

loosen vb liberate, relax, release, separate, slacken, unbind, unloose, untie.

loot vb pillage, plunder, ransack, rifle, rob, sack. • n booty, plunder, spoil.

lordly adj aristocratic, dignified, exalted, grand, lofty, majestic, noble; arrogant, despotic, domineering, haughty, imperious, insolent, overbearing, proud, tyrannical; large, liberal, noble.

lose vb deprive, dispossess, forfeit, miss; dislodge, displace, mislay, misspend, squander, waste; decline, fall, succumb, yield.

loss n deprivation, failure, forfeiture, privation; casualty, damage, defeat, destruction, detriment, disadvantage, injury, overthrow, ruin.

lost adj astray, missing; forfeited, missed, unredeemed; dissipated, misspent, squandered, wasted; bewildered, confused, distracted, perplexed, puzzled; absent, absentminded, abstracted, dreamy, napping, preoccupied; abandoned, corrupt, debauched, depraved, dissolute, graceless, hardened, incorrigible, irreclaimable, licentious, obdurate, profligate, reprobate, shameless, unchaste, wanton; destroyed, ruined.

lot n allotment, apportionment, destiny.

loud adj high-sounding, noisy, resounding, sonorous; deafening, stentorian, strong, stunning; boisterous, clamorous, obstreperous, tumultuous, turbulent, uproarious, vociferous; emphatic, impressive, positive, vehement; flashy, gaudy, glaring, ostentatious, showy, vulgar.

love vb adore, like, worship. • n affection, amity, courtship, delight, fondness, friendship, kindness, regard, tenderness, warmth; adoration, amour, attachment, passion; devotion, fondness, inclination, liking; benevolence, charity.

lovely adj beautiful, charming, delectable, delightful, enchanting, exquisite, graceful, pleasing, sweet, winning; admirable, adorable.

low[1] vb bellow, moo.

low[2] adj basal, depressed, profound; gentle, grave, soft, subdued; cheap, humble, mean, plebeian, vulgar; abject, base, base-minded, degraded, dirty, grovelling, ignoble, low-minded, menial, scurvy, servile, shabby, slavish, vile; derogatory, disgraceful, dishonourable, disreputable, unbecoming, undignified, ungentlemanly, unhandsome, unmanly; exhausted, feeble, reduced, weak; frugal, plain, poor, simple, spare; humble, lowly, reverent, submissive; dejected, depressed, dispirited.

lower vb depress, drop, sink, subside; debase, degrade, disgrace, humble, humiliate, reduce; abate, decrease, diminish, lessen. • adj baser, inferior, less, lesser; subjacent, under.

lowly adj gentle, humble, meek, mild, modest, plain, poor, simple, unassuming, unpretending, unpretentious; low-born, mean, servile.

loyal adj constant, devoted, faithful, patriotic.

loyalty n allegiance, constancy, devotion, faithfulness, fealty, fidelity, patriotism.

luck n accident, casualty, chance, fate, fortune, hap, haphazard, hazard, serendipity, success.

lucky adj blessed, favoured, fortunate, happy, successful; auspicious, favourable, fortunate.

lucrative adj advantageous, gainful, paying, profitable, remunerative.

ludicrous adj absurd, burlesque, comic, comical, droll, farcical, funny, laughable, odd.

lukewarm adj blood-warm, tepid, thermal; apathetic, cold, dull, indifferent, listless.

lull vb calm, compose, hush, quiet, still, tranquillise; abate, cease, decrease, diminish, subside. • n calm, calmness, cessation.

luminous adj effulgent, incandescent, radiant, refulgent, resplendent, shining; bright, brilliant, clear; clear, lucid, lucent, perspicuous, plain.

lunacy n aberration, craziness, crack, derangement, insanity, madness, mania.

lunatic adj crazy, deranged, insane, mad. • n madman, maniac, psychopath.

lure vb allure, attract, decoy, entice, inveigle, seduce, tempt. • n allurement, attraction, bait, decoy, enticement, temptation.

lurid adj dismal, ghastly, gloomy, lowering, murky, pale, wan; glaring, sensational, startling.

lurk vb hide, prowl, skulk, slink, sneak, snoop.

luscious adj delicious, delightful, palatable.

lush adj fresh, juicy, luxuriant, moist, sappy, succulent, watery.

lust vb covet, crave, desire, hanker, need, want, yearn. • n cupidity, desire, longing; carnality, concupiscence, lasciviousness, lechery, lewdness, lubricity, salaciousness.

lustful adj carnal, concupiscent, hankering, lascivious, lecherous, licentious, libidinous.

lustre n brightness, brilliance, splendour.

lusty adj healthful, lively, robust, stout, strong, sturdy, vigorous; bulky, burly, corpulent, fat.

luxuriant adj exuberant, plenteous, plentiful, profuse, superabundant.

luxuriate *vb* abound, delight, enjoy, flourish, indulge, revel.

luxurious *adj* epicurean, opulent, pampered, self-indulgent, sensual, sybaritic, voluptuous.

luxury *n* epicureanism, epicurism, luxuriousness, opulence, sensuality, voluptuousness; delicacy, treat.

lyrical *adj* ecstatic, enthusiastic, expressive; mellifluous, melodic, musical, poetic.

M

macabre *adj* cadaverous, deathlike, deathly, dreadful, eerie, frightening, frightful, ghoulish, grim, grisly, gruesome, hideous, horrid, morbid.

machine *n* instrument, puppet, tool; machinery, organisation, system; engine.

mad *adj* crazed, crazy, delirious, demented, deranged, distracted, insane, irrational, lunatic, maniac, maniacal; enraged, furious, rabid, raging, violent; angry, enraged, exasperated, furious, incensed, provoked, wrathful; distracted, infatuated, wild; frantic, frenzied, raving.

madden *vb* annoy, craze, enrage, exasperate, inflame, infuriate, irritate, provoke.

madness *n* aberration, craziness, derangement, insanity, lunacy, mania; delirium, frenzy, fury.

magic *adj* bewitching, charming, enchanting, fascinating, magical, miraculous, spellbinding. • *n* conjuring, enchantment, necromancy, sorcery, witchcraft; fascination, witchery.

magician *n* conjurer, enchanter, juggler, magus, necromancer, shaman, sorcerer, wizard.

magisterial *adj* august, majestic, dignified, pompous; authoritative, despotic, domineering.

magnanimity *n* chivalry, disinterestedness, forbearance, high-mindedness, generosity, nobility.

magnificent *adj* elegant, grand, majestic, noble, splendid, superb; brilliant, gorgeous, imposing, lavish, luxurious, pompous, showy, stately.

magnify *vb* amplify, augment, enlarge; bless, celebrate, elevate, exalt, extol, glorify, laud, praise; exaggerate.

magnitude *n* bulk, dimension, extent, mass, size, volume; consequence, greatness, importance; grandeur, loftiness, sublimity.

maim *vb* disable, disfigure, mutilate.

main[1] *adj* capital, cardinal, chief, leading, principal; essential, important, indispensable, necessary, requisite, vital; enormous, huge, mighty, vast. • *n* force, might, power, strength.

main[2] *n* high seas, ocean; continent, mainland.

maintain *vb* keep, preserve, support, sustain, uphold; hold, possess; defend, vindicate, justify; carry on, continue, keep up; feed, provide, supply; allege, assert, declare; affirm, allege, aver, contend, declare, hold, say.

maintenance *n* defence, justification, preservation, support, sustenance, vindication; food, livelihood, provisions, subsistence, sustenance.

majestic *adj* august, dignified, imperial, imposing, lofty, noble, pompous, princely, stately, regal, royal; grand, magnificent, splendid.

majority *n* bulk, greater, mass, more, most, plurality, preponderance, superiority; adulthood.

make *vb* create; fashion, figure, form, frame, mould, shape; cause, construct, effect, establish, fabricate, produce; do, execute, perform, practice; acquire, gain, get, raise, secure; cause, compel, constrain, force, occasion; compose, constitute, form; go, journey, move, proceed, tend, travel; conduce, contribute, effect, favour, operate; estimate, judge, reckon, suppose, think. • *n* brand, build, constitution, construction, form, shape, structure.

maker *n* creator, god; builder, constructor, fabricator, framer, manufacturer; author, composer.

malady *n* affliction, ail, ailment, complaint, disease, disorder, illness, indisposition, sickness.

malevolent *adj* evil-minded, hateful, hostile, ill-natured, malicious, malignant, mischievous, rancorous, spiteful, venomous, vindictive.

malice *n* animosity, bitterness, enmity, grudge, hate, ill will, malevolence, maliciousness, malignity, spite, venom, vindictiveness.

malicious *adj* bitter, envious, evil-minded, ill-disposed, ill-natured, invidious, malevolent, malignant, mischievous, spiteful, vicious.

malign *vb* abuse, asperse, blacken, calumniate, defame, disparage, revile, scandalise, slander, traduce, vilify. • *adj* malevolent, malicious, malignant, ill-disposed; baneful, injurious, pernicious, unfavourable, unpropitious.

malignant *adj* bitter, envious, hostile, inimical, malevolent, malicious, malign, spiteful, rancorous, resentful, virulent; heinous, virulent, pernicious; ill-boding, unfavourable, unpropitious; dangerous, fatal, virulent.

mammoth *adj* colossal, enormous, gigantic.

man *vb* crew, garrison, furnish; fortify, reinforce, strengthen. • *n* adult, being, body, human, individual, one, person, personage, somebody;

soul; humanity, humankind, mankind; attendant, butler, dependant, liege, servant, subject, valet, vassal; employee, workman.

manage vb administer, conduct, direct, guide, handle, operate, order, regulate, superintend, supervise, transact, treat; control, govern, guide, rule; handle, manipulate, train, wield; contrive, economise, husband, save.

manageable adj controllable, docile, easy, governable, tamable, tractable.

management n administration, care, charge, conduct, control, direction, disposal, economy, government, guidance, superintendence, supervision, surveillance, treatment.

manager n comptroller, conductor, director, executive, governor, impresario, overseer, superintendent, supervisor.

mandate n charge, command, commission, edict, injunction, order, precept, requirement.

mangle[1] vb hack, lacerate, mutilate, rend, tear; cripple, crush, destroy, maim, mutilate, mar.

mangle[2] vb calender, polish, press, smooth.

mania n aberration, craziness, delirium, dementia, derangement, frenzy, insanity, lunacy, madness; craze, desire, enthusiasm, fad, fanaticism.

manifest vb declare, demonstrate, disclose, discover, display, evidence, evince, exhibit, express, reveal, show. • adj apparent, clear, conspicuous, distinct, evident, glaring, indubitable, obvious, open, palpable, patent, plain, visible.

manifold adj complex, diverse, many, multifarious, multiplied, multitudinous, numerous, several, sundry, varied, various.

manipulate vb handle, operate, work.

manner n fashion, form, method, mode, style, way; custom, habit, practice; degree, extent, measure; kind, kinds, sort, sorts; air, appearance, aspect, behaviour, carriage, demeanour, deportment, look, mien; mannerism, peculiarity, style.

manners npl conduct, habits, morals; air, bearing, behaviour, breeding, carriage, comportment, deportment, etiquette.

manoeuvre vb contrive, finesse, intrigue, manage, plan, plot, scheme. • n evolution, exercise, movement, operation; artifice, finesse, intrigue, plan, plot, ruse, scheme, stratagem, trick.

manufacture vb build, compose, construct, create, fabricate, forge, form, make, mould, produce, shape. • n constructing, fabrication, making, production.

many adj abundant, diverse, frequent, innumerable, manifold, multifarious, multifold, multiplied, multitudinous, numerous, sundry, varied.

map vb chart, draw up, plan, plot, set out, sketch. • n chart, diagram, outline, plot, sketch.

mar vb blot, damage, harm, hurt, impair, injure, ruin, spoil, stain; deface, deform, disfigure.

march vb go, pace, parade, step, tramp, walk. • n

hike, tramp, walk; parade, procession; gait, step, stride; advance, evolution, progress.

margin n border, brim, brink, confine, edge, limit, rim, skirt, verge; latitude, room, space.

marital adj connubial, conjugal, matrimonial.

mark vb distinguish, earmark, label; betoken, brand, characterise, denote, designate, engrave, impress, imprint, indicate, print, stamp; evince, heed, note, notice, observe, regard, remark, show, spot. • n brand, character, characteristic, impression, impress, line, note, print, sign, stamp, symbol, token, race; evidence, indication, proof, symptom, token, trace, track, vestige; badge, sign; footprint, trace, track, vestige; bull's-eye, butt, object, target; consequence, distinction, eminence, fame, importance, position.

marked adj conspicuous, distinguished, eminent, notable, noted, outstanding, prominent.

marriage n espousals, nuptials, spousals, wedding; matrimony, wedlock; union; alliance, association, confederation.

marshal vb arrange, array, dispose, gather, muster, range, order, rank; guide, herald, lead. • n conductor, director, master of ceremonies, regulator; harbinger, herald, pursuivant.

martial adj brave, heroic, military, warlike.

marvel vb gape, gaze, goggle, wonder. • n miracle, prodigy, wonder.

marvellous adj amazing, astonishing, extraordinary, miraculous, prodigious, strange, stupendous, wonderful, wondrous; improbable, incredible, surprising, unbelievable.

masculine adj bold, hardy, manful, manlike, manly, mannish, virile; powerful, robust, strong.

mask vb cloak, conceal, cover, disguise, hide, screen, shroud, veil. • n blind, cloak, disguise, screen, veil; evasion, pretence, plea, pretext, ruse, shift, subterfuge, trick; masquerade.

mass vb accumulate, amass, assemble, collect, gather, rally, throng. • adj extensive, general, large-scale, widespread. • n cake, clot, lump; assemblage, collection, combination, congeries, heap; bulk, dimension, magnitude, size; accumulation, aggregate, body, sum, total, whole.

massacre vb annihilate, butcher, exterminate, kill, murder, slaughter, slay. • n annihilation, butchery, carnage, extermination, killing, murder, pogrom, slaughter.

massive adj big, bulky, colossal, enormous, heavy, huge, immense, ponderous, solid, substantial, vast, weighty.

master vb conquer, defeat, direct, govern, overcome, overpower, rule, subdue, subjugate, vanquish; acquire, learn. • adj cardinal, chief, especial, grand, great, main, leading, prime, principal; adept, expert, proficient. • n director, governor, lord, manager, overseer, superintendent, ruler; captain, commander; instructor, pedagogue, preceptor, schoolteacher, teacher, tutor; holder, owner, possessor, proprietor; chief, head, leader.

masterly adj adroit, clever, dextrous, excellent, expert, finished, skilful, skilled.

mastery n command, dominion, mastership, power, rule, supremacy, sway; ascendancy, conquest, leadership, preeminence, superiority, supremacy, upper-hand, victory; acquisition, acquirement, attainment; ability, skill.

match vb equal, rival; adapt, fit, harmonise, proportion, suit; marry, mate; combine, couple, join, sort; oppose, pit; correspond, suit, tally. • n companion, equal, mate, tally; competition, contest, game, trial; marriage, union.

matchless adj consummate, excellent, exquisite, incomparable, inimitable, peerless, perfect, surpassing, unequalled, unparalleled.

mate vb marry, match, wed. • n associate, companion, compeer, consort, crony, friend, fellow, intimate; companion, equal, match; assistant, subordinate; husband, wife.

material adj bodily, corporeal, nonspiritual, physical, temporal; essential, important, momentous, relevant, vital, weighty. • n body, element, stuff, substance.

maternal adj motherlike, motherly.

matrimonial adj conjugal, connubial, marital.

matter vb import, signify, weigh. • n body, content, sense, substance; difficulty, distress, trouble; material, stuff; question, subject, subject matter, topic; affair, business, concern, event; consequence, import, importance, moment, significance; discharge, purulence, pus.

mature vb develop, perfect, ripen. • adj complete, fit, full-grown, perfect, ripe; completed, prepared, ready, well-considered, well-digested.

maze vb amaze, bewilder, confound, confuse, perplex. • n intricacy, labyrinth, meander; bewilderment, embarrassment, intricacy, perplexity.

meagre adj emaciated, gaunt, lank, lean, poor, skinny, starved, spare, thin; barren, poor, sterile, unproductive; bald, barren, dry, dull, mean, poor, prosy, feeble, insignificant, jejune, scanty.

mean[1] vb contemplate, design, intend, purpose; connote, denote, express, imply, import, indicate, purport, signify, symbolise.

mean[2] adj average, medium, middle; intermediate, intervening. • n measure, mediocrity, medium, moderation; average.

mean[3] adj coarse, common, humble, ignoble, low, ordinary, plebeian, vulgar; abject, base, base-minded, beggarly, contemptible, degraded, dirty, dishonourable, disingenuous, grovelling, low-minded, pitiful, rascally, scurvy, servile, shabby, sneaking, sorry, spiritless, unfair, vile; illiberal, mercenary, miserly, narrow, narrow-minded, niggardly, parsimonious, penurious, selfish, sordid, stingy, ungenerous, unhandsome;

contemptible, despicable, diminutive, insignificant, paltry, petty, poor, small, wretched.

meaning n acceptation, drift, import, intention, purport, purpose, sense, signification.

means npl instrument, method, mode, way; appliance, expedient, resource; property, resources, revenue, substance, wealth.

measure vb mete; adjust, gauge, proportion; appraise, appreciate, estimate, gauge, value. • n gauge, meter, rule, standard; degree, extent, length, limit; allotment, share, proportion; degree; means, step; foot, metre, rhythm, tune.

meddle vb interfere, interpose, intrude.

meddlesome adj interfering, intrusive, officious, prying.

mediation n arbitration, intercession, interposition, intervention.

mediator n advocate, arbitrator, interceder, intercessor, propitiator, umpire.

mediocre adj average, commonplace, indifferent, mean, medium, middling, ordinary.

meditate vb concoct, contrive, design, devise, intend, plan, purpose, scheme; chew, contemplate, ruminate, study; cogitate, muse, ponder.

meditation n cogitation, contemplation, musing, pondering, reflection, study, thought.

medium adj average, mean, mediocre, middle. • n agency, channel, intermediary, instrument, instrumentality, means, organ; conditions, environment, influences; average, means.

medley n confusion, farrago, hodgepodge, hotchpotch, jumble, mass, melange, miscellany.

meek adj gentle, humble, lowly, mild, modest, pacific, soft, submissive, unassuming, yielding.

meet vb cross, intersect, transact; confront, encounter, engage; answer, comply, fulfil, gratify, satisfy; converge, join, unite; assemble, collect, convene, congregate, forgather, muster, rally. • adj adapted, appropriate, befitting, convenient.

meeting n encounter, interview; assemblage, assembly, audience, company, concourse, conference, congregation, convention, gathering; assignation, encounter, introduction, rendezvous; confluence, conflux, intersection, joining, junction, union; collision.

melancholy adj blue, dejected, depressed, despondent, desponding, disconsolate, dismal, dispirited, doleful, downcast, downhearted, dumpish, gloomy, glum, hypochondriac, low-spirited, lugubrious, moody, mopish, sad, sombre, sorrowful, unhappy; afflictive, calamitous, unfortunate, unlucky; dark, gloomy, grave, quiet, sad. • n blues, dejection, depression, despondency, dismals, dumps, gloom, gloominess, sadness.

mellow vb mature, ripen; improve, smooth, soften, tone; pulverise; perfect. • adj mature, ripe; dulcet, mellifluous, mellifluent, silver-toned, rich, silvery, smooth, soft; delicate, rich, soft;

genial, good-humoured, jolly, jovial, matured, softened; perfected, well-prepared; fuddled, intoxicated, tipsy.

melodious *adj* euphonious, harmonious, mellifluous, musical, sweet, tuneful.

melt *vb* dissolve, fuse, liquefy, thaw; mollify, relax, soften, subdue; dissipate, waste; blend, pass.

member *n* arm, leg, limb, organ; component, constituent, element, part, portion; branch, clause, division, head.

memento *n* remembrance, reminder, souvenir.

memoir *n* account, autobiography, biography, journal, narrative, record, register.

memorable *adj* celebrated, distinguished, extraordinary, famous, great, illustrious, important, notable, noteworthy, remarkable, significant.

memorandum *n* minute, note, record.

memorial *adj* commemorative, monumental. • *n* cairn, commemoration, memento, monument, plaque, record, souvenir; memorandum, remembrance.

memory *n* recollection, remembrance, reminiscence; celebrity, fame, renown, reputation; commemoration, memorial.

menace *vb* alarm, frighten, intimidate, threaten. • *n* danger, hazard, peril, threat, warning; nuisance, pest, troublemaker.

mend *vb* darn, patch, rectify, refit, repair, restore, retouch; ameliorate, amend, better, correct, emend, improve, meliorate, rectify, reform; advance, help, improve; augment, increase.

mendacious *adj* deceitful, deceptive, fallacious, false, lying, untrue, untruthful.

menial *adj* base, low, mean, servile, vile. • *n* attendant, bondsman, domestic, flunkey, footman, lackey, serf, servant, slave, underling.

mental *adj* ideal, immaterial, intellectual, psychiatric, subjective.

mention *vb* acquaint, allude, cite, communicate, declare, disclose, divulge, impart, inform, name, report, reveal, state, tell. • *n* allusion, citation, designation, notice, noting, reference.

mentor *n* adviser, counsellor, guide, instructor.

mercantile *adj* commercial, marketable.

mercenary *adj* hired, paid, purchased, venal; avaricious, covetous, grasping, mean, niggardly, parsimonious, penurious, sordid, stingy. • *n* hireling, soldier.

merchandise *n* commodities, goods, wares.

merchant *n* dealer, retailer, shopkeeper, trader.

merciful *adj* clement, compassionate, forgiving, gracious, lenient, pitiful; benignant, forbearing, gentle, gracious, humane, kind, mild, tender.

merciless *adj* barbarous, callous, cruel, fell, hard-hearted, inexorable, pitiless, relentless, remorseless, ruthless, savage, severe, uncompassionate, unfeeling, unmerciful, unrelenting.

mercurial *adj* active, lively, nimble, prompt,

quick, sprightly; cheerful, light-hearted, lively; changeable, fickle, flighty, volatile.

mercy *n* benevolence, clemency, compassion, gentleness, kindness, lenience, leniency, lenity, mildness, pity, tenderness; blessing, favour, grace; discretion, disposal; forgiveness, pardon.

mere *adj* bald, bare, naked, plain, sole, simple. • *n* lake, pond, pool.

merge *vb* bury, dip, immerse, involve, lose, plunge, sink, submerge.

merit *vb* deserve, earn, incur; acquire, desert, gain, profit, value. • *n* claim, right; credit, desert, excellence, goodness, worth, worthiness.

merry *adj* agreeable, brisk, delightful, exhilarating, lively, pleasant, stirring; airy, blithe, blithesome, buxom, cheerful, comical, droll, facetious, frolicsome, gladsome, gleeful, hilarious, jocund, jolly, jovial, joyous, light-hearted, lively, mirthful, sportive, sprightly, vivacious.

mess *n* company, set; farrago, hodgepodge, hotchpotch, jumble, medley, mass, melange, miscellany, mishmash, mixture; confusion, muddle, perplexity, pickle, plight, predicament.

message *n* communication, dispatch, intimation, letter, missive, notice.

metaphorical *adj* allegorical, figurative.

method *n* course, manner, means, mode, procedure, process, rule, way; arrangement, classification, disposition, order, plan, system.

methodical *adj* orderly, regular, systematic.

mettle *n* constitution, element, material, stuff; character, disposition, spirit, temper; ardour, courage, fire, hardihood, life, nerve, pluck, spirit, sprightliness, vigour.

microscopic *adj* infinitesimal, minute, tiny.

middle *adj* central, halfway, mean, medial, mid; intermediate. • *n* centre, halfway, mean.

might *n* ability, capacity, efficacy, efficiency, force, main, power, prowess, strength.

mighty *adj* able, bold, courageous, potent, powerful, puissant, robust, strong, sturdy, valiant, valorous, vigorous; bulky, enormous, huge, immense, monstrous, stupendous, vast.

mild *adj* amiable, clement, compassionate, gentle, indulgent, kind, merciful, pacific, tender; bland, gentle, pleasant, soft, suave; calm, gentle, kind, placid, pleasant, soft, tranquil; assuasive, demulcent, emollient, lenitive, soothing.

militant *adj* belligerent, combative, contending.

military *adj* martial, soldier, soldierly, warlike. • *n* army, militia, soldiers.

mill *n* factory, manufactory; grinder; crowd, throng.

mimic *vb* ape, counterfeit, imitate, impersonate, mime, mock, parody. • *adj* imitative, mock, simulated. • *n* imitator, impersonator, parrot.

mince[1] *vb* chop, cut, hash, shatter. • *n* forcemeat, hash, mash, mincemeat.

mince² vb attenuate, diminish, extenuate, mitigate, palliate, soften; pose, sashay, simper.

mind¹ vb attend, heed, mark, note, notice, regard, tend, watch; obey, observe, submit; design, incline, intend, mean; recall, recollect, remember, remind; beware, look out, watch out. • n soul, spirit; brains, common sense, intellect, reason, understanding; belief, consideration, contemplation, judgement, opinion, reflection, sentiment, thought; memory, recollection, remembrance; bent, desire, disposition, inclination, intention, leaning, purpose, tendency, will.

mind² vb balk, begrudge, grudge, object, resent.

mindful adj attentive, careful, heedful.

mindless adj dull, heavy, insensible, senseless, sluggish, stupid, unthinking; careless, forgetful, heedless, neglectful, negligent, regardless.

mine vb dig, excavate, quarry, unearth; sap, undermine, weaken; destroy, ruin. • n colliery, deposit, lode, pit, shaft.

mingle vb blend, combine, commingle, compound, intermingle, intermix, join, mix, unite.

miniature adj diminutive, little, small, tiny.

minister vb administer, afford, furnish, give, supply; aid, assist, contribute, help, succour. • n agent, assistant, servant, subordinate, underling; administrator, executive; ambassador, delegate, envoy, plenipotentiary; chaplain, churchman, clergyman, cleric, curate, divine, ecclesiastic, parson, pastor, preacher, priest, rector, vicar.

ministry n agency, aid, help, instrumentality, interposition, service, support; administration, cabinet, council, government.

minor adj less, smaller; inferior, junior, secondary, subordinate, younger; inconsiderable, petty, unimportant, small.

mint vb coin, stamp; fabricate, fashion, forge, invent, make, produce. • adj fresh, new, perfect, undamaged. • n die, punch, seal, stamp; fortune, (inf) heap, million, pile, wad.

minute¹ adj diminutive, fine, little, microscopic, miniature, slender, slight, small, tiny; circumstantial, critical, detailed, exact, fussy, meticulous, nice, particular, precise.

minute² n account, entry, item, memorandum, note, proceedings, record; instant, moment, second, trice, twinkling.

miracle n marvel, prodigy, wonder.

miraculous adj amazing, extraordinary, incredible, marvellous, supernatural, unaccountable, unbelievable, wondrous.

mirror vb copy, echo, emulate, reflect, show. • n looking-glass, reflector, speculum; archetype, exemplar, example, model, paragon, pattern.

mirth n cheerfulness, festivity, frolic, fun, gaiety, gladness, glee, hilarity, festivity, jollity, joviality, joyousness, laughter, merriment.

misadventure n accident, calamity, catastrophe, cross, disaster, failure, ill-luck, infelicity, mischance, misfortune, mishap, reverse.

miscellaneous adj confused, diverse, diversified, heterogeneous, indiscriminate, jumbled, many, mingled, mixed, promiscuous, various.

miscellany n collection, diversity, farrago, gallimaufry, hodgepodge, hotchpotch, jumble, medley, mishmash, melange, variety.

mischief n damage, detriment, disadvantage, evil, harm, hurt, ill, injury, prejudice; ill-consequence, misfortune, trouble; devilry.

mischievous adj destructive, detrimental, harmful, hurtful, injurious, noxious, pernicious; malicious, sinful, vicious, wicked; annoying, impish, naughty, troublesome, vexatious.

misconduct n misbehaviour, misdemeanour, rudeness, transgression; ill-management, mismanagement.

misconstrue vb misread, mistranslate; misapprehend, misinterpret, mistake, misunderstand.

miser n money-grabber, niggard, skinflint.

miserable adj afflicted, broken-hearted, comfortless, disconsolate, distressed, forlorn, heartbroken, unhappy, wretched; calamitous, hapless, ill-starred, pitiable, unfortunate, unhappy, unlucky, wretched; poor, valueless, worthless; abject, contemptible, despicable, low, mean.

miserly adj avaricious, beggarly, close, closefisted, covetous, grasping, mean, niggardly, parsimonious, penurious, stingy, tight-fisted.

misery n affliction, agony, anguish, calamity, desolation, distress, grief, heartache, heavyheartedness, misfortune, sorrow, suffering, torment, torture, tribulation, unhappiness, woe.

misfortune n adversity, affliction, bad luck, blow, calamity, casualty, catastrophe, disaster, distress, hardship, harm, ill, infliction, misadventure, mischance, mishap, reverse, scourge, stroke, trial, trouble, visitation.

misgiving n apprehension, distrust, doubt, hesitation, suspicion, uncertainty.

mishap n accident, calamity, disaster, ill luck, misadventure, mischance, misfortune.

mislead vb beguile, deceive, delude, misdirect.

misrepresent vb belie, caricature, distort, falsify, misinterpret, misstate, pervert.

miss¹ vb blunder, err, fail, fall short, forgo, lack, lose, miscarry, mistake, omit, overlook, trip; avoid, escape, evade, skip, slip; feel the loss of, need, want, wish. • n blunder, error, failure, fault, mistake, omission, oversight, slip, trip.

miss² n damsel, girl, lass, maid, maiden.

mission n commission, legation; business, charge, commission, duty, errand, office, trust; delegation, deputation, embassy.

mist vb cloud, drizzle, mizzle, smog. • n cloud, fog, haze; bewilderment, obscurity, perplexity.

mistake vb misapprehend, miscalculate, misconceive, misjudge, misunderstand; confound, take; blunder, err. • n misapprehension, misconception, mistaking, misunderstanding; blunder, error, fault, inaccuracy, oversight, slip, trip.

mistrust vb distrust, doubt, suspect; apprehend, fear, surmise, suspect. • n doubt, distrust.

misty adj cloudy, clouded, dark, dim, foggy.

misunderstanding n error, misapprehension, misconception, mistake; difference, difficulty, disagreement, discord, dissension, quarrel.

misuse vb desecrate, misapply, misemploy, pervert, profane; abuse, ill-treat, maltreat, ill-use; fritter, squander, waste. • n abuse, perversion, profanation, prostitution; ill-treatment, ill-use, ill-usage, misusage; misapplication, solecism.

mitigate vb abate, alleviate, assuage, diminish, lessen, moderate, palliate, relieve; allay, appease, calm, mollify, pacify, quell, quiet, soften, soothe; moderate, temper; diminish, lessen.

mix vb alloy, amalgamate, blend, commingle, combine, compound, incorporate, interfuse, interlard, mingle, unite; associate, join, unite. • n alloy, amalgam, blend, combination, compound.

mixture n admixture, association, intermixture, union; compound, farrago, hash, hodgepodge, hotchpotch, jumble, medley, melange, mishmash; diversity, miscellany, variety.

moan vb bemoan, bewail, deplore, grieve, groan, lament, mourn, sigh, weep. • n groan, lament, lamentation, sigh, wail.

mob vb crowd, jostle, surround, swarm, pack, throng. • n assemblage, crowd, rabble, multitude, throng, tumult; dregs, canaille, populace.

mobile adj changeable, fickle, expressive, inconstant, sensitive, variable, volatile.

mock vb ape, counterfeit, imitate, mimic, take off; deride, flout, gibe, insult, jeer, ridicule, taunt; balk, cheat, deceive, defeat, disappoint, dupe, elude, illude, mislead. • adj assumed, counterfeit, fake, false, feigned, make-believe, pretended, spurious.

mockery n contumely, counterfeit, deception, derision, imitation, jeering, mimicry, ridicule, scoffing, scorn, sham, travesty.

model vb design, fashion, form, mould, plan, shape. • adj admirable, archetypal, estimable, exemplary, ideal, meritorious, paradigmatic, praiseworthy, worthy. • n archetype, design, mould, original, pattern, protoplast, prototype, type; dummy, example, mould; copy, facsimile, image, imitation, representation.

moderate vb abate, allay, appease, assuage, blunt, dull, lessen, soothe, mitigate, mollify, pacify, quell, quiet, reduce, repress, soften, still, subdue; diminish, qualify, slacken, temper; control, govern, regulate. • adj abstinent, frugal, sparing, temperate; limited, mediocre; abstemi-

ous, sober; calm, cool, judicious, mild, reasonable, sedate; gentle, mild, temperate.

moderation n abstemiousness, forbearance, frugality, restraint, sobriety, temperance; calmness, composure, coolness, deliberateness, equanimity, mildness, sedateness.

modern adj fresh, late, latest, new, novel, present, recent, up-to-date.

modest adj bashful, coy, diffident, humble, meek, reserved, retiring, shy, unassuming, unobtrusive, unostentatious, unpretending, unpretentious; chaste, proper, pure, virtuous.

modification n alteration, change, qualification, reformation, variation; form, manner, mode.

modify vb alter, change, qualify, reform, shape, vary; lower, moderate, qualify, soften.

modulate vb attune, harmonise, tune; inflict, vary; adapt, adjust, proportion.

molest vb annoy, badger, bore, bother, chafe, discommode, disquiet, disturb, harass, harry, fret, gull, hector, incommode, inconvenience, irritate, oppress, pester, plague, tease, torment.

mollify vb soften; appease, calm, compose, pacify, quiet, soothe, tranquillise; abate, allay, assuage, blunt, dull, ease, lessen, mitigate, moderate, relieve, temper; qualify, tone down.

moment n flash, instant, jiffy, second, trice, twinkling, wink; avail, consequence, consideration, force, gravity, importance, significance, value, weight.

momentous adj grave, important, serious, significant, vital, weighty.

monarch n chief, dictator, emperor, king, potentate, prince, queen, ruler, sovereign.

monitor vb check, observe, oversee, supervise, watch. • n admoniser, admonitor, adviser, counsellor, instructor, mentor, overseer.

monopolise vb control, dominate, engross.

monotonous adj boring, dull, tedious, tiresome, undiversified, uniform, unvaried.

monotony n boredom, dullness, sameness, tedium, tiresomeness, uniformity, wearisomeness.

monster n enormous, gigantic, huge, immense, mammoth, monstrous. • n enormity, marvel, prodigy, wonder; brute, demon, fiend, miscreant, ruffian, villain, wretch.

monstrous adj abnormal, preternatural, prodigious, unnatural; colossal, enormous, extraordinary, huge, immense, prodigious, stupendous, vast; marvellous, strange, wonderful; dreadful, flagrant, frightful, hateful, hideous, horrible, shocking, terrible.

monument n memorial, record, remembrance, testimonial; cairn, cenotaph, gravestone, mausoleum, memorial, pillar, tomb, tombstone.

mood n disposition, humour, temper, vein.

moody adj capricious, humoursome, variable; angry, crabbed, crusty, fretful, ill-tempered, irascible, irritable, passionate, pettish, peevish, petulant, snappish, snarling, sour, testy; cross-grained, dogged, frowning, glowering, glum, intractable, morose, perverse, spleeny, stubborn, sulky, sullen, wayward; abstracted, gloomy.

moral *adj* ethical, good, honest, honourable, just, upright, virtuous; abstract, ideal, intellectual, mental. • *n* intent, meaning, significance.

morals *npl* ethics, morality; behaviour, conduct.

morbid *adj* ailing, corrupted, diseased, sick, sickly, tainted, unhealthy, unsound, vitiated; depressed, downcast, gloomy, pessimistic.

moreover *adv, conj* also, besides, further, furthermore, likewise, too.

morning *n* daybreak, dawn, morningtide.

morose *adj* austere, churlish, crabbed, crusty, dejected, desponding, downcast, downhearted, gloomy, glum, melancholy, moody, sad, severe, sour, sullen, surly.

morsel *n* bite, mouthful, titbit; bit, fragment, morceau, part, piece, scrap.

mortal *adj* deadly, destructive, fatal, final, human, lethal, perishable, vital. • *n* being, earthling, human, man, person, woman.

mortality *n* corruption, death, destruction.

mortify *vb* annoy, chagrin, depress, disappoint, displease, disquiet, dissatisfy, harass, humble, plague, vex, worry; abase, abash, confound, humiliate, restrain, shame, subdue; corrupt, fester.

mostly *adv* chiefly, customarily, especially, generally, mainly, particularly, principally.

motherly *adj* affectionate, kind, maternal.

motion *vb* beckon, direct, gesture, signal. • *n* action, change, drift, flux, movement, passage, transit; gesture, impulse, suggestion; proposal, proposition.

motive *adj* activating, driving, moving, operative. • *n* cause, consideration, ground, impulse, incentive, incitement, inducement, influence, occasion, prompting, purpose, reason, spur.

mould[1] *vb* carve, cast, fashion, form, make, model, shape. • *n* cast, character, fashion, form, matrix, pattern, shape; material, matter.

mould[2] *n* blight, mildew, mouldiness, must, mustiness, rot; fungus, lichen, mushroom, puffball, rust, smut, toadstool; earth, loam, soil.

mouldy *adj* decaying, fusty, mildewed, musty.

mount[1] *n* hill, mountain, peak.

mount[2] *vb* arise, ascend, climb, rise, soar, tower; ascend, climb, escalate, scale; embellish, ornament; bestride, get upon. • *n* horse, ride, steed.

mountain *n* alp, height, hill, mount, peak; abundance, heap, mound, stack.

mourn *vb* bemoan, bewail, deplore, grieve, lament, sorrow, wail.

mournful *adj* afflicting, afflictive, calamitous, deplorable, distressed, grievous, lamentable, sad, woeful; doleful, heavy, heavy-hearted, lugubrious, melancholy, sorrowful, tearful.

mouth *vb* clamour, declaim, rant, roar, vociferate. • *n* chaps, jaws; aperture, opening, orifice; entrance, inlet; mouthpiece, spokesman.

move *vb* dislodge, drive, impel, propel, push, shift, start, stir; actuate, incite, instigate, rouse; determine, incline, induce, influence, persuade, prompt; affect, impress, touch, trouble; agitate, awaken, excite, incense, irritate; propose, recommend, suggest; go, march, proceed, walk; act, live; flit, remove. • *n* action, motion.

movement *n* change, move, motion, passage; emotion, motion; crusade, drive.

moving *adj* impelling, influencing, instigating, persuading, persuasive; affecting, impressive, pathetic, touching.

muddle *vb* confuse, disarrange, disorder; fuddle, inebriate, stupefy; muff, mull, spoil.

muffle *vb* cover, envelop, shroud, wrap; conceal, disguise, involve; deaden, soften, stifle.

multiply *vb* augment, extend, increase, spread.

multitude *n* numerousness; host, legion; army, assemblage, assembly, collection, concourse, congregation, crowd, horde, mob, swarm, throng; commonality, herd, mass, pack.

mundane *adj* earthly, secular, sublunary, temporal, terrene, terrestrial, worldly.

murder *vb* assassinate, butcher, destroy, dispatch, kill, massacre, slaughter, slay; abuse, mar, spoil. • *n* assassination, butchery, destruction, homicide, killing, manslaughter, massacre.

murderer *n* assassin, butcher, cut-throat, killer, manslaughterer, slaughterer, slayer.

murky *adj* cheerless, cloudy, dark, dim, dusky, gloomy, hazy, lowering, lurid, obscure, overcast.

murmur *vb* croak, grumble, mumble, mutter, rapine; hum, whisper. • *n* complaint, grumble, mutter, plaint, whimper; hum, undertone.

muscular *adj* sinewy; athletic, brawny, powerful, lusty, stalwart, stout, strong, sturdy.

muse *vb* brood, cogitate, consider, contemplate, deliberate, dream, meditate, ponder, reflect, ruminate, speculate, think. • *n* abstraction, musing.

music *n* harmony, melody, symphony.

musical *adj* dulcet, harmonious, melodious, sweet, sweet-sounding, symphonious, tuneful.

musing *adj* absent-minded, meditative, preoccupied. • *n* absent-mindedness, abstraction, contemplation, daydreaming, meditation, muse, reflection, reverie, rumination.

muster *vb* assemble, collect, congregate, convene, convoke, gather, marshal, meet, rally, summon.

musty *adj* fetid, foul, fusty, mouldy, rank, spoiled; hackneyed, old, stale, trite; ill-favoured, insipid, stale, vapid; dull, heavy.

mutable *adj* alterable, changeable, variable; changeful, fickle, inconstant, irresolute, mutational, unsettled, unstable, unsteady, vacillating.

mute vb dampen, lower, moderate, muffle, soften. • adj dumb, voiceless; silent, speechless, still, taciturn.

mutilate vb cripple, damage, disable, disfigure, hamstring, injure, maim, mangle, mar.

mutinous adj contumacious, insubordinate, rebellious, refractory, riotous, tumultuous, turbulent, unruly; insurgent, seditious.

mutiny vb rebel, revolt, rise, resist. • n insubordination, insurrection, rebellion, revolt, revolution, riot, rising, sedition, uprising.

mutter vb grumble, muffle, mumble, murmur.

mutual adj common, correlative, interchangeable, interchanged, reciprocal, requited.

myriad adj innumerable, manifold, multitudinous, uncounted. • n host, million(s), multitude, score(s), sea, swarm, thousand(s).

mysterious adj abstruse, cabbalistic, concealed, cryptic, dark, dim, enigmatic, enigmatical, hidden, incomprehensible, inexplicable, inscrutable, mystic, mystical, obscure, occult, puzzling, recondite, secret, sphinx-like, unaccountable, unfathomable.

mystery n enigma, puzzle, riddle, secret.

mystical adj abstruse, cabbalistic, dark, enigmatical, esoteric, hidden, inscrutable, mysterious, obscure, occult, recondite, transcendental.

mystify vb befog, bewilder, confound, confuse, dumbfound, embarrass, obfuscate, perplex.

myth n fable, legend, tradition; allegory, fiction, invention, parable, story; falsehood, fancy, figment, lie, untruth.

mythical adj allegorical, fabled, fabulous, fanciful, fictitious, imaginary, legendary.

N

nab vb catch, clutch, grasp, seize.

nag vb carp, fuss, hector, henpeck, pester.

naive adj artless, candid, ingenuous, natural, plain, simple, unaffected, unsophisticated.

naked adj bare, nude, uncovered; denuded, unclad, unclothed, undressed; defenceless, exposed, open, unarmed, unguarded, unprotected; evident, manifest, plain, stark, unconcealed, undisguised; bare, mere, sheer, simple; destitute, rough, rude, unfurnished, unprovided; plain, uncoloured, unexaggerated, unvarnished.

name vb call, christen, denounce, dub, entitle, phrase, style, term; mention; denominate, designate, indicate, nominate, specify. • n appellation, cognomen, denomination, designation, epithet, nickname, surname, sobriquet, title; character, credit, reputation, repute; celebrity, distinction, eminence, fame, honour, note, praise, renown.

narrate vb chronicle, describe, detail, enumerate, recite, recount, rehearse, relate, tell.

narrow vb confine, contract, cramp, limit, restrict, straiten. • adj circumscribed, confined, contracted, cramped, incapacious, limited, pinched, scanty, straitened; bigoted, hidebound, illiberal, ungenerous; close, near.

nasty adj defiled, dirty, filthy, foul, impure, loathsome, polluted, squalid, unclean; gross, impure, indecent, indelicate, lewd, loose, obscene, smutty, vile; disagreeable, disgusting, nauseous, odious, offensive, repulsive, sickening.

nation n commonwealth, realm, state; community, people, population, race, stock, tribe.

native adj aboriginal, autochthonal, autochthonous, domestic, home, indigenous, vernacular; genuine, intrinsic, natural, original, real; congenital, inborn, inbred, inherent, innate, natal, natural. • n aborigine, autochthon, inhabitant, national, resident.

natural adj indigenous, native, original; characteristic, essential, native; legitimate, normal, regular; artless, genuine, ingenious, simple, spontaneous, unaffected; bastard, illegitimate.

nature n universe, world; character, constitution, essence; kind, quality, species, sort; disposition, grain, humour, mood, temper; being, intellect, intelligence, mind.

naughty adj bad, corrupt, mischievous.

nauseous adj abhorrent, disgusting, distasteful, loathsome, offensive, repulsive, revolting.

naval adj marine, maritime, nautical.

navigate vb cruise, direct, guide, sail, steer.

near vb approach, draw close. • adj adjacent, close, contiguous, neighbouring, nigh; approaching, forthcoming, imminent, impending; dear, familiar, intimate; close, direct, immediate; close, narrow, parsimonious.

nearly adv almost, approximately, well-nigh.

neat adj clean, cleanly, orderly, tidy, trim, unsoiled; nice, smart, spruce, trim; chaste, pure, simple; excellent, pure, unadulterated; adroit, clever, exact, finished; dainty, nice.

nebulous adj cloudy, hazy, misty.

necessary adj inevitable, unavoidable; essential, expedient, indispensable, needful, requisite; compelling, compulsory, involuntary. • n essential, necessity, requirement, requisite.

necessitate vb compel, constrain, demand, force, impel, oblige.

necessitous adj destitute, distressed, indigent, moneyless, needy, penniless, pinched, poor.

necessity n inevitability, inevitableness, unavoidability, unavoidableness; compulsion, destiny, fatality, fate; emergency, urgency; exigency, indigence, indispensability, indispensableness, need, needfulness, poverty, want; essentiality, essentialness, requirement, requisite.

need vb demand, lack, require, want. • n emergency, exigency, extremity, necessity, strait, urgency, want; destitution, distress, indigence, neediness, penury, poverty, privation.

needless adj superfluous, unnecessary, useless.

needy adj destitute, indigent, necessitous, poor.

negation n denial, disavowal, disclaimer, rejection, renunciation.

neglect vb condemn, despise, disregard, forget, ignore, omit, overlook, slight. • n carelessness, default, failure, heedlessness, inattention, omission, remissness; disregard, disrespect, slight; negligence.

negligence n carelessness, disregard, heedlessness, inadvertency, inattention, indifference, neglect, remissness, slackness, thoughtlessness; defect, fault, inadvertence, omission.

negotiate vb arrange, bargain, deal, debate, sell, settle, transact, treat.

neighbourhood n district, environs, locality, vicinage, vicinity; adjacency, nearness, propinquity, proximity.

neighbourly adj attentive, civil, friendly, kind.

nerve vb brace, energise, fortify, invigorate, strengthen. • n force, might, power, strength, vigour; coolness, courage, endurance, firmness, fortitude, hardihood, manhood, pluck, resolution, self-command, steadiness.

nervous adj forcible, powerful, robust, strong, vigorous; irritable, fearful, shaky, timid, timorous, weak, weakly.

nestle vb cuddle, harbour, lodge, nuzzle.

nettle vb chafe, exasperate, fret, harass, incense, irritate, provoke, ruffle, sting, tease, vex.

neutral adj impartial, indifferent; colourless.

neutralise vb cancel, counterbalance, counterpoise, invalidate, offset.

nevertheless adv however, nonetheless, notwithstanding, yet.

new adj fresh, latest, modern, novel, recent, unused; additional, another, further.

nice adj accurate, correct, critical, definite, delicate, exact, exquisite, precise, rigorous, strict; dainty, difficult, exacting, fastidious, finical, punctilious, squeamish; discerning, discriminating, particular, precise, scrupulous; neat, tidy, trim; fine, minute, refined, subtle; dainty, delicate, delicious, luscious, palatable, savoury, soft, tender, agreeable, delightful, good, pleasant.

nicety n accuracy, exactness, niceness, precision, truth, daintiness, fastidiousness, squeamishness; discrimination, subtlety.

nimble adj active, agile, alert, brisk, lively, prompt, quick, speedy, sprightly, spry, swift.

noble adj dignified, elevated, eminent, exalted, generous, great, honourable, illustrious, magnanimous, superior, worthy; choice, excellent; aristocratic, gentle, high-born, patrician; grand, lofty, lordly, magnificent, splendid, stately. • n aristocrat, grandee, lord, nobleman, peer.

noise vb bruit, gossip, repeat, report, rumour. • n ado, blare, clamour, clatter, cry, din, fuss, hubbub, hullabaloo, outcry, pandemonium, racket, row, sound, tumult, uproar, vociferation.

noisy adj blatant, blustering, boisterous, brawling, clamorous, loud, riotous, tumultuous.

nomadic adj migratory, vagrant, wandering.

nominal adj formal, inconsiderable, minimal, ostensible, pretended, professed, so-called, titular.

nominate vb appoint, choose, designate, name, present, propose.

nonchalant adj apathetic, careless, cool, indifferent, unconcerned.

nondescript adj amorphous, characterless, commonplace, dull, indescribable, odd, ordinary, unclassifiable, uninteresting.

nonentity n cipher, futility, inexistence, inexistency, insignificance, nobody, nonexistence.

nonplus vb astonish, bewilder, confound, confuse, discomfit, disconcert, embarrass, floor, gravel, perplex, pose, puzzle.

norm n model, pattern, rule, standard.

normal adj analogical, legitimate, natural, ordinary, regular, usual; erect, perpendicular.

notable adj distinguished, extraordinary, memorable, noted, remarkable, signal; conspicuous, evident, noticeable, observable, plain, prominent, striking; notorious, rare, well-known. • n celebrity, dignitary, notability, worthy.

note vb heed, mark, notice, observe, regard, remark; record, register; denote, designate. • n memorandum, minute, record; annotation, comment, remark, scholium; indication, mark, sign, symbol, token; account, bill, catalogue, reckoning; billet, epistle, letter; consideration, heed, notice, observation; celebrity, consequence, credit, distinction, eminence, fame, notability, notedness, renown, reputation, respectability; banknote, bill, promissory note; song, strain.

noted adj celebrated, conspicuous, distinguished, eminent, famed, famous, illustrious, notable, notorious, remarkable, renowned.

nothing n inexistence, nihilism, nihilist, nonentity, nullity; bagatelle, trifle.

notice vb mark, note, observe, perceive, regard, see; comment on, mention, remark; attend to, heed. • n cognisance, heed, note, observation, regard; advice, announcement, information, intelligence, mention, news, notification; communication, intimation, premonition, warning; attention, civility, consideration, respect.

notify vb advertise, announce, declare, publish, promulgate; acquaint, apprise, inform.

notion n concept, conception, idea; apprehension, belief, conceit, conviction, expectation, estimation, impression, judgement, opinion.

notoriety n celebrity, fame, figure, name, note, publicity, reputation, repute, vogue.

notorious adj apparent, egregious, evident, notable, obvious, open, overt, manifest, patent, well-known; celebrated, conspicuous, distinguished, famed, famous, flagrant, infamous.

nourish vb feed, nurse, nurture; maintain, supply, support; breed, educate, instruct, train; cherish, encourage, foment, foster, promote, succour.

nourishment n aliment, diet, food, nutriment, nutrition, sustenance.

novel adj fresh, modern, new, rare, recent, strange, uncommon, unusual. • n fiction, romance, story.

novice n convert, proselyte; initiate, neophyte, novitiate, probationer; apprentice, beginner.

nude adj bare, denuded, exposed, naked, uncovered, unclothed, undressed.

nuisance n annoyance, bore, bother, infliction, offence, pest, plague, trouble.

nullify vb abolish, abrogate, annul, cancel, invalidate, negate, quash, repeal, revoke.

numb vb benumb, deaden, stupefy. • adj benumbed, deadened, dulled, insensible.

number vb calculate, compute, count, enumerate, numerate, reckon, tell; account, reckon. • n digit, figure, numeral; horde, multitude, numerousness, throng; aggregate, collection, sum.

numerous adj abundant, many, numberless.

nuptial adj bridal, conjugal, connubial, hymeneal, matrimonial.

nurse vb nourish, nurture; rear, suckle; cherish, encourage, feed, foment, foster, pamper, promote, succour; economise, manage; caress, dandle, fondle. • n auxiliary, orderly, sister; amah, au pair, babysitter, nanny, nursemaid.

nurture vb feed, nourish, nurse, tend; breed, discipline, educate, instruct, rear, school, train. • n diet, food, nourishment; breeding, discipline, education, instruction,schooling,training, tuition; attention, nourishing, nursing.

nutrition n diet, food, nourishment, nutriment.

nutritious adj invigorating, nourishing, strengthening, supporting, sustaining.

O

oaf n blockhead, dolt, dunce, fool, idiot.

oath n blasphemy, curse, expletive, imprecation, malediction; affirmation, pledge, promise.

obdurate adj hard, harsh, rough, rugged; callous, cantankerous, dogged, firm, hardened, inflexible, insensible, obstinate, pigheaded, unfeeling, stubborn, unbending, unyielding; depraved, graceless, lost, reprobate, shameless, impenitent, incorrigible, irreclaimable.

obedience n acquiescence, agreement, compliance, duty, respect, reverence, submission.

obedient adj compliant, deferential, duteous, dutiful, observant, submissive, regardful, respectful, subservient, yielding.

obese adj corpulent, fat, fleshy, gross, plump.

obey vb comply, conform, heed, keep, mind, observe, submit, yield.

obfuscate vb cloud, darken, obscure; bewilder.

object[1] vb cavil, contravene, demur, deprecate, disapprove of, oppose, protest, refuse.

object[2] n particular, phenomenon, precept, reality, thing; aim, butt, destination, end, mark, recipient, target; design, drift, goal, intention, motive, purpose, use, view.

objection n censure, difficulty, doubt, exception, protest, remonstrance, scruple.

obligation n accountability, accountableness, ableness, responsibility; agreement, bond, contract, covenant, engagement, stipulation; debt, indebtedness, liability.

oblige vb bind, coerce, compel, constrain, force, necessitate, require; accommodate, benefit, convenience, favour, gratify, please; obligate, bind.

obliging adj accommodating, civil, complaisant, considerate, kind, friendly, polite.

oblique adj aslant, inclined, sidelong, slanting, indirect, obscure.

obliterate vb cancel, delete, destroy, efface, eradicate, erase, expunge.

oblivious adj careless, forgetful, heedless, inattentive, mindless, negligent, neglectful.

obnoxious adj blameworthy, censurable, faulty, reprehensible; hateful, objectionable, obscene, odious, offensive, repellent, repugnant, repulsive, unpleasant, unpleasing.

obscene adj broad, coarse, filthy, gross, immodest, impure, indecent, indelicate, ribald, unchaste, lewd, licentious, loose, offensive, pornographic, shameless, smutty; disgusting, dirty.

obscure vb becloud, befog, cloud, darken, eclipse, dim, obfuscate, obnubilate, shade; conceal, cover, discover, hide. • adj dark, darksome, dim, dusky, gloomy, lurid, murky, rayless, shadowy, sombre, unenlightened, unilluminated; abstruse, blind, cabbalistic, difficult, doubtful, enigmatic, high, incomprehensible, indefinite, indistinct, intricate, involved, mysterious, mystic, recondite, undefined, unintelligible, vague; remote, secluded; humble, inglorious, nameless.

obsequious adj cringing, deferential, fawning, flattering, servile, slavish, supple, subservient, sycophantic, truckling.

observant adj attentive, heedful, mindful, perceptive, quick, regardful, vigilant, watchful.

observation n attention, cognition, notice, observance; annotation, note, remark.

observe vb eye, mark, note, notice, remark, watch; behold, detect, discover, notice, perceive, see; express, mention, remark, say, utter; comply, follow, fulfil, obey; celebrate, keep, regard.

obsolete adj ancient, antiquated, antique, archaic, disused, neglected, old, old-fashioned, obsolescent, out-of-date, past, passé.

obstacle n barrier, check, difficulty, hindrance, impediment, interference, interruption, obstruction, snag, stumbling block.

obstinate adj cross-grained, contumacious, dogged, firm, headstrong, inflexible, immovable, intractable, mulish, obdurate, opinionated, persistent, pertinacious, perverse, resolute, self-willed, stubborn, unyielding, wilful.

obstruct vb bar, barricade, block, blockade, block up, choke, clog, close, glut, jam, obturate, stop; hinder, impede, oppose, prevent, stop.

obtain vb achieve, acquire, attain, bring, contrive, earn, elicit, gain, get, induce, procure, secure; hold, prevail, stand, subsist.

obtrusive adj forward, interfering, intrusive, meddling, officious.

obvious adj exposed, liable, open, subject; apparent, clear, distinct, evident, manifest, palatable, patent, perceptible, plain, self-evident, unmistakable, visible.

occasion vb breed, cause, create, originate, produce; induce, influence, move, persuade. • n event, incident, occurrence; conjuncture, convenience, juncture, opening, opportunity; condition, necessity, need, requirement, want; cause, ground, reason; inducement, influence; circumstance, exigency.

occasional adj accidental, casual, incidental, infrequent, irregular, uncommon.

occupation n holding, occupancy, possession, tenure, use; avocation, business, calling, craft, employment, engagement, job, post, profession, trade, vocation.

occupy vb capture, hold, keep, possess; cover, fill, garrison, inhabit, take up, tenant.

occur vb appear, arise, offer; befall, chance, eventuate, happen, result, supervene.

occurrence n accident, adventure, affair, casualty, event, happening, incident.

odd adj additional, redundant, remaining; casual, incidental; inappropriate, queer, unsuitable; comical, droll, erratic, extravagant, extraordinary, fantastic, grotesque, irregular, peculiar, quaint, singular, strange, uncommon, uncouth, unique, unusual, whimsical.

odds npl difference, disparity, inequality; advantage, superiority, supremacy.

odious adj abominable, detestable, execrable, hateful, shocking; hated, obnoxious, unpopular, disagreeable, forbidding, loathsome, offensive.

odorous adj aromatic, balmy, fragrant, perfumed, redolent, scented, sweet-scented.

odour n aroma, fragrance, scent, smell.

offence n aggression, attack, assault; anger, displeasure, indignation, pique, resentment, umbrage, wrath; affront, harm, injury, injustice, insult, outrage, wrong; crime, delinquency, fault, misdeed, misdemeanour, sin, transgression.

offend vb affront, annoy, chafe, displease, fret, gall, irritate, mortify, nettle, provoke, vex; annoy, molest, pain, shock, wound; fall, sin.

offender n convict, criminal, culprit, delinquent, felon, malefactor, sinner, transgressor.

offensive adj aggressive, attacking, invading; disgusting, loathsome, nauseating, nauseous, repulsive, sickening; abominable, detestable, disagreeable, displeasing, execrable, hateful, obnoxious, repugnant, revolting, shocking, unpalatable, unpleasant, repugnant; abusive, disagreeable, impertinent, insolent, insulting, irritating, opprobrious, rude. • n attack, onslaught.

offer vb present, proffer, tender; exhibit; furnish, propose, propound, show; volunteer; dare, essay, endeavour, venture. • n overture, proffering, proposal, proposition, tender, overture; attempt, bid, endeavour, essay.

offhand adj abrupt, brusque, casual, curt, extempore, impromptu, informal, unpremeditated, unstudied. • adv carelessly, casually, clumsily, haphazardly, informally, slapdash; ad-lib, extemporaneously, extemporarily, impromptu.

office n duty, function, service, work; berth, place, position, post, situation; business, capacity, charge, employment, function, service, trust; bureau, room.

officious adj busy, dictatorial, forward, impertinent, interfering, intermeddling, meddlesome, meddling, obtrusive, pushing, pushy.

offset vb balance, counteract, counterbalance, counterpoise. • n branch, offshoot, scion, shoot, slip, sprout, twig; counterbalance, counterpoise, set-off, equivalent.

offspring n brood, children, descendants, issue, litter, posterity, progeny; cadet, child, scion.

often adv frequently, generally, repeatedly.

ogre n bugbear, demon, devil, goblin, hobgoblin, monster, spectre.

old adj aged, ancient, antiquated, antique, archaic, elderly, obsolete, olden, old-fashioned, superannuated; decayed, done, senile, worn-out; original, primitive, pristine; former, preceding.

omen n augury, auspice, foreboding, portent, presage, prognosis, sign, warning.

ominous adj inauspicious, monitory, portentous, premonitory, threatening, unpropitious.

omit vb disregard, drop, eliminate, exclude, miss, neglect, overlook, skip.

omnipotent adj almighty, all-powerful.

onerous adj burdensome, difficult, hard, heavy, laborious, oppressive, responsible, weighty.

only adj alone, single, sole, solitary. • adv barely, merely, simply.

onset n assault, attack, charge, onslaught.

ooze vb distil, drip, drop, shed; drain, exude, filter, leak, percolate, stain, transude.

opaque adj dark, dim, hazy, muddy; abstruse, cryptic, enigmatic, enigmatical, obscure.

open vb expand, spread; begin, commence, initiate; disclose, exhibit, reveal, show; unbar, unclose, uncover, unlock, unseal, untie. • adj expanded, extended, unclosed, spread wide; aboveboard, artless, candid, cordial, fair, frank, guileless, hearty, honest, sincere, openhearted, single-minded, undesigning, undisguised, undissembling, unreserved; bounteous, bountiful, free, generous, liberal, munificent; ajar, unclosed, uncovered; exposed, undefended, unprotected; clear, unobstructed; accessible, public, unenclosed, unrestricted; mild, moderate; apparent, debatable, evident, obvious, patent, plain.

opening adj commencing, first, inaugural, initiatory, introductory. • n aperture, breach, chasm, cleft, fissure, flaw, gap, gulf, hole, interspace, loophole, orifice, perforation, rent, rift; beginning, commencement; chance, vacancy.

openly adv candidly, frankly, publicly.

operate vb act, function, work; cause, effect, occasion, produce; manipulate, use, run, work.

operation n manipulation, performance, procedure, proceeding, process; action, affair, manoeuvre, motion, movement.

operative adj active, effective, effectual, efficient, serviceable, vigorous; important, indicative, influential, significant. • n artisan, employee, labourer, mechanic, worker, workman.

opinion n conception, idea, impression, judgement, notion, sentiment, view; belief, persuasion, tenet; esteem, estimation.

opinionated adj biased, bigoted, cocksure, conceited, dictatorial, dogmatic, stubborn.

opponent n adversary, antagonist, competitor, contestant, counteragent, enemy, foe, opposite, opposer, party, rival.

opportune adj appropriate, auspicious, convenient, favourable, felicitous, fit, fitting, fortunate, lucky, propitious, seasonable, suitable, timely.

opportunity n chance, convenience, moment.

oppose vb combat, contravene, counteract, dispute, obstruct, oppugn, resist, thwart, withstand; check, prevent, obstruct, withstand; confront.

opposite adj facing, fronting; conflicting, contradictory, contrary, different, diverse, incompatible, inconsistent, irreconcilable; adverse, antagonistic, hostile, inimical, opposed, opposing, repugnant. • n contradiction, contrary, converse.

opposition n antagonism, antimony, contrariety, inconsistency, repugnance; counteraction, counterinfluence, hostility, resistance; hindrance, obstacle, obstruction, prevention.

oppress vb burden, crush, depress, harass, load, maltreat, overburden, overpower, overwhelm, persecute, subdue, suppress, tyrannise, wrong.

oppressive adj close, muggy, stifling, sultry.

option n choice, discretion, election, preference.

optional adj discretionary, elective, nonobligatory, voluntary.

opulent adj affluent, flush, luxurious, moneyed, plentiful, rich, sumptuous, wealthy.

oral adj nuncupative, spoken, verbal, vocal.

oration n address, declamation, discourse, harangue, speech.

orbit vb circle, encircle, revolve around. • n course, path, revolution, track.

ordain vb appoint, call, consecrate, elect, experiment, constitute, establish, institute, regulate; decree, enjoin, enact, order, prescribe.

order vb adjust, arrange, methodise, regulate, systematise; carry on, conduct, manage; bid, command, direct, instruct, require. • n arrangement, disposition, method, regularity, symmetry, system; law, regulation, rule; discipline, peace, quiet; command, commission, direction, injunction, instruction, mandate, prescription; class, degree, grade, kind, rank; family, tribe; brotherhood, community, class, fraternity, society; sequence, succession.

orderly adj methodical, regular, systematic; peaceable, quiet, well-behaved; neat, shipshape.

ordinary adj accustomed, customary, established, everyday, normal, regular, settled, wonted, everyday, regular; common, frequent, habitual, usual; average, commonplace, indifferent, inferior, mean, mediocre, second-rate, undistinguished; commonplace, homely, plain.

organisation n business, construction, constitution, organism, structure, system.

organise vb adjust, constitute, construct, form, make, shape; arrange, coordinate, correlate, establish, systematise.

orgy n carousal, debauch, debauchery, revel.

origin *n* beginning, birth, commencement, cradle, derivation, foundation, fountain, fountainhead, original, rise, root, source, spring, starting point; cause, occasion; birth, heritage, lineage.

original *adj* aboriginal, first, primary, primeval, primitive, primordial, pristine; fresh, inventive, novel; eccentric, odd, peculiar. • *n* cause, commencement, origin, source, spring; archetype, exemplar, model, pattern, prototype, protoplast.

originate *vb* arise, begin, emanate, flow, proceed, rise, spring; create, discover, form, invent.

ornament *vb* adorn, beautify, bedeck, bedizen, decorate, deck, emblazon, garnish, grace. • *n* adornment, bedizenment, decoration, design, embellishment, garnish, ornamentation.

ornate *adj* beautiful, bedecked, decorated, elaborate, elegant, embellished, florid, flowery, ornamental, ornamented.

orthodox *adj* conventional, correct, sound, true.

ostensible *adj* apparent, assigned, avowed, declared, exhibited, manifest, presented, visible; plausible, professed, specious.

ostentatious *adj* boastful, dashing, flaunting, pompous, pretentious, showy, vain, vainglorious; gaudy.

ostracise *vb* banish, boycott, exclude, excommunicate, exile, expatriate, expel, evict.

oust *vb* dislodge, dispossess, eject, evict, expel.

outbreak *n* ebullition, eruption, explosion, outburst; affray, broil, conflict, commotion, fray, riot, row; flare-up, manifestation.

outcast *n* exile, expatriate; castaway, pariah, reprobate, vagabond.

outcome *n* conclusion, consequence, event, issue, result, upshot.

outcry *n* cry, scream, screech, yell; bruit, clamour, noise, tumult, vociferation.

outdo *vb* beat, exceed, excel, outgo, outstrip, outvie, surpass.

outlandish *adj* alien, exotic, foreign, strange; barbarous, bizarre, queer, strange, uncouth.

outlaw *vb* ban, banish, condemn, exclude, forbid, make illegal, prohibit. • *n* bandit, brigand, crook, freebooter, highwayman, lawbreaker, marauder, robber, thief.

outline *vb* delineate, draft, draw, plan, silhouette, sketch. • *n* contour, profile; delineation, draft, drawing, plan, rough draft, silhouette.

outlive *vb* last, live longer, survive.

outlook *n* future, prospect, sight, view; lookout.

outrageous *adj* abusive, frantic, furious, frenzied, mad, raging, turbulent, violent, wild; atrocious, enormous, flagrant, heinous, monstrous, nefarious, villainous; excessive, extravagant, unwarrantable.

outset *n* beginning, commencement, entrance, opening, start, starting point.

outspoken *adj* abrupt, blunt, candid, frank, plain, plainspoken, unceremonious, unreserved.

outstanding *adj* due, owing, uncollected, ungathered, unpaid, unsettled; conspicuous, eminent, prominent, striking.

outward *adj* exterior, external, outer, outside.

outwit *vb* cheat, circumvent, deceive, defraud, diddle, dupe, gull, outmanoeuvre, overreach, swindle, victimise.

overawe *vb* affright, awe, browbeat, cow, daunt, frighten, intimidate, scare, terrify.

overbearing *adj* oppressive, overpowering; arrogant, dictatorial, dogmatic, domineering, haughty, imperious, overweening, proud.

overcast *vb* cloud, darken, overcloud, overshadow, shade, shadow. • *adj* cloudy, darkened, hazy, murky, obscure.

overcome *vb* beat, choke, conquer, crush, defeat, discomfit, overbear, overmaster, overpower, overthrow, overturn, overwhelm, rout, subdue, subjugate, vanquish; conquer, prevail.

overflow *vb* brim over, fall over, pour over, pour out, shower, spill; deluge, inundate, submerge. • *n* deluge, inundation, profusion.

overhaul *vb* overtake; check, examine, inspect, repair, survey.

overlook *vb* inspect, oversee, superintend, supervise; disregard, miss, neglect, slight; condone, excuse, forgive, pardon, pass over.

overrule *vb* control, govern, sway; annul, cancel, nullify, recall, reject, repeal, repudiate, rescind, revoke, reject, set aside, supersede.

oversight *n* care, charge, control, direction, inspection, management, superintendence, supervision, surveillance; blunder, error, fault, inadvertence, inattention, lapse, miss, mistake, neglect, omission, slip, trip.

overt *adj* apparent, glaring, open, manifest, notorious, patent, public, unconcealed.

overthrow *vb* overturn, upset, subvert; demolish, destroy, level; beat, conquer, crush, defeat, discomfit, foil, master, overcome, overpower, overwhelm, rout, subjugate, vanquish, worst. • *n* downfall, fall, prostration, subversion; destruction, demolition, ruin; defeat, discomfiture, dispersion, rout.

overturn *vb* invert, overthrow, reverse, subvert, upset.

overture *n* invitation, proposal, proposition.

overwhelm *vb* drown, engulf, inundate, overflow, submerge, swallow up, swamp; conquer, crush, defeat, overbear, overcome, overpower, subdue, vanquish.

overwrought *adj* overdone, overelaborate; agitated, excited, overexcited, overworked, stirred.

own¹ *vb* have, hold, possess; acknowledge, avow, confess; acknowledge, admit, allow, concede, confess.

own² *adj* particular, personal, private.

P

pace *vb* go, hasten, hurry, move, step, walk. • *n* amble, gait, step, walk.

pacify *vb* appease, conciliate, harmonise, tranquillise; allay, appease, assuage, calm, compose, hush, lay, lull, moderate, mollify, quell, quiet, smooth, soften, soothe, still, tranquillise.

pack *vb* compact, compress, crowd, fill; bundle, burden, load, stow. • *n* bale, budget, bundle, package, packet, parcel; burden, load; assemblage, assembly, assortment, collection, set; band, bevy, clan, company, crew, gang, squad.

pact *n* agreement, alliance, bargain, bond, compact, concordat, contract, convention, covenant, league, stipulation.

pagan *adj* heathen, heathenish, idolatrous, irreligious, paganistic. • *n* heathen, idolater.

pain *vb* agonise, bite, distress, hurt, rack, sting, torment, torture; afflict, aggrieve, annoy, bore, chafe, displease, disquiet, distress, fret, grieve, harass, incommode, plague, tease, trouble, vex, worry; rankle, smart, shoot, sting, twinge. • *n* ache, agony, anguish, discomfort, distress, gripe, hurt, pang, smart, soreness, sting, suffering, throe, torment, torture, twinge; affliction, anguish, anxiety, bitterness, care, chagrin, disquiet, distress, dolour, grief, heartache, misery, punishment, solicitude, sorrow, trouble, uneasiness, unhappiness, vexation, woe, wretchedness.

pains *npl* care, effort, labour, task, toilsomeness, trouble; childbirth, labour, travail.

painstaking *adj* assiduous, careful, conscientious, diligent, hardworking, industrious, laborious, persevering, plodding, sedulous, strenuous.

paint *vb* delineate, depict, describe, draw, figure, pencil, portray, represent, sketch; adorn, beautify, deck, embellish, ornament. • *n* colouring, dye, pigment, stain; cosmetics, greasepaint, make-up.

pair *vb* couple, marry, mate, match. • *n* brace, couple, double, duo, match, twosome.

pale *vb* blanch, lose colour, whiten. • *adj* ashen, ashy, blanched, bloodless, pallid, sickly, wan, white; blank, dim, obscure, spectral.

pall[1] *n* cloak, cover, curtain, mantle, pallium, shield, shroud, veil.

pall[2] *vb* cloy, glut, gorge, satiate, surfeit; deject, depress, discourage, dishearten, dispirit; cloak, cover, drape, invest, overspread, shroud.

pallid *adj* ashen, ashy, cadaverous, colourless, pale, sallow, wan, whitish.

palpable *adj* corporeal, material, tactile, tangible; evident, glaring, gross, intelligible, manifest, obvious, patent, plain, unmistakable.

palpitate *vb* flutter, pulsate, throb; quiver, shiver, tremble.

paltry *adj* diminutive, feeble, inconsiderable, insignificant, little, miserable, petty, slender, slight, small, sorry, trifling, trivial, unimportant.

pamper *vb* coddle, fondle, gratify, spoil.

pang *n* agony, anguish, distress, gripe, pain, throe, twinge.

panic *vb* affright, alarm, scare, startle, terrify; become terrified, overreact. • *n* alarm, consternation, fear, fright, jitters, terror.

pant *vb* blow, gasp, puff; heave, palpitate, pulsate, throb; gasp, languish; desire, hunger, long, sigh, thirst, yearn. • *n* blow, gasp, puff.

parable *n* allegory, fable, story.

parade *vb* display, flaunt, show, vaunt. • *n* ceremony, display, flaunting, ostentation, pomp, show; array, pageant; mall, promenade.

parallel *vb* be alike, compare, conform, correlate, match. • *adj* abreast, concurrent; allied, analogous, correspondent, equal, like, resembling, similar. • *n* conformity, likeness, resemblance, similarity; analogue, counterpart.

paraphernalia *n* accoutrements, appendages, appurtenances, baggage, belongings, effects, equipage, equipment, ornaments, trappings.

parasite *n* bloodsucker, fawner, flatter, flunky, hanger-on, leech, spaniel, sycophant, toady.

pardon *vb* condone, forgive, overlook, remit; absolve, acquit, clear, discharge, excuse, release. • *n* absolution, amnesty, condonation, discharge, excuse, forgiveness, grace, mercy, release.

parentage *n* ancestry, birth, descent, extraction, family, lineage, origin, parenthood, pedigree.

parity *n* analogy, correspondence, equality, equivalence, likeness, sameness, similarity.

parody *vb* burlesque, caricature, imitate, lampoon, mock, ridicule, satirise, travesty.

part *vb* break, dismember, dissever, divide, sever, subdivide, sunder; detach, disconnect, disjoin, dissociate, disunite, separate; allot, apportion, distribute, divide, mete, share; secrete. • *n* crumb, division, fraction, fragment, moiety, parcel, piece, portion, remnant, scrap, section, segment, subdivision; component, constituent, element, ingredient, member, organ; lot, share; concern, interest, participation; allotment, apportionment; dividend; business, charge, duty, function, office, work; concern, faction, interest, party, side; character, cue, lines, role.

partial *adj* component, fractional, imperfect, incomplete, limited; biassed, influential, interested, one-sided, prejudiced, prepossessed, unfair, unjust, warped; fond, indulgent.

participate vb engage in, partake, share.

particle n atom, bit, corpuscle, crumb, drop, glimmer, grain, granule, iota, jot, mite, molecule, morsel, mote, scrap, shred, snip.

particular adj especial, special, specific; distinct, individual, respective, separate, single, special; characteristic, distinctive, peculiar; individual, intimate, own, peculiar, personal, private; notable, noteworthy, special; circumstantial, definite, detailed, exact, minute, narrow, precise; careful, close, conscientious, critical, fastidious, nice, scrupulous, strict; marked, notable, odd, peculiar, singular, strange, uncommon. • n circumstance, detail, feature, instance, item, particularity, regard, respect.

parting n breaking, dividing, separating; final, last, valedictory; declining, departing. • n breaking, disruption, rupture, severing; detachment, division, separation; death, departure, farewell.

partisan adj biased, factional, interested, partial, prejudiced. • n adherent, backer, champion, disciple, follower, supporter, votary.

partition vb apportion, distribute, divide, portion, separate, share. • n division, separation; barrier, division, screen, wall; allotment, apportionment, distribution.

partner n associate, colleague, copartner, partaker, participant, participator; accomplice, ally, confederate; companion, consort, spouse.

partnership n association, company, copartnership, firm, house, society; connection, interest, participation, union.

party n alliance, association, cabal, circle, clique, combination, confederacy, coterie, faction, group, junta, league, ring, set; body, company, detachment, squad, troop; assembly, company, gathering; partaker, participant, participator, sharer; defendant, litigant, plaintiff; individual, one, person, somebody; cause, division, interest, side.

pass[1] vb devolve, fall, go, move, proceed; change, elapse, flit, glide, lapse, slip; cease, die, fade, expire, vanish; happen, occur; convey, deliver, send, transmit, transfer; disregard, ignore, neglect; exceed, excel, surpass; approve, ratify, sanction; answer, do, succeed, suffice, suit; deliver, express, pronounce, utter; beguile, wile.

pass[2] n avenue, ford, road, route, way; defile, gorge, passage, ravine; authorisation, licence, passport, permission, ticket; condition, conjecture, plight, situation, state; lunge, push, thrust, tilt; transfer, trick.

passable adj admissible, allowable, mediocre, middling, moderate, ordinary, so-so, tolerable; acceptable; navigable, traversable.

passage n going, passing, progress, transit;

evacuation, journey, migration, transit, voyage; avenue, channel, course, pass, path, road, route, thoroughfare, vennel, way; access, currency, entry, reception; act, deed, event, feat, incidence, occurrence, passion; corridor, gallery, gate, hall; clause, paragraph, sentence, text; course, death, decease, departure, expiration, lapse; affair, brush, change, collision, combat, conflict, contest, encounter, exchange, joust, pass, skirmish.

passenger n fare, itinerant, tourist, traveller, voyager, wayfarer.

passionate adj animated, ardent, burning, earnest, enthusiastic, excited, fervent, fiery, furious, glowing, hot-blooded, impassioned, impetuous, impulsive, intense, vehement, warm, zealous; hot-headed, irascible, quick-tempered, tempestuous, violent.

passive adj inactive, inert, quiescent, receptive; apathetic, enduring, long-suffering, nonresistant, patient, stoical, submissive, suffering.

past adj accomplished, elapsed, ended, gone, spent; ancient, bygone, former, obsolete, outworn. • adv above, extra, beyond, over. • prep above, after, beyond, exceeding. • n antiquity, heretofore, history, olden times, yesterday.

pastime n amusement, diversion, entertainment, hobby, play, recreation, sport.

pat[1] vb hit, rap, tap; caress, chuck, fondle, pet.

pat[2] adj appropriate, apt, fit, pertinent, suitable. • adv aptly, conveniently, fitly, opportunely.

patch vb mend, repair. • n repair; parcel, plot, tract.

patent adj expanded, open, spreading; apparent, clear, conspicuous, evident, glaring, indisputable, manifest, notorious, obvious, public, open, palpable, plain, unconcealed, unmistakable. • n copyright, privilege, right.

path n access, avenue, course, footway, passage, pathway, road, route, track, trail, way.

pathetic adj affecting, melting, moving, pitiable, plaintive, sad, tender, touching.

patience n endurance, fortitude, long-sufferance, resignation, submission, sufferance; calmness, composure, quietness; forbearance, indulgence, leniency; assiduity, constancy, diligence, indefatigability, perseverance, persistence.

patient adj meek, passive, resigned, submissive, uncomplaining, unrepining; calm, composed, contented, quiet; indulgent, lenient, long-suffering; assiduous, constant, diligent, indefatigable, persevering, persistent. • n case, invalid, subject, sufferer.

patron n advocate, defender, favourer, guardian, helper, protector, supporter.

pattern vb copy, follow, imitate. • n archetype, exemplar, last, model, original, paradigm, plan, prototype; example, guide, sample, specimen; mirror, paragon; design, figure, shape, style.

pause *vb* breathe, cease, delay, desist, rest, stay, stop, wait; delay, forbear, intermit, stay, stop, tarry, wait; deliberate, demur, hesitate, waver. • *n* break, caesura, cessation, halt, intermission, interruption, interval, remission, rest, stop, stoppage, stopping, suspension; hesitation, suspense, uncertainty; break, paragraph.

pawn[1] *n* cat's-paw, dupe, plaything, puppet, stooge, tool, toy

pawn[2] *vb* bet, gage, hazard, lay, pledge, risk, stake, wager. • *n* assurance, bond, guarantee, pledge, security.

pay *vb* defray, discharge, discount, foot, honour, liquidate, meet, quit, settle; compensate, recompense, reimburse, requite, reward; punish, revenge; give, offer, render. • *n* allowance, commission, compensation, emolument, hire, recompense, reimbursement, remuneration, requital, reward, salary, wages.

peace *n* calm, calmness, quiet, quietness, repose, stillness; accord, amity, friendliness, harmony; composure, equanimity, imperturbability, placidity, quietude, tranquillity; accord, agreement, armistice.

peaceable *adj* pacific, peaceful; amiable, amicable, friendly, gentle, inoffensive, mild; placid, peaceful, quiet, serene, still, tranquil.

peaceful *adj* quiet, undisturbed; amicable, concordant, friendly, gentle, harmonious, mild, pacific, peaceable; calm, composed, placid, serene.

peak *vb* climax, culminate, top; dwindle, thin. • *n* acme, apex, crest, crown, pinnacle, summit, top, zenith.

peculiar *adj* appropriate, idiosyncratic, individual, proper; characteristic, eccentric, exceptional, extraordinary, odd, queer, rare, singular, strange, striking, uncommon, unusual; especial, particular, select, special, specific.

peculiarity *n* appropriateness, distinctiveness, individuality, speciality; characteristic, idiosyncrasy, individuality, singularity.

pedantic *adj* conceited, fussy, officious, ostentatious, over-learned, particular, pedagogical, pompous, pragmatical, precise, pretentious, priggish, stilted.

pedigree *adj* purebred, thoroughbred. • *n* ancestry, breed, descent, extraction, family, genealogy, house, line, lineage, race, stock, strain.

peer[1] *vb* gaze, look, peek, peep, pry.

peer[2] *n* associate, co-equal, companion, compeer, equal, equivalent, fellow, like, mate, match; aristocrat, baron, count, duke, earl, grandee, lord, marquis, noble, nobleman, viscount.

pelt[1] *vb* assail, batter, beat, belabour, bombard, pepper, stone, strike; cast, hurl, throw; hurry, rush, speed, tear.

pelt[2] *n* coat, hide, skin.

pen[1] *vb* compose, draft, indite, inscribe, write.

pen[2] *vb* confine, coop, encage, enclose, impound, imprison, incarcerate. • *n* cage, coop, corral, crib, hutch, enclosure, paddock, pound.

penalty *n* chastisement, fine, forfeiture, mulct, punishment, retribution.

penetrate *vb* bore, burrow, cut, enter, invade, penetrate, percolate, perforate, pervade, pierce, soak, stab; affect, sensitise, touch; comprehend, discern, perceive, understand.

penetrating *adj* penetrative, permeating, piercing, sharp, subtle; acute, clear-sighted, discerning, intelligent, keen, sagacious, shrewd.

penetration *n* acuteness, discernment, insight.

penitent *adj* compunctious, conscious-stricken, contrite, regretful, remorseful, repentant, sorrowful. • *n* penitentiary, repentant.

penniless *adj* destitute, distressed, impecunious, indigent, moneyless, pinched, poor, necessitous, needy, pensive, poverty-stricken.

pensive *adj* contemplative, dreamy, meditative, reflective, sober, thoughtful; grave, melancholic, melancholy, mournful, sad, serious, solemn.

people *vb* colonise, inhabit, populate. • *n* clan, country, family, nation, race, state, tribe; folk, humankind, persons, population, public; commons, community, democracy, populace, proletariat; mob, multitude, rabble.

perceive *vb* behold, descry, detect, discern, discover, discriminate, distinguish, note, notice, observe, recognise, remark, see, spot; appreciate, comprehend, know, understand.

perceptible *adj* apparent, appreciable, cognisable, discernible, noticeable, perceivable, understandable, visible.

perception *n* apprehension, cognition, discernment, perceiving, recognition, seeing; apprehension, comprehension, conception, consciousness, discernment, perceptiveness, perceptivity, understanding, feeling.

peremptory *adj* absolute, authoritative, categorical, commanding, decisive, express, imperative, imperious, positive; determined, resolute, resolved; arbitrary, dogmatic, incontrovertible.

perennial *adj* ceaseless, constant, continual, deathless, enduring, immortal, imperishable, lasting, never-failing, permanent, perpetual, unceasing, undying, unfailing, uninterrupted.

perfect *vb* accomplish, complete, consummate, elaborate, finish. • *adj* completed, finished; complete, entire, full, utter, whole; capital, complete, consummate, excellent, exquisite, faultless, ideal; accomplished, disciplined, expert, skilled; blameless, faultless, immaculate, pure.

perform *vb* accomplish, achieve, compass, consummate, do, effect, transact; complete, discharge, execute, fulfil, meet, observe, satisfy; act, play, represent.

performance *n* accomplishment, achievement,

completion, consummation, discharge, doing, execution, fulfilment; achievement, act, action, deed, exploit, feat, work; composition, production; acting, entertainment, exhibition, play, representation, hold; execution, playing.

perfume n aroma, bouquet, fragrance, odour, redolence, scent, smell, sweetness.

perfunctory adj careless, formal, heedless, indifferent, mechanical, negligent, reckless, slight, slovenly, thoughtless, unmindful.

peril vb endanger, imperil, jeopardise, risk. • n danger, hazard, insecurity, jeopardy, pitfall, risk, snare, uncertainty.

perilous adj dangerous, hazardous, risky.

period n aeon, age, cycle, date, eon, epoch, season, span, spell, stage, term, time; continuance, duration; bound, conclusion, determination, end, limit, term, termination.

periodical adj cyclical, incidental, intermittent, recurrent, recurring, regular, seasonal, systematic. • n magazine, paper, review, serial, weekly.

periphery n boundary, circumference, outside, perimeter, superficies, surface.

perish vb decay, moulder, shrivel, waste, wither; decease, die, expire, vanish.

perishable adj decaying, decomposable, destructible; dying, frail, mortal, temporary.

permanent adj abiding, constant, continuing, durable, enduring, fixed, immutable, invariable, lasting, perpetual, persistent, stable, standing, steadfast, unchangeable, unchanging.

permissible adj admissible, allowable, free, lawful, legal, legitimate, proper, sufferable.

permission n allowance, authorisation, consent, dispensation, leave, liberty, licence, permit, sufferance, toleration, warrant.

permit vb agree, allow, let, suffer, tolerate; admit, authorise, consent, empower, license, warrant. • n leave, liberty, licence, passport, permission, sanction, warrant.

perpetrate vb commit, do, execute, perform.

perpetual adj ceaseless, continual, constant, endless, enduring, eternal, ever-enduring, everlasting, incessant, interminable, never-ceasing, never-ending, perennial, permanent, sempiternal, unceasing, unending, unfailing.

perplex vb complicate, encumber, entangle, involve, snarl, tangle; beset, bewilder, confound, confuse, corner, distract, embarrass, fog, mystify, nonplus; annoy, bother, disturb, harass, molest, pester, plague, tease, vex, worry.

persecute vb afflict, distress, harass, molest, oppress, worry; annoy, beset, importune, pester.

persevere vb continue, determine, endure, maintain, persist, remain, resolve, stick.

persist vb continue, endure, last, remain; insist.

persistent adj constant, continuing, enduring, fixed, immovable, persevering, persisting,

steady, tenacious; contumacious, dogged, indefatigable, obdurate, obstinate, pertinacious, perverse, pigheaded, stubborn.

personable adj comely, good-looking, graceful, seemly, well-turned-out.

personal adj individual, peculiar, private.

perspective n panorama, prospect, view, vista; proportion, relation.

perspire vb exhale, glow, sweat, swelter.

persuade vb allure, actuate, entice, impel, incite, induce, influence, lead, move, prevail upon, urge; advise, counsel; convince, satisfy.

persuasion n incitement, inducement, influence; belief, conviction, opinion; belief, creed, doctrine, dogma, tenet; kind, sort.

persuasive adj cogent, convincing, inducing, inducible, logical, plausible, sound, valid.

pert adj brisk, dapper, lively, nimble, smart, sprightly, perky; bold, flippant, forward, free, impertinent, impudent, smart, saucy.

pertinent adj adapted, applicable, apposite, appropriate, apropos, apt, fit, germane, pat, proper, relevant, suitable; appurtenant, belonging, concerning, pertaining, regarding.

perturb vb agitate, disquiet, distress, disturb, excite, trouble, unsettle, upset, vex, worry.

pervade vb affect, animate, diffuse, extend, fill, imbue, impregnate, infiltrate, permeate.

perverse adj bad, disturbed, oblique, perverted; contrary, dogged, headstrong, mulish, obstinate, pertinacious, perversive, stubborn, ungovernable, intractable, unyielding, wayward, wilful; cantankerous, churlish, crabbed, cross, cross-grained, crusty, cussed, morose, peevish, petulant, snappish, snarling, spiteful, spleeny, surly, testy, touchy, wicked, wrong-headed; inconvenient, troublesome, untoward, vexatious.

perversion n abasement, corruption, debasement, impairment, injury, prostitution, vitiation.

perverted adj corrupt, debased, distorted, evil, impaired, vitiated, wicked.

pessimistic adj cynical, dark, dejected, depressed, despondent, downhearted, gloomy, glum, melancholy, melancholic, morose, sad.

pest n disease, epidemic, infection, pestilence, plague; annoyance, bane, curse, infliction, nuisance, scourge, trouble.

pestilent adj contagious, infectious, malignant, pestilential; deadly, evil, injurious, malign, mischievous, noxious, poisonous; annoying, corrupt, pernicious, troublesome, vexatious.

petition vb ask, beg, crave, entreat, pray, solicit, sue, supplicate. • n address, appeal, application, entreaty, prayer, request, solicitation, suit.

petrify vb calcify, fossilise, lapidify; benumb, deaden; amaze, appal, astonish, astound, confound, dumbfound, paralyse, stun, stupefy.

petty adj diminutive, frivolous, inconsiderable,

inferior, insignificant, little, mean, slight, small, trifling, trivial, unimportant.

petulant *adj* acrimonious, captious, cavilling, censorious, choleric, crabbed, cross, crusty, forward, fretful, hasty, ill-humoured, ill-tempered, irascible, irritable, peevish, perverse, pettish, querulous, snappish, testy, touchy.

phantom *n* apparition, ghost, illusion, phantasm, spectre, vision, wraith.

phenomenal *adj* marvellous, miraculous, prodigious, wondrous.

philanthropy *n* altruism, benevolence, charity, humanitarianism, humanity, kindness.

philosophical, philosophic *adj* rational, reasonable, sound, wise; calm, collected, composed, cool, imperturbable, sedate, serene, stoical, tranquil, unruffled.

phlegmatic *adj* apathetic, calm, cold, cold-blooded, dull, frigid, heavy, impassive, indifferent, inert, sluggish, stoical, tame, unfeeling.

phobia *n* aversion, detestation, dislike, distaste, dread, fear, hatred.

phrase *vb* call, christen, denominate, designate, describe, dub, entitle, name, style. • *n* diction, expression, phraseology, style.

physical *adj* material, natural; bodily, corporeal, external, sensible, substantial, tangible.

pick *vb* peck, pierce, strike; cut, detach, gather, pluck; choose, cull, select; acquire, collect, get; pilfer, steal. • *n* pickaxe, pike, spike, toothpick.

picture *vb* delineate, draw, imagine, paint, represent.

picturesque *adj* beautiful, charming, colourful, graphic, scenic, striking, vivid.

piece *vb* mend, patch, repair; augment, complete, enlarge, increase; cement, join, unite. • *n* amount, bit, chunk, cut, fragment, hunk, part, quantity, scrap, shred, slice; portion; article, item, object; composition, work, writing.

pierce *vb* gore, impale, prick, prick, stab, transfix; bore, drill, excite, penetrate, perforate, puncture; affect, move, rouse, strike, thrill, touch.

piety *n* devotion, devoutness, holiness, godliness, grace, religion, sanctity.

pile[1] *vb* accumulate, amass; collect, gather, heap, load. • *n* accumulation, collection, heap, mass, stack; fortune, wad; building, edifice, erection, fabric, pyramid, skyscraper, structure, tower; reactor, nuclear reactor.

pile[2] *n* beam, column, pier, pillar, pole, post.

pile[3] *n* down, feel, finish, fur, fluff, fuzz, grain, nap, pappus, shag, surface, texture.

pilfer *vb* filch, purloin, rob, steal, thieve.

pilgrim *n* journeyer, sojourner, traveller, wanderer, wayfarer; crusader, devotee, palmer.

pillar *n* column, pier, pilaster, post, shaft, stanchion; maintainer, prop, support, supporter.

pilot *vb* conduct, control, direct, guide, navigate,

steer. • *adj* experimental, model, trial. • *n* helmsman, navigator, steersman; airman, aviator, conductor, director, flier, guide.

pinch *vb* compress, contract, cramp, gripe, nip, squeeze; afflict, distress, famish, oppress, straiten, stint; frost, nip; apprehend, arrest; economise, spare, stint.

pine *vb* decay, decline, droop, fade, flag, languish, waste, wilt, wither; desire, long, yearn.

pinnacle *n* minaret, turret; acme, apex, height, peak, summit, top, zenith.

pious *adj* filial; devout, godly, holy, religious, reverential, righteous, saintly.

pirate *vb* copy, crib, plagiarise, reproduce, steal. • *n* buccaneer, corsair, freebooter, marauder.

pit *vb* match, oppose; dent, gouge, hole, mark, nick, notch, scar. • *n* cavity, hole, hollow; crater, dent, depression, dint, excavation, well; abyss, chasm, gulf; pitfall, snare, trap; auditorium.

pitch *vb* fall, lurch, plunge, reel; light, settle, rest; cast, dart, fling, heave, hurl, lance, launch, plunge, send, toss, throw; erect, establish, fix, locate, place, plant, set, settle, station. • *n* degree, extent, height, intensity, measure, modulation, rage, rate; declivity, descent, inclination, slope; cast, jerk, plunge, throw, toss; place, position, spot; field, ground; line, patter.

piteous *adj* affecting, distressing, doleful, grievous, mournful, pathetic, rueful, sorrowful, woeful; deplorable, lamentable, miserable, pitiable, wretched; compassionate, tender.

pithy *adj* cogent, energetic, forcible, powerful; compact, concise, brief, laconic, meaty, pointed, short, sententious, substantial, terse.

pitiable *adj* deplorable, lamentable, miserable, pathetic, piteous, pitiable, woeful, wretched; abject, base, contemptible, despicable, disreputable, insignificant, low, paltry, mean, sorry.

pitiful *adj* compassionate, kind, lenient, merciful, mild, sympathetic, tender, tenderhearted; deplorable, lamentable, miserable, pathetic, piteous, pitiable, wretched; abject, base, contemptible, despicable, disreputable, insignificant, mean, paltry, rascally, sorry, vile, worthless.

pitiless *adj* cruel, hardhearted, implacable, inexorable, merciless, unmerciful, relentless, remorseless, unfeeling, unpitying, unrelenting.

pity *vb* commiserate, condole, sympathise. • *n* clemency, commiseration, compassion, condolence, fellow-feeling, grace, humanity, leniency, mercy, quarter, sympathy, tenderheartedness.

place *vb* arrange, bestow, commit, deposit, dispose, fix, install, lay, locate, lodge, orient, orientate, pitch, plant, pose, put, seat, set, settle, situate, stand, station, rest; allocate, arrange, class, classify, identify, order, organise, recognise; appoint, assign, commission, establish, induct, nominate. • *n* area, courtyard, square; bounds, district, division, locale, locality, location, part, position, premises, quarter, region, scene, site, situation, spot, station, tract, whereabouts; calling, charge, employment, function, occupation, office, pitch, post; calling, condition, grade, precedence, rank, sphere, stakes, standing; abode, building, dwelling, habitation, mansion, residence, seat; city, town, village; fort, fortress, stronghold; paragraph, part, passage, portion; ground, occasion, opportunity, reason, room; lieu, stead.

placid *adj* calm, collected, composed, cool, equable, gentle, peaceful, quiet, serene, tranquil, undisturbed, unexcitable, unmoved, unruffled.

plague *vb* afflict, annoy, badger, bore, bother, pester, chafe, disquiet, distress, disturb, embarrass, harass, fret, gall, harry, hector, incommode, irritate, molest, perplex, tantalise, tease, torment, trouble, vex, worry. • *n* disease, pestilence, pest; affliction, annoyance, curse, molestation, nuisance, thorn, torment, trouble, vexation, worry.

plain *adj* dull, even, flat, level, plane, smooth, uniform; clear, open, unencumbered, uninterrupted; apparent, certain, clear, conspicuous, evident, distinct, glaring, manifest, notable, notorious, obvious, open, overt, palpable, patent, unmistakable, transparent, visible; explicit, intelligible, perspicuous, unambiguous, unequivocal; homely, ugly; aboveboard, blunt, crude, candid, direct, downright, frank, honest, ingenuous, sincere, straightforward, undesigning, unreserved, unsophisticated; artless, common, natural, simple, unaffected, unlearned, unsophisticated; absolute, mere, unmistakable; clear, direct, easy, frugal, homely, simple; artless, natural, simple, unaffected, unlearned; unadorned, unfigured, unornamented, unvariegated. • *n* grassland, plateau, prairie, steppe.

plan *vb* arrange, calculate, concert, delineate, devise, diagram, figure, premeditate, project, represent, study; concoct, conspire, contrive, design, digest, hatch, invent, manoeuvre, machinate, plot, prepare, project, scheme. • *n* chart, delineation, diagram, draught, drawing, layout, map, plot, sketch; arrangement, conception, contrivance, design, device, idea, method, programme, project, proposal, proposition, scheme, system; cabal, conspiracy, intrigue, machination; custom, process, way.

plane *vb* flatten, even, level, smooth; float, fly, glide, skate, skim, soar. • *adj* even, flat, horizontal, level, smooth. • *n* degree, evenness, level, levelness, smoothness; aeroplane, aircraft; groover, jointer, rabbet, rebate, scraper.

plant *vb* bed, sow; breed, engender; direct, point, set; colonise, furnish, inhabit, settle; establish, introduce; deposit, establish, fix, found, hide. • *n* herb, organism, vegetable; establishment, equipment, factory, works.

plaster *vb* bedaub, coat, cover, smear, spread. • *n* cement, gypsum, mortar, stucco.

plastic *adj* ductile, flexible, formative, mouldable, pliable, pliant, soft.

platitude *n* dullness, flatness, insipidity, mawkishness; banality, commonplace, truism.

plausible *adj* believable, credible, probable, reasonable; bland, glib, smooth, suave.

play *vb* caper, disport, frisk, frolic, gambol, revel, romp, skip, sport; dally, flirt, idle, toy, trifle, wanton; flutter, hover, wave; act, impersonate, perform, personate, represent; bet, gamble, stake, wager. • *n* amusement, exercise, frolic, gambol, game, jest, pastime, prank, romp, sport; gambling, gaming; act, comedy, drama, farce, performance, tragedy; action, motion, movement; elbowroom, freedom, latitude, movement, opportunity, range, scope, sweep, swing, use.

playful *adj* frisky, frolicsome, gamesome, jolly, kittenish, merry, mirthful, rollicking, sportive; amusing, arch, humorous, jolly, lively, mirthful, mischievous, roguish, sprightly, vivacious.

plead *vb* answer, appeal, argue, reason; argue, defend, discuss, reason, rejoin; appeal, beg, beseech, entreat, implore, petition, sue, supplicate.

pleasant *adj* acceptable, agreeable, delectable, delightful, enjoyable, grateful, gratifying, nice, pleasing, pleasurable, prepossessing, seemly.

please *vb* charm, delight, elate, gladden, gratify, pleasure, rejoice; content, oblige, satisfy.

pleasure *n* cheer, comfort, delight, delectation, elation, enjoyment, exhilaration, joy, gladness, gratification, gratifying, gusto, relish, satisfaction, solace; amusement, diversion, entertainment, indulgence, refreshment, treat; gratification, luxury, sensuality, voluptuousness; choice, desire, preference, purpose, will, wish.

pledge *vb* hypothecate, mortgage, pawn, plight; affiance, bind, contract, engage, plight, promise. • *n* collateral, deposit, gage, pawn; earnest, guarantee, security; hostage, security.

plentiful *adj* abundant, ample, copious, full, enough, exuberant, fruitful, luxuriant, plenteous.

plenty *n* abundance, adequacy, affluence, amplitude, copiousness, enough, exuberance, fertility, fruitfulness, fullness, overflow, plenteousness, plentifulness, plethora, profusion.

plethora *n* fullness, plenitude, repletion; excess, redundance, redundancy, superabundance.

pliable *adj* flexible, limber, lithe, lithesome, pliable, pliant, supple; adaptable, compliant, docile, ductile, facile, manageable, obsequious, tractable, yielding.

plight¹ *n* case, category, complication, condition, dilemma, imbroglio, mess, muddle, pass, predicament, scrape, situation, state, strait.

plight² *vb* avow, contract, covenant, engage, honour, pledge, promise, propose, swear, vow.

plod vb drudge, lumber, persevere, persist

plot[1] vb connive, conspire, intrigue, machinate, scheme; brew, concoct, contrive, devise, frame, hatch, compass, plan, project; chart, map. • n blueprint, chart, diagram, draft, outline, plan, scenario, skeleton; cabal, combination, complicity, connivance, conspiracy, intrigue, plan, project, scheme, stratagem; script, story, subject, theme, thread, topic.

plot[2] n field, lot, parcel, patch, piece, tract.

pluck[1] vb cull, gather, pick; jerk, pull, snatch, tear, tug, twitch.

pluck[2] n backbone, bravery, courage, daring, determination, energy, force, grit, hardihood, heroism, resolution, spirit, valour.

plump[1] adj bonny, bouncing, buxom, chubby, corpulent, fat, fleshy, full-figured, well-rounded.

plump[2] vb dive, drop, plank, plop, plunge, plunk, put; choose, favour, support • adj blunt, complete, direct, downright, unreserved.

plunder vb desolate, despoil, devastate, fleece, forage, harry, loot, maraud, pillage, raid, ransack, ravage, rifle, rob, sack, spoil, spoliate, plunge. • n freebooting, marauding, rapine, robbery; booty, pillage, prey, spoil.

ply[1] vb apply, employ, exert, manipulate, wield; exercise, practise; assail, belabour, beset, press; importune, solicit, urge; offer, present.

ply[2] n fold, layer, plait, twist.

pocket vb appropriate, steal; bear, endure, suffer, tolerate. • n cavity, cul-de-sac, hollow, pouch, receptacle.

poignant adj bitter, intense, penetrating, severe, sharp; acrid, biting, mordacious, piquant, prickling, pungent, sharp, stinging; caustic, irritating, keen, mordant, pointed, satirical, severe.

point vb acuminate, sharpen; aim, direct, level; designate indicate, show; punctuate. • n apex, needle, nib, pin, prong, spike, stylus, tip; cape, headland, projection, promontory; eve, instant, moment, period, verge; place, site, spot, stage, station; condition, degree, grade, state; aim, design, end, intent, limit, object, purpose; nicety, pique, punctilio, trifle; position, proposition, question, text, theme, thesis; aspect, matter, respect; characteristic, peculiarity, trait; character, mark, stop; dot, jot, speck; epigram, quip, quirk, sally, witticism; poignancy, sting.

point-blank adj categorical, direct, downright, explicit, express, plain, straight. • adv categorically, directly, flush, full, plainly, right, straight.

pointless adj blunt, obtuse; aimless, dull, flat, fruitless, futile, meaningless.

poise vb balance, float, hang, hover, support, suspend. • n aplomb, balance, composure, dignity, equanimity, equilibrium, equipoise, serenity.

poison vb adulterate, contaminate, corrupt, defile, embitter, envenom, impair, infect, intoxi-

cate, pollute, taint, vitiate. • adj deadly, lethal, poisonous, toxic. • n bane, canker, contagion, pest, taint, toxin, venom, virulence, virus.

poisonous adj baneful, corruptive, deadly, fatal, noxious, pestilential, toxic, venomous.

poke vb jab, jog, punch, push, shove, thrust; interfere, meddle, pry, snoop. • n jab, jog, punch, push, shove, thrust; bag, pocket, pouch, sack.

policy n administration, government, management, rule; plan, plank, platform, role; art, address, cunning, discretion, prudence, shrewdness, skill, stratagem, strategy, tactics; acumen, astuteness, shrewdness, wisdom, wit.

polish vb brighten, buff, burnish, furbish, glaze, gloss, scour, shine, smooth; civilise, refine. • n brightness, brilliance, brilliancy, lustre, splendour; accomplishment, elegance, refinement.

polite adj attentive, accomplished, affable, chivalrous, civil, complaisant, courtly, courteous, cultivated, elegant, gallant, genteel, gentle, gentlemanly, gracious, mannerly, polished, refined, suave, urbane, well-mannered.

politic adj civic, civil, political; astute, discreet, judicious, long-headed, noncommittal, provident, prudent, prudential, sagacious, wary, wise; artful, crafty, cunning, diplomatic, expedient, foxy, ingenious, intriguing, Machiavellian, shrewd, skilful, sly, subtle, strategic, timeserving, unscrupulous, wily.

political adj civic, civil, national, politic, public.

pollute vb defile, foul, soil, taint; contaminate, corrupt, debase, demoralise, deprave, impair, infect, pervert, poison, stain, tarnish, vitiate; desecrate, profane; abuse, debauch, defile, deflower, dishonour, ravish, violate.

pollution n abomination, contamination, corruption, defilement, foulness, impurity, pollutedness, taint, uncleanness, vitiation.

pomp n display, flourish, grandeur, magnificence, ostentation, pageant, pageantry, parade, show, splendour, state, style.

pompous adj august, boastful, bombastic, dignified, gorgeous, grand, inflated, lofty, ostentatious, pretentious, vainglorious.

ponder vb cogitate, consider, contemplate, deliberate, examine, meditate, muse, reflect, study.

poor adj indigent, necessitous, pinched, straitened; destitute, distressed, impecunious, insolvent, moneyless, penniless, poverty-stricken, reduced, seedy; emaciated, gaunt, spare, lean, lank, shrunk, skinny, spare, thin; barren, fruitless, sterile, unfertile, unfruitful, unproductive, unprolific; flimsy, inadequate, insignificant, insufficient, paltry, slender, slight, small, trifling, trivial, unimportant, valueless, worthless; delicate, feeble, frail, infirm, unsound, weak; inferior, seedy, shabby, valueless; bad, beggarly, contemptible, despicable, humble, low, mean, paltry, pitiful, sorry; bald, barren, mean, meagre, prosaic, prosing, spiritless, tame, vapid, weak; ill-fated, ill-starred, luckless, miserable, pitiable, unfortunate, unhappy, unlucky, wretched; deficient, imperfect, inadequate, insufficient, faulty, unsatisfactory.

popular *adj* lay, plebeian, public; comprehensible, easy, familiar, plain; acceptable, accepted, accredited, admired, approved, favoured, liked, pleasing, praised; received; common, current, prevailing, prevalent; cheap, inexpensive.

port *n* anchorage, harbour, haven, shelter; door, entrance, gate, passageway; porthole.

portable *adj* convenient, handy, light, manageable, movable, portative, transmissible.

portent *n* augury, omen, presage, prognosis, sign, warning; marvel, phenomenon, wonder.

portion *vb* allot, distribute, divide, parcel; endow, supply. • *n* bit, fragment, morsel, part, piece, scrap, section; allotment, contingent, dividend, division, lot, measure, quantity, quota, ration, share; inheritance, share.

portray *vb* act, draw, depict, delineate, describe, represent, paint, picture, sketch, pose, position.

pose *vb* bewilder, confound, dumbfound, embarrass, mystify, nonplus, perplex, puzzle, set, stagger; affect, attitudinise. • *n* attitude, posture; affectation, air, pretence, role.

position *vb* arrange, array, fix, locate, place, put, set, site, stand. • *n* locality, place, post, site, situation, spot, station; relation; attitude, bearing, posture; affirmation, assertion, doctrine, predication, principle, proposition, thesis; caste, dignity, honour, rank, standing, status; circumstance, condition, state; berth, billet, incumbency, situation.

positive *adj* categorical, clear, defined, definite, direct, determinate, explicit, express, expressed, precise, unequivocal, unmistakable, unqualified; absolute, actual, real, substantial, true, veritable; assured, certain, confident, convinced, sure; decisive, incontrovertible, indisputable, indubitable, inescapable; imperative, unconditional, undeniable; decided, dogmatic, emphatic, obstinate, overbearing, overconfident, stubborn.

possess *vb* control, have, hold, keep, obtain, occupy, own, seize.

possession *n* monopoly, ownership, proprietorship; control, occupation, occupancy, retention, tenancy, tenure; bedevilment, lunacy, madness, obsession; (*pl*) assets, effects, estate, property, wealth.

possible *adj* conceivable, contingent, imaginable, potential; accessible, feasible, likely, practical, practicable, workable.

post[1] *vb* advertise, announce, inform, placard, publish; brand, defame, disgrace, vilify; enter, slate, record, register. • *n* column, picket, pier, pillar, stake, support.

post[2] *vb* establish, fix, place, put, set, station. • *n* billet, employment, office, place, position, quarter, seat, situation, station.

post[3] *vb* drop, dispatch, mail. • *n* carrier, courier, express, mercury, messenger, postman.

posterity *n* descendants, offspring, progeny, seed; breed, brood, children, family, heirs, issue.

postpone *vb* adjourn, defer, delay, procrastinate, prorogue, retard.

posture *vb* attitudinise, pose. • *n* attitude, pose, position.

potent *adj* efficacious, forceful, forcible, intense, powerful, strong; able, capable, efficient, mighty; cogent, influential.

potential *adj* able, capable, inherent, latent, possible. • *n* ability, capability, dynamic, possibility.

pound[1] *vb* beat, strike, thump; bray, bruise, comminute, crush, levigate, pulverise, triturate.

pound[2] *n* enclosure, fold, pen.

pour *vb* cascade, emerge, flood, flow, issue.

poverty *n* destitution, difficulties, distress, impecuniosity, impecuniousness, indigence, necessity, need, neediness, penury, privation, straits, want; beggary, mendicancy, pauperism, pennilessness; dearth, jejuneness, lack, scantiness, sparingness, meagreness; exiguity, paucity, poorness, smallness; humbleness, lowliness; barrenness, sterility, unfruitfulness.

power *n* ability, ableness, capability, cogency, competency, efficacy, faculty, might, potency, validity, talent; energy, force, strength, virtue; capacity, susceptibility; endowment, faculty, gift, talent; ascendancy, authoritativeness, authority, carte blanche, command, control, domination, dominion, government, influence, omnipotence, predominance, prerogative, pressure, proxy, puissance, rule, sovereignty, sway, warrant; army, host, troop.

powerful *adj* mighty, potent, puissant; ablebodied, herculean, muscular, nervous, robust, sinewy, strong, sturdy, vigorous, vivid; able, commanding, dominating, forceful, forcible, overpowering; cogent, effective, effectual, efficacious, efficient, energetic, influential.

practicable *adj* achievable, attainable, bearable, feasible, performable, possible, workable.

practical *adj* hardheaded, matter-of-fact, pragmatic; able, experienced, practised, proficient, qualified, trained, skilled; effective, workable.

practice *n* custom, habit, manner, method, repetition; procedure, usage, use; application, drill, exercise, pursuit; action, acts, behaviour, conduct, dealing, proceeding.

practise *vb* apply, do, exercise, follow, observe, perform, perpetrate, pursue.

practised *adj* able, accomplished, experienced, instructed, practical, proficient, qualified, skilled, thoroughbred, trained, versed.

pragmatic *adj* impertinent, interfering, intrusive, meddlesome, obtrusive, officious; earthy, hard-headed, matter-of-fact, practical, realistic, sensible.

praise *vb* approbate, acclaim, applaud, approve, commend; celebrate, compliment, eulogise, extol, flatter, laud; adore, bless, exalt, glorify, magnify, worship. • *n* acclaim, approbation, approval, commendation; encomium, eulogy, glorification, laud, laudation, panegyric; exaltation, extolling, glorification, homage, tribute, worship; celebrity, distinction, fame, glory, honour, renown; desert, merit, praiseworthiness.

prank *n* antic, caper, escapade, frolic, trick.

pray *vb* ask, beg, beseech, conjure, entreat, implore, importune, invoke, petition, request, solicit, supplicate.

prayer *n* beseeching, entreaty, imploration, petition, request, supplication; adoration, devotion(s), litany, invocation, orison, praise.

preach *vb* declare, deliver, proclaim, pronounce, publish; inculcate, press, teach, urge; exhort, lecture, moralise, sermonise.

precarious *adj* critical, doubtful, dubious, equivocal, hazardous, insecure, perilous, unassured, risky, uncertain, unsteady.

precaution *n* care, caution, circumspection, foresight, forethought, providence, prudence, safeguard, wariness.

precede *vb* antedate, forerun, head, herald, introduce, lead, utter.

precedence *n* advantage, antecedence, lead, pre-eminence, preference, priority.

precedent *n* antecedent, authority, custom, example, instance, model, pattern, standard.

precept *n* behest, bidding, cannon, charge, command, commandment, decree, dictate, edict, injunction, instruction, law, mandate, ordinance, ordination, order, regulation; direction, doctrine, maxim, principle, teaching, rubric, rule.

precinct *n* border, bound, boundary, confine, environs, frontier, enclosure, limit, list, march, neighbourhood, purlieus, area, district.

precious *adj* costly, inestimable, invaluable, priceless, prized, valuable; adored, beloved, cherished, darling, dear, idolised, treasured; fastidious, overnice, over-refined, precise.

precipitate *vb* advance, accelerate, dispatch, expedite, forward, further, hasten, hurry, plunge, press, quicken, speed. • *adj* hasty, hurried, headlong, impetuous, indiscreet, overhasty, rash, reckless; abrupt, sudden, violent.

precipitous *adj* abrupt, cliffy, craggy, perpendicular, uphill, sheer, steep.

precise *adj* accurate, correct, definite, distinct, exact, explicit, express, nice, pointed, severe, strict, unequivocal, well-defined; careful, exact, scrupulous, strict; ceremonious, finical, formal, prim, punctilious, rigid, starched, stiff.

precision *n* accuracy, correctness, definiteness, distinctness, exactitude, exactness, nicety.

precocious *adj* advanced, forward, overforward, premature.

precursor *n* antecedent, cause, forerunner, predecessor; harbinger, herald, messenger.

predatory *adj* greedy, pillaging, plundering, predacious, rapacious, ravaging, voracious.

predicament *n* attitude, case, condition, plight, position, posture, situation, state; conjecture, corner, dilemma, emergency, exigency, fix, hole, impasse, mess, pass, pinch, push, quandary.

predict *vb* augur, betoken, bode, divine, forebode, forecast, foresee, foretell, forewarn, portend, prognosticate, prophesy.

predominant *adj* ascendant, controlling, dominant, overruling, prevailing, prevalent, reigning, ruling, sovereign, supreme.

predominate *vb* dominate, prevail, rule.

pre-eminent *adj* chief, conspicuous, consummate, controlling, distinguished, excellent, excelling, paramount, peerless, predominant, renowned, superior, supreme, unequalled.

preface *vb* begin, introduce, induct, launch, open, precede. • *n* exordium, foreword, induction, introduction, preamble, preliminary, prelude, prelusion, premise, proem, prologue.

prefer *vb* address, offer, present, proffer, tender; advance, elevate, promote, raise; adopt, choose, elect, fancy, pick, select, wish.

preference *n* advancement, choice, election, estimation, precedence, priority, selection.

preferment *n* advancement, benefice, dignity, elevation, exaltation, promotion.

pregnant *adj* big, enceinte, parturient, fraught, full, important, replete, significant, weighty; fecund, fertile, fruitful, generative, impregnating, potential, procreant, procreative, productive.

prejudice *vb* bias, incline, influence, turn, warp; damage, diminish, hurt, impair, injure. • *n* bias, intolerance, partiality, preconception, predilection, prejudgement, prepossession, unfairness; damage, detriment, disadvantage, harm, hurt.

preliminary *adj* antecedent, initiatory, introductory, precedent, precursive, precursory, prefatory, prelusive, prelusory, preparatory, previous, prior, proemial. • *n* beginning, initiation, introduction, opening, preamble, preface, prelude.

prelude *n* introduction, opening, overture, prelusion, preparation, voluntary; exordium, preamble, preface, preliminary, proem.

premature *adj* hasty, ill-considered, precipitate, unmatured, unprepared, unripe, untimely.

premeditation *n* deliberation, design, forethought, intention, prearrangement.

premise *vb* introduce, preamble, preface, prefix. • *n* affirmation, antecedent, argument, assertion, assumption, basis, foundation, ground, hypothesis, position, premiss, presupposition, proposition, support, thesis, theorem.

premium n bonus, bounty, encouragement, fee, gift, guerdon, meed, payment, prize, recompense, remuneration, reward; appreciation, enhancement.

premonition n caution, foreboding, foreshadowing, forewarning, indication, omen, portent, presage, presentiment, sign, warning.

preoccupied adj absent, absentminded, abstracted, dreaming, engrossed, inadvertent, inattentive, lost, musing, unobservant.

prepare vb adapt, adjust, fit, qualify; arrange, concoct, fabricate, make, order, plan, procure.

prepossessing adj alluring, amiable, attractive, bewitching, captivating, charming, engaging, fascinating, inviting, taking, winning.

preposterous adj absurd, excessive, exorbitant, extravagant, foolish, improper, irrational, monstrous, nonsensical, perverted, ridiculous.

prescribe vb advocate, appoint, command, decree, dictate, direct, enjoin, establish, institute, ordain, order.

presence n attendance, company, inhabitance, inhabitancy, nearness, neighbourhood, occupancy, propinquity, proximity, residence, ubiquity, vicinity; air, appearance, carriage, demeanour.

present[1] adj near; actual, current, existing, happening, immediate, instant, living; available, quick, ready. • n now, time being, today.

present[2] n benefaction, boon, donation, favour, gift, grant, gratuity, largesse, offering.

present[3] vb introduce, nominate; exhibit, offer; bestow, confer, give, grant; deliver, hand; advance, express, prefer, proffer, tender.

presently adv anon, directly, forthwith, immediately, shortly, soon.

preservation n cherishing, conservation, curing, maintenance, protection, support; safety, salvation, security; integrity, keeping.

preserve vb defend, guard, keep, protect, rescue, save, secure, shield; maintain, uphold, sustain, support; conserve, economise, husband, retain. • n comfit, compote, confection, confiture, conserve, jam, jelly; enclosure, warren.

preside vb control, direct, govern, manage.

press vb compress, crowd, crush, squeeze; flatten, iron, smooth; clasp, embrace, hug; force, compel, constrain; emphasise, enforce, enjoin, inculcate, stress, urge; hasten, hurry, push, rush; crowd, throng; entreat, importune, solicit. • n crowd, crush, multitude, throng; hurry, pressure, urgency; case, closet, cupboard, repository.

pressure n compressing, crushing, squeezing; influence, force; compulsion, exigency, hurry, persuasion, press, stress, urgency; affliction, calamity, difficulty, distress, embarrassment, grievance, oppression, straits.

prestige n credit, distinction, importance, influence, reputation, weight.

presume vb anticipate, apprehend, assume, believe, conjecture, deduce, expect, infer, surmise, suppose, think; consider, presuppose, suppose; dare, undertake, venture.

presumption n anticipation, assumption, belief, concession, conclusion, condition, conjecture, deduction, guess, hypothesis, inference, opinion, supposition, understanding; arrogance, assurance, audacity, boldness, brass, effrontery, forwardness, haughtiness; probability.

presumptuous adj arrogant, assuming, audacious, bold, brash, forward, irreverent, insolent, intrusive, presuming; foolhardy, overconfident.

pretence n affectation, cloak, colour, disguise, mask, semblance, show, simulation, veil, window dressing; excuse, evasion, fabrication, feigning, makeshift, pretext, sham, subterfuge.

pretend vb affect, counterfeit, deem, dissemble, fake, falsify, feign, sham, simulate; act, imagine, lie, profess; aspire, claim.

pretentious adj affected, arrogant, conceited, conspicuous, ostentatious, presuming, priggish.

pretty adj attractive, beautiful, bonny, comely, elegant, fair, handsome, neat, pleasing, trim; affected, foppish. • adv fairly, moderately, quite.

prevailing adj controlling, dominant, effectual, efficacious, general, influential, operative, overruling, persuading, predominant, preponderant, prevalent, ruling, successful.

prevalent adj ascendant, compelling, efficacious, governing, predominant, prevailing, successful; superior; extensive, general, rife.

prevaricate vb cavil, deviate, dodge, equivocate, evade, palter, pettifog, quibble, shift.

prevent vb bar, check, debar, deter, forestall, help, hinder, impede, inhibit, intercept, interrupt, obstruct, obviate, preclude, prohibit, restrain.

prevention n anticipation, determent, deterrence, deterrent, frustration, hindrance, interception, interruption, obstruction, preclusion, prohibition, restriction, stoppage.

previous adj antecedent, anterior, earlier, foregoing, foregone, former, preceding, prior.

prey vb devour, eat, feed on, live off; exploit, intimidate, terrorise; burden, distress, haunt, oppress, trouble, worry. • n booty, loot, pillage, plunder, prize, rapine, spoil; food, game, kill, quarry, victim; depredation, ravage.

price vb assess, estimate, evaluate, rate, value. • n amount, cost, expense, outlay, value; appraisal, charge, estimation, excellence, figure, rate, quotation, valuation, value, worth; compensation, guerdon, recompense, return, reward.

priceless adj dear, expensive, precious, inestimable, invaluable, valuable; amusing, comic.

prick vb perforate, pierce, puncture, stick; drive,

goad, impel, incite, spur, urge; cut, hurt, pain, sting, wound; hasten, post, ride, spur. • *n* mark, perforation; point, puncture; prickle, sting.

pride *vb* boast, brag, crow, preen, revel in. • *n* conceit, egotism, self-complacency, self-esteem, self-exaltation, self-importance, self-sufficiency, vanity; arrogance, assumption, disdain, haughtiness, hauteur, insolence, loftiness, lordliness, pomposity, presumption, superciliousness, vainglory; decorum, dignity, elevation, loftiness, self-respect; decoration, glory, ornament, show.

prim *adj* demure, formal, nice, precise, prudish, starch, starched, stiff, strait-laced.

primary *adj* aboriginal, earliest, first, initial, original, prime, primitive, primeval, primordial, pristine; chief, main, principal; basic, elementary, fundamental, preparatory: radical.

prime[1] *adj* aboriginal, basic, first, initial, original, primal, primary, primeval, primitive, primordial, pristine; chief, foremost, highest, leading, main, paramount, principal; blooming, early; capital, cardinal, dominant, predominant; excellent, first-class, first-rate, optimal, optimum, quintessential; beginning, initial, opening. • *n* beginning, dawn, morning, opening; spring, youth; bloom, cream, flower, height, heyday, optimum, perfection, quintessence, zenith.

prime[2] *vb* charge, load, prepare, undercoat; coach, groom, train, tutor.

primitive *adj* aboriginal, first, original, primal, primary, prime, primitive, primordial, pristine; antiquated, crude, old-fashioned, quaint, simple, unsophisticated; formal, grave, prim, solemn.

princely *adj* imperial, regal, royal; august, generous, grand, liberal, magnanimous, magnificent, majestic, munificent, noble, splendid, superb, titled; dignified, elevated, high-minded, lofty, stately.

principal *adj* capital, cardinal, chief, essential, first, foremost, highest, leading, main, pre-eminent, prime. • *n* chief, head, leader; master.

principle *n* cause, fountain, fountainhead, groundwork, mainspring, nature, origin, source, spring; basis, constituent, element, essence, substratum; assumption, axiom, law, maxim, postulation; doctrine, dogma, impulse, maxim, opinion, precept, rule, tenet, theory; conviction, ground, motive, reason; equity, goodness, honesty, honour, incorruptibility, integrity, justice, probity, rectitude, righteousness, trustiness, truth, uprightness, virtue, worth; faculty, power.

print *vb* engrave, impress, imprint, mark, stamp; issue, publish. • *n* book, periodical, publication; copy, engraving, photograph, picture; characters, font, fount, lettering, type, typeface.

prior *adj* antecedent, anterior, earlier, foregoing, precedent, preceding, precursory, previous.

priority *n* antecedence, anteriority, precedence, pre-eminence, pre-existence, superiority.

pristine *adj* ancient, earliest, first, former, old, original, primary, primeval, primitive.

privacy *n* concealment, secrecy; retirement, retreat, seclusion, solitude.

private *adj* retired, secluded, sequestrated, solitary; individual, own, particular, peculiar, personal, special, unofficial; confidential, privy; clandestine, concealed, hidden, secret.

privilege *n* advantage, charter, claim, exemption, favour, franchise, immunity, leave, liberty, licence, permission, prerogative, right.

prize[1] *vb* appreciate, cherish, esteem, treasure.

prize[2] *adj* best, champion, first-rate, outstanding, winning. • *n* guerdon, honours, meed, premium, reward; cup, decoration, medal, laurels, palm, trophy; booty, capture, lot, plunder, spoil; advantage, gain, privilege.

probable *adj* apparent, credible, likely, presumable, reasonable.

probably *adv* apparently, likely, maybe, perchance, perhaps, presumably, possibly.

probation *n* essay, examination, ordeal, proof, test, trial; novitiate.

probe *vb* examine, explore, fathom, investigate, measure, prove, scrutinise, search, sift, sound.

probity *n* candour, conscientiousness, equity, fairness, faith, goodness, honesty, honour, incorruptibility, integrity, justice, loyalty, morality, principle, rectitude, righteousness, sincerity, soundness, trustworthiness, truth, truthfulness, uprightness, veracity, virtue, worth.

problem *adj* difficult, intractable, uncontrollable, unruly. • *n* dilemma, dispute, doubt, enigma, exercise, proposition, puzzle, riddle.

problematic *adj* debatable, disputable, doubtful, dubious, enigmatic, uncertain.

procedure *n* conduct, course, custom, management, method, operation, policy, practice, process; act, action, deed, measure, performance.

proceed *vb* advance, continue, go, pass, progress; accrue, arise, come, emanate, ensue, flow, follow, issue, originate, result, spring.

proceeds *npl* balance, earnings, effects, gain, income, profits, receipts, returns, yield.

process *n* advance, course, progress, train; action, conduct, management, measure, mode, operation, performance, practice, procedure, proceeding, step, transaction, way; action, case, suit, trial; outgrowth, projection, protuberance.

procession *n* cavalcade, cortege, file, march, parade, retinue, train.

proclaim *vb* advertise, announce, broach, broadcast, circulate, cry, declare, herald, promulgate, publish, trumpet; ban, outlaw, proscribe.

procrastinate *vb* adjourn, defer, delay, postpone, prolong, protract, retard; neglect; lag.

procure *vb* acquire, gain, get, obtain; cause.

prodigal *adj* abundant, dissipated, excessive,

extravagant, generous, improvident, lavish, profuse, reckless, squandering, thriftless, unthrifty, wasteful. • n spendthrift, squanderer, waster.

produce vb exhibit, show; bear, beget, breed, conceive, engender, furnish, generate, hatch, procreate, yield; accomplish, achieve, cause, create, effect, make, occasion, originate; accrue, afford, give, impart, make, render; extend, lengthen, prolong, protract; fabricate, fashion, manufacture. • n crop, fruit, greengrocery, harvest, product, vegetables, yield.

product n crops, fruits, harvest, outcome, proceeds, yield; consequence, effect, issue, performance, production, result.

production n fruit, produce, product; construction, creation, erection, fabrication, making, performance; completion, fruition; birth, breeding, development, growth, propagation; opus, publication, work.

productive adj copious, fertile, fruitful, luxuriant, plenteous, prolific, teeming; causative, constructive, creative, efficient, life-giving.

profane vb defile, desecrate, pollute, violate; abuse, debase. • adj godless, heathen, idolatrous, impure, pagan, secular, temporal, unconsecrated, unhallowed, unholy, unsanctified.

profess vb acknowledge, affirm, allege, aver, avouch, avow, confess, declare, own, proclaim, state; affect, feign, pretend.

profession n acknowledgement, assertion, avowal, claim, declaration; avocation, evasion, pretence, pretension, protestation, representation; business, calling, employment.

proficiency n advancement, forwardness, improvement; accomplishment, skill.

proficient adj able, accomplished, adept, competent, conversant, dextrous, expert, finished, masterly, practised, skilled, skilful, thoroughbred, trained, qualified, well-versed.

profit vb advance, benefit, gain, improve. • n aid, clearance, earnings, emolument, fruit, gain, lucre, produce, return; advancement, advantage, benefit, interest, perquisite, service, use, utility.

profitable adj advantageous, beneficial, desirable, gainful, productive, useful; lucrative.

profound adj abysmal, deep, fathomless; heavy, undisturbed; erudite, learned, penetrating, sagacious, skilled; far-reaching, heartfelt, intense; abstruse, obscure, complete, thorough.

profuse adj abundant, bountiful, copious, excessive, extravagant, exuberant, generous, improvident, lavish, overabundant, plentiful.

progress vb advance, continue, proceed; better, gain, improve, increase. • n advance, advancement, progression; course, headway, ongoing, passage; betterment, development, growth, improvement, increase, reform: circuit, procession.

prohibit vb debar, hamper, hinder, preclude, prevent; ban, disallow, forbid, inhabit, interdict.

prohibition n ban, bar, disallowance, embargo, forbiddance, inhibition, interdict, interdiction, obstruction, prevention, proscription, taboo.

prohibitive adj forbidding, prohibiting.

project vb cast, eject, fling, hurl, propel, shoot, throw; brew, concoct, contrive, design, devise, intend, plan, plot, scheme; delineate, draw, exhibit; bulge, extend, jut, protrude. • n contrivance, design, device, intention, plan, proposal, purpose, scheme.

projection n delivery, ejection, emission, propulsion, throwing; contriving, designing, planning, scheming; bulge, extension, outshoot, process, prominence, protuberance, salience, saliency, salient, spur; delineation, map, plan.

prolific adj abundant, fertile, fruitful, generative, productive, teeming.

prologue n foreword, introduction, preamble, preface, preliminary, prelude, proem.

prolong vb continue, extend, lengthen, protract, sustain; defer, postpone.

prominent adj convex, embossed, jutting, projecting, protuberant, raised, relieved; celebrated, conspicuous, distinguished, eminent, famous, foremost, influential, leading, main, noticeable, outstanding; conspicuous, important, salient.

promiscuous adj confused, heterogeneous, indiscriminate, intermingled, mingled, miscellaneous, mixed; abandoned, dissipated, dissolute, immoral, licentious, loose, unchaste, wanton.

promise vb covenant, engage, pledge, subscribe, swear, underwrite, vow; assure, attest, guarantee, warrant; agree, bargain, engage, stipulate, undertake. • n agreement, assurance, contract, engagement, oath, parole, pledge, vow.

promising adj auspicious, encouraging, hopeful, likely, propitious.

promote vb advance, aid, assist, cultivate, encourage, further, help, promote; dignify, elevate, exalt, graduate, honour, pass, prefer, raise.

prompt vb actuate, dispose, impel, incite, incline, induce, instigate, stimulate, urge; remind; dictate, hint, influence, suggest. • adj active, alert, apt, quick, ready; forward, hasty; disposed, inclined, prone; early, exact, immediate, instant, precise, punctual, seasonable, timely. • adv apace, directly, forthwith, immediately, promptly. • n cue, hint, prompter, reminder, stimulus.

prone adj flat, horizontal, prostrate, recumbent; declivitous, inclined, inclining, sloping; apt, bent, disposed, inclined, predisposed, tending.

pronounce vb articulate, enunciate, frame, say, speak, utter; affirm, announce, assert, declare.

proof adj firm, fixed, impenetrable, stable, steadfast. • n essay, examination, ordeal, test, trial; attestation, certification, conclusion, conclusiveness, confirmation, corroboration, demonstration, evidence, ratification, substantiation, testimony, verification.

prop vb bolster, brace, buttress, maintain, shore, stay, support, sustain, truss, uphold. • n brace, support, stay; buttress, fulcrum, pin, strut.

propel vb drive, force, impel, push, urge; cast, fling, hurl, project, throw.

proper adj individual, inherent, natural, original, particular, peculiar, special, specific; adapted, appropriate, becoming, befitting, convenient, decent, decorous, demure, fit, fitting, legitimate, meet, pertinent, respectable, right, seemly, suitable; accurate, correct, fair, fastidious, formal, just, precise; actual.

property n attribute, characteristic, disposition, mark, peculiarity, quality, trait, virtue; appurtenance, assets, belongings, chattels, circumstances, effects, estate, goods, possessions, resources, wealth; ownership, possession, proprietorship, tenure; claim, copyright, right, title.

prophecy n augury, divination, forecast, foretelling, portent, prediction, premonition, presage, prognostication.

prophesy vb augur, divine, foretell, predict.

proportion vb adjust, graduate, regulate; form, shape. • n arrangement, relation; adjustment, commensuration, dimension, distribution, symmetry; lot, part, portion, quota, ratio, share.

proposal n design, motion, offer, overture, proffer, proposition, recommendation, scheme, statement, suggestion, tender.

propose vb move, offer, pose, present, propound, proffer, put, recommend, state, submit, suggest, tender; design, intend, mean, purpose.

proposition vb accost, proffer, solicit. • n offer, overture, project, proposal, suggestion, tender, undertaking; affirmation, assertion, axiom, declaration, dictum, doctrine, position, postulation, predication, statement, theorem, thesis.

propriety n accuracy, adaptation, appropriation, aptness, becomingness, consonance, correctness, fitness, justness, reasonableness, rightness, seemliness, suitableness; conventionality, decency, decorum, demureness, fastidiousness, formality, modesty, properness, respectability.

prosaic adj commonplace, dull, flat, humdrum, matter-of-fact, pedestrian, plain, prolix, prosing, sober, stupid, tame, tedious, tiresome, unentertaining, unimaginative, unromantic, vapid.

proscribe vb banish, doom, exile, expel, ostracise, outlaw; exclude, forbid, interdict, prohibit; censure, condemn, curse, denounce, reject.

prosecute vb conduct, continue, exercise, follow, persist, pursue; arraign, indict, sue.

prospect vb explore, search, seek, survey. • n display, field, landscape, outlook, perspective, scene, show, sight, spectacle, survey, view, vision, vista; picture, scenery; anticipation, calculation, contemplation, expectance, expectancy, expectation, foreseeing, foresight, hope, presumption, promise, trust; likelihood, probability.

prosper vb aid, favour, forward, help; advance, flourish, grow rich, thrive, succeed; increase.

prosperity n affluence, blessings, happiness, felicity, good luck, success, thrift, weal, welfare.

prostrate vb demolish, destroy, fell, level, overthrow, overturn, ruin; depress, exhaust, overcome, reduce. • adj fallen, prostrated, prone, recumbent, supine; helpless, powerless.

protect vb cover, defend, guard, shield; fortify, harbour, house, preserve, save, screen, secure, shelter; champion, foster, patronise.

protest vb affirm, assert, asseverate, attest, aver, avow, declare, profess, testify; demur, expostulate, object, remonstrate, repudiate. • n complaint, declaration, disapproval, objection.

prototype n archetype, copy, exemplar, example, ideal, model, original, paradigm, precedent.

protract vb continue, extend, lengthen, prolong; defer, delay, postpone.

protrude vb beetle, bulge, extend, jut, project.

proud adj assuming, conceited, contended, egotistical, overweening, self-conscious, self-satisfied, vain; arrogant, boastful, haughty, high-spirited, highly strung, imperious, lofty, lordly, presumptuous, supercilious, uppish, vainglorious.

prove vb ascertain, conform, demonstrate, establish, evidence, evince, justify, manifest, show, substantiate, sustain, verify; assay, check, examine, experiment, test, try.

proverb n adage, aphorism, apothegm, byword, dictum, maxim, precept, saw, saying.

provide vb arrange, collect, plan, prepare, procure; gather, keep, store; afford, contribute, feed, furnish, produce, stock, supply, yield; cater, purvey; agree, bargain, condition, contract, covenant, engage, stipulate.

province n district, domain, region, section, territory, tract; colony, dependency; business, calling, capacity, charge, department, duty, employment, function, office, part, post, sphere.

provision n anticipation, providing; arrangement, care, preparation, readiness; equipment, fund, grist, hoard, reserve, resources, stock, store, supplies, supply; clause, condition, prerequisite, proviso, reservation, stipulation.

provocation n incentive, incitement, provocativeness, stimulant, stimulus; affront, indignity, insult, offence; angering, vexation.

provoke vb animate, arouse, awaken, excite, impel, incite, induce, inflame, instigate, kindle, move, rouse, stimulate; affront, aggravate, anger, annoy, chafe, enrage, exacerbate, exasperate, incense, infuriate, irritate, nettle, offend, pique, vex; cause, elicit, evoke, instigate, occasion, produce, promote.

prudent adj cautious, careful, circumspect, considerate, discreet, foreseeing, heedful, judicious, politic, provident, prudential, wary, wise.

prudish *adj* coy, demure, modest, perjink, precise, prim, reserved, strait-laced.

prune *vb* abbreviate, clip, cut, dock, lop, thin.

pry *vb* examine, ferret, inspect, investigate, peep, peer, question, scrutinise, search.

public *adj* civil, common, countrywide, general, national, political, state; known, notorious, open, popular, published, well-known. • *n* citizens, community, country, everyone, masses, nation, people, population; audience, buyers.

publication *n* advertisement, announcement, blazon, disclosure, divulgement, divulgation, proclamation, promulgation, report; edition, issue, issuance, printing.

publicity *n* daylight, currency, limelight, notoriety, spotlight; outlet, vent.

publish *vb* advertise, air, bruit, announce, blaze, blazon, broach, communicate, declare, diffuse, disclose, disseminate, impart, placard, post, proclaim, promulgate, reveal, tell, utter, vent.

pull *vb* drag, draw, haul, row, tow, tug; cull, extract, gather, pick, pluck; detach, rend, tear, wrest. • *n* pluck, shake, tug, twitch, wrench; contest, struggle; attraction, gravity, magnetism; graft, influence, power.

pulsate *vb* beat, palpitate, throb, vibrate.

pun *n* assonance, alliteration, conceit, paranomasia, quip, rhyme, witticism, wordplay.

punctual *adj* exact, nice, precise, punctilious; early, prompt, ready, regular, seasonable, timely.

puncture *vb* bore, penetrate, perforate, pierce, prick. • *n* bite, hole, sting, wound.

pungent *adj* acid, acrid, biting, burning, caustic, hot, mordant, penetrating, peppery, piercing, piquant, prickling, racy, salty, seasoned, sharp, smart, sour, spicy, stimulating, stinging; acute, acrimonious, cutting, distressing, irritating, keen, painful, peevish, piquant, poignant, pointed, satirical, severe, smart, tart, trenchant.

punish *vb* beat, castigate, chasten, chastise, correct, discipline, flog, lash, scourge, torture.

punishment *n* castigation, chastening, chastisement, correction, discipline, infliction, retribution, scourging, trial; judgment, nemesis.

puny *adj* feeble, inferior, weak; dwarf, dwarfish, insignificant, diminutive, little, petty, pygmy, small, stunted, tiny, undersized.

purchase *vb* buy, gain, get, obtain, pay for, procure; achieve, attain, earn, win. • *n* acquisition, buy, gain, possession, property; advantage, foothold, grasp, hold, influence, support.

pure *adj* clean, clear, fair, immaculate, spotless, stainless, unadulterated, unalloyed, unblemished, uncorrupted, undefiled, unpolluted, unspotted, unstained, unsullied, untainted, untarnished; chaste, continent, guileless, guiltless, holy, honest, incorrupt, innocent, modest, sincere, true, uncorrupt, uncorrupted, upright, virgin, virtuous, white; clear, genuine, perfect, real, simple, true; absolute, mere, sheer; attic, classic.

purge *vb* cleanse, clear, purify; clarify, defecate, evacuate; deterge, scour; absolve, pardon, shrive. • *n* elimination, eradication, expulsion, removal, suppression; emetic, laxative.

purify *vb* clean, cleanse, clear, depurate, expurgate, purge, refine, wash; clarify, defecate, fine.

puritanical *adj* ascetic, narrow-minded, overscrupulous, prim, prudish, rigid, severe, strict.

purpose *vb* contemplate, design, intend, mean, meditate; determine, resolve. • *n* aim, design, drift, end, intent, intention, object, resolution, resolve, view; plan, project; meaning, purport, sense; consequence, end, effect.

pursue *vb* chase, dog, follow, hound, hunt, shadow, track; conduct, continue, cultivate, maintain, practise, prosecute; seek, strive;.

pursuit *n* chase, hunt, race; conduct, cultivation, practice, prosecution, pursuance; avocation, calling, business, employment, occupation.

push *vb* elbow, crowd, hustle, impel, jostle, shoulder, shove, thrust; advance, drive, hurry, propel, urge; importune, persuade, tease. • *n* pressure, thrust; determination, perseverance; emergency, exigency, extremity, pinch, strait, test, trial; assault, attack, charge, endeavour.

put *vb* bring, collocate, deposit, impose, lay, locate, place, set; enjoin, impose, inflict, levy; offer, present, propose, state; compel, constrain, force, oblige; induce, urge; utter.

puzzle *vb* bewilder, confound, confuse, embarrass, gravel, mystify, nonplus, perplex, pose, stagger; complicate, entangle. • *n* conundrum, enigma, labyrinth, maze, paradox, poser, problem, riddle; bewilderment, complication, confusion, difficulty, dilemma, embarrassment, mystification, perplexity, point, quandary, question.

Q

quail *vb* blench, cower, droop, faint, flinch, shrink, tremble.

quaint *adj* antiquated, antique, archaic, curious, droll, extraordinary, fanciful, old-fashioned, queer, singular, uncommon, unique, unusual; affected, fantastic, farfetched, odd.

quake *vb* quiver, shake, shiver, shudder; move, vibrate. • *n* earthquake, shake, shudder.

qualification n ability, accomplishment, capability, competency, eligibility, fitness, suitability; condition, exception, limitation, modification, proviso, restriction, stipulation; abatement, allowance, diminution, mitigation.

qualify vb adapt, capacitate, empower, entitle, equip, fit; limit, modify, narrow, restrain, restrict; abate, assuage, ease, mitigate, moderate, reduce, soften; diminish, modulate, temper.

quality n affection, attribute, characteristic, colour, distinction, feature, flavour, mark, nature, peculiarity, property, singularity, timbre, tinge, trait; character, characteristic, condition, disposition, humour, mood, temper; brand, calibre, capacity, class, condition, description, grade, kind, rank, sort, stamp, standing, station, status; aristocracy, gentry, noblesse, nobility.

qualm n agony, pang, throe; nausea, queasiness; compunction, remorse, uneasiness, twinge.

quandary n bewilderment, difficulty, dilemma, doubt, embarrassment, perplexity, pickle, plight, predicament, problem, puzzle, uncertainty.

quantity n content, extent, greatness, measure, number, portion, share, size; aggregate, batch, amount, bulk, lot, mass, quantum, store, sum, volume; duration, length.

quarrel vb altercate, bicker, brawl, carp, cavil, clash, contend, differ, dispute, fight, jangle, jar, scold, scuffle, spar, spat, squabble, wrangle.

quarrelsome adj argumentative, choleric, combative, contentious, cross, discordant, disputatious, dissentious, fiery, irascible, irritable.

quarter vb billet, lodge, post, station; allot, furnish, share. • n abode, billet, dwelling, habitation, lodgings, posts, quarters, stations; direction, district, locality, location, lodge, position, region, territory; clemency, mercy, mildness.

quell vb conquer, crush, overcome, overpower, subdue; bridle, check, curb, extinguish, lay, quench, rein in, repress, restrain, stifle; allay, calm, compose, hush, lull, pacify, quiet, quieten, still, subdue, tranquillise; alleviate, appease, blunt, deaden, dull, mitigate, mollify, soothe.

quench vb extinguish, put out; check, destroy, repress, satiate, stifle, still, suppress; allay, cool, dampen, extinguish, slake.

query vb ask, enquire, inquire, question; dispute, doubt. • n enquiry, inquiry, interrogatory, issue, problem, question.

quest n expedition, journey, search, voyage; pursuit, suit; examination, enquiry, inquiry; demand, desire, invitation, prayer, request.

question vb ask, catechise, enquire, examine, inquire, interrogate, quiz, sound out; doubt, query; challenge, dispute. • n examination, enquiry, inquiry, interpellation, interrogation; query; debate, discussion, disquisition, examination, investigation; issue, trial; controversy, dispute, doubt; motion, mystery, point, poser, problem, proposition, topic.

questionable adj ambiguous, controversial, controvertible, debatable, doubtful, disputable, equivocal, problematic, suspicious.

quick adj active, agile, alert, animated, brisk, lively, nimble, prompt, ready, smart, sprightly; expeditious, fast, fleet, flying, hasty, hurried, rapid, speedy, swift; adroit, apt, clever, dextrous, expert, skilful; choleric, hasty, impetuous, irascible, irritable, passionate, peppery, petulant, precipitate, sharp, unceremonious, testy, touchy, waspish; alive, animate, live, living.

quicken vb animate, energise, resuscitate, revivify, vivify; cheer, enliven, invigorate, reinvigorate, revive, whet; accelerate, dispatch, expedite, hasten, hurry, speed; actuate, excite, incite, kindle, refresh, sharpen, stimulate.

quiet adj hushed, motionless, quiescent, still, unmoved; calm, contented, gentle, mild, meek, modest, peaceable, peaceful, placid, silent, smooth, tranquil, undemonstrative, unobtrusive, unruffled; contented, patient; retired, secluded. • n calmness, peace, repose, rest, silence.

quieten vb arrest, discontinue, intermit, interrupt, still, stop, suspend; allay, appease, calm, compose, lull, pacify, sober, soothe, tranquillise; hush, silence, still; alleviate, assuage, blunt, dull, mitigate, moderate, mollify, soften.

quit vb absolve, acquit, deliver, free, release; clear, deliver, discharge from, free, liberate, relieve; acquit, behave, conduct; carry through, perform; discharge, pay, repay, requite; relinquish, renounce, resign, stop, surrender; depart from, leave, withdraw from; abandon, desert, forsake, forswear.

quite adv completely, entirely, exactly, perfectly, positively, precisely, totally, wholly.

quiz vb examine, question; peer at; banter, hoax, puzzle, ridicule.

quotation n citation, clipping, cutting, extract, excerpt, reference, selection; estimate, tender.

quote vb adduce, cite, excerpt, extract, illustrate, instance, name, repeat; estimate, tender.

R

race¹ n ancestry, breed, family, generation, house, kindred, line, lineage, strain; clan, folk, nation, people, tribe; children, descendants, issue, stock.

race² vb career, compete, contest, course, hasten, hurry, run, speed. • n career, chase, competition, contest, course, dash, heat, match, pursuit, run.

rack vb agonise, distress, excruciate, rend, torment, torture, wring; exhaust, force, harass, oppress, strain, stretch, wrest. • n agony, anguish, pang, torment, torture; crib, manger; neck, crag; dampness, mist, moisture, vapour.

racket n clamour, clatter, din, dissipation, disturbance, fracas, frolic, hubbub, noise, outcry, tumult, uproar; game, graft, scheme.

radiant adj beaming, brilliant, effulgent, glittering, glorious, luminous, lustrous, resplendent, shining, sparkling, splendid; ecstatic, happy.

radiate vb beam, gleam, glitter, shine; emanate, emit; diffuse, spread.

radical adj constitutional, deep-seated, essential, fundamental, ingrained, inherent, innate, native, natural, organic, original, uncompromising; original, primitive, simple, uncompounded, underived; complete, entire, extreme, fanatic, fundamental, insurgent, perfect, rebellious, thorough, total. • n etymon, radix, root; fanatic.

rage vb bluster, boil, chafe, foam, fret, fume, ravage, rave. • n excitement, frenzy, fury, madness, passion, rampage, raving, vehemence, wrath; craze, fashion, mania, mode, style.

raid vb assault, forage, invade, pillage, plunder. • n attack, foray, invasion, inroad, plunder.

raise vb boost, construct, erect, heave,hoist, lift, uplift, upraise, rear; advance, elevate, ennoble, exalt, promote; advance, aggravate, amplify, augment, enhance, heighten, increase, invigorate; arouse, awake, cause, effect, excite, originate, produce, rouse, stir up, occasion, start; assemble, collect, get, levy, obtain; breed, cultivate, grow, propagate, rear; ferment, leaven.

ramble vb digress, maunder, range, roam, rove, saunter, straggle, stray, stroll, wander. • n excursion, roving, tour, trip, stroll, wandering.

rancid adj bad, fetid, foul, fusty, musty, offensive, rank, sour, stinking, tainted.

random adj accidental, casual, chance, fortuitous, haphazard, irregular, stray, wandering.

range vb course, cruise, extend, ramble, roam, rove, straggle, stray, stroll, wander; bend, lie, run; arrange, class, dispose, rank. • n file, line, row, rank, tier; class, kind, order, sort; excursion, expedition, ramble, roving, wandering; amplitude, bound, command, compass, distance, extent, latitude, scope; compass, register.

rank[1] vb arrange, class, classify, range. • n file, line, order, range, row, tier; class, division, group, order, series; birth, blood, caste, degree, estate, grade, position, quality, sphere, stakes, standing; distinction, eminence, nobility.

rank[2] adj dense, exuberant, luxuriant, overabundant, overgrown, vigorous, wild; excessive, extreme, extravagant, flagrant, gross, rampant, sheer, unmitigated, utter, violent; fetid, foul, fusty, musty, offensive, rancid.

ransack vb pillage, plunder, ravage, rifle, sack, strip; explore, overhaul, rummage.

ransom vb deliver, emancipate, free, liberate, redeem, rescue, unfetter. • n deliverance, liberation, redemption, release.

rapid adj fast, fleet, quick, swift; brisk, expeditious, hasty, hurried, quick, speedy.

rapture n delight, exultation, enthusiasm, rhapsody; beatification, beatitude, bliss, ecstasy, felicity, happiness, joy, transport.

rare[1] adj sparse, subtle, thin; extraordinary, infrequent, scarce, singular, strange, uncommon, unique, unusual; choice, excellent, exquisite, fine, incomparable, inimitable.

rare[2] adj bloody, underdone.

rascal n blackguard, caitiff, knave, miscreant, rogue, reprobate, scallywag, scapegrace, scamp, scoundrel, vagabond, villain.

rash[1] adj adventurous, audacious, careless, foolhardy, hasty, headlong, headstrong, heedless, incautious, inconsiderate, indiscreet, injudicious, impetuous, impulsive, incautious, precipitate, quick, rapid, reckless, temerarious, thoughtless, unguarded, unwary, venturesome.

rash[2] n breaking-out, efflorescence, eruption; epidemic, flood, outbreak, plague, spate.

rate[1] vb appraise, compute, estimate, value. • n cost, price; class, degree, estimate, rank, value, valuation, worth; proportion, ration; assessment, charge, impost, tax.

rate[2] vb abuse, berate, censure, chide, criticise, find fault, reprimand, reprove, scold.

ratify vb confirm, corroborate, endorse, establish, seal, settle, substantiate; approve, bind, consent, sanction.

ration vb apportion, deal, distribute, dole, restrict. • n allowance, portion, quota, share.

rational adj intellectual, reasoning; equitable, fair, fit, just, moderate, natural, normal, proper, reasonable, right; discreet, enlightened, intelligent, judicious, sagacious, sensible, sound, wise.

raucous adj harsh, hoarse, husky, rough.

ravenous adj devouring, ferocious, gluttonous, greedy, insatiable, omnivorous, voracious.

raving adj delirious, deranged, distracted, frantic, frenzied, furious, infuriated, mad, phrenetic, raging. • n delirium, frenzy, fury, madness, rage.

raw adj fresh, inexperienced, unpractised, unprepared, unseasoned, untried, unskilled; crude, green, immature, unfinished, unripe; bare, chaffed, excoriated, galled, sensitive, sore; bleak, chilly, cold; uncooked.

ray n beam, emanation, gleam, moonbeam, radiance, shaft, streak, sunbeam.

reach vb extend, stretch; grasp, hit, strike, touch; arrive at, attain, gain, get, obtain, win. • n capability, capacity, grasp.

ready vb arrange, equip, organise, prepare. • adj

alert, expeditious, prompt, quick, punctual, speedy; adroit, apt, clever, dextrous, expert, facile, handy, keen, nimble, prepared, prompt, ripe, quick, sharp, skilful, smart; cheerful, disposed, eager, free, inclined, willing; accommodating, available, convenient, near, handy; easy, facile, fluent, offhand, opportune, short, spontaneous.

real *adj* absolute, actual, certain, literal, positive, practical, substantial, substantive, veritable; authentic, genuine, true; essential.

realise *vb* accomplish, achieve, discharge, effect, effectuate, perfect, perform; apprehend, comprehend, experience, recognise, understand; externalise, substantiate; acquire, earn, gain, get, net, obtain, produce, sell.

really *adv* absolutely, actually, certainly, indeed, positively, truly, verily, veritably.

rear[1] *adj* aft, back, following, hind, last. • *n* background, reverse, setting; heel, posterior, rear end, rump, stern, tail; path, trail, train, wake.

rear[2] *vb* construct, elevate, erect, hoist, lift, raise; cherish, educate, foster, instruct, nourish, nurse, nurture, train; breed, grow; rouse, stir up.

reason *vb* argue, conclude, debate, deduce, draw from, infer, intellectualise, think, trace. • *n* faculty, intellect, intelligence, judgment, mind, principle, sanity, sense, thinking, understanding; account, argument, basis, cause, consideration, excuse, explanation, gist, ground, motive, occasion, pretence, proof; aim, design, end, object, purpose; argument, reasoning; common sense, reasonableness, wisdom; equity, fairness, justice, right; exposition, rationale, theory.

reasonable *adj* equitable, fair, fit, honest, just, proper, rational, right, suitable; enlightened, intelligent, judicious, sagacious, sensible, wise; considerable, fair, moderate, tolerable; credible, intellectual, plausible, well-founded; sane, sober, sound; cheap, inexpensive, low-priced.

rebel *vb* mutiny, resist, revolt, strike. • *adj* insubordinate, insurgent, mutinous, rebellious.

rebellion *n* anarchy, insubordination, insurrection, mutiny, resistance, revolt, revolution.

rebellious *adj* contumacious, defiant, disloyal, disobedient, insubordinate, intractable, obstinate, mutinous, rebel, refractory, seditious.

recall *vb* abjure, abnegate, annul, cancel, countermand, deny, nullify, overrule, recant, repeal, repudiate, rescind, retract, revoke, swallow, withdraw; commemorate, recollect, remember, retrace, review, revive.

recapitulate *vb* epitomise, recite, rehearse, reiterate, repeat, restate, review, summarise.

receive *vb* accept, acquire, derive, gain, get, obtain, take; admit, shelter, take in; entertain, greet, welcome; allow, permit, tolerate; adopt, approve, believe, credit, embrace, follow, learn, understand; accommodate, admit, carry, contain,

hold, include, retain; bear, encounter, endure, experience, meet, suffer, sustain.

recent *adj* fresh, new, novel; latter, modern, young; deceased, foregoing, late, preceding.

reception *n* acceptance, receipt, receiving; entertainment, greeting, welcome; levee, soiree, party; admission, belief, recognition.

reckless *adj* breakneck, careless, desperate, devil-may-care, flighty, foolhardy, giddy, harebrained, headlong, heedless, inattentive, improvident, imprudent, inconsiderate, indifferent, indiscreet, mindless, negligent, rash, regardless.

reckon *vb* calculate, cast, compute, consider, count, enumerate, guess, number; account, class, esteem, estimate, regard, repute, value.

reclaim *vb* amend, correct, reform; recover, redeem, regenerate, regain, reinstate, restore.

recline *vb* couch, lean, lie, lounge, repose, rest.

reclusive *adj* recluse, retired, secluded, sequestered, sequestrated, solitary.

recognise *vb* apprehend, identify, perceive, remember; acknowledge, admit, avow, confess, own; allow, concede, grant; greet, salute.

recognition *n* identification, memory, recollection, remembrance; acknowledgement, appreciation, avowal, comprehension, confession, notice; allowance, concession.

recoil *vb* react, rebound, reverberate; retire, retreat, withdraw; blench, fail, falter, quail, shrink.

recollect *vb* recall, remember, reminisce.

recommend *vb* approve, commend, endorse, praise, sanction; commend, commit; advise, counsel, prescribe, suggest.

reconcile *vb* appease, conciliate, pacify, placate, propitiate, reunite; content, harmonise, regulate; adjust, compose, heal, settle.

record *vb* chronicle, enter, note, register. • *n* account, annals, archive, chronicle, diary, docket, enrolment, entry, file, list, minute, memoir, memorandum, memorial, note, proceedings, registry, report, roll, score; mark, memorial, relic, trace, track, trail, vestige; memory, remembrance; achievement, career, history.

recover *vb* recapture, reclaim, regain; rally, recruit, repair, retrieve; cure, heal, restore, revive; redeem, rescue, salvage, save; convalesce, rally.

recreation *n* amusement, cheer, diversion, entertainment, fun, game, leisure, pastime, play, relaxation, sport.

recruit *vb* repair, replenish; recover, refresh, regain, reinvigorate, renew, renovate, restore, retrieve, revive, strengthen, supply. • *n* auxiliary, beginner, helper, learner, novice, tyro.

rectify *vb* adjust, amend, better, correct, emend, improve, mend, redress, reform, regulate.

rectitude *n* conscientiousness, equity, goodness, honesty, integrity, justice, principle, probity, right, righteousness, uprightness.

recur *vb* reappear, resort, return, revert.

redemption *n* buying, compensation, recovery, repurchase, retrieval; deliverance, liberation, ransom, release, rescue, salvation; discharge, fulfilment, performance.

reduce *vb* bring, reduce; form, make, model, mould, remodel, render, resolve, shape; abate, abbreviate, abridge, attenuate, contract, curtail, decimate, decrease, diminish, lessen, minimise, shorten, thin; abase, debase, degrade, depress, dwarf, impair, lower, weaken; capture, conquer, master, overpower, overthrow, subject, subdue, subjugate, vanquish; impoverish, ruin; resolve.

redundant *adj* copious, excessive, exuberant, fulsome, inordinate, lavish, needless, overflowing, overmuch, plentiful, prodigal, superabundant, replete, superfluous, unnecessary, useless; diffuse, tautological, verbose, wordy.

reel[1] *n* capstan, winch, windlass; bobbin, spool.

reel[2] *vb* falter, flounder, heave, lurch, pitch, plunge, rear, rock, roll, stagger, sway, toss, totter, tumble, wallow, welter, vacillate; spin, swing, turn, twirl, wheel, whirl. • *n* gyre, pirouette, spin, turn, twirl, wheel, whirl.

refer *vb* commit, consign, direct, leave, relegate, send, submit; ascribe, assign, attribute, impute; appertain, belong, concern, pertain, point, relate, respect, touch; appeal, apply, consult; advert, allude, cite, quote.

referee *vb* arbitrate, judge, umpire. • *n* arbiter, arbitrator, judge, umpire.

reference *n* concern, connection, regard, respect; allusion, ascription, citation, hint, intimation, mark, reference, relegation.

refine *vb* clarify, cleanse, defecate, fine, purify; cultivate, humanise, improve, polish, rarefy.

refined *adj* courtly, cultured, genteel, polished, polite; discerning, discriminating, fastidious, sensitive; filtered, processed, purified.

reflect *vb* copy, imitate, mirror, reproduce; cogitate, consider, contemplate, deliberate, meditate, muse, ponder, ruminate, study, think.

reflection *n* echo, shadow; cogitation, consideration, contemplation, deliberation, idea, meditation, musing, thought; aspersion, blame, censure, criticism, disparagement, reproach, slur.

reform *vb* amend, ameliorate, better, correct, improve, mend, meliorate, rectify, reclaim, redeem, regenerate, repair, restore; reconstruct, remodel, reshape. • *n* amendment, correction, progress, reconstruction, rectification.

refrain[1] *vb* abstain, cease, desist, forbear, stop, withold.

refrain[2] *n* chorus, song, undersong.

refresh *vb* air, brace, cheer, cool, enliven, exhilarate, freshen, invigorate, reanimate, recreate, recruit, reinvigorate, revive, regale, slake.

refuge *n* asylum, covert, harbour, haven, protection, retreat, safety, sanction, security, shelter.

refund *vb* reimburse, repay, restore, return. • *n* reimbursement, repayment.

refuse[1] *n* chaff, discard, draff, dross, dregs, garbage, junk, leavings, lees, litter, lumber, offal, recrement, remains, rubbish, scoria, scum, sediment, slag, sweepings, trash, waste.

refuse[2] *vb* decline, deny, withhold; decline, disallow, disavow, exclude, rebuff, reject, renege, renounce, repel, repudiate, revoke, veto.

regal *adj* imposing, imperial, kingly, noble, royal, sovereign.

regard *vb* behold, gaze, look, notice, mark, observe, remark, see, view, watch; attend to, consider, heed, mind, respect; esteem, honour, respect, revere, reverence, value; account, believe, consider, estimate, deem, hold, imagine, reckon, suppose, think, treat, use. • *n* gaze, look, view; attention, care, concern, consideration, heed, notice, observance; account, reference, relation, respect, view; affection, attachment, concern, consideration, deference, esteem, estimation, honour, interest, liking, love, reverence, sympathy, value; account, eminence, note, reputation, repute; condition, consideration, point.

regardless *adj* careless, disregarding, heedless, inattentive, indifferent, mindless, neglectful, negligent, unconcerned, unmindful, unobservant. • *adv* however, irrespectively, nevertheless, none the less, notwithstanding.

region *n* climate, clime, country, district, division, latitude, locale, locality, province, quarter, scene, territory, tract; area, neighbourhood, part, place, portion, spot, space, sphere, vicinity.

register *vb* delineate, portray, record, show. • *n* annals, archive, catalogue, chronicle, list, record, roll, schedule; compass, range.

regret *vb* bewail, deplore, grieve, lament, repine, sorrow; bemoan, repent, mourn, rue. • *n* concern, disappointment, grief, lamentation, rue, sorrow, trouble; compunction, contrition, penitence, remorse, repentance, repining.

regular *adj* conventional, natural, normal, ordinary, typical; correct, customary, cyclic, established, fixed, habitual, periodic, periodical, usual, recurring, reasonable, rhythmic, seasonal, stated, usual; steady, constant, uniform, even; just, methodical, orderly, punctual, systematic, uniform, unvarying; complete, genuine, indubitable, out-and-out, perfect, thorough; balanced, consistent, symmetrical.

regulate *vb* adjust, arrange, dispose, methodise, order, organise, settle, standardise, time, systematise; conduct, control, direct, govern, guide.

regulation *n* adjustment, arrangement, control, disposal, disposition, law, management, order, ordering, precept, rule, settlement.

reign vb administer, command, govern, influence, predominate, prevail, rule.

rein vb bridle, check, control, curb, guide, harness, hold, restrain, restrict. • n bridle, check, curb, harness, restraint, restriction.

reject vb cashier, discard, dismiss, eject, exclude, pluck; decline, deny, disallow, despise, disapprove, disbelieve, rebuff, refuse, renounce, repel, repudiate, scout, slight, spurn, veto. • n cast-off, discard, failure, refusal, repudiation.

rejoice vb cheer, delight, enliven, enrapture, exhilarate, gladden, gratify, please, transport; crow, exult, delight, gloat, glory, jubilate.

rejoin vb answer, rebut, respond, retort.

relate vb describe, detail, mention, narrate, recite, recount, report, tell; apply, connect.

relation n account, chronicle, description, detail, explanation, history, mention, narration, narrative, recital, rehearsal, report, statement, story, tale; affinity, application, bearing, connection, correlation, dependency, pertinence, relationship; concern, reference, regard, respect; alliance, connection, nearness, propinquity, rapport; affinity, blood, consanguinity, kin, kinship, relationship; kinsman.

relax vb loose, loosen, slacken, unbrace, unstrain; debilitate, enervate, enfeeble, prostrate, unbrace, unstring, weaken; abate, diminish, lessen, mitigate, reduce, remit; amuse, divert, ease, entertain, recreate, unbend.

release vb deliver, discharge, disengage, exempt, extricate, free, liberate, loose, unloose; acquit, discharge, quit, relinquish, remit.

relentless adj cruel, hard, impenitent, implacable, inexorable, merciless, obdurate, pitiless, rancorous, remorseless, ruthless, unappeasable, uncompassionate, unfeeling, unforgiving, unmerciful, unpitying, unrelenting, unyielding.

relevant adj applicable, appropriate, apposite, apt, apropos, fit, germane, pertinent, proper.

reliable adj authentic, certain, constant, dependable, sure, trustworthy, trusty, unfailing.

reliance n assurance, confidence, credence, dependence, hope, trust.

relief n aid, alleviation, amelioration, assistance, assuagement, comfort, deliverance, ease, easement, help, mitigation, reinforcement, respite, rest, succour, softening, support; indemnification, redress, remedy; embossment, projection, prominence, protrusion; clearness, distinction.

relieve vb aid, comfort, free, help, succour, support, sustain; abate, allay, alleviate, assuage, cure, diminish, ease, lessen, lighten, mitigate, remedy, remove, soothe; indemnify, redress, right, repair; disengage, free, release, remedy.

religious adj devotional, devout, god-fearing, godly, holy, pious, prayerful, spiritual; conscientious, exact, rigid, scrupulous, strict; canonical, divine, theological.

relinquish vb abandon, desert, forsake, forswear, leave, quit, renounce, resign, vacate; abdicate, cede, forbear, forego, give up, surrender.

relish vb appreciate, enjoy, like, prefer; season, flavour, taste. • n appetite, appreciation, enjoyment, fondness, gratification, gusto, inclination, liking, partiality, predilection, taste, zest; cast, manner, quality, savour, seasoning, sort, tinge, tang; appetiser, condiment; flavour.

reluctant adj averse, backward, disinclined, hesitant, indisposed, loath, unwilling.

rely vb confide, count, depend, hope, lean, reckon, repose, trust.

remain vb abide, continue, endure, last, stay; exceed, survive; abide, continue, dwell, halt, rest, sojourn, stay, stop, tarry, wait.

remainder n balance, excess, leavings, remains, remnant, residue, rest, surplus.

remark vb heed, notice, observe, regard; comment, express, mention, observe, say, state, utter. • n consideration, heed, notice, observation, regard; annotation, comment, gloss, note, stricture; assertion, averment, declaration, saying, statement, utterance.

remarkable adj conspicuous, distinguished, eminent, extraordinary, famous, notable, noteworthy, noticeable, pre-eminent, rare, singular, strange, striking, uncommon, unusual.

remedy vb cure, heal, help, palliate, relieve; amend, correct, rectify, redress, repair, restore, retrieve. • n antidote, antitoxin, corrective, counteractive, cure, help, medicine, nostrum, panacea, restorative, specific; redress, reparation, restitution, restoration; aid, assistance, relief.

remiss adj backward, behindhand, dilatory, indolent, languid, lax, slack, slow, tardy; careless, dilatory, heedless, idle, inattentive, neglectful, negligent, shiftless, slack, slothful, slow.

remission n abatement, diminution, lessening, mitigation, moderation, relaxation; cancellation, discharge, release, relinquishment; intermission, interruption, rest, stop, stoppage, suspense, suspension; absolution, acquittal, discharge, excuse, exoneration, forgiveness, pardon.

remorse n compunction, contrition, penitence, qualm, regret, repentance, reproach, sorrow.

remorseless adj cruel, barbarous, hard, harsh, implacable, inexorable, merciless, pitiless, relentless, ruthless, savage, unrelenting.

remote adj distant, far, out-of-the-way; alien, far-fetched, foreign, inappropriate, unconnected, unrelated; abstracted, separated; inconsiderable, slight; isolated, removed, secluded.

removal n abstraction, departure, dislodgement, displacement, relegation, remove, shift, transference; elimination, extraction, withdrawal; abatement, destruction; discharge, dismissal, ejection.

remove vb carry, dislodge, displace, shift, transfer, transport; abstract, extract, withdraw; abate, banish, destroy, suppress; cashier, depose, discharge, dismiss, eject, expel, oust; depart, move.

render vb restore, return, surrender; assign, deliver, give, present; afford, contribute, furnish, supply, yield; construe, interpret, translate.

renounce vb abjure, abnegate, decline, deny, disclaim, disown, forswear, neglect, recant, repudiate, reject, slight; abandon, abdicate, drop, forego, forsake, desert, leave, quit, relinquish.

renovate vb reconstitute, re-establish, refresh, refurbish, renew, restore, revamp; reanimate, recreate, regenerate, reproduce, revive.

renown n celebrity, distinction, eminence, fame, figure, glory, honour, greatness, name, note, notability, notoriety, reputation, repute.

rent[1] n breach, break, crack, cleft, crevice, fissure, flaw, fracture, gap, laceration, opening, rift, rupture, separation, split, tear; schism.

rent[2] vb hire, lease, let. • n income, rental.

repair[1] vb mend, patch, piece, refit, retouch, tinker, vamp; correct, recruit, restore, retrieve.

repair[2] vb betake oneself, go, move, resort, turn.

repay vb refund, reimburse, restore, return; compensate, recompense, remunerate, reward, satisfy; avenge, retaliate, revenge.

repeal vb abolish, annul, cancel, recall, rescind, reverse, revoke.

repeat vb double, duplicate, iterate; cite, narrate, quote, recapitulate, recite, rehearse; echo, renew, reproduce. • n duplicate, duplication, echo, iteration, recapitulation, reiteration.

repel vb beat, disperse, repulse, scatter; check, confront, oppose, parry, rebuff, resist, withstand; decline, refuse, reject; disgust, revolt, sicken.

repellent adj abhorrent, disgusting, forbidding, repelling, repugnant, repulsive, revolting.

repent vb atone, regret, relent, rue, sorrow.

repentance n compunction, contriteness, contrition, penitence, regret, remorse.

repentant adj contrite, penitent, regretful, remorseful, rueful, sorrowful, sorry.

repetition n harping, iteration, recapitulation, reiteration; diffuseness, redundancy, tautology, verbosity; narration, recital, rehearsal, relation, retailing; recurrence, renewal.

replace vb re-establish, reinstate, reset; refund, repay, restore; succeed, supersede, supplant.

replenish vb fill, refill, renew, re-supply; enrich, furnish, provide, store, supply.

replica n autograph, copy, duplicate, facsimile, reproduction.

reply vb answer, echo, rejoin, respond. • n acknowledgement, answer, rejoinder, repartee, replication, response, retort.

report vb announce, annunciate, communicate, declare; advertise, broadcast, bruit, describe, detail, herald, mention, narrate, noise, promulgate, publish, recite, relate, rumour, state, tell; minute,

record. • n account, announcement, communication, declaration, statement; advice, description, detail, narration, narrative, news, recital, story, tale, tidings; gossip, hearsay, rumour; clap, detonation, discharge, explosion, noise, repercussion, sound; fame, reputation, repute; account, bulletin, minute, note, record, statement.

repose[1] vb compose, recline, rest, settle; couch, lie, recline, sleep, slumber; confide, lean. • n quiet, recumbence, recumbency, rest, sleep, slumber; breathing time, inactivity, leisure, respite, relaxation; calm, ease, peace, peacefulness, quiet, quietness, quietude, stillness, tranquillity.

repose[2] vb place, put, stake; deposit, lodge.

reprehensible adj blameable, blameworthy, censurable, condemnable, culpable, reprovable.

represent vb exhibit, express, show; delineate, depict, describe, draw, portray, sketch; act, impersonate, mimic, personate, personify; exemplify, illustrate, image, portray, reproduce.

representation n delineation, exhibition, show; impersonation, personation, simulation; account, description, narration, narrative, relation, statement; image, likeness, model, portraiture, resemblance, semblance; sight, spectacle; expostulation, remonstrance.

representative adj figurative, illustrative, symbolic, typical; delegated, deputed, representing. • n agent, commissioner, delegate, deputy, emissary, envoy, legate, lieutenant, messenger, proxy.

repress vb choke, crush, dull, overcome, overpower, silence, smother, subdue, suppress, quell; bridle, chasten, chastise, check, control, curb, restrain; appease, calm, quiet.

reprimand vb admonish, blame, censure, chide, rebuke, reprehend, reproach, reprove, upbraid.

reproach vb blame, censure, rebuke, reprehend, reprimand, reprove, upbraid; abuse, accuse, asperse, condemn, defame, discredit, disparage, revile, traduce, vilify.

reproduce vb copy, duplicate, emulate, imitate, print, repeat, represent; breed, generate, procreate, propagate.

reproof n admonition, animadversion, blame, castigation, censure, chiding, condemnation, correction, criticism, lecture, monition, objurgation, rating, rebuke, reprehension, reprimand, reproach, reproval, upbraiding.

repudiate vb abjure, deny, disavow, discard, disclaim, disown, nullify, reject, renounce.

repugnant adj incompatible, inconsistent, irreconcilable; adverse, antagonistic, contrary, hostile, inimical, opposed, opposing, unfavourable; detestable, distasteful, offensive, repellent.

repulse vb check, defeat, refuse, reject, repel. • n repelling, repulsion; denial, refusal; disappointment, failure.

repulsion n abhorrence, antagonism, anticipation, aversion, discard, disgust, dislike, hatred, hostility, loathing, rebuff, rejection, repugnance, repulse, spurning.

repulsive *adj* abhorrent, cold, disagreeable, disgusting, forbidding, frigid, harsh, hateful, loathsome, nauseating, nauseous, odious, offensive, repellent, repugnant, reserved, revolting, sickening, ugly, unpleasant.

reputable *adj* creditable, estimable, excellent, good, honourable, respectable, worthy.

reputation *n* account, character, fame, mark, name, repute; celebrity, credit, distinction, eclat, esteem, estimation, fame, glory, honour, prestige, regard, renown, report, repute, respect.

request *vb* ask, beg, beseech, call, claim, demand, desire, entreat, pray, solicit, supplicate. • *n* asking, entreaty, importunity, invitation, petition, prayer, solicitation, suit, supplication.

require *vb* beg, beseech, bid, claim, crave, demand, dun, importune, invite, pray, requisition, request, sue, summon; need, want; direct, enjoin, exact, order, prescribe.

requirement *n* claim, demand, exigency, market, need, needfulness, requisite, requisition, request, urgency, want; behest, bidding, charge, claim, command, decree, exaction, injunction, mandate, order, precept.

rescue *vb* deliver, extricate, free, liberate, preserve, recover, redeem, release, save.

research *vb* analyse, examine, explore, inquire, investigate, probe, study. • *n* analysis, examination, exploration, inquiry, investigation.

resemblance *n* affinity, agreement, analogy, likeness, semblance, similarity, similitude; counterpart, facsimile, image, likeness.

resentful *adj* angry, bitter, choleric, huffy, hurt, irascible, irritable, malignant, revengeful, sore.

resentment *n* acrimony, anger, annoyance, bitterness, choler, displeasure, dudgeon, fury, gall, grudge, heartburning, huff, indignation, ire, irritation, pique, rage, soreness, spleen, sulks, umbrage, vexation, wrath.

reservation *n* reserve, suppression; appropriation, booking, exception, restriction, saving; proviso, salvo; custody, park, reserve, sanctuary.

reserve *vb* hold, husband, keep, retain, store. • *adj* alternate, auxiliary, spare, substitute. • *n* reservation; aloofness, backwardness, closeness, coldness, concealment, constraint, suppression, reservedness, retention, restraint, reticence, uncommunicativeness, unresponsiveness; coyness, demureness, modesty, shyness, taciturnity; park, reservation, sanctuary.

reserved *adj* coy, demure, modest, shy, taciturn; aloof, backward, cautious, cold, distant, incommunicative, restrained, reticent, self-controlled, unsociable, unsocial; bespoken, booked, excepted, held, kept, retained, set apart, taken.

reside *vb* abide, domicile, domiciliate, dwell, inhabit, live, lodge, remain, room, sojourn, stay.

residence *n* inhabitance, inhabitancy, sojourn, stay, stop, tarrying; abode, domicile, dwelling, habitation, home, house, lodging, mansion.

resign *vb* abandon, abdicate, abjure, cede, commit, disclaim, forego, forsake, leave, quit, relinquish, renounce, surrender, yield.

resignation *n* abandonment, abdication, relinquishment, renunciation, retirement, surrender; acquiescence, compliance, endurance, forbearance, patience, submission, sufferance.

resist *vb* assail, attack, baffle, block, check, confront, counteract, disappoint, frustrate, hinder, impede, impugn, neutralise, obstruct, oppose, rebel, rebuff, stand against, stem, stop.

resolute *adj* bold, constant, decided, determined, earnest, firm, fixed, game, hardy, inflexible, persevering, pertinacious, relentless, resolved, staunch, steadfast, steady, stout, stouthearted, sturdy, tenacious, unalterable, unbending, undaunted, unflinching, unwavering.

resolution *n* boldness, disentanglement, explication, unravelling; backbone, constancy, courage, decision, determination, earnestness, energy, firmness, fortitude, grit, hardihood, inflexibility, intention, manliness, pluck, perseverance, purpose, relentlessness, resolve, resoluteness, stamina, steadfastness, steadiness, tenacity.

resolve *vb* analyse, disperse, scatter, separate, reduce; change, dissolve, liquefy, melt, reduce, transform; decipher, disentangle, elucidate, explain, interpret, unfold, solve, unravel; conclude, decide, determine, fix, intend, purpose, will. • *n* conclusion, decision, determination, intention, will; declaration, resolution.

resort *vb* frequent, haunt; assemble, congregate, convene, go, repair. • *n* application, expedient, recourse; haunt, refuge, rendezvous, retreat, spa; assembling, meeting; recourse, reference.

resource *n* dependence, resort; appliance, contrivance, expedient, instrumentality, means.

resources *npl* capital, funds, income, money, property, reserve, supplies, wealth.

respect *vb* admire, esteem, honour, prize, regard, revere, reverence, spare, value, venerate; consider, heed, notice, observe. • *n* attention, civility, courtesy, consideration, deference, estimation, homage, honour, notice, politeness, recognition, regard, reverence, veneration; consideration, favour, goodwill, kind; aspect, bearing, connection, feature, matter, particular, point, reference, regard, relation.

respectable *adj* considerable, estimable, honourable, presentable, proper, upright, worthy; considerable, mediocre, moderate.

respectful *adj* ceremonious, civil, courteous, decorous, deferential, dutiful, formal, polite.

respond vb answer, reply, rejoin; accord, correspond, suit.

responsible adj accountable, amenable, answerable, liable, trustworthy.

rest¹ vb cease, desist, halt, hold, pause, repose, stop; breathe, relax, repose, unbend; repose, sleep, slumber; lean, lie, lounge, perch, recline, ride; acquiesce, confide, trust; confide, lean, rely, trust; calm, comfort, ease. • n fixity, immobility, inactivity, motionlessness, quiescence, quiet, repose; hush, peace, peacefulness, quiet, quietness, relief, security, stillness, tranquillity; cessation, intermission, interval, lull, pause, relaxation, respite, stop, stay; siesta, sleep, slumber; death; brace, prop, stay, support.

rest² vb be left, remain. • n balance, remainder, remnant, residuum; overplus, surplus.

restive adj mulish, obstinate, unwilling; impatient, recalcitrant, restless, uneasy, unquiet.

restless adj disquieted, disturbed, restive, sleepless, uneasy, unquiet, unresting; changeable, inconstant, irresolute, unsettled, unstable, unsteady, vacillating; active, astatic, roving, transient, unsettled, unstable, wandering; agitated, fidgety, fretful, turbulent.

restorative n corrective, curative, cure, healing, medicine, remedy, reparative, stimulant.

restore vb refund, repay, return; caulk, cobble, emend, heal, mend, patch, reintegrate, re-establish, rehabilitate, reinstate, renew, repair, replace, retrieve, splice, tinker; cure, heal, recover, revive; resuscitate, revive.

restraint n bridle, check, coercion, control, compulsion, constraint, curb, discipline, repression, suppression; arrest, deterrence, hindrance, inhibition, limitation, prevention, prohibition, restriction, stay, stop; confinement, detention, imprisonment, shackles; constraint, reserve.

restrict vb bound, circumscribe, confine, limit, qualify, restrain, straiten.

result vb accrue, arise, come, ensue, flow, follow, issue, originate, proceed, spring, rise; end, eventuate, terminate. • n conclusion, consequence, deduction, inference, outcome; consequence, corollary, effect, end, event, eventuality, fruit, issue, outcome, product, sequel, termination; conclusion, decision, determination, finding, resolution, resolve, verdict.

resume vb continue, recommence, restart.

résumé n abstract, curriculum vitae, epitome, recapitulation, summary, synopsis.

retain vb detain, hold, husband, keep, preserve, recall, recollect, remember, reserve, save, withhold; engage, maintain.

retainer n adherent, attendant, dependant, follower, hanger-on, servant.

retaliate vb avenge, match, repay, requite, retort, return, turn.

reticent adj close, reserved, secretive, silent, taciturn, uncommunicative.

retinue n bodyguard, cortege, entourage, escort, followers, household, ménage, suite, tail, train.

retire vb discharge, remove, shelve, superannuate, withdraw; depart, leave, remove, retreat.

retired adj abstracted, removed, withdrawn; apart, private, secret, sequestrated, solitary.

retiring adj coy, demure, diffident, modest, reserved, retreating, shy, withdrawing.

retreat vb recoil, retire, withdraw; recede. • n departure, recession, recoil, retirement, withdrawal; privacy, seclusion, solitude; asylum, habitat, haunt, recess, refuge, resort, shelter.

retribution n compensation, desert, judgement, nemesis, penalty, recompense, repayment, requital, retaliation, revenge, vengeance.

retrieve vb recall, recover, recoup, recruit, reestablish, regain, repair, restore.

return vb reappear, recoil, recur, revert; answer, reply, respond; recriminate, retort; convey, give, communicate, reciprocate, recompense, refund, remit, repay, report, requite, send, tell, transmit; elect. • n payment, reimbursement, remittance, repayment; recompense, recovery, recurrence, renewal, repayment, requital, restitution, reward; advantage, benefit, interest, profit.

reveal vb announce, communicate, confess, declare, disclose, discover, display, divulge, expose, impart, open, publish, tell, uncover.

revel vb carouse, disport, riot, roister, tipple; delight, indulge, luxuriate, wanton. • n carousal, feast, festival, saturnalia, spree.

revenge n malevolence, rancour, reprisal, requital, retaliation, retribution, vengeance, vindictiveness.

revenue n fruits, income, produce, proceeds, receipts, return, reward, wealth.

revere vb adore, esteem, hallow, honour, reverence, venerate, worship.

reverse vb invert, transpose; overset, overthrow, overturn, quash, subvert, undo, unmake; annul, countermand, repeal, rescind, retract, revoke; back, back up, retreat. • adj back, converse, contrary, opposite, verso. • n back, calamity, check, comedown, contrary, counterpart, defeat, opposite, tail; change, vicissitude; adversity, affliction, hardship, misadventure, mischance, misfortune, mishap, trial.

revert vb repel, reverse; backslide, lapse, recur, relapse, return.

review vb inspect, overlook, reconsider, re-examine, retrace, revise, survey; analyse, criticise, discuss, edit, judge, scrutinise, study. • n reconsideration, re-examination, re-survey, retrospect, survey; analysis, digest, synopsis; commentary, critique, criticism, notice, review, scrutiny.

revile vb abuse, asperse, backbite, calumniate,

defame, execrate, malign, reproach, slander, traduce, upbraid, vilify.

revise vb reconsider, re-examine, review; alter, amend, correct, edit, overhaul, polish, review.

revive vb reanimate, reinspire, reinspirit, reinvigorate, resuscitate, revitalise, revivify; animate, cheer, comfort, invigorate, quicken, reawaken, recover, refresh, renew, renovate, rouse, strengthen; reawake, recall.

revoke vb abolish, abrogate, annul, cancel, countermand, invalidate, quash, recall, recant, repeal, repudiate, rescind, retract.

revolt vb desert, mutiny, rebel, rise; disgust, nauseate, repel, sicken.

revolution n coup, disobedience, insurrection, mutiny, outbreak, rebellion, sedition, strike, uprising; change, innovation, reformation, transformation, upheaval; circle, circuit, cycle, lap, orbit, rotation, spin, turn.

revolve vb circle, circulate, rotate, swing, turn; devolve, return; consider, ponder, study.

revulsion n abstraction, shrinking, withdrawal; change, reaction, reversal, transition; abhorrence, disgust, loathing, repugnance.

reward vb compensate, gratify, indemnify, pay, punish, recompense, remember, remunerate, requite. • n compensation, gratification, guerdon, indemnification, pay, recompense, remuneration, requital; bounty, bonus, fee, gratuity, honorarium, meed, perquisite, premium, remembrance, tip; punishment, retribution.

rhythm n cadence, lilt, pulsation, swing; measure, metre, number, rhyme, verse.

rich adj affluent, flush, moneyed, opulent, prosperous, wealthy; costly, estimable, gorgeous, luxurious, precious, splendid, sumptuous, superb, valuable; delicious, luscious, savoury; abundant, ample, copious, enough, full, plentiful, plenteous, sufficient; fertile, fruitful, luxuriant, productive, prolific; bright, dark, deep, exuberant, vivid; harmonious, mellow, melodious, soft, sweet; comical, funny, humorous.

rid vb deliver, free, release; clear, disburden, disencumber, scour, sweep; disinherit, dispatch, dissolve, divorce, finish, sever.

riddle[1] n conundrum, enigma, mystery.

riddle[2] vb sieve, sift, perforate, permeate, spread. • n colander, sieve, strainer.

ridicule vb banter, burlesque, chaff, deride, disparage, jeer, mock, lampoon, satirise, taunt.

ridiculous adj absurd, amusing, comical, droll, eccentric, fantastic, farcical, funny, laughable, ludicrous, nonsensical, odd, outlandish, preposterous, queer, risible, waggish.

right vb adjust, correct, regulate, settle, straighten, vindicate. • adj direct, rectilinear, straight; erect, perpendicular, plumb, upright; equitable, even-handed, fair, just, justifiable, honest, lawful, legal, legitimate, rightful, square, unswerving; appropriate, becoming, correct, conventional, fit, fitting, meet, orderly, proper, reasonable, seemly, suitable, well-done; actual, genuine, real, true, unquestionable. • n authority, claim, liberty, permission, power, privilege, title; equity, good, honour, justice, legality, propriety, reason, righteousness, truth.

righteous adj devout, godly, good, holy, honest, incorrupt, just, pious, religious, saintly, uncorrupt, upright, virtuous.

rightful adj lawful, legitimate, true; appropriate, correct, deserved, due, equitable, fair, fitting, honest, just, lawful, legal, legitimate, merited, proper, reasonable, suitable, true.

rigid adj firm, hard, inflexible, stiff, stiffened, unbending, unpliant, unyielding; bristling, erect, precipitous, steep, stiff; austere, conventional, correct, exact, formal, harsh, precise, rigorous, severe, sharp, stern, strict, unmitigated.

rigour n hardness, inflexibility, rigidity, rigidness, stiffness; asperity, austerity, harshness, severity, sternness; evenness, strictness.

rim n brim, brink, border, confine, curb, edge, flange, girdle, margin, ring, skirt.

ring[1] n circle, circlet, girdle, hoop, round, whorl; cabal, clique, combination, confederacy, coterie, gang, junta, league, set.

ring[2] vb chime, clang, jingle, knell, peal, resound, reverberate, sound, tinkle, toll; call, phone, telephone.

riot n affray, altercation, brawl, broil, commotion, disturbance, fray, outbreak, pandemonium, quarrel, squabble, tumult, uproar; dissipation, excess, luxury, merrymaking, revelry.

riotous adj boisterous, luxurious, merry, revelling, unrestrained, wanton; disorderly, insubordinate, lawless, mutinous, rebellious, refractory, seditious, tumultuous, turbulent, ungovernable, unruly, violent.

ripe adj advanced, grown, mature, mellow, seasoned, soft; fit, prepared, ready; accomplished, complete, consummate, finished, perfect.

ripen vb burgeon, develop, mature, prepare.

rise vb arise, ascend, clamber, climb, levitate, mount; excel, succeed; enlarge, heighten, increase, swell, thrive; revive; grow, kindle, wax; begin, flow, head, originate, proceed, spring, start; mutiny, rebel, revolt; happen, occur. • n ascension, ascent, rising; elevation, grade, hill, slope; beginning, emergence, flow, origin, source, advance, expansion, increase.

risk vb bet, endanger, hazard, jeopardise, peril, speculate, stake, venture, wager. • n chance, danger, hazard, jeopardy, peril, venture.

rite n ceremonial, ceremony, form, formulary, ministration, observance, ordinance, ritual, rubric, sacrament, solemnity.

ritual *adj* ceremonial, conventional, formal, habitual, routine, stereotyped. • *n* ceremonial, ceremony, liturgy, observance, rite, sacrament, service; convention, form, formality, habit, practice.

rival *vb* emulate, match, oppose. • *n* antagonist, competitor, emulator, opponent.

roam *vb* jaunt, prowl, ramble, range, rove, straggle, stray, stroll, wander.

roar *vb* bawl, bellow, cry, howl, vociferate, yell; boom, peal, rattle, resound, thunder. • *n* bellow, roaring; rage, resonance, storm, thunder; cry, outcry; shout; laugh, laughter, shout.

rob *vb* despoil, fleece, pilfer, pillage, plunder, rook, strip; appropriate, deprive, embezzle.

robber *n* bandit, brigand, desperado, depredator, despoiler, footpad, freebooter, highwayman, marauder, pillager, pirate, plunderer, rifler, thief.

robe *vb* array, clothe, dress, invest. • *n* attire, costume, dress, garment, gown, habit, vestment; bathrobe, dressing gown, housecoat.

robust *adj* able-bodied, athletic, brawny, energetic, firm, forceful, hale, hardy, hearty, iron, lusty, muscular, powerful, seasoned, self-assertive, sound, stalwart, stout, strong, sturdy.

rock[1] *n* boulder, cliff, crag, reef, stone; asylum, defence, foundation, protection, refuge, strength, support; gneiss, granite, marble, slate.

rock[2] *vb* calm, cradle, lull, quiet, soothe, still, tranquillise; reel, shake, sway, teeter, totter.

rogue *n* beggar, vagabond, vagrant; caitiff, cheat, knave, rascal, scamp, scapegrace, scoundrel, sharper, swindler, trickster, villain.

role *n* character, function, impersonation, task.

roll *vb* gyrate, revolve, rotate, turn, wheel; curl, muffle, swathe, wind; bind, involve, enfold, envelop; flatten, level, smooth, spread; bowl, drive; trundle, wheel; gybe, lean, lurch, stagger, sway, yaw; billow, swell, undulate; wallow, welter; flow, glide, run. • *n* document, scroll, volume; annals, chronicle, history, record, rota; catalogue, inventory, list, register, schedule; booming, resonance, reverberation, thunder; cylinder, roller.

romance *vb* exaggerate, fantasise. • *n* fantasy, fiction, legend, novel, story, tale; exaggeration, falsehood, lie; ballad, idyll, song.

romantic *adj* extravagant, fanciful, fantastic, ideal, imaginative, sentimental, wild; chimerical, fabulous, fictitious, imaginary, improbable, legendary, picturesque, quixotic, sentimental. • *n* dreamer, idealist, visionary.

romp *vb* caper, gambol, frisk, sport.

room *n* accommodation, capacity, compass, elbowroom, expanse, extent, field, latitude, leeway, play, scope, space; place; apartment, chamber, lodging; chance, occasion, opportunity.

roomy *adj* ample, broad, capacious, comfortable, commodious, expansive, extensive, large.

root[1] *vb* anchor, embed, fasten, implant, place, settle; confirm, establish. • *n* base, bottom, foundation; cause, occasion, motive, origin, reason, source; etymon, radical, radix, stem.

root[2] *vb* destroy, eradicate, extirpate, exterminate, remove, unearth, uproot; burrow, dig, forage, grub, rummage; applaud, cheer, encourage.

rot *vb* corrupt, decay, decompose, degenerate, putrefy, spoil, taint.

rotten *adj* carious, corrupt, decomposed, fetid, putrefied, putrescent, putrid, rank, stinking; defective, unsound; corrupt, deceitful, immoral, treacherous, unsound, untrustworthy.

rough *adj* bumpy, craggy, irregular, jagged, rugged, scabrous, scraggy, scratchy, stubby, uneven; approximate, cross-grained, crude, formless, incomplete, knotty, rough-hewn, shapeless, sketchy, uncut, unfashioned, unfinished, unhewn, unpolished, unwrought, vague; bristly, bushy, coarse, disordered, hairy, hirsute, ragged, shaggy, unkempt; austere, bearish, bluff, blunt, brusque, burly, churlish, discourteous, gruff, harsh, impolite, indelicate, rude, rugged, surly, uncivil, uncourteous, ungracious, unpolished, unrefined; harsh, severe, sharp, violent; astringent, crabbed, hard, sour, tart; discordant, grating, inharmonious, jarring, raucous, scabrous, unmusical; boisterous, foul, inclement, severe, stormy, tempestuous, tumultuous, turbulent, untamed, violent, wild; acrimonious, brutal, cruel, disorderly, hard, riotous.

round *vb* curve; circuit, encircle, encompass, surround. • *adj* bulbous, circular, cylindrical, globular, orbed, orbicular, rotund, spherical; complete, considerable, entire, full, great, large, unbroken, whole; chubby, corpulent, full, plump, stout, swelling; continuous, flowing, full, harmonious, smooth; brisk, full, quick; blunt, candid, fair, frank, honest, open, plain, upright. • *adv* around, circularly, circuitously. • *prep* about, around. • *n* bout, cycle, game, lap, revolution, rotation, succession, turn; cannon, catch, dance; ball, circle, circumference, cylinder, globe, sphere; circuit, compass, perambulation, routine, tour, watch.

rouse *vb* awaken, raise, shake, wake; animate, bestir, brace, excite, inspire, kindle, rally, stimulate, whet; startle, surprise.

rout *vb* beat, conquer, defeat, discomfit, overcome, overpower, overthrow, vanquish; chase away, dispel, disperse, scatter. • *n* defeat, discomfiture, flight, ruin; concourse, multitude, rabble; brawl, disturbance, noise, roar, uproar.

route *n* course, circuit, direction, itinerary, journey, march, road, passage, path, way.

routine *adj* conventional, familiar, habitual, ordinary, standard, typical, usual; boring, dull, humdrum, predictable, tiresome. • *n* beat, custom, method, practice, procedure, rut.

row¹ *n* file, line, queue, range, rank, series, string, tier; alley, street, terrace.

row² *n* affray, altercation, brawl, commotion, dispute, disturbance, noise, outbreak, quarrel, riot, squabble, tumult, uproar.

royal *adj* august, courtly, dignified, generous, grand, imperial, kingly, kinglike, magnanimous, magnificent, majestic, monarchical, noble, princely, regal, sovereign, splendid, superb.

rub *vb* abrade, chafe, grate, graze, scrape; burnish, clean, massage, polish, scour, wipe; apply, put, smear, spread. • *n* caress, massage, polish, scouring, shine, wipe; catch, difficulty, drawback, impediment, obstacle, problem.

rubbish *n* debris, detritus, fragments, refuse, ruins, waste; dregs, dross, garbage, litter, lumber, refuse, scoria, scum, sweepings, trash, trumpery.

rude *adj* coarse, crude, ill-formed, rough, rugged, shapeless, uneven, unfashioned, unformed, unwrought; artless, barbarous, boorish, clownish, ignorant, illiterate, loutish, raw, savage, uncivilised, uncouth, uncultivated, undisciplined, unpolished, ungraceful, unskilful, unskilled, untaught, untrained, untutored; awkward, barbarous, bluff, blunt, boorish, brusque, brutal, churlish, coarse, gruff, ill-bred, impertinent, impolite, impudent, insolent, insulting, rough, saucy, savage, uncivil, uncivilised, uncourteous, unrefined; boisterous, fierce, harsh, severe, tumultuous, turbulent, violent; artless, crude, inelegant, raw, rustic, unpolished.

rudimentary *adj* elementary, embryonic, fundamental, initial, primary, undeveloped.

ruffian *n* bully, caitiff, cutthroat, hoodlum, miscreant, monster, murderer, rascal, robber, roisterer, rowdy, scoundrel, villain, wretch.

ruffle *vb* damage, derange, disarrange, dishevel, disorder, ripple, roughen, rumple; agitate, confuse, discompose, disquiet, disturb, excite, harass, irritate, molest, plague, perturb, torment, trouble, vex, worry; flounce, pucker, wrinkle.

rugged *adj* austere, bristly, coarse, crabbed, cragged, craggy, hard, hardy, irregular, ragged, robust, rough, rude, scraggy, severe, seamed, shaggy, uneven, unkempt, wrinkled; boisterous, inclement, rude, stormy, tempestuous, tumultuous, turbulent, violent, grating, harsh, inharmonious, unmusical, scabrous.

ruin *vb* crush, damn, defeat, demolish, desolate, destroy, devastate, overthrow, overturn, overwhelm, seduce, shatter, smash, subvert, wreck; beggar, impoverish.

ruinous *adj* decayed, demolished, dilapidated;

baneful, calamitous, damnatory, destructive, disastrous, mischievous, noisome, noxious, pernicious, subversive, wasteful.

rule *vb* bridle, command, conduct, control, direct, domineer, govern, judge, lead, manage, reign, restrain; advise, guide, persuade; adjudicate, decide, determine, establish, settle; obtain, prevail, predominate. • *n* authority, command, control, direction, domination, dominion, empire, government, jurisdiction, lordship, mastery, mastership, regency, reign, sway; behaviour, conduct; habit, method, order, regularity, routine, system; aphorism, canon, convention, criterion, formula, guide, law, maxim, model, precedent, precept, standard, system, test, touchstone; decision, order, prescription, regulation, ruling.

ruler *n* chief, governor, king, lord, master, monarch, potentate, regent, sovereign; director, head, manager, president; controller, guide, rule, straightedge.

rumour *vb* bruit, circulate, report, tell. • *n* bruit, gossip, hearsay, report, talk; news, report, story, tidings; celebrity, fame, reputation, repute.

rumple *vb* crease, crush, corrugate, crumple, disarrange, dishevel, pucker, ruffle, wrinkle.

run *vb* bolt, career, course, gallop, haste, hasten, hie, hurry, lope, post, race, scamper, scour, scud, scuttle, speed, trip; flow, glide, go, move, proceed, stream; fuse, liquefy, melt; advance, pass, proceed, stream; extend, lie, spread, stretch; circulate, go, pass, press; average, incline, tend; flee; pierce, stab; drive, force, propel, push, thrust, turn; cast, form, mould, shape; follow, perform, pursue, take; discharge, emit; direct, maintain, manage. • *n* race, running; course, current, flow, motion, passage, progress, way, wont; continuance, currency, popularity; excursion, gallop, journey, trip, trot; demand, pressure; brook, burn, flow, rill, rivulet, runlet, runnel, stream.

rupture *vb* break, burst, fracture, sever, split. • *n* breach, break, burst, disruption, fracture, split; contention, feud, hostility, quarrel, schism.

rural *adj* agrarian, bucolic, country, pastoral, rustic, sylvan.

rush *vb* attack, career, charge, dash, drive, gush, hurtle, precipitate, surge, sweep, tear.

ruthless *adj* barbarous, cruel, fell, ferocious, hardhearted, inexorable, inhuman, merciless, pitiless, relentless, remorseless, savage, truculent, uncompassionate, unmerciful, unpitying, unrelenting, unsparing.

S

sacred adj consecrated, dedicated, devoted, divine, hallowed, holy; inviolable, inviolate.

sacrifice vb forgo, immolate, surrender. • n immolation, oblation, offering; destruction, devotion, loss, surrender.

sacrilegious adj impious, irreverent, profane.

sad adj sober, sombre; dejected, depressed, doleful, gloomy, melancholic, miserable, mournful, sorrowful.

saddle vb burden, charge, clog, encumber, load.

safe adj undamaged, unharmed, unhurt, unscathed; guarded, protected, secure, snug, unexposed; certain, dependable, reliable, sure, trustworthy; good, harmless, sound, whole. • n chest, coffer, strongbox.

safeguard vb guard, protect. • n defence, protection, security; convoy, escort, guard, safeconduct; pass, passport.

sage adj acute, discerning, intelligent, prudent, sagacious, sapient, sensible, shrewd, wise; prudent, judicious, well-judged; grave, serious, solemn. • n philosopher, pundit, savant.

saintly adj devout, godly, holy, pious, religious.

sale n auction, demand, market, vendition, vent.

salt adj saline, salted; bitter, pungent, sharp. • n flavour, savour, seasoning, smack, relish, taste; humour, piquancy, poignancy, sarcasm, smartness, wit, zest; mariner, sailor, seaman, tar.

salvation n deliverance, escape, preservation, redemption, rescue, saving.

same adj ditto, identical, selfsame; corresponding, like, similar.

sample vb savour, sip, smack, sup, taste; test, try; demonstrate, exemplify, illustrate, instance. • adj exemplary, illustrative, representative. • n demonstration, exemplification, illustration, instance, piece, specimen; example, model.

sanctimonious adj affected, devout, holy, hypocritical, pharisaical, pious, self-righteous.

sanction vb authorise, countenance, encourage, support; confirm, ratify. • n approval, authority, authorisation, confirmation, countenance, endorsement, ratification, support, warranty; ban, boycott, embargo, penalty.

sanctity n devotion, godliness, goodness, grace, holiness, piety, purity, religiousness, saintliness.

sanctuary n altar, church, shrine, temple; asylum, protection, refuge, retreat, shelter.

sane adj healthy, lucid, normal, rational, reasonable, sober, sound.

sanitary adj clean, curative, healing, healthy, hygienic, remedial, therapeutic, wholesome.

sarcastic adj acrimonious, biting, cutting, mordacious, mordant, sardonic, satirical, sharp, severe, sneering, taunting.

sardonic adj bitter, derisive, ironical, malevolent, malicious, malignant, sarcastic.

satirical adj abusive, biting, bitter, censorious, cutting, invective, ironical, keen, mordacious, poignant, reproachful, sarcastic, severe, sharp.

satisfaction n comfort, complacency, contentment, ease, enjoyment, gratification, pleasure, satiety; amends, appeasement, atonement, compensation, indemnification, recompense, redress, remuneration, reparation, requital.

satisfy vb appease, content, fill, gratify, please, sate, satiate, suffice; indemnify, compensate, liquidate, pay, recompense, remunerate, requite; discharge, pay, settle; assure, convince, persuade; answer, fulfil, meet.

savage vb attack, lacerate, mangle, maul. • adj rough, sylvan, uncultivated, wild; rude, uncivilised, unpolished, untaught; bloodthirsty, feral, ferine, ferocious, fierce, rapacious, untamed, beastly, brutal, brutish, inhuman; atrocious, barbarous, bloody, cruel, fell, hardhearted, heathenish, merciless, murderous, pitiless, relentless, ruthless, sanguinary, truculent; native, rough, rugged, uncivilised.

save vb keep, liberate, preserve, rescue; salvage, recover, redeem; economise, gather, hoard, husband, reserve, store; hinder, obviate, prevent, spare. • prep but, deducting, except.

saviour n defender, deliverer, guardian, protector, preserver, rescuer, saver.

savour vb affect, appreciate, enjoy, like, partake, relish; flavour, season. • n flavour, gust, relish, smack, taste; fragrance, odour, smell, scent.

say vb declare, express, pronounce, speak, tell, utter; affirm, allege, argue; recite, rehearse, repeat; assume, presume, suppose. • n affirmation, declaration, speech, statement; decision, voice.

saying n declaration, expression, observation, remark, speech, statement; adage, aphorism, byword, dictum, maxim, proverb, saw.

scan vb examine, investigate, scrutinise, search.

scandalous adj defamatory, libellous, opprobrious, slanderous; atrocious, disgraceful, disreputable, infamous, inglorious, ignominious, odious, opprobrious, shameful.

scanty adj insufficient, meagre, narrow, scant, small; hardly, scarce, short, slender; niggardly, parsimonious, penurious, skimpy, sparing.

scar vb hurt, mark, wound. • n seam; blemish, defect, disfigurement, flaw, injury, mark.

scarce adj deficient, wanting; infrequent, rare, uncommon. • adv barely, hardly, scantily.

scare vb affright, alarm, appal, daunt, fright, frighten, intimidate, shock, startle, terrify. • n alarm, fright, panic, shock, terror.

scatter vb broadcast, sprinkle, strew; diffuse, disperse, disseminate, dissipate, distribute, separate, spread; disappoint, dispel, frustrate.

scent vb breathe in, inhale, nose, smell, sniff; detect, smell out, sniff out; aromatise, perfume. • n aroma, fragrance, odour, perfume, smell.

sceptical adj doubtful, doubting, dubious, hesitating, incredulous, questioning, unbelieving.

schedule vb line up, list, plan, programme, tabulate. • n document, scroll; catalogue, inventory, list, plan, record, register, roll, table, timetable.

scheme vb contrive, design, frame, imagine, plan, plot, project.

school vb drill, educate, exercise, indoctrinate, instruct, teach, train; admonish, control, chide, discipline, govern, reprove, tutor. • adj academic, collegiate, institutional, scholastic, schoolish. • n academy, college, gymnasium, institute, institution, kindergarten, lyceum, manège, polytechnic, seminary, university; adherents, camarilla, circle, clique, coterie, disciples, followers; body, order, organisation, party, sect

scintillate vb coruscate, flash, gleam, glisten, glitter, sparkle, twinkle.

scoff vb deride, flout, jeer, mock, ridicule, taunt; gibe, sneer.

scold vb berate, blame, censure, chide, rate, reprimand, reprove; blowup, rail, rate, reprimand, upbraid, vituperate. • n shrew, termagant, virago.

scope n aim, design, drift, end, intent, intention, mark, object, purpose, tendency, view; amplitude, field, latitude, liberty, margin, opportunity, purview, range, room, space, sphere, vent; extent, length, span, stretch, sweep.

scorch vb blister, burn, char, parch, roast, sear.

score vb cut, furrow, mark, notch, scratch; charge, note, record; charge, impute, note; enter, register. • n incision, mark, notch; account, bill, charge, debt, reckoning; consideration, ground, motive, reason.

scorn vb condemn, despise, disregard, disdain, scout, slight, spurn. • n contempt, derision, disdain, mockery, slight, sneer; derision, mockery.

scoundrel n cheat, knave, miscreant, rascal, reprobate, rogue, scamp, trickster, villain.

scowl vb frown, glower, lower.

scrap¹ vb discard, junk, trash. • n bit, fragment, modicum, particle, piece, snippet; bite, crumb, fragment, morsel, mouthful; debris, junk, litter, rubbish, rubble, trash, waste.

scrap² vb altercate, bicker, dispute, clash, fight, hassle, quarrel, row, spat, squabble, tiff, tussle. • n affray, altercation, bickering, clash, dispute, fight, fray, hassle, melee, quarrel, row, run-in, set-to, spat, squabble, tiff, tussle, wrangle.

scrape vb bark, grind, rasp, scuff; accumulate, acquire, collect, gather, save; erase, remove. • n difficulty, distress, embarrassment, perplexity, predicament.

scream vb screech, shriek, squall, ululate.

screen vb cloak, conceal, cover, defend, fence, hide, mask, protect, shelter, shroud. • n blind, curtain, lattice, partition; defence, guard, protection, shield; cloak, cover, veil, disguise; riddle.

screw vb force, press, pressurise, squeeze, tighten, twist, wrench; oppress, rack; distort. • n extortioner, extortionist, miser, scrimp, skinflint; prison guard; sexual intercourse.

scrimp vb contract, curtail, limit, pinch, reduce, scant, shorten, straiten.

scrupulous adj conscientious, fastidious, nice, precise, punctilious, rigorous, strict; careful, cautious, circumspect, exact, vigilant.

scrutiny n examination, exploration, inquisition, inspection, investigation, search, sifting.

scuffle vb contend, fight, strive, struggle. • n altercation, brawl, broil, contest, encounter, fight, fray, quarrel, squabble, struggle, wrangle.

scurry vb bustle, dash, hasten, hurry, scamper, scud, scutter.

seal vb close, fasten, secure; attest, authenticate, confirm, establish, ratify, sanction; confine, enclose, imprison. • n fastening, stamp, wafer, wax; assurance, attestation, authentication, confirmation, pledge, ratification.

sear vb blight, brand, cauterise, dry, scorch, wither. • adj dried up, dry, sere, withered.

search vb examine, explore, ferret, inspect, investigate, overhaul, probe, ransack, scrutinise, sift; delve, hunt, forage, inquire, look, rummage. • n examination, exploration, hunt, inquiry, inspection, investigation, pursuit, quest, research, seeking, scrutiny.

searching adj close, keen, penetrating, trying; examining, exploring, inquiring, investigating, probing, seeking.

season vb acclimatise, accustom, form, habituate, harden, inure, mature, qualify, temper, train; flavour, spice. • n interval, period, spell, term, time, while.

seasonable adj appropriate, convenient, fit, opportune, suitable, timely.

secluded adj close, covert, embowered, isolated, private, removed, retired, screened, sequestrated, withdrawn.

second¹ n instant, jiffy, minute, moment, trice.

second² vb abet, advance, aid, assist, back, encourage, forward, further, help, promote, support, sustain; approve, favour, support. • adj inferior, second-rate, secondary; following, next, subsequent; additional, extra, other; double, duplicate. • n another, other; assistant, backer, supporter.

secondary *adj* collateral, inferior, minor, subsidiary, subordinate. • *n* delegate, deputy, proxy.

secret *adj* close, concealed, covered, covert, cryptic, hid, hidden, mysterious, privy, shrouded, veiled, unknown, unrevealed, unseen; cabbalistic, clandestine, furtive, privy, sly, stealthy, surreptitious, underhand; confidential, private, retired, secluded, unseen; abstruse, latent, mysterious, obscure, occult, recondite, unknown. • *n* confidence, enigma, key, mystery.

secretive *adj* cautious, close, reserved, reticent, taciturn, uncommunicative, wary.

sect *n* denomination, faction, schism, school.

section *n* cutting, division, fraction, part, piece.

secure *vb* guard, protect, safeguard; assure, ensure, guarantee, insure; fasten; acquire, gain, get, obtain, procure. • *adj* assured, certain, confident, sure; insured, protected, safe; fast, firm, fixed, immovable, stable; careless, easy, undisturbed.

security *n* bulwark, defence, guard, palladium, protection, safeguard, safety, shelter; bond, collateral, deposit, guarantee, pawn, pledge, stake, surety, warranty; assurance, assuredness, certainty, confidence, ease.

sedate *adj* calm, collected, composed, contemplative, cool, demure, grave, placid, philosophical, quiet, serene, serious, sober, still, thoughtful, tranquil, undisturbed, unemotional.

sedative *adj* allaying, anodyne, assuasive, balmy, calming, composing, demulcent, lenient, lenitive, soothing, tranquillising. • *n* anaesthetic, anodyne, hypnotic, narcotic, opiate.

sediment *n* dregs, grounds, lees, precipitate, residue, residuum, settlings.

seduce *vb* allure, attract, betray, corrupt, debauch, deceive, decoy, deprave, ensnare, entice, inveigle, lead, mislead.

seductive *adj* alluring, attractive, enticing.

see *vb* behold, contemplate, descry, glimpse, survey; comprehend, conceive, distinguish, espy, know, notice, observe, perceive, remark, understand; beware, consider, envisage, regard; experience, feel, know, suffer; consider, distinguish, examine, inspire, notice, observe; discern, look, penetrate, perceive, understand.

seek *vb* hunt, look, search; court, follow, prosecute, pursue, solicit; attempt, endeavour, strive.

seem *vb* appear, assume, look, pretend.

segment *n* bit, division, part, piece, portion.

segregate *vb* detach, disconnect, disperse, insulate, part, separate.

seize *vb* capture, catch, clutch, grab, grapple, grasp, grip, gripe, snatch; confiscate, impress, impound; apprehend, comprehend; arrest, capture, take.

seldom *adv* infrequently, occasionally, rarely.

select *vb* choose, cull, pick, prefer. • *adj* choice, chosen, excellent, exquisite, good, picked, rare.

selection *n* choice, election, pick, preference.

self-conscious *adj* awkward, diffident, embarrassed, insecure, nervous.

self-control *n* restraint, willpower.

self-important *adj* assuming, consequential, proud, haughty, lordly, overbearing.

selfish *adj* egoistic, egotistical, greedy, illiberal, mean, narrow, self-seeking, ungenerous.

self-possessed *adj* calm, collected, composed, cool, placid, sedate, undisturbed, unruffled.

self-willed *adj* contumacious, dogged, headstrong, obstinate, pig-headed, stubborn, wilful.

sell *vb* barter, exchange, hawk, market, peddle, trade, vend.

semblance *n* likeness, resemblance, similarity; air, appearance, aspect, bearing, exterior, figure, form, mien, seeming, show; image, likeness.

send *vb* cast, drive, emit, fling, hurl, impel, lance, launch, project, propel, throw, toss; delegate, depute, dispatch; forward, transmit; bestow, confer, give, grant.

senile *adj* aged, doddering, superannuated; doting, imbecile.

senior *adj* elder, older; higher, superior.

sensation *n* feeling, sense, perception; excitement, impression, thrill.

sensational *adj* exciting, melodramatic, startling, thrilling.

sense *vb* appraise, appreciate, estimate, notice, observe, perceive, suspect, understand. • *n* brains, intellect, mind, reason, understanding; appreciation, apprehension, discernment, feeling, perception, recognition, tact, understanding; idea, judgement, notion, opinion, sentiment, view; import, interpretation, meaning, purport, significance; good, judgement, reason, sagacity, soundness, understanding, wisdom.

sensible *adj* apprehensible, perceptible; aware, cognisant, conscious, convinced, persuaded, satisfied; discreet, intelligent, judicious, rational, reasonable, sagacious, sage, sober, sound, wise; observant, understanding.

sensitive *adj* perceptive, sentient; affected, impressible, impressionable, responsive, susceptible; delicate, tender, touchy.

sensual *adj* animal, bodily, carnal, voluptuous; gross, lascivious, lewd, licentious, unchaste.

sentence *vb* condemn, doom, judge. • *n* decision, determination, judgement, opinion; doctrine, dogma, opinion, tenet; condemnation, doom, judgement; period, proposition.

sentiment *n* judgement, notion, opinion; maxim, saying; emotion, tenderness; disposition, feeling, thought.

sentimental *adj* impressible, impressionable, over-emotional, romantic, tender.

separate *vb* detach, disconnect, disjoin, disunite, dissever, divide, divorce, part, sever, sunder; eliminate, remove, withdraw; cleave, open.

sequel n close, conclusion, denouement, end, termination; consequence, event, issue, result.

sequence n following, graduation, progression, succession; arrangement, series, train.

serene adj calm, collected, placid, peaceful, quiet, tranquil, sedate, undisturbed, unperturbed, unruffled; bright, calm, clear, fair, unclouded.

series n chain, concatenation, course, line, order, progression, sequence, succession, train.

serious adj earnest, grave, demure, pious, sedate, sober, solemn, staid, thoughtful; grave, great, important, momentous, weighty.

servant n attendant, dependant, factotum, helper, henchman, retainer, servitor, subaltern, subordinate, underling; domestic, drudge, flunky, lackey, menial, scullion, slave.

serve vb aid, assist, attend, help, minister, oblige, succour; advance, benefit, forward, promote; content, satisfy, supply; handle, officiate, manage, manipulate, work.

service vb check, maintain, overhaul, repair. • n labour, ministration, work; attendance, business, duty, employ, employment, office; advantage, benefit, good, gain, profit; avail, purpose, use, utility; ceremony, function, observance, rite.

set[1] vb lay, locate, mount, place, put, stand, station; appoint, determine, establish, fix, settle; risk, stake, wager; adapt, adjust, regulate; adorn, stud, variegate; arrange, dispose, pose, post; appoint, assign, predetermine, prescribe; estimate, prize, rate, value; embarrass, perplex, pose; contrive, produce; decline, sink; congeal, concern, consolidate, harden, solidify; flow, incline, run, tend; (with **about**) begin, commence; (with **apart**) appropriate, consecrate, dedicate, devote, reserve, set aside; (with **aside**) abrogate, annul, omit, reject; reserve, set apart; (with **before**) display, exhibit; (with **down**) chronicle, jot down, record, register, state, write down; (with **forth**) display, exhibit, explain, expound, manifest, promulgate, publish, put forward, represent, show; (with **forward**) advance, further, promote; (with **free**) acquit, clear, emancipate, liberate, release; (with **off**) adorn, decorate, embellish; define, portion off; (with **on**) actuate, encourage, impel, influence, incite, instigate, prompt, spur, urge; attack, assault, set upon; (with **out**) display, issue, publish, proclaim, prove, recommend, show; (with **right**) correct, put in order; (with **to rights**) adjust, regulate; (with **up**) elevate, erect, exalt, raise; establish, found, institute; (with **upon**) assail, assault, attack, fly at, rush upon. • adj appointed, established, formal, ordained, prescribed, regular, settled; determined, fixed, firm, obstinate, positive, stiff, unyielding; immovable, predetermined; located, placed, put.

set[2] n assortment, collection, suit; class, circle,

clique, cluster, company, coterie, division, gang, group, knot, party, school, sect.

setback n blow, hitch, hold-up, rebuff; defeat, disappointment, reverse.

settle vb adjust, arrange, compose, regulate; account, balance, close up, conclude, discharge, liquidate, pay, pay up, reckon, satisfy, square; allay, calm, compose, pacify, quiet, repose, rest, still, tranquillise; confirm, decide, determine, make clear; establish, fix, set; fall, gravitate, sink, subside; abide, colonise, domicile, dwell, establish, inhabit, people, place, plant, reside; (with on) determine on, fix on, fix upon.

sever vb divide, part, rend, separate, sunder; detach, disconnect, disjoin, disunite.

several adj distinct, exclusive, independent, separate; different, diverse, many, sundry, various.

severe adj austere, bitter, dour, hard, harsh, inexorable, morose, relentless, rigid, rigorous, rough, sharp, stern, stiff, strait-laced, unmitigated, unrelenting, unsparing; accurate, exact, methodical, strict; chaste, plain, restrained, simple, unadorned; biting, bitter, caustic, cruel, cutting, harsh, keen, sarcastic, satirical, sharp, trenchant; acute, afflictive, distressing, extreme, intense, sharp, stringent, violent; critical, exact, hard.

sew vb baste, bind, hem, stitch, tack.

shabby adj faded, mean, poor, ragged, seedy, threadbare, worn, worn-out; beggarly, mean, paltry, penurious, stingy.

shackle vb chain, fetter, gyve, hamper, manacle; bind, clog, confine, cumber, embarrass, encumber, impede, obstruct, restrict, trammel.

shade vb cloud, darken, dim, eclipse, ofuscate, obscure; cover, ensconce, hide, protect, screen, shelter. • n darkness, dusk, duskiness, gloom, obscurity, shadow; cover, protection, shelter; awning, blind, curtain, screen, shutter, veil; degree, difference, kind, variety; cast, colour, complexion, dye, hue, tinge, tint, tone; apparition, ghost, manes, phantom, shadow, spectre, spirit.

shadow vb becloud, cloud, darken, obscure, shade; adumbrate, foreshadow, symbolise, typify; conceal, cover, hide, protect, screen, shroud. • n penumbra, shade, umbra, umbrage; darkness, gloom, obscurity; cover, protection, security, shelter; adumbration, foreshowing, image, prefiguration, representation; apparition, ghost, phantom, shade, spirit.

shake vb quake, quaver, quiver, shiver, shudder, totter, tremble; agitate, convulse, jar, jolt, stagger; daunt, frighten, intimidate; endanger, move, weaken; oscillate, vibrate, wave; move, put away, remove, throw off.

shallow adj flimsy, foolish, frivolous, puerile, trashy, trifling, trivial; empty, ignorant, silly.

sham vb ape, feign, imitate, pretend; cheat, deceive, delude, dupe, impose, trick. • adj assumed, counterfeit, false, feigned, mock, make-believe, pretended, spurious. • n delusion, feint, fraud, humbug, imposition, imposture, pretence.

shame vb debase, degrade, discredit, disgrace, dishonour, stain, sully, taint, tarnish; abash, confound, confuse, discompose, disconcert, humble, humiliate; deride, flout, jeer, mock, ridicule, sneer. • n contempt, degradation, derision, discredit, disgrace, dishonour, disrepute, ignominy, infamy, obloquy, odium, opprobrium, reproach, scandal; abashment, chagrin, confusion, humiliation, mortification; disgrace, dishonour, reproach, scandal; decency, decorum, modesty.

shameful adj atrocious, base, disgraceful, dishonourable, disreputable, heinous, ignominous, infamous, nefarious, opprobrious, outrageous, scandalous, vile, villainous, wicked.

shameless adj assuming, audacious, bold-faced, brazen, brazen-faced, cool, immodest, impudent, indecent, indelicate, insolent, unabashed, unblushing; abandoned, corrupt, depraved, dissolute, graceless, hardened, incorrigible, irreclaimable, lost, obdurate, profligate, reprobate, sinful, unprincipled, vicious.

shape vb create, form, make, produce; fashion, form, model, mould; adjust, direct, frame, regulate; conceive, conjure up, figure, image, imagine. • n appearance, aspect, fashion, figure, form, guise, make; build, cast, cut, fashion, model, mould; pattern; apparition, image.

share vb apportion, distribute, divide, parcel out, portion, split; partake, participate; experience, receive. • n part, portion, quantum; allotment, allowance, contingent, deal, dividend, division, interest, lot, proportion, quantity, quota.

sharp adj acute, cutting, keen, keen-edged, trenchant; acuminate, needle-shaped, peaked, pointed, ridged; acute, apt, astute, canny, clear-sighted, clever, cunning, discerning, discriminating, ingenious, inventive, keen-witted, penetrating, perspicacious, quick, ready, sagacious, sharp-witted, shrewd, smart, subtle, witty; acid, acrid, biting, bitter, burning, high-flavoured, high-seasoned, hot, piquant, poignant, pungent, sour, stinging; acrimonious, biting, caustic, cutting, harsh, keen, mordant, pointed, sarcastic, severe, tart, trenchant; cruel, hard, rigid, severe; acute, afflicting, distressing, excruciating, intense, keen, painful, piercing, poignant, severe, shooting, sore, violent; biting, nipping, piercing, pinching; ardent, eager, fervid, fierce, fiery, impetuous, strong, violent; high, piercing, shrill; attentive, vigilant; keen, penetrating, piercing, severe; close, exacting, shrewd. • adv abruptly, sharply, suddenly; exactly precisely, punctually.

sharpen vb edge, intensify, point.

shatter vb break, burst, crack, rend, shiver, smash, splinter, split; break up, derange, disorder, overthrow.

shave vb crop, cut off, mow, pare; slice; graze, skim, touch.

sheen n brightness, gloss, glossiness, shine.

sheepish adj bashful, diffident, overmodest, shamefaced, timid, timorous.

sheer[1] adj perpendicular, precipitous, steep, vertical; clear, downright, mere, pure, simple, unadulterated, unmingled, unmixed, unqualified, utter; clear, pure; fine, transparent.

sheer[2] vb decline, deviate, move aside, swerve.

shelter vb cover, defend, ensconce, harbour, hide, house, protect, screen, shield, shroud. • n asylum, cover, covert, harbour, haven, refuge, retreat, sanctuary; cover, defence, protection, safety, screen, security, shield.

shield vb cover, defend, guard, protect, shelter; repel, ward off; avert, forbid, forfend. • n aegis, buckler, escutcheon, targe; bulwark, cover, defence, guard, protection, security, shelter.

shift vb alter, change, fluctuate, move, vary; chop, dodge, gype, swerve, veer; contrive, devise, manage, plan, scheme, shuffle. • n change, substitution, turn; contrivance, expedient, means, resort, resource; artifice, craft, device, dodge, evasion, fraud, mask, ruse, stratagem, subterfuge, trick, wile; chemise, smock.

shiftless adj improvident, imprudent, negligent, slack, thriftless, unresourceful.

shifty adj tricky, undependable, wily.

shimmer vb flash, glimmer, glisten, shine. • n blink, glimmer, glitter, twinkle.

shine vb beam, blaze, coruscate, flare, give light, glare, gleam, glimmer, glisten, glitter, glow, lighten, radiate, sparkle; excel. • n brightness, brilliancy, glaze, gloss, polish, sheen.

shiny adj bright, clear, luminous, sunshiny, unclouded; brilliant, burnished, glassy, glossy.

shipshape adj neat, orderly, tidy, trim.

shirk vb avoid, dodge, evade, malinger, quit, slack; cheat, shark, trick.

shiver[1] vb break, shatter, splinter. • n bit, fragment, piece, slice, sliver, splinter.

shiver[2] vb quake, quiver, shake, shudder, tremble. • n shaking, shivering, shuddering, tremor.

shock vb appall, horrify; disgust, disquiet, disturb, nauseate, offend, outrage, revolt, scandalise, sicken; astound, stagger, stun; collide with, jar, jolt, shake, strike against; encounter, meet. • n agitation, blow, offence, stroke; assault, brunt, conflict; clash, collision, concussion, impact, percussion.

shoot vb catapult, expel, hurl, let fly, propel; discharge, fire, let off; dart, fly, pass, pelt; extend, jut, project, protrude, protuberate, push, put forth, send forth, stretch; bud, germinate, sprout; (with up) grow increase, spring up, run up, start up. • n branch, offshoot, scion, sprout.

shore¹ *n* beach, brim, coast, seabord, seaside, strand, waterside.

shore² *vb* brace, buttress, prop, stay, support.

short *adj* brief, curtailed; direct, near, straight; brief, compendious, concise, condensed, laconic, pithy, terse, sententious, succinct, summary; abrupt, curt, petulant, pointed, sharp, snappish, uncivil; defective, deficient, inadequate, insufficient, niggardly, scanty, scrimpy; contracted, desitute, lacking, limited, minus, wanting; dwarfish, squat, undersized, vertically challenged; brittle, crisp, crumbling, friable. • *adv* abruptly, at once, forthwith, suddenly.

shortcoming *n* defect, deficiency, delinquency, error, failing, failure, fault, imperfection, inadequacy, remissness, slip, weakness.

shorten *vb* abbreviate, abridge, curtail, cut short; contract, diminish, lessen, retrench, reduce; cut off, dock, lop, trim.

shoulder *vb* bear, bolster, carry, hump, maintain, pack, support, sustain, tote; crowd, elbow, jostle, press forward, push, thrust.

shout *vb* bawl, cheer, clamour, exclaim, halloo, roar, vociferate, whoop, yell.

shove *vb* jostle, press against, propel, push, push aside; (*with* off) push away, thrust away.

show *vb* blazon, display, exhibit, flaunt, parade, present; indicate, mark, point out; disclose, discover, divulge, explain, make clear, make known, proclaim, publish, reveal, unfold; demonstrate, evidence, manifest, prove, verify; conduct, guide, usher; direct, inform, instruct, teach; explain, expound, elucidate, interpret; (*with* off) display, exhibit, make a show, set off; (*with* up) expose. • *n* array, exhibition, representation, sight, spectacle; blazonry, bravery, ceremony, dash, demonstration, display, flourish, ostentation, pageant, pageantry, parade, pomp, splendour, splurge; likeness, resemblance, semblance; affectation, appearance, colour, illusion, mask, plausibility, pose, pretence, pretext, simulation, speciousness; entertainment, production.

showy *adj* bedizened, dressy, fine, flashy, flaunting, garish, gaudy, glaring, gorgeous, loud, ornate, smart, swanky, splendid; grand, magnificent, ostentatious, pompous, pretentious.

shred *vb* tear. • *n* bit, fragment, piece, rag, scrap.

shrewd *adj* arch, artful, astute, crafty, cunning, Machiavellian, sly, subtle, wily; acute, astute, canny, discerning, discriminating, ingenious, keen, knowing, penetrating, sagacious, sharp.

shriek *vb* scream, screech, squeal, yell, yelp.

shrill *adj* acute, high, high-toned, high-pitched, piercing, piping, sharp.

shrink *vb* contract, decrease, dwindle, shrivel, wither; balk, blench, draw back, flinch, give way, quail, recoil, retire, swerve, wince.

shrivel *vb* dry, dry up, parch; contract, decrease, dwindle, shrink, wither, wrinkle.

shroud *vb* bury, cloak, conceal, cover, hide, mask, muffle, protect, screen, shelter, veil. • *n* covering, garment; grave clothes, winding sheet.

shudder *vb* quake, quiver, shake, shiver.

shuffle *vb* confuse, disorder, intermix, jumble, mix, shift; cavil, dodge, equivocate, evade, prevaricate, quibble; make shift, shift, struggle.

shun *vb* avoid, elude, eschew, escape, evade.

shut *vb* close, close up, stop; confine, coop up, enclose, imprison, lock up, shut up; (*with* in) enclose, enclose; (*with* off) bar, exclude, intercept; (*with* up) close up, shut; confine, enclose, fasten in, imprison, lock in, lock up.

shy *vb* cast, chuck, fling, hurl, jerk, pitch, sling, throw, toss; boggle, sheer, start aside. • *adj* bashful, coy, diffident, reserved, retiring, sheepish, shrinking, timid; cautious, chary, distrustful, heedful, wary. • *n* start; fling, throw.

sick *adj* ailing, ill, indisposed, laid-up, unwell, weak; nauseated, queasy; disgusted, revolted, tired, weary; diseased, distempered, disordered, feeble, morbid, unhealthy, unsound, weak.

sicken *vb* ail, fall sick, make sick; nauseate; disgust, weary; decay, droop, languish.

side *vb* border, bound, edge, flank, frontier, march, rim, skirt, verge; avert, turn aside; (*with* with) befriend, favour, flock to, join with, second, support. • *adj* flanking, later, skirting; indirect, oblique; extra, odd, off, spare. • *n* border, edge, flank, margin, verge; cause, faction, interest, party, sect.

sift *vb* part, separate; bolt, screen winnow; analyse, canvass, discuss, examine, fathom, follow up, inquire into, investigate, probe, scrutinze.

sigh *vb* complain, grieve, lament, mourn. • *n* long breath, sough, suspiration.

sight *vb* get sight of, perceive, see. • *n* cognisance, ken, perception, view; beholding, eyesight, seeing, vision; exhibition, prospect, representation, scene, show, spectacle.

sign *vb* indicate, signal, signify; countersign, endorse, subscribe. • *n* emblem, index, indication, manifestation, mark, note, proof, signal, signification, symbol, symptom, token; beacon, signal; augury, auspice, foreboding, miracle, omen, portent, presage.

signal *vb* flag, glance, hail, nod, nudge, salute, sign, signalise, sound, speak, touch, wave, wink. • *adj* conspicuous, eminent, extraordinary, memorable, notable, noteworthy, remarkable. • *n* cue, indication, mark, sign, token.

significant *adj* betokening, expressive, indicative, significative, signifying; important, material, momentous, portentous, weighty; forcible, emphatic, expressive, telling.

signify *vb* betoken, communication, express, indicate, intimate; denote, imply, import, mean, purport, suggest; announce, declare, give notice of, impart, make known, manifest, proclaim, utter; augur, foreshadow, indicate, portend, represent, suggest; import, matter, weigh.

silence vb hush, muzzle, still; allay, calm, quiet. • interj be silent, be still, hush, soft, tush, tut, whist. • n calm, hush, lull, noiselessness, peace, quiet, quietude, soundlessness, stillness; dumbness, muteness, reticence, speechlessness.

silly adj brainless, childish, foolish, inept, senseless, shallow, simple, stupid, weak-minded, witless; absurd, frivolous, imprudent, indiscreet, nonsensical, preposterous, trifling, unwise.

similar adj analogous, duplicate, like, resembling, twin; homogeneous, uniform.

similarity n agreement, analogy, correspondence, likeness, parallelism, parity, resemblance, sameness, semblance, similitude.

simmer vb boil, bubble, seethe, stew.

simple adj bare, elementary, homogeneous, incomplex, mere, single, unalloyed, unblended, uncombined, uncompounded, unmingled, unmixed; chaste, plain, homespun, inornate, natural, neat, unadorned, unaffected, unembellished, unpretentious, unstudied, unvarnished; artless, downright, frank, guileless, inartificial, ingenuous, naive, open, plain, simple-hearted, simpleminded, sincere, single-minded, straightforward, true, unaffected, unconstrained, undesigning, unsophisticated; credulous, fatuous, foolish, shallow, silly, unwise; clear, intelligible, plain, understandable, uninvolved, unmistakable.

simplicity n chasteness, homeliness, naturalness, neatness, plainness; artlessness, frankness, naivety, openness, simplesse, sincerity; clearness, plainness; folly, silliness, weakness.

simultaneous adj coeval, coincident, concomitant, concurrent, synchronous.

sin vb do wrong, err, transgress, trespass. • n delinquency, depravity, guilt, iniquity, misdeed, offence, transgression, wickedness, wrong.

since conj as, because, considering, seeing that. • adv before this; from that time. • prep after, from the time of, subsequently to.

sincere adj pure, unmixed; genuine, honest, inartificial, real, true, unaffected, unfeigned, unvarnished; artless, candid, direct, frank, guileless, hearty, honest, ingenuous, open, plain, single, straightforward, true, truthful, undissembling, upright, whole-hearted.

sincerity n artlessness, candour, earnestness, frankness, genuineness, guilelessness, honesty, ingenuousness, probity, truth, truthfulness.

sinful adj bad, criminal, depraved, immoral, iniquitous, mischievous, peccant, transgressive, unholy, unrighteous, wicked, wrong.

singe vb burn, scorch, sear.

single vb (with out) choose, pick, select, single. • adj alone, isolated, one only, sole, solitary; individual, particular, separate; celibate, unmarried, unwedded; pure, simple, uncompounded.

singular adj eminent, exceptional, extraordinary, rare, remarkable, strange, uncommon, unusual, unwonted; exceptional, particular, remarkable, unexampled, unparalleled, unprecedented; strange, unaccountable; bizarre, eccentric, fantastic, odd, peculiar; individual, single; not complex, single, uncompounded.

sinister adj baleful, injurious, untoward; boding ill, ominous; left, on the left hand.

sink vb droop, drop, fall, founder, go down, submerge, subside; enter, penetrate; collapse, fail; decay, decline, decrease, dwindle, give way, languish, lose strength; engulf, immerse, merge, submerge, submerse; dig, excavate, scoop out; abase, bring down, crush, debase, degrade, depress, diminish, lessen, lower, overbear; destroy, overthrow, overwhelm, reduce, ruin, swamp, waste. • n basin, cloaca, drain, sewer.

sinner n criminal, delinquent, evildoer, offender, reprobate, wrongdoer.

sip vb drink, suck up, sup; absorb, drink in. • n small draught, taste.

sit vb abide, be, remain, repose, rest, stay; bear on, lie, rest; abide, dwell, settle; perch; brood, incubate; become, be suited, fit.

site vb locate, place, position, situate, station. • n ground, locality, location, place, position, seat, situation, spot, station, whereabouts.

situation n ground, locality, location, place, position, seat, site, spot, whereabouts; case, category, circumstances, condition, juncture, plight, predicament, state; employment, office, place.

size n amplitude, bigness, bulk, dimensions, expanse, greatness, largeness, magnitude, mass, volume.

sketch vb design, draft, draw out; delineate, depict, paint, portray, represent. • n delineation, design, draft, drawing, outline, plan, skeleton.

skilful adj able, accomplished, adept, adroit, apt, clever, competent, conversant, cunning, deft, dexterous, dextrous, expert, handy, ingenious, masterly, practised, proficient, qualified, quick, ready, skilled, trained, versed.

skill n ability, address, adroitness, aptitude, aptness, art, cleverness, deftness, dexterity, expertise, expertness, facility, ingenuity, knack, quickness, readiness, skilfulness; discernment, discrimination, knowledge, understanding, wit.

skim vb brush, glance, graze, kiss, scrape, scratch, sweep, touch lightly; coast, flow, fly, glide, sail, scud, whisk; dip into, glance at, scan, skip, thumb over, touch upon.

skin vb pare, peel; decorticate, excoriate, flay. • n cuticle, cutis, derm, epidermis, hide, integument, pellicle, pelt; hull, husk, peel, rind.

skip vb bound, caper, frisk, gambol, hop, jump,

leap, spring; disregard, intermit, miss, neglect, omit, pass over, skim.

skirmish *vb* battle, brush, collide, combat, contest, fight, scuffle, tussle. • *n* affair, affray, battle, brush, collision, combat, conflict, contest, encounter, fight, scuffle, tussle.

skirt *vb* border, bound, edge, fringe, hem, march, rim; circumnavigate, circumvent, flank, go along.

slack *vb* ease off, let up; abate, ease up, relax, slacken; malinger, shirk; choke, damp, extinguish, smother, stifle. • *adj* backward, careless, inattentive, lax, negligent, remiss; abated, dilatory, diminished, lingering, slow, tardy; loose, relaxed; dull, idle, inactive, quiet, sluggish. • *n* excess, leeway, looseness, play; coal dust, culm.

slacken *vb* abate, diminish, lessen, lower, mitigate, moderate, neglect, remit, relieve, retard, slack; loosen, relax; flag, slow down; bridle, check, control, curb, repress, restrain.

slander *vb* asperse, backbite, belie, brand, calumniate, decry, defame, libel, malign, reproach, scandalise, traduce, vilify; detract from, disparage. • *n* aspersion, backbiting, calumny, defamation, detraction, libel, obloquy, scandal.

slanderous *adj* calumnious, defamatory, false, libellous, malicious, maligning.

slant *vb* incline, lean, lie obliquely, list, slope. • *n* inclination, slope, steep, tilt.

slap *vb* dab, clap, pat, smack, spank, strike.

slapdash *adv* haphazardly, hurriedly.

slash *vb* cut, gash, slit. • *n* cut, gash, slit.

slaughter *vb* butcher, kill, massacre, murder, slay. • *n* bloodshed, butchery, carnage, havoc, killing, massacre, murder, slaying.

slay *vb* assassinate, butcher, dispatch, kill, massacre, murder, slaughter; destroy, ruin.

sleek *adj* glossy, satin, silken, silky, smooth.

sleep *vb* catnap, doze, drowse, nap, slumber. • *n* dormancy, hypnosis, lethargy, repose, rest.

sleepwalker *n* night-walker, noctambulist, somnambulist.

sleepy *adj* comatose, dozy, drowsy, heavy, lethargic, nodding, somnolent; narcotic, opiate, slumberous, somniferous, somnific, soporiferous, soporific; dull, heavy, inactive, lazy, slow.

slender *adj* lank, lithe, narrow, skinny, slim, slight, spindly, thin; feeble, fine, flimsy, fragile, slight, tenuous, weak; inconsiderable, moderate, small, trivial; exiguous, inadequate, insufficient, lean, meagre, pitiful, scanty, small; abstemious, light, meagre, simple, spare, sparing.

slice *vb* cut, divide, part, section; cut off, sever.

slick *adj* glassy, glossy, polished, sleek, smooth; alert, clever, cunning, shrewd, slippery.

slide *vb* glide, move smoothly, slip. • *n* glide, glissade, skid, slip.

slight *vb* cold-shoulder, disdain, disregard, ne-

glect, snub; overlook; scamp, skimp, slur. • *adj* inconsiderable, insignificant, little, paltry, petty, small, trifling, trivial, unimportant, unsubstantial; delicate, feeble, frail, gentle, weak; careless, cursory, desultory, hasty, hurried, negligent, scanty, superficial; flimsy, perishable; slender, slim. • *n* discourtesy, disregard, disrespect, inattention, indignity, neglect.

slim *vb* bant, lose weight, reduce, slenderise. • *adj* gaunt, lank, lithe, narrow, skinny, slender, spare; inconsiderable, paltry, poor, slight, trifling, trivial, unsubstantial, weak; insufficient.

slimy *adj* miry, muddy, oozy; clammy, gelatinous, glutinous, gummy, lubricious, mucilaginous, mucous, ropy, slabby, viscid, viscous.

sling *vb* cast, fling, hurl, throw; suspend.

slink *vb* skulk, slip away, sneak, steal away.

slip[1] *vb* glide, slide; err, mistake, trip; lose, omit; disengage, throw off; escape, let go, loose, loosen, release. • *n* glide, slide, slipping; blunder, error, fault, lapse, misstep, mistake, oversight, peccadillo, trip; backsliding, error, fault, impropriety, indiscretion, transgression; desertion, escape; cord, leash, strap, string; case, covering.

slip[2] *n* cutting, scion, shoot, twig; piece, strip.

slippery *adj* glib, slithery, smooth; changeable, insecure, mutable, perilous, shaky, uncertain, unsafe, unstable, unsteady; cunning, dishonest, elusive, faithless, false, perfidious, shifty.

slipshod *adj* careless, shuffling, slovenly.

slit *vb* cut; divide, rend, slash, split, sunder.

slope *vb* incline, slant, tilt. • *n* acclivity, cant, declivity, glacis, grade, gradient, incline, inclination, obliquity, pitch, ramp.

slouch *vb* droop, loll, slump; shamble, shuffle. • *n* malingerer, shirker, slump; shamble, shuffle.

slovenly *adj* unclean, untidy; blowsy, disorderly, dowdy, frowsy, loose, slatternly, tacky, unkempt, untidy; careless, heedless, negligent.

slow *vb* abate, brake, check, decelerate, diminish, lessen, mitigate, moderate, modulate, reduce, weaken; delay, detain, retard; ease, ease up, relax, slack, slacken, slack off. • *adj* deliberate, gradual; dead, dull, heavy, inactive, inert, sluggish, stupid; behindhand, late, tardy, unready; delaying, dilatory, lingering, slack.

sludge *n* mire, mud; slosh, slush.

sluggish *adj* dronish, drowsy, idle, inactive, indolent, inert, languid, lazy, listless, lumpish, phlegmatic, slothful, torpid; slow; dull, stupid.

slumber *vb* doze, nap, repose, rest, sleep.

slump *vb* droop, drop, fall, flop, founder, sag, sink, sink down; decline, depreciate, deteriorate, ebb, fall, fall, fall away, lose ground, recede, slide, slip, subside, wane. • *n* droop, drop, fall, flop, lowering, sag, sinkage; decline, depreciation, deterioration, downturn, downtrend, subsidence, ebb, falling off, wane; crash, recession.

slur vb asperse, calumniate, disparage, depreciate, reproach, traduce; conceal, disregard, gloss over, obscure, pass over, slight. • n mark, stain; brand, disgrace, reproach, stain, stigma.

sly adj artful, crafty, cunning, insidious, subtle, wily; astute, cautious, shrewd; arch, knowing, clandestine, secret, stealthy, underhand.

smack¹ vb smell, taste. • n flavour, savour, tang, taste, tincture; dash, infusion, little, space, soupçon, sprinkling, tinge, touch; smattering.

smack² vb slap, strike; crack, slash, snap; buss, kiss. • n crack, slap, slash, snap; buss, kiss.

small adj diminutive, Lilliputian, little, miniature, petite, pygmy, tiny, wee; infinitesimal, microscopic, minikin, minute; inappreciable, inconsiderable, insignificant, petty, trifling, trivial, unimportant; moderate, paltry, scanty, slender; faint, feeble, puny, slight, weak; illiberal, mean, narrow, narrow-minded, paltry, selfish, sorded, ungenerous, unworthy.

smart¹ vb hurt, pain, sting; suffer.

smart² adj active, agile, brisk, fresh, lively, nimble, quick, spirited, sprightly, spry; effective, efficient, energetic, forcible, vigorous; adroit, alert, clever, dexterous, dextrous, expert, intelligent, quick, stirring; acute, apt, pertinent, ready, witty; chic, dapper, fine, natty, showy, spruce.

smash vb break, crush, dash, mash, shatter. • n crash, debacle, destruction, ruin; bankruptcy.

smattering n dabbling, sciolism, smatter.

smear vb bedaub, begrime, besmear, daub, plaster, smudge; contaminate, pollute, smirch, smut, soil, stain, sully, tarnish. • n blot, blotch, daub, patch, smirch, smudge, spot, stain; calumny, defamation, libel, slander.

smell vb scent, sniff, stench, stink. • n aroma, bouquet, fragrance, fume, odour, perfume, redolence, scent, stench, stink; sniff, snuff.

smile vb grin, laugh, simper, smirk.

smoke vb emit, exhale, reek, steam; fumigate, smudge; discover, find out, smell out. • n effluvium, exhalation, fume, mist, reek, smother, steam, vapour; fumigation, smudge.

smooth vb flatten, level, plane; ease, lubricate; extenuate, palliate, soften; allay, alleviate, assuage, calm, mitigate, mollify. • adj even, flat, level, plane, polished, unruffled, unwrinkled; glabrous, glossy, satiny, silky, sleek, soft, velvet; euphonious, flowing, liquid, mellifluent; fluent, glib, voluble; bland, flattering, ingratiating, insinuating, mild, oily, smooth-tongued, soothing, suave, unctuous.

smother vb choke, stifle, suffocate; conceal, deaden, extinguish, hide, repress, suppress.

smudge vb besmear, blacken, blur, smear, smut, smutch, soil, spot, stain.

smug adj complacent, self-satisfied.

smutty adj coarse, gross, immodest, impure, indecent, indelicate, loose, nasty; dirty, foul, nasty, soiled, stained.

snag vb catch, enmesh, entangle, hook, snare, sniggle, tangle. • n knarl, knob, knot, projection, protuberance, snub; catch, difficulty, drawback, hitch, rub, shortcoming, weakness; obstacle.

snap vb break, fracture; bite, catch at, seize, snatch at, snip; crack; crackle, crepitate, decrepitate, pop. • adj casual, cursory, hasty, offhand, sudden, superficial. • n bite, catch, nip, seizure; catch, clasp, fastening, lock.

snare vb catch, ensnare, entangle, entrap. • n catch, gin, net, noose, springe, toil, trap, wile.

snarl¹ vb girn, gnarl, growl, grumble, murmur.

snarl² vb complicate, disorder, entangle, knot; confuse, embarrass, ensnare. • n complication, disorder, entanglement, tangle; difficulty, embarrassment, intricacy.

snatch vb catch, clutch, grasp, grip, pluck, pull, seize, snip, twich, wrest, wring. • n bit, fragment, part, portion; catch, effort.

sneak vb lurk, skulk, slink, steal; crouch, truckle. • adj clandestine, concealed, covert, hidden, secret, sly, underhand. • n informer, telltale.

sneer vb flout, gibe, jeer, mock, rail, scoff; (with at) deride, despise, disdain, laugh at, mock.

snip vb clip, cut, nip; snap, snatch. • n bit, fragment, particle, pice, shred; share, snack.

snooze vb catnap, doze, drowse, nap, sleep.

snub¹ vb abash, cold-shoulder, cut, discomfit, humble, humiliate, mortify, slight, take down. • n check, rebuke, slight.

snub² vb check, clip, cut short, dock, nip, prune, stunt. • adj pug, retroussé, snubbed, squashed, squat, stubby, turned-up.

snug adj close, concealed; comfortable, compact, convenient, neat, trim.

snuggle vb cuddle, nestle, nuzzle.

so adv thus, with equal reason; in such a manner; in this way, likewise; as it is, as it was, such; for this reason, therefore; be it so, thus be it. • conj in case that, on condition that, provided.

soak vb drench, moisten, permeate, saturate, wet; absorb, imbibe; imbue, macerate, steep.

soar vb ascend, fly aloft, glide, mount, rise.

sob vb cry, sigh convulsively, weep.

sober vb (with up) calm down, collect oneself, compose oneself, control oneself, cool off, master, moderate, simmer down. • adj abstemious, abstinent, temperate, unintoxicated; rational, reasonable, sane sound; calm, collected, composed, cool, dispassionate, moderate, rational, reasonabler, regular, steady, temperate, unimpassioned, unruffled, well-regulated; demure, grave, quiet, sedate, serious, solemn, sombre, staid; dark, drab, dull-looking, quiet.

sociable adj affable, communicative, companionable, friendly, genial.

social adj civic, civil; accessible, affable, communicative, companionable, familiar, friendly, hospitable, neighbourly, sociable; convivial, festive, gregarious. • n conversazione, gathering, get-together, party, reception, soiree.

society n association, companionship, company, converse, fellowship; the community, the public, the world; elite, *monde*; association, body, brotherhood, copartnership, corporation, club, company, fellowship, fraternity, partnership, sodality, union.

sodden adj drenched, saturated, soaked, steeped, wet; boiled, decocted, seethed, stewed.

soft adj impressible, malleable, plastic, pliable, yielding; downy, fleecy, velvety, mushy, pulpy, squashy; compliant, facile, irresolute, submissive, undecided, weak; bland, mild, gentle, kind, lenient, tender; delicate, tender; easy, even, gentle, quiet, smooth-going, steady; effeminate, luxurious, unmanly; dulcet, gentle, mellifluous.

soften vb intenerate, mellow, melt, tenderise; abate, allay, alleviate, appease, assuage, attemper, balm, blunt, calm, dull, ease, lessen, make easy, mitigate, moderate, mollify, qualify, quell, quiet, relent, relieve, soothe, still, temper; extenuate, modify, palliate.

soil[1] n earth, ground loam, mould; country, land.

soil[2] vb bedaub, begrime, bemire, besmear, bespatter, contaminate, daub, defile, dirty, foul, pollute, smirch, stain, sully, taint, tarnish.

sole adj alone, individual, one, only, single.

solemn adj ceremonial, formal, ritual; devotional, devout, religious, reverential, sacred; earnest, grave, serious, sober; august, awe-inspiring, awful, grand, imposing, impressive.

solicit vb appeal to, ask, beg, beseech, conjure, crave, entreat, implore, importune, petition, pray, press, request, supplicate, urge; arouse, entice, excite, invite, summon; canvass, seek.

solicitous adj anxious, apprehensive, careful, concerned, disturbed, eager, troubled, uneasy.

solid adj congealed, firm, hard, impenetrable; compact, dense, impermeable, massed; cubic; firm, sound, stable, stout, strong, substantial; firm, just, real, sound, strong, substantial, true, valid, weighty; reliable, safe, trustworthy.

solidarity n communion of interests, community, consolidation, fellowship, joint interest, mutual responsibility.

solidify vb compact, congeal, consolidate, harden, petrify.

solitary adj alone, companionless, lone, lonely, only, separate, unaccompanied; individual, single, sole; desert, deserted, desolate, isolated, remote, retired, secluded, unfrequented. • n anchoret, anchorite, eremite, hermit, recluse.

solution n answer, clue, disentanglement, elucidation, explication, explanation, key, resolution,

unravelling, unriddling; disintegration, dissolution, liquefaction, melting, resolution, separation; breach, disconnection, discontinuance.

solve vb clear, clear up, disentangle, elucidate, explain, expound, interpret, make plain, resolve.

sombre adj cloudy, dark, dismal, dull, dusky, gloomy, murky, overcast, rayless, shady, sombrous, sunless; doleful, funereal, grave, lugubrious, melancholy, mournful, sad, sober.

something n part, portion, thing; somebody; affair, event, matter, thing.

sometime adj former, late. • adv formerly, once; now and then, at one time or other.

sometimes adv at intervals, at times, now and then, occasionally.

somewhat adv in some degree, more or less, rather, something.

somewhere adv here and there, in one place or another, in some place.

song n aria, ballad, canticle, canzonet, carol, ditty, glee, lay, lullaby, snatch; descant, melody; anthem, hymn, lay, poem, psalm, strain.

soon adv anon, before long, by and by, in a short time, presently, shortly; betimes, earth, forthwith, promptly, quick; gladly, readily, willingly.

soothe vb cajole, flatter, humour; appease, assuage, balm, calm, compose, lull, mollify, pacify, quiet, soben, soften, still, tranquillise; allay, alleviate, blunt, check, deaden, dull, ease, lessen, mitigate, moderate, palliate, qualify, relieve.

soporific adj hypnotic, narcotic, opiate, sleepy, slumberous.

sorcerer n charmer, conjurer, diviner, enchanter, juggler, magician, necromaners, seer, shaman, soothsayer, thaumaturgist, witch, wizard.

sordid adj base, degraded, low, mean, vile; avaricious, close-fisted, covetous, illiberal, miserly, niggardly, penurious, stingy, ungenerous.

sore adj irritated, painful, raw, tender, ulcerated; aggrieved, galled, grieved, hurt, irritable, painted, tender, vexed; afflictive, distressing, severe, sharp, violent. • n abscess, boil, gathering, pustule, ulcer; affliction, grief, pain, sorrow, trouble.

sorrow vb bemoan, bewail, grieve, lament, mourn, weep. • n affliction, dolour, grief, heartache, mourning, sadness, trouble, woe.

sorrowful adj afflicted, dejected, depressed, grieved, grieving, heartsore, sad; baleful, distressing, grievous, lamentable, melancholy, mournful, painful, sad; disconsolate, dismal, doleful, dolorous, drear, dreary, lugubrious, melancholy, piteous, rueful woebegone, woeful.

sorry adj afflicted, dejected, grieved, pained, poor, sorrowful; distressing, pitiful; chagrined, mortified, pained, regretful, remorseful, sad, vexed; abject, base, beggarly, contemptible, despicable, low, mean, paltry, poor, insignificant, miserable, pitiful, shabby, worthless, wretched.

sort vb arrange, assort, class, classify, distribute, order; conjoin, join, put together; choose, elect, pick out, select. • n character, class, denomination, description, kind, nature, order, race, rank, species, type; manner, way.

soul n mind, psyche, spirit; being, person; embodiment, essence, personification, spirit, vital principle; ardour, energy, fervour, inspiration.

sound[1] adj entire, intact, unbroken, unhurt, unimpaired, uninjured, unmutilated, whole; hale, hardy, healthy, hearty, vigorous; good, perfect, undecayed; perfect, sane, well-balanced; correct, orthodox, right, solid, valid, well-founded; legal, valid; deep, fast, profound, unbroken, undisturbed; forcible, lusty, severe, stout.

sound[2] n channel, narrows, strait.

sound[3] vb resound; appear, seem; play on; express, pronounce, utter; announce, celebrate, proclaim, publish, spread. • n noise, note, tone, voice, whisper.

sound[4] vb fathom, gauge, measure, test; examine, probe, search, test, try.

sour vb acidulate; embitter, envenom. • adj acetose, acetous, acid, astringent, pricked, sharp, tart, vinegary; acrimonious, crabbed, cross, crusty, fretful, glum, ill-humoured, ill-natured, ill-tempered, peevish, pettish, petulant, snarling, surly; bitter, disagreeable, unpleasant; austere, dismal, gloomy, morose, sad, sullen; bad, coagulated, curdled, musty, rancid, turned.

source n beginning, fountain, fountainhead, head, origin, rise, root, spring, well.

souvenir n keepsake, memento, remembrance.

sovereign adj imperial, monarchical, princely, regal, royal, supreme; chief, commanding, excellent, highest, paramount, predominant, principal, supreme, utmost; efficacious, effectual. • n autocrat, monarch, suzerain; emperor, empress, king, lord, potentate, prince, princess, queen.

sovereignty n authority, dominion, empire, power, rule, supremacy, sway.

sow vb scatter, spread, strew; disperse, disseminate, propagate, plant.

space n expanse, expansion, extension, extent, proportions, spread; accommodation, capacity, room, place; distance, interspace, interval.

spacious adj extended, extensive, vast, wide; ample, broad, capacious, commodious, large.

span vb compass, cross, encompass, measure, overlay. • n brief period, spell; pair, team, yoke.

spare vb lay aside, lay by, reserve, save, set apart, set aside; dispense with, do without, part with; forbear, omit, refrain, withhold; exempt, forgive, keep from; afford, allow, give, grant; preserve, save; economise, pinch. • adj frugal, scanty, sparing, stinted; chary, parsimonious,

sparing; emaciated, gaunt, lank, lean, meagre, poor, thin, scraggy, skinny, raw-boned; additional, extra, supernumerary.

sparing adj little, scanty, scarce; abstemious, meagre, scanty, spare; chary, economical, frugal, parsimonious, saving; compassionate, forgiving, lenient, merciful.

spark vb scintillate, sparkle; begin, fire, incite, instigate, kindle, light, set off, start, touch off, trigger. • n scintilla, scintillation, sparkle; beginning, element, germ, seed.

sparkle vb coruscate, flash, gleam, glisten, glister, glitter, radiate, scintillate, shine, twinkle.

sparse adj dispersed, infrequent, scanty, scattered, sporadic, thin.

spasmodic adj erratic, fitful, intermittent, irregular, sporadic; convulsive, paroxysmal.

spatter vb bespatter, besprinkle, plash, splash, sprinkle; spit, sputter.

speak vb articulate, deliver, enunciate, express, pronounce, utter; announce, confer, declare, disclose, mention, say, tell; announce, celebrate, declare, make known, proclaim, speak abroad; accost, address, greet, hail; declare, exhibit, make known; argue, converse, dispute, say, talk; discourse, hold forth, harangue, mention, orate, plead, spout, tell, treat.

speaker n discourse, elocutionist, orator, prolocutor, spokesman; chairman, presiding officer.

special adj specific, specifical; especial, individual, particular, peculiar, unique; exceptional extraordinary, marked, particular, uncommon; appropriate, especial, express, peculiar.

speciality n particularity; feature, forte.

species n assemblage, class, collection, group; description, kind, sort, variety; (law) fashion, figure, form, shape.

specific adj characteristic, especial, particular, peculiar; definite, limited, precise, specified.

specify vb define, designate, detail, indicate, individualise, name, show, particularise.

specimen n example, model, pattern, sample.

speck n blemish, blot, flaw, speckle, spot, stain; atom, bit, corpuscle, mite, mote, particle.

spectacle n display, exhibition, pageant, parade, representation, review, scene, show, sight; curiosity, marvel, phenomenon, sight, wonder.

spectator n beholder, bystander, looker-on, observer, onlooker, witness.

spectre n apparition, banshee, ghost, goblin, hobgoblin, phantom, shade, shadow, spirit.

speculate vb cogitate, conjecture, contemplate, imagine, meditate, muse, ponder, reflect, ruminate, theorise, think; bet, gamble, hazard, risk.

speculative adj contemplative, philosophical, speculatory, unpractical; ideal, imaginary, theoretical; hazardous, risky, unsecured.

speech n articulation, language, words; dialect,

idiom, language, locution, tongue; conversation, parlance, talk, verbal intercourse; talk, address, discourse, harangue, oration.

speed vb hasten, hurry, rush, scurry; flourish, prosper, succeed, thrive; accelerate, dispatch, expedite, hasten, hurry, quicken, press forward, urge on; carry through, dispatch, execute; advance, aid, assist, help; favour, prosper. • n acceleration, celerity, dispatch, expedition, fleetness, haste, hurry, quickness, rapidity, swiftness, velocity; good fortune, good luck, prosperity.

spell[1] n charm, exorcism, hoodoo, incantation, jinx, witchery; allure, bewitchment, captivation, enchantment, entrancement, fascination.

spell[2] vb interpret, read, unfold, unravel.

spell[3] n fit, period, season, stint, term, turn.

spellbound adj bewitched, charmed, enchanted, entranced, enthralled, fascinated.

spend vb disburse, dispose of, expend, lay out, part with; consume, dissipate, exhaust, lavish, squander, use up, wear, waste; apply, bestow, devote, employ, pass.

spendthrift n prodigal, squanderer, waster.

spent adj exhausted, fatigued, played out, used up, wearied, worn out.

sphere n ball, globe, orb, spheroid; ambit, beat, bound, circle, circuit, compass, department, function, office, orbit, province, range, walk; country, domain, quarter, realm, region.

spherical adj bulbous, globular, orbicular, rotund, round, spheroid; planetary.

spice n flavour, flavouring, relish, savour, taste; admixture, dash, grain, infusion, particle.

spicy adj aromatic, balmy, fragrant; keen, piquant, pointed, pungent, sharp; indelicate, off-colour, racy, risqué, sensational, suggestive.

spill vb effuse, pour out, shed. • n accident, fall.

spin vb twist; draw out, extend; lenthen, prolong, protract, spend; pirouette, turn, twirl, whirl. • n drive, joyride, ride; autorotation, gyration, loop, revolution, rotation, turning, wheeling; pirouette, reel, turn, wheel, whirl.

spine n barb, prickle, thorn; backbone; ridge.

spirit vb animate, encourage, excite, inspirit; carry off, kidnap. • n immaterial substance, life, vital essence; person, soul; angel, apparition, demon, elf, fairy, genius, ghost, phantom, shade, spectre, sprite; disposition, frame of mind, humour, mood, temper; spirits; ardour, cheerfulness, courage, earnestness, energy, enterprise, enthusiasm, fire, force, mettle, resolution, vigour, vim, vivacity, zeal; animation, cheerfulness, enterprise, esprit, glow, liveliness, piquancy, spice, spunk, vivacity, warmth; drift, gist, intent, meaning, purport, sense, significance, tenor; character, characteristic, complexion, essence, nature, quality, quintessence; alcohol, liquor.

spirited adj active, alert, animated, ardent, bold,

brisk, courageous, earnest, frisky, high-mettled, high-spirited, lively, mettlesome, vivacious.

spiritual adj ethereal, ghostly, immaterial incorporeal, psychical, supersensible; ideal, moral, unwordly; divine, holy, pure, sacred.

spit[1] vb impale, thrust through, transfix.

spit[2] vb eject, throw out; drool expectorate, salivate, splutter. • n saliva, spittle, sputum.

spite vb injure, mortify, thwart; annoy, offend, vex. • n grudge, hate, hatred, ill-nature, ill-will, malevolence, malice, maliciousness, malignity, pique, rancour, spleen, venom, vindictiveness.

spiteful adj evil-minded, hateful, ill-disposed, ill-natured, malevolent, malicious, malign.

splash vb dabble, dash, plash, spatter, splurge.

splendid adj beaming, bright, brilliant, effulgent, glowing, lustrous, radiant, refulgent, resplendent, shining; dazzling, gorgeous, imposing, kingly, magnificent, pompous, showy, sumptuous, superb; brilliant, celebrated, conspicuous, distinguished, eminent, famous, glorious, illustrious, noble, pre-eminent, remarkable, signal; grand, heroic, lofty, noble, sublime.

splendour n brightness, brilliance, brilliancy, lustre, radiance, refulgence; display, éclat, gorgeousness, grandeur, magnificence, parade, pomp, show, stateliness; celebrity, eminence, fame, glory, renown.

splinter n fragment, piece.

split vb cleave, rive; break, burst, rend, splinter; divide, part, separate, sunder. • n crack, fissure, rent; breach, division, separation.

spoil vb despoil, fleece, loot, pilfer, plunder, ravage, rob, steal, strip, waste; corrupt, damage, destroy, disfigure, harm, impair, injure, mar, ruin, vitiate; decay, decompose.

spokesman n mouthpiece, prolocutor, speaker.

sponge vb cleanse, wipe; efface, expunge, obliterate, rub out, wipe out.

spongy adj absorbent, porous, spongeous; rainy, showery, wet; drenched, marshy, saturated, soaked, wet.

sponsor vb back, capitalise, endorse, finance, guarantee, patronise, promote, support, stake, subsidise, take up, underwrite. • n angel, backer, guarantor, patron, prompter, supporter, surety, underwriter; godfather, godmother, godparent.

spontaneous adj free, gratuitous, impulsive, improvised, instinctive, unbidden, unconstrained, voluntary, willing.

sport vb caper, disport, frolic, gambol, have fun, make merry, play, romp, skip; trifle; display, exhibit. • n amusement, diversion, entertainment, frolic, fun, gambol, game, jollity, joviality, merriment, merry-making, mirth, pastime, pleasantry, prank, recreation; jest, joke; derision, jeer, mockery, ridicule; monstrosity.

sportive adj frisky, frolicsome, gamesome, hilarious, lively, merry, playful, prankish, rollicking, sprightly, tricksy; comic, facetious, funny, humorous, jocose, jocular, lively, ludicrous, merry, mirthful, vivacious, waggish.

spot vb besprinkle, dapple, dot, speck, stud, variegate; blemish, disgrace, soil, splotch, stain, sully, tarnish; detect, discern, espy, make out, observe, see, sight. • n blot, dapple, fleck, freckle, maculation, mark, mottle, patch, speck, speckle; blemish, blotch, flaw, pock, splotch, stain; place, site.

spotless adj perfect, undefaced, unspotted; blameless, immaculate, innocent, irreproachable, pure, stainless, unblemished.

spouse n companion, consort, husband, wife.

spout vb gush, jet, pour out, spirit, spurt, squirt; declaim, mouth, speak, utter. • n ajutage, conduit, tube; beak, gargoyle, nose, nozzle.

sprain vb overstrain, rick, strain, twist, wrench.

spray[1] vb atomise, besprinkle, douche, gush, jet, shower, splash, splatter, spout, sprinkle, squirt. • n aerosol, atomiser, douche, foam, froth, shower, sprinkler, spume.

spray[2] n bough, branch, shoot, sprig, twig.

spread vb dilate, expand, extend, mantle, stretch; diffuse, disperse, distribute, radiate, scatter, sprinkle, strew; broadcast, circulate, disseminate, divulge, make known, make public, promulgate, propagate, publish; open, unfold, unfurl; cover, extend over, overspread. • n compass, extent, range, reach, scope, stretch; expansion, extension; circulation, dissemination, propagation; cloth, cover; banquet, feast, meal.

spree n bacchanal, carousal, debauch, frolic, jollification, orgy, revel, revelry, saturnalia.

sprig n shoot, spray, twig; lad, youth.

sprightly adj airy, animated, blithe, blithesome, brisk, buoyant, cheerful, debonair, frolicsome, joyous, lively, mercurial, vigorous, vivacious.

spring vb bound, hop, jump, leap, prance, vault; arise, emerge, grow, issue, proceed, put forth, shoot forth, stem; derive, descend, emanate, flow, originate, rise, start; rebound, recoil; bend, warp; grow, thrive, wax. • n bound, hop, jump, leap, vault; elasticity, flexibility, resilience, resiliency, springiness; fount, fountain, fountainhead, geyser, springhead, well; cause, origin, principle, source; springtime.

springy adj bouncing, bounding, elastic, rebounding, recoiling, resilient.

sprinkle vb scatter, strew; bedew, besprinkle, dust, powder, sand, spatter; wash, cleanse.

sprinkling n affusion, baptism, bedewing, spattering, splattering, spraying, wetting; dash, scattering, seasoning, smack, soupçon, suggestion, tinge, touch, trace, vestige.

sprout vb bourgeon, burst forth, germinate, grow, pullulate, push, put forth, ramify, shoot, shoot forth. • n shoot, sprig.

spruce vb preen, prink; adorn, deck, dress, smarten, trim. • adj dandyish, dapper, fine, foppish, jaunty, natty, neat, nice, smart, tidy, trig.

spry adj active, agile, alert, brisk, lively, nimble, prompt, quick, ready, smart, sprightly.

spur vb gallop, hasten, press on, prick; animate, arouse, drive, goad, impel, incite, induce, instigate, rouse, stimulate, urge forward. • n goad, point, prick, rowel; fillip, goad, impulse, incentive, incitement, inducement, instigation, motive, provocation, stimulus, whip; gnarl, knob, knot, projection, snag.

spurious adj bogus, counterfeit, deceitful, false, feigned, fictitious, make-believe, meretricious, mock, pretended, sham, unauthentic.

spurn vb drive away, kick; contemn, despise, disregard, flout, scorn, slight; disdain, reject.

spurt vb gush, jet, spirt, spout, spring out, stream out, well.

spy vb behold, discern, espy, see; detect, discover, search out; explore, inspect, scrutinize, search; shadow, trail, watch. • n agent, detective, double agent, mole, scout.

squabble vb brawl, fight, quarrel, scuffle, struggle, wrangle; altercate, bicker, contend, dispute, jangle.

squalid adj dirty, filthy, foul, mucky, slovenly, unclean, unkempt.

squander vb dissipate, expend, lavish, lose, misuse, scatter, spend, throw away, waste.

square vb make square, quadrate; accommodate, adapt, fit, mould, regulate, shape, suit; adjust, balance, close, make even, settle; accord, chime in, cohere, comport, fall in, fit, harmonise, quadrate, suit. • adj four-square, quadrilateral, quadrate; equal, equitable, exact, fair, honest, just, upright; adjusted, balanced, even, settled; just, true, suitable. • n four-sided figure, rectangle, tetragon; parade, piazza, plaza.

squat vb cower, crouch; occupy, plant, settle. • adj cowering, crouching; dumpy, pudgy, short.

squeal vb creak, cry, howl, scream, screech, shriek, squawk, yell; betray, inform on.

squeamish adj nauseated, qualmish, queasy, sickish; dainty, delicate, fastidious, finical, hypercritical, nice, over-nice, particular, priggish.

squeeze vb clutch, compress, constrict, grip, nip, pinch, press; drive, force; crush, harass, oppress; crowd, force through, press; (with out) extract. • n congestion, crowd, crush, throng.

squirm vb twist, wriggle, writhe.

stab vb broach, gore, jab, pierce, pink, spear, stick, transfix, transpierce; wound. • n cut, jab, prick, thrust; blow, dagger-stroke, injury.

stable adj established, fixed, immovable, immutable, invariable, permanent, unalterable, unchangeable; constand, firm, staunch, steadfast, steady, unwavering; abiding, durable, enduring, fast, lasting, permanent, perpetual, secure, sure.

staff n baton, cane, pole, rod, stick, wand; bat, bludgeon, club, cudgel, mace; prop, stay, support; employees, personnel, work force.

stage vb dramatise, perform, present, produce, put on. • n dais, platform, rostrum, scaffold, staging, stand; arena, field; boards, playhouse, theatre; degree, point, step; stagecoach.

stagger vb reel, sway, totter; alternate, fluctuate, overlap, vacillate, vary; falter, hesitate, waver; amaze, astonish, astound, confound, dumbfound, nonplus, pose, shock, surprise.

stagnant adj close, motionless, quiet, standing; dormant, dull, heavy, inactive, inert, sluggish.

stagnate vb decay, deteriorate, languish, rot, stand still, vegetate.

staid adj calm, composed, demure, grave, sedate, serious, settled, sober, solemn, steady.

stain vb blemish, blot, blotch, discolour, maculate, smirch, soil, splotch, spot, sully, tarnish; colour, dye, tinge; contaminate, corrupt, debase, defile, deprave, disgrace, dishonour, pollute, taint. • n blemish, blot, defect, discoloration, flaw, imperfection, spot, tarnish; contamination, disgrace, dishonour, infamy, pollution, reproach, shame, taint, tarnish.

stake[1] vb brace, mark, prop, secure, support. • n pale, palisade, peg, picket, post, stick.

stake[2] vb finance, pledge, wager; hazard, imperil, jeopardize, peril, risk, venture. • n bet, pledge, wager; adventure, hazard, risk, venture.

stale adj flat, fusty, insipid, mawkish, mouldy, musty, sour, tasteless, vapid; decayed, effete, faded, old, time-worn, worn-out; common, commonplace, hackneyed, stereotyped, trite.

stalk[1] n culm, pedicel, peduncle, petiole, shaft, spire, stem, stock.

stalk[2] vb march, pace, stride, strut, swagger; follow, hunt, shadow, track, walk stealthily.

stall[1] n stable; cell, compartment, recess; booth, kiosk, shop, stand.

stall[2] vb block, delay, equivocate, filibuster, hinder, postpone, procrastinate, temporise; arrest, check, conk out, die, fail, halt, stick, stop.

stalwart adj able-bodied, athletic, brawny, lusty, muscular, powerful, robust, sinewy, stout, strapping, strong, sturdy, vigorous; bold, brave, daring, gallant, indomitable, intrepid, redoubtable, resolute, valiant, valorous. • n backer, member, partisan, supporter.

stamina n energy, force, lustiness, power, stoutness, strength, sturdiness, vigour.

stammer vb falter, hesitate, stutter.

stamp vb brand, impress, imprint, mark, print. • n brand, impress, impression, print; cast, character, complexion, cut, description, fashion, form, kind, make, mould, sort, type.

stampede vb charge, flee, panic. • n charge, flight, rout, running away, rush.

stand vb be erect, remain upright; abide, be fixed, continue, endure, hold good, remain; halt, pause, stop; be firm, be resolute, stand ground, stay; be valid, have force; depend, have support, rest; bear, brook, endure, suffer, sustain, weather; abide, admit, await, submit, tolerate, yield; fix, place, put, set upright; (with against) oppose, resist, withstand; (with by) be near, be present; aid, assist, defend, help, side with, support; defend, make good, justify, maintain, support, vindicate; (naut) attend, be ready; (with fast) be fixed, be immovable; (with for) mean, represent, signify; aid, defend, help, maintain, side with, support; (with off) keep aloof, keep off; not to comply; (with out) be prominent, jut, project, protrude; not comply, not yield, persist; (with up for) defend, justify, support, sustain, uphold; (with with) agree. • n place, position, post, station; halt, stay, stop; dais, platform, rostrum; booth, stall; opposition, resistance.

standard adj average, conventional, customary, normal, ordinary, regular, usual; accepted, approved, authoritative, orthodox, received; formulary, prescriptive, regulation. • n canon, criterion, model, norm, rule, test, type; gauge, measure, model, scale; support, upright.

standing adj established, fixed, immovable, settled; durable, lasting, permanent; motionless, stagnant. • n position, stand, station; continuance, duration, existence; footing, ground, hold; condition, estimation, position, rank, reputation.

standpoint n point of view, viewpoint.

standstill n cessation, interruption, stand, stop.

staple adj basic, chief, essential, fundamental, main, primary, principal.

star vb act, appear, feature, headline, lead, perform, play; emphasise, highlight, stress, underline. • adj leading, main, paramount, principal; celebrated, illustrious, well-known. • n heavenly body, luminary; aserisk, pentacle, pentagram; destiny, doom, fate, fortune, lot; diva, headliner, hero, heroine, lead, principal, protagonist.

stare vb gape, gaze, look intently, watch.

stark adj rigid, stiff; absolute, bare, downright, entire, gross, mere, pure, sheer, simple. • adv absolutely, completely, entirely, fully, wholly.

starry adj astral, sidereal, star-spangled, stellar; bright, brilliant, lustrous, shining, sparkling.

start vb begin, commence, inaugurate, initiate, institute; discover, invent; flinch, jump, shrink, startle, wince; alarm, disturb, fright, rouse, scare, startle; depart, set off, take off; arise, call forth, evoke, raise; dislocate, move suddenly, spring, startle. • n beginning, commencement, inauguration, outset; fit, jump, spasm, twitch.

startle vb flinch, shrink, start, wince; affright, alarm, fright, frighten, scare, shock.

starvation n famine, famishment.

starve *vb* famish, perish; lack, want.

state *vb* affirm, assert, declare, explain, expound, express, narrate, propound, recite, say, set forth, specify, voice. • *adj* civic, national, public. • *n* case, circumstances, condition, pass, phase, plight, position, posture, predicament, situation, status; condition, guise, mode, quality, rank; dignity, glory, grandeur, magnificence, pageantry, parade, pomp, spendour; body politic, civil community, commonwealth, nation.

stately *adj* august, dignified, elevated, grand, imperial, imposing, lofty, magnificent, majestic, noble, princely, royal; ceremonious, formal.

statement *n* account, allegation, announcement, communiqué, declaration, description, exposition, mention, narration, narrative, recital, relation, report, specification; assertion, predication, proposition, pronouncement, thesis.

station *vb* establish, fix, locate, place, post, set. • *n* location, place, position, post, seat, situation; business, employment, function, occupation, office; character, condition, degree, dignity, rank, state, status; depot, stop, terminal.

stationary *adj* fixed, motionless, permanent, quiescent, stable, standing, still.

stature *n* height, physique, size, tallness; altitude, consequence, elevation, eminence.

status *n* caste, condition, footing, position, rank, standing, station.

stay *vb* abide, dwell, lodge, rest, sojourn, tarry; continue, halt, remain, stand still, stop; attend, delay, linger, wait; arrest, check, curb, hold, keep in, prevent, rein in, restrain, withhold; delay, detain, hinder, obstruct; hold up, prop, shore up, support, sustain, uphold. • *n* delay, repose, rest, sojourn; halt, stand, stop; bar, check, curb, hindrance, impediment, interruption, obstacle, obstruction, restraint, stumbling block; buttress, dependence, prop, staff, support, supporter.

steady *vb* balance, counterbalance, secure, stabilise, support. • *adj* firm, fixed, stable; constant, equable, regular, undeviating, uniform, unremitting; constant, persevering, resolute, stable, staunch, steadfast, unchangeable, unwavering.

steal *vb* burglarise, burgle, crib, embezzle, filch, peculate, pilfer, plagiarise, purloin, peculate, poach, shoplift, thieve; creep, sneak.

stealthy *adj* clandestine, furtive, private, secret, skulking, sly, sneaking, surreptitious.

steam *vb* emit vapour, fume; evaporate, vaporise; coddle, cook, poach; navigate, sail; be hot, sweat. • *n* vapour; effluvium, exhalation, fume, mist, reek, smoke.

steel *vb* case-harden, edge; brace, fortify, harden, make firm, nerve, strengthen.

steep¹ *adj* abrupt, declivitous, precipitous, sheer, sloping, sudden. • *n* declivity, precipice.

steep² *vb* digest, drench, imbrue, imbue, soak.

steer *vb* direct, conduct, govern, guide, pilot.

stem¹ *vb* (with **from**) bud, descend, generate, originate, spring, sprout. • *n* axis, stipe, trunk; pedicel, peduncle, petiole, stalk; branch, descendant, offspring, progeny, scion, shoot; ancestry, descent, family, generation, line, lineage, pedigree, race, stock; (*naut*) beak, bow, cutwater, forepart, prow; helm, lookout; etymon, radical, radix, origin, root.

stem² *vb* breast, oppose, resist, withstand; check, dam, oppose, staunch, stay, stop.

step *vb* pace, stride, tramp, tread, walk. • *n* footstep, pace, stride; stair, tread; degree, gradation, grade, interval; advance, advancement, progression; act, action, deed, procedure, proceeding; footprint, trace, track, vestige; footfall, gait, pace, walk; expedient, means, measure, method; round, rundle, rung.

sterile *adj* barren, infecund, unfruitful, unproductive, unprolific; bare, dry, empty, poor.

stern¹ *adj* austere, dour, forbidding, grim, severe; bitter, cruel, hard, harsh, inflexible, relentless, rigid, rigorous, severe, strict, unrelenting; immovable, incorruptible, steadfast.

stern² *n* behind, breach, hind part, posterior, rear, tail; (*naut*) counter, poop, rudderpost, tailpost; butt, buttocks, fundament, rump.

stew *vb* boil, seethe, simmer, stive. • *n* ragout, stewed meat; confusion, difficulty, mess.

stick¹ *vb* gore, penetrate, pierce, puncture, spear, stab, transfix; infix, insert, thrust; attach, cement, glue, paste; fix in, set; adhere, cleave, cling, hold; abide, persist, remain, stay, stop; doubt, hesitate, scruple, stickle, waver; (*with* by) adhere to, be faithful, support.

stick² *n* birch, rod, switch; bat, bludgeon, club, cudgel, shillelah; cane, staff, walking stick; cue, pole, spar, stake.

sticky *adj* adhesive, clinging, gluey, glutinous, gummy, mucilaginous, tenacious, viscid.

stiff *adj* inflexible, rigid, stark, unbending, unyielding; firm, tenacious, thick; obstinate, pertinacious, strong, stubborn, tenacious; absolute, austere, dogmatic, inexorable, peremptory, positive, rigorous, severe, straitlaced, strict, stringent, uncompromising; ceremonious, chilling, constrained, formal, frigid, prim, punctilious, stately, starchy, stilted:

stifle *vb* choke, smother, suffocate; check, deaden, destroy, extinguish, quench, repress, stop, suppress; conceal, gag, hush, muffle, muzzle, silence, smother, still.

stigma *n* blot, blur, brand, disgrace, dishonour, reproach, shame, spot, stain, taint, tarnish.

still¹ *vb* hush, lull, muffle, silence, stifle; allay, appease, calm, compose, lull, pacify, quiet, smooth, tranquillise; calm, check, immobilise, quiet, restrain, stop, subdue, suppress. • *adj* hushed, mum, mute, noiseless, silent; calm, placid, quiet, serene, stilly, tranquil, unruffled; inert, motionless, quiescent, stagnant, stationary.

still² *adv, conj* till now, to this time, yet; however, nevertheless, notwithstanding; always, continually, ever, habitually, uniformly; again.

stimulate *vb* animate, arouse, awaken, brace, encourage, energise, excite, fire, foment, goad, impel, incite, inflame, inspirit, instigate, kindle, prick, prompt, provoke, rally, rouse, set on, spur, stir up, urge, whet, work up.

stimulus *n* encouragement, fillip, goad, incentive, incitement, motivation, motive, provocation, spur, stimulant.

sting *vb* hurt, nettle, prick, wound; afflict, cut.

stingy *adj* avaricious, close, close-fisted, covetous, grudging, mean, miserly.

stink *vb* emit a stench, reek, smell bad. • *n* bad smell, fetor, offensive odour, stench.

stint *vb* bound, confine, skimp, limit, restrain; begrudge, pinch, scrimp, skimp, straiten; cease, desist, stop. • *n* bound, limit, restraint; lot, period, quota, share, shift, task, time, turn.

stipulate *vb* agree, bargain, condition, contract, covenant, engage, provide, settle terms.

stir *vb* budge, change place, go, move; agitate, bestir, disturb, prod; argue, discuss, moot, raise, start; animate, arouse, awaken, excite, goad, incite, instigate, prompt, provoke, quicken, rouse, spur, stimulate; appear, happen, turn up; get up, rise; (*with up*) animate, awaken, incite, instigate, move, provoke, quicken, rouse, stimulate. • *n* activity, ado, agitation, bustle, confusion, excitement, fidget, flurry, fuss, hurry, movement; commotion, disorder, disturbance, tumult, uproar.

stock *vb* fill, furnish, store, supply; accumulate, garner, hoard, lay in, reposit, reserve, save, treasure up. • *adj* permanent, standard, standing. • *n* assets, capital, commodities, fund, principal, shares; accumulation, hoard, inventory, merchandise, provision, range, reserve, store, supply; ancestry, breed, descent, family, house, line, lineage, parentage, pedigree, race; cravat, neckcloth; butt, haft, hand; block, log, pillar, post, stake; stalk, stem, trunk.

stockstill *adj* dead-still, immobile, motionless, stationary, still, unmoving.

stocky *adj* chubby, chunky, dumpy, plump, short, stout, stubby, thickset.

stoic, stoical *adj* imperturbable, passionless, patient, philosophic, phlegmatic.

stolid *adj* blockish, doltish, dull, foolish, heavy, obtuse, slow, stockish, stupid.

stomach *vb* abide, bear, brook, endure, put up with, stand, submit to, suffer, swallow, tolerate. • *n* abdomen, belly, gut, paunch, pot, tummy; appetite, desire, inclination, keenness, liking.

stone *vb* free from stones, stein; brick, cover,

face, slate, tile; lapidate, pelt. • *n* boulder, cobble, gravel, pebble, rock; gem, jewel, precious stone; cenotaph, gravestone, monument, tombstone; nut, pit; adamant, agate, flint, gneiss, granite, marble, slate, etc.

stony *adj* gritty, hard, lapidose, lithic, petrous, rocky; adamantine, flinty, hard, inflexible, obdurate; cruel, hard-hearted, inexorable, pitiless.

stoop *vb* bend forward, bend down, bow, lean, sag, slouch, slump; abase, cower, cringe, give in, submit, succumb, surrender; condescend, deign, descend, vouchsafe; fall, sink.

stop *vb* block, blockade, close, close up, obstruct, occlude; arrest, block, check, halt, hold, pause, stall, stay; bar, delay, embargo, hinder, impede, intercept, interrupt, obstruct, preclude, prevent, repress, restrain, staunch, stay, suppress, thwart; break off, cease, desist, discontinue, forbear, give over, leave off, refrain from; arrest, intermit, quiet, quiten, terminate; lodge, stay, tarry. • *n* halt, intermission, pause, respite, rest, stoppage, suspension, truce; block, cessation, check, hindrance, interruption, obstruction, repression; bar, impediment, obstacle, obstruction; full stop, point.

store *vb* accumulate, amass, cache, deposit, garner, hoard, husband, lay by, lay in, lay up, put by, reserve, save, store up, stow away, treasure up; furnish, provide, replenish, stock, supply.

storm *vb* assail, assault, attack; blow violently; fume, rage, rampage, rant, rave, tear. • *n* blizzard, gale, hurricane, squall, tempest, tornado, typhoon, whirlwind; agitation, clamour, commotion, disturbance, insurrection, outbreak, sedition, tumult, turmoil; adversity, affliction, calamity, distress; assault, attack, brunt, onset.

stormy *adj* blustering, boisterous, gusty, squally, tempestuous, windy; passionate, riotous, rough, turbulent, violent, wild.

story *n* annals, chronicle, history, record; account, narration, narrative, recital, record, rehearsal, relation, report, statement, tale; fable, fiction, novel, romance; anecdote, incident, legend, tale; canard, fabrication, falsehood, fib, fiction, figure, invention, lie, untruth.

stout *adj* able-bodied, athletic, brawny, lusty, robust, sinewy, stalwart, strong, sturdy, vigorous; courageous, hardy, indomitable, stouthearted; contumacious, obstinate, proud, resolute, stubborn; compact, firm, hardy, solid, staunch, strong, sturdy; bouncing, burly, chubby, corpulent, fat, jolly, large, obese, plump, portly, stocky, strapping, thickset.

stow *vb* load, pack, put away, store, stuff.

straggle *vb* rove, wander, deviate, digress, bafdaboutt, ramble, range, roam, rove, stray.

straight *adj* direct, near, rectilinear, right, short, undeviating, unswerving; erect, perpendicular, plumb, right, upright, vertical; equitable, fair, honest, honourable, just, square.

straightaway, straightway adv at once, directly, forthwith, immediately, speedily.

straighten vb arrange, neaten, order, tidy.

strain¹ vb draw tightly, make tense, stretch, tighten; injure, sprain, wrench; exert, overexert, overtax, rack; embrace, fold, hug, press, squeeze; compel, constrain, force; dilute, distill, drain, filter, filtrate, ooze, percolate, purify, separate; fatigue, overtask, overwork, task, tax, tire. • n stress, tenseness, tension, tensity; effort, exertion, force, overexertion; burden, task, tax; sprain, wrench; lay, melody, snatch, song.

strain² n manner, style, tone, vein; disposition, tendency, trait, turn; descent, extraction, family, lineage, pedigree, race, stock.

strand vb abandon, beach, be wrecked, cast away, go aground, ground, maroon, run aground, wreck. • n beach, coast, shore.

strange adj alien, exotic, far-fetched, foreign, outlandish, remote; new, novel; curious, exceptional, extraordinary, irregular, odd, particular, peculiar, rare, singular, surprising, uncommon, unusual; abnormal, anomalous, extraordinary, inconceivable, incredible, inexplicable, marvellous, mysterious, preternatural, unaccountable, unbelievable, unheard of, unique, unnatural, wonderful; bizarre, droll, grotesque, odd, quaint, queer, peculiar; inexperienced, unacquainted, unfamiliar, unknown; bashful, distant, shy.

stranger n alien, foreigner, newcomer, immigrant, outsider; guest, visitor.

strangle vb choke, contract, smother, squeeze, stifle, suffocate, throttle, tighten; keep back, quiet, repress, still, suppress.

strap vb beat, thrash, whip; bind, fasten, sharpen, strop. • n thong; band, ligature, strip, tie.

stratagem n artifice, cunning, device, dodge, finesse, intrigue, machination, manoeuvre, plan, plot, ruse, scheme, trick, wile.

strategic adj calcuated, deliberate, diplomatic, manoeuvering, planned, politic, tactical; critical, decisive, key, vital.

strategy n generalship, manoeuvering, plan, policy, stratagem, strategetics, tactics.

stray vb deviate, digress, err, meander, ramble, range, roam, rove, straggle, stroll, swerve, transgress, wander. • adj abandoned, lost, strayed, wandering; accidental, erratic, random.

streak vb band, bar, striate, stripe, vein; dart, dash, flash, hurtle, run, speed, sprint, stream, tear. • n band, bar, belt, layer, line, strip, stripe, thread, trace, vein; cast, grain, stripe, tone, touch, vein; beam, bolt, dart, dash, flare, flash.

stream vb course, flow, glide, pour, run, spout; emit, pour out, shed; emanate, go forth, issue, radiate; extend, float, stretch out, wave. • n

brook, burn, race, rill, rivulet, run, runlet, runnel, trickle; course, current, flow, flux, race, rush, tide, torrent, wake, wash; beam, gleam, patch.

strength n force, might, main, nerve, potency, power, vigour; hardness, solidity, toughness; impregnability, proof; brawn, grit, lustiness, muscle, robustness, sinewy, stamina, thews; animation, courage, determination, firmness, fortitude, resolution, spirit; cogency, efficacy, soundness, validity; emphasis, energy; brilliance, clearness, intensity, vitality, vividness; body, excellence, potency, spirit, virtue; force, impetuosity, vehemence, violence; boldness, energy.

strengthen vb buttress, recruit, reinforce; fortify; brace, energise, harden, nerve, steel, stimulate; freshen, invigorate, vitalise.

strenuous adj active, ardent, eager, earnest, energetic, resolute, vigorous, zealous; bold, determined, doughty, intrepid, resolute, spirited.

stress vb accent, accentuate, emphasise, highlight, point up, underline, underscore; bear, bear upon, press, pressurise; pull, rack, strain, stretch, tense, tug. • n accent, accentuation, emphasis; effort, force, pull, strain, tension, tug; boisterousness, severity, violence; pressure, urgency.

stretch vb brace, screw, strain, tense, tighten; elongate, extend, lengthen, protract, pull; display, distend, expand, spread, unfold, widen; sprain, strain; distort, exaggerate, misrepresent. • n compass, extension, extent, range, reach, scope; effort, exertion, strain, struggle.

strict adj close, demand, tense, tight; accurate, careful, close, exact, literal, particular, precise, scrupulous; austere, inflexible, harsh, orthodox, puritanical, rigid, rigorous, severe, stern, strait-laced, stringent, uncompromising, unyielding.

strife n battle, combat, conflict, contention, contest, discord, quarrel, struggle, warfare.

strike vb bang, beat, belabour, box, buffet, cudgel, cuff, hit, knock, lash, pound, punch, rap, slap, slug, smite, thump, whip; impress, imprint, stamp; afflict, chastise, deal, give, inflict, punish, smite; affect, astonish, electrify, stun; clash, collide, dash, hit, touch; mutiny, rebel.

stringent adj binding, contracting, rigid, rigorous, severe, strict.

strip¹ n piece, ribbon, shred, slip.

strip² vb denude, hull, skin, uncover; bereave, deprive, deforest, desolate, despoil, devastate, disarm, dismantle, disrobe, divest, expose, fleece, loot, shave; plunder, pillage, ransack, rob, sack, spoil; disrobe, uncover, undress.

strive vb aim, attempt, endeavour, labour, strain, struggle, toil; contend, contest, fight, tussle, wrestle; compete, cope, struggle.

stroke¹ n blow, glance, hit, impact, knock, lash, pat, percussion, rap, shot, switch, thump; attack, paralysis, stroke; affliction, damage, hardship, hurt, injury, misfortune, reverse, visitation; dash, feat, masterstroke, touch.

stroke² vb caress, feel, palpate, pet, knead, massage, nuzzle, rub, touch.

stroll vb loiter, lounge, ramble, range, rove, saunter, straggle, stray, wander.

strong adj energetic, forcible, powerful, robust, sturdy; able, enduring; cogent, firm, valid.

structure vb arrange, constitute, construct, make, organise. • n arrangement, conformation, configuration, constitution, construction, form, formation, make, organisation; anatomy, composition, texture; building, edifice.

struggle vb aim, endeavour, exert, labour, strive, toil, try; battle, contend, contest, fight, wrestle; agonise, flounder, writhe.

stubborn adj contumacious, dogged, headstrong, heady, inflexible, intractable, mulish, obdurate, obstinate, perverse, positive, refractory, ungovernable, unmanageable, unruly, unyielding, willful; constant, enduring, firm, hardy, persevering, persistent, steady, stoical, uncomplaining, unremitting; firm, hard, inflexible, stiff.

studious adj contemplative, meditative, reflective, thoughtful; assiduous, attentive, desirous, diligent, eager, lettered, scholarly, zealous.

study vb cogitate, lubricate, meditate, muse, ponder, reflect, think; analyze, contemplate, examine, investigate, ponder, probe, scrutinise, search, sift, weigh. • n exercise, inquiry, investigation, reading, research, stumble; cogitation, consideration, contemplation, examination, meditation, reflection, thought; model, object, representation, sketch; den, studio.

stunning adj deafening, stentorian; dumbfounding, stupefying.

stunted adj checked, diminutive, dwarfed, dwarfish, lilliputian, small, undersized.

stupendous adj amazing, astonishing, astounding, marvellous, overwhelming, surprising, wonderful; enormous, huge, immense, monstrous, prodigious, towering, tremendous, vast.

stupid adj brainless, crass, doltish, dull, foolish, idiotic, inane, inept, obtuse, pointless, prosaic, senseless, simple, slow, sluggish, stolid, tedious, tiresome, witless.

sturdy adj bold, determined, dogged, firm, hardy, obstinate, persevering, pertinacious, resolute, stiff, stubborn, sturdy; athletic, brawny, forcible, lusty, muscular, powerful, robust, stalwart, stout, strong, thickset, vigorous, well-set.

style vb address, call, characterise, denominate, designate, dub, entitle, name, term. • n dedication, expression, phraseology, turn; cast, character, fashion, form, genre, make, manner, method, mode, model, shape, vogue, way; appellation, denomination, designation, name, title; chic, elegance, smartness; pen, pin, point, stylus.

stylish adj chic, courtly, elegant, fashionable, genteel, modish, polished, smart.

suave adj affable, agreeable, amiable, bland, courteous, debonair, delightful, glib, gracious, smooth, oily, unctuous, urbane.

subdue vb beat, bend, break, bow, conquer, control, crush, defeat, discomfit, foil, master, overbear, overcome, overpower, overwhelm, quell, rout, subject, subjugate, surmount, vanquish, worst; allay, choke, curb, mellow, moderate, mollify, reduce, repress, restrain.

subject vb control, master, overcome, reduce, subdue, subjugate, tame; enslave, enthral; abandon, refer, submit, surrender. • n dependent, henchman, liegeman, slave, subordinate; matter, point, subject matter, theme, thesis, topic; nominative, premise; case, object, patient, recipient; ego, mind, self.

sublime adj elevated, high, sacred; eminent, exalted, grand, great, lofty, noble; august, glorious, magnificent, majestic, noble, stately, solemn, sublunary.

submission n capitulation, cession, relinquishment, surrender, yielding; acquiescence, compliance, obedience, resignation; deference, homage, humility, lowliness, obeisance, passiveness.

submit vb cede, defer, endure, resign, subject, surrender, yield; commit, propose, refer; offer; acquiesce, bend, capitulate, comply, stoop.

subordinate adj ancillary, dependent, inferior, junior, minor, secondary, subject, subservient.

subscribe vb accede, approve, agree, assent, consent, yield; contribute, donate, give, offer.

subsequent adj after, attendant, ensuing, later, latter, following, posterior, sequent, succeeding.

subside vb settle, sink; abate, decline, decrease, diminish, drop, ebb, fall, intermit, lapse, lessen.

subsidiary adj adjutant, aiding, assistant, auxiliary, cooperative, corroborative, helping, subordinate, subservient.

subsidise vb aid, finance, fund, sponsor, support, underwrite.

subsidy n aid, bounty, grant, subvention, support, underwriting.

subsist vb be, breathe, consist, exist, inhere, live, prevail; abide, continue, endure, persist, remain; feed, maintain, ration, support.

substance n actuality, element, groundwork, hypostasis, reality, substratum; burden, content, core, drift, essence, gist, heart, import, meaning, pith, sense, significance, solidity, soul, sum, weight; estate, income, means, property.

substantial adj actual, considerable, existent, hypostatic, pithy, potential, real, subsistent, virtual; concrete, durable, positive, solid, tangible, true; corporeal, bodily, material; bulky, firm, goodly, heavy, large, massive, notable, significant, sizable, solid, sound, stable, stout, strong, well-made; cogent, just, efficient, influential, valid, weighty.

subterfuge n artifice, evasion, excuse, expedient, mask, pretence, pretext, trick.

subtle adj arch, artful, astute, crafty, crooked, cunning, designing, diplomatic, intriguing, insinuating, sly, tricky, wily; clever, ingenious, acute, deep, discerning, discriminating, keen, profound, sagacious, shrewd; airy, delicate, ethereal, light, nice, rare, refined, volatile.

subtract vb deduct, detract, diminish, remove, take, withdraw.

subvert vb invert, overset, overthrow, overturn, reverse, upset; demolish, destroy, extinguish, raze, ruin, overthrow; confound, corrupt, injure.

succeed vb ensue, follow, inherit, replace; flourish, gain, hit, prevail, prosper, thrive, win.

success n attainment, issue, result; fortune, happiness, hit, luck, prosperity, triumph.

successful adj auspicious, booming, felicitous, fortunate, happy, lucky, prosperous, victorious.

succession n chain, concatenation, cycle, consecution, following, procession, progression, rotation, round, sequence, series, suite; descent, entail, inheritance, lineage, race, reversion.

succinct adj brief, compact, compendious, concise, condensed, curt, laconic, pithy, short.

sudden adj abrupt, hasty, hurried, immediate, instantaneous, rash, unanticipated, unexpected, unforeseen, unusual; brief, momentary, quick.

sue vb charge, court, indict, prosecute, solicit, summon, woo; appeal, beg, demand, entreat, implore, petition, plead, pray, supplicate.

suffer vb feel, undergo; bear, endure, pocket, staunch, support, sustain, tolerate; admit, allow.

sufferance n endurance, inconvenience, misery, pain, suffering; long-suffering, moderation, patience, submission; allowance, permission.

sufficient adj adequate, ample, commensurate, competent, enough, full, plenteous, satisfactory; able, equal, fit, qualified, responsible.

suffocate vb asphyxiate, choke, smother, stifle.

suggest vb advise, allude, hint, indicate, insinuate, intimate, move, present, prompt, propose.

suggestion n allusion, hint, indication, insinuation, intimation, presentation, prompting, proposal, recommendation, reminder.

suit vb accommodate, adapt, adjust, fashion, fit, level, match; accord, become, befit, gratify, harmonise, please, satisfy, tally. • n appeal, entreaty, invocation, petition, prayer, request, solicitation, supplication; courtship, wooing; action, case, cause, process, prosecution, trial; clothing, costume, habit.

suitable adj adapted, accordant, agreeable, answerable, apposite, applicable, appropriate, apt, becoming, befitting, conformable, congruous, convenient, consonant, correspondent, decent,

due, eligible, expedient, fit, fitting, just, meet, pertinent, proper, relevant, seemly, worthy.

sulky adj aloof, churlish, cross, cross-grained, dogged, grouchy, ill-humoured, ill-tempered, moody, morose, perverse, sour, sullen, surly, vexatious.

sullen adj cross, crusty, glum, grumpy, ill-tempered, moody, morose, sore, sour, sulky; cheerless, cloudy, dark, depressing, dismal, foreboding, gloomy, lowering, sombre; dull, heavy, slow, sluggish; intractable, obstinate, perverse, refractory, stubborn, vexatious.

sully vb blemish, blot, contaminate, deface, defame, dirty, disgrace, dishonour, foul, smirch, soil, slur, spot, stain, tarnish.

sultry adj close, damp, hot, humid, muggy.

sum vb add, calculate, compute, reckon; collect, comprehend, condense, epitomise, summarise. • n aggregate, amount, total, totality, whole; compendium, substance, summary; acme, completion, height, summit.

summary adj brief, compendious, concise, curt, laconic, pithy, short, succinct, terse; brief, quick, rapid. • n abridgement, abstract, brief, compendium, digest, epitome, precis, résumé, synopsis.

summit n acme, apex, cap, climax, crest, crown, pinnacle, top, vertex, zenith.

summon vb arouse, bid, call, cite, invite, invoke, rouse; convene, convoke; charge, indict, prosecute, subpoena, sue.

sundry adj different, divers, several, some.

sunny adj bright, brilliant, clear, fine, luminous, radiant, shining, unclouded, warm; cheerful, genial, happy, joyful, mild, optimistic, pleasant.

superb adj august, beautiful, elegant, exquisite, grand, gorgeous, imposing, magnificent, majestic, noble, pompous, rich, showy, splendid.

superficial adj external, flimsy, shallow.

superfluous adj excessive, redundant.

superintend vb administer, conduct, control, direct, inspect, manage, oversee, supervise.

superior adj better, greater, high, higher, finer, paramount, supreme, ultra, upper; chief, foremost, principal; distinguished, matchless, noble, pre-eminent, preferable, sovereign, surpassing, unrivalled, unsurpassed; predominant, prevalent. • n boss, chief, director, head, leader.

supernatural adj abnormal, marvellous, metaphysical, miraculous, otherworldly, unearthly.

supersede vb displace, remove, replace, succeed, supplant.

supervise vb administer, conduct, control, direct, inspect, manage, overlook, oversee.

supple adj elastic, flexible, limber, lithe, pliable, pliant.

supplement vb add, augment, extend, reinforce, supply. • n addendum, addition, appendix, codicil, complement, continuation, postscript.

supply vb endue, equip, furnish, minister, outfit, provide, replenish, stock, store; afford, accommodate, contribute, give, grant, yield.

support vb brace, cradle, pillow, prop, sustain, uphold; bear, endure, undergo, suffer, tolerate; cherish, keep, maintain, nourish, nurture; act, assume, carry, perform, play, represent; accredit, corroborate, substantiate, confirm verify; abet, advocate, aid, approve, assist, back, befriend, champion, countenance, encourage, favour, float, hold, patronise, relieve, reinforce, succour, uphold, vindicate. • n bolster, brace, buttress, foothold, guy, hold, prop, purchase, shore, stay, substructure, supporter, underpinning; groundwork, mainstay, staff; base, basis, bed, foundation; keeping, living, livelihood, maintenance, subsistence, sustenance; confirmation, evidence; aid, assistance, backing, behalf, championship, comfort, countenance, encouragement, favour, help, patronage, succour.

suppose vb apprehend, believe, conceive, conclude, consider, conjecture, deem, imagine, judge, presume, presuppose, think; assume, hypothesise; imagine, imply, posit, predicate, think; fancy, opine, speculate, surmise.

suppress vb choke, crush, destroy, overwhelm, overpower, overthrow, quash, quell, quench, smother, stifle, subdue, withhold; arrest, inhibit, obstruct, repress, restraint, stop; conceal, extinguish, keep, retain, secrete, silence.

supreme adj chief, dominant, first, greatest, highest, leading, paramount, predominant, pre-eminent, principal, sovereign.

sure adj assured, certain, confident, positive; accurate, dependable, effective, honest, infallible, precise, reliable, trustworthy, undeniable, undoubted, unmistakable, well-proven; assured, guaranteed, inevitable, irrevocable; fast, firm, safe, secure, stable, steady.

surfeit vb cram, gorge, overfeed, sate, satiate; cloy, nauseate, pall. • n excess, fullness, glut, oppression, plethora, satiation, superfluity.

surge vb billow, rise, rush, sweep, swell, swirl.

surly adj churlish, crabbed, cross, crusty, discourteous, fretful, gruff, grumpy, harsh, ill-natured, ill-tempered, morose, peevish, perverse, pettish, petulant, rough, rude, snappish, snarling, sour, sullen, testy, touchy, uncivil, ungracious.

surpass vb beat, cap, eclipse, exceed, excel, outdo, outmatch, outnumber, outrun, outstrip, override, overshadow, overtop, outshine.

surplus adj additional, leftover, remaining, spare, superfluous, supernumerary, supplementary. • n balance, excess, overplus, remainder, residue, superabundance, surfeit.

surprise vb amaze, astonish, astound, bewilder, confuse, disconcert, dumbfound, startle, stun.

surrender vb cede, sacrifice, yield; abdicate,

abandon, forgo, relinquish, renounce, resign, waive; capitulate, comply, succumb.

surround vb beset, circumscribe, compass, embrace, encircle, encompass, environ, hem.

survey vb contemplate, observe, overlook, reconnoitre, review, scan, scout, view; examine, inspect, scrutinise; oversee, supervise; estimate, measure, plan, plot, prospect. • n prospect, retrospect, sight, view; examination, inspection, prospect, reconnaissance, review; estimating, measuring, planning, plotting, prospecting.

survive vb endure, last, outlast, outlive.

susceptible adj capable, excitable, impressible, inclined, predisposed, receptive, sensitive.

suspect vb believe, conclude, conjecture, fancy, guess, imagine, judge, suppose, surmise, think; distrust, doubt, mistrust. • adj doubtful, dubious, suspicious.

suspend vb append, hang, sling, swing; adjourn, arrest, defer, delay, discontinue, hinder, intermit, interrupt, postpone, stay, withhold; debar, dismiss, rusticate.

suspicion n assumption, conjecture, dash, guess, hint, inkling, suggestion, supposition, surmise, trace; apprehension, distrust, doubt, fear, jealousy, misgiving, mistrust.

sustain vb bear, bolster, fortify, prop, strengthen, support, uphold; maintain, nourish, perpetuate, preserve, support; aid, assist, comfort, relieve; brave, endure, suffer, undergo; approve, confirm, ratify, sanction, validate; confirm, establish, justify, prove.

swallow vb bolt, devour, drink, eat, englut, engorge, gobble, gorge, gulp, imbibe, ingurgitate, swamp; absorb, appropriate, arrogate, devour, engulf, submerge; consume, employ, occupy; brook, digest, endure, pocket, stomach.

swamp vb engulf, overwhelm, sink; capsize, embarrass, overset, ruin, sink, upset, wreck. • n bog, fen, marsh, morass, quagmire, slough.

swarm vb abound, crowd, teem, throng. • n cloud, concourse, crowd, drove, flock, hive, horde, host, mass, multitude, press, shoal.

sway vb balance, brandish, move, poise, rock, roll, swing, wave, wield; bend, bias, influence, persuade, turn, urge; control, dominate, direct, govern, guide, manage, rule; hoist, raise; incline, lean, lurch, yaw. • n ascendency, authority, command, control, domination, dominion, empire, government, mastership, mastery, omnipotence, predominance, power, rule, sovereignty; authority, bias, direction, influence, weight; preponderance, preponderation; oscillation, sweep, swing.

swear vb affirm, attest, avow, declare, depose, promise, testify, vow; blaspheme, curse.

sweep vb clean, brush; brush, graze, touch; rake, scour, traverse. • n amplitude, compass, drive, movement, range, reach, scope; destruction, devastation, havoc, ravage; curvature, curve.

sweeping *adj* broad, comprehensive, exaggerated, extensive, extravagant, general, unqualified, wholesale.

sweet *adj* candied, cloying, honeyed, luscious, nectareous, nectarous, sugary, saccharine; balmy, fragrant, odorous, redolent, spicy; harmonious, dulcet, mellifluous, mellow, melodious, musical, pleasant, soft, tuneful, silver-toned, silvery; beautiful, fair, lovely; agreeable, charming, delightful, grateful, gratifying, pleasant; affectionate, amiable, attractive, engaging, gentle, mild, lovable, winning; benignant, gentle, serene, soft; clean, fresh, pure, sound.

swell *vb* belly, bloat, bulge, dilate, distend, expand, inflate, intumesce, puff, turnefy; augment, enlarge, increase; heave, rise, surge; strut, swagger.

swift *adj* expeditious, fast, fleet, flying, quick, rapid, speedy; alert, eager, forward, prompt.

swindle *vb* cheat, con, cozen, deceive, defraud, diddle, dupe, embezzle, forge, gull, hoax, overreach, steal, trick, victimise.

swing *vb* oscillate, sway, vibrate, wave; dangle, depend, hang; brandish, flourish, wave, whirl;

administer, manage, ruin. • *n* fluctuation, oscillation, sway, undulation, vibration; elbow-room, play, range, scope, sweep; bias, tendency.

swoop *vb* descend, pounce, rush, seize, stoop.

symbol *n* badge, emblem, exponent, figure, mark, picture, representation, representative, sign, token, type.

symbolic(al) *adj* emblematic, figurative, hieroglyphic, representative, significant, typical.

symmetry *n* balance, congruity, evenness, harmony, order, proportion, regularity, shapeliness.

sympathetic *adj* affectionate, commiserating, compassionate, condoling, kind, pitiful, sympathetic, tender.

sympathy *n* accord, affinity, agreement, communion, concert, concord, congeniality, correlation, correspondence, harmony, reciprocity, union; commiseration, compassion, condolence, fellow-feeling, kindliness, pity, tenderness.

symptom *n* diagnostic, indication, mark, note, prognostic, sign, token.

symptomatic *adj* characteristic, indicative, symbolic, suggestive.

system *n* method, order, plan.

systematic *adj* methodic, methodical, orderly.

T

table *vb* enter, move, propose, submit, suggest. • *n* plate, slab, tablet; board, counter, desk, stand; catalogue, chart, compendium, index, list, schedule, syllabus, synopsis, tabulation; diet, fare, food, victuals.

taboo *adj* banned, forbidden, inviolable, outlawed, prohibited, proscribed. • *n* ban, interdict, prohibition, proscription.

tackle *vb* attach, grapple, seize; attempt, try, undertake. • *n* apparatus, cordage, equipment, gear, harness, implements, rigging, tools.

tact *n* address, adroitness, cleverness, dexterity, diplomacy, discernment, finesse, insight, knack, perception, skill, understanding.

tail *vb* dog, follow, shadow, stalk, track. • *n* appendage, conclusion, end, extremity, stub; flap, skirt; queue, retinue, train.

taint *vb* imbue, impregnate; contaminate, corrupt, defile, inflect, mildew, pollute, poison, spoil, touch; blot, stain, sully, tarnish. • *n* stain, tincture, tinge, touch; contamination, corruption, defilement, depravation, infection, pollution; blemish, defect, fault, flaw, spot.

take *vb* accept, obtain, procure, receive; clasp, clutch, grasp, grip, gripe, seize, snatch; filch, misappropriate, pilfer, purloin, steal; abstract,

apprehend, appropriate, arrest, bag, capture, ensnare, entrap; attack, befall, smite; capture, carry off, conquer, gain, win; allure, attract, bewitch, captivate, charm, delight, enchant, engage, fascinate, interest, please; consider, hold, interrupt, suppose, regard, understand; choose, elect, espouse, select; employ, expend, use; claim, demand, necessitate, require; bear, endure, experience, feel, perceive, tolerate; deduce, derive, detect, discover, draw; carry, conduct, convey, lead, transfer; clear, surmount; drink, eat, imbibe, inhale, swallow. • *n* proceeds, profits, return, revenue, takings; yield.

tale *n* account, fable, legend, narration, novel, parable, recital, rehearsal, romance, story.

talent *n* ableness, ability, aptitude, capacity, cleverness, declaim, endowment, faculty, forte, genius, gift, knack, parts, power, turn.

talk *vb* chatter, communicate, confer, confess, converse, declaim, discuss, gossip, pontificate, speak. • *n* chatter, communication, conversation, diction, rumour, speech, utterance.

tame *vb* domesticate, reclaim, train; conquer, master, overcome, repress, subdue, subjugate. • *adj* docile, domestic, domesticated, gentle, mild, reclaimed; broken, crushed, meek, subdued, unresisting, submissive; barren, commonplace, dull, feeble, flat, insipid, jejune, languid, lean, poor, prosaic, prosy, spiritless, tedious, vapid.

tamper vb alter, conquer, dabble, damage, interfere, meddle; intrigue, seduce, suborn.

tang n aftertaste, flavour, relish, savour, smack, taste; keenness, nip, sting.

tangible adj corporeal, material, palpable, tactile, touchable; actual, certain, embodied, evident, obvious, open, perceptible, plain, positive, real, sensible, solid, stable, substantial.

tangle vb complicate, entangle, intertwine, interweave, mat, perplex, snarl; catch, ensnare, entrap, involve; embarrass, embroil, perplex.

tap[1] vb knock, pat, rap, strike, tip, touch.

tap[2] vb broach, draw off, extract, pierce; draw on, exploit, mine, use, utilise; bug, eavesdrop, listen in. • n faucet, plug, spigot, spout, stopcock, valve; bug, listening device, transmitter.

tardy adj slow, sluggish, snail-like; backward, behindhand, dilatory, late, loitering, overdue.

tarnish vb blemish, deface, defame, dim, discolour, dull, slur, smear, soil, stain, sully.

tart adj acid, acidulous, acrid, piquant, pungent, sharp, sour; acrimonious, caustic, crabbed, curt, harsh, ill-humoured, ill-tempered, keen, petulant, sarcastic, severe, snappish, sharp, testy.

task n burden, overwork, strain, tax. • n drudgery, labour, toil, work; business, charge, chore, duty, employment, enterprise, job, mission, stint, undertaking, work; assignment, exercise, lesson.

taste vb experience, feel, perceive, undergo; relish, savour, sip. • n flavour, gusto, relish, savour, smack, piquancy; admixture, bit, dash, fragment, hint, infusion, morsel, mouthful, sample, shade, sprinkling, suggestion, tincture; appetite, desire, fondness, liking, partiality, predilection; acumen, cultivation, culture, delicacy, discernment, discrimination, elegance, fine-feeling, grace, judgement, polish, refinement; manner, style.

taunt vb censure, chaff, deride, flout, jeer, mock, scoff, sneer, revile, reproach, ridicule, twit, upbraid. • n censure, derision, gibe, insult, jeer, quip, quirk, reproach, ridicule, scoff.

taut adj strained, stretched, tense, tight.

tawdry adj flashy, gaudy, garish, glittering, loud, meretricious, ostentatious, showy.

tax vb burden, demand, exact, load, overtax, require, strain, task; accuse, charge. • n assessment, custom, duty, excise, impost, levy, rate, taxation, toll, tribute; burden, charge, demand, requisition, strain; accusation, censure, charge.

teach vb catechise, coach, discipline, drill, edify, educate, enlighten, inform, indoctrinate, initiate, instruct, ground, prime, school, train, tutor; communicate, disseminate, explain, expound, impart, implant, inculcate, infuse, instil, inter-

pret, preach, propagate; admonish, advise, counsel, direct, guide, signify, show.

teacher n coach, educator, inculcator, informant, instructor, master, pedagogue, preceptor, schoolteacher, trainer, tutor; adviser, counsellor.

tear vb burst, slit, rive, rend, rip; claw, lacerate, mangle, shatter, rend, wound; sever, sunder. • n fissure, laceration, rent, rip, wrench.

tease vb annoy, badger, beg, bother, chafe, chagrin, disturb, harass, harry, hector, importune, irritate, molest, pester, plague, provoke, tantalise, torment, trouble, vex, worry.

tedious adj dull, fatiguing, irksome, monotonous, tiresome, trying, uninteresting.

teem vb abound, bear, produce, swarm; discharge, empty, overflow.

tell vb compute, count, enumerate, number, reckon; describe, narrate, recount, rehearse, relate, report; acknowledge, announce, betray, confess, declare, disclose, divulge, own, reveal; acquaint, communicate, instruct, teach; discern, discover, distinguish; communicate, express, mention, publish, speak, state, utter.

temper vb modify, qualify; appease, assuage, calm, mitigate, mollify, moderate, pacify, restrain, soften, soothe; accommodate, adapt, adjust, fit, suit. • n character, constitution, nature, organisation, quality, structure, temperament, type; disposition, frame, grain, humour, mood, spirits, tone, vein; anger, ill-temper, irritation, spleen, passion.

temporary adj brief, ephemeral, evanescent, fleeting, impermanent, momentary, short-lived.

tempt vb prove, test, try; allure, decoy, entice, induce, inveigle, persuade, seduce; dispose, incite, incline, instigate, lead, prompt, provoke.

tenacious adj retentive, unforgetful; adhesive, clinging, cohesive, firm, glutinous, gummy, resisting, retentive, sticky, strong, tough, unyielding, viscous; dogged, fast, obstinate, opinionated, pertinacious, stubborn.

tend[1] vb accompany, attend, graze, guard, keep, protect, shepherd, watch.

tend[2] vb aim, exert, gravitate, head, incline, influence, lead, lean, point, trend, verge.

tendency n aim, aptitude, bearing, bent, bias, course, determination, disposition, direction, drift, gravitation, inclination, leaning, liability, predisposition, proclivity, proneness, propensity.

tender[1] n bid, offer, proffer, proposal; currency, money.

tender[2] adj callow, delicate, effeminate, feeble, feminine, fragile, immature, infantile, soft, weak, young; affectionate, compassionate, gentle, humane, kind, lenient, loving, merciful, mild, pitiful, sensitive, sympathetic; disagreeable, painful, unpleasant.

tense vb flex, strain, tauten, tighten. • adj rigid,

stiff, strained, stretched, taut, tight; excited, highly strung, intent, nervous, rapt.

tentative adj essaying, experimental, provisional, testing, toying.

term vb call, christen, denominate, designate, dub, entitle, name, phrase, style. • n bound, boundary, bourn, confine, limit, mete, terminus; duration, period, season, semester, span, spell, termination, time; denomination, expression, locution, name, phrase, word.

terminal adj bounding, limiting; final, terminating, ultimate. • n end, extremity, termination; bound, limit; airport, depot, station, terminus.

terminate vb bound, limit; end, finish, close, complete, conclude; eventuate, issue, prove.

termination n ending, suffix; bound, extend, limit; end, completion, conclusion.

terms npl conditions, provisions, stipulations.

terrible adj appalling, dire, dreadful, fearful, formidable, frightful, gruesome, hideous, horrible, horrid, shocking, terrific, tremendous; alarming, awe-inspiring, awful, dread, dreadful; great, excessive, extreme, severe.

terrify vb affright, alarm, appal, daunt, dismay, frighten, horrify, scare, shock, terrorise.

terror n affright, alarm, anxiety, awe, consternation, dismay, dread, fear, fright, horror, intimidation, panic, terrorism.

test vb assay; examine, prove, try. • n attempt, essay, examination, experiment, ordeal.

testify vb affirm, assert, asseverate, attest, avow, certify, corroborate, declare, depose, evidence.

testimonial n certificate, credential, recommendation, voucher; monument, record.

testimony n affirmation, attestation, confession, confirmation, corroboration, declaration, deposition, profession; evidence, proof, witness.

testy adj captious, choleric, cross, fretful, hasty, irascible, irritable, quick, peevish, peppery, pettish, petulant, snappish, splenetic, touchy.

text n copy, subject, theme, thesis, topic.

texture n fabric, web, weft; character, coarseness, composition, constitution, fibre, fineness, grain, make-up, nap, organisation, structure.

thankful adj appreciative, beholden, grateful.

thaw vb dissolve, liquefy, melt, soften, unbend.

theatrical adj dramatic, dramaturgic, dramaturgical, histrionic, scenic, spectacular; affected, ceremonious, meretricious, ostentatious, pompous, showy, stagy, stilted, unnatural.

theft n depredation, embezzlement, fraud, larceny, peculation, pilfering, purloining, robbery, spoliation, stealing, swindling, thieving.

theme n composition, subject, text, topic.

theoretical adj abstract, conjectural, doctrinaire, ideal, hypothetical, pure, speculative.

theory n assumption, conjecture, hypothesis, idea, plan, postulation, principle, scheme, speculation, surmise, system; doctrine, philosophy, science; explanation, exposition, rationale.

thick adj bulky, chunky, dumpy, plump, solid, squab, squat, stubby, thickset; clotted, coagulated, crass, dense, dull, gross, heavy, viscous; blurred, cloudy, dirty, foggy, hazy, indistinguishable, misty, obscure, vaporous; muddy, rolled, turbid; abundant, frequent, multitudinous, numerous; close, compact, crowded, set, thickset; confused, guttural, hoarse, inarticulate, indistinct; dim, dull, weak; familiar, friendly, intimate, neighbourly, well-acquainted. • adv fast, frequently, quick; closely, densely, thickly. • n centre, middle, midst.

thief n depredator, filcher, pilferer, lifter, marauder, purloiner, robber, shark, stealer; burglar, corsair, defaulter, defrauder, embezzler, footpad, highwayman, housebreaker, kidnapper, pickpocket, swindler, peculator.

thieve vb cheat, embezzle, peculate, pilfer, plunder, purloin, rob, steal, swindle.

thin vb attenuate, dilute, diminish, prune, reduce, refine, weaken. • adj attenuated, bony, emaciated, fine, fleshless, flimsy, gaunt, haggard, lank, lanky, lean, meagre, peaked, pinched, poor, scanty, scraggy, scrawny, slender, slight.

thing n being, body, contrivance, creature, entity, object, something, substance; act, action, affair, arrangement, circumstance, concern, deed.

think vb cogitate, contemplate, dream, meditate, muse, ponder, reflect, ruminate, speculate; consider, deliberate, reason, undertake; apprehend, believe, conceive, conclude, deem, determine, fancy, hold, imagine, judge, opine, presume, reckon, suppose, surmise; design, intend, mean, purpose; account, believe, consider, count, deem, esteem, hold, regard, suppose.

thirst n appetite, craving, desire, hunger, longing, yearning; aridity, drought, dryness.

thorough adj absolute, arrant, complete, downright, entire, exhaustive, finished, perfect, radical, sweeping, unmitigated, total; accurate, correct, reliable, trustworthy.

thought n absorption, cogitation, engrossment, meditation, musing, reflection, reverie, rumination; contemplation, intellect, ratiocination, thinking, thoughtfulness; application, conception, consideration, deliberation, idea, pondering, speculation, study; consciousness, imagination, intellect, perception, understanding; conceit, fancy, notion; conclusion, fancy, idea, judgement, motion, opinion, sentiment, supposition, view; anxiety, attention, care, concern, consideration, deliberation, provision, solicitude; design, expectation, intention, purpose.

thoughtful adj absorbed, contemplative, deliberative, dreamy, engrossed, introspective, pensive, philosophic, reflecting, reflective, sedate, speculative; attentive, careful, cautious, circumspect, considerate, discreet, heedful, friendly, kind-hearted, kindly, mindful, neighbourly, provident, prudent, regardful, watchful, wary; quiet, serious, sober, studious.

thoughtless *adj* careless, casual, flighty, heedless, improvident, inattentive, inconsiderate, neglectful, negligent, precipitate, rash, reckless, regardless, remiss, trifling, unmindful, unthinking.

thrash *vb* beat, bruise, conquer, defeat, drub, flog, lash, maul, pummel, punish, trounce.

thread *vb* course, direction, drift, tenor; reeve, trace. • *n* cord, fibre, filament, hair, line, twist.

threadbare *adj* napless, old, seedy, worn; common, commonplace, hackneyed, stale, trite.

threaten *vb* denounce, endanger, fulminate, intimidate, menace, thunder; augur, forebode, foreshadow, indicate, portend, presage, prognosticate, warn.

thrift *n* economy, frugality, parsimony, saving, sparing.

thrifty *adj* careful, economical, frugal, provident, saving, sparing; flourishing, prosperous, thriving, vigorous.

thrill *vb* affect, agitate, electrify, inspire, move, penetrate, pierce, rouse, stir, touch. • *n* excitement, sensation, shock, tingling, tremor.

throng *vb* congregate, crowd, fill, flock, pack, press, swarm. • *n* assemblage, concourse, congregation, crowd, horde, host, mob, multitude.

throw *vb* cast, chuck, dart, fling, hurl, lance, launch, overturn, pitch, pitchfork, send, sling, toss, whirl. • *n* cast, fling, hurl, launch, pitch, sling, toss, whirl; chance, gamble, try, venture.

thrust *vb* clap, dig, drive, force, impel, jam, plunge, poke, propel, push, ram, run, shove.

thump *vb* bang, batter, beat, belabour, knock, punch, strike, thrash, whack.

tickle *vb* amuse, delight, divert, enliven, gladden, gratify, please, rejoice, titillate.

ticklish *adj* dangerous, precarious, risky, tottering, uncertain, unstable, unsteady; critical.

tidy *vb* clean, neaten, order, straighten. • *adj* clean, neat, orderly, shipshape, spruce, trig, trim.

tie *vb* bind, confine, fasten, knot, lock, manacle, secure, shackle, fetter, yoke; complicate, entangle, interlace, knit; connect, hold, join, link, unite; constrain, oblige, restrain, restrict. • *n* band, fastening, knot, ligament, ligature; allegiance, bond, obligation; bow, cravat, necktie.

tight *adj* close, compact, fast, firm; taut, tense, stretched; impassable, narrow, strait.

tilt *vb* cant, incline, slant, slope, tip; forge, hammer; point, thrust; joust, rush.

time *vb* clock, control, count, measure, regulate, schedule. • *n* duration, interim, interval, season, span, spell, term, while; aeon, age, date, epoch, eon, era, period, term; cycle, dynasty, reign; confinement, delivery, parturition; measure.

timely *adj* acceptable, appropriate, apropos, early, opportune, prompt, punctual, seasonable.

timid *adj* afraid, cowardly, faint-hearted, fearful, irresolute, nervous, pusillanimous, timorous, unadventurous; bashful, coy, diffident, modest, shrinking, retiring.

tinge *vb* colour, dye, stain, tincture, tint; imbue, impregnate, impress, infuse. • *n* cast, colour, dye, hue, shade, stain, tincture, tint; flavour, smack, spice, quality, taste.

tint *n* cast, colour, complexion, dye, hue, shade.

tiny *adj* diminutive, dwarfish, lilliputian, little, microscopic, miniature, minute, puny, pygmy.

tip[1] *n* apex, cap, end, extremity, peak, pinnacle.

tip[2] *vb* incline, overturn, tilt; dispose of, dump. • *n* donation, fee, gift, gratuity, perquisite, reward; inclination, slant; hint, pointer, suggestion.

tire *vb* exhaust, fag, fatigue, harass, jade, weary.

tiresome *adj* annoying, arduous, boring, dull, exhausting, fatiguing, fagging, humdrum, irksome, laborious, monotonous, tedious.

tissue *n* cloth, fabric; membrane, network, structure, texture, web; accumulation, chain, collection, combination, conglomeration, mass, network, series, set.

title *vb* call, designate, name, style, term. • *n* caption, legend, head, heading; appellation, application, cognomen, completion, denomination, designation, epithet, name; claim, due, ownership, part, possession, prerogative, right.

toast *vb* brown, dry, heat; honour, pledge, propose, salute. • *n* compliment, drink, pledge, salutation, salute; favourite, pet.

toil *vb* drudge, labour, strive, work. • *n* drudgery, effort, exertion, exhaustion, grinding, labour, pains, travail, work.

token *adj* nominal, superficial, symbolic. • *n* badge, evidence, index, indication, manifestation, mark, note, sign, symbol, trace, trait; keepsake, memento, memorial, reminder, souvenir.

tolerable *adj* bearable, endurable, sufferable, supportable; fair, indifferent, middling, ordinary.

tolerance *n* endurance, receptivity, sufferance.

tolerate *vb* admit, allow, indulge, let, permit, receive; abide, brook, endure, suffer.

toll[1] *n* assessment, charge, customs, demand, dues, duty, fee, impost, levy, rate, tax, tribute; cost, damage, loss.

toll[2] *vb* chime, knell, peal, ring, sound.

tomb *n* catacomb, charnel house, crypt, grave, mausoleum, sepulchre, vault.

tone *vb* blend, harmonise, match, suit. • *n* note, sound; accent, cadence, emphasis, inflection, intonation, modulation; key, mood, strain, temper; elasticity, energy, force, health, strength, tension, vigour; cast, colour, manner, hue, shade, style, tint; drift, tenor.

top *vb* cap, head, tip; ride, surmount; outdo, surpass. • adj apical, best, chief, culminating, finest, first, foremost, highest, leading, prime, principal, topmost, uppermost. • n acme, apex, crest, crown, head, meridian, pinnacle, summit.

topic n business, question, subject, text, theme, thesis; division, head, subdivision; commonplace, dictum, maxim, precept, proposition, principle, rule; arrangement, scheme.

topple vb fall, overturn, tumble, upset.

torment vb annoy, agonise, distress, excruciate, pain, rack, torture; badger, fret, harass, harry, irritate, nettle, plague, provoke, tantalise, tease, trouble, vex, worry.

tortuous adj crooked, curved, curvilineal, curvilinear, serpentine, sinuate, sinuated, sinuous, twisted, winding; ambiguous, circuitous, crooked, deceitful, indirect, perverse, roundabout.

torture vb agonise, distress, excruciate, pain, rack, torment. • n agony, anguish, distress, pain.

toss vb cast, fling, hurl, pitch, throw; agitate, rock, shake; disquiet, harass, try; roll, writhe.

total vb add, amount to, reach, reckon. • adj complete, entire, full, whole; entire, integral, undivided. • n aggregate, all, gross, lump, mass, sum, totality, whole.

touch vb feel, graze, handle, hit, pat, strike, tap; concern, interest, regard; affect, impress, move, stir; grasp, reach, stretch; melt, mollify, move, soften; afflict, distress, hurt, injure, molest, sting, wound. • n hint, smack, suggestion, suspicion, taste, trace; blow, contract, hit, pat, tap.

touchy adj choleric, cross, fretful, hot-tempered, irascible, irritable, peevish, petulant, quick-tempered, snappish, splenetic, tetchy, testy.

tough adj inflexible, intractable, rigid, stiff; callous, hard, obdurate, stubborn; difficult, formidable, hard, troublesome. • n brute, bully, hooligan, ruffian, thug.

tour vb journey, perambulate, travel, visit. • n circuit, course, excursion, expedition, journey, perambulation, pilgrimage, round.

tow vb drag, draw, haul, pull, tug.

tower vb mount, rise, soar, transcend. • n belfry, bell tower, column, minaret, spire, steeple, turret; castle, citadel, fortress, stronghold.

toy vb dally, play, sport, trifle, wanton. • n bauble, doll, gewgaw, gimmick, knick-knack, plaything, puppet, trinket; bagatelle, bubble, trifle.

trace vb follow, track, train; copy, deduce, delineate, derive, describe, draw, sketch. • n evidence, footmark, footprint, footstep, impression, mark, remains, sign, token, track, trail, vestige, wake; memorial, record; bit, dash, flavour, hint.

track vb chase, draw, follow, pursue, scent, track, trail. • n footmark, footprint, footstep, spoor, trace, vestige; course, pathway, rails, road, runway, trace, trail, wake, way.

trade vb bargain, barter, chaffer, deal, exchange,

interchange, sell, traffic. • n bargaining, barter, business, commerce, dealing, traffic; avocation, business, calling, craft, employment, occupation, office, profession, pursuit, vocation.

traditional adj accustomed, apocryphal, customary, established, historic, legendary, old, oral, transmitted, uncertain, unverified.

traffic vb bargain, barter, chaffer, deal, exchange, trade. • n barter, business, chaffer, commerce, exchange, intercourse, trade, transport.

tragedy n drama, play; adversity, calamity, catastrophe, disaster, misfortune.

tragic adj dramatic; calamitous, catastrophic, disastrous, dreadful, fatal, grievous, heart-breaking, mournful, sad, shocking, sorrowful.

trail vb follow, hunt, trace, track; drag, draw, float, flow, haul, pull. • n footmark, footprint, footstep, mark, trace, track.

train vb drag, draw, haul, trail, tug; allure, entice; discipline, drill, educate, exercise, instruct, school, teach; accustom, break in, familiarise, habituate, inure, prepare, rehearse, use. • n trail, wake; entourage, cortege, followers, retinue, staff, suite.

traitor n apostate, betrayer, deceiver, Judas, miscreant, quisling, renegade, turncoat; conspirator, deserter, insurgent, mutineer, revolutionary.

traitorous adj faithless, false, perfidious, recreant, treacherous; insidious, perfidious.

tramp vb hike, march, plod, trudge, walk. • n excursion, journey, march, walk; landloper, loafer, stroller, tramper, vagabond, vagrant.

trample vb crush, tread; scorn, spurn.

trance n dream, ecstasy, hypnosis, rapture; catalepsy, coma.

tranquil adj calm, hushed, peaceful, placid, quiet, serene, still, undisturbed, unmoved, unperturbed, unruffled, untroubled.

tranquillise vb allay, appease, assuage, calm, compose, hush, lay, lull, moderate, pacify, quell, quiet, silence, soothe, still.

transact vb conduct, dispatch, enact, execute, do, manage, negotiate, perform, treat.

transcend vb exceed, overlap, overstep, pass, transgress; excel, outstrip, outrival.

transfer vb convey, dispatch, move, remove, send, translate, transmit, transplant, transport; abalienate, alienate, assign, cede, confer, convey, consign, devise, displace, forward, grant, pass, relegate, transmit. • n abalienation, alienation, assignment, bequest, carriage, cession, change, conveyance, copy, demise, devisal, gift, grant, move, relegation, removal, shift, shipment, transference, transferring, transit, transmission, transportation.

transform vb alter, change, metamorphose, transfigure; convert, resolve, translate, transmogrify, transmute.

translate *vb* remove, transfer, transport; construe, decipher, decode, interpret, render, turn.

transmit *vb* forward, remit, send; communicate, conduct, radiate; bear, carry, convey.

transparent *adj* bright, clear, diaphanous, limpid, lucid; crystalline, hyaline, pellucid, serene, translucent, transpicuous, unclouded; open, porous, transpicuous; evident, obvious, manifest.

transpire *vb* befall, chance, happen, occur.

transport *vb* bear, carry, cart, conduct, convey, fetch, remove, ship, take, transfer, truck; banish, expel; beatify, delight, enrapture, enravish, entrance, ravish. • *n* carriage, conveyance, movement, transportation, transporting; beatification, beatitude, bliss, ecstasy, felicity, happiness, rapture, ravishment; frenzy, passion, vehemence.

trap *vb* catch, ensnare, entrap, noose, snare, springe; ambush, deceive, dupe, trick; enmesh, tangle. • *n* gin, snare, springe, toil; ambush, artifice, pitfall, stratagem.

trappings *npl* adornments, decorations, dress, embellishments, frippery, gear, livery, ornaments, paraphernalia, rigging; accoutrements.

trash *n* dregs, dross, garbage, refuse, rubbish, trumpery, waste; balderdash, nonsense, twaddle.

travel *vb* journey, peregrinate, ramble, roam, rove, tour, voyage, walk, wander; go, move.

traveller *n* excursionist, explorer, globe-trotter, itinerant, passenger, pilgrim, rover, sightseer, tourist, trekker, tripper, voyager, wayfarer.

treacherous *adj* deceitful, disloyal, faithless, false, false-hearted, insidious, perfidious, recreant, sly, traitorous, treasonable, unfaithful, unreliable, unsafe, untrustworthy.

treason *n* betrayal, disloyalty, lèse-majesté, perfidy, sedition, traitorousness, treachery.

treasonable *adj* disloyal, traitorous.

treasure *vb* accumulate, collect, garner, hoard, husband, save, store; cherish, idolise, prize, value, worship. • *n* cash, funds, jewels, money, riches, savings, valuables, wealth; abundance, reserve, stock, store.

treat *vb* entertain, feast, gratify, refresh; attend, doctor, dose, handle, manage, serve; bargain, covenant, negotiate, parley. • *n* banquet, entertainment, feast; delight, enjoyment, entertainment, luxury, pleasure, refreshment.

treatment *n* usage, use; dealing, handling, management, manipulation; doctoring, therapy.

treaty *n* agreement, alliance, bargain, compact, concordat, convention, covenant, entente.

tremble *vb* quake, quaver, quiver, shake, shiver, shudder, vibrate, wobble.

tremendous *adj* alarming, appalling, awful, dreadful, fearful, frightful; wonderful.

tremor *n* agitation, quaking, quivering, shaking, trembling, trepidation, tremulousness, vibration.

trend *n* bent, course, direction, drift, inclination, set, leaning, tendency.

trespass *vb* encroach, infringe, intrude, trench; offend, sin, transgress. • *n* encroachment, infringement, injury, intrusion, invasion; crime, delinquency, error, fault, sin, misdeed.

trial *adj* experimental, exploratory, testing. • *n* examination, experiment, test; experience, knowledge; aim, attempt, effort, endeavour, essay, exertion, struggle; assay, criterion, ordeal, prohibition, proof, test, touchstone; affliction, burden, chagrin, dolour, distress, grief, hardship, heartache, inclination, misery, mortification, pain, sorrow, suffering, tribulation, trouble, unhappiness, vexation, woe, wretchedness; action, case, cause, hearing, suit.

tribulation *n* adversity, affliction, distress, grief, misery, pain, sorrow, suffering, trial, trouble, unhappiness, woe, wretchedness.

tribute *n* subsidy, tax; custom, duty, excise, impost, tax, toll; contribution, grant, offering.

trice *n* flash, instant, jiffy, moment, second.

trick *vb* cheat, circumvent, cozen, deceive, defraud, delude, diddle, dupe, fob, gull, hoax, overreach. • *n* artifice, blind, deceit, deception, dodge, fake, feint, fraud, game, hoax, imposture, manoeuvre, shift, ruse, swindle, stratagem, wile; antic, caper, deftness, gambol, sleight.

trickle *vb* distil, dribble, drip, drop, ooze, percolate, seep. • *n* dribble, drip, percolation, seepage.

tricky *adj* artful, cunning, deceitful, deceptive.

trifle *vb* dally, dawdle, fool, play, potter, toy. • *n* bagatelle, bauble, bean, fig, nothing, triviality; iota, jot, modicum, particle, trace.

trifling *adj* empty, frippery, frivolous, inconsiderable, insignificant, nugatory, petty, piddling, shallow, slight, small, trivial, unimportant.

trill *vb* shake, quaver, warble.

trim *vb* adjust, arrange, prepare; balance, equalise, fill; adorn, array, bedeck, decorate, dress, embellish, garnish, ornament; clip, curtail, cut, lop, mow, poll, prune, shave, shear. • *adj* compact, neat, nice, shapely, snug, tidy, well-adjusted, well-ordered; chic, elegant, finical, smart, spruce. • *n* dress, embellishment, gear, ornaments, trappings, trimmings; case, condition, order.

trip *vb* caper, dance, frisk, hop, skip; misstep, stumble; bungle, blunder, err, fail, mistake; overthrow, supplant, upset; catch, convict, detect. • *n* hop, skip; lurch, misstep, stumble; blunder, bungle, error, failure, fault, lapse, miss, mistake, oversight, slip, stumble; circuit, excursion, expedition, jaunt, journey, ramble, route, tour.

triumph *vb* exult, rejoice; prevail, succeed, win; flourish, prosper, thrive; boast, brag, crow, gloat, swagger, vaunt. • *n* celebration, exultation, joy, jubilation, jubilee, ovation; accomplishment, achievement, conquest, success, victory.

triumphant *adj* boastful, conquering, elated, exultant, exulting, jubilant, rejoicing, successful.

trivial *adj* frivolous, gimcrack, immaterial, inconsiderable, insignificant, light, little, nugatory, paltry, petty, small, slight, slim, trifling.

troop *vb* crowd, flock, muster, throng. • *n* company, crowd, flock, herd, multitude, number, throng; band, body, party, squad; troupe.

trouble *vb* agitate, confuse, derange, disarrange, disorder, disturb; afflict, ail, annoy, badger, concern, disquiet, distress, disturb, fret, grieve, harass, molest, perplex, perturb, pester, plague, torment, vex, worry. • *n* adversity, affliction, calamity, distress, dolour, grief, hardship, misfortune, misery, pain, sorrow, suffering, tribulation, woe; ado, annoyance, anxiety, bother, care, discomfort, embarrassment, fuss, inconvenience, irritation, pains, perplexity, plague, torment, vexation, worry; disturbance, row; bewilderment, disquietude, embarrassment, perplexity.

troublesome *adj* annoying, distressing, disturbing, galling, grievous, harassing, painful, perplexing, vexatious, worrisome; burdensome, irksome, tiresome, wearisome; importunate, intrusive, teasing; arduous, difficult, hard.

truce *n* armistice, breathing space, cessation, delay, intermission, lull, pause, recess, reprieve.

truck *vb* barter, deal, exchange, trade, traffic. • *n* lorry, van, wagon.

true *adj* actual, unaffected, authentic, genuine, legitimate, pure, real, rightful, sincere, sound, truthful, veritable; substantial, veracious; constant, faithful, loyal, staunch, steady; equitable, honest, honourable, just, upright, trusty, trustworthy, virtuous; accurate, correct, even, exact.

trust *vb* confide, depend, expect, hope, rely; believe, credit; commit, entrust. • *n* belief, confidence, credence, faith; credit, tick; charge, deposit; charge, commission, duty, errand; assurance, belief, confidence, expectation, faith.

trustworthy *adj* confidential, constant, credible, dependable, faithful, firm, honest, incorrupt, upright, reliable, responsible, straightforward, staunch, true, trusty, uncorrupt, upright.

truth *n* fact, reality, veracity; actuality, authenticity, realism; cannon, law, oracle, principle; right, truthfulness, veracity; candour, fidelity, frankness, honesty, honour, ingenuousness, integrity, probity, sincerity, virtue; constancy, devotion, faith, fealty, loyalty, steadfastness; accuracy, correctness, exactness, nicety, precision.

truthful *adj* correct, reliable, true, trustworthy, veracious; artless, candid, frank, guileless, honest, ingenuous, open, sincere, straightforward, true, trustworthy, trusty.

try *vb* examine, prove, test; attempt, essay; adjudicate, adjudge, examine, hear; purify, refine; sample, sift, smell, taste; aim, attempt, endeavour, seek, strain, strive. • *n* attempt, effort, endeavour, experiment, trial.

trying *adj* difficult, fatiguing, hard, irksome, tiresome, wearisome; afflicting, afflictive, calamitous, deplorable, dire, distressing, grievous, hard, painful, sad, severe.

tug *vb* drag, draw, haul, pull, tow, wrench; labour, strive, struggle.

tuition *n* education, instruction, schooling, teaching, training.

tumble *vb* heave, pitch, roll, toss, wallow; fall, sprawl, stumble, topple, trip; derange, disarrange, dishevel, disorder, rumple, tousle.

tumult *n* ado, affray, agitation, altercation, bluster, brawl, disturbance, ferment, flurry, feud, fracas, fray, fuss, hubbub, hurly-burly, melee, noise, perturbation, pother, quarrel, racket, riot, row, squabble, stir, turbulence, turmoil.

tumultuous *adj* blustery, breezy, bustling, confused, disorderly, disturbed, riotous, turbulent.

tune *vb* accord, attune, harmonise, modulate; adapt, adjust, attune. • *n* air, aria, melody, strain, tone; agreement, concord, harmony; accord.

tuneful *adj* dulcet, harmonious, melodious.

turbulent *adj* agitated, disturbed, restless, tumultuous, wild; blatant, blustering, boisterous, brawling, disorderly, obstreperous, tumultuous, uproarious, vociferous; disorderly, factious, insubordinate, insurgent, mutinous, raging, rebellious, refractory, revolutionary, riotous, seditious, stormy, wild, violent.

turmoil *n* activity, agitation, bustle, commotion, confusion, disorder, disturbance, ferment, flurry, hubbub, hurly-burly, noise, trouble, tumult, turbulence, uproar.

turn *vb* revolve, rotate; bend, cast, defect, inflict, round, spin, sway, swivel, twirl, twist, wheel; crank, grind, wind; deflect, divert, transfer, warp; form, mould, shape; adapt, fit, manoeuvre, suit; adapt, alter, change, conform, metamorphose, transform, transmute, vary; convert, persuade, prejudice; construe, render, translate; depend, hang, hinge, pivot; eventuate, issue, result, terminate; acidify, curdle, ferment. • *n* cycle, gyration, revolution, rotation, round; bending, oil, deflection, deviation, diversion, doubling, flection, flexion, flexure, reel, retroversion, slew, spin, sweep, swing, swirl, swivel, turning, twist, twirl, whirl, winding; alteration, change, variation, vicissitude; bend, circuit, drive, ramble, run, round, stroll; bout, hand, innings, opportunity, round, shift, spell; act, action, deed, office; convenience, occasion, purpose; cast, fashion, form, guise, manner, mould, phase, shape; aptitude, bent, bias, faculty, genius, gift, inclination, proclivity, proneness, propensity, talent, tendency.

tussle *vb* conflict, contend, contest, scuffle, struggle, wrestle.

tutor *vb* coach, educate, instruct, teach; discipline, train. • n coach, governess, governor, instructor, master, preceptor, teacher.

tweak vb, n jerk, pinch, pull, twinge, twitch.

twin vb couple, link, match, pair. • adj double, doubled, duplicate, geminate, identical, matched, matching, second, twain. • n corollary, double, duplicate, fellow, likeness, match.

twine vb embrace, encircle, entwine, interlace, surround, wreathe; bend, meander, wind; coil, twist. • n convolution, coil, twist; embrace, twining, winding; cord, string.

twinge n tweak, twitch; pang, spasm.

twinkle vb blink, twink, wink; flash, glimmer, scintillate, sparkle.

twirl vb revolve, rotate, spin, turn, twist. • n convolution, revolution, turn, twist, whirling.

twist vb purl, rotate, spin, twine; complicate, contort, convolute, distort, pervert, screw, twine, wring; coil, writhe; encircle, wind, wreathe. • n coil, curl, spin, twine; braid, coil, curl, roll; change, complication, development, variation; bend, convolution, turn; defect, distortion, flaw,

imperfection; jerk, pull, sprain, wrench; aberration, characteristic, eccentricity, oddity, peculiarity, quirk.

twitch vb jerk, pluck, pull, snatch.

type n emblem, mark, stamp; adumbration, image, representation, representative, shadow, sign, symbol, token; archetype, exemplar, model, original, pattern, prototype, protoplast, standard; character, form, kind, nature, sort; figure, letter, text, typography.

typical adj emblematic, exemplary, figurative, ideal, indicative, model, representative.

typify vb betoken, denote, embody, exemplify, figure, image, indicate, represent, signify.

tyrannical adj absolute, arbitrary, autocratic, cruel, despotic, dictatorial, domineering, high, imperious, irresponsible, severe, unjust; cruel, inhuman, oppressive, severe.

tyranny n absolutism, arbitrations, autocracy, despotism, dictatorship, harshness, oppression.

tyrant n autocrat, despot, dictator, oppressor.

U

ubiquitous adj omnipresent, present, universal.

ugly adj ill-favoured, unlovely, unprepossessing, unshapely, unsightly; forbidding, frightful, gruesome, hideous, horrible, horrid, loathsome, monstrous, shocking, terrible, repellent, repulsive; bad-tempered, cantankerous, churlish, quarrelsome, spiteful, surly, spiteful, vicious.

ultimate adj conclusive, decisive, eventual, extreme, farthest, final, last. • n acme, consummation, culmination, height, peak, pink, quintessence, summit.

umbrage n shadow, shade; anger, displeasure, dissatisfaction, dudgeon, injury, offence, pique, resentment.

umpire vb adjudicate, arbitrate, judge, referee. • n adjudicator, arbiter, arbitrator, judge, referee.

unabashed adj bold, brazen, confident, unblushing, undaunted, undismayed.

unable adj impotent, incapable, incompetent, powerless, weak.

unaccommodating adj disobliging, noncompliant, uncivil, ungracious.

unanimity n accord, agreement, concert, concord, harmony, union, unity.

unanimous adj agreeing, concordant, harmonious, like-minded, solid, united.

unassuming adj humble, modest, reserved, unobtrusive, unpretending, unpretentious.

unbalanced adj unsound, unsteady; unadjusted, unsettled.

unbecoming adj inappropriate, indecent, indecorous, improper, unseemly, unsuitable.

unbending adj inflexible, rigid, stiff, unpliant, unyielding; firm, obstinate, resolute, stubborn.

unbridled adj dissolute, intractable, lax, licensed, licentious, loose, uncontrolled, ungovernable, unrestrained, violent, wanton.

uncanny adj inopportune, unsafe; eerie, eery, ghostly, unearthly, unnatural, weird.

uncertain adj ambiguous, doubtful, dubious, equivocal, indefinite, indeterminate, indistinct, questionable, unsettled; insecure, precarious, problematical; capricious, changeable, desultory, fitful, fluctuating, irregular, mutable, shaky, slippery, unreliable, unsettled, variable.

uncommon adj choice, exceptional, extraordinary, infrequent, noteworthy, odd, original, queer, rare, remarkable, scarce, singular, strange, unexampled, unfamiliar, unusual.

uncomplaining adj long-suffering, meek, patient, resigned, tolerant.

uncompromising adj inflexible, narrow, obstinate, orthodox, rigid, stiff, strict, unyielding.

unconditional adj absolute, categorical, complete, entire, free, full, positive, unlimited, unqualified, unreserved, unrestricted.

uncouth adj awkward, boorish, clownish, clumsy, gawky, inelegant, loutish, lubberly, rough, rude, rustic, uncourtly, ungainly, unpolished, unrefined, unseemly.

unctuous *adj* greasy, oily, fat, fatty, oleaginous, sebaceous; bland, smooth, slippery; fawning, glib, obsequious, oily, plausible, servile, suave, smooth, sycophantic; fervid, gushing.

under *prep* below, beneath, inferior to, lower than, subordinate to, underneath. • *adv* below, beneath, down, lower.

underestimate *vb* belittle, underrate.

undergo *vb* bear, endure, experience, suffer.

underhand *adj* deceitful, disingenuous, fraudulent, hidden, secret, sly, stealthy, unfair.

undermine *vb* excavate, mine, sap; demoralise, foil, frustrate, thwart, weaken.

understand *vb* apprehend, catch, comprehend, conceive, discern, grasp, know, penetrate, perceive, see, seize, twig; assume, interpret, take; imply, mean.

understanding *adj* compassionate, considerate, forgiving, kind, kindly, patient, sympathetic, tolerant. • *n* brains, comprehension, discernment, faculty, intellect, intelligence, judgement, knowledge, mind, reason, sense.

undertake *vb* assume, attempt, begin, embark on, engage in, enter upon, take in hand; agree, bargain, contract, covenant, engage, guarantee, promise, stipulate.

undertaking *n* adventure, affair, attempt, business, effort, endeavour, engagement, enterprise, essay, move, project, task, venture.

undo *vb* annul, cancel, frustrate, invalidate, neutralise, nullify, offset, reverse; disengage, loose, unfasten, unmake, unravel, untie.

undying *adj* deathless, endless, immortal.

unearthly *adj* preternatural, supernatural, uncanny, weird.

uneasy *adj* disquieted, disturbed, fidgety, impatient, perturbed, restless, restive, unquiet, worried; awkward, stiff, ungainly, ungraceful; constraining, cramping, disagreeable.

unending *adj* endless, eternal, everlasting.

unequalled *adj* exceeding, incomparable, inimitable, matchless, new, nonpareil, novel, paramount, peerless, pre-eminent, superlative, surpassing, transcendent, unique, unparalleled, unrivalled.

unexpected *adj* abrupt, sudden, unforeseen.

unfair *adj* dishonest, dishonourable, faithless, false, hypocritical, inequitable, insincere, oblique, one-sided, partial, unequal, unjust.

unfaithful *adj* false, perfidious, treacherous, unreliable; careless, negligent; changeable, inconstant, untrue.

unfeeling *adj* callous, heartless, insensible, numb, obdurate, torpid, unconscious, unimpressionable; cold-blooded, cruel, hard, merciless, unkind, unsympathetic.

unfit *adj* inappropriate, incompetent, inconsistent, unsuitable; ill-equipped, inadequate, incapa-

ble, incompetent, unqualified, useless; debilitated, feeble, flabby, unhealthy.

unfold *vb* display, expand, open, separate, unfurl, unroll; declare, disclose, reveal, tell; decipher, develop, disentangle, evolve, explain.

ungainly *adj* awkward, boorish, clownish, clumsy, gawky, inelegant, loutish, lubberly, lumbering, slouching, stiff, uncouthly, uncouth.

uniform *adj* alike, constant, even, equable, equal, smooth, steady, regular, unbroken, unchanged, undeviating, unvaried, unvarying. • *n* costume, dress, livery, outfit, regalia, suit.

union *n* coalescence, coalition, combination, conjunction, coupling, fusion, incorporation, joining, junction, unification, uniting; agreement, concert, concord, concurrence, harmony, unanimity, unity; alliance, association, club, confederacy, federation, guild, league.

unique *adj* choice, exceptional, matchless, only, peculiar, rare, single, sole, singular, unmatched.

unison *n* accord, agreement, harmony.

unite *vb* amalgamate, attach, blend, centralise, coalesce, confederate, consolidate, embody, fuse, incorporate, merge, weld; associate, conjoin, connect, couple, link, marry; combine, join; harmonise, reconcile; agree, concert, concur, cooperate, fraternise.

universal *adj* all-reaching, catholic, cosmic, encyclopedic, general, ubiquitous, unlimited; all, complete, entire, total, whole.

unjust *adj* inequitable, injurious, partial, unequal, unfair, unwarranted, wrong, wrongful; flagitious, heinous, iniquitous, nefarious, unrighteous, wicked, wrong; biased, partial.

unknown *adj* undiscovered, unexplored, uninvestigated; concealed, dark, enigmatic, hidden, mysterious, mystic; anonymous, incognito, inglorious, nameless, obscure.

unlimited *adj* boundless, infinite, interminable, limitless, measureless, unbounded; absolute, full, unconfined, unconstrained, unrestricted.

unmanageable *adj* awkward, cumbersome, inconvenient, unwieldy; intractable, unruly, unworkable, vicious; difficult, impractical.

unmitigated *adj* absolute, complete, consummate, perfect, sheer, stark, thorough, utter.

unnatural *adj* aberrant, abnormal, anomalous, foreign, irregular, prodigious, uncommon; brutal, cold, heartless, inhuman, unfeeling, unusual; affected, artificial, constrained, forced, insincere, self-conscious, stilted, strained; artificial.

unprincipled *adj* bad, crooked, dishonest, fraudulent, immoral, iniquitous, knavish, lawless, profligate, rascally, roguish, thievish, trickish, tricky, unscrupulous, vicious, villainous.

unqualified *adj* disqualified, incompetent, ineligible, unadapted, unfit; absolute, certain, consummate, decided, direct, downright, full, outright, unconditional, unmitigated.

unreal adj chimerical, dreamlike, fanciful, flimsy, ghostly, illusory, insubstantial, nebulous, shadowy, spectral, visionary, unsubstantial.

unreserved adj absolute, entire, full, unlimited; above-board, artless, candid, communicative, fair, frank, guileless, honest, ingenuous, open, sincere, single-minded, undesigning, undissembling; demonstrative, emotional, open-hearted.

unrivalled adj incomparable, inimitable, matchless, peerless, unequalled, unexampled, unique.

unroll vb develop, discover, evolve, open, unfold; display, lay open.

unruly adj disobedient, disorderly, fractious, headstrong, insubordinate, intractable, mutinous, obstreperous, rebellious, refractory, riotous, seditious, turbulent, ungovernable, unmanageable, wanton, wild; lawless, obstinate, rebellious, stubborn, ungovernable, unmanageable.

unsafe adj dangerous, hazardous, insecure, perilous, precarious, risky, treacherous, uncertain.

unsaid vb tacit, unmentioned, unspoken.

unsavoury adj flat, insipid, mawkish, savourless, tasteless, unflavoured, unpalatable, vapid; disagreeable, disgusting, distasteful, nasty, nauseating, nauseous, offensive, rank, revolting, sickening, uninviting, unpleasing.

unsay vb recall, recant, retract, take back.

unscrupulous adj dishonest, reckless, ruthless, unprincipled, unrestrained.

unseasonable adj ill-timed, inappropriate, inopportune, untimely; late, too late; ill-timed, inappropriate, unfit, ungrateful, unsuitable, untimely, unwelcome; premature.

unseasoned adj inexperienced, unaccustomed, unqualified, untrained; immoderate, inordinate, irregular; green; fresh, unsalted.

unseeing adj blind, sightless.

unseemly adj improper, indecent, inappropriate, indecorous, unbecoming.

unseen adj undiscerned, undiscovered, unobserved, unperceived; imperceptible, indiscoverable, invisible, latent.

unselfish adj altruistic, devoted, disinterested, generous, high-minded, impersonal, liberal, magnanimous, self-denying, self-forgetful, selfless, self-sacrificing.

unsettle vb confuse, derange, disarrange, disconcert, disorder, disturb, trouble, unbalance, unfix, unhinge, upset.

unshaken adj constant, firm, resolute, steadfast, steady, unmoved.

unshrinking adj firm, determined, persisting, resolute, unblenching, unflinching.

unsightly adj deformed, disagreeable, hideous, repellent, repulsive, ugly.

unsociable adj distant, reserved, retiring, solitary, standoffish, taciturn, uncommunicative; inhospitable, misanthropic, morose.

unsound adj imperfect, rotten, thin; disturbed; diseased, feeble, infirm, morbid, poorly, sickly, unhealthy, weak; deceitful, defective, erroneous, fallacious, false, faulty, hollow, illogical, incorrect, invalid, questionable, sophistical, unsubstantial, untenable, wrong; deceitful, dishonest, false, insincere, unfaithful, untrustworthy.

unsparing adj bountiful, generous, lavish, liberal, profuse, ungrudging.

unspeakable adj indescribable, inexpressible, unutterable.

unstable adj infirm, insecure, precarious, top-heavy, tottering, unbalanced, unballasted, unsafe, unsettled, unsteady; changeable, erratic, fickle, inconstant, irresolute, mercurial, mutable, unsteady, vacillating, variable, volatile.

unsteady adj fluctuating, oscillating, unsettled; insecure, precarious, unstable; changeable, desultory, ever-changing, fickle, inconstant, irresolute, mutable, unstable, variable, wavering; drunken, jumpy, tottering, vacillating.

unsuccessful adj abortive, bootless, fruitless, futile, ineffectual, profitless, unavailing, vain; ill-fated, ill-starred, luckless, unfortunate, unhappy, unlucky, unprosperous.

unsuitable adj ill-adapted, inappropriate, malapropos, unfit, unsatisfactory, unsuited; improper, inapplicable, inapt, incongruous, inexpedient, infelicitous, unbecoming.

unsuited adj unadapted, unfitted, unqualified.

unsurpassed adj matchless, peerless, unequalled, unexampled, unexcelled, unmatched, unparagoned, unparalleled, unrivalled.

unsuspecting adj credulous, trusting, unsuspicious.

unswerving adj direct, straight, undeviating; constant, determined, firm, resolute, staunch, steadfast, steady, stable, unwavering.

untamed adj fierce, unbroken, wild.

untenable adj indefensible, unmaintainable, unsound; fallacious, hollow, illogical, indefensible, insupportable, unjustifiable, weak.

unthinking adj careless, heedless, inconsiderate, thoughtless, unreasoning, unreflecting; automatic, mechanical.

untidy adj careless, disorderly, dowdy, frumpy, mussy, slatternly, slovenly, unkempt, unneat.

untie vb free, loose, loosen, unbind, unfasten, unknot, unloose; clear, resolve, solve, unfold.

until adv, conj till, to the time when; to the place, point, state or degree that; • prep till, to.

untimely adj ill-timed, inconvenient, inopportune, mistimed, premature, unseasonable, unsuitable; ill-considered, inauspicious, uncalled for, unfortunate.

untiring adj persevering, incessant, indefatigable, patient, tireless, unceasing, unfatiguing, unflagging, unremitting, wearied.

untold *adj* countless, incalculable, innumerable, uncounted, unnumbered; unrelated, unrevealed.

untoward *adj* adverse, froward, intractable, perverse, refractory, stubborn, unfortunate; annoying, ill-timed, inconvenient, unmanageable, vexatious; awkward, uncouth, ungainly, ungraceful.

untrue *adj* contrary, false, inaccurate, wrong; disloyal, faithless, false, perfidious, recreant, treacherous, unfaithful.

untrustworthy *adj* deceitful, dishonest, inaccurate, rotten, slippery, treacherous, undependable, unreliable; disloyal, false; deceptive, fallible, illusive, questionable.

untruth *n* error, faithlessness, falsehood, falsity, incorrectness, inveracity, treachery; deceit, deception, error, falsehood, fabrication, fib, fiction, forgery, imposture, invention, lie, misrepresentation, misstatement, story.

unusual *adj* abnormal, curious, exceptional, extraordinary, odd, peculiar, queer, rare, recherché, remarkable, singular, strange, unaccustomed, uncommon, unwonted.

unutterable *adj* incommunicable, indescribable, ineffable, inexpressible, unspeakable.

unvarnished *adj* unpolished; candid, plain, simple, true, unadorned, unembellished.

unveil *vb* disclose, expose, reveal, show.

unversed *adj* inexperienced, raw, undisciplined, undrilled, uneducated, unexercised, unpractised, unprepared, unschooled; unskilful.

unwelcome *adj* disagreeable, unacceptable, ungrateful, unpleasant, unpleasing.

unwell *adj* ailing, delicate, diseased, ill.

unwholesome *adj* baneful, deleterious, injurious, insalubrious, noisome, noxious, poisonous, unhealthful, unhealthy; injudicious, pernicious, unsound; corrupt, tainted, unsound.

unwieldy *adj* bulky, clumsy, cumbersome, cumbrous, elephantine, heavy, hulking, large, massy, ponderous, unmanageable, weighty.

unwilling *adj* averse, backward, disinclined, indisposed, laggard, loath, opposed, recalcitrant, reluctant; forced, grudging.

unwise *adj* brainless, foolish, ill-advised, illjudged, impolitic, imprudent, indiscreet, injudicious, inexpedient, senseless, silly, stupid.

unwittingly *adv* ignorantly, inadvertently, unconsciously, unintentionally, unknowingly.

unwrap *vb* open, unfold.

unwritten *adj* oral, traditional, unrecorded; conventional, customary.

unyielding *adj* constant, determined, indomitable, inflexible, pertinacious, resolute, staunch, steadfast, steady, tenacious, uncompromising, unwavering; headstrong, intractable, obstinate, perverse, self-willed, stiff, stubborn, wayward, wilful; adamantine, firm, grim, hard, immovable, implastic, inexorable, relentless, rigid, stiff.

upheaval *n* cataclysm, convulsion, disorder, eruption, explosion, outburst, overthrow.

uphill *adj* ascending, upward; arduous, difficult, hard, laborious, strenuous, toilsome, wearisome.

uphold *vb* elevate, raise; bear up, hold up, support, sustain; advocate, aid, champion, countenance, defend, justify, maintain, support, sustain, vindicate.

upon *prep* on, on top of, over; about, concerning, on the subject of, relating to; immediately after, with.

uppermost *adj* foremost, highest, loftiest, supreme, topmost, upmost.

upright *adj* erect, perpendicular, vertical; conscientious, equitable, fair, faithful, good, honest, honourable, incorruptible, just, pure, righteous, straightforward, true, trustworthy, upstanding.

uproar *n* clamour, commotion, confusion, din, disturbance, fracas, hubbub, hurly-burly, noise, pandemonium, racket, riot, tumult, turmoil.

uproarious *adj* boisterous, clamorous, loud, noisy, obstreperous, riotous, tumultuous.

uproot *vb* eradicate, extirpate, root out.

upset *vb* capsize, invert, overthrow, overtumble, overturn, spill, tip over, topple, turn turtle; agitate, confound, confuse, discompose, disconcert, distress, disturb, embarrass, excite, fluster, muddle, overwhelm, perturb, shock, startle, trouble; unnerve, unsettle; defeat, revolutionise, subvert; foil, frustrate, nonplus, thwart. • *adj* disproved, exposed, overthrown; bothered, confused, disconcerted, flustered, mixed-up, perturbed; shocked, startled, unsettled; beaten, defeated, overcome, overpowered, overthrown; discomfited, distressed, discomposed, overcome, overexcited, overwrought, perturbed, shaken, troubled, unnerved.

upshot *n* conclusion, consummation, effect, end, event, issue, outcome, result, termination.

upstart *n* adventurer, arriviste, parvenu, snob, social cimber, yuppie.

upturned *adj* raised, uplifted; retroussé.

upward *adj* ascending, climbing, mounting, rising, uphill. • *adv* above, aloft, overhead, up; heavenwards, skywards, up.

urbane *adj* civil, complaisant, courteous, courtly, elegant, mannerly, polished, polite, refined, smooth, suave, well-mannered.

urge *vb* crowd, drive, force on, impel, press, press on, push, push on; beg, beseech, conjure, entreat, exhort, implore, importune, ply, press, solicit, tease; animate, egg on, encourage, goad, hurry, incite, instigate, quicken, spur, stimulate. • *n* compulsion, desire, drive, impulse, longing, wish, yearning.

urgency *n* drive, emergency, exigency, haste, necessity, press, pressure, push, stress; clamorousness, entreaty, insistence, importunity, instance, solicitation; goad, incitement, spur.

urgent *adj* cogent, critical, crucial, crying, exigent, immediate, imperative, important, importunate, insistent, instant, pertinacious, pressing.

usage *n* treatment; consuetude, custom, fashion, habit, method, mode, practice, tradition.

use *vb* administer, apply, avail oneself of, drive, employ, handle, improve, make use of, manipulate, occupy, operate, ply, put into action, take advantage of, turn to account, wield, work; exercise, exert, exploit, practise, profit by, utilise; absorb, consume, exhaust, expend, swallow up, waste, wear out; accustom, familiarise, habituate, harden, inure, train; act toward, behave toward, deal with, handle, manage, treat; be accustomed, be wont. • *n* appliance, application, consumption, conversion, disposal, exercise, employ, employment, practice, utilisation; adaptability, advantage, avail, benefit, convenience, profit, service, usefulness, utility, wear; exigency, necessity, indispensability, need, occasion, requisiteness; custom, exercise, habit, handling, method, practice, treatment, usage, way.

useful *adj* active, advantageous, available, availing, beneficial, commodious, convenient, effective, good, helpful, instrumental, operative, practical, profitable, remunerative, salutary, suitable, serviceable, utilitarian.

useless *adj* abortive, bootless, fruitless, futile, idle, ineffective, ineffectual, inutile, nugatory, null, profitless, unavailing, unprofitable, unproductive, unserviceable, valueless, worthless.

usher *vb* announce, forerun, herald, induct, introduce, precede; conduct, direct, escort, shepherd, show. • *n* attendant, conductor, escort.

usual *adj* accustomed, common, customary, everyday, familiar, frequent, general, habitual, normal, ordinary, prevailing, prevalent, regular.

usurp *vb* appropriate, arrogate, assume, seize.

utilise *vb* employ, exploit, make use of, put to use, turn to account, use.

utility *n* advantageousness, avail, benefit, profit, service, use, usefulness; happiness, welfare.

utmost *adj* extreme, farthest, highest, last, main, most distant, remotest; greatest, uttermost. • *n* best, extreme, maximum, most.

utter[1] *adj* complete, entire, perfect, total; absolute, blank, diametric, downright, final, peremptory, sheer, stark, unconditional, total.

utter[2] *vb* articulate, breathe, deliver, disclose, divulge, emit, enunciate, express, give forth, pronounce, reveal, speak, talk, tell, voice; announce, circulate, declare, issue, publish.

utterance *n* articulation, delivery, disclosure, emission, expression, pronouncement, pronunciation, publication, speech.

V

vacant *adj* blank, empty, unfilled, void; disengaged, free, unemployed, unoccupied, unencumbered; thoughtless, unmeaning, unthinking, unreflective; uninhabited, untenanted.

vacate *vb* abandon, evacuate, relinquish, surrender; abolish, abrogate, annul, cancel, disannul, invalidate, nullify, overrule, quash, rescind.

vagabond *n* beggar, landloper, loafer, lounger, nomad, outcast, tramp, vagrant, wanderer.

vagrant *adj* erratic, itinerant, roaming, roving, nomadic, strolling, unsettled, wandering. • *n* beggar, castaway, landloper, loafer, lounger, nomad, outcast, tramp, vagabond, wanderer.

vague *adj* ambiguous, confused, dim, doubtful, indefinite, ill-defined, indistinct, lax, loose, obscure, uncertain, undetermined, unsettled.

vain *adj* baseless, delusive, dreamy, empty, false, imaginary, shadowy, suppositional, unsubstantial, unreal, void; abortive, bootless, fruitless, futile, ineffectual, nugatory, profitless, unavailing, unprofitable; trivial, unessential, unimportant, unsatisfactory, unsatisfying, useless, vapid, worthless; arrogant, conceited, egotistical, flushed, high, inflated, opinionated, ostentatious, overweening, proud, self-confident, self-opinionated, vainglorious.

valiant *adj* bold, brave, chivalrous, courageous, daring, dauntless, doughty, fearless, gallant, heroic, intrepid, lion-hearted, redoubtable.

valid *adj* binding, cogent, conclusive, efficacious, efficient, good, grave, important, just, logical, powerful, solid, sound, strong, substantial, sufficient, weighty.

valour *n* boldness, bravery, courage, daring, gallantry, heroism, prowess, spirit.

valuable *adj* advantageous, precious, profitable, useful; costly, expensive, rich; admirable, estimable, worthy. • *n* heirloom, treasure.

value *vb* account, appraise, assess, estimate, price, rate, reckon; appreciate, esteem, prize, regard, treasure. • *n* avail, importance, usefulness, utility, worth; cost, equivalent, price, rate; estimation, excellence, importance, merit, worth.

vandal *n* barbarian, destroyer, savage.

vandalism *n* barbarism, barbarity, savagery.

vanish *vb* disappear, dissolve, fade, melt.

vanity *n* emptiness, falsity, foolishness, futility, hollowness, insanity, triviality, unreality, worthlessness; arrogance, conceit, egotism, ostentation, self-conceit.

vanquish vb conquer, defeat, outwit, overcome, overpower, overthrow, subdue, subjugate; crush, discomfit, foil, master, quell, rout, worst.

vapour n cloud, exhalation, fog, fume, mist, rack, reek, smoke, steam; daydream, dream, fantasy, phantom, vagary, vision, whim, whimsy.

variable adj changeable, mutable, shifting; aberrant, alterable, capricious, fickle, fitful, floating, fluctuating, inconstant, mobile, mutable, protean, restless, shifting, unsteady, vacillating.

variance n disagreement, difference, discord, dissension, incompatibility, jarring, strife.

variation n alteration, change, modification; departure, deviation, difference, discrepancy, innovation; contrariety, discordance.

variety n difference, dissimilarity, diversity, diversification, medley, miscellany, mixture, multiplicity, variation; kind, sort.

various adj different, diverse, manifold, many, numerous, several, sundry.

vary vb alter, metamorphose, transform; alternate, exchange, rotate; diversify, modify, variegate; depart, deviate, swerve.

vast adj boundless, infinite, measureless, spacious, wide; colossal, enormous, gigantic, huge, immense, mighty, monstrous, prodigious, tremendous; extraordinary, remarkable.

vault[1] n arch, bend, curve, span. • n cupola, curve, dome; catacomb, cell, cellar, crypt, dungeon, tomb; depository, strongroom.

vault[2] vb bound, jump, leap, spring; tumble, turn. • n bound, leap, jump, spring.

veer vb change, shift, turn.

vegetate vb blossom, develop, flourish, flower, germinate, grow, shoot, sprout, swell; bask, hibernate, idle, stagnate.

vehement adj furious, high, hot, impetuous, passionate, rampant, violent; ardent, burning, eager, earnest, enthusiastic, fervid, fiery, keen, passionate, sanguine, zealous.

veil vb cloak, conceal, cover, curtain, envelop, hide, invest, mask, screen, shroud. • n cover, curtain, film, shade, screen; blind, cloak, cover, disguise, mask, muffler, screen, visor.

vein n course, current, lode, seam, streak, stripe, thread, wave; bent, character, faculty, humour, mood, talent, turn.

vend vb dispose, flog, hawk, retail, sell.

venerable adj grave, respected, revered, sage, wise; aged, old, patriarchal.

veneration n adoration, devotion, esteem, respect, reverence, worship.

vengeance n retaliation, retribution, revenge.

venom n poison, virus; acerbity, acrimony, bitterness, gall, hate, ill-will, malevolence, malice, maliciousness, malignity, rancour, spite.

venomous adj deadly, poisonous, septic, toxic, virulent; caustic, malicious, malignant.

vent vb emit, express, release, utter. • n air hole, hole, mouth, opening, orifice; air pipe, air tube, aperture, blowhole, bunghole, hydrant, plug, spiracle, spout, tap, orifice; effusion, emission, escape, outlet, passage.

ventilate vb aerate, air, freshen, oxygenate, purify; fan, winnow; canvas, comment, discuss, examine, publish, review, scrutinise.

venture vb adventure, dare, hazard, imperil, jeopardise, presume, risk, speculate, test, try, undertake. • n adventure, chance, hazard, jeopardy, peril, risk, speculation, stake.

verdict n answer, decision, finding, judgement.

verge vb bear, incline, lean, slope, tend; approach, border, skirt. • n mace, rod, staff; border, boundary, brink, confine, edge, extreme, limit, margin; edge, eve, point.

verify vb attest, authenticate, confirm, corroborate, prove, substantiate.

versatile adj capricious, changeable, erratic, mobile, variable; fickle, inconstant, mercurial, unsteady; adaptable, protean, plastic, varied.

versed adj able, accomplished, acquainted, clever, conversant, practised, proficient, qualified, skilful, skilled, trained.

version n interpretation, reading, rendering.

vertical adj erect, perpendicular, plumb, steep.

vertigo n dizziness, giddiness.

verve n animation, ardour, energy, enthusiasm, force, rapture, spirit.

very adv absolutely, enormously, excessively, hugely, remarkably, surpassingly. • adj actual, exact, identical, precise, same; bare, mere, plain, pure, simple.

vestige n evidence, footprint, footstep, mark, record, relic, sign, token.

veteran adj adept, aged, experienced, disciplined, seasoned, old. • n campaigner, old soldier; master, past master, old-timer, old-stager.

veto vb ban, embargo, forbid, interdict, negate, prohibit. • n ban, embargo, interdict, prohibition.

vex vb annoy, badger, bother, chafe, cross, distress, gall, harass, harry, hector, molest, perplex, pester, plague, tease, torment, trouble, roil, spite, worry; affront, displease, fret, irk, irritate, nettle, offend, provoke; agitate, disquiet, disturb.

vexation n affliction, agitation, chagrin, discomfort, displeasure, disquiet, distress, grief, irritation, pique, sorrow, trouble; affliction, annoyance, curse, nuisance, plague, torment.

vibrate vb oscillate, sway, swing, undulate, wave; impinge, quiver, sound, thrill.

vice n blemish, defect, failing, fault, imperfection, infirmity; badness, corruption, depravation, depravity, error, evil, immorality, iniquity, laxity, obliquity, sin, viciousness, vileness, wickedness.

vicinity n nearness, proximity; locality, neighbourhood, vicinage.

vicious adj abandoned, atrocious, bad, corrupt, degenerate, demoralised, depraved, devilish, diabolical, evil, flagrant, hellish, immoral, iniquitous, mischievous, profligate, shameless, sinful, unprincipled, wicked; malicious, spiteful, venomous; foul, impure; corrupt, debased, faulty, impure; contrary.

victim n martyr, sacrifice, sufferer; prey, sufferer; dupe, gull, prey, puppet.

victimise vb bamboozle, befool, beguile, cheat, circumvent, cozen, deceive, defraud, dupe, hoodwink, overreach, swindle, trick.

victor n champion, conqueror, winner.

victorious adj conquering, successful, triumphant, winning.

victory n conquest, mastery, triumph.

view vb behold, contemplate, eye, inspect, scan, survey; consider, contemplate, inspect, regard, study. • n inspection, observation, regard, sight; outlook, panorama, perspective, prospect, range, scene, survey, vista; aim, intent, intention, design, drift, object, purpose, scope; belief, conception, impression, idea, judgement, notion, opinion, sentiment, theory; appearance, aspect.

vigilant adj alert, attentive, careful, cautious, circumspect, observant, watchful.

vigorous adj lusty, powerful, strong; active, alert, cordial, energetic, forcible, vehement, vivid, virile, strenuous; brisk, hale, hardy, robust, sound, sturdy, healthy; fresh, flourishing; bold, emphatic, impassioned, lively, nervous, piquant.

vigour n activity, efficacy, energy, force, might, potency, power, spirit, strength; bloom, elasticity, haleness, health, heartiness, pep, punch, robustness, soundness, thriftiness, tone, vim, vitality; enthusiasm, freshness, fire, intensity.

vile adj abject, base, beastly, beggarly, brutish, contemptible, despicable, disgusting, grovelling, ignoble, low, mean, odious, paltry, pitiful, repulsive, scurvy, shabby, slavish, sorry, ugly; bad, base, evil, foul, gross, impure, iniquitous, lewd, obscene, sinful, vicious, wicked; cheap, mean, miserable, valueless, worthless.

vilify vb abuse, asperse, backbite, berate, blacken, blemish, brand, calumniate, decry, defame, disparage, lampoon, libel, malign, revile, scandalise, slander, slur, traduce, vituperate.

villain n blackguard, knave, miscreant, rascal, reprobate, rogue, ruffian, scamp, scoundrel.

vindicate vb defend, justify, uphold; advocate, avenge, assert, maintain, right, support.

vindictive adj avenging, grudgeful, implacable, malevolent, malicious, malignant, retaliative, revengeful, spiteful, unforgiving, unrelenting.

violate vb hurt, injure; break, disobey, infringe, invade; desecrate, pollute, profane; abuse, debauch, defile, deflower, outrage, ravish.

violent adj boisterous, demented, forceful, forcible, frenzied, furious, high, hot, impetuous, insane, intense, stormy, tumultuous, turbulent, vehement, wild; fierce, fiery, fuming, heady, heavy, infuriate, passionate, obstreperous, strong, raging, rampant, rank, rapid, raving, refractory, roaring, rough, tearing, towering, ungovernable; desperate, extreme, outrageous.

virile adj forceful, manly, masculine, robust.

virtual adj constructive, equivalent, essential, implicit, implied, indirect, practical, substantial.

virtue n chastity, goodness, grace, morality, purity; efficacy, excellence, honesty, integrity, justice, probity, quality, rectitude, worth.

virtuous adj blameless, equitable, exemplary, excellent, good, honest, moral, noble, righteous, upright, worthy; chaste, continent, immaculate, innocent, modest, pure, undefiled.

virulent adj deadly, malignant, poisonous, toxic, venomous; acrid, acrimonious, bitter, caustic.

visible adj perceivable, perceptible, seeable, visual; apparent, clear, conspicuous, discoverable, distinct, evident, manifest, noticeable, obvious, open, palpable, patent, plain.

vision n eyesight, seeing, sight; eyeshot, pen; apparition, chimera, dream, ghost, hallucination, illusion, phantom, spectre.

visionary adj imaginative, impractical, quixotic, romantic; chimerical, dreamy, fancied, fanciful, fantastic, ideal, illusory, imaginary, romantic, shadowy, unsubstantial, utopian, wild. • n dreamer, enthusiast, fanatic, idealist, optimist, theorist, zealot.

vital adj basic, cardinal, essential, indispensable, necessary; animate, alive, existing, life-giving, living; essential, paramount.

vitality n animation, life, strength, vigour.

vivacious adj active, animated, breezy, brisk, cheerful, frolicsome, gay, jocund, light-hearted, lively, merry, mirthful, spirited, sprightly.

vivid adj active, animated, bright, brilliant, clear, intense, fresh, lively, living, lucid, quick, sprightly, strong; expressive, graphic, striking.

vocation n call, citation, injunction, summons; business, calling, employment, occupation, profession, pursuit, trade.

vogue n custom, fashion, favour, mode, practice, repute, style, usage, way.

voice vb declare, express, say, utter. • n speech, tongue, utterance; sound; opinion, preference, suffrage, vote; accent, articulation, enunciation, inflection, intonation, modulation, pronunciation; expression, language, words.

void vb clear, eject, emit, empty, evacuate. • adj blank, empty, hollow, vacant; clear, destitute, devoid, free, lacking, wanting, without; inept, ineffectual, invalid, nugatory, null; imaginary, unreal, vain. • n abyss, blank, chasm, emptiness.

volatile *adj* gaseous, incoercible; airy, buoyant, frivolous, gay, jolly, lively, sprightly, vivacious; capricious, changeable, fickle, flighty, flyaway, giddy, harebrained, inconstant, light-headed, mercurial, reckless, unsteady, whimsical, wild.

volume *n* book, tome; amplitude, body, bulk, compass, dimension, size, substance, vastness; fullness, power, quantity.

voluminous *adj* ample, big, bulky, full, great, large; copious, diffuse, discursive, flowing.

voluntary *adj* free, spontaneous, unasked, unbidden, unforced; deliberate, designed, intended, purposed; discretionary, optional, willing.

volunteer *vb* offer, present, proffer, propose.

voracious *adj* devouring, edacious, greedy, hungry, rapacious, ravenous.

vote *vb* ballot, elect, opt, return; judge, pronounce, propose, suggest. • *n* ballot, franchise, poll, referendum, suffrage, voice.

vow *vb* consecrate, dedicate, devote; asseverate. • *n* oath, pledge, promise.

voyage *vb* cruise, journey, navigate, ply, sail. • *n* crossing, cruise, excursion, passage, sail.

vulgar *adj* base-born, common, ignoble, lowly, plebeian; boorish, cheap, coarse, discourteous, flashy, homespun, garish, gaudy, ill-bred, inelegant, loud, rustic, showy, tawdry, uncultivated, unrefined; general, ordinary, popular, public; base, broad, loose, low, gross, mean, ribald, vile.

vulnerable *adj* accessible, assailable, defenceless, exposed, weak.

W

waft *vb* bear, carry, convey, float, transmit.

wag[1] *vb* shake, sway, waggle; oscillate, vibrate.

wag[2] *n* humorist, jester, joker, wit.

wage *vb* conduct, undertake.

wager *vb* back, gamble, lay, pledge, risk, stake. • *n* bet, gamble, pledge, risk, stake.

wages *npl* allowance, compensation, earnings, emolument, hire, pay, payment, remuneration, salary, stipend.

wail *vb* bemoan, deplore, lament, mourn; cry, howl, weep. • *n* complaint, cry, lamentation.

wait *vb* delay, linger, pause, remain, rest, stay, tarry; attend, minister, serve; abide, await, expect, look for. • *n* delay, halt, holdup, pause, respite, rest, stay, stop.

waive *vb* defer, forego, surrender, relinquish, remit, renounce; desert, reject.

wake[1] *vb* arise, awake, awaken; activate, animate, arouse, awaken, excite, kindle, provoke, stimulate. • *n* vigil, watch, watching.

wake[2] *n* course, path, rear, track, trail, wash.

walk *vb* advance, depart, go, march, move, pace, saunter, step, stride, stroll, tramp. • *n* amble, carriage, gait, step; beat, career, course, department, field, province; conduct, procedure; alley, avenue, cloister, esplanade, footpath, path, pathway, pavement, promenade, range, sidewalk, way; constitutional, excursion, hike, ramble, saunter, stroll, tramp, turn.

wan *adj* ashen, bloodless, pale, pallid.

wander *vb* forage, prowl, ramble, range, roam, rove, stroll; deviate, digress, straggle, stray; moon, ramble, rave.

wane *vb* abate, decrease, ebb, subside; decline, fail, sink.

want *vb* crave, desire, need, require, wish; fail, lack, neglect, omit. • *n* absence, defect, default,

deficiency, lack; defectiveness, deficiency, failure, inadequacy, insufficiency, meagreness, paucity, poverty, scantiness, scarcity, shortness; necessity, need, craving, desire, longing, wish; destitution, distress, indigence, penury, straits.

war *vb* battle, campaign, combat, contend, crusade, engage, fight, strive. • *n* contention, enmity, hostility, strife, warfare.

warble *vb* sing, trill, yodel.

ward *vb* guard, watch; defend, fend, parry, protect, repel. • *n* care, charge, guard, guardianship, watch; defender, guardian, keeper, protector, warden; custody; defence, garrison, protection; minor, pupil; district, division, precinct, quarter; apartment, cubicle.

warehouse *n* depot, magazine, repository, store, storehouse.

warfare *n* battle, conflict, contest, discord, engagement, fray, hostilities, strife, struggle, war.

warm *vb* heat, roast, toast; animate, chafe, excite, rouse. • *adj* lukewarm, tepid; genial, mild, pleasant, sunny; close, muggy, oppressive; affectionate, ardent, cordial, eager, earnest, enthusiastic, fervent, fervid, genial, glowing, hearty, hot, zealous; excited, fiery, flushed, furious, hasty, keen, lively, passionate, quick, vehement.

warmth *n* glow, tepidity; ardour, fervency, fervour, zeal; animation, cordiality, eagerness, earnestness, enthusiasm, excitement, fervency, fever, fire, flush, heat, intensity, passion, spirit.

warn *vb* caution, forewarn; admonish, advise; apprise, inform, notify; bid, call, summon.

warning *adj* admonitory, cautionary, cautioning, monitory. • *n* admonition, advice, caveat, caution, monition; information, notice, augury, indication, intimation, omen, portent, presage, prognostic, sign, symptom; call, summons; example, lesson.

warrant *vb* answer for, certify, guarantee, secure; affirm, assure, attest, avouch, declare, justify, state; authorise, justify, license, maintain, sanction, support, sustain, uphold. • *n* guarantee, pledge, security, surety, warranty; authentication, authority, commission, verification; order, pass, permit, summons, subpoena, voucher, writ.

warrior *n* champion, fighter, hero, soldier.

wary *adj* careful, cautious, chary, circumspect, heedful, prudent, vigilant, watchful.

wash *vb* purify, purge; moisten, wet; bathe, clean, flush, irrigate, lap, lave, rinse, sluice; colour, stain, tint. • *n* ablution, bathing, cleansing, lavation, washing; bog, fen, marsh, swamp, quagmire; bath, lotion; laundry, washing.

waste *vb* consume, corrode, decrease, diminish, emaciate, wear; absorb, consume, deplete, devour, dissipate, drain, empty, exhaust, expend, lavish, lose, misspend, misuse, scatter, spend, squander; demolish, desolate, destroy, devastate, devour, dilapidate, harry, pillage, plunder, ravage, ruin, scour, strip; damage, impair, injure; decay, dwindle, perish, wither. • *adj* bare, desolated, destroyed, devastated, empty, ravaged, ruined, spoiled, stripped, void; dismal, dreary, forlorn; abandoned, bare, barren, uncultivated, unimproved, uninhabited, untilled, wild; useless, valueless, worthless; exuberant, superfluous. • *n* consumption, decrement, diminution, dissipation, exhaustion, expenditure, loss, wasting; destruction, dispersion, extravagance, loss, squandering, wanton; decay, desolation, destruction, devastation, havoc, pillage, ravage, ruin; chaff, debris, detritus, dross, husks, junk, matter, offal, refuse, rubbish, trash, wastrel, worthlessness; barrenness, solitude, wild, wilderness.

wasteful *adj* destructive, ruinous; extravagant, improvident, lavish, squandering, thriftless.

watch *vb* attend, guard, keep, oversee, protect, superintend, tend; eye, mark, observe. • *n* espial, guard, outlook, wakefulness, watchfulness, watching, vigil, ward; alertness, attention, inspection, observation, surveillance; guard, picket, sentinel, sentry, watchman; timepiece.

watchful *adj* alert, attentive, awake, careful, circumspect, guarded, heedful, observant, vigilant.

wave *vb* float, flutter, heave, shake, sway, undulate, wallow; brandish, flaunt, flourish, swing; beckon, signal. • *n* billow, bore, breaker, flood, flush, ripple, roll, surge, swell, tide, undulation; flourish, gesture, sway; convolution, curl, roll.

waver *vb* flicker, float, undulate, wave; reel, totter; falter, fluctuate, flutter, hesitate, oscillate.

wax *vb* become, grow, increase, mount, rise.

way *n* advance, journey, march, passage, progression, transit, trend; access, alley, artery, avenue, beat, channel, course, highroad, highway, passage, path, road, route, street, track, trail; fashion, manner, means, method, mode, system; distance, interval, space, stretch; behaviour, custom, fashion, form, guise, habit, habitude, manner, practice, process, style, usage; device, plan.

wayward *adj* capricious, captious, contrary, forward, headstrong, intractable, obstinate.

weak *adj* debilitated, delicate, enfeebled, enervated, exhausted, faint, feeble, fragile, frail, infirm, invalid, languid, languishing, shaky, sickly, spent, strengthless, tender, unhealthy, unsound, wasted, weakly; accessible, defenceless, unprotected, vulnerable; light, soft, unstressed; boneless, infirm; compliant, irresolute, pliable, pliant, undecided, undetermined, unsettled, unstable, unsteady, vacillating, wavering, yielding; childish, foolish, imbecile, senseless, shallow, silly, simple, stupid, weak-minded, witless; erring, foolish, indiscreet, injudicious, unwise; faint, feeble, gentle, indistinct, low, small; adulterated, attenuated, diluted, insipid, tasteless, thin, watery; feeble, flimsy, frivolous, poor, sleazy, slight, trifling; futile, illogical, inconclusive, ineffective, ineffectual, inefficient, lame, unconvincing, unsatisfactory, unsupported, unsustained, vague, vain; unsafe, unsound, unsubstantial, untrustworthy; helpless, impotent, powerless; breakable, brittle, delicate, frangible; inconsiderable, puny, slender, slight, small.

weaken *vb* cramp, cripple, debilitate, devitalise, enervate, enfeeble, invalidate, relax, sap, shake, stagger, undermine, unman, unnerve, unstring; adulterate, attenuate, debase, depress, dilute, exhaust, impair, impoverish, lessen, lower, reduce.

wealth *n* assets, capital, cash, fortune, funds, goods, money, possessions, property, riches, treasure; abundance, affluence, opulence.

wear *vb* bear, carry, don; endure, last; consume, impair, rub, use, waste. • *n* corrosion, deterioration, disintegration, erosion, wear and tear; consumption, use; apparel, array, attire, clothes.

wearisome *adj* annoying, boring, dull, exhausting, fatiguing, humdrum, irksome, monotonous, prolix, prosaic, slow, tedious, tiresome.

weary *vb* debilitate, exhaust, fag, fatigue, harass, jade, tire. • *adj* apathetic, bored, drowsy, exhausted, jaded, spent, tired, worn.

wed *vb* contract, couple, espouse, marry.

wedding *n* bridal, espousal, marriage, nuptials.

weep *vb* bemoan, bewail, complain, cry, lament.

weigh *vb* balance, counterbalance, lift, raise; consider, deliberate, esteem, examine, study.

weight *vb* ballast, burden, fill, freight, load; weigh. • *n* gravity, heaviness, heft, tonnage; burden, load, pressure; burden, consequence, efficacy, emphasis, importance, impressiveness, influence, moment, pith, power, significance, value.

weighty *adj* heavy, massive, onerous, ponderous, unwieldy; considerable, efficacious, forcible, grave, important, influential, serious.

weird *adj* eerie, ghostly, strange, supernatural, uncanny, unearthly, witching.

welcome *vb* embrace, greet, hail, receive. • *adj* acceptable, agreeable, grateful, gratifying, pleasant, pleasing, satisfying.

welfare *n* advantage, affluence, benefit, happiness, profit, prosperity, success, thrift, weal.

well[1] *vb* flow, gush, issue, jet, pour, spring. • *n* fount, fountain, reservoir, spring, wellhead, wellspring; origin, source; hole, pit, shaft.

well[2] *adj* hale, healthy, hearty, sound; fortunate, good, happy, profitable, satisfactory, useful. • *adv* accurately, adequately, correctly, efficiently, properly, suitably; abundantly, considerably, fully, thoroughly; agreeably, commendably.

wellbeing *n* comfort, good, happiness, health, prosperity, welfare.

wet *vb* dabble, damp, dampen, dip, drench, moisten, saturate, soak, sprinkle, water. • *adj* clammy, damp, dank, dewy, dripping, humid, moist; rainy, showery, sprinkly.

wheel *vb* gyrate, revolve, roll, rotate, spin, swing, turn, twist, whirl, wind. • *n* circle, revolution, roll, rotation, spin, turn, twirl.

whim *n* caprice, crochet, fancy, freak, frolic, humour, notion, quirk, sport, vagary, whimsy.

whimsical *adj* capricious, eccentric, erratic, fanciful, odd, peculiar, quaint.

whine *vb* cry, grumble, moan, mule, snivel, wail, whimper.

whip *vb* beat, lash, strike; beat, flagellate, flog, goad, horsewhip, lash, scourge, slash; hurt, sting; jerk, snap, snatch, whisk. • *n* cane, crop, horsewhip, lash, scourge, switch, thong.

whirl *vb* gyrate, pirouette, roll, revolve, rotate, turn, twirl, twist, wheel.

whole *adj* all, complete, entire, intact, integral, total, undivided; faultless, firm, good, perfect, strong, unbroken, undivided, uninjured; healthy, sound, well. • *adv* entire, in one. • *n* aggregate, all, amount, ensemble, entirety, gross, sum, total.

wholesome *adj* healthy, healthful, helpful, invigorating, nourishing, nutritious, salubrious, salutary; beneficial, good, helpful, improving, salutary; fresh, sound, sweet.

wicked *adj* abandoned, abominable, depraved, devilish, godless, graceless, immoral, impious, infamous, irreligious, irreverent, profane, sinful, ungodly, unholy, unprincipled, unrighteous, vicious, vile, worthless; atrocious, bad, black, criminal, dark, evil, heinous, ill, iniquitous, monstrous, nefarious, unjust, villainous.

wide *adj* ample, broad, capacious, comprehensive, distended, expanded, large, spacious, vast; distant, remote; prevalent, rife, widespread. • *adv* completely, farthest, fully.

wield *vb* brandish, flourish, handle, manipulate, ply, work; control, manage, sway, use.

wild *adj* feral, undomesticated, untamed; desert, desolate, native, rough, rude, uncultivated; barbarous, ferocious, fierce, rude, savage, uncivilised, untamed; dense, luxuriant, rank; disorderly, distracted, frantic, frenzied, furious, impetuous, irregular, mad, outrageous, raving, turbulent, ungoverned, uncontrolled, violent; dissipated, fast, flighty, foolish, giddy, harebrained, heedless, ill-advised, inconsiderate, reckless, thoughtless, unwise; boisterous, rough, stormy; crazy, extravagant, fanciful, grotesque, imaginary, strange. • *n* desert, waste, wilderness.

wilful *adj* cantankerous, contumacious, dogged, headstrong, heady, inflexible, intractable, mulish, obdurate, obstinate, perverse, pig-headed, refractory, self-willed, stubborn, unruly, unyielding; arbitrary, capricious, self-willed.

will *vb* bid, command, decree, direct, enjoin, ordain; choose, desire, elect, wish; bequeath, convey, demise, devise, leave. • *n* decision, determination, resoluteness, resolution, self-reliance; desire, disposition, inclination, intent, pleasure, purpose, volition, wish; behest, command, decree, demand, direction, order, request.

willing *adj* adaptable, amenable, compliant, desirous, disposed, inclined, minded; deliberate, free, intentional, spontaneous, unasked, unbidden, voluntary; eager, prompt, ready.

wily *adj* arch, artful, crafty, crooked, cunning, deceitful, designing, diplomatic, foxy, insidious, intriguing, politic, sly, subtle, treacherous.

win *vb* accomplish, achieve, acquire, catch, earn, effect, gain, gather, get, make, obtain, procure, reach, realise, reclaim, recover; gain, succeed, surpass, triumph; arrive, get; allure, attract, convince, influence, persuade. • *n* conquest, success, triumph, victory.

wind[1] *n* air, blast, breeze, draught, gust, hurricane, whiff, zephyr; breath, breathing, expiration, inspiration, respiration; flatulence, gas.

wind[2] *vb* coil, crank, encircle, involve, reel, roll, turn, twine, twist; bend, curve, meander, zigzag.

wipe *vb* clean, dry, mop, rub. • *n* blow, hit, strike; gibe, jeer, sarcasm, sneer, taunt.

wisdom *n* depth, discernment, far-sightedness, foresight, insight, judgement, judiciousness, prescience, profundity, prudence, sagacity, sapience, solidity, sense, understanding, wiseness; attainment, enlightenment, erudition, information, knowledge, learning, lore, scholarship.

wise *adj* deep, discerning, enlightened, intelligent, judicious, penetrating, philosophical, profound, rational, seasonable, sensible, sage, sapient, solid, sound; erudite, informed, knowing, learned, scholarly; crafty, cunning, designing, foxy, knowing, politic, sly, subtle, wary, wily.

wish *vb* covet, desire, hanker, list, long; bid, command, intend, mean, order, want. • *n* behest, desire, mind, pleasure, want, will; craving, hankering, longing, yearning.

wistful adj contemplative, engrossed, meditative, musing, pensive, reflective, thoughtful; desirous, eager, earnest, longing.

wit n genius, intellect, intelligence, reason, sense, understanding; brightness, banter, cleverness, drollery, facetiousness, fun, humour, jocularity, piquancy, point, raillery, satire, sparkle, whim; conceit, epigram, jest, joke, pleasantry, quip, quirk, repartee, sally, witticism; humorist.

witch n charmer, enchantress, fascinator, sorceress; crone, hag, sibyl.

witchcraft n conjuration, enchantment, magic, necromancy, sorcery, spell.

withdraw vb abstract, deduct, remove, retire, separate, sequester, sequestrate, subduct, subtract; disengage, wean; abjure, recall, recant, relinquish, resign, retract, revoke; abdicate, decamp, depart, dissociate, retire, shrink, vacate.

wither vb contract, droop, dry, sear, shrivel, wilt, wizen; decay, decline, droop, languish, pine.

withhold vb check, detain, hinder, repress, restrain, retain, suppress.

withstand vb confront, defy, face, oppose.

witness vb corroborate, mark, note, notice, observe, see. • n attestation, conformation, corroboration, evidence, proof, testimony; deponent, eyewitness, onlooker, spectator, testifier.

witty adj bright, clever, droll, facetious, funny, humorous, jocose, jocular, pleasant, waggish; alert, penetrating, quick, sparkling, sprightly.

wizard n charmer, diviner, conjurer, enchanter, magician, necromancer, seer, sorcerer.

woe n affliction, agony, anguish, bitterness, depression, distress, dole, grief, heartache, melancholy, misery, sorrow, torture, tribulation, trouble, unhappiness, wretchedness.

wonder vb admire, gape, marvel; conjecture, ponder, query, question, speculate. • n amazement, astonishment, awe, bewilderment, curiosity, marvel, miracle, prodigy, surprise.

wonderful adj amazing, astonishing, astounding, awe-inspiring, awesome, awful, extraordinary, marvellous, miraculous, portentous, prodigious, startling, stupendous, surprising.

word n expression, name, phrase, term, utterance; account, advice, information, intelligence, message, news, report, tidings; affirmation, assertion, averment, avowal, declaration, statement; conservation, speech; agreement, assurance, engagement, parole, pledge, plight, promise; behest, bidding, command, direction, order, precept; password, signal.

work vb act, operate; drudge, fag, grind, grub, labour, slave, sweat, toil; move, perform, succeed; aim, attempt, strive, try; effervesce, ferment, leaven; accomplish, beget, cause, effect, engender, rise; accomplish, beget, cause, effect, engender, manage, originate, produce; exert, strain; embroi-

der, stitch. • n exertion, drudgery, grind, labour, pain, toil; business, employment, function, occupation, task; action, accomplishment, achievement, composition, deed, feat, fruit, handiwork, opus, performance, product, production; fabric, manufacture; ferment, leaven; management, treatment.

worldly adj common, earthly, human, mundane, sublunary, terrestrial; carnal, fleshly, profane, secular, temporal; ambitious, grovelling, irreligious, selfish, proud, sordid, unspiritual.

worry vb annoy, badger, bait, beset, bore, bother, chafe, disquiet, disturb, fret, gall, harass, harry, hector, infest, irritate, molest, persecute, pester, plague, tease, torment, trouble, vex.

worship vb adore, esteem, honour, revere, venerate; deify, idolise; aspire, pray.

worst vb beat, choke, conquer, crush, defeat, discomfit, foil, master, overpower, overthrow, quell, rout, subdue, subjugate, vanquish.

worth n account, character, credit, desert, excellence, importance, integrity, merit, nobleness, worthiness, virtue; cost, estimation, price, value.

worthless adj futile, meritless, miserable, nugatory, paltry, poor, trifling, unproductive, unsalable, unserviceable, useless, valueless, wretched; abject, base, corrupt, degraded, ignoble, low.

worthy adj deserving, fit, suitable; estimable, excellent, exemplary, good, honest, honourable, reputable, righteous, upright, virtuous. • n celebrity, dignitary, luminary, notability, personage.

wound vb damage, harm, hurt, injure; cut, gall, harrow, irritate, lacerate, pain, prick, stab; annoy, mortify, offend. • n blow, hurt, injury; damage, detriment; anguish, grief, pain, pang, torture.

wrap vb cloak, cover, encase, envelope, muffle, swathe, wind. • n blanket, cape, cloak, cover.

wreath n chaplet, curl, festoon, garland, ring.

wreathe vb encircle, festoon, garland, intertwine, surround, twine, twist.

wreck vb founder, shipwreck, strand; blast, blight, break, devastate, ruin, spoil. • n crash, desolation, destruction, perdition, prostration, ruin, shipwreck, smash, undoing.

wrench vb distort, pervert, twist, wrest, wring; sprain, strain; extort, extract. • n twist, wring; sprain, strain; monkey wrench, spanner.

wrest vb force, pull, strain, twist, wrench.

wrestle vb contend, contest, grapple, strive.

wretched adj afflicted, comfortless, distressed, forlorn, sad, unfortunate, unhappy, woebegone; afflicting, calamitous, deplorable, depressing, pitiable, sad, saddening, shocking, sorrowful; bad, beggarly, contemptible, mean, paltry, pitiful, poor, shabby, sorry, vile, worthless.

wring vb contort, twist, wrench; extort, force, wrest; anguish, distress, harass, pain, rack, torture.

wrinkle[1] vb cockle, corrugate, crease, gather,

pucker, rumple. • *n* cockle, corrugation, crease, crimp, crinkle, crumple, fold, furrow, gather.
wrinkle² *n* device, tip, trick.
write *vb* compose, copy, indite, inscribe, pen, scrawl, scribble, transcribe.
writer *n* amanuensis, author, clerk, penman.
wrong *vb* abuse, encroach, injure, maltreat, oppress. • *adj* inequitable, unfair, unjust, wrongful; bad, criminal, evil, guilty, immoral, improper,

iniquitous, reprehensible, sinful, vicious, wicked; amiss, improper, inappropriate, unfit, unsuitable; erroneous, false, faulty, inaccurate, incorrect, mistaken, untrue. • *n* foul, grievance, inequity, injury, injustice, trespass, unfairness; blame, crime, dishonesty, evil, guilt, immorality, iniquity, misdeed, sin, transgression, vice, wickedness, wrongdoing; error, falsity.
wry *adj* askew, contorted, crooked, twisted.

XYZ

Xmas *n* Christmas, Noel, Yule, Yuletide.
X-ray *n* roentgen ray, röntgen ray.
xylograph *n* cut, woodcut, wood engraving.
yap *vb* bark, cry, yelp. • *n* bark, cry, yelp.
yard *n* close, compound, court, courtyard, enclosure, garden.
yarn *n* anecdote, boasting, fabrication, narrative, story, tale, untruth.
yawn *vb* dehisce, gape, open wide.
yearn *vb* crave, desire, hanker after, long for.
yell *vb* bawl, bellow, cry out, howl, roar, scream, screech, shriek, squeal.
yelp *vb* bark, howl, yap; complain, bitch.
yet *adv* at last, besides, further, however, over and above, so far, still, thus far, ultimately. • *conj* moreover, nevertheless, notwithstanding, now.
yield *vb* afford, bear, bestow, communicate, confer, fetch, furnish, impart, produce, render, supply; accede, accord, acknowledge, acquiesce, allow, assent, comply, concede, give, grant, permit; abandon, abdicate, cede, forego, give up, let go, quit, relax, relinquish, resign, submit, succumb, surrender, waive. • *n* earnings, income, output, produce, profit, return, revenue.
yielding *adj* accommodating, acquiescent, affable, compliant, complaisant, easy, manageable, obedient, passive, submissive, unresisting;

bending, flexible, flexile, plastic, pliant, soft.
yoke *vb* associate, bracket, connect, couple, harness, interlink, join, link, unite. • *n* bond, chain, ligature, link, tie, union; bondage, dependence, enslavement, service, servitude, subjection.
young *adj* green, ignorant, inexperienced, juvenile, new, recent, youthful. • *n* young people, youth; babies, issue, brood, offspring, progeny.
youth *n* adolescence, childhood, immaturity, juvenile, juvenility, minority, nonage, pupillage, wardship; boy, girl, lad, lass, youngster.
zany *adj* comic, comical, crazy, droll, eccentric, funny, imaginative, scatterbrained; clownish, foolish, ludicrous, silly.
zeal *n* alacrity, ardour, cordiality, devotedness, devotion, earnestness, eagerness, energy, enthusiasm, fervour, heartiness, intensity.
zealous *adj* ardent, burning, devoted, eager, earnest, enthusiastic, fervent, fiery, keen, passionate.
zenith *n* acme, apex, climax, culmination, heyday, pinnacle, prime, summit, top.
zero *n* cipher, naught, nadir, nil, nothing.
zest *n* appetite, enjoyment, exhilaration, gusto, liking, piquancy, relish, thrill; edge, flavour, salt, savour, tang, taste; appetiser, sauce.
zone *n* circuit, clime, region.